Annotated Instructor's Edition

PRODUCTION AND OPERATIONS MANAGEMENT

Focusing on Quality and Competitiveness

INSTRUCTOR'S SECTION

Annotated Instructor's Edition

PRODUCTION AND OPERATIONS MANAGEMENT

Focusing on Quality and Competitiveness

Roberta S. Russell
Professor
Virginia Polytechnic Institute and State University

Bernard W. Taylor III
R.B. Pamplin Professor
Virginia Polytechnic Institute and State University

Prentice-Hall, Inc.
Englewood Cliffs, New Jersey 07632

INSTRUCTOR'S SECTION

Library of Congress Cataloging-in-Publication Data
Russell, Roberta S.
Production and operations management : focusing on quality and competitiveness / by Roberta S. Russell and Bernard W. Taylor.
p. cm.
Includes bibliographical references and indexes.
ISBN 0-205-14733-X : $48.75. — ISBN 0-205-16340-8 (AIE)
1. Production management. 2. Quality control. I. Taylor, Bernard, 1931- . II. Title.
TS155.R755 1995
658.5—dc20 94-3609
CIP

Editor-in-Chief: Rich Wohl
Acquisitions Editor: Tom Tucker
Production Editor: Barbara Barg
Managing Editor: Joyce Turner
In-House Liaison: Penelope Linskey
Manufacturing Buyer: Marie McNamara
Editorial Assistant: Andrea Cuperman
Production Assistant: Renée Pelletier
Design Director: Patricia Wosczyk
Interior Design: Glenna Collett
Cover Design: Patricia Wosczyk
Cover Art: David M. Jones/© Uniphoto, Inc.
Photo Research: Sarah Evertson/Photosynthesis
Illustration: Precision Graphics, Inc.
Compositor: Omegatype Typography, Inc.
Printer/Binder: R. R. Donnelley

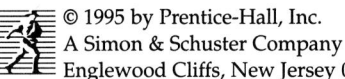

A Simon & Schuster Company
Englewood Cliffs, New Jersey 07632

Printed in the United States of America
10 9 8 7 6 5 4 3 2 1

ISBN 0-205-16340-8

Prentice-Hall International (UK) Limited, *London*
Prentice-Hall of Australia Pty. Limited, *Sydney*
Prentice-Hall Canada Inc., *Toronto*
Prentice-Hall Hispanoamericana, S.A., *Mexico*
Prentice-Hall of India Private Limited, *New Delhi*
Prentice-Hall of Japan, Inc., *Tokyo*
Simon & Schuster Asia Pte. Ltd., *Singapore*
Editora Prentice-Hall do Brasil, Ltda., *Rio de Janeiro*

INSTRUCTOR'S SECTION

INTRODUCTION

The *Annotated Instructor's Edition* (AIE) of *Production and Operations Management: Focusing on Quality and Competitiveness* is available only to instructors. The AIE includes an Instructor's Section followed by the complete student edition of the text with marginal annotations for the instructor. A Solutions Manual is provided separately. The AIE has a number of unique features designed to assist the instructor in teaching the introductory production and operations management course. The following is a description of the special features of the AIE that are not part of the student version.

ANNOTATIONS

The AIE version of this text makes extensive use of annotations that appear in the margins. These annotations do not appear in the student version. Included are annotations for the following features.

- *Abbreviated solutions* are given for homework problems at the end of each chapter.
- *Teaching notes* offer suggestions and material to facilitate the learning process.
- *Alternate examples* to the examples in the text.
- *Video titles* indicate that a video is available to complement the text material.
- *Transparency titles* indicate text material that is available on a transparency master.

TEACHING NOTES

Each chapter in the Instructor's Section begins with a list of teaching notes that suggests important points in the chapter deserving extra attention, helpful ways to approach a topic, ways to promote in-class discussion and possible useful exercises. Annotations in the margins of the AIE indicate reference points for the teaching notes.

ALTERNATE EXAMPLES

Each chapter in the text includes numbered examples that primarily demonstrate the use of the quantitative techniques introduced in the text. The AIE provides alternatives to many of these examples. These alternate examples generally follow the same format as the text examples with a problem statement followed by a detailed solution. They enable the instructor to introduce fresh material into his or her lecture that is not in the text. Annotations in the margins of the AIE at the location of the textual example indicate reference points for the alternate examples.

VIDEOS

Following the *Alternate Examples* for most chapters is a brief description of supplementary videos that are available to qualified adopters (ask your Prentice-Hall representative). Annotations in the text margins of the AIE indicate where the videos might be shown. In most cases the videos are tied to *Gaining the Competitive Edge* application boxes throughout the text. Nine video cassettes encompassing seventeen different programs that accompany the text can be used with most of the chapters. Following is a brief summary of each of the video cassettes.

Total Quality Management. (Volume I) This video is part of a series of tapes produced by the Society of Manufacturing Engineers. The tape's duration is 29 minutes. Its subject is the TQM program at Kurt Manufacturing Company, a midsize supplier of precision machine parts based in Minneapolis. This tape is used in conjunction with Chapter 3 ("Quality Management"), Chapter 4 ("Statistical Quality Control"), and Chapter 13 ("Material Requirements Planning").

The Allyn and Bacon Plant Tour Video. This video cassette includes three programs. The first program (1) is "Federal Express: Setting the Pace for the 90s." It has a duration of 15 minutes, and describes Federal Express's air freight package-handling and distribution terminal, called the "Superhub," in Memphis, Tennessee. It can be used in conjunction with Chapter 1 ("Operations, Competitiveness, and Strategy") and Chapter 8 ("Location Analysis and Logistics Management"). Program 2 is "Milliken & Company: The Baldrige Award." It has a duration of 14.5 minutes. This tape provides a brief overview of the two 1989 Malcolm Baldrige Award winners: Milliken and Xerox Business Products. It can be used in conjunction with Chapter 3 ("Quality Management"). Program 3 is "Volvo Torslanda Plant." It has a duration of 22 minutes and provides a comprehensive tour of the Volvo production process at its Torslanda plant. Included are Volvo's pressing, welding, and paint operations. It can be used with Chapter 6 ("Process Planning and Technology Decisions").

Harley-Davidson, Building Better Motorcycles the American Way. This tape's duration is approximately 25 minutes. It focuses on Harley-Davidson's manufacturing processes and its success as the only U.S. manufacturer of motorcycles. It particularly emphasizes the company's overall commitment to quality through such things as product design (CAD), engineering, and statistical process control. It can be used in conjunction with Chapter 1 ("Operations, Competitiveness, and Strategy"), Chapter 4 ("Statistical Quality Control"), Chapter 5 ("Product and Service Design"), and Chapter 7 ("Facility Layout").

Malcolm Baldrige Awards, Quest for Excellence. This video cassette is from a series of Baldrige Award videos presented by the U.S. Department of Commerce, the Technology Administration, the National Institute of Standards and Technology, and the American Society for Quality Control. It includes overviews of the three 1991 Malcolm Baldrige Award winners, Zytec Corporation, Solectron Corporation, and Marlow Industries, Inc. It has a duration of approximately 17 minutes and can be used in conjunction with Chapter 3 ("Quality Management") and Chapter 6 ("Process Planning and Technology Decisions").

Malcolm Baldrige Awards, Quest for Excellence V. This video cassette is another in the Malcolm Baldrige award-winner's series, including the 1992 winners, AT&T Network Systems Group, AT&T Universal Card Services, Granite Rock Company, Texas Instruments, Inc.—Defense Systems and Electronics Group and, the Ritz Carlton Hotel. The tape's duration is 18.5 minutes and it can be used in conjunction with Chapter 1 ("Operations, Competitiveness, and Strategy"), Chapter 3 ("Quality Management"), and Chapter 9 ("Jobs: Design, Analysis, and Measurement").

LTV's Flexible Manufacturing Cell. This video cassette describes the operation of a flexible manufacturing cell at LTV's Dallas, Texas, plant. It has a duration of 10 minutes. It can be used in conjunction with Chapter 7 ("Facility Layout").

CNN Work in Progress. This video cassette is a 1-hour documentary that appeared on the CNN network. It is hosted by CNN news anchor Bernard Shaw and the narrator is television news reporter Stephen Frazier. The documentary focuses on the future of the workplace and jobs in America. It includes short segments on different companies and employees, including a cartoonist for the Los Angeles Herald Examiner, Foundry Services Company, Harley-Davidson, the Ritz Carlton Hotel, IC Designs, and Microsoft, among others. One particular segment on Quad Graphics, Inc., a printing company in Milwaukee, focuses on job training and employee education. Another segment focuses on employee empowerment at Harley-Davidson and the Ritz Carlton Hotel. The final segment is on Microsoft and its unique corporate structure that has little bureaucracy and no middle management. Included are comments by Microsoft chairperson, William Gates. This tape can be used in conjunction with Chapter 9 ("Jobs: Design, Analysis, and Measurement").

Consortium for Mathematics and Its Applications (COMAP). This video was originally produced for the series "For All Practical Purposes," which was shown on public television and funded by the Annenberg/CPB Project. It includes five programs related to quantitative methods. Four of these programs (1, 2, 4, and 5) are directly applicable to material in this text. Program 1, "Management Science Overview," describes the use of various quantitative methods for operational decision making. Applications are provided for NASA's Apollo moon project, Avis Car Rental, and a convenience store in Boston. It has a duration of approximately 20 minutes. This tape can be used with Chapter 2 ("Operational Decision Making"). Program 2, "Juicy Problems," is an introductory overview of linear programming. It describes several applications of linear programming, including its use at American Airlines for airline scheduling. It has a duration of approximately 28 minutes. It can be used in conjunction with the Chapter 2 Supplement ("Linear Programming"). Program 3, "Juggling Machines," demonstrates how a news show gets everything put together in time for the broadcast. It can be used with Chapter 14 ("Scheduling"). Program 4, "Trains, Planes, and Critical Paths," is an introduction to network models and scheduling. It has a duration of 16 minutes and can be used with Chapter 17 ("Project Management"). Program 5, "Statistical Quality Control," describes how control charts are used at Frito-Lay to monitor the salt content of Ruffles potato chips. There is also a segment on W. E. Deming and his contributions to quality control with some historical footage. This tape is approximately 14 minutes long and can be used with Chapter 4 ("Statistical Quality Control").

TIMS Edelman Awards Tape. (Volume II) This video cassette includes three programs describing the application of management science techniques at Reynolds Metals Company, Citgo Petroleum, and L.L. Bean. Each of the programs is an edited version of a presentation made by the company for the TIMS/Franz Edelman Award competition. Program 1, "Reynolds Metals," describes the use of management science techniques on a broad scale for the development of a central dispatch facility for Reynolds' truck carriers. It has a duration of approximately 20 minutes and is used with Chapter 2 ("Operational Decision Making"), the Chapter 12 Supplement ("Simulation"), and Chapter 14 ("Scheduling"). Program 2, "Citgo Petroleum," is similar to the Reynolds Metals Co. tape in that it describes the widespread use of management science techniques in the company. It has a duration of about 20 minutes and can be used with the Chapter 2 Supplement ("Linear Programming") and Chapter 10 ("Forecasting"). Program 3, "L.L. Bean Company" describes the use of management science to solve problems in L.L. Bean's telephone catalog ordering service. It lasts about 20 minutes and is used with Chapter 11 ("Aggregate Production and Capacity Planning"), and Chapter 16 ("Waiting Line Models and Service Improvement").

Following is a summary of the videos that are used in the text and their location.

Chapter 1: Operations, Competitiveness, and Strategy

Video 1.1 1992 *Malcolm Baldrige Awards, Quest for Excellence V*

Video 1.2 *Harley-Davidson, Building Better Motorcycles the American Way*

Video 1.3 *The Allyn and Bacon Plant Tour Video,* Program 1: "Federal Express"

Chapter 2: Operational Decision Making
Video 2.1 *TIMS Edelman Awards Tape,* Program 1: "Reynolds Metals"
Video 2.2 *COMAP,* Program 1: "Management Science Overview"

Chapter 2 Supplement: Linear Programming
Video S2.1 *COMAP,* Program 2: "Juicy Petroleum"
Video S2.2 *TIMS Edelman Award Tape,* Program 2: "Citgo Petroleum"

Chapter 3: Quality Management
Video 3.1 *Total Quality Management*
Video 3.2 *The Allyn and Bacon Plant Tour Video,* Program 2: "Milliken & Company: The Baldrige Award"
Video 3.3 1991 *Malcolm Baldrige Awards, Quest for Excellence*
Video 3.4 1992 *Malcolm Baldrige Awards, Quest for Excellence V*

Chapter 4: Statistical Quality Control
Video 4.1 *Total Quality Management*
Video 4.2 *COMAP,* Program 5: "Statistical Quality Control"
Video 4.3 *Harley-Davidson, Building Better Motorcycles the American Way*

Chapter 5: Product and Service Design
Video 5.1 *Harley Davidson, Building Better Motorcycles the American Way*

Chapter 6: Process Planning and Technology Decisions
Video 6.1 1991 *Malcolm Baldrige Awards, Quest for Excellence*
Video 6.2 *The Allyn and Bacon Plant Tour Video,* Program 3: "Volvo Torslanda Plant"

Chapter 7: Facility Layout
Video 7.1 *Harley-Davidson, Building Better Motorcycles the American Way*
Video 7.2 *LTV's Flexible Manufacturing Cell*

Chapter 8: Location Analysis and Logistics Measurement
Video 8.1 *The Allyn and Bacon Plant Tour Video,* Program 1: "Federal Express"

Chapter 9: Jobs: Design, Analysis, and Measurement
Video 9.1 *CNN Work in Progress*
Video 9.2 *CNN Work in Progress*
Video 9.3 1992 *Malcolm Baldrige Awards, Quest for Excellence V*

Chapter 10: Forecasting
Video 10.1 *TIMS Edelman Awards Tape,* Program 2: "Citgo Petroleum"

Chapter 11: Aggregate Production and Capacity Planning
Video 11.1 *TIMS Edelman Awards Tape,* Program 3: "L.L. Bean"

Chapter 12 Supplement: Simulation
Video S12.1 *TIMS Edelman Awards Tape,* Program 1: "Reynolds Metals"

Chapter 13: Material Requirements Planning
Video 13.1 *Total Quality Management*

Chapter 14: Scheduling
Video 14.1 *COMAP,* Program 3: "Juggling Machines"
Video 14.2 *TIMS Edelman Awards Tape,* Program 1: "Reynolds Metals"

Chapter 16: Waiting Line Models and Service Improvement
Video 16.1 *TIMS Edelman Awards Tape,* Program 3: "L.L. Bean"

Chapter 17: Project Management
Video 17.1 *COMAP,* Program 4: "Trains, Planes, and Critical Paths"

THE SOLUTIONS MANUAL

Located in the Solutions Manual are "Answers to Questions" for the questions section that is found at the end of each chapter of the student edition. This text contains over 340 discussion questions.

Following the "Answers to Questions" are complete detailed solutions for all homework problems in the student edition. Approximately 375 end-of-chapter problems are included. Abbreviated solutions, where space allows, are found in the margins of the Instructor's Edition. Homework problems that are more difficult, that require more time, or that perhaps have a unique twist to them requiring a little additional thought are denoted by a star ★ in the AIE version of the text. This is meant as a guideline to help the instructor prepare homework assignments. Problems for which a computer solution is suggested or required are denoted by a personal computer icon in the margin of both the AIE and the student versions of the text. "Solutions to Problems" are followed by detailed "Case Solutions" for the 24 cases in the text.

Annotated Instructor's Edition

PRODUCTION AND OPERATIONS MANAGEMENT

Focusing on Quality and Competitiveness

1 OPERATIONS, COMPETITIVENESS, AND STRATEGY

TEACHING NOTES

Teaching Note 1.1 Class Participation

Give the students a list of operating systems and see whether they can identify the inputs, outputs, and transformation process. Try these: grade school, restaurant, sawmill, consultant, airlines, prison, taxi service, IRS, bank, university, physician. Then ask them what they expect to get out of this course (output), what they are willing to put into the course (input), and how they think the transformation process ought to occur.

Teaching Note 1.2 Student Assignments

Do your students seem at all concerned about international competition? Try these assignments to help make them more aware of their surroundings:

- Have students look up U.S. productivity figures, GDP/GNP, and any other measures of competitiveness they can find in *Statistical Abstracts of the United States, Monthly Labor Review, Quarterly National Accounts*, or *Fortune's World 500* (it comes out every summer). Have them show the results graphically and comment on any trends. Do the data differ from different sources?
- Have the students collect newspaper and magazine articles about competitiveness for just 2 weeks. How many different articles can they find? Are the views encouraging or discouraging?
- Ask the students why they think the United States has had (or does have) competitive problems, then have them find data to support their assumptions. How does their list compare to the MIT list in the text?

Teaching Note 1.3 A Video Suggestion

The "Made in America" four-tape video series, narrated by Robert Reich and originally shown on PBS, explores the industries referenced in the MIT Report on Competitiveness. At 58 minutes each, all four videos would probably take too long, but showing one video would give the students a good flavor for the state of industry. The titles of the videos are 1. *Who's the Enemy?* 2. *The Automobile Story*, 3. *Winners and Losers*, and 4. *National Industrial Policy*. They are available from Films for the Humanities and Sciences, Inc., Box 2053, Princeton, NJ 08543-2053. The copyright is 1992.

Teaching Note 1.4 An Industry Analysis

Cooperation within industries, along the logistical chain, between workers and management, between government and industry, and between companies and their customers have changed significantly over the past five to ten years. Divide the class into groups and assign a different industry to each group. Have them explore this issue and report back to class on their findings.

Teaching Note 1.5 Attitudes Toward Workers

The following quotes from Frederick Taylor and Konosuka Matsushita illustrate different views of the worker's role in operations. In fairness to Frederick Taylor, his quote was made more than 100 years ago, when workers were uneducated—and in many cases—did not even speak the same language. (More than fifty different languages were spoken at Ford's Rouge plant.) Still, his views are the mindset upon which American management has based its actions towards workers for almost 100 years.

> Hardly a competent workman can be found who does not devote a considerable amount of time to studying just how slowly he can work and still convince his employer that he is going at a good pace. Under our system a worker is told just what to do and how he is to do it. Any improvement he makes upon the orders given him is fatal to his success.
>
> —Frederick Taylor, Father of Scientific Management

> For you, the essence of management is getting the ideas out of the heads of the bosses and into the hands of labor. Your bosses do the thinking while the workers wield the screwdrivers. Business, we know, is now so complex and difficult, the survival of firms so hazardous in an environment increasingly unpredictable, competitive and fraught with danger, that our continued existence depends on the day-to-day mobilization of every ounce of intelligence.
>
> —Konosuka Matsushita, founder of Panasonic

Source: Robert Harvey, "Another Hero Comes Tumbling Down," *Metalworking News*, 1987.

Teaching Note 1.6 Attitudes Toward Manufacturing

Wickham Skinner, manufacturing strategist at Harvard University, (now retired) describes the attitude of top management toward manufacturing as follows:

> To many executives, manufacturing and the production function is a necessary nuisance—it soaks up capital in facilities and inventories, it resists changes in products and schedules, its quality is never as good as it should be, and its people are unsophisticated, tedious, detail-oriented and unexciting.

Source: Wickham Skinner, *Manufacturing: The Formidable Competitive Weapon*, New York: John Wiley, 1985.

Teaching Note 1.7 Realizing Manufacturing's Strategic Importance

The realization of manufacturing's strategic importance came slowly to U.S. firms. The following quote, taken from a Ford executive's testimony before Congress in 1978, reflects the typical corporate attitude toward manufacturing and the competitive challenge:

> All the products and processes used by the Japanese motor industry are known to us . . . their success depends on achieving *economies of scale* based on a large home market, on a different attitude adopted by labor in their industry, and also on their apparent success in containing inflation more effectively than we have been able to do in this country.

Source: Select Committee on Science and Technology, 1977/78, "Innovation, Research and Development in Japanese Science-Based Industry," August, 1978.

Five years later, after more than 250 visits to Japan, Ford acknowledged that the Japanese advantage came from a strategic focus on manufacturing. Their view is confirmed in the following summary from an analysis of the automobile industry:

> Most explanations of the Japanese advantage in production costs and product quality emphasize the impact of automation, the strong support of central government, and the pervasive influence of national culture. No doubt, these factors have played an important role, but the primary sources of this advantage are found instead in the Japanese execution of a well-designed *strategy* based on the shrewd use of manufacturing excellence. The Japanese cost and quality advantage originates in the painstaking strategic management of people, materials, and equipment—that is, in superior manufacturing performance.

Source: William Abernathy, Kim Clark, and Alan Kantrow, "The New Industrial Competition," Harvard Business Review, September/October 1983, pp. 73–74.

Teaching Note 1.8 Visions

Have the students collect corporate vision statements from annual reports. For example, Norfolk Southern's vision statement is: "Be the safest, most customer-focused, and successful transportation company in the world." Does your university publish a vision statement?

Teaching Note 1.9 Order Winners and Order Qualifiers

Ask the students to describe the selection process they used for a recent major purchase. What factors qualified a product or service to be considered? What was the one factor that made the difference in their purchasing decision? If they have trouble thinking of an example, ask them why they chose this university, this major, or the seat they are sitting in.

VIDEOS

Video 1.1 *1992 Malcolm Baldrige Awards, Quest For Excellence V*

This video profiles the 1992 Malcolm Baldrige Award Winners, AT&T UCS, AT&T Transmissions, Texas Instruments, and the Ritz-Carlton Hotel. It accompanies the lead-in to Chapter 1 and provides an upbeat way to begin the course and start the students thinking about quality.

Video 1.2 *Harley-Davidson, Building Better Motorcycles the American Way*

This video produced by Harley-Davidson can be used with the application box "U.S. Manufacturers Fight Back." It describes Harley's comeback and also shows quite a bit of their manufacturing operations.

Video 1.3 *The Allyn and Bacon Plant Tour Video,* Program 1: "Federal Express, Setting the Pace for the 90s"

This video can be used with the application box "The Technology Edge" to illustrate a successful strategy, competing on technology. The video highlights several of Federal Express's technological accomplishments, such as their distribution center, COSMOS network, and Super Trackers.

2 OPERATIONAL DECISION-MAKING TECHNIQUES

TEACHING NOTES

Teaching Note 2.1 Quality

As the title of this text suggests, there is a strong emphasis and focus on quality throughout the text. Instances in the text where quality is discussed relative to the topics in a chapter are highlighted by an icon—the letter Q—in the margin.

Teaching Note 2.2 Scanning the Text

It is beneficial to have the students scan the text and read a few homework problems from the chapters assigned on their course syllabus. This gives the students an idea of the kinds of operational problems they will be solving during the course, even though they do not yet know how to solve them, which can spur interest.

Teaching Note 2.3 Quantitative Techniques Involve a Logical, Systematic Approach to Problem Solving

Impress on the students that quantitative techniques provide a logical, systematic approach to decision making. As such, they are valuable in that they teach them a way in which to approach problems of all kinds. Although the students may not immediately perceive the relevance of these techniques, the techniques are still beneficial in that they teach students a logical approach to different problems. The approach to decision making as described in this section generally follows what is known as the "scientific" approach to problem solving.

Teaching Note 2.4 The Increasing Popularity of Quantitative Techniques

It is a good time to note that, because of the advances in computer technology, quantitative techniques are growing in popularity. Point out that only about ten years ago the applicability of models and techniques was somewhat limited because often no means were available to solve large, complex problems and computing systems were expensive. The rapid advances in computer technology have now made such computation not only possible, but also widespread because of the low cost. Even the smallest businesses now have the computing ability and inexpensive software to use these techniques. This is also a good time to mention the use of software in the text, if it is going to be used.

Teaching Note 2.5 Decision Analysis as a Reflection of How Decisions Are Made

There is a tendency for the teacher and the student to focus exclusively on the technical aspects of the decision-making criteria in this chapter. When that occurs, the students sometimes begin to question the applicability of the criteria in real-world situations—that is, they begin to ask if they would really sit down in a real decision-making situation, define the various states of nature and outcomes, construct a payoff table, apply one of the decision criteria, and make a decision based on the result. Actually, some decision makers or analysts do exactly that. However, whether or not the student will ever apply the actual criteria described in the chapter, this study of decision analysis has great benefit in that it describes decision situations and how people logically approach decisions. Students may not formally construct a payoff table or compute an expected value, but decision makers do (perhaps subconsciously) consider the outcomes of different decisions, given their "guess" as to what conditions will exist in the future. They also apply "criteria" (either risky or conservative) that reflect the mathematical criteria described in this chapter. So the students are not simply learning techniques in this chapter; they are studying a logical process of decision making so that they will be able to make more effective decisions by applying the logic, if not the actual techniques.

Teaching Note 2.6 Involving the Student

This is a relatively easy topic with which to involve the student in class discussion since everyone makes decisions on a daily basis. Ask the student to relate several recent (important) decisions and to describe the process they went through in making the decision. Ask students to categorize themselves as a conservative or risky decision maker, and ask why they place themselves in that category. Ask students if they ever try to predict the chances of what the future will bring. Set up hypothetical decision situations, such as investing money or making a major purchase, and have students assess the decisions. Have students make a decision for some of the chapter problems without applying the decision criteria and then compare their decision with the decision when the criteria are used.

Teaching Note 2.7 Determining Probabilities for States of Nature

A good starting point for decision making with probabilities is to ask students to identify real decision situations in which such probabilities are actually used and how probabilities are determined.

Teaching Note 2.8 The Value of Information

A good discussion point with the topic of expected value of information is to ask the students what types of information are paid for in the real world and how they think this information should be valued.

Teaching Note 2.9 AB:POM Computer Software

This text can be used with or without computer software. The chapters are structured so that sections and problems can be easily omitted if computer software is not used. However, if a software package is used in conjunction with the text, many of the chapters contain examples of computer usage, including example screens. If AB:POM is being used in this course, this is a good time to introduce the package through Appendix A. This appendix provides a tutorial on how to get started on AB:POM.

Teaching Note 2.10 *Gaining the Competitive Edge* Boxes

This chapter contains two *Gaining the Competitive Edge* boxes describing real-world applications. These applications, as well as others throughout the text, are adapted from articles in various journals, magazines, and videos. Since most real-world problems are too lengthy and complex to include in the text as examples and homework problems, these applications are important in showing the student real operational applications and their impacts. These applications are brief adaptations that focus on the problem, the general solution approach, and the outcome, *not* on the technical aspects of the application. The student should be encouraged to go to the library and read the articles from which these applications are adapted. In fact, a good extra assignment here or in any chapter is to have the students write a one-page summary of a journal application not included in this text. A number of these boxes in the text also have accompanying videos, which are identified by annotations located in the margin adjacent to the box in the Annotated Instructor's Edition.

Teaching Note 2.11 Applications of MIS and DSS

Decision support systems are sometimes difficult for the student to conceptualize. For that reason, applications can help the student understand how DSS and MIS are utilized in the real world. Numerous examples are available in the journal *Interfaces*, published by TIMS/ORSA.

ALTERNATE EXAMPLES

Alternate Example 2.1

The following alternative to Example 2.1 in the text employs three states of nature. An investor is going to purchase one of three types of real estate. The investor must decide among an apartment building, an office building, and a warehouse. The future states of nature that will determine how much profit the investor will make are good, fair, and poor economic conditions. The profits that will result from each decision in the event of each state of nature are shown in the following payoff table.

	States of Nature		
Decision (Purchase)	*Good Economic Conditions*	*Fair Economic Conditions*	*Poor Economic Conditions*
Apartment	$50,000	$25,000	$10,000
Office	100,000	30,000	–40,000
Warehouse	30,000	15,000	–10,000

The appropriate decisions according to the various decision-making criteria are as follows.

1. Maximax: office building, $100,000
2. Maximin: apartment building, $10,000
3. Minimax regret: warehouse, $20,000
4. Hurwicz ($\alpha = 0.40$): apartment building, $26,000
5. Equal likelihood: office building, $29,700

Alternate Example 2.2

The following example is an alternative to Example 2.2 in the text. Referring to Alternative Example 2.1, compute the expected value for each decision given. The probabilities of the three states of nature are as follows:

Good economic conditions = 0.20
Fair economic conditions = 0.70
Poor economic conditions = 0.10

The expected values are

EV (apartment building) = $28,500
EV (office building) = $37,000*
EV (warehouse) = $15,500

VIDEOS

Video 2.1 *TIMS Edelman Award Tape*, "Reynolds Metals"

The TIMS videos are edited versions of presentations made at an ORSA/TIMS national meeting as part of the Franz Edelman Award competition for outstanding applications of management science. The tapes typically consist of verbal presentations by one or more speakers, accompanied by visual aids such as videos and slides.

This video accompanies the introductory application at the beginning of this chapter describing the application of management science at Reynolds Metals Company. This application was selected for this chapter because it shows how quantitative techniques can be used for operational decision making. It focuses primarily on the central dispatch facility at Reynolds, which selects and schedules truck carriers. The tape is approximately 20 minutes in length and has minimal technical material; that is, it is mostly descriptive.

Video 2.2 *COMAP*, Program 1: "Management Science Overview"

Program 1 of the COMAP video is an overview of management science. It is 19 minutes long and is a good introduction to the use of quantitative techniques for operational decision making. It describes management science within the context of applications at NASA, Eastern Airlines, Avis Car Rental, and a convenience store in Boston; however, it is very nontechnical and quite appropriate for this stage of an introductory POM text.

2 SUPPLEMENT: LINEAR PROGRAMMING

TEACHING NOTES

Teaching Note S2.1 Achieving an Objective in a Resource-Constrained Environment

Explain the concept of attempting to achieve an objective in an environment where unlimited achievement is not possible because of resource constraints. Note that this is a frequent occurrence in businesses and organizations, and give examples. A good way to encourage discussion is to ask the class for an example of a product made by a specific company, such as cars by Chrysler, and then pose the question, "What is Chrysler's objective?" Next ask, "Why doesn't Chrysler make an unlimited number of cars?" Then ask, "Name as many constraints as you can think of that keeps it from making an unlimited number of cars."

Teaching Note S2.2 Formulating the Model

The student will have a tendency to try and "swallow a formulation problem whole." A systematic approach should be developed for attacking a formulation problem. One such approach is first to decide if it is a maximization or minimization problem and then to determine what decision the model requires. From that define the decision variables and then formulate the constraints. Students should be encouraged at first to just formulate the models without trying to convert them into proper form for eventual solution.

Teaching Note S2.3 Determining the Feasible Solution Space

After students learn how to plot the constraint lines, they sometimes have problems determining which side of the line corresponds to ≥ or ≤ and where the feasible solution space is. It helps to suggest to the students that they should test different values for the variables to see which points violate the constraints and which do not. (Note that the < and > inequality signs also can be thought of as arrows that point to the side of the constraint line that is feasible.)

Teaching Note S2.4 Locating the Optimal Extreme Point

After developing the graph of a linear programming problem and identifying the solution space, tell the class to imagine that the classroom in which they are sitting is the solution space, and stand in a corner at the front. Explain that you are at the origin, and start walking toward one of the classroom walls. Next, ask the class how far you can walk. The obvious answer is only to the wall; explain that the wall is like the boundary of the solution space containing the farthest points from the origin. Then ask, "If I go in any direction, what is the farthest point I can travel?" Students will indicate a corner of the room. Explain that the corner is a protrusion that represents the farthest point in the feasible solution space.

Teaching Note S2.5 Graphical Solution Methods

There are two basic methods for determining an optimal solution with a graph: solving for all corner point solutions or seeing which point the objective function line touches last as it leaves the solution area. It should be pointed out to the students that the graphical method, in general, is a poor way to find a solution to a linear programming problem and that the main value derived from graphical analysis is to see how a solution comes about. Allow students to use either method, whichever they are comfortable with, although experience shows that solving at every corner point is the most fail-safe method. Students can sometimes be poor at drawing graphs, which can make it difficult to determine the last point the objective function line touches.

Teaching Note S2.6 The Purpose of Adding Slack Variables

The students should not simply think slack variables are added to a ≤ constraint so that the problem can be solved. Slack variables have a meaning and their addition to a constraint reflects a real occurrence in the model, such as resources left unused.

Teaching Note S2.7 Computer Solution Versus the Simplex Method

It is difficult for students to solve even the smallest simplex problem without making an arithmetic error, at least when they first start out. In addition, although the simplex method is not overly complex, it requires a number of steps and has a number of variations for different problem types. As a result, several weeks during the term are normally required to learn adequately and practice the manual simplex method. Since most instructors do not wish to spend that much time on this type of topic in an introductory POM course, we have excluded it from this supplement on linear programming and rely instead on computer solution. For those interested in a detailed presentation of the simplex method, the "Just-in-Time" publishing feature offered by Allyn & Bacon will allow chapters on the simplex method from *Introduction to Management Science*, 4th edition, by Bernard W. Taylor III, to be included with this text.

VIDEOS

Video S2.1 *COMAP*, Program 2, "Juicy Problems"

The second COMAP program is an introduction to linear programming. It describes how linear programming is used at American Air Lines for flight scheduling. It also uses a mixture problem involving blending juices for New England Apple Products. Although this is a real company, the presentation is at a very basic level and provides an excellent general overview of linear programming. The tape is 28 minutes long; the first part deals with model formulation, whereas the second part deals with graphical solutions, followed by a brief, nonmathematical discussion of the simplex method.

Video S2.2 *TIMS Edelman Award Tape*, Program 2: "Citgo Petroleum"

This video accompanies the *Gaining the Competitive Edge* box in this chapter describing the application of linear programming for refinery blending at Citgo Petroleum. The presentation is approximately 20 minutes long and includes a description of other management science applications at Citgo besides linear programming.

3 QUALITY MANAGEMENT

TEACHING NOTES

Teaching Note 3.1 Quality After World War II

After World War II the demand for consumer goods increased dramatically, while at the same time manufacturers were shifting from military production to consumer production. This created large shortages for consumer goods. In a time of shortages, quality will almost always decline. In their desire to get products, consumers will accept lower quality, and in an effort to produce as much as possible and meet schedules, manufacturers will take shortcuts with quality. This is the situation that resulted in America at the end of World War II. In addition, there was little international competition, especially competition that was perceived to be of higher quality and that most Americans could afford. It was unfortunate and ironic that this situation arose, since the infrastructure for quality control and management was in place in many companies following the war because of the quality requirements set by the government and armed forces.

Teaching Note 3.2 Made in Japan

During the several decades preceding World War II the Japanese military establishment channeled most of the country's resources into building a military machine. Japanese armaments, which were subsequently used in World War II with devastating effect, were of high quality and competitive with military armaments produced by the allied nations. During this same period the Japanese civilian economy received low priorities for funds and materials, which seriously handicapped their ability to produce high-quality consumer products. The export of the resulting poor-quality products was so extensive that the Japanese gained a reputation for making cheap, shoddy products. The term *made in Japan* became synonymous with poor quality. After the war the Japanese found their reputation for poor quality to be a major obstacle in their ability to compete in world markets, so it became obvious to them that they would need a complete and total commitment to quality in order to change their image. This created an eager atmosphere of acceptance for the ideas and philosophies about quality provided by W. E. Deming when he visited Japan as a consultant after the war.

Teaching Note 3.3 Operational Functions and Quality Management

The impact of quality management on some of the operational functions discussed in these sections of the text are also addressed, often in greater detail, in other chapters of the text. For example, the relationship between quality management and product design is discussed in greater detail in Chapter 5 ("Product and Service Design"). The relationship of quality to job design, personnel, and employees is also considered in Chapter 9 ("Jobs: Design, Analysis, and Measurement"). Quality and inspection are discussed in greater depth in Chapter 4 ("Statistical Quality Control"), whereas quality and shipping are addressed in Chapter 8 ("Location Analysis and Logistics Management"). These topics can all be located and incorporated into lectures with Chapter 3 by using the index and Q, icons, which highlight points of quality focus in the text.

Teaching Note 3.4 Recycling

Important aspects in the design of a number of products in recent years are recyclability and/or environmental safety. Various types of packaging and containers are now designed so that the used product can be recycled or is not harmful to the environment. For example, soft drinks are designed with plastic containers that are recyclable, and products such as detergents and antifreeze are designed to be biodegradable. Many automobile companies now advertise "asbestos-free" brakes. Although these product features may not be thought of as strictly related to quality, consumers often connect products they perceive to be environmentally "friendly" with good quality. This aspect of product design is discussed in more detail in Chapter 5 ("Product and Service Design").

Teaching Note 3.5 Design Teams

A recent trend in TQM is to use design teams for product design. Design teams include members from various functions and operations in the organization that can effect product quality such as engineering, quality, purchasing, manufacturing and marketing. For example, members from purchasing can provide input on supplier capabilities, and frequently representatives from the actual suppliers are members of the team. Other members might include marketing representatives to indicate consumer preferences and the quality features most likely to appeal to consumer tastes and demands. In some cases important consumers are informal members of the design team. The use of design teams at Chrysler and Ford is described in the beginning applications section of Chapter 17 (Project Management), and it is also discussed in greater detail in Chapter 5 (Product and Service Design).

Teaching Note 3.6 Employee Involvement at Chrysler

At Chrysler a "reverse appraisal" program was initiated in 1988 to give employees a greater sense of involvement and participation in the workplace. With reverse appraisal, performance is appraised from the bottom up, enabling employees to provide direct feedback to managers on performance. The performance appraisal is conducted much like student evaluations of instructors at many universities. A questionnaire was developed with six categories of questions, including teamwork, communication, quality, leadership, planning, and workforce development. A sample question in the teamwork category is, "My supervisor promotes cooperation and teamwork within our work group." A sample question in the quality category is, "My supervisor demonstrates meaningful commitment to our work group." Questions are answered on a scale from 1 to 5, with 1 representing "almost never" and 5 representing "almost always." The anonymous appraisal results are seen only by the manager, his or her immediate boss, and a third party, who conducted the appraisal. Managers subsequently meet with their employees to discuss and clarify the appraisal results and develop an action plan for improvement.

Source: Santora, Joyce E., "Rating the Boss at Chrysler," *Personnel Journal* 71, no. 5 (May 1992): 38–45.

Teaching Note 3.7 W. E. Deming and Statistical Process Control

During the mid-1930s, W. E. Deming took a one-year leave of absence from the U.S. Department of Agriculture to study statistical theory under Ronald A. Fisher, as mentioned in the text. After he returned to the USDA, he organized a series of evening lectures on statistical theory for the USDA's graduate school of continuing education. Deming invited a number of prominent international scholars to lecture, and it was in this forum that Deming promoted Walter Shewhart's work on statistical process control. Shewhart delivered a four-part lecture, which Deming helped compile into the book that for many years was the bible of statistical quality control, *Statistical Method from the Viewpoint of Quality Control*. Through this lecture series, Deming became well known to many prominent individuals who attended the lectures, including Milton Friedman, the future Nobel laureate in Economics.

Source: Gabor, A., "Deming Demystifies the Black Art of Statistics," *Quality Progress* (December 1991): 26–28.

Teaching Note 3.8 Joseph Juran

Joseph Juran worked as an engineer at the Hawthorne Works at Western Electric Company, the manufacturing arm of the Bell Telephone System, in the 1920s. He worked in close association with some of the pioneers in quality at Bell Laboratories, including Walter Shewhart, Harold Dodge, and George Edwards. During World War II he worked as assistant lend-lease administrator and assistant foreign economic administrator.

Teaching Note 3.9 Readings About Baldrige Award Winners

A supplement available with this text is the book *Profiles of Malcolm Baldrige Award Winners*, published by Allyn and Bacon. This is a 127-page paperback that provides an overview of the Baldrige Award criteria, history, and objectives, followed by individual descriptions of the award-winning companies from 1988 through 1991. Also included are descriptions of an additional ten companies that did not win the award but whose participation in the competition enhanced their quality performance.

Teaching Note 3.10 Winning the Baldrige Award at Xerox

Xerox's receipt of the Malcolm Baldrige National Quality Award in 1989 was the culmination of a total quality management program initiated ten years earlier. The program began in 1979 with the establishment of benchmarks so that Xerox could measure its own products, services, and practices against their competitors as well as companies known as leaders in quality. This led to the development of the "Quality of Work Life Team" in 1980. In 1981 Xerox started training their suppliers in the use of statistical quality control methods. In 1982 employee-involvement groups, similar to the quality of work life team, were started for product development, and in 1983 these two team concepts were combined into a corporate-wide movement. In 1984 Xerox pulled its previous quality activities together to form its "Leadership Through Quality" program, and by 1985 all senior and middle managers had completed training in the program. By 1986 Xerox had more than 2,500 quality improvement teams in place throughout its organization. In 1987 company priorities were shifted to focus on customer satisfaction. By 1988 all 100,000 Xerox employees were trained in the "Leadership Through Quality" program and were performing under common goals and a quality environment. In 1989 Xerox established a team to prepare its application for the Baldrige Award, which it won, and in 1990 Xerox used the award findings to develop plans for future quality improvement.

Source: Fenwick, A. C., "Five Easy Lessons," *Quality Progress* 24, no. 10 (1991): 63–66.

Teaching Note 3.11 Additional Readings About ISO 9000

Profile of ISO 9000 is a 217-page paperback book published by Allyn and Bacon that offers an in-depth overview of ISO 9000. It describes the ISO 9000 standards and the accreditation process in detail and documents the experience of a number of companies that have sought and achieved ISO 9000 certification. It provides advice on how to achieve ISO 9000 certification and describes the impact ISO 9000 can have on companies who compete in international markets.

Teaching Note 3.12 The Origination of ISO 9000 Standards

Following World War II, the Air Force, in reviewing their military performance during the war, came to the conclusion that their reliance on inspection to ensure quality was not entirely effective. As a result the Air Force embarked on a new approach by establishing a plan for quality assurance and making sure contractors conformed to the plan via close surveillance. The Department of Defense later adopted this same concept in its standard MIL-Q-9858, which subsequently, in revised form, was embodied in the ISO 9000 series of standards.

Teaching Note 3.13 Personal Quality Management

An interesting student exercise for this chapter is to have students define a personal TQM program for themselves either as an individual or as a student. They should be encouraged to employ the principles and aspects of quality management discussed in this chapter. For example, they might analyze the costs of quality as they relate to themselves on a personal basis and how they might measure the impact of improved quality on their own productivity. A useful source of information on this topic is a series of five articles entitled "The Pursuit of Quality Through Personal Change," by Harry I. Forsha, that appeared in the first five 1992 issues (January–May) of *Quality Progress*. These articles are excerpted from this author's book of the same title. The articles consider the process of continuous quality improvement on a personal basis, including (1) problem identification, (2) problem analysis, (3) planning, (4) data collection, (5) interpretation, (6) action, and (7) appraisal.

VIDEOS

Video 3.1 *Total Quality Management*

This video is one of a series of tapes produced by the Society for Manufacturing Engineers (SME). Its subject is the TQM program at Kurt Manufacturing Company, a midsize manufacturer and supplier of precision machine parts based in Minneapolis. The program focuses on product design, engineering, and statistical process control and the necessity to satisfy the customer. It addresses many of the TQM concepts and principles introduced in this chapter. It lasts 29 minutes, and it accompanies the application box titled "TQM at Kurt Manufacturing" in this chapter.

Video 3.2 *The Allyn and Bacon Plant Tour Video,* Program 2: "Milliken & Company: The Baldrige Award"

This video provides a brief overview of the two winners of the 1989 Malcolm Baldrige Awards: Milliken and Xerox Business Products. Along with the other two Baldrige Award videos available with this text, it provides an excellent insight into the philosophies of companies that have been internationally recognized for the success of their TQM programs. The tape's duration is approximately 14.5 minutes.

Video 3.3 1991 *Malcolm Baldrige Awards, Quest for Excellence*

This video is the second in the Malcolm Baldrige series of tapes available with this text. It describes the three 1991 winners of the Baldrige Award: Zytec Corporation, Solectron Corporation, and Marlow Industries, Inc. It has a duration of approximately 17 minutes and provides an excellent overview of less well known and somewhat smaller companies recognized for their successful TQM programs.

Video 3.4 1992 *Malcolm Baldrige Awards, Quest For Excellence V*

This is the third and most recent of the Baldrige Award videos that are available with this text. It provides an overview of the five 1992 Baldrige Award winners: AT&T Network Systems Group, AT&T Universal Card Services, Granite Rock Company, Texas Instruments, Inc.—Defense Systems and Electronics Group, and the Ritz Carlton Hotel. This program is interesting because of the diversity of the companies—a rock company and an exclusive hotel. (The Ritz Carlton Hotel is also featured in the *CNN Work in Progress* video that accompanies Chapter 9.) Its duration is 18.5 minutes and it accompanies the application box in this chapter titled "The 1992 Malcolm Baldrige Award Winners."

4 STATISTICAL QUALITY CONTROL

TEACHING NOTES

Teaching Note 4.1 The Evolution of Statistical Quality Control

The popularity and use of statistical quality control techniques grew enormously in the United States during World War II. The government and armed forces greatly expanded the infrastructure for inspection and quality. This emphasis on quality spread throughout the private sector to companies who were contractors and suppliers for the military. The government trained thousands of engineers and managers in the use of statistical quality control techniques; these people subsequently created quality control departments in their own companies. However, following World War II there was a tremendous surge in demand for consumer goods, coupled with huge shortages. As a result many manufacturers shifted their priorities to production volume, and the emphasis on quality declined, as is normal in a period of shortages. Also, when the inevitable economic recession occurred after the war, many companies—in an effort to cut costs—eliminated quality departments. However, it is not true that U.S. companies completely abandoned statistical quality control techniques. Their use continued in many companies throughout the 1950s and 1960s, although an important and fateful exception was the U.S. automobile industry.

Source: Juran, J. M., "World War II and the Quality Movement," *Quality Progress* (December 1991): 19–24; "Statistical Quality Control in the World War II Years," *Quality Progress* (December 1991): 31–35.

Teaching Note 4.2 The Early Use of Control Charts

Joseph Juran indicates that during the 1920s the newly developed inspection sampling techniques had an impact on Bell system manufacturing practices. However, the control chart concept did not arouse much interest. W. E. Deming contends that Walter Shewhart was disappointed with the degree to which statistical process control charts were used at Western Electric.

Source: Juran, J. M., "World War II and Quality Movement," *Quality Progress* (December 1991): 19–24; Gabor, A., "Deming Demystifies the Black Art of Statistics," *Quality Progress* (December 1991): 26–28.

Teaching Note 4.3 The Derivation of MIL-STD-105 Tables

During World War II the U.S. government and armed forces faced an enormous problem in trying to ensure that the products they received from contractors was of the highest quality. It was a time of severe and widespread shortages, and in this type of environment, quality will always tend to decline. Before the war the government approach to quality was based on inspection. Often all product items delivered by contractors were inspected and tested to make sure they conformed to product specifications. This same basic approach was retained during World War II, requiring a large expansion of inspection personnel. This, in turn, resulted in problems of recruiting, training, and retaining inspection employees. The armed forces attempted to reduce these problems by greater use of sampling techniques. Their solution was to adapt sampling tables derived earlier at the Bell System in the 1920s and the 1930s by Walter Shewhart, Harold Dodge, George Edwards, and others. Specifically, Harold Dodge and George Edwards worked with the Army Ordinance Department to develop sampling procedures to ensure the quality of ammunition, and Ralph E. Wareham of General Electric and Hugh Smallwood of U.S. Rubber developed similar procedures for the U.S. Signal Corps. These tables were published by the government as MIL-STD-105 and were included in government contracts. In turn, contractors referred to these tables in their contracts with subcontractors and suppliers, so they became disseminated in the nonmilitary sectors of the economy.

Source: Wareham, R. E., and Stratton, B., "Standards Sampling and Schooling," *Quality Progress* (December 1991): 38–42; Juran, J. M., "World War II and the Quality Movement," *Quality Progress* (December 1991): 19–24.

ALTERNATE EXAMPLES

Alternate Example 4.1

Problem Statement:

The Jammin Shoe Company manufacturers athletic shoes. The company wants to establish a p-chart to monitor the production process using $z = 3.00$. The company has taken a sample of 50 shoes every 4 hours for a workweek of 5 days. Because the company runs two 8-hour shifts each day, this yields 20 samples. The sample results are as follows.

Sample	*Number of Defectives*	*Proportion Defective*	*Sample*	*Number of Defectives*	*Proportion Defective*
1	0	0.00	11	4	0.08
2	1	0.02	12	1	0.02
3	0	0.00	13	1	0.02
4	3	0.06	14	2	0.04
5	2	0.04	15	2	0.04
6	5	0.10	16	3	0.06
7	3	0.06	17	4	0.08
8	2	0.04	18	1	0.02
9	1	0.02	19	5	0.10
10	0	0.00	20	2	0.04

The population proportion defective is not known. Construct a p-chart to monitor this process.

Solution:

$$\bar{p} = \frac{42}{(20)(50)} = 0.042$$

$$\text{UCL} = \bar{p} + z\sqrt{\frac{\bar{p}(1-\bar{p})}{n}} = 0.042 + 3\sqrt{\frac{(0.042)(0.958)}{50}} = 0.127$$

$$\text{LCL} = \bar{p} - z\sqrt{\frac{\bar{p}(1-\bar{p})}{n}} = 0.042 - 3\sqrt{\frac{(0.042)(0.958)}{50}}$$

$= -0.043$ or 0.0 (since the control chart cannot go below zero).

The same data include no points outside the control limits.

Alternate Example 4.2

Problem Statement:

Freshly painted autos are inspected for blemishes. The company has established that the process average that meets their desired quality level is 8 blemishes per sample during the inspection process. Following are the results for inspecting 20 groups of 10 cars at random during a weeklong period.

Sample	*Blemishes*	*Sample*	*Blemishes*
1	8	11	6
2	12	12	8
3	9	13	9
4	11	14	15
5	6	15	7
6	12	16	10
7	10	17	11
8	8	18	12
9	14	19	9
10	7	20	6

Construct a c-chart using $z = 3.00$ and determine if the painting process is in control.

Solution:

$$\text{UCL} = c + z\sigma_c = 8 + 3\sqrt{8} = 16.5$$
$$\text{LCL} = c - z\sigma_c = 8 - 3\sqrt{8} \cong 0$$

The process appears to be in control.

Alternate Example 4.3

Problem Statement:

Ann's Snack Foods produces Bob's Potato Chips. The salt content of the chips is a very important taste feature. Every 15 minutes an inspector obtains three sample batches of chips, dissolves the chips in water, filters out the water, and analyzes it electronically to determine the percentage salt content. The average target salt content is 1.6 percent. The process samples have a standard deviation of 0.08 percent. Construct an $\bar{x}$-chart for this process.

Solution:

$$\text{UCL} = \mu + z\left(\frac{\sigma}{\sqrt{n}}\right) = 1.6 + 3\left(\frac{0.08}{\sqrt{3}}\right) = 1.73\%$$

$$\text{LCL} = \mu - z\left(\frac{\sigma}{\sqrt{n}}\right) = 1.6 - 3\left(\frac{0.08}{\sqrt{3}}\right) = 1.46\%$$

Alternate Example 4.4

Problem Statement:

Ten samples of three batches of Bob's Potato Chips have been taken during a 3-hour period to test for salt content of the chips. The individual observations from each sample are as follows.

	Observations (% salt content)				
Sample k	1	2	3	$\bar{x}$	*R*
1	1.2	1.4	1.6	1.40	0.4
2	1.1	1.5	1.3	1.30	0.4
3	1.2	0.9	1.5	1.20	0.6
4	1.0	1.5	1.6	1.36	0.6
5	1.7	1.4	1.6	1.56	0.3
6	1.3	2.0	1.5	1.60	0.7
7	1.3	2.1	1.7	1.70	0.8
8	1.7	1.6	1.3	1.53	0.4
9	1.5	2.3	1.2	1.66	1.1
10	1.2	1.5	1.6	1.43	0.4

Develop an *R*-chart to monitor process variability.

Solution:

$$\bar{R} = \frac{\Sigma R}{k} = \frac{5.7}{10} = 0.57$$

$D_3 = 0$ and $D_4 = 2.57$ (from Table 4.1 in the text)

$$\text{UCL} = D_4\bar{R} = (2.57)(0.57) = 1.47$$

$$\text{LCL} = D_3\bar{R} = (0)(0.57) = 0$$

The process appears to be in control.

Alternate Example 4.5

Problem Statement:

Develop an $\bar{x}$-chart to be used in conjunction with the *R*-chart developed in Alternate Example 4.4 for the production of Bob's Potato Chips.

Solution:

$$\bar{\bar{x}} = \frac{\Sigma\bar{x}}{10} = \frac{14.74}{10} = 1.47$$

From Table 4.1 in the text, $A_2 = 1.02$.

$$\text{UCL} = \bar{\bar{x}} + A_2\bar{R} = 1.47 + 1.02(0.57) = 2.05$$

$$\text{LCL} = \bar{\bar{x}} - A_2\bar{R} = 1.47 - (1.02)(0.57) = 0.89$$

The process appears to be in control.

Alternate Example 4.6

Problem Statement:

Perform above/below and up/down pattern tests for the $\bar{x}$ sample data shown in Alternate Example 4.4. Use a test statistic of $z = \pm 2.00$.

Solution:

Sample	*Above/Below*	*Up/Down*
1	B	—
2	B	D
3	B	D
4	B	U
5	A	U
6	A	U
7	A	U
8	A	D
9	A	U
10	B	D

$$z_{A/B} = \frac{3 - [(10/2) + 1]}{\sqrt{(10-1)/4}} = -2.00$$

$$z_{U/D} = \frac{5 - [(20-1)/3]}{\sqrt{(160-29)/90}} = -1.11$$

The $z_{A/B}$ pattern test statistic indicates the process may not be in control and requires further examination.

VIDEOS

Video 4.1 *Total Quality Management*

This video is one of a series of tapes produced by the Society of Manufacturing Engineers (SME) on different aspects of manufacturing operations. Its subject is the TQM program at Kurt Manufacturing, a midsize manufacturer and supplier of precision machine parts based in Minneapolis. The program describes a number of components of the company's successful TQM program, including the use of statistical process control, which is a major focus of the video. The tape has a duration of 29 minutes, and it accompanies the featured application section at the beginning of Chapter 4 titled "Statistical Process Control at Kurt Manufacturing."

Video 4.2 *COMAP*, Program 5: "Statistical Quality Control"

This program is one of the five programs on the COMAP video produced for the series "For All Practical Purposes." This program describes how control charts are used at the Frito-Lay Company to monitor the salt content of Ruffles Potato Chips. There is also a segment on W. E. Deming and his contributions to quality control. It includes some historical footage showing his work with the Japanese following World War II. The program is approximately 14 minutes long and accompanies the application box in this chapter titled, "Using $\bar{x}$-Charts at Frito Lay."

Video 4.3 *Harley-Davidson, Building Better Motorcycles the American Way*

This video tape focuses on Harley-Davidson's manufacturing processes and its success with its TQM program. It emphasizes the company's overall commitment to quality through product design (CAD), engineering, and statistical process control. It discusses the precision machinery done at Harley at state-of-the-art machine centers. The video's duration is approximately 25 minutes, and it accompanies the application box in this chapter titled "Achieving Design Tolerances at Harley-Davidson Company."

5 PRODUCT AND SERVICE DESIGN

TEACHING NOTES

Teaching Note 5.1 Interesting Design Stories

Here are several good references on product/service design that tell some interesting stories:

- Ira Flatow, *They All Laughed … From Light Bulbs to Lasers. The Fascinating Stories Behind the Great Inventions that Have Changed Our Lives*, New York: Harper Collins, 1992.
- Henry Petroski, *The Evolution of Useful Things*, New York: Knopf, 1993.
- Henry Petroski, *To Engineer is Human*, New York: Knopf, 1991
- Henry Petroski, *The Pencil*, New York: Knopf, 1992
- *Invention and Technology* magazine.

Teaching Note 5.2 The Product Concept for Honda's Accord

Honda's engineers were given the task of conceptualizing a new car that had the following meanings:

1. Open-minded
2. Friendly communication
3. Tough spirit
4. Stress-free
5. Love forever

The design team focused on an image of their customer as "a rugby player in a business suit." The new product even had a motto: "Man maximum, machine minimum." The result was Honda's popular Accord.

Source: The Power of Product Integrity, *Harvard Business Review* (November–December 1990): 110.

Teaching Note 5.3 A Benchmark Clearing House

There is now an International Clearinghouse for Benchmarking (IBC) located in Houston, Texas. The clearinghouse collects, compiles, and analyzes data from thousands of firms and industries. Here is an example of benchmarking for the automotive industry:

	GM	Best-in-Class	
Labor hours per vehicle	30	19	(Ford)
Defects per vehicle	3.1	1.0	(Toyota)
Warranty cost per car	$250	$170	(Toyota)
% First time paint OK	75%	90%	(Suzuki)
Product development (months)	60	30	(Honda)
Order response time (days)	10	2	(Toyota)
Die change time (min)	60	10	(Honda)
% External JIT parts	5%	70%	(Nummi)
% Internal JIT parts	5%	100%	(Nummi)
Fastener part numbers	700	330	(Nummi)
Fasteners per car	2000	1400	(Toyota)

You can even call up the Best Manufacturing Practices (BMPNET) data base from your PC (with a modem). Call 703-271-9055 for access information.

Source: Sprow, Eugene, "Benchmarking," *Manufacturing Engineering* (September 1993): 64.

Teaching Note 5.4 Marriott's Courtyard Design

There's an excellent reference on the design of Marriott's Courtyard line of hotels in Jerry Wind, et al., "Courtyard by Marriott: Designing a Hotel Facility," *Interfaces* (Jan.–Feb. 1989): 25–47. Marriott was one of the finalists in the Franz Edelman award for 1988.

Teaching Note 5.5 General Formulae for Reliability

The general formula for the system reliability of n components in *series* is:

$$Rs = R_1 \times R_2 \times R_3 \times \ldots \times R_n$$

R_1 — R_2 — R_3 · · · R_n

The general formula for the system reliability of n components in *parallel* is:

$$R_p = 1 - (1 - R_1) \times (1 - R_2) \times (1 - R_3) \times \ldots \times (1 - R_n)$$

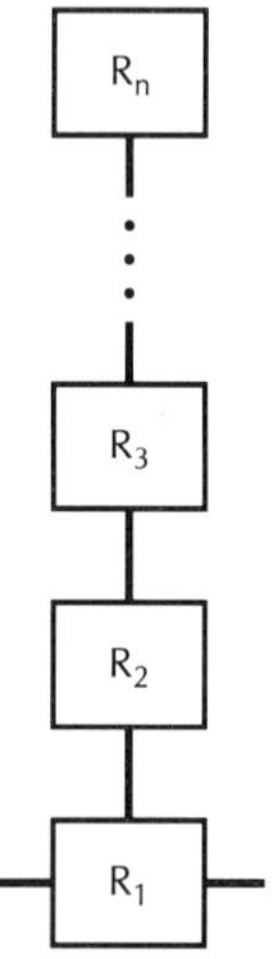

If $R_1 = R_2 = R_3 \ldots = R_n$, then $R_p = 1 - (1 - R_1)^n$

Teaching Note 5.6 AB:POM's Reliability Module

AB:POM's reliability module will compute the reliability of systems with up to 10 components in series and 12 components in parallel. The AB:POM solution to Example 5.1(b) is shown at the bottom of this page.

Teaching Note 5.7 Team Taurus

Ford Motor Company has been a leader in initiating the team approach to product design in the automotive industry and in U.S. industry as a whole. Taurus, the first automobile designed with quality as its overriding goal, came in $400 million under budget through the efforts of a design team called Team Taurus. Personnel from design engineering, marketing, and manufacturing were not the only members of Team Taurus—dealers, lawyers, insurance companies, suppliers, workers, and customers were also involved.

Dealers recounted the problems they faced on the sales floor and suggested how cars could be made more user-friendly. Lawyers informed the team of pending legislation so that safety features could be designed in instead of added on later. Insurance companies explained how changes in car design could minimize customer expense after an accident. (One result is

```
                         Reliability                        Solution
Number of systems in series (1-10) 3Max # of parallel components (1-12)  3
                          Example 5.1b
  Parll  Parll  Parll
  Sys 1  Sys 2  Sys 3
 0.9000 0.9000 0.9000
 0.9500 0.9500 0.9500
 0.9950 0.9950 0.9950
System reliability = .98507
```

that Taurus' engraved cross marks under the hood define the center of gravity and help align the front end properly after a collision.)

Supplier roles changed significantly. A frame manufacturer suggested that its engineers be allowed to design that portion of the car and submit the design to Ford for approval. Their design was accepted and, as a result, the supplier received a long-term contract for a part they *knew* could be manufactured successfully in their factories. On their own initiative, a lighting firm developed louvered interior lights that cut down reflection on the driver's side, a plastics company developed a foldout tray for tailgate parties, and a carpet manufacturer designed the carpeting layout so that all the fibers would lay in the same direction.

Input from workers and customers was solicited *during* the design process. The team visited stamping plants and assembly plants, presenting preliminary designs and gathering thousands of suggestions from hourly workers, most of which were incorporated in the final design. A prototype was built 9 months before scheduled production to be tested by potential customers. Customer comments were received, evaluated, and incorporated in the design before the first car was sold, instead of 3 months to a year after the car had been on the market. Prototypes of the complete car were taken to supplier factories around the world so that those workers could see how the component they manufactured fit into the overall product.

Not only has Taurus been a profitable venture for Ford, it has also started the company in a new direction. In that process, Team Taurus has become the new standard for design by multifunctional design teams.

Source: Walton, M., *The Deming Management Method*, New York: Putnam Publishers, 1986, 139–45.

Teaching Note 5.8 Tasks of Manufacturing Engineers

As part of their Profile 2000 study, SME surveyed the work tasks of manufacturing engineers in the United States versus Japan. Here are the results:

Top Three Functions of Manufacturing Engineers

United States	Japan
1. Shop floor problem-solving	1. Research and development
2. Design of tools, facilities, and equipment	2. Supervising production operations
3. Process planning	3. Product design

Clearly, the manufacturing engineers in Japan are performing the same duties as design engineers in the United States, with the exception that Japanese engineers have more exposure to manufacturing capabilities from their work-supervising operations. The results of this survey and a follow-up task force study prompted SME to recommend that U.S. engineering schools change how they educate their students by eliminating the category of manufacturing engineer entirely and adding more intense study of manufacturing to their curriculum for design engineers. This is quite a drastic recommendation, because most professional societies do not suggest actions that would lead to their own dissolution.

Teaching Note 5.9 Video Suggestions

Westinghouse has two short videos on design for manufacture produced for in-house use. The first video, *Design for Manufacture*, shows the advantages of IBM's ProPrinter design and encourages Westinghouse engineers to use the same concepts. The second video, *Design for Producibility*, introduces Westinghouse's three-pronged approach to design. The video can be used to accompany the Westinghouse application box in the chapter. Contact Westinghouse's Productivity and Quality Center, Pittsburgh, Pennsylvania, for more information.

SME also has several nice videos in the design area. The section on K-2 Skis in the video *CAD/CAM* and the Motorola and NCR sections of the video *Simultaneous Engineering* are especially good.

Contact: SME Videos
One SME Drive
Dearborn, MI 48121
(313) 271-1500

Teaching Note 5.10 A Car Door

Of all the features in an automobile, the quality of car doors is noticeably better in a Japanese or European car than in an American car. Consumers can't quantify the difference, but they say a foreign-made car has doors that are more solid, that sound right when you shut them, don't rattle, and seal tighter. When you consider that over 100 components come together in a single car door, a clue to the problem becomes evident. The possibility of assembly error or design incompatibility increases significantly with the number of components involved. Thus, any errors in design will be magnified in assemblies with numerous components. It's not coincidence that the first application of the house of quality at Ford concerned the design of a car door. See the classic *Harvard Business Review* article:

Hauser, J. R., and D. Clausing, "The House of Quality," *Harvard Business Review* (May–June 1988): 63–73.

Teaching Note 5.11 Tolerances, Control Limits, and Quality Loss

This is a good time to review the differences between control limits and tolerance limits discussed in Chapter 4. A graph of the actual Sony data discussed in Example 5.3 would look something like this:

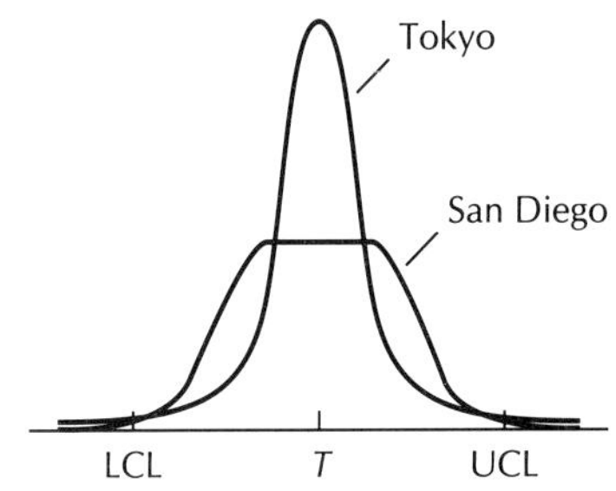

Have the students compare this graph to the quality loss curve shown in Figure 5.16.

Teaching Note 5.12 Taguchi and ASI

Genuchi Taguchi and his son, Shin Taguchi, now live in the United States and direct the American Supplier Institute (ASI) in Dearborn, Michigan. ASI is a good resource for many of the best concepts in manufacturing, such as JIT, TQM, and, of course, Taguchi methods. ASI originated as an organization for suppliers of Ford Motor Company.

Contact: ASI
15041 Commerce Drive South, Suite 401
Dearborn, MI 48120
(313) 336-8877

Teaching Note 5.13 Virtual Reality

Virtual reality techniques were used to check out the positioning of the corrective optics for fixing the Hubble space telescope. For some elegant photos, see Dennis Hancock, "Prototyping the Hubble Fix," *IEEE Spectrum* (October 1993): 34–39.

Other virtual reality references are as follows:

- Pimentel, Ken, and Kevin Teixeira, *Virtual Reality: Through the New Looking Glass*, New York: McGraw-Hill, 1993.
- Rheingold, Howard, *Virtual Reality: The Revolutionary Technology of Computer-Generated Artificial Worlds*, New York: Simon & Schuster, 1992.

Teaching Note 5.14 Example Specifications for Racing Skis

Performance Specs	*Design Specs*
• Fast	• P-9000 base, length 207 to 215 cm
• Durable, stiff	• Wood core for natural dampening
• Quick turning ability	• Edges of high quality carbon and stainless steel
	• S-curve-shaped profile

ALTERNATE EXAMPLES

Alternate Example 5.1

Problem Statement:

Determine the reliability of the systems shown.

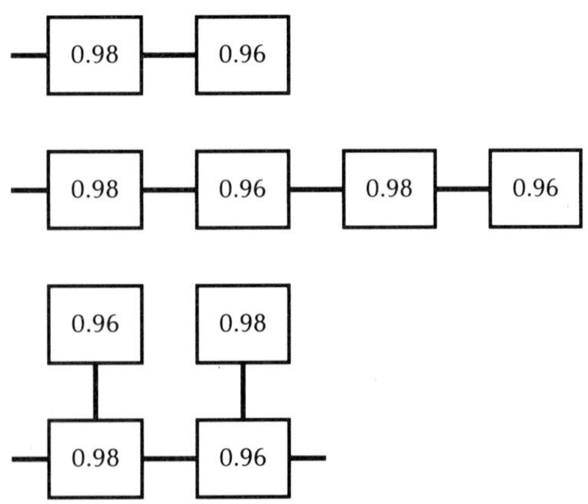

Solution:

a. $0.98 \times 0.96 = 0.9408$

b. $0.98 \times 0.96 \times 0.98 \times 0.96 = 0.8851$

c. $[0.98 + (1 - 0.98)0.96] \times [0.96 + (1 - 0.96)0.98] = 0.992 \times 0.992$
$= 0.9984$

Alternate Example 5.2

Problem Statement:

John is leaving home for college this fall. In preparation, his mother has given him a choice between two TV sets: 1. a five-year-old 13-inch color TV made by XYZ, a highly reputable manufacturer, and 2. a new 13-inch color TV made by ABC, a less reliable manufacturer. A leading consumer magazine estimates that XYZ TVs last an average of 10 years and ABC TVs, around 4 years. Given that the life of the TV sets follows an exponential distribution and all other characteristics are comparable, which set should John choose in each case?

a. If he wants the set to get him through his entire four years of college

b. If he wants the set to last five years

c. If he expects to give away the 13-inch set in two years and purchase a larger one with his own funds

Solution

a. For XYZ: MTBF $= 10$ years, $T = 5 + 4 = 9$ years,

$T/\text{MTBF} = 9/10 = 0.90$

From Table 5.1, $e^{-0.90} = 0.4066$.

For ABC: MTBF $= 4$ years, $T = 4$ years

$T/\text{MTBF} = 4/4 = 1.0$

From Table 5.1, $e^{-1.00} = 0.3679$.

There is a 41 percent chance that the XYZ TV set will last until John finishes college and a 37 percent chance that the ABC set will last that long. John should choose the old XYZ TV set.

b. For XYZ: MTBF $= 10$ years, $T = 5 + 5 = 10$ years

$T/\text{MTBF} = 10/10 = 1.0$

From Table 5.1, $e^{-1.00} = 0.3679$.

For ABC: MTBF $= 4$ years, $T = 5$ years

$T/\text{MTBF} = \frac{5}{4} = 1.25$

From Table 5.1, $e^{-1.25}$ is between 0.3012 and 0.2725.

Thus, there is a higher probability that the old TV set will last 5 years.

c. For XYZ: MTBF $= 10$ years, $T = 5 + 2 = 7$ years

$T/\text{MTBF} = \frac{7}{10} = 0.70$

From Table 5.1, $e^{-0.70} = 0.4966$.

For ABC: MTBF $= 4$ years, $T = 2$ years

$T/\text{MTBF} = \frac{2}{4} = 0.50$

From Table 5.1, $e^{-0.50} = 0.6065$.

There is a 50 percent probability that the old TV set will last until a larger TV is purchased, but there is a 60 percent probability that the new TV set will last until a larger TV can be purchased. Thus, John should choose the new TV.

Alternate Example 5.3

Problem Statement:

Odds and Ends Furniture Company makes occasional pieces for the home out of pine and oak wood. Bookshelves are one of its most popular items. From experience, the shelfmaker has learned that customers are unhappy when board lengths for the bookcases are ±1 inch off the specified length. Lengths shorter by more than 1 inch do not stay fastened, and lengths longer by more than 1 inch tend to warp. Both errors result in unsatisfied customers and a shelf replacement cost of $5 per shelf.

A recent audit of a day's production of 36-inch shelves yielded the following data:

Shelf Length (in.)	Frequency
38	2
37	10
36	15
35	15
34	3

What is the quality loss for the forty-five shelves produced?

Solution:

$$k = \frac{\$5}{1^2} = \$5$$

$$\begin{aligned}\text{Loss} &= 2(5 \times 2^2) + 10(5 \times 1^2) + 15(5 \times 0^2) + 15(5 \times 1^2) + 3(5 \times 2^2)\\ &= 40 + 50 + 0 + 75 + 60\\ &= \$225\end{aligned}$$

Alternate Example 5.4

Problem Statement:

The Odds and Ends Furniture Company from Alternate Example 5.3 wants to use tolerances to standardize shelf production. If it costs an average of $1 to fix a shelf that is too long or too short before assembly into the bookcase, how should the manufacturing tolerances be set for the 36-inch shelves?

Solution

$$\begin{aligned}L &= kd^2\\ 1 &= 5d^2\\ \frac{1}{5} &= d^2\\ 0.447 &= d\end{aligned}$$

The manufacturing tolerance for shelf length should be 36 inches ± 0.447 inch, or between 35.553 inches and 36.447 inches.

VIDEO

Video 5.1 *Harley-Davidson, Building Better Motorcycles the American Way*

This video focuses on Harley-Davidson's overall commitment to quality through product design (CAD), engineering, and statistical process control. It does a good job of showing the engineering-manufacturing interface through CAD/CAM.

6 PROCESS PLANNING AND TECHNOLOGY DECISIONS

TEACHING NOTES

Teaching Note 6.1 Some Assembly Required

Everyone has had the experience of trying to assemble something that is supposed to be easy but isn't. Bring a few examples for the students, or have them bring in examples to class. In fairness, it is not as easy to communicate assembly instructions as it might seem. Try this classroom exercise:

- Divide your class into groups of two to four students each.
- Divide each group into builders and designers.
- Give them each an identical set of five or six DUPLO (or Lego) blocks, and place the group members back to back. Designers make something out of their blocks and then try to get the builders to construct the same thing from verbal or written instructions (try with and without verbal feedback). Take turns playing the role of builder and designer.
- If you are limited in time or DUPLO resources, select a few students to demonstrate in front of the class.
- To complete the exercise, give blocks to the group members that are identical in size and shape but not color. How long does it take for each side to figure out something is wrong?

Teaching Note 6.2 Flowcharts

The process flowcharts described in this chapter use specific symbols. The symbols are useful because their shape identifies both productive and nonproductive activities. A work group or company should agree on the types of symbols used, but they can vary from the standard set.

Flowcharting, or "process mapping," has become very popular as companies try to reengineer the way work is done. More and more companies are starting from scratch, taking a clean-sheet approach to designing processes. The author who made reengineering a household word is Michael Hammer. See: *Reengineering the Corporation*, Michael Hammer and James Champy, New York: Harper-Collins, 1993.

Teaching Note 6.3 Vertical Integration Versus Supplier Partnerships

We used to teach the value of vertical integration for protecting the source of supply and speeding up the logistical chain from raw materials to components to finished product. Ford's Rouge plant did everything on site, from processing steel to final assembly, and the entire process took a matter of weeks. Now companies find they can move faster if suppliers take on more of the designing and building duties. There is one catch, though, the bond between supplier and producer must be strong.

To get a feel for early opinions in this area, see three articles in *Harvard Business Review* (September–October 1988): Markides and Berg, "Manufacturing Offshore is Bad Business," Kumpe and Bolwign, "Manufacturing: The New Case for Vertical Integration," and Johnston and Lawrence, "Beyond Vertical Integrations—The Rise of the Value Added Partnership."

Teaching Note 6.4 The Impact of Process Choice

It's sometimes hard for students to realize the enormous difference process choice can make in how work is done. Skinner gives a good example in *Manufacturing, The Formidable Competitive Weapon* (pp. 116–117) of different ways to manufacture a flashlight. An aluminum flashlight casing requires a deep-drawing process from sheet metal. A plastic casing is injection-molded in two halves and fit together. The summary chart from Skinner is shown at the top of the next column.

	Metal Drawing	*Plastic Molding*
Equipment	Massive press	Several smaller presses
Raw Materials	Metal sheets	Various plastics
Tools	Die set—male and female	Split halves
Building	Heavy foundations	Ordinary floor
Engineering expertise	Mechanical, metal	Plastics, hydraulics
Maintenance	Mechanical	Mechanical, hydraulic
Operator	Heavier work, higher skill	Lighter work, relatively lower skill
Inventory	Sheet metal; in-process	Plastic powder; finished goods
Operations	Several	One
Scheduling	Complex	Simple
Safety	Dangerous	Safer
Quality/ precision	Depends on die and physical setup	Depends on die and machine timing
Costs	Depends on die condition and setup skills	Depends on short cycle changeovers
Volume change	Add dies, machines, shifts, or move to higher speed equipment	Add dies, machines, shifts; cycle limited
Automation	Expensive; limited	Not so expensive already largely automatic

Teaching Note 6.5 Warnings about BE Analysis

We present break-even analysis as a simple, straightforward technique for process selection. However, BE analysis assumes that costs can be expressed as a linear relationship. It does not reflect step increases or synergistic effects common in process decisions.

Teaching Note 6.6 Activity-Based Costing

The Hewlett-Packard application box describes activity-based costing, although it does not refer to it by that name. This concept has revolutionized cost accounting and has had a major effect on the justification of new technology.

Teaching Note 6.7 Aversion to Technology

Aversion to technology is very common among business students. The typical attitude toward this whole chapter (and maybe the course) is 'Why do I have to learn about how things are made? That's the engineer's problem.' Skinner's five-question approach is very useful in convincing students that they can and should understand technology. To build student confidence in technology, try this series of exercises:

- Role play the purchase of a consumer item (CD player, computer, even athletic shoes). Have one student be the expert. Give him or her time to prepare (gather data, ask questions of an expert, etc.). Have another student be the consumer who comes in to purchase the item. This student should prepare by understanding clearly how he or she is going to use the product. The expert can respond only to questions asked by the consumer. Play it out until the class agrees the consumer has made a wise technology choice.
- Have the students explain to the class using analogies and nontechnical terms how a product is made or a machine operates. They can gather the information from research or viewing a process in operation.
- Test the student's technology smarts with this quiz:

Techno-type quiz

Do you thrive in a high-tech environment or avoid technology whenever possible? This quiz helps measure technical literacy. Circle the number that best describes your feelings about each statement below. Then total your score to find out your techno-type.

	N/A	← Agree				Disagree →
My VCR blinks "12:00" all the time	0	1	2	3	4	5
I enjoy using new software	0	1	2	3	4	5
I worry about deleting something I need on my computer	0	1	2	3	4	5
I miss my typewriter	0	1	2	3	4	5
A computer's winmark speed is important to me	0	1	2	3	4	5
I like to observe new technology, but I prefer not to use it until all bugs are out	0	1	2	3	4	5
I want the latest in technology, whatever the product	0	1	2	3	4	5
Setting the stations on my car radio is perplexing to me	0	1	2	3	4	5
Technology talk is boring	0	1	2	3	4	5
TOTAL SCORE	______					

0–22 (Techno-Phobe) You avoid technology whenever possible, preferring low-tech "uncomplicated" tools that have always served you well. You're a pencil-and-paper, dials-vs.-programmable buttons type all the way!

23–33 (Techno-Boomer or Techno-to-Go) You may not completely understand new technology, but you're not afraid to use it. You want a computer that's ready to run right out of the box. You don't often use an instruction manual, preferring to pick up the phone and call a customer assistance line for help when needed.

34-50 (Techno-Wizard) You thrive in a high-tech environment; the hotter and more challenging the technology, the better.

Source: Adapted from Squires, Paula Crawford, "Is Fear of Technology, the Phobia of the 1990s?" *Richmond Times Dispatch* (August 18, 1993).

Teaching Note 6.8 The American Robot Industry

There's a sad but telling story of how the United States lost the robot industry in an article in the *Wall Street Journal:* "How U.S. Robots Lost the Market to Japan in Factory automation," November 6, 1990, p. A12. Here are some highlights:

- In 1967, Joseph Engelberger appeared on "The Tonight Show" with a robot that opened a can of Budweiser and led the band. U.S. talent agents called to book the act, but the Japanese government flew Engelberger to Japan to address 700 industrialists and answer questions for 6 hours.
- The United States invested in hydraulic robots that were prone to leaks. When a robot broke down it took an electrician *and* a plumber to fix it. One $5 million order for Unimate robots included $160,000 for optional drip pans.

Teaching Note 6.9 Automation

Automated processes do not necessarily work like their manual counterparts. A good example is the sewing machine. Students can find how a sewing machine works in any encyclopedia. The needle does not follow the same path as in hand sewing. Investigate.

Teaching Note 6.10 STEP

STEP promises to settle the standardization argument for automation that MAP, TOP, IGES, PDES, and DMIS began. Ford Motor Co. cut powertrain design and manufacturing costs by 25 percent with STEP. The success of the Navy's RAMP (rapid acquisition of manufactured parts) system in reducing the lead-time of machined parts from 300 to 30 days is largely attributable to STEP.

Teaching Note 6.11 CIM and AI

GE Fanuc's CIMPLICITY system and Texas Instruments' THE WORKS contain fuzzy logic, expert systems, and neural networks. The IMS (Intelligent Manufacturing Systems) project is an international study of the interaction of people and intelligent machines to improve flexibility, agility, and quality in manufacturing. The United States, Japan, Canada, Australia, and the European Community are involved with the project, with Allen-Bradley leading the U.S. efforts.

ALTERNATE EXAMPLES

Alternate Example 6.1

Problem Statement:

Workplace, International, manufactures a variety of items to improve office efficiency. One of its simpler items is a three-hole paper punch assembled at the shop from parts provided by a supplier. The assembly process is as follows:

1. Assemble spring mechanism by attaching spring to metal post and inserting post into top hole of metal attachment.
2. Attach three spring mechanisms to the bottom plate of the hole punch with nuts and bolts.
3. Snap on the top plate of the hole punch.
4. Snap the chip collection tray onto the bottom of the hole punch assembly.
5. Place in box and seal.

Draw an assembly chart and construct a bill of material for the three-hole paper punch.

Solution:

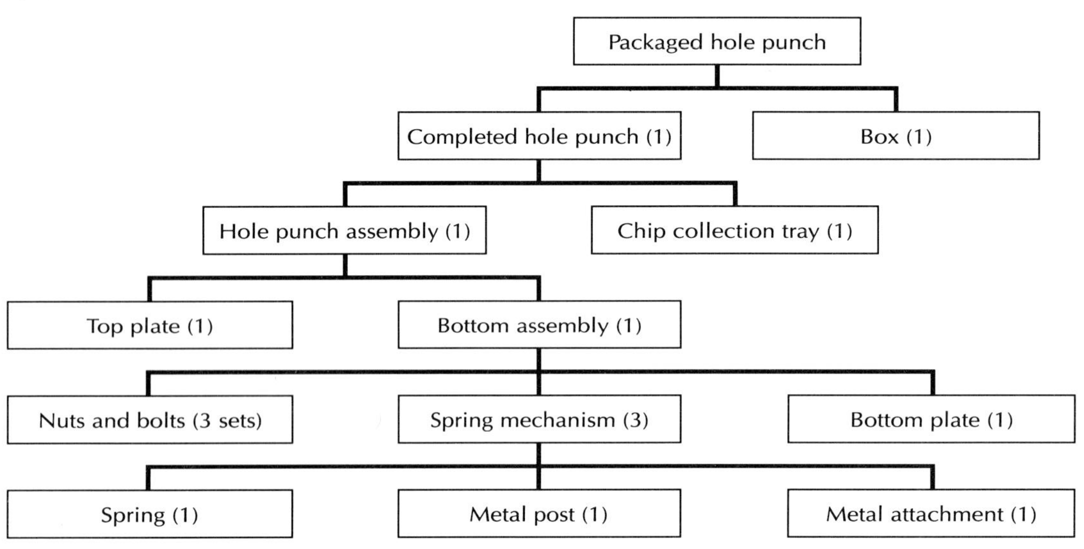

Bill of Material

Level	*Item*	*UM*	*QTY*
0	Packaged hole punch	Ea	1
— 1	Completed hole punch	Ea	1
—— 2	Hole punch assembly	Ea	1
——— 3	Top plate	Ea	1
——— 3	Bottom assembly	Ea	1
———— 4	Nuts and bolts	Set	3
———— 4	Spring mechanism	Ea	3
————— 5	Spring	Ea	1
————— 5	Metal post	Ea	1
————— 5	Metal attachment	Ea	1
———— 4	Bottom plate	Ea	1
—— 2	Chip collection tray	Ea	1
— 1	Box	Ea	1

Alternate Example 6.2

Problem Statement:

Workplace, International, is reevaluating the design, cost, and profitability of its line of office accessories. Currently, the items are constructed of metal-based parts for durable and consistent performance. At the time of the initial process decision, the metal-drawing process was also the most economical. Management now suspects that the cost advantage enjoyed by metal parts is highly dependent on the volume of parts produced. To confirm their suspicions, management would like you to compare the break-even volume for one of its products, the three-hole punch, when fabricated from metal versus plastic. What decision can be made based on the individual break-even points of each process?

	Metal Drawing Process	*Plastic Injection Molding*
Fixed Cost	$50,000	$100,000
Variable Cost	$5 per unit	$2 per unit
Selling Price	$10 per unit	$10 per unit

Solution:

$$\text{Break-even volume for metal} = \frac{50{,}000}{10-5} = 10{,}000 \text{ units}$$

$$\text{Break-even volume for plastic} = \frac{170{,}000}{10-2} = 21{,}250 \text{ units}$$

The break-even volumes indicated that the three-hole punch made out of metal should not be produced if the sales volume is lower than 10,000 units, and the three-hole punch should not be made out of plastic if the sales volume is less than 21,250 units.

Alternate Example 6.3

Problem Statement:

Referring to Alternate Example 6.2, workplace management wants more specific information regarding the volume at which the three-hole punch should be constructed from metal parts or from plastic parts. Management is also considering subcontracting out the production of the parts for $8 per unit. Which alternative would you recommend?

Solution:

Metal vs. Plastic

$$50{,}000 + 5x = 170{,}000 + 2x$$
$$3x = 120{,}000$$
$$x = 40{,}000$$

Metal vs. Buy

$$50{,}000 + 5x = 8x$$
$$50{,}000 = 3x$$
$$x = 16{,}666$$

Plastic vs. Buy

$$170{,}000 + 2x = 8x$$
$$170{,}000 = 6x$$
$$x = 28{,}333$$

If the sales volume is greater than or equal to 40,000, make the parts from plastic. If the sales volume is greater than or equal to 16,666 but less than 40,000, make the parts from metal. If the sales volume less than 16,666, purchase the parts.

VIDEOS

Video 6.1 1991 *Malcolm Baldrige Awards, Quest for Excellence*

This video is a short overview of the 1991 Malcolm Baldrige Award Winners, Zytec, Solectron, and Marlow. It contains some nice process footage from the high-tech electronics industry.

Video 6.2 *The Allyn and Bacon Plant Tour Video*, Program 3: "Volvo Torslanda Plant"

This video accompanies an application box in this chapter. The video is about 22 minutes long and shows a variety of operations at Volvo's Torslanda complex, such as pressing, welding, and painting. It also shows quite a bit of automation, mainly robots but also an AS/RS for body storage and a few AGVs.

7 *FACILITY LAYOUT*

TEACHING NOTES

Teaching Note 7.1 A Layout Experiment

Try an experiment with your students to see which kind of layout (and process) will perform the following arithmetic task quickly and correctly (without a calculator!).

Task: $[(72 + 4{,}237 + 419) \times (11{,}234 - 718)] \div 7{,}982$
$+ [(7{,}142 \times 0.378) - (157.32 \div 0.173)]$
$+ (1{,}411 + 1{,}235{,}175 + 827{,}134)$

Solution: 2,071,739.28

Alternate layouts:

1. *Fixed position:* One student does all the math.
2. *Process layout:* Divide task by function: one student does +, another −, another ×, another ÷. All can start at the same time, but work must be combined later.
3. *Product layout:* Set up an assembly line. Break up the problem into tasks from the beginning to the end of the process and assign certain tasks to different students along an assembly line.
4. *GT cell:* Break up the process into sections and arrange each section like an assembly line.

Teaching Note 7.2 Flexibility

Flexibility is the biggest issue in modern layouts. We see machines on wheels (even 40-ton presses) and collapsible, sectioned conveyor systems that can be assembled into different patterns like train tracks. Work cells "snake" through a plant so workers can shift their paths as demand changes. Machines are more general purpose, so they can adapt, too.

The original term *flexible manufacturing system* is what we discuss in the chapter as an automated random routing, computer-controlled production system. The popular literature, however, often speaks of flexible manufacturing in terms of any kind of production that can be changed over quickly.

Teaching Note 7.3 Mixed-Model Sequencing

Toyota originally used a process called goal chasing to sequence mixed-model assembly lines. The objective of the sequence is to minimize the deviation from linearity of production for components. The procedure was somewhat crude but worked well. Then researchers began to experiment with artificial intelligence methods.

Now, Toyota uses an expert system to sequence its mixed-model lines. Goal chasing is still a part of it but does not completely define the schedule. Commonsense rules such as the following are included: Do not send two models down the line that take longer than average to process. Put a short job after a long one, so the workers can catch up. See *Toyota Production System*, 1993 edition, by Monden, for details.

ALTERNATE EXAMPLES

Alternate Example 7.1

Problem Statement:

Use the following load summary chart to arrange departments 1 through 9 on a 3 × 3 grid so that the nonadjacent loads are minimized.

Dept.	*1*	*2*	*3*	*4*	*5*	*6*	*7*	*8*	*9*
1	—	50	100	25	60			65	
2	40	—	80			150	40		
3	10	65	—	55		40			
4	10		45	—	75			50	100
5	15			60	—		60		
6		25	50			—			
7		25			100		—		
8	10			65				—	
9				140					—

Solution:

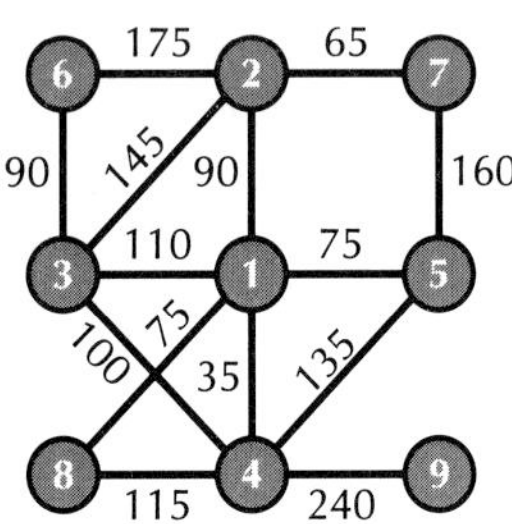

There are zero nonadjacent loads with this layout.

Alternate Example 7.2

Problem Statement:

Draw and label a precedence diagram from the following assembly information.

Work Element	*Predecessor*	*Time (min)*
a	—	4
b	a	2
c	a	1
d	b	1
e	b	5
f	d	3
g	c, e, f	4

Solution:

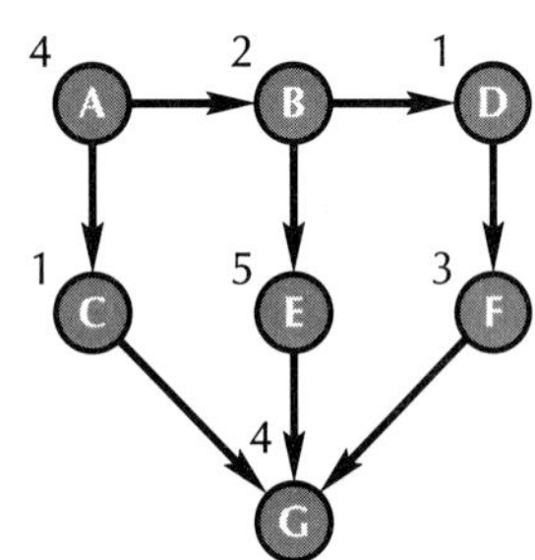

Alternate Example 7.3

Problem Statement:

Set up an assembly line for the assembly process described in Alternate Example 7.2 that will be capable of producing 120 units in a 10-hour day. Calculate the theoretical minimum number of workstations and the efficiency of the line. Why is there a discrepancy between the theoretical and actual number of workstations for this process? Would an assembly line in which the theoretical number of work stations equaled the actual number of work stations always be 100 percent efficient?

Solution:

$$\text{Cycle time} = \frac{10 \times 60}{120} = 5 \text{ min}$$

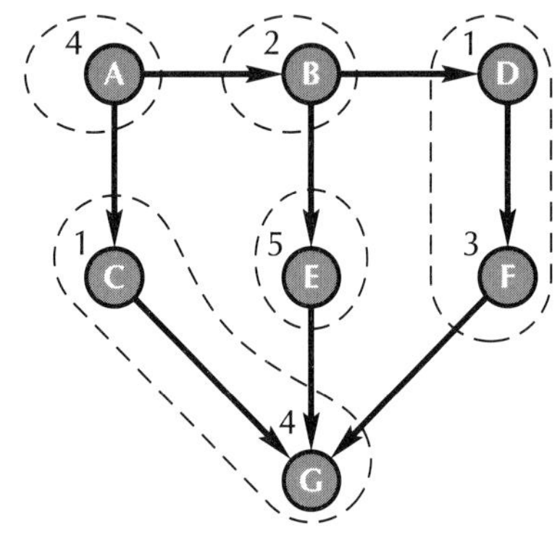

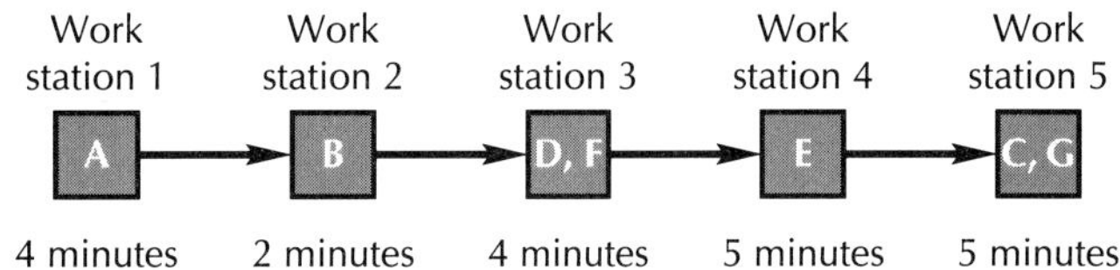

$$\begin{array}{c}\text{Theoretical minimum}\\ \text{number of workstations}\end{array} = \frac{4+2+1+1+5+3+4}{5} = 4$$

$$\text{Efficiency} = \frac{4+2+4+5+5}{5(5)} = \frac{20}{25}$$

$$= 0.80, \text{ or } 80\%$$

Precedence constraints prevent the actual number of workstations from reaching the theoretical number. An assembly line for which the actual number of workstations equals the theoretical minimum is not necessarily 100 percent efficient. The elemental times at each workstation must also be equal.

Alternate Example 7.4

Problem Statement:

Balance the assembly line from Example 7.3 by the technique of least number of following tasks. Calculate the efficiency of the line and determine how many claims can be processed in an 8-hour day.

Solution:

Element	*Number of Following Tasks*
A	4
B	2
C	1
D	1
E	0

- Assign element E to a workstation.
- Can elements C and/or D be added to the workstation? Yes, assign C, D, and E to the same workstation.
- Assign B to a workstation.
- Can element A be added? No, assign A to a separate workstation.

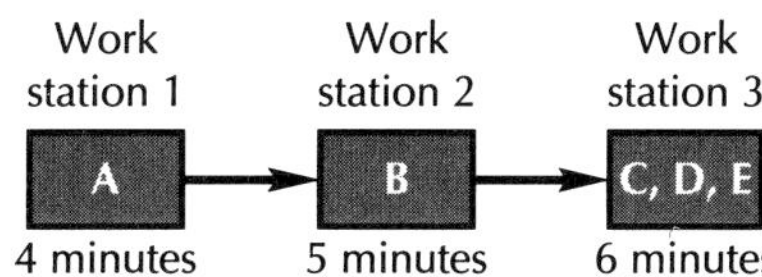

$$\text{Efficiency} = \frac{4+5+2+1+3}{3(6)}$$

$$= \frac{15}{18} = 0.833, \text{ or } 83.3\%$$

$$\text{No. of claims processed} = \frac{480}{6} = 80 \text{ per day}$$

VIDEOS

Video 7.1 *Harley-Davidson, Building Better Motorcycles the American Way*

This video has some good footage showing manufacturing cells in action and provides a nice balance between the need for automated versus manual work.

Video 7.2 *LTV's Flexible Manufacturing Cell*

This is an excellent video, showing LTV's advanced flexible manufacturing system. It is excerpted from a longer video produced as part of SME's Manufacturing Insights series. An application box in the chapter describes some of the equipment and systems you will see in the video.

8 LOCATION ANALYSIS AND LOGISTICS MANAGEMENT

TEACHING NOTES

Teaching Note 8.1 Inland Waterways and Floods

Of all the major transport systems in the United States, inland waterways, specifically the nation's river systems, comprise the only system subject to a period of long, sustained breakdown as a result of flooding. During the crippling floods of the summer of 1993 in the Midwest, barge traffic was at a standstill for several weeks, causing severe delays and spoilage that resulted in millions of dollars in losses. Although other forms of transport, such as rails and trucking, were delayed by the flood, they did not experience the total stoppage that occurred with barge traffic.

Teaching Note 8.2 The Transportation Problem Formulated as a Linear Programming Model

The transportation model is actually a special case of linear programming model with unique characteristics that allow it to be solved in a different manner than normal linear programming (lp) solution methods (i.e., simplex). The lp formulation minimizes transportation costs subject to constraints for supply and demand at the sources and destinations, respectively. The linear programming formulation for the transportation problem in Example 8.4 is as follows.

$$\text{Minimize } Z = \$6x_{1A} + 8x_{1B} + 10x_{1C} + 7x_{2A} + 11x_{2B} + 11x_{2C} + 4x_{3A} + 5x_{3B} + 12x_{3C}$$

subject to

$$x_{1A} + x_{1B} + x_{1C} = 150$$
$$x_{2A} + x_{2B} + x_{2C} = 175$$
$$x_{3A} + x_{3B} + x_{3C} = 275$$
$$x_{1A} + x_{2A} + x_{3A} = 200$$
$$x_{1B} + x_{2B} + x_{3B} = 100$$
$$x_{1C} + x_{2C} + x_{3C} = 300$$
$$x_{ij} \geq 0$$

The lp model can be solved using any linear programming software package or module.

ALTERNATE EXAMPLES

Alternate Example 8.1

Problem Statement:

The administration at State University wants to construct a new student athletic, shopping, and dining complex on campus. The university planning office is considering possible sites around the campus. They have studied a number of factors related to the location of the complex and they have scored the most important ones for each site as follows.

		Score (0 to 100)			
Location Factor	Weight	Site 1	Site 2	Site 3	Site 4
1. Auto traffic flow	0.25	70	75	84	68
2. Student/dorm concentration	0.20	65	91	85	96
3. Parking availability	0.15	100	83	90	92
4. Utilities	0.15	87	96	80	85
5. Proximity to local merchants	0.10	69	85	80	95
6. Drainage	0.10	50	68	92	77
7. Aesthetic considerations	0.05	86	100	95	80

Determine the best site using location factor rating.

Solution:

The weighted total scores for each factor for each site are summarized as follows.

	Site 1	Site 2	Site 3	Site 4
Score	74.75	84.10	85.45	83.95

The scores are so close for sites 2, 3, and 4 that the benefit of using this technique in this example may simply be to eliminate site 1 from further consideration.

Alternate Example 8.2

Problem Statement:

Bell Communications Company owns and operates cable television systems in five communities in the southwestern part of the state. They want to construct a centralized service facility from which to send out their service trucks for repair and installations. The communities have the following sets of location coordinates and annual number of repair truck visits.

A	B	C	D	E
$x_A = 20$	$x_B = 55$	$x_C = 25$	$x_D = 10$	$x_E = 60$
$y_A = 20$	$y_B = 30$	$y_C = 60$	$y_D = 40$	$y_E = 50$
$w_A = 420$	$w_B = 610$	$w_C = 505$	$w_D = 370$	$w_E = 570$

Using the center-of-gravity method determine the possible locations for the central service facility.

Solution:

$$x = \frac{92{,}475}{2{,}475} = 37.4$$

$$y = \frac{100{,}300}{2{,}475} = 40.5$$

Alternate Example 8.3

Problem Statement:

Wiley's Food Market owns grocery stores in four communities in a three-county area. They want to construct a centrally located warehouse to process, package, and distribute produce and other food items for their four stores. The items are transported in 40-foot trailer trucks. The stores have the following set of coordinates and annual shipments.

A	B	C	D
$x_A = 60$	$x_B = 110$	$x_C = 35$	$x_D = 70$
$y_A = 130$	$y_B = 40$	$y_C = 90$	$y_D = 50$
$w_A = 145$	$w_B = 210$	$w_C = 160$	$w_D = 95$

Three sites are being considered for the warehouse with the following coordinates:

Site 1: $x_1 = 50, y_1 = 60$
Site 2: $x_2 = 100, y_2 = 70$
Site 3: $x_3 = 40, y_3 = 90$

Using the load-distance technique, determine the best location for the warehouse.

Solution:

Site 1: $d_A = 70.7, d_B = 63.2, d_C = 33.5, d_D = 22.4$
Site 2: $d_A = 72.1, d_B = 31.6, d_C = 68, \ d_D = 36.1$
Site 3: $d_A = 44.7, d_B = 86.0, d_C = 5.0, \ d_D = 50.0$

$$\text{LD (site 1)} = (70.7)(145) + (63.2)(210) + (33.5)(160) + (22.4)(95) = 31{,}012$$

$$\text{LD (site 2)} = (72.1)(145) + (31.6)(210) + (68)(160) + (36.1)(95) = 31{,}400$$

$$\text{LD (site 3)} = (44.7)(145) + (86.0)(210) + (5)(160) + (50)(95) = 30{,}092$$

Site 3 has the lowest load-distance value.

VIDEO

Video 8.1: *The Allyn and Bacon Plant Tour Video,* Program 1: "Federal Express: Setting the Pace for the 90s"

This program describes Federal Express's airfreight packaging and handling distribution terminal, known as the *superhub,* in Memphis, Tennessee. The application box titled "The Federal Express Superhub" in this chapter complements this video. The video has a duration of 15 minutes and is completely nontechnical.

8 SUPPLEMENT: TRANSPORTATION MODEL SOLUTION METHODS

TEACHING NOTES

Teaching Note S8.1 The Stepping-Stone Method Versus MODI

In teaching the transportation method, we normally concentrate on becoming adept at only one of the two available solution methods, the stepping-stone technique or the modified distribution (MODI) technique. We have found that once students practice the stepping-stone method, they usually find it to be quicker; that is why we use it exclusively in this supplement and do not show MODI.

MODI is a modified version of the stepping-stone method, so there are close similarities. The MODI computations that result in the cell cost changes are a mathematical means for determining the same cell cost values found using the stepping-stone method. Essentially, MODI replicates the stepping-stone method. (See Teaching Note S8.2.)

Teaching Note S8.2 The MODI Solution

For those interested in using the MODI method we provide the solution for the transportation example shown in the text obtained with the MODI method. The tableau for the initial solution with the modifications required by MODI is shown as follows.

	v_j	$v_A =$	$v_B =$	$v_C =$	
u_i	From \ To	A	B	C	Supply
$u_1 =$	1	[6]	25 [8]	125 [10]	150
$u_2 =$	2	[7]	[11]	175 [11]	175
$u_3 =$	3	200 [4]	75 [5]	[12]	275
	Demand	200	100	300	600

The u_i and v_j values are computed for all cells with allocations by using the following formula.

$$u_i + v_j = c_{ij}$$

The formulas for the cells that presently contain allocations are

x_{1B}: $u_1 + v_B = 8$
x_{1C}: $u_1 + v_C = 10$
x_{2C}: $u_2 + v_C = 11$
x_{3A}: $u_3 + v_A = 4$
x_{3B}: $u_3 + v_B = 5$

There are five equations with six unknowns. To solve these equations, it is necessary to assign one of the unknowns a value of zero. Thus, if we let $u_1 = 0$, we can solve for all remaining values of u_i and v_j:

$$v_B = 8, \quad v_C = 10, \quad u_2 = 1, \quad u_3 = -3, \quad \text{and} \quad v_A = 7$$

Next, we use the following formula to evaluate all *empty* cells:

$$c_{ij} - u_i - v_j = k_{ij}$$

where k_{ij} equals the cost increase or decrease that would occur by allocating to a cell.

For the *empty cells* in the transportation tableau, this formula yields the following values:

x_{1A}: $k_{1A} = c_{1A} - u_1 - v_A = 6 - 0 - 7 = -1$
x_{2A}: $k_{2A} = c_{2A} - u_2 - v_A = 7 - 1 - 7 = -1$
x_{2B}: $k_{2B} = c_{2B} - u_2 - v_B = 11 - 1 - 8 = +2$
x_{3C}: $k_{3C} = c_{3C} - u_3 - v_C = 12 - (-3) - 10 = +5$

We can select either cell 1A or 2A to allocate to, since they are tied at −1. If cell 1A is selected as the entering nonbasic variable, then the stepping-stone path for that cell must be determined so that we know how much to reallocate. This is the same path previously identified in Table S8.10. Reallocating along this path results in the following tableau (shown in the text in Table S8.14).

	v_j	$v_A = 6$	$v_B = 7$	$v_C = 10$	
u_i	From \ To	A	B	C	Supply
$u_1 = 0$	1	25 [6]	[8]	125 [10]	150
$u_2 = 1$	2	[7]	[11]	175 [11]	175
$u_3 = -2$	3	175 [4]	100 [5]	[12]	275
	Demand	200	100	300	600

The u_i and v_j values for this table have been recomputed using our formula for the allocated-to cells, $u_i + v_j = c_{ij}$.

The cost changes for the empty cells are

x_{1B}: $k_{1B} = c_{1B} - u_1 - v_B = 8 - 0 - 7 = +1$
x_{2A}: $k_{2A} = c_{2A} - u_2 - v_A = 7 - 1 - 6 = 0$
x_{2B}: $k_{2B} = c_{2B} - u_2 - v_B = 11 - 1 - 7 = +3$
x_{3C}: $k_{3C} = c_{3C} - u_3 - v_C = 12 - (-2) - 10 = +4$

None of these values is negative, so this solution is optimal. However, as in the stepping-stone method, cell 2A with a zero cost change indicates a multiple optimal solution.

The steps of the modified distribution method can be summarized as follows.

1. Develop an initial solution using one of the three methods available.
2. Compute u_i and v_j values for each row and column by applying the formula $u_i + v_j = c_{ij}$ to each cell that has an allocation.
3. Compute the cost change, k_{ij}, for each empty cell using the formula $c_{ij} - u_i - v_j = k_{ij}$.
4. Allocate as much as possible to the empty cell that will result in the greatest net decrease in cost (most negative k_{ij}). Allocate according to the stepping-stone path for the selected cell.
5. Repeat steps 2 through 4 until all k_{ij} values are positive or zero.

Teaching Note S8.3 Integer Solution

The transportation method ensures integer solution values, something that should be pointed out to the student. The reason becomes apparent when considering the linear programming model formulation. All the constraint coefficients are 1s, meaning all solution values will be obtained by dividing by 1 in the simplex method.

Teaching Note S8.4 Degeneracy

Students can be quickly discouraged by the problem of degeneracy in transportation models. A problem is where to locate the ϕ. The first criteria is to put the ϕ in a cell that will ensure that all the stepping-stone paths (or MODI calculations) can be completed. Students need to be aware of when a problem becomes degenerate—that is, when row and column requirements are satisfied simultaneously. A good location for ϕ is in either that row or column that caused the degeneracy. A second criteria is locating the ϕ such that the number of solution iterations will be minimized. If there are several cell choices for ϕ, the one with the minimum cost should be selected to minimize the iterations.

Another problem with degeneracy is reallocating the ϕ along the stepping-stone path. Students are sometimes confused by this, and thus it should be carefully explained.

9 *JOBS: DESIGN, ANALYSIS, AND MEASUREMENT*

TEACHING NOTES

Teaching Note 9.1 Frederick W. Taylor

Frederick W. Taylor (1856–1915) started work at Midvale Steel Company in 1878 at the age of 22, earning a degree in mechanical engineering by attending Stevens Institute of Technology at night. In 1881 he employed a stopwatch to determine the proper output that should be produced per worker after analyzing and determining their jobs. For the next twenty years Taylor conducted experiments, primarily at Bethlehem Steel Company. From these experiments, his search for a means to set work standards and observations of management practices, Taylor developed his *principles of scientific management*. These principles sought to "develop a science for each element of a man's work, which replaces the old rule-of-thumb method" and "scientifically select, and then train, teach, and develop the workman, whereas previously he chose his own work methods and trained himself as best as he could."

Taylor has frequently been criticized as being "against labor" for establishing a system that seemed aimed at speeding up work. However, this criticism is unwarranted and misplaced. He believed that a worker should be able to work as hard and as fast as he could at his job and be rewarded accordingly. He believed workers should have the opportunity through piecework and wage incentives to earn more (up to 25 percent more) than the standard pay. To do so management had to know how much a worker should be able to produce *without fatigue*, hence his studies of jobs using a stopwatch. He was the first person to suggest that rest periods would improve productivity, and he included these in his time studies. Later industrialists who adopted time studies would frequently alter the output standards so that workers would derive no benefit from increased output, in direct opposition to what Taylor proposed.

Source: Emerson, H. P., and D. C. E. Naehring, *Origins of Industrial Engineering*, Atlanta, Ga.: Institute of Industrial Engineers, 1988.

Teaching Note 9.2 Job Training at Yamazaki Machinery UK Ltd.

At the time of its opening in 1987, the Yamazaki Machinery plant in Worcester, England, was the most technologically advanced machine tool plant in Europe. Although the plant made extensive us of "intelligent," automated equipment, a key objective was on hiring and training line employees to make sure they had the right skills, abilities, and attitudes to meet work requirements. Training at the plant was not a personnel function but was the responsibility of line management, who determined how much to invest in training, what to expect, and how to monitor future performance. Every job in the plant included a schedule of competencies (i.e., skills, abilities, and characteristics) rather than a job description. Training focused on reaching standard competency levels in three categories: basic competencies (skills necessary to do a job), breadth of competencies (skills across a variety of jobs), and future competencies (developing individual potential). The return on the investment in training was closely monitored by management as a measure of effectiveness.

Source: Lawrence, M., "Train the Troop," *Manufacturing Engineer*, 71, no. 3 (1992): 33.

Teaching Note 9.3 Frank and Lillian Gilbreth

Frank Gilbreth (1868–1924), thwarted in his plans to attend M.I.T. by his father's death, went to work as a bricklayer's apprentice at the age of 17. When he first started he noticed the bricklayer training him did his work in three different ways. Gilbreth also noticed that all the other bricklayers at the construction site had their own methods of laying bricks. At that time Gilbreth conceived the idea that there should be one best way to do a job, which became his lifelong goal. Gilbreth reduced the motions for laying a single brick from 18 to 4.5 and also invented the movable scaffold, which is still used today to keep the bricklayer at the proper level. His famous book *Motion Study*, published in 1911, deals mainly with bricklaying. Frank Gilbreth was 12 years younger than F. W. Taylor, and the two first met in 1907. Gilbreth was a supporter of Taylor's scientific management system and acknowledged the older engineer's initial contributions, although their relationship deteriorated in their later years. Gilbreth went into business for himself at age 26 and became one of the best-known building contractors in the world, with offices in London and New York. One reason for his success was the ability to build quickly.

Lillian Gilbreth (1878–1972) outlived her husband by 48 years and spent much of this time promoting the pioneering concepts of scientific management and industrial engineering. She was an important and equal contributor to the field of motion study and production management with her husband. She received a doctorate in psychology from Brown University, which she used to study problems in human relations and psychology in management. Excluded from even attending meetings of professional engineering societies in her youth because she was a woman, she was later bemedaled and feted by these same societies. She became known as the first lady of industrial engineering. She and her husband were the subject of a book by their children, *Cheaper by the Dozen*, which was made into a movie of the same name starring Clifton Webb and Myrna Loy.

Teaching Note 9.4 Performance Rating

A traditional "standard" for a performance rating of 1.00 is to deal a deck of 52 cards into four piles in 0.5 minutes. This is an interesting experiment to conduct in class. Have one student deal a deck of cards and the other students rate the subject's performance while the instructor times the "job" of dealing the cards. Students invariably rate the dealer too low, as 0.5 minutes is actually relatively slow. Another traditional standard for a performance rating of 1.00 is walking at a speed of 3 miles per hour. This is a harder experiment to conduct in class, since it requires a treadmill or pedometer.

Teaching Note 9.5 The Origination of Work Sampling

Work sampling originated in 1934 with a proposal by L. H. C. Tippet to measure delays in textile operations based on probability theory. The textile industry has historically relied on the use of work methods and time studies to set wages in a piece-rate system. A number of labor contracts in the textile industry have been and still are based on these piece-rate systems.

ALTERNATE EXAMPLE

Alternate Example 9.1

Problem Statement:

A grocery chain sells prewrapped flowers in its stores. The flowers are selected and wrapped in a central facility and then distributed to the stores in the area. A time study of the operation for assembling and wrapping a bouquet has been conducted, with the following results:

	Cycle Time (min)						*Performance*
Element	*1*	*2*	*3*	*4*	*5*	*6*	*Rating*
1. Prepare paper wrapping	0.05	0.61	1.26	2.00	2.61	3.22	1.10
2. Select flowers	0.22	0.75	1.47	2.18	2.72	3.37	0.95
3. Arrange flowers and secure	0.43	1.03	1.81	2.43	3.01	3.70	1.05
4. Place bouquet in box for transport	0.51	1.15	1.88	2.52	3.12	3.81	0.90

Determine the normal time, and, using a 15 percent allowance factor, find the standard time for this job. How many bouquets could be made in a 3-hour period?

Solution:

	Elemental Times (min)									
Element	*1*	*2*	*3*	*4*	*5*	*6*	$\sum t$	$\bar{t}$	*PF*	*Nt*
1. Prepare paper wrapping	0.05	0.10	0.11	0.12	0.09	0.11	0.58	0.096	1.10	0.106
2. Select flowers	0.17	0.14	0.21	0.18	0.11	0.25	1.06	0.176	0.95	0.167
3. Arrange flowers and secure	0.21	0.28	0.34	0.25	0.29	0.33	1.70	0.283	1.05	0.297
4. Place bouquet in box for transport	0.08	0.12	0.07	0.09	0.11	0.11	0.58	0.096	0.90	0.086
									NT =	0.656

INSTRUCTOR'S SECTION

$$\begin{aligned} ST &= (NT)(1 + AF) \\ &= (0.656)(1.15) \\ &= 0.754 \text{ min} \end{aligned}$$

$$\text{Production in 3 hours} = \frac{180}{0.754} = 238.7 \text{ bouquets}$$

VIDEOS

Video 9.1 *CNN Work in Progress*

This video is a 1-hour documentary, hosted by Bernard Shaw, that originally appeared on the CNN network in 1993. It focuses on the future of the workplace and jobs in the United States and the changes that are taking place. It includes a number of short segments of approximately 5 to 10 minutes on different companies and aspects of the workplace. One segment is on employment empowerment at Harley-Davidson, and it accompanies the application box in this chapter entitled "Worker Empowerment at Harley-Davidson."

Video 9.2 *CNN Work in Progress*

The second instance in this chapter where the *CNN Work in Progress* video is used is a segment on Quad Graphics, Inc., a large printing company in Milwaukee. This segment, one of the longer ones in the hour-long documentary, lasts approximately 10 minutes and focuses on the importance of job training and employee education at Quad Graphics. The video accompanies the application box in this chapter entitled "Employee Training at Quad Graphics, Inc."

Video 1.1 1992 *Malcolm Baldrige Awards, Quest For Excellence V*

This video includes overviews of the five 1992 Baldrige Award Winners, including AT&T Network Systems Group, AT&T Universal Card Services, Granite Rock Company, Texas Instruments, Inc.—Defense Systems and Electronics Group, and the Ritz Carlton Hotel. A consistent feature in the TQM program at all these companies is the emphasis on job training as compared to their competitors. The tape lasts 18.5 minutes, and it complements the application box in this chapter entitled "Employee Training at Quad Graphics, Inc."

10 FORECASTING

TEACHING NOTES

Teaching Note 10.1 Use of Forecasting

Forecasting is a pervasive activity in everyday life. We wake up in the morning to forecasts about the weather, eat lunch to forecasts on cable TV for the stock market, and go to bed to forecasts about the state of the world the next day. Virtually every business attempts to do some kind of forecasting on a regular basis. Students should be aware that if there is one quantitative technique from this text they are likely to encounter when they get a job, it is probably forecasting.

Teaching Note 10.2 Forecasting Terminology

Forecasting has a lot of unique terminology that initially confuses some students. Terms such as *short-term, long-term, pattern, trend, time series, regression,* and *smoothing* can temporarily overwhelm the student. The only way to sort this out is to have the students commit these different terms to memory; a brief in-class quiz is a good way to test this exercise.

Teaching Note 10.3 Forecasting Techniques Used in This Chapter

It is surprising how many businesses use the rather straightforward, uncomplicated forecasting techniques presented in this chapter. The authors have encountered several small firms that use moving averages just as they are shown in this chapter. Students are generally impressed by the fact that the techniques they learn in this chapter can—and most likely will—be directly applied in their future jobs.

Teaching Note 10.4 Data Collection

Example 10.1 includes only 10 months of historical data. However, the student should be reminded that in actual circumstances, a large amount of historical data would be used from at least several years in the past. By using only a few periods of data encompassing a year or less, it would be difficult to identify any seasonal trends. Note from Figure 10.2 that data collection and revision are important components of the forecasting process.

Teaching Note 10.5 The Moving Average

The moving average and other forecasts actually provide two kinds of forecasts. On the one hand, they provide a forecast for one period in the future; alternatively, the entire sequence of moving average values can provide a forecast for the same time periods the following year.

Teaching Note 10.6 Selecting α and β

As noted in the text, the selection of α and β are judgmental. The aim is to select values of α and β that will provide a forecast reflecting actual values as closely as possible. Computer software is useful in making this determination, since it allows the user to test different values of α and β very rapidly and easily.

Teaching Note 10.7 Forecast Accuracy

Forecasts are notoriously inaccurate; no technique can exactly predict the future. When students observe a series of forecasted values such as those shown in Table 10.1 and in Figure 10.3, they are sometimes dismayed by the fact that the forecast values differ from the actual values by so much. However, the accuracy of the forecast is determined by how well it predicts relative to some other device, including the decision maker's own judgment. Also, in many instances the purpose of the forecast is not necessarily to get an exact prediction of sales the next month (although that would be nice); rather, it is to discover a trend, a pattern, or some movement in a direction that will enable the manager to make an educated guess as to what sales might be in the future.

ALTERNATE EXAMPLES

Alternate Example 10.1

Problem Statement:

Gunn's Tannery supplies leather to the South Fork Boot Company on a monthly basis for manufacturing western-style cowboy boots. South Fork does not keep a large stock of inventory on hand, thus the tannery must provide sufficient leather to meet demand on a timely basis. Furthermore, the quality of the leather must be of the highest grade. The demand for cowboy boots is lowest in the late winter, increases during the summer and fall, and reaches its peak during the holiday season. The demand for leather follows the same general pattern. Gunn's Tannery has experienced the following monthly demand for the past 14 months.

Month	*Demand* (1,000 yd^2)	*Month*	*Demand* (1,000 yd^2)
January	1.3	August	2.0
February	1.1	September	2.9
March	0.9	October	3.2
April	1.6	November	3.7
May	1.5	December	2.4
June	2.1	January	1.6
July	2.4	February	1.0

Develop a forecast for March using a. a 3-month moving average and b. a 3-month weighted moving average with weights of 0.60, 0.30, and 0.10 for the most recent demand.

Solution:

Month	*MA(3) Forecast*	*WMA(3) Forecast*
April	1.10	1.00
May	1.20	1.34
June	1.33	1.47
July	1.73	1.87
August	2.00	2.22
September	2.16	2.13
October	2.43	2.58
November	2.70	2.99
December	3.26	3.47
January	3.10	2.87
February	2.56	2.05
March	1.66	1.32

Alternate Example 10.2

Problem Statement:

For the data provided in Alternate Example 10.1, develop an exponentially smoothed forecast with α = 0.4.

Solution:

Month	F_{t+1}	*Month*	F_{t+1}
January	1.30	September	1.97
February	1.30	October	2.34
March	1.22	November	2.68
April	1.09	December	3.09
May	1.29	January	2.81
June	1.37	February	2.32
July	1.66	March	1.79
August	1.95		

Alternate Example 10.3

Problem Statement:

For the data provided in Alternate Example 10.1, develop an adjusted exponentially smoothed forecast with α = 0.40 and β = 0.50.

Solution:

Month	F_{t+1}	*Month*	F_{t+1}
January	—	September	2.10
February	1.30	October	2.59
March	1.18	November	2.98
April	1.00	December	3.44
May	1.35	January	2.85
June	1.44	February	2.10
July	1.84	March	1.41
August	2.19		

Alternate Example 10.4

Problem Statement:

For the data provided in for Alternate Example 10.1, develop a linear trend line forecast.

Solution:

$$y = 1.31 + 0.088x$$
$$y \text{ (March)} = 2.64$$

Alternate Example 10.5

Problem Statement:

Compare the accuracy of the moving average, weighted moving average, exponential smoothing, adjusted exponential smoothing, and linear trend line forecasts developed in Alternate Examples, 10.1, 10.3, 10.4, and 10.5 using MAD, and indicate the forecast you would employ.

Solution:

Forecast	*MAD*
Moving average	0.787
Weighted moving average	0.693
Exponential smoothing	0.673
Adjusted exponential smoothing	0.575
Linear trend line	0.563

Although the linear trend line has the lowest MAD value, the adjusted exponentially smoothed forecast also has a low value for MAD and appears to give the most accurate forecast for March.

VIDEO

Video 10.1 *TIMS Edelman Award Tape,* Program 2: "Citgo Petroleum"

This video accompanies the application box in this chapter describing the use of forecasting at Citgo Petroleum for wholesale oil prices and product volume. This tape is approximately 20 minutes long, and the presentation is generally descriptive and nontechnical.

11 AGGREGATE PRODUCTION AND CAPACITY PLANNING

TEACHING NOTES

Teaching Note 11.1 Contingent Workers

The contingent work force in the United States, made up of part-time and temporary workers, is experiencing a dramatic increase. Part-time and temporary workers are more flexible and do not require expensive benefits (although the new National Health Care plan may change that). This trend makes aggregate planning more important, or at least an activity engaged in more frequently. Ask how many students in your class expect never to hold a full-time, permanent job. Probably no one will raise his or her hand. Statistics are moving toward 20 percent of the work force being permanently "temporary."

Teaching Note 11.2 Customer Expectations

Customer expectations are continually raising company performance as illustrated by the Henredon Furniture box. One of the slow service areas has traditionally been catalog sales. The standard promise date used to be 4 to 6 weeks to receive mail orders. Sometimes it took longer to ship the items to the customer than to make them at the factory. Look at the promise dates now—24 hours, within 3 days, order by December 22 for guaranteed delivery by Christmas. Things surely have changed.

Teaching Note 11.3 Tracking Peak Demand

Do you ever wonder how the Franklin Mint and those other places that offer limited editions of figurines, dolls, plates, or other collectibles figure out how many items there are in a limited edition? They have a sophisticated planning model that tries to predict from the first several days of orders when the peak will hit (and thus when demand will start to slide) so they can switch their capacity to start producing another limited edition. It's a tight call. Only a few copies are initially available, and in some cases the item is not physically produced until a market materializes.

Teaching Note 11.4 AB:POM for Aggregate Planning

AB:POM provides fast solutions to aggregate planning problems but does not guarantee optimality. Four planning strategies are available: 1. smooth production, 2. produce to demand, 3. constant regular time, then overtime and subcontracting, and 4. user defined (in which production amounts can be entered directly). The inputs to the program are the number of time periods, the planning method (by toggle), shortage type (by toggle), capacities, costs, and demand. Capacities are either given in the problem, or a result of the method chosen. For example, for smooth production, regular capacity must be set high enough to cover average demand. If no overtime or subcontracting is allowed, overtime and subcontracting capacities should be set to zero. All costs are given on a per unit basis, so hiring and firing costs per worker must be divided by the number of units each worker produces before entering into the program. Students should be advised to check their results carefully to ensure that the solution is feasible and within the guidelines of the problem. It is easy to forget about eliminating shortages and design a plan that is low cost but does not satisfy customer demand.

Teaching Note 11.5 The Transportation Method of APP

Two blank APP transportation tables are included for class handouts or overheads. We tried to make the concept simple by working with cases where demand does not exceed supply. The first version of the transportation tableau is presented in Chapter 11 of the textbook. The second version includes a dummy column called **unused capacity** that may be helpful in highlighting excesses in capacity. The problems in the text for the most part are optimal with the first tableau. Setting up the problem and converting the solution from the tableau to a production plan are the emphasized skills.

		Period of Production				
	Period of Use	1	2	3	4	Capacity
	Beginning Inventory					
1	Regular					
	Overtime					
	Subcontract					
2	Regular					
	Overtime					
	Subcontract					
3	Regular					
	Overtime					
	Subcontract					
4	Regular					
	Overtime					
	Subcontract					
	Demand					

		Period of Production					
	Period of Use	1	2	3	4	Unused Capacity	Capacity
	Beginning Inventory						
1	Regular						
	Overtime						
	Subcontract						
2	Regular						
	Overtime						
	Subcontract						
3	Regular						
	Overtime						
	Subcontract						
4	Regular						
	Overtime						
	Subcontract						
	Demand						

Teaching Note 11.6 Linear Decision Rule

The purpose of including the linear decision rule in this chapter is to encourage students to think about cost assumptions. If you briefly go over the graphs of each of the four cost components, students will probably agree that real-world costs are more quadratic than linear.

Teaching Note 11.7 A Video Suggestion

The *TIMS-CPMS Edelman Award for Management Science Achievement* video series includes a 1991 American Airline Decision Technologies presentation on yield management. Part of it is too technical for the students, but the description of yield management is good, and it is helpful to show the students how complicated the decisions really are. The system is written up in *Interfaces* (January–February 1991).

ALTERNATE EXAMPLES

Alternate Example 11.1

Problem Statement:

Consider the following modifications to Example 11.1 separately. How would the aggregate planning strategy change in each case?

a. Inventory carrying cost is reduced to $0.25 per pound per quarter.
b. The analysis is performed over a two-year planning horizon.
c. Sales promotions are successful in shifting demand of 25,000 pounds of candy from fall to spring and 20,000 pounds from winter to spring.

Solution:

a. The cost of the level production strategy would be cut in half, to $35,000, the same cost as the chase demand strategy.

b. The cost of the level production strategy would double, to $140,000. The cost of the chase demand strategy would more than double because 50 extra workers would need to be fired in moving from winter of the first year to spring of the second year. However, the resulting cost, ($35,000 × 2) + (50 × $500) = $95,000, is still the best choice.

c.

Level Production Strategy

Quarter	*Sales*	*Production*	*Inventory*
Spring	$100,000	100,000	0
Summer	75,000	100,000	25,000
Fall	95,000	100,000	30,000
Winter	130,000	100,000	0
			55,000

Cost = (55,000 × $0.50) = $27,500

Chase Demand Strategy

Quarter	*Sales*	*Production*	*Workers Needed*	*Workers Hired*	*Workers Fired*
Spring	$100,000	100,000	100	0	0
Summer	75,000	75,000	75	0	25
Fall	95,000	95,000	95	20	0
Winter	130,000	130,000	130	35	0
				55	25

Cost = (55 × $100) + (25 × $500) = $5,500 + $12,500 = $18,000

Thus, chase demand is still the preferred strategy.

Alternate Example 11.2

Problem Statement:

Given the following demand, cost, and operating data, evaluate the following production plans:

a. Produce to meet demand by varying the size of the work force. Satisfy demand for part-time work with overtime.

b. Produce with a fixed work force of 500. Subcontract excess demand.

c. Produce with a fixed work force of 400. Subcontract excess demand.

Manufacturing cost per unit	$100
Subcontracting cost per unit	$110
Regular hourly wage rate	$ 12
Overtime hourly wage rate	$ 18
Regular hours per day per worker	8
Labor hours per unit	4
Layoff cost per worker	$500
Hiring cost per worker	$400
Inventory holding cost per unit per month	$ 2
Initial work force	250

Month	*Demand*	*Working Days*
January	11,000	22
February	15,000	19
March	32,000	21
April	25,000	21
May	30,000	22
June	14,500	20

Solution:

a. Vary work force, use overtime:

Month	*Demand*	*Hours Req.*	*Hours Avail./ Worker*	*Workers Needed*	*Workers Hired*	*Workers Fired*
Jan	11,000	44,000	176	250		
Feb	15,000	60,000	152	394	144	
Mar	32,000	128,000	168	761	367	
Apr	25,000	100,000	168	595		166
May	30,000	120,000	176	681	86	
Jun	14,500	58,000	160	362		319
	127,500				597	485

Hours Required	*Regular Hours*	*Overtime Hours*
44,000	44,000	0
60,000	59,888	112
128,000	127,848	152
100,000	99,960	40
120,000	119,856	144
58,000	57,920	80
	509,472	528

Cost = (509,472 × $12) + (528 × $18)
+ (127,500 × $52) + (597 × $400) + (485 × $500)
= $6,113,664 + $9,504 + $6,630,000 + $238,800 + $242,500
= $13,234,468

b. 500 workers, subcontract:

Month	*Demand*	*Hours/ Worker*	*Production*	*Inventory*	*Subcontracted*
Jan	11,000	176	22,000	11,000	0
Feb	15,000	152	19,000	15,000	0
Mar	32,000	168	21,000	4,000	0
Apr	25,000	168	21,000	0	0
May	30,000	176	22,000	0	8,000
Jun	14,500	160	20,000	5,500	0
	127,500		125,000	35,500	8,000

Cost = (125,000 × $100) + (35,500 × $2) + (8,000 × $110)
= $12,500,000 + $71,000 + $880,000
= $13,451,000

c. 400 workers, subcontract:

Month	Demand	Hours/ Worker	Production	Inventory	Subcontracted
Jan	11,000	176	17,600	6,600	0
Feb	15,000	152	15,200	6,800	0
Mar	32,000	168	16,800	0	8,400
Apr	25,000	168	16,800	0	8,200
May	30,000	176	17,600	0	12,400
Jun	14,500	160	16,000	1,500	0
	127,500		100,000	14,900	29,000

$$\begin{aligned}\text{Cost} &= (100{,}000 \times \$100) + (14{,}900 \times \$2) + (29{,}000 \times \$110) \\ &= \$10{,}000{,}000 + \$29{,}800 + \$3{,}190{,}000 \\ &= \$13{,}219{,}800^*\end{aligned}$$

The best aggregate planning strategy is to employ a steady work force of 400 workers and subcontract excess demand.

Alternate Example 11.3

Problem Statement:

Formulate a linear programming model for Example 11.2 that will satisfy the demand for Quantum action toys at minimum cost.

Solution:

$$\text{Minimize } Z = \$10\sum_{n=1}^{12} R_n + \$15\sum_{n=1}^{12} O_n + \$25\sum_{n=1}^{12} S_n + \$1\sum_{n=1}^{12} I_n + \$10\sum_{n=1}^{12} H_n + \$20\sum_{n=1}^{12} F_n$$

subject to:

$$\begin{aligned} R_0 &= 500 \\ I_0 &= 50 \\ I_{n-1} + R_n + O_n + S_n - I_n &= D_n && \text{for all } n \\ O_n &\le 250 && \text{for all } n \\ S_n &\le 3{,}000 && \text{for all } n \\ R_n - R_{n-1} - H_n + F_n &= 0 && \text{for all } n \end{aligned}$$

where n = months 1 through 12
D_n = monthly demand (1,000, 250, 200, 300, 400, 500, 800, 400, 1,000, 1,500, 2,500, 3,000)
R_n = regular production in month n
O_n = overtime production in month n
S_n = production subcontracted in month n
H_n = no. of extra cases produced due to workers hired in month n
F_n = no. of fewer cases produced due to workers fired in month n

Alternate Example 11.4

Problem Statement:

Dunkirk Marine is in the process of developing their aggregate plan for fiberglass hull laminating material for the next 6 months. The same laminating material is used for all models of recreational boats produced and is manufactured or purchased by the linear foot. Forecasted demand requirements for the next 6 months are as follows:

Month	Forecast Demand (linear foot)
1	11,500
2	15,000
3	22,500
4	19,000
5	21,500
6	16,000

Currently, first-shift production capacity is 10,000 linear feet per month, at a cost of $100 per linear foot. Second-shift production capacity is 4,000 linear feet per month, at a cost of $120 per linear foot. Costs of production are expected to remain constant through the third month. However, due to governmental regulations, the cost of producing 1 linear foot of laminate is expected to increase by 10 percent in month 4 and then remain constant until the end of the planning horizon.

Two other alternatives are available for supplying laminate. First, production can be subcontracted out to a small fiberglass company that Dunkirk Marine has used in the past. The supplier can provide 2,200 linear feet of laminate per month for months 1 through 5 at a cost of $140 per linear foot. Due to other obligations, however, the supplier can provide only 1,000 linear feet of laminate in month 6, at a cost of $140 per linear foot. Second, laminate can be purchased from Dunkirk Marine's South American subsidiary at a cost of $150 per linear foot. The subsidiary can supply 1,500 linear feet of laminate per month.

There are currently 100 linear feet of laminate in stock. Inventory carrying costs are $1 per linear foot of laminate per month. Back-order costs are $5 per linear foot of laminate per month. Set up an aggregate production plan utilizing the transportation method that can be solved in order to meet anticipated demand.

Solution:

		Period of Production						
Period of Supply		1	2	3	4	5	6	Capacity
Beginning Inventory		0	1	2	3	4	5	100
1	First Shift	100	101	102	103	104	105	10,000
	Second Shift	120	121	122	123	124	125	4,000
	Sub-contract	140	141	142	143	144	145	2,200
	Sub-sidiary	150	151	152	153	154	155	1,500
2	First Shift	105	100	101	102	103	104	10,000
	Second Shift	125	120	121	122	123	124	4,000
	Sub-contract	145	140	141	142	143	144	2,200
	Sub-sidiary	155	150	151	152	153	154	1,500
3	First Shift	110	105	100	101	102	103	10,000
	Second Shift	130	125	120	121	122	123	4,000
	Sub-contract	150	145	140	141	142	143	2,200
	Sub-sidiary	160	155	150	151	152	153	1,500
4	First Shift	125	120	115	110	111	112	10,000
	Second Shift	147	142	137	132	133	134	4,000
	Sub-contract	155	150	145	140	141	142	2,200
	Sub-sidiary	165	160	155	150	151	152	1,500
5	First Shift	130	125	120	115	110	111	10,000
	Second Shift	152	147	142	137	132	133	4,000
	Sub-contract	160	155	150	145	140	141	2,200
	Sub-sidiary	170	165	160	155	150	151	1,500
6	First Shift	135	130	125	120	115	110	10,000
	Second Shift	157	152	147	142	137	132	4,000
	Sub-contract	165	160	155	150	145	140	1,000
	Sub-sidiary	175	170	165	160	155	150	1,500
Unmet demand		0	0	0	0	0	0	400
Units demanded		11,500	15,000	22,500	19,000	21,500	16,000	105,500

VIDEO

Video 11.1 *TIMS Edelman Awards Tape,* Program 3: "L.L. Bean"

This is an excellent tape dealing with resource allocation and capacity in a highly seasonal business. The presentation is well done, and the results are impressive. Students can relate to this tape because almost everyone knows L.L. Bean and their reputation for quality service.

12 INVENTORY MANAGEMENT

TEACHING NOTES

Teaching Note 12.1 Real-World Examples

A good in-class exercise is to have students identify as many examples as they can of the types of inventory different businesses maintain and to identify the different purposes of inventory. They should also distinguish types of inventory that are required and those that simply serve as a mask for production problems, poor management, and poor quality.

Teaching Note 12.2 Dependent Versus Independent Demand

A good class exercise is to have students identify examples of dependent and independent demand items. For example, the demand for airline tickets is independent, whereas the demand for airplanes is dependent.

Teaching Note 12.3 Quality Service

Ask students to identify examples of how inventory impacts on the ability of a business or operation to provide quality service. Obvious examples include various retail operations.

Teaching Note 12.4 EOQ Experimentation with the Computer

The AB:POM computer package can be used to demonstrate the robust nature of the EOQ model mentioned previously in the text. The various model parameters, D, C_o, C_c, and C_s, can be altered and the resulting impact on optimal Q and total cost can be observed.

Teaching Note 12.5 Single-Period Model for Limited Demand

A single-period model is a special-purpose inventory model used to determine the order size for an inventory system in which the product is limited to a brief time span, such as perishable goods (e.g., food or flowers) or items whose usefulness is limited, such as a newspaper or a magazine such as *TV Guide*. This type of inventory problem is sometimes referred to as the "newsboy" problem, reflecting a carrier's determination of how many papers to order each day.

This type of problem is frequently solved within the framework of the type of *payoff table* used in decision analysis (see Chapter 2). The "payoffs" in this case usually are in the form of a cost or profit equation reflecting a trade-off between the cost of ordering too much of a perishable or limited-use item and having to throw it away or sell it at a reduced price and a shortage cost resulting from a loss in customer goodwill and lost current and future sales. The basic structure of the payoff table for this type of inventory problem is shown as follows.

	States of Nature Demand, D				
Decision	D_1	D_2	D_3	...	D_n
(Order size, Q)	p_1	p_2	p_3	...	p_n
Q_1	c_{11}	c_{12}	c_{13}	...	c_{1n}
Q_2	c_{21}	c_{22}	c_{23}	...	c_{2n}
Q_3	c_{31}	c_{32}	c_{33}	...	c_{3n}
⋮	⋮	⋮	⋮	⋮	⋮
Q_n	c_{n1}	c_{n2}	c_{n3}	...	c_{nn}

In this general payoff table structure, each demand value, D_j, has a probability of occurrence, P_j, and each order size, Q_i, represents a potential decision. The optimal order size is determined by selecting the order size that has the minimum expected cost, where expected cost is computed as follows.

$$E(Q_i) = \sum p_j c_{ij}$$

Problems 2-7 and 2-8 are examples of this type of problem.

ALTERNATE EXAMPLES

Alternate Example 12.1

Problem Statement:

Sunshine Motors is a large car dealership. Its most popular car is a four-wheel drive, sports utility vehicle. The new-year models are available, and the dealer must determine how many of these vehicles to order from the car manufacturer. Demand is estimated at 160 vehicles per year. The annual carrying cost is \$650 per car, and the ordering cost is \$700 per order. Determine the optimal order size, total annual inventory cost, and the order cycle time.

Solution:

$$Q = \sqrt{\frac{2C_oD}{C_c}} = \sqrt{\frac{2(700)(160)}{650}} = 18.56 \text{ cars}$$

$$\text{TC} = C_o\frac{D}{Q} + C_c\frac{Q}{2}$$

$$= \frac{(700)(160)}{18.56} + \frac{(650)(18.56)}{2} = \$12{,}066.48$$

$$\text{Order cycle time} = \frac{365}{D/Q} = \frac{365}{160/18.56} = 42.34 \text{ days}$$

Alternate Example 12.2

Problem Statement:

For the inventory system described in Alternate Example 12.2 for Sunshine Motors, determine the optimal order quantity and total cost if shortages are allowed and C_s = \$250.

Solution:

$$Q = \sqrt{\frac{2C_oD}{C_c}\left(\frac{C_s + C_c}{C_s}\right)} = \sqrt{\frac{2(700)(160)}{650}\left(\frac{250 + 650}{250}\right)} = 35.22$$

$$S = Q\left(\frac{C_c}{C_c + C_s}\right) = 35.22\left(\frac{650}{650 + 250}\right) = 25.44$$

$$\begin{aligned} TC &= \frac{C_sS^2}{2Q} + \frac{C_c(Q - S)^2}{2Q} + \frac{C_oD}{Q} \\ &= \frac{250(25.44)^2}{2(35.22)} + \frac{650(35.22 - 25.44)^2}{2(35.22)} + 700\left(\frac{160}{35.22}\right) \\ &= \$6,359.59 \end{aligned}$$

Alternate Example 12.3

Problem Statement:

For Sunshine Motors (Alternate Examples 12.2 and 12.4), the car manufacturer has offered the following price discount schedule.

Order Size	*Price*
0–99	$16,000
100–149	15,700
150+	15,500

Determine the optimal order size and total cost.

Solution:

$$Q = 150$$
$$TC = \$2,529,496.75$$

INSTRUCTOR'S SECTION

12 SUPPLEMENT: SIMULATION

TEACHING NOTES

Teaching Note S12.1 Popularity of Simulation

Simulation is an enormously popular technique, made even more so in recent years because of the availability of low-cost personal computers and the fact that simulation is now being taught to more students. Various surveys mentioned indicate simulation ranks very high—and often first—among applied management science techniques with business firms.

Teaching Note S12.2 Examples of Simulation

It is useful to describe several physical systems that are simulated with other physical systems. The text mentions weightlessness for crewed space flight, wind tunnels, and treadmills. Other examples include simulating crowd noise at a football practice with audio tapes, all kinds of product testing, and simulated battles and war games.

Teaching Note S12.3 History of the Monte Carlo Method

The mathematics of the Monte Carlo method has been known for years; British mathematician Lord Kelvin used the technique in a paper in 1901. However, it was formally identified and given this name by the Hungarian mathematician John von Neumann while he was working on the Los Alamos atomic bomb project during World War II. During this project physicists confronted a problem in determining how far neutrons would travel through various materials (i.e., neutron diffusion in fissile material). The Monte Carlo process was suggested to von Neumann by a colleague at Los Alamos, Stanislas Ulam, as a means to solve this problem—that is, by selecting random numbers to represent the random actions of neutrons. However, the Monte Carlo method as used in simulation did not gain widespread popularity until the development of the modern electronic computer after the war. Interestingly, this remarkable man, John von Neumann, is credited with being the key figure in the development of the computer.

Teaching Note S12.4 Manual Versus Computer Simulation

The simulation examples in this chapter must by necessity be done manually. Developing computer simulation models is a skill in itself and is beyond the scope of this text. Therefore, the objective is to provide students with a general understanding of how simulation models can be constructed and the advantages of simulation. However, it should be stressed that for real-world applications, manual simulation is not a satisfactory substitute for computer simulation. Although manual simulations are useful initially in constructing models, the actual simulation results must be obtained from many repetitions of the simulation, which is not possible when done manually.

Teaching Note S12.5 Computer Software for Simulation

Very few POM or management science software packages have simulation programs; and when they do, they generally only apply to one specific type of problem or application, such as a specific queuing problem or inventory problem. The reason is that there is no set format or generic model for simulation; each model is uniquely constructed. This makes it virtually impossible for software packages to include much on simulation. Alternatively, simulation models are typically programmed individually using a general-purpose language such as BASIC or FORTRAN or a language specifically developed for simulation, such as GPSS, SIMSCRIPT, or SLAM. For students, this means that if they perceive that they might eventually want to use simulation in some future employment activity, they cannot anticipate that easily applied software packages will be available.

Teaching Note S12.6 Areas of Application

The student might notice from the different examples in this chapter that simulation can be used instead of a technique described in another chapter to solve problems. For example, simulation is often applied to queuing problems that cannot be solved by traditional queuing models and to inventory models when the same condition results. A good class exercise is to have students check the journal *Interfaces* and report on the different simulation applications they can identify.

Teaching Note S12.7 Student Simulation

As with queuing, there are a number of everyday situations of which the students are aware that can be simulated. A good class exercise is to have students (individually or in groups) identify systems with which they are familiar at school, home, or workplace, explain why they could be simulated, and describe how simulation models should be constructed. Following is an example of a simulation that students find of interest.

The Bolder Boulder, a popular 10-kilometer race held each Memorial Day in Colorado, attracts many of the world's best runners among its 20,000 participants. The race starts at the Bank of Boulder at the northeastern corner of the city, winds through the city streets, and ends at the University of Colorado's football stadium in the center of the city. As the race grew in size (from 2,200 participants in 1979 to 20,000 in 1985), its quality suffered from overcrowding problems, especially at the finish line, where runners are individually tagged as they finish. Large waiting lines built up at the finish line, causing many complaints from the participants.

To correct this problem, race management implemented an interval-start system in 1986, wherein 24 groups of up to 1,000 runners each were started at 1-minute intervals. Although this solution alleviated the problem of street crowding, it did not solve the queuing problem at the finish line.

A simulation model of the race was then developed to evaluate several possible solutions—specifically, increasing the number of finish-line chutes from the 8 used previously to either 12 or 15. The model also was used to identify a set of block-start intervals that would eliminate finish line queuing problems with either chute scenario. Recommendations based on the simulation model were for a 12-chute finish line configuration and specific block-start intervals. The race conducted using the recommendations from the simulation model was flawless. The actual race behavior was almost identical to the simulation results. No overcrowding or queuing problems occurred at the finish line. The simulation model was used to fine-tune the 1986 and 1987 races, which also were conducted with virtually no problems.

Source: Farina R., et al., "The Computer Runs the Bolder Boulder: A Simulation of a Major Running Race," *Interfaces* 19, no. 2 (March–April 1989): 48–55.

VIDEO

Video S12.1 *TIMS Edelman Award Tape*, Program 1: "Reynolds Metals"

This video accompanies the application box in this chapter describing the use of simulation at Reynolds Metals for truck carrier selection and deployment at its central dispatch facility. The tape is approximately 20 minutes long, and the presentation is generally descriptive and nontechnical.

13 MATERIAL REQUIREMENTS PLANNING

TEACHING NOTES

Teaching Note 13.1 The Beginnings of MRP

Time-phased ordering of material from a standard bill of material has been practiced as far back as the 1930s, but MRP as we know it did not begin until the advent of computers. In 1972, a team of IBM employees, including Joseph Orlicky, wrote a series of "concept" books about "an integrated approach to computer-based manufacturing control" along the lines of "wouldn't it be nice if we could do this . . . ." The eight-volume series of publications known as COPICS (Communications Oriented Production Information and Control System) generated a lot of interest and actually preceded by several years the software known as COPICS. The COPICS software is still in operation and is still marketed for large manufacturers (and some large services, like hospitals), but the MRP market has shifted to smaller MRP systems, such as IBM's MAPICS, and even PC versions.

Teaching Note 13.2 MPS and FAS

Students may ask why the text keeps referring to *end item* rather than final product. Aren't they the same? Although a detailed explanation is beyond the scope of this text (and teaching note), here is a short version:

- Some companies do master schedule the final product.
- Other companies master schedule major components or subassemblies (called end items) and then have another schedule for the final product, usually assembled to customer order. This other schedule is called the final assembly schedule (FAS).

Teaching Note 13.3 Adjusting Bills of Material for JIT

The introduction of JIT production has changed the manner in which bills of material are constructed. If an item is not inventoried or ordered, it is not specified in the bill. Many subassemblies "flow through" JIT systems and are never explicitly identified. Shortening the bills also eliminates a lot of the reporting requirements of MRP. Flow lines and manufacturing cells can operate with kanbans, rather than dispatch lists from production control. Supply chain management is also enhanced with MRP and EDI technology.

Teaching Note 13.4 The MRP Matrix

The MRP matrix shown in the text does not match the AB:POM version, but the names of the entries are similar, so the students should be able to figure it out. AB:POM does not show a past-due bucket, so problem orders are not immediately evident, but it does enter in the scheduled receipt row when the past-due order would arrive.

Some professors prefer to use a matrix with Planned Order Receipts and Planned Order Releases rows; others prefer just Planned Order Releases. Both versions are provided for class handouts (see next page).

Teaching Note 13.5 The MRP II Award

Every year R.D. Garwood, an Atlanta-based consulting firm, gives an award for manufacturing excellence called the MRPII Award. In 1993, Interbake Foods of Richmond, VA, won the award. Interbake is best known as the producer of Girl Scout cookies, although they do make other products, such as ice cream sandwich wafers. With MRPII, Interbake saved more than $500,000 in inventory and was able to re-engineer most of their processes. Look for the recipient of next year's award around September or October.

Teaching Note 13.6 MRP Implementation

Here are some interesting statistics on MRPII:

- MRPII software accounts for one-third of the total U.S. market for computer services.
- One-half of all MRP installations fail.

Teaching Note 13.7 MRP and CIM

Although MRP has gotten poor press in comparison with JIT, it remains an essential part of computer-integrated manufacturing systems. IBM has a video called *The CIM Imperative* that describes the production of their proprinter in an automated factory. MAPICS (an MRPII software system) is shown as the driving force for CIM integration. MRP, in its many forms, has had remarkable longevity in manufacturing because the system has grown and been adapted for new technologies, management philosophies, and production environments. Today's MRPII systems include mixed mode options, manufacturing execution systems (MES), efficient customer response (ECR) capabilities, sales and operations planning (SOP), and knowledge-based reasoning. For an up-to-date assessment of MRP, see the March 1994 issue of *APICS, The Performance Advantage*.

Teaching Note 13.8 Advanced MRP Problem

Problem 13-19 is more of a real-world MRP application. The answer is not clear-cut; it's not just a matter of manipulating numbers. The students are asked to make trade-off decisions based on their current knowledge of the situation.

The MRP Matrix

Item: LLC: Lot Size: LT:	PD	1	2	3	4	5	6	7	8	9	10
Gross requirements											
Scheduled receipts											
Projected on hand											
Net requirements											
Planned order receipts											
Planned order releases											

Item: LLC: Lot Size: LT:	PD	1	2	3	4	5	6	7	8	9	10
Gross requirements											
Scheduled receipts											
Projected on hand											
Net requirements											
Planned order receipts											
Planned order releases											

Item: LLC: Lot Size: LT:	PD	1	2	3	4	5	6	7	8	9	10
Gross requirements											
Scheduled receipts											
Projected on hand											
Net requirements											
Planned order receipts											
Planned order releases											

Item: LLC: Lot Size: LT:	PD	1	2	3	4	5	6	7	8	9	10
Gross requirements											
Scheduled receipts											
Projected on hand											
Net requirements											
Planned order receipts											
Planned order releases											

The MRP Matrix

Item: LLC: Lot Size: LT:	PD	1	2	3	4	5	6	7	8	9	10
Gross requirements											
Scheduled receipts											
Projected on hand											
Net requirements											
Planned order releases											

Item: LLC: Lot Size: LT:	PD	1	2	3	4	5	6	7	8	9	10
Gross requirements											
Scheduled receipts											
Projected on hand											
Net requirements											
Planned order releases											

Item: LLC: Lot Size: LT:	PD	1	2	3	4	5	6	7	8	9	10
Gross requirements											
Scheduled receipts											
Projected on hand											
Net requirements											
Planned order releases											

Item: LLC: Lot Size: LT:	PD	1	2	3	4	5	6	7	8	9	10
Gross requirements											
Scheduled receipts											
Projected on hand											
Net requirements											
Planned order releases											

ALTERNATE EXAMPLES

Alternate Example 13.1

Problem Statement:

Play Bricks is a classic U.S. toy made from reinforced cardboard. A 24-inch slab of cardboard is cut from a 4-foot sheet, trimmed and scored (to be folded later by the customer), and coated with 2 ounces of wax. One coated slab is used for the front of the brick and one coated slab is used for the back of the brick. Front sides require about 2 ounces of paint; back sides are unpainted. The front and back are pressure-glued together to make one complete (but unassembled) brick. Twenty unassembled bricks are packaged to a box. The wax and paint are purchased in gallon containers and take about 2 days to get from the supplier. The box is special ordered with a lead time of 5 days. All other processes require a 1-day lead time.

a. Construct a product structure diagram for Play Bricks.
b. Assuming no stock on hand, plan the purchase and work orders necessary to produce a standard lot size of 50 boxes of Play Bricks by period 7.

Solution:

a. Product structure diagram:

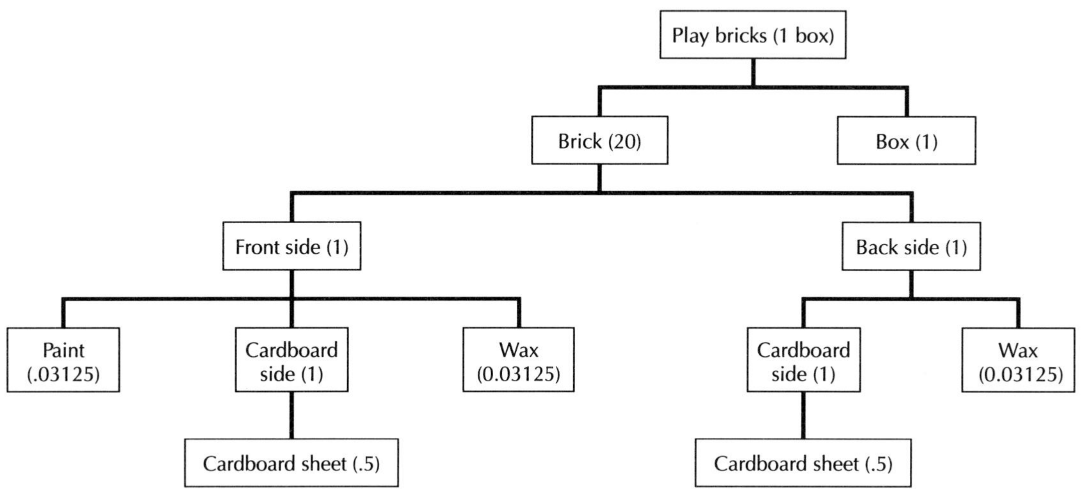

b. MRP calculations:

Item: Play Bricks LLC: 0 Lot Size: 1 LT: 1	PD	1	2	3	4	5	6	7	8	9	10
Gross requirements								50			
Scheduled receipts											
Projected on hand											
Net requirements								50			
Planned order releases							50				

Item: Box LLC: 1 Lot Size: 1 LT: 5	PD	1	2	3	4	5	6	7	8	9	10
Gross requirements							50				
Scheduled receipts											
Projected on hand											
Net requirements							50				
Planned order releases		50									

$50 \times 1 = 50$ boxes

Item: Brick LLC: 1 Lot Size: 1 LT: 1	PD	1	2	3	4	5	6	7	8	9	10
Gross requirements							1,000				
Scheduled receipts											
Projected on hand											
Net requirements							1,000				
Planned order releases						1,000					

$50 \times 20 = 1{,}000$ bricks

Item: Front side LLC: 2 Lot Size: 1 LT: 1	PD	1	2	3	4	5	6	7	8	9	10
Gross requirements						1,000					
Scheduled receipts											
Projected on hand											
Net requirements						1,000					
Planned order releases					1,000						

$1{,}000 \times 1 = 1{,}000$ sides

Item: Back side LLC: 2 Lot Size: 1 LT: 1	PD	1	2	3	4	5	6	7	8	9	10
Gross requirements						1,000					
Scheduled receipts											
Projected on hand											
Net requirements						1,000					
Planned order releases					1,000						

$1{,}000 \times 1 = 1{,}000$ sides

Item: Paint LLC: 3 Lot Size: 1 LT: 2	PD	1	2	3	4	5	6	7	8	9	10
Gross requirements					31.25						
Scheduled receipts											
Projected on hand					0.75						
Net requirements					31.25						
Planned order releases			32								

$1{,}000 \times 0.03125 = 31.25$ gallons

a b c d

(Continues on next page)

INSTRUCTOR'S SECTION

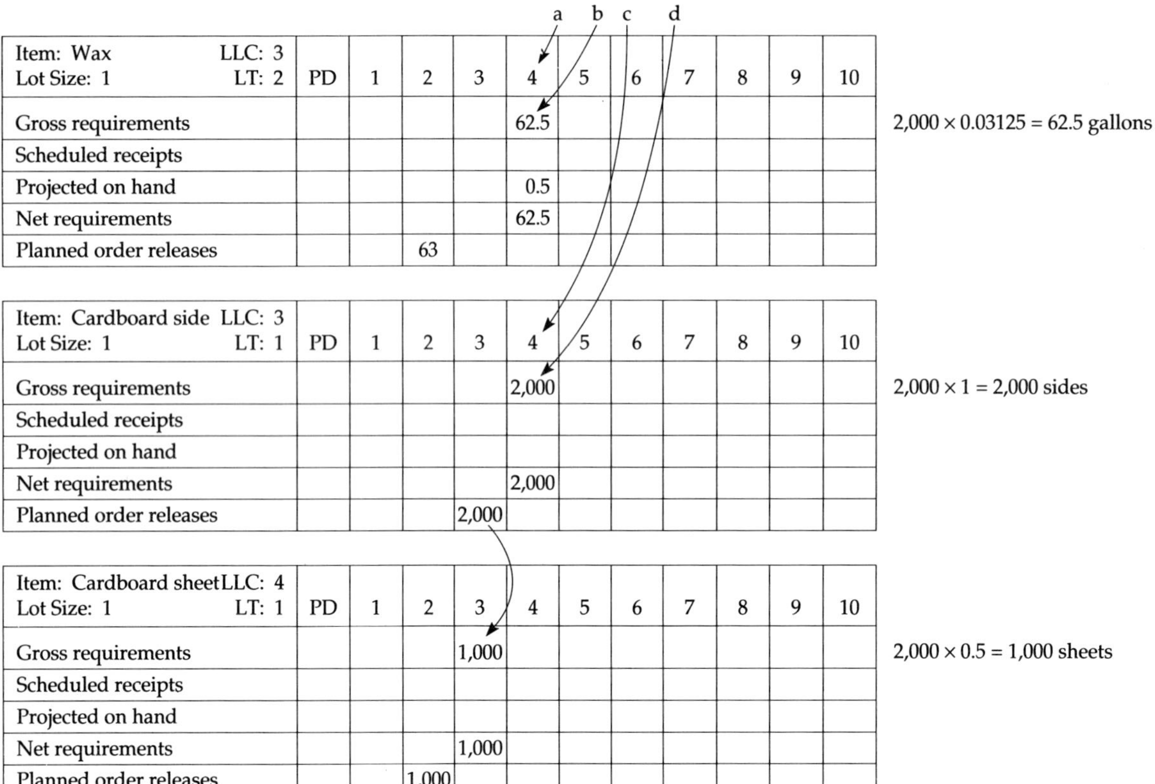

Item: Wax LLC: 3 Lot Size: 1 LT: 2	PD	1	2	3	4	5	6	7	8	9	10
Gross requirements					62.5						
Scheduled receipts											
Projected on hand					0.5						
Net requirements					62.5						
Planned order releases			63								

2,000 × 0.03125 = 62.5 gallons

Item: Cardboard side LLC: 3 Lot Size: 1 LT: 1	PD	1	2	3	4	5	6	7	8	9	10
Gross requirements					2,000						
Scheduled receipts											
Projected on hand											
Net requirements					2,000						
Planned order releases				2,000							

2,000 × 1 = 2,000 sides

Item: Cardboard sheet LLC: 4 Lot Size: 1 LT: 1	PD	1	2	3	4	5	6	7	8	9	10
Gross requirements				1,000							
Scheduled receipts											
Projected on hand											
Net requirements				1,000							
Planned order releases			1,000								

2,000 × 0.5 = 1,000 sheets

Planned Order Releases

Period	*Item*	*UM*	*Quantity*
1	Box	Ea	50
2	Paint	Gal	32
	Wax	Gal	65
	Cardboard Sheet	Ea	1,000
3	Cardboard Side	Ea	2,000
4	Front Side	Ea	1,000
	Back Side	Ea	1,000
5	Brick	Ea	1,000
6	Play Bricks	Bx	50

Alternate Example 13.2

Problem Statement:

Work center A has two machines that are operated for one 8-hour shift, 5 days a week. The utilization of the work center is 80 percent and the efficiency is 90 percent. Use the following work load information to calculate the load percent for work center A each week. How would you propose to level the load?

Week	*Job*	*No. of units*	*Setup Time (minutes)*	*Run Time (minutes per unit)*
1	147	50	20	5
	152	100	30	2
	137	75	45	9
	175	125	60	4
2	234	300	90	5
	217	85	30	3
	265	100	75	2
	235	50	60	6
3	310	60	30	8
	325	90	45	1
	330	100	50	5
	335	500	90	3
	342	300	60	6

Solution:

$$\text{Capacity} = 2 \times 5 \times 8 \times 0.80 \times 0.90 = 57.6 \text{ hours}$$
$$= 3{,}456 \text{ minutes}$$

Week	*Job*	*Total Time*	*Cum. Load*	*Load %*
1	147	20 + (50 × 5) = 270	270	8%
	152	30 + (100 × 2) = 230	500	14
	137	45 + (75 × 9) = 720	1,220	35
	175	60 + (125 × 4) = 560	1,780	52
2	234	90 + (300 × 5) = 1,590	1,590	46
	217	30 + (85 × 3) = 285	1,875	54
	265	75 + (100 × 2) = 275	2,150	62
	235	60 + (50 × 6) = 360	2,510	73
3	310	30 + (60 × 8) = 510	510	15
	325	45 + (90 × 1) = 135	645	19
	330	50 + (100 × 5) = 550	1,195	36
	335	90 + (500 × 3) = 1,590	2,695	78
	342	60 + (300 × 6) = 1,860	4,555	132

The work center is underloaded in the first two weeks and overloaded in the third week. One possible remedy is to move job 234 into week 1 and job 335 into week 2. This would bring the load percents to 98 percent, 73 percent, and 88 percent for weeks 1, 2, and 3, respectively.

Alternate Example 13.3

Problem Statement:

Salespersons at NAPCO, Inc., learn by doing. A novice salesperson accompanies a veteran salesperson for a week on his or her rounds. During the second week, client visits are split equally between the two employees. Although NAPCO is pleased with the training acquired through this approach, the company always experiences a drop in sales during the second week. Some clients do not even get a visit. Upon further investigation, it was determined that novice and veteran salespeople spend a different amount of time preparing for each sales call and making the sale. Veterans take about 30 minutes to prepare for each call and 10 minutes to make the call. Novices spend 1 hour preparing for each call and an average of 20 minutes making the call. Use these data to design an optimal split of sales calls between the two salespersons in a territory of 100 clients.

Solution:

$$30 + 10x = 60 + 20(100 - x)$$
$$30 + 10x = 60 + 2{,}000 - 20x$$
$$30x = 2{,}030$$
$$x = 68$$
$$100 - x = 100 - 68 = 32$$

The veteran salesperson should make 68 calls. The novice sales person should make 32 calls.

Alternate Example 13.4

Problem Statement:

Given the following demand and cost data for item X, determine whether lot-for-lot, EOQ, or POQ lot sizing would be more appropriate. Assume negligible lead time and zero beginning inventory.

Period	*Demand*
1	100
2	50
3	75
4	125
5	35
6	50
	435

Ordering cost = $300

Holding cost = $2 per unit per week

Solution:

Lot-for-lot: Order the exact amount needed every period for a cost of

$$0 + 6(\$300) = \$1{,}800$$

$$\text{EOQ:} \quad \sqrt{\frac{2(300)(435/6)}{2}} = 147 \text{ units}$$

Period	1	2	3	4	5	6
Requirements	100	50	75	125	35	50
Projected on hand	47	144	69	91	56	6
Planned order release	147	147		147		

Order 147 units in periods 1, 2, and 4 for a cost of:

$$(3 \times \$300) + [(47 + 144 + 69 + 91 + 56 + 11) \times \$2] = \$900 + \$848$$
$$= \$1{,}748$$

$$\text{POQ:} \quad \frac{147}{72.5} = 2.03$$

Place an order every 2 periods.

Period	1	2	3	4	5	6
Requirements	100	50	75	125	35	50
Projected on hand	50	0	125	0	50	0
Planned order release	150		200		85	

Order 147 units in periods 1, 2, and 4 for a cost of:

$$(3 \times \$300) + [(50 + 125 + 50) \times \$2] = \$900 + \$450$$
$$= \$1{,}350$$

The POQ lot-sizing technique results in the lowest total cost.

INSTRUCTOR'S SECTION

Alternate Example 13.5

Problem Statement:

Use the part-period balancing lot-sizing technique to plan orders for item *X* of Alternate Example 13.4.

Solution:

$$\text{EPP} = \frac{300}{2} = 150$$

Period	1	2	3	4	5	6
Demand	100	50	75	125	35	50
GPP	0	50	150	125	70	50
CGPP	0*	50	200*	125	195*	50
Order quantity	150		200		85	

Order 150 units in period 1, 200 in period 3, and 85 in period 5 for a total cost of:

$$(3 \times \$300) + [(50 + 125 + 50) \times \$2] = \$900 + \$450 = \$1{,}350$$

Alternate Example 13.6

Problem Statement:

Use the Wagner-Whitin lot-sizing technique to plan orders for item *X* of Alternate Example 13.4.

Solution:

Period	*Alternative*	*Ordering Cost*	*Holding Cost*	*Total Cost*
1	(1)	300	0	300*
2	(1)(2)	600	0	600
	(1, 2)	300	100	400*
3	(1, 2)(3)	600	100	700*
	(1, 2, 3)	300	400	700*
	(1)(2, 3)	600	150	750
4	(1, 2, 3)(4)	600	400	1,000
	(1, 2, 3, 4)	300	1,150	1,450
	(1, 2)(3, 4)	600	350	950*
	(1, 2)(3)(4)	900	100	1,000
5	(1, 2)(3, 4)(5)	900	350	1,250
	(1, 2)(3, 4, 5)	600	560	1,160
	(1, 2)(3)(4, 5)	900	170	1,070*
6	(1, 2)(3)(4, 5)(6)	1,200	170	1,370
	(1, 2)(3)(4, 5, 6)	900	350	1,250*

Order 150 units in period 1, 75 units in period 3, and 210 units in period 4 for a total cost of $1,250.

VIDEO

Video 13.1 *Total Quality Management*

This tape is part of SME's Manufacturing Insight Series. Although its major topic is TQM, it also talks about the success of MRP as its manufacturing control system.

14 SCHEDULING

TEACHING NOTES

Teaching Note 14.1 AB:POM for Scheduling

AB:POM will schedule one machine with a choice of several sequencing rules or two serial machines with Johnson's rule. It is still useful, however, to have the students solve some problems by hand and chart out the answers on a Gantt chart. That way they can get a feel for why each rule produces different results. For example, you might ask the student how they think Johnson came up with his rule. (It's basically SPT adapted for two centers.)

Teaching Note 14.2 Example of Johnson's Rule for More Than Two Machines

Consider a batch of four jobs that must be processed through three machines in 1, 2, 3 order. Processing times are given as follows:

Job	*Machine 1*	*Machine 2*	*Machine 3*
1	10	4	6
2	7	6	7
3	8	3	5
4	9	5	4

INSTRUCTOR'S SECTION

To modify Johnson's rule, add the processing times for each job for machines 1 and 2 and for machines 2 and 3. Then solve the problem with Johnson's rule.

Job	*Machines 1 and 2*	*Machines 2 and 3*
1	14	10
2	13	13
3	11	8
4	14	9

Gantt charts:

Machine 1

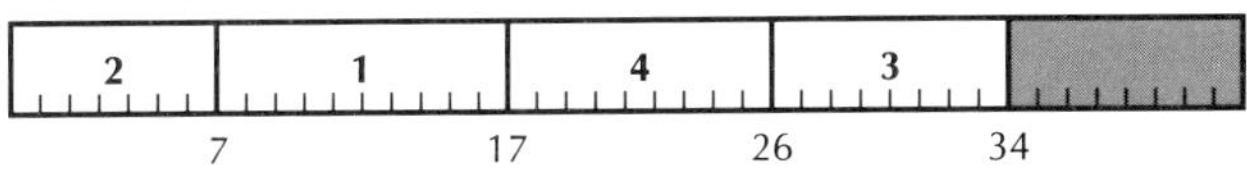

Machine 2

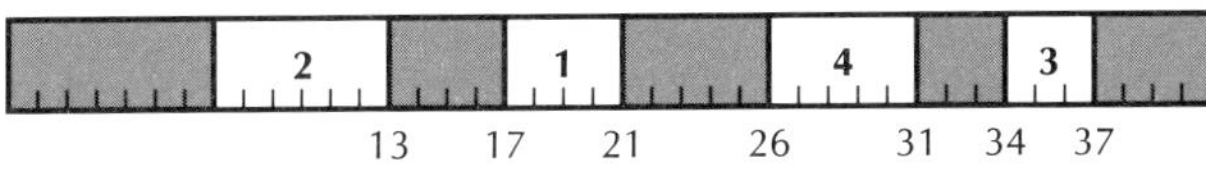

Machine 3

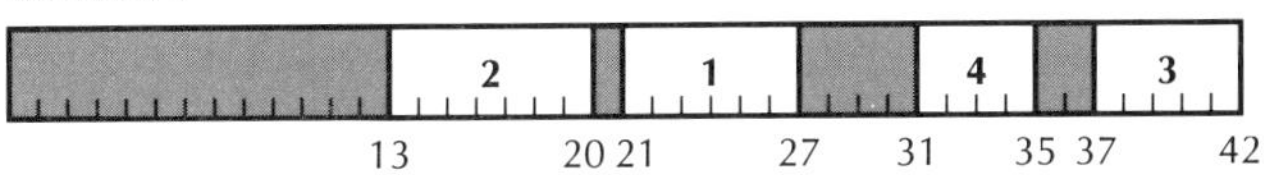

Teaching Note 14.3 *The Goal*

The Goal is a novelized account of a production manager trying to turn around both his life and his plant's performance. It's actually interesting and gets across the points of synchronous manufacturing, too. Students love it.

Source: Goldratt, E., and J. Cox, *The Goal*, Croton-on-Hudson, New York: North River Press, 1984.

Teaching Note 14.4 The $5,000 Problem

Example 14.6 is an adaptation of a problem that appeared in industrial magazines in the 1980s as part of a contest to test the validity of OPT (and get lots of publicity). The person who could schedule the most units through production won $5,000. It took the winner several weeks to come up with the solution. OPT, of course, could solve the problem in seconds.

Teaching Note 14.5 TPM

Total productive maintenance is a hot topic in Japan, as hot as TQM is here. Watch for more press about life-cycle maintenance and maximizing the productive life of machines (and people).

Teaching Note 14.6 Decision Support Systems for Scheduling

Computerized employee scheduling systems are blossoming on the market now. Some just make nice output reports; others have a quantitative basis and allow specific employee information to be considered. In addition to the videos that accompany this text, the *TIMS Edelman Award Tapes* have several videos that describe scheduling scenarios. One of them illustrates the benefits of a visual representation of schedules for the San Francisco Police Department (1989). An article on the system also appears in *Interfaces* (January–February 1989): 4–24.

ALTERNATE EXAMPLES

Alternate Example 14.1

Problem Statement:

Given the following jobs, machines, and processing times, use the index method to assign jobs to machines so that the set of jobs is processed as quickly as possible. No order splitting is allowed. Only one job may be assigned to each machine.

	Machine				
Job	*1*	*2*	*3*	*4*	*5*
A	10	15	13	10	12
B	8	10	12	6	5
C	5	10	7	8	6
D	15	20	16	18	17
E	22	25	23	19	20

Solution:

Matrix of row indices:

1.00	1.50	1.30	1.00	1.20
1.60	2.00	2.40	1.20	1.00
1.00	2.00	1.40	1.60	1.20
1.00	1.33	1.07	1.20	1.13
1.16	1.32	1.21	1.00	1.05

Assign job A to machine 4,
job B to machine 5,
job C to machine 1,
job D to machine 3,
job E to machine 2.

The jobs will require 10 + 5 + 5 + 16 + 25 = 61 minutes of processing time and will be completed in 25 minutes.

Alternate Example 14.2

Problem Statement:

Solve Alternate Example 14.1 by the assignment method.

How does the solution compare with that of the index method?

Solution:

Row reduction:

0	5	3	0	2
3	5	7	1	0
0	5	2	3	1
0	5	1	3	2
3	6	4	0	1

Column reduction:

0	0	2	0	2
3	0	6	1	0
0	0	1	3	1
0	0	0	3	2
3	1	3	0	1

Cover all zeros:

— [0] — 0 — 2 — 0 — 2
— 3 — 0 — 6 — 1 — [0]
— 0 — [0] — 1 — 3 — 1
— 0 — 0 — [0] — 3 — 2
— 3 — 1 — 3 — [0] — 1

Assign job A to machine 1,
job B to machine 5,
job C to machine 2,
job D to machine 3,
job E to machine 4.

The five jobs will require 10 + 5 + 10 + 16 + 19 = 60 minutes of processing time and will be completed in 19 minutes. The assignment method gives a better solution than the index method.

Alternate Example 14.3

Problem Statement:

Sequence the following list of jobs by a. FCFS, b. SPT, c. DDATE, and d. SLACK. Calculate the mean flow time, mean tardiness, and maximum tardiness for each sequencing rule. Are the results surprising to you? Which sequencing rule would you recommend?

Job	*Processing Time*	*Due Date*
A	20	20
B	10	15
C	30	50
D	15	30

Solution:

a. FCFS

Sequence	*Proc. Time*	*Completion*	*Due Date*	*Tardiness*
A	20	20	20	0
B	10	30	15	15
C	30	60	50	10
D	15	75	30	45
		185		70
	Average	46.25		17.5

b. SPT

Sequence	*Proc. Time*	*Completion*	*Due Date*	*Tardiness*
B	10	10	15	0
D	15	25	30	0
A	20	45	20	25
C	30	75	50	25
		155		50
	Average	38.75		12.5

c. DDATE

Sequence	*Proc. Time*	*Completion*	*Due Date*	*Tardiness*
B	10	10	15	0
A	20	30	20	10
D	15	45	30	15
C	30	75	50	25
		160		50
	Average	40		12.5

d. SLACK

Sequence	*Proc. Time*	*Completion*	*Due Date*	*Tardiness*
A	20	20	20	0
B	10	30	15	15
D	15	45	30	15
C	30	75	50	25
		170		55
	Average	42.5		13.75

SPT and DDATE produce the smallest mean tardiness values and SPT produces the smallest mean flow time. SPT, DDATE, and SLACK have the same maximum tardiness figure. FCFS is the worst performer. SPT is probably the best overall rule, but the importance of completing specific jobs on time may favor DDATE. It is surprising that SPT, which does not take due date into account, can perform so well on tardiness measures.

Alternate Example 14.4

Problem Statement:

Jane and Jake do yardwork throughout the year to earn extra money. One of their busiest times is in the fall, when leaves must be raked before the grass can be cut. The relationship between raking and mowing is not always clear cut. Some lawns, which have a lot of trees, take a long time to rake but a very short time to mow. Jane and Jake have found that customers are plentiful and their income is bounded only by the time they have available to work. This Saturday, they have six lawns to mow. The estimated time to rake and mow each yard is shown here. How should Jane and Jake schedule their yardwork to that it can be completed in the shortest amount of time?

	Rake	*Mow*
Yard 1	30	90
Yard 2	60	45
Yard 3	45	45
Yard 4	15	60
Yard 5	40	60
Yard 6	90	30

Solution:

Applying Johnson's Rule, Jane and Jake should do yard 4 first and then yards 1, 5, 3, and 2. It will take 345 minutes, or 5.75 hours, to complete the six yards.

VIDEOS

Video 14.1 *COMAP*, Program 3, "Juggling Machines"

The 16-minute video demonstrates the concept of sequencing jobs at machines with an illustration from TV broadcasting. Like all the videos in this series, it's well done.

Video 14.2 *TIMS Edelman Awards Tape*, Program 1: "Reynolds Metals"

This 20-minute tape shows how Reynolds Metals used simulation to dispatch its truck carriers. It highlights some of the issues involved in scheduling.

15 *JUST-IN-TIME AND CONTINUOUS IMPROVEMENT*

TEACHING NOTES

Teaching Note 15.1 Ford's Rouge Plant, the Original JIT?

Many JIT concepts have been around a long time, at least since the 1920s and the days of Henry Ford. Ford's huge Rouge complex had everything—a steel plant, a glass plant, and a mile-long assembly line. On Monday morning a barge bearing iron ore would arrive and be met at the docks by huge cranes. The cranes would unload the ore and take it to the blast furnace. On Tuesday, it would be poured into a foundry mold, and by that afternoon it would be an engine. Ford could convert "raw material to cash in 33 hours."

Source: Halberstam, David, *The Reckoning*, New York: Morrow, 1986.

Teaching Note 15.2 Elements of JIT

Since JIT is an evolving system and a philosophy of management, it's difficult to nail down all its elements. This is a representative list. One entry that sometimes confuses students (and teachers) is continuous improvement. JIT is a system of continuous improvement *and* continuous improvement is an integral part of JIT.

Teaching Note 15.3 Big JIT and Little jit

Some sources reference big JIT as a philosophy of continuous improvement and little jit as the kanban system for controlling inventory. We don't make that distinction because we want students to learn it as big JIT from the start.

Teaching Note 15.4 A Video Suggestion

HP has a training video produced in the 1980s when the company was trying to explain the pull concept to its workers. It's a short demonstration (20 minutes or so) of the push versus the pull system. Afterwards it shows an assembly cell with andons, kanban squares, and improvement boards. The only drawback of the video is that students might think this is all there is to JIT, and we know it's so much more.

Teaching Note 15.5 A Kanban Demonstration

In Chapter 5, we proposed an exercise for designing a triangular porthole. You can use that product now if you wish to demonstrate push versus pull, much like the HP video discussed in Teaching Note 15.4.

This time make the triangular porthole with one side yellow, one side green, and one side red. Since it will stand on all sides, students can use the finished product as an andon during class to let you know how well they are following your lecture. If you were to look up and see a "sea of red," you may need to go over that lecture again.

Set up an assembly line with kanban squares marked on each desk (or station) with masking tape. Let any student stop the line when they feel it is necessary (by shouting "jidoka," of course). The discipline that kanbans enforce on the system will become evident.

Teaching Note 15.6 Poka-Yokes

There are many examples of poka-yokes in our everyday environment. One of which you may not be aware is the use of check digits for identification numbers.

Here is how a check digit works: The last digit of an ID number is the result of a mathematical function of all the other digits in the ID. A typical check-digit function is one that divides the ID number by 11 and uses the remainder as the check digit (a remainder of 10 converts to 0). Using this function, the ID number 123456789 would have a check digit of 5, making 1234567895 the full ID.

Using check digits, machines can be programmed to help ensure that correct ID numbers are being entered. Using a single check digit makes the probability 0.1 that an erroneous entry will pass. To make the odds better, increase the number of check digits. The federal government probably wishes it had used such poka-yokes in constructing Social Security numbers.

Teaching Note 15.7 An Idea Fair

Everyone's heard of suggestion boxes, surveys, and town meetings to encourage employee involvement, but an idea fair? That's what Canon does each year. It's similar to our science fairs, with cardboard displays and demonstrations. It's also a traveling road show that visits not only Canon factories but schools and other public places. There are judging and awards too, and short videos are made of the inventor and his or her idea.

Then there's the one-idea-a-day program, where a company tries to encourage participation by distributing a special note pad for workers to write down their ideas. The goal is for every worker to come up with one idea every day for the duration of the "idea drive." Ideas are immediately posted on the bulletin board under each person's name so that a visual histogram is formed for all to see.

ALTERNATE EXAMPLES

Alternate Example 15.1

Problem Statement:

Consider a finishing operation that can process 200 units an hour. Completed units are placed in a container with a capacity of 50 before being transported to the packing station. It takes about an hour to receive input from the previous workstation. If one kanban is attached to each container and the factory uses no safety factor, how many kanbans are needed for the finishing operation?

Solution:

$$N = \frac{(200 \times 1) + 0}{50} = \frac{200}{50} = 4 \text{ kanbans, or containers}$$

Alternate Example 15.2

Problem Statement:

A & B Publishing is reissuing three previously published works of one of its authors, Russell Taylor. Production is planned for 12,000 *Quality Always* books, 6,000 *Quality's Best* books, and 4,000 *Quality Counts* books. In order to ensure the widest possible availability of all three publications, A & B has decided to apply mixed-model sequencing to its printing line. The line to which these publications have been assigned operates 10 hours a day, 20 days a month. Determine a mixed sequence of books for the final printing line that will provide a steady stream of the publications to the retail outlets.

Solution:

Book	*Monthly Requirements*	*Daily Requirements*	*Cycle Time*
QA	12,000	$\frac{12{,}000}{20} = 600$	$\frac{10 \times 60}{600} = 1$
QB	6,000	$\frac{6{,}000}{20} = 300$	$\frac{10 \times 60}{300} = 2$
QC	4,000	$\frac{4{,}000}{20} = 200$	$\frac{10 \times 60}{200} = 3$

QA should be printed every minute, QB, every 2 minutes, and QC, every 3 minutes. In a 6-minute time span, 6 QAs, 3 QBs, and 2 QCs should be produced. The following sequence satisfies those requirements and should be repeated 100 times a day to meet demand.

$$QA - QC - QA - QB - QA - QB - QA - QB - QA - QC - QA$$

INSTRUCTOR'S SECTION

16 QUEUING ANALYSIS

TEACHING NOTES

Teaching Note 16.1 Waiting Lines in Everyday Life

Waiting in line is a topic that is pervasive in everyday life as well as in business, so it is not difficult for students to relate to it. It is suggested that class discussion be initiated at the beginning of this chapter about the different queuing situations with which students are confronted. Because examples of queuing are so widespread and readily available, it is possible and beneficial to have students analyze queuing situations with which they are familiar as class exercises.

Teaching Note 16.2 Poisson and Exponential Distributions

The Poisson distribution as it relates to arrival rates and the exponential distribution as it relates to service times are not covered in depth in this chapter. The aspects of the derivation of queuing models (to us) is secondary to the use of queuing for decision-making purposes, especially for undergraduates. However, it is important to emphasize to the student that although these distributions are very common in the real world—and that is why the basic single-server model is constructed based on them—other distributions for arrival rates and service times also exist.

Teaching Note 16.3 Queuing Results

Queuing analysis provides only information about systems and does not provide a recommended decision, as do many of the prior techniques in this text. Therefore, decision making often requires weighing the queuing information for several alternate system configurations.

Teaching Note 16.4 Computer Software

The AB:POM software demonstrated in this chapter is very easy to use and can make solving the homework problems, especially the multiple-server models, a lot less tedious and time-consuming. Most other POM and quantitative methods software packages have similar queuing modules.

Teaching Note 16.5 Homework Assignments

Some of the problems in this chapter can be lengthy because of the queuing formulas and analysis involved. Thus, if computer software is not used, care should be given when selecting the number of problems to include in homework assignments.

ALTERNATE EXAMPLES

Alternate Example 16.1

Problem Statement:

An airline terminal has several terminal gates at the Hartsfield International Airport in Atlanta. Under normal conditions the airline assigns one operator to the desk at each gate to serve passengers, including making seat assignments, checking passengers in, rerouting passengers, and solving customer problems. At one specific gate that is in constant use throughout the day, passengers arrive at the desk at the rate of 80 per hour according to a Poisson distribution. The airline agent is able to serve passengers in an average time of 0.667 minutes, exponentially distributed. Determine L, L_q, W, and W_q for this waiting line system, and indicate if it seems adequate to be perceived as quality service.

Solution:

$$\lambda = 80, \qquad \mu = 90$$

$$L = \frac{\lambda}{\mu - \lambda} = \frac{80}{10} = 8 \text{ customers}$$

$$L_q = \frac{\lambda^2}{\mu(\mu - \lambda)} = \frac{(80)^2}{90(10)} = 7.1 \text{ customers}$$

$$W = \frac{1}{\mu - \lambda} = \frac{1}{10} = 0.1 \text{ hr} = 6 \text{ minutes}$$

$$W_q = \frac{\lambda}{\mu(\mu - \lambda)} = \frac{80}{90(10)} = 0.089 \text{ hr} = 5.33 \text{ minutes}$$

Passengers probably wait too long in the system for the service to be viewed as good.

Alternate Example 16.2

Problem Statement:

The manager of a video game arcade has installed a new video game that makes use of virtual reality. The game requires a constant 2.6 minutes to play. Customers arrive to play the game at an average rate of 20 per hour (Poisson distributed). The manager wants to know the average length of the waiting line and the average waiting time for a customer to play the game.

Solution:

$$\lambda = 20, \qquad \mu = 23.1$$

$$L_q = \frac{\lambda^2}{2\mu(\mu - \lambda)} = \frac{(20)^2}{2(23.1)(3.1)} = 2.79 \text{ customers}$$

$$W_q = \frac{L_q}{\lambda} = \frac{2.79}{20} = 0.14 \text{ hr} = 8.37 \text{ minutes waiting}$$

Alternate Example 16.3

Problem Statement:

A bank drive-in teller window can serve an average of 25 customers per hour (Poisson distributed). Customers arrive in their cars at a rate of 20 per hour (Poisson distributed). The driveway for the teller window can accommodate only three cars (two waiting and one being served). Determine the average waiting time, the average queue length, and the probability that a customer will have to drive on.

Solution:

$$\lambda = 20, \quad \mu = 25, \quad M = 3$$

$$P_0 = \frac{1 - \lambda/\mu}{1 - (\lambda/\mu)^{M+1}} = \frac{1 - \frac{20}{25}}{1 - \left(\frac{20}{25}\right)^4}$$

$$= 0.34 \text{ probability of no cars}$$

$$P_3 = (P_0)\left(\frac{\lambda}{\mu}\right)^3 = (0.34)\left(\frac{20}{25}\right)^3$$

$$= 0.17 \text{ probability that a customer must drive on}$$

$$L = \frac{\lambda/\mu}{1 - \lambda/\mu} - \frac{(M+1)(\lambda/\mu)^{M+1}}{1 - (\lambda/\mu)^{M+1}}$$

$$= \frac{\frac{20}{25}}{1 - \left(\frac{20}{25}\right)} = \frac{(4)\left(\frac{20}{25}\right)^4}{1 - \left(\frac{20}{25}\right)^4} = 1.23$$

$$L_q = L - \frac{\lambda(1 - P_m)}{\mu} = 1.23 - \frac{20(1 - 0.17)}{25}$$

$$= 1.20 \text{ customers waiting}$$

Alternate Example 16.4

Problem Statement:

Mary Richards is a full-time academic tutor for the State University football team. She has 10 players assigned to her for tutoring. A player visits her for tutoring an average of every 16 hours (assuming a 40-hour week), exponentially distributed. When a player visits, she spends an average of 1.5 hours with him. She is able to tutor only one player at a time, and players study while they are waiting. Determining the percentage of time Mary is busy tutoring and how long a player must wait to see her. Does the system seem adequate?

Solution (computer solution):

$\lambda = 0.625/\text{hour}$, $\mu = 0.67/\text{hour}$, $N = 10$

$L_q = 1.177$ players waiting

$L = 1.93$ players in the system

$W_q = 2.33$ hours waiting

$W = 3.82$ hours in the system

Mary's utilization rate seems reasonable, but the waiting time is probably excessive.

Alternate Example 16.5

Problem Statement:

At the Hartsfield International Airport there is one booth leading into the MARTA rapid transit system. The booth has two windows for selling tokens and providing information for arriving transit passengers, who form a single line and are served by the first available agent. Customers arrive at the average rate of 100 per hour. Each window agent is able to service customers at the average rate of 70 per hour. (Both arrival rate and service rate are Poisson distributed.) Determine the average number of passengers waiting and the average waiting time.

Solution (computer solution):

$\lambda = 100$, $\mu = 70$, $s = 2$

$L = 2.91$ customers in the system

$L_q = 1.49$ customers waiting

$W = 0.029$ hr $= 1.74$ minutes in the system

$W_q = 0.015$ hr $= 0.9$ minutes waiting

VIDEO

Video 16.1 *TIMS Edelman Awards Tape*, Program 3: "L.L. Bean"

This video accompanies the application at the start of this chapter describing the use of queuing at L.L. Bean. It is an excellent video that is presented in a mostly nontechnical manner. L.L. Bean is a company with which most students are familiar, and many of them have probably used its catalog service. Therefore, it is easy for students to visualize the type of queuing-related problems L.L. Bean might have. The tape lasts about 20 minutes. It is highly recommended. It brings out a number of issues related to queuing systems and problems that cannot be conveyed in a textbook presentation, and it demonstrates the major impact the application of quantitative techniques can have on profitability and cost savings.

17 PROJECT MANAGEMENT

TEACHING NOTES

Teaching Note 17.1 CPM/PERT Use in the Real World

CPM/PERT is an extremely popular and widely used management science technique. There is hardly a major construction project undertaken that does not have a CPM/PERT network as a requirement. If there is any building construction taking place on your campus (or in your town), the project manager would probably be very willing to display the CPM/PERT network to your class and provide some explanation. A good exercise is to have the class identify the activities and build a network in class for a familiar project such as building a house.

Teaching Note 17.2 Event Versus Activity Scheduling

A primary reason activity-on-arrow scheduling is used in this text is because it is the convention in most quantitative methods and POM software packages, including AB:POM.

Teaching Note 17.3 The Beta Distribution

Although it has become traditional to use the beta distribution for determining probabilistic activity times, several research studies have clearly shown that the beta provides no better results than several other distributions, including the normal and the simple triangular. Another important point to note to the student is that the formulas for the mean and variance are estimates and are not the true mean and variance of the beta.

Teaching Note 17.4 Project Crashing with Linear Programming

Project crashing, as well as general CPM scheduling, can be accomplished by using linear programming. A linear programming model for the project network must first be formulated. Using linear programming for project crashing enables us to use a linear programming software module rather than project crashing software. The interested reader is referred to Chapter 20, "CPM and PERT Network Analysis," in *Introduction to Management Science*, 4th ed., by Bernard W. Taylor III, published by Allyn and Bacon.

The general linear programming model of formulation of a CPM/PERT network can be summarized as

Minimize $Z = x_m$

subject to

$$x_j - x_i \geq t_{ij}, \text{ for all activities } i \rightarrow j$$
$$x_i, x_j \geq 0$$

x_i = earliest event time of node i

x_j = earliest event time of node j

t_{ij} = time of activity $i \rightarrow j$

m = number of the last node in the network

The linear programming model for the network in Figure 17.12 is

Minimize $Z = x_7$

subject to

$$x_2 - x_1 \geq 12$$
$$x_3 - x_2 \geq 8$$
$$x_4 - x_2 \geq 4$$
$$x_4 - x_3 \geq 0$$
$$x_5 - x_4 \geq 4$$
$$x_6 - x_4 \geq 12$$
$$x_6 - x_5 \geq 4$$
$$x_7 - x_6 \geq 4$$
$$x_i, x_j \geq 0$$

To crash a network, the objective must be to minimize the cost of crashing and the amount of time by which activity $i \rightarrow j$ is crashed (i.e., reduced).

The complete linear programming model for crashing the house-building network in Example 17.4 is as follows.

$$\text{Minimize } Z = \$400y_{12} + 500y_{23} + 3{,}000y_{24} + 200y_{45} + 7{,}000y_{46} + 200y_{56} + 7{,}000y_{67}$$

$$y_{12} \leq 5$$
$$y_{23} \leq 3$$
$$y_{24} \leq 1$$
$$y_{34} \leq 0$$
$$y_{45} \leq 3$$
$$y_{46} \leq 3$$
$$y_{56} \leq 3$$
$$y_{67} \leq 1$$
$$x_1 + 12 - y_{12} \leq x_2$$
$$x_2 + 8 - y_{23} \leq x_3$$
$$x_2 + 4 - y_{24} \leq x_4$$
$$x_3 + 0 - y_{34} \leq x_4$$
$$x_4 + 4 - y_{45} \leq x_5$$
$$x_4 + 12 - y_{46} \leq x_6$$
$$x_5 + 4 - y_{56} \leq x_6$$
$$x_6 + 4 - y_{67} \leq x_7$$
$$x_i, x_j, y_{ij} \geq 0$$

ALTERNATE EXAMPLE

Alternate Example 17.1

Following is a list of the activities for Example 17.1 and the figure on page 842 of the text, in a different format than shown in the text. A good exercise is to require the students to construct the network using only the activity letters and precedents. Students typically find it more difficult to construct a network in this manner, which is actually closer to the way it is done in the real world. They should not be told in advance that the network they are constructing is the same as the figure shown in the text.

Activity Nos.	*Activity*	*Predecessor(s)*
1-2	a	—
1-3	b	—
1-4	c	—
2-6	d	a
2-5	e (dummy)	a
3-5	f	b
4-5	g	c
4-8	h	c
5-7	i	e, f, g
5-8	j	e, f, g
8-7	k (dummy)	h, j
6-9	l	d
7-9	m	i, k

VIDEO

Video 17.1 *COMAP,* Program 4: "Trains, Planes, and Critical Paths"

Program 4 is an introductory tutorial on network scheduling and the critical path method. It includes examples of network scheduling for building contractors and Eastern Airlines. The tape is approximately 16 minutes long and is an excellent introduction to network models.

PRODUCTION AND OPERATIONS MANAGEMENT

Focusing on Quality and Competitiveness

Roberta S. Russell
Professor
Virginia Polytechnic Institute and State University

Bernard W. Taylor III
R.B. Pamplin Professor
Virginia Polytechnic Institute and State University

Prentice-Hall, Inc.
Englewood Cliffs, New Jersey 07632

Library of Congress Cataloging-in-Publication Data
Russell, Roberta S.
Production and operations management : focusing on quality and competitiveness / by Roberta S. Russell and Bernard W. Taylor.
p. cm.
Includes bibliographical references and indexes.
ISBN 0-205-14733-X : $48.75. — ISBN 0-205-16340-8 (AIE)
1. Production management. 2. Quality control. I. Taylor, Bernard, 1931- . II. Title.
TS155.R755 1995
658.5—dc20 94-3609
CIP

Editor-in-Chief: Rich Wohl
Acquisitions Editor: Tom Tucker
Production Editor: Barbara Barg
Managing Editor: Joyce Turner
In-House Liaison: Penelope Linskey
Manufacturing Buyer: Marie McNamara
Editorial Assistant: Andrea Cuperman
Production Assistant: Renée Pelletier
Design Director: Patricia Wosczyk
Interior Design: Glenna Collett
Cover Design: Patricia Wosczyk
Cover Art: David M. Jones/© Uniphoto, Inc.
Photo Research: Sarah Evertson/Photosynthesis
Illustration: Precision Graphics, Inc.
Compositor: Omegatype Typography, Inc.
Printer/Binder: R. R. Donnelley

Printed in the United States of America
10 9 8 7 6 5 4 3 2 1

ISBN 0-205-14733-X

Photo Credits are found on page 917, which should be considered an extension of the copyright page.

Prentice-Hall International (UK) Limited, *London*
Prentice-Hall of Australia Pty. Limited, *Sydney*
Prentice-Hall Canada Inc., *Toronto*
Prentice-Hall Hispanoamericana, S.A., *Mexico*
Prentice-Hall of India Private Limited, *New Delhi*
Prentice-Hall of Japan, Inc., *Tokyo*
Simon & Schuster Asia Pte. Ltd., *Singapore*
Editora Prentice-Hall do Brasil, Ltda., *Rio de Janeiro*

To my children
Travis and Amy Russell

■

To my parents
Jean V. Taylor and Bernard W. Taylor, Jr.
with love and appreciation.

ABOUT THE AUTHORS

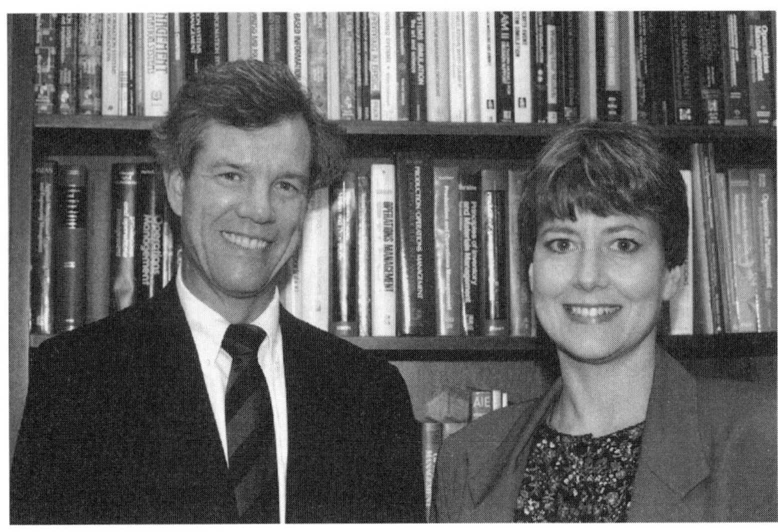

Bernard W. Taylor, III, is the R. B. Pamplin Professor of Management Science and Head of the Department of Management Science in the Pamplin College of Business at Virginia Polytechnic Institute and State University. He received the Ph.D. and M.B.A. from the University of Georgia and B.I.E. from the Georgia Institute of Technology. He is the author of the book *Introduction to Management Science* (4th ed.) and co-author of *Management Science* (4th ed.), both published by Prentice-Hall. Dr. Taylor has published over seventy-five articles in such journals as *Operations Research, Management Science, Decision Sciences, IIE Transactions, Journal of the Operational Research Society, Computers and Operations Research, Omega,* and the *International Journal of Production Research* among others. His paper in *Decision Sciences* (with P. Y. Huang and L. P. Rees) on the Japanese kanban production system received the Stanley T. Hardy Award for its contribution to the field of production and operations management. He has served as President of the Decision Sciences Institute (DSI) as well as Associate Program Chair, Council Member, Vice President, Treasurer, and as the Editor of *Decision Line,* the newsletter of DSI. He is a Fellow of DSI and a recipient of their Distinguished Service Award. He is a former President, Vice-President, and Program Chair of the Southeast Decision Sciences Institute and a recipient of their Distinguished Service Award. He teaches management science and production and operations management courses at both the undergraduate and graduate level. He has received the University Certificate of Teaching Excellence on four occasions, the R. B. Pamplin College of Business Certificate of Teaching Excellence Award, and the R. B. Pamplin College of Business Ph.D. Teaching Excellence Award at Virginia Tech.

Roberta S. Russell is Professor of Management Science. She received the Ph.D. from Virginia Polytechnic Institute and State University, an M.B.A. from Old Dominion University and a B.S. degree from Virginia Polytechnic Institute and State University. Dr. Russell's primary research and teaching interests are in the areas of production and operations management, service operations management, simulation, and quality. She has published in *Decision Sciences, IIE Transactions, The International Journal of Production Research, Material Flow, Business Horizons, Computers, Environment and Urban Systems, Computers and Operations Research* and others. She is also co-author of the Prentice-Hall text, *Service Operations Management.* Dr. Russell is a member of DSI, TIMS, ASQC, and IIE, and a certified fellow of APICS. She is Past President of the Southwest Virginia Chapter of APICS and has held numerous offices in Southeast DSI. She has received the R. B. Pamplin College of Business Certificate of Teaching Excellence, the University Certificate of Teaching Excellence, and the MBA Association's Outstanding Professor Award. She is also listed in Outstanding Young Women of America and is a recipient of the Virginia Tech Outstanding Young Alumna Award.

BRIEF CONTENTS

CONTENTS

1 OPERATIONS, COMPETITIVENESS, AND STRATEGY 1

2 OPERATIONAL DECISION MAKING 29

2 SUPPLEMENT LINEAR PROGRAMMING 61

3 QUALITY MANAGEMENT 85

4 STATISTICAL QUALITY CONTROL 145

5 PRODUCT AND SERVICE DESIGN 209

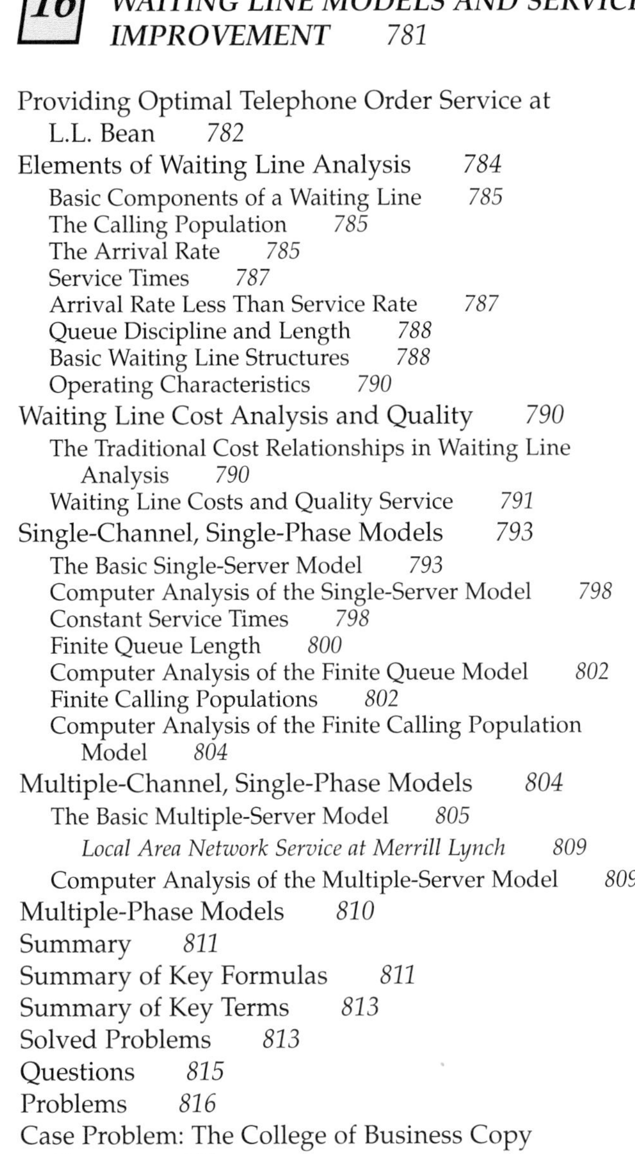

16 WAITING LINE MODELS AND SERVICE IMPROVEMENT 781

17 PROJECT MANAGEMENT 823

EPILOGUE: CHANGE 873

APPENDICES

PREFACE

We embarked on this project to create a new text in production and operations management with several objectives in mind. First, we want the text to be eminently readable for the student—clear, concise, and organized. We want to include lots of features and examples to make the topics interesting. We want the concepts we describe to be logical and easily understood. We want to make efficient use of the English language to avoid drowning straightforward topics in a sea of verbiage. And most important, we want the student to feel excited about production and operations management because we live in an exciting time with many new, unique, and interesting changes occurring in manufacturing and service operations around the world. We hope and believe we have accomplished this objective but the reader must be the ultimate judge on this account.

A second objective is to make the text contemporary and comprehensive. There are many new and important changes taking place in production and operations management today, and we want to make sure that they are conspicuously integrated with the more traditional topics in POM. That is why we focused our attention on quality management and competitiveness as consistent themes throughout the text. We do not believe that quality is simply a recent trend, but rather a pervasive philosophy that impacts on and influences all the other topics and functions in production and operations management. Quality especially impacts on the ability of firms to compete in today's global market. As the student and instructor proceed through this text, they will see how decision making for all operations has quality as a consistent and ultimate objective. Traditional functions such as planning, product and service design, facility layout and location, scheduling, and job design are considered by operations managers based on how effectively they fit in with an overall program of quality management, and thus, how effectively they enhance the firm's competitiveness. In the oft-used term *total quality management,* or *TQM,* the key word is *total.* The pursuit of quality has become all encompassing in today's management of operations, and that totality of commitment is reflected in our text.

A third objective is to strike a balance between the quantitative and managerial (or behavioral) aspects of production and operations management. Too often in the past, POM texts have seemed to be simply a loose compilation of different quantitative techniques applied to various functional topics. In the contemporary world of operations management, the quantitative and technological aspects are probably more important than ever. However, the ability to manage people and resources effectively, to motivate, organize, control, evaluate, and particularly to adapt to change, have become critical to achieving total quality and to competing in today's international markets. Thus, throughout this text we seek to explain and demonstrate how the successful operations manager manages, and when quantitative techniques are applicable, how they are used to manage and make decisions.

We also have attempted to strike a balance between manufacturing and service operations in our text. Traditionally when one thought of operations management it was in terms of manufacturing, and POM texts frequently reflected this bias. However, in the United States today there has been a perceptible shift in the economy toward service industries and away from manufacturing. Thus, managing service operations has become equally as important as managing manufacturing operations. In many cases, management techniques and processes are indistinguishable between service and manufacturing operations. However, in numerous other cases, service operations present unique situations and problems that require focused attention and unique solutions.

Another important objective is to have a well-organized text that flows smoothly and follows a logical progression of topics that places the different functions in operations management in their proper perspective. Although we have not formally subdivided our book into groupings or sections, it does have a logical organizational structure. The first two chapters introduce the subject of production and operations management and the environment for making decisions and managing operations. These chapters seek to place POM in a proper perspective and emphasize its importance in today's highly competitive world marketplace, as well as provide an overview of what is to come in the remainder of the text. The next two chapters focus on quality management from both the managerial perspective in Chapter 3 and the quantitative perspective in Chapter 4. These chapters set the tone and form the basis for our emphasis on quality management in the chapters that follow. Chapters 5 through 9 comprise a group that addresses the design of operations, while chapters 10 through 17 focus on operating functions. Thus, a logical flow is created from establishing the operating environment, to setting the quality program, to designing the operation to meet the objectives for quality, and finally to producing the service or product that will achieve the quality objectives and compete in the world market.

In order to help us achieve these objectives we have included a number of features in the text, which we will describe as follows.

LEARNING FEATURES

Focus on Quality Management

Throughout the text, icons in the margins identify locations where we specifically discuss how the topic under discussion relates to, and is impacted by, quality management.

Global and Service Highlights

In addition to the icon, we also use several other icons throughout the text to highlight topics related to the global market or competitiveness, and to service operations. The icon is employed to identify global topics, specifically when we are discussing POM or a company in a country other than the United States; and the icon is used when we are talking about a specific service operation or company.

"Gaining the Competitive Edge" Application Boxes

These boxes are located in every chapter and supplement in the text. They describe how a company, organization, or agency uses the particular management technique or function being discussed in the chapter to compete in a global environment. There are more than 60 of these boxes throughout the text and they encompass a broad range of service and manufacturing operations, foreign and domestic.

Introductory Applications

Each chapter begins with a description relating the subject of the chapter to an actual application in a company. These applications are provided first to give the reader a realistic perspective of the topic prior to embarking on its discussion.

Photos

The text includes a variety of color photographs that enhance and complement the presentation of the written textual material. These photos accompany the introductory application that starts off each chapter, and they are located at other points of interest in the chapters.

Quantitative Supplements

The text includes three chapter supplements that address three of the more traditional and mathematically rigorous quantitative techniques used in production and operations management: linear programming, transportation solution methods, and simulation. These topics have been segregated from the normal chapters because in many instances students already will have studied them in a separate quantitative methods course. In addition, their study can be time consuming and often the instructor will prefer not to take time from the coverage of other important POM topics.

Margin Notes

Notes are included in the margins that serve the same basic function as notes that students themselves might write in the margin. They highlight certain topics to make it easier for the student to locate them, they summarize topics and important points, and they provide brief definitions of key terms and concepts.

Examples

Examples are liberally inserted throughout the text, primarily to demonstrate quantitative techniques and to make them easier to understand. The examples illustrate how the results of the quantitative technique may be used to help the manager make decisions. The examples are organized into a "problem statement" and "solution" format. We also make frequent use of real world applications, often citing the experiences of companies as they relate to individual topics.

AB:POM Computer Software

The computer software package that accompanies this text, AB:POM, is very user friendly. It is easy to understand and use, requiring virtually no preliminary instruction, although a tutorial on its use that describes its features is included in Appendix A. It is used whenever possible in the text to show how to solve example problems on the computer. Also a portion of the homework problems require computer solutions and are so designated by a personal computer icon in the margin. This text can also be packaged with QSOM or STORM software.

Summary of Key Formulas

Following the summary at the end of each chapter is a "Summary of Key Formulas" that provides a list of the most important formulas derived in the presentation of any quantitative techniques introduced in the chapter. These enable the student to turn to a specific location to refresh their memories about a formula without having to search through the chapter.

Summary of Key Terms

Following the "Summary of Key Formulas" at the end of each chapter is a "Summary of Key Terms." It provides a list of the most important terms for the chapter and their definitions. This list enables the student to access a specific location to refresh their memories about an important term without having to search through the chapter or marginal notes.

Solved Example Problems

At the end of each chapter just prior to the homework questions and problems, there is a section with solved examples that serve as a guide for doing the homework problems. These examples are solved in a detailed, step-by-step fashion.

Supplemental Items

The text is accompanied by a number of supplemental items that the instructor may wish to use in the course. These supplements include a set of videos that complement the textual presentation of material in a number of locations throughout the text. The locations where these videos might be used, and a description of each video, is provided in the Annotated Instructor's Edition (AIE) of this text. The AIE also includes teaching notes for the instructor, alternate examples to those examples provided in the text, and summaries of the videos that can be used in these chapters. Also included with this text is the Solutions Manual detailing answers to end-of-chapter questions, homework problems, and case problems; a Text Bank; and Transparency Masters. Other available supplements include a Study Guide and the books *Profiles of Malcolm Baldrige Award Winners, Profile of ISO 9000, Games and Exercises in Production and Operations Management,* and *Cases and Readings in Production and Operations Management,* all published by Prentice-Hall.

ACKNOWLEDGMENTS

The writing of a textbook, like any large project, requires the help of many people and this is certainly not the exception. We especially appreciate the guidance, support, ideas, suggestions, and help of our editor, Rich Wohl. We willingly acknowledge that this book was his suggestion, and we especially appreciate his confidence in us that we could carry his idea to fruition. We also thank the various support personnel at our publisher, including Mark Palmer, Jennifer Strada, Marjorie Payne, Joyce Turner, and numerous other people who work behind the scenes and whom we never saw or talked to. We would also like to thank Barbara Barg for all of her help and suggestions during the editing and production process. We are indebted to the reviewers of the initial draft of this text, including: Dennis Krumwiede, Kansas State University; Reino V. Warren, Eastern Michigan University; Ramesh G. Soni, Indiana University of Pennsylvania, Michael S. Spencer, University of Northern Iowa; Lance Heiko, Bryant College; Craig Cowles, Bridgewater State University; Ali Behnezhad, California State University, Northridge; Richard A. Reid, University of New Mexico, Albuquerque. They contributed numerous suggestions, comments, and ideas that dramatically changed and improved on our original effort. We offer our sincere thanks to these colleagues and hope that they can take some satisfaction in their contribution to our final product. We wish to thank our students who have class-tested, critiqued, and contributed to the material from a consumer's point of view. We are especially grateful to Tracy Black and Jay Teets for their contributions to specific homework and example problems. Last, but certainly not least, we would like to thank Tracy McCoy at Virginia Tech for her unstinting help, hard work, and patience.

1

OPERATIONS, COMPETITIVENESS, AND STRATEGY

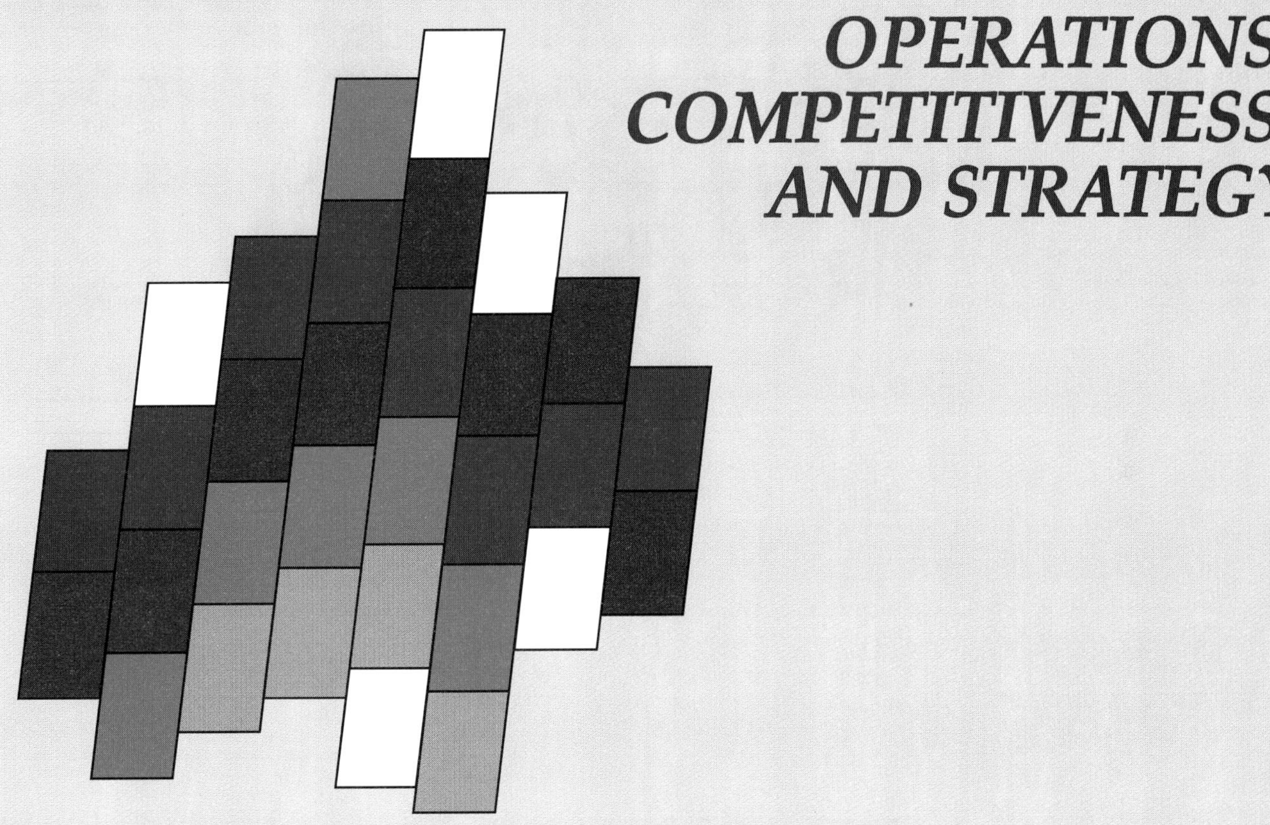

CHAPTER OUTLINE

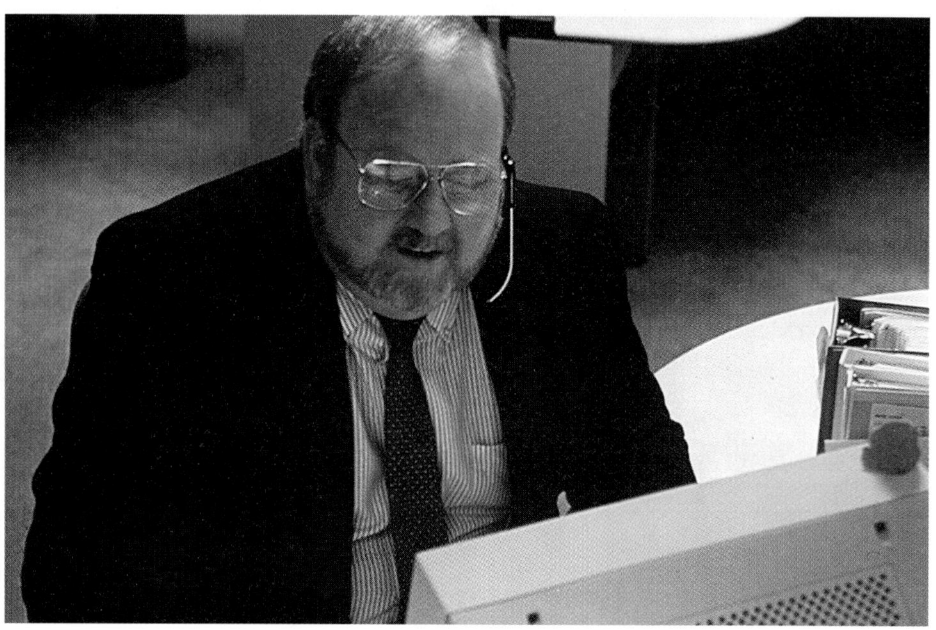

AT&T Universal Card Services (UCS) won the Malcolm Baldrige National Quality Award as a young company built on a set of quality values that guide both long range planning and day-to-day operations. These values include: customer delight, commitment, teamwork, continuous improvement, trust and integrity, mutual respect, and a sense of urgency. Going beyond rhetoric, UCS collects data daily on over 100 measurements of customer satisfaction and creates a monthly list of "Ten Most Wanted" quality improvements. A Service Quality Warranty promises customers courteous treatment, 100% error-free service, continuous availability, quick replacement of lost or stolen cards, and an advocate in billing disputes with merchants and banks. Ten dollar service guarantee certificates (to be applied toward UCS bill) are given on the spot to customers who are not happy with the service provided.

THEY ALL BELIEVE IN QUALITY

What do a credit card company, a hotel, a rock quarry, a defense contractor, and an electronics manufacturer have in common? They are the five recipients of the 1992 Malcolm Baldrige National Quality Award and role models for excellence in operations.

Video 1.1 1992 *Malcolm Baldrige Awards, Quest for Excellence V*

AT&T Universal Card Services (UCS) entered the very competitive credit card industry in 1990 and within three years was the second largest competitor (out of a field of 6000). How did UCS get so good so fast? Through excellent "product" design and impeccable employee performance.

Every detail is carefully planned at the Ritz Carlton Hotels—carefully planned and measured. The hotel gathers data daily on more than 720 measurements of performance. Each employee receives more than 136 hours of training to become "quality engineers." Customers are not just satisfied; they describe staying at the Ritz-Carlton as a "memorable experience."

It may not seem possible to differentiate one's product in the quarry business, but Granite Rock found a way. Their quality is the standard for the industry, and their operations are innovative. For example, an ATM-like system is used by customers to order and receive customized mixtures automatically, cutting the service time to a mere 9 minutes.

The defense and electronics group of Texas Instruments stands out in a shrinking market. Their concurrent design process has given them an edge in finding new markets for their products.

All 10,000 employees at AT&T Transmission Systems are involved in quality planning. A system called policy deployment links corporate goals with customer satisfiers and individual actions with departmental and corporate goals.[1]

These companies represent the kind of excellence in production/operations of which the United States can be proud. In this opening chapter we talk about operations management, the drive for competitiveness, and strategy issues. Henry Ford once remarked that working in a factory was like working in the future. We hope that your journey through this chapter—and the textbook as a whole—will challenge your imagination (as was Henry Ford's) and open your eyes to future possibilities in the way work is organized, performed, and improved.

Traditionally, *production* has been defined as a transformation process. As shown in Figure 1.1, *inputs* (such as material, machines, labor, management, and capital) are transformed into *outputs* (goods and services). Feedback from the output stage is used to adjust factors in the input or transformation stage. In production/operations management, we try to ensure that the transformation process is performed efficiently and that the output is of greater *value* than the sum of the inputs. Thus, in a sense, production is the creation of value.

The input-transformation-output process is characteristic of a wide variety of operating systems. In an automobile factory, sheet steel is formed into different shapes, painted and finished, and then assembled with thousands of component parts to produce a working automobile. In an aluminum factory, various grades of crushed coke are mixed, heated, and molded into anode blocks of different sizes. In a hospital, patients are restored into healthier individuals through special care, meals, medication, lab procedures, and surgical procedures. Obviously, "production" can take many different forms. The transformation process can be

Teaching Note 1.1 Class Participation

Production can be viewed as a transformation process.

Physical, as in manufacturing operations,
Locational, as in transportation or warehouse operations,
An *exchange,* as in retail operations,
Physiological, as in healthcare,
Psychological, as in entertainment, or
Informational, as in communications.

Transparency 1.1 Production as a Transformation Process

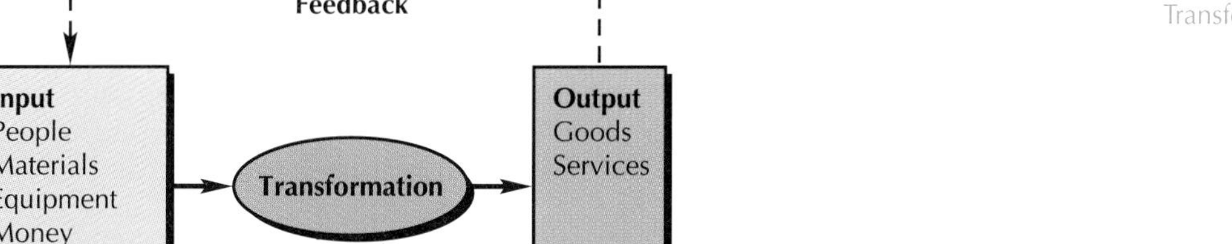

FIGURE 1.1 Production as a Transformation Process

[1]*Quest for Excellence V,* American Society of Quality Control Video Series, 1993.

Production is a function or system that transforms inputs into outputs of greater value.

Production is often used to describe the transformation process in manufacturing firms, whereas *operations* is more prevalent in services. The acronym POM (for production/operations management) describes the entire field of study. We will use the terms *production, operations,* and *production/operations* interchangeably in this text.

THE OPERATIONS FUNCTION

The types of activities involved in POM include organizing work, selecting processes, arranging layouts, locating facilities, designing jobs, measuring performance, controlling quality, scheduling work, managing inventory, and planning production. Operations managers deal with people, technology, and deadlines. These managers need good technical, conceptual, and behavioral skills. Their activities are closely intertwined with other functional areas in a firm.

Production can be viewed as a function.

As shown in Figure 1.2, the three primary functions of a firm are 1. marketing, 2. finance, and 3. production. Other areas, such as personnel, engineering, accounting, and purchasing, support the three main functions. In simplified form, *marketing* establishes the demand for goods or services, *finance* provides the capital, and *production* actually makes the goods or provides the service. Of the three functions, production typically employs the greatest number of people and requires the largest investment in assets. For these reasons, management of the production function has often been viewed as an opportunity to improve a firm's efficiency and gain higher profits. Seldom, however, has the production function been seen as an avenue to increase sales, gain market share, or eliminate the competition—that is, until foreign competitors did just that.

Production can be viewed as the technical core.

Figure 1.3 views production from another perspective, as the *technical* core of an organization. In this scenario, production is the central function of an organization. The organization exists to provide goods and services. All other functions exist to support the operations function. Operations interacts with *marketing* to receive estimates of customer demand and customer feedback on problems, *finance* for capital investments, budgets, and stockholder requirements, *personnel* to train, hire, and fire workers, and *purchasing* to order needed materials for production. The operations function is purposely isolated from contact with outside influences, such as customers and financial markets, so that a stable environment for top efficiency can be created and maintained. However, this very isolation contributed to the competitive problems experienced by U.S. manufacturers in the 1970s and 1980s. We will learn that successful operations managers do more than efficiently convert inputs to outputs. As part of the management team, they must be in direct contact with internal and external customers and be responsive to their needs. In order to understand better the role of operations and the operations manager, let's briefly review the historical evolution of POM.

Transparency 1.2 Production as a Basic Function

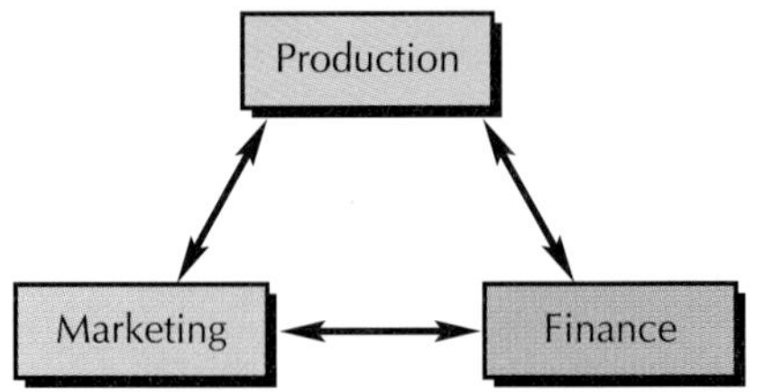

FIGURE 1.2 Production as a Basic Function

Transparency 1.3 Production as the Technical Core

FIGURE 1.3 Production as the Technical Core

THE EVOLUTION OF PRODUCTION/OPERATIONS MANAGEMENT

Although history is full of amazing production feats—the pyramids of Egypt, the Great Wall of China, the roads and aqueducts of Rome—the widespread production of consumer goods (and thus, production/operations management) did not begin until the Industrial Revolution in the 1700s. Prior to that time, skilled craftspersons and their apprentices fashioned goods for individual customers from studios in their own homes. For the most part, every piece was unique, hand-fitted, and made from start to finish by one person. Then, the invention of an improved steam engine in 1782 by James Watt and the availability of coal and iron ore set into motion a series of impressive industrial inventions that revolutionized the way work was performed. Great mechanical-powered machines made of iron replaced the laborer as the primary factor of production and brought scores of workers to a central location to perform tasks under the direction of an "overseer" in a place called a "factory." The revolution first took hold in the textile mills, grain mills, metalworking, and machine-making facilities.

Around the same time, Adam Smith's *Wealth of Nations* (1776) proposed the concept of *division of labor,* in which the production process was broken down into a series of small tasks, each performed by a different worker. The specialization of the worker on limited, repetitive tasks allowed him or her to become very proficient at those tasks and further encouraged the development of specialized machinery. The introduction of *interchangeable parts* by Eli Whitney (1790s) allowed the manufacture of firearms, clocks, watches, sewing machines, and other goods to shift from customized one-at-a-time production to volume production of standardized parts. This meant that the factory now needed a system of measurements and inspection, a standard method of production, and extra supervisors to check the quality of the worker's production. Advances in technology continued at an unprecedented rate through the 1800s. Cost accounting and other control systems were developed, but management theory and practice were virtually nonexistent.

From the Industrial Revolution to the Quality Revolution

The void was filled in the early 1900s by an enterprising laborer (and later chief engineer) at Midvale Steel Works named Frederick W. Taylor. Taylor believed that the management of work should be approached as a science. That is, based on observation, measurement, and analysis, the very best method for performing each job should be identified. Once determined, the methods should be standardized for all workers and economic incentives established to encourage workers to follow the standards. Taylor's philosophy became known as *scientific management.* His ideas were embraced and extended by efficiency experts Frank and Lillian

Gilbreth, Henry Gantt, and many others. One of Taylor's biggest advocates was Henry Ford.

Henry Ford applied scientific management to the production of the Model T in 1913 and came up with a system that reduced the time required to assemble a car from a high of 728 hours to 1½ hours. In this system, a Model T chassis moved slowly down a conveyor belt with six workers walking along beside it, picking up parts from carefully spaced piles on the floor and fitting them to the chassis.[2] The short assembly time per car allowed the Model T to be produced in high volumes, or "en masse," thus yielding the name **mass production.**

Mass production is high-volume production of a standardized product for a mass market.

American manufacturers became very adept at mass production over the next fifty years and easily dominated manufacturing worldwide. The human relations movement of the 1930s, led by Elton Mayo and the Hawthorne studies, introduced the idea that worker motivation, as well as the technical aspects of work, affected productivity. Theories of motivation were developed by Herzberg, Maslow, McGregor, and others. Quantitative models and techniques spawned by the operations research groups of World War II continued to develop and were applied successfully to manufacturing. Computers and automation led still another upsurge in technological advancements applied to operations. See Table 1.1.

From the industrial revolution through the 1960s, the United States was the world's greatest producer of goods and services, as well as the major source of

Transparency 1.4 Some Historical Events in POM

TABLE 1.1 Some Historical Events in POM

Era	*Events/Concepts*	*Dates*	*Originator*
Industrial Revolution	Steam engine	1769	James Watt
	Division of labor	1776	Adam Smith
	Interchangeable parts	1790	Eli Whitney
Scientific Management	Principles of scientific management	1911	Frederick W. Taylor
	Time and motion studies	1911	Frank and Lillian Gilbreth
	Activity scheduling chart	1912	Henry Gantt
	Moving assembly line	1913	Henry Ford
Human Relations	Hawthorne studies	1930	Elton Mayo
	Motivation theories	1940s, 1950s, 1960s	Abraham Maslow Frederick Hertzberg Douglas McGregor
Management Science	Linear programming	1947	George Dantzig
	Digital computer	1951	Remington Rand
	Simulation, waiting line theory, decision theory, PERT/CPM	1950s, 1960s	Operations research groups
 Quality Revolution	Lean production, JIT (just-in-time)	1970s, 1980s	Taiichi Ohno (Toyota)
	TQM (Total quality management)	1980s, 1990s	W. Edwards Deming, Joseph Juran, and others
	CIM (computer-integrated manufacturing)	1980s, 1990s	Numerous individuals and companies

[2]David Halberstam, *The Reckoning*, New York: Morrow, 1986, pp. 79–81.

managerial and technical expertise. Looking back, 1960 was probably the heyday for American manufacturing. From then on, industry by industry, U.S. manufacturing superiority was challenged. By the 1970s and 1980s, the world had become a very competitive place. Foreign manufacturers, led by Japan, changed the rules of production with an adaptation of mass production known as *lean production.* Lean production prized flexibility (rather than efficiency) and quality (rather than quantity). The "total quality" fervor has since spread across the globe and is the focus of operations today in a highly competitive world of global enterprises.

This text discusses many of the issues, approaches, and techniques mentioned in our brief overview of POM history, with a focus on quality. In this first chapter, we lay the groundwork for your study of operations by addressing the issue of competitiveness. In the process, it is necessary to review the sometimes painful problems faced by U.S. industry in the past ten to twenty years. By the end of the chapter, it should be abundantly clear that the United States is in the midst of a long-term, high-stakes battle called "competitiveness," and to succeed we must maintain an unswerving dedication to excellence in operations.

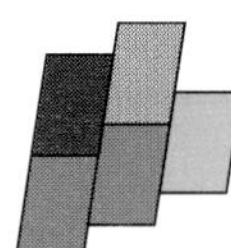

U.S. COMPETITIVENESS

Competitiveness is defined as "the degree to which a nation can, under demanding and rapidly changing market conditions, produce goods and services that meet the test of international markets while simultaneously maintaining or expanding the real incomes of its citizens."[3] The United States is the world's largest exporter and the most productive country in the world (as measured by GDP and per capita GDP/GNP), and yet we speak of U.S. problems with competitiveness.[4] So where is the competitive problem? The problem comes from the difficulty of "maintaining or expanding" the standard of living to which U.S. residents have become accustomed. One critical measure of competitiveness is *productivity growth.* The United States' productivity increased less than 3 percent per year in the early 1990s, whereas Japan's increased over 4 percent per year and Germany's, nearly 3 percent per year. The real winners were the newly industrialized economies (called NIE) of South Korea, Hong Kong, Taiwan, and Singapore, with increases nearing 5 percent.

Competitiveness is the degree to which a nation can produce goods and services that meet the test of international markets while simultaneously maintaining or expanding the real income of its citizens.

Teaching Note 1.2 Student Assignments

Competitiveness can be measured as *productivity growth.*

Is a 3 percent growth in productivity bad? Actually, 3 percent is a significant comeback for U.S. industry. In the 1970s the annual productivity growth averaged 1.3 percent, and, in the 1980s, it was 0.2 percent (with some years negative). Several studies were published during those years that bemoaned the United States' lack of competitiveness. The studies confirmed what the U.S. consumer already knew—U.S.-made products of that era were inferior and could not compete on the world market. Table 1.2 shows damaging comparisons of product performance for U.S. versus Japanese automobiles, semiconductors, air conditioners, and color televisions.

Early rationalizations that the Japanese success was a cultural phenomenon were disproved by the successes of Japanese-owned plants in this country. A prime example is the Matsushita purchase from Motorola of a failing Quasar television plant in Chicago. Part of the purchase contract specified that Matsushita had to retain the entire hourly work force of 1000 persons. After only two years,

[3] *Report of the President's Commission on Industrial Competitiveness,* chaired by John A. Young, President and CEO, Hewlett-Packard, 1985.

[4] The statistics in this section are from "The World Economy in Charts," *Fortune,* July 26, 1993, pp. 88–96. GDP stands for gross domestic product and GNP, gross national product.

TABLE 1.2 A Comparison of American and Japanese Products in the 1970s and 1980s

Quality of Automobiles	*TGWs (things gone wrong) in First 8 Months per 100 cars*	
Chrysler	285	
GM	256	
Ford	214	
Japanese (avg.)	132	
Toyota	55	
Quality of Semiconductors	***U.S. Companies***	***Japanese Companies***
Defective on delivery	16%	0%
Failure after 1000 hours	14%	1%
Quality of Room Air Conditioners	***U.S. Companies***	***Japanese Companies***
Fabrication defects	4.4%	<0.1%
Assembly line defects	63.5%	0.9%
Service calls	10.5%	0.6%
Warranty cost (as % of sales)	2.2%	0.6%
Quality of Color TVs	***U.S. Companies***	***Japanese Companies***
Assembly line defects per set	1.4–2.0	0.01–0.03
Service calls per set	1.0–2.0	0.09–0.26

Sources: National Academy of Engineering, *The Competitive Status of the U.S. Auto Industry,* Washington, D.C.: National Academy Press, 1982, pp. 90–108; A.L. Robinson, "Perilous Times for U.S. Microcircuit Makers," *Science,* May 9, 1980, pp. 582–586; D. Garvin, "Quality on the Line," *Harvard Business Review,* Sept.–Oct. 1983, pp. 64–75; I. Magaziner and R. Reich, *Minding America's Business,* New York: Harcourt Brace Jovanovich, 1982, p. 176; M. Porter, *Cases in Competitive Strategy,* New York: The Free Press, 1983, p. 511.

with the identical workers, half the management staff, and little or no capital investment, Matsushita doubled production, cut assembly repairs from 130 percent to 6 percent, and reduced warranty costs from $16 million a year to $2 million a year. You can bet Motorola took notice. (Not surprisingly, today Motorola is one of the success stories of American manufacturing.)

Transparency 1.5 U.S. Problems with Competitiveness

Teaching Note 1.3 A Video Suggestion

How did this come about? How did a country that dominated manufacturing for most of the twentieth century suddenly become no good at it? One of the most comprehensive studies of competitiveness was conducted by the MIT Commission on Industrial Productivity. The study identified the following weaknesses across eight industries:[5]

Competitive weaknesses

1. Short-term financial orientation
2. Lack of cooperation
3. Weaknesses in human resources management
4. Recurring weaknesses in technological practice
5. Strategic weaknesses

We discuss each of these weaknesses in turn.

[5]The material in the following sections is adapted from Michael Dertouzos, Richard Lester, and Robert Solow, *Made in America,* Cambridge, Mass.: MIT Press, 1989.

Short-term Financial Orientation

There is an old saying that no one wants to plant the crops if they won't be around for the harvest. That saying is certainly true in the business world. The typical U.S. manager stays in his or her position for five years or less. This fact does not encourage long-term thinking, since any programs or activities in which the manager is involved will have to yield a return within five years, or someone else will end up getting the credit for it. In addition, workers, managers, and CEOs are very mobile across firms. This fact, coupled with incentive pay schemes, such as profit sharing and stock options, further encourages the pursuit of short-term profits at the expense of long-term survival.

ROI versus market share

Corporate performance in the United States is measured internally by return on investment (ROI) and, externally, by earnings per share. In Germany and Japan, market share is a more important performance measure, and earnings per share is rarely considered. The overreliance on ROI discourages investment, especially if some risk is involved. Decisions with consequences extending far into the future are risky. Top management inexperience with R&D and technology and the uncertainty of the outcomes make decisions in those areas especially risky. The risk is incorporated in higher hurdle rates for ROI, which, in turn, reduces the likelihood that the proposal will be accepted.

Risk and time also have the potential to affect negatively the financial market's assessment of the firm in terms of earnings per share. Waiting for long-term strategies or investments to pay off might trigger stockholder unrest, hostile takeovers, or leveraged buyouts. This was especially true in the 1980s.

Teaching Note 1.4 An Industry Analysis

The decline of the steel industry is a prime example of the results of short-term thinking. It took the U.S. steel industry six to seven years to begin investing in the new technologies of oxygen furnaces, continuous casters, and computer controls. By then, they were hopelessly behind their foreign competitors. Consumer electronics is another example. U.S. manufacturers were not willing to wait out the periods of low profit as new products were being introduced to the market. U.S. manufacturers "gave away" production of the VCR, camcorder, CT scanner (used in medical diagnosis), and fax (facsimile machine)—all products that were invented in the United States—because initial profits were marginal and many years of development work were required. U.S. automakers followed a similar approach, conceding the low end of the automobile market to Japanese producers because profits were low. This is classic Japanese strategy—enter the market at the low end, establish position, refine product and process knowledge, and advance little by little over an extended period of time. The success of this strategy is symbolized by Toyota's Lexus, which captured almost 8 percent of the lucrative luxury car market in the United States within three years of its introduction.

In terms of manufacturing, pressure to optimize short-term performance translates into high-volume production, low labor costs, stability, and operational efficiency rather than strategic effectiveness. As we shall see later, the strategy of *economies of scale* is no longer appropriate for most operations.

Lack of Cooperation

Teaching Note 1.5 Attitudes Toward Manufacturing

U.S. individualism does not encourage cooperation. This is nowhere more evident than in the corporate structure. In many industries, management and workers have an adversarial relationship. Workers compete for wages and have trouble working together in groups. Different departments within the same firm are often at odds. Functional areas in a firm are clearly delineated and make decisions separately. Government is viewed as an obstacle to competitiveness (with its taxes and regulations) rather than a source of support. Consumers mistrust corporations, and corporations are wary of consumers. Suppliers are not partners, but competitors for profits. Companies do not share information or strategies in the same industry or across industries. In sum, relationships between people, departments, and firms are often more competitive than cooperative.

Cooperation is needed between all groups.

A more constructive and profitable basis for relationships is cooperation: management and labor working together; integrated decision making within a firm; companies that listen to their customers; manufacturers that listen to their suppliers, learn their technology, and work together to synchronize production; firms in the same industry that establish common standards and pool resources for R&D; and a government that supports long-term investment, provides quality education, and keeps the country's infrastructure up-to-date.

U.S. companies have made gigantic strides in the areas of cooperation and coordination in reaction to tough foreign competition. But this is a difficult area in which to make lasting changes because it requires changes in attitudes as well as in practices. One example of effective cooperation is the textile industry's *quick response program,* designed to improve the flow of information, standardize recoding systems, and reduce turnaround time along the entire logistical chain from fiber to textiles, apparel, and retailing.

Human Resource Management

Human resource management in the United States suffers from many deficiencies. Layers upon layers of management reach from the worker level to the top management level. The decision-making process is slow and not necessarily effective. By the time a proposal has passed through several layers of management, approval is inevitable, whether the proposal makes sense anymore or not. Labor is viewed as a factor of production, to be acquired at the lowest possible cost. Skill development is more the responsibility of the individual than the corporation. Management sees its role as planning and controlling work and the worker's job as completing manual tasks and following orders from management.

Many of our ideas about management and modern production systems come from Frederick Taylor, who methodically studied how work could best be performed. Workers using his methods saw dramatic increases in their efficiency and productivity. Their extra work was rewarded by increased pay based on the number of pieces produced. Although Taylor's work methods and analytic approach still play an important role in production today, his view that workers should "check their brains at the door" is outdated and is an obstacle to the effective management of human resources. In today's competitive world, companies have learned that labor is a valuable asset that should be utilized to the fullest extent—and that means brains as well as brawn.

Teaching Note 1.6 Attitudes Toward Workers

People are a valuable asset.

So how do you obtain the best from your work force? You can invest in training, give workers more responsibilities and less supervision, use problem-solving teams, and create an environment in which suggestions for improvement are encouraged, valued, and acted upon. AT&T Universal Card Services received 10,000 suggestions for improvement last year. That's an average of almost 5 suggestions per employee. After 90 line workers put together the first production prototypes of the Chrysler Neon, the designers asked for their suggestions—and got 4000 of them! At North American Tool and Die, worker involvement became the competitive edge the company needed to survive. With worker ownership, productivity rose 480 percent, and absenteeism dropped to less than 1 percent, turnover to less than 4 percent, and rejects to less than 0.10 percent. On the bottom line, pretax earnings were twenty-five times greater than previous years and the company's stock prices grew by 47 percent.[6]

Managers who doubt the abilities of their workers to make good decisions and to contribute to workplace management need only look at their communities and take note of who runs the volunteer fire and rescue squads, PTAs, and little

[6]M. Ray and A. Rinzler, *The New Paradigm in Business,* New York: Perigee Books, 1993, p. 120.

leagues. There are a lot of good ideas and many talented people among us living ordinary lives and accomplishing extraordinary tasks.

Technological Practice

American firms tend to concentrate on product innovation at the expense of process innovation. This was a wise strategy thirty years ago. In the 1960s, the rate of return on product R&D was always higher than on process R&D. The inventors of new products were the winners in the marketplace because they had monopoly power to set prices and earn hefty profits. Americans were known for their innovation in product design. In fact, the United States had such a technological advantage in the development of new products that Japan and Germany were forced to focus their efforts on process technology.

Thirty years later, technology and the competitive environment have changed the manner and speed with which new products are designed and produced. Whether the product itself is high-tech or low-tech, the processes by which it is produced are increasingly high-tech. New product designs can be easily reproduced; new processes take more time and capital to match. Companies that can *make* a product better or cheaper take the advantage away from the inventor. Thus, the invention and perfecting of new processes has replaced the invention of new products as the primary source of competitive advantage.

Process technology becomes a competitive advantage.

Strategic Weaknesses

After World War II, the United States had an enormous consumer market that could best be supplied by the rapid production of standardized products. Henry Ford's assembly line concept was the basis for mass production, which relied on **economies of scale** to produce large quantities of output cheaply. The highly effective Japanese production systems of today were fashioned after Ford's assembly line, with one exception—the Japanese systems are flexible.

In **economies of scale,** as the number of units produced increases, the cost of producing each individual unit decreases.

After years of decline, the U.S. has become the leader in low-cost production of many products and services, from motorcycles to finances. Companies that focused on quality, streamlined their workforce, and reengineered their processes in the latter half of the 1980s are now reaping their rewards. Even industries we thought were gone forever, such as automobiles, machine tools, steel, and computer chips are back with a vengeance. Shown in this photo are completed Harley-Davidson motorcycles ready for a 28-test inspection process. Harley is representative of American firms that have worked hard to find success once again.

GAINING THE COMPETITIVE EDGE

U.S. Manufacturers Fight Back

Whirlpool's Benton Harbor facility turns metal rods into parts for washers and dryers. In the mid-1980s, Whirlpool closed down the main portion of the Benton Harbor plant, eliminating 1000 jobs. What remained was a small tooling and plating shop that wasn't exactly high-tech. Instead of building a state-of-the-art facility or sending the jobs elsewhere, Whirlpool decided to overhaul the manufacturing process and teach its workers to improve quality. The gamble paid off. Labor productivity grew by nearly 20 percent in just four years and the number of rejects fell from 800 per million to 10 per million. An innovative gain-sharing agreement helped convince the workers that the company was serious about improving operations. The concept was simple: the bigger the gain in output, the larger the pool of money for the workers and the company to share. This may not seem much different from other profit-sharing plans, but under this system the precise percentage of the pool is determined by the quality of the output (as measured by the number of rejects). The workers divide their share of the pool evenly. The company's share is divided between shareholders and consumers, thus balancing profits and prices. Over the past several years, Whirlpool's bottom line has improved significantly and its market share has also increased. All this has occurred in a highly competitive market during a time when major productivity improvements were evident throughout the appliance industry.

Cincinnati Milicron was a leading manufacturer of advanced automation when companies had little interest in or couldn't afford the new technology. In the meantime, aggressive Japanese producers seized half of the U.S. market in more conventional machinery. After ten years without an acceptable profit, Milicron decided to make a major strategic move. They sold their line of heavy robots to Asea Brown Boveri, a Swiss manufacturer, and concentrated instead on three basic product lines: machine tools, plastics machinery, and consumable accessories (such as grinding wheels). The restructuring itself helped the company, but if they were going to compete in this arena, costs had to be reduced drastically. Milicron set to work redesigning the machines it produced with fewer parts, thereby cutting its manufacturing costs 40 percent. The next step was an additional 15 percent reduction through automation and streamlined assembly. Finally, Milicron reorganized its entire company along customer lines, such as lathes or machining centers. This meant that the designers, manufacturers, and service personnel for each product type were working together on a day-to-day basis and were more knowledgeable and accessible to customers.

Video 1.2 *Harley-Davidson, Building Better Motorcycles the American Way*

Currently, Harley-Davidson is the only U.S. manufacturer of motorcycles. Some fifteen years ago they took their Japanese competitors to court, accusing them of selling motorcycles on the U.S. market below cost to capture market share (and drive Harley out of business). They lost the suit—the competitors proved that their costs really were that low. Faced with the threat of bankruptcy, Harley used advanced technology, excellence in design, attention to operations, and their people's love for the product to come fighting back. Today, one of the biggest markets for "hogs" is Japan!

Sources: Based on Rick Wartzman, "A Whirlpool Factory Raises Productivity—and Pay of Workers," *The Wall Street Journal*, May 4, 1992; "Milicron Wolfpack Goes in for the Kill," *The Wall Street Journal*, August 14, 1990; and "Building Better Motorcycles the American Way," Allyn and Bacon Video Series, Harley-Davidson Company, 1991.

Misfit between the market and production

Mass production can produce large volumes of goods quickly, but it cannot adapt very well to changes in demand. The consumer market of the last ten years or so has been characterized by product proliferation, shortened product life-cycles, shortened product development times, changes in technology, more customized products, and segmented markets. Mass production does not "fit" that type of environment. Why did it take U.S. managers so long to see the misfit?

Quite simply, they weren't paying attention. From the 1950s onward, U.S. companies thought mass production had solved the "problem" of production, so they delegated the function of manufacturing to technical specialists (usually engineers). A firm's direction was determined by financial or marketing concerns; the strategic impact of manufacturing was ignored. Manufacturing was placed in a subordinate role to marketing and finance. Its influence was limited to "reacting" to demands, and often those reactions were seen as bothersome complaints.

The realization of manufacturing's strategic importance has come slowly to U.S. firms. Now most firms seem convinced. Discussions about quality, cycle time, and process analysis are taking place in boardrooms across the United States.

Teaching Note 1.7 Realizing Manufacturing's Strategic Importance

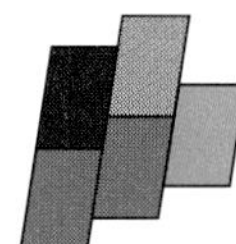

STRATEGY

The 1990s are a good time to study operations. The 1970s and 1980s were our reality check, our "wake-up call," a time when we discovered that strategies successful in the past were no longer appropriate in today's competitive environment. Given the importance of strategy to our economic survival, let's spend some time going over the basics of formulating strategy.

Strategy can be defined in many ways. In simple terms, strategy is a framework for planning. Strategy focuses on what is needed for survival. In more comprehensive terms, strategy consists of a shared vision that unites an organization, provides for consistent decision making, and keeps it moving in the right direction.

Strategy is a common vision that unites an organization, provides consistency in decisions, and keeps the organization moving in the right direction.

Strategy formulation consists of four basic steps:

1. *Defining a primary task* (what are you in the business of doing?) The **primary task** should not be defined too narrowly. Norfolk & Southern Railways is in the business of transportation, not railroads. Paramount is in the business of communications, not making movies. Disney goes one step further—its primary task is making people happy! For diverse corporations, the primary task is also referred to as the *core business* of the firm. Often, the primary task is expressed in a firm's vision or mission statement. From the primary task, competitors and positions in the marketplace can be determined.

The **primary task** is the one most central to the operation of a firm.

Teaching Note 1.8 Visions

2. *Assessing distinctive competence* (what do you do better than anyone else?). Also called *competitive advantage,* this can be experienced only in comparison with competitors. A company's **distinctive competence** can be providing a product or service quicker than anyone else or providing superior service, higher quality, or lower cost. It can involve superior performance, better reliability, more features, more variety, or simply being most convenient. One company may relish its reputation for being first to the market with innovative designs, whereas another may be content with arriving later to the market but with consistently better quality. A company that cannot identify its distinctive competence and capitalize on it will not stay in business for long.

Transparency 1.6 Strategy Formulation

Distinctive competence is what an entity does better than anyone else.

3. *Determining order winners and order qualifiers* (what wins orders in the marketplace? what qualifies a product or service to be considered by the customer?). There is typically only one **order winner** for a product but many **order qualifiers.** For example, when you purchase a CD player, you may determine a price range (order qualifier) and then choose the product with the most features (order winner) in that price range. Or you may have a set of features in mind (order qualifiers) and then select the cheapest CD player (order winner) that has all the required features.

An **order winner** is the characteristic of a product or service that wins orders in the marketplace.

Order qualifiers are a characteristic of a product or service that qualifies it to be considered for purchase by a customer.

This step in formulating strategy looks toward the customer in an attempt to determine whether a firm's distinctive competence will, in fact, pay off. A firm is

Teaching Note 1.9 Order Winners and Order Qualifiers

in trouble if the things it does best are of no importance to the customer. Ideally, a firm's distinctive competence should match the market's order winner. If the market is not homogeneous, individual market segments can be targeted.

Chase an effective positioning strategy.

4. *Positioning the firm* (for what do you want to be known? on what do you wish to compete?). An effective positioning strategy will consider the strengths and weaknesses of the company, the needs of the marketplace, and the position of competitors (in other words, everything we've discussed in Steps 1 through 3). It is important for the manufacturing system to reflect the positioning strategy. For example, U.S. manufacturers are known for their ability to mass-produce standard items at low cost. This is an appropriate strategy if the market volume is high and if product design does not change often. If, however, the market is volatile or segmented into smaller volumes, mass production would be a mistake.

There can be a progression in strategic focus, just as order winners and order qualifiers can evolve over time, and competencies can be gained and lost. Japanese automakers initially competed on price, but they had to assure certain levels of quality before the U.S. consumer would consider their product. Over time, the consumer was willing to pay a higher price (within reason) for the assurance of a superior-quality Japanese car. Price became a qualifier, but quality won the orders. Now, Japanese luxury cars are known for their innovative design as well as their high quality and reasonable cost.

It is important for a firm to keep track of the order winners and order qualifiers of their products to constantly position itself in the marketplace. Companies need to make sure their products are meeting all qualifiers and be able to sense when changes in order-winning criteria occur. A significant change for many American companies occurred in the 1970s and 1980s when manufacturing (through superior quality, fast delivery, low cost, etc.) became the distinctive competence of many foreign competitors and won orders for them in the marketplace. Let's examine further the role of operations in corporate strategy.

Federal Express began operations in 1973 with a fleet of eight small aircraft. Five years later, the company employed 10,000 people to handle 35,000 daily deliveries. Today, over 90,000 FedEx employees process 1.5 million shipments daily, all of which must be tracked, sorted, and delivered in a short amount of time. The SuperTracker, shown here, is a hand-held computer used for scanning a shipment's bar code every time a package changes hands between pickup and delivery. It provides valuable input data for locating the root causes of problems and calculating the company's 12-component Service Quality Indicator (SQI).

GAINING THE COMPETITIVE EDGE

Technology as a Distinctive Competence

For many companies, technology is an integral part of corporate strategy. Xerox has long recognized that its survival in the arena of communications depends on the strategy of successfully integrating paper-based and electronic information technology. One product designed to complement that strategy is *PaperWorks*, a $250 software package that allows users to access their PCs from any fax machine in the world. With special paper forms, an individual can instruct his or her computer to store, retrieve, and distribute files without having to be at the computer itself. A PC at home or the office could forward faxes, store newspaper articles and fax copies to a mailing list, or receive and resend images sent from far distances. The product was developed in a scant 15 months and signifies the strategic shift from Xerox as "the document company" to Xerox as the company for "productive work communities."

Service companies seldom come to mind as examples of high-tech operations, but Federal Express was built on advanced technology. Their hub-and-spokes transportation system has been copied by every major airline in the world. Manufacturers often benchmark against FedEx's specially designed package-sortation system that processes 1 million packages in less than 3 hours. FedEx also has one of the most sophisticated computer information systems in the world. The COSMOS network can receive information from transfer terminals in delivery vans and in customer facilities and from hand-held computers called SuperTrackers. They use the information to track customer orders, adjust delivery routes, determine load factors and docking sequences for aircraft, schedule maintenance activities, and maintain a sufficient inventory of service parts. Federal Express even designs and operates inventory-management and distribution centers for their customers. Clearly, technology gives them a competitive edge.

Video 1.3 *The Allyn and Bacon Plant Tour Video, Program 1: "Federal Express"*

AT&T, Sony, and Matsushita look at long-term strategies. One of the promising future developments in entertainment technology is the fusion of audio and video hardware with the software of creativity and artistry. Virtual reality home theatres is one example. Sony's purchase of Columbia Pictures and Matsushita's purchase of MCA is part of the positioning strategy of those companies in the emerging market of technology-based entertainment.

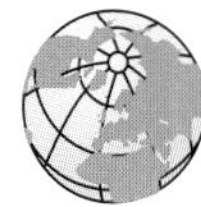

Sources: Based on Robert Howard, "The CEO as Organizational Architect: An Interview with Xerox's Paul Allaire," *Harvard Business Review,* Sept.–Oct. 1992, pp. 107–121; "Federal Express: Setting the Pace for the Nineties," Allyn and Bacon Video Series; and Fumio Kodama, "Technology Fusion and The New R&D," *Harvard Business Review,* July–Aug. 1992, pp. 70–78.

Operations Strategy

Hayes and Wheelwright describe the role that operations can play on corporate strategy as evolving through four stages:[7]

Neutral operations strategies

Transparency 1.7 Operations Strategy

1. *Internally neutral*—"Just don't mess up." These companies are highly marketing oriented and either view their products and processes as low-tech or concentrate on product improvements in lieu of process improvement. They rely on sophisticated performance-measurement systems to warn of manufacturing blunders. Companies unchallenged by significant competition can stay in this stage for decades.

2. *Externally neutral*—"Be as good or as bad as the competition." These companies follow industry practice. Comparative advantages are obtained from capital investments and are thus short-lived, because the competition upgrades its technology also. Traditional industries in the United States (such as steel, heavy

[7]Robert Hayes and Steven Wheelwright, *Restoring Our Competitive Edge: Competing Through Manufacturing,* New York: John Wiley & Sons, 1984, pp. 395–403.

equipment, automobiles, and appliances) were typical believers in this type of strategy.

Supportive operations strategies

3. *Internally supportive*—"Understand and support the needs of the other functional areas." Corporate strategy is translated into implications and terminology that are meaningful to manufacturing. Manufacturing is expected to screen its decisions to make sure they are consistent with corporate strategy. Investment in technology is pursued as part of an overall corporate strategy. Many U.S. firms moved from stage 2 to this stage in the 1980s when competitive pressures became intense.

4. *Externally supportive*—"Manufacturing is a source of competitive advantage." In this stage, manufacturing is a full partner in formulating corporate strategy. New manufacturing practices and technologies are pursued in anticipation of their advantage in the marketplace (i.e., the firm's external environment). Other functions cooperate to support manufacturing initiatives. Movement to this stage requires a fundamental change in attitudes toward manufacturing. U.S. companies who have made successful comebacks against foreign competition (such as Motorola, Ford, Miliken, and GE) operate at this stage.

Ideally, companies should operate at stage 3 or 4 of the strategy phases just described, where the operations function can play two important roles in corporate strategy: 1. to provide *support* for the strategy of a firm (help with order qualifiers), and 2. to serve as a firm's *distinctive competence* (win orders). We have selected four such "order winners"—cost, quality, flexibility, and speed—to discuss in the next few sections.

Competing on Cost

Cost: Eliminate all waste.

Companies that compete on cost relentlessly pursue the elimination of all waste. In the past, companies in this category produced standardized products for large markets. They improved yield by stabilizing the production process, tightening productivity standards, and investing in automation. Today, the entire cost structure is examined for reduction potential, not just direct labor costs, and high-volume production and automation may or may not provide the most cost-effective alternative.

Take the example of Lincoln Electric, a manufacturer that has reduced costs by \$10 million a year for the past 10 years. As one example of their cost-cutting measures, air currents from ducts behind a waterfall draw paint that has missed its mark during the painting process and carry it into a filtering system so that it can be reused at a later date. Skilled machine operators work on a strict piece-rate system and earn around \$80,000 a year. They make their own tools, maintain and repair the equipment themselves, and check their own quality. Called "million-dollar men," these workers have saved the company millions of dollars that would otherwise have been spent on new equipment.

Another example is Chaparrel Steel of Texas. Chaparrel Steel runs the lowest-cost minimill in the industry with state-of-the-art technology. It produces 1 ton of steel with only 1.8 worker-hours and staffs its entire assembly line with only two workers. The company uses its factory as an R&D facility, experimenting with new ways to improve the production process and reduce costs. It has made tremendous strides in productivity with small, continuous improvements in operations. Chaparrel also uses its personnel in unconventional ways. Its sales staff has been eliminated, with production personnel making all sales calls. Not only did this move save costs, it made the company more responsive to customer needs. Also, customers showed renewed confidence in the company's ability to follow through on promises. Along the same lines, security personnel are trained as emergency medical technicians and keyboard operators (they input data in their spare time).

Companies that compete on cost should realize that low cost cannot be sustained as a competitive advantage if increases in productivity are obtained by short-term cost reductions alone. A long-term productivity "portfolio" is required that trades off current expenditures for future reductions in operating cost. The portfolio should consist of investments in 1. updated facilities and equipment, 2. programs and systems to streamline operations, and 3. training and development that enhances the skills and capabilities of people. Investments should be consistent and provide a synergistic effect on productivity as well as reduce costs.

Competing on Quality

Most companies approach quality in a defensive or reactive mode; quality is confined to minimizing defect rates or conforming to design specifications. To compete on quality, companies must view quality as an opportunity to please the customer, not just a way to avoid problems or reduce rework costs. Table 1.2

GAINING THE COMPETITIVE EDGE

Wal-Mart Brings It All Together

Wal-Mart has a corporate strategy not unlike most retailers—its goal is to provide customers access to quality goods at competitive prices. The key to Wal-Mart's phenomenal success is the vigor with which it has pursued its goal and the support structure it has built. "Access" to Wal-Mart means providing the right goods when and where the customers want them. This requires a sophisticated logistics infrastructure and decentralized stocking decisions by store managers.

Wal-Mart ships goods from warehouses to stores in less than 48 hours. Store shelves are replenished twice a week, in contrast to the industry average of every 2 weeks. The company has 19 distribution centers and nearly 2000 company-owned trucks. Wal-Mart's private satellite communication system sends point-of-sales data directly to its 4000 vendors. The satellite system also serves as a video link connecting individual stores to corporate headquarters and to each other. Store managers frequently hold conferences to exchange information on what is and isn't selling and which promotions are working. Each store manager decides how to stock his or her store. The job of senior management is to create an environment in which the managers can learn from the market and from each other. Store managers are provided with detailed information about customer behavior. Within the store, 36 separate merchandising departments (compared to K-Mart's 5) are run by employees trained to be attuned to the customer and provide input to stocking decisions.

Wal-Mart practices an interesting logistics technique known as *cross-docking*. In this system, goods delivered to Wal-Mart warehouses are selected, repacked, and dispatched to stores without ever sitting in inventory. Goods cross from one loading dock to another in 48 hours or less. Cross-docking allows Wal-Mart to order merchandise in full truckloads from suppliers and save on freight charges, but it is a difficult system to manage. Information must flow smoothly and quickly between the stores, distribution centers, and suppliers. The satellite communications network connected to data-collection cash registers and knowledgeable store managers support the information requirements.

Wal-Mart's strategy, supported by its operations (i.e., information system, logistics/inventory replenishment system, and decentralization), has enabled the company to locate equally successful stores in the rural South and urban North and to expand into new retail sectors, such as pharmacies, warehouse clubs, and superstores.

Source: Based on George Stalk, Philip Evans, and Lawrence Shulman, "Competing on Capabilities: The New Rules of Corporate Strategy," *Harvard Business Review*, March–April 1992, pp. 57–69.

showed quality comparisons of several U.S. and Japanese products. It is obvious from those figures that superior quality can provide a significant competitive advantage.

David Garvin, a Harvard quality expert, cites the following tenets for companies that compete on quality:

Quality: Please the customer.

1. Quality is defined from the customer's point of view.
2. Quality is linked with profitability on both the market and cost sides.
3. Quality is viewed as a competitive weapon.
4. Quality is built into the strategic planning process.
5. Quality receives organizationwide commitment.

An annual survey by the American Society for Quality Control (ASQC) provides some insight into consumer preferences for quality. A recent survey found that Americans were willing to spend 33 percent more for a better-quality car, 50 percent more for a better-quality dishwasher, 65 percent more for a better TV, 70 percent more for a better sofa, and more than twice as much for a better pair of shoes. It is important to understand the customer's attitude toward and expectations of quality.

The pursuit of the quality advantage can be quite tough in today's competitive environment. For example, Corning Glass discovered in the early 1980s that its 2 percent defect rate was no longer acceptable, since its Japanese competitors achieved a 0.04 percent defect rate. After several years of hard work, Corning was pleased with its remarkable 0.02 percent defect rate until it examined its competitor's newly achieved masterpiece—0.00008 percent defective. That's about as close to zero defects as you can get!

Quality is such an important competitive tool that we have included it in virtually every chapter of this book. Look for the Q icon wherever quality is discussed.

Competing on Flexibility

Marketing always wants more variety to offer its customers. Manufacturing resists this trend because variety upsets the stability (and efficiency) of a production system and increases costs. The ability of manufacturing to respond flexibly to marketing's request for variation has opened up a new level of competition. **Flexibility** has become a powerful competitive weapon. It includes the ability to produce a wide variety of products, to introduce new products and modify existing products quickly, and, in general, to respond to customer needs.

Flexibility is the ability to adjust to changes in product mix, production volume, or design.

Flexibility: Many choices are available.

A prime example of the strategic importance of flexibility is provided by the so-called H-Y war in Japan in the early 1980s, when Yamaha challenged Honda's dominance of the motorcycle market. At the initiation of the challenge, both companies offered about 60 different models of motorcycles. Within 18 months, Honda had introduced and retired 113 models. Yamaha was able to introduce only 37 new models in that time frame. Honda's new models had four-valve engines, composites, direct drive, and other innovations. Compared to a Honda, a Yamaha motorcycle was perceived as old and outdated. Two years later, with their complete field inventory rendered obsolete, Yamaha conceded defeat. Honda "won" the war with innovation and variety in the marketplace. Their key to achieving market dominance was flexibility through superior methods for developing, manufacturing and introducing new products.

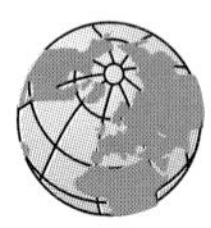

Technology can also provide the tools for flexibility. Allen-Bradley offers its customers more than 900 variations of electric contactors. Its automated production facility can receive, manufacture, and ship customized orders within 24 hours of order placement. The facility produces 600 contactors per hour, and since

Automation is the key to Allen-Bradley's flexibility. Their "factory within a factory" CIM (computer-integrated manufacturing) line has been in operation since 1982. New functions added to the factory in 1985, 1990, and 1992 have kept it productive and state-of-the-art. The line shown in the picture above is self-contained; no human hands touch the product from when it enters the line until exit. The line produces contactors, a device for repeatedly interrupting or establishing a power circuit. Each contactor contains about 76 parts, 22 of which are unique to a particular option. Production is initiated by laser markings on the contactor's base which call up a preprogrammed assembly sequence for over 900 contactor variations. The initial investment of $15 million has been returned several fold in profits from product sales, as well as in the promotion of Allen-Bradley control systems that operate the line.

changeover from one type of product to another takes only 6 seconds, all 600 could be different items! The National Bicycle Industrial Company fits bicycles to exact customer measurements. Bicycle manufacturers typically offer customers a choice between 20 or 30 different models. National offers 11,231,862 variations and delivers within 2 weeks at costs only 10 percent above standard models. In both cases, computerized design and computer-controlled machinery allow customized products to be essentially mass produced.

Competing on Speed

Speed has become a new source of competitive advantage. Service organizations such as McDonald's, LensCrafters, and Federal Express have always competed on speed. Citicorp advertises a 15-minute mortgage approval, L.L. Bean ships orders the day they are received, and Wal-Mart replenishes its stock twice a week instead of the industry average of every 2 weeks. Now manufacturers are discovering the advantages of time-based competition. In the garment industry, Saks Fifth Avenue has terminals from the French national Videotex system that link retailers to manufacturers abroad. Tailors in New York send suit measurements via satellite to France, where a laser cuts the cloth and tailors begin their work. The suit is completed and shipped back to New York within 4 days. That's about the same amount of time required for alterations in most clothing stores. The standard for custom-made suits is 10 weeks.

GAINING THE COMPETITIVE EDGE

Mitsubishi's "Slow-and-Steady" Strategy Leapfrogs the Competition

The effects of strategy are not immediate. Sometimes a competitor's strategy, which has been pursued for a period of time, comes as a surprise when it catches up with you and surpasses you. That's what happened in the residential air-conditioning business.

Mitsubishi Electric is a small Japanese producer of heat pumps for residential air conditioners. Its strategy of incremental innovations over a ten-year period virtually captured the air conditioning market. Let's look at the progression.

From 1975 to 1979, the product design remained stable. In 1980, Mitsubishi introduced integrated circuits to control the air-conditioning cycle of its heat pumps. In 1981, the integrated circuits were replaced with microprocessors that were simple to install and very reliable. In 1982, a high-energy rotary compressor replaced the reciprocating compressor. Since the balance of the system changed, all the electronics had to be redesigned. In 1983, Mitsubishi expanded the electronic control capabilities by adding sensors and more computing power. In 1984, an inverter was added to control the motor speed. By 1990, logic circuits were installed that enabled the machine to "learn" its defrost cycles and perform them automatically. Electronic air purification packs were also added. The company is currently working on smart controllers that will learn the user's pattern for adjusting temperature and will mimic that pattern.

Meanwhile, in 1985, U.S. producers were just beginning to consider whether to use integrated circuits in their heat pumps. Given the five-year development cycle typical for the industry, the innovation would not be ready until 1990. By then the technology of U.S.-made heat pumps would be 10 years behind the Japanese version. The U.S. companies followed the lead of many other U.S. industries and decided its only option was to subcontract air conditioners and components from their Japanese competitors.

Source: Based on George Stalk, Jr., "The Strategic Value of Time," Chapter 4 in *Time-Based Competition: The Next Battleground in American Manufacturing*, J. Blackburn, ed., Homewood, IL: Irwin, 1991.

In 5 days, Hewlett-Packard can produce electronic testing equipment that used to take 4 weeks to produce. General Electric has reduced the time of manufacture for circuit-breaker boxes from 3 weeks to 3 days and the manufacture of dishwashers from 6 days to 18 hours. Motorola now needs 90 minutes to build to order and ship pagers that used to take 3 weeks! Reductions in the time required to get new products to the market is also improving. For the past decade Japanese automakers have held a two-year advantage in new product development. Now U.S. automakers have closed that gap.

Tom Peters calls speed "the hustle strategy" and says it requires a new type of organization characterized by fast moves, fast adaptations, and tight linkages.[8] To compete on speed, companies must

Speed: Fast moves, fast adaptations, and tight linkages are vital.

- Flatten the organization,
- Defunctionalize,
- Create autonomous teams,
- Be flexible,
- Practice forward (to the customer) and backward (to the supplier) integration,
- Colocate electronically and physically,
- Create a sense of urgency,

[8]The material is adapted from Tom Peters, *Thriving on Chaos*, New York: Alfred A. Knopf, 1987, Chapter C-4.

In the 1980s, as a competitive response to comparable but cheaper products from foreign manufacturers, Motorola began assembling products offshore in Singapore, Puerto Rico, and the South Pacific. Production costs were lower, but the speed of production was insufficient to meet customer demands. Motorola decided to change manufacturing strategies and create a state-of-the-art production facility onshore for its paging products. Within 18 months of the decision, the so-called Bandit project (because it borrowed the best technology) successfully completed the design of a new production system that was fast and cost competitive. The photo above shows part of the carefully designed assembly line. Pagers that used to take 3 weeks to manufacture took 2 hours on the new line. Further improvements reduced the leadtime for customized pagers to less than 90 minutes from order placement to order shipment. It is no surprise that Motorola currently dominates the pager market.

- Be willing to accept risks and failures,
- Develop quick feedback mechanisms, and
- Expect radical change.

Clearly, competing on speed requires a special type of corporate culture, supported by flexible operations.

Policy Deployment

Strategic planning has never been more important than in today's business environment. Every recipient of the Deming Prize[9] over the past twenty years has used a strategic planning system called *hoshin kanri. Hoshin kanri* roughly translates as "shining metal, pointing direction," something similar to a straight arrow. Americans using similar planning systems call the process hoshin planning, policy deployment, management by policy, management by planning, or other company-specific names. (We will use the term **policy deployment.**)

Policy deployment is a Japanese approach to planning that focuses a company's strategy and converts the strategic plan to manageable objectives from the top to the bottom of the organization.

Believing that it is impossible to concentrate on everything at once, *policy deployment* focuses a company's efforts. In a company that effectively uses policy deployment, everyone in the organization understands the company's 5-year plan, the three or four goals they have to achieve to move the plan along, and how each goal ties into their daily activities.[10] The process involves converting the company's 5-year strategic plan into a series of 1-year plans and converting company ini-

[9]The Deming Prize is Japan's top quality award, named for their American friend and teacher, W. Edwards Deming.

[10]Bob King, *Policy Deployment: The Developmental Approach,* Springfield, Mass.: GOAL/QPC, 1989.

TABLE 1.3 A Quality-Planning Matrix for Policy Deployment

Transparency 1.8 A Quality Planning Matrix for Policy Deployment

Top Management Directive	*Functional Objective*	*Departmental Objective*	*Individual Objective*
1.0 Enhance quality	1.1 Improve key processes	1.1.1 Improve manufacturing process A by 1 sigma	1.1.1.1 Redesign fixtures 1.1.1.2 Analyze process flow
		1.1.2 Improve manufacturing process B by 1 sigma	1.1.2.1 Work with suppliers
2.0 Reduce time to market	2.1 Shorten cycle time	2.1.1 Shorten cycle time for product by 30%	2.1.1.2 Reduce setup time 2.1.1.2 Change sequencing procedures 2.1.1.3 Reduce lot sizes

tiatives to departmental and individual initiatives. Individual and departmental goals are aligned with corporate objectives through the use of planning tools such as affinity charts, matrix diagrams, and project planning. Table 1.3 shows a quality-planning matrix for policy deployment.

Monthly and annual assessments of the plans ensure that they are being followed. Florida Power and Light, the only non-Japanese company to win the Deming Prize, was one of the first American companies to use policy deployment. Hewlett-Packard, Procter and Gamble, Ford, ITT, and others were early adopters of the planning system. Now, most of the top U.S. corporations are using policy deployment in some form to ensure that their strategies are indeed being carried out as effectively as possible.

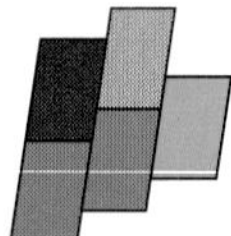

ISSUES AND TRENDS IN OPERATIONS

Operations is a field that is rapidly changing and growing in importance. Current issues and future trends in operations include the following:

Future trends: More, better, quicker, cheaper, anywhere, anytime

1. *Intense competition.* The intensity of worldwide competition will increase. Economist Lester Thurow predicts that the military warfare of the twentieth century will be replaced by economic warfare in the twenty-first century. Head-to-head competition between the European Community (led by Germany), Japan, and the United States is on the horizon.

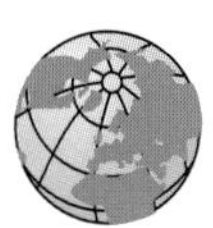

2. *Global markets, global sourcing, and global financing.* Few companies will be able to survive by competing in the domestic market alone. Companies need to learn about foreign societies, understand foreign customers, build networks, and forge partnerships. Production will take place wherever in the world it can be done the cheapest. Access to capital markets will be worldwide.

3. *Importance of strategy.* Companies will need long-term global strategies to survive in the marketplace. Vertically integrated partnerships, partnerships with other companies in the same industry, partnerships with educational institutions, and partnerships with government will be needed to strengthen competitive positions. A new type of capitalism based on cooperative specialization within industries may become a necessity.

4. *Product variety and customization.* An increasing variety of products and services will be offered to the customer. In many cases, customization for the individual will be possible. This means that the expected life of products on the market will continue to decrease, and product and service innovations will hit the market at an increasing rate.

5. *More services.* The rapid growth in services throughout the 1980s slowed in the 1990s. Regardless of whether the service sector continues to increase, the level of service associated with the service sector and the manufacturing sector will increase. Customer service is destined to become another competitive battleground.

6. *Emphasis on quality.* The quality of products and services will continue to improve as customer expectations of quality grow. Zero defects will be the norm. Quality that delights the customer will be the goal.

7. *Flexibility.* The most successful production systems will be those that are most flexible. Flexibility will be measured by the ability to adjust to changes in product design, changes in product mix, changes in the volume of demand, and changes in process technology.

8. *Advances in technology.* Technology will continue to advance at a rapid rate, particularly in the areas of advanced materials (metal-based composites, polymer-based composites, high-tech ceramics, and smart materials), advanced machining (EDM, lasers, electron beams, plasma flame cutting, flexible tooling and fixturing), intelligent sensors, smart robots, biotechnology, digital imaging, artificial intelligence, superconductors, and supercomputing.

Needed: Brainpower

9. *Worker involvement.* The empowerment of the work force has had a significant impact on operations in the past decade. Predictions of the key industries for the next few decades include: 1. microelectronics, 2. biotechnology, 3. new materials, 4. aviation, 5. telecommunications, 6. robots and advanced machine tools, and 7. computers plus software.[11] It is clear that success in these industries will be based on *brainpower.* Countries that perform the best in the world market will be those that have the best R&D, the best education system, the brightest people, and the savvy to use those assets to their fullest advantage.

10. *Environmental concerns.* Companies and industries will increasingly consider the environmental impact of the design, manufacture, distribution, use, and disposal of their products and services. The impetus for environmental responsibility will shift from government regulations to customer requirements.

PURPOSE AND ORGANIZATION OF THIS BOOK

The purpose of this text is threefold:

1. *To ensure that business students are "operations literate."* Regardless of your major or career aspiration, as a business student, it is important that you understand the basic issues, capabilities, and limitations of the operations function. Especially relevant are issues related to quality, strategy, and technology.

2. *To instill in students a healthy respect for operations.* By the conclusion of this course, you should be able to describe the impact of operations on other functions within a firm as well as on the competitive position of the firm.

3. *To encourage students to apply the concepts and methods they learn in this course.* The ability to conceptualize how systems are interrelated, to organize activities effectively, to analyze processes critically, to make decisions based on data, and to push for continual improvement can revolutionize jobs, industries, and society. It

[11]Lester Thurow, *Head to Head,* New York: William Morrow and Company, 1992, p. 45.

is our hope that you will become proficient with these skills and see yourself as a conduit for that revolution.

There are many issues, concepts, and techniques associated with the field of production/operations management. This text is designed as an introductory survey course in POM that covers many different topics. In organizing this text, we envisioned three phases to the learning process: understanding, designing, and operating productive systems. The chapters included in each phase are outlined next.

Transparency 1.9 Organization of Text

Understanding Productive Systems	*Designing Productive Systems*	*Operating Productive Systems*
1 Operations, Competitiveness, and Strategy	5 Product and Service Design	10 Forecasting
2 Operational Decision Making	6 Process Planning and Technology Decisions	11 Aggregate Production and Capacity Planning
3 Quality Management	7 Facility Layout	12 Inventory Management
4 Statistical Quality Control	8 Location Analysis and Logistics Management	13 Material Requirements Planning
	9 Jobs: Design, Analysis, and Measurement	14 Scheduling
		15 Just-In-Time and Continuous Improvement
		16 Waiting Line Models and Service Improvement
		17 Project Management

The material contained in Chapters 1 through 4 was placed first because the concepts and skills contained therein are needed throughout the course. Chapters 5 through 9 relate primarily to the *design* of productive systems, and Chapters 10 through 17 relate primarily to the *operation* of productive systems.

SUMMARY

In this chapter, we presented a simple definition of operations, examined the operations function, and briefly reviewed the history of production/operations management. We discussed changes in the global business environment and identified several sources of America's past problems with competitiveness: 1. short-term financial orientations of American management, 2. failure to regard manufacturing as a source of competitive advantage, 3. lack of cooperation (between workers and management, among departments within the same firm, between firms and their customers, and between firms and their suppliers), 4. weaknesses in human resource management, and 5. a preference for product innovation at the expense of process innovation.

We also discussed the steps involved in formulating strategy, including 1. defining the primary task, 2. identifying distinctive competence, 3. determining order winners and order qualifiers, and 4. positioning the firm. The role of operations strategy was discussed, then several examples of competitive strategies were given. Finally, an integrated approach to implementing strategy, called *policy deployment,* was presented.

The chapter concluded with a list of issues and trends in operations and a statement of purpose for the text.

SUMMARY OF KEY TERMS

competitiveness: the degree to which a nation can produce goods and services that meet the test of international markets while simultaneously maintaining or expanding the real incomes of its citizens.

distinctive competence: what an entity does better than anyone else; in the marketplace, the competitive advantage.

economies of scale: an advantage that accrues from high-volume production; as the number of units produced increases, the cost of producing each individual unit decreases.

flexibility: in manufacturing, the ability to adjust to changes in product mix, production volume, or product or process design.

mass production: high-volume production of a standardized product for a mass market.

order qualifiers: the characteristics of a product or service that qualify it to be considered for purchase by a customer.

order winner: the characteristic of a product or service that wins orders in the marketplace.

policy deployment: a Japanese approach to planning that focuses a company's strategy and converts the strategic plan to manageable objectives from the top to the bottom of the organization.

primary task: the task that is most central to the operation of a firm; it defines the business that a firm is in.

production: a function or system that transforms inputs into outputs of greater value; often referred to as *operations* in a service firm.

strategy: a common vision that unites an organization, provides consistency in decisions, and keeps the organization moving in the right direction.

QUESTIONS

1-1. What activities are involved in the production/operations function?

1-2. Name several causes of the United States' competitive problems.

1-3. How can a short-term financial orientation affect competitiveness?

1-4. What weaknesses have become evident in the choice of strategy, technology, and management of human resources in U.S. firms?

1-5. Why do U.S. workers, companies, and industries find it difficult to cooperate?

1-6. Using outside resources, assess the competitiveness of U.S. firms in the following industries:
  a. Textiles
  b. Chemicals
  c. Commercial aircraft
  d. Machine tools
  e. Computers

1-7. What role can operations play in corporate strategy?

1-8. Why has manufacturing been ignored as a source of competitive advantage?
1-9. List and explain the four steps of strategy formulation.
1-10. What is the difference between an order winner and an order qualifier?
1-11. Discuss the requirements from an operations perspective of competing on
   a. Quality
   b. Cost
   c. Flexibility
   d. Speed
   e. Dependability
   f. Service
1-12. Give examples of manufacturing or service firms that successfully compete on each of the criteria listed in Question 11.
1-13. Describe policy deployment. What advantages does it provide over traditional methods of planning?
1-14. Examine the annual reports of a company of your choosing over a number of years. Use quotes from the reports to describe the company's overall strategy and their specific goals each year.
1-15. What are your expectations regarding this course? What are your instructor's expectations? Use a quality planning matrix to reconcile the differences.
1-16. List several issues and trends in operations for the future. What actions do you recommend to prepare for the future challenges?

CASE PROBLEM

Whither an MBA at Strutledge?

Strutledge is a small private liberal arts school located within 50 miles of a major urban area in the southeast United States. As with most institutions of higher education, Strutledge's costs are rising, and its enrollments are decreasing. In an effort to expand its student base, build valuable ties with area businesses, and simply survive, the Board of Regents is considering a proposal to establish an MBA program.

Currently, no undergraduate degree is given in business, although business courses are taught. The dean of the school visualizes the MBA as an interdisciplinary program with emphasis on problem solving, communication, and global awareness. Faculty expertise would be supplemented by instructors from local industry. The use of local faculty would also better connect the university with the business community and provide opportunities for employment of the program's graduates.

In terms of competition, a major state-funded university that offers an MBA is located in the adjacent urban area. Strutledge hopes that state budget cutbacks and perceptions of overcrowded classrooms and overworked professors at public institutions would open the door for a new entrant into the market. They also feel that their small size would allow them to tailor the MBA program more closely to area business needs.

Several members of the Board are concerned about recent reports of the dwindling value of an MBA and are wondering if a better niche could be found with another graduate degree, perhaps a master of science in business or something in the education or health-care field.

See Solutions Manual.

1. What action would you recommend to the Board of Regents?
2. How should Strutledge go about making a strategic decision such as this?

REFERENCES

Abernathy, William, Kim Clark, and Alan Kantrow, *Industrial Renaissance,* New York: Basic Books, 1983.

Blackburn, J., ed., *Time-Based Competition: The Next Battleground in American Manufacturing,* Homewood, Ill.: Irwin, 1991.

Dertouzos, Michael, Richard Lester, and Robert Solow, *Made in America,* Cambridge, Mass.: MIT Press, 1989.

Garvin, David, *Operations Strategy: Text and Cases,* Englewood Cliffs, N.J.: Prentice Hall, 1992.

Hayes, Robert and Steven Wheelwright, *Restoring Our Competitive Edge: Competing Through Manufacturing,* New York: John Wiley, 1984.

Hill, Terry, *Manufacturing Strategy: Text and Cases,* Homewood, Ill.: Irwin, 1989.

Hoerr, John, *And the Wolf Finally Came: The Decline of the American Steel Industry,* Pittsburgh, Penn.: University of Pittsburgh Press, 1988.

Holland, Max, *When the Machine Stopped: A Cautionary Tale from Industrial America,* Boston, Mass.: Harvard Business School Press, 1988.

King, Bob, *Policy Deployment: The Developmental Approach,* Springfield, Mass.: GOAL/QPC, 1989.

Manufacturing Studies Board, *Towards a New Era in Manufacturing: The Need for a National Vision,* Washington, D.C.: National Academy Press, 1986.

Peters, Tom, *Thriving on Chaos,* New York: Alfred A. Knopf, 1987.

Skinner, Wickham, *Manufacturing: The Formidable Competitive Weapon,* New York: John Wiley, 1985.

Thurow, Lester, *Head to Head: The Coming Economic Battle Among Japan, Europe, and America,* New York: William Morrow, 1992.

Womack, James, Daniel Jones, and Daniel Roos, *The Machine that Changed the World,* New York: Macmillan, 1990.

2
OPERATIONAL DECISION MAKING

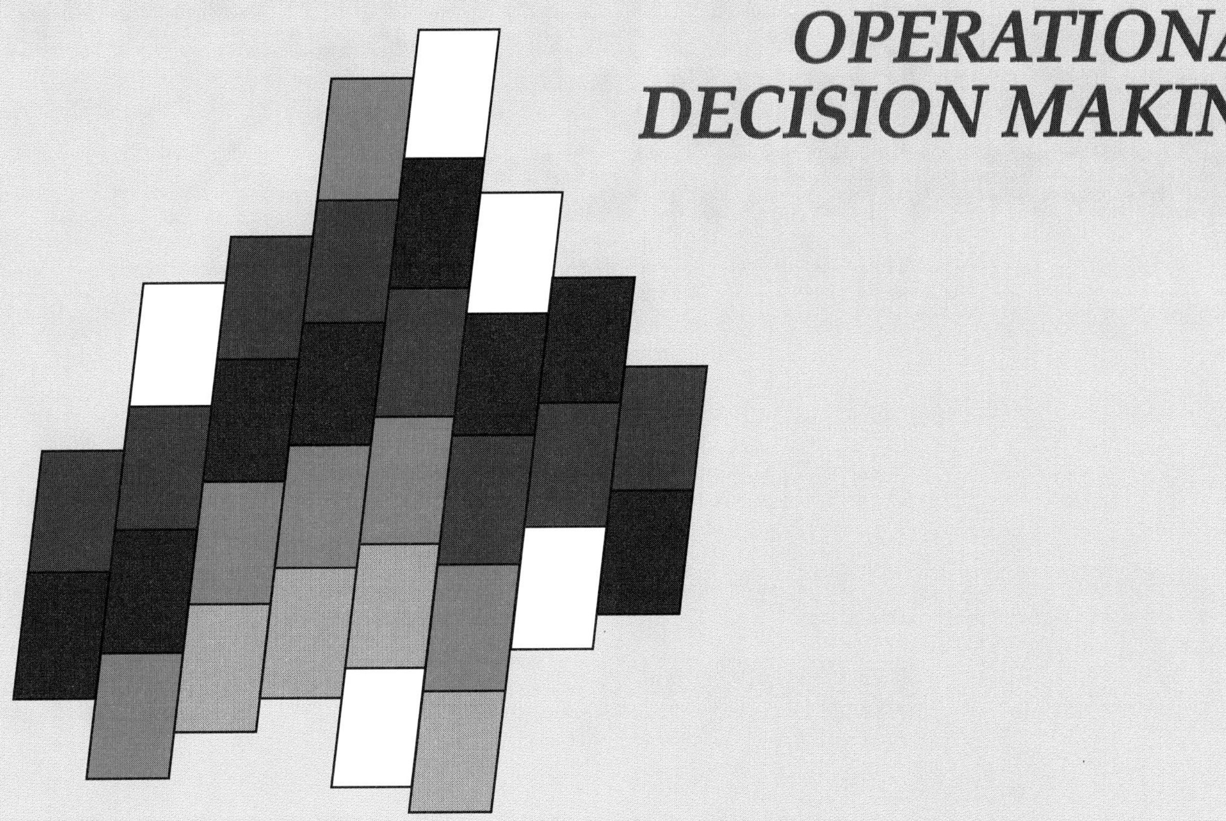

CHAPTER OUTLINE

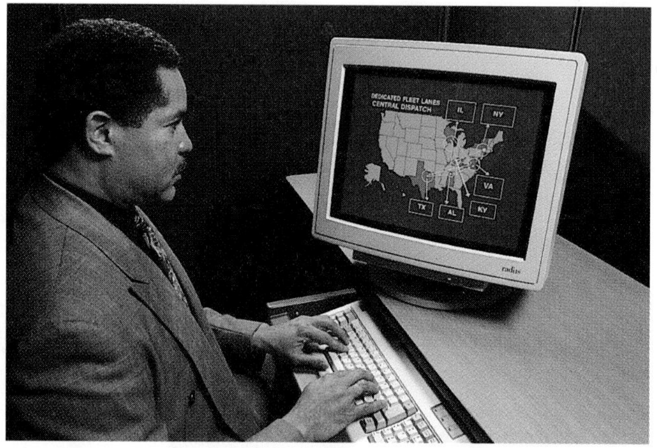

Reynolds Metals Company sends its truck to pick up and make deliveries from a computerized control dispatch facility in Richmond, Virginia. At one time Reynolds allowed each of its more than 200 plants, warehouses, and suppliers to select their own trucking firms. However, this decentralization of shipping responsibility resulted in uneven service quality and was believed to be financially wasteful. As a result, Reynolds developed their central dispatch facility which dispatches trucks to locations using a sophisitcated computer system. The system works with the help of several operational decision-making techniques such as simulation and mathematical programming to determine when and where different trucks are needed to make pick ups and deliveries. The new system reduced the number of trucking firms Reynolds deals with from over 200 to just 14, improved service from 80 percent on-time deliveries to 95 percent, and saved the company $7 million annually in shipping costs. This is just one example of how operational decision-making techniques can be used by companies to improve quality for services and products and reduce costs.

OPERATIONAL DECISION MAKING AT REYNOLDS METALS COMPANY

Video 2.1 *TIMS Edelman Awards Tape, "Reynolds Metals"*

Reynolds Metals Company is an international aluminum company with sales (in 1989) of $6.2 billion, 12 decentralized operating divisions, several subsidiaries, and 60 domestic manufacturing facilities. They spend more than $.25 billion annually on truck, rail, ship, and air transportation costs from more than 120 shipping locations, including plants, warehouses, and suppliers, to more than 5,000 shipping destinations, including plants, warehouses, subsidiaries, and customers. Reynolds incurs annual truck freight bills in excess of $80 million. Consistent with its decentralized operating philosophy, the company's divisions and plants were traditionally responsible for their own freight operations. Plants selected their own carriers, negotiated rates, and arranged shipments. However, because of variability in service and quality standards and concerns about costs, Reynolds decided to centralize the management and operations of its interstate truck shipments with a central dispatch facility in Richmond, Virginia, that oversees the scheduling and servicing of truck shipments, both internally and from suppliers.

The company was able to reduce the more than 200 carriers it used to 14 core carriers who were strong financially, had good drivers, were well maintained, and had good and sufficient equipment. The new central dispatch facility improved quality; customer service was increased from 80 percent on-time deliveries to 95 percent on-time deliveries. The central dispatch system has given Reynolds a competitive advantage and has helped attract new customers. The cost of developing

the system was $618,000, and the savings in freight costs is over $7 million annually.

The primary tools used in the development of the central dispatch system were operational decision-making techniques, simulation, and mathematical programming. These techniques were used to select core carriers, identify shipments, dispatch trucks, establish and communicate shipping volumes, and estimate costs within a support system framework.[1]

Operations management is a business function based essentially on decision making. An operations manager is required to make decisions and carry out decisions made by others. The various topics and areas in production and operations management differ from each other according to the types of decisions that are required. For example, in inventory management key decisions include how much and when to order to replenish inventory levels, whereas in quality management a key decision is the level of quality to seek.

For many topics in production and operations management, there are quantitative models and techniques available that help managers make decisions. Some techniques simply provide information that the operations manager might use to help come to a decision, whereas other techniques provide a recommended decision for the manager. Some techniques are specific to a particular aspect of operations management, and others are more generic and can be applied to a variety of different decision-making categories. These different models and techniques are, in effect, the "tools" of the operations manager. Simply having these tools does not make someone an effective operations manager, just as owning a saw and a hammer does not make someone a carpenter. To be an operations manager, a person must know how to use the available decision-making tools. However, these techniques and how they are used in the decision-making process are an important and necessary part of the study of production and operations management.

Quantitative methods are the tools of the operations manager.

In this chapter we examine several different aspects of operational decision making. First, we look at the focus of decision making, the goals of the firm that drive the decision-making process. Second, we describe the different categories of operational decision making, which also provides an overview of the topics covered in this text. Next, we look more closely at the actual process of making decisions and provide an example of how quantitative methods are used to help in decision making. Finally, we look at systems that are used to provide information and support for operational decision making.

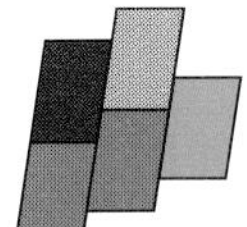

THE FOCUS OF OPERATIONAL DECISION MAKING

Decision making at the operational level involves many different types of decisions that have a common thread, in that they all seek to achieve the strategic goals of the organization. For businesses, whether manufacturing or service, the ultimate goal is usually to make as much profit as possible. However, in the short run a company will occasionally accept less profit in order to achieve some other goal, such as market share. For example, some competitors have effectively followed a strategy of pricing their products low in the short run in order to capture market share and establish a customer base. These firms attract and retain customers by combining competitive pricing with attractive product features and high quality.

The long-run goal for a business is to make a profit.

[1]E. W. Moore, Jr., "The Indispensable Role of Management Science in Centralizing Freight Operations at Reynolds Metals Company," *Interfaces* 21, no. 1 (January–February 1991): 107–129.

In the long run, this results in higher profits. Alternatively, a company may have a short-run goal of introducing a new product with the expectation of reaping profits in the long run.

At the operational level hundreds of decisions are made in order to achieve local outcomes that contribute to the achievement of the company's overall strategic goal. These local outcomes are usually not measured directly in terms of profit, but instead are measured in terms of quality, cost effectiveness, efficiency, productivity, etc. Achieving good results for local outcomes is an important objective for individual operational units and individual operations managers. However, all these decisions are interrelated and must be coordinated for the purpose of attaining the overall company goals. Decision making is analogous to a great stage play or opera, in which all the actors, the costumes, the props, the music, the orchestra, and the script must be choreographed and staged by the director, the stage managers, the author, and the conductor so that everything comes together for the performance.

Production and operations management includes many different areas of decision making at different levels of the organization. Thus, the study of POM—and the purpose of this text, to a large extent—is learning what decisions must be made, how to make good decisions, and how these decisions all fit together. As already mentioned, various quantitative techniques are frequently available to help operations managers make decisions, often by providing information on which decisions can be based. Thus, part of learning about operational decision making is learning about the techniques that are available, learning how to use them, and becoming aware not only of their usefulness, but also of their limitations. However, operational decision making and managing also requires a knowledge of production systems, the context within which decisions are made, and the interrelationship of different operations functions. In the final analysis, the success of an operations manager will be determined by how well he or she uses knowledge of operations, experience, quantitative tools, and available information to make good decisions.

In the following section we provide a brief overview of the primary areas of operational decision making. It is not a coincidence that these are the topics of the chapters that follow, in the order in which they are presented. There appears to be a natural order, or progression, in operational decision making, which the following discussion and the text follow.

Transparency 2.1 Areas of Operational Decision Making

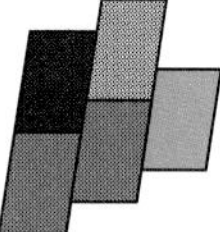

AREAS OF OPERATIONAL DECISION MAKING

The types of decisions that comprise production and operations management fall into categories that support and complement each other in the eventual production of a product or service. These interrelated categories of decision making are summarized as follows.

Quality

Chapters 3 and 4: Quality is the focus of operational decision making for many businesses.

Teaching Note 2.1 Quality

For an increasing number of companies in today's world, quality is the driving force for subsequent operational decisions. The level of quality a company seeks to achieve is a strategic or top-management decision that eventually determines how a product is made or a service is delivered. As such, quality has come to permeate the delivery of services and the production process and thus to dictate much of operational decision making. Designing products and services, designing and planning the production process, locating and developing the production facility, designing jobs and work activities, and planning and scheduling the flow of prod-

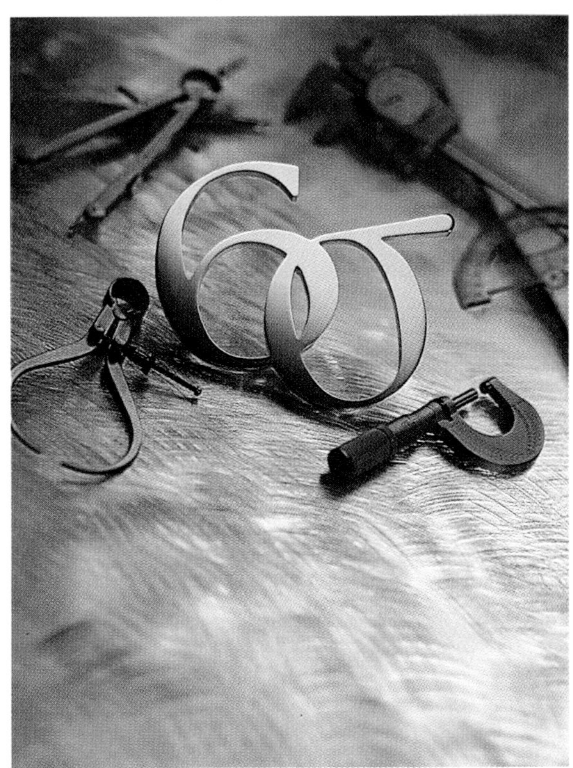

Motorola's Six Sigma symbol represents their commitment to producing quality products and customer satisfaction. Technically six sigma performance is a level of statistical variation in product quality that translates to only a little over 3 defects for every million parts produced, or virtually no defects. The six sigma performance program is part of the Motorola Corporate Quality Council (MCQC) which was established to coordinate and manage Motorola's corporate-wide quality program. Motorola's goal from this program has been to instill a commitment to absolute quality performance and total customer satisfaction throughout all areas of the company from purchasing to engineering and design to manufacturing to sales. Its MCQC program and its goal of six sigma performance enabled Motorola, Inc. to be among the first U.S. companies to receive the coveted Malcolm Baldrige National Quality Award from the U.S. Department of Commerce in 1988. The philosophy of total quality management (TQM) with zero defects has been adopted by numerous companies that hope to survive in today's highly competitive global business environment. The topics of total quality management and statistical quality control will be addressed specifically in Chapters 3 and 4, however, quality is focused on throughout the text.

ucts throughout the production process or the delivery of a service are all areas of decision making that are increasingly being dominated by quality. For this reason this text focuses on quality management, and the first two topics presented after this initial discussion of decision making are *quality management* and *statistical quality control.*

Designing Products and Services

The traditional starting point in the production process is designing the product or service. On one hand, a product or service must be designed to attract customers, whereas on the other hand, it must also be cost effective. Products and services can be well designed, but if the design is so costly to produce that it results in a price that is too high to be competitive, and hence a price that customers refuse to pay, the design process has failed. Decisions related to design include the product features to include, the desired level of quality, the materials to use, and the resulting production costs. This specific topic is referred to in the text as *product and service design.*

Chapter 5: Designing quality into the product is the first step in the production process.

Planning the Production Process

Once the product or service has been designed, the next related area of decision making is designing and constructing the physical process that will produce the product or deliver the service. This stage includes acquiring materials, determining the types of job skills, equipment, and technology required for producing the product, and managing the process. This area of decision making is essentially concerned with developing a process to turn materials into a final product or service; the topic is referred to as *process planning and technology decisions.*

Chapter 6: Developing the physical process to implement the design

Laying Out the Facility

Chapter 7: The process must be set up so that it works smoothly and efficiently.

The production process that has been designed must be physically housed in a facility and laid out in an effective manner so that the product can be produced as efficiently and as cheaply as possible. Although people tend to think of a facility as being a manufacturing plant, a service operation such as McDonald's either is performed in a facility or emanates from one. Decision making focuses on where to locate different parts of the process in the facility in order to ensure that the production process flows smoothly and has adequate space, proper ventilation, adequate heating, air conditioning, and power, adequate room for storage, and unencumbered traffic flow, among other things. The title of this area of operational decision making is *facility layout.*

Locating the Facility and Transporting Materials and Products

Chapter 8: Location of the business to meet company needs

Once the production process is designed and a proper facility has been laid out to house it, decisions must be made regarding where to locate the facility. This process is referred to as *location analysis and logistics management.* Factors that relate to the location decision include its proximity to customers, the availability of resources, the cost of the facility, the environment, governmental restrictions, and modes of transport available for receiving materials and parts and for delivering the final product or service.

Designing Jobs and Work

Chapter 9: One component is designing jobs and work to produce quality products.

A primary component of the production process is the work performed by people, alone or together (as in some service operations), or with machines and equipment (as in manufacturing and service operations). The work activity of these people define their jobs. *Job design, analysis, and measurement* is the area of POM concerned with making sure that jobs meet the requirements of the production process in the most efficient manner possible.

Forecasting Demand for Products and Services

Chapter 10: Predicting demand in order to know how much to produce and when to produce it

Once the physical facility and production process are in place to produce a product or deliver a service, a host of planning decisions are required to determine how much to produce and when to produce it. These decisions are based on how much demand for the product there will be from customers. *Forecasting* involves using a number of different methods and quantitative techniques in order to provide accurate forecasts for demand, which are subsequently used to make the necessary planning decisions to produce enough of the product or service to meet the demand.

Production Planning and Scheduling

Chapters, 11, 12, 13, 14, 15, and 16: Production must be planned and scheduled to meet demand.

Once management has determined how much product or service is needed to meet the demand, production schedules are developed that involve a myriad of decisions. These decisions include how much material or how many parts to order, when material or parts should be ordered, how many workers to hire, and how these workers should be scheduled on jobs and machines. Decisions must also be made to ensure the amount of inventory available at each stage of the production process is sufficient to avoid work stoppages and delays and to maintain a steady production flow, and the amount of final inventory to keep on hand is sufficient to meet customer demand and avoid turning customers away. For service operations, the number of servers required to serve customers in a timely manner must be established. Production planning represents a major area of decision making in operations management and includes the topics of *aggregate production planning, inventory management, materials requirement planning, scheduling, just-in-time and continuous improvement,* and *service improvement.*

QUANTITATIVE TECHNIQUES FOR DECISION MAKING

Video 2.2 *COMAP, Program 1: "Management Science Overview"*

Quantitative techniques are mathematical procedures for solving a model.

Teaching Note 2.2 Scanning the Text

As we have previously noted, various **quantitative techniques** are available that assist the manager in making many of the decisions in these categories of operational decision making. For example, methods for determining product yield and productivity are used to measure the effectiveness of quality management efforts, and several statistical methods are used to monitor product quality in production processes and to inspect products for quality. A variety of quantitative methods, including location factor rating and center-of-gravity and load-distance techniques, are available to assist in location analysis decisions, and transportation models are used to determine the least costly transportation routes or modes of transportation. Various mathematical and statistical methods, including time and motion studies, work sampling, and learning curves, are used to measure job performance and work activity. Aggregate production planning, materials requirement planning, and scheduling all are based on mathematical procedures. Inventory management makes use of several traditional models and formulas for determining how much to order and when to order under different operating conditions. Waiting line formulas and models are used to analyze service delivery, and several network techniques are used to plan and schedule projects.

Many of these quantitative techniques tend to be applicable only to a specific category of decision making. For example, the models used in inventory management are used almost exclusively for making decisions relevant to inventory control. Alternatively, some techniques are more generic and can be applied to several different decision-making categories. Statistical methods fall into this technique classification. For example, statistical methods can be used for decision making in quality control, job analysis, forecasting, and inventory control, among other areas. Other generic quantitative techniques that can be applied to different decision-making categories include *linear programming* and *simulation.* Linear programming is a technique wherein mathematical models made up of linear equations are constructed to replicate decision situations in which some objective, such as profit, is constrained by limited resources. These models are then solved using mathematical techniques. Linear programming models are used for such decision situations as determining blends or mixes—for example, cereal or gasoline—or finding a mix of different products to produce. Simulation is a computer-based tool of analysis in which real-world decision situations are replicated using mathematical models that are analyzed on the computer. Such techniques are applicable to a wide variety of different operational problems and are used extensively by businesses to help make decisions.

Computer software is available for solving quantitative models.

Virtually all the quantitative techniques used to help make operational decisions—and examined in this text—can be applied using a computer, in most cases a personal computer. Although there are many different computer software packages that include quantitative techniques for operational decision making, we primarily use two in this text, AB:POM and STORM. Both are well-known software packages that are low in cost and are easy to learn and use. In those instances in the text where we demonstrate a quantitative technique for decision making, we also show the computer application of the technique.

Teaching Note 2.3 Quantitative Techniques Involve a Logical, Systematic Approach to Problem Solving

Transparency 2.2 The Decision-Making Process

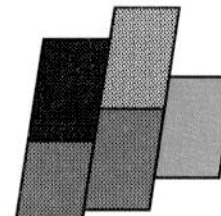

THE DECISION-MAKING PROCESS

Although only some operational decisions are made using quantitative techniques or models, the decision-making process used in applying quantitative models is generally applicable to most decision-making situations. As such, we will use this same process in this section to demonstrate a systematic approach to operational decision making.

Everyone is familiar with toy cars, airplanes, and dolls, which are simplified versions of real objects and are commonly called *models.* A quantitative model is a mathematical representation of a real thing, and although not always simple, it is generally easier and quicker to analyze and to experiment on than the physical entity it represents. The application of quantitative models encompasses a logical, systematic approach to decision making that follows a generally recognized ordered set of steps: observation, problem definition, model construction, experimentation and solution, decision making, and implementation. The objective of this systematic approach is to make good choices from existing decision alternatives by utilizing a systematic means of generating information and of learning about the decision environment and then to be able to evaluate the range of decision alternatives in a logical, precise manner.

Observation

The steps of the decision-making process

The first step in a systematic approach to decision making is the identification of a problem that exists in the operation. The operation must be continuously and closely observed so that problems can be identified as soon as they occur or are anticipated. Problems are not always the result of a crisis to which one must react; instead, they frequently involve an anticipatory or planning situation. The operations manager is frequently the person who identifies a problem, since the manager is the one who works in the vicinity of places where problems might occur.

Identification and Definition of the Problem

Once it has been determined that a problem or decision-making situation exists, the problem must be clearly and concisely *defined.* Improperly defining a problem can easily result in no solution or an inappropriate solution. Attention must be focused on the cause of the problem rather than on simply eliminating the symptoms. The limits of the problem and the degree to which it pervades other units of the organization must be included in the problem definition. Since the existence of a problem implies that the objectives of the firm are not being met in some way, the goals (or objectives) of the organization must also be clearly defined. A stated objective helps to focus attention on what the problem actually is, and it defines the standards by which the solution or decision will be judged.

Teaching Note 2.4 The Increasing Popularity of Quantitative Techniques

Model Formulation

A **quantitative model** is an abstract representation of an existing problem situation.

A **variable** is a mathematical model symbol that has no predetermined numerical value.

As we mentioned, a **quantitative model** is an abstract representation of an existing problem situation. It can be in the form of a graph, a chart, or, most frequently, a set of mathematical relationships made up of numbers and symbols. The symbols are often referred to as **variables** because they have no predetermined numerical value, and they usually represent the solution or decision. The numerical values in a mathematical relationship are referred to as *parameters,* and they usually remain constant during the problem-solving process. Parameters are generally derived from information called *data* from the decision-making environment. The model itself consists of one or more mathematical relationships that relate variables and parameters to each other. Sometimes data are not as readily available to the manager or firm, and the parameters must be either estimated or based on a combination of the available data and estimates. In such cases, the model is only as accurate as the data used in constructing the model.

Models may be categorized into two groups: deterministic models and probabilistic models. **Deterministic models** are models developed under conditions of assumed certainty. They are necessarily simplifications of reality, since certainty is rare. The advantage of such models is that they can generally be manipulated and solved with relative ease. Thus, complicated systems can often be modeled and analyzed if it can be assumed that all the numerical components of the system are known with certainty. **Probabilistic models** are those in which uncertainty is assumed. Although incorporating uncertainty into a model may yield a more realistic representation of the situation, such a model is generally more difficult to analyze. Statistically based models are typically used to analyze probabilistic decision-making situations.

Deterministic models are models under conditions of assumed certainty.

A **probabilistic model** is a model for which uncertainty is assumed and probabilities are assigned to the decision outcomes.

Model Solution

Once models have been constructed, they are solved using quantitative techniques. A solution technique usually applies to a specific type of model. Thus, the model type and solution method are often referred to as part of the technique. For this reason the terms *model* and *technique* are frequently used interchangeably. We are able to say that a *model is solved,* since the model represents a problem. When we refer to model solution, we also mean problem solution.

Model solutions can take several forms. In some cases the results will be in the form of a specific answer to a problem that serves as a recommended decision or guideline for the operations manager. Alternatively, some quantitative techniques do not generate an answer; instead, they provide information or descriptive results that fit the operational decision-making environment. In this case the operations manager uses the information as input into the decision-making process. Often the model is the basis for experimentation, where the results of one experiment provide the input for a second experiment, and so on, so that a variety of solutions and scenarios are tested.

Decision Making

Using model results

Operations managers do not normally take model results and apply them directly without careful consideration and evaluation. Decision making encompasses a combination of quantitative results and managerial skills, abilities, and experience. The operations manager typically must consider several alternative choices before making a decision, some of which may not be the result of a quantitative model but might be intuitive or experimental. Sometimes the modeling results are nothing more than one piece of information that must be considered along with many other pieces of information before a decision can be made. Although the use of quantitative models and a systematic problem-solving approach can enhance and improve the decision-making process, decision making is still very much an art or skill predicated on experience and ability.

Implementation of Results

The final use of the model results in an operation called *implementation.* Occasionally there is a hesitancy to use quantitative model results even though they may give the correct decision or benefit the decision-making process. The mathematics of quantitative models is sometimes so complex that the operations manager may not understand where the results come from or how they were derived and, as a result, will not trust them. For that reason some of the most popular quantitative methods are those that are the easiest to understand by the individuals who ultimately make the decisions. Alternatively, in many instances the manager is prudent not to implement directly the results of a model. No matter how much effort goes into the development of a mathematical model, it is very difficult to construct a true and accurate representation of a real-life situation. Thus, models frequently have limitations that must be recognized before the results are blindly implemented. Operations managers often use models simply for experimentation and to evaluate different decision alternatives.

Completion of the steps in the systematic approach just described does not necessarily mean that the process has been completed. The model results and the decisions based on the results provide *feedback* to the original model, which can be modified to test different conditions and decisions the manager thinks might occur in the future. Or, the results may indicate that a problem exists that had not been considered previously; if so, the original model can be altered or reconstructed. Because models can be modified or reconstructed, the decision-making process can be continuous rather than simply providing one solution to one problem.

As we noted previously, a variety of quantitative techniques are available for a wide range of different operational decision-making situations. In the next section, we demonstrate the decision-making process using a quantitative technique known as decision analysis.

Teaching Note 2.5 Decision Analysis as a Reflection of How Decisions Are Made

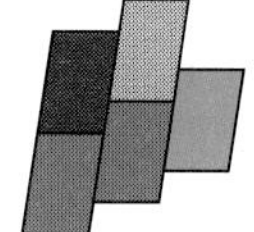

DECISION ANALYSIS

Decision analysis is a set of quantitative decision-making techniques for decision situations in which uncertainty exists.

In this section we demonstrate the use of the quantitative technique known as **decision analysis** for decision-making situations where uncertainty exists. Decision analysis is a generic technique that can be applied to a number of different types of operational decision-making areas. However, besides simply being a quantitative technique that can be applied to a specific problem, it also illustrates the logic a decision maker often uses in decision making.

Many decision-making situations occur under conditions of *uncertainty.* For example, the demand for a product may not be 100 units next week but may vary between 0 and 200 units, depending on the state of the market (which is uncertain). Decision analysis is a set of quantitative decision-making techniques to aid the decision maker in dealing with the type of decision situation in which there is uncertainty. However, besides the basic usefulness of decision analysis for decision making, it is also a beneficial topic to study because it reflects a structured, systematic approach to decision making that many decision makers follow intuitively without ever consciously thinking about it. Thus, decision analysis represents not only a collection of decision-making techniques, but also an analysis of logic underlying decision making.

Decision Making Without Probabilities

Teaching Note 2.6 Involving the Student

A decision-making situation includes several components—the decisions themselves and the actual events that may occur in the future, known as *states of nature.* Future states of nature may be high demand or low demand for a product or good economic conditions or bad economic conditions. At the time a decision is made, the decision maker is uncertain which state of nature will occur in the future and has no control over these states of nature.

TABLE 2.1 Payoff Table

	STATES OF NATURE	
Decision	*a*	*b*
1	Payoff 1a	Payoff 1b
2	Payoff 2a	Payoff 2b

When probabilities can be assigned to the occurrence of states of nature in the future, the situation is referred to as *decision making under risk,* whereas when probabilities cannot be assigned to the occurrence of future events, the situation is called *decision making under uncertainty.* We discuss this latter case first in this section.

To facilitate the analysis of decision situations so that the best decisions result, they are organized into **payoff tables.** A payoff table is a means of organizing and illustrating the payoffs from the different decisions, given the various states of nature, and has the general form shown in Table 2.1.

A **payoff table** is a method for organizing and illustrating the payoffs from different decisions given various states of nature.

Each decision, 1 or 2, in Table 2.1 will result in an outcome, or *payoff,* for the particular state of nature that will occur in the future. Payoffs are typically expressed in terms of profit, revenues, or cost (although they may be expressed in terms of a variety of quantities). For example, if decision 1 is to expand a production facility and state of nature *a* is good economic conditions, payoff 1a could be $100,000 in profit.

A **payoff** is the outcome of the decision.

Decision-making criteria

Once the decision situation has been organized into a payoff table, several criteria are available that reflect how the decision maker arrives at a decision, including maximax, maximin, minimax regret, Hurwicz, and equal likelihood. These criteria reflect different degrees of decision-maker conservatism or liberalism. On occasion they will result in the same decision; however, they will often yield different results. These decision-making criteria are demonstrated within the context of the following example.

Alternate Example 2.1

EXAMPLE 2.1.
Decision-Making Criteria Under Uncertainty

Problem Statement:

The Southern Textile Company is contemplating the future of one of its major plants, which is located in South Carolina. Three alternative decisions are being considered: 1. expand the plant and produce lightweight, durable materials for possible sales to the military, a market with little foreign competitions, 2. maintain the status quo at the plant, continuing production of textile goods that are subject to heavy foreign competition, or 3. sell the plant now. If one of the first two alternatives is chosen, the plant will still be sold at the end of the year. The amount of profit that could be earned by selling the plant in a year depends on foreign market conditions, including the status of a trade embargo bill in Congress. The following payoff table describes this decision situation.

Transparency 2.3 Payoff Table for Example 2.1

	STATES OF NATURE	
Decision	*Good Foreign Competitive Conditions*	*Poor Foreign Competitive Conditions*
Expand	$ 800,000	$ 500,000
Maintain status quo	1,300,000	–150,000
Sell now	320,000	320,000

Determine the best decision using the following decision criteria.

1. Maximax
2. Maximin
3. Minimax regret
4. Hurwicz
5. Equal likelihood

Solution:

1. Maximax criterion

The **maximax criterion** is a decision criterion that results in the maximum of the maximum payoffs.

With the **maximax criterion,** the decision maker selects the decision that will result in the maximum of the maximum payoffs. (In fact, this is how this criterion derives its name—the maximum of the maxima.) The maximax criterion is very optimistic. The decision maker assumes that the most favorable state of nature for each decision alternative will occur. Thus, for this example, the company would optimistically assume that good competitive conditions will prevail in the future, which will result in the following maximum payoffs and decisions:

Expand:	$ 800,000	
Status quo:	1,300,000	← Maximum
Sell:	320,000	

Decision: Maintain status quo

2. Maximin criterion

The **maximin criterion** is a decision criterion that results in the maximum of the minimum payoffs.

In contrast to the maximax criterion, which is very optimistic, the **maximin criterion** is pessimistic. With the **maximin criterion,** the decision maker selects the decision that will reflect the *maximum* of the *minimum* payoffs. For each decision alternative, the decision maker assumes that the minimum payoff will occur; of these, the maximum is selected as follows:

Expand:	$500,000	← Maximum
Status quo:	–150,000	
Sell:	320,000	

Decision: Expand

3. Minimax Regret Criterion

The **minimax regret criterion** is a decision criterion that results in the minimum of the maximum regrets for each alternative.

With the **minimax regret criterion,** the decision maker attempts to avoid *regret* by selecting the decision alternative that minimizes the maximum regret. To use the minimax regret criterion, a decision maker first selects the maximum payoff under each state of nature; then all other payoffs under the respective states of nature are subtracted from these amounts, as follows:

Good Competitive Conditions	*Poor Competitive Conditions*
$1,300,000 – 800,000 = 500,000	$500,000 – $500,000 = 0
1,300,000 – 1,300,000 = 0	500,000 – (–150,000) = 650,000
1,300,000 – 320,000 = 980,000	500,000 – 320,000 = 180,000

These values represent the regret for each decision that would be experienced by the decision maker if a decision were made that resulted in less than the maximum payoff. In order to make the decision according to the minimax regret criterion, the maximum regret for *each decision* must be determined. The decision corresponding to the minimum of these regret values is then selected as follows:

	Regret Value
Expand:	\$500,000 ← Minimum
Status quo:	650,000
Sell:	980,000

Decision: Expand

4. Hurwicz criterion

The **Hurwicz criterion** strikes a compromise between the maximax and maximin criteria. The principle underlying this decision criterion is that the decision maker is neither totally optimistic (as the maximax criterion assumes) nor totally pessimistic (as the maximin criterion assumes). With the Hurwicz criterion, the decision payoffs are weighted by a **coefficient of optimism,** a measure of the decision maker's optimism. The coefficient of optimism, which we will define as α, is between 0 and 1 (i.e., $0 < \alpha < 1.0$). If $\alpha = 1.0$, then the decision maker is said to be completely optimistic, and if $\alpha = 0$, then the decision maker is said to be completely pessimistic. (Given this definition, if α is the coefficient of optimism, $1 - \alpha$ is the *coefficient of pessimism.*) The Hurwicz criterion requires that for each decision alternative, the maximum payoff is multiplied by α and the minimum payoff is multiplied by $1 - \alpha$. For our investment example, if α equals 0.3 (i.e., the company is slightly pessimistic), $1 - \alpha = 0.7$, and the following values and decision will result:

The **Hurwicz criterion** is a decision criterion in which the decision payoffs are weighted by a coefficient of optimism, α.

The **coefficient of optimism (α)** is a measure of a decision maker's optimism, from 0 (completely pessimistic) to 1 (completely optimistic).

Expand:	\$ 800,000(0.3) + 500,000(0.7)	= \$590,000 ← Maximum
Status quo:	1,300,000(0.3) – 150,000(0.7)	= 285,000
Sell:	320,000(0.3) + 320,000(0.7)	= 320,000

Decision: Expand

5. Equal Likelihood criterion

When the maximax criterion is applied to a decision situation, the decision maker implicitly assumes that the most favorable state of nature for each decision will occur. Alternatively, when the maximin criterion is applied, the least favorable states of nature are assumed. The **equal likelihood** (or **LaPlace**) **criterion** weights each state of nature equally, thus assuming that the states of nature are equally likely to occur. Since there are two states of nature in our example, we assign a weight of 0.50 to each one. Next, we multiply these weights by each payoff for each decision and select the alternative with the maximum of these weighted values.

The **equal likelihood (La Place) criterion** is a decision criterion in which each state of nature is weighted equally.

Expand:	\$ 800,000(0.50) + 500,000(0.50)	= \$650,000 ← Maximum
Status quo:	1,300,000(0.50) – 150,000(0.50)	= 575,000
Sell:	320,000(0.50) + 320,000(0.50)	= 320,000

Decision: Expand

The decision to expand the plant was designated most often by the various decision criteria. Notice that the decision to sell was never indicated by any criterion. This is because the payoffs for expansion, under either set of future economic conditions, are always better than the payoffs for selling. Thus, given any situation with these two alternatives, the decision to expand will always be made over the decision to sell. In fact, the sell decision alternative could have been eliminated from consideration under each of our criteria. The alternative of selling is said to be *dominated* by the alternative of expanding. In general, dominated decision alternatives can be removed from the payoff table and not considered when the various decision-making criteria are applied, which reduces the complexity of the decision analysis.

The use of several decision criteria often results in a mix of decisions, with no one decision being selected more than the others. The criterion or collection of criteria used and the resulting decision depend on the characteristics and philosophy of the decision maker. For example, the extremely optimistic decision maker might eschew the majority of the preceding results and make the decision to maintain the status quo, because the maximax criterion most closely reflects his or her personal decision-making philosophy.

Teaching Note 2.7 Determining Probabilities for States of Nature

Risk involves assigning probabilities to states of nature.

Decision Making with Probabilities

The decision-making criteria just presented were based on the assumption that no information regarding the probability of the states of nature was available. However, it is often possible for the decision maker to know enough about the future states of nature to assign probabilities to their occurrence, which is known as decision making under conditions of *risk*. The most widely used decision-making criterion under risk is **expected value,** which is computed by multiplying each outcome by the probability of its occurrence and then summing these products according to the following formula:

The **expected value** is a weighted average of decision outcomes in which each future state of nature is assigned a probability of occurrence.

$$EV(x) = \sum_{i=1}^{n} p(x_i)x_i$$

where

$$x_i = \text{outcome } i$$
$$p(x_i) = \text{probability of outcome}$$

Alternate Example 2.2

EXAMPLE 2.2.
Expected Value

Problem Statement:
Assume that it is now possible for the Southern Textile Company in Example 2.1 to estimate a probability of 0.70 that good foreign competitive conditions will exist and a probability of 0.30 that poor conditions will exist in the future. Determine the best decision using expected value.

Solution:
The expected values for each decision alternative are computed as follows.

EV(expand) = \$800,000(0.70) + 500,000(0.30) = \$710,000
EV(status quo) = 1,300,000(0.70)– 150,000(0.30) = 865,000 ← Maximum
EV(sell) = 320,000(0.70) + 320,000(0.30) = 320,000

The decision according to this criterion is to maintain the status quo, since it has the highest expected value.

Teaching Note 2.8 The Value of Information

Expected Value of Perfect Information

Occasionally additional information will become available or can be purchased regarding future events, thus enabling the decision maker to make a better decision. For example, a company could hire an economic forecaster to perform an analysis of the economy in order to determine more accurately the economic conditions that will occur in the future. However, they would be foolish to pay more for this information than they stand to gain in extra profit from having the information. That is, the information has some maximum value that represents the limit of what the decision maker would be willing to spend. This value of information can be computed as an expected value—hence its name, the **expected value of perfect information** (also referred to as **EVPI**).

Expected value of perfect information (EVPI) is the maximum value of perfect information to the decision maker.

In order to compute the expected value of perfect information, one first looks at the decisions under each state of nature. If information that assured us which state of nature was going to occur (i.e., perfect information) could be obtained, the best decision for that state of nature could be selected. For example, in the textile company example, if the company executives knew for sure that good competitive conditions would prevail, then they would maintain the status quo. Similarly, if they knew for sure that poor competitive conditions will occur, then they would expand.

The probabilities of each state of nature (i.e., 0.70 and 0.30) indicate that good competitive conditions will prevail 70 percent of the time and poor competitive conditions will prevail 30 percent of the time (if this decision situation is repeated many times). In other words, even though perfect information enables the investor to make the right decision, each state of nature will occur only a certain portion of the time. Thus, each of the decision outcomes obtained using perfect information must be weighted by its respective probability:

$$\$1{,}300{,}000(0.70) + (500{,}000)(0.30) = \$1{,}060{,}000$$

The amount $1,060,000 is the expected value of the decision *given perfect information,* not the expected value of perfect information. The expected value of perfect information is the maximum amount that would be paid to gain information that would result in a decision better than the one made *without perfect information.* Recall that the expected-value decision without perfect information was to maintain status quo and the expected value was $865,000.

The expected value of perfect information is computed by subtracting the expected value without perfect information from the expected value given perfect information:

EVPI = expected value given perfect information – expected value without perfect information.

For our example, the EVPI is computed as,

$$\text{EVPI} = \$1{,}060{,}000 - 865{,}000 = \$195{,}000$$

The expected value of perfect information, $195,000, is the maximum amount that the investor would pay to purchase perfect information from some other source, such as an economic forecaster. Of course, perfect information is rare and is usually unobtainable. Typically, the decision maker would be willing to pay some smaller amount, depending on how accurate (i.e., close to perfection) the information is believed to be.

Sequential Decision Trees

A payoff table is essentially limited to a single decision situation. If a decision requires a series of decisions, then a payoff table cannot be created, and a **sequential decision tree** must be used. We demonstrate the use of a decision tree within the context of the following example.

A **sequential decision tree** is a graphical method for analyzing decision situations that require a sequence of decisions over time.

EXAMPLE 2.3.
A Sequential Decision Tree

Problem Statement:

The Southern Textile Company from Example 2.1 is considering two decision alternatives: to expand its existing production operation in order to manufacture a new line of lightweight material or to purchase land to construct a new facility on in the future. Each of these decisions has outcomes based on product market growth in the future that result in another set of decisions (during a ten-year planning horizon), as shown in the following figure of a sequential decision tree. In this figure the square nodes represent decisions and the circle nodes reflect different states of nature.

Transparency 2.4 The Sequential Decision Tree for Example 2.3

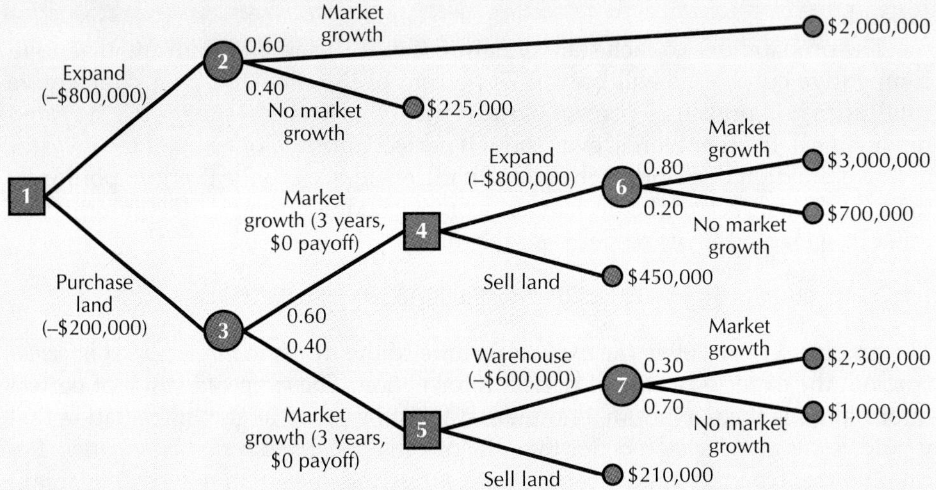

The first decision facing the company is whether to expand or buy land. If the company expands, two states of nature are possible. Either the market will grow (with a probability of 0.60) or it will not grow (with a probability of 0.40). Either state of nature will result in a payoff. On the other hand, if the company chooses to purchase land, three years in the future another decision will have to be made regarding the development of the land.

At decision node 1 in the above figure, the decision choices are to expand and to purchase land. Notice that the costs of the ventures ($800,000 and $200,000, respectively) are shown in parentheses. If the plant is expanded, two states of nature are possible at probability node 2: The market will grow, with a probability of 0.60, or it will not grow or will decline, with a probability of 0.40. If the market grows, the company will achieve a payoff of $2,000,000 over a ten-year period. However, if no growth occurs, a payoff of only $225,000 will result.

If the decision is to purchase land, two states of nature are possible at probability node 3. These two states of nature and their probabilities are identical to those at node 2; however, the payoffs are different. If market growth occurs for a three-year period, no payoff will occur, but the company will make another decision at node 4 regarding development of the land. At that point, either the plant will be expanded at a cost of $800,000 or the land will be sold, with a payoff of $450,000. Notice that the decision situation at node 4 can occur only if market growth occurs first. If no market growth occurs at node 3, there is no payoff, and another decision situation becomes necessary at node 5: A warehouse can be constructed at a cost of $600,000 or the land can be sold for $210,000. (Notice that the sale of the land results in less profit if there is no market growth than if there is growth.)

If the decision at decision node 4 is to expand, two states of nature are possible; the market may grow, with a probability of 0.80, or it may not grow, with a probability of 0.20. The probability of market growth is higher (and the probability of no growth is lower) than before because there has already been growth for the first three years, as shown by the branch from node 3 to node 4. The payoffs for these two states of nature at the end of the ten-year period are $3,000,000 and $700,000, respectively, as shown in the figure on page 44.

If the company decides to build a warehouse at node 5, then two states of nature can occur. Market growth can occur, with a probability of 0.30 and an eventual payoff of $2,300,000, or no growth can occur, with a probability of 0.70 and a payoff of $1,000,000. The probability of market growth is low (i.e., 0.30) because there has already been no market growth, as shown by the branch from node 3 to node 5.

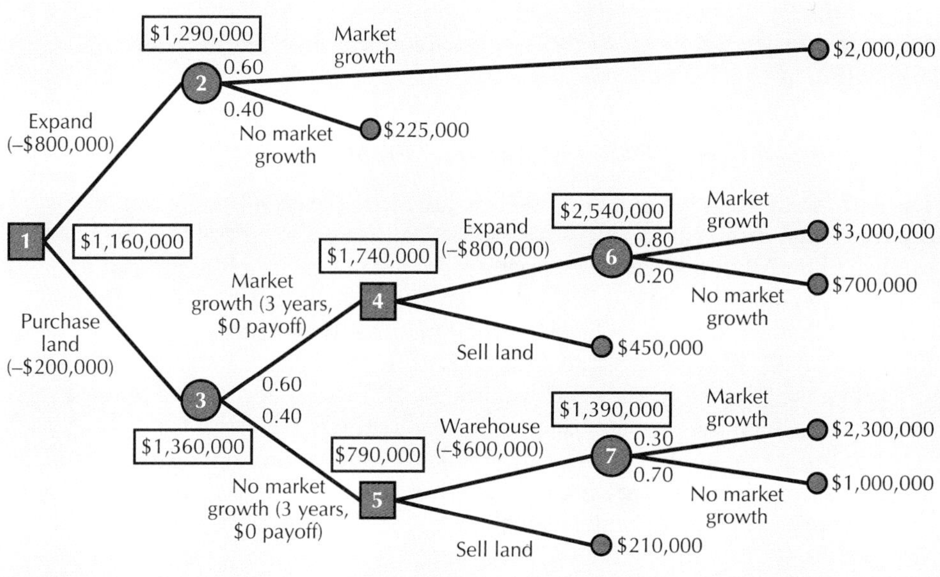

Solution:

We start the decision analysis process at the end of the decision tree and work backward toward a decision at node 1.

First, we must compute the expected values at nodes 6 and 7.

$$\text{EV(node 6)} = 0.80(\$3{,}000{,}000) + 0.20(\$700{,}000) = \$2{,}540{,}000$$
$$\text{EV(node 7)} = 0.30(\$2{,}300{,}000) + 0.70(\$1{,}000{,}000) = \$1{,}390{,}000$$

These expected values (as well as all other nodal values) are shown in boxes in the figure above.

At decision nodes 4 and 5, a decision must be made. As with a normal payoff table, the decision is made that results in the greatest expected value. At node 4 the choice is between two values: $1,740,000, the value derived by subtracting the cost of expanding ($800,000) from the expected payoff of $2,540,000, and $450,000, the expected value of selling the land computed with a probability of 1.0. The decision is to expand, and the value at node 4 is $1,740,000.

This same process is repeated at node 5. The decisions at node 5 result in payoffs of $790,000 (i.e., $1,390,000 – 600,000 = $790,000) and $210,000. Since the value $790,000 is higher, the decision is to build a warehouse.

Next the expected values at nodes 2 and 3 are computed.

EV(node 2) = 0.60($2,000,000) + 0.40($225,000) = $1,290,000
EV(node 3) = 0.60($1,740,000) + 0.40($790,000) = $1,360,000

(Note that the expected value for node 3 is computed from the decision values previously determined at nodes 4 and 5.)

Now the final decision at node 1 must be made. As before, we select the decision with the greatest expected value after the cost of each decision is subtracted.

Expand: $1,290,000 – 800,000 = $490,000
Land: $1,360,000 – 200,000 = $1,160,000

Since the highest *net* expected value is $1,160,000, the decision is to purchase land, and the payoff of the decision is $1,160,000.

Example 2.3 demonstrates the usefulness of decision trees for decision analysis. The decision tree allows the decision maker to see the logic of decision making, because it provides a picture of the decision process. Decision trees can be used for decision problems more complex than this example without too much difficulty.

Teaching Note 2.9 AB:POM Computer Software

Computer Solution of Decision Analysis Problems

Decision analysis with AB:POM

Throughout this text we will demonstrate how to solve quantitative models using the computer, primarily with the AB:POM software package by Howard J. Weiss, published by Allyn and Bacon. Appendix A contains a complete tutorial on how to get started and use the AB:POM software; however, it is a user-friendly, menu-driven package and requires little instruction, other than knowledge of the quantitative method. We demonstrate AB:POM using Examples 2.1 and 2.2.

When the "Decision Analysis" module in AB:POM is accessed, a blank screen appears on which the problem data is input, as shown in Exhibit 2.1.

The input display has a series of menu selection commands listed across the bottom of the screen. By pressing the F2 or the "N" key, a new set of problem data can be entered. The model can subsequently be solved by pressing the F10 or the "R" key. Brief descriptions for all the commands at the bottom of the screen are provided on the F1, or Help, screen. Exhibit 2.2 is the model solution output, which also shows the input data, in response to running the program module.

```
                    Decision and Breakeven Analysis               Data Screen
Number of alternatives (2-10) 3                  Number of nature states (1-8) 2
Profits     - maximize profits

                                    Example 2.1

Probability->       0.000        0.000
                  state 1      state 2
alternatv 1             0            0
alternatv 2             0            0
alternatv 3             0            0

F1=Help F2=New F3=Load F4=Main F5=Util F6=Quit F7=Save F9=Prnt F10=Run    Esc
Enter the probability for this state of nature
```

EXHIBIT 2.1

Transparency 2.5 AB:POM Computer Solution for Decision Analysis

```
                        Decision and Breakeven Analysis                 Solution
Number of alternatives (2-10) 3                   Number of nature states (1-8) 2
Profits    - maximize profits
                           Example 2.1 and 2.2

Probability->   0.700        0.300
                 Good         Poor          EMV       Row Min      Row Max
Expand          800000       500000       720000       500000       800000
Status quo     1300000      -150000       865000      -150000      1300000
Sell            320000       320000       320000       320000       320000
             column maximum->             865000       500000      1300000
The maximum expected monetary value is 865000 given by Status quo
The maximin is   50000 given by Expand
The maximax is 1300000 given by Status quo
```

EXHIBIT 2.2

The output includes the maximax and maximin decisions as well as the expected value for Examples 2.1 and 2.2. To print the solution, press the F9 or the "P" key, as instructed at the bottom of the output screen. To save the problem data, press the ESC key and return to the input screen; then press the F7 or the "S" key.

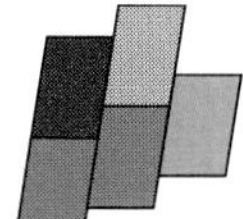

SUPPORT SYSTEMS FOR DECISION MAKING

Information for decision making

Quantitative techniques such as decision analysis do not actually make decisions, but they provide information that can aid the operations manager in making decisions. However, where in the organization is information generated, how does it get to the operations manager, and how does the manager use it to make decisions? Many organizations employ some form of computer-based information system to accumulate, organize, and distribute information for decision-making purposes. In this section we will present and discuss two types of information systems, a *management information system* and a *decision support system.*

Teaching Note 2.10 Applications of MIS and DSS

Management Information Systems

Management information system (MIS) is a computer system designed to channel large quantities of different types of information, organized into reports, through an organization.

A **management information system** (also known as an **MIS**) is a system specifically designed to channel large quantities and numerous types of information through an organization. In a management information system, data are collected, organized, processed, and made conveniently accessible to the manager so that the information will be of assistance in making decisions and carrying out routine functions. Much of this information is in the form of reports that are posted according to a predetermined schedule. Examples include payroll and sales reports generated on a weekly or monthly basis and monthly inventory reports. Such reports enable the company to maintain control and also serve as a communication system, linking the various units (or departments) of an organization so that decision making is coordinated.

A *data base* is an organized collection of numerical information.

The first component in a management information system is the *data base,* which is an organized collection of numerical information. Prices, production output and rates, cost data, inventory, numbers of orders, available resources, capacities, and labor rates are examples of the pieces of information that form a data base.

For a management information system to be efficient and effective, the data base must contain the right amount and the right type of relevant, high-quality in-

Teaching Note 2.11 "Gaining the Competitive Edge" Boxes

GAINING THE COMPETITIVE EDGE

Selecting Health-Care Providers for a Bank's Employees

An increasingly popular means for employers to cut personnel costs is to contract for discounted health services, which the employee receives incentives to use. An anonymous bank was considering such an arrangement with a preferred health-care provider (PPO). With the bank's existing health plan, employees could use any physician of their choice and could, after a deductible, submit bills to the bank for partial reimbursement. The bank was self-insured and thus paid for actual health expenses, whereas employees paid relatively small premiums that accounted for less than 15 percent of the cost of the plan. The PPO plan required the employee to use a clinic with a large number of physicians but discounted clinic charges by 15 percent and hospital charges by 10 percent to the employee and bank. The health benefits coverage would not change with the PPO. A decision analysis model was constructed to help the bank decide if it should join the PPO. The model included two decision alternatives: to join the PPO or continue with the current health-care plan. The decision model computes the expected savings to the bank for an employee who joins the PPO. It was determined that joining the PPO would result in more frequent clinic visits and hospitalizations but would lower hospitalization charges. Specifically, the decision to join the PPO would be more cost-effective if the expected cost was lower than $1,383. Costs for the PPO were computed to be $640 lower per family than the current plan. Since an independent conclusion indicated that approximately 25 percent of the bank's 992 employees might join the PPO, total savings to the bank were projected to be approximately $160,000 annually. This decision analysis enabled the bank's benefit manager to negotiate favorable contract terms with the preferred provider that was subsequently offered to employees.

Source: Based on F. Alemi and J. Agliato, "Restricting Patients' Choices of Physicians: A Decision Analytic Evaluation of Costs," *Interfaces*, 19, no. 2 (March–April 1989): 20–28.

formation. In addition, this information must be properly organized. The vast amounts of data available to organizations make the computer an essential component of most management information systems (although manual systems do exist in smaller organizations). Frequently, a company will develop a management information system from a combination of commercially available computer software packages and internally developed programs. These information systems are customized to fit the company's specific needs. For example, a spreadsheet package like Lotus 1-2-3 might be a module in an information system.

The computer in a management information system processes data and generates information for use by the different units in the organization. The information flowing from the computer to the different departments and functions can take several forms. It can be in the form of *reports* that summarize and organize the data, such as reports about accounts receivable, work orders, work force, inventory level, resource level, market behavior, or production output. These reports can provide recent information or historical information that might be relevant for present or future decisions. Reports typically do not reflect any form of operations analysis but are simply collections of data organized so as to be useful and easily interpreted. They can be generated at the request of management or on a regular basis as a matter of policy. For example, the manager of a production department might request a report on the frequency of machine breakdowns during a particular month, whereas a report on monthly production output would be provided on a regular basis without request.

Information can also take the form of quantitative model results or solutions. Like reports, this information can be generated on a regular basis or by request. Most frequently, the information is compiled at the request of a manager who wants to solve a specific problem. However, it is important to point out that the management information system generally cannot formulate the model itself.

Decision Support Systems

A **decision support system (DSS)** is an information system with the capability of supporting the manager in the decision-making process. It differs from a management information system in that the manager typically acts as an *internal* component in a DSS, rather than an *external* component, as in an MIS. In other words, the operations manager interacts with the computer-based information system in order to reach a decision through an iterative process. Therefore, decision support systems are typically thought of as having interactive capabilities whereby the manager can establish a dialogue with the information system. In addition, a DSS frequently integrates quantitative models within its framework as a system component with which the decision maker interacts.

A **decision support system (DSS)** is a computerized information system with the capability to support a manager interactively in the decision-making process.

A general framework of a decision support system is illustrated in Figure 2.3. Notice that the blocks designated as *data, computer system—data processing,* and *information* and the various information flows to management comprise the management information system. The added components that form a DSS are the decision-making capabilities, the quantitative techniques, and the interactive capabilities (i.e., what-if? analysis). To clarify the operation of a decision support system, we will explain the interactive capabilities of a DSS in greater detail.

Interactive Decision Making

The information flows shown in Figure 2.3 reflect the interaction between the operations manager and the computer system, or what is more commonly referred to as *what-if? analysis.* That is, the computer system generates the results of a quantitative model and the manager asks the computer, "What if something were changed in the model?" For example, the computer system might generate an order quantity based on data provided in an inventory model. The manager might then anticipate that the cost of ordering might change and ask the computer for new results based on the change. Such experimentation with possible changes educates the manager regarding the possible courses of action that can be taken as a

The manager and DSS interacting to analyze an operation

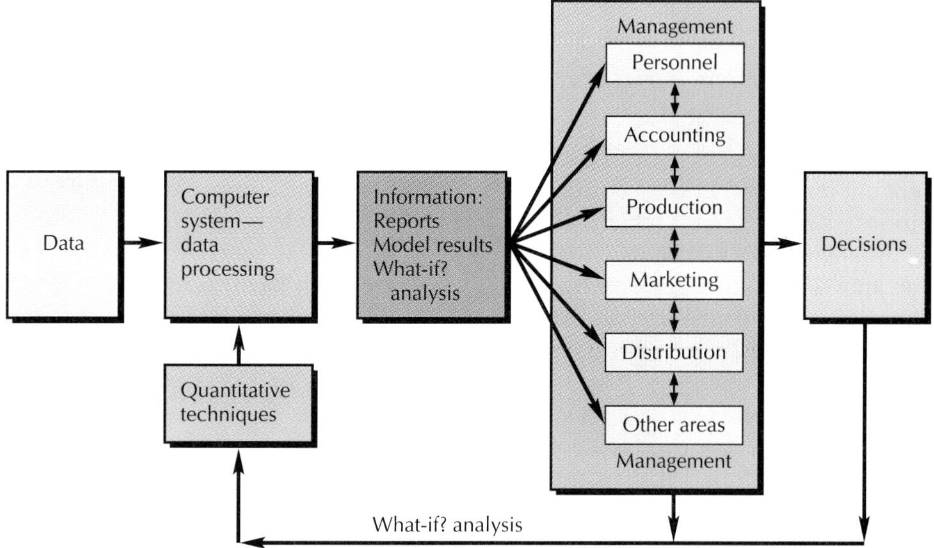

FIGURE 2.1 A Decision Support System

Transparency 2.6 A Decision Support System

result of occurrences in the future. The manager can also test possible decisions to see their potential results before actually making them.

As in the case of management information systems, a number of interactive software packages are commercially available for use on mainframe or personal computers. Some of these packages serve only as decision support systems. In other cases, these packages can be integrated within a company's own customized DSS to perform specific operations. Examples of such commercially available decision support systems include IFPS and Lotus 1-2-3.

These programs are designed to request the necessary input data from the manager by asking questions. The computer actually carries on a dialogue with the manager. For example, if the manager is performing inventory analysis, the computer might print the following question on the terminal screen:

WHAT IS THE ORDER COST PER UNIT?

The manager would then type in the order cost,

200

and the computer would type out the optimal order quantity on the screen:

500

One additional aspect of a decision support system is the interaction between departments. Notice in Figure 2.3 that information flows between the departments or business functions. Decisions rarely affect only one unit in an organization. For example, inventory decisions affect not only the production operation but also the marketing department (which wants to be able to promise customers immediate delivery), the distribution department (because the availability of units of product affects shipping loads), and accounting (because the inventory on hand represents both an investment and a cost). The flow of information between areas must be coordinated in order to develop cooperative decisions.

The final stage in the decision support system shown in Figure 2.3 reflects the actual decisions made by management. Based on the information contained in reports, the solution results from quantitative models, and what-if? analysis, managers make decisions. However, these decisions are not ends in themselves; the decisions and their results in the form of *feedback* provide additional data for the data base. An ideal decision support system is an ongoing, dynamic system that continuously updates itself.

Expert Systems and Artificial Intelligence

An **expert system** is a computer system that includes an expert's knowledge about a problem.

A decision support system has already been defined as an interactive, computer-based information system that uses models and data to assist decision makers in making decisions. In comparison, an **expert system** is a computer system that includes a *knowledge base,* which contains an expert's knowledge on a particular type of problem, and a mechanism for reasoning that allows inferences to be made from the knowledge base. An expert system provides the user with some detail about the reasoning process and advises users on specific problem areas. Hence, these systems are often referred to as intelligent DSS.

Because a knowledge base is central to the concept of an expert system, such a system is often called a *knowledge-based expert system.* The knowledge base is a large amount of knowledge about the problem that is stored in the system. Researchers have found that using masses of knowledge in an effective manner is more conducive to success than using a specific solution technique. The term *expert* is used because the system addresses problems typically thought to require an expert or specialist to solve. Expert systems can be viewed as computerized "consultants" for decision making that have a collection of facts, knowledge, and rules

GAINING THE COMPETITIVE EDGE

A DSS for Evaluating Freight Transportation Alternatives at Heinz

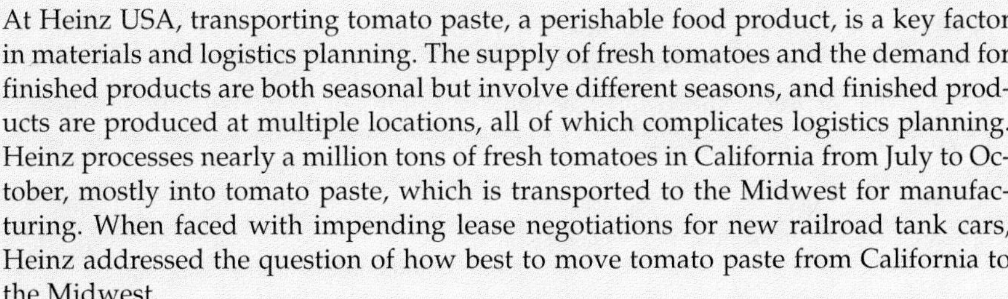

At Heinz USA, transporting tomato paste, a perishable food product, is a key factor in materials and logistics planning. The supply of fresh tomatoes and the demand for finished products are both seasonal but involve different seasons, and finished products are produced at multiple locations, all of which complicates logistics planning. Heinz processes nearly a million tons of fresh tomatoes in California from July to October, mostly into tomato paste, which is transported to the Midwest for manufacturing. When faced with impending lease negotiations for new railroad tank cars, Heinz addressed the question of how best to move tomato paste from California to the Midwest.

A task force identified three alternatives: Invest in the newly designed railroad tank cars, use a giant pouch called a Scholle bag that holds over 300 gallons of tomato paste and ship in regular boxcars, or use a combination of these two alternatives. A decision support system was developed to evaluate these options and perform a variety of sensitivity analysis. The primary components of the DSS were parameters for such items as freight costs, demand rate, and capital cost for the alternatives. These were inputs into economic cost models that computed the least cost solution (alternative) for each manufacturing location. As a result of the DSS analysis, Heinz opted not to acquire new tank cars and to satisfy demand with Scholle bags instead, which, compared with the original lease proposal arrangement, lowered operating costs by $1 million annually. The DSS had the added benefit of more fully educating managers about railroad costs, which strengthened their negotiating position with the railroad about rates.

Source: Based on S. Kekre, et al., "A Logistics Analysis at Heinz," *Interfaces* 20, no. 5 (September–October 1990): 1–13.

used to make inferences about a problem area. In effect, an expert system can diagnose problems and then suggest alternate solutions.

Artificial Intelligence (AI) is a concept that is difficult to define specifically, yet it appears to have certain characteristics. The objective of those interested in artificial intelligence is to study and understand human thought processes (i.e., intelligence) and to develop computational processes (using computers, robots, etc.) that will simulate those thought processes. Artificial intelligence allows machines to exhibit behavior such as solving problems or carrying out tasks that is similar to the behavior of human beings. Such behavior would be viewed as intelligent if a human rather than a machine exhibited it. Some of the earliest (and still most popular) examples of artificial intelligence are the use of computers to play games like chess and checkers. In general, expert systems are viewed as a subspecialty of artificial intelligence.

Artificial Intelligence (AI) is a computer system that attempts to replicate human thought processes to diagnose and solve problems.

The use of artificial intelligence and its subset of expert systems merges with and affects operations management in several ways. Expert systems with heuristic reasoning have been applicated in such areas as developing, reviewing, and monitoring plans; production and manufacturing; and maintenance.

SUMMARY

In this chapter we have provided a general overview of the process of operational decision making. To a limited extent we have shown how operational decisions are interrelated to achieve company strategic goals. In the chapters to come we will provide a more in-depth look at how decisions are made in each functional area in operations management and describe their interrelationships in greater detail. The area in operations that has become most important in recent years—or at least garnered the most attention—is quality management, the subject of our next chapter.  Quality management has become such a pervasive issue for most companies in their quest to remain competitive in a global economy that decisions related to quality now affect virtually every other operational function. In effect, contemporary approaches to quality management have essentially become programs for managing all operational functions.

 SUMMARY OF KEY FORMULAS

Expected Value

$$EV(x) = \sum_{i=1}^{n} p(x_i)x_i$$

Expected Value of Perfect Information

EVPI = expected value given perfect information – expected value without perfect information

 SUMMARY OF KEY TERMS

artificial intelligence (AI): a computer system that attempts to replicate human thought processes to diagnose and solve problems.

coefficient of optimism (α): a measure of a decision maker's optimism, from 0 (completely pessimistic) to 1 (completely optimistic), used in the Hurwicz decision criterion.

decision analysis: a set of quantitative decision-making techniques to aid the decision maker in dealing with decision situations in which uncertainty exists.

decision support system (DSS): a computerized information system with the capability to support a manager interactively in the decision-making process.

deterministic models: models under conditions of assumed certainty.

equal likelihood (La Place) criterion: a decision criterion in which each state of nature is weighted equally.

expected value: a weighted average of decision outcomes in which each future state of nature is assigned a probability of occurrence.

expected value of perfect information: the maximum value that a decision maker would be willing to pay for perfect information about future states of nature.

expert system: a computer system that includes an expert's knowledge about a particular problem area and that can diagnose problems and recommend solutions.

Hurwicz criterion: a decision criterion in which the decision payoffs are weighted by a coefficient of optimism, α.

management information system (MIS): a computer system designed to channel large quantities of different types of information, organized into reports, through an organization.

maximax criterion: a decision criterion that results in the maximum of the maximum payoffs.

maximin criterion: a decision criterion that results in the maximum of the minimum payoffs.

minimax regret criterion: a decision criterion that results in the minimum of the maximum regrets for each alternative.

parameter: numerical values in a mathematical relationship
payoff table: a means of organizing and illustrating the payoffs from different decisions given various states of nature.
probabilistic models: models for which uncertainty is assumed and probabilities are assigned to the decision outcomes.
quantitative model: an abstract representation of an existing problem situation.
quantitative technique: a mathematical procedure for solving a model.
sequential decision tree: a graphical method for analyzing decision situations that require a sequence of decisions over time.
variable: a mathematical model symbol that has no predetermined numerical value.

SOLVED PROBLEM

Problem Statement:

Consider the following payoff table for three product decisions (A, B, and C) and three future market conditions (payoffs = $ millions).

	MARKET CONDITIONS		
DECISION	1	2	3
A	$1.0	$2.0	$0.5
B	0.8	1.2	0.9
C	0.7	0.9	1.7

Determine the best decision using the following decision criteria.

1. Maximax
2. Maximin
3. Minimax regret
4. Hurwicz ($\alpha = 0.2$)
5. Equal likelihood
6. Expected value; $p(1) = 0.3$, $p(2) = 0.5$, $p(3) = 0.2$

Solution:

Step 1. Maximax criterion

	Maximin payoffs
A	$2.0 ← Maximum
B	1.2
C	1.7

Decision: Product A

Step 2. Maximin criteria

	Minimum payoffs
A	0.5
B	0.8 ← Maximum
C	0.7

Decision: Product B

Step 3. Minimax regret

	Minimax regrets
A	1.2
B	0.8 ← Minimum
C	1.1

Decision: Product B

Step 4: Hurwicz criterion ($\alpha = 0.2$)

A: 2.0(0.2) + 0.5(0.8) = \$0.80 million
B: 1.2(0.2) + 0.8(0.8) = \$0.88 million
C: 1.7(0.2) + 0.7(0.8) = \$0.90 million ← Maximum

Decision: Product C

Step 5. Equal likelihood

A: 1.0(0.33) + 2.0 (0.33) + 0.5(0.33) = \$1.16 million ← Maximum
B: 0.8(0.33) + 1.2(0.33) + 0.9(0.33) = \$0.96 million
C: 0.7(0.33) + 0.9(0.33) + 1.7(0.33) = \$1.09 million

Decision: Product A

Step 6. Expected value

A: 1.0(0.3) + 2.0(0.5) + 0.5(0.2) = \$1.4 million ← Maximum
B: 0.8(0.3) + 1.2(0.5) + 0.9(0.2) = \$1.02 million
C: 0.7(0.3) + 0.9(0.5) + 1.7(0.2) = \$1.00 million

Decision: Product A

QUESTIONS

2-1. Describe situations of your own that you can classify as decision making without probabilities and decision making with probabilities.
2-2. Explain the concept of *regret.*
2-3. What is the expected value of perfect information and how does it differ from the expected value of a decision given perfect information and the expected value of sample information?
2-4. When is a decision tree a better method for analyzing a decision situation than a payoff table?
2-5. What is a management information system?
2-6. Explain the function of a data base in a management information system.
2-7. Why are management information systems typically computerized?
2-8. Define *decision support system,* and describe the difference between an MIS and a DSS.
2-9. Explain what the term *what-if? analysis* means.
2-10. Explain what an interactive computer program does.
2-11. What is the function of information feedback in a decision support system?
2-12. Using the general form of Figure 2.3, design a theoretical decision support system that encompasses one or more quantitative techniques and assists the operations manager in making a specific decision.
2-13. Define *expert system.*
2-14. Discuss the differences between a decision support system and an expert system.

PROBLEMS

2-1. The owner of the Burger Doodle Restaurant is considering two ways to expand operations: opening a drive-up window or serving breakfast. The increase in profits resulting from these proposed expansions depends on whether a competitor opens a franchise down the street. The possible profits from each expansion in operations given both future competitive situations are shown in the following payoff table.

	COMPETITOR	
DECISION	*Open*	*Not Open*
Drive-up window	–$6,000	$20,000
Breakfast	4,000	8,000

Select the best decision using the following decision criteria.

a. Maximax
b. Maximin
c. Minimax regret
d. Hurwicz ($\alpha = 0.6$)
e. Equal likelihood

2.1. a. Drive-up window, $20,000
b. Breakfast, $4,000
c. Drive-up window, $10,000
d. Drive-up window, $9,600
e. Drive-up window, $7,000

2-2. The owner of the Columbia Construction Company must decide among building a housing development, constructing a shopping center, or leasing all the company's equipment to another company. The profit that will result from each alternative will be determined by whether material costs remain stable or increase. The profit from each alternative given the two possibilities for material costs is shown in the following payoff table.

	MATERIAL COSTS	
DECISION	*Stable*	*Increase*
Houses	$ 70,000	$30,000
Shopping center	105,000	20,000
Leasing	40,000	40,000

Determine the best decision using the following decision criteria.

a. Maximax
b. Maximin
c. Minimax regret
d. Hurwicz ($\alpha = 0.2$)
e. Equal likelihood

2.2. a. Shopping center, $105,000
b. Lease equipment, $40,000
c. Shopping center, $20,000
d. Lease equipment, $40,000
e. Shopping center, $62,500

2-3. A shopping complex is considering three alternate construction projects: a motel, a theater, or a restaurant. Profits from the motel or restaurant will be affected by future economic conditions in the area. The following payoff table shows the monthly profit or loss that could result from each investment.

	ECONOMY CONDITIONS		
INVESTMENT	*Poor*	*Fair*	*Good*
Motel	–$8,000	$15,000	$20,000
Restaurant	2,000	8,000	6,000
Theater	6,000	6,000	5,000

Determine the best investment using the following decision criteria.

2-3. a. Motel, $20,000
b. Theater, $5,000
c. Motel or restaurant, $14,000
d. Theater, $5,400
e. Motel, $9,000

a. Maximax
b. Maximin
c. Minimax regret
d. Hurwicz (α = 0.4)
e. Equal likelihood

★ 2-4. Ann Tyler has come into an inheritance from her grandparents. She is attempting to decide between several investment alternatives. The return after one year is primarily dependent on the interest rate during the next year. The rate is currently 7 percent, and she anticipates it will stay the same or go up or down by at most 2 points. The various investment alternatives plus their returns ($10,000) given the interest rate changes are shown in the following table.

	INTEREST RATES				
INVESTMENTS	*5%*	*6%*	*7%*	*8%*	*9%*
Money market fund	2	3.1	4	4.3	5
Stock growth fund	–3	–2	2.5	4	6
Bond fund	6	5	3	3	2
Government fund	4	3.6	3.2	3	2.8
Risk fund	–9	–4.5	1.2	8.3	14.7
Savings bonds	3	3	3.2	3.4	3.5

Determine the best investment using the following decision criteria.

2-4. a. Risk fund, $147,000
b. Savings bonds, $30,000
c. Growth stocks, $90,000
d. Bond fund, $38,000
e. Risk fund, $75,900
f. Bond fund, $41,000

a. Maximax
b. Maximin
c. Minimax regret
d. Equal likelihood
e. Hurwicz (α = 0.7)
f. Assume that Ann Tyler, with the help of a financial newsletter and some library research, has been able to assign probabilities to each of the possible interest rates during the next year as follows:

Interest Rate	5%	6%	7%	8%	9%
Probability	0.2	0.3	0.3	0.1	0.1

Using expected value, determine her best investment decision.

★ 2-5. The Tech football coaching staff has six basic plays it runs every game. Tech has an upcoming game against State on Saturday and the coaches know State employs five different defenses. The coaches have estimated the number of yards Tech will gain with each play against each defense, as shown in the following payoff table.

	DEFENSE				
PLAY	*54*	*63*	*Wide Tackle*	*Nickel*	*Blitz*
Off tackle	3	–2	9	7	–1
Option	–1	8	–2	9	12
Toss sweep	6	16	–5	3	14
Draw	–2	4	3	10	–3
Pass	8	20	12	–7	–8
Screen	–5	–2	8	3	16

a. If the coaches employ an offensive game plan, they will use the maximax criterion. What will their best play be?
b. If the coaches employ a defensive plan, they will use the maximin criterion. What will their best play be?
c. What will their best play be if State is equally likely to use any of its defenses?
d. The Tech coaches have reviewed game films and have determined the following probabilities that State will use each of its defenses.

2-5. a. Pass, 20 yd
b. Off tackle or option, -2 yd
c. Toss sweep, 6.8 yd
d. Pass best; screen worst
Toss sweep, 10.4 yd

Defense	54	63	Wide Tackle	Nickel	Blitz
Probability	0.40	0.10	0.20	0.20	0.10

Using expected value, rank Tech's plays from best to worst. During the actual game, Tech has a third down and 10 yards to go and the coaches are 60 percent certain State will blitz, with a 10 percent chance of any of the other four defenses. What play should Tech run, and is it likely they will make the first down?

2-6. The Miramar Company is going to introduce one of three new products: a widget, a hummer, or a nimnot. The market conditions (favorable, stable, or unfavorable) will determine the profit or loss the company realizes, as shown in the following payoff table.

	MARKET CONDITIONS		
PRODUCT	*Favorable* 0.2	*Stable* 0.7	*Unfavorable* 0.1
Widget	$120,000	$70,000	–$30,000
Hummer	60,000	40,000	20,000
Nimnot	35,000	30,000	30,000

2-6. a. Widget, $70,000
b. EVPI = $6,000
c. Maximax: widget, 120,000
Maximin: nimnot, $30,000
Regret: widget or nimnot, $60,000
Equal likelihood: widget, $53,333

a. Compute the expected value for each decision and select the best one.
b. Determine how much the firm would be willing to pay to a market research firm to gain better information about future market conditions.
c. Assume that probabilities cannot be assigned to future market conditions, and determine the best decision using the maximax, maximin, minimax regret, and equal likelihood criteria.

2-7. The Steak and Chop Butcher Shop purchases steak from a local meat-packing house. The meat is purchased on Monday at $2.00 per pound, and the shop sells the steak for $3.00 per pound. Any steak left over at the end of the week is sold to a local zoo for $0.50 per pound. The possible demands for steak and the probability for each are as follows. ★

Demand (lb)	*Probability*
20	0.10
21	0.20
22	0.30
23	0.30
24	0.10
	1.00

a. The shop must decide how much steak to order in a week. Construct a payoff table for this decision situation and determine the amount of steak that should be ordered using expected value.

2-7. a. 22 lb, EV = $21
b. Maximax: 24 lb, EV = $24
Maximin: 20 lb, EV = $20

b. Assuming that probabilities cannot be assigned to the demand values, what would the best decision be using the maximax and maximin criteria?

★ 2-8. The manager of the greeting card section of Mazey's department store is considering her order for a particular line of holiday cards. The cost of each box of cards is $3; each box will be sold for $5 during the holiday season. After the holiday season, the cards will be sold for $2 a box. The card section manager believes that all leftover cards can be sold at that price. The estimated demand during the holiday season for the cards, with associated probabilities, is as follows:

Demand (boxes)	*Probability*
25	0.10
26	0.15
27	0.30
28	0.20
29	0.15
30	0.10

2-8. a. 28 boxes, EV = $53.30
b. EVPI = $1.60

a. Develop the payoff table for this decision situation and compute the expected value for each alternative and identify the best decision.
b. Compute the expected value of perfect information.

★ 2-9. The Americo Oil Company is considering making a bid for a shale oil development contract to be awarded by the federal government. The company has decided to bid $110 million. The company estimates that it has a 60 percent chance of winning the contract with this bid. If the firm wins the contract, it can choose one of three methods for getting the oil from the shale. It can develop a new method for oil extraction, use an existing (inefficient) process, or subcontract the processing out to a number of smaller companies once the shale has been excavated. The results from these alternatives are given as follows.

Develop New Process

Outcomes	*Probability*	*Profit (millions)*
Great success	0.30	$ 600
Moderate success	0.60	300
Failure	0.10	–100

Use Present Process

Outcomes	*Probability*	*Profit (millions)*
Great success	0.50	$ 300
Moderate success	0.30	200
Failure	0.20	–40

Subcontract

Outcomes	*Probability*	*Profit (millions)*
Moderate success	1.00	$250

2-9. Make bid, $142 million

The cost of preparing the contract proposal is $2,000,000. If the company does not make a bid, it will invest in an alternative venture with a guaranteed profit of $30 million. Construct a sequential decision tree for this decision situation and determine whether the company should make a bid.

CASE PROBLEM

Steeley Associates Versus Concord Falls

Steeley Associates, Inc., a property-development firm, purchased an old house near the town square in Concord Falls, where the state university was located. The old house was built in the mid-1800s; Steeley Associates restored it and, for almost a decade, leased it to the university for academic office space. The house was located on a wide lawn and became a town landmark.

However, in 1991, the lease with the university expired and Steeley Associates decided to use the site for high-density student apartments, which would use all the open space. The community was outraged and objected to the town council. The legal counsel for the town spoke with a representative from Steeley and hinted that if Steeley requested a permit, the town would probably reject it. Steeley had reviewed the town building code and felt confident that their plan was within the guidelines, but that did not necessarily mean that they could win a lawsuit against the town to force them to grant a permit.

The principals at Steeley Associates had a series of meetings to review their alternatives. They decided that they had three options: They could request the permit, they could sell the property, or they could request a permit for a low-density office building, which the town had indicated they would not fight. Regarding the last two options, if they sold the house and property, they thought they could get $900,000, whereas if they built a new office building, their return would depend on town business growth in the future. They felt there was a 70 percent chance of future growth, in which case they would see a return of $1,300,000 (over a ten-year planning horizon); if no growth (or erosion) occurred, they would make only $200,000.

If they requested a permit for the apartments, a host of good and bad outcomes would be possible. The immediate good outcome was approval of their permit, which they estimated would result in a return of $3 million. However, they gave that result only a 10 percent chance of occurring. Alternatively, they thought there was a 90 percent chance the town would reject their application, and that would result in another set of decisions.

They could sell the property at that point; however, the rejection of the permit would undoubtedly decrease the value to potential buyers, and they estimate they would only get $700,000. Alternatively, they could construct the office building and face the same potential outcomes as they did earlier—that is, a 30 percent chance of no town growth and a $200,000 return or a 70 percent chance of growth with a return of $1.3 million. A third option was to sue the town. On the surface their case looks good, but the town building code is vague and a sympathetic judge could throw out their suit. Regardless of the outcome, they estimated their possible legal fees to be $300,000, and they felt they had only a 40 percent chance of winning. However, if they did win, they estimate the award will be approximately $1 million, and they would also get their $3 million return for building the apartments. They also estimated that there was a 10 percent chance the suit could linger on in the courts for such a long time that any future return would be negated during their planning horizon and they would incur an additional $200,000 in legal fees.

If they lost the suit, they would then be faced with the same options of selling the property or constructing an office building. However, if the suit were carried this far into the future, they felt as if the selling price they could ask would be somewhat dependent on the town's growth prospects at that time, which they feel they can access at only 50-50. If the town were in a growth mode that far in the future, they thought that $900,000 would be a conservative estimate of the potential sale price, whereas if the town were not growing, they thought $500,000 would be a more likely estimate. Finally, if they constructed the office building, they felt the chance of town growth would be 50 percent, in which case the return would be only $1,200,000, whereas if no growth occurred, they conservatively estimated only a $100,000 return.

1. Request a permit, $1,767,000

2. See Solutions Manual.

1. Perform a decision tree analysis of the Steeley Associates decision situation using expected value and indicate the appropriate decision with this criteria.
2. Indicate the decision you would make and explain your reasons.

REFERENCES

Davis, G. B., *Management Information Systems: Conceptual Foundations, Structure and Development,* New York: McGraw-Hill, 1974.

Edelman, F., "Managers, Computer Systems, and Productivity," *Interfaces* 12, no. 5 (October 1982): 35–46; reprinted from *MIS Quarterly* 5, no. 3 (September 1981).

Holloway, C. A., *Decision Making Under Uncertainty,* Englewood Cliffs, N.J.: Prentice Hall, 1979.

Howard, R. A., "An Assessment of Decision Analysis," *Operations Research,* 28, no. 1 (January–February 1980): 4–27.

Keeney, R. L., "Decision Analysis: An Overview," *Operations Research* 30, no. 5 (September–October 1982): 803–38.

Luce, R. D., and H. Raiffa, *Games and Decisions,* New York: John Wiley, 1957.

Sprague, R. H., and H. J. Watson, "MIS Concepts," *Journal of Systems Management* (January and February 1985).

Turban, E., *Decision Support and Expert Systems,* New York: Macmillan, 1988.

Von Neumann, J., and O. Morgenstern, *Theory of Games and Economic Behavior,* 3d ed., Princeton, N.J.: Princeton University Press, 1953.

Williams, J. D., *The Complete Strategist,* rev. ed., New York: McGraw-Hill, 1966.

SUPPLEMENT

2

LINEAR PROGRAMMING

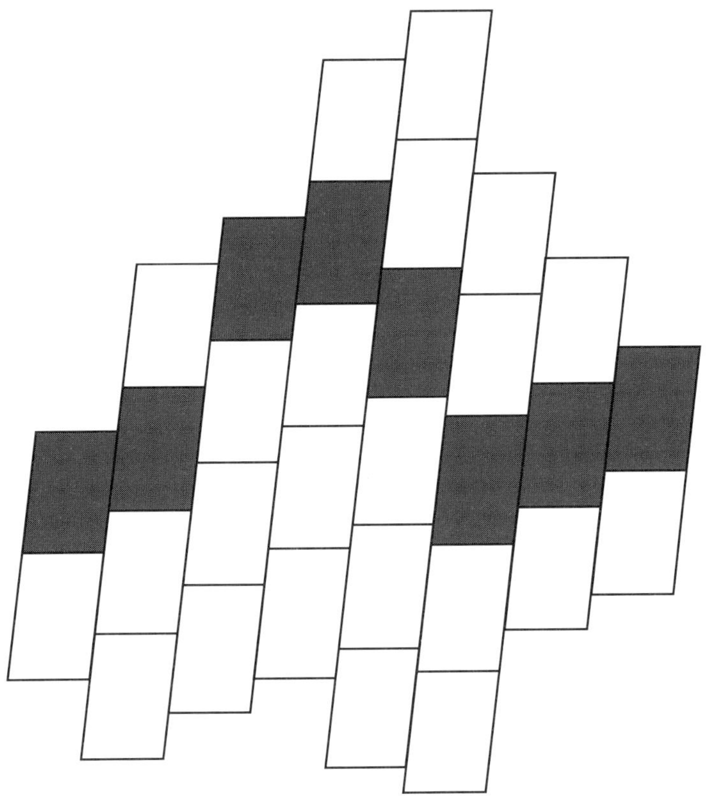

CHAPTER OUTLINE

LINEAR PROGRAMMING

Video S2.1 *COMAP, Program 2: "Juicy Problems"*

Linear programming is one of the most popular and widely used quantitative techniques for operational decision making. In a series of five-year surveys conducted from 1973 to 1988 by the Operations Research Society of America (ORSA), linear programming consistently ranked as the most useful of the quantitative techniques used by businesses and industry practitioners.[1] It has been used, for example, by virtually all major companies in the petroleum industry from the mid-1950s to the present for problems such as blending gasoline and scheduling refineries.[2]

Linear programming is a model consisting of linear relationships representing a firm's objective and resource constraints.

Teaching Note S2.1 Achieving an Objective in a Resource-Constrained Environment

Linear programming is a deterministic (i.e., does not use probabilities) modeling technique. It is used to solve problems in which the general decision is to determine a level of operational activity in order to achieve an objective, subject to restrictions. Many major decisions faced by an operations manager are centered around the best way to achieve the objectives of the firm subject to the restrictions placed on the manager by the operating environment. These restrictions can take the form of limited resources, such as time, labor, energy, materials, or money, or they can be in the form of restrictive guidelines, such as a recipe for making cereal, engineering specifications, or a blend for gasoline. In general, the most frequent objective of business firms is to gain the most profit possible—or, in other words, to *maximize* profit—whereas the objective of individual operational units within a firm (such as a production or packaging department) is often to *minimize* cost.

A common linear programming problem is to determine the number of units of product to produce in order to maximize profit subject to resource constraints such as labor and materials. All these components of the decision situation—the decisions, objectives and constraints—are expressed as mathematically linear relationships that together form a model.

Linear programming, as it is known today, was conceived by George B. Dantzig in 1947 while heading up the Air Force Statistical Control's Combat Analysis Branch at the Pentagon. The military referred to their plans for training, supplying, and deploying combat units as "programs." When Dantzig analyzed Air Force planning problems, he realized they could be formulated as a system of linear inequalities; hence, his original name for the technique was programming in a linear structure, which was later shortened to linear programming.

Teaching Note S2.2 Formulating the Model

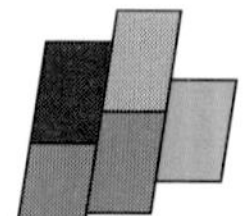

MODEL FORMULATION

Decision variables are mathematical symbols representing levels of activity of an operation.

A linear programming model consists of certain common components, including decision variables, an objective function, and model constraints. **Decision variables** are mathematical symbols that represent levels of activity by the operation.

[1] Lane, M. S., Mansow, A. H., and Harpell, J. L., "Operations Research Techniques: A Longitudinal Update 1973–1988," *Interfaces* 23, no. 2 (March–April 1993): 63–68.

[2] Bodington, C. E., and Baker, T. E., "A History of Mathematical Programming in the Petroleum Industry," *Interfaces* 20, no. 4 (July–August 1990): 117–127.

GAINING THE COMPETITIVE EDGE

A Refinery Linear Programming System at Citgo Petroleum

In 1983 Southland Corporation, the parent company of the 7-Eleven convenience store chain, acquired Citgo Petroleum Corporation. Prior to this acquisition, Citgo had lost money for several years; thus, a primary objective of Southland was to improve Citgo's profitability. The Southland Corporation invested in a number of management science applications to achieve this objective, and one of the largest and most important was a refinery linear programming system. The linear programming system allowed for effective management of crude stock acquisition, processing costs, and energy costs, which were almost $4 billion in 1984. The refinery linear programming system is used routinely to make decisions regarding crude selection and acquisition, refinery run levels, feedstock acquisitions, unit turnaround optics, and hydrocracker conversion. The linear programming system is now one of the primary corporation operational-planning tools. In 1985, Citgo achieved a pretax profit of over $70 million, and the linear programming system was cited as a significant contributor to this turnaround.

Source: Based on D. Klingman et. al., "The Successful Deployment of Management Science throughout Citgo Petroleum Corporation," *Interfaces* 17, no. 1 (January–February 1987): 4–25.

Video S2.2 *TIMS Edelman Award Tape, Program 2: "Citgo Petroleum"*

For example, an electrical manufacturing firm desires to produce radios, toasters, and clocks. The number of each item to produce is represented by symbols, x_1, x_2, and x_3. Thus x_1 = the number of radios, x_2 = the number of toasters, and x_3 = the number of clocks. The final values of x_1, x_2, and x_3, as determined by the firm, constitute a *decision* (e.g., $x_1 = 10$ radios is a decision by the firm to produce 10 radios).

The **objective function** is a linear mathematical relationship that describes the objectives of an operation in terms of the decision variables. The objective function always consists of either *maximizing* or *minimizing* some value (e.g., maximizing the profit or minimizing the cost of producing radios). For example, if the profit from a radio is $6, the profit from a toaster is $4, and the profit from a clock is $2, then the total profit, Z, is defined as $Z = \$6x_1 + 4x_2 + 2x_3$.

The **objective function** is a linear relationship reflecting the objective of an operation.

The model **constraints** are also linear relationships of the decision variables; they represent the restrictions placed on the decision situation by the operating environment. The restrictions can be in the form of limited resources or restrictive guidelines. For example, if it requires 2 hours of labor to produce a radio, 1 hour to produce a toaster, and 1.5 hours to produce a clock, and only 40 hours of labor are available, the constraint reflecting this is $2x_1 + 1x_2 + 1.5x_3 \leq 40$.

A **constraint** is a linear relationship representing a restriction on decision making.

The general structure of a linear programming model is as follows:

Maximize (or minimize) $Z = c_1x_1 + c_2x_2 + \ldots + c_nx_n$

subject to

$$\begin{aligned} a_{11}x_1 + a_{12}x_2 + \ldots + a_{1n}x_n &\ (\leq, =, \geq)\ b_1 \\ a_{21}x_1 + a_{22}x_2 + \ldots + a_{2n}x_n &\ (\leq, =, \geq)\ b_2 \\ &\ \vdots \\ a_{n1}x_1 + a_{n2}x_2 + \ldots + a_{nn}x_n &\ (\leq, =, \geq)\ b_n \\ x_i \geq 0 & \end{aligned}$$

where

x_i = decision variables
b_i = constraint levels
c_j = objective function coefficients
a_{ij} = constraint coefficients

EXAMPLE S2.1

Linear Programming Model Formulation

Problem Statement:

The Beaver Creek Pottery Company is a small craft operation run by a Native American tribal council. The company employs artisans to produce clay bowls and mugs with authentic Native American designs and colors. The two primary resources used by the company are special pottery clay and skilled labor. Given these limited resources, the company wants to know how many bowls and mugs to produce each day in order to maximize profit.

Transparency S2.1 Example S2.1, Model Formulation

The two products have the following resource requirements for production and selling price per item produced (i.e., the model parameters).

	RESOURCE REQUIREMENTS		
PRODUCT	*Labor (h/unit)*	*Clay (lb/unit)*	*Revenue ($/unit)*
Bowl	1	4	40
Mug	2	3	50

There are 40 hours of labor and 120 pounds of clay available each day for production. Formulate this problem as a linear programming model.

Solution:

The decision confronting management in this problem is how many bowls and mugs to produce represented by the following decision variables.

$$x_1 = \text{number of bowls to produce}$$
$$x_2 = \text{number of mugs to produce}$$

The objective of the company is to maximize total revenue computed as the sum of the individual profits gained from each bowl and mug:

$$\text{Maximize } Z = \$40x_1 + 50x_2$$

The model contains the constraints for labor and clay which are

$$x_1 + 2x_2 \le 40 \text{ hr}$$
$$4x_1 + 3x_2 \le 120 \text{ lb}$$

The less than or equal to inequality (≤) is employed instead of an equality (=) because 40 hours of labor is a maximum limitation that *can be used*, not an amount that *must be used*. However, constraints can be equalities (=) or greater than or equal to inequalities (≥).

The complete linear programming model for this problem can now be summarized as follows:

$$\text{Maximize } Z = 40x_1 + 50x_2$$

subject to

$$1x_1 + 2x_2 \le 40$$
$$4x_1 + 3x_2 \le 120$$
$$x_1, x_2 \ge 0$$

The solution of this model will result in numerical values for x_1 and x_2 that maximize total profit, Z, without violating the constraints. The solution that achieves this objective is $x_1 = 24$ bowls and $x_2 = 8$ mugs, with a corresponding revenue of $1,360, the determination of which we will discuss in the following sections.

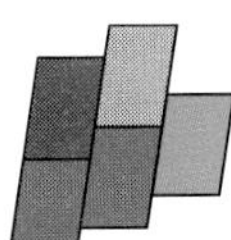

GRAPHICAL SOLUTION METHOD

The linear programming model in the previous section has certain characteristics that are common to all linear programming models: The mathematical relationships are additive, the model parameters are assumed to be known with certainty, the variable values are continuous (not restricted to integers), and the relationships are linear. Because of this last characteristic, linearity, models with two decision variables (corresponding to two dimensions) can be solved graphically. Although graphical solution is not very efficient and is cumbersome, it is useful in that it provides a picture of how a solution is derived.

A picture of how a solution is obtained for a linear programming model

The basic steps in the **graphical solution method** are to plot the model constraints on a set of Cartesian coordinates (i.e., a plane), and identify the area on the graph that satisfies all the constraints simultaneously. The point on the boundary of this space that maximizes (or minimizes) the objective function is the solution. The following example illustrates these steps.

The **graphical solution method** is a method for solving a linear programming problem using a graph.

EXAMPLE S2.2.

Graphical Solution

Problem Statement:

Determine the solution for the Beaver Creek Pottery Company formulated in Example S2.1:

$$\text{Maximize } Z = \$40x_1 + \$50x_2$$

subject to

$$x_1 + 2x_2 \leq 40$$
$$4x_1 + 3x_2 \leq 120$$
$$x_1, x_2, \leq 0$$

Solution:

The graph of the model constraints are shown in the following figure of the feasible solution space. The graph is produced in the positive quadrant since both decision variables must be positive or zero, i.e., $x_1,x_2 \geq 0$.

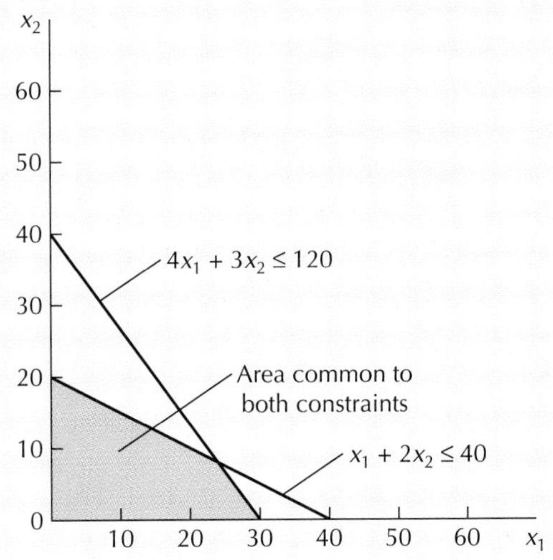

Transparency S2.2 Graphical Solution of Example S2.2

Teaching Note S2.3 Determining the Feasible Solution Space

The **feasible solution space** is an area bounded by the constraint equations.

The first step in drawing the graph of the model is to plot the constraints on the graph. This is done by treating both constraints as equations (or straight lines) and plotting each line on the graph. A simple procedure for plotting each line is to determine the two endpoints on the axis and draw a straight line connecting the points. The shaded area in this figure is the area that is common to both model constraints. Therefore, this is the only area on the graph that contains points (i.e., values for x_1 and x_2) that will satisfy both constraints simultaneously. This area is referred to as the **feasible solution space,** because it is the only area that contains solution values for the variables that are feasible, or do not violate the constraints.

The second step in the graphical solution method is to locate the point in the feasible solution area that will result in the greatest total revenue. To begin the solution analysis, we will first plot the objective function line for an *arbitrarily* selected level of revenue. For example, if revenue, Z, is \$800, the objective function is

$$\$800 = 40x_1 + 50x_2$$

Plotting this line just as we plotted the constraint lines results in the graph showing the determination of the optimal point in the following figure. Every point on this line is in the feasible solution area and will result in a revenue of \$800 (i.e., every combination of x_1 and x_2 on this line will give a Z value of \$800). As the value of Z increases, the objective function line moves out through the feasible solution space away from the origin until it reaches the last feasible point on the boundary of the solution space and then leaves the solution space.

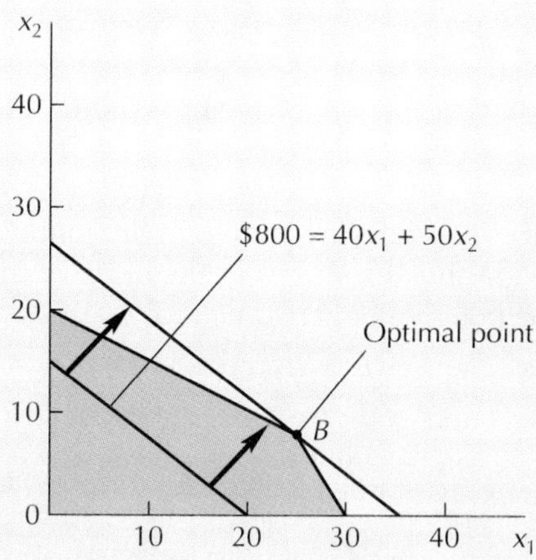

Teaching Note S2.4 Locating the Optimal Extreme Point

Extreme points are corner points on the boundary of the feasible solution space.

The **optimal solution** is the one best solution point.

The solution point is always on this boundary, because the boundary contains the points farthest from the origin (i.e., the points corresponding to the greatest profit). However, the solution point will not only be on the boundary of the feasible solution area, but it will be at one of the *corners* of the boundary where two constraint lines intersect. These corners (labeled *A*, *B*, and *C* in the following figure) are protrusions called **extreme points.** It has been proven mathematically that the optimal solution in a linear programming model will always occur at an extreme point. Therefore, in our example problem, the possible solution points are limited to the three extreme points, *A*, *B*, and *C*, and the **optimal,** or "one best," **solution** point is *B*, since the objective function touches it last as it leaves the feasible solution area.

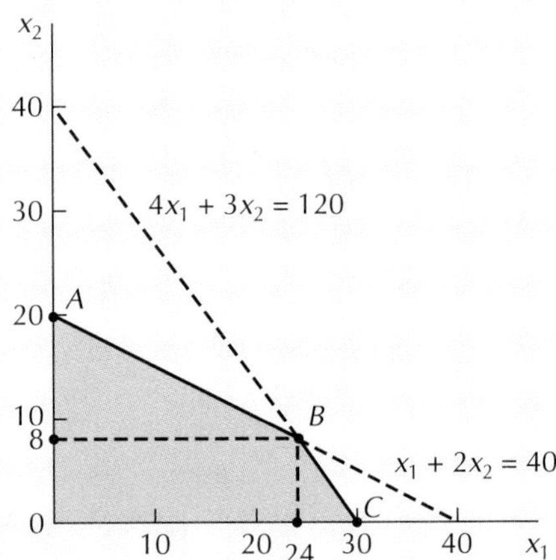

Because point B is formed by the intersection of two constraint lines, these two lines are *equal* at point B. Thus, the values of x_1 and x_2 at that intersection can be found by solving the two equations *simultaneously:*

$$\begin{aligned} x_1 + 2x_2 &= 40 \\ 4x_1 + 3x_2 &= 120 \\ \hline 4x_1 + 8x_2 &= 160 \\ -4x_1 - 3x_2 &= -120 \\ \hline 5x_2 &= 40 \\ x_2 &= 8 \end{aligned}$$

Thus

$$\begin{aligned} x_1 + 2(8) &= 40 \\ x_1 &= 24 \end{aligned}$$

The optimal solution at point B in Figure S2.3 is $x_1 = 24$ and $x_2 = 8$. Substituting these values into the objective function gives the maximum revenue,

$$\begin{aligned} Z &= \$40(24) + 50(8) \\ Z &= \$1{,}360 \end{aligned}$$

Given that the optimal solution will be at one of the extreme corner points A, B, or C you can find the solution by testing each of the three points to see which results in the greatest revenue rather than by graphing the objective function and seeing which point it last touches as it moves out of the feasible solution area. The figure below shows the solution values for all three points A, B, and C and the amount of revenue, Z, at each point.

Teaching Note S2.5 Graphical Solution Methods

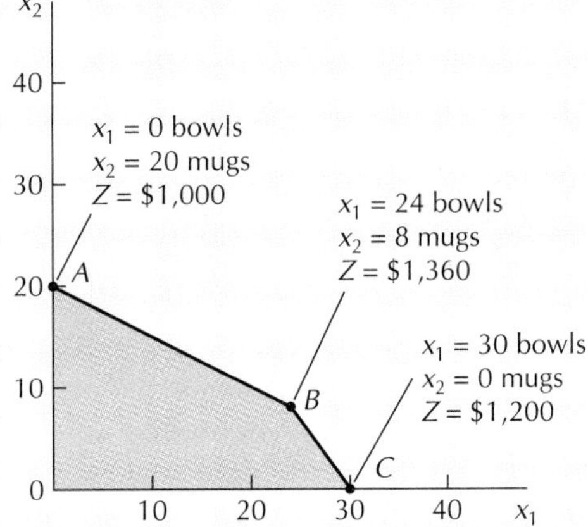

Transparency S2.3 Solutions at All Corner Points

The objective function determines which extreme point is optimal, because the objective function designates the revenue that will accrue from each combination of x_1 and x_2 values at the extreme points. If the objective function had had different coefficients (i.e., different x_1 and x_2 profit values), one of the extreme points other than *B* might have been optimal.

Assume for a moment that the revenue for a bowl is $70 instead of $40 and the revenue for a mug is $20 instead of $50. These values result in a new objective function, $Z = \$70x_1 + 20x_2$. If the model constraints for labor or clay are not changed, the feasible solution area remains the same, as shown in the figure below. However, the location of the objective function in this figure is different from that of the original objective function in the second figure on page 67 because the new profit coefficients give the linear objective function a new *slope*. The change results in point C becoming optimal, with Z = $2,100. This situation demonstrates one of the useful functions of linear programming—and model analysis in general—called *sensitivity analysis:* the testing of changes in the model parameters reflecting different operating environments in order to analyze the impact on the solution.

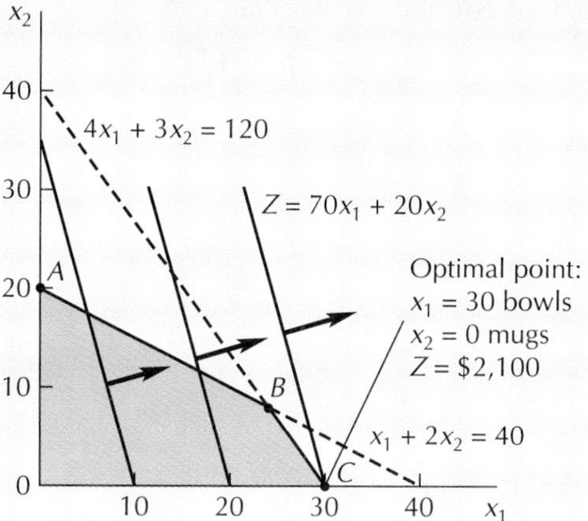

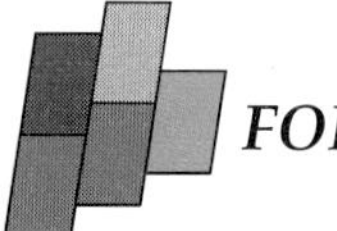

FORMAT FOR MODEL SOLUTION

The Simplex Method

The **simplex method** is a mathematical procedure for solving a linear programming problem according to a set of steps.

Graphically determining the solution to a linear programming model can provide insight into how a solution is derived, but it is not generally an effective or efficient solution approach. The traditional mathematical approach for solving a linear programming problem is a mathematical procedure called the **simplex method.** In the simplex method, the model is put into the form of a table, and then a number of mathematical steps are performed on the table. These mathematical steps replicate the process of moving from one extreme point on the solution boundary to another. However, unlike the graphical method, in which we simply searched through *all* the solution points to find the best one, the simplex method moves from one *better* solution to another until the best one is found, and then it stops.

The simplex method for solving linear programming problems is based, at least partially, on the solution of simultaneous equations and matrix algebra. In this supplement on linear programming we are not going to provide a detailed presentation of the simplex method. It is a mathematically cumbersome approach that is very time-consuming even for very small problems of two or three variables and a few constraints. It includes a number of mathematical steps and requires numerous arithmetic computations, which frequently result in simple arithmetic errors when done by hand. Alternatively, we will demonstrate how linear programming problems are solved on the computer. Depending on the software used, the computer solution to a linear programming problem may be in the same form as a simplex solution. As such, it is necessary for us to review the procedures for setting up a linear programming model in the simplex format for solution.

Converting Model Constraints

Recall that the solution to a linear programming problem occurs at an extreme point where constraint equation lines intersect with each other or with the axis. Thus, the model constraints must all be in the form of *equations* (=) rather than inequalities (≥ or ≤).

Teaching Note S2.6 The Purpose of Adding Slack Variables

The standard procedure for transforming ≤ inequality constraints into equations is achieved by adding a new variable, called a **slack variable,** to each constraint. For the Beaver Creek Pottery Company example, the addition of a unique slack variable (s_i) to each of the constraint inequalities results in the following equations:

A **slack variable** is a variable representing unused resources that is added to a ≤ constraint to make it an equality.

$$x_1 + 2x_2 + s_1 = 40 \text{ hr of labor}$$
$$4x_1 + 3x_2 + s_2 = 120 \text{ lb of clay}$$

The slack variables in these equations, s_1 and s_2, will take on any value necessary to make the left-hand side of the equation equal to the right-hand side. If slack variables have a value in the final solution, they generally represent unused resources. Since unused resources would contribute nothing to total revenue, they have a coefficient of zero in the objective function:

$$\text{Maximize } Z = \$40x_1 + 50x_2 + 0s_1 + 0s_2$$

The graph in Figure S2.1 shows all the solution points in our Beaver Creek Pottery Company example with the values for decision *and* slack variables. This example model is a maximization problem with all ≤ constraints. A minimization problem with ≥ and = constraints requires several different adjustments.

First, with a ≥ constraint, instead of adding a slack variable, we start by subtracting a **surplus variable.** Whereas a slack variable is added and reflects unused resources, a surplus variable is subtracted and reflects the excess above a minimum resource-requirement level. Like the slack variable, a surplus variable is represented symbolically by s_i and must be nonnegative. For example, consider the following constraint:

A **surplus variable** is a variable representing an excess above a resource requirement that is subtracted from a ≤ constraint to make it an equality.

$$2x_1 + 4x_2 \geq 16$$

Transparency S2.4 Extreme Point Solutions with Slack Variables

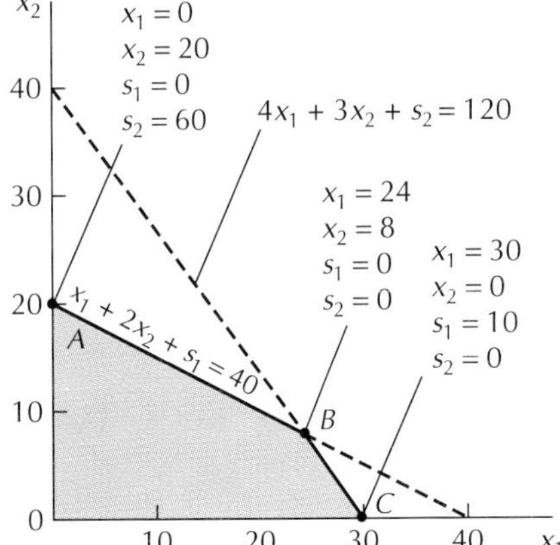

FIGURE S2.1 Solutions at Extreme Points

Subtracting a surplus variable would result in

$$2x_1 + 4x_2 - s_1 = 16$$

However, the simplex method requires that the initial basic feasible solution be at the origin, where x_1 and $x_2 = 0$. Testing these solution values, we have

$$\begin{aligned} 2x_1 + 4x_2 - s_1 &= 16 \\ 2(0) + 4(0) - s_1 &= 16 \\ s_1 &= -16 \end{aligned}$$

The idea of negative resources is illogical and violates the nonnegativity restriction of linear programming.

An *artificial variable* is a variable added to a constraint to give it a positive solution at the origin.

In order to alleviate this difficulty and get a solution at the origin, we add an *artificial variable* (A_i) to the constraint equation:

$$2x_1 + 4x_2 - s_1 + A_1 = 16$$

The artificial variable, A_1, does not have a meaning, as a slack variable or a surplus variable does. It is inserted into the equation simply to give a positive solution at the origin where all other values are zero.

$$\begin{aligned} 2x_1 + 4x_2 + s_1 + A_1 &= 16 \\ 2(0) + 4(0) - 0 + A_1 &= 16 \\ A_1 &= 16 \end{aligned}$$

All variables in a linear programming model must be included in the objective function, thus whenever an artificial variable is added to a ≥ constraint, it must also be included in the model objective function. However, an artificial variable cannot be assigned a profit (or cost) value equal to zero, as would be the case with a slack or surplus variable. Assigning a value of 0 to an artificial variable in the objective function would not prohibit it from being in the final optimal solution. However, if the artificial variable appeared in the solution, it would render the final solution meaningless, since an artificial variable has no meaning. Therefore, we must ensure that an artificial variable is *not* in the final solution. We can prohibit a variable from being in the final solution by assigning it a large negative profit in a maximization problem or a large cost in a minimization problem. Rather than assigning a dollar cost or profit to an artificial variable, the convention is to assign a value of M, representing a very large cost for a minimization problem, or $-M$, representing a very large negative profit (i.e., loss) for a maximization problem.

Next consider the case where a constraint is already an equation, for example,

$$x_1 + x_2 = 30$$

Since this constraint is already an equation it is not necessary to add a slack or subtract a surplus; in fact neither would be possible since the sum of x_1 and x_2 must exactly equal 30. However, the initial solution at the origin $x_1 = 0$, and $x_2 = 0$, is not feasible, i.e., $0 + 0 \neq 30$. In order to rectify this difficulty we can add an artificial variable, just as we did with an ≥ constraint. Now at the origin, where $x_1 = 0$ and $x_2 = 0$, we would have,

$$\begin{aligned} x_1 + x_2 + A_1 &= 30 \\ 0 + 0 + A_1 &= 30 \\ A_1 &= 30 \end{aligned}$$

Any time a constraint is initially an equation, an artificial variable is added.

The following table summarizes the rules for transforming all three types of model constraints

CONSTRAINT	ADJUSTMENT	OBJECTIVE FUNCTION COEFFICIENT	
		Maximization	*Minimization*
$\leq$	Add a slack variable	0	0
$=$	Add an artificial variable	$-M$	M
$\geq$	Subtract a surplus variable	0	0
	and add an artificial variable	$-M$	M

The following example illustrates the formulation of a minimization model with $\geq$ constraints.

EXAMPLE S2.3.

A Minimization Linear Programming Model

Problem Statement:

The Farmer's Hardware and Feed Store is preparing a fertilizer mix for a farmer who is preparing a field to plant a crop. The store will use two brands of fertilizer, Super-Gro and Crop-Quik, to make the proper mix for the farmer. Each brand yields a specific amount of nitrogen and phosphate, as follows.

BRAND	CHEMICAL CONTRIBUTION	
	Nitrogen (lb/bag)	*Phosphate (lb/bag)*
Super-Gro	2	4
Crop-Quik	4	3

The farmer's field requires at least 16 pounds of nitrogen and 24 pounds of phosphate. Super-Gro costs \$6 per bag, and Crop-Quik costs \$3. The store wants to know how many bags of each brand to purchase in order to minimize the total cost of fertilizing.

Formulate a linear programming model for this problem, and solve it using the graphical method.

Solution:

This problem is formulated as follows:

Transparency S2.5 Example S2.3, Model Formulation and Graphical Solution

$$\text{Minimize } Z = \$6x_1 + 3x_2$$

subject to

$$2x_1 + 4x_2 \geq 16 \text{ lb of nitrogen}$$
$$4x_1 + 3x_2 \geq 24 \text{ lb of phosphate}$$
$$x_1, x_2 \geq 0$$

The graphical solution of the problem is shown in the figure on page 72. The conversion of the model constraints and objective function is as follows.

$$\text{Minimize } Z = 6x_1 + 3x_2 + 0S_1 + 0S_2 + MA_1 + MA_2$$

subject to

$$2x_1 + 4x_2 - S_1 + A_1 = 16$$
$$4x_1 + 3x_2 - S_2 + A_2 = 24$$
$$x_1, x_2, S_1, S_2, A_1, A_2 \geq 0$$

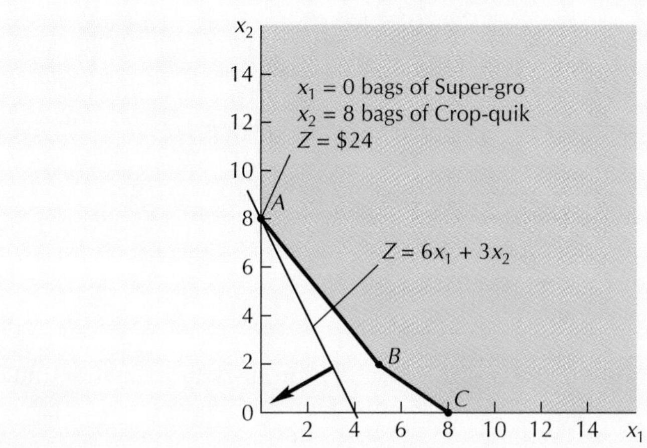

COMPUTER SOLUTION OF LINEAR PROGRAMMING MODELS

Teaching Note S2.7 Computer Solution Versus the Simplex Method

The ability to solve linear programming problems on the computer has greatly enhanced and popularized its use. Manual solution with the simplex method can become very tedious and cumbersome for a model with as few as three variables and five constraints, and most realistic problems are much larger than this. Virtually hundreds of mainframe and microcomputer linear programming software packages and general-purpose quantitative-method software packages that contain linear programming modules are in existence.

Computer solution using AB:POM

The AB:POM computer software package that we introduced in the section of Chapter 2 on decision analysis also includes a module for linear programming problems. Exhibit S2.1 is the solution output screen for Example S2.1.

A *dual value* is the value of one additional unit of a resource.

Notice the values 16 and 6 under the column labeled "Shadow" on the output. They are also called *dual values,* or *shadow prices,* and they reflect the marginal value of the resources in the model. For example, the first constraint is for labor; thus, the shadow price of 16 means that if one additional hour of labor could be secured by the company, it would increase revenue by $16. Likewise, if one additional pound of clay could be secured, it would increase revenue by $6. As a result, $16 and $6 are the marginal values of labor and clay, respectively, for the company. These values are valuable to the operations manager in pricing resources and making decisions about securing additional resources.

Transparency S2.6 AB:POM Computer Solution for Linear Programming

```
                          Linear Programming          Solution
Number of constraints (2-99) 2 Number of variables (2-99) 2
maximize

                           Example S2.1
Options ->  NO step  Cmputr     PrtOFF
                 x1      x2                    RHS
maximize         40      50                             Shadow
const 1           1       2        <          40.00     16.00
const 2           4       3        <         120.00      6.00
Values ->     24.00    8.00                $1,360.00
```

EXHIBIT S2.1 Solution for Example S2.1

SUMMARY

Linear programming is one of several related quantitative techniques that are generally classified as mathematical programming models. Other quantitative techniques that fall into this general category include integer programming, nonlinear programming, goal, or multiobjective, programming, and dynamic programming. These modeling techniques are capable of addressing a large variety of complex operational decision-making problems, and they are used extensively to do so by businesses and companies around the world. Computer software packages are available to solve most of these types of models, which greatly promotes their use.

SUMMARY OF KEY TERMS

constraints: linear relationships of decision variables representing the restrictions placed on the decision situation by the operating environment.

decision variables: mathematical symbols that represent levels of activity of an operation.

extreme points: corner points, or protrusions, on the boundary of the feasible solution space in a linear programming model.

feasible solution space: an area that satisfies all constraints in a linear programming model simultaneously.

graphical solution method: a method for determining the solution of a linear programming problem using a two-dimensional graph of the model.

linear programming: a deterministic modeling technique for general decision situations in which the decision is to determine a level of operational activity in order to achieve an objective subject to restrictions.

objective function: a linear mathematical relationship that describes the objective of an operation in terms of decision variables.

optimal solution: the single best solution to a problem.

simplex method: a series of mathematical steps conducted within a tabular structure for solving a linear programming model.

slack variable: a variable added to a linear programming $\leq$ constraint to make it an equality.

surplus variable: a variable subtracted from a $\geq$ model constraint in a linear programming model in order to make it an equality.

SOLVED PROBLEM

Problem Statement:

A leather shop makes custom-designed, hand-tooled briefcases and luggage. The shop makes a \$400 profit from each briefcase and a \$200 profit from each piece of luggage. (The profit for briefcases is higher because briefcases require more hand-tooling.) The shop has a contract to provide a store with exactly 30 items per month. A tannery supplies the shop with at least 80 square yards of leather per month. The shop must purchase at least this amount but can order more. Each briefcase requires 2 square yards of leather; each piece of luggage requires 8 square yards of leather. From past performance, the shop owners know they cannot make more than 20 briefcases per month. They want to know the number of briefcases and pieces of luggage to produce in order to maximize profit. Formulate a linear programming model for this problem and solve it graphically and using the computer.

Solution:

Step 1: Model formulation

$$\text{Maximize } Z = \$400x_1 + 200x_2$$

subject to

$$x_1 + x_2 = 30 \text{ contracted items}$$
$$2x_1 + 8x_2 \geq 80 \text{ yd}^2 \text{ of leather}$$
$$x_1 \leq 20 \text{ briefcases}$$
$$x_1, x_2 \geq 0$$

where

$$x_1 = \text{briefcases}$$
$$x_2 = \text{pieces of luggage}$$

Step 2: Graphical solution

See the following figure.

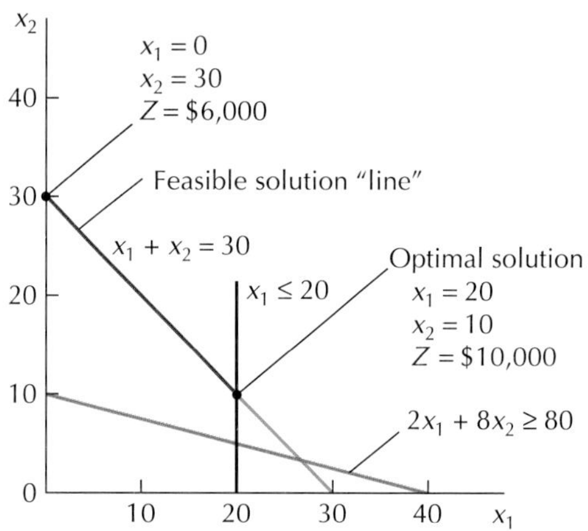

Step 3: Model solution format

The model in proper form for simplex solution is shown as follows.

$$\text{Maximize } Z = 400x_1 + 200x_2 + 0s_1 + 0s_2 - MA_1 - MA_2$$

subject to

$$x_1 + x_2 + A_1 = 30$$
$$2x_1 + 8x_2 - s_1 + A_2 = 80$$
$$x_1 + s_2 = 20$$
$$x_1, x_2, s_1, s_2, A_1, A_1, A_2 \geq 0$$

Step 4: Computer Solution with AB:POM as shown below.

```
                          Linear Programming          Solution
Number of constraints (2-99) 3 Number of variables (2-99) 2
maximize


                          Solved Problem
Options ->  NO step  Cmputr   PrtOFF
                 x1       x2                   RHS
maximize        400      200                             Shadow
const 1           1        1       =          30.00     200.00
const 2           2        8       >          80.00       0.00
const 3           1        0       <          20.00     200.00
Values ->     20.00    10.00               $10,000.00
```

QUESTIONS

2-1. Why is the term *linear* used in the name *linear programming?*

2-2. Describe the steps one should follow in formulating a linear programming model.

2-3. Summarize the steps for solving a linear programming model graphically.

2-4. In the graphical analysis of a linear programming model, what occurs when the slope of the objective function is the same as the slope of one of the constraint equations?

2-5. What are the benefits and limitations of the graphical method for solving linear programming problems?

2-6. What constitutes the feasible solution area on the graph of a linear programming model?

2-7. How is the optimal solution point identified on the graph of a linear programming model?

2-8. Why does the coefficient of a slack variable equal zero in the objective function?

PROBLEMS

S2-1. Irwin Textile Mills produces two types of cotton cloth—denim and corduroy. Corduroy is a heavier grade of cotton cloth and, as such, requires 7.5 pounds of raw cotton per yard, whereas denim requires 5 pounds of raw cotton per yard. A yard of corduroy requires 3.2 hours of processing time; a yard of denim requires 3.0 hours. Although the demand for denim is practically unlimited, the maximum demand for corduroy is 510 yards per month. The manufacturer has 6,500 pounds of cotton and 3,000 hours of processing time available each month. The manufacturer makes a profit of $2.25 per yard of denim and $3.10 per yard of corduroy. The manufacturer wants to know how many yards of each type of cloth to produce to maximize profit.

a. Formulate a linear programming model for this problem.
b. Solve this model using the graphical method.
c. Solve this problem using a computer.

S2-1. a. See Solutions Manual.
b. and c. $x_1 = 456$, $x_2 = 510$, $Z = \$2,607$

S2-2. The Pyrotec Company produces three electrical products—clocks, radios, and toasters. These products have the following resource requirements.

	RESOURCE REQUIREMENTS	
PRODUCT	*Cost/Unit*	*Labor Hours/Unit*
Clock	$ 8	2
Radio	10	3
Toaster	5	2

The manufacturer has a daily production budget of $2,000 and a maximum of 660 hours of labor. Maximum daily customer demand is for 200 clocks, 300 radios, and 150 toasters. Clocks sell for $15, radios, for $20, and toasters, for $12. The company desires to know the optimal product mix that will maximize profit.

a. Formulate a linear programming model for this problem.
b. Solve the problem using a computer.

S2-2. a. See Solutions Manual.
b. $x_1 = 178.57$, $x_3 = 150$, $Z = \$2,478.57$

S2-3. $x_{1b} = 30$, $x_{2a} = 30$, $x_{3c} = 30$, $Z = \$159{,}000$

S2-3. The Roadnet Transport Company has expanded its shipping capacity by purchasing 90 trucks and trailers from a competitor that went bankrupt. The company subsequently located 30 of the purchased trucks at each of its shipping warehouses in Charlotte, Memphis, and Louisville. The company makes shipments from each of these warehouses to terminals in St. Louis, Atlanta, and New York. Each truck is capable of making one shipment per week. The terminal managers have each indicated their capacity for extra shipments. The manager at St. Louis can accommodate 40 additional trucks per week, the manager at Atlanta can accommodate 60 additional trucks, and the manager at New York can accommodate 50 additional trucks. The company makes the following profit per truckload shipment from each warehouse to each terminal. The profits differ as a result of differences in products shipped, shipping costs, and transport rates.

	TERMINAL		
WAREHOUSE	*St. Louis*	*Atlanta*	*New York*
Charlotte	\$1,800	\$2,100	\$1,600
Memphis	1,000	700	900
Louisville	1,400	800	2,200

The company wants to know how many trucks to assign to each route (i.e., warehouse to terminal) to maximize profit. Formulate a linear programming model for this problem and solve using a computer.

S2-4. a. See Solutions Manual.
b. $x_1 = 40$, $Z = \$16{,}000$

S2-4. The Hickory Cabinet and Furniture Company produces sofas, tables, and chairs at its plant in Greensboro, North Carolina. The plant uses three main resources to make furniture—wood, upholstery, and labor. The resource requirements for each piece of furniture and the total resources available weekly are as follows.

	RESOURCE REQUIREMENTS		
FURNITURE PRODUCT	*Wood (lb)*	*Upholstery (yd)*	*Labor (hr)*
Sofa	7	12	6
Table	5	—	9
Chair	4	7	5
Total available resources	2,250	1,000	240

The furniture is produced on a weekly basis and stored in a warehouse until the end of the week, when it is shipped out. The warehouse has a total capacity of 650 pieces of furniture. Each sofa earns \$400 in profit, each table, \$275, and each chair, \$190. The company wants to know how many pieces of each type of furniture to make per week in order to maximize profit.

a. Formulate a linear programming model for this problem.
b. Solve the problem using a computer.

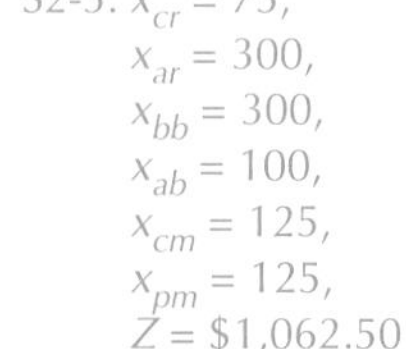
S2-5. $x_{cr} = 75$, $x_{ar} = 300$, $x_{bb} = 300$, $x_{ab} = 100$, $x_{cm} = 125$, $x_{pm} = 125$, $Z = \$1{,}062.50$

★ S2-5. The Oscar Maher meat-processing firm produces wieners from four ingredients: chicken, beef, pork, and a cereal additive. The firm produces three types of wieners: regular, beef, and all meat. The company has the following amounts of each ingredient available on a daily basis:

	Pounds/Day	*Cost/Pound*
Chicken	200	$0.20
Beef	300	0.30
Pork	150	0.50
Cereal additive	400	0.05

Each type of wiener has certain ingredient specifications.

Wiener	*Specifications*	*Selling Price/lb.*
Regular	Not more than 10% beef and pork combined; not less than 20% chicken	$0.90
Beef	Not less then 75% beef	1.25
All meat	No cereal additive; not more than 50% beef and pork combined	1.75

The firm wants to know the amount of wieners of each type to produce in order to maximize profits. Formulate a linear programming model for this problem and solve using a computer.

S2-6. A small metal-parts shop contains three machines—a drill press, a lathe, and a grinder—and has three operators, each certified to work on all three machines. However, each operator performs better on some machines than on others. The shop has contracted to do a big job that requires all three machines. The times required by the various operators to perform the required operations on each machine are summarized below.

S2-6. $x_1 = 1$, $x_5 = 1$, $x_9 = 1$, $Z = 70$

Operator	*Drill Press (min)*	*Lathe (min)*	*Grinder (min)*
1	22	18	35
2	41	30	28
3	25	36	18

The shop manager wants to assign one operator to each machine so that the total operating time for all three operators is minimized. Formulate a linear programming model for this problem and solve using a computer.

S2-7. The Bluegrass Distillery produces custom-blended whiskey. A particular blend consists of rye and bourbon whiskey. The company has received an order for a minimum of 400 gallons of the custom blend. The customer specified that the order must contain at least 40 percent rye and not more than 250 gallons of bourbon. The customer also specified that the blend should be mixed in the ratio of two parts rye to one part bourbon. The distillery can produce 500 gallons per week, regardless of the blend. The production manager wants to complete the order in 1 week. The blend is sold for $12 per gallon. The distillery company's cost per gallon is $4 for rye and $2 for bourbon. The company wants to determine the blend mix that will meet customer requirements and maximize profits.

a. Formulate a linear programming model for this problem.
b. Solve the problem using the graphical method.

S2-7. a. See Solutions Manual.
b. $x_1 = 333.33$, $x_2 = 166.67$, $Z = \$4{,}333.33$

S2-8. A manufacturer of bathroom fixtures produces fiberglass bathtubs in an assembly operation consisting of three processes: molding, smoothing, and

★

S2-8. $x_1 = 15.87$, $x_2 = 9.56$, $x_3 = 11.11$, $Z = \$19,444.45$

painting. The number of units that can be put through each process in an hour is as follows.

Process	*Output (units/hr)*
Molding	7
Smoothing	12
Painting	10

(*Note:* The three processes are continuous and sequential; thus, no more units can be smoothed or painted than have been molded.) The labor costs per hour are \$8 for molding, \$5 for smoothing, and \$6.50 for painting. The company's labor budget is \$3,000 per week. A total of 120 hours of labor is available for all three processes per week. Each completed bathtub requires 90 pounds of fiberglass, and the company has a total of 10,000 pounds of fiberglass available each week. Each bathtub earns a profit of \$175. The manager of the company wants to know how many hours per week to run each process in order to maximize profit. Formulate a linear programming model for this problem and solve using a computer.

S2-9. See Solutions Manual.

★ S2-9. A refinery blends four petroleum components into three grades of gasoline, regular, premium, and low-lead. The maximum quantities available of each component and the cost per barrel are as follows.

Component	*Maximum Barrels Available/Day*	*Cost (barrel)*
1	5,000	\$ 9.00
2	2,400	7.00
3	4,000	12.00
4	1,500	6.00

To ensure that each gasoline grade retains certain essential characteristics, the refinery has put limits on the percentage of the components in each blend. The limits as well as the selling prices for the various grades are as follows.

Grade	*Component Specifications*	*Selling Price (barrel)*
Regular	Not less than 40% of 1	\$12.00
	Not more than 20% of 2	
	Not less then 30% of 3	
Premium	Not less than 40% of 3	18.00
Low-lead	Not more than 50% of 2	10.00
	Not less than 10% of 1	

The refinery wants to produce at least 3,000 barrels of each grade of gasoline. Management wishes to determine the optimal mix of the four components that will maximize profit. Formulate a linear programming model for this problem and solve using a computer.

S2-10. a and b. See Solutions Manual.
c. $x_2 = 50$ bds., $x_4 = 600$ bds., $x_6 = 125$ bds., $Z = 775$ bds. and 675 ft

★ S2-10. The Cash and Carry Building Supply Company has received the following order for boards in three lengths.

Length	*Order (quantity)*
7 feet	700 boards
9 feet	1,200 boards
10 feet	300 boards

The company has 25-foot standard-length boards in stock. Therefore, the standard-length boards must be cut into the lengths necessary to meet order requirements. Naturally, the company wishes to minimize the number of standard-length boards used. The company must, therefore, determine how to cut up the 25-foot boards in order to meet the order requirements and minimize the number of standard-length boards used.

a. Formulate a linear programming model for this problem.
b. When a board is cut in a specific pattern, the amount of board left over is referred to as *trim loss*. Reformulate the linear programming model for this problem, assuming that the objective is to minimize trim loss rather than to minimize the total number of boards used.
c. Solve parts (a) and (b) using a computer.

S2-11. The production manager of Videotechnics Company is attempting to determine the upcoming five-month production schedule for video recorders. Past production records indicate that 2,000 recorders can be produced per month.

An additional 600 recorders can be produced monthly on an overtime basis. Unit cost is $10 for records produced during regular working hours and $15 for those produced on an overtime basis. Contracted sales per month are as follows:

Month	*Contracted Sales (units)*
1	1,200
2	2,100
3	2,400
4	3,000
5	4,000

Inventory carrying costs are $2 per recorder per month. The manager does not want any inventory carried over past the fifth month. The manager wants to know the monthly production that will minimize total production and inventory costs. Formulate a linear programming model for this problem and solve using the computer.

S2-12. The manager of the Ewing and Barnes Department Store has four employees available to assign to three departments in the store: lamps, sporting goods, and linen. The manager wants each of these departments to have at least one employee but not more than two. Therefore, two departments will be assigned one employee and one department will be assigned two. Each employee has different areas of expertise, which are reflected in the following daily sales each employee is expected to generate in each department.

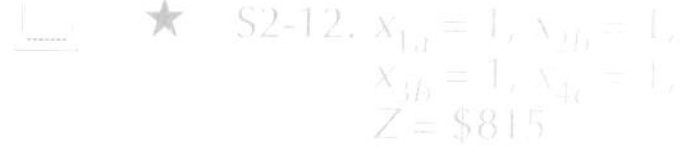

	DEPARTMENT		
Employee	*Lamps*	*Sporting Goods*	*Linen*
1	$130	$150	$ 90
2	275	300	100
3	180	225	140
4	200	120	160

The manager wishes to know which employee(s) to assign to each department in order to maximize expected sales. Formulate a linear programming model for this problem and solve using a computer.

S2-13. $x_1 = 90$, $x_2 = 250$, $x_4 = 175$, $x_5 = 125$, $Z = 640$

S2-13. Mazy's department store has decided to stay open for business on a 24-hour basis. The store manager has divided the 24-hour day into six 4-hour periods and determined the following minimum personnel requirements for each period.

Time	*Personnel Needed*
12:00 P.M. – 4:00 A.M.	90
4:00 A.M.– 8:00 A.M.	215
8:00 A.M.–12:00 A.M.	250
12:00 A.M.– 4:00 P.M.	65
4:00 P.M. – 8:00 P.M.	300
8:00 P.M. –12:00 P.M.	125

Store personnel must report for work at the beginning of one of the given time periods and must work for 8 consecutive hours. The store manager wants to know the minimum number of employees to assign to each 4-hour segment in order to minimize the total number of employees. Formulate a linear programming model for this problem and solve using a computer.

S2-14. $x_b = 200$, $y_1 = \$20{,}000{,}000$, $Z = \$31{,}200{,}000$

S2-14. A company that has a two-year contract to haul ore from an open-pit mine to loading docks needs 200 additional trucks. The company can purchase trucks only at the beginning of the two-year period. Alternatively, the company can lease trucks for $80,000 per year (paid at the beginning of the year). Trucks cost $140,000 each to purchase and have a useful life of two years. They have no salvage value at the end of the two years. The mining company has $8 million cash available to lease and/or buy trucks at the beginning of year 1. In addition, the company can obtain a loan each year for as much as $20 million at 16 percent interest per year. The loan agreement requires that the company repay the borrowed amount plus interest at the end of the year. Each truck will earn $120,000 per year, which becomes part of the flow of cash available to the company for truck leasing and loan repayment. The company wants to minimize the total cost of expanding its fleet of trucks over a two-year period. Formulate a linear programming model for this problem and solve it using a computer.

S2-15. $x_1 = 4$, $x_2 = 2$, $Z = \$22$

S2-15. The Kalo Fertilizer Company makes a fertilizer using two chemicals that provide nitrogen, phosphate, and potassium. The company wants to know how many pounds of each chemical ingredient (x_1 and x_2) to put into a bag of fertilizer to meet minimum requirements for nitrogen, phosphate, and potassium while minimizing cost. The following linear programming model has been developed.

$$\text{Minimize } Z = 3x_1 + 5x_2 \quad \text{(cost, \$)}$$

subject to

$$\begin{aligned} 10x_1 + 2x_2 &\geq 20 \quad \text{(nitrogen, oz)} \\ 6x_1 + 6x_2 &\geq 36 \quad \text{(phosphate, oz)} \\ x_2 &\geq 2 \quad \text{(potassium, oz)} \\ x_1, x_2 &\geq 0 \end{aligned}$$

a. Solve this model graphically.
b. Solve the model using a computer.

S2-16. a. $x_1 = 6$, $x_2 = 3.2$, $Z = \$2{,}720$
b. No labor, 4.8 lb of wood

S2-16. The Pinewood Furniture Company produces chairs and tables from two resources: labor and wood. The company has 80 hours of labor and 36 pounds of wood available each day. Demand for chairs is limited to 6 per day. The company has developed the following linear programming model for determining the number of chairs and tables (x_1 and x_2) to produce each day in order to maximize profit.

$$\text{Maximize } Z = 400x_1 + 100x_2 \quad \text{(profit, \$)}$$

subject to

$$\begin{aligned} 8x_1 + 10x_2 &\leq 80 \quad \text{(labor, hr)} \\ 2x_1 + 6x_2 &\leq 36 \quad \text{(wood, oz)} \\ x_1 &\leq 6 \quad \text{(demand, chairs)} \\ x_1, x_2, &\geq 0 \end{aligned}$$

a. Solve this model graphically.
b. How much labor and wood will be unused if the optimal numbers of chairs and tables are produced?

S2-17. A jewelry store makes necklaces and bracelets from gold and platinum. The store has developed the following linear programming model for determining the number of necklaces and bracelets (x_1 and x_2) to make in order to maximize profit.

S2-17. a. $x_1 = 4$, $x_2 = 3$, $Z = \$2{,}400$
b. No, 1 bracelet
c. \$600, $x_1 = 4$, $x_2 = 3$ and $x_1 = 6$, $x_2 = 0$

$$\text{Maximize } Z = 300x_1 + 400x_2 \quad \text{(profit, \$)}$$

subject to

$$\begin{aligned} 3x_1 + 2x_2 &\leq 18 \quad \text{(gold, oz)} \\ 2x_1 + 4x_2 &\leq 20 \quad \text{(platinum, oz)} \\ x_2 &\leq 4 \quad \text{(demand, bracelets)} \\ x_1, x_2 &\geq 0 \end{aligned}$$

a. Solve this model graphically.
b. The maximum demand for bracelets is 4. If the store produces the optimal number of bracelets and necklaces, will the maximum demand for bracelets be met? If not, by how much will it be missed?
c. What profit for a necklace would result in no bracelets being produced, and what would be the optimal solution for this problem?

S2-18. The Copperfield Mining Company owns two mines, which produce three grades of ore: high, medium, and low. The company has a contract to supply a smelting company with 12 tons of high-grade ore, 8 tons of medium-grade ore, and 24 tons of low-grade ore. Each mine produces a certain amount of each type of ore each hour it is in operation. The company has developed the following linear programming model to determine the number of hours to operate each mine (x_1 and x_2) so that contracted obligations can be met at the lowest cost.

S2-18. $x_1 = 1$, $x_2 = 3$, $Z = \$680$

$$\text{Minimize } Z = 200x_1 + 160x_2 \quad \text{(cost, \$)}$$

subject to

$$\begin{aligned} 6x_1 + 2x_2 &\geq 12 \quad \text{(high-grade ore, tons)} \\ 2x_1 + 2x_2 &\geq 8 \quad \text{(medium-grade ore, tons)} \\ 4x_1 + 12x_2 &\geq 24 \quad \text{(low-grade ore, tons)} \\ x_1, x_2 &\geq 0 \end{aligned}$$

a. Solve this model graphically.
b. Solve the model using a computer.

S2-19. A manufacturing firm produces two products. Each product must go through an assembly process and a finishing process. The product is then transferred to the warehouse, which has space for only a limited number of items. The following linear programming model has been

S2-19. a. $x_1 = 3.3$, $x_2 = 6.7$, $Z = \$568$
b. $-3/7$, $-9/7$

developed for determining the quantity of each product to produce in order to maximize profit.

$$\text{Maximize } Z = 30x_1 + 70x_2 \quad \text{(profit, \$)}$$

subject to

$$\begin{aligned} 4x_1 + 10x_2 &\le 80 \quad \text{(assembly, h)} \\ 14x_1 + 8x_2 &\le 112 \quad \text{(finishing, h)} \\ x_1 + x_2 &\le 10 \quad \text{(inventory, units)} \\ x_1, x_2 &\ge 0 \end{aligned}$$

a. Solve this model graphically.
b. Assume that the objective function has been changed to $Z = 90x_1 + 70x_2$. Determine the slope of each objective function and discuss what effect these slopes have on the optimal solution.

S2-20. $x_3 = 8$, $Z = \$96$ thousand

S2-20. The Eastern Iron and Steel Company makes nails, bolts, and washers from leftover steel and coats them with zinc. The company has 24 tons of steel and 30 tons of zinc. The following linear programming model has been developed for determining the number of batches of nails (x_1), bolts (x_2), and washers (x_3) to produce in order to maximize profit.

$$\text{Maximize } Z = 6x_1 + 2x_2 + 12x_3 \quad \text{(profit, \$1,000s)}$$

subject to

$$\begin{aligned} 4x_1 + x_2 + 3x_3 &\le 24 \quad \text{(steel, tons)} \\ 2x_1 + 6x_2 + 3x_3 &\le 30 \quad \text{(zinc, tons)} \\ x_1, x_2, x_3 &\ge 0 \end{aligned}$$

Solve this model using the computer.

S2-21. $x_1 = 2$, $x_2 = 3$, $Z = \$17$ hundred

S2-21. A custom tailor makes pants and jackets from imported Irish wool. In order to get any wool at all, the tailor must purchase at least 25 square feet each week. Each pair of pants and each jacket requires 5 square feet of material. The tailor has 16 hours available each week to make pants and jackets. The demand for pants is never more than 5 pairs per week. The tailor has developed the following linear programming model to determine the number of pants (x_1) and jackets (x_2) to make each week in order to maximize profit.

$$\text{Maximize } Z = x_1 + 5x_2 \quad \text{(profit, \$100s)}$$

subject to

$$\begin{aligned} 5x_1 + 5x_2 &\ge 25 \quad \text{(wool, ft}^2\text{)} \\ 2x_1 + 4x_2 &\le 16 \quad \text{(labor, hr)} \\ x_1 &\le 5 \quad \text{(demand, pants)} \\ x_1, x_2 &\ge 0 \end{aligned}$$

Solve this model using a computer.

★ ## CASE PROBLEM

See Solutions Manual.

Metropolitan Police Patrol

The Metropolitan Police Department had recently been criticized in the local media for not responding rapidly enough to police calls in the downtown area. In several recent cases, alarms had sounded during break-ins, but by the time the police car had arrived, the perpetrators had left, and in one instance a store owner had been shot. Sergeant Joe Davis had been assigned by the police chief as head of a task force to find a way to determine optimal patrol area (dimensions) for their cars that would minimize the average time it took to respond to a call in the downtown area.

Sergeant Davis solicited help from Angela Maris, an analyst in the operations area for the police department. Together they began to work through the problem.

Sergeant Davis noted to Angela that normal patrol sectors are laid out in rectangles, with each rectangle including a number of city blocks. For illustrative purposes, he defined the dimensions of the sector as x in the horizontal direction and y in the vertical direction. He explained to Angela that cars traveled in straight lines either horizontally or vertically and turned at right angles. Travel in a horizontal direction must be accompanied by travel in a vertical direction, and the total distance traveled is the sum of the horizontal and vertical segments. He further noted that past research on police patrolling in urban areas had shown that the average distance traveled by a patrol car responding to a call in either direction was one-third of the dimensions of the sector, or $x/3$ and $y/3$. He also explained that the travel time it took to respond to a call (assuming a car left immediately upon receiving the call) is simply the average distance traveled divided by the average travel speed.

Angela said that now that she understood how average travel time to a call was determined, she could see that it was closely related to the size of the patrol area. She asked Sergeant Davis if there were any restrictions on the size of the sectors that cars patrolled. He responded that for their city, the department believed the perimeter of a patrol sector should neither be less than 5 miles nor exceed 12 miles. He noted several policy issues and labor constraints that required these specifications. Angela wanted to know if any additional restrictions existed, and Sergeant Davis indicated that the distance in the vertical direction must be at least 50 percent more than the horizontal distance for the sector. He explained that laying out sectors in that manner meant the patrol areas would have a greater tendency to overlap different residential, income, and retail areas than if they ran the other way. He said these areas were layered from north to south in the city. So if a sector were laid out east to west, it would tend to all be in one demographic layer.

Angela indicated she had almost enough information to develop a model, except she also needed to know the average travel speed the patrol cars could travel. Sergeant Davis said cars moving vertically traveled an average of 15 miles per hour, whereas cars traveled horizontally at an average of 20 miles per hour. He said the difference was due to different traffic flows.

Develop a linear programming model for this problem and solve it using the graphical method.

CASE PROBLEM

The Big Country Amusement Park

The Big Country, a large amusement park in Texas, hires high school and college students to work during the summer months of May, June, July, and August. The students run virtually all the highly mechanized rides, are the entertainers, perform most of the custodial work during park hours, make up the work force for the restaurants, food service, retail shops and stores, drive trams, and park cars. Park management has assessed their monthly needs based on the previous summer's attendance at the park and employment patterns. They estimate that during May they will require 32,000 hours of student labor. In June they estimate they will need 48,000 hours, whereas in the peak month of park attendance, July, they will need 64,000 hours. In August attendance begins to decline, so they believe they will need only 48,000 hours.

Because the student employees are so visible, especially to parents, who are the park's biggest spenders and the most frequent return visitors, it is important that they are friendly, are well mannered, are well groomed, and are knowledgeable about their own jobs and the park as a whole. The park also has a policy of requiring the students to know multiple jobs, both as a hedge against absenteeism and to keep the students from getting bored and lackadaisical. Students typically work three or four different jobs in a single day. Because of all these job requirements, management provides a month of training before a student can work regularly at the park. As a result, the students must be hired at least 1 month before they are needed. Also, during their 1-month training period, each student requires 50 hours of direct supervision by an experienced employee (i.e., a student who has already completed the training period). During these 50 hours, the experienced employee is not available for work.

After the training period is completed, a student employee can work only 160 hours per month. Since the park is open every day, this means students will always work less than an eight-hour day and no more than 40 hours per week, eliminating any overtime for management. If more employees are available than are actually needed, each employee simply works less than 160 hours; no one is laid off. The park management feels this is a necessary condition of employment, since so many of the students move to the area during the summer just to work in the park. If anyone were laid off and had rent payments, travel home, etc., it would undoubtedly hurt employment efforts in the future.

Although the park does not lay off people, 15 percent of all experienced employees quit each month for a variety of reasons, including homesickness, illness, and personal reasons. However, one of the stipulations of employment is that the student agrees to work out the month in which he or she quits. The park pays the students on a 2-week delayed basis, and anyone who violates this agreement forfeits that pay.

The salary of an experienced employee is $800 per month, and the salary of a trainee is $500 per month. The park picks 250 of its best student employees from the previous summer to start out at the beginning of May.

The personnel manager at the park would like to know how many students to hire and train through July in order to minimize total salary costs.

1. Formulate a linear programming model for this problem.
2. Solve this model using a computer.

1. See Solutions Manual.
2. $x_1 = 250$, $x_2 = 335.8$, $x_3 = 400$, $x_4 = 340$, $y_1 = 123.3$, $y_2 = 114.6$, $Z = \$1,757,472$

REFERENCES

Charnes, A., and W. W. Cooper, *Management Models and Industrial Applications of Linear Programming*, New York: John Wiley, 1961.

Dantzig, G. B., *Linear Programming and Extensions*, Princeton, NJ: Princeton University, 1963.

Gass, S., *Linear Programming*, 4th ed., New York: McGraw-Hill, 1975.

Moore, L. J., S. M. Lee, and B. W. Taylor, *Management Science*, 4th ed., Needham Heights, MA: Allyn and Bacon, 1993.

Taylor, B. W., *Introduction to Linear Programming*, 4th ed., Needham Heights, Mass.: Allyn and Bacon, 1993.

Wagner, A. M., *Principles of Operations Research*, 2d ed., Englewood Cliffs, N.J.: Prentice Hall, 1975.

3
QUALITY MANAGEMENT

CHAPTER OUTLINE

IBM's Rochester plant shown here won the 1990 Malcolm Baldrige National Quality Award. IBM used the Baldrige award criteria and its own experiences in winning this award at Rochester to establish its corporate-wide Market Driven Quality (MDQ) Plan for competing in an international business environment through the 1990s. Many U.S. companies now use the Baldrige award criteria as guidelines to help them establish their own total quality management program.

MARKET-DRIVEN QUALITY AT IBM

IBM initiated its market-driven quality (MDQ) plan in 1990 as a renewed approach to competing in a changing international business environment. The ultimate goal of the program was to achieve 100 percent customer satisfaction. IBM examined more than 50 companies around the world that were known for high quality, including Milliken, Xerox, Motorola, and American Express, discovering that all perceived the quest for quality as a continuing, never-ending process. Additionally, all the companies borrowed the best ideas from each other. The MDQ plan includes three basic components: a quality self-assessment system, a process review system for constantly improving basic company business processes, and a set of five quality initiatives. The quality self-assessment system was adapted from the Malcolm Baldrige National Quality Award criteria and IBM Rochester's experiences as winners of this award in 1990. It measures and compares IBM's quality against internal and external standards over time. The process review system analyzes all systems to see where changes are needed. It requires that every IBM employee examine their own individual process or function for improvement. Quality initiatives include defining market needs, eliminating defects, and reducing cycle time for all functions (not just manufacturing), empowering employees to use their own initiative and talent to improve quality, and measuring progress in quality improvement for every function and unit. Regarding this last initiative, IBM established as an overall corporate goal the reduction of defects from 66,800 defects per million operations in 1990 to 3.4 defects per million by 1994. Achievement of this goal required a tenfold improvement in quality in 1991 and an improvement of ten times that by the end of 1993, leading to the final goal in 1994. During the 1980s, IBM improved quality by a factor of two; however, in the first two years of MDQ, IBM tripled quality improvement and achieved a sixfold improvement by 1992, an impressive achievement, although it fell short of the goal.[1]

Quality is a major focal point throughout this text. We emphasize its importance in the context of all the operational functions discussed in the text's chapters. The reason for this emphasis is simple: The importance of quality in today's international business environment is paramount. It cannot be underestimated or overlooked by any business firm, regardless of its size or assets. Business leaders and CEOs frequently cite quality as the most important factor in the long-term profitability and success of their firms.

Quality has become pervasive in our everyday life. We are exposed to it in a variety of forms, from product advertising with slogans like "Putting Quality on the Road" (General Motors) and "Quality is Job 1" (Ford) to newly coined phrases such as "quality of life" and "quality time." One almost gets the impression that the "pursuit of quality" would amply fit the U.S. lifestyle (and consumer) as this century draws to a close.

Teaching Note 3.1 Quality After World War II

Teaching Note 3.2 Made in Japan

The changing business environment of the 1970s: quality and foreign competition.

Why has quality become such a pervasive notion and become so important to businesses and consumers around the world? In the period following World War II, when the consumption of goods and services expanded dramatically in the United States, quality was neither a focal point nor a matter of overriding concern to consumers or producers. When consumers purchased U.S. goods and services, they assumed they were getting the best products available; that they were of good quality was accepted without question. "Made in Japan" was a term of derision. However, during the 1970s this business environment began to change, and the single most important factor that facilitated this change was foreign competition. Foreign companies, especially those from Japan, began to gain inroads in U.S. markets, primarily in markets for manufactured goods and electronic products. Consumers began to have more choices and, importantly, more information to help them make these choices. This resulted in higher expectations for products from consumers. Consumers found themselves in a position where they could demand—and expect to receive—products of high quality that were reliable and were priced affordably and competitively. In this new environment of increased

[1]Bemowski, K., "Big Q at Big Blue," *Quality Progress* 24, no. 5 (1991): 17–21; Akers, J.F., "World-Class Quality: Nothing Less Will Do," *Quality Progress* 24, no. 10 (1991): 26–27.

competition from foreign companies, quality has become not only a very real entity that allows for product discrimination, it also has become a potent marketing weapon.

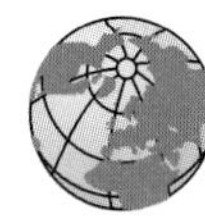

Quality was not the sole or even the predominant reason for the initial Japanese success in the U.S. market. High-quality products from foreign firms such as Rolls Royce and Mercedes Benz automobiles and Hasselblad cameras had been available in the United States for a number of years but had not altered consumers' preferences or perceptions. However, these products were very expensive, whereas Japanese products were more competitively priced. The Japanese were uniquely able to establish the concept of *value,* or the combination of price plus quality, and effectively change their product-design philosophy such that the cost of achieving better quality was not prohibitive.

Value: The combination of price plus quality.

How were Japanese firms able, in such a short period of time, to change their image from producers of inferior quality products to producers of high-quality products? The reasons are varied and complex; some were the result of fortuitous happenstance. A prolonged gasoline shortage in the mid-1970s turned consumer's attention to automobiles with high gas mileage at about the same time that the Honda Accord was being introduced in the United States, consequently Americans were introduced to the concept of high performance standards in Japanese cars. The growing media attention to consumer issues, particularly quality (exemplified by publications such as *Consumer Reports*), consumer advocates such as Ralph Nader, and various consumer affairs' shows and segments on radio and television provided consumers with information about the quality of products that was not previously available. However, the most important factor in changing consumer perspectives was that foreign competitors, and especially the Japanese, were able to produce goods equal or superior in quality to U.S. goods at a very competitive price; through word of mouth, effective marketing, and fortuitous circumstances, the U.S. consumer became quality and value conscious.

Japan adopted fundamentals of quality management from the United States.

The Japanese achieved enhanced product quality by adapting many of the principles of quality management originally developed in the United States, combined with their own management philosophies. As a competitive reaction, American firms have focused attention on quality as possibly the most important factor in their long-term profitability and survival. In this chapter we discuss some of the more prominent aspects of quality management that are now popular, as they apply to business organizations. In Chapter 4, "Statistical Quality Control," we present some of the classical technical procedures for monitoring and controlling quality within the production process. We begin this chapter by attempting to define quality.

THE MEANING OF QUALITY

What is quality?

In response to the question "What is quality?" one of our students said it is "getting what you pay for." Another student quickly added that to her, quality was "getting *more* than you paid for!" The *Oxford American Dictionary* defines quality as "a degree or level of excellence." The "official" definition of quality by the American National Standards Institute (ANSI) and the American Society for Quality Control (ASQC) is "the totality of features and characteristics of a product or service that bears on its ability to satisfy given needs." It is obvious that quality can be defined in many ways, depending on who is defining it and to what product or service it is related. In this section we attempt to gain a perspective on just what quality means to consumers and different people within a business organization.

Quality from the Consumer's Perspective

The objective of a business organization is to produce goods and services that meet their customers' needs. Quality is rapidly becoming a major factor (if not the primary factor) in a customer's choice of products and service. Customers now perceive that certain companies produce better-quality products than others, and they make decisions about which products to purchase accordingly. An important consideration, then, in producing quality products is how consumers make judgments as to what constitutes good quality; that is, how does the consumer define quality? The consumer can be a manufacturer purchasing raw materials or parts, a store owner or retailer purchasing products to sell, or someone who purchases retail products. W. Edwards Deming, the internationally famous author and consultant on quality, has made the frequent observation that "The consumer is the most important part of the production line. Quality should be aimed at the needs of the consumer, present and future." From this perspective, product quality is determined by what the consumer wants and is willing to pay for. Since individual consumers have different product needs and requirements, they will have different quality expectations. This results in a commonly used definition of quality as a product's *fitness for its intended use,* or **fitness for use.** In other words, how well does the product do what the consumer or user thinks it is supposed to do and wants it to do?

Fitness for use is how well the product does what it is supposed to.

Products are designed with intentional differences in quality to meet the different wants and needs of individual consumers. A Porshe and a Jeep are equally "fit for use," in the sense that they both provide automobile transportation for the consumer, and each product may meet the quality standards of its individual purchaser. However, the two products have obviously been designed differently for different types of consumers. This is commonly referred to as the **quality of design,** which is the degree to which quality characteristics are designed into the product. Although designed for the same use, the Porshe and Jeep differ in their performance, features, size, and various other quality characteristics.

Quality of design involves designing quality characteristics into a product.

David Garvin[2] has identified eight *dimensions of quality,* or product-quality characteristics, for which the consumer looks in a product.

Dimensions of quality for which a consumer looks

Transparency 3.1 Eight Dimensions of Quality

1. *Performance:* The basic operating characteristics of a product, for example, how well a car handles or its gas mileage.
2. *Features:* The "extra" items added to the basic features, such as a stereo CD or a leather interior in a car.
3. *Reliability:* The probability that a product will operate properly within an expected time frame.
4. *Conformance:* The degree to which a product meets preestablished standards.
5. *Durability:* How long the product lasts; its life span before replacement.
6. *Serviceability:* The ease of getting repairs, the speed of repairs, and the courtesy and competence of the repair person.
7. *Aesthetics:* How a product looks, feels, sounds, smells, or tastes.
8. *Other perceptions:* Subjective perceptions based on brand name, advertising, etc.

These quality characteristics are weighed by the customer relative to the cost of the product. In general, consumers will pay for the level of quality that they can afford. If consumers feel like they are getting what they paid for, then they tend to be satisfied with the quality of the product.

All the product characteristics just mentioned are important and must be considered in the product's design in order to meet the consumer's expectations for quality. This requires that a company, through its marketing department or some other avenue, accurately assess what the consumer wants and needs. Consumer research to determine what kind of products are desired and the level of quality

[2]Garvin,D.A., "What Does Quality Really Mean," *Sloan Management Review* 26, no. 1 (1984): 25–43.

that is expected is an important, major function of a company's quality management program. Once consumer needs and wants have been determined by marketing, they are then incorporated into the design of the product, and it is up to operations to ensure that the design is properly implemented, resulting in the final products that the consumers want at the quality level expected.

Quality from the Producer's Perspective

Quality of conformance is making sure the product is produced according to design.

A second point of view of quality derives from the producer's (or manufacturer's) vantage point. We have already mentioned how product development is a function of the level of quality characteristics (i.e., the product's fitness for use) that the consumer wants, needs, and can afford. Product design results in design specifications that, it is to be hoped, will achieve the desired quality characteristics. However, once the product design has been determined, the producer perceives quality to be how effectively the production process is able to conform to the specifications required by the design. This concept is referred to as the **quality of conformance.** Put another way, quality during the production process focuses on making sure that the product meets the specifications required by the design.

As an example of the quality of conformance, consider new tires that should be rounded within certain specifications. If they do not conform to specifications, the tires wobble. If a soft-drink bottle does not hold the volume of liquid it is designed to hold, it does not conform to specifications. If a hotel room is not clean when a guest checks in, the hotel is not functioning according to the specifications of its design; it is a faulty service. From this producer's perspective, good-quality products are ones that conform to specifications (i.e., they are well made),

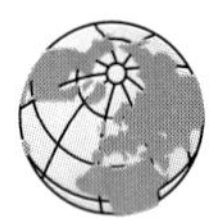

GAINING THE COMPETITIVE EDGE

Reflecting Customer Preferences at Germany's Rational Company

Rational is a German manufacturer of professional ovens for chefs and restaurants. The company is the exclusive producer of an oven that roasts, steams, bakes, stews, and poaches all in one unit. It combines dry heat for baking and roasting in combination with steam heat, hence its name, "combi-oven steamer." The oven sells for between \$6,000 and \$30,000 and is recognized around the world as the state-of-the-art restaurant cooking oven. Rational is the only producer of this type of oven, and the oven is their only product.

Rational reflects a trait of many German companies by combining sophisticated electronic and manufacturing technology with computer software and artisanry in a product that is recognized as top of the line in terms of quality and simplicity of use. The company's motto is posted approximately every 10 feet in the company's manufacturing plant. It is "Gut genug? Der kunde entscheidet!" which translates as, "Good enough? The customer will decide!" In order to find out what the customer wants, Rational employs eight professional chefs as part of its research and development department. These chefs are constantly on the road, visiting current and potential customers and learning what is wrong with their product, what features chefs would like, and how to improve the product. If something goes wrong with an oven, the company sends a researcher from the R&D department to listen and learn directly from the customer instead of having a member of the sales force relay the problem. Out of 300 total employees at Rational, 38 are in research and development, reflecting their commitment to continuous improvement of their product according to their customers' needs and wants.

Source: Based on Peters, Tom (narrator), "Germany's Quality Obsession." Video co-produced by The Tom Peters group, KERA, and Video Publishing House, Inc. Copyright: Video Publishing House, Inc., and Excell, A California Partnership, 1991.

whereas poor-quality products are not made well (i.e., they do not conform to specifications).

The ability to achieve quality of conformance is a function of a number of factors in the production process. These factors include the design of the production process itself (distinct from the product design), the performance level of machinery and equipment, the materials used, the training and supervision of operators, and the degree to which statistical quality control techniques are used. When machines fail or are maladjusted, when operators make mistakes, when material and parts are defective, and when supervision is lax, design specifications are generally not met. Key personnel in achieving conformance to specifications include the engineering staff and production supervisors and managers.

Achieving quality of conformance involves design, equipment, materials, training, supervision, and control.

In our previous discussion we noted that an important consideration from the consumer's perspective of product quality is the product price. Alternatively, from the producer's perspective an important consideration is achieving quality of conformance at an acceptable cost. Product cost is also an important design specification. If the production process cannot produce items at a cost that conforms to the product price, then the consumer will not perceive that the final product has acceptable value; that is, the price is more than the customer is willing to pay for the quality characteristics of the product. The quality characteristics included in the product design must be balanced against production costs.

In our effort to define the meaning of quality we approached quality from two perspectives, that of the consumer and that of the producer. However, it is important to recognize that these two perspectives are not independent of each other. Although product design is customer-motivated, it cannot be achieved without the coordination and participation of the production process. When a product is designed independently of production considerations, it may prove to be impossible for the production process to meet design specifications or so costly to do so that the final product must be priced prohibitively high.

Figure 3.1 summarizes our discussion of the meaning of quality from the consumer's and producer's perspectives. At the end of the diagram, note that the final determination of quality is "fitness for use," which you will recall is the consumer's view of quality. This is a natural conclusion, since ultimately it is the consumer who makes the final judgment regarding quality, and so it is the consumer's view that must be dominant.

Transparency 3.2 The Meaning of Quality

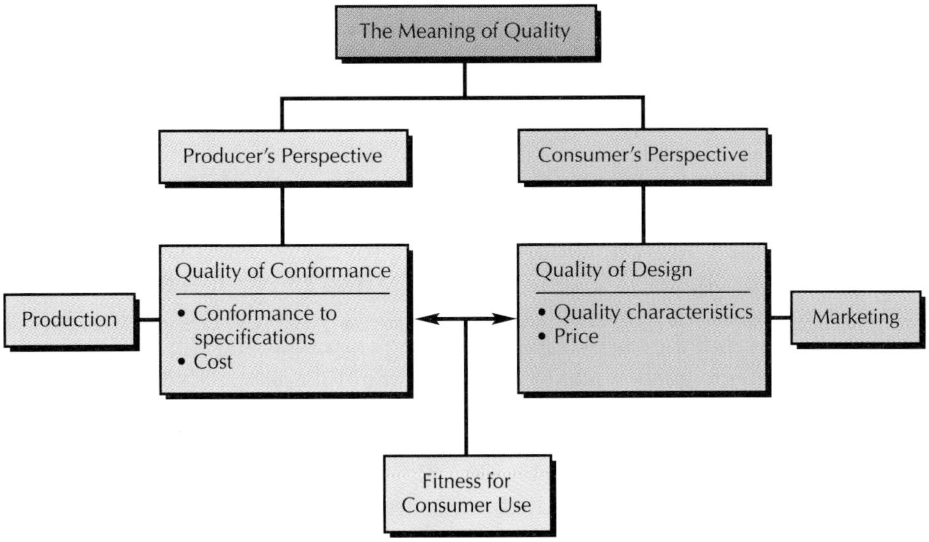

FIGURE 3.1 The Meaning of Quality

TOTAL QUALITY MANAGEMENT

In the previous section we approached quality from two perspectives, the consumer's and the producer's. In this section we explore how quality is managed in a business organization. Thus, our focus will be from the producer's perspective—on the production process and achieving quality of conformance. The production process is used here in a broad context to mean the conversion of resources (of any type) into goods and services; all the functions of a business that combine in the production process form the production system. In order to assure that the quality levels designed into products are achieved, a commitment to quality throughout the production system is required; that is, a systems approach to quality must be used. This approach to the management of quality throughout the entire production system—and thus the business organization—has evolved into what is currently referred to as **total quality management,** or **TQM.**

Total quality management is the management of quality throughout the organization.

The Evolution of Total Quality Management

Quality assurance was introduced at Bell Labs in the 1920s and is the management of quality throughout the organization.

The term **quality assurance** was first used at Bell Telephone Laboratories during the 1920s by a group of early pioneers in the field, including George Edwards, Harold Dodge, and Walter Shewhart. Many of the technical methods for statistical quality control, such as control charts and sampling techniques, were developed by these individuals. For almost five decades these technical methods formed the foundation for quality assurance, but in the early 1970s the focus of quality changed from the technical aspects to more of a managerial philosophy. Today, when the term quality assurance is used, it refers to a commitment to product or service quality throughout an entire organization, inclusive of all business functions. It is, generally speaking, any activity in a company aimed at providing quality goods and services to consumers.

Total quality control is a companywide commitment by management and employees to improving quality.

Over a decade ago A. V. Feigenbaum introduced the term **total quality control** to reflect a total commitment of effort on the part of management and employees throughout an organization to improving quality. A primary precept of total quality control is strong leadership from top management to improve quality and make it a continual process. The Japanese subsequently adopted this concept, referring to it as *companywide quality control.* Although the word *total* was replaced by *companywide,* the concept is the same—that all employees at all levels of the organization, led by top management, are responsible for quality. Furthermore, quality improvement is a continual process, giving rise to the term *continuous improvement,* which has become a fundamental principle of quality management.

In recent years the expression *TQM* has become popular. It embodies the same basic principles as quality assurance, total quality control, and companywide quality control. TQM emphasizes top management's predominant role in leading a total quality effort on which all employees at all levels must focus. All employees are responsible for continuous quality improvement, and that quality is the focal point of all organizational functions. TQM also emphasizes that quality is a strategic issue. The organization must determine what the customer wants in terms of quality and then use strategic planning encompassing all functional areas to achieve strategic goals related to quality. From this perspective, quality is the most important company issue. Because of its emphasis on the long-term strategic management aspects of quality, some individuals and companies consider TQM to be less concerned with the technical "control" aspects of quality than the more traditional approach embodied in quality assurance. However, this may be drawing too fine a line between obviously similar philosophies.

Principles of Total Quality Management

The different terms used to refer to an organization's approach to quality can be confusing. As noted, in many ways they mean the same thing and embody many of the same concepts. The same key terms are common to all: strategic goal, total commitment, continuous improvement, comprehensive focus, employee responsibility, job training, etc. In general, total quality management represents a set of management principles that focus on quality improvement as the driving force in all functional areas and at all levels in a company. These principles can be summarized as follows:

Transparency 3.3 The Principles of TQM

1. The customer defines quality, and the customer's needs are paramount.
2. Top management must provide the leadership for quality.
3. Quality is a strategic issue and a primary focus of strategic planning.
4. Quality is the responsibility of all employees at all levels of the organization.
5. All functions of the company must focus on continuous quality improvement to achieve strategic goals.
6. Quality problems are solved through cooperative effort involving employees and management.
7. Problem solving and continuous quality improvement are based on the use of statistical quality control methods.
8. Training and education of all employees are the basis for continuous quality improvement.

TQM Principles: Customer-defined quality, management leadership, strategic planning, employee responsibility, continuous improvement, cooperative effort, control, and training.

The general perception in the United States and even among the Japanese has been that cultural differences are a key factor in keeping U.S. companies from duplicating Japanese successes. However, irrefutable evidence exists to the contrary that management principles such as those embodied in TQM are the key determinants in achieving quality. Motorola, Nissan, and Honda plants in the United States are examples of Japanese companies following Japanese management principles with U.S. workers and managers, yet still achieving significantly higher quality than their competitors. There are other similar examples of U.S. companies, such as IBM, Xerox, Federal Express, and Ford, achieving success in quality improvement from applying TQM or similar management principles and practices.[3]

Japanese success is due to quality management practices, not cultural differences.

Thus, management principles and practices are the key to success in quality improvement. The approach embodied in TQM is that quality is built into the product by improving all activities in the production process from design to marketing. In the next few sections we briefly discuss how quality management impacts on the various functions that make up the production process.

Teaching Note 3.3 Operational Functions and Quality Management

Marketing, Sales, and Consumer Research

The marketing, sales, and research area of a business firm represents the primary point of contact with the consumer. The marketing staff is typically responsible for the consumer research that determines the quality characteristics that consumers want and need and the price they are willing to pay for the quality level that meets their fitness-for-use criteria. The sales force provides feedback information through its interaction with the consumer. This information is a primary determinant of product design. Marketing also has the responsibility of informing the consumer about the quality characteristics of a product—that is, that it meets their fitness-for-use criteria—through advertising and promotion. In many companies a research and development (R&D) department will explore new ideas for products and be actively involved in product innovation. R&D will use feedback and input from marketing to generate ideas for new products and product features.

Marketing, R&D, and consumer research help define what the customer wants.

[3]Flynn, B. B., "Managing for Quality in the U.S. and Japan," *Interfaces* 22, no. 5 (1992): 69–80.

Engineering creates the product design based on what the customer wants.

Teaching Note 3.4 Recycling

Teaching Note 3.5 Design Teams

Engineering and Product Design

The engineering staff is responsible for translating the product quality characteristics determined by marketing and top management into a product design, including technical specifications, material and parts requirements, equipment requirements, workplace and jobs design, and operator training and skills. This function must determine if the firm possesses the technology capable of conforming to quality specifications for the product demanded by the consumer, including overall product cost. Overdesigning the product such that it exceeds the consumer's fitness-for-use criteria is a drain on the company's resources and can erode profits, whereas underdesigned products will generally not meet the customer's quality expectations.

Genichi Taguchi, the well-known Japanese quality expert, estimates that poor product design is the cause of as much as 80 percent of all defective items. Because the Japanese recognize that it is much cheaper and easier to make changes at the design stage than at the production stage or after a product has been marketed, they focus on quality at all stages of the design process.[4]

Purchasing

Purchased materials have historically accounted for about 50 percent of U.S. and about 70 percent of Japanese manufacturing costs,[5] and most manufacturers purchase more than 50 percent of their parts.[6] As such, the purchasing function plays a crucial role in quality management. Purchasing must make sure that the parts and materials required by the product specifications are of the desired quality. Recall the old adage, "You can't make a silk purse out of a sow's ear." If poor-quality parts and materials are used in the production process, the final product will almost assuredly be of poor quality.

Selecting vendors that will provide quality parts, material, and service is essential.

Purchasing must select vendors that share the company's commitment to quality and that maintain their own quality assurance program for providing good quality materials and parts. As part of the traditional purchasing function, the company—through the *receiving* department—monitors the quality of incoming parts and materials. Statistical quality control techniques (described in Chapter 4) are used to accomplish this. However, under TQM a partnership exists between the supplier and the company. In this partnership the company expects and, in fact, demands that the supplier monitor its own quality so that it is unnecessary for the company to inspect incoming parts and materials. The supplier, in effect, becomes an integral part of the company's quality management program and is subject to the same quality goals and responsibilities as the other functional areas. More and more suppliers are recognizing that they must adopt TQM principles in order to do business with companies that have become quality conscious. In a very competitive global economy, this means that American suppliers often must adopt TQM principles and practices in order to do business with countries around the world. This is an important aspect of international quality certification known as ISO 9000, which we discuss at the end of this chapter.

In the past many manufacturing companies have purposefully purchased a part or material from a variety of different suppliers, and suppliers have contracted with a number of different firms. It was not unusual for a company to limit their purchases of a part from any single supplier to a maximum percentage, for example, 10 or 15 percent. The logic behind this practice was that the company would not be dependent on the uncertain performance of any one supplier. If a supplier was unable to meet delivery schedules, delivered a poor-quality batch, or

[4]Flynn, Barbara B., "Managing for Quality in the U.S. and in Japan," *Interfaces* 22, no. 5 (1992): 69–80.

[5]Reddy, J., and Berger, A., "Three Essentials of Product Quality," *Harvard Business Review* 61, no. 4 (1983): 153–9.

[6]Cole. R. E., "The Japanese Lesson in Quality," *Technology Review* 83, no. 7 (1981): 29–40.

even went out of business, the effect on the customer would be dampened by the other suppliers. However, TQM practices have resulted in a new approach called *single-sourcing*.

Single-sourcing limits suppliers to gain more control over quality.

With single-sourcing, a company purchases a particular part or material from very few suppliers, in many cases only one. The motivation for single-sourcing is that a company has more direct influence and control over the quality performance of a supplier if the company has a major portion of that supplier's volume of business. The company and supplier enter into a partnership, referred to as *partnering*, where the supplier agrees to meet the quality standards of the customer in terms of parts, materials, service, and delivery. Suppliers, in effect, become part of the TQM program of the customer. In return the company enters into a long-term purchasing agreement with the supplier that includes a stable order and delivery schedule. Every part except the engine block in General Motor's Quad 4 engine (its first new engine in several decades) is single-sourced, resulting in only 69 total suppliers, which is half the normal number for a production engine. In return for the suppliers' assurance of top quality and low cost, GM guaranteed the suppliers their jobs for the life of the engine.[7] In the development of its new LH cars, the Chrysler Concorde, the Dodge Intrepid, and the Eagle Vision, Chrysler has trimmed its supplier base from 3,000 to a few more than 1,000, with a goal of 750 suppliers by 1995.[8] Single-sourcing obviously creates an intensely competitive environment among suppliers, with high quality in parts and service being priority factors in the selection process.

In *partnering*, the supplier becomes part of the customer's TQM program.

An additional aspect of the partnering relationship is the involvement of the supplier in the product design process. In many cases the supplier is given the

A Chrysler LH car and the $1 billion Chrysler Technology Center at Auburn Hills, Michigan, where new and innovative ideas and designs for Chrysler automobiles originate, are tested, and brought to fruition. An on-site pilot plant at the Technology Center allows designers and engineers to observe the actual assembly process and make adjustments before the first vehicle comes off the production line. In the late 1980s Chrysler adopted the "platform" concept for new car design and development. The goal was to focus its resources in order to reduce product development lead times from five to three years, which would be more competitive with what Japanese automakers were achieving. The platform team is a completely self-contained entity with total responsibility for a new car program, from design through development, all under one roof at the Chrysler Technology Center. The team includes buyers, suppliers, designers and engineers. The platform team for the $1.6 billion Chrysler LH project developed the LH cars with their "cab forward" design from scratch, under budget, in 39 months, and with only about 200 suppliers (compared with the normal 700 for a new car program).

[7]Raia, E., "JIT in Detroit," *Purchasing* (September 15, 1988): 68–77.

[8]Raia, E., "The Extended Enterprise," *Purchasing* 114, no. 3 (March 4, 1993): 48–51.

GAINING THE COMPETITIVE EDGE

Achieving Supplier Quality

In a 1992 survey by *Purchasing* magazine of 400 large manufacturing companies, more than 93 percent indicated they actively promote quality-improvement programs, and in all these companies, purchasing is an important part of the program. Following are some examples of what some of the companies interviewed in the survey do to promote quality in the purchasing area. Perdue Farms, Inc., exercises a demanding set of controls over supplier operating procedures, which it closely monitors. As an example, approximately 2,000 farmers receive about 5,000 one-day-old chicks into 5,000 Perdue-built chicken houses especially equipped with individual clean-water nipples and feeders for Perdue-manufactured feed. To make sure the Perdue quality process is implemented properly, a team of 100 service agents visits the chicken flocks daily.

Monsanto Chemical Company initiated a supplier quality-upgrading program in 1987 called Total Quality/Total Partnership. Suppliers are rated according to specific sites, products, and, services. Quality-improvement teams include employees of the supplier manufacturing plant and the Monsanto plant, with a Monsanto purchasing manager as the facilitator. In the Monsanto program, suppliers climb four quality rating levels in the following order: supplier, approved, preferred, and, at the top, partner. Suppliers at the bottom level either move up or out.

Bethlehem Steel Corporation initiated its Supplier Excellence certification process in 1990 to evaluate and certify more than 1,250 suppliers and carriers. The certification process includes an evaluation of the supplier's quality system through a comprehensive questionnaire, an on-site audit, and a merit assessment by other major users of the supplier. The Supplier Excellence program has two levels of certification, qualified and preferred, depending on the numerical rating attained from the evaluation and a positive merit assessment. Suppliers must be certified or risk losing Bethlehem's business.

Union Camp Corporation looks favorably on suppliers who achieve ISO 9000 registration, a "third-party" quality certification process administered by the International Organization of Standards. An outside firm evaluates a supplier's quality management program using international standards.

Honda America's quality and purchasing departments work together to ensure supplier quality. The quality department reviews every supplier of Honda parts to make sure that good operations exist. Once this is done, suppliers are certified. Teams of three purchasing engineers are sent to Honda suppliers selected for their Best Position program and work with a three-person team from the supplier to brainstorm on new ways to improve product quality and productivity.

Source: Based on Morgan, J. P., and Cayer, S., "Quality: Up and Running," *Purchasing* 112, no. 1 (1992): 69–83.

responsibility of designing a new part or component to meet the quality standards and features outlined by the company. When Guardian Industries of Northville, Michigan, developed an oversized solar glass windshield for Chrysler's new LH cars, their engineers met on an almost daily basis with the Chrysler design team to make sure the quality, features, and cost of the windshield met Chrysler standards. To produce the windshields, Guardian opened a new $35 million plant in Ligonier, Indiana, in 1991.[9]

Industrial Engineering and Job Design

It is the responsibility of the industrial engineering staff to design the individual operator tasks and the workplace such that the product will meet quality specifi-

[9]Raia, E. "The LH Story," *Purchasing* 114, no. 2 (February 18, 1993): 55–57.

cations. This function focuses on making sure resources are used efficiently and waste is minimized.

In U.S. companies the industrial engineering (IE) staff has also traditionally been responsible for monitoring quality control and developing and implementing statistical process control procedures. However, under modern TQM initiatives, employees are now encouraged to provide input into their own job design and into improving the quality of their own work activities. As such, IEs now work in concert with employees in both job design and quality control. Further, industrial engineers have taken on responsibility for measuring the outcome of quality improvement in terms of increased productivity and lower cost.

IEs work with employees in job design and quality control.

Personnel

Operator or employee skills must be sufficient to perform the job tasks designed to meet quality specifications. The personnel department is responsible for hiring employees that have the prerequisite abilities and skills and for developing and training them for specific job tasks. Employees not well trained in their tasks will probably contribute to defective, poor-quality products. Personnel also has responsibility for educating and training employees about quality and ways to achieve quality in their own individual tasks as well as imbuing them with the company's commitment to quality.

Hiring employees with skills and providing training is the job of personnel.

Under the TQM philosophy, personnel recruits employees with broad-based general skills and the ability to learn new skills quickly. Employees are provided with extensive training not only for their jobs, but also in quality control methods. The average Japanese employee receives 50 days of training annually.[10] Performance appraisal and rework systems under TQM focus more on quality improvement and group and company achievement than on individual job performance. Profit-sharing plans and plans where employees share cost savings (called gainsharing) are examples of reward systems under a TQM approach.

Employees

TQM requires that all employees throughout the organization be responsible for quality. Employees, collectively and individually, are responsible for performing their tasks according to design specifications and exhibiting good artisanship. Further, employees are responsible for identifying poor quality or problems that may lead to poor quality and taking action to have these problems corrected. Labor unions now generally acknowledge the necessity of developing a strong group commitment to quality in order for their employers to remain competitive and provide jobs.

Employees have responsibility for quality.

Production Management

The actual making of a product is the responsibility of the management team. Managers must implement the product design according to quality specifications by effectively managing and controlling labor, materials, and equipment. They must maintain a smooth flow through the manufacturing process according to predetermined plans and schedules. Failure to manage effectively can result in operator errors, equipment breakdown, bottlenecks, slack time, etc., which contribute to poor quality. It is also the responsibility of the production managers and line supervisors to make sure the company's quality program is implemented at its most critical point, the making of the product.

Management responsibility is to maintain a smooth flow through the production process.

[10]Lee, S. M., and Ebrahimpow, M., "An Analysis of Japanese Quality Control Systems: Implications for American Manufacturing Firms," *SAM Advanced Management Journal* 50, no. 2 (1985): 24–31.

Product Inspection

TQM emphasizes inspection of the process.

Traditionally, it is the responsibility of product inspection to monitor incoming parts and material and final product quality, make certain items conform to the quality specifications included in the product design, and make sure inferior final products are not passed on to the consumer. It is also the responsibility of inspection to monitor the production process itself and to expose any deficiencies that cause defective products. Statistical quality control techniques are widely used for the inspection function. In the TQM approach, less emphasis is generally placed on inspection at the end of the production process. In TQM, quality improvement occurs at all stages of the production process and at all levels of the company, with the goal of virtually no defective items, thus obviating the need for final inspection. Although U.S. companies traditionally reported defectives in terms of very small percentages, under TQM Japanese and American companies have so few defectives that they cannot be effectively measured in terms of percentages but are instead often reported in terms of parts per million (PPM).[11]

Packaging, Storage, and Shipping

Product damage must be prevented.

It is the responsibility of packaging, storing, and shipping to make sure that good-quality final products are not damaged en route to the consumer. Packaging meth-

Video 3.1 *Total Quality Management*

GAINING THE COMPETITIVE EDGE

TQM at Kurt Manufacturing

Kurt Manufacturing Company, based in Minneapolis, is a midsize supplier of precision machine parts. It operates six plants and has approximately 1,100 employees. In order to remain competitive in international markets, Kurt has adopted a commitment to continuous improvement through total quality management principles and practices. Kurt's TQM program strives to eliminate quality and production problems by systematic, continuous improvement of its processes. Kurt's top management estimates that in the United States probably 15 to 25 percent of labor is spent producing scrap or rework. Profit in their market is typically between 3 and 10 percent. Thus, they must eliminate scrap and rework in order to survive in international markets, and survival is based on TQM.

A primary goal of top management is for customers to be loyal to Kurt. They want their customers to perceive them as a company committed to total quality. This is achieved by understanding what their customers want and being responsive to their needs and problems. In Kurt's TQM approach, even though they are a manufacturing firm, they interact with customers as if they were a service company. This means they must focus on the whole job transaction, from the actual sale to responsiveness to the problems and unique needs of the customers after the part has been delivered. It is Kurt's belief that even if they have their manufacturing process in place as they want it, they will still not be perceived as a total quality company if their service side is not in order.

Many of Kurt's customers have reduced their suppliers in recent years, some from as many as 3,000 to about 150. Kurt Manufacturing has survived these cuts because of its commitment to TQM.

Source: Based on *Total Quality Management*, a video produced by the Society of Manufacturing Engineers and distributed by Allyn and Bacon, 1993.

[11]Fawcett, S. E., "The Japanese Challenge: A Note on the Emergence of Japanese Competitiveness," *Operations Management Review* 7, no. 1 (1989): 46–52.

ods and materials, storage facilities and procedures, and shipping modes must be selected to ensure that products are protected following production and that the customer receives them on time.

Customer Service

After the consumer purchases the product, the company's role does not end. It has the responsibility of providing the customer with good instructions for the product's installation and use, with personal assistance if required. If the product fails to function properly (i.e., fulfill the use for which it was designed), the company is responsible for its repair or replacement. This function is of major importance in quality management, since it represents the other direct point of contact (in addition to marketing and sales) with the customer.

Providing quality service is as important as a quality product.

In order to have a successful quality management program, each of these areas in a business—as well as all other organizational support groups—must have a strong commitment to quality, and they each must assume individual responsibility for quality. However, this commitment will not emanate on its own from the functional areas; the commitment to quality begins from top management and spreads down through the organization. A successful total quality management program must be planned, established, and initiated by top management and then implemented by the various functions and employees in the organization. Although it is popular to say that quality is everyone's responsibility in a company, total quality management generally requires a total commitment from top management to monitor and maintain quality throughout the organization. Sometimes this commitment may include quality manager(s) or a quality department. The position of this function in the organizational structure and the degree of its autonomy usually reflect the company's commitment to quality. Staff personnel who work directly with the quality function are frequently certified by one of several professional organizations, indicating that they are trained in the methods of quality management. However, within some companies, the need for a specifically identified department or expert is unnecessary, since everyone in the company is an "expert" responsible for quality.

Commitment to quality begins at the top.

Figure 3.2 displays the relationship of the functional areas in a quality management program.

Transparency 3.4 Functional Relationships in Quality Management

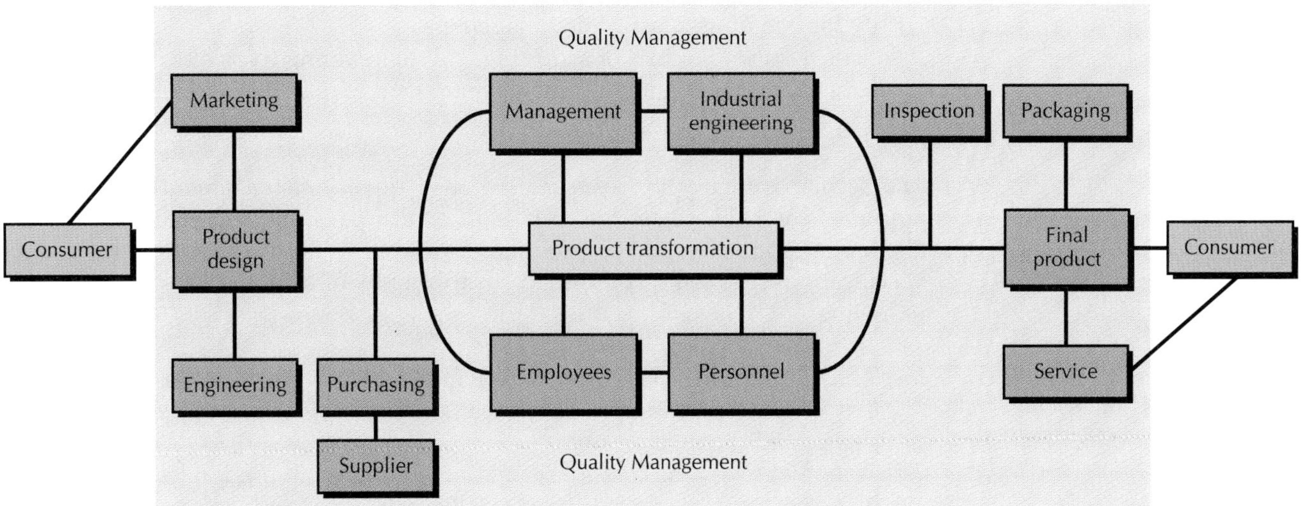

FIGURE 3.2 Quality Management

THE COST OF QUALITY

All the functional areas in the production system we described in the previous section incur costs as part of a quality management program. For example, the marketing area incurs a cost for performing consumer research to determine what quality characteristics the consumer wants; purchasing must monitor and test incoming parts and materials to make certain they conform to specifications resulting in costs; engineering incurs costs for designing in quality characteristics; personnel incurs costs for quality training programs; inspection is a direct cost for monitoring the quality of finished goods; costs are incurred by packaging for making sure products are not damaged in transit to the customer, and so on. Alternatively, poor-quality products result in costs for returned items, discarded products (including parts and material), and reworked products. In general, quality costs fall into two major categories, the cost of achieving good quality, also known as the *cost of quality assurance,* and the cost associated with poor-quality products, also referred to as the *cost of not conforming* to specifications.

Transparency 3.5 The Cost of Achieving Good Quality

The Cost of Achieving Good Quality

Prevention costs are costs incurred during product design.

The costs of preventing poor quality include planning, design, process, training, and information costs.

The costs of maintaining an effective quality management program can be divided into two categories, *prevention costs* and *appraisal costs.* **Prevention costs** result from the efforts of the company during product design and manufacturing that prevent nonconformance to specifications. Put simply, these are the costs of trying to prevent poor-quality products from reaching the consumer. Prevention reflects the quality philosophy of "do it right the first time," and it is the ultimate goal of most quality management programs. Examples of prevention costs include the following:

Quality planning costs: The costs of developing and implementing the quality management program.

Product design costs: The costs of designing products with quality control characteristics.

Process costs: The costs expended to make sure the production process conforms to quality specifications.

Training costs: The costs of developing and putting on training programs on quality for operators, staff, and management.

Information costs: The costs of acquiring and maintaining (typically on computers) data related to quality and the development and analysis of reports on quality performance.

Appraisal costs are costs of measuring, testing, and analyzing.

The second category of costs related to a quality management program are **appraisal costs.** These are the costs of measuring, testing, and analyzing materials, parts, products, and the production process to ensure that product quality specifications are being conformed to. Examples of appraisal costs include the following:

Costs of measuring quality include inspection, testing, equipment, and operator costs.

Inspection and testing: The costs of testing and inspecting materials and parts as they come from the supplier/vendor, the product at various work-in-process stages, and the final product.

Test equipment costs: The costs of maintaining equipment used in testing the quality characteristics of products in good working order.

GAINING THE COMPETITIVE EDGE

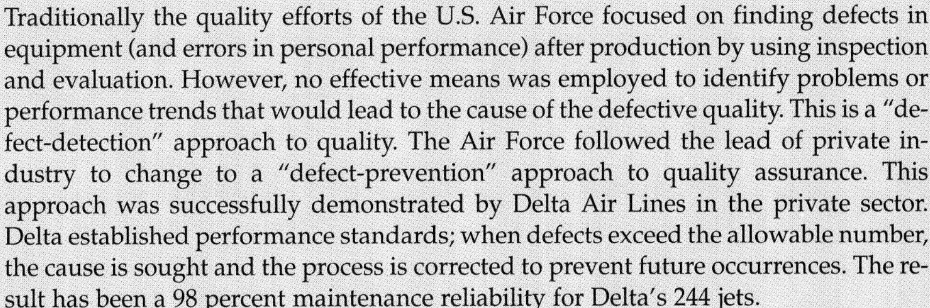

Defect Prevention in the U.S. Air Force

Traditionally the quality efforts of the U.S. Air Force focused on finding defects in equipment (and errors in personal performance) after production by using inspection and evaluation. However, no effective means was employed to identify problems or performance trends that would lead to the cause of the defective quality. This is a "defect-detection" approach to quality. The Air Force followed the lead of private industry to change to a "defect-prevention" approach to quality assurance. This approach was successfully demonstrated by Delta Air Lines in the private sector. Delta established performance standards; when defects exceed the allowable number, the cause is sought and the process is corrected to prevent future occurrences. The result has been a 98 percent maintenance reliability for Delta's 244 jets.

The Air Force's adoption of the defect-prevention approach increased inspections throughout the maintenance function from approximately 300 per month to 1,200 and resulted in the development of PEAP (Personnel Evaluation Analysis Program) to analyze the additional inspection data generated to monitor performance trends. The new approach successfully altered the Air Force's approach to quality management, increased quality in the maintenance program, and improved productivity.

Source: Based on Baysinger, S. M., "The U.S. Air Force is Changing the Way it Does Business," *Quality Progress* 24, no. 7 (1991): 36–38.

Operator costs: The cost of the time spent by operators to gather data for testing product quality, to make equipment adjustments to maintain quality, and to stop work to access quality.

The Cost of Poor Quality

The second major category of quality costs are the costs associated with poor quality, also referred to as the cost of nonconformance, or failure costs. In general, the cost of failures is the difference between what it actually costs to produce a product or deliver a service and what it would cost if there were no failures. This is generally the largest quality cost category in a company, frequently accounting for 70 percent to 90 percent of total quality costs. As a result, it is the area in which the greatest improvement is possible.

Transparency 3.6 The Cost of Poor Quality

The cost of poor quality can be categorized as *internal failure costs* and *external failure costs.* **Internal failure costs** are incurred when poor-quality products are discovered before they are delivered to the customer. Examples of internal failure costs include the following:

Internal failure costs include scrap, rework, process failure, downtime, and price reductions.

Scrap costs: The costs of poor-quality products that must be discarded, including labor, material, and indirect costs.

Rework costs: The costs of fixing defective products that do not conform to quality specifications.

Process failure costs: The costs of determining why the production process is producing poor quality products.

Process downtime costs: The costs of shutting down the manufacturing process to repair equipment, replace or train operators, or replace materials that are causing poor quality.

Price-downgrading costs: The costs of discounting poor-quality products—that is, selling products as "seconds."

External failure costs include complaints, returns, warranty claims, liability, and lost sales.

External failure costs are costs that are incurred after the customer has received a poor-quality product and are primarily related to customer service. Examples of external failure costs include the following:

Customer complaint costs: The costs of investigating and satisfactorily responding to a customer complaint resulting from a poor-quality product.

Product return costs: The costs of handling and replacing poor-quality products returned by the customer.

Warranty claims costs: The costs of complying with product warranties.

Product liability costs: The litigation costs resulting from product liability and customer injury.

Lost sales costs: The costs incurred because customers are dissatisfied with poor-quality products and do not make additional purchases.

Measuring and Reporting Quality Costs

Collecting data on quality costs is occasionally difficult. Many of the examples of quality costs mentioned in the previous section are not easy to measure, whereas the cost of other quality categories can be determined directly. The costs of lost sales, of responding to customer complaints, of process downtime, of operator testing, of quality information, and of quality planning and product design are all costs that may be difficult to measure and report on. These costs must generally be estimated by management. Alternatively, training costs, inspection and testing costs, scrap costs, the cost of product downgrading, product return costs, warranty claims and liability costs can usually be accurately measured. Many of these costs are collected as part of normal accounting procedures.

Index numbers are ratios that measure quality costs against a base value.

Management typically wants quality costs reported in a manner that can be easily interpreted and is meaningful. One popular format for reporting quality costs are with **index numbers,** or **indices.** Index numbers are usually in the form of ratios that measure quality costs relative to some base value, such as the ratio of quality costs to total sales revenue or the ratio of quality costs to units of final product. Management then uses these index numbers to compare quality management efforts between time periods or between departments or functions. Index numbers in and of themselves do not provide very much information to management about the effectiveness of a quality management program. They usually will not show directly that a company is producing good- or poor-quality products. These measures are informative only when they are compared to some standard or other index. Some of the more common index measures are defined as follows.

The **labor index** is the ratio of quality cost to labor hours.

Labor index: The ratio of quality cost to direct labor hours; it has the advantage of being easily computed (from accounting records) and easily understood, but it is not always effective for long-term comparative analysis when technological advances reduce labor usage.

The **cost index** is the ratio of quality cost to manufacturing cost.

Cost index: The ratio of quality cost to manufacturing cost (direct and indirect cost); it also has the advantage of being easy to compute from accounting records and is not affected by technological change.

The **sales index** is the ratio of quality cost to sales.

Sales index: The ratio of quality cost to sales; it can easily be computed and is a more visible measure, but it can be distorted by changes in selling price and costs.

The **production index** is the ratio of quality cost to units of final product.

Production index: The ratio of quality cost to units of final product; it is easy to compute from accounting records but is not effective if a number of different products exist.

The following example illustrates the reporting and use of several of these index numbers.

EXAMPLE 3.1

An Evaluation of Quality Costs and Quality Index Numbers

Problem Statement:

The H&S Motor Company produces small motors (3 hp, etc.) for use in lawnmowers and garden equipment. The company instituted a quality management program in 1993 and has recorded the following quality cost data and accounting measures for the past four years.

	YEAR			
	1991	*1992*	*1993*	*1994*
Quality Costs				
Prevention	$ 27,000	41,500	74,600	112,300
Appraisal	155,000	122,500	113,400	107,000
Internal failure	386,400	469,200	347,800	219,100
External failure	242,000	196,000	103,500	106,000
Total	$ 810,400	829,200	639,300	544,400
Accounting Measures				
Sales	$4,360,000	4,450,000	5,050,000	5,190,000
Manufacturing costs	1,760,000	1,810,000	1,880,000	1,890,000

The company wants to assess the impact of its quality assurance program and develop quality index numbers using sales and manufacturing cost bases for the four-year period.

Solution:

The H&S Company experienced many of the typical outcomes when its quality assurance program was instituted. Approximately 78 percent of H&S's total quality costs are a result of internal and external failures, not an uncommon result for many companies. Failure costs frequently contribute 50 to 90 percent of overall quality costs. The typical reaction to high failure costs is to increase product monitoring and inspection in order to eliminate poor-quality products resulting in high appraisal costs. This appeared to be the strategy employed by H&S when their quality management program was initiated in 1991. In 1992 H&S was able to identify more defective items, resulting in an apparent increase in internal failure costs and lower external failure costs (as fewer defective products reached the customer).

During 1991 and 1992 prevention costs were relatively modest. However, prevention is often a critical factor in reducing both internal and external failures. By instituting quality training programs, redesigning the production process, and planning how to build in product quality, companies are able to reduce poor-quality products within the production process and prevent them from reaching the customer. This was the case at H&S, because prevention costs increased by more than 400 percent during the four-year period. Since fewer poor-quality products are being made, less monitoring and inspection is necessary, and appraisal costs thus decline. Internal and external failure costs are also reduced by a reduction in defective products. In general, an increase in expenditures for prevention will result in a decrease in all other quality-cost categories. It is also not uncommon for a quality management program to isolate one or two specific quality problems that, when prevented, have a relatively large impact on overall quality cost reduction. Quality problems are not usually evenly distributed throughout the product process; a few isolated problems tend to result in the majority of poor-quality products.

The H&S Company also desired to develop index numbers using quality costs as a proportion of sales and manufacturing costs, generally two of the more popular quality indexes. These index numbers are computed as follows.

$$\text{Quality index} = \frac{\text{total quality costs}}{\text{base}}(100)$$

For example, the index number for 1991 sales is

$$\text{Quality cost per sale} = \frac{\$810{,}400(100)}{4{,}360{,}000}$$

$$= 18.58$$

The quality index numbers for sales and manufacturing costs for the four-year period are given in the following table.

Year	*Quality Sales Index*	*Quality Cost Index*
1991	18.58	46.04
1992	18.63	45.18
1993	12.66	34.00
1994	10.49	28.80

These index numbers alone provide little insight into the effectiveness of the quality management program; however, as a standard to make comparisons over time they can be useful. Clearly the H&S Company quality index numbers reflect dramatically improved quality during the four-year period. Quality costs as a proportion of both sales and manufacturing costs improved significantly. Quality index numbers do not provide information that will enable the company to diagnose and correct quality problems in the production process; however, they are useful in showing trends in product quality over time and reflecting the impact of product quality relative to accounting measures with which managers are usually familiar.

The Traditional Quality-Cost Trade-off

Transparency 3.7 The Traditional and Modified Quality-Cost Trade-off

In Example 3.1 we showed that when the sum of prevention and appraisal costs increased, internal and external failure costs decreased. Recall from our previous discussion that we had categorized prevention and appraisal costs as the cost of achieving good quality, whereas we referred to internal and external failure costs as the cost of poor quality. In general, when the cost of achieving good quality increases, the cost of poor quality declines. This relationship, considered to be the classical economic trade-off between quality costs, is depicted graphically in Figure 3.3.

In this diagram, cost is measured on the vertical axis and the percentage of good quality products is measured on the horizontal axis. As the cost of quality assurance rises (i.e., the quality assurance curve goes up), the percentage of good-quality products also increases. This has the effect of decreasing the cost resulting from poor quality in our figure. This is a classic economic relationship. Adding the two costs together produces a total cost curve; at the lowest point on this curve, the total quality cost is minimized. According to traditional quality philosophy, this is the level to which a quality management program should gravitate. Notice that the optimal point on the total cost of quality curve does not coincide with to-

The traditional approach to quality cost accepts a level of quality that coincides with the minimum cost level.

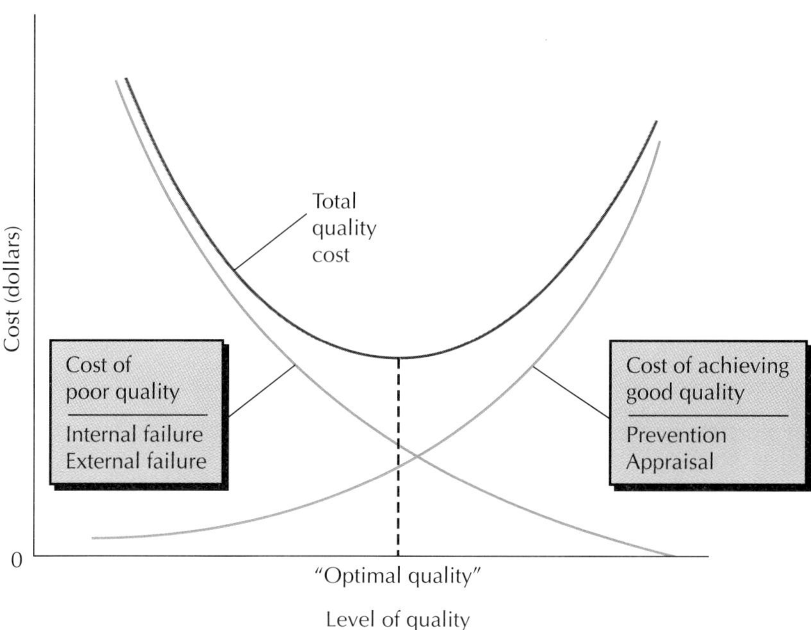

FIGURE 3.3 The Traditional Quality-Cost Trade-off

tally (100 percent) good-quality products. This fact seems to justify a level of quality assurance somewhat lower than "perfect" quality, where all products would conform to specifications. This conclusion is consistent with the traditional perception that 100 percent quality is not possible at any cost and even approaching perfect quality is too costly for most companies to attempt. Instead, based on this economic justification, companies seek a satisfactory level of product quality.

A number of Japanese firms (and subsequently U.S. companies) took exception to this economic justification for lower quality and the classic quality-cost trade-off relationship. In fact, some Japanese companies ignored this economic trade-off altogether and sought to attain 100 percent good quality, believing that the increase in sales and market share resulting from increased consumer confidence in the quality of their products would offset the higher quality costs. The premise for this Japanese approach offered by Hsiang and Lee[12] is that the classic quality-cost trade-off shown in Figure 3.3 does not reflect the increase in sales and market share that will result from better-quality products. Further, as a company focuses on improved quality, the cost of achieving good quality will be less because of the innovations in technologies, processes, and work methods that will result from the quality-improvement effort. This viewpoint is reflected in the modified version of the quality-cost trade-off curve shown in Figure 3.4. Notice that in this figure the cost of achieving good quality does not rise as rapidly as it does in Figure 3.3.[13] As a result, the total quality-cost curve has a different shape, and the minimum cost point occurs at the 100 percent quality level. This is the point of *zero defects* that has been popularized by the Japanese, and taken up by Americans.

Zero defects occur when minimum total quality cost coincides with perfect quality.

Although it may not always be feasible to achieve 100 percent quality and zero defects, Japanese firms have been very successful in exploiting this new philosophy (and refuting the traditional quality-cost trade-off) during the past two decades, especially in the expanding markets for many of the new products that

[12]Hsiang, T. C., and Lee, L., "Zero Defects: A Quality Costs Approach," *Communications in Statistics—Theory and Methods* 14, no. 11 (1985): 2641–55.

[13]Evans, J. R., and Lindsay, W. M., *The Management and Control of Quality,* 2d ed., St. Paul, Minn.: West Publishing Co., 1993.

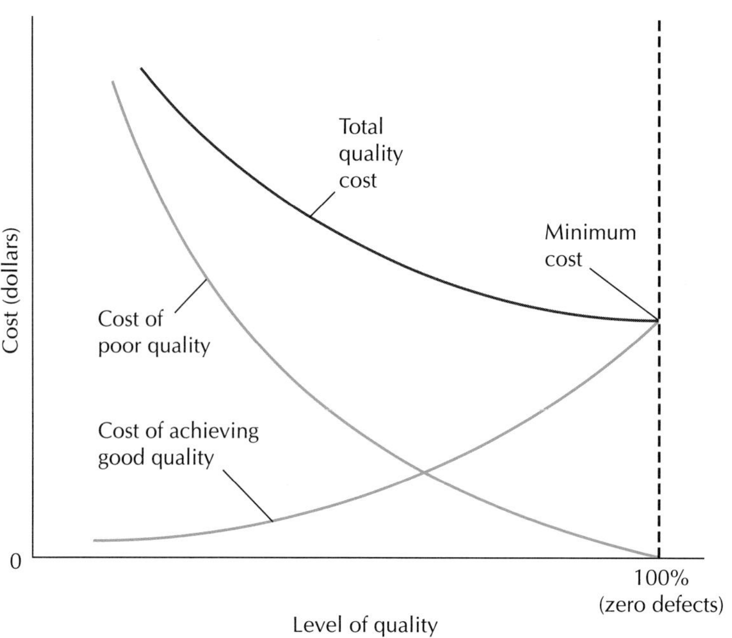

FIGURE 3.4 The Modified Quality-Cost Trade-off

have been introduced. Robert Cole[14] provides several reasons for the Japanese success in seemingly shifting the optimal point on the total quality-cost curve to the right toward the 100 percent quality level.

First, he suggests that the Japanese recognized that the costs of poor quality had been traditionally underestimated, since they did not take into account the customer losses that can be attributed to a negative quality reputation for a company. Such costs were hard to quantify, so they were virtually ignored. Alternatively, the Japanese view the cost associated with a reputation for poor quality among consumers to be quite high. Second, the traditional quality-cost relationship does not reflect the total impact on a company's performance of an effective quality management program. A 1991 General Accounting Office report on companies that were Baldrige (Quality) Award finalists showed that corporatewide quality improvement programs resulted in higher worker motivation, improved employee relations, increased productivity, higher customer satisfaction, and increased market share and profitability. The cost savings inherent in these improvements do not tend to be reflected in the traditional quality-cost trade-off relationship.

Japanese success: Better quality at lower cost.

Another reason for Japanese success has been their commitment to achieving better quality at minimum cost. One way they have done this is to focus more on improving the capabilities and training of production workers, thus getting them more involved in preventing poor quality, and to focus less on "engineering" solutions. The Japanese have also concentrated on improving quality at the new product development stage rather than attempting to build in quality during the production process for products already developed. This tends to reduce appraisal costs. Finally, the Japanese recognized that if they provided higher-quality products, they could charge higher prices than the traditional quality-cost relationship seemed to allow. The traditional approach implied that a "satisfactory" quality level was optimal because higher levels of quality would require prices higher than the customer was willing to pay in order to lower the increased costs. The Japanese have shown that this is not the case; in fact, they have created a market for higher quality, for which consumers are willing to pay.

[14]Cole, Robert E., "The Quality Revolution," *Production and Operations Management* 1, no. 1 (1992): 118–120.

Many U.S. firms have subsequently adopted the Japanese view of the quality-cost relationship. The experiences of Xerox Corporation during the 1980s is a good example of the impact of quality improvement on cost. Xerox's extensive quality improvement program initiated in the early 1980s resulted in a decline of 90 percent in defective items between 1982 and 1990. This, in turn, resulted in a 20 percent reduction in manufacturing cost and a 45 percent reduction in purchasing cost and purchased parts during the same period.

THE EFFECT OF QUALITY MANAGEMENT ON PRODUCTIVITY

In the previous section we indicated how an effective quality management program can have a very significant impact on the overall reduction of quality-related costs and potentially improve market share and sales. Quality management can also improve productivity—that is, the number of units produced from available resources.

Productivity

Productivity is a measure of a company's effectiveness in converting inputs into outputs. It is broadly defined as follows:

Productivity is the ratio of output to input.

$$\text{Productivity} = \frac{\text{output}}{\text{input}}$$

An output is usually defined as the final product from a service or production process, such as an automobile, a hamburger, or a customer. Inputs are the parts, material, labor, capital, etc., that go into the production of the product. Different productivity measures can be computed, depending on the type of outputs and inputs used, such as labor productivity (output per labor-hour) and machine productivity (output per machine-hour).

Improving quality can have a significant impact on productivity measures. Reducing defects will increase good output, whereas quality improvement efforts can reduce inputs. In fact, virtually all aspects of quality improvement have a favorable impact on different measures of productivity. Improving product designs and production processes, improving the quality of materials and parts, and improving job designs and work activity will all increase productivity as well as improve quality.

Quality impact on productivity: Fewer defects increase output and quality improvement reduces inputs.

Measuring Product Yield and Productivity

Product **yield** is a measure of output that is frequently used as an indicator of productivity. It can be computed for the entire production process (or for one stage in the process) as follows:

Yield is a measure of productivity.

$$\begin{aligned}\text{Yield} = {} & \text{(total input) (\% good products)} + \\ & \text{(total input) (1 – \% good parts) (\% reworked)}\end{aligned}$$

or

$$Y = (I)\,(\%G) + (I)\,(1 - \%G)\,(\%R)$$

where

I = planned number units of product started in the production process
$\%G$ = percentage of good units
$\%R$ = percentage of defective units

In this formula, yield is the sum of the percentage of products started in the process (or at a stage) that will turn out to be good quality plus the percentage of the defective (rejected) products that are reworked. Any increase in the percentage of good products through improved quality will increase product yield. The following example demonstrates the determination of product yield.

Improved quality increases product yield.

EXAMPLE 3.2

Computing Product Yield

Problem Statement:

The H&S Motor Company introduced in Example 3.1 starts their production process for a particular type of motor with a steel motor housing. The production process begins with 100 motors each day. The percentage of good motors produced each day averages 80 percent and the percentage of poor-quality motors that can be reworked is 50 percent. The company wants to know the daily product yield and the effect on productivity if the daily percentage of good-quality motors is increased to 90 percent.

Solution:

$$\text{Yield} = (I)(\%G) + (I)(1 - \%G)(\%R)$$
$$Y = 100\,(0.80) + 100\,(1 - 0.80)\,(0.50)$$
$$= 90 \text{ motors}$$

If product quality is increased to 90 percent good motors, the following yield will result:

$$Y = 100\,(0.90) + 100\,(1 - 0.90)(0.50)$$
$$= 95$$

Thus, a 10 percent increase in quality products results in a 5.5 percent increase in productivity output. If, in fact, the cost of achieving the quality was slight, the impact on productivity would be significant.

Now we will expand our discussion of productivity to include product manufacturing cost. The manufacturing cost per (good) product is computed by dividing the sum of total direct manufacturing cost and total cost for all reworked units by the yield, as follows.

$$\text{Product cost} = \frac{(\text{direct manufacturing cost})(\text{input}) + (\text{rework cost})(\text{reworked units})}{\text{yield}}$$

or

$$\text{Product cost} = \frac{(K_d)(I) + (K_r)(R)}{Y}$$

where

K_d = direct manufacturing cost
I = input
K_r = rework cost per unit
R = reworked units
Y = yield

EXAMPLE 3.3

Computing Product Cost Per Unit

Problem Statement:

The H&S Motor Company from Example 3.2 has a direct manufacturing cost per product of $30, and motors that are of inferior quality can be reworked for $12.

From Example 3.1, 100 motors are produced daily, 80 percent of which (on average) are of good quality and 20 percent of which are defective. Of the defective motors, half can be reworked to yield good-quality products. Through their quality management program, the company has discovered a problem in their production process that, when corrected (at a minimum cost), will increase the good-quality products to 90 percent. The company wants to assess the impact on the direct cost per product of their improvement in product quality.

Solution:
The original manufacturing cost per motor is

$$\text{Product cost} = \frac{(K_d)(I) + (K_r)(R)}{Y}$$

$$\text{Product cost} = \frac{(\$30)(100) + (\$12)(10)}{90}$$

$$= \$34.67$$

This product cost does not include the cost of the discarded, unreworkable units. The manufacturing cost per motor with the quality improvement is

$$\text{Product cost} = \frac{(\$30)(100) + (\$12)(5)}{95}$$

$$\text{Product cost} = \$32.21$$

The improvement in the production process as a result of the quality management program will result in a \$2.46 per-unit, or 7.1 percent, decrease in direct manufacturing cost per unit as well as a 5.5 percent increase in product yield (computed in Example 3.2) with virtually no investment in labor, plant, or equipment.

In Examples 3.2 and 3.3 we determined productivity measures in which we considered the production process to be a single entity; that is, we computed the yield based on process input and final output. However, in a quality management program, it is more likely that product quality would be monitored throughout the production process at various stages of product completion. In this scenario, each stage would result in a portion of good-quality, "work-in-process" products. For a production process with n stages, the yield, Y (without reworking), is computed as follows.

$$Y = (I)\,(\%g_1)\,(\%g_2)\,\ldots\,(\%g_n)$$

where

I = input of items to the production process that will result in finished products
g_i = good-quality, work-in-process products at stage i

EXAMPLE 3.4
Computing Product Yield for a Multistage Process

Problem Statement:
Returning to the H&S Motor Company, motors are produced in a four-stage process. Motors are inspected following each stage with percentage yields (on average) of good quality in process units as follows.

Stage	*Average Percentage Good Quality*
1	0.93
2	0.95
3	0.97
4	0.92

The company wants to know what the daily product yield will be for product input of 100 units per day. Further, H&S would like to know how many input units they would have to start with each day to result in a final yield of 100 good quality units.

Solution:

$$Y = (I)\,(\%g_1)\,(\%g_2)\,(\%g_3)\,(\%g_4)$$
$$= (100)\,(0.93)\,(0.95)\,(0.97)\,(0.92)$$
$$Y = 78.8 \text{ units}$$

Thus, the production process has a daily good-quality product yield of 78.8 units.

In order to determine the product input that would be required to achieve a product yield of 100 units, I is treated as a decision variable when Y equals 100:

$$I = \frac{Y}{(\%g_1)(\%g_2)(\%g_3)(\%g_4)}$$

$$I = \frac{100}{(0.93)(0.95)(0.97)(0.92)}$$

$$= 126.8 \text{ units}$$

Thus, in order to achieve the desired product output of 100 good-quality motors, the production process must start with approximately 127 motors.

Both these examples for computing yield and product input demonstrate the rather dramatic impact on productivity of modest but continued problems of poor quality. Defective rates of only 7 percent, 5 percent, 3 percent, and 8 percent at the four stages in the production process resulted in a product yield of only 78.8 percent.

The Quality-Productivity Ratio

The **quality-productivity ratio** is a productivity index that includes productivity and quality costs.

Another measure of the effect of quality on productivity, developed by Adam, Hershauer, and Rich,[15] combines the concepts of quality index numbers discussed earlier in this chapter and product yield presented in this section. This measure is called the **quality-productivity ratio** (QPR), and it is computed as follows:

$$\text{QPR} = \frac{\text{Good-quality units}}{(\text{input})(\text{processing cost}) + (\text{defective units})(\text{rework cost})}(100)$$

This is actually a quality index number that includes productivity and quality costs. The QPR increases if either processing cost or rework costs or both decrease. It also increases if more good-quality units are produced relative to total product input (i.e., the number of units that begin the production process). The following example will illustrate the use of the quality-productivity ratio.

EXAMPLE 3.5

Computing the Quality-Productivity Ratio (QPR)

Problem Statement:

The H&S Motor Company (from our previous examples) produces small motors at a processing cost of $30 per unit. Defective motors can be reworked at a cost of

[15]Adam, E. E., Hershauer, J. E., and Rich, W. A., Productivity and Quality: Measurement as a Basis of Improvement, 2d ed., Columbia, Mo.: Research Center, College of Business and Public Administration, University of Missouri, 1986.

\$12. The company produces 100 motors per day and averages a yield of 80 percent good-quality motors, resulting in 20 percent defects, all of which can be reworked prior to shipping to customers. The company wants to examine the effects of 1. increasing the production rate to 200 motors per day; 2. reducing the processing cost to \$26 and the rework cost to \$10; 3. increasing through quality improvement the product yield of good-quality products to 95 percent; and 4. the combination of 2 and 3.

Solution:
The QPR for the base case is computed as follows.

$$\text{QPR} = \frac{80}{(100)(\$30) + (20)(\$12)}(100) = 2.47$$

Case 1: Increase input to production capacity of 200 units.

$$\text{QPR} = \frac{160}{(200)(\$30) + (40)(\$12)}(100) = 2.47$$

Increasing production capacity alone has no effect on the QPR; it remains the same as the base case.

Case 2: Reduce processing cost to \$26 and rework cost to \$10.

$$\text{QPR} = \frac{80}{(100)(\$26) + (20)(\$10)}(100) = 2.86$$

These cost decreases caused the QPR to increase.

Case 3: Increase yield of good-quality units to 95 percent.

$$\text{QPR} = \frac{95}{(100)(\$30) + (5)(\$12)}(100) = 3.10$$

Again, the QPR increases as product quality improves.

Case 4: Decrease costs and increase good-quality yield.

$$\text{QPR} = \frac{95}{(100)(\$26) + (5)(\$10)} = 3.60$$

The largest increase in the QPR results from decreasing costs and increasing product yield through improved quality.

Just-in-Time and Productivity

JIT impact on productivity: JIT creates pressure to eliminate defects, which increases product output.

Just-in-time (JIT) is an approach to inventory control developed at Toyota that has had a significant role in quality improvement and increasing productivity in Japan

GAINING THE COMPETITIVE EDGE

Increasing Productivity Through Total Quality Management at ITT

ITT Electro-Optical Products Division in Roanoke, Virginia, is a major designer, developer, and producer of image-intensification devices used in night-vision products, such as helicopter pilot's goggles, aviator's night-vision imaging systems, and single-tube night goggles. Manufacturing the image intensifier is a complex operation, requiring over 400 different processes and 200 different chemicals, which combines the technologies of electronics, fiber optics, chemistry, optics, and semiconductors, among others. The production process is further complicated by the use of working vacuums that exceed NASA requirements and sophisticated test equipment of the type used by the National Institute of Standards and Technology. As a result, manufacturing yields are only 10 to 40 percent throughout the night-vision industry. In 1986 the company implemented a total quality management program that included continuous process improvement, statistical process control, Taguchi experiments, and employee involvement, including the use of cause-and-effect diagrams. In 1985, prior to the initiation of the TQM program, the company averaged a manufacturing yield of 35 percent, which increased to 75 percent by 1989 with the quality improvement program. In 1985 the company delivered only 500 image-intensifier tubes, but in 1990 deliveries exceeded 29,000 tubes, and during this same period, production capacity increased from 1,000 tubes to 35,000 tubes annually. As a result of this phenomenal success (unique in the night-vision industry) the ITT Electro-Optical Products Division received the 1990 U.S. Senate Productivity Award for Virginia Medallion and became the first and only Virginia company to be invited by the U.S. Army to apply for certification in its Contractor Performance Certification Program.

Source: Based on Kempster, J. E., "ITT Electro-Optical Products Division Roanoke, Virginia," *Quality and Productivity Management* 9, no. 2 (1991): 37–46.

and, more recently, in the United States. The basic objective of JIT is to attempt to eliminate inventory so that just enough units exist to keep each successive stage in the production process operational. As one partially completed unit is finished at a stage, the next unit arrives from the succeeding stage, without a stock of inventory between the stages.

The obvious immediate benefit from JIT is a significant reduction in inventory costs, since no extra inventory exists. However, JIT also has a significant impact on quality and productivity. JIT *cannot* work with poor-quality materials or parts from suppliers or with many defects at any stage of the production process. If a part or a partially completed product is defective, the production process simply stops, because there is no inventory to fall back on. Thus, JIT puts extreme pressure on the supplier and the producer to maintain high quality and few defects, which in turn increases productivity. If JIT were applied in Example 3.4, where we computed product yield for a multistage process, the percentage of good quality at each stage would have to be virtually 100 percent, thus resulting in almost a 100 percent yield. JIT is discussed in greater detail in Chapter 15.

QUALITY AND THE ROLE OF MANAGEMENT

The effectiveness of a quality management program in a business is largely dependent on how well the program is managed. In general, a business organization will have three levels of management: top middle, and supervisory. The managers at each of these levels must monitor, direct, and control the quality-management program as it applies to their areas of responsibility. In the next several sections we discuss the responsibilities of management at each of these organizational levels.

Top Management

In most businesses, top management has responsibility for setting organizational goals, including those for quality. These goals typically focus on broad-based, long-term issues and concerns of the firm such as profitability, market share, competition, and growth. To achieve these organizational goals, management also has the responsibility of developing strategic plans. Since, as we have discussed previously in this chapter, quality can have a significant impact on the enhancement of such things as profitability and market share, it is natural that quality and quality management are important aspects of the strategic planning process conducted by top management.

Most major decisions regarding overall product quality and the company's commitment to quality are made by top management through the strategic planning process. As part of this process, top management determines the markets the company will enter and the products that will be entered into those markets. As we have already discussed, quality is an integral part of product design and product quality is a major factor in defining the consumer markets in which the company will compete. Through the establishment of goals and the development of strategic plans to achieve those goals, top management ultimately determines the level of quality that is required in product design and the degree of commitment to quality management necessary to achieve this quality level in the final product.

A company's commitment to quality is a strategic management goal.

Top management must be committed to quality.

As an example of top management's role, consider an automaker contemplating the introduction of a new car. Top management must decide if the car should be aimed at the consumer in the Cadillac market or the Ford Escort market based on the company's goals for profitability, market share, and growth. The automaker then must determine a design for this car that will meet the consumer's fitness-for-use definition for this market—the quality characteristics the car will have. Top management must then commit to a quality management program that will achieve the level of quality dictated by the car design.

It will ultimately be up to middle management and the workers to put into operation the goals and plans developed by top management. However, top management must make the initial, strong commitment to quality management. Further, they must make sure that all areas and functions within the entire organization share a common commitment to quality management.

Middle Management

The role of middle managers in an organization is to implement the strategic plans developed by top management. Management at this level focuses on designing and controlling the production process according to the specifications laid out in the product's design; that is, middle managers must make sure the product conforms to specifications. As such, middle management has the responsibility for designing and implementing an effective quality management program that will ensure product conformance to specifications.

Middle managers help design and implement quality.

Middle managers must make sure that the quality management program is implemented throughout the organization and, in many cases, beyond it. For example, it is especially important that quality improvement efforts encompass vendor selection and the requisition of parts and materials. Extending quality management to include a company's suppliers has become a critical aspect of

GAINING THE COMPETITIVE EDGE

Strategic Planning at Union Carbide

At Union Carbide's Chemicals and Plastics Division, senior management focused on the improvement of the strategic planning process as a key component of the company's Excellence Through Quality (EQ) program.

The strategic plan provided a focus and motivation for the entire quality improvement effort. Strategic planning was the first step in the EQ process; it provided managers with an understanding of the EQ program and their role in EQ. Plans developed from the strategic plan outlined how EQ would work, and the plan's implementation demonstrated the company's commitment to their quality improvement philosophy and objectives.

The strategic planning process was based on five basic concepts, including realism, vision, flexibility, commitment to continuous change, and the hard work change requires. *Realism* required Union Carbide's senior managers to develop a realistic perception of the company's existing condition to assess accurately its standing in the industry and determine what it did well and did not do well. Once Union Carbide's management team had accessed the reality of its situation, they created a *vision* for the future that went beyond the current reality. This vision had to be challenging but also attainable. At this stage of the strategic planning process, management knew where it had been, where it wanted to go, and what it wanted to achieve. The strategic plan had to be *flexible* in order to react to changes in the competition and the company's own production process; that is, it was a dynamic process. In order for the strategic plan to work effectively, there had to be a *commitment to change*, and resistance to planned change must be overcome. Finally, everyone in the company had to be committed to *working hard* to affect the changes for which the strategic plan called in order to improve quality. To make the strategic plan work and the EQ program a success, top management had to maintain their commitment to the program and inspire commitment in others, be a role model dedicated to the planning and implementation process, and remain flexible.

Source: Based on Wall, S. T., and Zeynel, S. C., "The Senior Manager's Role in Quality Improvement," *Quality Progress* 24, no. 1 (1991): 66–68.

quality management in recent years. Middle management must design and implement an effective prevention and quality appraisal system for the various stages of the production process. Finally, management at this level has responsibility for customer service programs. Many of middle management's responsibilities relative to specific functions in the production process were discussed in the section on total quality management.

A quality manager or quality department is sometimes located at the middle management level. The quality management function has the responsibility of coordinating the quality management program among all other functions in the production process. The quality manager, in conjunction with industrial engineers, analyzes quality-cost information in the form of quality index numbers and/or productivity measures and current data about the ongoing quality of products obtained by monitoring and inspecting the production process. This information is used to identify quality improvement opportunities, which are shared with the appropriate middle manager for implementation. However, the quality manager is not solely responsible for quality; this is a shared responsibility with employees at every level and across all management functions.

Supervisory Management

Supervisors have responsibility for solving quality problems.

Supervisors have the responsibility for directing and controlling the operations in the production process designed by middle management. The supervisory level is

Transparency 3.8 Management Roles in Achieving Quality

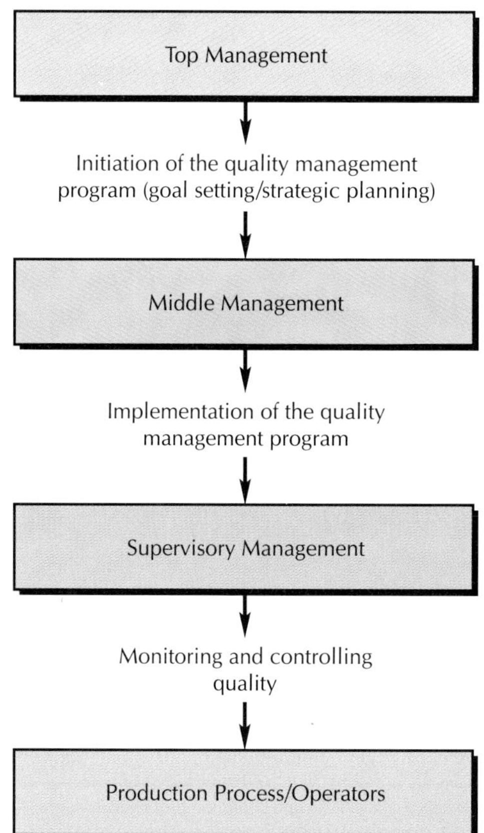

FIGURE 3.5 Management Roles In Achieving Quality

the first line of management, thus, much of a supervisor's time is spent managing personnel such as machine operators, servers, and clerical staff. Direct quality monitoring and control take place at this level. As a result, managers at the supervisory level have first responsibility for identifying and seeking solutions for quality problems.

When quality problems are identified, supervisory management works with middle management to correct and improve the production process. If operators are the cause of quality problems due to poor work methods or insufficient training, supervisors have responsibility for identifying these problems and taking the necessary action to have the problems corrected. In most quality management programs, supervisory management collects and reports quality-related data to the quality manager or appropriate middle manager. In many companies (especially Japanese), supervisors also set quality goals in conjunction with the workers in their area as part of participative quality management programs.

Figure 3.5 provides a summary outline of the role of each of the three levels of management in a total quality management program.

QUALITY IMPROVEMENT AND THE ROLE OF EMPLOYEES

Labor in the United States is changing from an adversarial relationship to employee involvement.

The relationship between labor and management in the United States has sometimes been adversarial. However, it has become clear in recent years that this type of operational environment is not conducive to effective quality management. In order to achieve high levels of product quality, it is absolutely necessary that management and labor cooperate and that each have an equally strong commitment

Mickey Mouse is not just a costumed character at the various Disney parks in the United States and abroad; he is a host who represents all the other costumed host and hostesses to Disney's thousands of "guests" each day. Every employee at a Disney park from janitors to Mickey has undergone extensive training to provide quality service to Disney's guests.

to quality. Cooperation and commitment is generally not possible, though, when management "dictates" quality to production employees. The Japanese have vividly demonstrated that true cooperation in a quality management program is achieved when employees are allowed to participate in the quality management process—that is, when they are given a voice.

In **participative problem solving,** employees are directly involved in the quality management process.

The type of approach wherein employees are directly involved in the quality management process is referred to as **participative problem solving.** Quality management programs in which employees participate in identifying and solving quality problems have been shown to be very effective not only in improving product quality, but also in increasing employee satisfaction and morale, improving job skills, reducing job turnover and absenteeism, and increasing productivity.

Teaching Note 3.6 Employee Involvement at Chrysler

Participative problem solving is usually carried out within the framework of an *employee-involvement* (EI) program, which is often in the form of a team approach. A number of different EI programs for improving quality have been developed in recent years, primarily by Japanese companies, who have been the innovators in these areas. In the remainder of this section we review some of these programs for involving employees in quality management, beginning with the most popular, *quality circles.*

Quality Circles

A **quality circle** is a group of workers and supervisors from the same area who address production problems.

Quality circles, originally referred to as quality control circles in Japan, where they originated during the 1960s, were introduced in the United States in the 1970s. A **quality circle** is a small, voluntary group of workers and their supervisor(s), who constitute a team of about eight to ten members from the same work area or department. The supervisor is typically the circle moderator, promoting group discussion but not directing the group or making decisions; decisions are the result of group consensus. A circle meets about once a week during company time in a room designated especially for that purpose, where the team works on problems

GAINING THE COMPETITIVE EDGE

Employee Quality Awareness at Disneyland

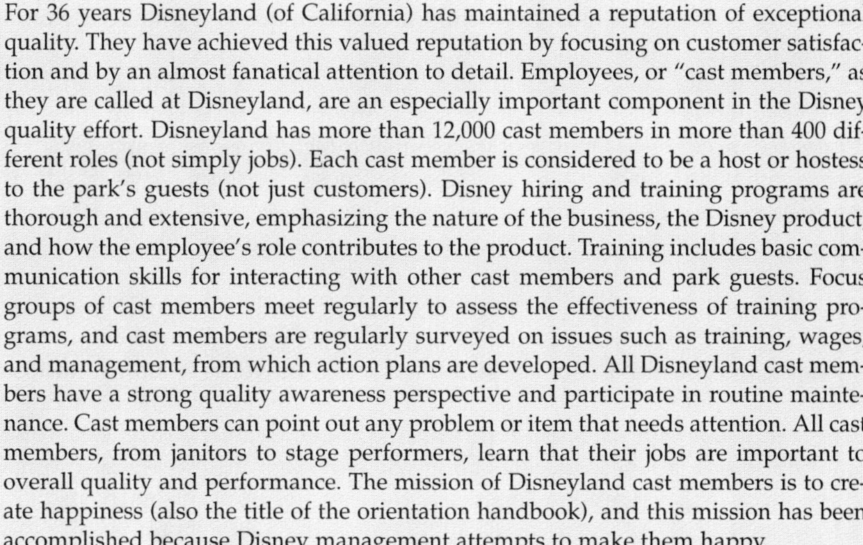

For 36 years Disneyland (of California) has maintained a reputation of exceptional quality. They have achieved this valued reputation by focusing on customer satisfaction and by an almost fanatical attention to detail. Employees, or "cast members," as they are called at Disneyland, are an especially important component in the Disney quality effort. Disneyland has more than 12,000 cast members in more than 400 different roles (not simply jobs). Each cast member is considered to be a host or hostess to the park's guests (not just customers). Disney hiring and training programs are thorough and extensive, emphasizing the nature of the business, the Disney product, and how the employee's role contributes to the product. Training includes basic communication skills for interacting with other cast members and park guests. Focus groups of cast members meet regularly to assess the effectiveness of training programs, and cast members are regularly surveyed on issues such as training, wages, and management, from which action plans are developed. All Disneyland cast members have a strong quality awareness perspective and participate in routine maintenance. Cast members can point out any problem or item that needs attention. All cast members, from janitors to stage performers, learn that their jobs are important to overall quality and performance. The mission of Disneyland cast members is to create happiness (also the title of the orientation handbook), and this mission has been accomplished because Disney management attempts to make them happy.

Source: Based on Stratton, B., "How Disneyland Works," *Quality Progress* 24, no. 7 (1991): 17–30.

and projects of their own choice. These problems may not always relate to quality issues; instead, they focus on productivity, costs, safety, or other work-related issues in the circle's area. Quality circles follow an established procedure for identifying, analyzing, and solving quality-related (or other) problems. Figure 3.6 provides a schematic of the quality circle process.

Transparency 3.9 The Quality Circle Process

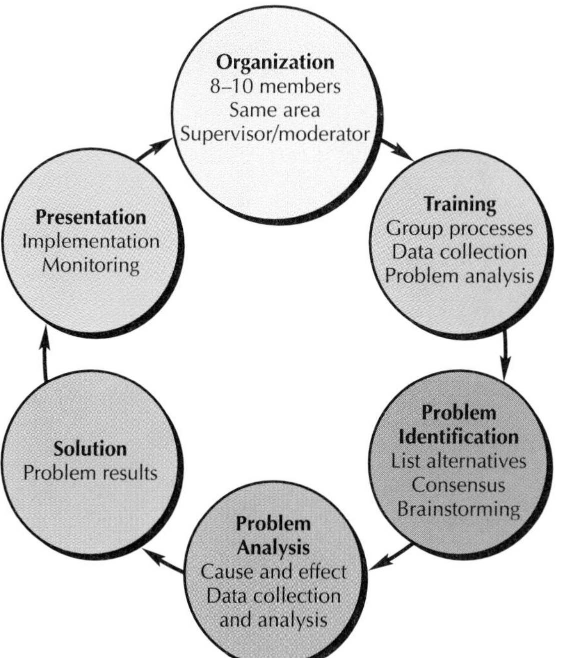

FIGURE 3.6 The Quality Circle Process

One particularly beneficial technique for identifying and solving problems is *brainstorming*. The objective of brainstorming is to generate a lot of ideas. Free expression of ideas is encouraged, and criticism is not allowed during brainstorming sessions. Only after brainstorming is completed are the ideas evaluated. We discuss some of the other most frequently used techniques for identifying quality problems and their causes later in this chapter.

When a quality circle is organized, the members receive training in how to conduct meetings and address problems as a group as well as how to collect data and analyze problems. When required, outside technical and managerial assistance is available to the circle. The circle sometimes includes an advisor, who provides guidance but is not a team member. When project results are achieved or problems are solved, presentations are made to management, who actually make decisions about the studies.

Quality circles were developed by Kaoru Ishikawa in Japan in the 1960s.

Quality circles have been very successful in Japan. The original development has been credited to Dr. Kaoru Ishikawa of the University of Tokyo, who adapted many of the approaches to quality promoted by W. Edwards Deming and Joseph Juran (of the United States) to the Japanese business environment during the 1960s. (We discuss all three individuals in greater detail in the next section). Today, millions of Japanese workers are involved in quality circles. It is estimated that approximately 10 million Japanese workers and supervisors have participated in quality circles, and several million projects have been undertaken, with an average return of several thousand dollars each since their inception in the 1960s.

The immense popularity of quality circles achieved in Japan has not been universally duplicated in the United States. The Japanese seem to have a cultural affinity for group participation that U.S. workers and supervisors do not always share. U.S. managers traditionally have been reluctant to share any of their functional responsibilities with workers. They have viewed the analysis and solution of problems and issues as a part of their own job domain that is not delegated. In addition, workers have frequently perceived themselves in an adversarial role with management and have not felt a responsibility to help managers improve quality performance.

A number of U.S. companies have adopted quality circle programs.

Despite these cultural obstacles, select U.S. firms such as Lockheed, Westinghouse, Ford Motor Company, Coors Beer Corporation, and General Electric,

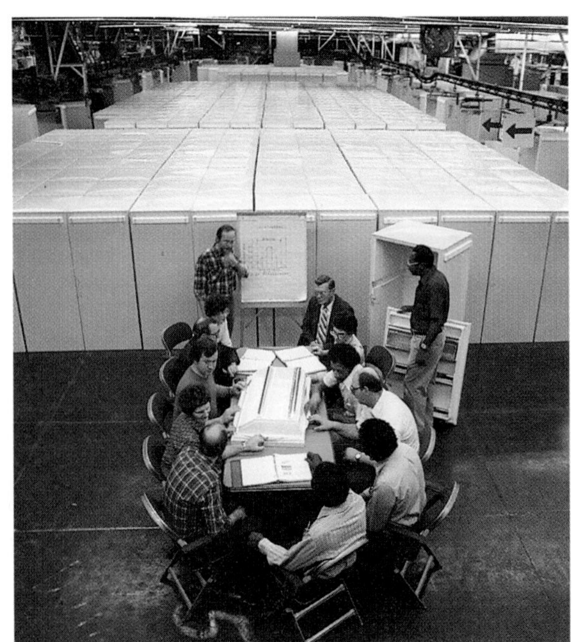

Quality circles like this one at a General Electric assembly plant are an important part of many TQM programs. They provide an organized format for allowing workers and supervisors to work together as a team to solve operational problems and improve quality. Quality circles originated in Japan where they have been immensely popular and successful. They subsequently were introduced in the United States, where they have been less popular but generally no less successful. Normally a circle consists of 8 to 10 members that meet once a week to address problems and projects of their own choosing. They frequently make use of various techniques and tools for identifying causes of quality problems including brainstorming, Pareto charts, fish bone diagrams, process control charts, scatter diagrams, check sheets, and histograms.

among others, have established successful quality circle programs. These successes have led to recent growth in this approach not only among business firms, but also in service organizations and government. As noted previously, it is misleading to attribute too much to the cultural factor in explaining the differences in the success of quality circles between Japanese and U.S. firms. It is probably more a function of different managerial practices.

A survey conducted by the International Association of Quality Circles in the mid-1980s showed that the most effective quality circle programs were in larger, nonmanufacturing organizations with older, more established programs. The average net savings contributed by circle members was estimated to be about $1000.

Employee Suggestions

Employee involvement in quality management need not be confined to group participative problem-solving approaches like quality circles. Employee involvement on an individual basis can be a very effective component of a quality management program. The time-tested, simple suggestion box is an example of a means for including employees in quality improvement efforts.

In many Japanese companies individual operators are encouraged and rewarded for stopping the production line or assembly process to correct a quality problem they have discovered. This strongly suggests that a key to any type of employee suggestion program is a strong commitment and reinforcement from management at all levels. Equally important, operators must be sufficiently trained to identify quality problems so that work will not be stopped needlessly. Overall, the traditional suggestion box is not sufficient to achieve active employee involvement in quality management. A structured program is required that provides a convenient means for making quality suggestions, a commitment from management, and a reward structure.

In the 1980s employees of Toyota averaged more than 30 suggestions per employee as a result of a program designating suggestion quotas for each work

GAINING THE COMPETITIVE EDGE

Employee Involvement at Molded Fiber Glass Company

Molded Fiber Glass Company of Ashtabula, Ohio, manufactures fiberglass products such as truck hoods, boats, and chair shells. Although the company had always been quality conscious, there had been little emphasis on employee involvement, minimal training, and few efforts at improving employee performance or motivation. In adopting a quality improvement program, the company used the General Motors' "Targets for Excellence" program as a model of an approach to quality management based on teamwork and employee involvement. An important component of the company's new quality program was a team structure for employee involvement that incorporated all levels and functions of the organization. Each team consisted of a small number of volunteers who led the quality improvement effort in an area. Teams from staff areas were known as resource teams, and teams from manufacturing were called process improvement teams. Extensive team training included courses on team skills (communication, decision making, etc.) and technical skills (process knowledge and skills for monitoring quality such as statistical quality control). Teams developed action plans and selected quality improvement projects. Results included increased profits at one of the company's two plants and more business with the quality-demanding automotive industry.

Source: Based on Sippola, K., "Eight Steps to a Quality Turnaround," *Quality Progress* 24, no. 4, (April 1991): 43–45.

GAINING THE COMPETITIVE EDGE

An Employee Suggestion Program at Atlantic Research Corporation

The Virginia Propulsion Division of Atlantic Research Corporation produces solid rocket-propulsion systems for guided missiles, including the Stinger and Tomahawk cruise missiles for the military. As an effort to improve quality and its competitive posture, the Virginia Propulsion Division instituted two programs to foster employee involvement, the ARC Suggestion Program and a Quality Circles Program. The suggestion program was aimed at those employees who might not be group-oriented and who catered to individualism. Collection sites were placed at ten strategic locations. Recognitions for accepted ideas was provided through a number of awards and acknowledgments in the company newsletter. In 1988, employee suggestions through this program resulted in savings estimated at $60,000.

Source: Based on Lewis, G. L., "Atlantic Research Corporation, Virginia Propulsion Division: High Tech and High Employee Investment," *Quality and Productivity Management* 7, no. 3 (1989): 24–25.

unit,[16] whereas U.S. auto makers did not fare nearly this well. Nevertheless, many U.S. companies and organizations have achieved some degree of employee involvement through suggestion programs for a number of years; in lieu of group participative programs, they are an effective alternative.

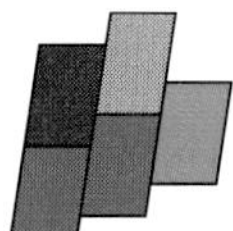

IDENTIFYING QUALITY PROBLEMS AND CAUSES

Some of the most frequently used techniques for identifying the causes of quality problems include Pareto charts, flowcharts, check sheets, histograms, cause-and-effect diagrams, scatter diagrams, and process control charts. These well-known simple tools for identifying quality problems and their causes and finding solutions are sometimes known as the "magnificent seven" or the "seven QC tools." We discuss them in a little more depth in the following sections.

Seven quality control tools for identifying quality problems and their causes

Pareto Analysis

Pareto analysis: Most quality problems result from a few causes.

In order to correct poor quality it is first necessary to identify the causes of quality problems. **Pareto analysis** is a method of identifying the causes of poor quality. It was devised in the early 1950s by the well-known quality expert Joseph Juran. He named this method after a turn-of-the-century Italian economist, Vilfredo Pareto, who determined that in Milan fewer than 20 percent of the people had more than 80 percent of the wealth. Pareto theorized that this was true of other economies as well. Pareto analysis is based on Juran's finding that most quality problems and costs resulted from only a few causes. For example, he discovered in a textile mill that almost 75 percent of all defective cloth was caused by only a few weavers, and in a paper mill he studied, more than 60 percent of the cost of poor quality was attributable to a single category of defects. In other words, he discovered that quality costs are not uniform across all causes. Thus, correcting the relatively few major causes of most of the quality problems will result in the greatest cost impact.

[16]Fujita, Y., "Participative Work Practices in the Japanese Auto Industry: Some Neglected Considerations," *The Quality Circles Journal* 6 (September 1983): 15–19.

Pareto analysis can be applied by simply tallying the number of defects for all the different possible causes of poor quality in a product and then developing a frequency distribution from the data. This frequency distribution is referred to as a *Pareto diagram,* and it is a very useful visual aid for focusing on major quality problems.

Consider a brief, general example of a manufactured product for which the different causes of poor quality have been identified.

Cause	*Number of Defects*	*Percentage*
Poor design	80	64%
Wrong part dimensions	16	13
Defective parts	12	10
Incorrect machine calibration	7	6
Operator errors	4	3
Defective material	3	2
Surface abrasions	3	2
	125	100

In this table, for each category of a potential cause of poor quality, the number of defects attributed to that cause has been tallied over a period of time. This information is then converted into the Pareto chart shown in Figure 3.7.

This Pareto diagram clearly identifies the major cause of poor quality to be poor design. It is assumed that correcting the design problem will result in the greatest possible quality cost savings with the least expenditure—that is, the greatest quality return on investment. However, this does not mean that the other causes of quality should be ignored. The principles of TQM teach us that total and continual quality improvement is the desirable long-term goal. Thus, the Pareto diagram simply identifies the quality problems that will result in the greatest immediate impact in quality improvement.

Transparency 3.10 A Pareto Chart

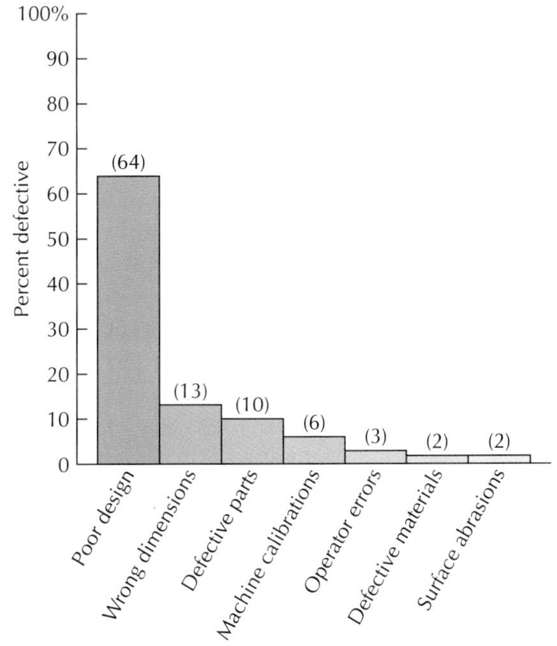

FIGURE 3.7 Pareto Chart

Flowcharts

A *flowchart* is a diagram of a job operation or process.

A *flowchart* is a diagram of the steps involved in a job, operation, or process. It enables all the participants involved in identifying and solving quality problems to have a clear picture of how a specific operation works and to have a common frame of reference. This helps the problem solver focus on where problems might occur in the process and if the process itself needs fixing. Development of the flowchart itself can help identify quality problems by helping the problem solvers better understand the operation. Flowcharts are described in greater detail in Chapter 6 ("Process Planning and Technology Decisions") and Chapter 9 ("Jobs: Design, Analysis, and Measurement").

Check Sheets and Histograms

A *check sheet* is a list of causes of quality problems with the number of defects resulting from each cause.

A *histogram* is a bar chart showing the frequency of occurrence of causes of defects.

Check sheets are frequently used in conjunction with histograms, as well as with Pareto diagrams. A *check sheet* is a fact-finding tool that is used to collect data about quality problems. A typical check sheet for quality defects tallies the number of defects for a variety of previously identified problem causes. When the check sheet is completed, after some length of time, the total tally of defects for each cause can be used to create a *histogram* or (as we demonstrated earlier) a Pareto chart.

Scatter Diagrams

A *scatter diagram* is a graph showing how two process variables relate to each other.

Scatter diagrams graphically show the relationship between two variables in a process, such as the brittleness of a piece of material and the temperature at which it is baked. One temperature reading should result in a specific degree of brittleness representing one point on the diagram. Many such points on the diagram visually show a pattern between the two variables and a relationship or lack of one. This relationship could then be used to identify a particular quality problem associated with the baking process. In effect, a scatter diagram is the graph of the data points used in regression analysis.

Process Control Charts and Statistical Quality Control

Process control involves monitoring a production process using statistical quality control methods.

We will discuss control charts and other statistical quality control methods in much greater detail in the next chapter, "Statistical Quality Control." For now, it is sufficient to say that a control chart includes a horizontal line through the middle of a chart representing the process mean or norm. It also has a line below this mean line representing the lower control limit and a line above it for the upper control limit. Samples from the process are then taken over time and measured according to some attribute. In its simplest form, if the measurement is within the control limits, the process is said to be in control and there is no quality problem, but if the measurement is outside the limits, then a problem probably exists and should be investigated.

In general, statistical quality control methods such as the process control chart are extremely important tools for quality improvement. Japanese employees at all levels of the company, and especially in production, are provided with extensive training in statistical quality control methods. This enables them to identify quality problems and their causes and to make suggestions for improvement, which they do very frequently.

Cause-and-Effect Diagrams

A cause-and-effect, or fishbone, diagram, is a chart showing the different categories of problem causes.

A **cause-and-effect diagram,** also called a "fishbone" diagram, is a graphical description of the elements of a specific quality problem and the relationship between those elements. It is used to identify the causes of a quality problem so

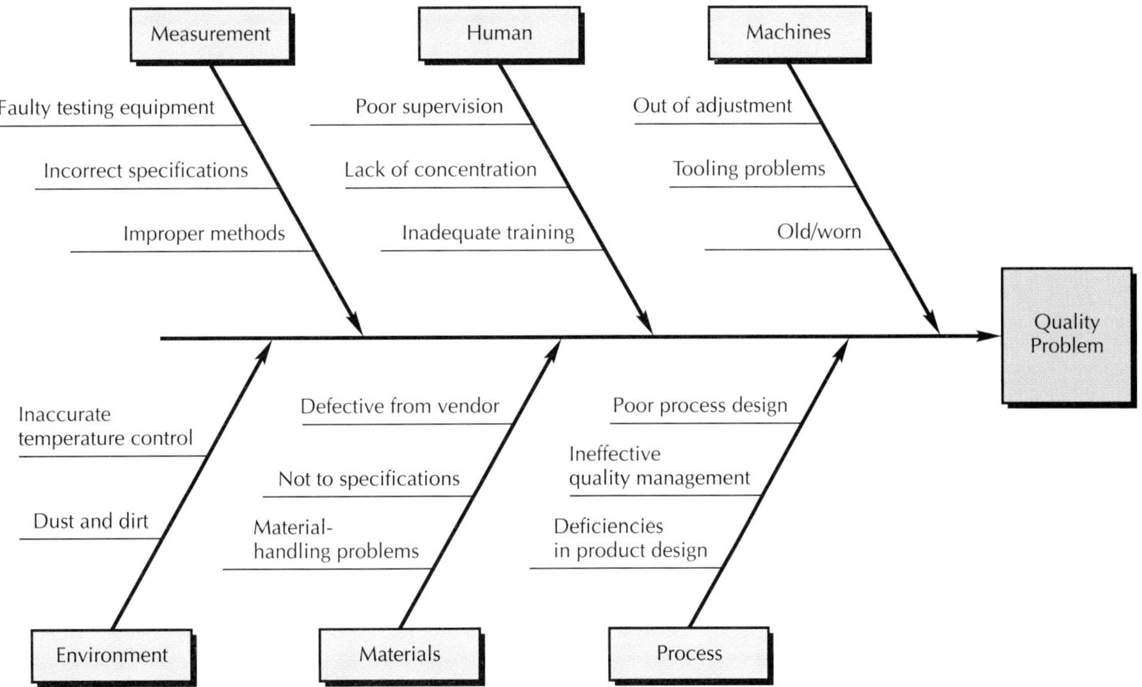

FIGURE 3.8 A General Cause-and-Effect Diagram

Transparency 3.11 A General Cause-and-Effect Diagram

that the problem can be corrected. Cause-and-effect diagrams are usually developed as part of a participative problem-solving activity to help a team of workers, supervisors, and managers identify causes of quality problems. This tool is a normal part of the problem-solving activity of quality circles in Japanese companies; however, in the United States it is often used separately, outside the quality circle program.

Figure 3.8 illustrates the general structure of the cause-and-effect diagram. The "effect" box at the end of the diagram is the quality problem that needs correction. A center line connects the effect box to the major categories of possible problem causes, displayed as branches off of the center line. The box at the end of each branch (or fishbone) describes the cause category. The diagram starts out in this form with only the major categories at the end of each branch. Individual causes associated with each category are attached as separate lines along the length of the branch during the brainstorming process. Sometimes the causes are rank-ordered along the branches in order to identify those that are most likely to impact on the problem. The cause-and-effect diagram is essentially a means for thinking through a problem and recording the possible causes in an organized and easily interpretable manner. The causes listed along the branches under each category in Figure 3.8 are generic, but for a specific quality problem with an actual product, the causes would be product- and problem-specific.

CURRENT TRENDS AND PHILOSOPHIES IN QUALITY MANAGEMENT

A handful of prominent individuals have had a dramatic impact on the rise of quality awareness in the United States, Japan, and other countries of the world. These individuals include W. Edwards Deming, Joseph Juran, Philip Crosby, and

Kaoru Ishikawa. In this section we review the contributions of these individuals and others and discuss their philosophies of quality management.

Walter Shewhart and Harold Dodge: Quality Pioneers

Shewhart developed statistical control charts.

Walter Shewhart and Harold Dodge were employees of Bell Telephone Laboratories during the 1920s where they developed the technical tools that formed the beginning of statistical quality control. These tools became the basic foundation of the modern quality management movement in Japan and later in the United States during the 1970s and 1980s. Walter A. Shewhart developed the concept of statistical process control (and control charts) in 1924 to control manufacturing quality at Western Electric, the manufacturing arm of the Bell Telephone system. Shewhart helped ignite a quality revolution at AT&T with his pioneering work and later became known as the father of statistical quality control. In 1937 Shewhart delivered a four-part lecture at the United States Department of Agriculture (arranged by W. E. Deming), which was later compiled into a book (with Deming's assistance), *Statistical Methods from the Viewpoint of Quality Control*, considered the bible of quality control for many years.

Dodge is known for acceptance sampling plans.

Although Shewhart's control charts provided a means for diagnosing quality problems and determining why specifications are not met, Harold F. Dodge developed acceptance sampling plans that forced movement toward managing quality in the late 1920s, as an alternative to 100 percent inspection. Dodge developed the Dodge-Romig tables in the 1920s at the Bell Labs with Harold G. Romig (Dodge was the architect of the tables and Romig supervised their construction), and the Army Ordinance tables at the outbreak of World War II. It was at Bell Laboratories during this time that the term *quality assurance* originated.

Although it may seem incongruous to begin this section on "current" philosophies with a brief review of these early quality pioneers, it was these technical methods and quality philosophies developed at Bell Laboratories that were embraced by the Japanese in the 1960s. The consultants and leaders on quality management who conveyed these methods and philosophies to the Japanese were W. Edwards Deming and Joseph Juran, both of whom were heavily influenced by Bell Labs' and Western Electric's pioneers and training.

W. Edwards Deming: The Fourteen Points

Teaching Note 3.7 W. E. Deming and Statistical Process Control

W. E. Deming was a protégé of Walter Shewhart in the 1920s.

W. Edwards Deming met Walter Shewhart in 1927 while working at the Department of Agriculture in Washington. Deming became a disciple of Shewhart's and often visited him at his home in New Jersey on weekends to discuss statistics. Deming later studied under the noted statistician Ronald A. Fisher and became a respected statistician in his own right. In 1940 Deming moved to the Census Bureau, where he introduced the use of statistical process control to monitor the mammoth operation of key punching data from census questionnaires onto millions of punch cards. During World War II Deming worked with economist (and future Nobel laureate) Milton Friedman in the Statistical Research Group at Columbia University on military-related problems. Beginning in 1942 Deming developed a national program of 8-and 10-day courses to teach statistical quality control techniques to executives and engineers of companies that were suppliers in the war effort. Over 10,000 engineers were trained in Shewhart's statistical process control techniques. Many of these individuals formed study groups at Deming's urging that eventually developed into the American Society for Quality Control. By the time World War II ended, Deming had gained an international reputation, and by the late 1940s he was accepting consulting assignments in Japan. In 1950 he began teaching statistical quality control to Japanese companies based on the series of training lectures he had developed over the years in his work with the U.S. government. Through his roles as a consultant to Japanese industries and a teacher, he was able to convince their management of the importance and benefits of statistical quality control. He has since come to be recognized as a major figure in the Japanese quality movement. In Japan he is frequently referred to as the father of quality control.

In the 1950s W. E. Deming began teaching quality control in Japan.

Deming's general approach to quality management advocates continuous improvement of the production process to achieve conformance to specifications and reduce variability. He identifies two primary sources of process improvement: eliminating common causes of quality problems, such as poor product design and insufficient worker training, and eliminating special causes, such as a specific machine or operator. Deming places great emphasis on the use of statistical quality control techniques (consistent with his training as a statistician), to reduce variability in the production process. Conversely, he dismisses the extensive use of final product inspection as being too late in the system to effectively reduce product defects to acceptable levels. Primary responsibility for quality improvement is management's and not the quality manager's and technician's. He promotes extensive employee involvement in the quality improvement program, and he recommends training for workers in quality control techniques and methods.

Deming's overall philosophy for achieving improvement is embodied in his fourteen points, summarized as follows.[17]

Deming's 14 points

Transparency 3.12 W. E. Deming's Fourteen Points

1. Create a constancy of purpose toward product improvement to achieve long-term organizational goals.
2. Adopt a philosophy of preventing poor-quality products instead of acceptable levels of poor quality as necessary to compete internationally.
3. Eliminate the need for inspection to achieve quality by relying instead on statistical quality control to improve product and process design.
4. Select a few number of suppliers or vendors based on quality commitment rather than competitive prices.
5. Constantly improve the production process by focusing on the two primary sources of quality problems, the system and workers, thus increasing productivity and reducing costs.
6. Institute worker training that focuses on the prevention of quality problems and the use of statistical quality control techniques.
7. Instill leadership among supervisors to help workers perform better.
8. Encourage employee involvement by eliminating the fear of reprisal for asking questions or identifying quality problems.
9. Eliminate barriers between departments, and promote cooperation and a team approach for working together.
10. Eliminate slogans and numerical targets that urge workers to achieve higher performance levels without first showing them how to do it.
11. Eliminate numerical quotas that employees attempt to meet at any cost without regard for quality.
12. Enhance worker pride, artisanry and self-esteem by improving supervision and the production process so that workers can perform to their capabilities.
13. Institute vigorous education and training programs in methods of quality improvement throughout the organization, from top management down, so that continuous improvement can occur.
14. Develop a commitment from top management to implement the previous thirteen points.

[17]W. Edwards Deming, "Transformation of Western Style Management," *Interfaces* 15, no. 3, (May–June 1985): 6–11.

Joseph M. Juran: Quality Control, Improvement, and Planning

Teaching Note 3.8 Joseph Juran

Joseph Juran, a highly respected author and consultant on quality, followed W. E. Deming to Japan in 1954, where he taught courses on the management of quality. Previously he had spent many years working in the quality program at Western Electric. Like Deming, he is credited with being a major contributor to the Japanese movement in quality improvement during the past three decades. As might be expected, there are similarities between the philosophies of Juran and Deming. For example, both believe that top management is ultimately responsible for quality improvement in the organization and that quality improvement is a continual, evolving process that goes on forever.

Juran is known for quality planning.

Juran's approach focuses on three elements of quality management: planning, control, and improvement. *Quality planning* is concerned with determining the product quality level and designing the production process in order to achieve the quality characteristics of the product. Strategic planning for quality is conducted within the framework of an annual quality program. It should involve management in setting goals and priorities, assessing the results of previous plans, and coordinating quality objectives with other company goals. *Quality control* uses statistical process control methods to make sure products are meeting quality standards as they move through the production process. When problems are identified, they are corrected. *Quality improvement* is achieved by focusing on chronic quality problems and applying a three-step process for securing a "breakthrough" solution: Study the problem symptoms, analyze the causes of the problem, and implement a remedy. Juran believes that at any time there should be hundreds (or perhaps even thousands) of quality improvement projects going on everywhere in the company where improvement is possible.

Phillip B. Crosby: Quality Is Free

Crosby identified the true cost of quality.

For fourteen years Phillip B. Crosby was a corporate vice president and director of quality at ITT. Now a prominent quality consultant, in 1979 he authored a popular book, *Quality is Free,* that changed the perceptions of many regarding the cost of quality. He pointed out that the costs of poor quality (including labor, machine time, lost sales, downtime, scrap, etc.) far outweigh the cost of preventing poor quality, a view not traditionally accepted by U.S. industry at that time.

Crosby promotes a quality improvement program based on what he refers to as "absolutes of quality management," which are summarized as follows. First, quality means conformance to requirements (that are set by management). Second, prevention is the means for achieving quality, which requires that the production process be analyzed and understood and all problem areas be eliminated with the aid of statistical quality control techniques. Next, Crosby believes zero defects is a reasonable and necessary quality performance standard. Finally, quality must be measured in order to access improvement. Crosby's approach for achieving quality improvement requires a commitment from top management and also that management throughout the organization understands what that commitment is and how it is to be achieved.

Armand V. Feigenbaum: Total Quality Control

Feigenbaum introduced total quality control.

Armand Feigenbaum is another noted management consultant and author on quality. He worked for a number of years in the quality area at General Electric. He introduced the concept of total quality control (TQC) and has a book by the same name, which advocates a total, companywide approach to quality management, where all members and areas of the organization are involved in quality improvement. Japanese companies in particular have adopted the TQC concept.

Total quality control, as practiced by the Japanese, requires that all areas and departments of the company, not just manufacturing, emphasize quality as the highest-priority goal. This emphasis extends to workers and supervisors, who individually have primary responsibility for quality improvement. As part of this responsibility, TQC focuses on "quality at the source," identifying quality problems at the job level or as early as possible in the production process. As a means of accomplishing quality at the source, workers and supervisors can stop an assembly line when a quality problem has been detected.

Kaoru Ishikawa: The Japanese Quality Movement

Kaoru Ishikawa developed quality circles and the fishbone diagram.

Dr. Kaoru Ishikawa of the University of Tokyo was strongly influenced by both W. Edwards Deming and Joseph Juran, and he has been instrumental in adapting the teachings and recommendations of these U.S. consultants to the Japanese culture. As mentioned previously, Dr. Ishikawa is credited with introducing quality circles as a means of involving workers and supervisors in the quality improvement process. He also developed the cause-and-effect (or fishbone) diagrams for group use in graphically analyzing quality problems. Ishikawa recognized the Japanese affinity for group participation and problem solving, which has resulted in the enormous success of quality circles in Japan. Through quality circles and such tools as cause-and-effect diagrams, he has shown how a total, companywide commitment to quality management at all levels and in all areas, as espoused by Deming, Juran, and Feigenbaum, can be accomplished.

Genichi Taguchi: The Taguchi Method

The **Taguchi method** advocates product uniformity as the key to quality.

The **Taguchi method,** developed by Dr. Genichi Taguchi, is an approach to product and process design that seeks to achieve high quality at reduced costs. In the Taguchi approach, quality is achieved with product uniformity around a target value for a quality characteristic rather than being achieved if the value of the quality characteristic simply conforms to specifications. Taguchi suggests it is more cost efficient for product quality to be consistently good—that is, near the target value, with an occasional poor-quality value—than to be always "just" within design specifications. The basis for this logic is the Taguchi loss function, which is a measure of the costs that result from poor quality (i.e., warranty costs, customer service, scrap, rework, etc.). Worker and supervisor teams cooperate to identify possible critical factors in product quality; then statistical methods are used to gather data and determine which factors are most important in achieving product quality. Settings for the production process are established based on this investigation, as are statistical experimental designs that reduce performance variation and result in product uniformity. The Taguchi method has been implemented with success by many companies in Japan and such companies as Ford, ITT, General Motors, Chrysler, and Xerox in the United States.

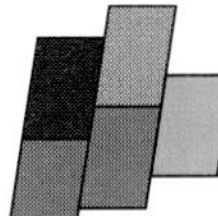

QUALITY AWARDS AND THE COMPETITIVE SPIRIT

In the previous section we presented the philosophies of well known quality pioneers, consultants, and teachers, individuals who are sometimes referred to as the "gurus" of quality. Alternatively, the Malcolm Baldrige Award, the Deming Prize, and other quality awards are entities, and, although they do not necessarily represent a "philosophy" of quality management, they have been instrumental in helping to establish a trend toward quality management in the United States.

Japanese companies did not simply adopt American quality management techniques in the early 1960s; they "adapted" them to their own unique culture and business environment. However, because of these cultural differences, many of the quality improvement approaches that have worked so well in Japan, such as extensive employee involvement through quality circles, have not been so easily adapted in America. The value of the Baldrige Award, Deming Prize, and other award competitions has been the impetus they have given American firms to commit to quality management programs because they appeal to the American competitive spirit. Americans, individuals and organizations, love contests, whether it be sporting events, beauty contests, or horse races. The Baldrige Award in America has become a valuable and coveted prize to American companies eager to benefit from the aura and reputation for quality that awaits the winners.

Americans love competition.

The Baldrige Award was created in 1987 to stimulate growth of quality management in the United States.

Video 3.2 *The Allyn and Bacon Plant Tour Video,* Program 2: "Milliken & Company: The Baldrige Award"

Video 3.3 1991 *Malcolm Baldrige Awards, Quest for Excellence*

Teaching Note 3.9 Readings About Baldrige Award Winners

The Malcolm Baldrige Award

The Malcolm Baldrige National Quality Award is given annually to a maximum of two companies in each of three categories: manufacturing companies, service companies, and small businesses (with less than 500 full-time employees). It was created by law in 1987 (named after former Secretary of Commerce Malcolm Baldrige, who died in 1987) to 1. stimulate U.S. companies to improve quality, 2. to establish criteria for businesses to use to evaluate their individual quality improvement efforts, 3. to set as examples those companies that were successful in improving quality, and 4. to help other U.S. organizations learn how to manage quality by disseminating information about the award winners' programs.

The award criteria, which are extensive, focus on the soundness of the approach to quality improvement, the overall quality management program as it is implemented throughout the organization, and customer satisfaction. (However, the award does not promote any particular philosophy, approach, or system.) The seven major categories of criteria over which companies are examined are leadership, information and analysis, strategic quality planning, human resource utilization, quality assurance of products and service, quality results, and customer satisfaction.

Teaching Note 3.10 Winning the Baldrige Award at Xerox

The Baldrige Award competition has had a marked influence on those companies who have been active participants, that is, the finalists and winners. According to a General Accounting Office report issued in 1990, the twenty-two companies who were finalists in 1988 and 1989 experienced overall corporate improvement in performance. Companies that adopted total quality management practices achieved higher productivity, better employee relations, increased market share, greater customer relations, and higher profitability. However, the Baldrige Award has also had a tremendous influence on U.S. companies, in general, promoting the need for quality improvement. Thousands of U.S. companies request applications from the government each year, primarily to obtain a copy of the award guidelines and criteria for internal use in establishing quality management programs. Many companies have made the Baldrige criteria for quality their own. Some companies have demanded that their suppliers submit applications for the Baldrige Award. Since its inception in 1987, companies that have won the Baldrige Quality Award and have become known as leaders in quality as a result include Motorola, Xerox, Cadillac, Milliken, Federal Express, and IBM, among others.

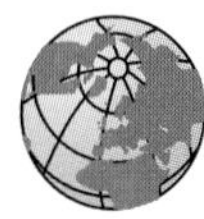

The Deming Application Prize

The Deming Prize was created in 1957 in Japan in honor of W. Edwards Deming. The purpose of the award is to recognize organizations that "successfully apply

GAINING THE COMPETITIVE EDGE

The 1992 Malcolm Baldrige Award Winners

The five recipients of the 1992 Malcolm Baldrige Awards were

AT&T Network Systems Group, Transmission Systems Business Unit, Morristown, N.J.
AT&T Universal Card Services, Jacksonville, Fla.
Granite Rock Company, Watsonville, Calif.
Texas Instruments Inc., Defense Systems and Electronics Group, Dallas, Texas
The Ritz Carlton Hotel Company, Atlanta, Ga.

Although this is a diverse group of companies, they all exhibit similar characteristics in their successful TQM programs. These characteristics include a commitment to change and to continuous improvement from top management down to all employees and workers, to product and process design that focuses on quality from the beginning, to employee education and training, to employee empowerment, to a reliance on customer input into design and feedback, to a team approach to problem solving, and to extensive use of statistical process control by all employees. All these companies experienced an improved bottom line and an enhanced ability to compete as a result of their TQM programs. The Baldrige principles provided a map to guide them toward quality improvement and customer satisfaction.

Source: Based on "Malcolm Baldrige Award, Quest for Excellence," video presented by the U.S. Department of Commerce, the Technology Administration, the National Institute of Standards and Technology, and, the American Society for Quality Control; produced by Image Associates, 1993. Distributed by Allyn and Bacon.

Video 3.4 1992 *Malcolm Baldrige Awards, Quest for Excellence V*

companywide quality control based on statistical quality control." The award is made annually to all companies who meet a set of standards. The Deming Prize is extremely prominent in Japan and, like the Baldrige award, is highly coveted and sought after.

Japan's top quality prize

There are three major award categories: (1) individuals in Japan who have made outstanding contributions in statistical quality control theory, application, or popularity; (2) organizations in Japan that achieve distinctive performance improvement through quality control; and (3) overseas companies examined according to the same criteria for Japanese companies. The ten major award criteria include policy and objectives, organization and operations, education, information, analysis, standardization, control, quality assurance, effects, and future plans. The first American company to receive the Deming Prize for Overseas Companies was the Florida Power and Light Company (in 1989).

The President's Award for Quality

The President's Award was established in 1988 to recognize federal government organizations with 500 or more employees that provide products or services to the public (except the Department of Defense). Award criteria include top management, leadership, strategic planning, customer focus, employee training, employee empowerment and teamwork, measurement and analysis, quality assurance, and quality improvement results. Two winners are selected annually. Past recipients include the Naval Air Systems Command and Air Force Logistics Command.

An award for quality within the U.S. government

A companion prize is the Quality Improvement Prototype Award for federal organizations with at least 100 employees. The President's Award represents a higher level of recognition, however, the criteria and evaluation period for the

Quality Improvement Prototype Award are similar. Past recipients include the Equal Employment Opportunity Commission, the Norfolk Naval Shipyard, the IRS Federal Tax Deposit System, and VA Kansas City Medical Center.

The IIE Award for Excellence in Productivity Improvement

Industrial Engineering prize for quality and productivity

The Award for Excellence in Productivity Improvement has been provided annually since 1980 by the Institute of Industrial Engineers (IIE) to recognize companies that have achieved a competitive advantage through productivity and quality programs. The award winner must have exceeded the norm for quality programs on a continuous basis. The four award categories include small companies/organizations, large companies/organizations, manufacturing companies, and service companies. The seven award criteria include strategic planning, leadership, management by data, productivity and quality management, training, measurement of results, and innovation. Past winners include Anheuser-Busch, Inc., Chrysler Corporation, Black and Decker Corporate Management, Norfolk Naval Shipyard, Ford Motor Company, and Texas Instruments (Johnson City, Tennessee).

NASA's Quality and Excellence Award

NASA award for quality among suppliers

The George M. Low trophy, NASA's Quality and Excellence Award, is awarded annually to current NASA contractors, subcontractors, and suppliers demonstrating excellence in quality and productivity for three or more years. The award may be given to any number of applicants who meet the standards for excellence over a specified period of time. The award criteria include customer satisfaction, quality, productivity, commitment and communication, and human resource activities. Past recipients include Thiokol Corporation and Grumman Corporation.

GAINING THE COMPETITIVE EDGE

Rockwell International and NASA's Quality and Excellence Award

The Space Systems Division (SSD) of Rockwell International Corporation has enjoyed a thirty-year relationship with NASA, working on some of the nations most important space projects, including the space shuttle program. Between 1987 and 1989, the SSD had twenty-eight NASA contracts from six different NASA centers. The quality of work performed by SSD earned it NASA's Quality and Excellence Award, the George M. Low Trophy, in 1990. SSD began its quality improvement program in 1982 and entered the award competition for the first time in 1985; it entered again in 1988 and 1989 before winning in 1990. Each time it entered, the company used the comments of the evaluators to alter its quality program. The result was not only the award but a significant improvement in SSD's competitive posture. Employee-initiated team excellence plans to improve performance saved $20 million in costs in 1989 alone, and an employee suggestion plan saved nearly $3 million between 1987 and 1990. SSD was also able to reduce nonconformance rates to a level twice as good as the industry average and reduced scrap cost to a level four times lower than the industry average.

Source: Based on Baker, C. O., "Rockwell's Space Systems Division—Striving for Excellence," *Quality and Productivity Management* 9, no. 2 (1991): 19–26.

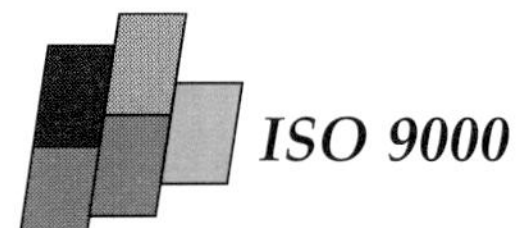

ISO 9000

The International Organization for Standardization (ISO), headquartered in Geneva, Switzerland, has as its members the national standards organizations for more than 90 countries. The ISO member for the United States is the American National Standards Institute, known as ANSI. The purpose of ISO is to seek to facilitate the development of global consensus agreements on international standards. For practical purposes, it has resulted in a system for certifying suppliers to make sure that they meet internationally accepted standards for quality management. It is a nongovernment organization and is not a part of the United Nations (although it does share some technical liaison committees with the UN).

The International Organization for Standardization

Teaching Note 3.11 Additional Readings About ISO 9000

ISO 9000 has evolved into a procedure for the international certification of suppliers.

During the decade of the 1970s it was generally acknowledged that the word *quality* had different meanings within and between industries and countries and around the world. In 1979 the ISO member representing the United Kingdom, the British Standard Institute (BSI), recognizing the need for standardization for quality management and assurance, submitted a formal proposal to ISO to form a technical committee to develop international standards for quality assurance techniques and practices. As a result ISO/Technical Committee 176, or ISO/TC 176, referred to as "Quality Assurance," was formed. Using standards that already existed in the United Kingdom and Canada as a basis, this committee set out to establish generic quality standards primarily for manufacturing firms that could be used worldwide.

The ISO 9000 series of quality management and assurance standards, developed by the ISO/TC 176 Committee over a period of seven years and first published in 1987, consists of four subsections, ISO 9001, 9002, 9003 and 9004. Following is a brief description of each of these subsections.

The ISO 9000 Series Standards

ISO 9000, the first standard in the series, titled *Quality Management and Quality Assurance Standards for Selection and Use,* is actually a guide for using the other four standards in the series, 9001, 9002, 9003 and 9004.

The ISO 9000 standards certify that suppliers have a quality management system that meets specified criteria; they do not certify individual products.

Teaching Note 3.12 The Origination of ISO 9000 Standards

ISO 9001, *Quality Systems—Model for Quality Assurance in Design/Development, Production, Installation, and Servicing,* is the standard with the widest scope of application. It applies to those instances where a supplier has responsibility for the design and development, production, installation, and servicing of a product. This standard includes a set of generic requirements for the quality management system of the supplier, beginning with top management responsibility and providing objective criteria to verify that key elements in the total quality management approach of the supplier are present. For example, ISO 9001 specifies minimum requirements for contract review procedures, design and process control, inspection, testing, etc. This standard also requires a documented system for the identification of tested products, the control of nonconforming products, and procedures for taking corrective action to avoid repeating nonconformance in processes. It further defines requirements for product handling, storage, packaging, and delivery and includes requirements for conducting internal quality audits to verify the effectiveness of the quality management system.

ISO 9002, *Quality Systems—Model for Quality Assurance in Production and Installation,* is very similar to ISO 9001 except that it is limited to cases where the supplier is not responsible for design, development, or servicing of the product. For a supplier that only produces and installs a product, ISO 9002 assures the customer that the supplier's quality system for production and installation meets basic requirements.

ISO 9003, *Quality Systems—Model for Quality Assurance in Final Inspection and Test,* is limited to cases where product design and installation is less relevant because of the relative simplicity of the product. As such, this standard is limited to providing guidelines for final inspection and testing. ISO 9003 gives a customer assurance that a supplier's final inspection and test area has quality system elements that guarantee the integrity of data about the quality of the product and actually reflect the quality of the product the customer is receiving. This standard shifts responsibility for quality to the supplier in that if the supplier's inspection and test process complies with ISO 9003, the customer is assured of that quality standard or level of quality when the product is received. Thus, it is not necessary for the customer to repeat the inspection and test process that the supplier has already done. The supplier simply provides the customer with the inspection and test data for the product.

ISO 9004, *Quality Management and Quality System Elements—Guidelines,* provides general guidelines for developing and implementing the kinds of quality management systems required in ISO 9001, 9002, and 9003. It considers management responsibility, principles of quality system development, system structure, auditing, and system review. In general, these guidelines and suggestions are aimed at helping management develop an effective quality management system so that their companies can be qualified to meet ISO 9001, 9002, and 9003 requirements. In 1991 the Technical Committee added a second part to ISO 9004, providing special attention to quality management in the service sector, since, as already mentioned, the original ISO 9000 series focused almost exclusively on the manufacturing sector. However, the ISO 9000 standards can generally be applied to the service sector by making such simple modifications as substituting terms, such as *process* for *production* and *service* for *product.*

The ISO series standards do not tell management how to meet requirements, rather they simply indicate what is required. For this reason the ISO 9000 documents are not very large. For example, 9001 and 9002 contain only seven pages of text, and 9003 has only two pages. In general, larger companies tend to use ISO 9001, and smaller companies tend to use 9002, since smaller companies are not as frequently involved in the product design process. Also, in some cases, smaller companies do not feel they can attain the type of pervasive total quality system required by 9001.

In addition to these main documents of the ISO 9000 standards, there are several supporting and complementary standards and parts, which rely heavily on existing international standards, many of which have been around for a long time. One set of documents, the three-part ISO 10011, focuses on the entire quality system auditing process. It deals with the management of the overall auditing program and specifically provides a detailed description of the objectives of quality system auditing, the role and responsibility of auditors, how the audit team is formed, how the audit should be carried out and reported, and how corrective action based on the audit should be taken. It also addresses the qualifications for auditors, including their education, training, and experience. Another document, "Application of Statistical Methods" includes basic standard techniques for statistical quality control, including sampling, inspection, control charts, and other process control methods.

Implications of ISO 9000 for U.S. Companies

The importance of ISO 9000 to companies in the United States cannot be underestimated. To understand fully the importance and significance of ISO 9000 for

United States firms, it is helpful to look briefly at the evolution of ISO 9000 since the standards were first published in 1987.

Currently, more than 50 countries have adopted the ISO 9000 standards. Originally, ISO 9000 was adopted by the twelve countries of the European Community (EC), which includes Belgium, Denmark, France, Germany, Greece, Ireland, Italy, Luxembourg, the Netherlands, Portugal, Spain, and the United Kingdom. In effect, the governments of the EC countries adopted ISO 9000 as a uniform quality standard to use for cross-border transactions within the EC and for international transactions. The EC was soon joined by the countries of the European Free Trade Association (EFTA), including Austria, Finland, Iceland, Liechtenstein, Norway, Sweden, and Switzerland, in adopting ISO 9000 standards. In addition Australia, Japan, and many other Pacific Rim countries plus South America and Africa have adopted ISO 9000.

By adopting the ISO 9000 standards, countries (especially those in the EC) are specifically acknowledging that they prefer suppliers with ISO 9000 certification. Thus, to remain competitive in international markets, U.S. companies must comply with the standards in the ISO 9000 series. Some products in the EC, for example, are "regulated" to the extent that the products must be certified to be in ISO 9000 compliance by an EC-recognized accreditation registrar. Most of these products have health and safety considerations. However, companies have discovered that in order to remain competitive and satisfy customer preferences, their products must be in compliance with ISO 9000 requirements even though these products are not specifically regulated.

Many companies overseas and in U.S. will not do business with a supplier unless it has ISO 9000 certification.

The United States exports more than $100 billion annually to the European Community market, most of it to the five EC countries France, Germany, Italy, Spain, and the United Kingdom. More than half of this $100 billion in exports is impacted by ISO 9000 standards by EC regulations requiring ISO 9000 compliance, by EC companies that prefer ISO 9000 standards, or by suppliers that voluntarily adopt ISO 9000 as a means to be more competitive.

However, companies are also being pressured within the United States to comply with ISO 9000 as more and more customers adopt ISO 9000 standards and/or certification procedures. For example, the United States Department of Defense, and specifically the Department of the Navy, has adopted ISO 9000, as have such private companies as DuPont, 3M, and AT&T. They recognize the value of these standards for helping to assure top-quality systems, products, and services and accordingly ask that their suppliers comply with ISO 9000.

Achieving ISO 9000 Accreditation

The ISO 9000 standards were originally developed according to a scheme in which customers would evaluate the quality systems of their suppliers. However, some of the EC countries, especially the United Kingdom, strongly desired a third-party appraisal system in which an accredited registrar would, for a fee, assess a company's quality system and determine whether it was in compliance with ISO 9001, 9002, or 9003 standards. If the company's quality system complied with the appropriate ISO 9000 standard, the registrar would issue it a certificate and register that certificate in a book that would be widely distributed.

ISO 9000 Certification is awarded by third-party quality assessors.

In the EC registration system, the third-party assessors of quality are referred to as *notified bodies;* that is, the twelve EC governments notify one another as to which organization in their country is the officially designated government-approved quality assessor. The notified bodies perform both product and process assessment and ultimately certify a company with a European Conformity (CE) mark. Fourteen of the twenty-three categories of products exported to the EC are currently regulated; for these products the CE mark is mandatory. The fourteen

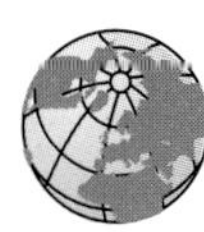

GAINING THE COMPETITIVE EDGE

The AT&T Quality Registrar

The AT&T Quality Registrar was one of the first registrars accredited by the RAB in the United States. Because of its extensive experience in working with the quality systems of its own suppliers and its experience with ISO 9000 standards, AT&T was ideally positioned to provide a great deal of knowledge to the development of the U.S. registration system. As a result, AT&T formed its own quality registrar and went through the RAB accreditation process in order to assist in the actual development of the process as it went through it. The AT&T quality registrar was accredited in 1991 and began to register companies in the United States. They could concentrate on a broad range of product areas because AT&T suppliers historically included many varied products, such as electronic components, textile products, printing products, chemicals and plastics, rubber products, and fabricated metal products.

The ISO 9000 registration process employed by AT&T includes nine steps. First, an application form is submitted by the supplier. This form includes a four-page questionnaire that provides general information about the company, including the type of product it makes, its locations, etc. Next, the company is provided with a "Quality Manual Desk Audit" in order to determine the current extent to which the company is complying with ISO 9000 standards. This step is followed by a preliminary audit, which may last from one to several days. The next step is a full audit, which typically requires two auditors and takes approximately three days. In this audit the auditors go through the whole facility to see if the company complies with ISO 9000 standards; the company is given verbal feedback immediately and a written report in a few weeks. The auditing team does not make the actual registration decision, but it presents a report to a registration board, which either approves or rejects the auditors' recommendation. The essential question the board members ask is, "If we were the customer, would we want this company to provide us with products or service?" If the board approves the company, it provides the company with a certificate and the right to use AT&T's mark and the RAB mark in its advertising and correspondence. However, the mark cannot be used on a product. The company receives a semiannual follow-up audit and a full audit every three years. Formal recognition of registration by the AT&T Quality Registrar has met with some resistance in the European Community. However, AT&T works with the supplier's European customers, explaining their registration process and credentials in order to obtain informal recognition with that particular company. They provide the supplier with whatever support is needed to prove to a European customer that they and the RAB are credible accreditation bodies. As the AT&T quality registrar and other U.S. registrars successfully convince more and more EC companies of their credibility, U.S. suppliers will find it easier to move products into and within EC markets.

Source: Based on "The AT&T Quality Registrar," *Profile of ISO 9000,* Needham Heights, Mass.: Allyn and Bacon, 1992, pp. 67–74.

regulated categories include toys, machinery, gas appliances, and many medical-related products, among others. In other words, the CE mark must be on any product exported from the United States that is ISO 9000–regulated. It is illegal to sell a regulated product in a store in the EC without the CE mark. Thus, in order for a supplier in the United States to export regulated products to an EC country, it must be accredited by European registrars that are recognized as notified bodies within the EC. However, more and more EC companies are requiring ISO 9000 certification for suppliers of products that fall in the unregulated categories, which will probably lead to a situation in the future in which virtually all products exported to the EC will require certification.

It is also important that U.S. companies obtain accreditation with a notified body that has widespread positive recognition in the EC so that they will have

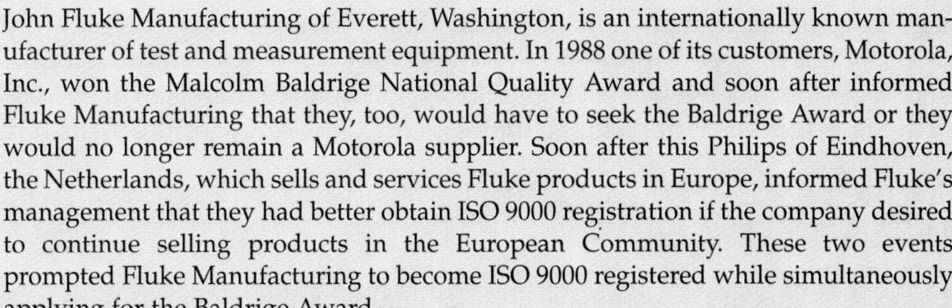

GAINING THE COMPETITIVE EDGE

Combining the Malcolm Baldrige Award and ISO 9000

John Fluke Manufacturing of Everett, Washington, is an internationally known manufacturer of test and measurement equipment. In 1988 one of its customers, Motorola, Inc., won the Malcolm Baldrige National Quality Award and soon after informed Fluke Manufacturing that they, too, would have to seek the Baldrige Award or they would no longer remain a Motorola supplier. Soon after this Philips of Eindhoven, the Netherlands, which sells and services Fluke products in Europe, informed Fluke's management that they had better obtain ISO 9000 registration if the company desired to continue selling products in the European Community. These two events prompted Fluke Manufacturing to become ISO 9000 registered while simultaneously applying for the Baldrige Award.

Management at Fluke discovered that many of the applicants for the Baldrige Award were also applying for ISO 9000 registration. The two seemed to complement each other, and both sought to achieve the same goal, a commitment to total quality. Fluke management viewed ISO 9000 as a base on which a company can build a good quality system. ISO 9000 requires documentation of processes that helps a company to understand all the quality elements of those processes. It also provides a good standard for the quality system, although standardization does not alone assure quality. The Baldrige criteria complement ISO 9000 standards by maintaining continuous improvement and by establishing measurement procedures for improving processes. To summarize, Fluke manufacturing perceives ISO 9000 as the documentation, the standardization, and the common language necessary to establish a quality management system, whereas the Baldrige criteria focus more on continuous improvement, measurement of processes, and strategic planning. They both have the common goal of customer satisfaction and an overall quality system.

Source: Based on "ISO 9000, MBNQA, and Total Quality: How They Interconnect at John Fluke Manufacturing," *Profile of ISO 9000*, Needham Heights, Mass.: Allyn and Bacon, 1992, pp. 115–120.

broad access to markets throughout the EC. In countries such as Germany and the United Kingdom, there appears to be preference for ISO registrars that are located within that country, whereas in other countries such as the Netherlands, France, and Spain there seems to be less prejudice over where certification is obtained.

Because the third-party quality registration system has become the accepted mode in the EC and because so many countries trade with EC countries, third-party registration has become important in the rest of the world, particularly the United States. However, it has not been quite as easy for the United States to initiate and develop a registration system because of the natural separation between government and business that exists in the United States but is not present in most EC countries.

As mentioned previously, the U.S. member of the ISO is the American National Standards Institute (ANSI), which designated the American Society for Quality Control (ASQC), a professional organization, as the sponsoring organization for ISO 9000 in the United States. Subsequently, ASQC negotiated with ANSI to create an independent subsidiary, the Registrar Accreditation Board (RAB), with whom ANSI subcontracted to act as the third-party registrar.

In 1992 RAB developed an auditing system for the registration of supplier companies and accreditation of registrars based on the ISO 10011 standard for quality systems auditing (which was mentioned previously). A registrar is an organization that conducts audits by individual auditors. Auditors are individuals skilled in quality systems and the manufacturing and service environments in which an audit will be performed. The registrar develops an audit team of one or more auditors to evaluate a company's quality system and then report back to the registrar. An organization that wants to become a registrar must go through a lengthy process to be accredited by RAB. Once RAB accredits a registrar by issuing a certificate, the registrar can then authorize its registered suppliers to use the RAB certificate in advertising, indicating compliance with ISO 9000. (Registrars assess companies' quality systems but not individual products; thus, the registration marks may not be used on products). In 1992 only a few RAB-approved quality system registrars existed in the United States and none of these had achieved EC accreditation. However, this list will undoubtedly grow dramatically in the future.

SUMMARY

A total commitment to quality is required throughout an organization.

In our discussions of the various aspects of quality management in this chapter, including the meaning of quality, total quality management, quality costs, productivity, the role of managers and employees, and different philosophies of quality management, certain consistencies or commonalities have surfaced. The most important perspective of product quality is the consumer's; products and processes must be designed to meet consumer expectations and needs for quality. A total commitment to quality is necessary throughout an organization for it to be successful in improving and managing product quality. This commitment must start with top management and filter down through all levels of the organization and across all areas and departments. Workers and supervisors need to be active participants in the quality-improvement process and must feel a responsibility for product quality. Workers must feel free to make suggestions to improve product quality without fear of reprisal, and some systematic procedure is necessary to involve workers and solicit their input. Improving product quality is cost effective; the cost of poor quality greatly exceeds the cost of attaining good quality. Quality costs can be minimized by seeking to improve the production process with the effective use of statistical quality control methods. In fact, the use of statistical quality control has been a pervasive part of our discussions on quality management, and it has been identified as an important part of any quality management program. In the following chapter we concentrate on statistical quality control methods and principles.

SUMMARY OF KEY FORMULAS

Quality index numbers

$$\text{Quality index} = \frac{\text{total quality costs}}{\text{base}}(100)$$

Product yield

$$Y = (I)\,(\%G) + (I)\,(1 - \%G)\,(\%R)$$

Manufacturing cost per product

$$\text{Product cost} = \frac{(K_d)(I) + (K_r)(R)}{Y}$$

Multistage product yield

$$Y = (I)\,(\%g_1)\,\ldots\,(\%g_2)$$

Quality-productivity ratio

$$\text{QPR} = \frac{\text{good-quality units}}{\text{(input)(processing cost)} + \text{(defective units)(rework cost)}}(100)$$

SUMMARY OF KEY TERMS

appraisal costs: costs of measuring, testing, and analyzing materials, parts, products, and the production process to make sure they conform to design specifications.

cause-and-effect diagram: a graphical description of the elements of a specific quality problem.

cost index: the ratio of quality cost to manufacturing cost.

external failure costs: costs of poor quality incurred after the product gets to the customer, that is, customer service, lost sales, etc.

fitness-for-use: a measure of how well a product does what the consumer thinks it is supposed to do and wants it to do.

index numbers: ratios that measure quality costs relative to some base accounting values such as sales or product units.

internal failure costs: costs of poor-quality products discovered during the production process, that is, scrap, rework, etc.

labor index: the ratio of quality cost to direct labor hours.

Pareto analysis: a method for identifying the causes of poor quality, which usually shows that most quality problems result from only a few causes.

participative problem solving: involving employees directly in the quality management process to identify and solve problems.

prevention costs: costs incurred during product design and manufacturing that prevent nonconformance to specifications.

production index: the ratio of quality cost to final product units.

productivity: a measure of effectiveness in converting resources into products, generally computed as output divided by input.

quality assurance: the management of quality throughout the organization.

quality circles: a small, voluntary group (team) of workers and supervisors formed to address quality problems in their area.

quality of conformance: the degree to which the product meets the specifications required by design during the production process.

quality of design: the degree to which quality characteristics are designed into a product.

quality-productivity ratio: a productivity index that includes productivity and quality costs.

sales index: the ratio of quality cost to sales.

Taguchi method: an approach to quality management that seeks to achieve high quality through product uniformity at low costs.

total quality control: a total, companywide systems approach to quality developed by Arnold V. Feigenbaum.

total quality management: the management of quality throughout the organization at all management levels and across all areas.

yield: a measure of productivity; the sum of good quality and reworked units.

SOLVED PROBLEMS

1. Product Yield

Problem Statement:

A manufacturing company has a weekly product input of 1,700 units. The average percentage of good-quality products is 83 percent. Of the poor-quality products, 60 percent can be reworked and sold as good-quality products. Determine the weekly product yield and the product yield if the good-product quality is increased to 92 percent.

Solution:

Step 1: Compute yield according to the formula:

$$Y = (I)\,(\%G) + (I)\,(1 - \%G)\,(\%R)$$
$$Y = (1{,}700)\,(0.83) + (1{,}700)\,(0.17)\,(0.60)$$
$$= 1{,}584.4 \text{ units}$$

Step 2: Increase %G to 92 percent:

$$Y = (1{,}700)\,(0.92) + (1{,}700)\,(0.08)\,(0.60)$$
$$= 1645.6 \text{ units}$$

2. *Quality-Productivity Ratio*

Problem Statement:

A retail telephone catalog company takes catalog orders from customers and then sends the completed orders to the warehouses to be filled. An operator processes an average of 45 orders per day. The cost of processing an order is \$1.15, and it costs \$0.65 to correct an order that has been filled out incorrectly by the operator. An operator averages 7 percent bad orders per day, all of which are reworked prior to filling the customer order. Determine the quality-productivity ratio for an operator.

Solution:

Compute the quality-productivity ratio according to the formulas,

$$QPR = \frac{\text{good-quality units}}{(\text{input})(\text{processing cost}) + (\text{defective units})(\text{rework cost})}(100)$$

$$QPR = \frac{41.85}{(45)(\$1.15) + (3.15)(\$0.65)}(100)$$

$$= 77.79$$

QUESTIONS

Teaching Note 3.13 Personal Quality Management

3-1. How does the consumer's perspective of quality differ from the producer's?
3-2. Briefly describe Garvin's *eight dimensions of quality,* for which a consumer looks in a product.
3-3. How does *quality of design* differ from *quality of conformance?*
3-4. How do the marketing and sales areas impact on product quality in a total quality management system? Purchasing?
3-5. Define the two major categories of quality cost and how they relate to each other.
3-6. What is the difference between internal and external failure costs?
3-7. A defense contractor manufactures rifles for the military. The military has exacting quality standards that the contractor must meet. The military is very pleased with the quality of the products provided by the contractor and rarely has to return products or has reason for complaint. However, the contractor is experiencing extremely high quality-related costs. Speculate on the reasons for the contractor's high quality-related costs.
3-8. Consider your school (university or college) as a production system in which the final product is a graduate. For this system:
   a. Define quality from the producer's and consumer's perspectives.

b. Develop a fitness-for-use description for final product quality.
c. Give examples of the cost of poor quality (internal and external failure costs) and the cost of quality assurance (prevention and appraisal) costs.
d. Describe how quality circles might be implemented in a university setting. Do you think they would be effective?

3-9. Explain how the Japanese perspective on the economics of quality differs from the traditional American perspective.

3-10. Describe the differences between the American and Japanese business environments and cultures that make it difficult for American companies to duplicate successfully Japan's quality management programs such as quality circles.

3-11. Describe how a quality assurance program might impact the different organizational functions shown in Figure 3.2 for a fast-food business (such as McDonald's or Burger King).

3-12. Discuss how a quality management program can affect productivity.

3-13. The Aurora Electronics Company has been receiving a lot of customer complaints and returns of a front-loading VCR that they manufacture. When a videotape is pushed into the loading mechanism, it can stick inside with the door open; the recorder cannot run, and it is difficult to get the tape out. Consumers will try to pull the tape out with their fingers or pry the tape out with an object such as a knife, pencil, or screwdriver, frequently damaging the VCR, tearing up the tape cartridge, or hurting themselves. What are the different costs of poor quality and costs of quality assurance that might be associated with this quality problem?

3-14. What are the different quality characteristics you (as a consumer) would expect to find in the following three products: a VCR, a pizza, running shoes?

3-15. AMERICARD, a national credit card company, has a toll-free, 24-hour customer service number. Describe the input for this system function and the final product. What quality-related costs might be associated with this function, and how might a quality management program impact on this area?

3-16. A number of quality management philosophies hold that prevention costs are the most critical quality-related costs. Explain the logic behind this premise.

3-17. Why is it important for companies to measure and report quality costs?

3-18. What traits of quality management are generally consistent among most current quality philosophies and trends?

3-19. Describe the primary contribution to quality management of each of the following: W. E. Deming, Joseph Juran, Phillip Crosby, Armand Feigenbaum, Kaoru Ishikawa, and Genichi Taguchi.

3-20. Describe the impact that the creation of the Malcolm Baldrige Award had on quality improvement in the United States.

3-21. Write a one- to two-page summary of an article from *Quality Progress*, *Quality Forum*, *Quality and Productivity Management*, or *Quality Review* about quality management in a company or organization.

PROBLEMS

3-1. Backwoods American, Inc., produces expensive water-repellant, down-lined parkas. The company implemented a total quality management program in 1991. Following are quality-related accounting data that have been accumulated for the past five-year period, or one year prior to the program's start.

3-1. a. 1990: 84.24%; 1991: 80.22%; 1992: 72.28%; 1993: 65.6%; 1994: 58.3%
b–d. See Solutions Manual.

	YEAR				
	1990	1991	1992	1993	1994
Quality Costs (000s)					
Prevention	$ 3.2	10.7	28.3	42.6	50.0
Appraisal	26.3	29.2	30.6	24.1	19.6
Internal failure	39.1	51.3	48.4	35.9	32.1
External failure	118.6	110.5	105.2	91.3	65.2
Accounting Measures (000s)					
Sales	$2,700.6	2,690.1	2,705.3	2,810.2	2,880.7
Manufacturing cost	420.9	423.4	424.7	436.1	435.5

a. Compute the company's total failure costs as a percentage of total quality costs for each of the five years. Does there appear to be a trend to this result? If so, speculate on what might have caused the trend.
b. Compute prevention costs and appraisal costs, each as a percentage of total costs, during each of the five years. Speculate on what the company's quality strategy appears to be.
c. Compute quality-sales indices and quality-cost indices for each of the five years. Is it possible to assess the effectiveness of the company's quality management program from these index values?
d. List several examples of each quality-related cost—that is, prevention, appraisal, and internal and external failure—that might result from the production of parkas.

3-2. a. 1990: 17,280; 1991: 17,600; 1992: 17,920; 1993: 18,240; 1994: 18,560
b. 1990: $24.83; 1991: $24.47; 1992: $24.05; 1993: $24.20; 1994: $23.70

3-2. The Backwoods American company in Problem 1 produces approximately 20,000 parkas annually. The quality management program the company implemented was able to improve the average percentage of good parkas produced by 2 percent each year, beginning with 83 percent good-quality parkas in 1990. Only about 20 percent of poor-quality parkas can be reworked.

a. Compute the product yield for each of the five years.
b. Using a rework cost of $12 per parka, determine the manufacturing cost per good parka for each of the five years. What do these results imply about the company's quality management program?

3-3. a. 139.8
b. 91.6%

3-3. The Colonial House Furniture Company manufacturers two-drawer oak file cabinets that are sold unassembled through catalogs. The company initiates production of 150 cabinet packages each week. The percentage of good-quality cabinets averages 83 percent per week, and the percentage of poor-quality cabinets that can be reworked is 60 percent.

a. Determine the weekly product yield of file cabinets.
b. If the company desires a product yield of 145 units per week, what increase in the percentage good-quality products must result?

3-4. $30; $28.63

3-4. In Problem 3, if the direct manufacturing cost for cabinets is $27 and the rework cost is $8, compute the manufacturing cost per good product. Determine the manufacturing cost per product if the percentage of good-quality file cabinets is increased from 83 percent to 90 percent.

3-5. 1991: $12.49; 1992: $11.57; 1993: $11.15; 1991–92: –7.37%; 1992–93: –3.63%

3-5. The Omega Shoe Company manufactures a number of different styles of athletic shoes. Its biggest seller is the X-Pacer running shoe. In 1991 Omega implemented a quality management program. The company's shoe production for the past three years and manufacturing costs are as follows.

	YEAR		
	1991	*1992*	*1993*
Units produced/input	32,000	34,600	35,500
Manufacturing cost	$278,000	291,000	305,000
Percent good quality	78%	83%	90%

Only one-quarter of the defective shoes can be reworked, at a cost of 20 percent of the total direct manufacturing cost.

Compute the manufacturing cost per good product for each of the three years and indicate the annual percentage of increase or decrease resulting from the quality management program.

3-6. The Colonial House Furniture Company manufactures four-drawer oak filing cabinets in six stages. In the first stage, the boards forming the walls of the cabinet are cut; in the second stage the front drawer panels are woodworked; in the third stage the boards are sanded and finished; in the fourth stage the boards are cleaned, stained, and painted with a clear finish; in the fifth stage the hardware for pulls, runners, and fittings is installed; and in the final stage the cabinets are assembled. Inspection occurs at each stage of the process, and the average percentages of good-quality units are as follows, ★

3-6. a. 185 cabinets
b. 486 cabinets

Stage	*Average Percentage Good Quality*
1	87%
2	91%
3	94%
4	93%
5	93%
6	96%

The cabinets are produced in weekly production runs with a product input for 300 units.

a. Determine the weekly product yield of good-quality cabinets.
b. What would weekly product input have to be in order to achieve a final weekly product yield of 300 cabinets?

3-7. In Problem 6, the Colonial House Furniture Company has investigated the manufacturing process to identify potential improvements that would improve quality. The company has identified four alternatives, each costing $15,000, as follows. ★

3-7. a. Alternative 2
b. Alternative 2

Alternative	*Quality Improvement*
1	Stage 1: 93%
2	Stage 2: 96%, Stage 4: 97%
3	Stage 5: 97%, Stage 6: 98%
4	Stage 2: 97%

a. Which alternative would result in the greatest increase in product yield?
b. Which alternative would be the most cost-effective?

3-8. 248

3-8. The Backwoods American company operates a telephone order system for a catolog of its outdoor clothing products. The catalog orders are processed in three stages. In the first stage the telephone operator enters the order into the computer; in the second stage the items are secured and batched in the warehouse; and in the final stage the ordered products are packaged. Errors can be made in orders at any of these stages, and the average percentage of errors that occurs at each stage are as follows.

Stage	*% Errors*
1	12%
2	8%
3	4%

If an average of 320 telephone orders are processed each day, how many errorless orders will result?

3-9. a. 4.97
b. 4.97
c. 5.51
d. 5.14

★ 3-9. The total processing cost for producing the X-Pacer running shoe in Problem 5 is $18. The Omega Shoe Company starts production of 650 pairs of the shoes weekly, and the average weekly yield is 90 percent, with 10 percent defective shoes. One-quarter of the defective shoes can be reworked at a cost of $3.75.

a. Compute the quality-productivity ratio (QPR).
b. Compute the QPR if the production rate is increased to 800 pairs of shoes per week.
c. Compute the QPR if the processing cost is reduced to $16.50 and the rework cost to $3.20.
d. Compute the QPR if the product yield is increased to 93 percent good quality.

3.10.a. 1.77
b. 2.19

★ 3-10. Airphone, Inc. manufactures cellular telephones at a processing cost of $47 per unit. The company produces an average of 250 phones per week and has a yield of 87 percent good-quality phones, resulting in 13 percent defective phones, all of which can be reworked. The cost of reworking a defective telephone is $16.

a. Compute the quality-productivity ratio (QPR).
b. Compute the QPR if the company increased the production rate to 320 phones per week while reducing the processing cost to $42, reducing the rework cost to $12, and increasing the product yield of good-quality telephones to 94 percent.

CASE PROBLEM

See Solutions Manual.

TQM at State University

As a result of several years of severe cuts to its operating budget by the state legislature, the administration at State University has raised tuition annually for the past five years. Whereas just five years ago an education at State was considered to be a bargain for both in-state and out-of-state students, it is now considered to be one of the more expensive state land-grant universities. An immediate repercussion of this policy has been a decline in applications for admission. Since a portion of state funding is tied to enrollments, State has kept its enrollments up at a constant level by going deeper into its pool of applications, taking some less qualified students.

The increase in the cost of a State degree has also caused legislators, parents, and students to be more conscious of the value of a State education—that is, the value parents and students are receiving for their money. This increased scrutiny has been fueled by numerous media reports about the decreased emphasis on teaching in universities, low teaching loads by faculty, and the large number of courses taught by graduate students. This, in turn, has led the state legislature committee on higher education to call for an "outcomes assessment program" to determine how well State University is achieving its mission of producing high-quality graduates.

On top of those problems, a substantial increase in the college-age population is expected in the next decade, resulting from a "baby boom" during the early 1980s. Key members of the state legislature have told the university administration that they will be expected to absorb their share of the additional students during the next decade. However, because of the budget situation, they should not expect any funding increases for additional facilities, classrooms, dormitory rooms, or faculty. In effect, they will be expected to do more with their existing resources. State already faces a classroom deficit, and faculty have teaching loads above the average of its peer institutions. Legislators are fond of citing a study that shows that if the university simply gets all the students to graduate within a four-year period or reduces the number of hours required for graduation, they can accommodate the extra students they will be expected to accommodate.

This entire scenario has made the university president, Fred McMahan, consider retirement. He has summarized the problems to his administration staff as "having to do more, better, with less." One of the first things he did to address these problems was to set up a number of task forces made up of faculty and administrators to brainstorm a variety of topics. Among the topics and problems these task forces addressed were quality in education, educational success, graduation rules, success rates in courses (i.e., the percentage of students passing), teaching, the time to graduation, faculty issues, student issues, facilities, class scheduling, admissions, and classroom space.

Several of the task forces included faculty from engineering and business. These individuals noted that many of the problems the university faced would benefit from the principles and practices of a total quality management (TQM) approach. This recommendation appealed to Fred McMahan and the academic vice president, Anne Baker.

Discuss in general terms how TQM philosophy and practices might be instituted at State University.

CASE PROBLEM

Product Yield at Continental Luggage Company

★ See Solutions Manual.

The Continental Luggage Company manufactures several different styles of soft- and hardcover luggage, briefcases, hanging bags, and purses. Their best-selling item is a line of hardcover luggage called the "Trotter." It is produced in a basic five-stage assembly process that can accommodate several different outer coverings and colors. The assembly process includes constructing a heavy-duty plastic and metal frame, attaching the outer covering, joining the top and bottom and attaching the hinge mechanism, attaching the latches, lock, and handle, and doing the finishing work, including the luggage lining.

The market for luggage is extremely competitive, and product quality is a very important component in product sales and market share. Customers normally expect luggage to be able to withstand rough handling, while at the same time retaining its shape and an attractive appearance and protecting the clothing and personal items inside the bag. They also prefer the bag to be lightweight and not cumbersome. Furthermore, customers expect the latches and locks to work properly over an extended period of time. Another key factor in sales is that the luggage must be stylish and visually appealing.

Because of the importance of quality, company management has established a process control procedure that includes inspection at each stage of the five major stages of the assembly process. The following table shows the percentage of good-quality units yielded at each stage of the assembly process and the percentage of bad units that can be reworked, on average.

Assembly Stage	*Average Percentage Good Quality*	*Average Percentage Reworked*
1	0.94	0.23
2	0.96	0.91
3	0.95	0.67
4	0.97	0.89
5	0.98	0.72

The first stage of the process is construction of the frame, and it is very difficult to rework the frame if an item is defective, which is reflected in the low percentage of reworked items.

Five hundred new pieces of luggage of a particular style and color are initiated through the assembly process each week. The company would like to know the weekly product yield and the number of input units that would be required to achieve a weekly yield of 500 units. Further, the company would like to know the impact on product yield (given 500 initial starting units) if a quality improvement program was introduced that would increase the average percentage of good-quality units at each stage by 1 percent.

REFERENCES

Crosby, P. B., *Quality is Free,* New York: McGraw-Hill, 1979.

Deming, W. E., *Out of the Crisis,* Cambridge, Mass.: M.I.T. Center for Advanced Engineering Study, 1986.

Evans, J. R., and W. M. Lindsay, *The Management and Control of Quality,* 2d ed., St. Paul, Minn.: West, 1993.

Feigenbaum, A. V., *Total Quality Control,* 3d ed., New York: McGraw-Hill, 1983.

Garvin, D. A., *Managing Quality,* New York: The Free Press/Macmillan, 1988.

Ishikawa, K., *Guide to Quality Control,* 2d ed., White Plains, N.Y.: Kraus International Publications, 1986.

Juran, J. M., *Juran of Planning for Quality,* New York: The Free Press/Macmillan, 1988.

Juran, J. M., and F. M. Gryna, Jr., *Quality Planning and Analysis,* 2d. ed., New York: McGraw-Hill, 1980.

Montgomery, D. C., *Introduction to Statistical Quality Control,* 2d ed., New York: John Wiley, 1991.

Profile of ISO 9000, Needham Heights, Mass.: Allyn and Bacon, 1992.

Taguchi, G., *Introduction to Quality Engineering,* Tokyo: Asian Productivity Organization, 1986.

4 STATISTICAL QUALITY CONTROL

CHAPTER OUTLINE

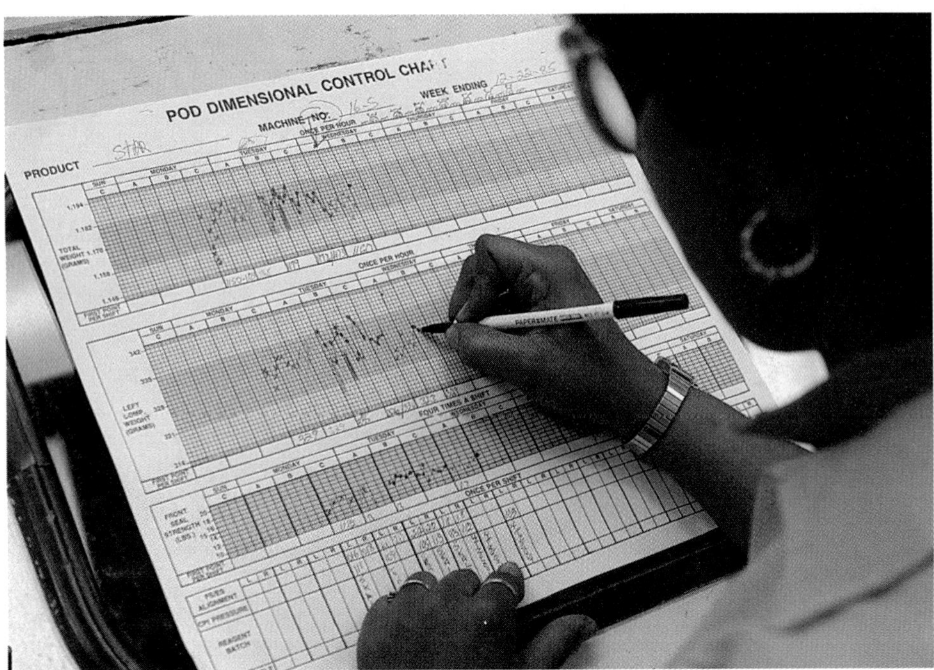

A statistical control chart like the one this factory worker is using is a graph to monitor a production process. Samples are taken from the process periodically and the results plotted on the graph. If the sample results move outside of the upper or lower limits on the graph it may indicate that something is wrong in the process, that is, it is not in control, which may result in defective or poor quality items. By monitoring the production process with a control chart the worker and management can detect problems quickly and prevent poor-quality items from passing on through the remainder of the process, and ending up as defective products that must be thrown away or reworked, thus wasting time and resources. Control charts have become one of the most important statistical tools in TQM for continuous quality improvement. Basic training in statistical process control for all workers and managers is now a fundamental educational activity at many companies that have adopted TQM.

STATISTICAL PROCESS CONTROL AT KURT MANUFACTURING

Video 4.1 *Total Quality Management*

Kurt Manufacturing Company, based in Minneapolis, is a midsize supplier of precision machine parts. It operates six plants with approximately 1,100 employees. In order to remain competitive in international markets Kurt has adopted a commitment to continuous quality improvement through TQM principles and practices. One of the primary tools Kurt employs in its TQM program is statistical process control (SPC). All Kurt employees at all six plants—from janitors to top managers—received 30 hours of basic training in SPC. SPC training was conducted by 20 employees within Kurt, who were taught SPC methods. Kurt wrote their own SPC manual using data from the plant floor for examples.

SPC is a primary tool for machine operators to monitor their process by measuring variability, reliability, repeatability, and predictability for their machines. Training stresses that SPC is a tool for operators to use in monitoring manufacturing processes and making quality improvement, not just for the sake of documentation. Operators control their own processes, and SPC charts are kept by the operator directly on the shop floor. When SPC charts show processes to be out of control, operators are taught to investigate the process to see what causes the out of control condition. Kurt has a firm policy that if a process is out of control, operators have the right and responsibility to shut down and make corrections. A problem within control limits of the SPC chart can be corrected by the operator, whereas a correction for a problem outside the control limits must be endorsed by a supervisor.

A number of Kurt's customers have reduced their suppliers in recent years, some from as many as 3,000 suppliers to around 150. In most cases Kurt Manufacturing has survived these cuts because of its commitment to TQM principles and continuous quality improvement.[1]

Teaching Note 4.1 The Evolution of Statistical Quality Control

After World Ward II W. E. Deming, the noted quality expert and consultant, was invited to Japan by the Japanese government to give a series of lectures on improving product reliability. This action was probably the single most important event that started the Japanese down the road that has ultimately led to a global quality revolution and the development of total quality management. The content of these lectures was based on statistical quality control. They included the principles and concepts of statistical quality control that Deming had originally learned from Walter Shewhart, the pioneer in statistical quality control at Bell Telephone Laboratories in the 1920s. Japanese companies adapted Deming's teachings on statistical quality control to their own needs and environments, and they became a cornerstone of their evolving commitment and approach to quality management.

The two primary topics in statistical quality control are *statistical process control (SPC)* and *acceptance sampling*. **Statistical process control (SPC)** is a statistical procedure using control charts to check a production process to see if any part of it is in some way not functioning properly, which could lead to poor quality. One of W. E. Deming's fourteen points for effective quality management is to use inspection methods for improving processes, which is what SPC does. In a TQM environment operators use SPC methods to inspect and measure items during the production process to see if the process is varying at all from what it is supposed to be doing. If there is unusual or unwarranted variability, the process is corrected so that defective items will not occur. In this way statistical process control is used to prevent poor quality before it occurs. It is such an important part of quality management in Japan that virtually all workers at all levels in Japanese companies are given extensive and continual training in SPC methods and concepts. Conversely, in the United States one of the main reasons cited for the past failure of companies to achieve high quality is the lack of comprehensive training for employees in SPC methods. U.S. companies that have enjoyed recent success in adopting a TQM approach train all their employees in SPC methods and make extensive use of SPC for continuous process improvement.

Statistical process control (SPC) involves monitoring the production process to prevent poor quality.

Employee training in SPC is a fundamental principle of TQM.

The other primary topic in statistical quality control, **acceptance sampling,** involves inspecting a sample of product input (i.e., raw materials or parts) and/or the final product and comparing it to a quality standard. If the sample fails the comparison, or test, then that is seen to imply poor quality, and the entire group of items from which the sample was taken is rejected. This traditional approach to quality control directly conflicts with the philosophy of TQM in that it assumes

Acceptance Sampling involves taking a random sample to determine if a lot is acceptable.

[1]*Total Quality Management*, video produced by the Society of Manufacturing Engineers (SME) and distributed by Allyn and Bacon, 1993.

that some degree of poor quality will occur and that it is acceptable. TQM, at least theoretically, seeks ultimately to have zero defects and absolute quality. Acceptance sampling is a statistical method for identifying defective items after the product is already finished, whereas TQM preaches the need to prevent defective items altogether. To disciples of TQM, acceptance sampling is simply a means of identifying the products to throw away or rework. It does nothing to prevent poor quality and to ensure good quality in the future. Nevertheless, acceptance sampling is still used by many firms that, for whatever reason, have not adopted a TQM approach. There may come a time in the future when TQM becomes so pervasive that acceptance sampling will be used not at all or to a very limited extent. However, that time has not yet arrived, and until it does acceptance sampling still is an important topic to study.

INSPECTION

Traditional role of inspection—at beginning and end of the production process

Inspection in the past traditionally focused on incoming parts and materials and the final product. When materials were received from the supplier, mass inspections were undertaken by inspectors. If a certain number of defective items were found, whole shipments would be returned to the supplier. This approach reflected virtually no confidence in the ability of the supplier to deliver quality parts or material. It delayed the production process, making it more difficult to manage; it created waste, and the expense of inspecting added cost to the product but no value. Inspection of the final product before it was shipped had similar results. If a certain number of defective items were found, entire lots or batches would be scrapped or reworked, disrupting the production process, wasting parts and material, and adding unnecessary cost to the product.

Inspection also occasionally occurred during the production process, but it was usually minimal. When process inspection occurred, it was conducted by inspectors who would test parts in an area away from the process, separate from the operators. This form of inspection and testing was slow, allowing the process to continue to produce defective items while testing was being conducted. Furthermore, it separated the detection of quality problems from those individuals most likely to understand the cause of the problem and be able to make corrections rapidly, the operators. This method of inspection (at least psychologically) relieved the operator from the responsibility of detecting defective items and quality problems; that was inspection's job.

The Changing Role of Inspection

In TQM, inspection is part of process.

With the advent of TQM principles and practices, the traditional role of inspection has largely been discredited. W. E. Deming has as one of his tenets that mass inspection is an ineffective and inefficient means of quality control. In an ideal TQM environment suppliers are expected to deliver quality parts and materials, making local inspection unnecessary. TQM practices focus on making certain that quality is achieved during the production process by continuous quality improvement, thus obviating the need for final inspection. Once a product is finished and it is found to be defective, the damage has already been done. All inspection does is identify a problem that should have been corrected much earlier in the process, as soon as it occurred. With the TQM approach the operator ideally serves as the inspector, identifying quality problems and causes and making the necessary corrections. Operators inspect items and use SPC methods to determine if the process is in control or not. If it is not, the operator either corrects the problem or works with other employees and managers to make corrections. This approach serves to eliminate defective items during the process, making final inspection unnecessary.

However, an ideal TQM environment does not exist universally for all companies. As a result, initial and final inspections are still a major and important function for many companies. In addition, there are instances where inspection of materials and final inspection are necessary even in a TQM environment. Government regulations sometimes require inspection to ensure quality, such as with military equipment or in the space program. Customers may require independent inspections to guarantee quality, such as with critical medical supplies or equipment where a defective part could be life-threatening. Some items may require inspection with specially designed equipment and trained inspectors.

How Much to Inspect

At the extreme, management can individually inspect each unit that is produced, which is known as complete, or 100 percent, inspection. If the cost of delivery (or of accepting) a defective item is very high when compared to the cost of inspecting every item, then complete inspection is a viable—and possibly preferred—alternative. For example, a company that produces canisters for poison gas might be compelled to inspect each unit, since the cost of inspecting the canisters is relatively less expensive than that of the possible catastrophe, injury, or even death that might result from a defective canister. However, 100 percent inspection does not guarantee that no defective items will result. Human or equipment error in the testing process can allow a defective item to escape.

For most companies, the cost of complete inspection is prohibitive or complete inspection is not necessary. Instead, only partial inspection, or the inspection of some portion of the units produced, is required. In partial inspection the number of items inspected is called a *sample.* The statistical quality control procedures in this chapter are based on taking samples for inspection purposes. One of the primary considerations in designing these procedures is determining the size of the sample. The sample size must be of sufficient size to assess accurately the quality of the process, part, or product. However, the larger the sample and the more frequently a sample is taken, the higher the cost will be and the more time it will take.

A *sample* is a portion of the items produced, which are used for inspection.

Inspection Location

Traditionally, inspection occurred at the end of the production process, just before the finished product was passed on to the retail store or customer. However, in a TQM approach inspection occurs throughout the production process. Inspection at the beginning of the production process involves checking the raw materials or purchased parts from suppliers from which the final product is produced. If the materials are bad to begin with, the final product will be of poor quality, and the resources that went into the production process will have been wasted.

Inspection occurs during the production process itself as the product passes through the various stages of work-in-process. One objective of inspection at workstations is to determine if the production process is functioning properly, that is, if it is *in control* or *out of control.* An out-of-control process can signify that machinery is malfunctioning or not set properly; operators are fatigued, careless, or not operating properly; poor-quality work-in-process units are being fed into the workstation; or the measurement process is faulty. Correcting a quality problem during the production process is the primary focus of TQM, and it will ideally reduce the number of potentially defective units of finished product to zero.

In TQM, inspection occurs throughout the production process.

In TQM, the operator is ideally the inspector.

As we mentioned, in an ideal TQM environment the operator serves as the inspector, inspecting items as they come through the workstation and taking immediate corrective action. However, this is not always feasible. Inspecting parts may be time-consuming and slow down the process too much if the operator inspects, or it may require special skills or training. In these cases, inspection stations are necessary.

Ideally, inspection would take place before all operations. However, it may be expensive to inspect before or after each processing station, in which case companies must locate inspection stations where they will have the greatest effect. A key location for an inspection station during the production process is before an irreversible operation, after which the product cannot be reworked but must be discarded. Other locations are prior to a costly operation that requires a large relative expenditure of time, labor, or resources or before an assembly or painting operation that might mask a defect. Another key location is after an operation that is likely to generate a large number of defects.

Final inspection takes place at the end of the production process, prior to the customer's receiving the product. Typically, the final product is subject to a quality standard set by the customer, directly or indirectly. The customer may have specified an expected quality level in a contract or an informal agreement. In a TQM environment the company knows what level of quality its customers expect and the amount of business they will lose if they do not meet those expectations. However, discovery of defective items during final inspection results in scrap and rework, which is very costly. This fact is an important consideration when determining at what stage in the production process to inspect. The earlier in the production process that defective items are detected, the fewer the resources that will be wasted in subsequent stages in the process on products that may ultimately be thrown away.

The earlier in the process that poor quality is detected, the fewer the resources that are wasted.

In this chapter we will focus on two statistical procedures for inspecting samples. The first method, statistical process control, is used to monitor the production process that transforms materials, parts, or people into a finished product or service. SPC is now clearly recognized as one of the most important tools in TQM for achieving quality improvement. The second method, acceptance sampling, is used to determine the quality of the raw materials and purchased parts prior to the beginning of the production process and to check the quality of finished goods at the end of the production process. Since acceptance sampling allows for some acceptable level of poor quality, it conflicts with the contemporary philosophy of TQM. As a result it is no longer as popular as it once was. Nevertheless, there are many companies who have not yet adopted TQM, and for them acceptance sampling is still used as a quality control method.

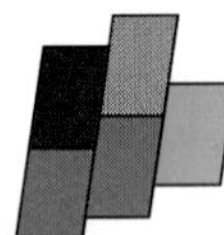

STATISTICAL PROCESS CONTROL

Teaching Note 4.2 The Early Use of Control Charts

Statistical process control focuses on the product while it is being produced—that is, during the production process—in order to ensure that good-quality final items result. In general terms, process control is achieved by taking periodic samples from the process and seeing if the process average is within statistical control limits. If the process average is outside the limits, the process is determined to be out of control, and the cause is sought so that the problem can be corrected. If the process average is within the control limits, the process simply continues without interference but with continued monitoring. Applied in this manner, SPC is a means of preventing quality problems by correcting the process before it starts producing defective items.

No production process produces exactly identical items, one after the other. All production processes contain a certain amount of variability that renders some degree of variation between units inevitable. This variation may be very slight or pronounced. There are essentially two reasons why a production process might vary. The first reason is simply the inherent random variability of the process, which depends on the equipment and machinery, engineering, and the system used for measurement. Variability because of this reason is a result of natural common occurrences. The other reason for variability is unique or special causes that are identifiable and that management can seek to correct. These causes tend to be nonrandom and, if left unattended, will continue to cause variability and poor quality. These might include, among other causes, equipment that is out of adjustment, defective materials, changes in parts of materials, broken machinery or equipment, operator fatigue or poor work methods, or errors due to lack of training.

All processes have variability—random and nonrandom (identifiable, correctable).

SPC in a TQM Environment

In a TQM operating environment, SPC is used primarily by operators to test their own process to see if it is in control—that is, working properly. This procedure requires that all operators or workers be trained in the use of SPC methods and concepts. In general, companies adopting TQM provide such training on a continuing basis. TQM training normally stresses that SPC is a tool for operators to use to monitor their part of the production process *for the purpose of making improvements.* SPC is not just a means of collecting information about the process; it has a function. Through the use of statistical process control, the workers are made responsible for quality in their area. It is the operator's responsibility to identify problems and either correct them or seek help in correcting them. By continually monitoring the production process and making improvements, the operator contributes to the overall TQM goal of continuous improvement and zero defects.

SPC is a tool for identifying problems in order to make improvements.

Although in TQM operators ideally employ SPC methods to monitor their own areas of responsibility in the production process, in some cases an inspector or inspection station may be required. If the inspection and measurement process is abnormally time-consuming, then it may slow down the operator too much to perform these activities. Also, the inspection and measurement process may be very complex, with elaborate measuring equipment that requires specially trained inspectors with special technical skills.

As mentioned, when SPC methods indicate that a process is out of control, it is the responsibility of the operator either to correct the problem or initiate the correction process. The first step in correcting the problem is identifying the causes. In Chapter 3 we briefly described several quality control tools used for identifying causes of problems, including brainstorming, Pareto charts, histograms, check sheets, quality circles, and fishbone (cause-and-effect) diagrams.

When an operator is unable to individually correct a problem, the supervisor is typically notified who might initiate a group problem-solving process. This group may be in the form of a quality circle or it may be less formal including other operators, engineers, quality experts, and the supervisor. This group would brainstorm the problem to seek out possible causes. They might use a technique such as a fishbone diagram to assist in identifying problem causes. Sometimes this process requires experiments to be conducted under controlled conditions to isolate the cause of a problem.

Quality Measures: Attributes and Variables

An **attribute** is a product characteristic that can be evaluated with a discrete response (good/bad, yes/no).

The quality of a product can be evaluated using either an *attribute* of the product or a *variable measure.* An **attribute** is a product characteristic such as color, surface

GAINING THE COMPETITIVE EDGE

Statistical Process Control at ITT

ITT Electro-Optical Products Division in Roanoke, Virginia, is a major designer, developer, and producer of night-vision image-intensification devices for use in such products as helicopter pilot's goggles. The manufacturing process for these devices is extremely complex, requiring more than 400 processes, 200 chemicals, and the combination of such technologies as fiber optics, electronics, chemistry and semiconductors. In 1986 the company implemented a TQM program that increased manufacturing yield from 35 percent to more than 75 percent by 1989. A significant component in the successful quality management program was the use of statistical process control methods for sampling and statistical analysis of the process output. Statistical process control methods were used to reduce variation in raw material, subassembly purchases, internal processing, and assembly operations that affected final product quality. All senior managers and supervisors were trained in the use of statistical process control techniques by the ITT Statistical Program Group.

Source: Based on Kempster, J.E., "ITT Electro-Optical Products Division, Roanoke, Virginia," *Quality and Productivity Management* 9, no. 2 (1991): 37–46.

texture, or perhaps even smell or taste. Attributes can be evaluated quickly with a simple discrete response such as good or bad, acceptable or not acceptable, or yes or no. Even if quality specifications are very extensive, an attribute test might be used to determine if a product is or is not defective. For example, an operator or inspector might test a television set by simply turning it on and seeing if it has a picture and sound. If it does not work, it can be examined to find out the exact technical cause for failure, but for inspection purposes, the fact that it is defective has been determined.

A **variable measure** is a product characteristic that can be measured (weight, length).

A **variable measure** is a product characteristic that is measured on a continuous scale such as length, weight, volume, or time. For example, the amount of liquid detergent in a plastic container can be measured according to weight (or volume) to see if it conforms to the company's product specifications. If the weight of the liquid detergent is outside of specified limits for several containers in a production lot, then the whole lot might be rejected. Since a variable evaluation is the

This Goodyear employee is using a dial caliper to measure variations in tire tread in a tire mold. The dial caliper is a mechanical device, or gage, in which movable contacts touch the object to be measured and, using a gear train, translate the dimensions to the dial where it can be read by the operator. Measurements from a gage like this are accurate to within 0.001 inch. Digital gages, that perform the same function electronically, are generally more accurate than a mechanical gage. Measuring instruments like the dial caliper are used by operators to take sample measurements during the inspection process for use with a process control chart.

result of some form of measurement, it is sometimes referred to as a *quantitative* classification method. Alternatively, an attribute evaluation is sometimes referred to as a *qualitative* classification, since the response is not measured. Because it is a measurement, a variable classification typically provides more information about the product; that is, the weight of a product is more informative than simply saying the product is good or bad.

CONTROL CHARTS

The primary tool used in SPC to determine if processes are in control or not is the *control chart.* **Control charts** are graphs that visually show if sample results are within statistical **control limits.** They have two basic purposes, to establish the control limits for a process and then to monitor the process to indicate when it is out of control. Control charts exist for attributes and variables; within each category there are several different types of control charts. We will present four commonly used control charts, two in each category: *mean* ($\bar{x}$) and *range (R)* control charts for variables and *p*-charts and *c*-charts for attributes. Even though these control charts differ in how they measure process control, they all have certain similar characteristics. They all are visually alike, with a line through the center of the graph that indicates the process average and lines above and below the center line that represent the upper and lower limits of the process, as shown in Figure 4.1.

A **control chart** is a graph that establishes the control limits of a process.

Control limits are the upper and lower bands of a control chart.

Types of charts: variables, $\bar{x}$ and R, and attributes, p and c

Each time a sample is taken, the sample average is recorded as shown in Figure 4.1. In general, a process is *in control* if the following occur:

Characteristics of a process "in control"

1. There are no sample points outside the control limits.
2. Most points are near the process average (i.e., the control line), without too many close to the control limits.
3. Approximately equal numbers of sample points occur above and below the center line.
4. The points appear to be randomly distributed around the center line (i.e., no discernible pattern).

If any of these guidelines are violated the process may be *out of control.* Thus, the reason must be determined, and if the cause is not random, the problem must be corrected.

Transparency 4.1 Process Control Chart and Control Criterion

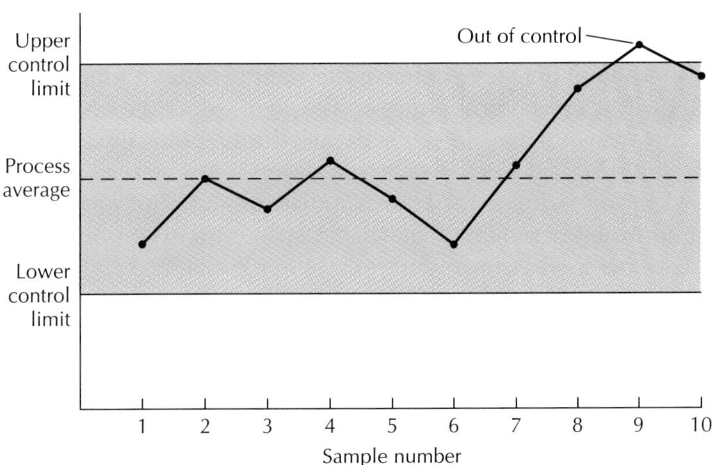

FIGURE 4.1 Process Control Chart

Since the sample average obtained for sample 9 in Figure 4.1 is beyond the upper control limit, the control chart suggests the process is out of control. The cause for this occurrence is not likely to be random, so management should attempt to find out what is wrong with the process and bring it back in-control. Note that, although the results for all the other samples generally display some degree of variation from the process average, they are usually considered to be caused by normal, random variability in the process and are thus in control. However, it is possible for sample observations to be within the control limits and for the process to be out of control anyway, if the observations display a discernible, abnormal pattern of movement. We discuss such patterns in a later section.

The development of a control chart

Theoretically, a process control chart should be based only on sample observations from when the process is in control so that the control chart reflects a true benchmark for an in-control process. However, it is not known whether the process is in control or not until the control chart is initially constructed. Therefore, when a control chart is first developed and the process is found to be out of control, if nonrandom causes are the reason for the out-of-control observations, these observations (and any others influenced by the nonrandom causes) should be discarded. A new center line and control limits should then be determined from the remaining observations. This "corrected" control chart is then used to monitor the process. It may not be possible to discover the cause(s) for the out-of-control sample observations. In this case a new set of samples can be taken, and a completely new control chart can be constructed. Alternatively it may be decided to simply use the initial control chart assuming that it accurately reflects the process variation.

Control Charts for Attributes

A ***p-chart*** uses the proportion defective in a sample.

A ***c-chart*** uses the number of defective items in a sample.

The quality measures used in *attribute control charts* are discrete values reflecting a simple-decision criterion such as good or bad. As we mentioned earlier, we will present two of the more commonly used attribute control charts, *p*-charts and *c*-charts. A ***p*-chart** uses the proportion defective items in a sample as the sample statistic, whereas a ***c*-chart** uses the actual number of defective items in a sample. A *p*-chart can be used when it is possible to distinguish between defective and nondefective items. In such cases it is possible to state the number of defectives as a percentage of the whole. However, in some processes, the proportion defective cannot be determined. For example, when counting the number of blemishes on a roll of upholstery material (at periodical intervals), it is not possible to compute a proportion. In this case a *c*-chart is required.

p-Chart

With a *p*-chart a sample is taken periodically from the production process and the proportion of defective items in the sample is determined to see if the proportion falls within the control limits on the chart. Since a *p*-chart employs a discrete attribute measure (i.e., defective items), it is theoretically based on the binomial distribution. However, as the sample size gets larger, the normal distribution can be used to approximate the binomial distribution. This enables us to use the following formulas based on the normal distribution to compute the upper control limit (UCL) and lower control limit (LCL) of a *p*-chart.

Control limits of a *p*-chart

$$\text{UCL} = p + z\sigma_p$$
$$\text{LCL} = p - z\sigma_p$$

where

z = the number of standard deviations from the process average

p = the population proportion defective, also referred to as the process average
σ_p = the standard deviation of the sample proportion

The sample standard deviation is computed as

$$\sigma_p = \sqrt{\frac{p(1-p)}{n}}$$

where n is the sample size.

If the population proportion defective, p, is not known, then an estimate of the proportion defective, $\bar{p}$, can be computed from the samples. In that case, $\bar{p}$ would replace p in the preceding formulas for control limits and standard deviation.

In the control limit formulas for p-charts (and other control charts), z is occasionally equal to 2.00 but most frequently is 3.00. A z value of 2.00 corresponds to an overall normal probability of 95 percent and $z = 3.00$ corresponds to a normal probability of 99.74 percent. The smaller the value of z, the more narrow the control limits are and the more sensitive the chart is to changes in the production process. Control charts using $z = 2.00$ are often referred to as having "2-sigma" (2σ) limits (referring to two standard deviations), whereas $z = 3.00$ means "3-sigma" (3σ) limits.

Sigma limits are the number of standard deviations.

Management usually selects $z = 3.00$ because if the process is in control they want a high probability that the sample values will fall within the control limits. In other words, with wider limits management is less likely to (erroneously) conclude that the process is out of control when points outside the control limits are due to normal, random variations. Alternatively, wider limits make it harder to detect changes in the process that are not random and have an assignable cause. A process might change because of a nonrandom, assignable cause and be detectable with the narrower limits but not with the wider limits. However, as we mentioned, management traditionally uses the wider control limits.

The following example demonstrates how a p-chart is constructed.

EXAMPLE 4.1

Alternate Example 4.1

Construction of a p-chart

Problem Statement:

The Western Jeans Company produces denim jeans. The company wants to establish a p-chart to monitor the production process and maintain high quality. They believe that approximately 99.74 percent of the variability in the production process (corresponding to 3-sigma limits, or $z = 3.00$) is random and thus should be within control limits, whereas .26 percent of the process variability is not random and suggests that the process is out of control.

The company has taken 20 samples (one per day for 20 days), each containing 100 pairs of jeans ($n = 100$), and inspected them for defects, the results of which are as follows.

Sample	*Number of Defectives*	*Proportion Defective*
1	6	.06
2	0	.00
3	4	.04
4	10	.10
5	6	.06

Table continues

Sample	*Number of Defectives*	*Proportion Defective*
6	4	.04
7	12	.12
8	10	.10
9	8	.08
10	10	.10
11	12	.12
12	10	.10
13	14	.14
14	8	.08
15	6	.06
16	16	.16
17	12	.12
18	14	.14
19	20	.20
20	18	.18
	200	

The proportion defective for the population is not known. The company wants to construct a p-chart in order to determine when the production process might be out of control.

Solution:

Since p is not known, it can be estimated from the total sample:

$$\bar{p} = \frac{\text{total defectives}}{\text{total sample observations}}$$

$$= \frac{200}{20(100)}$$

$$= 0.10$$

The control limits are computed as follows.

$$\text{UCL} = \bar{p} + z\sqrt{\frac{\bar{p}(1-\bar{p})}{n}}$$

$$= 0.10 + 3.00\sqrt{\frac{0.10(1-0.10)}{100}} = 0.190$$

$$\text{LCL} = \bar{p} - z\sqrt{\frac{\bar{p}(1-\bar{p})}{n}}$$

$$= 0.10 - 3.00\sqrt{\frac{0.10(1-0.10)}{100}} = 0.010$$

The resulting p-chart, including the sample points, is shown in the following figure.

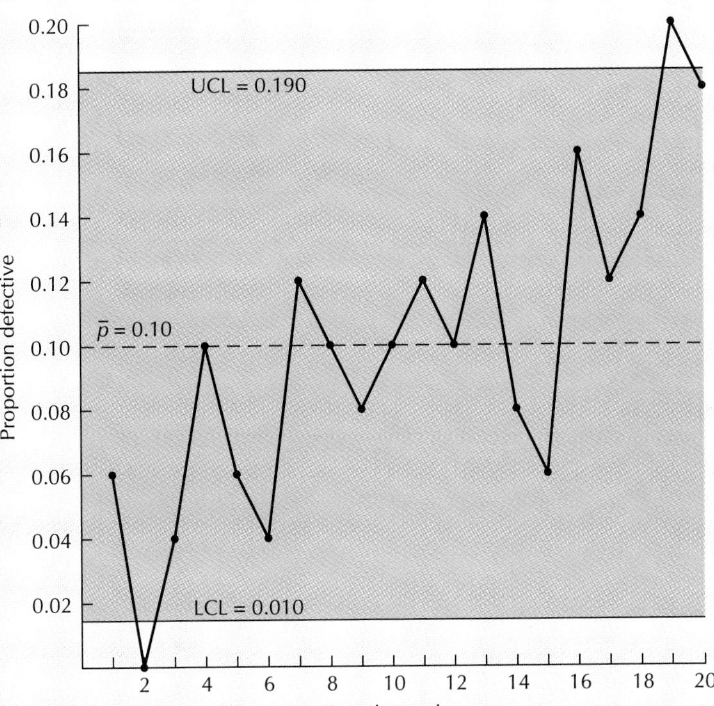

Transparency 4.2 *p*-Chart for Example 4.1

Observe that the process was below the lower control limits for sample 2 (i.e., during day 2). Although this could be perceived as a "good" result, it might also suggest to management that something was wrong with the inspection process during that week that should be checked out. If there is no problem with the inspection process, then management would probably be interested in what caused the quality of the process to improve. Perhaps "better" denim material from a new supplier was used or a different operator was working that day.

The process was above the upper limit during day 19. This suggests that the process may not be in control and the cause should be investigated. The cause could be defective or maladjusted machinery or a problem with an operator, defective materials (i.e., denim cloth), or a number of other correctable problems. In fact, there is an upward trend in the number of defectives throughout the 20-day test period that becomes distinct at week 15. This indicates the process was consistently moving toward an out-of-control situation. This trend represents a pattern in the observation, which suggests a nonrandom cause. If this was the actual control chart used to monitor the process (and not the initial chart), it is likely this pattern would have indicated an out-of-control situation before week 19, which would have alerted the operator to make corrections. Patterns are discussed in a separate section later in this chapter.

Patterns indicating a nonrandom cause; see page 166.

The initial construction of this control chart shows two out-of-control observations and a distinct pattern of increasing defects. Thus, management would probably want to discard this set of samples and develop a new center line and control limits from a different set of sample values after the process has been corrected. If the pattern had not existed and only the two out-of-control observations were present, these two observations could be discarded, and a control chart could be developed from the remaining sample values, if the problem is corrected.

GAINING THE COMPETITIVE EDGE

Process Control Charts at P*I*E Nationwide

P*I*E Nationwide, formed by the merger of Ryder Truck Lines and Pacific Intermountain Express, is the nation's fourth-largest trucking company. An important part of the company's "Blueprint for Quality" program is the extensive use of statistical process control charts. A *p*-chart was initially used to monitor the proportion of daily defective freight bills. This resulted in a reduction in the error rate in freight bills from 10 percent per day to 0.8 percent within one year, and the subsequent reduction in inspection time increased productivity by 30 percent. Although the freight bill–rating process was in control, the company continued to evaluate the causes of the remaining errors. Using a *p*-chart for the proportion of bill of lading defects, the company found that 63 percent of the bills of lading P*I*E received from its customers contained errors. Many of the errors were corrected by employees (at a rework cost of $1.83 per error); however, some errors were not corrected, causing eventual service problems. Eventual correction of the process dropped the error rate from 63 percent to 8 percent, and savings at a single trucking terminal were greater than $38,000.

Source: Based on Dondero, C., "SPC Hits the Road," *Quality Progress* 24, no. 1 (1991): 43–44.

Once a control chart is accurately established—that is, it is based solely on natural, random variation in the process—it is used to monitor the process, just as shown in this example. Samples are taken periodically, and the observations are checked on the control chart to see if the process is in control.

c-Chart

A *c*-chart is used when it is not possible to compute a proportion defective and the actual number of defects must be used instead. For example, when automobiles are inspected, the number of blemishes (i.e., defects) in the paint job can be counted for each car, but the proportion of blemishes cannot be computed, since the total number of possible blemishes is not known (i.e., it is infinite).

Since the number of defects per sample is assumed to derive from some extremely large population or continuous region, the probability of a single defective item is very small. These characteristics allow for the use of the Poisson distribution. However, as with the *p*-chart, the normal distribution can be used to approximate the Poisson distribution. The process average for the *c*-chart is the mean number of defects per sample, c, and the sample standard deviation, σ_c, is $\sqrt{c}$. When c is not known directly, the sample mean, $\bar{c}$, can be estimated by dividing the total number of defects by the number of samples. The value of $\bar{c}$ can also be used to estimate the standard deviation. The following formulas for the control limits are used:

Control limits of a *c*-chart

$$\text{UCL} = c + z\sigma_c$$
$$\text{LCL} = c - z\sigma_c$$

Alternate Example 4.2

EXAMPLE 4.2

Construction of a *c*-chart

Problem Statement:

Barrett Mills in North Carolina produces denim cloth used by manufacturers (such as the Western Jeans Company) to make jeans. The denim cloth is woven from thread on a weaving machine, and the thread occasionally breaks and is repaired by the operator, sometimes causing blemishes (called "picks"). The operator inspects rolls of denim on a daily basis as they come off the loom and counts the number of blemishes. Following are the results from inspecting 15 rolls of denim during a 3-week period.

Sample	*Number of Defects*
1	12
2	8
3	16
4	14
5	10
6	11
7	9
8	14
9	13
10	15
11	12
12	10
13	14
14	17
15	15
	190

The company believes that approximately 99 percent of the defects (corresponding to 3-sigma limits) are caused by natural, random variations in the weaving process, with 1 percent caused by nonrandom variability. They want to construct a *c*-chart to monitor the weaving process.

Solution:

Since c, the population process average, is not known, the sample estimate, $\bar{c}$, can be used instead:

$$\bar{c} = \frac{190}{15} = 12.67$$

The control limits are computed using $z = 3.00$, as follows.

$$\text{UCL} = \bar{c} + z\sqrt{\bar{c}} = 12.67 + 3\left(\sqrt{12.67}\right) = 23.35$$

$$\text{LCL} = \bar{c} - z\sqrt{\bar{c}} = 12.67 - 3\left(\sqrt{12.67}\right) = 1.99$$

The resulting *c*-chart, including the sample points, is shown in the following figure on page 160.

All the sample observations are within the control limits, which suggests that the weaving process is in control. This chart would be considered reliable to monitor the weaving process in the future.

Transparency 4.3 *c*-Chart for Example 4.2

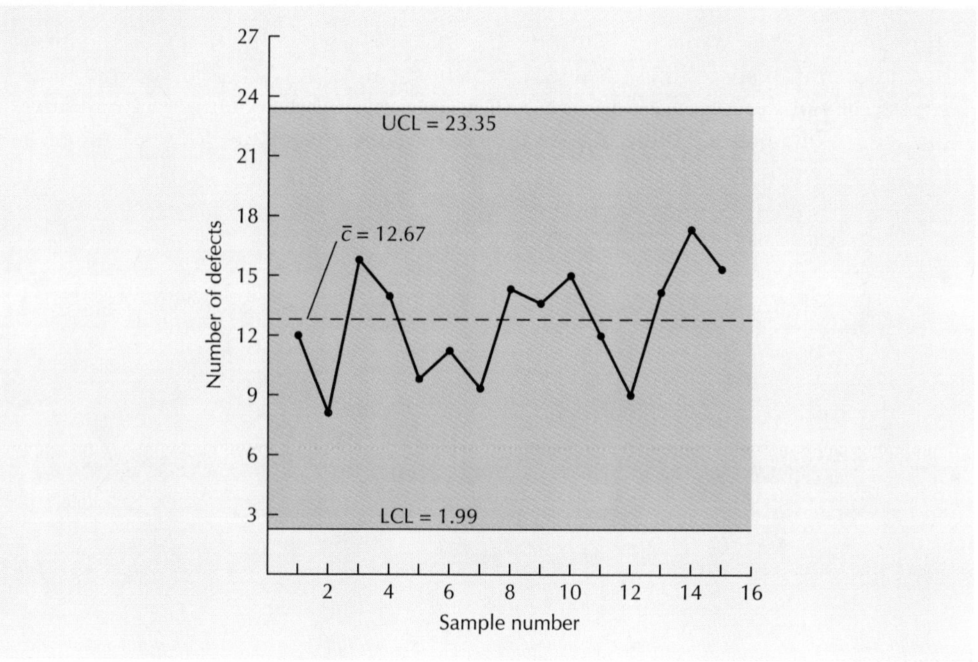

Control Charts for Variables

An **$\bar{x}$-chart** uses the process average of a sample.

An *R*-chart uses the amount of dispersion in a sample.

The quality measures used in variable control charts are for continuous variables reflecting measurements, such as weight or volume. Two of the more commonly used variable control charts are the mean chart, also known as the $\bar{x}$-chart, and the range chart, or *R*-chart. A **mean ($\bar{x}$-) chart** indicates how sample results relate to the process average or mean, whereas a **range (*R*-) chart** reflects the amount of dispersion that is present in each sample. These charts are normally used in conjunction to determine if a process is in control.

Mean ($\bar{x}$-) Chart

For an $\bar{x}$-chart, each time a sample is taken, the mean of the sample is computed and plotted on the chart; that is, the control points are the sample means. Each sample mean is another value of $\bar{x}$. The samples taken tend to be small, usually around 4 or 5. The center line of the chart is the overall process average.

The $\bar{x}$-chart is theoretically based on the normal distribution. It is assumed, from the central limit theorem, that the sample means are normally distributed if the process distribution is also normal. Even if the process is not normal, the distribution of the sample means will be if the sample size is sufficiently large. This enables us to use the following formulas for constructing control limits for an $\bar{x}$-chart (where z occasionally equals 2, but is most frequently 3, standard deviations):

$$\text{UCL} = \mu + z\sigma_{\bar{x}} \qquad \text{LCL} = \mu - z\sigma_{\bar{x}}$$

The sample standard deviation, $\sigma_{\bar{x}}$

These formulas assume that the process average, μ, and the standard deviation, σ, are both known. In this case the sample standard deviation, $\sigma_{\bar{x}}$, is computed as

$$\sigma_{\bar{x}} = \frac{\sigma}{\sqrt{n}}$$

When the process mean, μ, is not known, the average of the sample means, $\bar{\bar{x}}$, can be used instead:

$$\bar{\bar{x}} = \frac{\bar{x}_1 + \bar{x}_2 + \cdots + \bar{x}_n}{n}$$

GAINING THE COMPETITIVE EDGE

Using $\bar{x}$-charts at Frito-Lay

Since the Frito-Lay Company implemented statistical process control techniques, it has experienced a 50 percent improvement in the variability of bags of potato chips. As an example, the company uses $\bar{x}$-charts to monitor and control salt content, an important taste feature in Ruffles potato chips. Three batches of finished Ruffles are obtained every 15 minutes. Each batch is ground up, weighed, dissolved in distilled water, and filtered into a beaker. The salt content of this liquid is determined using an electronic salt analyzer. The salt content of the three batches is averaged to get a sample mean, which is plotted on an $\bar{x}$-chart with a center line (target) salt content of 1.6 percent.

Source: Based on "Against All Odds, Statistical Quality Control," COMAP Program 3, Annenberg/CPB Project, 1988. Allyn and Bacon.

Video 4.2 *COMAP, Program 5: "Statistical Quality Control"*

In most cases, an *R*-chart and an $\bar{x}$-chart are used in conjunction with each other. In those cases the computation of the $\bar{x}$-chart is based on the range values. We provide an example of the joint application of these two charts following our presentation of the range chart in the next section. For now, we demonstrate the use of the mean chart alone in the following example.

The *R*-chart and $\bar{x}$-chart are typically used together.

EXAMPLE 4.3

Constructing a Mean Chart

Alternate Example 4.3

Problem Statement:

The Goliath Tool Company produces slip-ring bearings. These bearings (as opposed to more familiar ball bearings) look like flat doughnuts or washers. They fit around shafts or rods, such as drive shafts in machinery or motors. The production process for a particular slip-ring bearing that fits around the drive shaft of a large truck motor has a mean diameter of 5 centimeters and a standard deviation of 0.04 centimeters. The company wants to develop a mean chart for this production process that will include 99.74 percent (i.e., three standard deviations) of the process variability using samples of size 20.

Solution:

The control limits are computed as follows:

$$\text{UCL} = \mu + z\left(\frac{\sigma}{\sqrt{n}}\right) = 5 + (3)\left(\frac{0.04}{\sqrt{20}}\right) = 5.027 \text{ cm}$$

$$\text{LCL} = \mu - z\left(\frac{\sigma}{\sqrt{n}}\right) = 5 - (3)\left(\frac{0.04}{\sqrt{20}}\right) = 4.973 \text{ cm}$$

If a sample is taken and the sample mean falls outside of these control limits, it suggests that the process is out of control, so the cause is probably nonrandom and should be investigated.

Range (R-)Chart

In an R-chart, the *range* is the difference between the smallest and largest values in a sample. This range reflects the process variability instead of the tendency toward a mean value, as the $\bar{x}$-chart does. However, the distribution of sample ranges cannot be assumed to be normally distributed as in the $\bar{x}$-chart, although the formula for determining control limits are somewhat similar:

The *range* is the difference between the smallest and largest values in a sample.

$$\text{UCL} = D_4\bar{R} \qquad \text{LCL} = D_3\bar{R}$$

A conveyor of potato chips at a Frito-Lay plant. Periodically samples of chips will be taken from the conveyor and tested for salt content, thickness, crispness, and other product variables. The sample results will be plotted on a control chart to see if the production process is in control. If the process is discovered not to be in control, it will be corrected before a large number of defective chips are produced thereby preventing costly waste.

In these formulas $\bar{R}$ is the average range for the samples taken. D_3 and D_4 are table values for determining control limits that have been developed based on range values rather than standard deviations. They generally provide control limits comparable to three standard deviations for different sample sizes. These tables are readily available from a variety of sources and are included in many texts on operations management and quality control. Table 4.1 includes values for D_3 and D_4 for sample sizes up to 25.

Alternate Example 4.4

EXAMPLE 4.4

Constructing an *R*-Chart

Problem Statement:

Consider again the Goliath Tool Company from Example 4.3. The company has taken 10 samples (during a 10-day period) of 5 slip-ring bearings (i.e., $n = 5$). The individual observations from each sample are shown as follows

	OBSERVATIONS (SLIP-RING DIAMETER, cm)						
SAMPLE k	1	2	3	4	5	$\bar{x}$	R
1	5.02	5.01	4.94	4.99	4.96	4.98	0.08
2	5.01	5.03	5.07	4.95	4.96	5.00	0.12
3	4.99	5.00	4.93	4.92	4.99	4.97	0.08
4	5.03	4.91	5.01	4.98	4.89	4.96	0.14
5	4.95	4.92	5.03	5.05	5.01	4.99	0.13
6	4.97	5.06	5.06	4.96	5.03	5.01	0.10
7	5.05	5.01	5.10	4.96	4.99	5.02	0.14
8	5.09	5.10	5.00	4.99	5.08	5.05	0.11
9	5.14	5.10	4.99	5.08	5.09	5.08	0.15
10	5.01	4.98	5.08	5.07	4.99	5.03	0.10
						50.09	1.15

TABLE 4.1 Factors for Determining Control Limits for $\bar{x}$- and R-Charts

Sample Size n	*Factor for $\bar{x}$-Chart* A_2	*Factors for R-Chart* D_3	D_4
2	1.88	0	3.27
3	1.02	0	2.57
4	0.73	0	2.28
5	0.58	0	2.11
6	0.48	0	2.00
7	0.42	0.08	1.92
8	0.37	0.14	1.86
9	0.34	0.18	1.82
10	0.31	0.22	1.78
11	0.29	0.26	1.74
12	0.27	0.28	1.72
13	0.25	0.31	1.69
14	0.24	0.33	1.67
15	0.22	0.35	1.65
16	0.21	0.36	1.64
17	0.20	0.38	1.62
18	0.19	0.39	1.61
19	0.19	0.40	1.60
20	0.18	0.41	1.59
21	0.17	0.43	1.58
22	0.17	0.43	1.57
23	0.16	0.44	1.56
24	0.16	0.45	1.55
25	0.15	0.46	1.54

The company wants to develop an R-chart to monitor the process variability.

Solution:

$\bar{R}$ is computed by first determining the range for each sample by taking the difference between the highest and lowest values. These ranges are summed and then divided by the number of samples, k, as follows:

$$\bar{R} = \frac{\sum R}{k} = \frac{1.15}{10} = 0.115$$

$D_3 = 0$ and $D_4 = 2.11$ from Table 4.1 for $n = 5$. Thus, the control limits are computed as

$$\text{UCL} = D_4\bar{R} = 2.11\ (0.115) = 0.243$$
$$\text{LCL} = D_3\bar{R} = 0\ (0.115) = 0$$

These limits define the R-chart shown in the following figure. The R-chart indicates that the process seems to be in control; that is, the variability observed is a result of natural random occurrences.

Transparency 4.4 *R*-Chart for Example 4.4

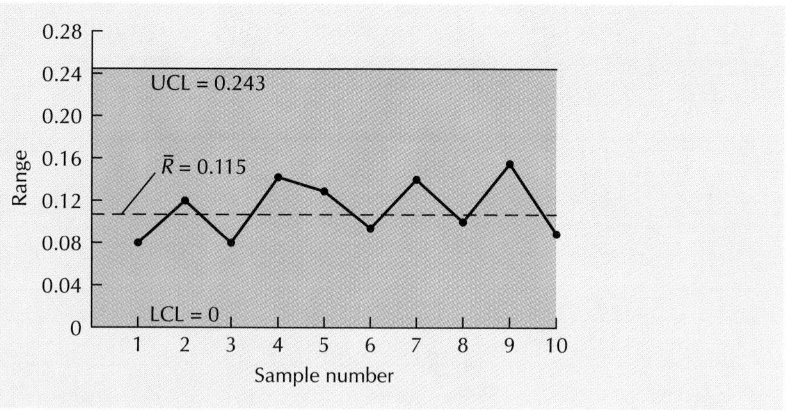

Using $\bar{x}$- and R-Charts Together

Both the process average and variability must be in control.

As mentioned previously, the $\bar{x}$-chart is frequently used in conjunction with the *R*-chart under the premise that both the process average and variability must be in control for the process to be in control. This is a logical assumption. The two charts measure the process differently. It is quite possible for samples to have very narrow ranges, suggesting little process variability, but the sample averages might be beyond the control limits. For example, the ranges for two samples could both be 0.10 centimeter, and be within the control limits. However $\bar{x}$ could be 5.01 for the first sample and 5.12 for the second, suggesting the process is out of control for the second sample. Conversely, it is possible for the sample averages to be in control, but the ranges might be very large. For example, two samples could both have $\bar{x}$ = 5.01 centimeters, but sample 1 could have a range between 4.95 and 5.05 (R = 0.10 centimeter) and sample 2 could have a range between 4.80 and 5.20 (R = 0.40 centimeter). Sample 2 suggests the process is out of control.

It is also possible for an *R*-chart to exhibit a distinct downward trend in the range values, indicating that the ranges are getting narrower and there is less variation. This would be reflected on the $\bar{x}$-chart by mean values closer to the center line. Although this occurrence does not indicate that the process is out of control, it does suggest that some nonrandom cause is reducing process variation. This cause needs to be investigated to see if it is sustainable. If so, new control limits would need to be developed.

Control limits when $\bar{x}$-and *R*-charts are used together

When an $\bar{x}$-chart is used in conjunction with an *R*-chart, the following formulas for control limits are used:

$$\text{UCL} = \bar{\bar{x}} + A_2\bar{R}$$
$$\text{LCL} = \bar{\bar{x}} + A_2\bar{R}$$

where $\bar{\bar{x}}$ is the average of the sample means and $\bar{R}$ is the average range value. These formulas assume that neither the process average, $\bar{x}$, nor the standard deviation is known. As a result $\bar{\bar{x}}$, the average of the sample means, is used instead of the process average, $\bar{R}$ is the average range value, and A_2 is a tabular value like D_3 and D_4 that is used to establish the control limits. Values of A_2 are included in Table 4.1. They were developed specifically for determining the control limits for $\bar{x}$-charts and are comparable to 3-standard-deviation (3-σ) limits.

Alternate Example 4.5

EXAMPLE 4.5

An $\bar{x}$-Chart and $\bar{R}$-Chart Used Together

Problem Statement:

The Goliath Tool Company, described in Examples 4.3 and 4.4, now desires to develop an $\bar{x}$-chart to be used in conjunction with the *R*-chart developed in Example 4.4. It is assumed that neither the process average nor the standard deviation are known, and only the sample data provided in the Example 4.4 problem statement are available.

Solution:

The data provided in Example 4.4 for the various samples taken allow us to compute $\bar{\bar{x}}$ as follows:

$$\bar{\bar{x}} = \frac{\sum \bar{x}}{10} = \frac{50.09}{10} = 5.01 \text{ cm}$$

Using the value of $A_2 = 0.58$ for $n = 5$ from Table 4.1 and $\bar{R} = 0.115$ from Example 4.4, the control limits are computed as

$$\begin{aligned} \text{UCL} &= \bar{\bar{x}} + A_2\bar{R} \\ &= 5.01 + (0.58)(0.115) = 5.08 \\ \text{LCL} &= \bar{\bar{x}} - A_2\bar{R} \\ &= 5.0 - (0.58)(0.115) = 4.94 \end{aligned}$$

The $\bar{x}$-chart defined by these control limits is shown in the following figure. Notice that the process is out of control for sample 9; in fact, samples 8, 9, 10, all are close to the upper limit. This would suggest that the process variability is subject to nonrandom causes and should be investigated.

Transparency 4.5 $\bar{x}$-Chart for Example 4.5

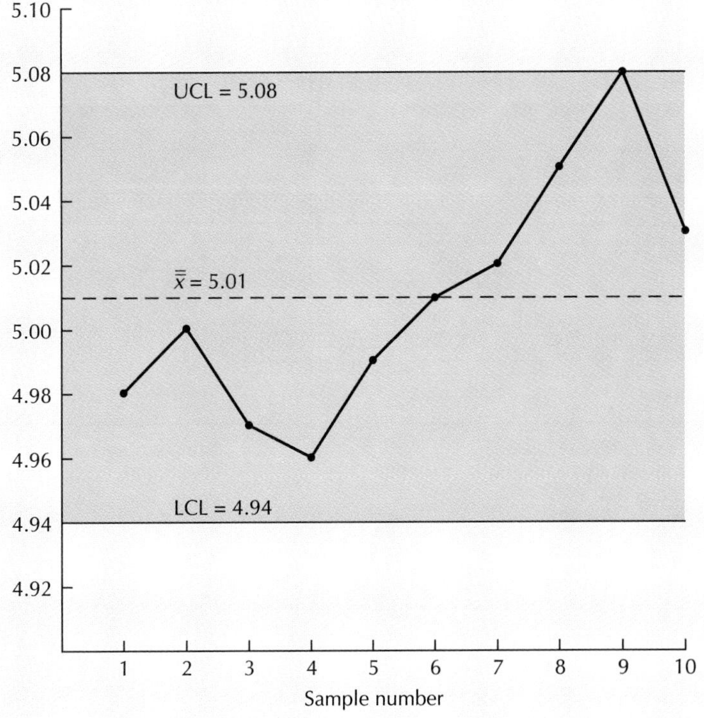

This example illustrates the need to employ the R-chart and the $\bar{x}$-chart together. The R-chart in Example 4.4 suggested that the process was in control, and none of the ranges for the samples were close to the control limits. However, the $\bar{x}$-chart suggests that the process is not in control. In fact, the ranges for samples 8 and 10 were relatively narrow, whereas the means of both samples were relatively high. The use of both charts together provided a more accurate picture of the overall process variability.

The decision whether to use a single chart or both charts is usually based on knowledge of the tendencies of the process. Experience may indicate that when the process moves out of control, the sample ranges tend to remain narrow and the sample means provide a more accurate indication of process control, as in this example. In such cases, it would be more economical and efficient to employ a single chart, because control charts are often time-consuming and tedious to construct and maintain. However, as we mentioned, common practice is to use both charts together. In fact, in order to save time and effort, it is frequently suggested that the *R*-chart be developed first to make sure it is in control before developing the $\bar{x}$-chart.

Control Chart Patterns

A pattern can indicate an out-of-control process even if sample values are within control limits.

Even though a control chart may indicate that a process is in control, it is still possible that the sample variations within the control limits are not random. If the sample values (i.e., sample ranges or means) display a consistent pattern, even though the values are within the control limits, it suggests that this pattern has a nonrandom cause that might warrant investigation. In other words, we expect the sample values in a control chart to "bounce around" above and below the center line, reflecting the natural, random variation in the process we know will be present. However, if the sample values are consistently above (or below) the center line for an extended number of samples or if they move consistently up or down, we would suspect that there is a reason for this behavior; that is, it is not random. Example of these patterns are shown in Figure 4.2.

Transparency 4.6 Control Chart Patterns

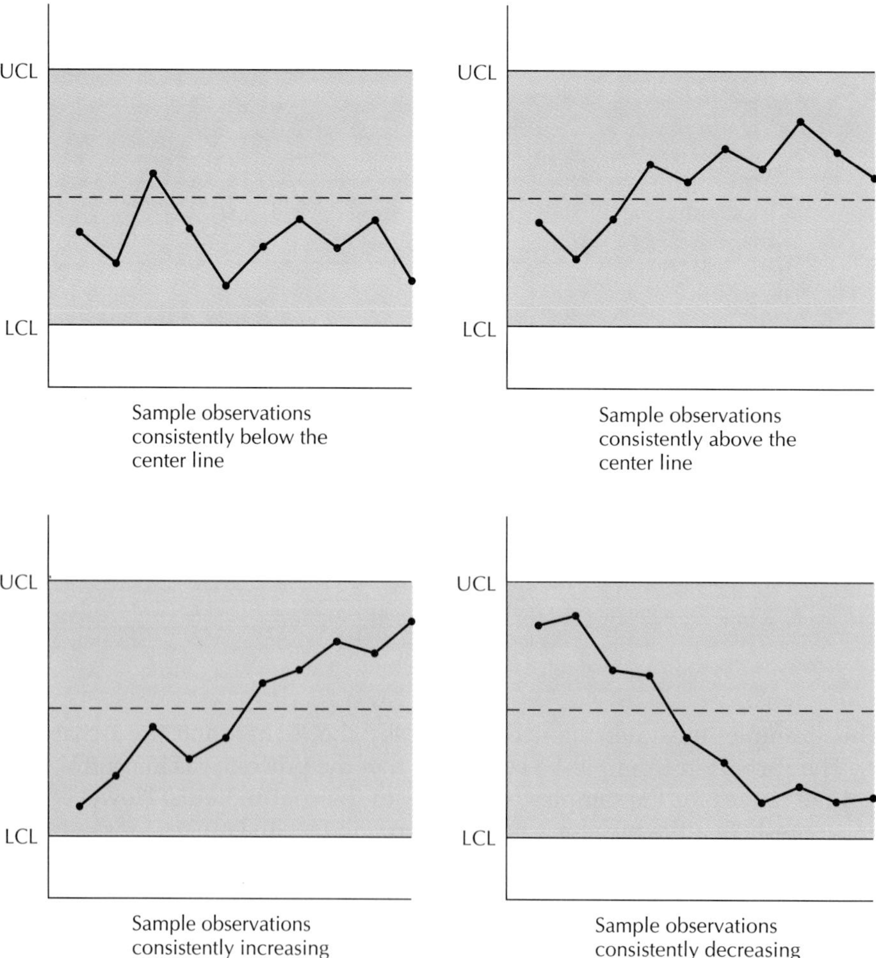

FIGURE 4.2 Control Chart Patterns

A pattern in a control chart is characterized by a sequence of sample observations that display the same characteristics (also called a *run*). One type of pattern is a sequence of observations either above or below the center line in a control chart. For example, three values above the center line followed by two values below the line represent two runs of a pattern. Another type of pattern is a sequence of sample values that consistently go up or go down within the control limits. In both cases, a test is available to determine if the pattern is nonrandom or random.

A *run* is a sequence of sample values that display the same characteristic.

The z **pattern test,** or *run test* determines the number of standard deviations the observed number of pattern runs in a control chart is from an expected number of runs. The z test is computed according to the following general formula:

The **pattern test** determines if the observations within the limits of a control chart display a nonrandom pattern.

$$z_{\text{test}} = \frac{\textit{observed runs} - \textit{expected runs}}{\sigma}$$

Substituting various formulas for the expected number of pattern runs and the standard deviation into this formula results in the following computation for each type of pattern: runs above and below (A/B) the center line and runs up and down (U/D) within the control limits.

$$z_{A/B} = \frac{r - [(N/2) + 1]}{\sqrt{(N-1)/4}}$$

$$z_{U/D} = \frac{r - [(2N-1)/3]}{\sqrt{(16N-29)/90}}$$

where

r = the observed number of runs
N = sample size

These computed test values are subsequently compared to a z value for a specified level of variability. For example, if it is assumed that 95 percent of the pattern runs are the result of random causes and are thus acceptable, then the situation coincides with a range of values of ±1.96 (from Table A.3 in Appendix A).

A second type of pattern test divides the control chart into three "zones" on each side of the center line, where each zone is one standard deviation wide. These are often referred to as 1-sigma, 2-sigma, and 3-sigma limits. The pattern of sample observations in these zones is then used to determine if any nonrandom patterns exist. Recall that the formula for computing an $\bar{x}$-chart uses A_2 from Table 4.1, which assumes 3-standard deviation control limits (or 3-sigma limits). Thus, to compute the dividing lines between each of the three zones for an $\bar{x}$-chart, we use $\frac{1}{3}A_2$. The formulas to compute these zone boundaries are shown in Figure 4.3.

There are several well-known general rules associated with the zones for identifying patterns in a control chart, where none of the observations are beyond the control limits:

Rules for identifying patterns

1. Eight consecutive points on one side of the center line
2. Eight consecutive points up or down across zones
3. Fourteen points alternating up or down
4. Two out of three consecutive points in zone A but still inside the control limits
5. Four out of five consecutive points in zone B or beyond the 1-sigma limits

If any of these rules apply to the sample observations in a control chart, it would imply that a nonrandom pattern exists and the cause should be investigated.

Transparency 4.7 Rules and Zones for Pattern Tests

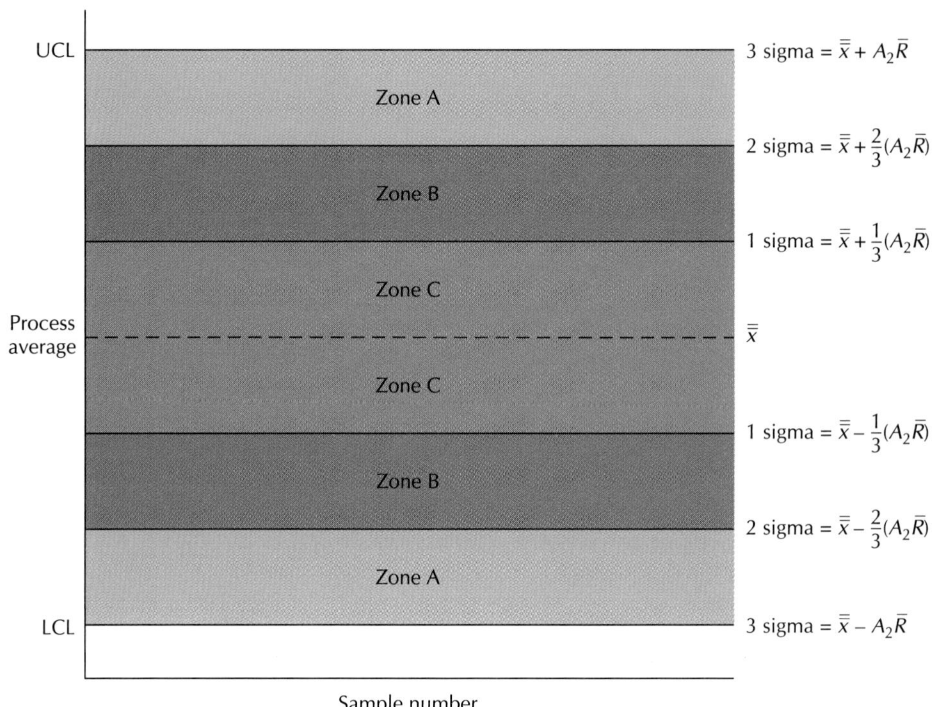

FIGURE 4.3 Zones for Pattern Tests

Alternate Example 4.6

EXAMPLE 4.6

Performing Run Tests

Problem Statement:

The Goliath Tool Company has developed the *R*-chart shown in Figure 4.4 on page 170, which indicates that the process is in control. However, the company wants to perform run tests to see if there is a pattern of nonrandomness exhibited within the control limits. It wants to use a test statistic consistent with a 95 percent probability that the nonrandom patterns exist.

Solution:

The first step for performing the pattern tests is to identify the runs that exist in the sample data for Example 4.4, as follows.

Sample	*Above/Below*	*Up/Down*
1	B	—
2	A	U
3	B	D
4	A	U
5	B	D
6	B	D
7	A	U
8	B	D
9	A	U
10	B	D

In the first case there are nine "above/below" runs, and in the second case there are eight "up/down" runs. The *z* tests for both cases are computed as

$$z_{A/B} = \frac{9 - [(10/2) + 1]}{\sqrt{(10 - 1)/4}} = 2.00$$

$$z_{U/D} = \frac{8 - [(20 - 1)/3]}{\sqrt{(160 - 29)/90}} = 1.38$$

The test statistic is $z = \pm 1.96$ (for a probability of 95 percent). One of the pattern tests, $z_{A/B} = 2.00$, is slightly out of this range, indicating that there may be some discernible, nonrandom pattern in the samples. Thus, the variation within the control limits may not be totally random. In this case the process should be checked.

Sample Size Determination

In our discussions of the various control charts for attributes and variables, sample sizes varied significantly. For *p*-charts and *c*-charts, we typically used sample sizes in the hundreds, whereas for $\bar{x}$- and *R*-charts we used samples of four or five. In general, larger sample sizes are needed for attribute charts because more observations are required to develop a usable quality measure. A process with a population proportion defective of only 5 percent would require 5 defective items from a sample of 100 to reach this value. Conversely, a sample of 10 does not even permit a result with 5 percent defective items. Alternatively, variable control charts require much smaller sample sizes because each sample observation provides usable information—for example, weight, length, or volume. Thus, after only a few sample observations (i.e., as few as two), it is possible to compute a range or a sample average that probably accurately reflects the sample characteristics. It is desirable to take as few sample observations as possible, because they require the operator's or inspector's time to take them.

Attribute charts require larger sample sizes; variable charts require smaller samples.

It is interesting to note that some Japanese companies use sample sizes of just two. They inspect only the first and last items in a production lot under the premise that if neither is out of control, then the process is in control. This requires the production of small lots (which are characteristic of some Japanese companies), so that the process will not be out of control for too long before a problem is discovered.

Size may not be the only consideration in sampling. It may also be important that the samples come from a homogeneous source so that if the process is out of control, the cause can be accurately determined. If production takes place on either one of two machines (or two sets of machines), mixing the sample observations between them makes it difficult to ascertain which machine operator or machine caused the problem. Similarly, if the production process encompasses more than one shift, mixing the sample observation between shifts may make it more difficult to discover which shift caused the process to move out of control.

Design Tolerances and Process Capability

Control limits are occasionally mistaken for tolerances, however, they refer to quite different things. Control limits, as we have shown, provide a means for determining natural variation in a production process. They are statistical results based on sampling. **Tolerances** are design or engineering specifications reflecting customer requirements for a product. As such, they are not statistically determined and are not a direct result of the production process. Tolerances are externally imposed, whereas control limits are determined internally. It is possible for a process to be in control according to control charts, yet not meet product tolerances. In order to avoid such a situation, the process must be evaluated to see if it can meet product specifications before the process is initiated and control charts

Tolerances are design specifications reflecting product requirements.

are established. This is one of the principles of TQM discussed in Chapter 3 ("Quality Management")—that is, that products must be designed so that they will meet reasonable and cost-effective standards.

Process capability is the range of natural variability in a process—what we measure with control charts.

Another possible use of control charts that we have not previously mentioned is to determine what is known as *process capability*. **Process capability** is technically the range of natural variation in a process, essentially what we have been measuring with control charts. It is sometimes also referred to as the *natural tolerances* of a process. It is used by product designers and engineers to determine how well a process will fall within design specifications. In other words, charts can be used for process capability to determine if an existing process is capable of meeting the specifications for a newly designed product. Design specifications are sometimes referred to as specification limits, or *design tolerances,* as opposed to the natural limits of the control chart. The two sets of limits have no statistical relationship to each other.

If the natural variability in a process exceeds tolerances, the process cannot meet design specifications.

If the natural variation of an existing process is greater than the specification limits of a newly designed product, the process is not capable of meeting specifications. This situation will result in a large proportion of defective parts or products. In other words, if the limits of a control chart measuring natural variation exceed the specification limits or designed tolerances of a product, the process cannot produce the product according to specifications. The variation that will occur naturally, at random, is greater than the designed variation. This situation is depicted graphically in Figure 4.4(a).

Transparency 4.8 Process Capability

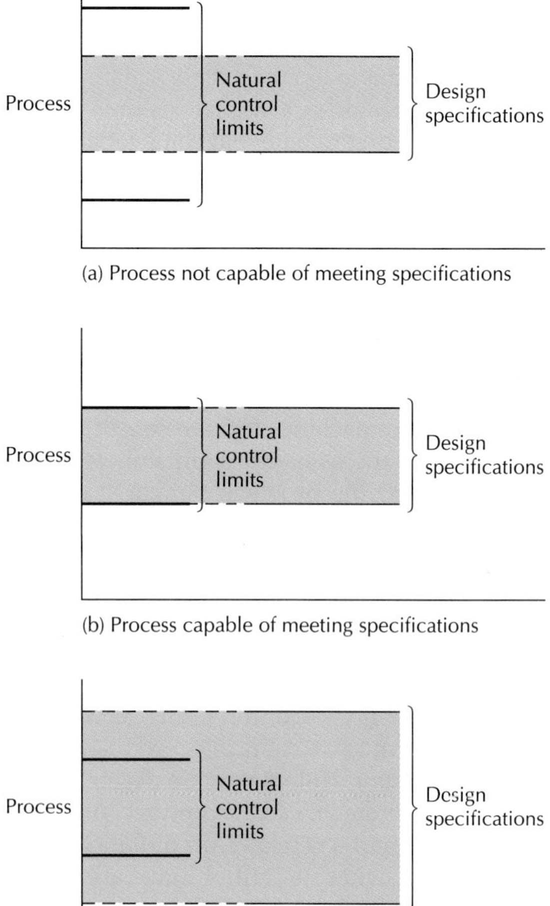

FIGURE 4.4 Process Capability

GAINING THE COMPETITIVE EDGE

Achieving Design Tolerances at Harley-Davidson Company

The Harley-Davidson Company is the only manufacturer of motorcycles in the United States. Once at the brink of going out of business, it is now a thriving, successful company known for high quality. It has achieved this comeback by combining the classic styling and traditional features of its motorcycles with advanced engineering technology and a renewed commitment to continuous improvement. Harley-Davidson's highly computerized manufacturing process incorporates computer-integrated manufacturing (CIM) techniques with state-of-the-art computerized numerical control (CNC) machining stations. These CNC stations are capable of performing dozens of machining operations and provide the operator with computerized data for statistical process control.

Harley-Davidson uses a statistical operator control (SOC) quality improvement program to reduce parts variability to only a fraction of design tolerances. SOC ensures precise tolerances during each manufacturing step and predicts out-of-control components before they occur. Statistical operator control is especially important when dealing with complex components such as transmission gears.

The tolerances for Harley-Davidson cam gears are extremely close, and the machinery is especially complex. CNC machinery allows the manufacturing of gear centers time after time with tolerances as close as 0.0005 inch. Statistical operator control ensures the quality necessary to turn the famous Harley-Davidson Evolution engine shift after shift, mile after mile, year after year.

Source: Based on *Harley-Davidson, Building Better Motorcycles the American Way,* video, Allyn and Bacon, 1991.

Video 4.3 *Harley-Davidson, Building Better Motorcycles the American Way*

Parts that do not meet specifications (i.e., they are within the control limits but outside the design specification) can be scrapped or reworked. This solution can be very costly and wasteful, and it conflicts with the basic principles of TQM. More viable alternatives include developing a new process or redesigning the product. However, these solutions can also be costly. As such it is important that process capability studies be done during product design, and before contracts for new parts or products are entered into.

Figure 4.4(b) shows the situation where the natural control limits and specification limits are the same. This will result in only a very small number of defective items, essentially only the few items that will fall outside the natural control limits due to random causes. For many companies, this is a reasonable quality goal. If the process distribution is normally distributed and the natural control limits are three standard deviations from the process average—that is, they are 3-sigma limits—then the probability between the limits is 0.9973. This is the possibility of a good item. This means the area, or probability, outside the limits is 0.0027, which translates to 2.7 defects per thousand or 2,700 defects out of one million items. According to strict TQM philosophy, this is not an appropriate quality goal. As Evans and Lindsay point out in the book *The Management and Control of Quality,* this level of quality corresponding to 3-sigma limits is comparable to at least 20,000 wrong drug prescriptions each year, more than 15,000 babies accidentally dropped by nurses and doctors each year, 500 incorrect surgical operations each week, and 2,000 lost pieces of mail each year."[2]

In TQM, 3-sigma limits do not provide good quality.

As a result, a number of companies have adopted what is advertised in the media as "6-sigma" quality. This situation represents product design specifications that are twice as large as the natural variations reflected in 3-sigma control

In 6-sigma quality, we have 3.4 defective PPM, or zero defects.

[2]Evans, J. R., and Lindsay, W. M., *The Management and Control of Quality,* 2d ed. Minneapolis, Minn.: West Publishing Co., 1993, p. 438.

limits. This type of situation, where the design specifications exceed the natural control limits, is shown graphically in Figure 4.4(c). Six-sigma limits correspond to 3.4 defective parts per million (very close to zero defects) instead of the 2.7 defective parts per thousand with 3-sigma limits. In fact, under Japanese leadership, the number of defective parts per million, or PPM, has become the international measure of quality, supplementing the traditional measure of a percentage of defective items. Percentages reflect a numerical magnitude deemed too high to measure quality according to TQM adherents, which is one reason acceptance sampling, the next statistical quality control topic in this chapter, is perceived as being incompatible with good quality.

COMPUTERIZED STATISTICAL PROCESS CONTROL

A number of computer software packages are available that perform statistical quality control analysis, including the development of process control charts. One example is AB:POM[3] by Howard J. Weiss, published by Allyn and Bacon. AB:POM is a general software package for production and operations management that includes modules for various production and operations management techniques, including statistical quality control. AB:POM is used extensively throughout this text.

AB:POM has the capability to develop process control charts for p, $\bar{x}$ and R. Exhibit 4.1 shows the computer output for the R-chart developed originally in Example 4.4 and the $\bar{x}$-chart developed in Example 4.5. The only input requirements are the sample mean and range values.

Exhibit 4.2 shows the p-chart developed in Example 4.1.

Transparency 4.9 AB:POM $\bar{x}$-Chart, R-Chart, and p-Chart

```
                          Quality Control              Solution
Number of samples (1-36) 10       Sample Size (n) (2-25) 5
                       Examples 4.4 and 4.5
Sample                  Sample                Sample
number                   Mean                  Range
   1                     4.98                   0.08
   2                     5.00                   0.12
   3                     4.97                   0.08
   4                     4.96                   0.14
   5                     4.99                   0.13
   6                     5.01                   0.10
   7                     5.02                   0.14
   8                     5.05                   0.11
   9                     5.08                   0.15
  10                     5.03                   0.10
                              Xbar             Range
Upper Control Limit       5.075355          0.243225
Center Line (ave)            5.009             0.115
Lower Control Limit       4.942645              0.00
```

EXHIBIT 4.1

[3]Weiss, Howard J., *AB:POM, Version 3.32*. Needham Heights, Mass: Allyn & Bacon, 1993.

```
                                      Quality Control                            Solution
Number of samples (1-36) 20                               Sample size (n) (2-9999) 100
                                        Example 4.1
Sample     Number of        Percent     Sample    Number of        Percent
number       Defects        Defects     number      Defects        Defects
  1                3         0.0300       13              7         0.0700
  2                0         0.0000       14              4         0.0400
  3                2         0.0200       15              3         0.0300
  4                5         0.0500       16              8         0.0800
  5                3         0.0300       17              6         0.0600
  6                2         0.0200       18              7         0.0700
  7                6         0.0600       19             10         0.1000
  8                5         0.0500       20              9         0.0900
  9                4         0.0400
 10                5         0.0500
 11                6         0.0600
 12                5         0.0500
                              95%          98%          99%         99.7%
Upper Control Limit          .09272       .10078       .10623       .11538  |   Std dev
Center Line (p-bar)          0.0500       0.0500       0.0500       0.0500  |   σp-bar=
Lower Control Limit          .00728       0.0000       0.0000       0.0000  |   .021794
```

EXHIBIT 4.2

In order to acquaint you with the capability of different computer software packages, we will employ STORM[4] by Emmons, Flowers, Khot, and Mathur to develop a process control chart. We will use Example 4.2 for the Barrett Mills to demonstrate a *c*-chart using STORM. Exhibit 4.3 gives the computer output for this example, showing the number of defective jeans found in each sample and the *c*-chart (using 3-sigma limits). Note the control limits, UCL = 23.34 and LCL = 1.99, are the same as computed in Example 4.2.

Transparency 4.10 STORM *c*-Chart

```
                                      Example 4.5
                                   ATTRIB 1 : C CHART
                     LCL = 1.9896  Center = 12.6667    UCL = 23.3437
Sample                 Value    LCL                C                  UCL 0
--------------------------------------------------------------------------------
SAMPLE  1               12       |   .              *|             .    |
SAMPLE  2                8       |   .     *         |             .    |
SAMPLE  3               16       |   .               |      *      .    |
SAMPLE  4               14       |   .               |   *         .    |
SAMPLE  5               10       |   .          *    |             .    |
SAMPLE  6               11       |   .            *  |             .    |
SAMPLE  7                9       |   .       *       |             .    |
SAMPLE  8               14       |   .               | *           .    |
SAMPLE  9               13       |   .               *             .    |
SAMPLE 10               15       |   .               |  *          .    |
SAMPLE 11               12       |   .              *|             .    |
SAMPLE 12               10       |   .            *  |             .    |
SAMPLE 13               14       |   .               | *           .    |
SAMPLE 14               17       |   .               |     *       .    |
SAMPLE 15               15       |   .               |  *          .    |
```

EXHIBIT 4.3

[4]Emmons, H., Flower, A. D., Khot, C. and Mathur, K., *STORM, Personal Version 3.1, Quantitative Modeling for Decision Support*. Needham Heights, Mass.: Allyn and Bacon, 1992

ACCEPTANCE SAMPLING

Acceptance sampling is accepting or rejecting a production lot based on the number of defects in a sample.

In **acceptance sampling,** a random sample of the units produced is inspected, and the quality of this sample is assumed to reflect the overall quality of all items or a particular group of items, called a *lot.* Acceptance sampling is a statistical method, so if a sample is random, it ensures that each item has an equal chance of being selected and inspected. This enables statistical inferences to be made about the population (i.e., the lot) as a whole. If a sample has an acceptable number or percentage of defective items, it is accepted, but if it has an unacceptable number of defects, it is rejected.

Acceptance sampling is a traditional approach to quality control based on the premise that some number of defective items will result from the production process. This acceptable number of defects is agreed upon by the producer and customer. The number of acceptable defects is normally measured in terms of a percentage. However, in the remarks introducing this chapter and at other points, we have noted that the notion of a producer or customer agreeing to any defects at all is anathema to the adherents of TQM. The primary focus for companies that have adopted the TQM philosophy and management principles is to achieve zero defects.

Acceptance sampling is not consistent with the philosophy of TQM and zero defects.

TQM companies measure defects as PPM, not percent.

TQM companies do not even report the number of defective parts in terms of a percentage because the proportion of defective items they expect to produce is so small that a percentage is meaningless. As we noted previously, the international measure for reporting defects has become defective parts per million, or PPM.[5] For example, a defect rate of 2 percent, which is frequently used in acceptance sampling and has traditionally been considered a high-quality standard, is still 20,000 defective parts per million. This would be a totally unacceptable level of quality for firms using TQM that are continuously trying to achieve zero defects. Three or four defects would be a more acceptable level of quality for these companies.

Nevertheless, acceptance sampling is still used as a statistical quality control method by many companies who have either not yet adopted a TQM approach or are required by customer demands or government regulations to use acceptance sampling. Thus, since this method does still enjoy wide application, it is beneficial and necessary for it to be studied.

Acceptance sampling has traditionally been used when the cost of inspection is very high relative to the cost of allowing a defective item to escape. The inspection cost may not be simply the cost of the inspectors or the machinery used for inspection, but may also be a result of the inspection process. It may require units of the product to be destroyed, such as when a sample of food is tasted, a bottle of wine is opened, a battery is used up, or a roll of film is exposed.

When a sample is taken and inspected for quality, the items in the sample are being checked to see if they conform to some predetermined specification. The evaluation of these specifications generally take one of two forms, either attributes or variable measures.

A **sampling plan** provides the guidelines for accepting a lot.

A **sampling plan** establishes the guidelines by which a sample is taken and the criteria for making a decision regarding the quality of a product lot. A sampling plan can be developed for either attributes or variable measures and for one or more samples. In the following discussion, we focus on the simplest form of sampling plan, a single-sample attribute plan.

[5]Flynn, B. B. "Managing for Quality in the U.S. and in Japan," *Interfaces* 22, no. 5 (1992): 69–80.

Single-Sample Attribute Plan

A single-sample attribute plan has as its basis an attribute that can be evaluated with a simple, discrete decision, such as defective or not defective or good or bad. The plan includes the following structural components:

Components of a sampling plan

N = the lot size
n = the sample size (selected randomly)
c = the acceptable number of defective items in a sample
d = the actual number of defective items in a sample

The decision-making criteria in such a plan are straightforward. A single sample of size n is selected randomly from a larger lot, and each of the n items is inspected. If the sample contains $d \leq c$ defective items, the entire lot is accepted; alternatively, if $d > c$, the lot is rejected.

However, although the sampling plan includes only a few components, which are not difficult to understand, management must still decide the values of these components that will result in the most effective sampling plan. In addition, management must also determine what constitutes an effective plan. These are all design considerations. The design of a sampling plan includes both the structural components (the sample size, n, the decision criteria, etc.) and performance measures. These performance measures include the *producer's* and *consumer's risks*, the *acceptable quality level*, and the *lot tolerance percent defective*. In the following section we discuss these measures individually.

Producer's and Consumer's Risks

When a sample is drawn from a production lot and the items in the sample are inspected, management hopes that if the actual number of defective items exceeds the predetermined acceptable number of defective items (i.e., $d > c$) and the entire lot is rejected, then the sample results have accurately portrayed the quality of the entire lot. Management would hate to think that the sample results were not indicative of the overall quality of the lot and a lot that was actually acceptable was erroneously rejected and wasted. Conversely, management hopes that an actual bad lot of items is not erroneously accepted if $d \leq c$. An effective sampling plan attempts to minimize the possibility of wrongly rejecting good items or wrongly accepting bad items.

When an acceptance-sampling plan is designed, management specifies a quality standard commonly referred to as the **acceptable quality level,** or **AQL.** The AQL reflects the consumer's willingness to accept lots with a small proportion of defective items. The AQL is the fraction of defective items in a lot that is deemed acceptable. For example, the AQL might be two defective items in a lot of 500, or 0.004. The AQL may be determined by management to be the level that is generally acceptable in the marketplace and will not result in a loss of customers. Or, it may be dictated by an individual customer as the quality level it will accept. In other words, the AQL is negotiated.

The **AQL** is an acceptable proportion of defects in a lot to the consumer.

As indicated previously, management hopes that the sampling results will not result in a lot that meets the AQL being erroneously rejected. The probability of rejecting a production lot that has an acceptable quality level is referred to as the **producer's risk** and is commonly designated by the Greek symbol α. In statistical jargon, α is the probability of committing a type I error.

Producer's risk is the probability of rejecting a lot that has an AQL.

There will be instances in which the sample will not accurately reflect the quality of a lot and a lot that does not meet the AQL will pass on to the consumer. Although the consumer expects to receive some of these lots, there is a limit to the number of defective items the consumer will accept. This upper limit is known as the **lot tolerance percent defective,** or **LTPD** (LTPD is also generally negotiated

The **LTPD** is the maximum number of defective items a consumer will accept in a lot.

between the producer and consumer). The probability of accepting a lot in which the fraction of defective items exceeds the LTPD is referred to as the **consumer's risk** and is designated by the Greek symbol β. In statistical jargon, β is the probability of committing a type II error.

Consumer's risk is the probability of accepting a lot in which the fraction of defective items exceeds LTPD.

α- producer's risk and β- consumer's risk

In general, the customer would like for the quality of a lot to be as good or better than the AQL but is willing to accept some lots with quality levels no worse than the LTPD. Frequently, sampling plans are designed with the producer's risk (α) about 5 percent and the consumer's risk (β) around 10 percent. Be careful not to confuse α with the AQL or β with the LTPD. If α equals 5 percent and β equals 10 percent, then management expects to reject lots that are as good or better than the AQL about 5 percent of the time, whereas the customer expects to accept lots that exceed the LTPD about 10 percent of the time.

The Operating Characteristic Curve

An **OC curve** is a graph that shows the probability of accepting a lot for different quality levels with a specific sampling plan.

The performance measures we described in the previous section for a sampling plan can be represented graphically with an **operating characteristic curve (OC).** The OC curve measures the probability of accepting a lot for different quality (proportion defective) levels given a specific sample size (n) and acceptance level (c). Management can use such a graph to determine if their sampling plan meets the performance measures they have established for AQL, LTPD, α, and β. Thus, the OC curve indicates to management how effective the sampling plan is in distinguishing (more commonly known as *discriminating*) between good and bad lots. The shape of a typical OC curve for a single-sample plan is shown in Figure 4.5.

In Figure 4.5 the percentage defective in a lot is shown along the horizontal axis whereas the probability of accepting a lot is measured along the vertical axis.

Transparency 4.11 An Operating Characteristic Curve

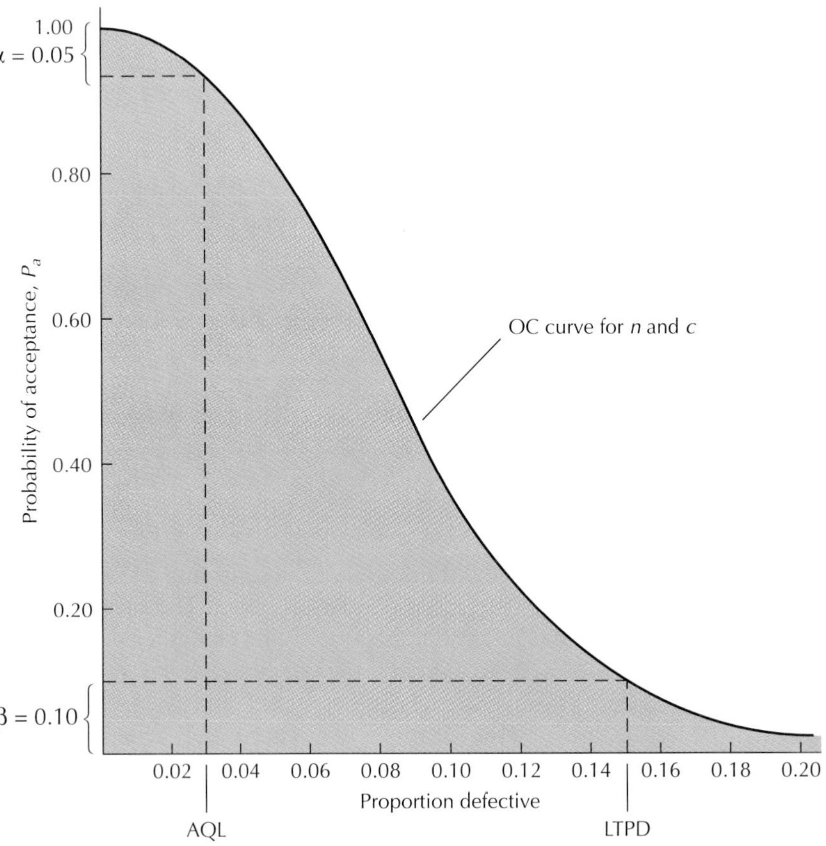

FIGURE 4.5 An Operating Characteristic Curve

The exact shape and location of the curve is defined by the sample size (n) and acceptance level (c) for the sampling plan.

Observing Figure 4.5, if a lot has 3 percent defective items, for example, the probability of accepting the lot (based on the sampling plan defined by the OC curve) is 0.95. If management defines the AQL as 3 percent, then the probability that an acceptable lot will be rejected (α) is 1 minus the probability of accepting a lot or $1 - 0.95 = 0.05$. If management is willing to accept lots with a percentage defective up to 15 percent (i.e., the LTPD), this corresponds to a probability that the lot will be accepted (β) of 0.10. A frequently used set of performance measures is $\alpha = 0.05$ and $\beta = 0.10$.

Although the OC curve in Figure 4.5 illustrates the relationship of the performance measures in a single-sampling plan, we have not shown how the sampling plan that will result in desirable performance measures is developed. This is demonstrated in Example 4.7.

EXAMPLE 4.7
Developing an Operating Characteristic Curve

Problem Statement:

The Anderson Bottle and China Company (the ABC Company) produces a specific style of solid-colored blue china. The china is produced exclusively for a large department store chain. The china includes a number of complementary items that are sold in open stock in the stores, including coffee mugs. For a production lot of 1,000 coffee mugs, a quality control inspector takes a sample of 50 mugs and checks them for defects and color. Performance measures for the quality of coffee mugs sent to the stores require a producer's risk (α) of 0.05 with an AQL of 1 percent defective and a consumer's risk (β) of 0.10 with a LTPD of 5 percent defective.

Solution:

Initially the ABC Co. does not know what size sample, n, to take or what the acceptance number, c, should be in order to achieve the performance measures. A trial-and-error process is required to determine n and c. As a starting point, we will consider a sample size of 20 and $c \leq 1$ (i.e., a lot is accepted if no more than one defective item is found in the sample).

In order to develop the operating characteristic curve, we must determine the probabilities of accepting a lot for various lot percentage defective values. This scenario reflects the properties that correspond to a discrete probability distribution, specifically the *binomial probability distribution.* The binomial distribution can be used to determine the probability of a number of successes (or failures) in n trials. The trials are discrete and independent and for each trial there are only two outcomes, success or failure, or—for our purposes—defective or not defective. The formula for the binomial distribution is

$$P(c) = \frac{n!}{c!(n-c)!}p^c q^{n-c}$$

where

p = probability of a success (i.e., a defective item)
$q = 1 - p$ = probability of a failure (i.e., a good item)
n = number of trials (i.e., the sample size)
c = number of successes in n trials (i.e., the acceptance number)

Thus, for our example, the probability of finding 1 defective item or fewer in a sample of 20 given an actual percentage of lot defectives of 0.05 is actually the cumulative probability of 0 defective items plus 1 defective item:

$$P(c \le 1) = P(c = 0) + P(c = 1)$$
$$= \frac{20!}{0!\,(20-0)!}(0.05)(0.95)^{20-0} + \frac{20!}{1!\,(20-1)!}(0.05)^{1}(0.95)^{20-1}$$
$$= 0.3585 + 0.3774$$
$$= 0.7359$$

Thus, the probability of finding 1 or fewer defective items in a sample of 20 units and accepting the lot, given that the actual percentage of defective items in the lot, is 0.05, is 0.7359.

In order to plot an OC curve we need to compute several more probability values. These values can be computed using the preceding formulas and an electronic calculator; however, values for the binomial distribution for various levels of p, n, and c are also contained in Table B.1 in Appendix B. The probabilities for several values of p (for $n = 20$ and $c \le 1$) are as follows:

% Defective p	$P(c \le 1)$
0.01	0.9831
0.02	0.9401
0.03	0.8802
0.04	0.8103
0.05	0.7359
0.10	0.3917

These values result in the OC curve shown in the following figure.

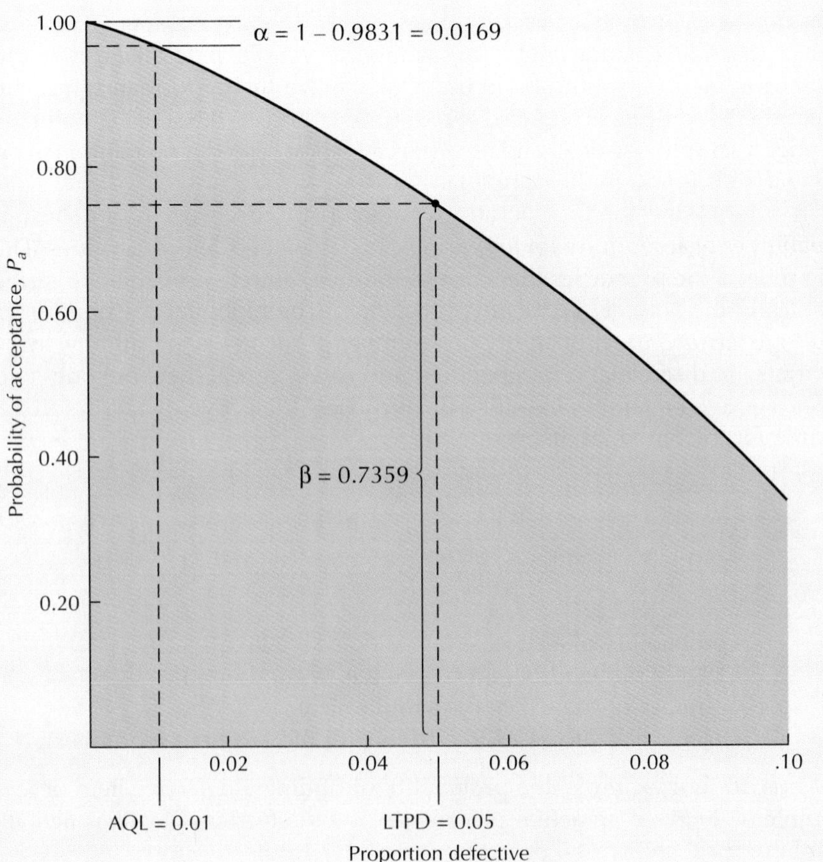

This curve, and hence the sampling plan, clearly does not conform to the set of performance measures management desires! For an AQL of 0.01, the producer's risk (α) is only 0.0169 and for an LTPD of 0.05, the consumer's risk (β) is 0.7359. These values are not close to our specified values of $\alpha = 0.05$ and $\beta = 0.10$. The shape of this OC curve does not even look like the typical OC curve in Figure 4.5. It is much flatter and less steep. We have obviously selected inappropriate values for both n and c.

Since the values for n and c we initially selected do not conform to the values for α and β we want, we increase n to 100, let $c \leq 2$, and see how these changes effect the OC curve. In general, a sample size of 20 is too small for a single-sampling plan. Increasing the sample size will have the effect of making the probability of acceptance smaller for our range of p values and the OC curve steeper. This can be seen by a closer examination of the binomial table; as n is increased for $c \leq 1$, the probability of acceptance gets smaller.

These changes also allow us to use a different probability distribution. When $p < 0.10$ and $n > 20$, such that $np > 5$, we can use the *Poisson* distribution to approximate the binomial distribution. In the Poisson distribution, the mean of the binomial distribution, np, is treated as the mean of the Poisson, λ. The Poisson distribution has the following formula:

$$P(x) = \frac{\lambda^x e^{-\lambda}}{x!}$$

where

$$\lambda = np$$
$$e = 2.71828\ldots$$

Table B.2 in Appendix B also provides probability values for different levels of c and λ.

For example, with $n = 100$ and $p = 0.01$, $\lambda = 1.00$ and the probability of $c \leq 2$ is computed using the Poisson formula:

$$P(c \leq 2) = P(c = 0) + P(c = 1) + P(c = 2)$$

$$= \frac{(1)^0(2.718)^{-1}}{0!} + \frac{(1)^1(2.718)^{-1}}{1!} + \frac{(1)^2(2.718)^{-1}}{2!}$$

$$= 0.3679 + 0.3679 + 0.1839$$

$$= 0.920$$

We can determine the additional $P(c \leq 2)$ values we need for different values of p to develop an OC curve using either the Poisson formula (and an electronic calculator) or Table A.2. These values are as follows.

% Defective, p	$np = \lambda$	$P\ (c \leq 2)$
0.01	1	0.920
0.02	2	0.677
0.03	3	0.423
0.04	4	0.238
0.05	5	0.125
0.06	6	0.062
0.07	7	0.038
0.08	8	0.014
0.09	9	0.006
0.10	10	0.003

These values are plotted in the OC curve in the following figure.

Transparency 4.12 An OC Curve for a Single-Sampling Plan with $n = 100$ and $c \leq 2$

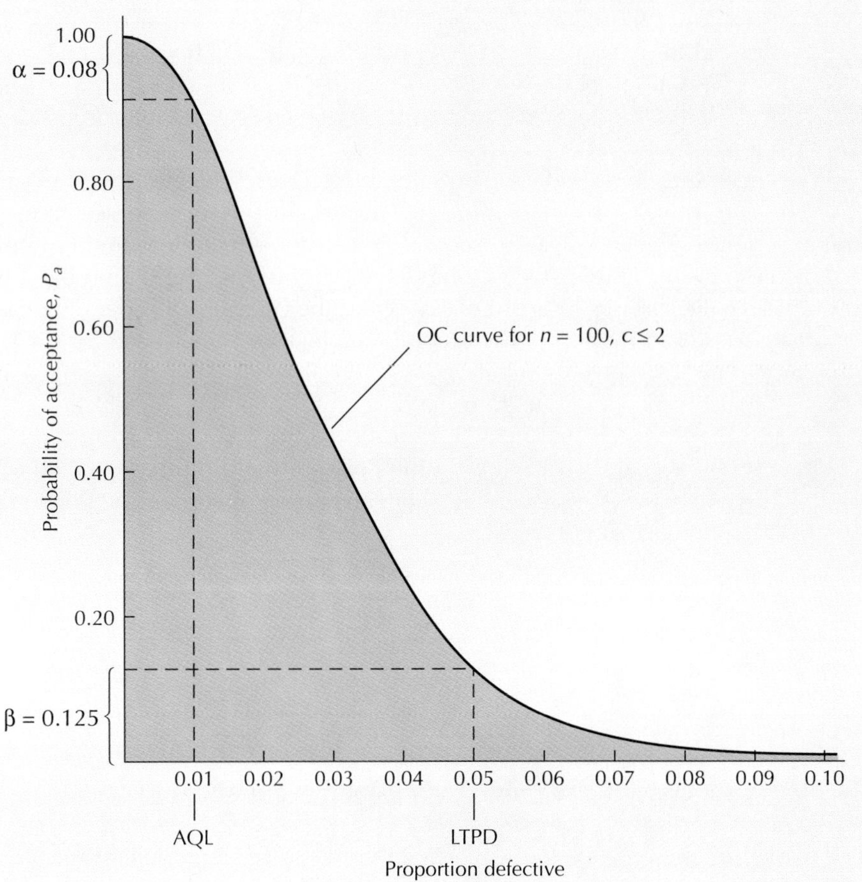

This sampling plan comes much nearer to the performance measures we seek. Observing this figure, for an AQL of 0.01, $\alpha = 0.08$ (i.e., $1 - 0.920$), as compared to $\alpha = 0.05$, which is sought. For the LTPD of 0.05, $\beta = 0.125$, in contrast to $\beta = 0.10$ that management wants. Using a trial-and-error approach and further altering the values for n and c, we can determine that values of $n = 130$ and $c \leq 3$ closely approximate our desired performance measures. For this sampling plan, $\alpha = 0.05$ and $\beta = 0.10$.

Guidelines for developing an OC curve

You will notice that determining a sampling plan using this trial-and-error approach required that n and c be progressively changed until we obtained a sampling plan that met our performance measures. In general, OC curves have certain characteristics that can be used as guidelines for focusing in on "good" values of n and c.

- Holding c constant, the OC curve is more likely to be flatter for a small sample size (as in the figure on page 178) and steeper for larger values of n. The OC curve becomes more "discriminating" between good and bad lots when the sample size is larger and the curve steeper.
- Holding n constant, the producer's risk, α, is more likely to be high for a low value of c, and the consumer's risk is likely to be higher for a higher value of c. This is a logical result; the higher the acceptance number, the greater the probability that a bad lot will be wrongly accepted.

A selection of OC curves with different values of n and c (including the OC curve for our example) is shown in Figure 4.6. These different OC curves reflect

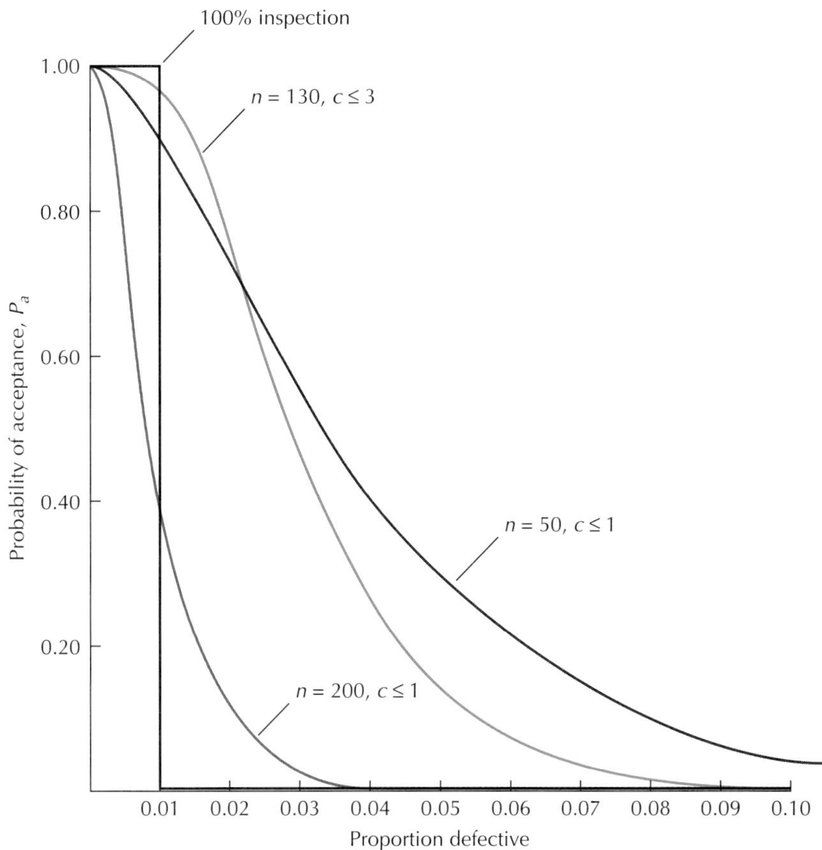

FIGURE 4.6 Selected Operating Characteristic Curves for Different Sample Sizes

the characteristics described here. Note that in the case where the sample size is the same as the lot size (i.e., $n = N$) the curve is completely vertical, indicating 100 percent inspection. In this case there are no producer's and consumer's risks; that is, since everything is inspected, neither good lots nor bad lots will be erroneously rejected.

Standardized Sampling Plans

The objective of Example 4.7 was primarily to provide an understanding of how a sampling plan is developed. Actually developing an OC curve to reflect a sampling plan that meets a set of quality performance standards using a trial-and-error approach can be a tedious and time-consuming task. Fortunately, standardized tables from several sources exist that provide sampling plans for a variety of performance measure combinations. These include *Sampling Inspection Tables, Single and Double Sampling* (2d ed., New York: Wiley, 1959) by Dodge and Romig, and *Sampling Procedures and Tables for Inspection of Attributes,* known more commonly as MIL-STD-105E (prepared by the Department of Defense and published by the U.S. Navy Printing Office). In addition, a number of texts devoted exclusively to quality control have examples of standardized tables.

Teaching Note 4.3 The Derivation of MIL-STD-105E Tables

MIL-STD-105E is actually a collection of sampling schemes constituting an attribute-sampling system developed during World War II for government procurement. There have been several revisions of the system (labeled from A to E), the last in 1989. In 1981 MIL-STD-105E was adopted by the American National Standards Institute (ANSI) and the American Society for Quality Control (ASQC). MIL-STD-105E focuses on the AQL, which ranges from 0.10 percent to 10 percent in the system. The sample size used in the MIL-STD-105E schemes is determined by the lot size and one of three levels of inspection: I (reduced inspection), II (normal inspection), and III (tightened inspection). MIL-STD-105E will provide a sampling plan for achieving AQL quality or better given the AQL, the inspection level (I, II or III), and the lot size.

Figure 4.7 provides an example of one of the sampling plan tables from MIL-STD-105E. This table is for the normal level of inspection (II). The code letters from A to S along the left-hand side of Table II-A are determined by lot size. For example, consider a lot size of 1,000 in which a normal level of inspection and an AQL of 1 percent are desired. A lot size between 501 and 1,200 for level II inspection corresponds to letter J (from Table I), which corresponds to a sample size of 80 as shown in the second column of Table II-A. Acceptable quality level values are shown across the top of the table as percentages. For an AQL of 1 percent (shown as a value of 1.0) and a sample size of 80, the acceptance number is 2 and the rejection number is 3, meaning if the sample contains 2 or fewer defectives, it is accepted; the lot is rejected if there are 3 or more defectives. Notice that there is no LTPD producer's risk or consumer's risk included in this sampling plan. To a certain extent these parameters are part of the "normal" level of inspection or classification.

There are also several computer software packages for both statistical quality control and production and operations management that will develop sampling plans given values for AQL, LTPD, α, and β. An example of the use of a computer software package for developing a sampling plan is provided in the section titled "Computerized Acceptance Sampling" at the end of this chapter.

Average Outgoing Quality

The **AOQ** is the expected number of defective items that the consumer will receive with a specific sampling plan.

The shape of the operating characteristic curve shows that lots with a low percentage of defective items have a high probability of being accepted, and lots with a high percentage of defectives have a low probability of being accepted, just as one would expect. For example, using the OC curve for our sampling plan developed in Figure 4.6 ($n = 130$, $c \leq 3$) for $p = 0.01$, the probability the lot will be accepted is 0.95, whereas for $p = 0.08$, the probability of accepting a lot is very small, 0.005. However, all lots, whether they are accepted or not, will pass on some defective items to the customer. The **average outgoing quality (AOQ)** is a measure of the expected number of defective items that will pass on to the customer with the sampling plan selected.

When a lot is rejected as a result of the sampling plan, it is assumed that it will be subjected to a complete inspection, and all defective items will be replaced with good ones. Also, even when a lot is accepted, the defective items found in the sample will be replaced. Thus, some portion of all the defective items contained in all the lots produced will be replaced before they are passed on to the customer. The remaining defective items that make their way to the customer are contained in lots that are accepted. The following formula for AOQ reflects the replacement of the defective items in rejected (and thus completely inspected) lots and in samples.

$$\text{AOQ} = pP_a\left(\frac{N-n}{N}\right)$$

where

p = percentage defective (the horizontal axis on the OC curve)
P_a = probability of accepting a lot (the vertical axis on the OC curve)
N = lot size
n = sample size

Sample size code letters

Lot or batch size			Special inspection levels				General inspection levels		
			S-1	S-2	S-3	S-4	I	II	III
2	to	8	A	A	A	A	A	A	B
9	to	15	A	A	A	A	A	B	C
16	to	25	A	A	B	B	B	C	D
26	to	50	A	B	B	C	C	D	E
51	to	90	B	B	C	C	C	E	F
91	to	150	B	B	C	D	D	F	G
151	to	280	B	C	D	E	E	G	H
281	to	500	B	C	D	E	F	H	J
501	to	1200	C	C	E	F	G	J	K
1201	to	3200	C	D	E	G	H	K	L
3201	to	10000	C	D	F	G	J	L	M
10001	to	35000	C	D	F	H	K	M	N
35001	to	150000	D	E	G	J	L	N	P
150001	to	500000	D	E	G	J	M	P	Q
500001	and	over	D	E	H	K	N	Q	R

Single sampling plans for normal inspection (Master table)

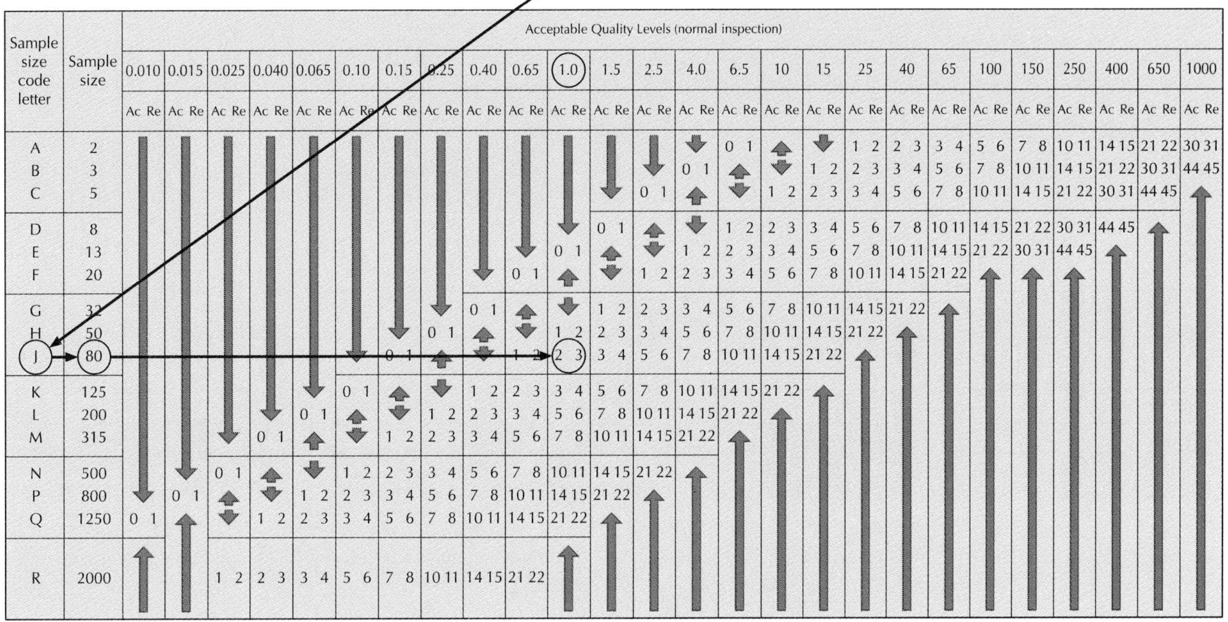

Sample size code letter	Sample size	Acceptable Quality Levels (normal inspection) 0.010	0.015	0.025	0.040	0.065	0.10	0.15	0.25	0.40	0.65	1.0	1.5	2.5	4.0	6.5	10	15	25	40	65	100	150	250	400	650	1000
		Ac Re	Ac Re	Ac Re	Ac Re	Ac Re	Ac Re	Ac Re	Ac Re	Ac Re	Ac Re	Ac Re	Ac Re	Ac Re	Ac Re	Ac Re	Ac Re	Ac Re	Ac Re	Ac Re	Ac Re	Ac Re	Ac Re	Ac Re	Ac Re	Ac Re	Ac Re
A	2														↓	0 1	↑	↓	1 2	2 3	3 4	5 6	7 8	10 11	14 15	21 22	30 31
B	3													↓	0 1	↑	↓	1 2	2 3	3 4	5 6	7 8	10 11	14 15	21 22	30 31	44 45
C	5												↓	0 1	↑	↓	1 2	2 3	3 4	5 6	7 8	10 11	14 15	21 22	30 31	44 45	↑
D	8											↓	0 1	↑	↓	1 2	2 3	3 4	5 6	7 8	10 11	14 15	21 22	30 31	44 45	↑	
E	13										↓	0 1	↑	↓	1 2	2 3	3 4	5 6	7 8	10 11	14 15	21 22	30 31	44 45	↑		
F	20									↓	0 1	↑	↓	1 2	2 3	3 4	5 6	7 8	10 11	14 15	21 22	↑	↑	↑			
G	32								↓	0 1	↑	↓	1 2	2 3	3 4	5 6	7 8	10 11	14 15	21 22	↑						
H	50							↓	0 1	↑	↓	1 2	2 3	3 4	5 6	7 8	10 11	14 15	21 22	↑							
J	80						↓	0 1	↑	↓	1 2	2 3	3 4	5 6	7 8	10 11	14 15	21 22	↑								
K	125					↓	0 1	↑	↓	1 2	2 3	3 4	5 6	7 8	10 11	14 15	21 22	↑									
L	200				↓	0 1	↑	↓	1 2	2 3	3 4	5 6	7 8	10 11	14 15	21 22	↑										
M	315			↓	0 1	↑	↓	1 2	2 3	3 4	5 6	7 8	10 11	14 15	21 22	↑											
N	500		↓	0 1	↑	↓	1 2	2 3	3 4	5 6	7 8	10 11	14 15	21 22	↑												
P	800	↓	0 1	↑	↓	1 2	2 3	3 4	5 6	7 8	10 11	14 15	21 22	↑													
Q	1250	0 1	↑	↓	1 2	2 3	3 4	5 6	7 8	10 11	14 15	21 22	↑														
R	2000	↑		1 2	2 3	3 4	5 6	7 8	10 11	14 15	21 22	↑															

↓ = Use first sampling plan below arrow. If sample size equals, or exceeds, lot or batch size, do 100 percent inspection.
↑ = Use first sampling plan above arrow.
Ac = Acceptance number.
Re = Rejection number.

FIGURE 4.7 MIL-STD-105E Tables

In most cases, the term $\frac{(N-n)}{N}$ will approach 1.0 when N is very large compared to n, and in those cases it can effectively be omitted from the formula, so that

$$AOQ = pP_a$$

EXAMPLE 4.8
Computing the Average Outgoing Quality

Problem Statement:

In order to demonstrate how to compute the AOQ, we use the example for the ABC Co. described in Example 4.7. The company wants to determine the AOQ for its sampling plan, which has $N = 1{,}000$, $n = 130$, and $c \leq 3$.

Solution:

The AOQ values are estimated for various levels of p using the Poisson tables in Appendix Table B.2.

Percent Defective p	λ np	P_a	$\left(\frac{N-n}{N}\right)$	*AOQ*
0.01	1.3	0.957	0.870	0.008
0.02	2.6	0.736	0.870	0.013
0.03	3.9	0.453	0.870	0.012
0.04	5.2	0.238	0.870	0.008
0.05	6.5	0.112	0.870	0.005
0.06	7.8	0.049	0.870	0.002
0.07	9.1	0.020	0.870	0.001
0.08	10.4	0.008	0.870	0.001
0.09	11.7	0.003	0.870	0.000
0.10	13.0	0.001	0.870	0.000

A curve is plotted in the following figure for these AOQ values in the same manner that an OC curve was developed previously.

Transparency 4.13 An AOQ Curve

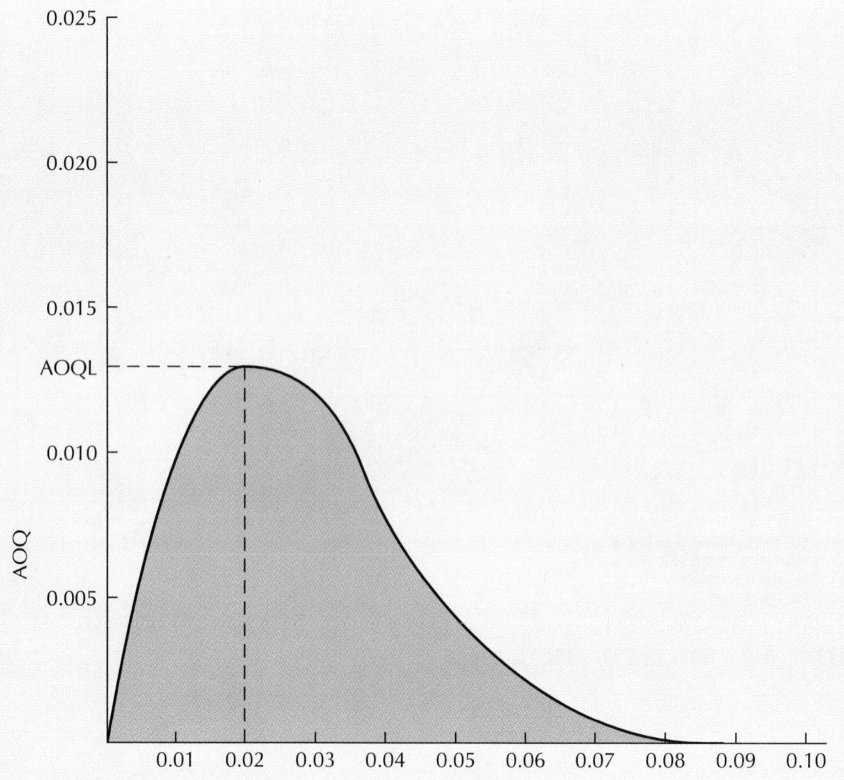

The maximum point on the curve is referred to as the *average outgoing quality limit* (AOQL). For our example, the AOQL is approximately 1.3 percent defective when the actual proportion defective of the lot is 2 percent. This is the worst level of outgoing quality that management can expect on average, and if this level is acceptable, then the sampling plan is deemed acceptable. Notice that as p increases and the quality of the lots deteriorate, the AOQ improves. This occurs because as the quality of the lots becomes poorer, it is more likely that bad lots will be identified and rejected, and any defective items in these lots will be replaced with good ones.

Double-Sampling Plans

In a *double-sampling plan*, a smaller sample is taken first; if the quality is very good, the lot is accepted, and if the sample is very poor, the lot is rejected. However, if the initial sample is inconclusive, a second sample is taken and the lot is either accepted or rejected based on the combined results of the two samples. The objective of such a sampling procedure is to save costs relative to a single-sampling plan. For very good or very bad lots, the smaller, less expensive sample will suffice and a larger, more expensive sample is avoided.

Double-sampling plans are less costly than single-sampling plans.

The steps of a double-sampling process are outlined as follows:

1. From a (smaller) sample, n_1, determine the number of defective items, d_1.
2. If $d_1 \leq c_1$ (where c_1 reflects very good quality), accept the lot; if $d_1 > c_2$ (where c_2 reflects very poor quality), reject the lot.
3. If $c_1 < d_1 \leq c_2$, take a second sample, n_2, and determine d_2.
4. If $d_1 + d_2 \leq c_3$ (an acceptable quality level for the combined sample), accept the lot, otherwise reject.

Multiple-Sampling Plans

A *multiple-sampling plan*, also referred to as a sequential-sampling plan, generally employs the smallest sample size of any of the sampling plans we have discussed. In its most extreme form, individual items are inspected sequentially, and the decision to accept or reject a lot is based on the cumulative number of defective items. As such, a multiple-sampling plan can result in small samples and, consequently, can be the least expensive of the sampling plans.

A *multiple-sampling plan* uses the smallest sample size of any sampling plan.

The steps of a multiple-sampling plan are similar to those described for a double-sampling plan. An initial sample (which can be as small as one unit) is taken. If the number of defective items is less than or equal to a lower limit, the lot is accepted, whereas if it exceeds a specified upper limit, the lot is rejected. If the number of defective items falls in between the two limits, a second sample is obtained. The cumulative number of defects is then compared to an increased set of upper and lower limits, and the decision rule used in the first sample is applied. If the lot is neither accepted or rejected with the second sample, a third sample is taken, with the acceptance/rejection limits revised upward. These steps are repeated for subsequent samples until the lot is either accepted or rejected. An example of this type of sampling plan is depicted graphically in Figure 4.8.

Steps of a multiple-sampling plan

In Figure 4.8, samples of size 10 are progressively taken. In the first sample, 2 defective items were found. However, since this number was not less than or equal to the acceptable limit of 0 items, nor did it exceed the upper limit of 3 items, the lot was neither accepted nor rejected, and a second sample of 10 items was taken. For the second sample the lower and upper limits increased to 1 unit and 4 units, respectively, and, although the cumulative number of defective items increased to 3, this was still within the revised upper and lower limits. Third and fourth samples were taken with no increase in the cumulative number of defective items, so the lot was accepted on the fourth sample.

Transparency 4.14 Multiple-Sampling Plan

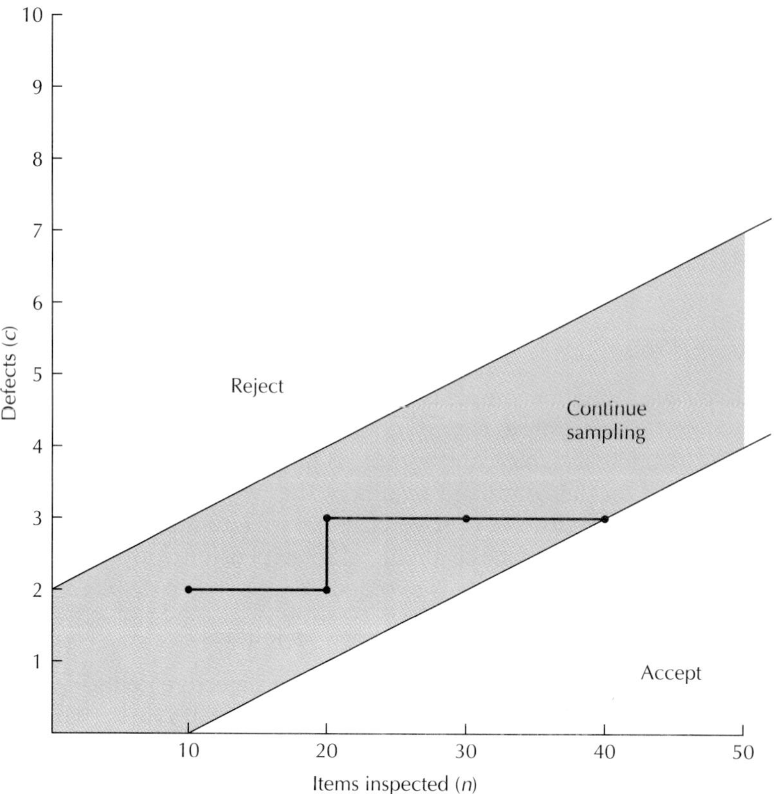

FIGURE 4.8 Multiple-Sampling Plan

Selecting an Attribute Plan

Choosing between single-, double-, or multiple-sampling plans is typically an economic decision. When the cost of obtaining a sample is very high compared to the inspection cost, a single-sampling plan is usually preferred. For example, if a petroleum company is analyzing soil samples from various locales around the globe, it is probably more economical to take a single, large sample in Brazil than to return for additional samples if the initial sample is inconclusive. Alternatively, if the cost of sampling is low relative to inspection costs, a double- or multiple-sampling plan may be preferred. For example, if a winery is sampling bottles of wine, it may be more economical to use a sequential sampling plan, tasting individual bottles, than to test a large single sample containing a number of bottles, since each bottle sampled is, in effect, destroyed. In most cases where quality control requires destructive testing, the inspection costs are high compared to sampling costs.

Variable-Sampling Plans

In our discussion of acceptance sampling so far, we have focused on attribute plans, in which a discrete decision criterion for determining product quality has been used. The other form of acceptance sampling entails measurement of a continuous variable, such as weight, length, or volume, and is thus referred to as a *variable-sampling plan.*

A *variable-sampling plan* measures a continuous variable, such as length or volume.

A variable-sampling plan is very similar in principle to an attribute plan. The objective is to develop a plan that meets performance standards for producer's (α) and consumer's (β) risks. The construction of a variable plan requires the determination of a sample size, n, and an acceptance value, c. In an attribute plan, c referred to a number of defective items, but in a variable plan, c is a measure designating acceptance and rejection limits. Assuming a normal probability distribution, acceptance and rejection values for c are set a number of sample standard deviations from the mean, such that the probability of rejecting a good lot (α) and the probability of accepting a bad lot (β) conform to the specifications of the sampling plan.

You will recall that in an attribute plan, discrete probability distributions, the binomial and the Poisson, were employed. For a variable-sampling plan, a normal distribution is usually assumed, especially if the sample is relatively large (i.e., greater than 30). In the following example we use the normal distribution to develop a variable-sampling plan.

EXAMPLE 4.9

Constructing a Variable-Sampling Plan

Problem Statement:

The Kalo Fertilizer Company produces Crop-Quik Fertilizer and packages it in what are supposed to be 50-pound bags. However, because of variances in their packaging equipment, the bags do not always contain exactly 50 pounds of fertilizer. The weights of these bags are assumed to be normally distributed with a standard deviation of $\sigma = 1.2$ pounds. Bag lots that average 50 pounds are considered to be of good quality and are thus acceptable, whereas lots averaging 49 pounds or less are not acceptable. The Kalo Company's quality control program requires that the probability that a lot with an average weight of 50 pounds is rejected be no more than 0.05 and the probability that a lot with an average weight of 49 pounds is accepted be no more than 0.10 (i.e., $\sigma = 0.05$ and $\beta = 0.10$). The company wants to design a variable-sampling plan that will achieve these performance standards. This will require the determination of the acceptance value, c, and the sample size, n.

Solution:

The construction of the sampling plan requires that we consider the achievement of α and β simultaneously. The figure below displays this situation graphically. The normal distribution at the top of this figure represents the sampling distribution for good lots, where $\alpha = 0.05$, whereas the sampling distribution on the bottom reflects bad lots and $\beta = 0.10$. The point where the two distributions intersect (i.e., where α and β are simultaneously achieved) is at the acceptance value, c.

Transparency 4.15 Variable-Sampling Plan

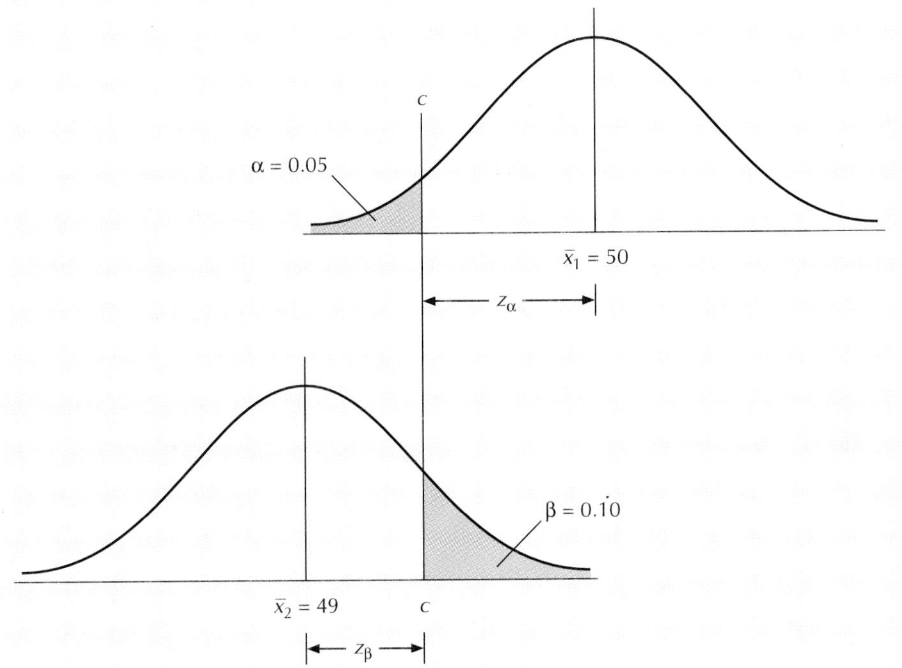

The value of c for each distribution is expressed mathematically as

$$c = \bar{x}_1 - z_\alpha \frac{\sigma}{\sqrt{n}} = 50 - 1.65\frac{(1.2)}{\sqrt{n}}$$

$$c = \bar{x}_2 - z_\beta \frac{\sigma}{\sqrt{n}} = 49 + 1.28\frac{(1.2)}{\sqrt{n}}$$

z represents the number of standard deviations a point is from the mean in a normal distribution. The values for z_α and z_β are obtained from the normal table (A.3) in Appendix A. z_α for a probability of 0.95 is 1.65, whereas z_β for a probability of 0.90 is 1.28. Since both equations equal c, they can be set equal to each other and solved simultaneously for n.

$$50 - 1.65\frac{(1.2)}{\sqrt{n}} = 49 + 1.28\frac{(1.2)}{\sqrt{n}}$$

$$1 = (1.65 + 1.28)\frac{(1.2)}{\sqrt{n}}$$

$$n = (3.516)^2$$

$$n = 12.36$$

Since a fractional sample size cannot be taken, n is rounded to 12. Substituting this into one of the equations for c yields

$$c = 50 - 1.65\frac{(1.2)}{\sqrt{12}}$$

$$= 49.42 \text{ lb}$$

Thus, the sampling plan requires a sample of size 12 to be taken, and if the sample mean is 49.42 pounds or greater, the lot is accepted.

Standardized Variable Plans

Although a variable-sampling plan does not require the tedious trial and error approach necessary for developing an attribute-sampling plan, standardized variable sampling plans are available. The companion sampling system to MIL-STD-105E is MIL-STD-414 (*Sampling Procedures and Tables for Inspection by Variables for Percent Defective*, provided by the Department of Defense). MIL-STD-414 focuses on AQL values ranging from 0.04 percent to 15 percent and includes five general levels of inspection.

COMPUTERIZED ACCEPTANCE SAMPLING

Transparency 4.16 AB:POM Statistical Sampling Plan

We will demonstrate AB:POM by developing a statistical sampling plan for the problem described in Example 4.7. Recall that the ABC Company wanted to develop a sampling plan using the following guidelines: AQL = 0.01, LTPD = 0.05,

$\alpha = 0.05$ and $\beta = 0.10$. These values are input into the AB:POM program in response to menu questions, and the output screen in Exhibit 4.4 is provided.

The output shows a sampling plan with $n = 137$ and $c \leq 3$, which is approximately what we determined using a trial-and-error approach. The computer output also will display the OC curve for Example 4.7 (similar to the one shown in Figure 4.6), as shown in Exhibit 4.5.

The AB:POM program will also display the AOQ curve. The computer-generated curve corresponding to Example 4.8 and Figure 4.7 is shown as in Exhibit 4.6.

```
                    Quality Control      Solution
                      Example 4.7
            Attributes sampling -determine the plan
AQL          .010         The sample size   (n) = 137
LTPD         .050         The critical value(c) = 3
α            .05          (Upper limit on producer's risk)
β            .10          (Upper limit on consumer's risk)
Actual Producer's risk (α) = .050
Actual Consumer's risk (β) = .084
```

EXHIBIT 4.4

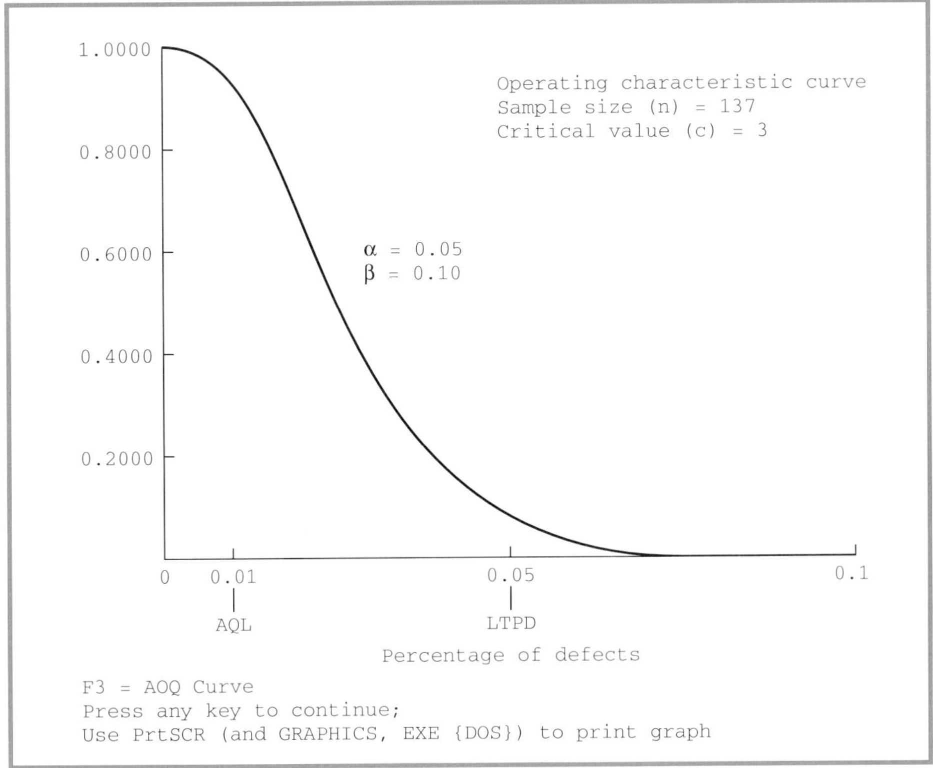

EXHIBIT 4.5

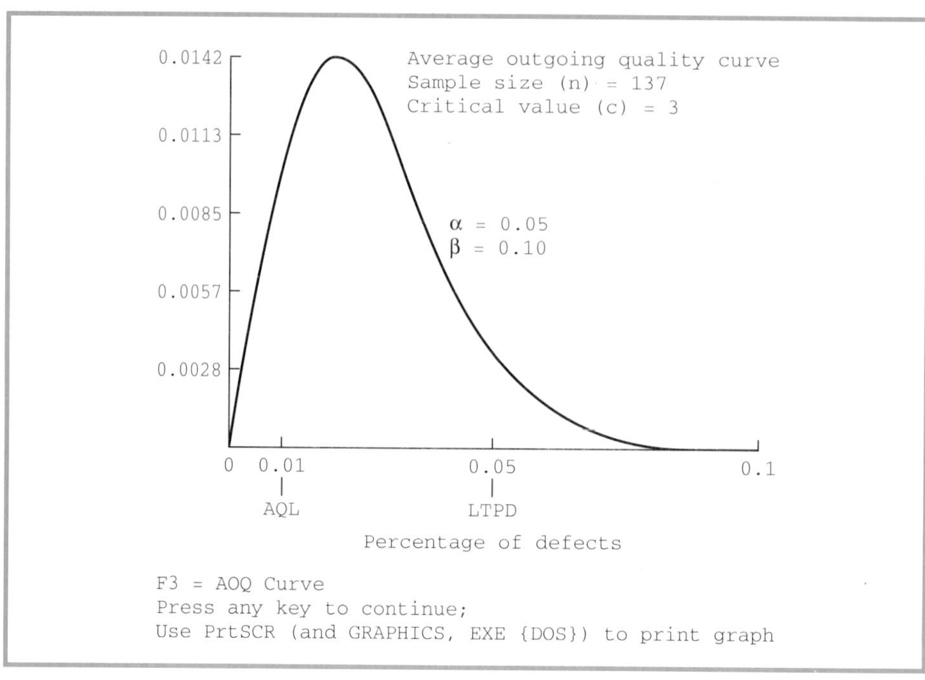

EXHIBIT 4.6

GAINING THE COMPETITIVE EDGE

A Quality Control Decision-Support System for a Farm Implements Business

Hay and Forage Industries (HFI) is a farm implement company that manufactures items such as tractors, balers, mowers, backhoes, tillers, forage harvesters, and hay-handling equipment. During the 1980s many U.S. farm implement companies failed or were greatly reduced. In order to survive and grow in this type of business environment, HFI focused on product quality and implemented an aggressive program of quality control in the late 1980s. The objective of the quality control program was to develop a process control decision-support system (PCDSS) that would merge information system capabilities with the quality control function and would integrate quality control information throughout the company.

The development of the PCDSS required an enormous data base encompassing such items as quality characteristic measures, inspection standards, acceptance/rejection criteria, process control statistics, design specifications, and quality program costs, all of which change continuously. These data are necessary for both vendor-supplied raw materials and parts. They are analyzed in the PCDSS and statistical sampling plans, and process control charts are developed for each part; the resulting quality-related information is linked to the corporate information system for other areas in the organization, such as engineering and marketing. The PCDSS generates OC and AOQ curves for single- and double-sampling plans and also determines sample sizes and acceptance criteria for attributes and variable-sampling plans.

The initial implementation of the PCDSS required a high start-up cost for training quality control personnel (including inspectors) during an 18-month period to meet American Society for Quality Control (ASQC) standards and a cost for establishing the system and data base. However, the PCDSS has resulted in numerous benefits. Overall, the system has reduced the fraction of defective items by 30 percent for most parts and by more than 60 percent in some cases. The sampling plans

continues

now developed are more efficient, resulting in the appropriate number of items to inspect (rather than too few or too many, as was done in the past). The PCDSS has reduced the time quality control managers previously spent on designing sampling plans and control charts and training inspectors by more than 50 percent. This has allowed them to redirect their efforts to analyzing statistical results and quality control costs and to developing more efficient quality control and inspection plans. The quality of incoming material and outgoing products is effectively monitored, and immediate shifts in the production process are detected by control charts. It is anticipated that the long-term result of the PCDSS will be a reduction of total quality cost.

Source: Based on Hosseini, J., and Fard, N. S., "A System for Analyzing Information to Manage the Quality Control Process," *Interfaces* 21, no. 2 (1991): 48–55.

SUMMARY

In this chapter we presented the topic of statistical process control, which is the main quantitative tool used in the TQM approach to quality management. Companies that have adopted TQM provide extensive training in SPC methods and concepts for all employees at all levels. Japanese companies have provided such training for many years, whereas U.S. companies have only recently embraced the need for this type of comprehensive training. One of the major reasons U.S. companies have traditionally cited for not training their workers in SPC methods was their general lack of mathematical knowledge and skills. However, U.S. companies are now beginning to follow the Japanese trend in upgrading hiring standards for workers and giving workers more responsibility for controlling their own work activity. In this environment workers recognize the usefulness and need for SPC for accomplishing a major part of their job, product quality. It is not surprising that when workers are provided with adequate training and understand what is expected of them, they have little difficulty using statistical process control methods.

SUMMARY OF KEY FORMULAS

Average Outgoing Quality

$$\text{AOQ} = pP_a\left(\frac{N-n}{N}\right)$$

Control Limits for p-Charts

$$\text{UCL} = \bar{p} + z\sqrt{\frac{\bar{p}(1-p)}{n}}$$

$$\text{LCL} = \bar{p} - z\sqrt{\frac{\bar{p}(1-p)}{n}}$$

Control Limits for c-Charts

$$\text{UCL} = \bar{c} + z\sqrt{\bar{c}}$$

$$\text{LCL} = \bar{c} - z\sqrt{\bar{c}}$$

Control Limits for $\bar{x}$ Charts

$$\text{UCL} = \mu + z\frac{\sigma}{\sqrt{n}}$$

$$\text{LCL} = \mu - z\frac{\sigma}{\sqrt{n}}$$

or

$$\text{UCL} = \bar{\bar{x}} + A_2\bar{R}$$

$$\text{LCL} = \bar{\bar{x}} - A_2\bar{R}$$

Control Limits for R-Charts

$$\text{UCL} = D_4\bar{R}$$

$$\text{LCL} = D_3\bar{R}$$

Pattern Run Tests

$$z_{A/B} = \frac{r - [(N/2) + 1]}{\sqrt{(N-1)/4}}$$

$$z_{U/D} = \frac{r - [(2N-1)/3]}{\sqrt{(16N-29)/90}}$$

SUMMARY OF KEY TERMS

acceptable quality level (AQL): the fraction of defective items deemed acceptable in a lot.

acceptance sampling: a statistical procedure for taking a random sample in order to determine whether or not a lot should be accepted or rejected.

attributes: a product characteristic that can be evaluated with a discrete response such as yes or no, good or bad.

average outgoing quality: the expected number of defective items that will be passed on to the customer with a sampling plan.

***c*-chart:** a control chart based on the number of defects in a sample.

consumer's risk (β): the probability of accepting a lot in which the fraction of defective items exceeds the most (LTPD) the consumer is willing to accept.

control chart: a graph that visually shows if sample results are within statistical limits for defective items.

control limits: the upper and lower bands of a control chart.

lot tolerance percent defective (LTPD): the maximum percentage defective items in a lot that the consumer will knowingly accept.

mean ($\bar{x}$-chart): a control chart based on the means of the samples taken.

operating characteristic (OC) curve: a graph that measures the probability of accepting a lot for different proportions of defective items.

***p*-chart:** a control chart based on the proportion defective of the samples taken.

pattern test: a statistical test to determine if the observations within the limits of a control chart display a nonrandom pattern.

process capability: the capability of a process to accommodate design specifications of a product.

producer's risk (α): the probability of rejecting a lot that has an acceptable quality level (AQL).

range: the difference between the smallest and largest values in a sample.

range (*R*-) chart: a control chart based on the range (from the highest to the lowest values) of the samples taken.

run: a sequence of sample values that display the same tendency in a control chart.
sample: a portion of the items produced used for inspection.
sampling plan: the guidelines for taking a sample including the AQL, LTPD, n, and c.
statistical process control (SPC): a statistical procedure for monitoring the quality of the production process using control charts.
tolerances: product design specifications required by the customer.
variable measure: a product characteristic that can be measured such as weight or length.

 SOLVED PROBLEMS

1. *p*-Charts

Problem Statement:
Twenty samples of $n = 200$ were taken at an inspection station between two crucial workstations in a production process. The number of defective items in each sample were recorded as follows.

Sample	*Number Defective*	*p*	*Sample*	*Number Defective*	*p*
1	12	0.060	11	16	0.080
2	18	0.090	12	15	0.075
3	10	0.050	13	13	0.065
4	15	0.075	14	16	0.080
5	16	0.080	15	18	0.090
6	19	0.095	16	17	0.085
7	17	0.085	17	18	0.090
8	12	0.060	18	20	0.100
9	11	0.055	19	21	0.105
10	14	0.070	20	22	0.110

Management wants to develop a p-chart based on these data that assigns 95 percent (2-sigma limits) of the variability to random causes. Set up the p-chart and plot the observations to determine if the process was out of control at any point.

Solution:
Step 1: Compute $\bar{p}$:

$$\bar{p} = \frac{\text{total number of defectives}}{\text{total number of observations}} = \frac{320}{(20)(200)} = 0.08$$

Step 2: Determine the control limits:

$$\text{UCL} = \bar{p} + z\sqrt{\frac{\bar{p}(1-p)}{n}} = 0.08 + (2.00)(0.019) = 0.118$$

$$\text{LCL} = \bar{p} - z\sqrt{\frac{\bar{p}(1-p)}{n}} = 0.08 - (2.00)(0.019) = 0.042$$

Step 3: Construct the $\bar{p}$-chart with $\bar{p} = 0.08$, UCL = 0.118, and LCL = 0.042.

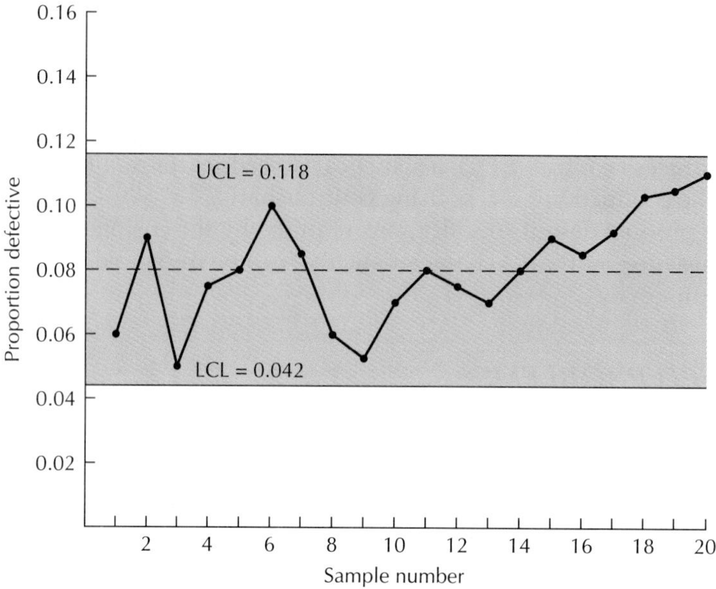

The process does not appear to be out of control.

2. *Pattern Tests*

Problem Statement:

In the preceding problem, even though the control chart indicates that the process is in control, management is not totally sure. Use pattern run tests to further determine if the process is in control with 95 percent probability.

Solution:

Step 1. Determine the "up-and-down" and "above-and-below" runs in the observation:

Sample	*Above/Below* $\bar{p} = 0.08$	*Up/Down*	*Sample*	*Above/Below* $p = 0.08$	*Up/Down*
1	B	—	11	A	U
2	A	U	12	B	D
3	B	D	13	B	D
4	B	U	14	A	U
5	A	U	15	A	U
6	A	U	16	A	D
7	A	D	17	A	U
8	B	D	18	A	U
9	B	D	19	A	U
10	B	U	20	A	U

(*Note:* Ties are broken in favor of A and U.)

Step 2: Perform the z tests for 1.96 and $N = 20$:

$$z_{A/B} = \frac{r - [(N/2)+1]}{\sqrt{(N-1)/4}} = \frac{8-(11)}{\sqrt{19/4}} = -1.38$$

$$z_{U/D} = \frac{r - [(2N-1)/3]}{\sqrt{(16N-29)/90}} = \frac{8-(13)}{1.80} = -2.78$$

The first $z_{A/B}$ test value of −1.38 is within the z range of ±1.96; however, the second $z_{U/D}$ test value of −2.78 is outside the ± range. This indicates that there is a pattern to the observations and the process is likely not in control—that is, that there are some nonrandom causes for the process behavior. In fact, it can be seen that the observations continuously increase from sample 14 through 20, indicating the process is out of control.

3. *Single-Sample, Attribute Plan*

Problem Statement:

A product lot of 2,000 items is inspected at a station at the end of the production process. Management and the product's customer have agreed to a quality control program whereby lots that contain no more than 2 percent defectives are deemed acceptable, whereas lots with 6 percent or more defectives are not acceptable. Further, management desires to limit the probability that a good lot will be rejected to 6 percent, and the customer wants to limit the probability that a bad lot will be accepted to 10 percent. Management is considering a sampling plan of $n = 150$ and $c \leq 5$. Develop an OC curve for this plan and determine if it satisfies the requirements of the quality program established by management.

Solution:

Step 1: Summarize the quality parameters:

$$\text{AQL} = 0.02, \quad \text{LTPD} = 0.06, \quad \alpha = 0.06, \quad \alpha = 0.10$$

Step 2: For selected percent defectives (p), determine $P\ (c \leq 5)$ using the Poisson distribution (Table A.2, Appendix A).

Percent Defective, p	$\lambda = np$	$P(c \leq 5)$
0.01	1.5	0.996
0.02	3.0	0.916
0.03	4.5	0.703
0.04	6.0	0.446
0.05	7.5	0.241
0.06	9.0	0.116
0.07	10.5	0.050
0.08	12.0	0.020
0.09	13.5	0.008
0.10	15.0	0.003

Step 3: Construct the OC curve using the values for p and $P(c \leq 5)$.

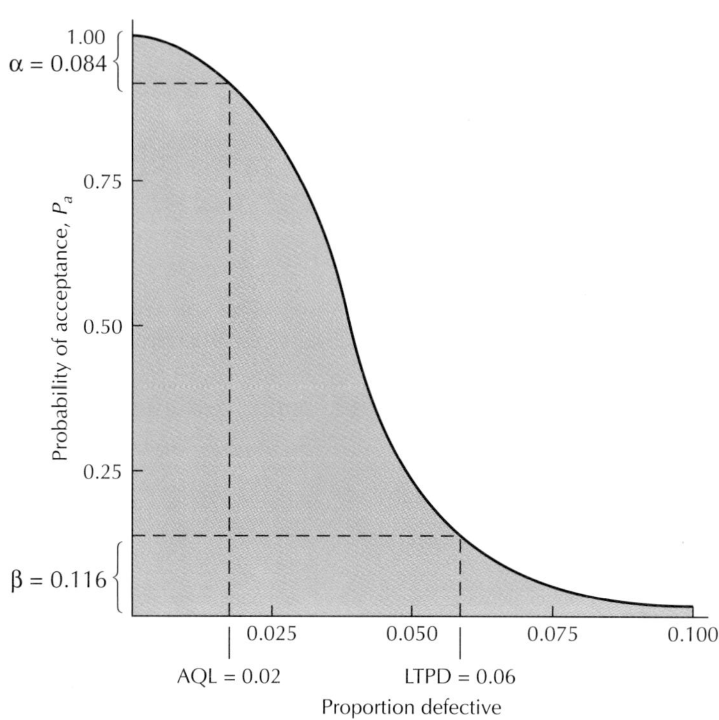

Step 4: Determine α and β for this OC curve:

$$\alpha = 0.084 \quad \text{and} \quad \beta = 0.116$$

The plan calls for $\alpha = 0.06$ and $\beta = 0.10$, so the current plan is not quite satisfactory. A trial-and-error approach would have to be used in order to determine the correct values for n and c that will result in $\alpha = 0.06$ and $\beta = 0.10$. In this case, a sampling plan with $n = 194$ and $c = 7$ will approximately achieve the quality criteria.

4. *Average Outgoing Quality*

Problem Statement:

In the preceding problem, management is considering adopting the sampling plan with $n = 150$ and $c \leq 5$ (and $\alpha = 0.08$ and $\beta = 0.12$), even though it does not quite meet their original requirements, if the average outgoing quality is not greater than 3 percent. Construct an AOQ curve for this problem and determine if the plan can be adopted.

Solution:

Step 1: For selected values of p (% defective), compute the AOQ values, where

$$\text{AOQ} = pP_a\left(\frac{N-n}{N}\right), \qquad N = 2{,}000, \quad \text{and} \quad n = 150$$

p	np	P_a	*AOQ*
0.01	1.5	0.996	0.009
0.02	3.0	0.916	0.016
0.03	4.5	0.703	0.020
0.04	6.0	0.446	0.016
0.05	7.5	0.241	0.011
0.06	9.0	0.116	0.006

Table continues

p	np	P_a	AOQ
0.07	10.5	0.050	0.005
0.08	12.0	0.020	0.001
0.09	13.5	0.008	0.001
0.10	15.0	0.003	0.000

Step 2: Construct the AOQ curve using the values for p and AOQ.

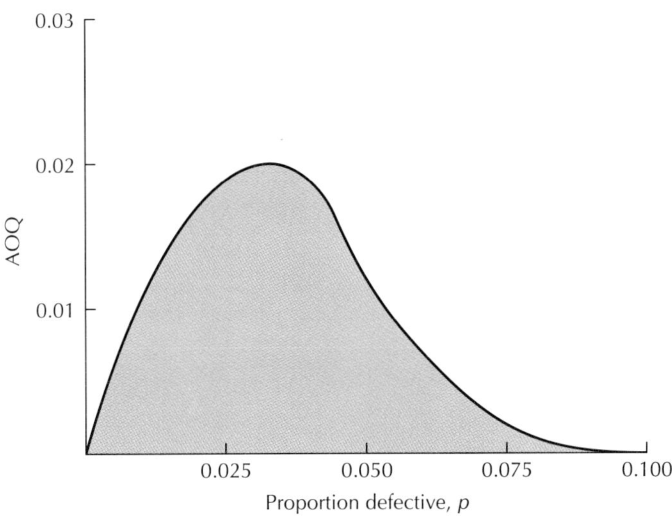

Since the AOQ limit is 2 percent, the modified sampling plan appears to be satisfactory.

QUESTIONS

4-1. What is the difference between acceptance sampling and process control?
4-2. Explain the difference between attribute control charts and variable control charts.
4-3. How are mean ($\bar{x}$-) and range (R-) charts used together?
4-4. Why are sample sizes for attributes necessarily larger than sample sizes for variables?
4-5. How is the sample size determined in a single-sample attribute plan?
4-6. What is the purpose of a pattern test?
4-7. What determines the width of the control limits in a process chart?
4-8. Explain how the sample size, n, and the acceptance level, c, are determined in a variable-sampling plan.
4-9. Explain the difference between attribute- and variable-sampling plans.
4-10. How does the acceptable quality level (AQL) relate to producer's risk (α) and the lot tolerance percent defective (LTPD) relate to consumer's risk (β)?
4-11. What factors determine the construction of an operating characteristic (OC) curve?
4-12. What factors determine how much to inspect and where to inspect?
4-13. Under what circumstances should a c-chart be used instead of a p-chart?
4-14. What is the difference between tolerances and control limits?
4-15. Explain the difference between single-, double- and multiple-sampling plans.

PROBLEMS

4-1. $\bar{p} = 0.151$, UCL = 0.258, LCL = 0.044

4-1. The Great North Woods Clothing Company sells specialty outdoor clothing through its catalog. A quality problem that generates customer complaints occurs when a warehouse employee fills an order with the wrong items. The company has decided to implement a process control plan by inspecting the ordered items after they have been obtained from the warehouse and before they have been packaged. The company has taken 30 samples (during a 30-day period), each for 100 orders, and recorded the number of "defective" orders in each sample, as follows.

Sample	*Number of Defectives*	*Sample*	*Number of Defectives*
1	12	16	6
2	14	17	3
3	10	18	7
4	16	19	10
5	18	20	14
6	19	21	18
7	14	22	22
8	20	23	26
9	18	24	20
10	17	25	24
11	9	26	18
12	11	27	19
13	14	28	20
14	12	29	17
15	7	30	18

Construct a *p*-chart for the company that describes 99.74 percent (3σ) of the random variation in the process, and indicate if the process seems to be out of control at any time.

4-2. $\bar{p} = 0.153$, UCL = 0.225, LCL = 0.081

4-2. The Road King Tire Company in Birmingham wants to monitor the quality of the tires it manufactures in its production process. Each day the company quality control manager takes a sample of 100 tires, tests them, and determines the number of defective tires. The results of 20 samples have been recorded as follows.

Sample	*Number of Defectives*	*Sample*	*Number of Defectives*
1	14	11	18
2	12	12	10
3	9	13	19
4	10	14	20
5	11	15	17
6	7	16	18
7	8	17	18
8	14	18	22
9	16	19	24
10	17	20	23

Construct a *p*-chart for this process using 2σ limits, and describe the variation in the process.

4-3. The Commonwealth Banking Corporation issues a national credit card through its various bank branches in five southeastern states. The bank credit card business is highly competitive and interest rates do not vary substantially, so the company decided to attempt to retain its customers by improving customer service through a reduction in billing errors. The credit card division monitored its billing department process by taking daily samples of 200 customer bills for 30 days and checking their accuracy. The sample results are as follows.

4-3. $\bar{p}$ = 0.053, UCL = 0.101, LCL = 0.005

Sample	*Number of Defectives*	*Sample*	*Number of Defectives*	*Sample*	*Number of Defectives*
1	7	11	9	21	13
2	12	12	6	22	9
3	9	13	3	23	10
4	6	14	2	24	12
5	5	15	8	25	15
6	8	16	10	26	14
7	10	17	12	27	16
8	11	18	14	28	12
9	14	19	16	29	15
10	10	20	15	30	14

Develop a *p*-chart for the billing process using 3σ control limits and indicate if the process is out of control.

4-4. In the assembly process for automobile engines, at one stage in the process a gasket is placed between the two sections of the engine block before they are joined. If the gasket is damaged (bent, crimped, etc.), oil can leak from the cylinder chambers and foul the spark plugs, in which case the entire engine has to be disassembled and a new gasket inserted. The company wants to develop a *p*-chart with 2σ limits to monitor the quality of the gaskets prior to the assembly stage. Historically, 2 percent of the gaskets have been defective, and management does not want the upper control limit to exceed 3 percent defective. What sample size will be required to achieve this control chart?

4-4. n = 784

4-5. The Great Northwoods Clothing Company is a mail-order company that processes thousands of mail and telephone orders each week. They have a customer service number to handle customer order problems, inquiries, and complaints. The company wants to monitor the number of customer calls that can be classified as complaints. The total number of complaint calls the customer service department has received for each of the last 30 weekdays are shown as follows.

4-5. a. $\bar{c}$ = 24.73, UCL = 39.65, LCL = 9.81
b. See Solutions Manual.

Day	*Complaint Calls*	*Day*	*Complaint Calls*	*Day*	*Complaint Calls*
1	27	11	26	21	31
2	15	12	42	22	14
3	38	13	40	23	18
4	41	14	35	24	26
5	19	15	25	25	27
6	23	16	19	26	35
7	21	17	12	27	20
8	16	18	17	28	12
9	33	19	18	29	16
10	35	20	26	30	15

a. Construct a c-chart for this process with 3σ control limits, and indicate if the process was out of control at any time.
b. What nonrandom (i.e., assignable) causes might result in the process being out of control?

4-6. $\bar{c} = 4.3$, UCL = 10.52, LCL = 0

4-6. One of the stages in the process of making denim cloth at the Southern Mills Company is to spin cotton yarn onto spindles for subsequent use in the weaving process. Occasionally the yarn breaks during the spinning process, and an operator ties it back together. Some number of breaks is considered normal, however, too many breaks may mean that the yarn is of poor quality. In order to monitor this process, the quality control manager randomly selects a spinning machine each hour and checks the number of breaks during a 15-minute period. Following is a summary of the observations for the past 20 hours.

Sample	*Number of Breaks*	*Sample*	*Number of Breaks*
1	3	11	3
2	2	12	4
3	4	13	6
4	1	14	7
5	5	15	8
6	3	16	6
7	2	17	5
8	4	18	7
9	0	19	8
10	2	20	6

Construct a c-chart using 3σ limits for this process and indicate if the process was out of control at any time.

4-7. $\bar{c} = 10.67$, UCL = 17.20, LCL = 4.14

4-7. The Xecko Film Company manufactures color photographic film. The film is produced in large rolls of various lengths before it is cut and packaged as the smaller rolls purchased in retail stores. The company wants to monitor the quality of these rolls of film using a c-chart. Twenty-four rolls have been inspected at random, and the numbers of defects per roll are as follows.

Roll	*Number of Defects*	*Roll*	*Number of Defects*	*Roll*	*Number of Defects*
1	12	9	8	17	7
2	8	10	6	18	11
3	5	11	15	19	9
4	7	12	10	20	13
5	14	13	12	21	17
6	9	14	13	22	16
7	10	15	9	23	12
8	11	16	8	24	14

Construct a c-chart with 2σ limits for this process and indicate if the process was out of control at any time.

4-8. a. $\mu = 9$ in., UCL = 9.57, LCL = 8.43 ★
b. Yes
c. None

4-8. The Stryker Baseball Bat Company manufactures wooden and aluminum baseball bats at its plant in New England. Wooden bats produced for the mass market are turned on a lathe, where a piece of wood is shaped into a bat with a handle and barrel. The bat is cut to its specified length and then finished in subsequent processes. Once bats are cut to length, it is difficult to rework them into a different style, so it is important to catch defects before this step. As such, bats are inspected at this stage of the process. A specific style of wooden bat has a mean barrel circumference of 9 inches at its thickest point with a standard deviation of 0.6 inches. (The process variability is assumed to be normally distributed.)

a. Construct a mean control chart for this process for 3σ limits and a sample size of 10 bats.
b. Three samples are taken, and they have average bat diameters of 9.05 inches, 9.10 inches, and 9.08 inches. Is the process in control?
c. What effect will increasing the sample size to 20 bats have on the control charts? Will the conclusions reached in part (b) change for this sample size?

4-9. A machine at the Pacific Fruit Company fills boxes with raisins. The labeled weight of the boxes is 10 ounces. The company wants to construct an *R*-chart to monitor the filling process and make sure the box weights are in control. The quality control department for the company sampled five boxes every 2 hours for three consecutive working days. The sample observations are as follows. ★

4-9. a. $\bar{R} = 0.57$, UCL = 1.21, LCL = 0
b. in control

Sample	*Box Weights (oz)*					*Sample*	*Box Weights (oz)*				
1	9.06	9.13	8.97	8.85	8.46	7	9.00	9.21	9.05	9.23	8.78
2	8.52	8.61	9.09	9.21	8.95	8	9.15	9.20	9.23	9.15	9.06
3	9.35	8.95	9.20	9.03	8.42	9	8.98	8.90	8.81	9.05	9.13
4	9.17	9.21	9.05	9.01	9.53	10	9.03	9.10	9.26	9.46	8.47
5	9.21	8.87	8.71	9.05	9.35	11	9.53	9.02	9.11	8.88	8.92
6	8.74	8.35	8.50	9.06	8.89	12	8.95	9.10	9.00	9.06	8.95

a. Construct an *R*-chart from these data with 3σ control limits, and plot the sample range values.
b. What does the *R*-chart suggest about the process variability?

4-10. The City Square Grocery and Meat Market has a large meat locker in which a constant temperature of approximately 40°F should be maintained. The market manager has decided to construct an *R*-chart to monitor the temperature inside the locker. The manager had one of the market employees take sample temperature readings randomly five times each day for 20 days in order to gather data for the control chart. Following are the temperature sample observations. ★

4-10. a. $\bar{R} = 6.24$, UCL = 13.17, LCL = 0
b. See Solutions Manual.

Sample	*Temperature (°F)*					*Sample*	*Temperature (°F)*				
1	46.3	48.1	42.5	43.1	39.6	11	42.6	43.5	35.4	36.1	38.2
2	41.2	40.5	37.8	36.5	42.3	12	40.5	40.4	39.1	37.2	41.6
3	40.1	41.3	34.5	33.2	36.7	13	45.3	42.0	43.1	44.7	39.5
4	42.3	44.1	39.5	37.7	38.6	14	36.4	37.5	36.2	38.9	40.1
5	35.2	38.1	40.5	39.1	42.3	15	40.5	34.3	36.2	35.1	36.8
6	40.6	41.7	38.6	43.5	44.6	16	39.5	38.2	37.6	34.1	38.7
7	33.2	38.6	41.5	40.7	43.1	17	37.6	40.6	40.3	39.7	41.2
8	41.8	40.0	41.6	40.7	39.3	18	41.0	34.3	39.1	45.2	43.7
9	42.4	41.6	40.8	40.9	42.3	19	40.9	42.3	37.6	35.4	34.8
10	44.7	36.5	37.3	35.3	41.1	20	37.6	39.2	39.3	41.2	37.6

a. Construct an R-chart based on these data using 3σ limits, and plot the 20 sample range values.
b. Does it appear that the temperature is in control according to the criteria establishment by management?

4-11. a. $\bar{R} = 2$, UCL = 4.56, LCL = 0
b. See Solutions Manual.

★ 4-11. The Oceanside Apparel Company manufactures expensive, polo-style men's and women's short-sleeve knit shirts at its plant in Jamaica. The production process requires that material be cut into large patterned squares by operators, which are then sewn together at another stage of the process. If the squares are not of a correct length, the final shirt will be either too large or too small. In order to monitor the cutting process, management takes a sample of four squares of cloth every other hour and measures the length. The length of a cloth square should be 36 inches, and historically, the company has found the length to vary across an acceptable average range of 2 inches.

a. Construct an R-chart for the cutting process using 3σ limits.
b. The company has taken ten additional samples with the following results.

Sample	*Measurements (in.)*			
1	37.3	36.5	38.2	36.1
2	33.4	35.8	37.9	36.2
3	32.1	34.8	39.1	35.3
4	36.1	37.2	36.7	34.2
5	35.1	38.6	37.2	33.6
6	33.4	34.5	36.7	32.4
7	38.1	39.2	35.3	32.7
8	35.4	36.2	36.3	34.3
9	37.1	39.4	38.1	36.2
10	32.1	34.0	35.6	36.1

Plot the new sample data on the control chart constructed in (a) and comment on the process variability.

4-12. $\bar{\bar{x}} = 9.00$, UCL = 9.33, LCL = 8.67

4-12. For the sample data provided in Problem 9, construct an $\bar{x}$-chart in conjunction with the R-chart, plot the sample observations, and, using both $\bar{x}$- and R-charts, comment on the process control.

4-13. $\bar{\bar{x}} = 39.7$, UCL = 43.32, LCL = 36.08

4-13. For the sample data provided in Problem 10, construct an $\bar{x}$-chart in conjunction with the R-chart, plot the sample observations, and, using both $\bar{x}$- and R-charts, comment on the process control.

4-14. $\bar{\bar{x}} = 35.9$, UCL = 37.36, LCL = 34.44

4-14. Using the process information provided in Problem 11, construct an $\bar{x}$-chart in conjunction with the R-chart, plot the sample observations provided in part (b), and, using both the $\bar{x}$- and R-charts, comment on the process control.

4-15. $z_{A/B} = -0.603$, $z_{U/D} = -0.50$, $z = \pm 1.96$, no pattern

4-15. Use z run tests and a test statistic of $z = \pm 1.96$ to determine if the sample observations used in the $\bar{x}$-chart in Problem 12 reflect any nonrandom patterns.

4-16. $z_{A/B} = -2.23$, $z_{U/D} = -2.09$, $z = \pm 1.96$, pattern exists

4-16. Use z tests and a test statistic of $z = \pm 1.96$ to determine if the sample observations in Problem 5 reflect any nonrandom patterns.

4-17. $z_{A/B} = -0.45$, $z_{U/D} = -1.11$, $z = \pm 2.33$, no pattern

4-17. Use z tests and a test statistic of z ± 2.33 to determine if the sample observations in Problem 10 reflect any nonrandom patterns.

4-18. $z_{A/B} = -0.46$, $z_{U/D} = -0.56$, $z = \pm 1.96$, no pattern

4-18. Use z run tests and a test statistic of $z = \pm 1.96$ to determine if the sample observations used in the $\bar{x}$-chart in Problem 13 reflect any nonrandom patterns.

4-19. $z_{A/B} = -3.71$, $z_{U/D} = -2.08$, $z = \pm 1.96$, pattern exists

4-19. Use z run tests and a test statistic of $z = \pm 1.96$ to determine if the sample observations used in the $\bar{p}$-chart in Problem 1 reflect any nonrandom patterns.

4-20. A single-sampling plan for attributes has a sample size of 10, and the acceptance level is 1 defective item. If the percent defective items in the lot is 4 percent, what is the probability of accepting the lot?

4-20. 0.9418

4-21. A single-sample plan for attributes has a sample size of 100 and the acceptance level is 2 defective items. If the percent defective items in the lot is 4 percent, what is the probability of accepting the lot?

4-21. 0.2381

4-22. Draw an operating characteristics curve for a single-sample plan with $n = 150$, $c \leq 2$, AQL = 0.02, and LTPD = 0.07. What are the producer's risk (α) and consumer's risk (β) for this plan? Show the effect of reducing the sample size to 50.

★ 4-22. $\alpha = 0.577$, $\beta = 0.002$

4-23. The Great Lakes Company, a grocery store chain, purchases apples from a produce distributor in Virginia. The grocery company has an agreement with the distributor that it desires shipments of 10,000 apples with no more than 2 percent defectives (i.e., severely blemished apples), although it will accept shipments with up to a maximum of 8 percent defective. The probability of rejecting a good lot is set at 0.05 whereas the probability of accepting a bad quality lot is 0.10.

a. Determine a sampling plan that will approximately achieve these quality performance criteria.
b. Draw the operating characteristics curve for the sampling plan in (a) and label AQL, LTPD, α, and β.
c. Compute the average outgoing quality limit for this plan.

★ 4-23. a. $n = 131$, $c = 5$
b. See Solutions Manual.
c. 0.0242

4-24. The Academic House Publishing Company sends out the textbooks it publishes to an independent book binder. When the bound books come back, they are inspected for defective bindings (warped boards, ripples, cuts, poor adhesion, etc.). The publishing company has an acceptable quality level of 4 percent defectives but will tolerate lots of up to 10 percent defective. What (approximate) sample size and acceptance level would result in a probability of 0.05 that a good lot will be rejected and a probability of 0.10 that a bad lot will be accepted?

★ 4-24. $n = 155$, $c = 10$

4-25. For Problem 24, draw the operating characteristics curve.

★ 4-25. See Solutions Manual.

4-26. The Metro Packaging Company in Richmond produces clear plastic bottles for the Kooler Cola Company, a soft-drink manufacturer. Metro inspects each lot of 5,000 bottles before they are shipped to the Kooler Company. The soft-drink company has specified an acceptable quality level of 0.06 and a lot tolerance percent defective of 0.12. Metro currently has a sampling plan with $n = 150$ and $c \leq 4$. The two companies have recently agreed that the sampling plan should have a producer's risk of 0.05 and a consumer's risk of 0.10. Will the current sampling plan used by Metro achieve these levels of α and β?

★ 4-26. No, $n = 208$, $c \leq 18$

4-27. The Fast Break Computer Company assembles personal computers and sells them to retail outlets. It purchases keyboards for its PCs from a manufacturer in the Orient. The keyboards are shipped in lots of 1,000 units, and when they arrive at the Fast Break Company samples of 100 units are inspected. Fast Break's contract with the overseas manufacturer specifies that the quality level that they will accept is 4 percent defectives.

a. The personal computer company wants to avoid sending a shipment back because the distance involved would delay and disrupt the assembly process, thus, they want only a 2 percent probability of sending a good lot back. What acceptance value should the company use?
b. Using the acceptance criteria determined in (a), if the worst level of quality the Fast Break Company will accept is 12 percent defective items, what

4-27. a. $c = 8$
b. $\beta = 0.155$

is the probability that a shipment with a percent defective worse than this will be accepted?

4-28. a. $\alpha = 0.442$, $\beta = .092$
b. No
c. AOQL (a) = 0.015, and AOQL (b) = 0.007

★ 4-28. Viking Electronics manufactures low-cost, hand-held electronic calculators that are supplied to grocery, discount, and drug stores. The company has a sampling plan for inspection with AQL = 0.03, LTPD = 0.08, $n = 50$, and $c \leq 1$.

a. Compute the producer's and consumer's risks for this sampling plan.
b. In part (a), the company would like to reduce the producer's risk and is considering an increase in the sample size to 100. Would this change accomplish the company's objective?
c. Assuming a lot size of 500 units, compute the AOQL for the sampling plans in parts (a) and (b) and indicate which would result in the lowest AOQL.

4-29. a. No
b. AOQL = 0.015

★ 4-29. A department store chain in Atlanta has arranged to purchase specially designed sweatshirts with the Olympic logo from a clothing manufacturer in Hong Kong. When the sweatshirts arrive in Atlanta in lots of 2,000 units, they are inspected. The store's management and manufacturer have agreed on quality criteria of AQL = 2 percent defective and LTPD = 8 percent defective. Because sending poor-quality shipments back to Hong Kong would disrupt sales at the stores, management has specified a low producer's risk of 0.03 and will accept a relatively high consumer's risk of 0.15.

a. The store's quality control manager has suggested a sampling plan of $n =$ 150 and $c \leq 4$ defectives. Do you think this plan will be satisfactory to the store's management?
b. Determine the AOQ curve for this sampling plan and indicate the AOQL.

4-30. $c = 95.55$ in.

4-30. A lumber company supplies 8-foot boards to a chain of home-improvement stores in the Southwest. The boards have a standard deviation of 1.5 inches. Boards with a length of less than 8 feet are considered poor quality. The store management samples 30 boards from each shipment it receives and measures them. Determine an acceptance level that limits the probability of rejecting a shipment that does not average 8 feet to 0.05.

4-31. $c = 4.83$ min

4-31. The Quik Wheels Car Wash washes cars in an automated process and then cleans the interior manually. The interior cleaners receive a tip from every customer, so it is advantageous for them to clean cars as quickly as possible. As a result, the manual cleaners occasionally do a poor-quality job of cleaning. Based on historical analysis, the car-wash manager knows that the interior cleaning takes an average of 5 minutes, with a standard deviation of 0.6 minutes. Every hour the manager times the interior cleaning of twenty cars to see if the quality is being maintained. If the manager times the cleaning for a specific hour, what would the acceptable average time be for the sample that would limit the probability of wrongly believing that the average time was less than 5 minutes to 0.10?

4-32. $c = 31.12$ oz

★ 4-32. The Ritz Candy Company produces individually wrapped chocolate truffles and packages them in 2-pound tins, which it supplies to candy stores and department stores. The weight of the tins is normally distributed with a standard deviation of 1.5 ounces. Design a sampling plan that has a probability of 0.05 of rejecting a shipment with an average weight per tin of 2 pounds and, a probability of 0.10 of accepting a shipment with an average weight of 1.9 pounds per tin.

4-33. $c = 97.78$ lb

★ 4-33. A metal products firm manufactures nails, which it packs in wooden kegs and ships to building-supply stores. The keg's average weight is 100 pounds, with a standard deviation of 3 pounds. Design a sampling plan for which there is a 0.07 probability of rejecting a shipment with an average weight per keg of 100 pounds and a 0.15 probability of accepting a shipment with an average weight of 96 pounds per keg.

4-34. The South Fork Feed Company produces a liquid vitamin supplement that is added to feed mix. The supplement is packaged in heavy plastic 5-gallon containers. The volume is normally distributed with a standard deviation of 0.20 gallon. The feed company samples ten containers from each lot it produces and rejects lots that have an average sample value of less than 4.85 gallons. What is the probability that a good lot will be rejected? ★ **4-34.** 0.009

CASE PROBLEM

See Solutions Manual.

Quality Control at Rainwater Brewery

Bob Raines and Megan Waters are former students at State University. While at State they began experimenting with brewing beer in their apartment, and by their senior year they were not only brewing enough beer for themselves, they were also informally supplying their friends and neighbors with home brew. By the time they graduated with a degree in business, they had garnered quite a reputation among the student body for the quality of their beer. In fact, it was frequently suggested to Bob and Megan that they should go into business and sell their beer. After a while they began to take this suggestion seriously, and the summer after they graduated they formed the Rainwater Brewery in Whitesville, the town where State University is located.

Whitesville has a number of bars and restaurants that are patronized by the student body at State and the local resident population. In fact, Whitesville has the highest per capita beer consumption in the state. In setting up their small brewery, Bob and Megan decided that they would target their sales toward individuals who would pick up their orders directly from the brewery and toward restaurants and bars, where they would deliver orders on a daily or weekly basis.

The brewery process essentially occurs in three stages. First, the mixture is cooked in a vat according to a recipe; then it is placed in a stainless-steel container, where it is fermented for several weeks. During the fermentation process the specific gravity, temperature, and pH need to be monitored on a daily basis. The specific gravity starts out at about 1.006 to 1.008 and decreases to around 1.002, and the temperature must be between 50° and 60°F. After the brew ferments, it is filtered into another stainless-steel pressurized container, where it is carbonated and the beer ages for about a week (with the temperature monitored), after which it is bottled and is ready for distribution. Megan and Bob brew a batch of beer each day, which will result in about 1,000 bottles for distribution after the approximately 3-week fermentation and aging process.

In the process of setting up their brewery, Megan and Bob agreed they had already developed a proven product with a taste that was appealing, so the most important factor in the success of their new venture would be maintaining high quality. Thus, they spent a lot of time discussing what kind of quality control techniques they should employ. They agreed that the chance of brewing a "bad," or "spoiled," batch of beer was extremely remote, plus they really could not financially afford to reject a whole batch of 1,000 bottles of beer if the taste or color was a little "off" the norm. So they felt as if they needed to focus more on process control methods to identify quality problems that would enable them to adjust their equipment, recipe, or process parameters rather than to use some type of acceptance sampling plan.

Describe the different quality control methods that Rainwater Brewery might use to ensure good-quality beer and how these methods might fit into an overall TQM program.

$\bar{c} = 4.15$, UCL = 8.22, LCL = 0.076

CASE PROBLEM

Quality Control at Grass, Unlimited

Mark Sumansky owns and manages the Grass, Unlimited, lawn-care service in Middleton. His customers include individual homeowners and businesses that subscribe to his service during the winter months for lawn care beginning in the spring and ending in the fall with leaf raking and disposal. Thus, when he begins his service in April he generally has a full list of customers and does not take on additional customers unless he has an opening. However, if he loses a customer anytime after the first of June, it is difficult to find new customers, since most people make lawn-service arrangements for the entire summer.

Mark employs five crews, with between three to five workers each, to cut grass during the spring and summer months. A crew normally works 10-hour days and can average cutting about 25 normal-size lawns of less than a half-acre each day. A crew will normally have one heavy-duty, wide-cut riding mower, a regular power mower, and trimming equipment. When a crew descends on a lawn, the normal procedure is for one person to mow the main part of the lawn with the riding mower, one or two people to trim, and one person to use the smaller mower to cut areas the riding mower cannot reach. Crews move very fast, and they can often cut a lawn in 15 minutes.

Unfortunately, although speed is an essential component in the profitability of Grass, Unlimited, it can also contribute to quality problems. In his or her haste, a mower might cut flowers, shrubs, or border plants, nick and scrape trees, "skin" spots on the lawn creating bare spots, trim too close, scrape house paint, cut or disfigure house trim, destroy toys and lawn furniture, among other things. When these problems occur on a too-frequent basis, a customer cancels service, and Mark has a difficult time getting a replacement customer. In addition, he gets most of his subscriptions based on word-of-mouth recommendations and retention of previous customers who are satisfied with his service. As such, quality is a very important factor in his business.

In order to improve the quality of his lawn-care service, Mark has decided to use a process control chart to monitor defects. He has hired Lisa Anderson to follow the teams and check lawns for defects after the mowers have left. A defect is any abnormal or abusive condition created by the crew, including those items just mentioned. It is not possible for Lisa to inspect the more than 100 lawns the service cuts daily, so she randomly picks a sample of 20 lawns each day and counts the number of defects she sees at each lawn. She also makes a note of each defect, so that if there is a problem, the cause can easily be determined. In most cases the defects are caused by haste, but some defects can be caused by faulty equipment or by a crew member using a poor technique or not being attentive.

Over a 3-day period Lisa accumulated the following data on defects.

DAY 1		*DAY 2*		*DAY 3*	
Sample	*Number of Defects*	*Sample*	*Number of Defects*	*Sample*	*Number of Defects*
1	6	1	2	1	5
2	4	2	5	2	5
3	5	3	1	3	3
4	9	4	4	4	2
5	3	5	5	5	6
6	8	6	3	6	5
7	6	7	2	7	4

Table continues

DAY 1		DAY 2		DAY 3	
Sample	*Number of Defects*	*Sample*	*Number of Defects*	*Sample*	*Number of Defects*
8	1	8	2	8	3
9	5	9	2	9	2
10	6	10	6	10	2
11	4	11	4	11	2
12	7	12	3	12	4
13	6	13	8	13	1
14	5	14	5	14	5
15	8	15	6	15	9
16	3	16	3	16	4
17	5	17	4	17	4
18	4	18	3	18	4
19	3	19	3	19	1
20	2	20	4	20	3

Develop a process control chart for Grass, Unlimited, to monitor the quality of their lawn service using 2 σ limits. Describe any other quality control or quality management procedures you think Grass, Unlimited, might employ to improve the quality of their service.

REFERENCES

Montgomery, D. C., *Introduction to Statistical Quality Control*, 2d ed., New York: John Wiley, 1991.

Evans, James R., and Lindsay, William M., *The Management and Control of Quality*, 2d ed., St. Paul, Minn.: West, 1993.

Grant, E. L., and Leavenworth, R. S., *Statistical Quality Control*, 5th ed., New York: McGraw-Hill, 1980.

Charbonneau, H. C., and Webster, G. L., *Industrial Quality Control*, Englewood Cliffs, N.J.: Prentice-Hall, 1978.

Dodge, H. F., and Romig, H. G., *Sampling Inspection Tables—Single and Double Sampling*, 2d ed., New York: John Wiley, 1959.

Fetter, R. B., *The Quality Control System*, Homewood, Ill.: Irwin, 1967.

Duncan, A. J., *Quality Control and Industrial Statistics*, 4th ed., Homewood, Ill.: Irwin, 1974.

5
PRODUCT AND SERVICE DESIGN

CHAPTER OUTLINE

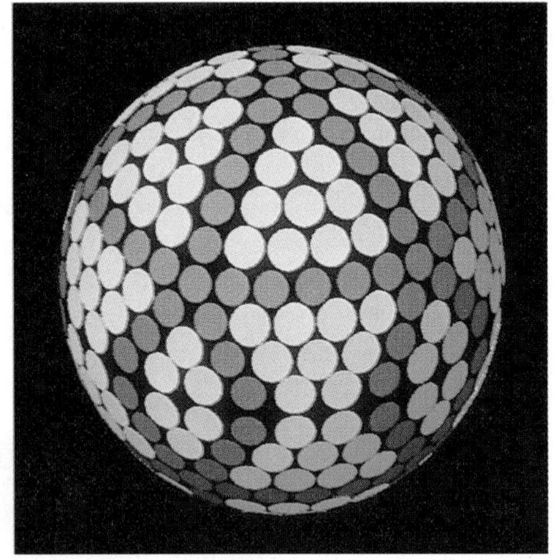

Computer-aided design (CAD) is used to design everything from pencils to submarines. Some of our everyday products are more difficult to design than you may think. Potato chips with ridges, the top of a soda can, a 2-liter bottle of soft drink, a car door, and golf balls are examples of simple products that require the sophistication of CAD for effective design and testing. Shown here are two examples of dimple design on Titleist golf balls. The number, size, and patterns of dimples on a golf ball can affect the distance, trajectory, and accuracy of play. The advent of CAD has allowed many more designs to be tested. Today, over 200 different dimple patterns are used by golfball manufacturers. Golf clubs and golf courses are also designed with CAD.

DESIGNING A BETTER GOLF BALL

Do you ever wonder where the ideas for some of our everyday products and services come from? The evolution of design is a fascinating topic. Consider the design history of the golf ball. Golf began in Scotland in the 1400s with a wooden ball and wooden clubs. Things did not change much until the 1800s, when a "feathery" was introduced. The feathery was made from pieces of bull's hide that had been soaked in water and alum, sewn together, and stuffed with a hatful of goose or chicken feathers. The feathery was then banged into a somewhat round shape, and several coats of paint were applied. This was such a time-consuming process that a golfball maker could make only four balls a day. The feathery didn't last very long either, one or two rounds—unless it got wet. Then it swelled up and wouldn't budge. The feathery's performance wasn't great, but it had a lasting impact on the game. Its fragility encouraged the graceful, sweeping swing of the golfer and the use of long, wispy clubs.

In the mid-1800s a Scottish divinity student introduced a gutta-perch ball made from the latex of a tree by the same name. The ball was waterproof, more durable, and easier to make than the feathery. Players soon discovered, however, that the smooth "guttie" did not fly well until it was old and pitted. Golfers and golfball makers alike began to age the gutties by marking their surfaces.

In the 1930s, an amateur golfer and owner of a molded-rubber company developed a ball with a noncompressible liquid center encased in a thin shell of rubber. The manufacturer, Titleist, used new and different winding patterns and X-rayed every ball to ensure that its core was round and on-center. The covers of the new ball had a mesh pattern, but soon manufacturers were experimenting with all types of markings—raised round bumps (called brambles), grids, square indentations, and even a map of the world. A breakthrough came when someone reversed the brambles mold, producing "dimples" instead. This improved the game so much that golfing authorities put a limit on the initial velocity of the ball (no greater than 250 feet per second).

Later it was discovered that dimple patterns can be designed to optimize the benefits of lift and minimize the problems associated with drag. Throughout the 1960s the most popular dimple configuration was a 336-dimple octahedron running in straight lines around the ball. In the 1970s, when computer-aided design became available, more than 200 dimple shapes and configurations were tested. One pattern, called the icosahedron, divided the surface into twenty triangular regions. Today there are dozens of different patterns and different-sized dimples (even on the same ball). Golfers can choose a dimple pattern to match their specific needs. For example, a player might choose a golf ball that provides a high trajectory and short roll or one with a low trajectory and long roll.

One particular golfball design (by a small company) was so effective that even an average golfer could hit drives of 300 yards; a pro could probably reach 500 yards. This kind of performance may be great for the individual golfer, but it would quickly make the golf courses around the world obsolete. (It would be like building a mousetrap that worked so well it endangered the species.) Predictably, the golf authorities saved their investment in golf courses and set a distance standard on golf balls of no longer than 296.8 yards per shot.[1]

Teaching Note 5.1 Interesting Design Stories

The basic purpose of any organization is to provide products or services to their customers. Thus, the *design* of these products and services is essential to the livelihood of a company. Effective designs must satisfy customer requirements, facilitate cost-effective and quality-effective manufacture or delivery, sell in the marketplace, and make a profit for the company. Organizations can gain a competitive edge through designs that bring new ideas to the market quickly, do a better job of satisfying customer needs, and are easier to manufacture, use, and repair than existing products.

Design can provide a competitive edge.

Transparency 5.1 Effective Designs

Product design specifies which materials are to be used, determines dimensions and tolerances, defines the appearance of the product, and sets standards for performance. *Service design* specifies what physical items, sensual benefits, and psychological benefits the customer is to receive from the service.

Clearly, design has a tremendous impact on the quality of a final product or service. However, conforming to design specifications may not be enough to ensure quality. What if the design does not meet customers needs or the design is difficult or costly to make? What if the design process takes so much time that a competitor is able to introduce new products, services, or features before us? What if, in rushing to be first to the market, our design is not as "clean" as we wish it to be and it requires numerous revisions that are frustrating to the consumer and costly to management? Quality in the design process involves matching product or service characteristics with customer requirements, ensuring that customer requirements are met in the simplest and least costly manner, reducing the time required to design a new product or service, and minimizing the revisions necessary to make a design workable. In this chapter we examine the design process with an eye toward ensuring quality in the final product or service. The impact of quality

[1]Stuller, J., "Better Golfing Through Chemistry," *Invention and Technology* (Summer 1993): 47–53.

and technology on design are discussed in separate sections. The chapter ends with a discussion of the differences between product and service design.

THE DESIGN PROCESS

There are four steps in the design process.

The design process involves four basic steps: 1. generating ideas, 2. conducting a feasibility study, 3. developing and testing a preliminary design, and 4. creating a detailed final design of the product or service. Traditionally, the design process has been performed sequentially by different personnel from separate departments in a firm. As shown in Figure 5.1, ideas for new products or improvements to existing products can be generated from a myriad of sources, including a company's own R&D department, customer complaints or suggestions, marketing research, suppliers, salespersons in the field, factory workers, actions by competitors, and new technological developments. It is normally the marketing department's job to take these ideas, form a *product concept* (or a series of alternative concepts), and conduct a study on the feasibility of the proposed product or service. If the proposed product meets certain market and economic expectations, *performance specifications* for the product are developed and sent to the company's design engineers to be developed into preliminary technical specifications and then detailed *design specifications.* The design specifications are sent to the manufacturing engineers, who develop a *process plan* that includes specific requirements for equip-

Teaching Note 5.2 The Product Concept for Honda's Accord

Transparency 5.2 The Sequential Design Process

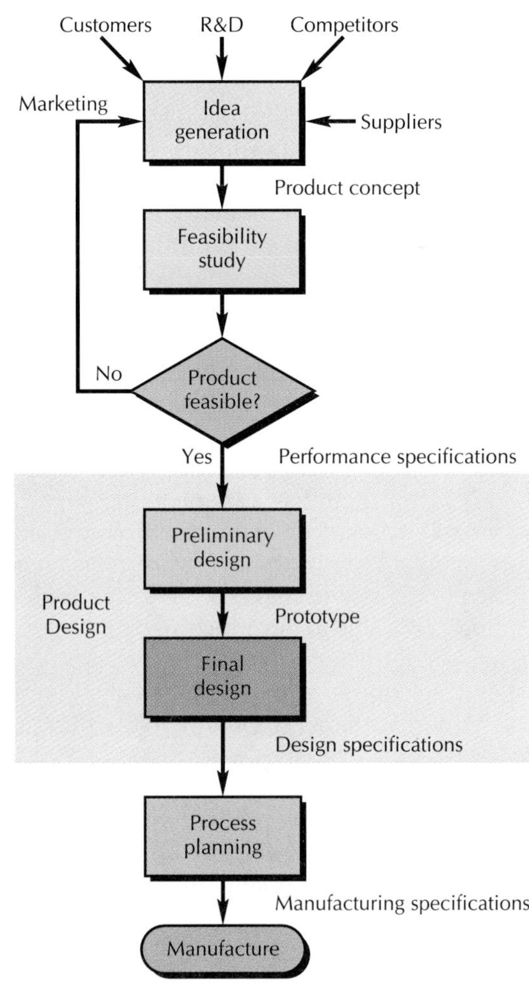

FIGURE 5.1 The Sequential Design Process

ment, tooling, and fixtures. These *manufacturing specifications* are passed on to production personnel on the factory floor, where production of the new product can be scheduled.

Although the steps in this process are valid, the sequential order in which decisions are made is *not*. What typically occurs is the buildup of physical or mental "walls" between functional areas and departments, causing the output from one design stage to be "thrown over the wall" to the next stage, with little discussion or feedback. A more enlightened view of product and service design brings representatives from the various functions and departments *together* to work on the design simultaneously (see Figure 5.2). We consider the order in which design decisions are made later in the chapter, but first, we need to examine each stage of the design process in more detail.

Idea Generation

Product innovation comes from understanding the customer and actively identifying customer needs. The primary source of new product ideas depends in large part on a company's strategy in the marketplace. For example, if a company is known for its innovation, ideas may be derived primarily from in-house research and development teams or funded research at universities. If a company's strength lies in manufacture rather than design, ideas for new products may consist mainly of analyzing competitors' wares and trying to improve on their

(a) Sequential design: Walls between functional areas

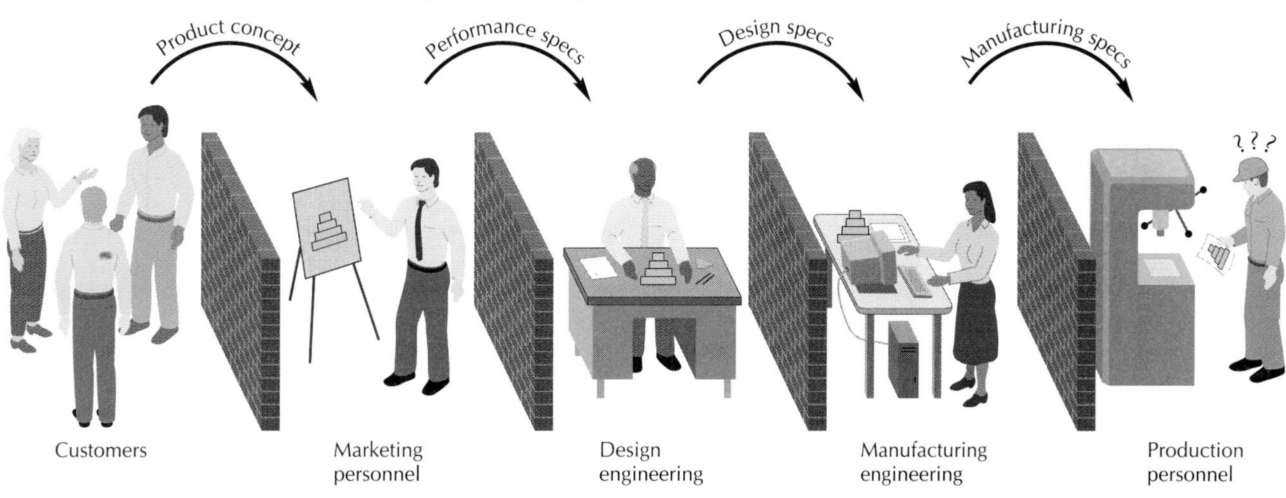

(b) Concurrent design: Walls broken down

FIGURE 5.2 Breaking Down the Barriers to Effective Design

offerings. Today, the competitive environment for new products is so fierce that many companies are exploring every conceivable avenue for generating new ideas. Ideas are derived from the following places:

Ideas come from many sources, including customers, competitors, and R&D.

1. Surveying suppliers, distributors, and salespersons
2. Monitoring trade journals and other published material
3. Analyzing warranty claims, customer complaints, and other failures
4. Conducting customer surveys, focus groups, and individual customer interviews
5. Field testing and evaluating trial users
6. Constructing perceptual maps and cluster charts of customer preferences
7. Benchmarking, reverse engineering, and creative swiping
8. Extensive research and development activities

Anyone who comes in contact with a company's product is a source of ideas. A formal channel for inputting ideas from suppliers, distributors, salespersons, and workers should be established and used frequently. Companies also need to *use* the information that is readily available to them through printed media and careful analysis of their own successes and failures. Of course, *customers* should be the focus of new ideas, and there are a variety of ways to garner their input. Would-be customers as well as existing customers should be surveyed. The toughest and more exacting customers provide the most useful information. Customer surveys should be followed up with smaller focus groups or individual customer interviews. Field testing is imperative and should be done as soon as possible. Pilots and prototypes are many times more powerful than abstract proposals for getting new ideas approved.

A **perceptual map** is a visual method of comparing customer perceptions of different products or services.

Competitors are also an excellent source of ideas and impetus to action. **Perceptual maps** compare customer perceptions of a company's products with competitor products. Consider the perceptual map of breakfast cereals in terms of taste and nutrition shown in Figure 5.3. The lack of an entry in the high-taste–high-nutrition category suggests that opportunities exist in this quadrant of the market. To capitalize on that fact, Cheerios introduced honey-nut and apple-cinnamon versions while promoting its "oat" base. Fruit bits and nuts were added to wheat flakes to make them more tasty and nutritious. Shredded Wheat opted for more taste by reducing its size and adding a sugar frosting or berry filling. Rice Krispies,

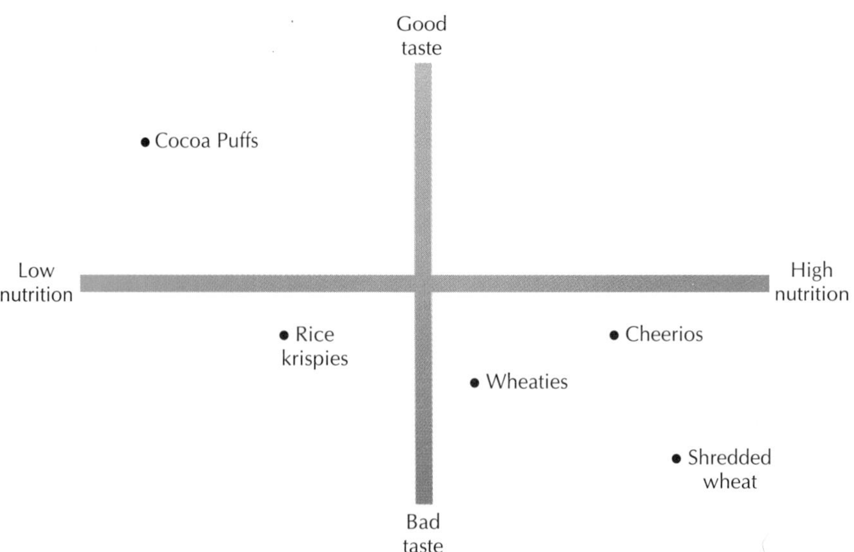

FIGURE 5.3 A Perceptual Map of Breakfast Cereals

on the other hand, sought to challenge Cocoa Puffs in the "more tasty" market quadrant with marshmallow and fruit-flavored versions.

Cluster charts help to identify market segments and profile customer preferences. Figure 5.4 shows two clear clusters of customers in the breakfast cereal market classified by their preference of the factors taste and nutrition. As might be expected, youngsters are more concerned with taste, whereas adults emphasize nutrition. To be useful, any mode of customer input (surveys, interviews, etc.) needs to recognize and segregate the responses from these distinct market segments.

A **cluster chart** is a graphical approach to profiling customer preferences.

Benchmarking refers to finding the best-in-class part, product, or process, measuring one's performance against it, and making recommendations for improvement based on the results. The benchmarked company may be in an entirely different line of business. For example, American Express is well-known for its ability to get customers to pay up quickly, Disney World, for its employee commitment, Federal Express, for its speed, McDonald's, for its consistency, and Xerox, for its benchmarking techniques.

Benchmarking is comparing a product or process against the best-in-class product.

Teaching Note 5.3 Benchmark Clearinghouse

Reverse engineering refers to the procedure of carefully dismantling and inspecting a competitor's product to look for design features that can be incorporated into one's own product. Ford used this approach successfully in its design of the Taurus automobile, assessing 400 features of competitor products and copying, adapting, or enhancing more than 300 of them, including Audi's accelerator pedal, Toyota's fuel-gauge accuracy, and BMW's tire and jack storage.

Reverse engineering refers to carefully dismantling a competitor's product in order to improve one's own product.

Creative swiping is a term used by author Tom Peters to describe the process of aggressively seeking out the knowledge of competitors and interesting noncompetitors. He suggests turning everyone in an organization (not just marketers and design engineers) into "vacuum cleaners" to try to understand the best of what others are offering. Marriott did just that in the design of its line of economy hotels. Teams of marketing, finance, human resources, and operations personnel were sent out to nearly 400 competing hotels to test their facilities (beds, size of rooms, thickness of walls, adjoining restaurants, etc.), their service (reservations, personal attention, room policies, etc.), and their management (operations, prices, morale, etc.). The result was a well-designed network of inexpensive hotels, called Courtyard Hotels, geared to the frequent business traveler. The design included such amenities as easy access to rooms, early breakfast times, superfast checkout, and an availability of dinner reservations at a variety of area restaurants to which customers might wish to take clients.

Teaching Note 5.4 Marriott's Courtyard Design

Awareness of competitive position is important, but for many products and services, following consumer or competitor leads is not enough; customers are attracted by superior technology and creative ideas. In these industries, research and development is the primary source of new product ideas. Expenditures for these efforts can be enormous ($2 million a day at Kodak) and investment risky (only

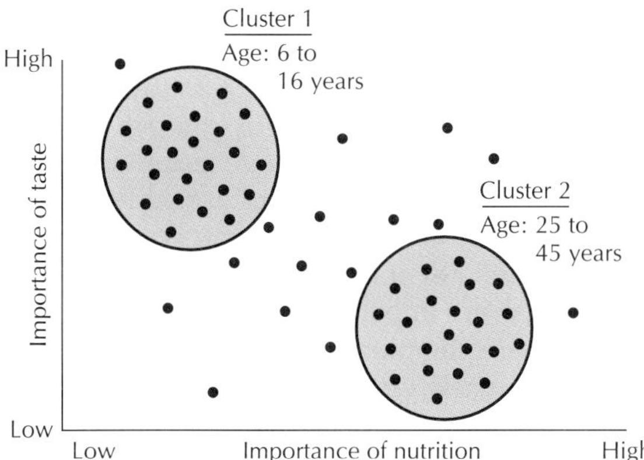

FIGURE 5.4 A Cluster Chart of Breakfast Cereal Customers

one in every twenty ideas ever becomes a product and only one of every ten new products is successful). In addition, ideas generated by R&D tend to follow a long path to commercialization.

Since a large percentage of R&D in the United States is government-funded by military or space agencies, American researchers are not as quick to see the commercial applications of their ideas as are researchers in other countries. For example, new discoveries in flexible metal alloys were used by the United States for pipe joints in fighter airplanes and by Japan for eyeglasses, air-conditioner louvers, and children's toys. Lightweight but strong graphite composite materials created in U.S. laboratories were applied to aerospace and aircraft design by this country and to tennis racquets, golf clubs, and other sports equipment by Japan. The United States used its discovery of solar electricity generation to power satellites, whereas Japan made enormous profits from solar-powered calculators.

Another potential problem is company attitudes toward research personnel. American firms are said to take the "Silicon Valley" approach to innovation: Put a few bright people in a dark room, pour in money, and hope. R&D staffs are purposely isolated from the rest of the organization so that their creativity is not compromised by everyday business activities. General Motor's technical center outside of Detroit and Xerox's Palo Alto Research Center (PARC) are examples. The results of this approach have not been particularly successful. Many feel that GM's scientists have not produced a steady stream of new ideas in recent years precisely *because* they are insulated from the crisis situation facing U.S. automakers. In the case of Xerox, its researchers created the basis for the PC revolution—graphics display terminal screens, pop-up windows, the point-and-click mouse, local area networks, and object-oriented programming—10 years before the concepts were ever applied—by others, not Xerox. The research was brilliant, but there was no appreciation of its market potential. Today, PARC researchers are teaming up with employees and customers to gain new insights into the *use* of technology.[2] And U.S. companies in general are engaged in more productive research. In 1993, IBM was the first U.S. company in a decade to receive the most patents from the U.S. government.

Feasibility Study

Marketing takes the ideas that are generated and the customer needs that are identified from the first stage of the design process and formulates alternative product concepts. The most promising concepts undergo a feasibility study that includes several types of analyses, beginning with a *market analysis*. Most companies have extensive staffs of market researchers who can design and evaluate customer surveys, interviews, focus groups, or market tests. Sometimes product concepts are tested; other times, physical prototypes or product samples are developed for the tests. The market analysis assesses whether sufficient demand for the proposed product exists to merit investment in its further development.

A feasibility study consists of a *market analysis*, an *economic analysis*, and a *technical/strategic analysis*.

If the demand potential exists, an *economic analysis* is conducted that looks at estimates of production and development costs and compares them to estimated sales volume. A price range for the product is discussed that is compatible with the market segment and image of the new product. Quantitative techniques such as cost/benefit analysis, decision theory, net present value, or internal rate of return are commonly used to evaluate the profit potential of the project. The data used in the analysis are far from certain. Estimates of risk in the new product venture and the company's attitude toward risk are important considerations.

Finally, *technical and strategic analyses* are completed that answer such questions as these: Does the new product require new technology? Is the risk or capi-

[2]Brown, J. S., "Research That Reinvents the Corporation," *Harvard Business Review* (January–February 1991): 102–11.

tal investment excessive? Does the company have sufficient labor and management skills to support the technology required? Is sufficient capacity available for production? Does the new product provide a competitive advantage for the company? Does it draw on corporate strengths? Is it compatible with the core business of the firm?

Product concepts that pass the feasibility study and are approved for development are sent to design engineering, where preliminary and detailed designs are developed. Performance specifications are provided by marketing that describe the function of the product—that is, what the product should do to satisfy customer needs.

Preliminary and Final Design

Design engineers take the performance specifications provided by marketing (which are usually quite general in nature) and translate them into technical specifications. The process involves creating a preliminary design, building a prototype, testing the prototype, revising the design, retesting, and so on, until a viable preliminary design is determined. Once a preliminary design is agreed upon, the final design can be developed. The final design stage refines, documents, and details the preliminary design through three phases: 1. functional, 2. form, and 3. production design.

Preliminary design involves testing and revising a prototype.

Final design includes functional, form, and production design.

Functional Design

Functional design is concerned with how the product performs. It is the first phase in the final design process and has the highest priority for the design engineer. Functional design seeks to meet the performance specifications provided by marketing for fitness of use to the customer. Two major performance characteristics are considered during this phase of design, reliability and maintainability.

Functional design is concerned with how the product will perform.

Reliability is the probability that a given part or product will perform its intended function for a specified length of time under normal conditions of use. Note that reliability refers to the *parts* of a product as well as the product as a whole and that the function of each part or product must be specified before reliability can be measured. Expected length of life, known as *durability*, must also be specified for each part or product. How long the part or product lasts depends on the definition of failure and the conditions defined as "normal." These conditions are inputs to the design process, not outputs. They are decided beforehand by marketing and are influenced by customer expectations, cost, and target market-quality levels.

Reliability is the probability that a product will perform its intended function for a specified period of time.

You may be familiar with reliability information from product warranties. For example, a hair dryer might be guaranteed to function (i.e., blow air with a certain force at a certain temperature) for one year under normal conditions of use (defined to be 300 hours of operation). Similarly, a car warranty might extend for three years or 50,000 miles. Normal conditions of use would include regularly scheduled oil changes and other minor maintenance activities. A missed oil change or mileage in excess of 50,000 miles in a three-year period would not be considered "normal" and would nullify the warranty.

Finally, note that reliability is expressed as a probability of performance. This probability can be interpreted in two ways, 1. the probability that a product will perform on a *given trial* or 2. the probability that a product will perform *after a length of time*.

The probability that a product will perform on a given trial is a function of the reliabilities of its component parts and how the parts are related. If all parts must function for the product or system to operate, then the system reliability is the *product* of the component part reliabilities. For example, if two component parts

Reliability may be viewed as performance on a given trial.

are required and they each have a reliability of 0.90, the reliability of the system is 0.90 x 0.90 = 0.81, or 81 percent. The system can be visualized as a *series* of components as follows:

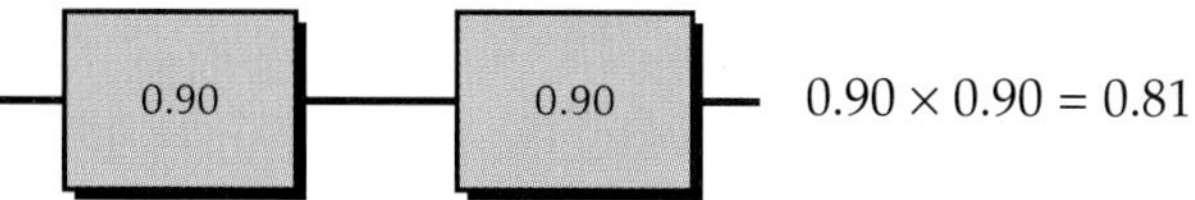

Teaching Note 5.5 General Formulae for Reliability

Note that the system reliability of 0.81 is considerably less than the component reliabilities of 0.90. As the number of serial components increases, system reliability will continue to deteriorate. This makes a good argument for simple designs with fewer components!

Failure of some components in a system is more critical than others—the brakes on a car, for instance. To increase the reliability of individual parts (and thus the system as a whole), *redundant* parts can be built in to back up a failure. Providing emergency brakes for a car is an example. Consider the following redundant design with R_1 representing the reliability of the original component and R_2 the reliability of the backup component.

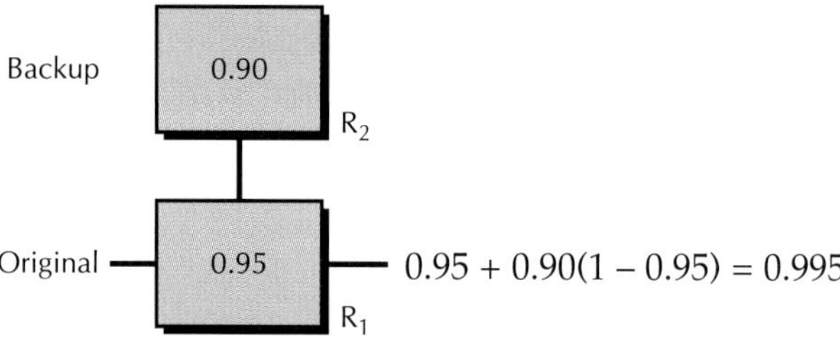

These components are said to operate in *parallel.* If the original component fails (a 5 percent chance), the backup component will automatically kick in to take its place—but only 90% of the time. Thus, the reliability of the system is the 0.95 reliability of the original component *plus* the 0.90 reliability of the backup component, which is called in (1 – 0.95) of the time, or $R_1 + R_2 (1 - R_1) = 0.95 + 0.90 (1 - 0.95) = 0.995$.

Alternate Example 5.1

EXAMPLE 5.1

Calculating System Reliabilities

Problem Statement:

Determine the reliability of the systems shown here.

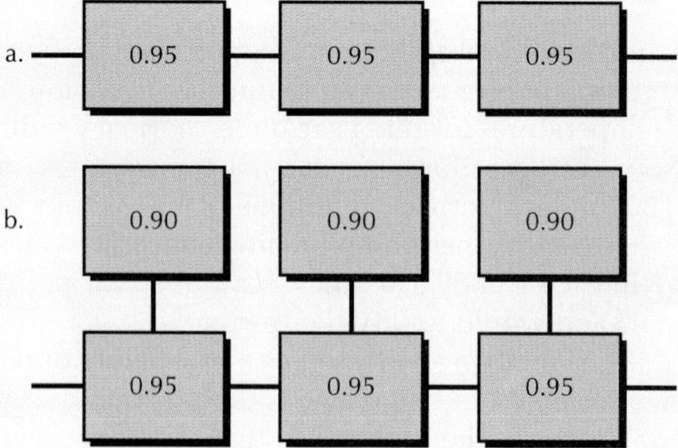

Solution:

a. The system reliability is the product of serial component reliabilities:
0.95 x 0.95 x 0.95 = 0.857

b. The system can be reduced to the following series of components.

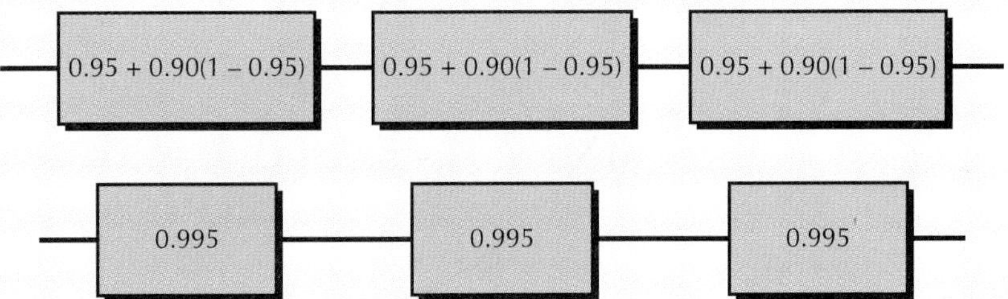

System reliability can now be calculated as the product of the serial component reliabilities, or 0.995 x 0.995 x 0.995 = 0.985

Teaching Note 5.16 AB:POM's Reliability Module

The alternate view of reliability considers the length of time a product is in operation as a factor in its ability to perform. In this case, we are concerned with a *failure rate,* that is, a distribution of failures over time. Failure rates tend to resemble the curve shown in Figure 5.5 with peaks on either end and a very flat bottom (sometimes called a bathtub curve). More failures can be expected toward the beginning of product use due to defective parts and again toward the end of the product's life as parts begin to wear out. Failures in between these extremes are usually attributed to chance occurrences.

The actual distribution of failure rates is determined through empirical testing of the part or product. The *mean time between failures* (MTBF) can be calculated as the reciprocal of the failure rate of a part. Very often MTBF will follow a negative exponential distribution, as shown in Figure 5.6 on page 220. Some interesting probability statements can be made using this distribution. The area under the curve to the left of time T is the probability that a given part or product will fail before time T. Thus, the area under the curve to the right of time T is the probability that a given part or product will *not* fail before time T—that is, the product's reliability. If we substitute the values for T and MTBF into the formula for the exponential distribution we get the following:

Reliability may be viewed as performance over time or mean time between failures (MTBF).

$$P(\text{no failure before } T) = e^{-T/\text{MTBF}}$$
$$P(\text{failure before } T) = 1 - e^{-T/\text{MTBF}}$$

where

$$e = 2.7183$$
$$T = \text{time of interest}$$
$$\text{MTBF} = \text{mean time between failures}$$

Most financial calculators have an e^x function. In addition, Table 5.1 lists some common values of $e^{-T/\text{MTBF}}$.

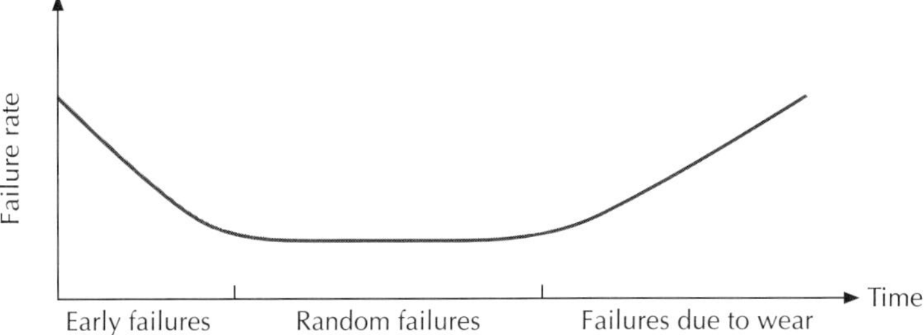

FIGURE 5.5 Distribution of Failure Rates

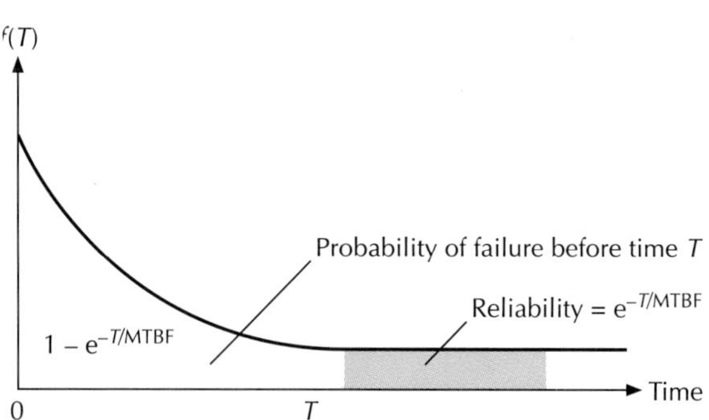

FIGURE 5.6 Time Between Failures as an Exponential Distribution

Alternate Example 5.2

EXAMPLE 5.2

Determining Probabilities of Failure

Problem Statement:

Diane Jones is a college student who has learned from experience to plan for financial contingencies. She has just purchased a new car that she hopes will last her through the completion of her undergraduate and master's degrees, about four more years. Her car has an extended five-year complete warranty on all parts. She recently read a Consumer Reports that claims car batteries have an average life of five years. Assuming that the life of a car battery follows an exponential distribution, determine: a. the probability that her car battery will last until the warranty expires, and b. the probability that her car battery will need to be replaced before she graduates.

Solution:

a. Average life of battery = MTBF = 5 years
 Time until warranty expires = T = 5 years

To calculate the battery's reliability, calculate MTBF and then use Table 5.1.

$$\frac{T}{\text{MTBF}} = \frac{5}{5} = 1.00$$

From Table 5.1, $e^{-1.00} = 0.3679$. There is a 37 percent probability that Diane's battery will last until the warranty expires.

b. Average life of battery = MTBF = 5 years
 Time until graduation = T = 4 years

$$\frac{T}{\text{MTBF} = \frac{4}{5} = 0.80}$$

From Table 5.1, reliability = $e^{-0.80} = 0.4493$. The probability of failure is $1 - 0.4493 = 0.5507$. There is a 55 percent probability that Diane will need to buy a new battery before she graduates.

Reliability can be improved by simplifying product design, improving the reliability of individual components, or adding redundant components. Products that are easier to manufacture or assemble, are well maintained, and have users who are trained in proper use have higher reliability.

Maintainability refers to ease of repair.

Another issue in functional design is the maintainability of the product. **Maintainability** (also called serviceability) refers to the ease and/or cost with which a product is maintained or repaired. Thus, servicing a product is considered in the

TABLE 5.1 Selected Values of $e^{-T/MTBF}$

$T/MTBF$	$e^{-T/MTBF}$	$T/MTBF$	$e^{-T/MTBF}$	$T/MTBF$	$e^{T/MTBF}$
0.10	0.9048	2.10	0.1255	4.10	0.0166
0.20	0.8187	2.20	0.1108	4.20	0.0150
0.30	0.7408	2.30	0.1003	4.30	0.0136
0.40	0.6703	2.40	0.0907	4.40	0.0123
0.50	0.6065	2.50	0.0821	4.50	0.0111
0.60	0.5488	2.60	0.0743	4.60	0.0101
0.70	0.4966	2.70	0.0672	4.70	0.0091
0.80	0.4493	2.80	0.0608	4.80	0.0082
0.90	0.4066	2.90	0.0550	4.90	0.0074
1.00	0.3679	3.00	0.0498	5.00	0.0067
1.10	0.3329	3.10	0.0450	5.10	0.0061
1.20	0.3012	3.20	0.0408	5.20	0.0055
1.30	0.2725	3.30	0.0369	5.30	0.0050
1.40	0.2466	3.40	0.0334	5.40	0.0045
1.50	0.2231	3.50	0.0302	5.50	0.0041
1.60	0.2019	3.60	0.0273	5.60	0.0037
1.70	0.1827	3.70	0.0247	5.70	0.0033
1.80	0.1653	3.80	0.0224	5.80	0.0030
1.90	0.1496	3.90	0.0202	5.90	0.0027
2.00	0.1353	4.00	0.0183	6.00	0.0025

design stage. Design engineers must specify maintenance schedules for the product and decide such issues as these: Will the consumer be able to maintain this product? Can any technician service this product, or will the product require service from specially trained technicians? Should the product be sent back to the factory for repair? Will service representatives visit the client site? What type of service contracts should be offered?

Maintainability should be viewed in relation to other design factors. For example, if a product is cheap to manufacture and priced so low that customers throw it away when it fails (such as calculators, telephones, and watches), maintainability may be a moot issue. Similarly, if a product is so reliable that it rarely breaks down, then ease of repair many not be important. On the other hand, it may be less costly to make a product easy to maintain than to increase its reliability. And for some products, both reliability and maintainability are very important (e.g., office machines, computers).

Products can be made easier to maintain by assembling them in modules, like computers, so that entire control panels, cards, or disk drives can be replaced when they malfunction. The location of critical parts or parts subject to failure affects the ease of disassembly and, thus, repair. Instructions that teach consumers how to anticipate malfunctions and correct them themselves can be included with the product. Specifying regular maintenance schedules is part of maintainability, as is proper planning for the availability of critical replacement parts.

Maintainability can be expressed quantitatively as the mean time to repair (MTTR) a product. Combined with the reliability measure of MTBF, the average availability, or "uptime," of a system can be determined. To lengthen uptime, a product should be designed to function under a variety of operating and environmental conditions, many of them not ideal. In a later section, we discuss

Taguchi's methods for lengthening uptime, which he terms making a design "robust."

Form Design

Form design refers to how the product will look.

Form design refers to the physical appearance of a product—its shape, color, size, and style. Aesthetics such as image, market appeal, and personal identification are also part of form design. In many cases, functional design must be adjusted to make the product look or feel right. For example, when Mazda designed its Miata sports car, it knew the car should be reminiscent of the classic Porsche 356 and MG open sports cars. But the form design went further than looks—the exhaust had to have a certain "sound," the gearshift lever a certain "feel," and the seat and window arrangement the proper dimensions to encourage passengers to ride with their elbows out.[3] For this product offering, form design was every bit as important as functional design.

Fashions are the best example of form design dominating the design process. Clothing can have many forms to be functional, but sales are defined by what's "in." Obviously, form design is more relevant for consumer goods than industrial goods, but industrial goods also have an image to maintain. The appearance of a finished product (the smoothness of the paint job, the attention to detail) projects a quality image to the firm buying the product and the workers who make the product. This is becoming more important, because workers are taking more pride in and ownership of their work.

Production Design

Production design refers to how the product will be made.

Production design is concerned with the ease and cost of manufacturing the product. Designs that are difficult to make often result in poor-quality products. Engineers tend to overdesign products with too many parts or tolerances that are too tight. Lack of knowledge of manufacturing capabilities can result in designs that are impossible to make or require skills and resources not currently available. Many production personnel find themselves redesigning products on the factory floor so that the product can be produced.

In the past, production design has been considered during the third phase of final product design, after functional and form decisions have been through at least one iteration. This phase normally consists of reviewing the existing design for manufacturing feasibility and cost reduction. Recommended approaches to production design include simplification, standardization, and modular design.

Simplification is reducing the number of parts, assemblies, or options in a product.

Simplify, standardize, and use modules.

Simplification attempts to reduce the number of parts and assemblies in a design and make the remaining parts compatible. Consider the assembly shown in part (a) of Figure 5.7. It consists of 24 parts (lots of fasteners) and takes 84 seconds to assemble. The design is typical, in that the parts are common and cheap and nuts and bolts are used as fasteners. It does not appear to be overly complex, unless the assembly task is automated. For a robot to assemble this item, the method of fastening needs to be revised. The design shown in Figure 5.7(b) has been simplified by molding the base as one piece and eliminating the fasteners. Plastic inserts snap over the spindle to hold it into place. The number of parts has been reduced to four, and the assembly time has been cut to 12 seconds. This represents a significant gain in productivity, from 43 assemblies per hour to 300 assemblies per hour. Figure 5.7(c) shows an even simpler design consisting of only two parts, a base and spindle. The spindle is made of flexible material, allowing a quick, one-motion assembly: Snap the spindle downward into place. Now the assembly task seems too simple for a robot. Indeed, many U.S. manufacturers have followed this

[3]Garwood, D., and M. Bane, *Shifting Paradigms: Reshaping the Future of Industry,* Marietta, Ga.: Dogwood Publishing Co., 1990, p. 160.

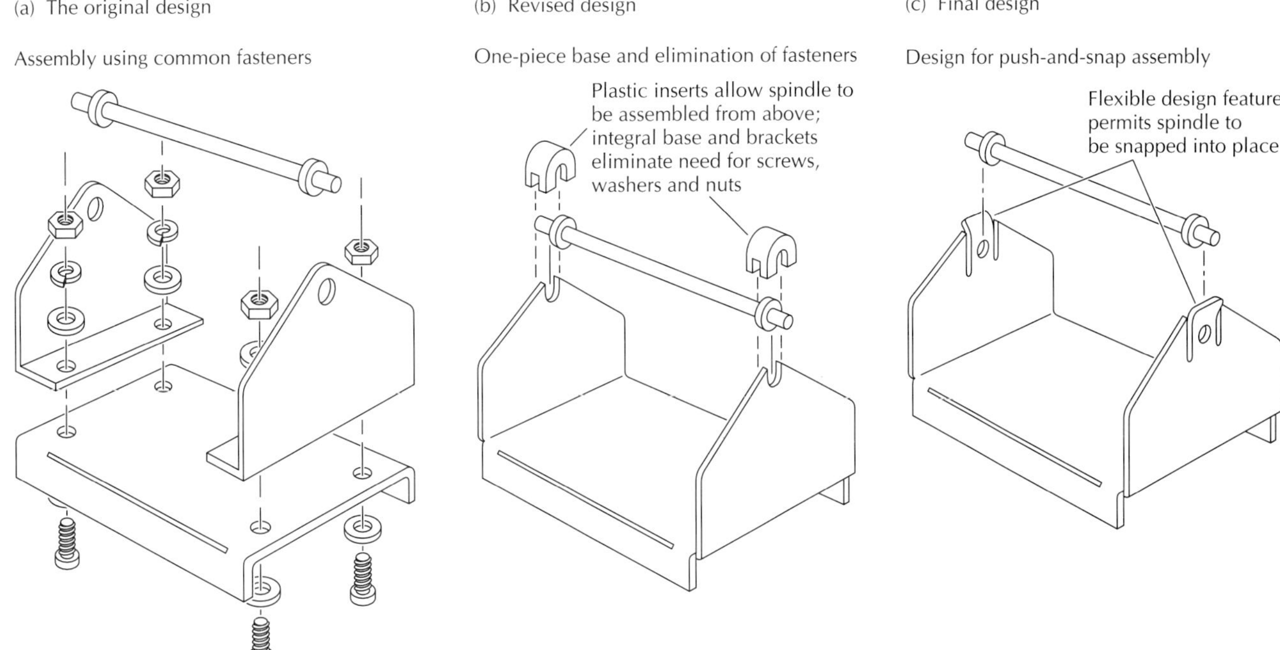

FIGURE 5.7 Design Simplification

Source: Adapted from G. Boothroyd and P. Dewhurst, "Product Design . . . Key to Successful Robotic Assembly," *Assembly Engineering,* (September 1986): 90–93.

process in rediscovering the virtues of simplification—in redesigning a product for automation, they have found that automation isn't necessary!

Using standard parts in a product or throughout many products saves design time, tooling costs, and production worries. **Standardization** makes possible the interchangeability of parts among products, resulting in higher-volume production and purchasing, lower investment in inventory, easier purchasing and material handling, fewer quality inspections, and fewer difficulties in production. Some products, such as light bulbs, batteries, and VCR tapes, benefit from being totally standardized. For others, a nonstandardized product, such as Macintosh's user-friendly operating system (which later became the industry standard), is a competitive advantage. The question becomes how to gain the cost benefits of standardization without losing the market advantage of variety and uniqueness.

With **standardization,** commonly available and interchangeable parts are used.

One solution is **modular design.** Modular design consists of combining standardized building blocks, or *modules,* in a variety of ways to create unique finished products. Modular design is common in the electronics industry and the automobile industry. Even Campbell's Soup Company practices modular design by producing large volumes of four basic broths (beef, chicken, tomato, and seafood bisque) and then adding special ingredients to produce 125 varieties of final soup products.

Modular design combines standardized building blocks or modules to create unique finished products.

The output of product design consists of detailed drawings and design specifications. These are passed on to manufacturing for the next stage of design, process planning.

Process Planning

Process planning is typically conducted by manufacturing engineers and production planners within the manufacturing function. Since it is the topic of the next chapter, we discuss it only briefly here. Process planning is concerned with how the product is to be made. It involves converting product designs into workable

Manufacturing's traditional role in product design is limited.

instructions for product manufacture, selecting equipment (purchasing new equipment, if necessary), deciding which components will be made in-house and which will be purchased from a supplier, ordering any tooling necessary for production, determining the order of operations and assembly, preparing job descriptions and procedures for workers, and programming automated machines. When process planning is complete, these manufacturing specifications are issued to manufacturing, and production of the new product can be scheduled.

GAINING THE COMPETITIVE EDGE

Making Xerox Copiers Easier to Use

A classic example of design overkill can be found in the Xerox products of the 1970s. Xerox at that time had a cadre of extremely bright engineers and no significant competition. So the engineers used their talents to design "incredibly complex machines" that "no mere mortals" could develop. Every nut and bolt had to be specially designed. Using standard parts was unheard of. The complex designs meant the machines were difficult to make correctly, difficult to operate, and difficult to maintain.

Like the rest of U.S. industry, Xerox faced severe competitive challenges in the 1980s. Canon dominated the market for low- to midrange copiers and was advancing rapidly on Xerox's share of the high-end market. At the same time, calls for service for existing products increased, as customer complaints charged that Xerox copiers were unreliable.

This charge puzzled the design engineers, who claimed that their machines were "idiot-proof." They had tried to foresee every possible failure and either design it out of the system or provide detailed instructions in case the failure occurred. After some investigation, they concluded that the machines weren't breaking down more often. Instead, customers just didn't know how to operate them. So Xerox researchers decided to watch exactly how customers used their machines, only the customers this time were the researchers themselves. The researchers were required to do their own copying and they were videotaped in the process.

Just as the ordinary customers claimed, these machines were exceedingly difficult to operate. If something went wrong, the machine would flash a code number, which required the user to flip through a stack of cards attached to the machine to explain the problem. This became very frustrating, and sometimes the user would leave the machine in the middle of a procedure. This is probably what happened in the field when a service call was placed unnecessarily.

In the next round of designs, the engineers did not try to make the copier error-free (there were too many user variables to control). Instead, they concentrated on making the copier easier to operate. From the video, they observed users having a mock conversation with the machine. So, they put short, computerized instructions on a display panel that would respond to various procedures or problems. When something went wrong, the display panel would show a picture of the machine, highlight the problem area, and give instructions for how to solve the problem. Paper-jamming problems that had taken an average of 28 minutes to correct took 20 seconds with the new design. Because problems were easier to fix, customers were less bothered by them. A new feature on Xerox copiers takes the maintainability of the machine one step further. A remote interactive communication (RIC) capability has been added to the copier that monitors system use and predicts when the next breakdown will occur. When the conditions exist for a probable malfunction, RIC automatically places a call to a local field office and downloads its prediction and the reasoning behind it to the computer there, which does further analysis and schedules a repairperson to visit the site *before* a breakdown ever occurs. An added plus for Xerox is that the enormous amount of data collected by RIC at various customer sites can be used to guide future designs of the product.

Source: Based on Jacobson, G., and J. Hillkirk, *Xerox: American Samurai,* New York: Macmillan, 1986, pp. 178–79; Brown, J. S., "Research That Reinvents the Corporation," *Harvard Business Review* (January–February 1991): 102–11.

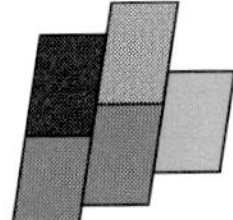

IMPROVING THE DESIGN PROCESS

American engineers are known for their creativity and innovation in product design but are notoriously slow and ineffective at getting new products to market. Consider the list of products that were invented in the United States, such as phonographs, tape recorders, VCRs, machine tool centers, semiconductors, and computers, that are now predominantly produced elsewhere. Clearly, we have problems converting ideas to finished products, but are the problems solely caused by poor manufacturing practices?

Design decisions affect sales strategies, efficiency of manufacture, speed of repair, and product cost. The impact on product cost is significant. It has been estimated that from 60 percent to 80 percent of the costs involved in producing a part or product are fixed during the design process, typically *before* manufacturing has had a chance to see the design. Manufacturing requests for changes in product design are not well received because of the high cost of changes and the inherent interdependency of design decisions; that is, an adjustment in one part may cause an adjustment in other parts, and the entire product design may begin to "unravel." Changes in design, known as *engineering change orders* (ECOs), increase dramatically in cost as the product is closer to production. For example, a report from the research firm DataQuest estimates that the cost of a major design change for an electronics product increases from $1,000 during the design phase to $100,000 during the planning stage for manufacture and to $10,000,000 during final production. With those cost differentials in mind, examine Figure 5.8, which shows two scenarios for the distribution of engineering changes in product design. For Company 1, 90 percent of the changes were initiated a full year before production, whereas for Company 2, changes surge 1 to 3 months prior to production of the first job and again during final production, a few months after the first job has been completed. Which scenario is more descriptive of sequential design decisions? Which scenario is preferable from a cost point of view?

Problems and limitations of the traditional design process.

The problems in design experienced by U.S. firms (and others) during the 1970s and 1980s involved both flaws in the sequential design process and poor ex-

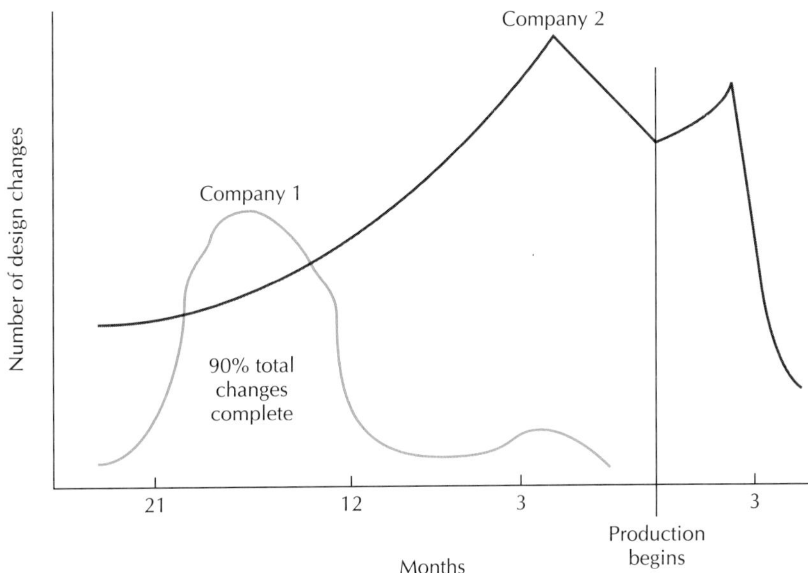

FIGURE 5.8 Distribution of Design Changes for Two Companies

Transparency 5.3 Problems With the Design Process

ecution of the process. The traditional design process of sequential decision making is inherently slow. This slowness was exacerbated by the business environment of the 1970s and 1980s, during which companies grew larger, products proliferated, and product designs became more complex. The job of designing a product was increasingly segregated among more specialized engineers and managers, lengthening the series of decisions that had to be made. The design function further distanced itself from manufacturing. Designing a product and making the product were separated by buildings, by management, and by time. The results were predictable—conflicts, numerous revisions, long development times, and high development costs.

In addition to the inefficiency of the design process, the quality of designs was also suspect. Products were too complicated for the worker to make or the customer to use. Engineers were lax in using design procedures they knew to be effective.[4] Although project groups were established for new product development, they did not operate as teams. The work was divided and doled out to individual members, who worked separately on their particular areas of expertise. In an attempt to get products to the market quickly, the production design phase of product design was ignored. Simplification and standardization, if considered at all, meant using parts and design procedures with which engineers were comfortable, not improving the design. One of the worst cases of lack of communication between design and manufacturing occurred in the aerospace industry. A well-established aerospace company designed an airplane with a wing span too long to fit into its manufacturing facility—and the problem was not discovered until midway through production!

Improving the design process to remain competitive in the world market involves completely restructuring the decision-making process and the participants in that process. The series of *walls* between functional areas portrayed in Figure 5.2 must be broken down and replaced with new alliances and modes of interaction. This feat can be accomplished by:

Transparency 5.4 Improving the Design Process

1. Establishing multifunctional design teams;
2. Making product and process design decisions *concurrently* instead of sequentially;
3. Changing the role of design engineers;
4. Utilizing new and existing tools and techniques to *design for manufacture;*
5. Designing for the environment;
6. Measuring design quality.

Design Teams

Design-build teams find success in U.S. industry.

The team approach to product design has proved to be highly successful worldwide. Full-time team participants from marketing, manufacturing, and engineering are essential to effective product design. Customers, dealers, suppliers, lawyers, accountants, and others are also useful team members. A recent study of new product launchings in high technology firms concluded that the critical factor between success and failure was the involvement and interaction of the "create, make, and market" functions from the beginning of the design project. Ford Motor Company has been a leader in initiating the team approach to product design in the automotive industry and in U.S. industry as a whole. Team design of the Taurus automobile beat all previous development efforts by coming in well before schedule and $400 million under budget. Other automobile manufacturers followed suit.

Teaching Note 5.7 Team Taurus

[4] For example, an exhaustive study of the air conditioning industry by David Garvin found that in ten out of eleven companies, there was no attempt to manage product reliability.

GAINING THE COMPETITIVE EDGE

Team Viper and Team Neon

Team Viper, initiated several years after Team Taurus' success, allowed Chrysler to bring the Viper sports car from concept to full production in less than three years and $2 million under budget. Working in a team was a cultural change for Chrysler engineers. The team (ranging from 20 to 85 members) met in one large room of a refurbished warehouse. Walls were literally torn down to encourage team members to communicate and work together. Private conversations were impossible; eavesdropping was encouraged. If someone overheard a discussion that might affect them, he or she was expected to jump right in and make his or her views known. This was a far cry from the "stay out of my territory" culture that dominated Chrysler at the time.

Except for the team leader, there were no managers present. A technical policy committee gave Team Viper its budget for capital expenditures and operating expenses. How the budget was split between functional areas or overtime was up to the team. The team reported its progress quarterly to the policy committee. As the project evolved, three engineering subgroups were formed: 1. chassis, 2. body, and 3. synthesis. The synthesis group wasn't charged with designing part of the car; it had the task of making sure every design decision was coordinated.

Vendors and production workers were treated differently in the revised design process. Requests for bids on Viper parts were released to vendors with only functional dimensions. Vendors were given a Team Viper list and expected to contact team members directly if they ran into any problems. Four assembly line workers, called craftpersons, were trained at each manufacturing station of a mock assembly line set up in the design facility. By field-testing each work station as it was developed, the workers were able to point out potential assembly problems to the engineers before a design was committed. When the testing was complete, each worker had received more than 600 hours of training and could assemble the car from scratch.

One final note: The design team was not dismantled when the design was finished. Although smaller in size, it exists to this day and will remain intact for the life of the product to work on continuous improvements, either for ease of manufacture or to increase the product's fitness for use by the customer.

With their new approach to design in place, Chrysler wanted to try its hand at both design and manufacture of small cars and make a profit doing so. American carmakers traditionally have priced small cars below cost to generate sales that could be averaged with their large cars in meeting government gas-mileage standards. Thus, Robert Marcell, head of Chrysler's small-car division, was faced with something Detroit had never done before—designing a *profitable* small car. Marcell knew he would have to do things differently to succeed. He formed a design team, involved suppliers, manufacturing, and workers early in the process, and used design for manufacture concepts. As early as the fall of 1990, the UAW was called in to help make the car easy to build, and they responded. Line workers came up with more than 4,000 suggestions, including making the assembly-line height adjustable and improving the door-installation equipment. The team used a technique called *quality function deployment* to convert customer needs into design specifications. From this they learned that consumers wanted a small car that felt like a big one and was reliable, fun to drive, and safe. Power windows and four-speed transmission weren't important, but standard dual airbags and reinforced doors were. Costs (but not corners) were cut by selling identical cars at Chrysler and Dodge dealerships (a $10 million savings in tooling costs) and allowing only one exterior molding (a savings of $50 per car). The team looked at cost in a broader sense. In one case, they chose a higher-cost folddown seat because it saved $1.1 million in simplified final assembly.

Was the design team successful? The Neon design was finished 3 months ahead of schedule and right on its $1.3 billion budget (in comparison, Saturn took seven years to develop and cost $5 billion). The car went into production in November of 1993, costing $500 less to build than any competing subcompact. However, the most important results are not in yet; to turn a profit, 300,000 Neons must be sold each year.

Sources: Based on Sprow, E., "Chrysler's Concurrent Engineering Challenge," *Manufacturing Engineering* (April 1992): 35–42; "Chryler's Neon, Is This the Small Car Detroit Couldn't Build?" *Business Week* (May 3, 1993): 116–26.

Concurrent Design

Concurrent design is a new approach to design that integrates product design and process planning.

Concurrent design changes the design process from a sequential one, where decisions are made by separate departments, to simultaneous decision making by design teams. The concept is also known as *simultaneous,* or *concurrent,* engineering. Figure 5.9 shows the concept graphically. Concurrent design attempts to integrate product design and process planning into a common activity. It helps improve the quality of early design decisions and thereby reduces the length and cost of the design process. Product-design decisions are extended to process decisions whenever possible. In this manner, one stage of design is not completely finished before another stage begins.

For example, consider the process of making car bodies.[5] Every car and light truck produced today has a body constructed of stamped steel panels. Heavy metal forms, called dies, are needed to press the finished body panels out of sheets of steel. These dies are very expensive to make and must be machined exactly to match design specifications. In the sequential design process, the dies cannot be manufactured until the final detailed design specifications for stamped doors are issued. Then, a block of steel can be ordered for the die-making department, and the die can be cut from it using a series of several expensive die-cutting machines, usually computer-driven. The process is lengthy and tedious and, because of the bottleneck of die-cutting machines, can take more than two years to complete.

Transparency 5.5 The Concurrent Design Process

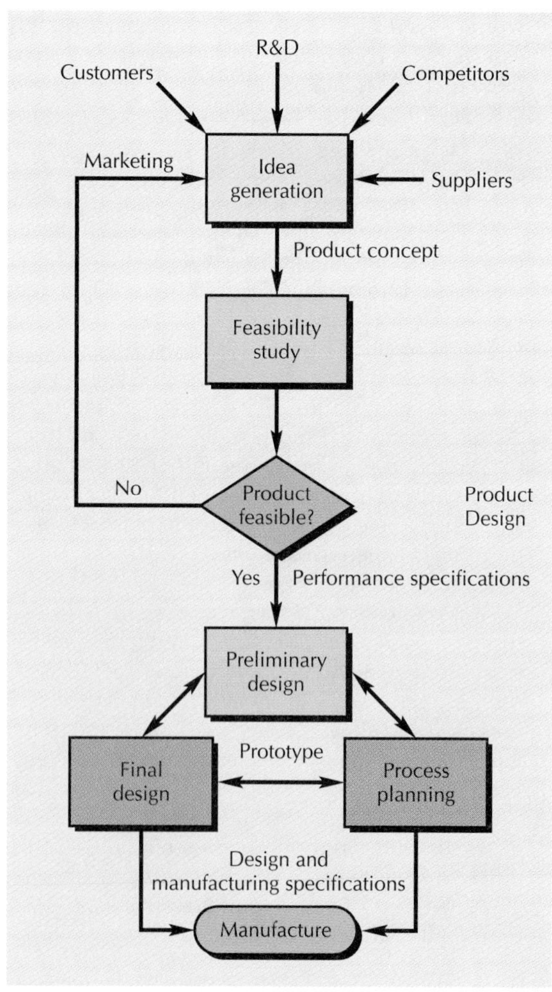

FIGURE 5.9 The Concurrent Design Process

[5]Adapted from Womack, J. P., D. T. Jones, and D. Roos, *The Machine that Changed the World,* New York: Macmillan, 1990, pp. 116–17.

Companies using concurrent design can begin die production at the same time they start body design because the die designers and the body designers are in direct contact on the design team. Once the die designers know the approximate size of the new car and the approximate number of panels needed, they can order the blocks of die steel and begin to make rough cuts. Final cutting, as before, must await the final detailed panel design. The simultaneous development of body design and die design saves more than a year in die production.

Another example of concurrent design concerns suppliers who complete the detailed design for the parts they will supply.[6] Suppliers are an important part of the design team often ignored by U.S. manufacturers. A study of product development in automobile manufacturing revealed that Japanese firms prepare an engineering design for only 30 percent of their parts (suppliers do the rest), whereas American firms design 81 percent of their component parts. In the traditional design process, U.S. manufacturers determine component design in detail, down to the fraction of an inch, including the specific material to be used. Detailed engineering drawings are made, and only then are the supplier organizations that will actually make the part called in to submit their bids. Japanese manufacturers, on the other hand, provide general performance specifications to their component suppliers, such as these: Design a set of brakes that can stop a 2200-pound car from 60 miles per hour in 200 feet ten times in succession without fading. The brakes should fit into a space 6 inches x 8 inches x 10 inches at the end of each axle and be delivered to the assembly plant for $40 a set. The supplier is asked to prepare a prototype for testing. Detailed design decisions are left up to the supplier, as a member of the design team who is the expert in that area. This approach saves considerable development time and resources.

Price-minus rather than cost-plus pricing is prefered.

One more difference between sequential design and concurrent design is the manner in which prices are set and costs are determined. In the traditional process, the feasibility study includes some estimate of price to be charged to the customer, but that selling price is not firmed up until the end of the design process, when all the product costs are accumulated, a profit margin is attached, and it is determined whether the original price estimate and the resulting figure are close. This is a *cost-plus* approach. If there are discrepancies, either the product is sold at the new price, a new feasibility study is made, or the designers go back and try to cut costs. Remember that design decisions are interrelated; the further back in the process one goes, the more expensive are the changes. Concurrent design uses a *price-minus* system. A selling price (that will give some advantage in the marketplace) is determined before design details are developed. Then a *target cost* of production is set and evaluated at every stage of product and process design. Techniques such as value analysis (which we discuss later) are used to keep costs in line.

Even with concurrent design, product design and development can be a long and tedious process. Because concurrent design requires that more tasks be performed in parallel, the scheduling of those tasks is even more complex than ever. Project-scheduling techniques, such as PERT/CPM discussed in Chapter 17, are being used to coordinate the myriad of interconnected decisions that constitute concurrent design. Other approaches involve changing the role of persons involved in design, assessing the effectiveness of the design process, and utilizing different tools and techniques. These approaches are discussed in the following sections.

The Role of Design Engineer

The role of design engineer is both expanded and curtailed in the concurrent design process. Design engineers are no longer *totally* responsible for the design of

[6] Ibid, pp. 157, 60.

the product. At the same time, they are responsible for more than what was traditionally considered "design." Their responsibilities extend to the manufacture and continuous improvement of the product as well.

Design engineers should be knowledgeable about manufacturing.

In many cases, design engineers do not have a good understanding of the capabilities or limitations of their company's manufacturing facilities. Increased contact with manufacturing can sensitize them to the realities of making a product. Simply consulting manufacturing personnel early in the design process about critical factors or constraints can dramatically improve the quality of product design. This is where most companies begin their efforts in changing the corporate culture from a separated design function to one that is more integrated with operations. IBM called their efforts in this area EMI, for *early manufacturing involvement*. Initially, one manufacturing engineer was assigned to each product-development group. Later, more staff were reassigned and physically relocated. In at least one instance, new design facilities were built within walking distance of where manufacturing occurred. The increased communication between design and manufacturing so improved the quality of the final product that IBM quickly threw out the term EMI and adopted CMI, for *continuous manufacturing involvement*.

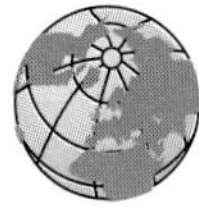

Teaching Note 5.8 Tasks of Manufacturing Engineers

In other countries, it is not uncommon for engineers to begin their careers with a two-year stint as an assembly line worker. Honda requires that even its most advanced engineers spend at least one month of every year working in another functional area of the firm, such as sales, purchasing, or operations. Engineers are often physically located on or near to the factory floor. Those engineers who work on designing a product (called design engineers in the United States) are often the same ones who design the system to produce the product (called manufacturing engineers in the United States). Professional societies in the United States (Society of Manufacturing Engineers [SME], for example) are calling for an integration of the design and manufacturing engineers in collegiate curriculums. While industry waits for the academic community to adjust to changing requirements for engineers, the two groups of engineers can be brought closer together by rotating job assignments, working in teams, and reporting to the same boss.

Design for Manufacture

Production design is included in the traditional product design process, as discussed earlier in this chapter. However, this phase of the design process has not received the emphasis it deserves. New methods, tools, and techniques for explicitly placing manufacture in the design of products are needed. **Design for manufacture (DFM)** is the new term used to describe designing a product so that it can be produced easily and economically. The concept of DFM begins with the view that product design is the first step in manufacturing a product. DFM identifies product-design characteristics that are inherently easy to manufacture, focuses on the design of component parts that are easy to fabricate and assemble, and integrates product design with process planning. When successful, DFM not only improves the quality of product design but also reduces the time and cost of both product design and manufacture.

Design for manufacture involves designing a product so that it can be produced easily and economically.

Transparency 5.6 Design for Manufacture

The development and use of design methodologies to ensure systematically that manufacturing concerns are incorporated into the design process is an important part of DFM. Several tools are available to help with the process of design for manufacture:

1. Design axioms
2. DFM guidelines
3. Design for assembly (DFA)
4. Failure mode and effect analysis (FMEA)
5. Fault tree analysis (FTA)
6. Value analysis (VA)

Use of *design axioms* begins with identifying the functional requirements of a product, eliminating those that are redundant, and reconciling those that are inconsistent. The functional requirements are then ordered from most important to least important, and the design axioms are applied to each one. The axioms attempt to mimic the expertise of an experienced designer or process planner. For example, the axioms might lead to such actions as avoiding side holes and depressions too close to the bend line of a sheet metal component, specifying hole diameters that fit available drill sizes, or matching the physicians on a preferred provider list with those certified to practice at approved hospitals. Although the axioms do a fairly good job on optimizing the design of individual components or decisions, they do not consider compromises or trade-offs between components or decisions, and they cannot be expected to cover all aspects of a design.

Identify functional requirements.

DFM guidelines are statements of good design practice that can lead to good—but not necessarily optimum—designs. Examples include the following:

1. Minimize the number of parts.
2. Develop a modular design.
3. Design parts for many uses.
4. Avoid separate fasteners.
5. Eliminate adjustments.
6. Make assembly easy and foolproof. If possible, design for top-down assembly.
7. Design for minimal handling and proper presentation.
8. Avoid tools.
9. Minimize subassemblies.
10. Use standard parts when possible.
11. Simplify operations.
12. Design for efficient and adequate testing and replacement of parts.
13. Use repeatable, well-understood processes.
14. Design for robustness.

Use good design practices.

These guidelines were used in the design of IBM's Proprinter, often considered a benchmark for successful product design. When introduced, the proprinter had 65 percent fewer parts and could be assembled 90 percent faster than its Japanese competitor. General Motors discovered the usefulness of DFM in a comparison of similar cars produced in similar factories by Ford. Ford's front bumper had ten parts to GM's one hundred. Ford's parts also fit together better, and its final product required fewer labor hours than any other automobile manufacturer worldwide.

Teaching Note 5.9 Video Suggestions

Design for assembly (**DFA**) is a set of procedures for reducing the number of parts in an assembly, evaluating methods for assembly, and determining an assembly sequence. DFA was developed by Professors Boothroyd and Dewhurst at the University of Massachusetts. It provides a catalog of generic part shapes classified by means of assembly, along with estimates of assembly times. For example, some parts are assembled by pushing; others, by pushing and twisting or pushing, twisting, and tilting. Guidelines are given for choosing manual versus automated assembly, avoiding part tangling or nesting in feeding operations, achieving the fewest number of reorientations of the parts during assembly, finding the fewest assembly steps, and determining the most foolproof sequence of assembly. The best sequence of assembly differs considerably for manual versus automated assembly. Manual assembly is concerned with maintaining a balance between operations on the assembly line; automated assembly is concerned with minimizing the reorientation of parts or assembly. Common assembly mistakes include hiding parts that later need to be inspected, disassembling already assembled parts to fit new parts in, and making it difficult to access parts that need maintenance or repair.

Design for assembly is a procedure for reducing the number of parts in an assembly, evaluating methods for assembly, and determining an assembly sequence.

Recognize that some assembly methods are easier than others.

Another approach to DFA, called the *assembly evaluation method,* was developed by Hitachi. It assigns penalty points for each assembly step. Some steps are

penalized more than others. For example, a twist-and-turn operation is penalized more than a straight push. Assemblies that exceed the maximum allowable number of penalty points must be redesigned.

Failure mode and effects analysis is a systematic method of analyzing product failures.

Failure mode and effects analysis (FMEA) is a systematic approach to analyzing the causes and effects of product failures. It begins with listing the functions of the product and each of its parts. Failure modes, such as fatigue, leakage, buckling, binding, or excessive force required, are then defined. All failure modes are ranked in order of their seriousness and likelihood of failure. Failures are addressed one by one (beginning with the most catastrophic), causes are hypothesized, and design changes are made to reduce the chance of failure. The objective of FMEA is to anticipate failures and design them out of the system. Table 5.2 shows a partial FMEA for potato chips.

Fault tree analysis is a visual method for analyzing the interrelationships among failures.

FMEA prioritizes failures and attempts to eliminate their causes but **fault tree analysis (FTA)** emphasizes the *interrelationship* between failures. FTA lists failures and their causes in a tree format using two hatlike symbols, one with a straight line on the bottom representing *and* and one with a curved line on the bottom for *or*. Figure 5.10 shows a partial FTA for a food manufacturer who has a problem with potato chip breakage. In this analysis, potato chips break because they are too thin *or* because they are too brittle. The options for fixing the problem of too-thin chips, increasing thickness or reducing size, are undesirable, as indicated by the Xs. The problem of too-brittle chips can be alleviated by adding more moisture, *or* having fewer ridges, *or* adjusting the frying procedure. We choose to adjust the frying procedure, which leads to the question of how hot the oil should be *and* how long to fry the chip. Once these values are determined, the issue of too-brittle chips (and thus chip breakage) is solved, as indicated by the rough circles.

Value analysis helps eliminate unnecessary features and functions.

Value analysis (VA; also known as value engineering) was developed by General Electric in 1947 to eliminate unnecessary features and functions in product designs. It has reemerged as an excellent technique for use by multifunctional design teams. The design team defines the essential functions of a component, assembly,

Analyze failures.

TABLE 5.2 Failure Mode and Effects Analysis for Potato Chips

Failure Mode	*Cause of Failure*	*Effect of Failure*	*Corrective Action*
Stale	Low moisture content, expired shelf life, poor packaging	Tastes bad, won't crunch, thrown out, lost sales	Add moisture, cure longer, better package seal, shorter shelf life
Broken	Too thin, too brittle, rough handling, rough use, poor packaging	Can't dip, poor display, injures mouth, choking, perceived as old, lost sales	Change recipe, change process, change packaging
Too salty	Outdated recipe, process not in control, uneven distribution of salt	Eat less, drink more, health hazard, lost sales	Experiment with recipe, experiment with process, introduce low salt version

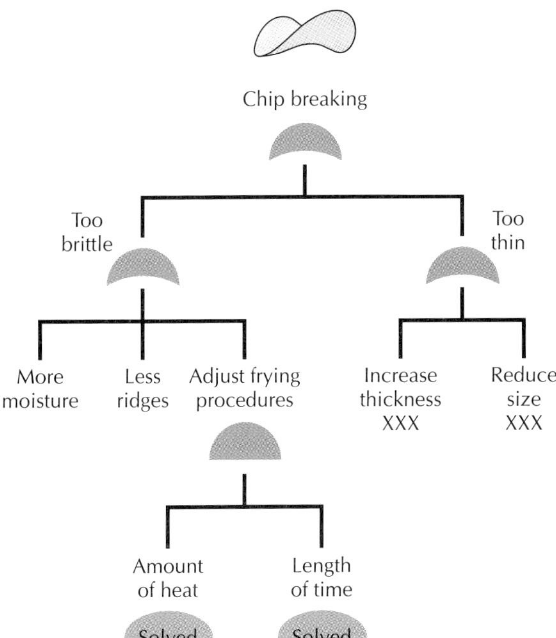

FIGURE 5.10 Partial Fault Tree Analysis for Potato Chips

or product using two words, a noun and a verb. For example, the function of a container might be described as *holds fluid*. Then the team assigns a value to each function and determines the cost of providing the function. With that information, a ratio of value to cost can be calculated for each item. The team attempts to improve the ratio by either reducing the cost of the item or increasing its worth. Every material, every part, and every operation is subjected to a rigorous analysis that includes questions such as these:

1. Can we do without it?
2. Does it do more than is required?
3. Does it cost more than it is worth?
4. Can something else do a better job?
5. Can it be made by a less costly method? With less costly tooling? With less costly material?
6. Can it be made cheaper, better, or faster by someone else?

Design for Environment

Design for Environment (DFE) involves designing products from recycled material, using materials or components that can be recycled, designing a product so that it is easier to repair than discard, and minimizing unnecessary packaging. It also includes minimizing material and energy usage during manufacture, consumption, and disposal. DFE is not exactly new. U.S. businesses already plan to invest more than $200 billion in the 1990s to prevent pollution, to make their products environmentally sound, and to reduce their use of hazardous material. Some obviously wasteful products have been redesigned due to consumer pressure. Remember the pop-top beverage can? The engineer that invented the current stay-on tab did so after seeing a picnic area strewn with literally hundreds of discarded tabs and rings. That example illustrates that if waste is to be dramatically reduced, producers must start considering issues of recycling and disposal at the product-design phase. From a cost standpoint, the earlier in the design stage the environment is considered, the better. Reengineering a design late in the product development cycle can be very costly.

Consider recycling at the design stage.

Transparency 5.7 Design for Environment

GAINING THE COMPETITIVE EDGE

Westinghouse's Design Calculator

Westinghouse has designed an assembly calculator to help its engineers design a part or product that is easier to assemble. A basic principle of design for assembly is that bringing parts to the assembly point (called acquisition) and bringing them together (called assembly) should be as simple as possible. Keeping the index of difficulty as low as possible helps to reduce product cost, improve quality, reduce cycle time, and facilitate the introduction of automated assembly in the future.

Westinghouse quantified the difficulty of acquisition and difficulty of assembly as a composite of a number of factors. Acquisition is affected by the part shape, part size, handling distance, handling conditions, part features, and feature size. Assembly is affected by the fastening method, component clearances, component features, feature size, and direction of assembly. The DFA calculator is a hand-held movable "wheel" that illustrates and helps add up the cumulative difficulty indices. With this device, the overall difficulty index of each part being designed can be quickly determined, and design trade-offs can be evaluated.

Westinghouse also uses design for value to evaluate the goodness of a design. Design for value refers to the cost of different assembly options when a line of products is considered. For example, it may be more cost-effective to design a component that can be used in several options of a product than to design slightly different components for each option.

Source: Based on *Design for Assembly Calculator Instructions,* Westinghouse Productivity and Quality Center, 1986.

Factors such as product life, recoverable value, ease of service, and disposal cost affect decisions on disposal, continued use, and recycling. Many products are discarded because they are difficult or expensive to repair. Materials from discarded products may not be recycled for a similar reason—the product is difficult to disassemble. Previous guidelines for ease of assembly may actually make disassembly more difficult. Aids to green design include Volvo's "environmental load units," which guide materials' selection, Siemens' "eco-balance" system, which includes both environmental and economic design requirements, and ATC DFE software that rates the environmental preferability of designs (similar to DFA software).

Peter Dewhurst (of DFA fame) proposes a measure of recycling efficiency as follows:[7]

$$I_r = \frac{[C_v - C_d - TL]}{C_{vm}}$$

where

C_v = value of recycled parts

C_{vm} = maximum value that can be obtained from recycling

C_d = cost of disposal

T = disassembly time

L = labor rate

The recycling index helps determine the time that can profitably be spent on disassembly. Dewhurst predicts that products of the future will be designed for ex-

[7]Dewhurst, P., "Product Design and Manufacture: Design for Disassembly," *Industrial Engineering* 25, no. 9 (September 1993): 26–28.

tremely rapid disassembly. For example, it should take only 15 minutes to completely disassemble an automobile.

The trend to reduce waste and consider recycling at the design stage is not just an attempt by corporations to be socially responsible. Some legislators believe that manufacturers should be responsible for the life cycle of a product. In other words, whoever sells a product should be responsible for the product when it becomes waste (a policy currently followed in Germany). Eventually manufacturers might be required to include the cost of disposal in a product's price or pay a tax for recycling. A 1994 German law mandates the collection, recycling, and safe disposal of personal computers and household appliances, including stereos and video appliances, television sets, washing machines, dishwashers, and refrigerators. The Netherlands recently announced that a color TV set would be considered chemical waste and should be treated as such. Seven U.S. states now have "take-back" laws that require the return and recycling of batteries. Japan is developing energy-consumption limits for information technology products as well as business enterprises. The European Community currently has a policy for green labeling, and ISO standards for environmental attributes are due out soon.

U.S. companies getting a head start on probable environmental legislation have discovered some surprising benefits. For example, companies as diverse as McDonald's and Chrysler are saving millions of dollars through a waste audit process that concentrates on reducing the amount of waste generated in the first place. McDonald's permanently eliminated 40 percent of its garbage costs. Similarly, a Chrysler Jeep plant eliminated 70 percent of the trash it used to send to landfills. Xerox's program to recycle copier parts (cartridges, power supplies, motors, paper-transport systems, printed wiring boards, and metal rollers), called *design for reassembly,* saves the company more than $200 million annually. The process involves disassembling a machine, replacing worn-out parts with new, remanufactured, or used components, cleaning the machine, and then testing it to make sure it meets the same quality and reliability standards as a newly manufactured machine. Xerox's goal is zero waste. Whether consumers will buy (or pay full price for) refurbished products is yet to be seen. In addition, before large num-

GAINING THE COMPETITIVE EDGE

Giving It Back

Each year Americans dispose of 350 million home and office appliances (50 million of them hair dryers) and more than 10 million PCs. At the current rate of discard, it's not hard to visualize rows of warehouses or city dumps filled with old refrigerators and outdated computers. That image prompted a joint industry-government commission to recommend the development of "green workstations," which are easier to upgrade or recycle than discard. IBM's green PS/2 primarily uses one polymer and snaps together for ease of disassembly and recycling. The computer industry's willingness to consider the environmental impact of design and manufacture decisions serves as a model for the EPA's "Design for Environment" initiative, in which business and government collaborate early to *prevent* pollution, rather than clean it up after damage to the environment has occurred.

Technology is also changing the way we deal with waste. The catalytic extraction process (CEP) uses a molten metal bath to convert hazardous and nonhazardous waste into its original gas and methal elements. No by-products are released, and the system can be integrated directly into a manufacturing process. CEP is truly an on-site, closed-loop recyling system.

Source: Based on "Redefining Waste," *Industrial Engineering* (September 1993): 23–24; Lohr, Steve, "Obsolete Computers Join Throwaway Age," *New York Times,* (April 18, 1993).

bers of companies begin remanufacture efforts, several consumer-protection and government procurement laws would have to be changed.[8]

Measures of Design Quality

Design engineers need to be aware of the importance of the production phase of product design and the ramifications of a design that is difficult to produce. One way to get this message across is to evaluate the *long-term quality* of an engineer's design. Traditionally, a product design is evaluated in terms of the cost of materials and the adherence to performance specifications provided by marketing. After a design is released to manufacturing, the responsibility of producing the product to design specifications is assigned to the manufacturing group. A more useful evaluation of design effectiveness that recognizes the impact of design specifications on the ease of manufacture (and thus on conforming to specifications) would include such measures as the following:[9]

Long-term measures of design quality are needed.

Transparency 5.8 Measures of Design Quality

1. Number of component parts and product options
2. Percentage of standard parts
3. Use of existing manufacturing resources
4. Cost of first production run
5. Cost of engineering changes during the first 6-months
6. First-year cost of field service and repair
7. Total product cost
8. Total product sales
9. Sustainable development

The first three measures of design quality refer to the simplicity of design. A design with a small number of parts, one with a large percentage of standard parts, and one that uses existing processes already familiar to manufacturing is cheaper and easier to produce.

The cost of the first production run measures how realistic the initial design is—that is, how well the design matches production capabilities. At the conclusion of the first production run, a design is certified to be "producible," but changes in the design can still be requested by manufacturing that would make the product easier or cheaper to produce. Fewer engineering changes in the first 6 months of production indicate a more thorough and better quality design.

The cost of field service and repair is a measure of design quality that originates from the customer. It takes into consideration both the frequency and severity of product failure. Product recalls, warranty requests, and liabilities are included in this category.

Total product cost includes not only the cost of materials, but also manufacturing costs (such as cost of assembly and investment in new equipment or processes) and development costs (such as cost of design revisions). One of the best examples of a seemingly innocuous part that significantly affects total product cost is the lowly screw. Although screws and bolts cost only pennies apiece, the assembly requirements of aligning the parts, inserting and tightening the screw, and threading the bolt can account for 75 percent of the cost of assembly. For its electronic cash registers, NCR estimates that over the lifetime of a product, each screw contributes $12,500 toward total product cost.[10] Total product sales indicate the marketability of the product design and the initial level of customer satisfaction.

[8]Holusha, John, "Who Foots the Bill for Recycling?" *New York Times* (April 25, 1993).

[9]Adapted from Waliszewski, D. A., "The JIT Starter Kit for Design Engineering," *Conference Proceedings of the American Production and Control Society* (1986): 358–60.

[10]Port, O., "The Best-Engineered Part Is No Part at All," *Business Week* (May 8, 1989): 150.

The last item in the list refers to the environmental soundness of a design. Sustainable development is defined as "a form of development or progress that meets the needs of the present without compromising the ability of future generations to meet their own needs."[11] This is a somewhat esoteric definition that, in its current form, is difficult to quantify. It may be that ATC DFE index will provide suitable guidelines for evaluation, or the EPA may come up with its own measures. Irregardless, be assured that the "greenness" of a design is becoming a major concern in design quality.

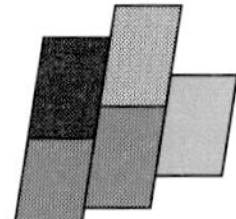

QUALITY OF DESIGN

Designing quality into a product is important, both in terms of how the product performs and how it is produced. The measures of design quality suggested in the previous section emphasize the ease and cost of manufacture and repair. However, *quality of design* also refers to the degree to which quality characteristics, as defined from the customer's point of view, are designed into a product or service. There are many different techniques available for ensuring that the customer's needs are properly converted into design specifications. We have selected three methods to discuss in this section: quality classifications, quality function deployment, and the Taguchi method for robust design.

Quality Classifications

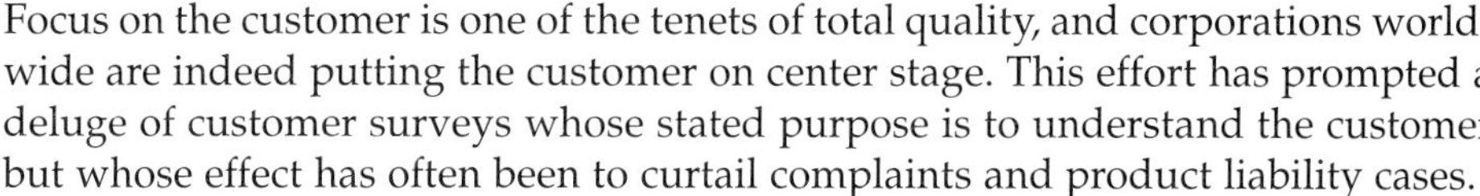

Focus on the customer is one of the tenets of total quality, and corporations worldwide are indeed putting the customer on center stage. This effort has prompted a deluge of customer surveys whose stated purpose is to understand the customer but whose effect has often been to curtail complaints and product liability cases.

In terms of product design, most surveys are too general, do not ask the right questions, and fail to reveal many things that are important to customers. In addition, those working in design fields often have access to possibilities of which the consumer would never dream. To gather more useful information from surveys, Professor Noritaki Kano suggests restructuring survey questions and classifying the responses into three quality categories.[12]

Quality expectations can be one-dimensional, expected, or attractive.

1. *One-dimensional quality:* what the customers tell you they want, which you give them.
2. *Expected quality:* what the customers do *not* tell you they want but assume they will get.
3. *Attractive quality:* what the customers did not expect or imagine but which pleases them.

One-dimensional quality can usually be identified in traditional customer surveys. If the item is present, the customer is happy; if the item is missing, the customer is unhappy. *Expected quality* is often hidden from the designer and may be discovered only by accident or through experience. For example, pencil manufacturers have learned through trial and error that customers prefer the color of their pencils to be yellow. Customers never told researchers that fact, they just do not buy many pencils in other colors. Expected quality items are dissatisfiers, never satisfiers. The last category, *attractive quality,* is what can set apart one product or

[11]Bendz, Diana, "Green Products for Green Profits," *IEEE Spectrum* (September 1993): 63–66.

[12]Kano, N., N. Seraku, F. Takahashi, and S. Tsuji, "Attractive and Must Be Quality," *Quality* 14, no. 2 (1984): 39–48.

service from another. The absence of these features or characteristics does not make customers dissatisfied, but their presence delights them, excites them, and encourages them to buy the product.

Consider the following example of a set of structured questions appearing in a newspaper publisher's survey. Notice that each question is asked in a positive and negative form and that the responses represent a broad range of attitudes.

Positive Question How do you feel when your newspaper arrives on time?	*Negative Question* How do you feel when your newspaper does *not* arrive on time?
A. I like it.	1. I like it.
B. I expect it.	2. I expect it.
C. I'm indifferent.	3. I'm indifferent.
D. It's the only possibility.	4. It's the only possibility.
E. I don't like it.	5. I don't like it.

A matrix showing the responses to these questions in shown in Figure 5.11. Responses in cells A2, A3, or A4 represent attractive quality, responses in cells A5 or E1 represent one-dimensional quality, and responses in cells B5, C5, or D5 represent expected quality. Responses in the other cells are either inconsistent or show a disinterest in the item being examined. From this we can deduce that for the largest number of respondents, timely delivery is a one-dimensional quality. Results of a more complete survey might show that accurate information is also a one-dimensional quality, comics and sports coverage are expected, and no-smudge ink and clear color pictures have attractive qualities. By learning which characteristics are absolutely required, which lose customers, and which gain customers, the newspaper publisher can design a more satisfying experience for the paper's customers and attract more business for the newspaper.

Companies in many industries are just beginning to see the significance of delighting the customer with attractive quality. Product designs are being evaluated on the degree to which they provide attractive quality. Quality classifications and structured surveys help to bridge the gap between what a customer wants or needs and what is communicated through marketing to design. The next technique facilitates interaction throughout the design and manufacturing process, beginning with the customer. It ensures that customer requirements are understood and that design decisions are consistent with customer requirements as well as manufacturing capabilities.

Newspaper arrives on time	Responses to negative question: 1: I like it.	2: I expect it.	3: I'm indifferent	4: It's the only possibility.	5: I don't like it.
Responses to positive question: A: I like it.		4	5	3	50
B: I expect it.			2	5	20
C: I'm indifferent.			3	4	10
D: It's the only possibility.			1		1
E: I don't like it.					

Attractive quality (A2–A4); One-dimensional quality (A5); Expected quality (B5–D5)

One-dimensional quality: A5 = 50

Expected quality: B5 + C5 + D5 = 20 + 10 + 1 = 31

Attractive quality: A2 + A3 + A4 = 4 + 5 + 3 = 12

Therefore, "newspaper arriving on time" is a one-dimensional quality characteristic.

FIGURE 5.11 Newspaper Survey Results

Quality Function Deployment

We have discussed the merits of making design decisions *concurrently* rather than *sequentially*. However, we must emphasize that concurrent design requires superior coordination among the parties involved. Consider, for example, the design of a new car. Even for the best Japanese manufacturers, the design of an automobile can take several years and involve hundreds of design engineers. The task of coordinating the design decisions of that many individuals can be monumentous. Now imagine that two engineers are working on two different components of a car sunroof simultaneously but separately.[13] The "insulation and sealing" engineer develops a new seal that will keep out rain, even during a blinding rainstorm. The "handles, knobs, and levers" engineer is working on a simpler lever that will make the roof easier to open. The new lever is tested and works well with the old seal. Neither engineer is aware of the activities of the other. As it turns out, the combination of heavier roof (due to the increased insulation) and lighter lever means that the driver can no longer open the sunroof with one hand, thereby violating a quality characteristic *expected* by the consumer. It is to be hoped that the problem will be detected in prototype testing before the car is put into production. At that point, one or both components will need to be *redesigned*. Otherwise, cars already produced will need to be *reworked* and cars already sold, *recalled*. None of these alternatives is pleasant; they all involve considerable cost.

Teaching Note 5.10 A Car Door

One remedy to this problem is to have engineers work in teams and share information. This is certainly beneficial, but there is no guarantee that all decisions will be coordinated. A formal method is needed for making sure that everyone working on a design project knows the design objectives and is aware of the interrelationships of the various parts of the design. Similar communications are needed between the customer and marketing, between marketing and engineering, between engineering and production, and between production and the worker. In broader terms, then, a structured process is needed that will translate the *voice of the customer* to technical requirements at every stage of design and manufacture. Such a process is called **quality function deployment (QFD)**.

Quality function deployment (QFD) translates the voice of the customer into technical design requirements.

The idea of QFD began in Japan in the late 1960s but was not formalized until Professor Akao introduced the first quality table at Mitsubishi's Kobe shipyard in 1972. The first quality table, dubbed the *house of quality*, converted customer requirements into product design characteristics. Three other tables were subsequently added to convert (i.e., deploy) product characteristics into part characteristics, part characteristics into process parameters, and process parameters into operating instructions for workers or machines.

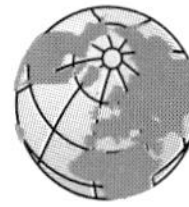

Toyota and its suppliers began using QFD in the late 1970s. By the mid-1980s Toyota had reduced the cost of new product designs by 61 percent and cut production start-up time by one-third. New tables were added to deploy cost, technology, reliability, and new concepts in the same manner as quality. In all, twenty houses, or matrices, were constructed to monitor and direct every aspect of design, from customer to manufacturing.

QFD came to America in 1984 via Ford, Omark Industries, and 3M. Today, QFD is widely used in the United States by such corporations as GM, Chrysler, GE, DEC, HP, AT&T, ITT, IBM, Procter and Gamble, and others. Services such as health care, software development, airlines, facility design, and education have also begun to apply the technique. The QFD process is continuing to evolve as companies adapt the concept to their needs. Most companies do not utilize the entire spectrum of matrices. The first matrix, the house of quality, continues to be the most popular.

[13]Adapted from King, Bob, *Better Designs in Half the Time*, Methuen, Mass.: GOAL/QPC, 1989, pp. 1.1–1.3.

As shown in Figure 5.12, the house of quality has six basic sections: a customer requirements section, a competitive assessment section, a product characteristics section, a relationship matrix, a roof matrix, and a technical assessment/target values section. Let's see how these sections interrelate by examining the completed House of Quality shown in Figure 5.13 for the redesign of a household steam iron.

1. *Customer requirements.* The customer requirements section listed on the left side of the house drives the entire QFD process. It lists, in customer terminology, the attributes of the product that are important to the customer (as revealed by market research). These attributes can get quite lengthy, so they are grouped into bundles (e.g., irons well, easy and safe to use) by consensus of the design team or by more formal nonparametric statistics techniques (such as factor analysis or cluster analysis). The smokestack of the house shows the weight, or relative importance, customers attach to each attribute. Larger numbers denote greater importance.

2. *Competitive assessment.* On the right side of the house is a perceptual map comparing customer perceptions of competitive products for each customer requirement. This information is used to determine which customer needs will yield a competitive advantage and thus should be pursued. In this example, our iron already excels in "removes wrinkles," "provides adequate steam," and "doesn't break when dropped," so we do not need to improve those factors. However, we are rated poorly on "heats quickly," "quick cool-down," "doesn't spot," and "doesn't stick." Also, we could gain some competitive advantage with an iron that "doesn't burn when touched," since no manufacturer does a good job on that point.

The information discussed so far has been the responsibility of marketing and has focused on the customer. Now, we move to design engineering and consider how the product can be changed based on customer input.

3. *Product characteristics.* The product characteristics, expressed in engineering terms, are located on the top floor of the house ("energy needed to press," "friction with cloth," "time to reach 450°," etc.). These characteristics may be bundled just like the customer attributes, except that the terminology reflects more of an engineering orientation. The objective measures toward the bottom of the house provide the technical data to support or refute customer perceptions. For example, the customer is correct, our iron does take longer to cool down than our competitors'.

4. *Relationship matrix.* The relationship matrix, located in the middle of the house, correlates customer attributes with product characteristics. We can see that

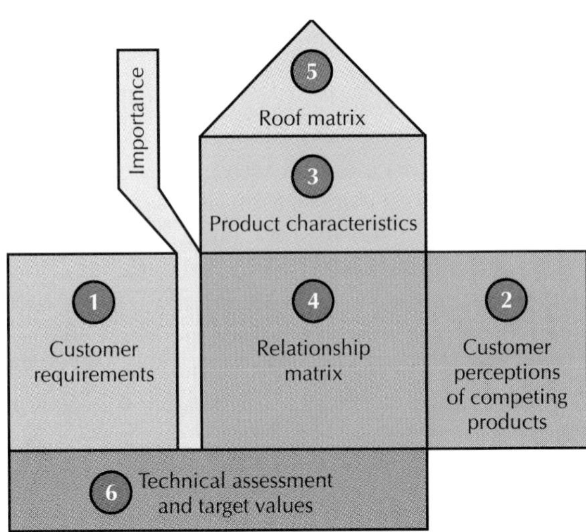

FIGURE 5.12 Outline of the House of Quality

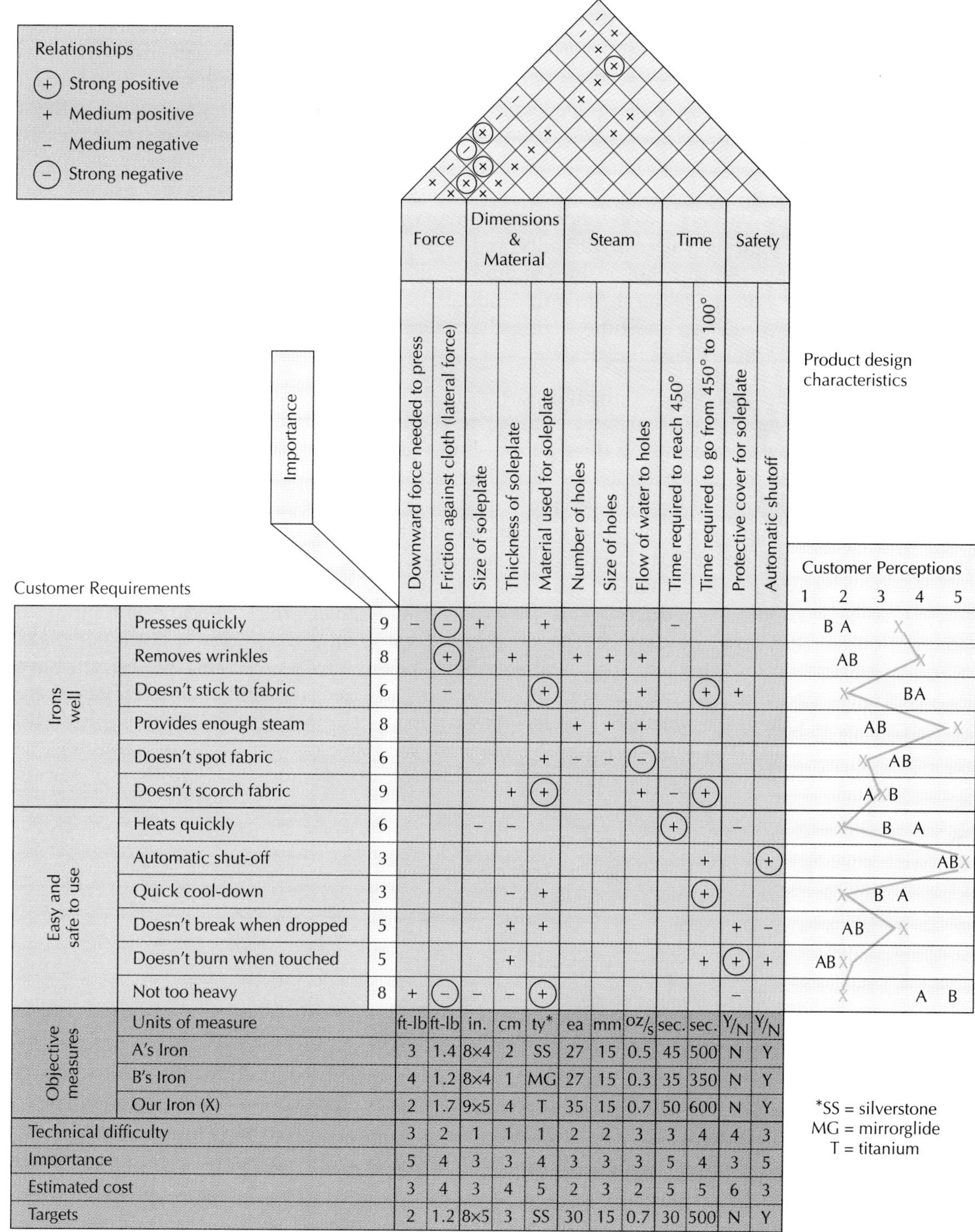

Customer Requirements		Importance	Downward force needed to press	Friction against cloth (lateral force)	Size of soleplate	Thickness of soleplate	Material used for soleplate	Number of holes	Size of holes	Flow of water to holes	Time required to reach 450°	Time required to go from 450° to 100°	Protective cover for soleplate	Automatic shutoff
Irons well	Presses quickly	9	–	⊖	+		+				–			
	Removes wrinkles	8		⊕		+		+	+	+				
	Doesn't stick to fabric	6		–			⊕			+		⊕	+	
	Provides enough steam	8						+	+	+				
	Doesn't spot fabric	6					+	–	–	⊖				
	Doesn't scorch fabric	9				+	⊕			+	–	⊕		
Easy and safe to use	Heats quickly	6			–	–					⊕		–	
	Automatic shut-off	3										+		⊕
	Quick cool-down	3				–	+					⊕		
	Doesn't break when dropped	5				+	+						+	–
	Doesn't burn when touched	5				+						+	⊕	+
	Not too heavy	8	+	⊖	–	–	⊕						–	
Objective measures	Units of measure		ft-lb	ft-lb	in.	cm	ty*	ea	mm	oz/s	sec.	sec.	Y/N	Y/N
	A's Iron		3	1.4	8×4	2	SS	27	15	0.5	45	500	N	Y
	B's Iron		4	1.2	8×4	1	MG	27	15	0.3	35	350	N	Y
	Our Iron (X)		2	1.7	9×5	4	T	35	15	0.7	50	600	N	Y
Technical difficulty			3	2	1	1	1	2	2	3	3	4	4	3
Importance			5	4	3	3	4	3	3	3	5	4	3	5
Estimated cost			3	4	3	4	5	2	3	2	5	5	6	3
Targets			2	1.2	8×5	3	SS	30	15	0.7	30	500	N	Y

FIGURE 5.13 The House of Quality for a Steam Iron

Transparency 5.9 Quality Function Deployment

a strong positive relationship exists between the customer attribute "doesn't break when dropped" and the product characteristic "thickness of soleplate," but a strong negative relationship exists between "quick cool-down" and "thickness of soleplate." This information is useful in coordinating design changes in response to one customer attribute that may be in conflict with others.

5. *Roof matrix.* The roof matrix looks at the interaction between product characteristics. For example, if the thickness of the soleplate is increased, the time required to heat up and cool down the iron will also increase, but the iron will press better and the steam will flow more evenly. All these characteristics will need to be monitored as design changes are made in soleplate thickness to maintain them at their desired level. This is not an easy task, but at least we are aware of the potential problems.

6. *Technical assessments and design targets.* The bottom portion of the house contains various factors important to management in determining target values for design, such as cost, difficulty, and importance. The target row is the *output* of the house—measurable values of product characteristics that are to be achieved in the new design of the steam iron. Notice that our efforts are directed at the dimension, performance, and time-saving characteristics, and no changes are undertaken in the safety characteristics.

To understand the full power of QFD, we need to consider (briefly) the additional houses that can be linked to the house of quality. Figure 5.14 shows the flow of information through four houses in the redesign of our steam iron. Recall that in our example the first house took the customer requirement "presses quickly" and converted it to a quantitative engineering goal expressed as "foot-pounds of pressing energy." The second house, *parts deployment,* examines which component parts are critical to meeting the engineering goal of decreased downward pressing energy. Suppose it is decided that the thickness of the soleplate should be reduced. This new part characteristic then becomes an input to the third house, *process planning.* In order to change the thickness of the soleplate, the dies used by the metal-stamping machine to produce the plates will have to change, and the stamping machine will require adjustments. Given these changes, a fourth house, *operating requirements,* prescribes how the fixtures and instructions to the stamping machine will be set, what additional training the operator of the machine needs, and how process control and preventive mainte-

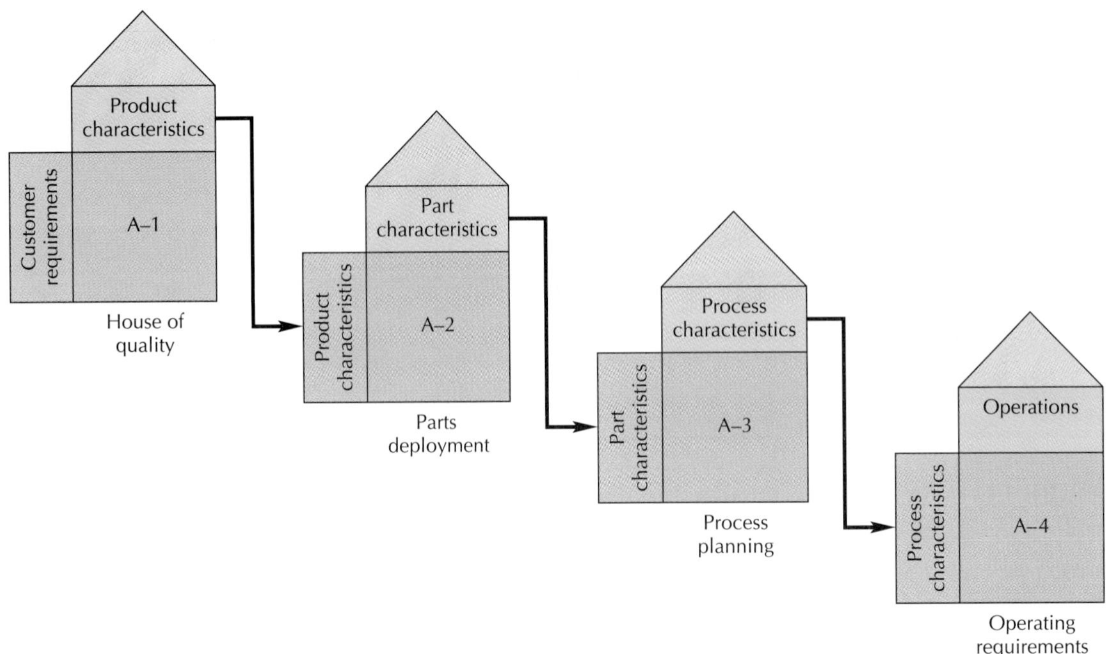

FIGURE 5.14 A Series of Connected QFD Houses

nance procedures need to be adjusted. Nothing is left to chance—all bases are covered from customer to design to manufacturing.

In comparison with traditional design approaches, QFD forces management to spend more time defining the new product changes and examining the ramifications of those changes. More time spent in the early stages of design means less time is required later to revise the design and make it work. This reallocation of time shortens the design process considerably. Some experts suggest that QFD can produce better product designs in *half* the time as conventional design processes. In summary, QFD is a communications tool that

QFD is a communications tool.

- Promotes better understanding of customer demands;
- Promotes better understanding of design interactions;
- Involves manufacturing in the design process;
- Breaks down barriers between functions and departments;
- Focuses the design effort;
- Fosters teamwork;
- Improves documentation of the design and development process;
- Provides a database for future designs;
- Increases customer satisfaction;
- Reduces the number of engineering changes;
- Brings new designs to the market faster; and
- Reduces the cost of design and manufacture.

Taguchi Methods for Robust Design

A product can fail because it was manufactured wrong in the factory (quality of conformance) or because it was designed incorrectly (quality of design). Taguchi suggests that product failure is primarily a function of design. Quality control techniques such as statistical process control (SPC) concentrate on quality of conformance. We discuss three of Taguchi's ideas for improving quality of design: 1. the concepts of robust design and consistency, 2. the quality loss function (QLF), and 3. design of experiments (DOE).

Superior quality is derived from a robust design.

Consumers typically subject products to a wide variety of operating conditions and still expect the product to function normally. The steering and brakes of a car, for example, should continue to perform their function even on wet, winding roads or when the tires are not inflated properly. A product designed to withstand variations in environmental and operating conditions is said to be *robust* or possess *robust quality*. Taguchi believes that superior quality is derived from products that are more robust and that robust products come from **robust design.**

Robust design yields a product or service designed to withstand variations.

As part of the design process, design engineers must specify certain *tolerances*, or allowable ranges of variation in the dimension of a part. It is assumed that producing parts within those tolerance limits will result in a quality product. That assumption is the basis for statistical process control. Taguchi, however, suggests that *consistency* is more important to quality than being within tolerances. He supports this view with the following observations: Consistent errors can be more easily corrected than random errors, *parts* within tolerance limits may produce *assemblies* that are not within limits, and consumers have a strong preference for product characteristics near their ideal values. Let's examine each of these observations in turn.

If an output value is consistent, its errors can be more easily corrected. Consider the professor who always starts class 5 minutes late. Students can adjust their arrival patterns to coincide with the professor's, or the professor's clock can be set ahead by 5 minutes. But if the professor sometimes starts class a few minutes early, sometimes on time, and other times 10 minutes late, the students are more apt to be frustrated, and the professor's behavior will be more difficult to change.

Consistency is important to quality.

Consistency is especially important for assembled products. The assembly of two parts that are near opposite tolerance limits may result in *tolerance stack-ups* and poor quality. For example, a button diameter that is small (near to the lower tolerance limit) combined with a buttonhole that is large (near to its upper tolerance limit) results in a button that won't stay fastened. Although it is beyond the scope of this text, Taguchi advises how to set tolerance limits so that tolerance stack-up can be avoided.

Manufacturing tolerances (or specification limits) define what is acceptable or unacceptable quality. Parts or products measured outside tolerance limits are considered defective and are either reworked or discarded. On the other hand, parts or products within the limits are considered "good," that is, *fit to use* by the next stage of production or *fit to sell* to the consumer. Taguchi asserts that although all the parts or products within tolerances may be acceptable, they are not all of the same quality. Consider a student who earns an average grade of 60 in a course. He or she will pass, whereas a student who earns an average grade of 59 will fail. A student with a 95 average will also pass the course. Taguchi would claim that there is negligible difference between the quality of the students with averages of 59 and 60, even though one was "rejected" and the other was not. There is, however, a great deal of difference in the quality of the student with an average of 60 and the student with an average of 95. Further, a professor in a subsequent class or a prospective employer will be able to detect the difference in quality and will overwhelmingly prefer the student who passed the course with a 95 average.

The **quality loss function** quantifies customer preferences toward quality.

Taguchi quantified customer preferences toward on-target quality in the **quality loss function** (QLF). The function, graphed in Figure 5.15, is a quadratic function, which implies that a customer's dissatisfaction (or quality loss) increases geometrically as the actual value deviates from the target value.

Mathematically, the function defines loss as

$$L = kd^2$$

where

L = quality loss

k = cost coefficient = $\dfrac{\text{consumer loss}}{(\text{functional tolerance})^2}$

d = deviation from target value = $x_i - T$

x_i = measure of item i

T = target value

The quality loss function is a simple cost estimate used to emphasize that customer preferences are strongly oriented toward *consistently* meeting quality expectations.

Transparency 5.10 Taguchi's Quality Loss Function

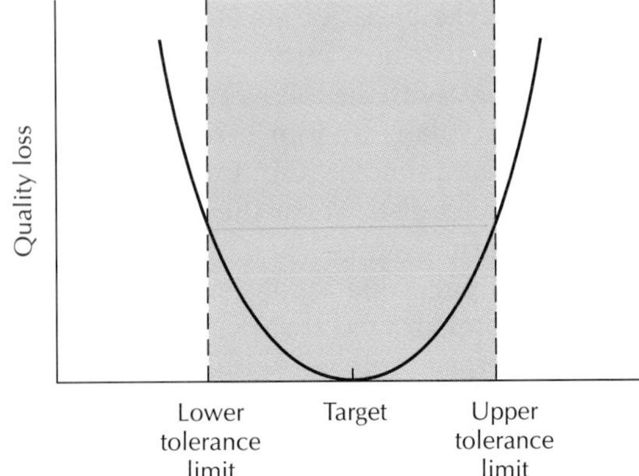

FIGURE 5.15 Taguchi's Quality Loss Function

Quality is expressed from the consumer's point of view. The cost coefficient, k, determines the steepness of the QLF curve. Larger k values produce QLF curves that rise more rapidly. The value of k is calculated as a ratio of the consumer's loss to the functional tolerance for error squared. *Consumer loss* consists primarily of the cost of repairing or replacing a product. Costs incidental to product failure may also be included, such as the cost of correcting the results of a failure, the cost of taking the product to be repaired, and the cost of not being able to use the product while it's in repair. *Functional tolerance* is the deviation from a target value at which most consumers will demand repair or replacement.

Teaching Note 5.11 Tolerances, Control Limits, and Quality Loss

One of the first publicized cases noting the difference between consistent quality and quality within specs occurred in 1979 when Sony used QLF to compare the quality of television sets produced in its Tokyo and San Diego plants. The following example is based on the Sony experience; however, the numbers have been changed to make the calculations easier.[14]

EXAMPLE 5.3

Calculating Quality Loss

Alternate Example 5.3

Problem Statement:

In the 1970s, Sony manufactured color television sets at factories located in Tokyo and San Diego. When both U.S. and Japanese customers showed a distinct preference toward the Tokyo-produced sets, management decided to investigate the reasons for the preference. They found that customer preference was related to the sharpness of the color image, defined in engineering terms as color density. The target for color density used by both plants was 10, with a range of 8 to 12 being acceptable. Both plants used statistical process control to keep the production of their sets within the tolerance limits of 10 ± 2. However, as shown in the following table, the San Diego plant produced sets with color density uniformly distributed across the range of acceptable values, whereas the Tokyo plant centered its production around the target value. If Sony estimates that it costs $40 to repair a set with inferior color density, what is the quality loss for each plant?

Color Density	*Tokyo Plant*	*San Diego Plant*
8	5	20
9	20	20
10	50	20
11	20	20
12	5	20

Solution:

The quality loss per television set is kd^2. The cost coefficient, k, is calculated as

$$k = \frac{\text{consumer loss}}{(\text{functional tolerance})^2} = \frac{\$40}{2^2} = \$10$$

To calculate the quality loss for each plant, calculate the quality loss per set for each level of color density, multiply by the number of sets produced at each level, and then sum over all levels produced at a particular plant.

[14]The Sony example was first published in the Japanese journal *Asahi* on April 17, 1979. It is discussed in L. Ealey, *Quality by Design: Taguchi Methods and U.S. Industry,* Dearborn, Mich.: ASI Press, 1988, pp. 261–263, and G. Taguchi and D. Clausing, "Robust Quality," *Harvard Business Review* (January–February 1990): 68–69.

$$\text{Loss}_{\text{Tokyo}} = 5(\$10 \times 2^2) + 20(\$10 \times 1^2) + 50(\$10 \times 0^2) + 20(\$10 \times 1^2) + 5(\$10 \times 2^2)$$
$$= 200 + 200 + 0 + 200 + 200 = \$800$$

$$\text{Loss}_{\text{San Diego}} = 20(\$10 \times 2^2) + 20(\$10 \times 1^2) + 20(\$10 \times 0^2) + 20(\$10 \times 1^2) + 20(\$10 \times 2^2)$$
$$= 800 + 200 + 0 + 200 + 800 = \$2{,}000$$

The television sets from both plants were within specifications, signifying that both plants produced quality products from the designer's point of view. However, the quality loss function shows a large difference in quality from the consumer's point of view. It would cost $2,000 to satisfy the customers who purchased television sets produced at the San Diego plant, but only $800 to satisfy those who purchased sets originating from the Tokyo plant.

The quality loss function does more than evaluate quality performance. It can be used to set more precise quality parameters, such as manufacturing tolerances, assembly tolerances, and inspection frequency. Let's look at an example of setting manufacturing tolerances.

Alternate Example 5.4

EXAMPLE 5.4

Calculating Manufacturing Tolerances

Problem Statement:

As an extension of Example 5.3, suppose it costs Sony $20 to rework an inferior television set prior to shipping (or to improve the production process so that inferior sets are not produced). How should Sony set its manufacturing tolerances to balance the cost of *rework* before an item is shipped with the cost of *repair* after an item is returned?

Solution:

Recall from Example 5.3 that it costs $40 to repair an inferior set returned by the customer and that a customer becomes dissatisfied at a color density deviation of ±2 from the target value. The cost coefficient, k, was calculated as $\$40/2^2 = \$10$. To use QLF in calculating manufacturing tolerances, we begin with knowledge of the cost coefficient, k, and the loss to the producer, L. We solve for the tolerance or deviation, d, as follows:

$$L = kd^2$$
$$20 = 10\, d^2$$
$$2 = d^2$$
$$1.41 = d$$

Thus, the manufacturing tolerance for color density should be 10 ± 1.41, or between 8.59 and 11.41. This tighter tolerance better reflects the trade-offs between the cost of reworking or scrapping an item before shipping and the cost of repairing or replacing an item that is returned from a disgruntled customer.

Much of Taguchi's work is directed toward convincing managers and design engineers that robustness and consistency are essential to design quality and thus product quality. But Taguchi's methods also specify *how* to make designs more robust by testing different design options under various operating and environmental conditions. This concept, called **design of experiments (DOE)**, begins with the identification of factors which can affect a product's performance.

Design of experiments helps determine design parameters that will make a product more robust.

The conditions that cause a product to operate poorly (called noise) can be separated into controllable and uncontrollable factors. From a designer's point of view, the controllable factors are design parameters such as material used, dimensions, and form of processing. Uncontrollable factors are under the user's control (length of use, maintenance, settings, etc.) or occur in the user's environment (heat, humidity, excess demand, etc.). The designer's job is to choose values for the control variables that react in a robust fashion to the possible occurrences of uncontrollable factors.

Suppose a group of engineers has identified thirteen critical factors that affect steering performance (such as spring stiffness, tire pressure, steering geometry, etc.) and they wish to test the factors at three levels each, a high, a medium, and a low level.[15] If the designers test the interaction of each factor at each level with every other factor, they would have to consider 3^{13}, or 1,594,323, design options. This is clearly too great a task, so most engineers will select one factor to vary, keeping all others constant. When the best level of that factor has been determined, it will be fixed and another factor will be chosen for analysis. This process reduces the number of experiments to 39 (i.e., 3 x 13), but it also ignores many possible interactions among factors. Taguchi recommends a design of experiments that is more efficient than the two just listed—it tests fewer options but examines interactions more uniformly. The Taguchi method would reduce the number of required experiments from 1,594,323 to 27. Table 5.3 describes the twenty-seven

TABLE 5.3 An Efficient Experimental Design for 13 Factors at Three Levels Each

Experiment No.	*A*	*B*	*C*	*D*	*E*	*F*	*G*	*H*	*I*	*J*	*K*	*L*	*M*
1	1	1	1	1	1	1	1	1	1	1	1	1	1
2	1	1	1	1	2	2	2	2	2	2	2	2	2
3	1	1	1	1	3	3	3	3	3	3	3	3	3
4	1	2	2	2	1	1	1	2	2	2	3	3	3
5	1	2	2	2	2	2	2	3	3	3	1	1	1
6	1	2	2	2	3	3	3	1	1	1	2	2	2
7	1	3	3	3	1	1	1	3	3	3	2	2	2
8	1	3	3	3	2	2	2	1	1	1	3	3	3
9	1	3	3	3	3	3	3	2	2	2	1	1	1
10	2	1	2	3	1	2	3	1	2	3	1	2	3
11	2	1	2	3	2	3	1	2	3	1	2	3	1
12	2	1	2	3	3	1	2	3	1	2	3	1	2
13	2	2	3	1	1	2	3	2	3	1	3	1	2
14	2	2	3	1	2	3	1	3	1	2	1	2	3
15	2	2	3	1	3	1	2	1	2	3	2	3	1
16	2	3	1	2	1	2	3	3	1	2	2	3	1
17	2	3	1	2	2	3	1	1	2	3	3	1	2
18	2	3	1	2	3	1	2	2	3	1	1	2	3
19	3	1	3	2	1	3	2	1	3	2	1	3	2
20	3	1	3	2	2	1	3	2	1	3	2	1	3
21	3	1	3	2	3	2	1	3	2	1	3	2	1
22	3	2	1	3	1	3	2	2	1	3	3	2	1
23	3	2	1	3	2	1	3	3	2	1	1	3	2
24	3	2	1	3	3	2	1	1	3	2	2	1	3
25	3	3	2	1	1	3	2	3	2	1	2	1	3
26	3	3	2	1	2	1	3	1	3	2	3	2	1
27	3	3	2	1	3	2	1	2	1	3	1	3	2

Source: Ealey, L., *Quality by Design: Taguchi Methods and U.S. Industry*, Dearborn, Mich.: ASI Press, 1988, p. 115. © Copyright, American Supplier Institute, Dearborn, Michigan (U.S.A.). Reproduced by permission under license No. 100293.

[15]This example is adapted from L.A. Ealey, *Quality by Design: Taguchi Methods and U.S. Industry*, Dearborn, Mich.: ASI Press, 1988, p. 115.

experiments with the critical factors listed across the top as letters, and the factor levels listed in the body as 1, 2, or 3 for high, medium, or low. The objective is to expose each performance level (1, 2, and 3) to every other performance level an equal number of times (thus, 3 x 3 x 3 = 27). If you examine each column of numbers under the factors, you will find 9 one's, 9 two's, and 9 three's. (The count for factor A is obvious; look more carefully at the other factors.) When this experimental design is followed, all three levels of spring stiffness will be exposed to all three levels of tire pressure, steering geometry, and so forth. How to choose the exact arrangement of factor levels in each experiment is described in more advanced texts.

GAINING THE COMPETITIVE EDGE

DEC Designs Better Products in Half the Time at Half the Cost

When DEC decided to enter the workstation market in the late 1980s, it expected its world-class manufacturing operations to help it win considerable market share. After a disappointing performance, the company realized that "the best products don't count if they don't show up on time," and they began to examine their process for designing new products. Successful application of three new techniques—quality function deployment, design for manufacture, and Taguchi methods—significantly improved the design process and enabled DEC's new workstations to 1. hit the market in less than half the time, 2. cut product costs in half while increasing customer options by fourfold, and 3. capture twice the market share with life-cycle profits several times greater.

QFD was used as a conduit to drive the "voice of the customer" through design requirements, part characteristics, process control characteristics, and operating instructions. QFD readjusted the design team's approach by forcing team members to listen to the customer, reducing many misconceptions and unproductive debates within the team, encouraging greater competitive awareness, and focusing the team on design target values instead of acceptable limits. More than 100 QFD studies have since been conducted, resulting in a 75 percent reduction in the time spent on the concept phase of design, a 40 percent reduction in the total engineering changes needed to get the product to market, and a 25 percent reduction in product features (mainly by designing what the customer wanted, rather than overdesigning what the design team *believed* the customer wanted).

Applying design for manufacture concepts resulted in a reduction in the number of parts, a simpler bill of materials with fewer levels, shorter assembly times, simpler production control, less inventory, and less operations and material costs. Specifically, the number of parts was cut in half (for a 40 percent cost savings), the number of assembly operations was reduced by 33 percent, and the assembly time was reduced by 65 percent—all this when the design cycle time was shortened by more than 70 percent.

Better quality used to mean tighter specifications and tolerances, but that's not necessarily the case with Taguchi methods. After a limited number of analyses à la Taguchi, an optimum set of parameter values can be determined for maximum design robustness. At DEC these more robust designs reduced rework by 60 percent, increased machine utilization by 44 percent, reduced the cost of quality by 25 percent, and increased the operational life of the product by 50 percent.

DEC continues to improve its product development process to achieve earlier-to-market and less-cost-to-market goals. The company measures the success of its design process by its accuracy of cost and time predictions, the number of engineering changes required, "ramp-up" time, the number of phase reworks, and break-even time.

Source: Based on Nichols, Keith, "Better, Cheaper, Faster Products—by Design," *Journal of Engineering Design* 3, no. 3 (1992): 217–28.

Taguchi's methods are widely used in Japan and are gaining acceptance in U.S. firms. Marketing and manufacturing appreciate his insight into customer preferences for robust quality and the role of design in determining product quality. His methodical approach for determining design parameters and tolerance ranges appeals to design engineers.

Teaching Note 5.12 Taguchi and ASI

TECHNOLOGY IN DESIGN

The environment for new products has changed dramatically over the past decade. New products for more segmented markets have proliferated. Changes in product design are more frequent and product life cycles are shorter. Hewlett-Packard derives more than 50 percent of its sales from products developed within the past three years. IBM estimates the average life of its new product offerings is about 6 months. Sony has introduced more than 160 different models of its Walkman over the past ten years. The ability to get new products to the market quickly has revolutionized the competitive environment and changed the nature of manufacturing.

Part of the impetus for the deluge of new products is the advancement of technology available for designing products. It begins with computer-aided design (CAD) and includes related technologies such as computer-aided engineering (CAE), computer-aided design for manufacture (CADFM), computer-aided process planning (CAPP), and computer-aided manufacturing (CAM).

Computer-Aided Design

Computer-aided design (**CAD**) is a software system that uses computer graphics to assist in the creation, modification, and analysis of a design. Design engineers input design features into a CAD system with a specially equipped graphics terminal and a mouse, joystick, light pen, track ball, keyboard, digitizing tablet, or magnetic field sensor. The mouse is popular because of its widespread use in PCs. Joysticks are used primarily in CAD systems that simulate action, such as aircraft flight simulators. Light pens are used as drawing pens to place points and lines directly on a special monitor. The track ball operates like an upside-down mouse but is more sensitive to movement than the mouse. Keyboards are useful for inputting certain kinds of input data, such as numbers and descriptions. The digitizing tablet is the most common device for CAD input. It consists of a flat surface tablet and a stylus or puck with small cross hairs. The tablet can digitize existing design blueprints into the CAD system or allow new three-dimensional designs to be entered. (The third dimension is derived from sound emitted by the stylus as it is moved vertically.) Magnetic field sensors, such as data gloves and helmets, are used in advanced CAD systems (called virtual reality) to manipulate objects in a three-dimensional environment. Monitors, printers, and plotters are common output devices.

CAD assists in the creation, modification, and analysis of a design.

CAD can be used for geometric modeling, automated drafting and documentation, engineering analysis, and design analysis. *Geometric modeling* uses basic lines, curves, and shapes to generate the geometry and topology of a part. The part may appear as a wire mesh image or as a shaded, solid model. Once an object has been input into the system, it can be displayed and manipulated in a variety of ways. The design can be rotated for a front, side, or top view, separated into different parts, enlarged for closer inspection, or shrunk back so that another feature can be highlighted. The CAD database created from the geometric design includes not only the dimensions of the product, but also tolerance information and

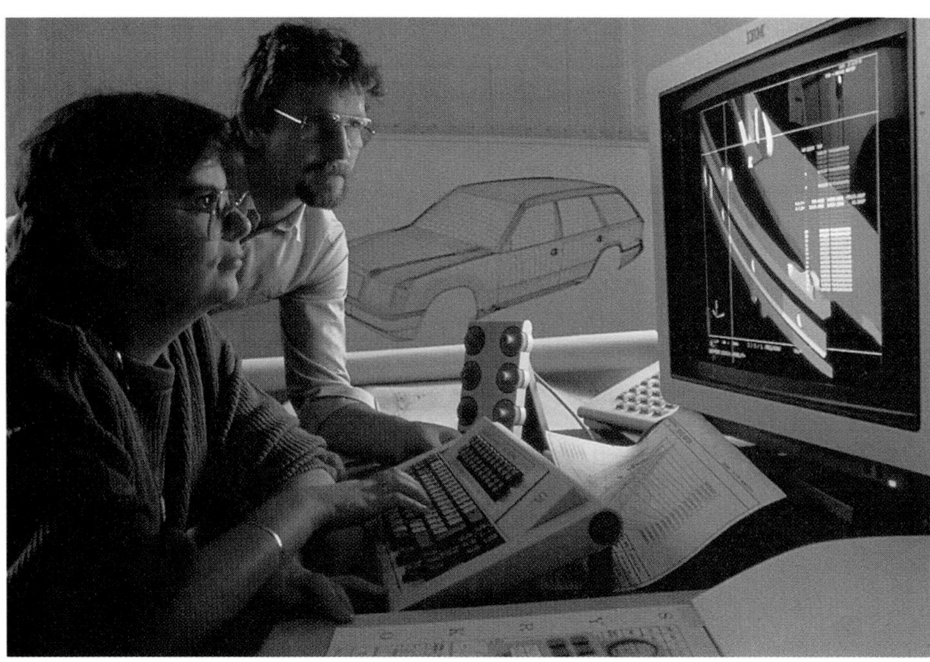

The operator of this CAD workstation can use a digitizing tablet (shown on the right), a standard keyboard (in the middle), track balls (on the left), and a special function keyboard (on the upper left) to input and edit data.

material specifications. Libraries of designs can be accessed so that designers can modify existing designs instead of building new ones from scratch.

Group technology groups parts into families for easy retrieval by the CAD database.

To enable the retrieval of similar designs from the CAD "library" or database, designs are coded and classified. *Group technology* (GT) is a common approach for grouping parts into families based on similar shapes or processing requirements. A GT parts classification code assigns numbers to part characteristics of an item, such as the shape, size, material composition, surface finish, dimensions, and tolerance ranges. Elaborate codes could specify a 30- to 40-digit part number. GT uses the codes to group parts into families, assuming that similar parts will have similar designs and be manufactured in similar ways.

Automated drafting produces hard-copy engineering drawings directly from the CAD database. It involves both the oldest and newest CAD technology. Computer plotting of engineering drawings is more than 20 years old and is standard practice today. More advanced documentation merges text and graphics to produce assembly drawings, bills of material, instruction manuals and reports, parts catalogues, and sales brochures. Automatic dimensioning, crosshatching, scaling, and sectional or enlarged parts detail are drafting options available in most CAD software.

CAE tests and analyzes designs on the computer screen.

Although the ability to combine, copy, translate, scale, and rotate designs or portions of designs is impressive, CAD is more than a drafter's version of a word processor. Its real power is derived from the ability to electronically link design with other automated systems. Engineering analysis, when performed at a computer terminal with a CAD system, is called **computer-aided engineering (CAE)**. CAE is an important extension of CAD. The description and geometry of a part are retrieved from the CAD database and subjected to testing and analysis on the computer screen without physically building a prototype. Analysis is usually of three types, 1. mass property analysis, 2. finite element analysis, or 3. kinematics. Analysis of mass properties includes such calculations as surface area, weight, volume, center of gravity, and moment of inertia. This is the most common CAE application. It could be used for such tasks as maximizing the volume of a fuel tank or the storage space in a car trunk.

Finite element analysis (FEA) analyzes stress, strain, or heat transfer in irregularly shaped, solid model designs. The three-dimensional design is subdivided into small rectangles, called *elements*, on which standard stress formulas are applied. After constraints, loads, and material properties are defined, CAE software calculates the stress on each element and maps the results onto the meshed figure. Each individual element is colored according to the stress that is exerted on it or the heat it absorbs. Red usually represents an area of concern (i.e., higher heat or more stress). Finite element analysis can be used to detect whether plastic parts are cooling evenly, how much stress will cause a bridge to crack, or if a potato chip will break when the number of "ridges" is increased.

Figure 5.16 shows a series of CAD drawings of an imaginary product. Part (a) is a conceptual design in wireframe format. Part (b) is a solids model of the part created by shading the wireframe image. Part (c), derived from the solids model, shows a minimal drawing of the part, the beginning of automated drafting. Drawing notes, a drawing format, and more dimensions are needed to complete the design documentation. Part (d) shows the results of a finite element analysis in color-coded format. Red represents areas of high stress, orange through yellow represent reduced stress, and the blue areas represent low stress. A prototype of the electronically generated part can be produced on a sterolithography machine with information sent directly from the CAD database. The prototype is constructed from a solidified liquid plastic that communicates the form of the design, but not always the function. It can be used as a concept model or as a pattern for molds that will make a working prototype or final product. Sterolithography has been called an "enabling technology" for concurrent design, because it creates a quick, inexpensive prototype that speeds up the design process.

Kinematics is the study of movement and the forces and moments that cause movement. A design engineer could use this analysis to test the stability of a boat, the operation of a hacksaw, or the path of a projectile. The results can be displayed as graphs (e.g., motion over time or velocity versus applied force) or in animated form. Animation would allow the design team to watch a car bump along a rough road, a combine strain its wheels over mud and ice, the pistons of an engine move up and down, or a golf ball soar through the air.

Other specialized CAD-based analyses are available. In the field of chemistry, for example, reactions of chemicals can be analyzed on the computer screen. And, in medicine, the effects of new drugs can be tested on computer-generated DNA molecules. Aerodynamics CAD/CAE packages can replace expensive wind tunnels. *Cyberman*, a computer mannequin, tests the ergonomics of a design by examining arm reach, pedal position, and steering-column angle for Chrysler cars.

CAD-related systems can also review designs to analyze accuracy, manufacturability, and processing detail. *Layering* overlaps part images to check for con-

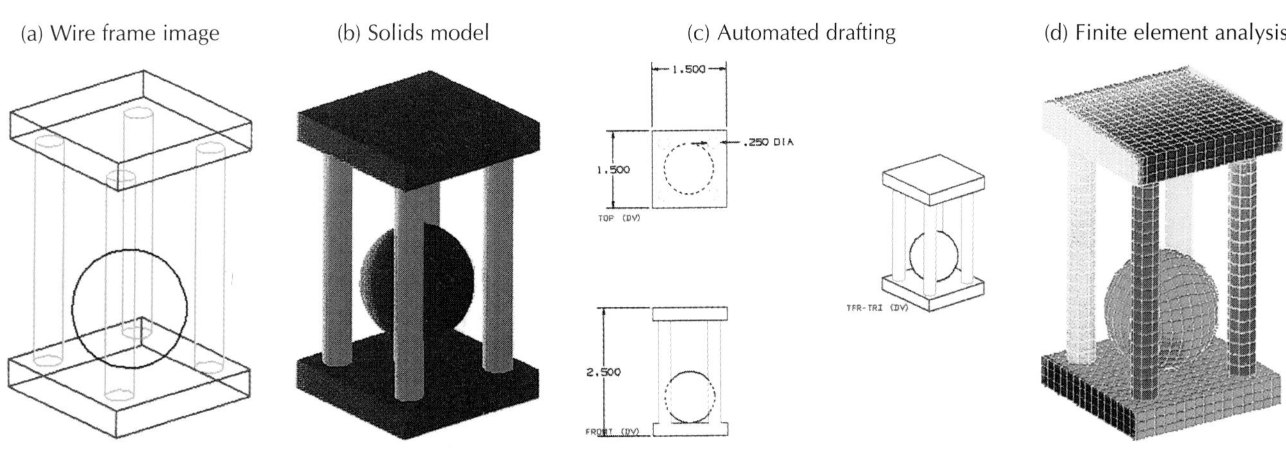

FIGURE 5.16 A CAD Example

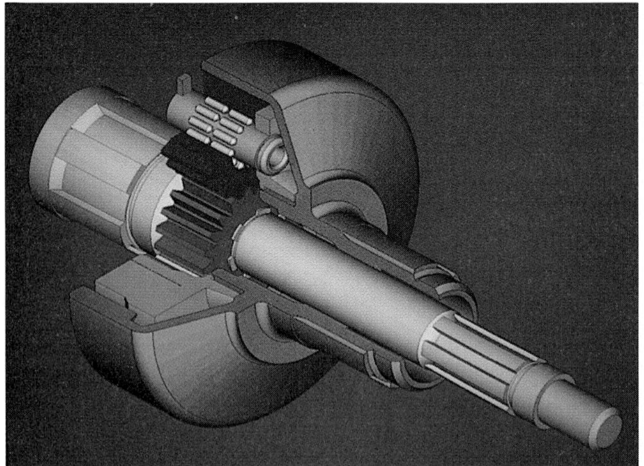

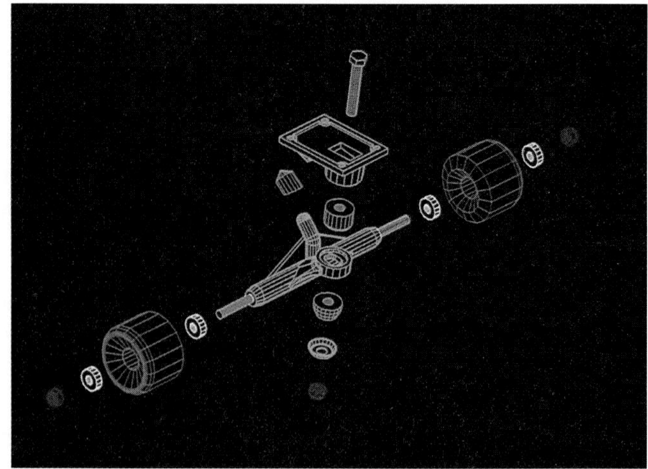

The gear case assembly shown on the left is a cutaway view of a solid model. The ability of CAD to reorient a design, to isolate and enlarge sections of a design, and to present different views of a design saves time in redrawing the image and improves the quality of the final design. Shown on the right is an assembly chart of a front axel. Parts lists and bills of material can be generated directly from the CAD file.

flicts in use or manufacture. For example, the geometric image of a part can be overlayed on its rough casting to determine final machining dimensions. Similarly, a tool path generated for a numerically controlled machine can be overlayed on a part to verify its accuracy. *Inference checking* examines assemblies to ensure that two components do not occupy the same space. Multilayered printed circuit boards can be examined to verify that connections are positioned correctly.

Specialized software packages for analyzing the manufacturability of a design, known as computer-aided DFM or designer tool kits, present guidelines and rules for using specific manufacturing processes (such as casting, injection molding, or metal stamping) and facilities (such as flexible assembly systems, triaxis transfer press lines, or flexible welding fixtures). The software guides the designer through various design options, is highly visual in nature, and may include specialized CAD, CAE, and simulation systems. Many of these packages use the latest knowledge-based technologies, including expert systems that capture the knowledge of expert designers and artisans, and neural networks that add to their knowledge base each time they are used.

CAD/CAM is the ultimate design-to-manufacture connection.

The ultimate connection to a CAD database is a CAD/CAM system. CAM is the acronym for computer-aided manufacturing. It basically refers to control of the manufacturing process by computers. CAD/CAM involves the automatic conversion of CAD design data into processing instructions for computer-controlled equipment and the subsequent manufacture of the part as it was designed. This integration of design and manufacture can save enormous amounts of time, ensure that parts and products are produced *precisely* as intended, and facilitate revisions in design or customized production.

Benefits of CAD

CAD radically reduces the leadtime for new product introduction. CAD's time advantage is not being able to *draw* lines faster, but being able to *find* them faster. The drafting of an original design by computer is not significantly faster than drafting by hand, but revising and adapting existing designs is almost twelve times faster. The ability to sort, classify, and retrieve similar designs facilitates standardization of parts, prompts ideas, and eliminates building a design from scratch.

GAINING THE COMPETITIVE EDGE

Three Miles of Tubing

One of the early examples of CAD/CAM success occurred in the aerospace industry. In aircraft production, an especially difficult part to design and manufacture correctly is the 3-mile-long hydraulic tubing that must be twisted and bent to fit within an airplane. Previously, the process involved building master tubes and bending them by hand to fit within the aircraft. The master tubes were then stored in a warehouse to serve as templates for production. During production, twelve artisans spent 6 weeks bending and fitting the tubes properly to each aircraft. On the average, 100 tubes per aircraft had to be adjusted because they would not fit the plane as designed.

Enter the world of CAD/CAM. Master tubes are stored in a computer database instead of a warehouse. A designer calls up the master design on a computer terminal and makes adjustments to sections of the tubing by touching a fiber optics light pen to the terminal screen. When the design is set, the punch of a button converts the design into machine instructions and sends those instructions to a tube-bending machine nearby. As bent sections of the tubing emerge from the machine, they are assembled by hand with other tube sections by two assemblers. The entire process involves three people and 18 minutes. This is quite a reduction from the 12-person, 3-week original process. Even more impressive is the quality of the CAD/CAM produced tubing. Typically, only four tubes per aircraft need to be readjusted.

Source: Based on Bylinsky, G., "A New Revolution is on the Way," *Fortune* (October 5, 1981): 106–15.

CAD produces better designs faster.

CAD-generated products can be introduced faster to the market because they can be tested quicker. CAE systems interacting with CAD databases can test the functioning of a design so thoroughly that a prototype may never be built. Costly mistakes in design or production can be avoided because materials, parts fit, and conditions of use can be tested on the screen. Time to manufacture can also be reduced with CAD-initiated designs of molds, dies, and processing instructions. Documentation of CAD designs allows the information to be printed out in various forms for multiple users—as a parts list, sales catalog, or assembly instructions.

Although the time savings from CAD have been significant, CAD and its related technologies have also significantly improved the *quality* of designs and the products manufactured from them. The communications capabilities of CAD may be more important than its processing capabilities in terms of design quality. CAD systems enhance communication and promote innovation in multifunctional design teams by providing a visual, interactive focus for discussion. Watching a vehicle strain its wheels over mud and ice prompts ideas on product design and customer use better than stacks of consumer surveys or engineering reports. New ideas can be suggested and tested immediately, allowing more alternatives to be evaluated. To facilitate discussion or clarify a design, CAD data can be sent electronically between designer and supplier or viewed simultaneously on computer screens by different designers in physically separated locations. Prototypes can be tested more thoroughly with CAD/CAE capabilities. More prototypes can be tested as well. As you can see, CAD improves every stage of product design—functional, form, and production design. It has been especially useful as a means of integrating design and manufacture.

Video 5.1 *Harley-Davidson, Building Better Motorcycles the American Way*

Future Developments in Technology

CAD systems have become less costly, more powerful, and more accessible in recent years. The related technologies for testing the function and planning the

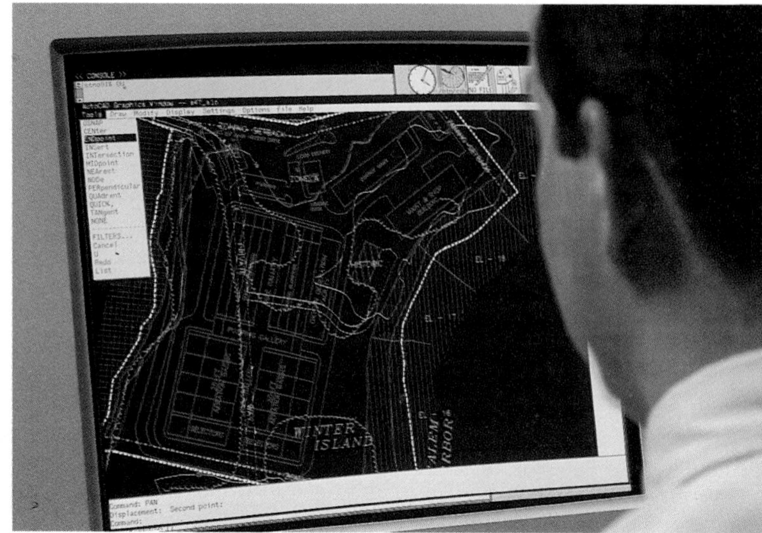

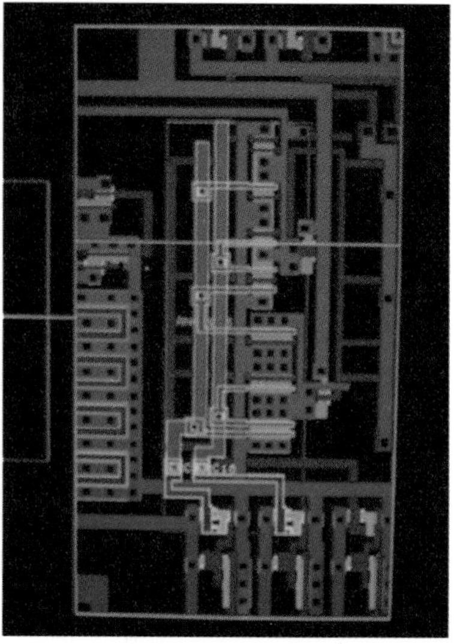

CAD systems have become widely used in architectural design and urban planning. It is common for a building's layout to be digitized as well as the layout of a city or town. Circuit boards contain dozens of layers that must connect in the right places. CAD allows the designer to examine one layer of the board at a time and test the accuracy of the design. Since most circuit boards are populated with automated equipment (usually robots), the CAD design also serves as an important input to programming automation or CAM. Today's CAD/CAM systems can handle designs with over 250 layers.

manufacture of specialized systems are also becoming more sophisticated. Although it is hard to predict exactly what lies in store for the future, two specific technologies deserve comment: imaging and virtual reality.

CAD systems continue to evolve with *imaging* and *virtual reality.*

Imaging is basically digital copying. Pictures or documents can be electronically copied and transmitted from one computer to another. For CAD users, imaging is an alternate form of transferring information. A CAD drawing can be imaged and sent to various sites for others to review. In this format, their comments can be entered right on the drawing without altering the original design. Imaging can also increase the transportability of designs from one CAD system to another, between manufacturer and supplier, for example, who may have purchased their CAD systems from different vendors. Simulations of product performance can also be enhanced with imaging. A flight simulation is much more realistic over imaged topography.

Image rendering is a sophisticated process of adding lighting, shading, reflection, transparency, and other surface attributes to a computerized picture to make it appear lifelike, like a photograph. Military applications have produced computer-generated pictures that are indistinguishable from photographs. Photographs can be altered with this technique, and negatives can even be produced, so that reality is not always a certainty.

Teaching Note 5.13 Virtual Reality

Virtual reality allows the user to experience animation as an active participant. With specialized gloves and helmets that contain fiber optic sensors, the user enters into a three-dimensional simulated world that reacts to his or her movement. This technology has been used in the architectural design of buildings, where the client can walk through the design, look out a window, tour the second floor, etc. Creative uses include medical researchers, who enter themselves into a simulated human body to *experience* the clogging of arteries and other maladies as a method of prompting ideas for solving the problems.

GAINING THE COMPETITIVE EDGE

Ford Engages in Long-Distance Design

Ford Motor Company has consolidated its European, North American, and Asian design operations into a single international network. Design sites on the network include Dearborn, Michigan; Dunton, England; Cologne, Germany; Turin, Italy; Valencia, California; Hiroshima, Japan; and Melbourne, Australia. The sites are connected via satellite links, undersea cables, and land lines purchased from telecommunications carriers.

Using a sophisticated CAD system and imaging software, a 3-D drawing of a new-car design can be sent from Dearborn to Dunton, where two colleagues can look at the design simultaneously and discuss changes to be made. The image can be enlarged, shrunk, rotated, run through tests, modified, and then sent on to a computerized milling machine in Turin, where a clay or plastic foam model can be produced in a few hours.

What's the advantage of such a system? Worldwide design means fewer repeated efforts by designers and better-quality designs by getting input from the expert wherever he or she might be. These experts include suppliers, manufacturers, and customers. Forty percent of the development costs of a new car are spent modifying the design after production has begun. Ford hopes the worldwide network will cut down on the number of changes in a new car's initial design and shorten the design cycle to two years or less.

Source: Based on Halpert, J., "One Car, Worldwide, With Strings Pulled From Michigan," *New York Times* (August 29, 1993).

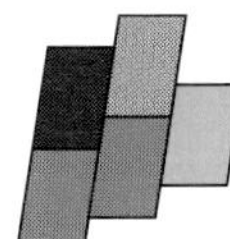

SERVICE DESIGN

The design of services has not received as much attention as the design of products. This is unfortunate, because services that are allowed just to "happen" rarely meet customer needs. Too often companies rely on the individual service provider to figure out what the customer wants and how the service should be provided without sufficient support from management, policies and procedures, or physical surroundings. The world-class services that come to mind—McDonald's, Nordstrom, Federal Express, Disney World—are all characterized by impeccable design. McDonald's plans every action of its employees (e.g., forty-nine steps to making perfect french fries), Nordstrom creates a pleasurable shopping environment with well-stocked shelves, live music, fresh flowers in the dressing rooms, and legendary salespersons, Federal Express designs every stage of the delivery process for efficiency and speed, and Disney World in Japan was so well designed that it impressed even the zero-defect Japanese.

Services need to be carefully designed.

Can services be designed in the same manner as products? Certainly, many of the techniques we have discussed (FMEA, FTA, QFD, etc.) can be used for either products or services. If we substitute the word *service* for *product* and *delivery* for *manufacture* in Figure 5.9, the design process would *look* much the same, but there are some important differences. Let's examine some characteristics of services that impact the design process.

Characteristics of Services

In this section we list eight common characteristics of services and discuss their implications for service design. Although not all services possess each of these characteristics, they do exhibit at least some of them to a varying degree.

Characteristics distinguish services from manufacturing.

1. *Services are intangible.* It is difficult to design something that you cannot see, touch, store on a shelf, or try on for size. Services are *experienced*, and that experience may be different for each individual customer. Designing a service involves describing what the customer is supposed to "experience," which can be a difficult task. Designers begin by compiling information on the way people think, feel, and behave (called *psychographics*).

Because of its intangibility, consumers perceive that a service is more risky to purchase than a product. Cues (such as physical surroundings, server's demeanor, service guarantees, etc.) need to be included in service design to help form or reinforce accurate perceptions of the service experience and reduce the consumer's risk.

The quality of a service experience depends in large measure on the customer's service *expectations*. Expectations can differ according to a customer's knowledge, experience, and self-confidence. The medical profession has done a masterful job of conditioning patients to be told little, accept what happens to them on faith, and not to be disappointed when medical problems are not corrected. In essence, patients expect to be treated like small children. Medical personnel who exceed these expectations, even by a small margin, are perceived as delivering outstanding service.[16]

Customers also have different expectations of different types of service providers. For example, you probably expect more from a department store than a discount store or from a car dealer's service center than an independent repair shop. Understanding the customer and his or her expectations is essential in designing good service.

2. *Service output is variable.* This statement is true because of the various service providers employed and the variety of customers they serve, each with their own special needs. Even though customer demands vary, the service experience is expected to remain consistent. According to a recent survey, reliability and consistency are the most important measures of service quality to the customer.[17] Service design, then, must strive for predictability or robustness. Examples of services known for their consistency include McDonald's, Holiday Inn, and ServiceMaster. Extensive employee training, set operating procedures, and standardized materials, equipment, and physical environments are used by these companies to increase consistency.

3. *Services have high customer contact.* The service "encounter" between service provider and customer *is* the service in many cases. Making sure the encounter is a positive one is an important part of service design. This involves giving the service provider the skills and authority necessary to complete a customer transaction successfully. Studies show a direct link between service provider motivation and customer satisfaction. Moreover, service providers are motivated primarily not by compensation but rather by concurrence with the firm's "service concept" and being able to perform their job competently.[18]

High customer contact can interfere with the efficiency of a service and make it difficult to control its quality (i.e., there is no opportunity for testing and rework). However, direct contact with customers can also be an advantage for services. Observing customers experiencing a service generates new service ideas and facilitates feedback for improvements to existing services.

[16]Heskett, J. L., W. E. Sasser, and C. Hart, *Service Breakthroughs: Changing the Rules of the Game,* New York: The Free Press, 1990, p. 7.

[17]Berry, L., A. Parasuraman, and V. Zeithaml, "The Service Quality Puzzle," *Business Horizons,* (September–October 1988): 37.

[18]Heskett, J. L., W. E. Sasser, and C. Hart, *Service Breakthroughs: Changing the Rules of the Game,* New York: Macmillan, 1990, p.15.

4. *Services are perishable.* Since services can't be saved until later, the timing and location of delivery is also important. Thus, service design should define not only *what* is to be delivered but also *where* and *when*.

5. *Consumers do not separate the service from the delivery of the service.* For services, product (i.e., service) design and process design must occur concurrently. (This is one area in which services have an advantage over manufacturing—it has taken manufacturing a number of years to realize the benefits of concurrent design.) Thus, in addition to deciding "what, where, and when," service design also specifies *how* the service should be provided. "How" decisions include the degree of customer participation in the service process, which tasks should be done in the presence of the customer (called front-room activities) and which should be done out of the customer's sight (back-room activities), the role and authority of the service provider in delivering the service, and the balance of "touch" versus "tech" (i.e., how automated the service should be).

6. *Services tend to be decentralized and geographically dispersed.* Many service employees are on their own to make decisions. Although this can present problems, careful service design will help employees deal successfully with contingencies. Multiple service outlets can be a plus in terms of rapid prototyping. New ideas can be field-tested with a minimum disturbance to operations. McDonald's considers each of its outlets a "laboratory" for new ideas.

7. *Services are consumed more often than products,* so there are more opportunities to succeed or fail with the customer. Jan Carlzon of SAS Airlines calls these opportunities "moments of truth." In a sense, the service environment lends itself more readily to continuous improvement than does the manufacturing environment.

8. *Services can be easily emulated.* Competitors can copy new or improved services quickly. New ideas are constantly needed to stay ahead of the competition. As a result, new service introductions and service improvements occur even more rapidly than new product introductions.

From the preceding discussion, we can conclude that service design is more comprehensive and occurs more often than product design. The process of generating the design, however, can be quite similar. Service design begins with a service concept and ends with design specifications to communicate the concept.

The Service Concept

The service concept involves creating a **service package,** or *bundle,* that meets certain customer needs. The package consists of a mixture of physical items, sensual benefits, and psychological benefits.[19] For example, for a restaurant the physical items consist of the facility, food, drinks, tableware, napkins, and other touchable commodities. The sensual benefits include the taste and aroma of the food and the sights and sounds of the people. Psychological benefits could be rest and relaxation, comfort, status, or a sense of well-being.

A **service package** includes physical items, sensual benefits, and psychological benefits.

The key to effective service design is to recognize and define *all* the components of a service package—none of the components should be left to chance. Finding the appropriate mix of physical items and sensual and psychological benefits and designing them to be consistent with each other is also important. For example, a fast-food restaurant promises nourishment with speed. The customer is served quickly and is expected to consume the food quickly. Thus, the tables, chairs, and booths are not designed to be comfortable, nor does their arrangement encourage lengthy or personal conversations. The service package is consistent.

[19]The concept of a service package and its contents comes from Sasser, W. E., R. P. Olsen, and D. Wyckoff, *Management of Service Operations,* Boston: Allyn and Bacon, 1978, pp. 8–10.

This is not the case for an up-scale restaurant located in a renovated train station. The food is excellent, but it is difficult to enjoy a full-course meal sitting on wooden benches in a drafty facility, where conversations echo and tables shake when the trains pass by.

Sometimes services are successful because their service concept fills a previously unoccupied niche or differs from the generally accepted mode of operation. For example, ClubMed perfected the "packaged vacation" concept for a carefree vacation experience. Citicorp offers 15-minute mortgage approvals through online computer networks with real estate offices, credit bureaus, and builder's offices, and an expert system loan-application adviser. Shouldice Hospital performs only inguinal hernia operations, for which its doctors are very experienced and its facilities carefully designed. Local anesthesia is used, patients walk into and out of the operating room under their own power, and telephones, televisions, and dining facilities are located in a communal area some distance from patient rooms. As a result, patients become ambulatory much earlier than in traditional hospitals, are discharged after 72 hours (compared to normal week-long stays), and pay one-third less for their operations.

Performance and Design Specifications

Teaching Note 5.14 Specifications for Racing Skis

From the service concept, *performance specifications* are determined to meet customer requirements (in general and for specific customers). The performance specifications are then converted into *design specifications* and, finally, into *service delivery specifications* (in lieu of manufacturing specifications).

Performance, design, and *delivery specifications* allow a service to be replicated at different locations and times.

In services, the design process incorporates both service design and delivery. Design specifications must describe the service in sufficient detail for the desired service experience to be replicated for different individuals at numerous locations. The specifications typically consist of drawings, physical models, and narrative descriptions of the service package. Employee training or guidelines for service providers may also be included. Finally, service delivery specifications outline the steps required in the work process.

GAINING THE COMPETITIVE EDGE

UCS Creates Customer Delight

Within three years of entering the crowded credit card market, AT&T Universal Card Services (UCS) emerged second out of 6,000 competitors and became the proud recipient of a Malcolm Baldrige National Quality Award. In a market that others viewed as saturated, Paul Kahn, CEO of UCS, saw unmet customer needs and "room in the business to give something back to the customer." He set out to become a major contender in the marketplace by startling customers with service that went far beyond what they had come to expect. The "product" design included a variable interest rate linked to the prime rate; no annual fee for life; an unconditional service guarantee ($10 for every mistake or inconvenience); customer service available 24 hours a day, 7 days a week; commitment to act as the customer's advocate in billing disputes; a combination credit card/calling card with 10 percent discount on calls; a standard card with the same features as gold cards; and rapid application approval (completed over the phone is less than 4 minutes). Kahn read the public correctly—the innovative design delighted the customer and attracted one million accounts in just 78 days.

Source: Based on *Universal Card Services Summary of 1992 Application for Malcolm Baldrige National Quality Award,* AT&T, 1993.

For example, suppose a house-painting service based on the concept of fast, guaranteed work receives the following *performance specifications* from a customer:[20]

> Paint the exterior of the house grey with white trim. Get rid of mildew stains on the north side of the house and use a type of paint that is resistant to peeling and fading from the sun. Complete the work as soon as possible for an amount not to exceed $2,500.

The service provider, in turn, translates the performance specifications into the following *design specifications:*

> Paint exterior of house with 10 gallons of SwissBoy oil-base enamel, color Driftwood. Paint house trim with 3 gallons of SwissBoy White Smoke. Put two coats on all outside surfaces, including the garage. Trim does not include gutters, downspouts, or cement foundation. Scrape and sand surfaces to prevent peeling. Treat north-facing surfaces with 3 gallons of RotAway as primer coat. Begin job on Monday and complete within 10 working days (weather permitting). Provide three-year guarantee against peeling but not fading. Cost: $2,750 payable upon completion by personal check.

At this point, the customer and the service provider obviously have some negotiation to do. Cost and guarantees will have to be reconciled. The customer will need to approve a color swatch and may request testimonials or opinions of others who have used RotAway. The painter may suggest painting the garage first to identify any potential areas of discrepancy between the design specifications and service delivery. After reaching agreement, the service provider creates the following service *delivery specifications:*

1. Order consumable materials (see design specifications).
2. Contract labor (three full-time workers for 8 days each).
3. Deliver materials to site (three ladders, six brushes, six cloths).
4. Scrape loose paint and sand and fill holes.
5. Apply RotAway primer.
6. Apply first white trim coat and first grey coat.
7. Apply second trim coat.
8. Apply second grey coat.
9. Scrape windows and clean up.
10. Collect fee and evaluate accuracy of time and cost estimates.

Taking the time to design a service carefully (often with direct customer participation) helps to prevent disagreements between customer and service provider and results in higher levels of customer satisfaction.

SUMMARY

New products are exciting. They enhance a company's image, invigorate employees, and help a firm to grow and prosper. Product design and development, however, can be a long and tedious process. The traditional serial design process is outdated. The new paradigm for design makes product and process decisions concurrently, utilizes design teams and design for manufacture concepts, and calls for changes in the role of design engineers. Methods for improving the quality of design include quality classifications, quality function deployment, and Taguchi methods for robust design.

[20]This example is adapted from module 10 of Xerox's *New Employee Quality Training Workbook,* 1988.

Technology, in the form of CAD and its variants (CAE, CADFM, CAD/CAM), has dramatically changed the design process. CAD allows better-quality products to be designed, revised, tested, and produced with record speed.

Service design is more comprehensive than product design because the customer considers service delivery as part of the service itself. Thus, service design includes such factors as physical surroundings and the role of the service provider as well.

Designs define what goods or services are to be provided to the customer. We must now decide how to provide them. The next chapter describes the decisions involved in planning the production process.

SUMMARY OF KEY FORMULAS

Reliability

$$P(\text{no failure before } T) = e^{-T/MTBF}$$

$$P(\text{failure before } T) = 1 - e^{-T/MTBF}$$

Quality Loss Function

$$L = kd^2$$

$$k = \frac{\text{consumer loss}}{(\text{functional tolerance})^2}$$

SUMMARY OF KEY TERMS

benchmarking: finding the best-in-class part, product, or process, measuring one's performance against it, and making recommendations for improvements based on the results.

cluster chart: a graphical approach to profiling customer preferences in order to identify market segments.

computer-aided design (CAD): a software system that uses computer graphics to assist in the creation, modification, and analysis of a design.

computer-aided engineering (CAE): engineering analysis performed at a computer terminal with information from a CAD database. It includes mass property analysis, finite element analysis, and kinematics.

concurrent design: a new approach to design that involves the simultaneous design of products and processes by design teams.

design for assembly (DFA): a set of procedures for reducing the number of parts in an assembly, evaluating methods of assembly, and determining an assembly sequence.

design for environment (DFE): designing a product from recycled materials, that can be recycled or easily repaired rather than discarded.

design for manufacture (DFM): designing a product so that it can be produced easily and economically; the concept is supported by DFM axioms, guidelines, and other analytical techniques.

design of experiments (DOE): a procedure for making designs more robust by efficiently testing the interactions of various design options under difficult operating conditions.

failure mode and effects analysis (FMEA): a systematic approach for analyzing the causes and effects of product failures.

fault tree analysis (FTA): a visual method for analyzing the interrelationships among failures.

form design: the phase of product design concerned with how the product looks.
functional design: the phase of product design concerned with how the product performs.
group technology: a common approach for grouping parts into coded and classified families for easy retrieval from the CAD database.
maintainability: the ease with which a product is maintained or repaired.
modular design: combining standardized building blocks or modules in a variety of ways to create unique finished products.
perceptual map: a visual method for comparing customer perceptions of different products or services.
production design: the phase of product design concerned with how the product will be manufactured.
quality function deployment (QFD): a structured process that will translate the voice of the customer into technical design requirements.
quality loss function: a mathematical relationship that quantifies the loss to the customer of quality that is off target.
reliability: the probability that a given part or product will perform its intended function for a specified period of time under normal conditions of use.
reverse engineering: the procedure of carefully dismantling and inspecting a competitor's product to look for design features that can be incorporated into one's own product.
robust design: the design of a product or a service that can withstand variations in environmental and operating conditions.
service package: the mixture of physical items, sensual benefits, and psychological benefits provided to the customer.
simplification: reducing the number of parts, assemblies, or options in a product.
standardization: using commonly available parts that are interchangeable among products.
value analysis (VA): an analytical approach for eliminating unnecessary design features and functions.

SOLVED PROBLEMS

1. Reliability

Problem Statement:

Jack McPhee, a production supervisor for McCormick, Inc., is committed to the company's new quality effort. Part of the program encourages making product components in-house to ensure higher quality levels and instill worker pride. The system seems to be working well. One assembly, which requires a reliability of 0.95, is normally purchased from a local supplier. Now it is being assembled in-house from three parts that each boast reliabilities of 0.96. However, customer complaints have risen in the last 12 months since McCormick started doing its own assembly work. Can you explain why? What can be done to correct the situation?

Solution:

The reliability of an assembly is the product of the reliabilities of its components. Thus, for the in-house assembly, the reliability is

$$0.96 \times 0.96 \times 0.96 = 0.8847$$

which is considerably less than the purchased assembly's reliability of 0.95. No wonder the customers are complaining.

To correct the situation, Jack could start purchasing the assembly again, redesign the product so that the number of components is reduced, increase the reliabilities of the individual components, or build in redundant components. To match an assembly reliability of 0.95, the individual reliabilities would need to be 0.983 for three components or 0.975 for two components.

The same effect could be achieved with the following backup system:

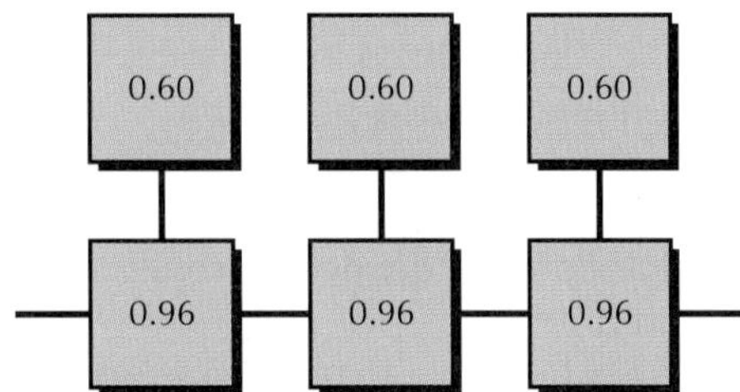

[0.96 + (0.04)(0.60)] x [0.96 + (0.04)(0.60)] x [0.96 + (0.04)(0.60)] = 0.84 x 0.984 x 0.984 = 0.95

There are many possible answers to this question. Jack's decision will depend on the difficulty and cost of implementing the options you suggest.

2. *Design of Experiments*

Problem Statement:

The energy department is investigating options for conserving fossil fuels. Their research staff has identified three critical factors that affect the fuel economy of automobiles: 1. driving speed, 2. tire pressure, and 3. engine displacement. They wish to test these factors at three levels each, high (H), medium (M), and low (L).

a. If the agency tests all possible combinations of factors and levels, how many experiments will it perform?
b. If the agency uses the one-factor-at-a-time method, how many experiments will it perform? Give an example.
c. Design a series of experiments using Taguchi's method in which all factors and levels are exposed once to every other factor and level. (There are several correct answers).

Solution:

a. $3^3 = 27$ experiments
b. One factor-at-a-time method (3 x 3 = 9 experiments):

Experiment	*Speed*	*Tire Pressure*	*Engine Displacement*
1	L	L	L
2	M[a]	L	L
3	H	L	L
4	M	L	L
5	M	M[a]	L
6	M	H	L
7	M	M	L
8	M	M	M
9	M	M	H

[a]Assume this is the best result of varying that factor and keeping other factors constant.

c. Taguchi method (3 x 3 x 1 = 9 experiments):

Experiment	*Speed*	*Tire Pressure*	*Engine Displacement*
1	L	L	L
2	L	M	M
3	L	H	H
4	M	M	L
5	M	H	M
6	M	L	H
7	H	H	L
8	H	L	M
9	H	M	H

Note: This is one of many possible answers. Each factor is tested three times at its low level, three at its medium level, and three at its high level. Each factor level is exposed to each other factor level one time. This design doesn't test all possible interactions, but it is more representative than the one-factor-at-a-time method.

QUESTIONS

5-1. Look around your classroom and make a list of items that impede your ability to learn. Classify them as problems in *quality of design* or *quality of conformance.*
5-2. How can organizations gain a competitive edge with product or service design?
5-3. Briefly describe the traditional sequential design process. What problems does it present?
5-4. Differentiate between performance specifications, design specifications, and manufacturing specifications.
5-5. Discuss several methods for generating new product ideas.
5-6. How are perceptual maps and cluster charts used?
5-7. Construct a perceptual map and cluster chart for the following products or services: a. business schools in your state or region, b. word-processing packages, and c. video rental stores. Label the axes with the dimensions you feel are most relevant.
5-8. Describe benchmarking and reverse engineering.
5-9. Find out if your university benchmarks itself against other universities. If so, write a summary of the characteristics that are considered, the measures that are used, and the results. Do the data support your views as a customer?
5-10. What kinds of analyses are conducted in a feasibility study for new products?
5-11. Discuss the objectives of form design, functional design, and production design.
5-12. Define reliability. What are the two ways reliability can be expressed?
5-13. Define maintainability. How are reliability and maintainability related?
5-14. Explain how simplification and standardization can improve designs.
5-15. How does modular design differ from standardization?

5-16. What types of decisions are involved in process planning?
5-17. How does the role of the design engineer change under concurrent design?
5-18. In what ways should design quality be measured?
5-19. What does design for manufacture entail? List several techniques that can facilitate the DFM process.
5-20. How does design for assembly (DFA) differ from design for manufacture (DFM)? What does design for environment (DFE) involve?
5-21. Describe the objectives of failure mode and effects analysis, fault tree analysis, and value analysis.
5-22. Prepare a fault tree analysis for a project, computer assignment, or writing assignment you have recently completed.
5-23. How can design teams improve the quality of design?
5-24. Discuss the concept of concurrent design. What are the advantages of this approach?
5-25. What is the purpose of quality classifications? Describe the three categories.
5-26. Compose a structured survey that will test ten characteristics of physician's services. Give the survey to your classmates, co-workers, or friends. Classify the quality characteristics and comment on the results.
5-27. What is the purpose of quality function deployment (QFD)? How does it accomplish that purpose?
5-28. Create a house of quality for a word-processing software. Include the following customer attribute bundles: ease of use, cost, desired capabilities, and software interface. The customer requirements should be a "wish list" stated in nontechnical terms.
5-29. Students often complain that the requirements of assignments or projects are unclear. From the student's perspective, whoever can guess what the professor wants wins the highest grade. Thus, grades appear to be assigned somewhat arbitrarily. If you have ever felt that way, here is your chance to clarify that next project or assignment.

    Construct a house of quality for a paper or project. View the professor as the customer. For the perceptual map, have your professor compare one of your papers with typical A, B, or C papers. When you have completed the exercise, give your opinion on the usefulness of QFD for this application.
5-30. Create a QFD example from your own experience. Describe the product or service to be designed and then complete a house of quality using representative data. Explain the entries in the house and how target values were reached. Also, describe how other houses might flow from the initial house you built. Finally, relate how QFD improves the design process for the example you chose.
5-31. Discuss the concept of robust design. What role does design of experiments play in achieving robust design?
5-32. Explain Taguchi's quality loss function in your own words. (An example might help.)
5-33. How has technology changed the manner in which products are designed?
5-34. What types of analyses can be performed with CAE?
5-35. Discuss the benefits of CAD.
5-36. List eight characteristics of services and explain how each characteristic impacts the design process.
5-37. How do product and service designs differ?
5-38. Describe the service package for a. a bank, b. an airline, and c. a lawn service.
5-39. Generate as many ideas as you can for additional services or improvements in service delivery for a. automated banking, b. higher education, and c. healthcare.

PROBLEMS

5-1. Use the following instructions to construct and test a prototype paper airplane. Are the instructions clear? How would you improve the design of the airplane or the manner in which the design is communicated?

- Begin with an $8^1/_2$-inch by 11-inch sheet of paper.
- Fold the paper together lengthwise to make a center line.
- Open the paper and fold the top corners to the center line.
- Fold the two top sides to the center line.
- Fold the airplane in half.
- Fold back the wings to meet the center line
- Hold the plane by the center line and let it fly.

5-1. See Solutions Manual.

5-2. An alternate airplane design is given here. Follow the assembly instructions and test the airplane. Are the instructions clear? Compare the performance of this airplane design with the one described in problem 5-1. Which plane was easier to construct? How would you improve the design of this plane or the manner in which the design is communicated?

- Begin with an $8^1/_2$-inch by 11-inch sheet of paper.
- Fold it lengthwise in alternating directions. The folds should be about 1 inch wide.
- Hold the top of the folded paper in one hand and fan out the back portion with the other hand.
- Make a small fold in the nose of the plane to hold it together, and let it fly.

5-2. See Solutions Manual.

5-3. You are a member of a group of engineers, production managers, financial analysts and marketing representatives. Your company has decided to produce a new product, the revolutionary triangular porthole, and each of you has been chosen to contribute your special knowledge and skills toward the product's design. You are given the following information about the new product:

- A triangular porthole consists of three sides with an empty area in the middle.
- The porthole must be able to stand on each side.
- The triangle formed must be isosceles. The sides should be straight and taut.
- The area in the middle should be large enough to enable an average size hand to pass through.
- Each side must be composed of the same material, with top sides facing out.

You have access to the following materials: index cards, construction paper, stapler with staples, tape, paper clips, ruler, and scissors.

The results of your deliberations should include a list of materials to be used, a diagram of the product at different stages of assembly (with dimensions and other specifications marked), and a sample triangular porthole. Your design must take into account how the product will look, how it will perform, and how it will be produced. Remember to consider such factors as market appeal, quality level, cost, reliability, maintainability, simplification, and standardization.

5-3. See Solutions Manual.

5-4. A broadcasting station has five major subsystems that must all be operational before a show can go on the air. If each subsystem has the same reliability, what reliability would be required to be 95 percent certain of broadcast success? 98 percent certain? 99 percent certain?

5-4. a. 0.990
b. 0.996
c. 0.998

5-5. 0.998

5-5. Competition for a new generation of computers is so intense that MicroTech has funded three separate design teams to create the new systems. Due to varying capabilities of the team members, it is estimated that team A has a 95 percent probability of coming up with an acceptable design before the competition, team B has an 85 percent chance, and team C has a 75 percent chance. What is the probability that MicroTech will beat the competition with its new computers?

5-6. a. Vendor 2
b. Yes

5-6. MagTech assembles tape players from four major components arranged as follows:

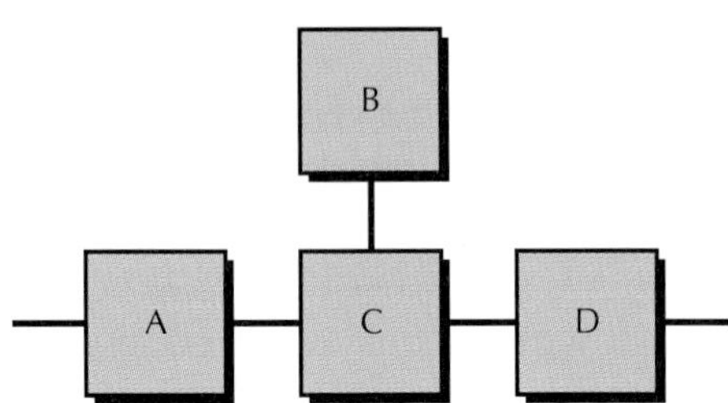

The components can be purchased from three different vendors, who have supplied the following reliability data:

	VENDOR		
Component	*1*	*2*	*3*
A	0.94	0.95	0.92
B	0.86	0.80	0.90
C	0.90	0.93	0.95
D	0.93	0.95	0.95

a. If MagTech has decided to use only one vendor to supply all four components, which vendor should be selected?
b. Would your decision change if all the components were assembled in series?

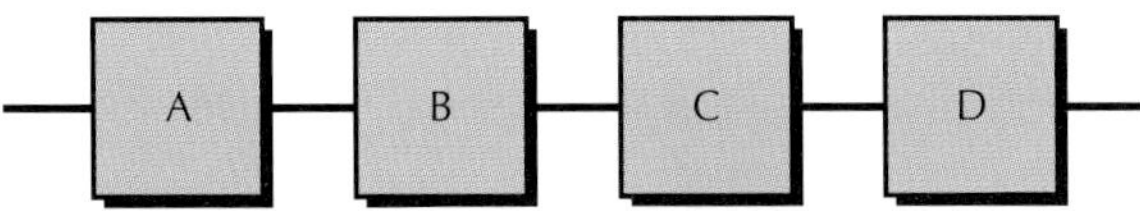

5-7. a. 74%
b. Every 4 months

5-7. Joe Powers is in charge of safety and security for a twelve-story office building. One of his most time-consuming functions involves replacing batteries in the six smoke detectors on each floor. Joe has learned that the average life of an alkaline battery is 3.33 years and that the warranty for batteries is one year beyond the last-sale date printed on the battery package. Joe is wondering if he needs to replace the batteries once a year or every 6 months (his current policy.)

a. What is the probability that a battery will last for a year before it needs to be replaced?
b. If management is comfortable with a smoke alarm reliability of 90 percent, how often should Joe replace the batteries?

5-8. a. No
b. Add redundancy.

5-8. Glen Evans is an emergency medical technician for a local rescue team and is routinely called upon to render emergency care to citizens facing crisis situations. Although Glen has received extensive training, he also relies heavily on his equipment for support. During a normal call, Glen uses five essential pieces of equipment, whose individual reliabilities are 0.98, 0.975, 0.99, 0.96, and 0.995, respectively.

a. Glen claims his equipment has a maximum probability of failure of 4 percent. Is he correct?
b. What can be done to increase the reliability of Glen's equipment to 96 percent?

5-9. Lisa Garrett has been a shift scheduler at a local fast-food chain for the past three years. Although the restaurant's patronage is relatively stable, employee attendance is not. For the most part, the restaurant employs students from a nearby high school. Experience has taught Lisa that both the age of the employee and the season of the year affect the reliability of employee attendance. During the school year, seniors are the most responsible and report to work 97 percent of the time, whereas juniors report only 95 percent of the time, and sophomores report 90 percent of the time. After graduation, however, students' thoughts turn to fun and freedom, and everyone's attendance drops to 90 percent.

5-9. a. 20%; 34%
b. 97%; 98%

a. If a shift consists of two seniors, one junior and one sophomore, what is the probability that Lisa will have to operate without a full shift during the school year? During the summer months?
b. Suppose, during the summer months, Lisa can find a replacement worker 95 percent of the time. However, during the school years she is successful only 87 percent of the time. How does the employee reliability change during the summer months? During the school year?

5-10. Carlotta Sanchez, a twenty-four-year-old college graduate, recently finished SCUBA training and obtained her diving certification. She has already purchased a new mask for her first SCUBA vacation. The mask has a three-year life expectancy and an 18-month warranty. Carlotta plans to continue scuba diving as a hobby until she is thirty years old.

5-10. a. 61%
b. 37%
c. 86%

a. What is the likelihood that the mask will outlast the warranty period?
b. What is the probability that the mask will last beyond the three-year life expectancy?
c. What is the likelihood that Carlotta's mask will fail before she gives up scuba diving?

5-11. Ben and Tina are excited about buying their first house. After months of searching, they have finally settled on a three-bedroom rambler in a quiet neighborhood. Tina loves the practical floor plan and the wooded lot. Ben is looking forward to tinkering at the built-in workbench, but he is concerned about the air conditioner. The engineer who examined the house estimated that the unit was five years old but in good condition. Since the average life expectancy of an air conditioner is only ten years, Ben is concerned that it will need to be replaced soon. Purchasing the house will leave Ben and Tina with a limited cash flow for the next year, and predictions suggest a hot summer ahead.

★ 5-11. a. 90%
b. 39%

a. What is the probability that the unit will last another year?
b. What is the probability that the unit will fail within the next five years?

5-12. Cellular Two, a manufacturer of cellular telephones, is trying to determine a reasonable length of time to offer free service for its new X28 portable model. The expected life of the X28 is approximately five years.

5-12. a. 18%
b. 6 mo

a. What is the probability that the X28 will fail within a one-year free service period?
b. If the company is willing to accept a 10 percent failure rate during the free service period, how long should the free service period be?

5-13. a. 10%, 16%, 18%
b. 63%
c. 50%, 69%, 75%
d. 26%

★ 5-13. Travis is an eleven-year-old video game expert who cannot survive without at least one video game system operational at all times. He received a regular system at the age of five, a hand-held model at eight, and a super system when he was ten years old. The systems have expected lives of ten years, six years, and five years, respectively.

a. What is the probability that any given system will fail this year?
b. What is the probability that Travis will be able to play all three video systems the entire year?
c. What is the probability that any given system will fail before Travis enters college (at age eighteen)?
d. What is the probability that all the systems will fail before Travis enters college?

5-14. a. 18%
b. 6 mo
c. 2.5 y

5-14. One of the video stores that Travis (Problem 5-13) frequents offers a one-year warranty on video games. If the game fails within a year, the store will replace the game at no charge.

a. Assuming a five-year average life, what is the probability that a game will fail during the warranty period?
b. If the video store can afford only a 10 percent probability of failure, how should the warranty period be set?
c. If the video store can afford a 40 percent probability of failure, how should the warranty period be set?

5-15. See Solutions Manual.

5-15. A recent survey of college students yielded the following reasons for frequenting local nightspots:

- Meet current friends and hang out with your crowd
- Meet new people
- Music format played
- Drink prices
- "Unwind" and drink
- Dance
- Promotions/giveaways/contests
- Something to do when nothing else is happening

Use this information and your own insight to build a house of quality for a nightspot in your area.

5-16. a. 0.55; 0.65
b. A

5-16. A soft-drink bottling company in Pennsylvania is requesting bids from vendors to supply metal twist-off caps. Two manufacturers have expressed interest in the contract. Since both are reputable, the soft-drink company solicited a sample of 200 caps from each manufacturer to test for quality. The company supplying the glass bottles targets the size of the bottleneck at $1 \pm \frac{1}{8}$ inch. The quality adjustment cost is \$0.01 per cap. The results of the quality sample are as follows.

Cap Size	*Manufacturer A*	*Manufacturer B*
$\frac{7}{8}$	15	20
$\frac{15}{16}$	47	54
1	68	67
$1\frac{1}{16}$	56	36
$1\frac{1}{8}$	14	23

a. What is the quality loss for each manufacturer?
b. Which manufacturer should receive the contract?

5-17. The PlayBetter Golf Company has experienced a steady decline in sales of golf bags over the past five years. The basic golf bag design has not changed over that time period, and PlayBetter's CEO, Jack Palmer, has decided that the time has come for a customer-focused overhaul of the product. Jack read about a new design methodology called QFD in one of his professional magazines (it was used to design golf balls), and he commissioned a customer survey to provide data for the design process. The design team's partially completed house of quality is given below. Complete the house and write a brief report to Mr. Palmer recommending revisions to the current golf bag design and explaining how those recommendations were determined.

5-17. See Solutions Manual.

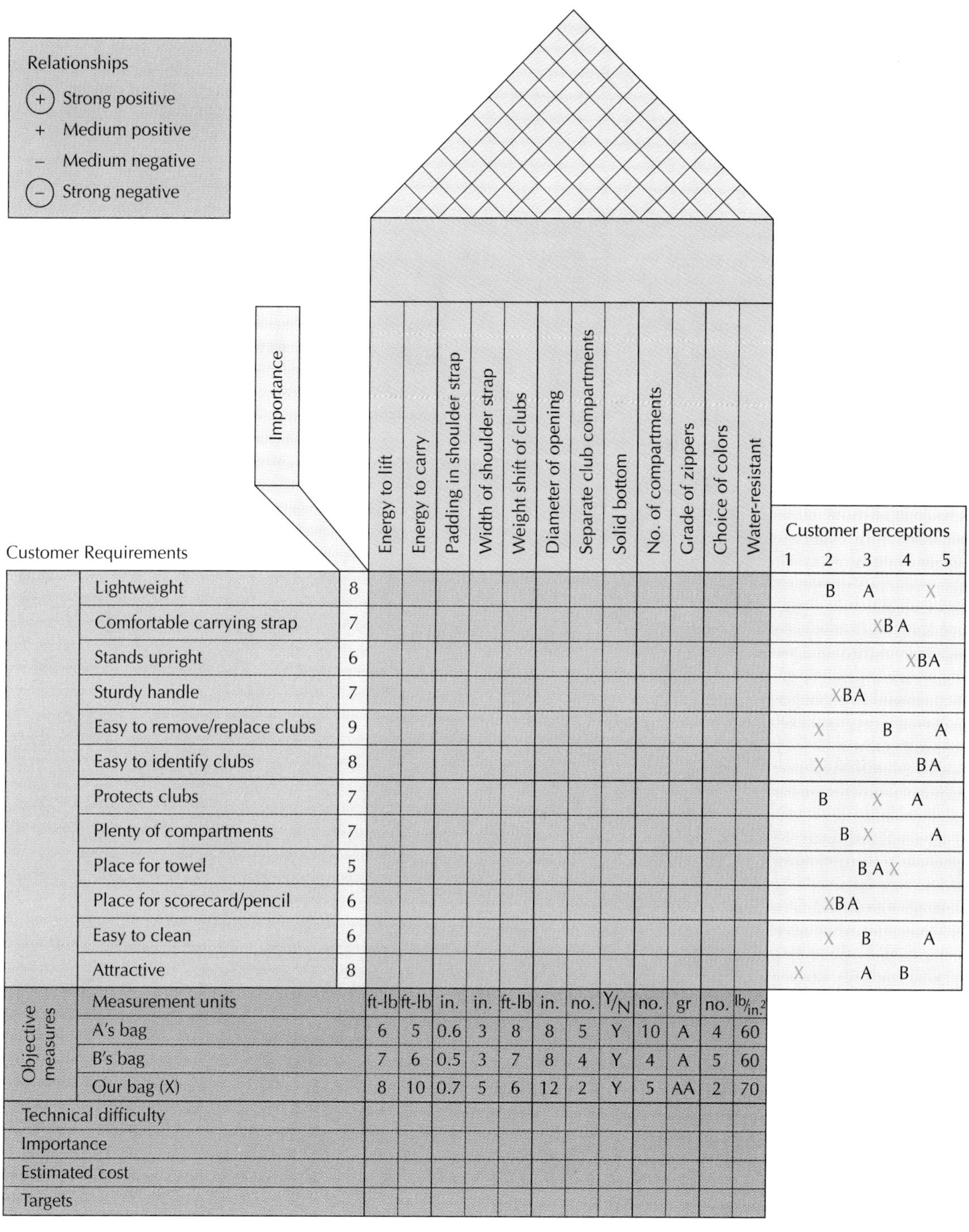

Customer Requirements	Importance	Customer Perceptions (1 2 3 4 5)
Lightweight	8	B A X
Comfortable carrying strap	7	XB A
Stands upright	6	XBA
Sturdy handle	7	XBA
Easy to remove/replace clubs	9	X B A
Easy to identify clubs	8	X BA
Protects clubs	7	B X A
Plenty of compartments	7	B X A
Place for towel	5	B A X
Place for scorecard/pencil	6	XBA
Easy to clean	6	X B A
Attractive	8	X A B

	Energy to lift	Energy to carry	Padding in shoulder strap	Width of shoulder strap	Weight shift of clubs	Diameter of opening	Separate club compartments	Solid bottom	No. of compartments	Grade of zippers	Choice of colors	Water-resistant
Measurement units	ft-lb	ft-lb	in.	in.	ft-lb	in.	no.	Y/N	no.	gr	no.	lb/in.²
A's bag	6	5	0.6	3	8	8	5	Y	10	A	4	60
B's bag	7	6	0.5	3	7	8	4	Y	4	A	5	60
Our bag (X)	8	10	0.7	5	6	12	2	Y	5	AA	2	70
Technical difficulty												
Importance												
Estimated cost												
Targets												

5-18. See Solutions Manual.

5-18. Lean and Mean (L&M), a weight-reduction company, is considering entering the frozen-dinner market with a line of pricey, nutritious, low-calorie frozen dinners. Help Lean and Mean find its competitive niche by completing the following house of quality. Choose three similar products currently on the market and assume that the most expensive product will most closely resemble L&M's new offering. What product design characteristics would you recommend for L&M? Why?

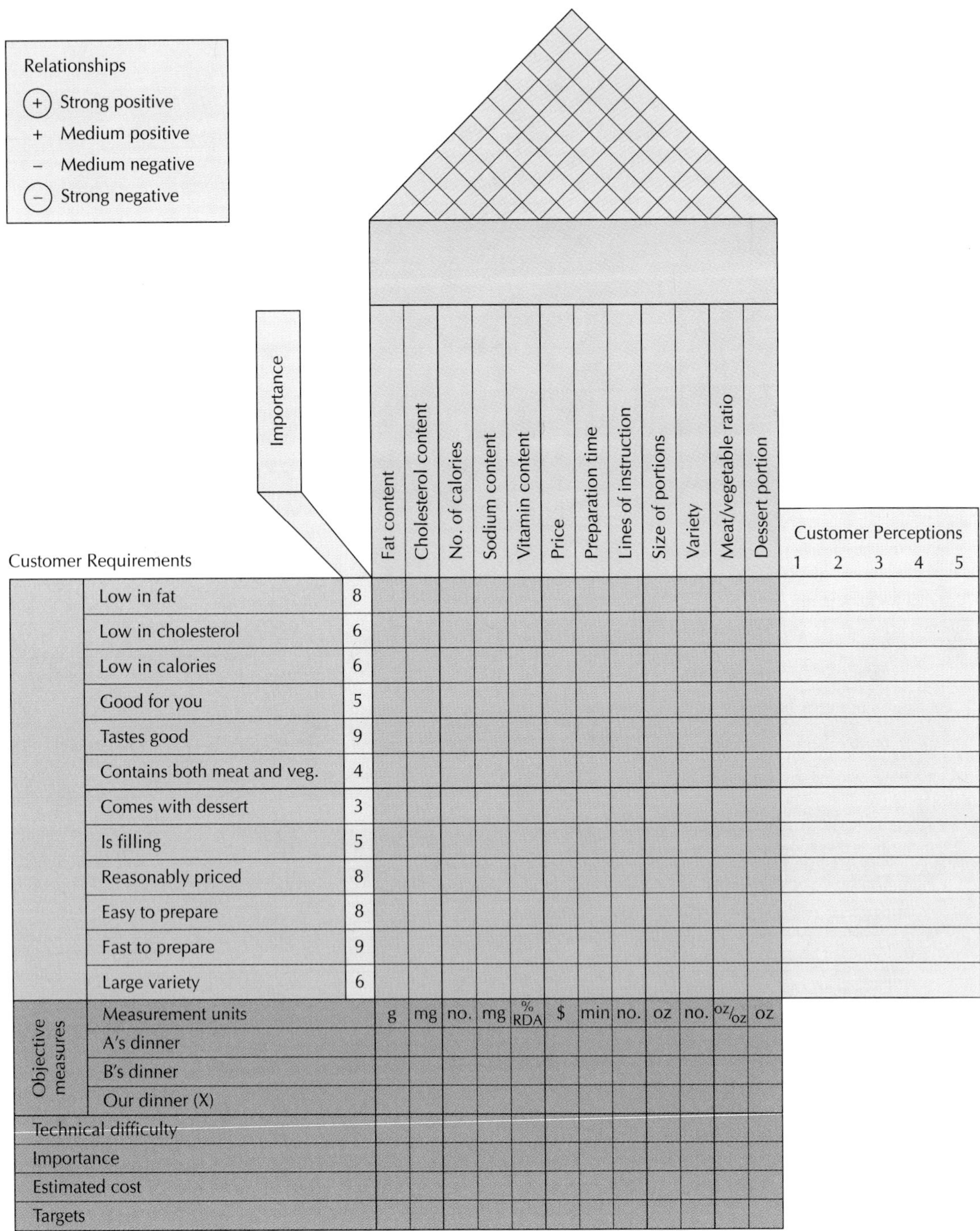

5-19. Home Cooking is a small country restaurant that has a reputation for serving inexpensive, hearty meals. At the present time, customers can select one meat and two vegetables from the following lists: ★ 5-19. a. 27 wks b. See Solutions Manual. c. 9 wks d. See Solutions Manual.

Meat	*Vegetable 1*	*Vegetable 2*
Meat loaf	Mashed potatoes	Green beans
Fried chicken	Fried apples	Black eyed peas
Pork chops	Macaroni and cheese	Salad

In order to handle the large crowds at lunchtime, conserve food, and save money, the restaurant wants to offer a blue plate special, for which the menu options (i.e., one meat and two vegetables) would be preselected by the cooking staff. However, in the process, it doesn't want to lose customers by offering unpopular combinations of meat and vegetables or by limiting variety. The cook suggested that she be allowed to test out customer preferences with trial blue plate specials offered once a week for a limited period of time.

a. If the cook tests all possible combinations of meats and vegetables, how long will it take to complete the experiment?
b. If the cook uses the one-factor-at-a-time method, how long will the experiment take? Give an example of this type of experimental design.
c. If the cook uses Taguchi's method and tests every factor level with every other factor level once, how long will the experiment take?
d. Based on your own cullinary preferences, design an experiment by Taguchi's method. Compare your design with the designs of other's in the class.

5-20. Jane Weathers, the Graduate Studies Program Director at Quality University, is concerned about the low grades (and student complaints) among first-year students in the quantitative methods class. She has surmised that the following factors have a bearing on student performance: 5-20. See Solutions Manual.

a. Undergraduate major (engineering, business, or other)
b. Instructor (Professor A, B, or C)
c. Semester (fall, spring, or summer)

Design an experiment for Dr. Weathers that would compare student performance at every factor level with every other factor level once.

5-21. In order better to understand student concern over the QM class discussed in Problem 5-20, Dr. Weathers talked at length with several students and gathered the following information: 5-21. \$0, \$500, \$2,000, \$4,500

- Although an A is definitely preferred, most students do not get upset until a grade of C is given.
- Although A, B, C, and D are considered passing grades, most employers will not reimburse their employees for courses in which they received a C or below.
- The cost of a semester course is \$500.

Construct a quality loss function for student performance. What is the quality loss for a grade of A, B, C, or D? (*Hint:* Consider B to be one grade level different from A, C to be two grade levels different, etc.)

See Solutions Manual.

CASE PROBLEM

In Search of Perfectly Popped Popcorn

Jenny Moseley knew before she opened the bag that the popcorn was burned again—that familiar odor filled the air. "You should have followed the instructions," her helpful boyfriend, Bob Townsend, told her.

"A lot of good these instructions do," replied Jenny. "Listen to this."

> Unfold popcorn bag and place in center of microwave. Set power on HIGH and timer to 4 minutes. Do not leave microwave unattended as popping time may vary between 2 minutes and 4 minutes, depending on your microwave. LISTEN CAREFULLY. Stop microwave when rapid popping slows to 2 to 3 seconds between pops. Warning: Popcorn will scorch when overcooked."

"Now who's going to count the seconds between pops? And what do they mean by "rapid popping slowing"? I want to turn my microwave on and pull out a bag of perfectly popped popcorn when the buzzer sounds, just like I do with everything else I cook."

"Come on, Jenny. Haven't you cooked enough popcorn to know how to set your own microwave?" chided her boyfriend.

"You just don't get it . . . you see, buttered popcorn seems to take more time than regular popcorn, and regular popcorn cooks differently than this bargain stuff you bought from the Boy Scouts," Jenny replied. "And besides, I seem to be the one who cooks the popcorn at your apartment, too, and at work. The microwave at work is old and slow, the one my Mom bought me is way too big and very powerful, and we all know how cheap your microwave is."

"Now wait a minute, you make it sound like it's all my fault. Let's calm down and approach this thing scientifically," retorted Bob. "We have three different microwaves and three types of popcorn. If we conduct an experiment varying popping time by 1 minute from 2 minutes to 4 minutes for every combination of oven and type of popcorn, we could find out how to set each oven and quit arguing."

"So how long would this take and how many bags would we have to pop? I'm short on money, you know."

"Let's see . . . 3 ovens x 3 types of popcorn x 3 time settings is 27 bags of popcorn. At 50¢ a bag and two bags a night, we'd spend $13.50 and about 2 more weeks together."

"Well, if it will keep us together . . . but you conduct the experiment. I'll rent the movies."

"Deal."

Is Jenny being reasonable to expect clearer popping instructions? What Taguchi concept does this popcorn problem illustrate? Design an experiment using Taguchi's method to test every factor level with every other factor level once. How many bags will Jenny and Bob have to pop with your design? What criteria would you use to evaluate the popped popcorn? If you have the facilities, actually perform the experiment and report on your results.

See Solutions Manual.

CASE PROBLEM

Sure, the Highway May Be Intelligent, But What Can It Do for ME?

Amy Russell was still arranging her overheads as the planning commission filed into the room. She hated project-review time, but at least it happened only once a year. After everyone was seated and niceties had been exchanged, she began her presentation in a clear, strong voice.

"Let me begin by summarizing the significance and focus of the intelligent highway project. Highways are one of America's greatest assets. They give us the freedom to live, work, and play as we choose. However, as you know, they also present problems in the form of traffic congestion, safety, and air quality. The old "let's build more roads" philosophy is not the answer to these problems given current budget constraints, land and fuel scarcities, and environmental restrictions. Fortunately, advancements in computer capabilities and accessibility, coupled with the information explosion, have provided us with new avenues for applying advanced technology to highways and transportation in general. The intelligent highway project is divided into five technology groups: 1. advanced traffic only management systems (ATMS), 2. advanced traveler information systems (ATIS), 3. advanced public transportation systems (APTS), 4. commercial vehicle operations (CVO), and 5. advanced vehicle control systems (AVCS). These technology groups provide the . . . "

"Now, hold on Amy," interrupted one of her listeners. "I know these acronyms and technology wonders make a lot of sense to you—after all, you're an engineer. But what do they mean to us as drivers on the highway, I mean to us as customers?"

"That's an interesting question, Earl," countered Amy. Thankful for a recent seminar on customer focus, she continued, "What uses would you and the other members of the commission make of an intelligent highway?" She looked out at blank stares.

"Let me put it another way," Amy added, "what *information* would help you in your highway travels and what delays do you experience in driving that you would like to eliminate?"

"Well, I'd like to know the best route to take on my vacation," spoke up Eliza Boone.

"As a commuter, I'd like information on traffic conditions and weather conditions up ahead and some guidance on what alternate route I could take to avoid delays," Hubert Banks commented.

"I'm a salesperson, so I travel alot. When I'm sent to a new city on business, I'd like to know how to get around," volunteered Felipe Guzman.

Not to be outdone, Stuart Schwartz added, "I'm a professional truck driver, and I hate to stop at those highway checkpoints. I figure it costs me about $1000 for every 15 minutes I wait, and I can't see any use for it. It's just harassment. Can anything be done about that?"

"This might sound picky," Mary Higgins thought aloud, "but I can't understand what takes so long at those tollbooths downtown. The congestion adds 30 minutes to my drive to work. Isn't there a better way to assess drivers than by physically taking their coins?"

After recording the group's comments on a spare transparency, Amy faced the group. "That's quite a list there. Let me convert what you've said into what we call *user services.* Eliza, I'd call your request pretrip planning. Hubert and Felipe, you need *route guidance.*"

"If you say so, Amy," laughed Hubert.

"Stuart, we can help you out with *commercial vehicle preclearance,* and Mary, what you'd like is an *electronic payment system.* I also see four categories of customers here," Amy continued somewhat excited by her discovery, "tourists, commuters, business travelers, and professional travelers."

"Don't forget a miscellaneous group," Earl added.

"Okay Earl, as the instigator of all this, you can represent the miscellaneous traveler," Amy sighed.

"That's the spirit," Earl smiled. "Now what do we do?"

"Well, if we have enough time, let me describe in very nontechnical terms some alternate means of delivering the available technologies and get you to help me match up needs with appropriately designed services," replied Amy. "I see two basic categories of service delivery: automated information with or without selection capability and personalized information delivered by service providers. Does that make sense?" queried Amy.

The group nodded and Earl added, "Let's get to work."

Amy wondered what her boss was going to think about her spontaneous session with the commission.

How does the commission's approach to designing intelligent highways differ from Amy's approach? Do you think Amy will be able to bring back useful information to her boss?

For each of the five customer types identified, make a more complete list of their information needs. (This will serve as the basis for performance specifications for the intelligent highway service.) Then, for each type of service delivery, suggest alternate designs that would appropriately meet the performance specifications. (These are the start of design specifications for the intelligent highway service.)

REFERENCES

Abernathy, W., *The Productivity Dilemma: Roadblock to Innovation in the Auto Industry,* Baltimore: Johns Hopkins University Press, 1978.

Bedworth, D., M. Henderson, and P. Wolfe, *Computer-Integrated Design and Manufacturing,* New York: McGraw-Hill, 1991.

Berry, L., A. Parasuraman, and V. Zeithaml, "The Service Quality Puzzle," *Business Horizons,* (September–October 1988): 35-43.

Blackburn, J., (ed.), *Time-Based Competition: The Next Battleground,* Homewood, Ill.: Irwin, 1991.

Brown, J. S., "Research That Reinvents the Corporation," *Harvard Business Review* (January/February 1991): 102–111.

Dumaine, B., "Closing the Innovation Gap," *Fortune* (December 2, 1991): 56–62.

Ealey, L., *Quality by Design: Taguchi Methods and U.S. Industry,* Dearborn, Mich.: ASI Press, 1988.

Garvin, D., *Managing Quality,* New York: Macmillan, 1988.

Garwood, D., and M. Bane, *Shifting Paradigms: Reshaping the Future of Industry,* Marietta, Ga.: Dogwood Publishing Co., 1990.

Hauser J. R., and D. Clausing, "The House of Quality," *Harvard Business Review,* (May–June 1988): 63–73.

Heskett, J. L., W. E. Sasser, and C. Hart, *Service Breakthroughs: Changing the Rules of the Game,* New York: Macmillan, 1990.

Jacobson, G., and J. Hillkirk, *Xerox: American Samurai,* New York: Macmillan, 1986, 178–79.

Kanter, R. M., *When Elephants Learn to Dance,* New York: Simon and Schuster, 1989.

King, B., *Better Designs in Half the Time,* Methuen, Mass.: GOAL/QPC, 1989.

Nevens, J., D. Whitney, T. DeFazio, A. Edsall, R. Gustavson, R. Metzinger, and W. Dvorak, *Concurrent Design of Products and Processes: A Strategy for the Next Generation in Manufacturing,* New York: McGraw-Hill, 1989.

Port, O. "Back to the Basics," *Business Week Special Report on Innovation in America,* (June 16, 1989): 15.

Profile 2000, Society of Manufacturing Engineers, Dearborn, Michigan, 1988.

Stoll, H., "Design for Manufacture," *Manufacturing Engineering,* (January 1988): 67–73.

Sullivan, L. P. "Quality Function Deployment," *Quality Progress* 19, no. 6 (1986): 39.

Sprow, E., "Chrysler's Concurrent Engineering Challenge," *Manufacturing Engineering* (April 1992): 35–42.

Taguchi, G., and D. Clausing, "Robust Quality," *Harvard Business Review* (January–February 1990): 65–75.

Walton, M., *The Deming Management Method,* New York: Putnam Publisher, 1986.

Whitney, D., "Manufacturing By Design," *Harvard Business Review,* (July–August 1988): 83–91.

Womack, J. P., D. T. Jones, and D. Roos, *The Machine that Changed The World,* New York: Macmillan, 1990, 118–19.

6 PROCESS PLANNING AND TECHNOLOGY DECISIONS

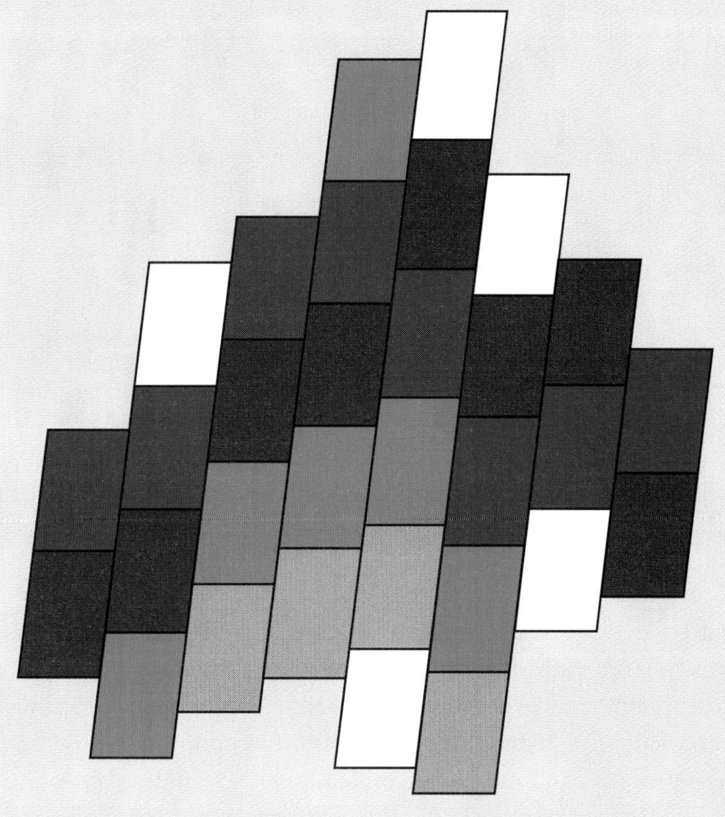

CHAPTER OUTLINE

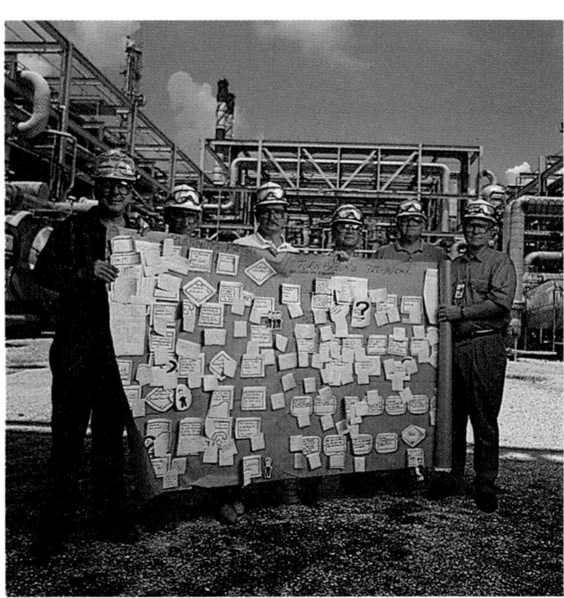

These workers at a Union Carbide Chemical plant are displaying a flowchart they developed to analyze an existing process. The chart is not neat and tidy, but it does offer some obvious candidates for improvement. U.S. workers and managers in both industry and government are examining their processes in an attempt to reengineer work for high quality, less waste, and speedier operation. This chapter begins with a description of an assembly process that was simplified through process analysis.

ASSEMBLING LASER PRINTERS IS A SNAP

Lexmark International develops, manufactures, and markets IBM printers, typewriters, and keyboards. The design of their newest laser printer mirrors the landmark design of IBM's "snap-together" Proprinter. The plastic cover set of the laser printer, for example, contains only one screw, compared with more than 40 screws in a competitor's product. All together, the laser printer has about half the number of parts of similar products and can be assembled in 30 percent less time. The assembly is easier, too. It is so easy, in fact, that the processes used to assemble the printers have been brought together on one assembly line.

Lexmark used to maintain five separate subassembly areas in different buildings and then move the subassemblies by forklift to the final assembly line. Now both subassembly and assembly is performed on one J-shaped, 30-station assembly line. The integrated workflow arrangement has reduced in-process time by 86%. The line is staffed with 50 workers, assembly is manual rather than automated, and each work station is responsible for up to 10 operations. Workers receive production instructions from a LAN (local area network) located on the factory floor. The LAN also has a notepad, so that information can more easily be passed from worker to supervisor or shift to shift. Repair personnel, technicians, and engineers have access to real-time data on production and quality measurements from the LAN. These measurements go into a database that, among other things, feeds the "line-down" process. If the same problem occurs three times in a shift, the line is automatically shut down until the problem is solved.[1]

[1]Huber, Daniel, "Laser Printer Assembly is a Snap at Lexmark International," *Industrial Engineering* (August 1993): 37–38.

Quality is the result of both a well-designed *product* and a well-designed *process*. This chapter discusses two areas of decision making that form the basis for process design, planning the production process and making wise technology choices. In basic terms, **process planning** determines *how* a product is to be produced. It converts designs into workable instructions for manufacture, decides which components will be made in-house and which will be purchased from a supplier, selects processes and specific equipment (purchasing new equipment, if necessary), and develops and documents the specifications for manufacture. These decisions are necessary whether or not they are made *concurrently* with product design (as suggested in the previous chapter) or after product design has been completed. Process planning is discussed in the first half of this chapter.

Process planning converts designs into workable instructions for manufacture.

Technology decisions are presented separately so that we can describe in more detail the levels of technology available to operations managers and the implications of technology choice. The technology half of the chapter begins with a discussion of management's aversion to technology and then describes some basic manufacturing processes and how they might be automated. The chapter continues with automation from the perspective of computer-integrated manufacturing (CIM), specifically examining the role of CAD/CAM, robotics, and flexible manufacturing systems in CIM. It ends with a discussion of technology adoption.

PROCESS PLANNING

Figure 6.1 outlines the elements involved in process planning: product analysis, make-or-buy decisions, process and equipment selection, and the development of process plans. These elements are discussed in the sections that follow.

Product Analysis

The first stage of process planning involves analyzing product design specifications and creating documents (diagrams, charts, etc.) to communicate how the product is to be manufactured. We have chosen three such documents to examine: 1. the assembly chart, 2. the operations process chart, and 3. the process flowchart.

Process planning documents include assembly charts, operations process charts, and process flowcharts.

As you may recall, product design provides either preliminary specifications (in the case of concurrent design) or detailed drawings and specifications of what to make. The drawings, generated manually in the form of a blueprint or electronically on a CAD system, show the entire product as well as the parts that make up the product. A **bill of material (BOM)** may also be included. The bill of material lists the materials and components that go into a product, provides a brief description, and specifies the quantity required for assembly. The drawings and BOM are usually constructed from the design engineer's point of view and may need to be redone for use in manufacturing. For example, design engineers may not differentiate between a raw casting and a machined casting or between an unpainted assembly and a finished, painted one. Subassemblies are rarely labeled, because what constitutes a subassembly can vary depending on the process chosen for manufacture and the order of assembly.

A **bill of material** lists materials and components that go into a product.

Figure 6.2, on page 279, shows an exploded view of a lawnmower as an example of the type of assembly diagrams typically included in the package of design specifications. If we could animate the diagram, we could imagine the parts coming together to form the final product. However, the picture is not accurate

Transparency 6.1 Process Planning

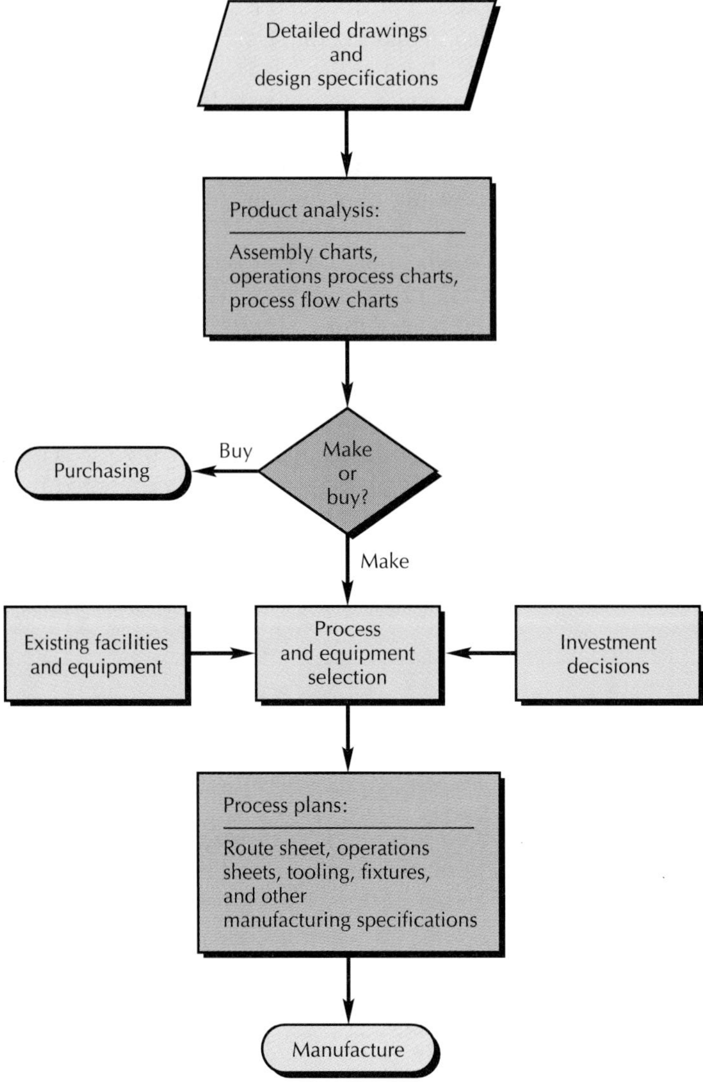

FIGURE 6.1 Process Planning
Reproduced by permission of Sears, Roebuck and Co. Copyright Sears, Roebuck and Co.

Teaching Note 6.1 Some Assembly Required

Assembly charts show how a product is to be assembled.

enough to communicate exactly how to assemble the product. If you have tried to assemble a bicycle from similar instructions, you know what we mean. We need to construct a schematic diagram that shows the relationship of each component part to its parent assembly, the grouping of parts that make up a subassembly, and the overall sequence of assembly. Such a document is called a product structure diagram, or **assembly chart.**

Figure 6.3, on page 280, shows an assembly chart for a Big Mac. Beginning at the top of the chart, the person assembling the burger grabs a bottom bun and then looks for a beef patty to which salt and cheese have been added. The beef-salt-cheese combination is a subassembly, preassembled when the beef was cooked. After the beef subassembly, the lettuce, special sauce, and onions are added to complete the first-layer assembly. A similar procedure is followed for the second-layer assembly. Finally, the first-layer assembly, second-layer assembly, and top bun, are wrapped together for a completed Big Mac.

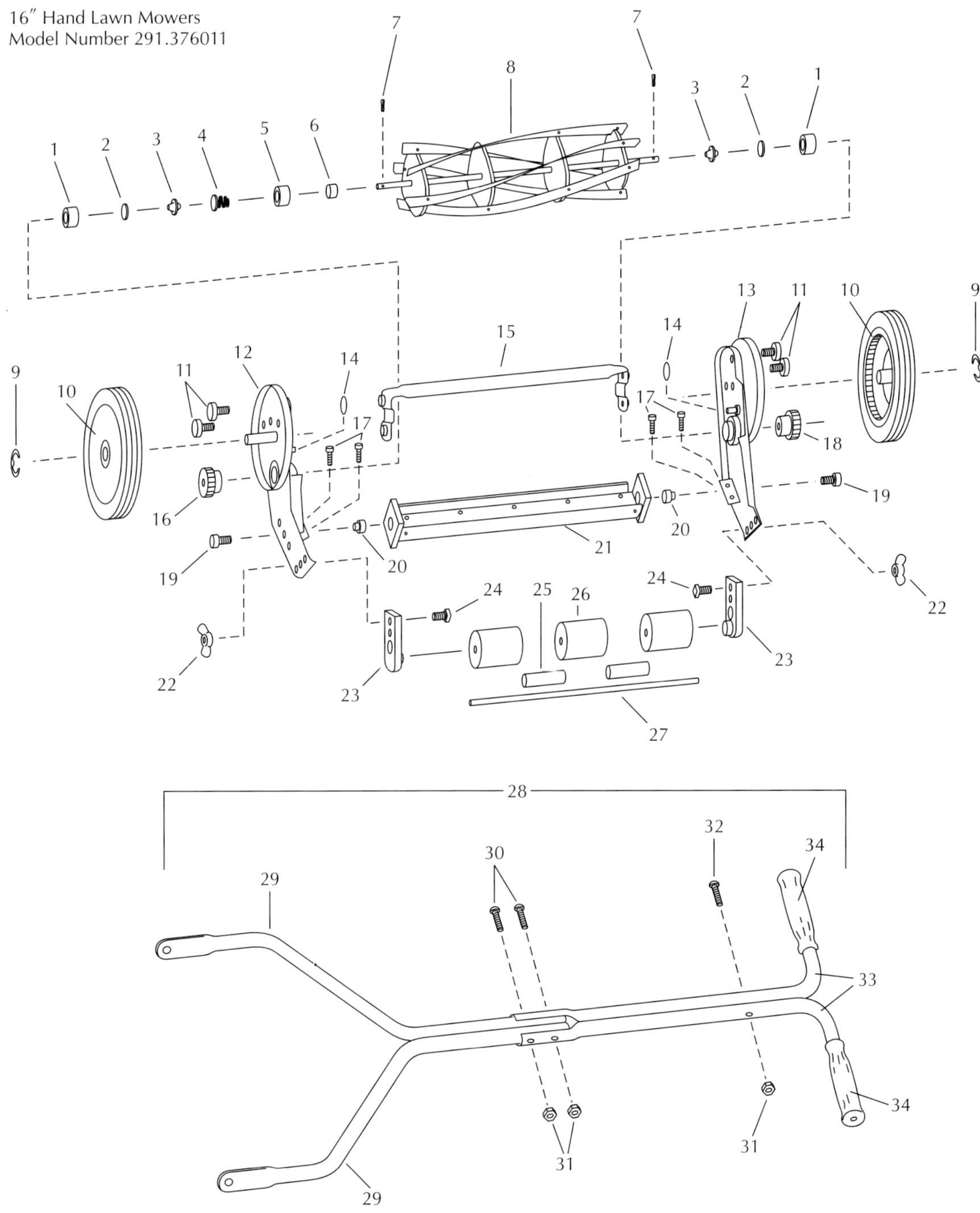

FIGURE 6.2 An Assembly Diagram
Reprinted by permission of Sears, Roebuck and Co. Copyrighted Sears, Roebuck and Co.

Notice that the assembly chart does not include instructions for preparing each item (such as cook beef patty, add two squirts of sauce, wrap burger); rather, its purpose is to show the *assembly flow.* Adding too many details would obscure the flow of the assembly process. Now let's look at an example that illustrates different options for constructing the assembly chart and communicating the assembly information.

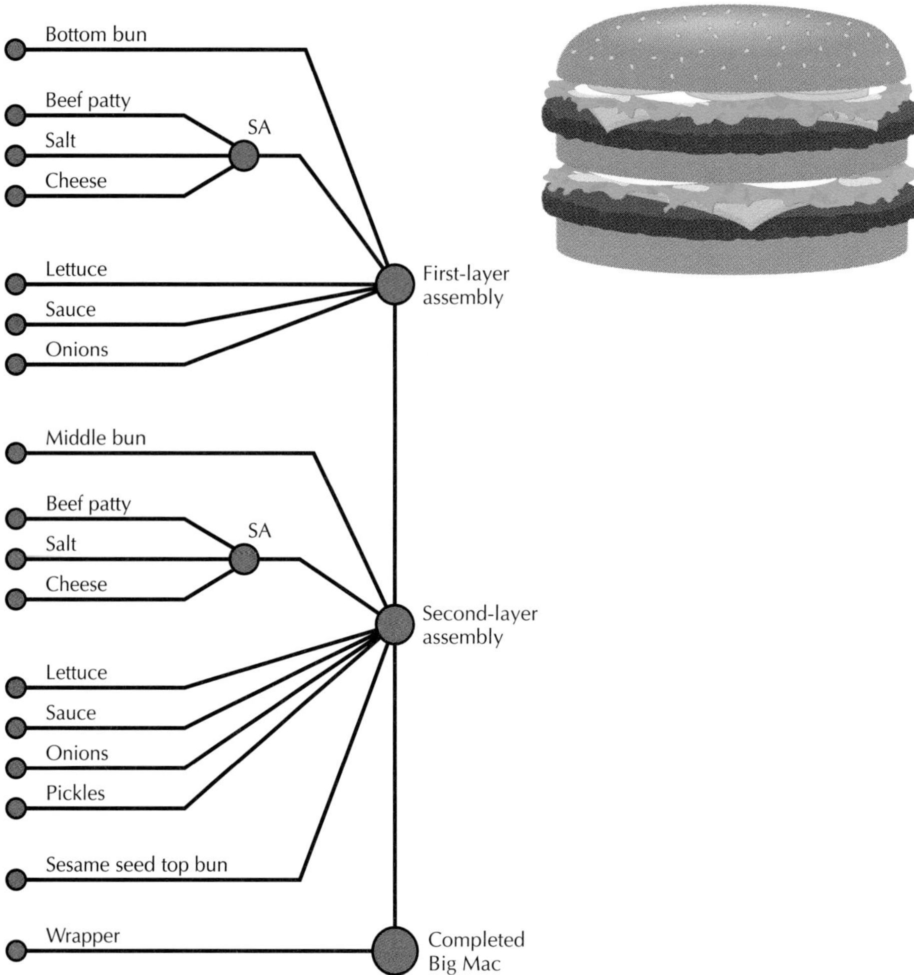

FIGURE 6.3 Assembly Chart for Big Mac

Alternate Example 6.1

EXAMPLE 6.1

Easy Assembly

Problem Statement:

Construct an assembly chart for the tree stand shown here. Assembly instructions are provided to help you understand the sequence of assembly.

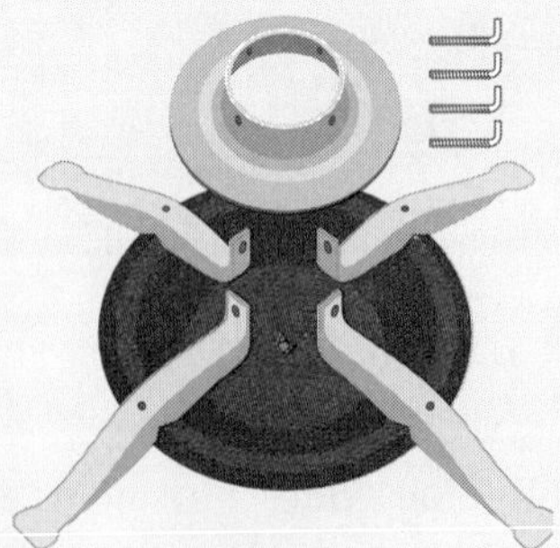

Assembly Instructions

1. Hook all four legs onto the edge of the bowl, where four indentations appear.
2. Place the top ring over the legs. Line up the holes in the ring and the legs, and press the ring down into position.

3. Insert the four screws through the holes in the ring and legs. The assembly should now be complete.

Solution:

First, list the materials used in the tree stand: four legs, one bowl, one ring, and four screws. Next, place them in the assembly chart in the order they are used, and connect them as an assembly.

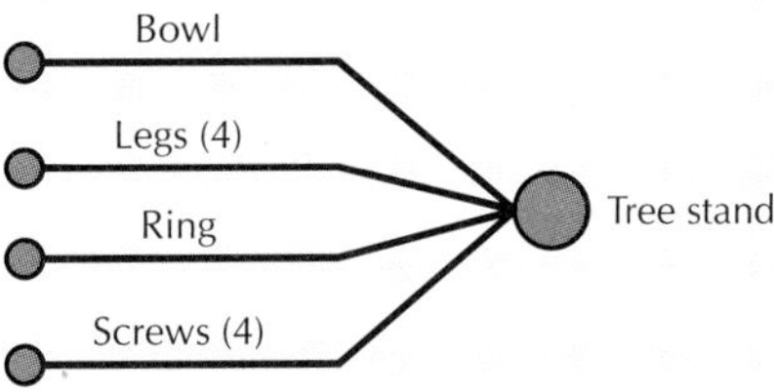

The assembly chart shown here assumes that one person is assembling the tree stand and that all the component parts are available at one workstation. The numbers in parentheses indicate the quantity of each item needed for the assembly.

Now suppose the tree stand will be assembled by three workers on an assembly line. The first worker takes the bowl and snaps the four legs into place. He or she passes the subassembly (we'll call it a base) to the next worker, who places the ring on top, aligns it, and presses it into position. The second worker then passes the assembly to the last worker, who inserts the four screws. The assembly chart for this process is a bit more complicated than the previous chart. Because of the different stages of assembly, we use a different format. In this format, the assembly chart is constructed of linked boxes instead of circles, and the flow is presented vertically instead of horizontally.

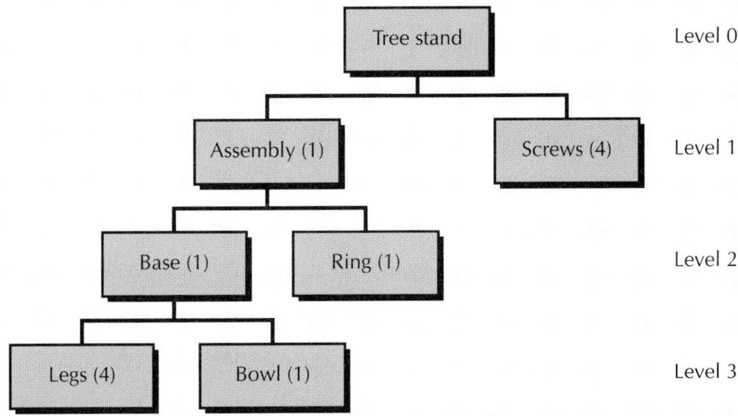

To interpret this assembly chart, begin at the bottom of the diagram and work upward. Notice that there are several levels of assembly and that each assembly is uniquely identified (as base and assembly). The levels of assembly (labeled at the right of the diagram) are assigned from the top of the product structure downward, so that the final product always appears at level 0 and the level numbers increase level by level down the product structure. Items that are assembled together appear on the same level and are connected by a line segment to each other and their parent item.

Labeling the levels of a product structure is helpful in converting the assembly chart into a form that can be stored and retrieved from a computer. A multilevel BOM for the tree stand is as follows:

MULTILEVEL INDENTED BOM			
Level	*Item*	*UM*	*QTY*
0	Tree Stand	Ea	1
–1	Screws	Ea	4
–1	Assembly	Ea	1
=2	Base	Ea	1
≡3	Legs	Ea	4
≡3	Bowl	Ea	1
=2	Ring	Ea	1

The tree stand is listed at the top of the BOM at level 0. The rest of the BOM tells what is needed to make one tree stand. The levels are indented so that it is easy to see which components belong to which assemblies. We interpret the bill of material by examining the items that appear indented beneath each item at the next level down. Thus, the tree stand is assembled from four screws and one assembly (i.e., the level 1 items), the assembly is put together from one base and one ring (the level 2 items), and the base is assembled from four legs and one bowl (the level 3 items). Once the product structure is converted to a computerized bill of material, it can be used to help schedule production and order materials. We discuss bills of material again in the chapter on material requirements planning.

Operations process charts show how a product is to be fabricated.

Other useful documents include the operations process chart and process flowchart. The **operations process chart,** as shown in Figure 6.4, resembles an assembly chart but includes more information. For each item listed in the assembly chart, a series of operations is added that describe how each item is to be fabricated. For example, the table leg in Figure 6.4 requires five operations, 1. sawing to rough length, 2. planing to size, 3. sawing to finished length, 4. measuring dimensions, and 5. sanding. These operations are performed on different machines, probably by different workers. The time required to complete each operation, special tools, fixtures, and gauges needed, and where the operation is to be performed may also be included in the chart. The chart is constructed for the entire product. Purchased items are designated as such. Later, the operations process chart is used as a source of operations requirements for job design.

Process flowcharts highlight nonproductive activities.

Process flowcharts (also known as flow process charts) look at the manufacture of a product or delivery of a service from a broader perspective. The chart

Transparency 6.2 An Operations Process Chart

Part name: Table leg
Part No.: 2410
Usage: Table
Assembly No.: 437

Oper. No.	Description	Dept.	Machine	Time	Tools
10	Saw to rough length	041			
20	Plane to size	043			
30	Saw to finished length	041			
40	Measure dimensions	051			
50	Sand	052			

FIGURE 6.4 Operations Process Chart

uses five standard symbols, shown in Figure 6.5, to describe the processes that are performed. *Operations* are designated by a circle, *inspections,* by a square, *transportation,* by an arrow, *delay,* by a capital D, and *storage,* by an inverted triangle. The details of each process are not necessary for this chart; however, the time required to perform each process and the distance between processes are often included. Notice that the chart incorporates nonproductive activities (inspection, transportation, delay, storage), as well as productive activities (operations). Thus, process flowcharts may be used to highlight the nonproductive activities, analyze the efficiency of a series of processes, and suggest improvements. They also provide a standardized method for documenting the steps in a process and can be used as a training tool. Automated versions of these charts are available that will superimpose the charts on floor plans of facilities. In this fashion, bottlenecks can be identified and layouts can be adjusted.

Teaching Note 6.2 Flowcharts

Process flowcharts are widely used in both manufacturing and service operations. We see them again in the chapter on job design.

Make-or-Buy Decisions

Not all the components that make up a product are produced in-house. Some may be purchased from a supplier. The decision concerning which items will be purchased and which items will be made is called a *make-or-buy decision.*

Components of a product may be purchased from a supplier or produced in-house.

The make-or-buy decision rests on an evaluation of the following factors:

1. *Cost:* Would it be cheaper to make the item or buy it, to perform the service in-house or subcontract it out? This is the primary consideration in most make-or-buy decisions. Although the cost of *buying* the item is relatively straightforward (i.e., the purchase price), the cost of *making* the item includes overhead allocations that may not accurately reflect the cost of manufacture. In addition, there are situations in which a company may decide to buy an item rather than make it (or vice versa) when, from a cost standpoint, it would be cheaper to do otherwise. The remaining factors in this list represent noneconomic factors that can influence or dominate the economic considerations.

Teaching Note 6.3 Vertical Integration Versus Supplier Partnerships

Transparency 6.3 A Process Flowchart

Date: 9-30-95 Analyst: TLR						Location: Graves Mountain Process: Apple sauce		
Step	Operation	Transport	Inspect	Delay	Storage	Description of process	Time (min)	Distance (feet)
1	●	⇨	□	D	▽	Unload apples from truck	20	
2	O	➡	□	D	▽	Move to inspection station		100 ft
3	O	⇨	■	D	▽	Weigh, inspect, sort	30	
4	O	➡	□	D	▽	Move to storage		50 ft
5	O	⇨	□	D	▼	Wait until needed	360	
6	O	➡	□	D	▽	Move to peeler		20 ft
7	●	⇨	□	D	▽	Apples peeled and cored	15	
8	O	⇨	□	D	▼	Soak in water until needed	20	
9	●	⇨	□	D	▽	Place on conveyor	5	
10	O	➡	□	D	▽	Move to mixing area		20 ft
11	O	⇨	■	D	▽	Weigh, inspect, sort	30	
	Page 1 of 3					Total	480	190 ft

FIGURE 6.5 Process Flowchart of Apple Processing

2. *Capacity:* Companies that are operating at less than full capacity usually opt to make components rather than buy them. This is particularly true if maintaining a level work force is important. Sometimes the available capacity is not sufficient to make all the components, so choices have to be made. The stability of demand is also important. Typically, it is better to produce in-house those parts or products with steady demand that consume a set capacity, whereas those whose demand patterns are uncertain or volatile are usually subcontracted.

3. *Quality:* The capability to provide quality parts consistently is certainly an important consideration in the make-or-buy decision. In general, it is easier to control the quality of items produced in one's own factory. However, standardization of parts, supplier certification, and supplier involvement in design can improve the quality of supplied parts. Poor manufacturing practices in the 1970s forced many U.S. companies in the 1980s to purchase major components from foreign competitors in order to meet customer quality expectations. This led to the creation of "hollow" corporations that farmed out every task except putting the final label on.

4. *Speed:* Sometimes components are purchased because a supplier can provide goods in shorter periods of time than the manufacturer. The smaller supplier is often more flexible, too, and can adapt quickly to design and technology changes. Of course, speed is useful only if one can rely on it.

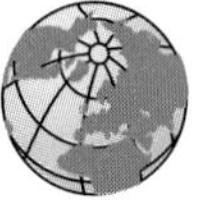

5. *Reliability:* Suppliers need to be reliable both in terms of the quality and timing of parts that are supplied. Unexpected delays in shipments or partial orders because of quality rejects can wreak havoc with the manufacturing system. Many companies today are requiring their suppliers to meet certain quality and delivery standards to be certified as an approved supplier. ISO 9000 is the European Market's quality certification program. Those foreign companies that are not certified simply may not trade in Europe. Other companies assess huge penalties for unreliable supply. Chrysler, for example, fines its suppliers $30,000 for each *hour* an order is late.

6. *Expertise:* Companies that are especially good at making or designing certain items may want to keep control over their production. Coca-Cola would not want to release its formula to a supplier, even if there were guarantees of secrecy. Although automakers might source many of their component parts, they need proprietary control over major components such as engines, transmissions, and electronic guidance systems. Japanese, Taiwanese, and Korean firms are currently learning American expertise in aircraft design and manufacture by serving as suppliers of component parts. The decision of whether or not to share one's expertise with a supplier for economic gains is a difficult one.

Companies that control the production of virtually all of their component parts, including the source of raw materials, are said to be *vertically integrated.* This strategy was popular for many years when companies did not want to be dependent on others for their livelihood. Today, buying components and raw materials from vendors is more common, but relationships with vendors have been strengthened. Termed *supplier partnerships,* networks of one-source suppliers are becoming valuable assets in corporate strategies to regain competitiveness.

Types of Processes

A **project** is a one-at-a-time production of a product to customer order.

Production processes are traditionally categorized into four basic types: 1. projects, 2. batch production, 3. mass production, and 4. continuous production. A **project** takes a long time to complete, involves a large investment of funds and resources, and produces one item at a time to customer order. Examples include construction projects, shipbuilding, new-product development, and aircraft manufacturing. Projects can be exciting because they typically involve cutting-edge technology,

The construction of an aircraft carrier is an enormous project. The U.S. NIMITZ, *shown in the first photo, accommodates a crew of more than 6,000 people and a full-load displacement of 91,000 tons. Each of the ship's four propellers weighs over 66,000 pounds. A single link in the anchor chain weighs 360 pounds. The carrier also houses two nuclear reactors enabling it to operate for 13 years without refueling. Modular construction, in which a ship is built in huge subassemblies or modules, has cut the production time of carriers and other ships in half. This is accomplished by outfitting several modules at one time, then adding them to the hull. Extensive use of CAD/CAM, precise tolerances, and careful quality control ensure that the modules fit together perfectly. The second photo shows an "island house" being lifted onto the deck of a carrier. The island house is the aircraft carrier's control center and contains the bridge and flight operations. The third photo shows a huge gantry crane putting a completed module (or appropriately named, superlift) into place. Superlifts, such as the one shown, weigh as much as 900 tons and are added to the hull almost weekly for the three years it takes to bring a ship from keel laying to launch.*

project teams, and close customer contact. The disadvantages of projects include the lengthy duration of the process during which customer preferences, technology, and costs can change; the large investment in resources, huge swings in resource requirements as new projects begin or old ones end; a slow learning curve inherent in nonrepetitive work; and industry dependence on a small customer base. Projects are managed very differently from other types of processes. We discuss project management in detail in Chapter 16.

Batch production typically processes many different jobs through the production system at the same time in groups (or batches). It is also known as *intermittent*, or *job shop, production*. Products are made to customer order, volume (in terms of customer order size) is low, and demand fluctuates. To allow for a variety of items to be produced, the equipment tends to be general purpose and the workers, highly skilled.

Batch production systems process many different jobs at the same time in groups (or batches).

Mass production is common for products that appeal to a mass market and exhibit high volume, stable demand. Examples include automobiles, industrial equipment, televisions, and computers. This photo shows a Nissan truck at an inspection station undergoing computerized tests. The tests are part of the Vehicle Evaluation System (VES) that provides statistical quality audits on each product as it moves through the assembly line. All of Nissan's trucks are manufactured at the Smyrna, Tennessee plant. The plant produces almost 100 vehicles each day.

Most of the operations in batch production involve fabrication (e.g., machining) rather than assembly. Jobs are sent through the system based on their processing requirements, so that those jobs requiring lathe work are sent to one location, those requiring painting to another, etc. A job may be routed through many different machine centers before it is completed. Because of this, if you were to track the flow of a particular customer order through the system, you would see a lot of stopping and starting as jobs queue at different machines, waiting to processed. Thus, work on a particular product is not continuous; it is *intermittent.* Examples of intermittent processes include machine shops, printers, bakeries, education, and furniture making. Advantages of this type of system are its flexibility, the customization of output, and the reputation for quality that customization implies. Disadvantages include high per-unit costs, frequent changes in product mix, complex scheduling problems, variations in capacity requirements, and slow speed of manufacture.

Mass production produces large volumes of a standard product for a mass market.

Mass production concentrates on producing large volumes of a standard product for a mass market. Product demand is stable, and product volume is high. Because of the stability and size of demand, the production system can afford to dedicate equipment to the production of a particular product. Thus, this type of system tends to be capital-intensive, with specialized equipment and limited labor skills.

Video 6.1 1991 *Malcolm Baldrige Awards, Quest for Excellence* 

Mass production is usually associated with *flow lines* or *assembly lines.* The term *flow* describes how a product moves through the system from one workstation to the next in order of the processing requirements for that particular product. (Batch production cannot be set up in this way because the processing requirements are different for each customer order.) The phrase *assembly line* is descriptive of the way mass production is typically arranged; that is, most of the operations required are assembly-oriented and are performed in a line. Goods that are mass-produced include automobiles, televisions, personal computers, fast food, and most consumer goods. Advantages of mass production are its efficiency, low per-unit cost, ease of manufacture and control, and speed. Disadvantages include the high cost of equipment, underutilization of human resources, the difficulties of adapting to changes in demand, technology, or product design, and the lack of responsiveness to individual customer requests.

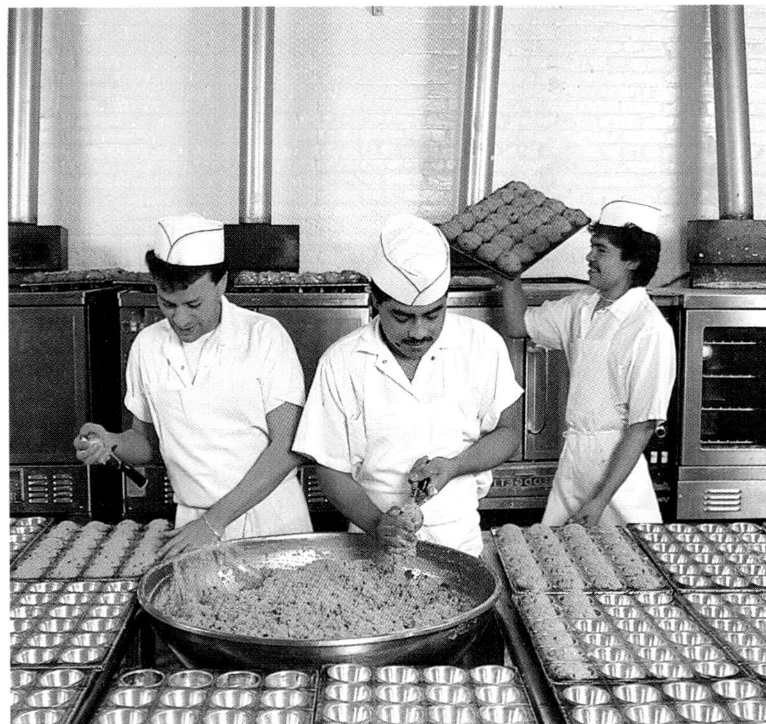

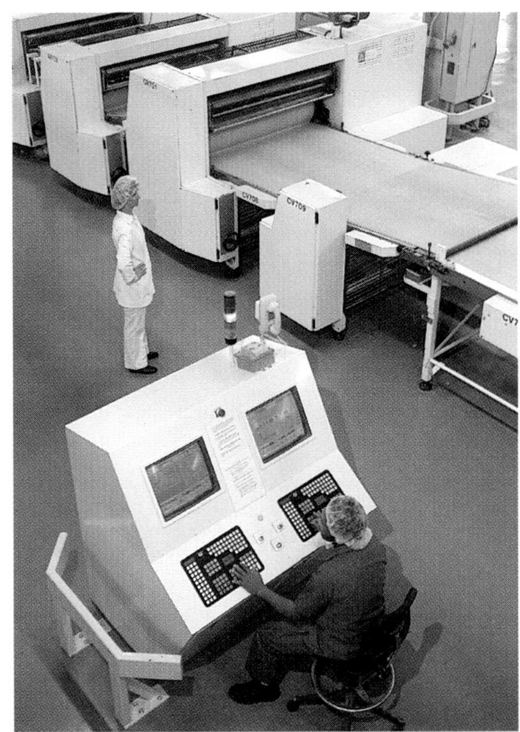

These photos highlight the differences between batch production and continuous production. In the first photo, oat bran muffins are made in batches according to the supply of dough and capacity of pans and ovens. With the exception of cooking and possibly mixing, the work is done by hand. The volume and type of goods produced by this bakery varies throughout the day from day to day. In the seecond photo, dough for graham crackers is mixed and rolled out into one continuous sheet by a series of machines. An elongated oven further down the line cooks the dough for the length of time it takes to pass through the oven area. More automated equipment on the same line cuts and scores the cooked dough, then separates, wraps, and packs it into boxes. The process is monitored by workers and computers. This plant produces graham crackers continuously every day of the year.

Continuous processes are used for very high volume commodity products that are very standardized. The system is highly automated (the worker's role is to monitor the equipment) and is typically in operation continuously 24 hours a day. The output is also continuous, not discrete—meaning individual units are measured, rather than counted. Refined oil, treated water, paints, chemicals, and foodstuffs are produced by continuous production. Companies that operate in this fashion are referred to as *process industries.* Advantages of this type of system are its efficiency, ease of control, and enormous capacity. Disadvantages include the large investment in plant and equipment, the limited variety of items that can be processed, the inability to adapt to volume changes, the cost of correcting errors in production, and the difficulties of keeping pace with new technology.

Continuous processes are used for very high volume commodity products.

Process Selection

From our discussion of the types of processes, which are summarized in Table 6.1 on page 289, it should be apparent that no one process is inherently better than another. However, it is very important that the process selected *match* certain product characteristics. Process selection is primarily dependent on two product characteristics, degree of standardization and demand volume. Products with low standardization require flexible processing, whereas products with high stan-

GAINING THE COMPETITIVE EDGE

Making Salsas Simple

La Victoria Foods, located in Rosemead, California, makes salsas, jalapenos, nachos, and tomatillo entero in a factory that operates 16 to 18 hours a day, 5 to 6 days a week. What's different about food processing? For one thing, fresh produce is perishable. When the chiles and tomatoes arrive for processing (usually from July to December), the plant operates at full speed. Breakdowns and work stoppages cannot be tolerated. A few hours of delay can make the product unuseable and destroy an entire day's work.

Another problem is that the inputs to the production process are not standardized. Tomatoes come in different sizes and textures; they vary in their degree of ripeness. The peeling process can differ based on the particular input ingredients, as can mixing. For example, one batch of salsas may require 30 pounds of tomatoes, whereas the next might need 34 pounds, depending on the characteristics of the particular tomatoes used in the mixture. Human experts are essential for these tasks. From the cooking kettles a batch of salsas is relayed to a holding tank, which keeps the mixture at a predetermined temperature until it can be released to the mechanical fillers that fill the glass jars. If the size of the jars is changed, then the filling rate of the jars also changes, and the mixture stays in the holding tank for a different length of time. This, in turn, affects the operation of the cooker. In this particular system, the cooker is the limiting factor, and the other operations are set to operate at a speed that matches the cooker capacity.

The jars are filled and labeled along three 300-foot conveyor-driven lines. The lines are controlled by PLCs (programmable logic controllers), as are individual machines on the line. In all, there are 35 PLCs in the plant. Everything has to be kept synchronized so that the filler does not get ahead of the capper and the line does not shut down because of inadequate cooking capacity. Because many of the PLCs are connected together and can be run using the PC in the production manager's office, a decision on the length of time required to cook a particular batch, the type of product to be bottled, and the size of the jars can be translated into the appropriate speed of the filling line, speed of the cappers, and length of time in the holding tank.

Source: Based on Stevenson, Blake, "Keeping it Simple to Reduce Spoiled Efficiency in the Food Industry," *Industrial Engineering* (June 1992): 29–32.

dardization can benefit from the efficiency of dedicated processing. Low-volume production is generally labor intensive, and high-volume production can provide the capital to invest in more automated equipment. Figure 6.6 summarizes the relationship between product characteristics and process choice.

Teaching Note 6.4 The Impact of Process Choice

It is important to obtain a good product-process match.

The proper product-process match occurs along the diagonal, as indicated by the types of processes that are shown. Companies or products that are off the diagonal have either made poor process choices or have found a means to execute a competitive advantage. For example, technological advancements in flexible automation allow Motorola to mass-produce customized pagers. Similarly, Toyota has perfected a hybrid manufacturing system in JIT (Just-in-Time) that allows different models of cars to be produced on the same assembly line. Volvo and Rolls Royce, on the other hand, occupy a special market niche by producing cars in a crafted, customized fashion. Examples of poor process choice include Texas Instrument's attempt to produce consumer products for mass markets by the same process that had been successful in the production of scientific products for specialized markets and Corning Glass' production of low-volume consumer items, such as range covers, with the same continuous process used for other items formed from glass.

TABLE 6.1 Types of Processes

	Project	*Batch production*	*Mass Production*	*Continuous Production*
Type of product	Unique	Made to order (customized)	Made to stock (standardized)	Commodity
Type of customer	One-at-a-time	Few individual customers	Mass market	Mass market
Product demand	Infrequent	Fluctuates	Stable	Very stable
Demand volume	Very low	Low to medium	High	Very high
No. of different products	Infinite variety	Many, varied	Few	Very few
Production system	Long-term project	Intermittent, job shops	Flow lines, assembly lines,	Process industry
Production equipment	Varied	General-purpose	Special-purpose	Highly automated
Primary type of work	Specialized contracts	Fabrication	Assembly	Mixing, treating, refining
Worker skills	Experts, craftspersons	Wide range of skills	Limited range of skills	Equipment monitors
Advantages	Custom work, latest technology	Flexibility, quality	Efficiency, speed, low cost	Highly efficient, large capacity, ease of control
Disadvantages	Nonrepetitive; small customer base, expensive	Costly, slow, difficult to manage	Capital investment; lack of responsiveness	Difficult to change; far-reaching errors, limited variety
Examples	Construction, shipbuilding, aircraft	Machine shops, print shops, bakeries, education	Automobiles, televisions, computers, fast food	Paint, chemicals, foodstuffs

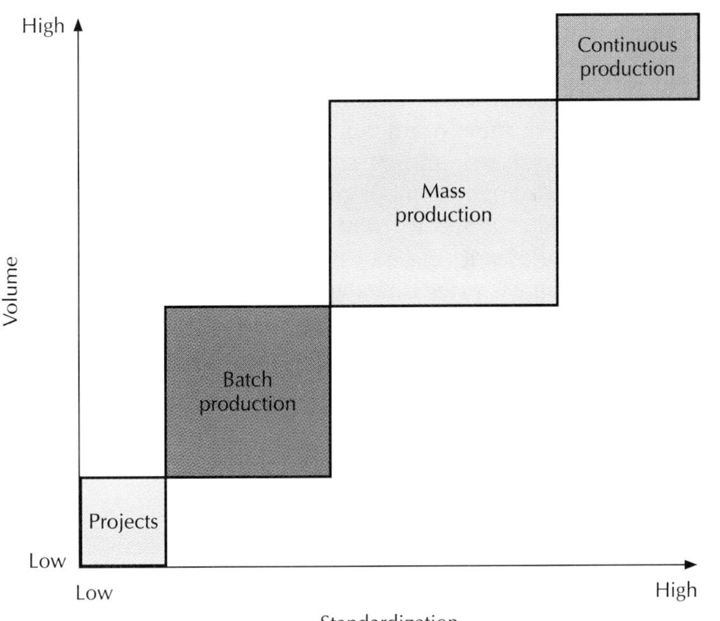

Transparency 6.4 Matching Product and Process Choice

FIGURE 6.6 Matching Product Characteristics with Process Choice

Video 6.2 *The Allyn and Bacon Plant Tour Video,* Program 3: "Volvo Torslanda Plant"

GAINING THE COMPETITIVE EDGE

Volvo's Torslanda Plant Stands Out

Volvo's manufacturing facility in Torslanda, Sweden, employs 10,000 workers and produces 150,000 cars a year. The facility consists of several plants that perform body work and assembly. The process begins at the pressing plant, where 20-ton rolls of sheet metal are cut into suitable sizes and then pressed into various shapes. The stamping presses themselves are as tall as a four-story building. Next, the pressed pieces are moved to the jig factory, where welding, grinding (i.e., finishing), and inspection take place. The jig factory consists of three workshops for welding the car sides, the underbody unit, and the car body. A Volvo requires more than 5,000 spot welds, 98 percent of which are performed by robots, but grinding, brushing, and adjusting the car bodies are done by hand. In the paint factory, car bodies move on a pallet in and out of electrodipping sections and drying ovens through 50 separate processes. About 40,000 of the completed car bodies are sent to other assembly plants. Six hundred bodies are kept in a sophisticated automatic storage and retrieval system as buffer inventory. The rest remain at the Torslanda site for final assembly. At final assembly, the body and drive line are combined. Parts, large and small, roll in from more than 600 suppliers. The assembly line is nontraditional in that cars move on separate battery-operated pallets whose speed is controlled by the workers. Assemblers work in pairs and take about 2 hours to complete their tasks at each station. Each car is customized from a selection of engines, gearboxes, upholstery, and special equipment. Since much of the quality of the final product is dependent on manual labor, Volvo tries to tailor the work environment to worker needs. For instance, a "tilt track" device tilts the car on its side so that a worker can make adjustments underneath the car while standing upright (rather than have the worker crawl under the car to make adjustments while lying on his or her back).

Source: Based on "Volvo's Torslanda Plant," *Allyn and Bacon Plant Tour Video,* Program 3.

Break-Even Analysis

Break-even analysis examines the cost trade-offs associated with demand volume.

Teaching Note 6.5 Warnings about Break Even Analysis

There are several quantitative techniques available for selecting a particular process among a list of alternatives. A popular technique that bases its decision on the cost trade-offs associated with demand volume is **break-even analysis.** The components of break-even analysis are volume, cost, revenue, and profit. *Volume* is the level of production, usually expressed as the number of units produced and sold. We assume that the number of units produced can be sold. *Cost* is divided into two categories, *fixed costs,* or costs that remain constant regardless of the number of units produced, such as plant and equipment and other elements of overhead, and *variable costs,* or costs that vary with the volume of units produced, such as labor and material. The total cost of a process is the sum of its fixed cost and its total variable cost (defined as volume times per unit variable cost). *Revenue* on a per-unit basis is simply the price at which an item is sold. *Total revenue* is price times volume sold. *Profit* is the difference between total revenue and total cost. These components can be expressed mathematically as follows:

$$\begin{aligned}\text{Total cost} &= \text{total fixed cost} + \text{total variable cost}\\ \text{TC} &= c_f + vc_v\\ \text{Total revenue} &= \text{volume} \times \text{price}\\ \text{TR} &= vp\\ \text{Total profit} &= \text{total revenue} - \text{total cost}\\ Z &= \text{TR} - \text{TC}\\ &= vp - (c_f + vc_v)\end{aligned}$$

where

c_f = fixed cost
v = volume (i.e., number of units)
c_v = variable cost per unit
p = price per unit

In selecting a process, it is useful to know at what volume of sales and production we can expect to earn a profit. In other words, we want to make sure that the cost of producing the product does not exceed the revenue we will receive from the sale of the product. By equating total revenue with total cost and solving for v, we can find the volume at which profit is zero. This is called the *break-even point.* At any volume above the break-even point, we will make a profit. A mathematical formula for the break-even point can be determined as follows:

$$\text{TR} = \text{TC}$$

$$vp = (c_f + vc_v)$$

$$vp - vc_v = c_f$$

$$v(p - c_v) = c_f$$

$$v = \frac{c_f}{p - c_v}$$

EXAMPLE 6.2

Alternate Example 6.2

Break-Even Analysis

Problem Statement:

Several enterprising graduate students at Whitewater University are interested in forming a company, aptly called the New River Rafting Company, to produce rubber rafts for rafting along the New River. The initial investment in plant and equipment is estimated to be \$2,000. Labor and material cost is approximately \$5 per raft. If the rafts can be sold for \$10 each, what volume of demand would be necessary for the New River Rafting Company to break even?

Solution:

Given,

Fixed cost = c_f = \$2,000
Variable cost = c_v = \$5 per raft
Price = \$10 per raft

Then, the break-even point is

$$v = \frac{c_f}{p - c_v}$$

$$= \frac{2{,}000}{10 - 5} = 400 \text{ rafts}$$

The solution is shown graphically in the following figure. The x-axis represents production or demand volume and the y-axis represents dollars of revenue, cost, or profit. The total revenue line extends from the origin, with a slope equal to the unit price of a raft. The total cost line intersects the y-axis at a level corresponding to the fixed cost of the process and has a slope equal to the per-unit variable cost. The break-even point can be found at the intersection of these two lines. If demand is less than the break-even point, the company will operate at a loss. But if demand exceeds the break-even point, the company will be profitable. Thus, the New River Rafting Company needs to sell more than 400 rafts to make a profit.

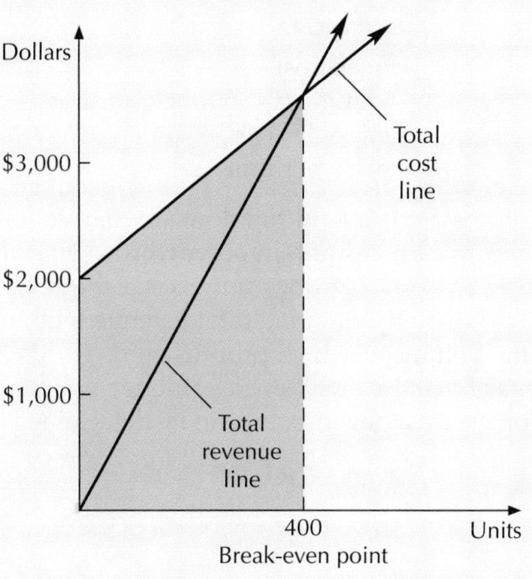

Break-even analysis can be used for evaluating alternative processes.

Break-even analysis is especially useful when evaluating different degrees of automation. More-automated processes have higher fixed costs but lower variable costs. The selection of the "best" process depends on the anticipated volume of demand for the product and the trade-offs between fixed and variable costs. Let's see how the concept of break-even analysis can be adapted to guide the selection of a process among several alternatives.

Alternate Example 6.3

EXAMPLE 6.3

Process Selection

Problem Statement:

The students from the New River Rafting Company are confident that demand for their product will substantially exceed the break-even point identified in Example 6.2. They are now contemplating a larger initial investment of $10,000 for more-automated equipment that would reduce the variable cost of manufacture to $2 per raft.

a. What is the break-even point for this new process?
b. Compare the process described in Example 6.2 with the process proposed here. For what volume of demand should each process be chosen?

Solution:

a. The break-even point for the new process is

$$v = \frac{10{,}000}{10 - 2} = 1{,}250 \text{ rafts}$$

b. Let's label the process in Example 6.2 Process A and the new process proposed here, Process B. In comparing the two processes, we note that the break-even point for process B of 1,250 rafts is larger than the break-even point for process A of 400 rafts. With this information we can conclude that if demand is less than 400 units, the students should not go into business. In addition, if demand is greater than 400 units but less than 1,250 units, process A should be selected. But what if demand is above 1,250? Let's try different demand volumes greater than 1,250 units and calculate which process gives the lowest total cost. (Because the rafts will be sold for $10 apiece regardless of which process is used to manufacture them, we will reach the same conclusion whether we use total profit or total cost as a decision criteria.)

First, we need to construct a mathematical formula for the total cost of each process as the sum of fixed costs plus variable costs. If v represents the volume of rafts demanded (and, we assume, produced), then

$$\text{Total cost for process A} = \$2{,}000 + \$5v$$
$$\text{Total cost for process B} = \$10{,}000 + \$2v$$

Next, we substitute different values for v and calculate the total cost of each process. Let's arbitrarily choose 2,000 units and 5,000 units.

For a demand volume of 2,000 units,

$$\begin{aligned}\text{Total cost for process A} &= \$2{,}000 + \$5(2{,}000)\\ &= \$2{,}000 + \$10{,}000 = \$12{,}000\\ \text{Total cost for process B} &= \$10{,}000 + \$2(2{,}000)\\ &= \$10{,}000 + \$4{,}000 = \$14{,}000\end{aligned}$$

For a demand volume of 5,000 units,

$$\begin{aligned}\text{Total cost for process A} &= \$2{,}000 + \$5(5{,}000)\\ &= \$2{,}000 + \$25{,}000 = \$27{,}000\\ \text{Total cost for process B} &= \$10{,}000 + \$2(5{,}000)\\ &= \$10{,}000 + \$10{,}000 = \$20{,}000\end{aligned}$$

Thus, for 2,000 rafts, process A is preferred, but for 4,000 rafts, process B is preferred. This is confusing—no one process is dominant above the 1,250 break-even point. Let's graph the problem and see if that helps to analyze the trade-offs between the two processes.

The problem is graphed in the following figure. We can see that the total cost lines for process A and process B intersect at approximately 2,666 units. The intersection point is called the *point of indifference,* because at that point the costs of the two processes are equal and we are indifferent as to which one to choose. However, if we look above the point of indifference, the total cost line for process B is always lower than for process A. Conversely, below the point of indifference, the total cost line for process A is always lower than process B.

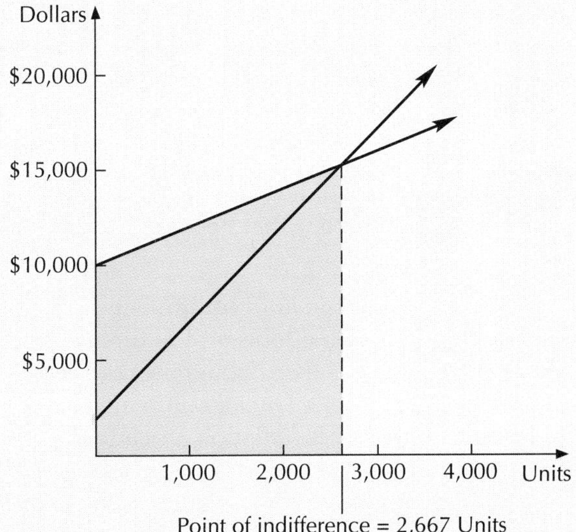

From the graphical solution to the problem, we might surmise that there is a quicker and more exact solution procedure than simply trying different levels of demand and calculating the total cost of each alternative process. The procedure evaluates the trade-offs between fixed and variable costs among the alternative processes and uses a set of decision rules to suggest a solution. Four steps are required.

1. Formulate a total cost equation for each process considered.
2. Calculate the *point of indifference* between two alternatives by equating the total cost of each alternative and solving for v, the demand volume.
3. Above the point of indifference, choose the alternative with the lowest variable cost.
4. Below the point of indifference, choose the alternative with the lowest fixed cost.

For this example, the point of indifference is

$$\begin{aligned} &\textit{Process A} \qquad \textit{Process B} \\ \$2{,}000 + \$5v &= \$10{,}000 + \$2v \\ \$3v &= \$8{,}000 \\ v &= 2{,}667 \text{ rafts} \end{aligned}$$

If the demand for rafts is 2,667 units, we can choose either process A or process B. If demand is less than 2,667 rafts, the alternative with the lowest fixed cost, process A, should be chosen. If demand is greater than 2,667 rafts, the alternative with the lowest variable cost, process B, is preferred.

The break-even model of AB:POM will find and graph the point of indifference (termed the break-even point) between two or three processes, but it will not find the break-even point for a single process. To reach a final solution, examine the graph and apply the decision rules as we discussed.

Specific Equipment Selection

After a process has been selected, specific equipment decisions can be made. Alternatives include using, replacing, or upgrading existing equipment, adding additional capacity, or purchasing new equipment. Any alternative that involves an outlay of funds is considered a *capital investment.* Capital investments involve the commitment of funds in the present with an expectation of returns over some future time period. The expenditures are usually large and can have a significant effect on the future profitability of a firm. Thus, these decisions are carefully analyzed and typically require top management approval.

The most effective quantitative techniques for capital investment consider the time value of money as well as the risks associated with benefits that will not accrue until the future. These techniques, known collectively as capital budgeting techniques, include payback period, net present value, and internal rate of return. Detailed descriptions can be found in any basic finance text.

Although capital budgeting techniques are beyond the scope of this text, we do need to comment on several factors that are often overlooked in a financial analysis of equipment purchases:

Several factors are often overlooked in a financial justification of new equipment.

1. *Purchase cost:* The initial investment in equipment consists of more than the basic purchase price. The cost of special tools and fixtures, installation, and engineering or programming adjustments (i.e., debugging) can represent a significant additional investment. This is especially true of automated equipment. For example, it is common for the cost of robot installation and added-on accessories to exceed the purchase price of the robot.

2. *Operating costs:* The annual cost of operating a machine includes direct labor, indirect labor (e.g., for programming, setups, material handling, or training), power and utilities, supplies, tooling, property taxes and insurance, and maintenance. In many cases indirect labor is underestimated, as are maintenance and tooling costs. In order to assess more accurately the requirements of the new equipment, it is useful to consider, step by step, how the machine will be operated, started, stopped, loaded, unloaded, changed over to another product, maintained, repaired, cleaned up, speeded up, and slowed down and what resources (i.e., labor, material, or equipment) will be needed for each step.

3. *Annual savings:* Most new equipment is justified based on direct labor savings. However, other savings can actually be more important. For example, a more efficient process may be able to use less material and require less machine time or fewer repairs, so that downtime is reduced. A process that produces a better-quality product can result in fewer inspections and less scrap and rework. Finally, new processes (especially those that are automated) may significantly reduce safety costs, in terms of compliance with required regulations, as well as fines or compensation for safety violations.

4. *Revenue enhancement:* Increases in revenue due to equipment upgrades or new-equipment purchases are often ignored in financial analysis because they are difficult to predict. New equipment can expand capacity and, assuming the extra units can be sold, increase revenue. Improvements in product quality, price reductions due to decreased costs, and more rapid or dependable delivery can increase market share and, thus, revenue. Flexibility of equipment can also be important in adapting to the changing needs of the customer. These are strategic advantages that have long-term implications. Unfortunately, most quantitative analyses are oriented toward short-term measures of performance.

5. *Replacement analysis:* As existing equipment ages, it may become slower, less reliable, and even obsolete. The decision to replace old equipment with state-of-the-art equipment depends in large measure on the competitive environment. If a major competitor upgrades to a newer technology that improves quality, cost, or flexibility and you do not, your ability to compete will be severely damaged. Deciding when to invest in new equipment can be a tricky task.

A hidden cost in replacement analysis is the opportunity cost of not investing in new equipment when upcoming technology will make the equipment obsolete. Part of the analysis should include estimates of salvage value reductions, operating cost inferiority, quality inferiority, and flexibility inferiority as compared with state-of-the-art technology. Salvage value, similar to the trade-in value of an automobile, decreases every year a company waits to replace equipment. In some industries, technology changes so rapidly that a replacement decision also involves determining whether this generation of equipment should be purchased or if it would be better to wait for the next generation. Replacement analysis maps out different schedules for equipment purchases over a five- to ten-year period and selects a replacement cycle that will minimize cost.

6. *Risk and uncertainty:* Investment in new equipment, especially if it represents an untested technology, can be risky. Estimates of equipment capabilities, length of life, and operating cost may be uncertain. Because of the risk involved, financial analysts tend to assign higher hurdle rates (i.e., required rates of return) to technology investments, making it difficult to gain approval for them. Management's general lack of understanding of new technology and its potential impact does not help the situation. Later in the chapter, we look more closely at technology-related decisions.

7. *Piecemeal analysis:* Investment in equipment and technology is expensive. Rarely can a company afford completely to automate a plant all at once. Rather, a *strategy* for capital investment is needed. This has led to the proposal and evaluation of equipment purchases in a piecemeal fashion. Technology plans are frequently abandoned, however, when pieces of technology don't fit into the existing system and fail to deliver the expected returns. There is a synergistic benefit to a well-designed technology plan that is too often ignored.

Process Plans

The output of process planning consists of a set of documents that specify how a product and its component parts are to be manufactured. These documents typically consist of blueprints or part drawings, assembly charts or bills of material, routing sheets (that show which machines are to be used in what order), opera-

Teaching Note 6.6 Activity-Based Costing

GAINING THE COMPETITIVE EDGE

Hewlett-Packard Rereads the Numbers

What happens when manufacturing, marketing, and design come up with vastly different costs for producing the same product? Most companies argue it out, and the most powerful entity wins. The Roseville Networks Division of Hewlett-Packard decided, instead, to completely overhaul the cost accounting system and determine more accurate sources of information. They formed a "Simple Six" task force (made up of representatives from manufacturing, design, procurement, accounting, sales, and information systems) to identify exactly what factors drove cost for their products. Direct materials remained a valid contributor to product cost, but not direct labor (on which, by the way, they were spending 30 minutes a day tracking). Accounting for less than 2 percent of product cost, direct labor was the first category eliminated by the Simple Six (it was lumped into overhead). Of course, a different manner of allocating overhead then had to be determined. First, two major categories, procurement and production overhead, were designated. Costing procurement overhead was relatively easy; it varied by the number of pieces in each order. Costing production overhead took more analysis. In the end, eight separate measures of production overhead were determined. The activities at the beginning of the process and during soldering were costed by the number of boards processed. The cost of insertions varied by the number of insertions per board and the type of insertion (axial, dip, manual, or backload). Finally, the cost of testing and rework was allocated by the amount of time spent in each process.

The new costing system is more complicated than the old formula of direct materials, direct labor, and overhead, but HP says it gives the company a solid base on which to make intelligent and informed manufacturing, marketing, and design decisions.

Source: Based on Berlant, Debbie, Reese Browning, and George Foster, "How Hewlett-Packard Gets Numbers It Can Trust," *Harvard Business Review,* (January–February 1990): 178–83.

The entire set of documents that details manufacturing specifications is called a *process plan.*

tions sheets (that show the steps the operator is to perform at each machine or workstation), and other manufacturing specifications such as tooling and fixture requirements. The entire set of documents is called a *process plan.*

For mass production and continuous production, a process plan may be developed only once, when the assembly line is set up or the process plant is built. For batch production, a process plan must be developed for every job that enters the shop or part that is produced. For projects, process plans are usually associated with each activity in the project network. (Project networks such as PERT/CPM are discussed in Chapter 16.)

Process planning can be a difficult, lengthy, and tedious task. It requires the skills of an individual (usually a manufacturing engineer or machinist) who is knowledgeable about the manufacturing capabilities of the factory, machine and process characteristics, tooling, materials, standard practices, and cost trade-offs. Very little of this information is documented; it may exist only in the mind of the process planner. Sometimes, workbooks used to store process information can serve as a reference to previous plans, but usually the ability to modify existing plans for new parts relies solely on the memory of the planner. In addition to these difficulties, process plans can be quite lengthy. It is not uncommon in the aerospace industry for the process plan of a single part to contain more than 100 pages.[2]

CAPP is a specialized software system for process planning.

Fortunately, **computer-aided process planning (CAPP)** is now available to alleviate some of the difficulties associated with the manual preparation of process

[2]Bedworth, D., M. Henderson, and P. Wolfe, *Computer-Integrated Design and Manufacturing,* New York: McGraw-Hill, 1991, p. 238.

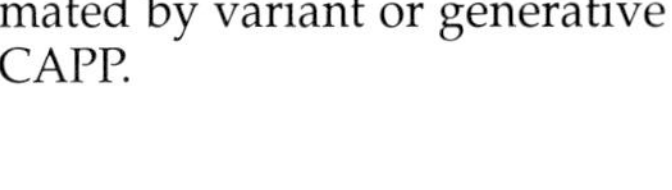
Process planning can be automated by variant or generative CAPP.

plans. CAPP is a specialized software system that attempts to automate process planning. Two types of systems are common, variant and generative. A *variant system* retrieves a standard process plan from a CAPP database and allows the planner or engineer to modify it for the new part. The database is organized by group technology into families of parts with similar processing requirements. Group technology can also be used to organize CAD databases into families of parts based on shape and other physical features related to design, but CAD and CAPP part families are not necessarily the same.

A *generative system* creates an individual process plan from scratch with the help of an expert system and four databases: machines, tooling, speed/feed rates, and time standards. Given user-input data on the size, shape, and material composition of a part, the generative system accesses a machine database to match part requirements to machine capabilities. For example, the system may determine that a table leg should be shaped on turret lathe 1 because that machine is capable of processing material between 3 inches and 56 inches long with a maximum diameter of 4 inches. Next, the proper tool is selected based on part geometry, physical and mechanical properties, and type of material to be processed. Tool characteristics include such factors as the hardness or wear resistance of a drill bit and the number of teeth in a cutter tool. After the tool has been selected, the speed at which to operate the machine and the manner in which the part is fed into the machine must be determined. Finally, the standard time needed to perform each operation is calculated from the time standards database, and the process plan is printed out in the form of several reports (routing sheets, operation sheets, etc.) that are used to manufacture the parts.

Manual process planning is very time-consuming, subjective, and error-prone because of the number of interrelated variables involved. Generative CAPP systems use a knowledge base of rules gathered from expert machinists to ensure good decisions. These knowledge bases have been difficult to develop and currently are available only for a limited class of items, such as cylindrical parts. Ideally, CAPP output could be used to program automated equipment electronically. In practice, this has proved difficult. Another difficulty is the transfer of CAD data directly to CAPP. In most cases, the user must again input part characteristics or part codes (from the group technology part family classification), which are then interpreted by the CAPP system. Current research in the field of artificial intelligence has led to the development of prototype *feature-recognition systems* that can automatically distinguish the features of a part from the CAD database and eliminate the reentry of part data by the process planner. Although not yet fully operational, these recognition systems hold promise for solving one of the major integration problems between CAD and CAM.

Problems of integration are common as new technology is introduced into a system. In the next section, we discuss some of the issues involved in making wise technology choices.

TECHNOLOGY DECISIONS

Teaching Note 6.7 Aversion to Technology

The MIT study on competitiveness (presented in the opening chapter) pointed out that American firms spend twice as much on product innovation as they do on process innovation, whereas the Germans and Japanese do just the opposite. Management analyst Peter Drucker says we must become "managers of technology," not merely "users of technology." Wickham Skinner, a former Harvard professor and authority on manufacturing practices, describes many U.S. managers as "technology-averse." This aversion can create a *technology trap:*

- Managers assume that many years of training and intense study are required to become competent in a technology; therefore, technological decisions are best delegated to experts, such as scientists and engineers.

Managers fall into the technology trap.

- Managers are reluctant to ask these experts questions about technology because they already feel inadequate in those matters and don't want to reinforce that feeling by appearing stupid.
- Managers fail to learn about technology because they are already so far behind that it would take too much time to catch up and keep up.
- Lack of knowledge breeds lack of confidence. As managers fall behind in managing technology, they make poor technology decisions and become personally obsolete.

Technology decisions typically involve large sums of money, are difficult to reverse, and have a long-term effect on the competitiveness of a firm. It is dangerous to delegate those types of decisions to specialists who lack the strategic, long-term vision to make wise technology choices. But how can a manager possibly master complex technologies to which engineers and scientists have devoted their entire professional lives? Skinner says they don't have to, but they do need to visualize the process taking place and obtain the answer to five simple questions:

A manager needs to ask five key questions to understand technology.

1. What will the new technology do?
2. What will it *not* do?
3. What will it require?
4. What will it cost?
5. How certain are the above?

Pictures, diagrams, and analogies help the manager visualize a process. The manager should be able to understand why the process is necessary, what changes take place as a result of the process, what actions are performed by the equipment and what role an operator plays, what must be done *before* the process begins, what must be done *after* the process ends, what can go wrong, and what usually does go wrong.

To illustrate the concept, let's consider the process of mowing grass.[3] Suppose a medium-priced lawn mower made by a well-known manufacturer is purchased to mow a residential yard. The mower has a gasoline engine and cuts a 24-inch swath of grass. The buyer gets home to his 8-inch-high grass and finds the following:

- The cutting technology is based on a reel moving past a cutter bar and thus will not cut grass much higher than one-half the reel diameter. Instead of cutting the grass, the mower pushes the 8-inch grass forward and down.
- The mower is self-propelled but has no effective free-wheeling device, so it is impossible to work close to and around a formal garden.
- It takes 30 minutes to change the cutting height for cutting the hillside grass longer than the lawn grass.
- The mower is not powerful enough to cut wet, thick grass going uphill.
- The mower does not mulch leaves.
- The mower has a two-cycle engine, which means that oil and gas have to be mixed each time the tank is filled.

The buyer has obviously made a poor technology choice. Before purchasing the mover, he or she needed a mental picture of the process of cutting grass, with the mower operating on a hillside, on level ground, and around the house and gardens. The buyer needed to consider how often he or she plans to cut the grass,

[3]Adapted from Skinner, W., *Manufacturing: The Formidable Competitive Weapon,* New York: John Wiley, 1985, pp. 113–21.

and his or her time, money, and skills. Then he or she could begin to ask the right questions and, it is to be hoped, purchase a more appropriate machine, such as an extra-powerful, four-cycle, self-propelled rotary mower with easy handling for tight maneuvering and with a simple height-adjustment mechanism.

Many technology decisions are made in a manner similar to the lawn-mower example. Equipment is purchased that performs some tasks well but does not perform the tasks that are needed. Similarly, it is not unusual for technology to cost more than anticipated, not be as reliable as it should be, or, in general, be more trouble than it is worth. You can probably think of examples from your own experiences in which you purchased a computer, camcorder, or athletic shoes that did not match your needs or expectations. General Motors made a poor technology choice in the 1980s when it invested millions of dollars on an automated factory that didn't work and had to be closed down. Blue Cross and Blue Shield of Wisconsin spent $20 million on an automated claims process that sent out $60 million in overpayments and lost the company over 35,000 members.

In order to understand how technology has changed manufacturing, we must first have some knowledge of basic manufacturing processes. The next two sections briefly discuss manufacturing processes and how these processes have been automated.

Manufacturing Processes

There are many different kinds of manufacturing processes. Most of them can be differentiated by the type of material that is being processed. Plastic and ceramic parts are extruded or molded, composite material is layered, and metal parts are formed by casting, forging, and machining. Machining processes are very common. They represent an old and well-understood technology performed at various levels of automation. Let's examine machining processes in more detail.

The machining process begins with a block or bar of standard metal stock, as shown in Figure 6.7.

Transparency 6.5 Basic Machining Operations

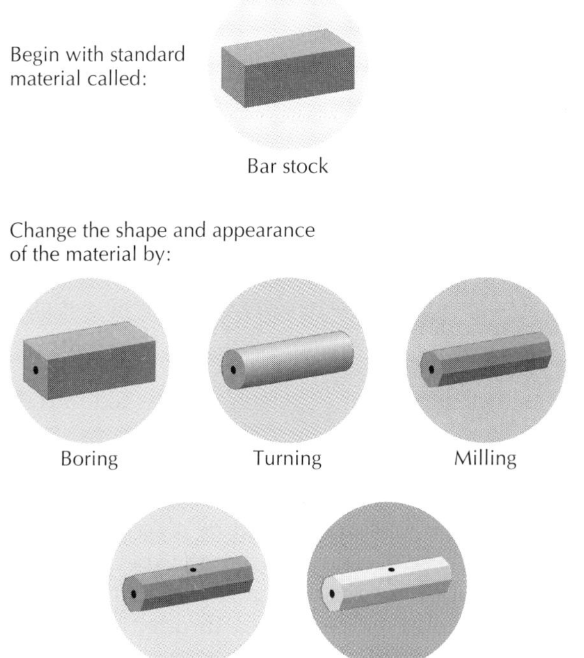

FIGURE 6.7 A Series of Machining Operations

Machining cuts away portions of the metal to bring it to an exact shape and size. Just about any contour can be produced with combinations of four basic machining processes:

Basic machining processes include turning, drilling, milling, and shaping.

1. *Turning:* In this operation, the workpiece revolves on a spindle while a cutting tool is moved along its surface, cutting away a portion of the material. Turning produces a cylindrical shape and is performed on a lathe.
2. *Drilling:* In drilling, the tool revolves and is fed into the material, cutting a cylindrical hole in the workpiece. There are, of course, a multitude of hole sizes that can be cut by changing the size of the drill bit. Different materials and thicknesses of material require specialized drill bits.
3. *Milling:* Milling changes the shape of an item by cutting chips away from its surface. The cutter tool rotates, progressively removing chips of material as the workpiece is fed into the cutter.
4. *Shaping:* Shaping produces smooth flat surfaces such as dovetail angles, gears, and keyways. Typically, the work table to which the workpiece is attached moves backward and forward, while the tool is being fed into the material.

A series of machining operations may be required to form the finished part. The number of operations performed and machine tools used is primarily a function of the part's geometry. For example, cylindrical parts are machined on lathes, whereas prismatic parts (those with flat outer surfaces) are produced on shapers. Simple parts can be machined in a few minutes; large or complex parts can take days or weeks. During this time, a partially machined part (called a workpiece) waiting to be processed can represent a substantial investment in work-in-process inventory for the manufacturer.

As machining removes material from a workpiece, chips or shavings are produced that must be cleared from the machine and recycled or discarded. Finishing of the part may be necessary to remove burrs or make the surface smooth. The part may also be washed, polished, painted, plated, or coated. Finished parts may represent the final product or they may be joined with other parts or subassemblies to create the final product. Assembly operations are usually the least automated of the processes.

Levels of Automation

The machines on which basic machining operations are performed, collectively called *machine tools,* have been in existence in some form for more than 200 years. Machine tools are an example of conventional, general-purpose equipment. Although they can be dedicated to processing items of the same shape and size repetitively, their advantage is derived from their ability to produce a multitude of different shapes and sizes by changing the *tool* used to cut the material. This flexibility also requires that the operator know how to set up or arrange the machine to process the material as desired. The proper tool must be selected and installed, the depth of cut must be determined, and a mechanism must be developed for stopping the tool when the desired cut is achieved. The operator must set the speed at which the tool operates as well as the rate at which work is fed into the machine. The workpiece must be secured and positioned with jigs, clamps, or fixtures so that the cut is taken in the exact location specified. Finally, the operator must be able to detect tool wear and determine when the tool needs to be replaced, when more coolant is needed, or when the machine should be stopped and adjusted. Skilled machinists usually make these decisions based on experience with no written instructions other than a blueprint of the designed part. Often this involves setting up the machine tool, running a few pieces through to test the arrangement, and then adjusting the setup until an acceptable part is produced. This can be a time-consuming and tedious process.

Numerically controlled (NC) machines were developed at MIT in the mid-1950s. With NC machines, machine motion is controlled by instructions contained on a punched tape. Operators no longer have to determine machine settings, but they must still select and install the tools and load and unload the machine. It is also the operator's job to monitor the operation of the machine tool to make sure the tape has been programmed properly and is in good condition and to listen for signs of excessive tool wear.

NC machines are machines whose motion is numerically controlled by instructions on a punched tape.

NC programs are written in a language called APT (automatically programmed tools), which was developed by the Air Force. The services of a trained programmer are usually required in addition to the machine operator. The high capital cost of the equipment plus the technical expertise required of an NC programmer have discouraged the use of NC technology. In the United States, NC machines are concentrated mainly in large firms or with smaller subcontractors in the aerospace or defense industries. It should be noted, however, that the machine tool population in the United States is significantly older than that of most other countries, and even though the numbers are low, NC machines are used more often than conventional machine tools. Technological enhancements to NC machining (such as ATC, CNC, DNC, and FMS) have made automated production more flexible and productive and, hence, more attractive to manufacturers. We discuss each of these enhancements next.

The addition of an automatic tool changer (ATC) to an NC machine can significantly increase the machine's flexibility, while reducing setup time and operator requirements. In this system, the punched tape not only guides the machine's operation, but it also selects the right tool from a bank of 20 to 100 available tools. Tools can be changed in as little as 2 seconds.

Advances in computer technology since the mid-1970s have allowed the punched tape of NC machines to be replaced with software instructions stored in the memory of a computer. These **computer numerical controlled** (**CNC**) machine tools are equipped with a screen and keyboard for writing and editing NC programs at the machine. This facilitates the access, editing, and loading of operating instructions and also encourages the collection of processing information and the control of processing quality. For example, records of tool use can be used to predict tool wear and generate replacement schedules before a substandard part is produced.

CNC machines are NC machines controlled by software instructions in the memory of a computer.

The control of several NC machines by a larger single computer is referred to as **direct numerical control** (**DNC**). DNC can also refer to distributed numerical control, in which each machine tool has its own microcomputer and the systems are linked to a central controlling computer. DNC machine tools can be of different types and can be programmed to carry out different tasks. When an automated material handling system is installed to link these machine tools together physically, a **flexible manufacturing system** (**FMS**) results.

DNC machines are several NC machines under direct or distributed numerical control by a single computer.

A **flexible manufacturing system** results from physically connecting DNC machines with an automated material handling system.

Automated Material Handling

Conveyors are probably the type of material handling system most associated with manufacturing. Of course, today's conveyor systems are much different than the belt or chain conveyors of Henry Ford's era. Modern conveyor systems are both fast and flexible. They can move in both directions, "read" parts or packages (via a bar code) and direct them to specific locations, and move on the floor, overhead, or underground.

Conveyors, AGVs, and AS/RS are examples of automated material handling.

An *automated guided vehicle* (*AGV*) is a driverless truck that typically follows a path of rails or wires imbedded in the floor or specially painted tape placed on the floor. Now available are AGVs that sport a small antenna and are radio controlled by a computer that emits FM radio frequencies. A fleet of AGVs can be directed by computer to virtually any location on the factory floor from any location. AGVs

GAINING THE COMPETITIVE EDGE

Automated Machining Center at Ingersol-Rand

Components for a family of large centrifugal pumps, formerly produced offshore, are now being manufactured at Ingersol-Rand's Allentown, Pennsylvania, plant. Production was brought back to the home plant because of the efficiency and improved quality provided by the plant's new horizontal CNC machining center. The center consists of one machine with three machining stations, a 120-tool automatic tool changer, and a rail-mounted AGV system with dual pallet changers and eight pallets. One machining station performs boring, drilling, milling, and tapping operations on a spindle, whereas two others are slide-mounted cutting stations for turning, boring, facing, threading, and contouring.

Each pump assembly is made up of a housing, a support head and a casing. The center is designed to machine the pump components in complete sets. A set of pump parts can be completed in 2 hours 45 minutes, as compared to the 2-week normal lead time. With this system, it is now economical to produce individual pump orders on demand.

Source: Based on "Cellular System Creativity Brings Pump Production Back to U.S.," *Industrial Engineering* (June 1992): 16.

come in different shapes and sizes and can transport a wide variety of containers and pallets of material. Some AGVs even have microprocessor-based intelligence to handle unanticipated events. AGVs are considered the most flexible type of material handling system.

Automated storage and retrieval systems (AS/RS) are basically automated warehouses, although their size has been considerably reduced in recent years. Parts stored in bins are retrieved by automated equipment (usually a stacker crane) and delivered to different collection and distribution points. The bins are typically stored in a carousel-type storage system that rotates to make the desired bin accessible for the "picking" equipment. A computer keeps track of how many items are stored in which bins and controls the system that selects the desired bin. Older AS/RSs were quite large, some extending several stories beyond the factory floor. Newer, smaller AS/RSs tend to use minibins and are located within easy reach of the assembly area. AS/RSs provide a space efficient, fast, and accurate way of storing and retrieving material.

Flexible Manufacturing Systems

An FMS can process hundreds of different items efficiently. Tools change automatically from large storage carousels at each machine that hold 100 or more tools. The material handling system (usually conveyors or automated guided vehicles) carries workpieces on pallets, which can be locked into a machine for processing. Pallets are transferred between the conveyor and machine automatically. Computer software keeps track of the routing and processing requirements for each pallet. Pallets communicate with the computer controller by way of bar codes or radio signals.

An FMS operates very differently from traditional fixed, or "hard," automation. Ford's engine transfer line performs 150 separate machining operations on an engine block.[4] Bar stock is fed in at one end of the line and is transferred from one machine to the next as it is automatically machined on specialized machine

[4]Schroeder, R., *Operations Management: Decision Making in the Operations Function,* New York: McGraw-Hill, 1989, p. 1973.

tools. The line is particular to one type of engine block, and a change in product design would require extensive changes in the transfer line and its equipment. The line is very efficient and can produce high volumes, but it is not flexible.

An FMS, on the other hand, combines flexibility with efficiency. Flexibility is derived from ease of parts transfer and the use of programmable automation. Parts can be transferred on the automated material handling system between *any* two machines in *any* routing sequence. With a variety of programmable machine tools and large tool banks, an FMS can theoretically produce thousands of different items, but it may take longer to write the computer program for a new item than to manufacture it. For this reason, an FMS is usually limited to producing families of parts or selected families of parts, whose basic process plans are stored in the computer database. As process planning becomes more automatic and versatile, flexible manufacturing systems will become even more flexible.

An FMS can process hundreds of different items efficiently.

The efficiency of an FMS is derived from reductions in setup and queue times. Setup activities take place *before* the part reaches the machine. A machine is presented only with parts and tools that are ready for immediate processing. Queuing areas at each machine hold pallets that are ready to move in the moment the machine finishes with the previous piece. The pallet also serves as a work platform, so no time is lost transferring the workpiece from pallet to machine or positioning and fixturing the part. Advanced FMSs may contain a second material handling system, whose job consists of replacing old tools with new ones and, when possible, taking worn tools away to be sharpened or repaired. The machines in an advanced FMS may also be more sophisticated, such as five-axis CNC *machining centers* that simultaneously perform up to five operations on a workpiece that would normally require a series of operations on individual milling machines, drill presses, and other machine tools.

Figure 6.8 (see page 304) is a schematic diagram of Ingersol-Rand's FMS in Roanoke, Virginia. Installed in the early 1970s, it was one of the first flexible manufacturing systems in the United States and is still in operation today. Originally designed to manufacture parts for hoists and winches, it currently produces rock drill bits for oil exploration. The system was flexible enough to adapt when the company went into an entirely new line of business. Flexible automation has become more important in today's manufacturing environment of rapidly changing and customized products. IBM's manufacturing facility for laptop PCs in Austin, Texas, can assemble any electronic product that will fit in the 2-foot by 2-foot by 14-inch cube that serves as a pallet and workspace for the system.

Robotics

Robots are manipulators that can be programmed to move workpieces or tools along a specified path. Contrary to popular images in science fiction, industrial robots show little resemblance to humans and, at their best, provide only a fraction of the dexterity, flexibility, and intelligence of human beings. Robots do not necessarily perform a job faster than human workers, but they can tolerate hostile environments, work longer hours, and do the job more consistently. The first applications of robots were for unpleasant, hazardous, or monotonous jobs, such as loading and unloading die-casting machines (where it is very hot), welding, and spray painting. Currently, robots are used for a wide range of applications, including material handling, machining, assembly, and inspection. Applications are shifting from simple to more complex operations. For example, in the 1980s, almost 50 percent of robots sold were used for welding and painting operations. In this decade, robots purchased for assembly and inspection have already more than doubled, exceeding those purchased for welding and painting.[5]

Robots are programmable manipulators.

[5]Farnum, G., "Industrial Robots—The Next Ten Years," *Manufacturing Engineering* (December 1985); Robot Institute of America, *Worldwide Robotics Survey and Directory, 1991.*

Transparency 6.6 A Flexible Manufacturing System

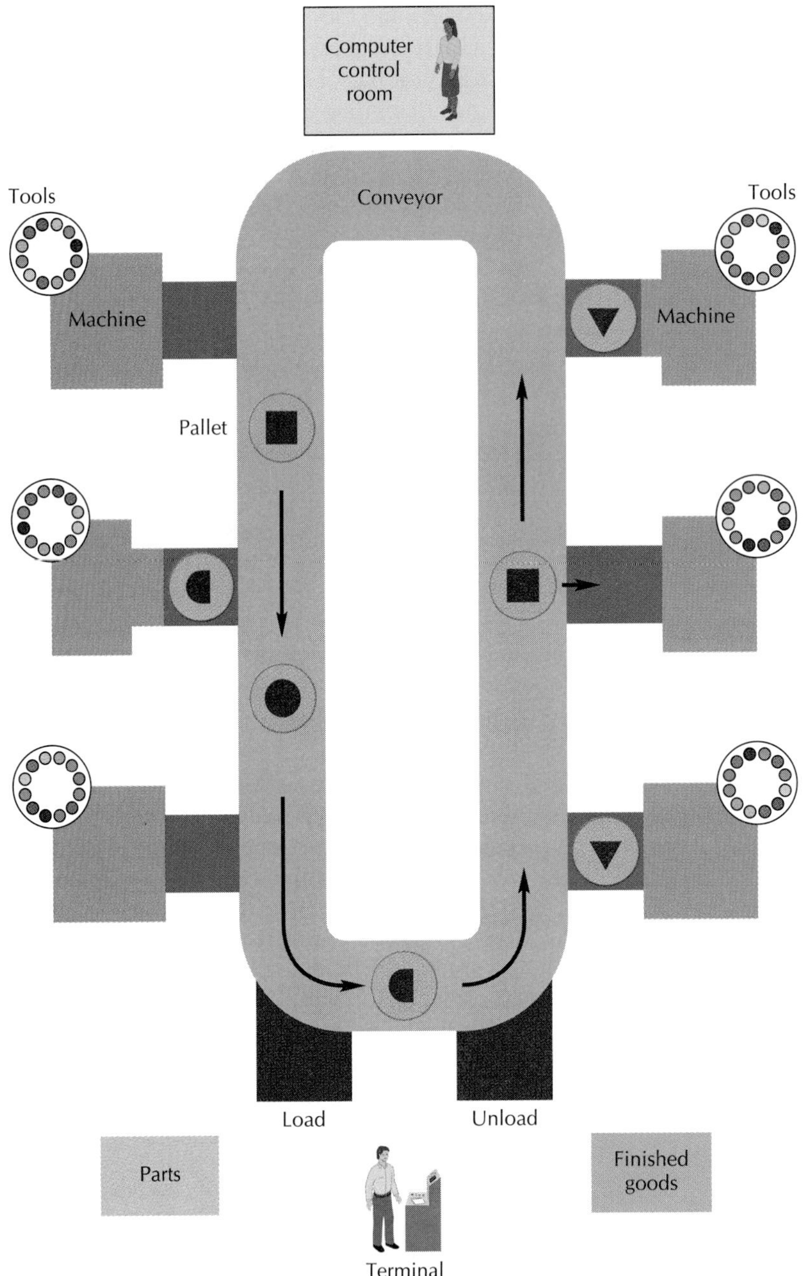

FIGURE 6.8 A Flexible Manufacturing System

Robots consist of three main parts, 1. the controller, 2. the manipulator, and 3. the end-effector.

The three main parts of a robot are its controller, its manipulator, and its end-effector.

1. *Controller:* The controller comprises the hardware, software, and power source through which the robot is programmed and by which the robot's motions are directed. The level of sophistication of a controller depends on the type of manipulator, end-effector, and sensor used by the robot. For instance, "pick-and-place" robots do not require a computer at all. Instead, these robots move their arms or grippers in one direction until pressure builds up to stop the motion. Most robots are controlled by *programmable logic controllers* (PLC), a specialized industrial version of the PC that uses ladder logic, similar to an electrician's relay dia-

Robots come in a variety of shapes and sizes. Some have the strength to lift and transport heavy loads; others can perform complex and precise tasks. The robots in the first photo are installing car windows on an assembly line. Notice the flexibility of the robot arms in assuming a variety of unusual positions. These robots are classified as "articulated robots" because of their extensive range of movement. The second photo shows a robot used in circuit board assembly. Often electronics assembly can be accomplished with "rectilinear robots" that require only pick-and-place movement.

gram. Programming can take place off-line at a PC and then be uploaded to the robot controller, or the robot can be guided through the desired path with a *teach pendant* and the path recorded for future use. Showing the robot what to do is a simple way to program the robot for continuous or imprecise movements, such as spray painting, but editing the robot path can be tedious because the entire path must be rerecorded, and the robot is down (i.e., unavailable for use) during that time.

Robots can be powered hydraulically, pneumatically, or electrically. *Hydraulic power,* derived from fluids under pressure, is used for large, powerful robots that must lift heavy loads or operate at high speeds. These robots require a lot of space, are noisy, dirty, and very expensive, and tend to break down often. *Pneumatic power,* based on compressed air, is most useful for smaller robots that are inexpensive and perform ordinary repetitive tasks, such as pick-and-place operations or machine loading and unloading. This type of power is not recommended when delicate positioning is required. Electrically powered robots are not as strong or fast as hydraulic robots; however, they are quiet, smaller, cheaper, and much more accurate. Thus, *electric power* should be used for precision jobs or jobs that require complicated paths of motion.

Teaching Note 6.8 The American Robot Industry

As you might have guessed, the trend for the future is electrically powered robots. Unfortunately, the American robot industry invested heavy in hydraulically powered robots. As a result, there are currently no major American manufacturers of robotic equipment.

2. *Manipulator:* The manipulator refers to the robot arm, which can be configured in a variety of ways to execute particular patterns of motion. Manipulator movement is described as *linear* (i.e., vertical or horizontal) or *rotational* (i.e., around) for armlike joints, such as the shoulder, elbow, and wrist. The flexibility of a robot's joints, called *degrees of freedom,* determines its dexterity and, to a large extent, its cost. Robot arm movements have three degrees of freedom, as do wrist movements. Robots are often classified by their patterns of movement, as shown in Figure 6.9.

Robots can be classified according to their pattern of movement as *rectilinear, cylindrical, spherical,* or *articulated.*

Rectilinear robots have three linear joints for moving vertically or horizontally. They are easy to program, have high repeatability, and have good lifting capabilities, but they take up a lot of space. The work envelope, or area of reach for the robot, forms a rectangle. *Cylindrical robots* have two linear joints and one rotational joint. The rotational joint allows the robot to rotate about its base. Cylindrical robots can handle heavy loads and reach deep into bins or machines, but their left and right movement is limited. The cylinder-shaped work envelope does not require much space.

Spherical robots have two rotational joints and one linear joint. They have good lifting capabilities and can reach into tight places. As expected, their work envelope resembles a portion of a sphere. *Articulated robots* most closely resemble the

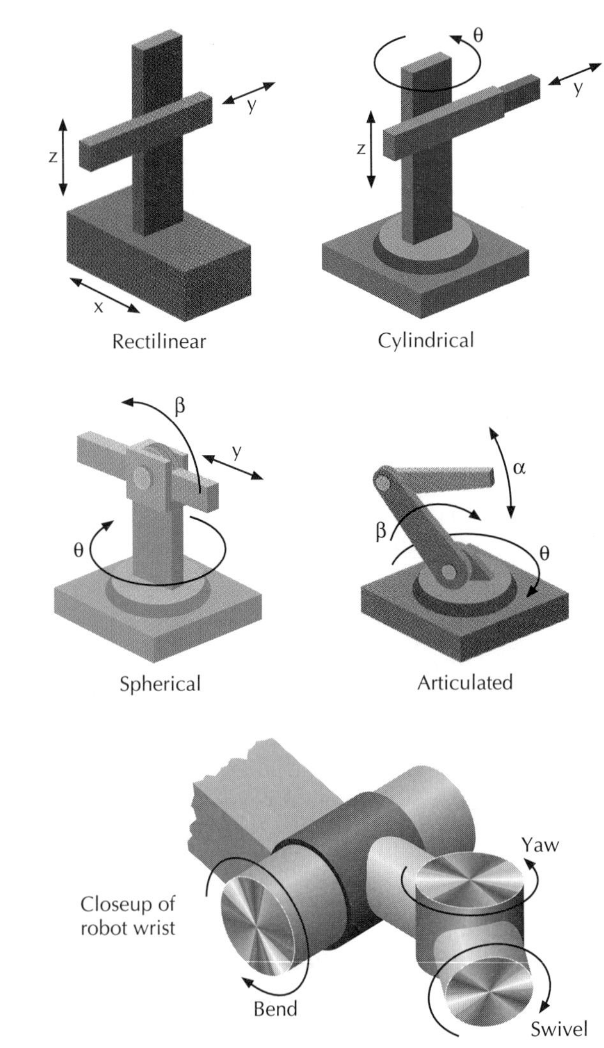

FIGURE 6.9 Robot Configurations

Reproduced by permission. ADVANCED MANUFACTURING TECHNOLOGY, by D.L. Goetsch. Delmar Publishers, Inc., Albany, N.Y., Copyright 1990.

human arm, with all joints (three or more) rotational. Less space is required and movement is very flexible. Another robot configuration is the *SCARA robot,* which combines an articulated arm with a cylindrical robot. It has found widespread use in electronics assembly.

3. *End-effectors:* End-effectors, the "hands" of the robot, can take many different forms, including guns for spray painting or glue application, torches for welding, saws for cutting, and grippers, vacuums, or magnets for grasping. End effectors are not permanently attached to the robot and can be changed to make it more flexible. Sensing devices, such as force sensors, presence and proximity sensors, and vision or tactile sensors, enhance the use of end-effectors.

The simplest sensing device on a robot is the *force sensor,* which enables a gripper to detect pressure between its fingertips. The force sensor consists of a limit switch that trips when a preset grip pressure is reached and stops the robot gripper from closing further. Photoelectric cells can be used as *presence sensors* so that when the path of the end-effector is crossed, the robot detects that an object is ready to be picked up. *Proximity sensors* bounce sound off objects to estimate how far away they are and prompt the robot to respond accordingly. Force, presence, and proximity sensing are fairly well developed technologies. Vision and tactile sensors are in their infancy. *Tactile sensors* involve end-effectors that can feel the difference between various textures and surface shapes. These types of sensors are used in *coordinate measuring machines,* which equip the end-effector with an electronic needlelike probe to measure precisely internal and external surfaces. *Vision sensors* use computers to process images from a video camera and recognize patterns or shapes. Vision sensors are popular for parts inspection or for orienting a part for automated moving or processing operations.

The use of robots has been both exciting and disappointing. Robots perform over 98 percent of the welding for Ford Taurus, drill 550 holes in 3 hours (versus the 24 hours worth of manual drilling) for General Dynamic's F-16 fighter planes, install disk drives in personal computers, snap keys onto electronic keyboards, and assemble electronic equipment with a feather-light touch. However, widespread adoption of robotics in the United States has been limited to larger industries. For example, the automobile industry alone accounts for over half of the robots in use in this country. One reason for the slow diffusion of robotic technology may be the ineffective integration of robots into existing design and manufacturing systems or the failure to adapt those systems to the unique requirements of automation. The next section addresses the issues involved in integrating manufacturing technologies.

Computer-Integrated Manufacturing

CNC machines, DNC machines, FMSs, robots, and automated material handling systems are part of the collection of technologies that are referred to as **computer-aided manufacturing (CAM)**. The integration of these and other technologies is called **computer-integrated manufacturing (CIM)**. CIM is often perceived as the ultimate in automated processing—the lights-out factory of the future with no human interference. But a more accurate description of CIM is the use of computer technology to tie together the design, production, marketing, and delivery of a product into a totally integrated system. Thus, CIM is a *strategy* for organizing and controlling a factory rather than specific technology that can be purchased. To put CIM in perspective, let's examine in general terms the evolution of manufacturing technology.

CAM is the use of programmable automation in manufacturing a product.

CIM is the total integration of design, manufacture, and delivery through the use of computer technology.

Throughout history, technology has outpaced our ability to manage it. This is especially true in the field of production. Figure 6.10 shows four steps in the evolution of manufacturing technology, from artisanship to mechanization, automation, and, finally, integration.

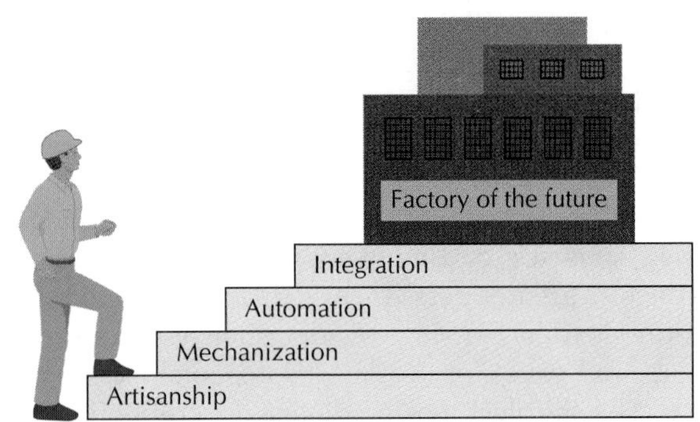

FIGURE 6.10
The Evolution of Manufacturing Technology

Manufacturing technology has evolved from *artisanship* to *mechanization* to *automation* to *integration.*

1. *Artisanship:* When manufacturing was performed by individuals with simple hand tools, all the information needed to design, produce, and deliver a product was contained in the mind of the artisan who performed all those tasks. There was no gap in communication because one individual was responsible for the entire cycle of production.

2. *Mechanization:* During the industrial revolution, machines were introduced on a large scale, and hundreds of workers were brought under one roof to manufacture a product. Production tasks were broken down and allocated to different groups of workers. Workers began specializing in certain areas of production. Communication among these specialists was achieved with drawings, specifications, job orders, and process plans. Quality control was introduced to ensure that the finished product matched the designed product.

Teaching Note 6.9 Automation

3. *Automation:* Automation improved the performance and enhanced the capabilities of both people and machines, but in isolation. CAD improved design, NC machines improved manufacturing, and robots speeded up certain processes, but islands of automation soon became apparent. Designers could conceive of parts with CAD that the factory could not make. NC and CNC machines could machine parts, but the cost of programming and debugging the programs to run the machines was exorbitant. The speed of robots at one stage of production often caused bottlenecks elsewhere.

4. *Integration:* The concept of CIM was suggested by Joseph Harrington in 1974 as a level of manufacturing achievement beyond automation. CIM's job is to develop linkages between people, machines, data bases, and decisions. The major components of CIM are shown in Figure 6.11. Each CIM component represents a different type of linkage.

Group technology is the grouping of parts into families.

CAD can physically link different design components together to create new or modified designs and communicate electronically to other systems. **Group technology (GT)** classifies existing designs so that new designs can incorporate the expertise of earlier designs. CAE (computer-aided engineering) links the functional design of the product to the CAD-generated form design. CAPP converts design specifications from CAD into instructions for manufacture for CAM. CAD/CAM describes the direct physical link between design and manufacturing.

Within the manufacturing function, CAM technologies (e.g., CNC machines, robots, automatic tool changers) facilitate remote control and integration of operations. Different operations may be physically linked with automated material handling (AMH) systems. In advanced CAM systems (i.e., DNC machines and flexible manufacturing systems), automated machines communicate directly with each other, work together, and are centrally controlled.

An important thrust in achieving a CIM environment is the development of shared data bases, standards, and networking within the manufacturing function. For example, MAP (manufacturing automation protocol), originally developed by

Transparency 6.7 Components of CIM

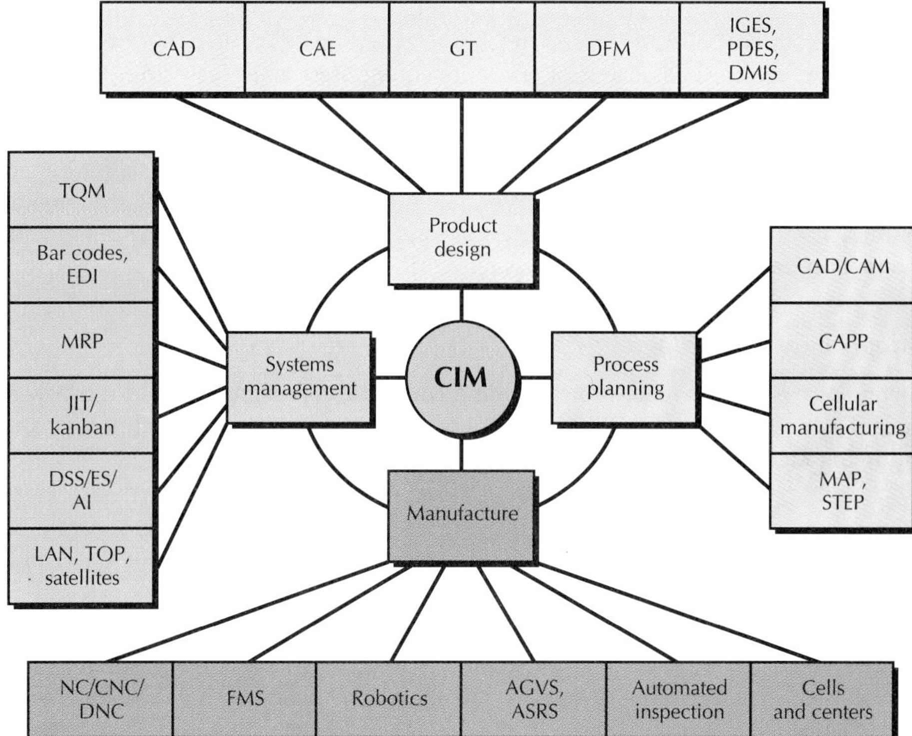

FIGURE 6.11 Components of CIM

General Motors to solve its automation headaches, sets standards for communication between pieces of automated equipment produced by different vendors. TOP (technical and office protocol) serves the same function in an office environment. IGES (initial graphics exchange specification) translates graphics data (mainly wireframe models) between different CAD systems. PDES (product data exchange specification) translates additional aspects of CAD design, such as solid modeling data, part features, tolerance specifications, surface finishes, and material specifications in the same manner. DMIS (dimensional measuring interface specification) provides a standard medium for exchanging inspection information between CAD systems and computerized inspection equipment. STEP (standard for the exchange of product model data) is the European version of MAP, TOP, IGES, PDES, and DMIS, combined and extended. It is currently being developed in conjunction with ISO 10303. When completed, STEP will be able to represent all critical product specifications (such as shape, material, tolerances, behavior, function, and structure), consider the entire product life-cycle (from development to manufacture through use and disposal), and specify process sequences for specific production systems (such as automobiles, shipbuilding, architectural engineering, or plant engineering).

Teaching Note 6.10 STEP

CIM also reaches outside of the manufacturing function. Electronic data interchange (EDI) allows information to be sent from computer to computer between customer and manufacturer or between manufacturer and supplier. Other technological advancements that enhance communication and speed up activity completions include electronic funds transfer (EFT), electronic mail (E-mail), teleconferencing, and telecommuting. Automated order entry by customers uses some of these technologies. In the process of manufacturing a product, materials need to be ordered, workers scheduled, demand forecasted, customer orders received and entered into the manufacturing system, production planned, progress reports issued, costs and quality documented, and customers billed. Computerized manufacturing control systems developed to collect, store, and display this information are an integral part of CIM. Manufacturing resources planning, an advanced version of MRP discussed in Chapter 13, is an example of such a system.

Teaching Note 6.11 CIM and AI

To summarize the concept of computer-integrated manufacturing, we might look at CIM's mission from two vantage points: For existing systems, CIM serves as a translator between the different languages of automated design and automated manufacture, and for future systems, CIM can provide the basis for an automation strategy that takes *integration* into account. Hence, CIM makes manufacturers aware of the capabilities of integrated manufacture and the type of interaction that can be expected between various systems.

Adoption of Technology

Technology is not a panacea for regaining competitiveness, nor should it be overlooked as a source of competitive advantage. When adopting new technology, the following factors should be carefully considered:

GAINING THE COMPETITIVE EDGE

Motorola's Latest CIM Project Is Pure "Fusion"

In the mid-1980s, Motorola changed its offshore manufacturing strategy and brought back pager manufacturing to their Boynton Beach facility in the United States. The celebrated "Bandit" project used the best of available technologies to automate production of a pager redesigned for automation. Bandit validated the flexibility and cost competitiveness of the CIM approach to manufacturing. It also provided the base for future, more advanced CIM systems.

Motorola's latest CIM project, called *Fusion*, is even more integrated (as the name implies) and flexible than Bandit. Before Fusion, Motorola factories could manufacture product variations such as housing covers, vibration options, altering options, and frequencies, but the products remained basically the same. The Fusion line can manufacture physically different pagers with different circuit board configurations. In fact, Fusion can manufacture any portable electronic product (from calculator to pager to personal digital communicator), as long as the design can be represented on the computer system and the parts are available to the assembly robot. At an engineer's or customer's request, Fusion can build products that have never before been built.

The system begins with a phone call from the customer. The customer orders a pager over the hot line, describing the features he or she wants in plain English. The order is automatically translated into a customized bill of materials in terms the factory (and the computer) can understand. The computer takes a few microseconds to then virtually build the product requested, verifying the availability of materials and processes. Once the computer is assured that the manufacturing system has the capability to build the item, it releases the order to the factory floor—while the customer is still on the line.

The first station on the line marks a printed circuit board with a machine-readable customer serial number. As the board flows down the line, the number is read by each machine. A Motorola-designed robot assembles different units, choosing parts from the appropriate bins. The assembly line is set up in tandem, with two parallel sections in the front end to populate, reflow, and solder circuit boards and two parallel sections in the back end for assembly, testing, and packing. Each downstream robot can do the job of its upstream counterpart if the latter goes down. If an entire section goes down, Fusion automatically routes the products to a parallel section. This is accomplished in the middle of the line at a singulation area (similar to a railyard switching station), where individual boards are directed along the most efficient path.

Source: Based on Strobel, Russ, and Andy Johnson, "Pocket Pagers in Lots of One," *IEEE Spectrum* (September 1993): 29–32.

- *Technology readiness:* Automation does not have the ability to grant exceptions, tweak a process, or modify a design. Poorly designed products and inefficient processes are often revealed when automation is introduced. This can be a learning experience (albeit an expensive one) for management. Unfortunately, many managers blame automation for causing problems revealed through automation that had always been present.
- *Technology design:* Automation's advantage comes not from its ability to mimic humans, but from the ability to do things that humans cannot do. For example, people have difficulty returning a hand or tool to exactly the same spot (i.e., poor repeatability), but they have very good sensors that can be used to search for the correct spot. Machines, on the other hand, have good repeatability, so sophisticated sensors are not needed. Manual assembly of high-tech products is almost obsolete due to the ability of robots to perform their task with higher quality, uniformity, and cleanliness.

  The most successful technologies look for the best way to perform a task and are not constrained by the limitations of the human body. Current experimentation with free-moving robots is patterned after insect movement, not human movement.
- *Technology selection:* The level of automation selected must match the requirements of the manufacturing system, the product being produced, and the competitive environment. Human-directed work is preferable in situations where sensing, judgment, or intelligence is required or in environments that change so frequently that the expense of programming automated equipment would be uneconomical. Specific guidelines can be found in the literature for when to use different types of manufacturing technologies. This makes the task of technology selection appear straightforward. However, even in those cases when it is a simple task to select a technology appropriate for the current product market, one must realize that the market may well change over the life of the technology. For example, if a formerly diverse market becomes large and homogeneous, flexible manufacturing may add undue cost to production. Similarly, if a focused market becomes more diverse, fixed automation will not be able to meet the varied demand requirements.
- *Technology integration:* Technology is so expensive that many firms can afford to automate only incrementally. Without a sound strategy for automation, it is difficult to ensure that the individual systems purchased can be integrated. GM, at one point, had 40,000 pieces of automated equipment, only 15 percent of which could communicate with each other or use the same data base.

Technology *readiness, design, selection,* and *integration* should be considered before adopting new technology.

It is difficult to predict the wonders that new technology will bring our way. However, it is generally agreed that technology in the future will become more powerful, more flexible, easier to use, more intelligent, and better integrated.

SUMMARY

This chapter discussed two important issues in manufacturing system design: process planning and technology decisions. Process planning consists of converting product designs into workable instructions for manufacture. These instructions may include the sequence of assembly, sequence of operations, machine assignments, tooling, machine settings, machine operating parameters, inspection criteria, operating procedures, and processing details. They often appear in the form of assembly charts, flow process charts, operations process charts, and manufacturing specifications. On a broader scale, process planning may involve decisions such as process selection, equipment purchases, and whether to make or buy product components.

Obviously, process planning is an important function that can significantly affect the cost and quality of manufacture. However, process planning did not receive much attention until the late 1970s, when automated systems formally required an extra planning step from design to manufacture. It was at this point that managers began to realize the impact of process decisions on manufacturing cost and performance. In today's environment of complex designs, advanced machining technologies, new materials, less skilled operators, and increasing product variety, process planning is viewed as essential to competitive success.

The second half of this chapter described technology decisions. Technology decisions typically involve large sums of money and can have a tremendous impact on the cost, speed, quality, and flexibility of manufacture. More importantly, however, they define the future capabilities of a firm and set the stage for competitive interactions. Thus, it is dangerous to delegate technology decisions to technical experts. A manager's ability to ask questions and understand the basic thrust of proposed technology is invaluable in making wise technology choices. For that reason, we spent some time in this chapter discussing several basic manufacturing processes and their different levels automation. Discussions of CAD/CAM, robotics, FMS, and CIM helped to explain the types of technology choices available to managers.

SUMMARY OF KEY TERMS

assembly chart: a schematic diagram of a product that shows the relationship of component parts to parent assemblies, the groupings of parts that make up a subassembly, and the overall sequence of assembly.

batch production: the low-volume production of customized products.

bill of material: a document that lists the materials and components that go into a product, provides a brief description, and specifies the quantities required for assembly.

break-even analysis: a technique that determines the volume of demand needed to be profitable; it takes into account the trade-off between fixed and variable costs.

CNC machines: NC machines that are controlled by software instructions stored in the memory of a computer.

computer-aided manufacturing (CAM): the use of programmable automation in the manufacture of a product.

computer-aided process planning (CAPP): a specialized software system that attempts to automate the development of process plans.

computer-integrated manufacturing (CIM): the total integration of design, manufacture, and delivery of a product through the use of computer technology.

continuous process: the production of a very high-volume commodity product with highly automated equipment.

DNC machines: several NC machines under direct or distributed numerical control of a single computer.

flexible manufacturing system: a versatile system that results from the physical connection of DNC machines with an automated material handling system.

group technology (GT): the grouping of parts into families based on similar shapes or processing requirements.

mass production: the high-volume production of a standard product for a mass market.

numerically controlled (NC) machines: machines whose motion is numerically controlled by instructions contained on a punched tape.

operations process chart: a document that shows the series of operations necessary to make each item listed on the assembly chart.
process flowchart: a document that uses standardized symbols to chart the productive and nonproductive flow of activities involved in a process; it may be used to document current processes or as a vehicle for process improvement.
process planning: the conversion of designs into workable instructions for manufacture, along with associated decisions on component purchase or fabrication and process and equipment selection.
project: the one-at-a-time production of a product to customer order that requires a long time to complete and a large investment of funds and resources.
robots: manipulators that can be programmed to move workpieces or tools along a specified path.

SOLVED PROBLEM

Process Selection

Problem Statement:
Texloy Manufacturing Company must select a process for its new product, TX142, from among three different alternatives. The following cost data have been gathered:

	Process A	*Process B*	*Process C*
Fixed cost	\$10,000	\$20,000	\$50,000
Variable cost	\$5/unit	\$4/unit	\$2/unit

For what volume of demand would each process be desirable?

Solution:
First, we need to construct a mathematical formula for the total cost of each process alternative as the sum of fixed costs and variable costs. If v represents the number of TX142s demanded (and, we assume, produced), then

$$\text{Total cost for process A} = \$10{,}000 + \$5v$$
$$\text{Total cost for process B} = \$20{,}000 + \$4v$$
$$\text{Total cost for process C} = \$50{,}000 + \$2v$$

Next, we calculate the points of indifference between the processes by equating their total costs and solving for demand volume, v. Note that in this problem there are three processes to consider, but we can compare only two at a time. Let's begin by comparing the alternative with the lowest fixed cost to the alternative with the next-lowest fixed cost.

Comparison 1: Process A versus process B

$$\begin{array}{ccc} \textit{Process A} & & \textit{Process B} \\ \$10{,}000 + \$5v & = & \$20{,}000 + \$4v \\ & v = & 10{,}000 \text{ units} \end{array}$$

Thus, if the demand for units is 10,000 units, we can choose either process A or process B. But if demand is less than 10,000, we should choose the alternative with the lowest fixed cost, process A. Conversely, if demand is greater than 10,000, we should choose the alternative with the lowest variable cost, process B.

Comparison 2: Process B versus process C

$$\begin{aligned} &\textit{Process B} \qquad \textit{Process C} \\ \$20{,}000 + \$4v &= \$50{,}000 + \$2v \\ 2v &= 30{,}000 \\ v &= 15{,}000 \text{ units} \end{aligned}$$

If demand is 15,000 units, we are indifferent between process B and process C. If demand is greater than 15,000 units, we should choose process C. If demand is less than 15,000 but greater than 10,000 (see comparison 1), we should choose process B.

Comparison 3: Process A versus process C

$$\begin{aligned} &\textit{Process A} \qquad \textit{Process C} \\ \$10{,}000 + \$5v &= \$50{,}000 + \$2v \\ 3v &= 40{,}000 \\ v &= 13{,}333 \text{ units} \end{aligned}$$

This comparison is not really necessary, because we were careful in ordering the previous comparisons. We have already concluded that process B should be selected between 10,000 and 15,000 units. Therefore, this point of indifference can be ignored.

The graph of the problem is shown here.

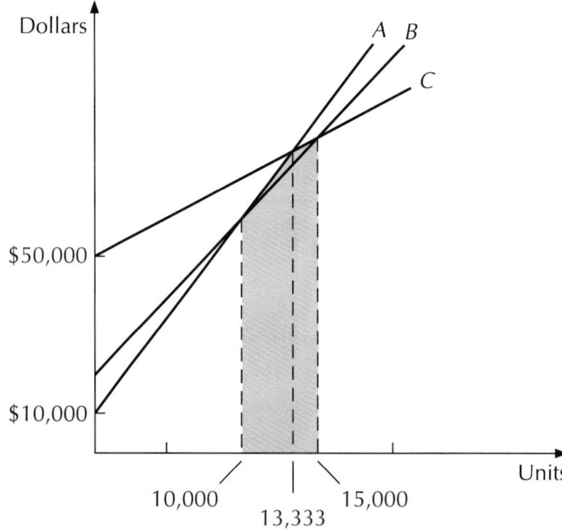

To summarize, from the graph and our decision rules, we can recommend the following process selection.

- Below 10,000 units, choose process A.
- Between 10,000 and 15,000 units, choose process B.
- Above 15,000 units, choose process C.

QUESTIONS

6-1. What kind of information do the following documents communicate?
   a. Assembly chart
   b. Operations process chart
   c. Process flowchart

6-2. List and explain five factors that affect the make-or-buy decision.
6-3. Differentiate between batch production, mass production, and continuous production.
6-4. How is break-even analysis used for process selection?
6-5. List several factors that are often overlooked in a financial analysis of equipment purchases.
6-6. Describe the output of process planning. How does process planning differ by type of process?
6-7. Describe the two approaches to computer-aided process planning. What are the advantages of each?
6-8. Why are many managers technology-averse?
6-9. What level of understanding is required for managers to make wise technology choices?
6-10. How do the four basic machining processes, turning, milling, drilling, and shaping, change the shape of material?
6-11. Describe several levels of automation for machine tools. How does the role of the operator change?
6-12. Give an example of an automated material handling system.
6-13. Define flexible manufacturing system. What are the advantages of an FMS?
6-14. How are robots controlled and powered?
6-15. How can manipulator movement be used to classify robots?
6-16. Describe several functions of robot end-effectors.
6-17. Briefly discuss the evolution of manufacturing technology.
6-18. What are the major impediments to CIM today?
6-19. List and explain four factors that should be considered in the adoption of technology.
6-20. Construct a process flowchart of a process with which you are familiar. Identify bottlenecks, potential failure points, and opportunities for improvement.

PROBLEMS

6-1. Create an assembly chart from the following multilevel bill of material:

6-1. See Solutions Manual.

LEVEL	*ITEM*	*QUANTITY*
0	XYZ Assembly	1
–1	X101	1
=2	Y110	1
=2	Y220	2
–1	X201	3
=2	Y330	2
–1	X301	4
=2	Y440	3
=2	Y550	1
≡3	Z111	2

6-2. Construct a multilevel bill of materials from the following assembly chart:

6-2. See Solutions Manual.

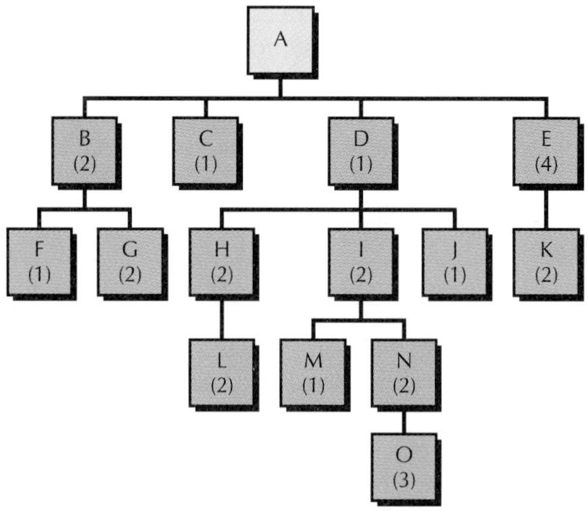

6-3. See Solutions Manual.

6-3. Bayside General is trying to streamline its operations. A problem-solving group consisting of a nurse, a technician, a doctor, an administrator, and a patient is examining outpatient procedures in an effort to speed up the process and make it more cost-effective. Listed here are the steps that a typical patient follows for diagnostic imaging. Create a process flowchart of the procedure and identify opportunities for improvement.

- Patient enters main hospital entrance.
- Patient registers at central reception.
- Patient taken to diagnostic imaging department.
- Patient registers at diagnostic imaging reception.
- Patient sits in department waiting area until dressing area clear.
- Patient changes in dressing area.
- Patient waits in dressing area.
- Patient taken to exam room.
- Exam performed.
- Patient taken to dressing area.
- Patient dresses.
- Patient leaves.

6-4. See Solutions Manual.

6-4. Newman & Sons assembles bedroom furniture for a major manufacturer. The business has grown in spurts, and, as with many small businesses, the manner in which work is performed is more a matter of convenience than careful planning.

Consider the process of assembling drawers. Three drawer-clamp machines put the drawer together by pressing the dovetails in the drawer sides into the slots in the drawer fronts and backs. The drawer subassembly is then placed on a roller line and transported to a stop, where it waits to be placed on a motorized conveyor line. On the conveyor line, the bottom of the drawer is stapled on, drawer guides are installed, and glue blocks are added. The drawers encounter another stop until one of two sander operators removes them. The dovetail joints are then sanded on a belt sander and loaded onto a hanger conveyor. The hanger conveyor transports the drawer through a spray booth, where the finish is applied. The finished drawer then winds its way to the chest assembly area downstairs, by which time the finish has dried.

a. Construct an assembly chart for a drawer, as described here.
b. Map out the flow of the process in a process flowchart. Do you have any suggestions for improving the process flow?

6-5. Mikey W. Smitty, an emerging rapper, is getting ready to cut his first CD, called "Western Rap." The cost of recording the CD is $5,000, but copies are $5 apiece. If the CDs can be sold for $15 each, how many CDs must be sold to break even? What is the break-even point in dollars?

6-5. 500; $7,500

6-6. Mikey W. Smitty is confident that demand for his "Western Rap" CD will substantially exceed the break-even point computed in Problem 6-5. So, Mikey is contemplating having his CD cut at a classier (and pricier) studio. The cost to record the CD would rise to $9,000. However, since this new studio works with very high volume, production costs would fall to $2 per CD.

a. What is the break-even point for this new process?
b. Compare this process to the process proposed in the previous problem. For what volume of demand should Mikey choose the classier studio?

6-6. a. 692
b. > 1,333

6-7. Patricia Zell, a dollmaker from Olney, Maryland, is interested in the mass marketing and production of a ceramic doll of her own design called Tiny Trisha. The initial investment required for plant and equipment is estimated at $25,000. Labor and material costs are approximately $10 per doll. If the dolls can be sold for $50 each, what volume of demand is necessary for the Tiny Trisha doll to break even?

6-7. 625

6-8. Although it will fulfill her lifelong dream, Patricia is not confident that demand for her Tiny Trisha doll will exceed the break-even point computed in Problem 6-7. If she chooses a less appealing site and does more of the work by hand, her initial investment cost can be reduced to $5,000, but her per-unit cost of manufacture will rise to $15 per doll.

a. What is the break-even point for this new process?
b. Compare this process to the process proposed in the previous problem. For what volume of demand should Patricia choose this process?

6-8. a. 143
b. < 1,334

6-9. The editors at Allyn and Bacon are trying to decide whether to offer a laser disk or a CD-ROM with its Russell and Taylor POM text. It costs $1800 to press a one-sided master disk but only $25 to reproduce each disk. CD-ROMs are less expensive to make, but there are no significant reductions in price for copies. A 75-image CD-ROM costs $1.59 per image to make and $99.00 per disk to reproduce.

Both the laser disk and CD-ROM would be provided free to adopters of the textbook. Assuming that the format of the images is not critical to sales, compare the laser disk cost with the cost of the CD-ROM. How many textbook adoptions would be required to justify investment in a laser disk instead of a CD-ROM?

6-9. > 22

6-10. David Austin recently purchased a chain of dry cleaners in northern Wisconsin. Although the business is making a modest profit now, David suspects that if he invests in a new press, he could recognize a substantial increase in profits. The new press costs $15,400 to purchase and install and can press 40 shirts an hour (or 320 per day). David estimates that with the new press, it will cost $0.25 to launder and press each shirt. Customers are charged $1.10 per shirt.

a. How many shirts will David have to press to break even?
b. So far, David's workload has varied from 50 to 200 shirts a day. How long would it take to break even on the new press at the low-demand estimate? At the high-demand estimate?
c. If David cuts his price to $0.99 a shirt, he expects to be able to stabilize his customer base at 250 shirts per week. How long would it take to break even at the reduced price of $0.99?

6-10. a. 18,118 shirts
b. 362 days, 961 days
c. 84 days

6-11. > 151 make; ≤ 151, buy

6-11. The school cafeteria can make pizza for approximately $0.30 a slice. The cost of kitchen use and cafeteria staff runs about $200 per day. The Pizza Den nearby will deliver whole pizzas for $9.00 per pizza. The cafeteria staff cuts the pizza into 8 pieces and serves them in the usual cafeteria line. With no cooking duties, the staff can be reduced by half, for a fixed cost of $75 per day. Should the school cafeteria make or buy its pizzas?

6-12. a. 242 boxes
b. 337 boxes
c. $v \leq 100$, current; $100 < v < 160$, supplier 1; $v \geq 160$, supplier 2

6-12. ComputerEase supply store sells both 5⁄-inch and 3fi-inch diskettes. Over the last few years the demand for each type of diskette has changed dramatically. The store purchases 5⁄-inch diskettes for $9.95 a box and sells them for $13.60. The 3fi-inch diskettes are purchased for $17.00 a box and sold for $19.70. The store needs to clear $1,000 per month in profit on diskettes.

a. If ComputerEase sells 95 boxes of 5⁄-inch diskettes, how many boxes of 3fi-inch diskettes must be sold to meet the profit objective?
b. If the demand for 5⁄-inch diskettes falls to 25 per month, how many boxes of 3fi-inch diskettes must be sold?
c. To remain competitive, ComputerEase feels it cannot raise its prices on diskettes, but with the decline in 5⁄-inch sales, it is difficult to reach the monthly profit goal. A survey of new supplier sources yielded the following options:
   - Supplier 1 Fixed order of 100 boxes/month of 3fi-inch diskettes, $1,700 plus $15/box for every box over 100
   - Supplier 2 Fixed order of 100 boxes/month of 3fi-inch diskettes, $2,000 plus $10/box for every box over 100

   Assuming that the market for 5⁄-inch diskettes disappears, should ComputerEase try supplier 1, try supplier 2, or stick with its current supplier? How does the monthly demand for diskettes affect your recommendation?

6-13. pages ≥ 100, A; 40 < pages < 100; pages ≤ 40, B

6-13. The office administrator of a large public accounting firm is calculating the cost of word processing a client's financial statements. The alternatives are to have the work done by the accounting firm's data-processing staff, which precludes the need for final review by an accountant (process A), have the client perform his or her own word processing, which requires extensive review by an accountant (process B) or contract out the work to a professional service, which requires some review by an accountant (process C). The cost of each alternative is outlined next.

	Process A	*Process B*	*Process C*
Word Processing	$3,000	$2,300	$2,500
Accountant Review	$0 per page	$10 per page	$5 per page

The office administrator has asked you to prepare a chart for the firm's clients that outlines the various word-processing costs and makes recommendations based on differing page lengths.

6-14. 187; 226

★ 6-14. Alma McCoy has decided to purchase a cellular phone for her car, but she is confused about which rate plan to choose. The "occasional-user" plan is $0.50/minute, regardless of how many minutes of air time are used. The "frequent-user" plan charges a flat rate of $55/month for 70 minutes of air time plus $0.33/minute for any time over 70 minutes. The "executive" plan charges a flat fee of $75 per month for 100 minutes of air time plus $0.25/minute over 100 minutes. In the interest of simplicity, Alma has decided to go with the occasional-user plan to start with and then upgrade as she sees fit at a later date.

How much air time per month would Alma need to use before she upgrades from the occasional-user plan to the frequent-user plan? At what usage rate should she switch from the frequent user plan to the executive plan?

6-15. Merrimac Manufacturing Company has always purchased a certain component part from a supplier on the East coast for \$50 per part. The supplier is reliable and has maintained the same price structure for years. Recently, improvements in operations and reduced product demand have cleared up some capacity in Merrimac's own plant for producing component parts. The particular part in question could be produced at \$40 per part, with an annual fixed investment of \$25,000. Currently, Merrimac needs 300 of these parts per year.

a. Should Merrimac make or buy the component part?
b. As another alternative, a new supplier located nearby is offering volume discounts for new customers of \$50 per part for the first 100 parts ordered and \$45 per part for each additional unit ordered. Should Merrimac make the component in-house, buy it from the new supplier, or stick with the old supplier?
c. Would your decision change if Merrimac's demand increased to 2,000 parts per month? Increased to 5,000 per month?
d. Develop a set of rules that Merrimac can use to decide when to make this component, when to buy it from the old supplier, or when to buy it from the new supplier.

6-15. a. Buy
b. Supplier 2
c. Supplier 2; make
d. $v \leq 100$, old; $4{,}900 < v < 100$, new; $v \geq 4{,}900$, make

6-16. Prydain Pharmaceuticals is reviewing its employee health-care program. Currently, the company pays a fixed fee of \$300 per month for each employee, regardless of the number or dollar amount of medical claims filed. Another health-care provider has offered to charge the company \$100 per month per employee and \$30 per claim filed. A third insurer charges \$200 per month per employee and \$10 per claim filed. Which health-care program should Prydain join? How would the average number of claims filed per employee per month affect your decision?

6-16. Provider 1 if claims ≥ 10, Provider 2 if claims ≤ 5, Provider 3 if $5 \leq$ claims ≤ 10

6-17. Gemstone Quarry is trying to decide whether or not to invest in a new material handling system. The current system (which is old and completely paid for) has an annual maintenance cost of \$10,000 and costs approximately \$25 to transport each load of material. The two new systems that are being considered vary both in sophistication and cost. System 1 has a fixed cost of \$40,000 and a cost per load estimated at \$10. System 2 has a fixed cost of \$100,000 but a per-load cost of \$5. At what volume of demand (i.e., number of loads) should Gemstone purchase System 1? System 2?

6-17. $v > 2{,}000$; $v > 12{,}000$

6-18. Tribal Systems, Inc., is opening a new plant and has yet to decide on the type of process to employ. A labor-intensive process would cost \$10,000 for tools and equipment and \$14 for labor and materials per item produced. A more automated process costs \$50,000 in plant and equipment but has a labor/material cost of \$8 per item produced. A fully automated process costs \$300,000 for plant and equipment and \$2 per item produced. If process selection were based solely on lowest cost, for what range of production would each process be chosen?

6-18. Labor intensive if demand $\leq 6{,}666$, Fully automated if demand $\geq 41{,}666$, Automated if $6{,}666 <$ demand $< 41{,}666$

6-19. Lydia and Jon order their holiday gifts through the mail. They have spent many evenings at home comparison-shopping through gift catalogs and have found all the things they need from three mail-order houses, B.B. Lean, Spoogle's, and Sea's End. The purchase price for their selections from each catalog is given here. The shipping and handling charge per item is also given. If Lydia and Jon want to order all their gifts from the same source,

6-19. B. B. Lean if order ≤ 30, Sea's End if $30 <$ order < 40, Spoogle's if order ≥ 40

which catalog should they choose? How does the number of items ordered affect your recommendation?

	B.B. Lean	*Spoogle's*	*Sea's End*
Purchase price	$400	$500	$460
Shipping/handling per item	$6	$3	$4

See Solutions Manual.

CASE PROBLEM

Streamlining the Refinancing Process

First National Bank has been swamped with refinancing requests this year. In order to handle the increased volume, they divided the process into five distinct phases and assigned several persons to each stage. (Each stage, in fact, became a department.)

The process begins with a customer completing a loan application for a *loan agent.* The loan agent discusses the refinancing options with the customer and performs quick calculations based on customer-reported data to see if the customer qualifies for loan approval. If the numbers work, the customer signs a few papers to allow a credit check and goes home to wait for notification of the loan's approval.

The customer's file is then passed on to a *loan processor,* who requests a credit check, verification of loans or mortgages from other financial institutions, an appraisal of the property, and employment verification. If any problems are encountered, the loan processor goes to the loan agent for advice. If items appear on the credit report that are not on the application or if other agencies have requested the credit report, the customer is required to explain the discrepancies in writing. If the explanation is acceptable, the letter is placed in the customer's file and the file is sent to the loan agent (and sometimes the bank's board) for final approval.

The customer receives a letter of loan approval and is asked to call the *closing agent* to schedule a closing date and to lock in a loan rate if the customer has not already done so.

The closing agent requests the name of the customer's attorney in order to forward the loan packet. The attorney is responsible for arranging a termite inspection, a survey, a title search, and insurance and for preparing the closing papers. The attorney and the closing agent correspond back and forth to verify exact fees, payment schedules, and payoff amounts.

The *loan-servicing specialist* makes sure the previous loan is paid off and the new loan is set up properly. After the closing takes place, the bank's *loan-payment specialist* takes care of issuing payment books or setting up the automatic drafting of mortgage fees and calculating the exact monthly payments, including escrow amounts. The loan-payment specialist also monitors late payment of mortgages.

It is difficult to evaluate the success or failure of the reengineered process, since the volume of refinancing requests is so much greater than it has ever been before. However, customer comments solicited by the loan-servicing specialist have been disturbing to management. In light of the customer comments listed here, evaluate First National's refinancing process and recommend improvements. What additional information would be helpful in your analysis?

Customer Comments:

- I decided to refinance with the same bank that held my original loan, thinking erroneously that I could save some time and money. You took 2 months longer proccessing my loan than the other bank would have and the money I saved on closing costs was more than eaten up by the extra month's higher mortgage payments.

- I just got a call from someone at your bank claiming my mortgage payment was overdue. How can it be overdue when you draft it automatically from my checking account?
- How come you do everything in writing and through the mail? If you would just call and ask me these questions instead of sending forms for me to fill out, things would go much quicker.
- If I haven't made any additions to my house or property in the past year, you appraised it last year, and you have access to my tax assessment, why bother with another appraisal? You guys just like to pass around the business.
- I never know who to call for what. You have so many people working on my file. I know I've repeated the same thing to a dozen different people.
- It took so long to get my loan approved that my credit report, appraisal report, and termite inspection ran out. I think you should pay for the new reports, not me.
- I drove down to your office in person today to deliver the attorney's papers, and I hoped to return them with your signature and whatever else you add to the closing packet. The loan specialist said that the closing agent wouldn't get to my file until the morning of the scheduled closing and that if she hit a snag, the closing could be postponed! I'm taking off half a day from work to attend the closing and "rescheduling" is not convenient. I know you have lots of business, but I don't like being treated this way.
- I received a letter from one of your loan-payment specialists today, along with a stack of forms to complete specifying how I want to set up my mortgage payments. I signed all these at closing—don't you read your own work? I'm worried that if I fill them out again you'll withdraw the payment twice from my account!

REFERENCES

Office of Technology Assessment, *Computerized Manufacturing Automation: Employment, Education, and the Workplace,* Washington, D.C.: Government Printing Office, 1984.

Bedworth, D., M. Henderson, and P. Wolfe, *Computer-Integrated Design and Manufacturing,* New York: McGraw-Hill, 1991.

Foston, L., *Fundamentals of Computer Integrated Manufacturing,* Englewood Cliffs, N.J.: Prentice Hall, 1991.

Goetsch, D., *Advanced Manufacturing Technology,* Albany, N.Y.: Delmar Publishers, 1990.

Gold, B., "CAM Sets New Rules for Production," *Harvard Business Review,* (November–December 1982): 88–94.

Groover, M., "Fundamental Operations," *IEEE Spectrum* 20, no. 5 (May 1983): 65–69.

Haas, E., "Breakthrough Manufacturing," *Harvard Business Review* (March–April 1987): 75–81.

Maus, R., and R. Allsup, *Robotics: A Manager's Guide,* New York: John Wiley, 1986.

Nevens, J., D. Whitney, T. DeFazio, A. Edsall, R. Gustavson, R. Metzinger, and W. Dvorak, *Concurrent Design of Products and Processes: A Strategy for the Next Generation in Manufacturing,* New York: McGraw-Hill, 1989.

Noori, H., *Managing the Dynamics of New Technology,* Englewood Cliffs, N.J.: Prentice Hall, 1990.

Robot Institute of America, *Worldwide Robotics Survey and Directory,* 1991.

Saporito, B., "IBM's No-Hands Assembly Line," *Fortune* (September 15, 1986).

Schroeder, R., *Operations Management: Decision Making in the Operations Function,* New York: McGraw-Hill, 1989.

Skinner, W., *Manufacturing: The Formidable Competitive Weapon,* New York: John Wiley, 1985.

Valery, N., "Factory of the Future," *The Economist* (May 30, 1987): 3–18.

7
FACILITY LAYOUT

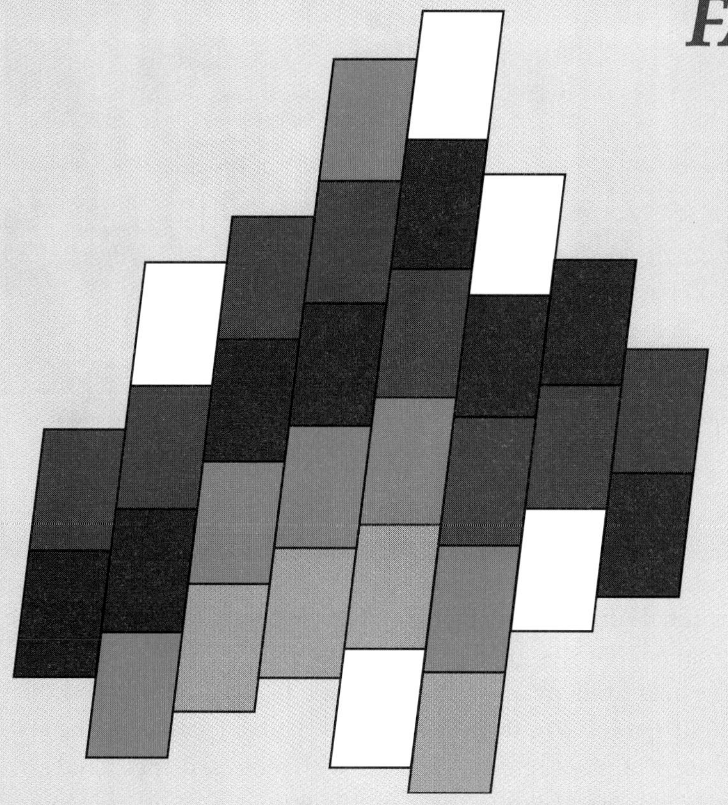

CHAPTER OUTLINE

Good Layouts can increase revenues, as well as save operating expenses. Pittsburgh airport's innovative X-design allows planes to approach the airport from any direction, significantly increasing the airspace capacity of the airport.

PITTSBURGH INTERNATIONAL: AN EFFICIENT LAYOUT

Pittsburgh International Airport is the first airport to be constructed from scratch since airline deregulation. It is designed to mesh with the "hub-and-spokes" system, in which passengers from a variety of cities come to a central hub and then transfer to other flights en route to their destinations. Hub airports must be able to handle large volumes of passengers and flights with increased speed and efficiency. At Pittsburgh, moving walkways and shuttle trains transport passengers to distant gates in 11 minutes or less. Gates are more spacious, too, to handle the larger crowds. Baggage is bar-coded and channeled by computerized laser scanners along 6 miles of conveyor belts from flight to flight. The terminal itself is X-shaped to allow planes to approach from any direction. Dual taxiways run in opposite directions around the terminal to reduce queuing time on takeoffs. USAIR estimates that the runway layout alone saves them more than $12 million in fuel costs each year.[1]

■■■

Facility layout is the arrangement of areas within a facility.

Facility layout refers to the arrangement of machines, departments, workstations, storage areas, aisles, and common areas within an existing or proposed facility. The basic objective of the layout decision is to arrange these elements to ensure a smooth flow of work, material, people, or information through the system. Effective layouts also seek to

Facility layout decisions involve multiple objectives.

- Minimize material handling costs;
- Utilize space efficiently;
- Utilize labor efficiently;

[1]McDowell, Edwin, "For Pittsburgh, a Model Airport at an Immodest Price," *The New York Times* (November 8, 1992).

- Eliminate bottlenecks;
- Facilitate communication and interaction between workers, between workers and their supervisors, or between workers and customers;
- Reduce manufacturing cycle time or customer service time;
- Eliminate wasted or redundant movement;
- Facilitate the entry, exit, and placement of material, products, or people;
- Incorporate safety and security measures;
- Promote product and service quality;
- Encourage proper maintenance activities;
- Provide a visual control of operations or activities;
- Provide flexibility to adapt to changing conditions.

This is quite a long list of objectives, and you might wonder how some of them are related to facility layout. For example, how can facility layout promote product and service quality? A department store that arranges cosmetics in several cage-like service areas, but does not (and never plans to) assign a salesperson to each island, encourages poor customer service. The salesperson cannot move freely from one island to another, and the probability of the salesperson being available at the particular counter where the customer needs service is slim. A layout that would encourage better service quality would link together several of the cosmetic islands so that the salesperson can float from counter to counter as needed. In a factory where items are worked on in sequence, it is better to locate operations physically close to one another. If there is a problem with the quality of work being passed to a station, the worker can simply walk over to the previous station (or better yet, turn around) and discuss the problem with his or her fellow worker. In this way, the quality problem can be fixed early and prevented from occurring again.

The inputs to layout decisions are the outputs from product and process decisions as well as characteristics of demand and the competitive environment. The type of layout chosen will be influenced by the process selected, the volume and variety of goods or services produced, the degree of customer interaction, the amount and type of equipment, the level of automation, the role of the worker, the availability of space, the stability of the system, and the objectives of the system.

Layout decisions significantly affect how efficiently workers can do their jobs, how fast goods can be produced, how difficult it is to automate a system, and how responsive the manufacturing system can be to changes in product design, product mix, or demand volume. For some types of operations, layouts can be changed without much expense. For others, a relayout is impossible or very expensive. For example, it can cost $10,000 or more to move one machine. In any case, the layout decision is an important one that has far-reaching implications for the productivity and competitiveness of a firm.

Layout decisions impact productive quality and competitiveness.

BASIC TYPES OF LAYOUTS

There are three basic types of layouts: 1. process, 2. product, and 3. fixed-position and three hybrid layouts: 1. cellular layouts, 2. flexible manufacturing systems, and 3. mixed-model assembly lines. We discuss each basic layout type in this section and hybrid layouts later in the chapter.

Process layouts, also known as *functional layouts,* group similar machines together in departments or work centers according to the process or function they perform. For example, all drills would be located in one work center, lathes in another work center, and milling machines in still another work center. All painting operations, of course, would be performed in the painting department. A department store is organized in this way, with women's clothes, men's clothes,

Process layouts group similar machines together according to the process they perform.

children's clothes, cosmetics, and shoes in separate departments. A process layout is characteristic of intermittent operations, job shops, or batch production, in which a variety of customers are served with different needs. The volume of each customer's order is relatively low, and the sequence of operations required to complete a customer's order can vary considerably. The equipment in a process layout is general purpose, and the workers are skilled at operating the equipment in their particular department. The main advantage of this layout is its flexibility. The main disadvantage is its inefficiency. Jobs do not flow through the system in an orderly manner, backtracking is common, movement from department to department can take a considerable amount of time, and queues tend to develop. In addition, each new job arrival to a work center may require that the machine be set up differently for its particular processing requirements. Although workers can operate a number of machines in a single department, their workload often fluctuates—from queues of jobs waiting to be processed to idle time between jobs. Figure 7.1 shows a schematic diagram of a process layout with sample job routings.

Product layouts arrange machines in a line according to the sequence of operations for a particular product.

Product layouts, primarily known as *assembly lines,* arrange machines in a line according to the sequence of operations that need to be performed to assemble a particular product. Thus, each product has its own "line" specifically designed to meet its requirements. The flow of work is very orderly and efficient, moving from one workstation to another down the assembly line until a finished product comes off the end of the line. Since the line is set up for one type of product, special machines can be purchased that match the specific processing requirements of the product. Product layouts are suitable for mass production or repetitive operations in which demand is stable and volume is high. The product is a standard one made for a general market, not for a particular customer. Because of the high level of demand, product layouts are typically more automated than process layouts, and the role of the worker is different. Workers perform narrowly defined fabrication or assembly tasks that do not demand as high a wage rate as those of the more versatile workers in a process layout.

Process layouts are flexible; product layouts are efficient.

The main advantage of the product layout is its efficiency and ease of use. The main disadvantage is its inflexibility. Significant changes in product design may require that a new assembly line be built and new equipment be purchased. This is what happened to U.S. automakers in the 1970s when demand shifted to smaller cars. The factories that could efficiently produce four-cylinder engines could not be adapted to produce six-cylinder engines. A similar inflexibility occurs when demand volume slows. The fixed costs of a product layout (mostly for equipment) allocated over fewer units can send the price of a product soaring. Figure 7.2

Transparency 7.1 A Process Layout

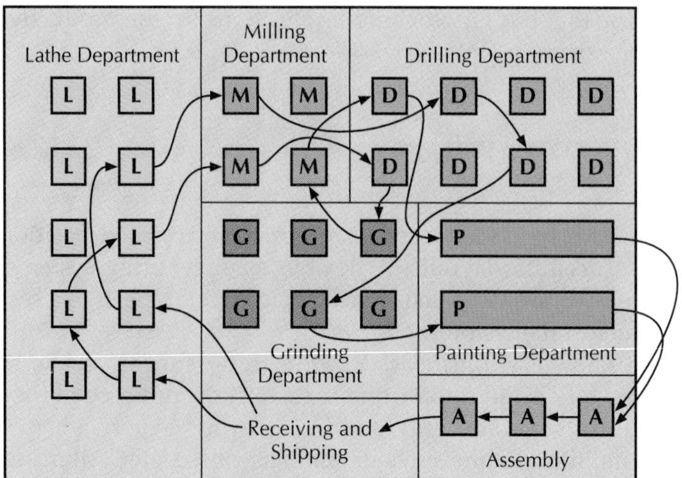

FIGURE 7.1 A Process Layout

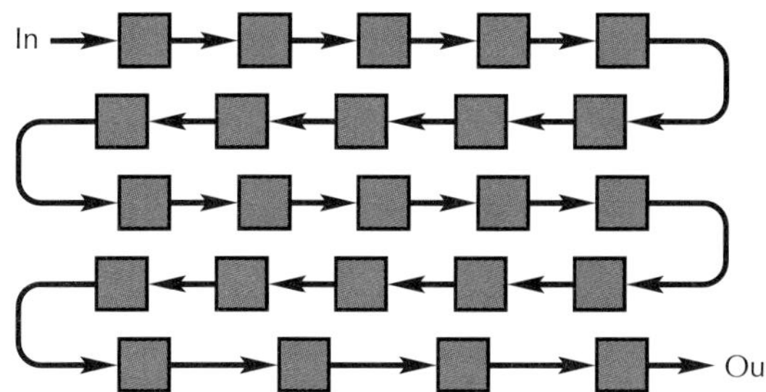

FIGURE 7.2 A Product Layout

Transparency 7.2 A Product Layout

shows a schematic diagram of a product layout and the flow of the products through the system. Contrast this with the flow of products through the process layout shown in Figure 7.1.

In addition to the flow of work and arrangement of machines, product and process layouts look very different in other ways. In-process inventory for a process layout is high because material moves from work center to work center in batches waiting to be processed. Finished goods inventory, on the other hand, is low because the goods are being made for a particular customer and are shipped out to that customer upon completion. The opposite is true of a product layout. In-process inventory is consumed in the assembly of the product as it moves down the assembly line, but finished goods inventory may stack up or require a separate warehouse for storage before the goods are shipped to dealers or stores to be sold. Storage space in the process layout is large to accommodate the large amount of in-process inventory. Some of these factories look like warehouses, with work centers strewn between storage aisles. In contrast, the storage space along an assembly line is usually quite small.

Product and process layouts look different.

Material handling methods are also different for the two layouts. Process layouts need flexible material handling equipment that can follow multiple paths, move in any direction, and carry large loads of in-process goods. A *forklift* fits that description and is typically used to move pallets of material from work center to work center in a process layout. A product layout needs material moved in one direction along the assembly line and always in the same pattern. *Conveyors* are the most common material handling equipment for product layouts. Conveyors can be paced (automatically set to control the speed of work) or unpaced (stopped and started by the workers according to their pace). Assembly work can be performed on-line (i.e., on the conveyor) or off-line (at a workstation serviced by the conveyor). The aisles in a process layout need to be wide to accommodate the two-way movement of forklifts. The aisles in a product layout can be narrow because the material is moved only one way, it is not moved very far, and the conveyor is an integral part of the assembly process, usually with workstations on either side. Scheduling of the conveyors, once they are installed, is simple—the only variable is how fast it should operate. Scheduling of forklifts is typically controlled by radio dispatch and varies from day to day and hour to hour. Routes have to be determined and priorities given to different loads competing for pickup.

Product and process layouts use different material handling methods.

The major problem in terms of layout for a process layout is where to locate the machine centers (i.e., groupings of similar machines) in relation to each other. Although each job potentially has a different route through the shop, there will be some paths between machines that are more common than others. Past information on customer orders and projections of customers orders are used to develop typical patterns of flow through the shop. For a product layout, the major layout problem is balancing the assembly line so that no one workstation becomes a bottleneck and holds up the flow of work through the line. Table 7.1, on page 330, summarizes the differences we have discussed between the product and process layouts.

Product and process layouts have different layout concerns.

The two photos highlight the material handling differences between process and product layouts. In the first photo, a forklift moves pallets of material from department to department in a stamping factory that makes automotive molding. In the second photo, partially completed units move by conveyor from one work station to the next on an electronics assembly line.

A combination of layout types in one facility

It is not uncommon for product and process layouts to be combined within a single manufacturing or service facility. Fabrication processes are normally handled with a process layout, whereas assembly operations fit nicely into a product layout. A hospital, which is predominantly a process layout, with separate patient-registration departments, X-ray departments, and radiology departments, still registers patients in an assembly line fashion and operates its cafeteria as a product layout. Figure 7.3, on page 330, shows a simplified drawing of a chain saw factory that includes both a product and process layout. The process layout is shown in areas A and B. In area A, four injection molding machines are used to form small plastic parts for the chain saw, such as the trigger. One worker operates the four machines by pouring in plastic bits in the top of the molding machines, inserting the proper molds, and starting the machines. Each machine chugs away, producing parts that fall into a basket beneath the machine. The operator takes the baskets and dumps them into the plastic-finishing area, where he or she breaks off rough edges by hand to make the parts smooth. The parts are then put into bins and taken to the assembly area or to the storeroom. Area B consists of four machines for preproduction machining and a parts washer. Two workers operate these machines, in which parts are welded together, holes are drilled, or other adjustments are made to components that have been supplied for the chain

Transparency 7.3 A Typical Factory Layout

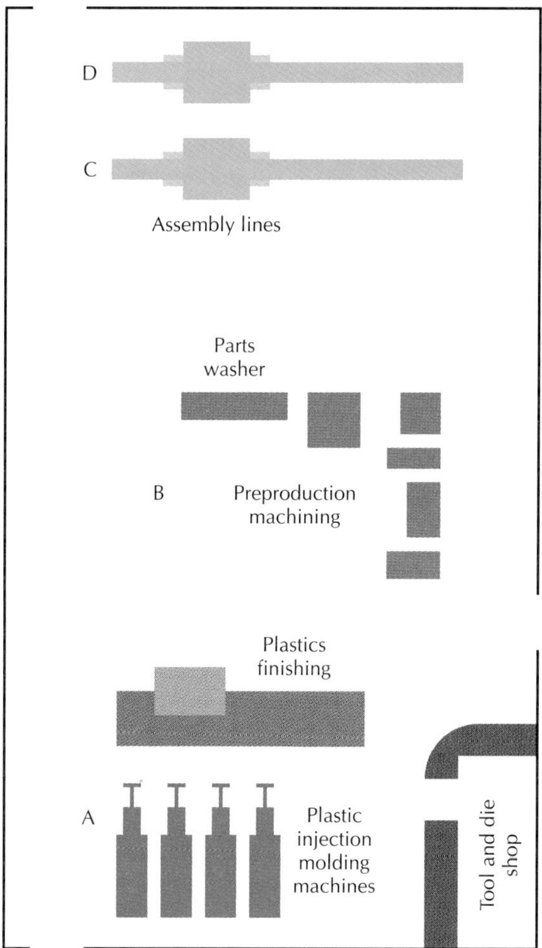

FIGURE 7.3 Factory Layout for a Chain Saw Manufacturer

saws. The processes often involve heat or metal chips as a by-product, so a parts washer is available to cool or cleanse the finished parts. As with the plastic parts, the finished parts are placed in bins and are moved to the assembly area or storeroom as needed.

The product layout portion of the factory is represented by two assembly lines at locations C and D. Each line produces a different-model chain saw. In contrast to the sizable area and small number of workers required for the process layout, each assembly line shown has 30 workers. Notice that the 60 assembly line workers take up less space than the 3 workers involved in machining and plastic parts production. The bulge in each assembly line, occurring near the end of the assembly process, is a test booth, where the chain saw is started up and put through a battery of tests. This testing process takes longer than the other operations on the assembly line, so two workers are assigned to each booth, and they alternate taking chain saws from the line to be tested. In this way the line can maintain a balanced workload between stations, and the testing booth does not become a bottleneck.

Fixed-position layouts are used in projects where the product cannot be moved.

The third basic type of layout is the fixed-position layout. **Fixed-position layouts** are typical of projects in which the product produced is too fragile, bulky, or heavy to move. Ships, houses, and aircraft are examples. As the name implies, in this layout, the product remains stationary for the entire manufacturing cycle. Equipment, workers, materials, and other resources are brought to the production site. Equipment utilization is low because it is often less costly to leave equipment idle at a location where it will be needed again in a few days, than to move it back and forth. Frequently, the equipment is leased or subcontracted, because it is used

Transparency 7.4 A Comparision of Product and Process Layouts

TABLE 7.1 A Comparison of Product and Process Layouts

	Product Layout	*Process Layout*
1. Description	Sequential arrangement of machines	Functional grouping of machines
2. Type of Process	Continuous, mass production, mainly assembly	Intermittent, job shop, batch production, mainly fabrication
3. Product	Standardized made to stock	Varied, made to order
4. Demand	Stable	Fluctuating
5. Volume	High	Low
6. Equipment	Special purpose	General purpose
7. Workers	Limited skills	Varied skills
8. Inventory	Low in-process, high finished goods	High in-process, low finished goods
9. Storage space	Small	Large
10. Material handling	Fixed path (conveyor)	Variable path (forklift)
11. Aisles	Narrow	Wide
12. Scheduling	Part of balancing	Dynamic
13. Layout decision	Line balancing	Machine location
14. Goal	Equalize work at each station	Minimize material handling cost
15. Advantage	Efficiency	Flexibility

for limited periods of time. The workers called to the work site are highly skilled at performing the special tasks they are requested to do. For instance, pipefitters may be needed at one stage of production and electricians or plumbers, at another. The wage rate for these workers is much higher than minimum wage. Thus, if we

The size and complexity of aircraft production requires a fixed-position layout. Construction takes place in stages at fixed locations. Rather than move the aircraft itself, crews of workers gather around each unit with their tools and equipment and move from site to site to complete their tasks. Notice the modular offices, and the various carts and bins with wheels for easy movement.

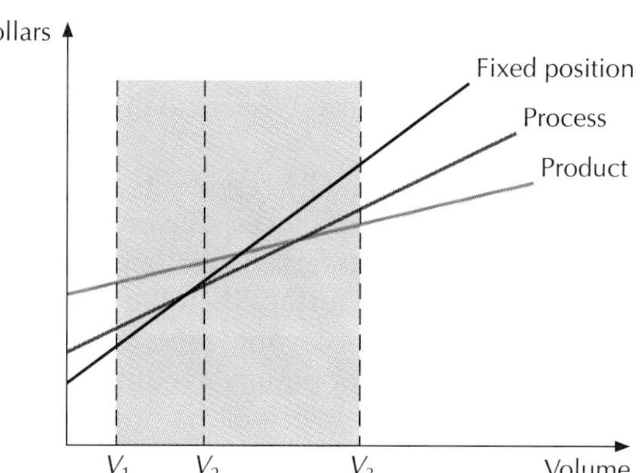

FIGURE 7.4 A Cost/Volume Comparison of Three Basic Layouts

Transparency 7.5 A Cost/Volume Comparison of Layout Types

were to look at the cost breakdown for fixed-position layouts, the fixed cost would be relatively low (equipment may not be owned by the company), whereas the variable costs would be high (due to high labor rates and the cost of leasing and moving equipment).

The fixed-position, process, and product layouts can be compared on the basis of cost in a break-even analysis format. Figure 7.4 is a graph of the three layouts, with representative values of fixed and variable costs. Examining the y-intercepts of the three layouts, the product layout has the highest fixed cost, followed by the process layout and then fixed-position layout. From the slope of the lines, we can see that the fixed-position layout has the highest variable costs, followed by the process layout and then product layout. A major determinant of the appropriate layout is demand volume. At volume v_1, a low-demand volume, the fixed-position layout would have the lowest total cost. But at volume v_2, a medium volume, the process layout would be preferred, and at volume v_3, a high demand volume, the product layout would be best.

Product layouts tend to have the highest fixed costs and fixed position layouts, the highest variable costs.

Because the fixed-position layout is quite specialized, we concentrate on the product and process layouts and their variations for the remainder of this chapter. In the sections that follow, we examine some quantitative approaches for designing product and process layouts.

DESIGNING PROCESS LAYOUTS

In designing a process layout, we are concerned with minimizing material handling cost, which is a function of the amount of material moved times the distance it is moved. This implies that departments that incur the most interdepartment movement should be located closest to each other, and those that do not interact should be located further away. The techniques used to design process layouts, like many techniques in the field of production/operations management, are based on logic and the visual presentation of data.

Process layout objective: Minimize material handling costs.

Block Diagramming

To begin the layout process, input is needed describing historical or predicted movement of material between departments in the existing or proposed facility. This information is typically provided in the form of a from/to chart, or *load summary chart*. The chart gives the average number of **unit loads** transported between the departments over a given period of time. A unit load can be a single unit, a pallet of material, a bin of material, or a crate of material—however material is normally moved from location to location. In automobile manufacturing, a single car represents a unit load. For a ball bearing producer, a unit load might consist of a bin of 100 or 1,000 ball bearings, depending on the size of the bearings.

A **unit load** is the quantity in which material is normally moved.

Block diagramming tries to minimize nonadjacent loads.

The next step in designing the layout is to calculate the *composite movements* between departments and rank them from most movement to least movement. Composite movement, represented by a two-headed arrow, refers to the back-and-forth movement between each pair of departments.

Finally, trial layouts are placed on a grid that visually represents the relative distances between departments in the form of uniform blocks. The objective is to assign each department to a block on the grid so that *nonadjacent loads* are minimized. The term *nonadjacent* is defined as a distance further than the next block, either horizontally, vertically, or diagonally. The trial layouts are scored on the basis of the number of nonadjacent loads. Ideally, the optimum layout would have zero nonadjacent loads. In practice, this is rarely possible, and the process of trying different layout configurations to reduce the number of nonadjacent loads continues until an acceptable layout is found.

Alternate Example 7.1

EXAMPLE 7.1

Process Layout

Problem Statement:

Barko, Inc., is a well-known manufacturer of *bark scalpers*, processing equipment that strips the bark off of trees and turns it into nuggets or mulch for gardens. The facility that makes bark scalpers is a small job shop that employs 50 workers and is arranged into five basic departments: 1. bar stock cutting, 2. sheet metal, 3. machining, 4. painting, and 5. assembly. The average number of loads transported between the five departments per month is given in the accompanying load summary chart. The current layout of the facility is shown schematically on the 2 x 3 grid. Notice that there is quite a bit of flexibility in the facility, as indicated by the six possible locations (i.e., blocks) available for five departments. In addition, the forklift used in the facility is very flexible, allowing horizontal, vertical, and diagonal movement of material.

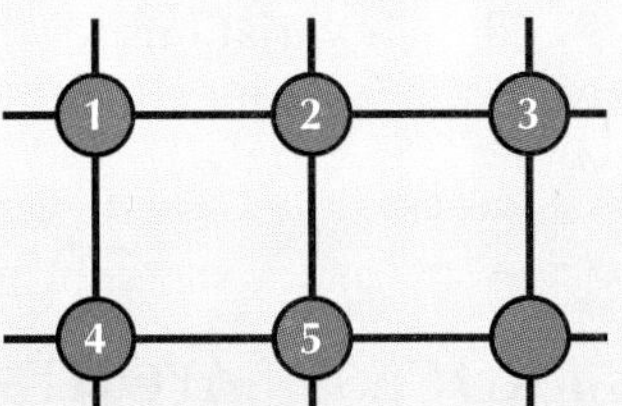

Barko management anticipates that a new bark scalper plant will soon be necessary and would like to know if a similar layout should be used or if a better layout can be designed. You are asked to do the following:

a. Evaluate the current layout in terms of nonadjacent loads.
b. If needed, propose a new layout on a 2 x 3 grid that will minimize the number of nonadjacent loads.

Load Summary Chart

From \ To DEPARTMENT	1	2	3	4	5
1		100	50		
2			200	50	
3	60			40	50
4		100			
5		50		60	

Solution:

a. In order to evaluate the current layout, we need to calculate the composite, or back-and-forth, movements between departments. For example, the composite movement between department 1 and department 3 is the sum of 50 loads moved from 1 to 3 plus 60 loads moved from 3 to 1, or 110 loads of material. If we continue to calculate composite movements in this manner, the following list results.

Composite Movements

2 ↔ 3	200 loads
2 ↔ 4	150 loads
1 ↔ 3	110 loads
1 ↔ 2	100 loads
4 ↔ 5	60 loads
3 ↔ 5	50 loads
2 ↔ 5	50 loads
3 ↔ 4	40 loads
1 ↔ 4	0 loads
1 ↔ 5	0 loads

Next, we evaluate the "goodness" of the layout by scoring it in terms of nonadjacent loads. The results are shown visually in grid 1.

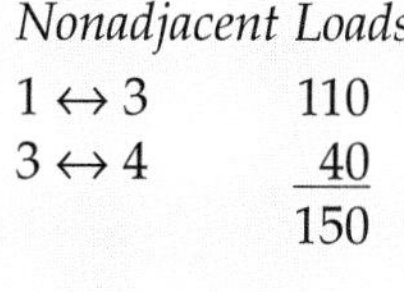

Nonadjacent Loads

1 ↔ 3	110
3 ↔ 4	40
	150

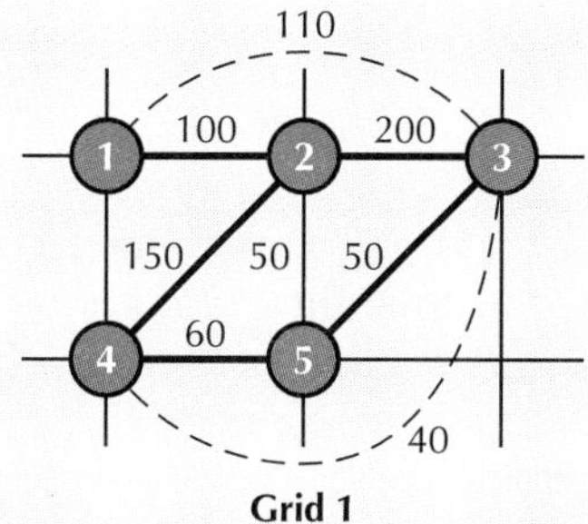

Grid 1

Following our composite movement list, 1 ↔ 2 is an adjacent move, but 1 ↔ 3 is not. The adjacent moves are marked with a solid line and the nonadjacent moves are shown with a curved dashed line to highlight the fact that material is required to move further than we would like. Our nonadjacent score starts with 110 loads of material from 1 ↔ 3. Continuing down our list, 2 ↔ 3 and 2 ↔ 4 are adjacent and are marked with solid lines. Movement 3 ↔ 4 is nonadjacent, so we designate it as such and add 40 loads to our nonadjacent score. The remaining movements are adjacent. Thus, our score for this layout is 110 + 40 = 150 nonadjacent loads.

b. To improve on this layout, we can look at our rankings of composite movements and conclude that departments 3 and 4 should be located adjacent to department 2 and that departments 4 and 5 may be located away from department 1 without adding to the score of nonadjacent loads. Let's put departments 4 and 5 on one end of the grid and department 1 on the other and then fill in departments 2 and 3 in the middle. The revised solution is shown in grid 2. The only nonadjacent moves are between departments 1 and 4 and 1 and 5. Since no loads of material are moved along those paths, the score for this layout is zero. It should be noted that there are multiple optimum solutions to this problem, although it may take several iterations before zero nonadjacent loads can be achieved.

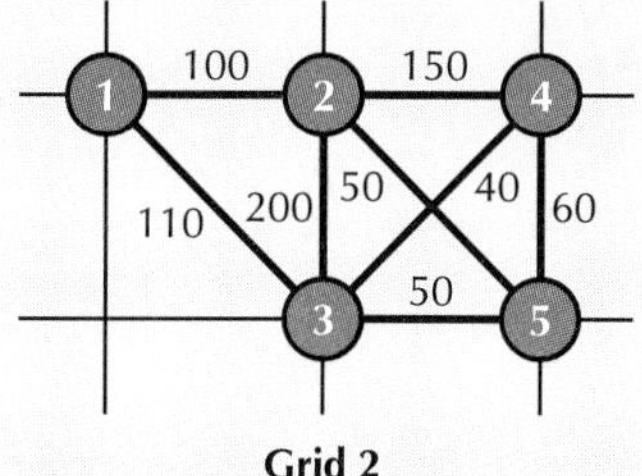

Grid 2

The layout solution shown in grid 2 is a typical schematic diagram that shows the relative position of each department. The next step in the layout process is to add information about the space required for each department. Recommendations for workspace around machines can be requested from equipment vendors or found in safety regulations or operating manuals. In some cases, vendors provide templates of equipment layouts, with work areas included. Workspace allocations for workers can be specified as part of job design (discussed in Chapter 10), recommended by professional groups, or agreed upon through union negotiations. A **block diagram** can be created by blocking in the work areas around the departments on a schematic diagram. The *final block diagram* adjusts the block diagram for the desired or proposed shape of the building. Standard building shapes include rectangles, L shapes, T shapes, and U shapes. Most manufacturing facilities and retail establishments are single-level facilities. Offices, hospitals, and banks tend to be multilevel. Multilevel buildings present special layout problems.

A **block diagram** is a type of schematic layout diagram that includes space requirements.

Figure 7.5(a) shows an initial block diagram for Example 7.1, and Figure 7.5(b) shows a final block diagram. Notice that the space requirements vary considerably from department to department, but the relative location of departments has been retained from the schematic diagram.

Relationship Diagramming

The preceding solution procedure is appropriate for designing process layouts when quantitative data are available. However, in situations for which quantitative data are difficult to obtain or do not adequately address the layout problem, the load summary chart can be replaced with subjective input from analysts or managers. Richard Muther developed a format for displaying manager preferences for departmental locations, known as **Muther's grid.**[2] The preference information is coded into six categories associated with the five vowels, A, E, I, O, and U, plus the letter X. As shown in Figure 7.6, the vowels match the first letter of the closeness rating for locating two departments next to each other. The diamond-shaped grid is read similar to mileage charts on a road map. For example, reading down the highlighted row in Figure 7.6, it is *okay* if the offices are located next to production, *absolutely necessary* that the stockroom be located next to production, *important* that shipping and receiving be located next to production, *especially important* for the locker room to be located next to production, and *absolutely necessary* that the toolroom be located next to production.

Muther's grid is a format for displaying manager's preferences for department locations.

The information from Muther's grid can be used to construct a **relationship diagram** that evaluates existing or proposed layouts. Consider the relationship

A **relationship diagram** is a schematic diagram that uses weighted lines to denote location preference.

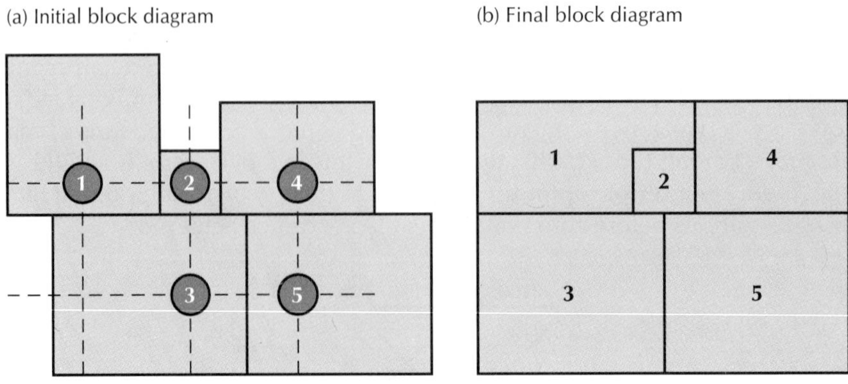

FIGURE 7.5 Block Diagrams

[2]Muther, R., *Systematic Layout Planning,* Boston: Industrial Education Institute, 1961.

diagram shown in Figure 7.7(a). A schematic diagram of the six departments from Figure 7.6 is given in a 2 x 3 grid. Lines of different thicknesses are drawn from department to department. The thickest lines (three, four, or five strands) identify the closeness ratings with the highest priority—that is, for which departments it is *important, especially important,* or *absolutely necessary* that they be located next to each other. The priority diminishes with line thickness. *Undesirable* closeness ratings are marked with a zigzagged line. Visually, the best solution would show short heavy lines and no zigzagged lines (undesirable locations are noted only if they are adjacent). Thin lines (one or two strands, representing *okay* or *unimportant*) can be of any length and for that reason are sometimes eliminated from the analysis. An

Manager preferences for department locations are displayed as A, E, I, O, U, or X.

Transparency 7.6 Muther's Grid

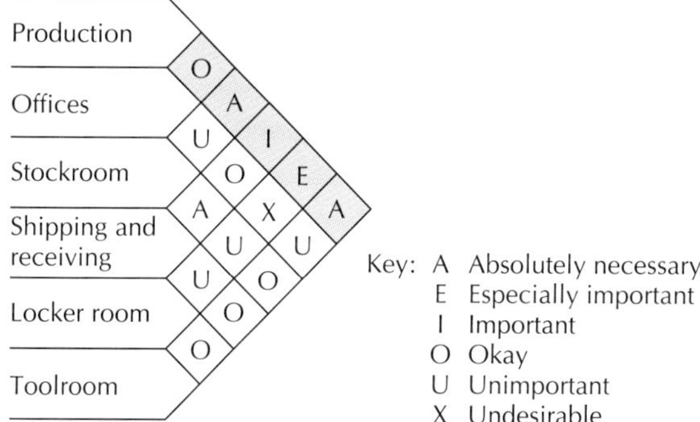

FIGURE 7.6 Muther's Grid

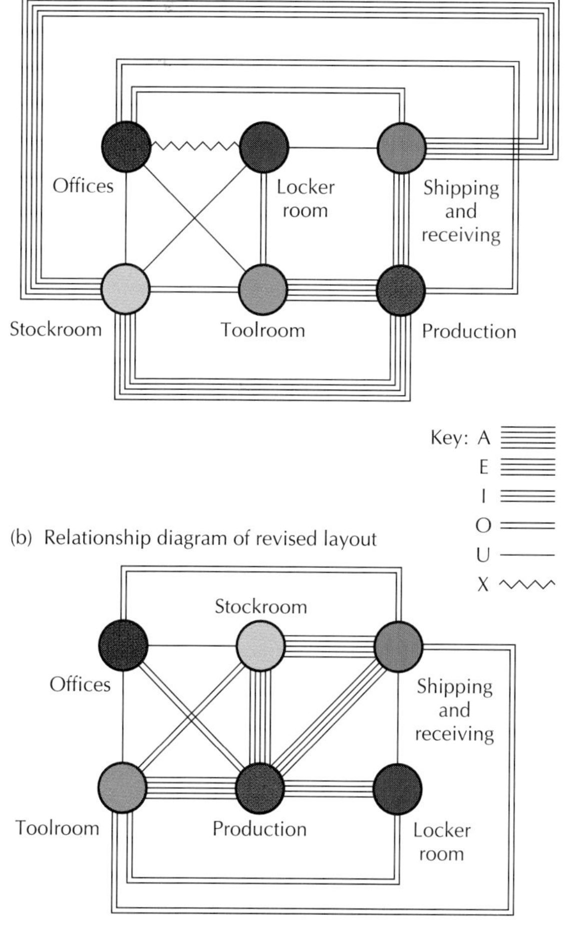

FIGURE 7.7 Relationship Diagrams

alternate form of relationship diagramming uses colors instead of line thickness to visualize closeness ratings.

From Figure 7.7(a), it is obvious that production and shipping and receiving are located too far from the stockroom and that the offices and locker room are located too close to one another. Figure 7.7(b) shows a revised layout, and evaluates the layout with a relationship diagram. The revised layout appears to satisfy the preferences expressed in Muther's grid. The heavy lines are short and within the perimeter of the grid. The lengthy lines are thin, and there are no zigzagged lines.

Computerized Layout Solutions

The visual diagrams just discussed help formulate ideas for the arrangement of departments in a process layout, but they can be cumbersome and far from optimal for large problems. Fortunately, several computer packages are available for designing process layouts. The best known is CRAFT (Computerized Relative Allocation of Facilities Technique). CRAFT takes a load summary chart and block diagram as input and then makes pairwise exchanges of departments until no improvements in cost or nonadjacency score can be found. The output is a revised

GAINING THE COMPETITIVE EDGE

Relationship Diagramming at Fairtron

Fairtron Fairplay, located in Des Moines, Iowa, manufactures scoreboards for high schools and colleges worldwide. The production process begins with sheets of aluminum routed, sheared, and pressed to form scoreboard cabinets. Next, component parts are assembled and then they are moved to paint and electronic assembly areas for final completion. In order to improve production efficiency, Fairtron decided to examine alternate layouts for its operation. In a 5-day period three feasible layouts were generated and analyzed using CAD software and a layout package called Factory Plan.

A nine-member team ranging from top management to machine operators performed the analysis. They decided to use an approach called relationship diagramming, which utilizes nonquantitative data because of the small number of processes, large variety of material flows, and the team's strong familiarity with the manufacturing process.

On day 1 the team was familiarized with layout techniques and software. On days 2 and 3, data were collected and used to generate a CAD layout drawing. This involved measuring and drawing 50 pieces of equipment and included the locations of cranes, fire extinguishers, lights, doors, windows, walls, and vents. On day 4, relationships between activity areas were developed and relationship diagrams generated. **A**'s were used for major flows, **E**'s were used when tight supervision or shared equipment was required, **I**'s were used for loose supervision and medium flows, **O**'s were used for shared utilities and minor flows, and **X**'s showed undesirable locations due to hazards, noise vibration, or fumes. The team had to be careful not to assign too many **A**'s and **O**'s. When completed, the initial diagram showed color-coded relationship lines between the various areas superimposed on the CAD floor plan according to the strengths of their relationships. The team examined the diagram, made suggestions for revisions in the layout, generated a revised relationship diagram, and made further revisions until a concensus was reached on the appropriateness of the proposed layout. In about 2 hours, three good layout alternatives were generated. On day 5, the three proposed layouts were presented to management, and a selection was made.

Source: Based on Sly, Dave, and Emit Polashek, "Fairtron Scores Big with New Cabinet Production Layout Redesign," *Industrial Engineering* (March 1993): 34–36.

block diagram after each iteration for a rectangular-shaped building, which may or may not be optimal. CRAFT is sensitive to the initial block diagram used; that is, different block diagrams as input will result in different layouts as outputs. For this reason, CRAFT is often used to improve upon existing layouts or to enhance the best manual attempts at designing a layout. Alternatively, several initial block diagrams can be submitted as starting points, and the final solutions of each can be compared.

PREP (Plant Relayout and Evaluation Package) is similar to CRAFT, except that it can handle more departments (ninety-nine instead of fourty), a multistory facility, and different material handling equipment. ALDEP (Automated Layout Design Program) and CORELAP (Computerized Relationship Layout Planning) use nonquantitative input and relationship diagramming to produce a feasible layout. ALDEP can handle sixty-three departments and a multistory facility. It begins with an initial random layout and seeks to improve upon the values in Muther's grid that are not satisfied. CORELAP can process forty-five departments and take into account different building shapes. It attempts to create an acceptable layout from the beginning by locating department pairs with *A* ratings first, then those with *E* ratings, and so on. All these computer packages are basically trial-and-error approaches to layout design that provide good—but not necessarily optimal—process layouts.

New software packages for layout analysis are appearing every day. Process layouts of limited size can be designed with several student-oriented computer packages, such as QSOM, STORM, or AB:POM. AB:POM will calculate the movement of material as load × distance for any layout you enter. In our examples, we have worked with relative distances on a grid instead of actual distances. Thus, distances should be entered as 1, 2, or 3 blocks away. The AB:POM input and total movement calculation for Barko, Inc., of Example 7.1 is shown in Exhibit 7.1.

Service Layouts

Most service organizations use process layouts. This makes sense because of the variability in customer requests for service. The general procedures for designing service layouts are the same as for process layouts in manufacturing firms, but the objectives may differ. For example, instead of minimizing the flow of materials

Department in Room

Dept 1 in Room 3
Dept 2 in Room 5
Dept 3 in Room 2
Dept 4 in Room 4
Dept 5 in Room 1

Flow matrix

	Dept 1	Dept 2	Dept 3	Dept 4	Dept 5
Dept 1	0	100	50	0	0
Dept 2	0	0	200	50	0
Dept 3	60	0	0	40	50
Dept 4	0	100	0	0	0
Dept 5	0	50	0	60	0

Distance Matrix

	Room 1	Room 2	Room 3	Room 4	Room 5
Room 1	0	1	2	1	1
Room 2	1	0	1	1	1
Room 3	2	1	0	2	1
Room 4	1	1	2	0	1
Room 5	1	1	1	1	0

The total movement is 760

EXHIBIT 7.1

GAINING THE COMPETITIVE EDGE

A Flexible Layout at the Ritz-Carlton Pavilion

Ritz-Carlton Hotels listen to their customers. When customers in Naples, Florida, wanted a less formal place to gather, the hotel put up a tent out back. When the tent was too hot, management air conditioned it. When the tent was too small, they decided to build a more permanent facility, a shell of a building called the Pavilion. Looking through his files to determine how customers had used the ballroom, the tent, and the grounds over the years, the general manager concluded that what the Pavilion needed was "extreme flexibility," so that each group could create whatever environment it wanted. Flexibility was provided—right down to the basic structure.

The Pavilion's flexibility is built into its ceiling and walls. The ceiling is painted midnight black with a unique lighting system of hundreds of tiny white lights that look like stars. Computer-operated, the ceiling consists of different motorized sections that can be raised or lowered to create a tiered effect and different degrees of formality. Fabric panels hang across the ceiling to form a visual curtain.

The lighting system can be adjusted and preprogrammed to highlight certain portions of the room or to pinpoint specific tables and speakers. At a moment's notice, the hotel's AV department can create templates of company logos and theme party decorations to be projected on the painted, unpapered walls. Spotlights with changing hues add to the variety of moods.

Source: Based on Wagner, Grace, "Customer-Driven Construction," *Lodging Hospitality* (November 1993): 23.

Service layouts may have different objectives than manufacturing layouts.

through the system, services may seek to minimize the flow of customers or the flow of paperwork. In retail establishments, the objective is usually related to maximizing profit per unit of display space. If one accepts the hypothesis that sales vary directly with customer exposure, then an effective layout would expose the customer to as many goods as possible. This means instead of minimizing a customer's flow, it would be more beneficial to maximize it (to a certain point). Grocery stores take this approach when they locate milk on one end of the store and bread on the other, forcing the customer to travel through aisles of merchandise that might prompt additional purchases. The other aspect of service layout that has not yet been discussed is the allocation of shelf space to various products. Industry-specific recommendations are available for layout and display decisions. Computerized versions, such as SLIM (Store Labor and Inventory Management) and COSMOS (Computerized Optimization and Simulation Modeling for Operating Supermarkets), consider shelf space, demand rates, profitability, and stockout probabilities in layout design. Finally, service layouts are often visible to the customer so they must be aesthetically pleasing as well as functional.

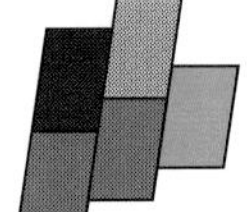

DESIGNING PRODUCT LAYOUTS

Product layout objective: Balance the assembly line.

Precedence requirements are physical restrictions in the order in which operations are performed.

The major concern in designing a product layout is balancing the assembly line. Recall that a product layout arranges machines or workers in a line according to the operations that need to be performed to assemble a particular product. From this description, it would seem that the layout could be determined quite simply by following the order of assembly as contained in the bill of material for the product. To some extent, this is true; **precedence requirements** specifying which operations must precede others, which can be done concurrently, and which must wait until later are an important input to the product layout decision, but there are other factors that make the decision more complicated.

Product layouts or assembly lines are used for high-volume production. One of the objectives of this system is to attain the required output rate as efficiently as possible. To do this, the jobs that must be performed are broken down into their smallest indivisible portions, called *work elements.* Work elements are so small that they cannot possibly be performed by more than one worker or at more than one workstation. But it is very common for one worker to perform several work elements as the product passes through his or her workstation. Part of the layout decision is concerned with grouping these work elements into workstations so products flow through the assembly line smoothly. A *workstation* is any area along the assembly line that requires at least one worker or one machine. If each workstation on the assembly line takes the same amount of time to perform the work elements that have been assigned, then products will move successively from workstation to workstation with no need for a product to wait or a worker to be idle. The process of equalizing the amount of work at each workstation is called **line balancing.**

Line balancing tries to equalize the amount of work at each workstation.

Line Balancing

Assembly line balancing operates under two constraints, precedence requirements and cycle-time restrictions. Precedence requirements, as we mentioned earlier, are physical restrictions on the *order* in which operations are performed on the assembly line. For example, we would not ask a worker to package a product before all the components were attached, even if he or she had the time to do so before passing the product to the next worker on the line. To facilitate the process of line balancing, precedence requirements are often expressed in the form of a precedence diagram. The precedence diagram is a network, with work elements represented by circles or nodes and precedence relationships represented by directed line segments connecting the nodes.

The precedence diagram is a network that describes any restrictions on the order in which work elements must be performed.

EXAMPLE 7.2

Precedence Diagramming

Alternate Example 7.2

Problem Statement:

Given the following information on work elements and time and precedence requirements, draw and label a precedence diagram for the assembly of fruit strip snacks.

	Work Element	*Precedence*	*Time (minutes)*
A	Press out sheet of fruit	—	0.1
B	Cut into strips	A	0.2
C	Outline fun shapes	A	0.4
D	Roll up and package	B, C	0.3

Solution:

Element A has no elements preceding it, so node A can be placed anywhere. Element A precedes element B, so the line segment that begins at node A must end at node B.

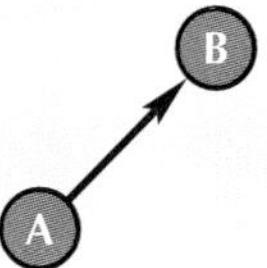

Element A precedes element C. Again, a line segment from node A must end at node C.

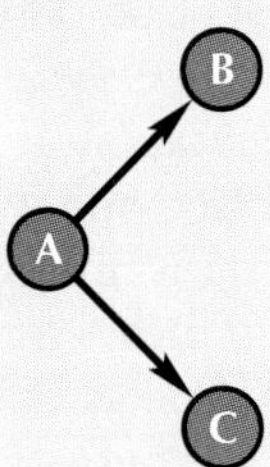

Elements A and C precede element D, so the line segments extending from nodes B and C must end at node D.

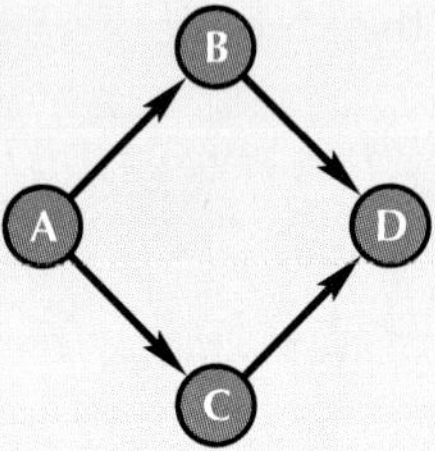

The precedence diagram is completed by adding the time requirements beside each node.

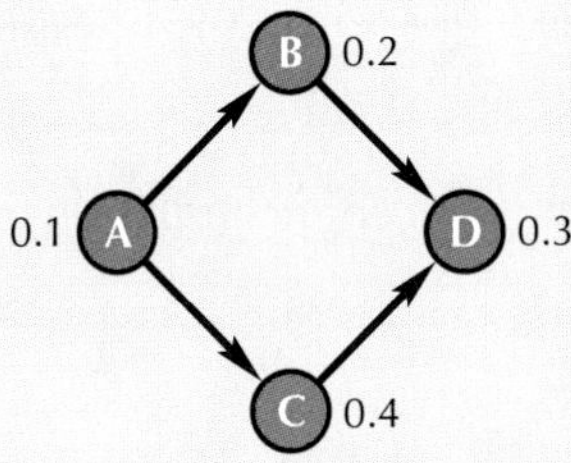

Cycle time is the maximum amount of time a product is allowed to spend at each workstation.

The second restriction on line balancing, **cycle time,** refers to the maximum amount of time the product is allowed to spend at each workstation if the targeted production rate is to be reached. Cycle time is calculated by dividing the time available for production by the number of units scheduled to be produced:

$$C = \frac{\text{production time available}}{\text{desired units of output}}$$

For example, suppose a company wanted to produce 120 units in an 8-hour day. The cycle time necessary to achieve that production quota is

$$C = \frac{(8 \text{ hours} \times 60 \text{ minutes/hour})}{(120 \text{ units})}$$

$$= \frac{480}{120} = 4 \text{ minutes}$$

Cycle time can also be viewed as the time between completed items rolling off the assembly line. For example, consider the three-station assembly line shown here.

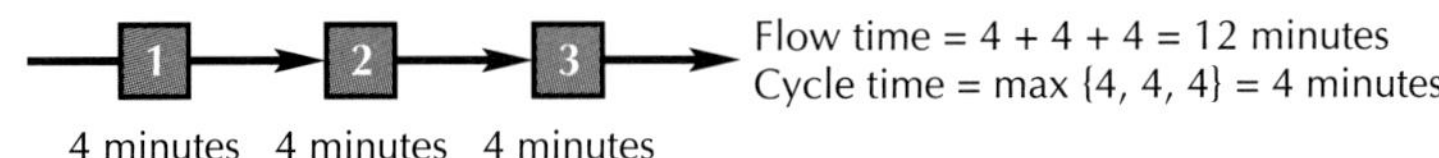

It takes 12 minutes (i.e., 4 + 4 + 4) for each item to pass completely through all three stations of the assembly line. The time required to complete an item is often referred to as its *flow time,* or *lead time.* However, the assembly line does not work on only one item at a time. In fact, when fully operational, the line will be processing three items at a time, one at each workstation, in various stages of assembly. Every 4 minutes a new item enters the line at workstation 1, an item is passed from workstation 1 to workstation 2, another item is passed from workstation 2 to workstation 3, and a completed item leaves the assembly line. Thus, a completed item rolls off the assembly line every 4 minutes. This 4-minute interval is the cycle time of the line.

Cycle time is different from flow time.

EXAMPLE 7.3

Line-Balancing Constraints

Alternate Example 7.3

Problem Statement:

Suppose the assembly process diagrammed in Example 7.3 requires the production of 6,000 fruit strips every 40-hour week. Group the elements into the smallest number of workstations that will achieve the production quota without violating the precedence constraints.

Solution:

First, we calculate cycle time as

$$C = \frac{40 \text{ hours} \times 60 \text{ minutes/hour}}{6{,}000 \text{ units}}$$

$$= \frac{2{,}400}{6{,}000} = 0.4 \text{ minute}$$

This result tells us that we must group elements into workstations so that the sum of the element times is less than or equal to 0.4 minutes.

Examining the precedence diagram, let's begin with element A since it is the only element that does not have a precedence. We assign A to workstation 1. Next, elements B and C are available for assignment. We assign B to workstation 1 (because it fits) and place C in a second workstation. No other element can be added to workstation 2, due to cycle time constraints. That leaves D for assignment to a third workstation. Elements grouped into workstations are circled on the precedence diagram.

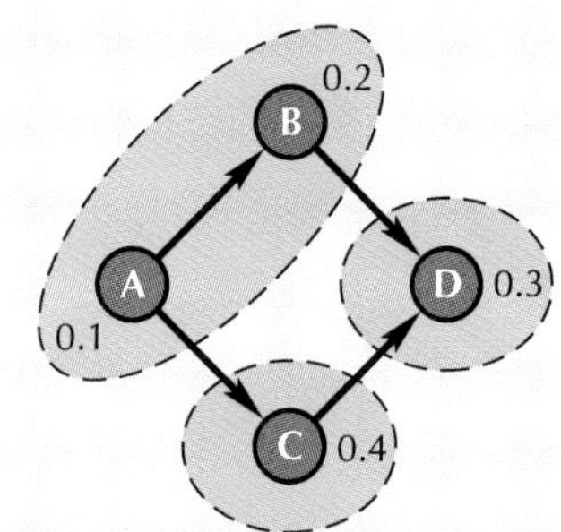

Our assembly line consists of three workstations, arranged as follows:

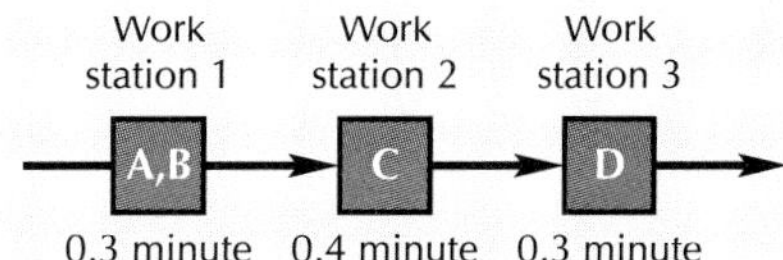

Calculate line efficiency and the theoretical minimum number of workstations.

The approach we used to solve the problem in Example 7.4 is a trial-and-error method of line balancing. We tried different combinations of work elements, recognizing time and precedence constraints. The problem was simple enough to evaluate all feasible groupings of elements. For a more complicated problem, we may need some guidance as to when to stop trying different workstation configurations. The *efficiency* of the line can provide one type of guideline; the *theoretical minimum number of workstations* provides another. The formulas for efficiency and minimum number of workstations are:

$$\text{Efficiency} = \frac{\sum_{i=1}^{j} t_i}{nC}$$

$$\text{Theoretical number of workstations} = \frac{\sum_{i=1}^{j} t_i}{C}$$

where

t_i = completion time for element i
j = number of work elements
n = actual number of workstations
C = cycle time

The assembly line in example 7.4 has an efficiency of

$$\text{Efficiency} = \frac{0.1 + 0.2 + 0.3 + 0.4}{3(0.4)}$$

$$= \frac{1.0}{1.2} = 0.833 = 83.3 \text{ percent}$$

Balance delay is the total idle time of the line.

The total idle time of the line, called **balance delay,** is calculated as (1 – efficiency), or for this example, 0.167, or 16.7 percent. Efficiency and balance delay are usually expressed as percentages.

The theoretical minimum number of workstations for Example 7.4 is

$$\frac{0.1 + 0.2 + 0.3 + 0.4}{0.4} = \frac{1.0}{0.4} = 2.5 \text{ workstations}$$

Since we cannot have half a workstation (or any portion of a work station), we round up the theoretical number to 3 workstations. Recall that our assembly line solution also consisted of three workstations, so we know we have balanced the line as efficiently as possible.

The trial-and-error method of line balancing can be summarized as follows:

Line balancing groups elements into workstations.

1. Draw and label a precedence diagram.
2. Calculate the cycle time required for the line.
3. Calculate the theoretical minimum number of workstations.
4. Group elements into workstations, recognizing cycle time and precedence constraints.
5. Calculate the efficiency of the line.
6. Determine if the theoretical minimum number of workstations or an acceptable efficiency level has been reached. If not, go back to step 4.

It should be noted that using the theoretical minimum number of workstations as a guideline can lead to erroneous groupings of elements if the precedence constraints are not closely monitored. In practice, it is very difficult to attain the theoretical number of workstations or 100 percent efficiency. Cycle time based on production quotas can also be misleading. Sometimes the production quota cannot be achieved because the time required for one work element is too large. To correct the situation, the quota can be revised downward or parallel stations can be set up for the bottleneck element, in much the same way as the chain saw manufacturer in Figure 7.4 assigned two workers to the test booth. At other times, the production quota may not match the maximum output attainable by the system, in which case the calculated cycle time and actual cycle time will be different. The actual cycle time is the maximum workstation time on the line. When calculating efficiency, most software packages use the *calculated cycle time.* To determine the *actual efficiency* of the line, the *actual cycle time* should be used in the efficiency formula.

Heuristic and Computerized Line Balancing

Line balancing by hand becomes unwieldy as the problems grow in size. Fortunately, there are software packages available that will balance large lines quickly. IBM's COMSOAL (Computer Method for Sequencing Operations for Assembly Lines) and GE's ASYBL (Assembly Line Configuration Program) can assign hundreds of work elements to workstations on an assembly line. These programs, and most of those that are commercially available, do not guarantee optimal solutions. They use various *heuristics,* or rules, to balance the line at an acceptable level of efficiency. The AB:POM software lets the user select from five different heuristics: ranked positional weight, longest operation time, shortest operation time, most number of following tasks, and least number of following tasks. These heuristics specify the *order* in which work elements are considered for allocation to workstations. Elements are assigned to workstations in the order given until the cycle time is reached or until all tasks have been assigned. The following example demonstrates the heuristic procedure using the ranked positional weight technique.

Line-balancing heuristics specify the order in which work elements are allocated to workstations.

EXAMPLE 7.4

Ranked Positional Weight Technique of Line Balancing

Alternate Example 7.4

Problem Statement:

The Costplus Corporation has set a processing quota of eighty insurance claims per 8-hour day. The claims process consists of five elements, which are detailed shortly. Costplus has decided to use an assembly line arrangement to process the forms and would like to make sure they have set up the line in the most efficient fashion.

a. Construct a precedence diagram for the claims process and calculate the cycle time required to meet the processing quota.
b. Balance the assembly line using the ranked positional weight technique and show your arrangement of workstations.
c. Calculate the efficiency of the line.
d. Determine how many claims can actually be processed on your line.

Element	*Predecessor*	*Performance Time (min.)*
A	—	4
B	A	5
C	B	2
D	A	1
E	C, D	3

Solution:

a. The precedence diagram is as follows:

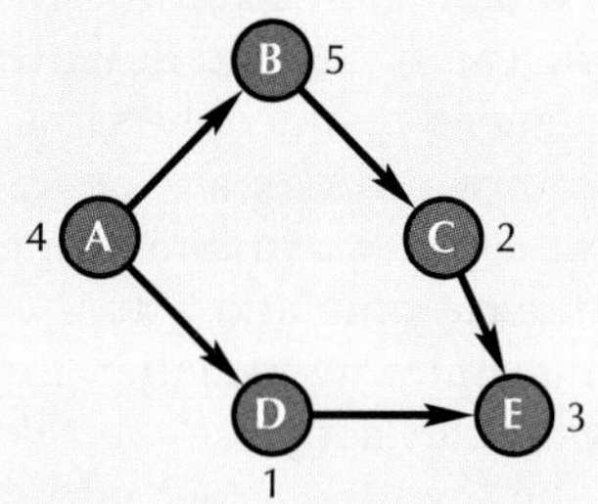

$$C = \frac{8 \text{ hours} \times 60 \text{ minutes/hour}}{80}$$

$$= \frac{480}{80} = 6.0 \text{ minutes}$$

b. The positional weight of an element is the element's operation time plus the operation time of all elements following that element in the network. The following positional weights are calculated for this problem:

Element A	4 + 5 + 2 + 1 + 3 = 15
Element B	5 + 2 + 3 = 10
Element C	2 + 3 = 5
Element D	1 + 3 = 4
Element E	3 = 3

The positional weights are used to construct a ranking—in this case, A, B, C, D, E—to use in considering elements for inclusion into workstations. After the ranking has been determined, the weights can be discarded. The heuristic balances the line in rank order as follows:

- A is the only element without a predecessor. Assign element A to workstation 1.
- Element B and D are now available for assignment.
- Element D can be added to workstation 1 (B cannot because its element time is too long).
- That leaves B as the only element available. Assign B to workstation 2.
- Now element C is available. It cannot be added to workstation 2 because of cycle-time restrictions. Assign C to workstation 3.
- The last available element is E. Assign element E to workstation 3.

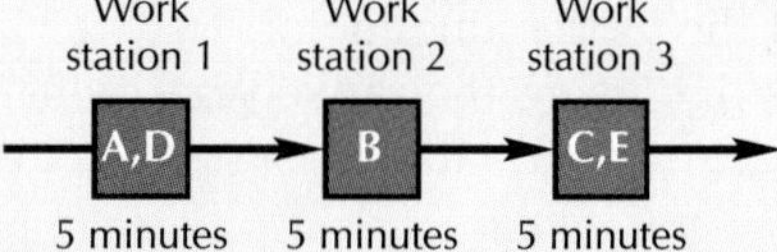

c. If we use the calculated cycle time in the efficiency formula, the efficiency is 83.3 percent.

$$\text{Efficiency} = \frac{4+5+2+1+3}{3(6)}$$

$$= \frac{15}{18} = 0.833, \text{ or } 83.3\%$$

But we know by looking at the line that it is 100 percent efficient. The line is perfectly balanced and there is no idle time. If we use the actual cycle time of 5.0 minutes in the efficiency formula, the efficiency of the line is, indeed, 100 percent.

d. A cycle time of 5 minutes means we can process a claim every 5 minutes. Thus, in an 8-hour day, we can process 480/5, or 96, claims on the line. We should inform Costplus management of our increased output.

The AB:POM solution to Example 7.4 is shown in Exhibit 7.2. Most of the computer output is self-explanatory, but a few items need clarification. The *Time left* column is the time remaining at a workstation that can be allocated without exceeding the cycle-time restrictions. *Ready tasks* are those elements for which precedence requirements have been met and thus are available for assignment to a workstation. *Cycle time* can be input as a constant value or can be calculated by the program from production quota or demand information. For this printout, cycle time was calculated, so the efficiency and idle-time calculations are based on the calculated, not actual, cycle time. To have these figures recalculated, input cycle time as the maximum workstation time of 5 minutes and rerun the program.

AB:POM produces a solution very quickly. If you are wondering which heuristic might be best to use, start with the default heuristic, longest operation time, and see if the theoretical number of workstations has been reached. If so, this is an optimal layout. If not, try running the problem with another heuristic.

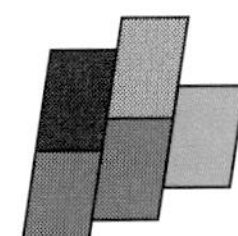

HYBRID LAYOUTS

Hybrid layouts modify and/or combine some aspects of the three basic layout types. The hybrid layouts that we discuss are cellular layouts, flexible manufacturing systems, and mixed-model assembly lines.

Cellular Layouts

Cellular layouts group dissimilar machines into work centers (called cells) that process families of parts with similar shapes or processing requirements.

Cellular layouts attempt to improve the efficiency of process layouts while maintaining their flexibility. Based on the concept of group technology (GT), dissimilar machines are grouped into work centers, called *cells*, that process parts with similar shapes or processing requirements. The manufacturing cells are viewed as more efficient alternatives to the functional departments of the process layout. The concept of manufacturing cells was first proposed in 1925 by an American engi-

```
                   Example 8.5—Ranked Positional Weight Technique
Ranked positional weight                                          Cycle time = 6 minutes
Station       task         Time       Time left    ready tasks
                                                   a
   1          a            4.00         2.00       b,d
              d            1.00         1.00       b
   2          b            5.00         1.00       c
   3          c            2.00         4.00       e
              e            3.00         1.00

Time allocated      (cyc*sta)= 18.00;                    Min (theoretical) # of stations = 3
Time needed    (sum task)  = 15.00;            EFFICIENCY = 83   BALANCE DELAY = 16.67%
Idle time  (alloc-needed)  = 3.00 minutes per cycle
```

EXHIBIT 7.2

neer[3] but did not gain prominence until the Japanese perfected its application as part of their just-in-time (JIT) production systems.

The procedure for developing a cellular layout involves the following steps:

1. Identifying families of parts that follow similar flow paths
2. Regrouping machines (from the process layout departments) into manufacturing cells according to the processing requirements of each part family
3. Arranging the manufacturing cells in relation to each other so that material movement is minimized
4. Locating large machines that cannot be split among cells near to the cells that use them, that is, at their *point of use*

Video 7.1 *Harley-Davidson, Building Better Motorcycles the American Way*

From this description, it should be obvious that the cellular layout contains elements of both product and process layouts. The layout of machines *within* each manufacturing cell resembles a small assembly line. Thus, line-balancing procedures, with some adjustment, can be used to arrange the machines within each cell. The layout *between* manufacturing cells is a process layout. Therefore, computer programs such as CRAFT can be used to locate cells and any leftover equipment in the facility. If group technology is successfully applied, cellular layouts should be able to combine the flexibility of a process layout with the efficiency of a product layout.

Consider the process layout shown in Figure 7.8. Machines are grouped by function into four separate departments. Component parts manufactured in the process layout section of the factory are later assembled into a finished product on

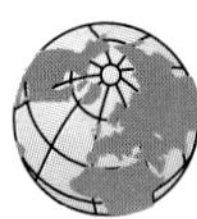

GAINING THE COMPETITIVE EDGE

A New Focused Factory for USRAC

U.S. Repeating Arms Co. (USRAC), a manufacturer of sporting arms (including the Winchester rifle), has a new owner, GIAT Industries of France, and will soon have a new facility. USRAC's current facility, built in New Haven, Connecticut, around the turn of the century and organized as a traditional process layout, has six stories, isolated rooms, long corridors, low ceilings, and narrow aisles. These outdated features do not lend themselves to the flexibility needs of modern manufacturing.

The new facility will be one-third smaller than the current one, will be all on one floor, and will have ceiling heights of 17 feet or more to accommodate overhead cranes. The biggest change, however, is in the *focused factory* concept around which the new factory will be organized. As if they were factories within a factory, the four product lines—model 9422, model 94, model 70, and shotguns—will each be housed in a separate area (or cell) of the facility with their own maintenance, engineering, tool control, and other support areas. Specialty processes, such as heat treatment and wood lacquering, will still be located in a centralized area. Bringing all the people and resources together to make the whole product, not just part of the product, will help the company better understand product cost, work flow, and resource needs. The focused factory concept is also expected to reduce leadtime from 8 weeks to 10 days, reduce facility cost by 40 percent, save 30 percent in energy consumption, reduce material handling costs by 20 percent, expand capacity, and improve communications.

One other change is management's attitude toward layout adjustments. Management now considers its layout to be dynamic, as if all "our machines are either on rollers or on wheels."

Source: Based on Ferguson, Gary, "U.S. Repeating Arms Sets Sights on World-Class Facility," *Industrial Engineering* (March 1993): 30–32.

[3]Flanders, R. E., "Design, Manufacture and Production Control of a Standard Machine," *Transactions*

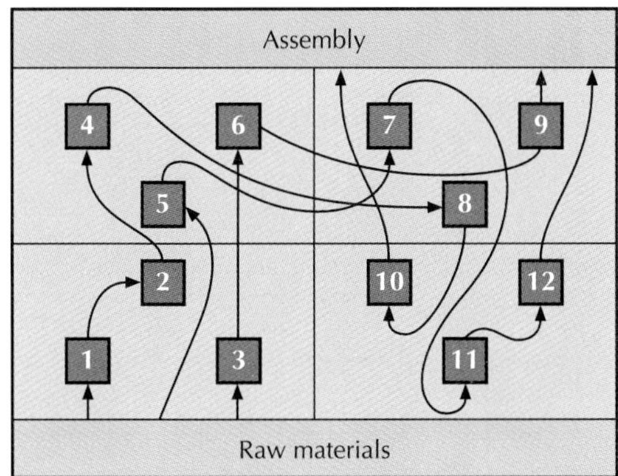

FIGURE 7.8 **Original Process Layouts**

the assembly line. The parts follow different flow paths through the shop. Three representative routings, for parts A, B, and C, are shown in the figure. Notice the distance that each part must travel before completion and the irregularity of the part routings. A considerable amount of shop "paper" is needed to direct the flow of each individual part and to confirm that the right operation has been performed. Workers are skilled at operating the types of machines within a single department and typically can operate more than one machine at a time.

Figure 7.9 gives the complete part routing matrix for the eight parts processed through the facility. In its current form, there is no apparent pattern to the routings. **Production flow analysis (PFA)** is a group technology technique that reorders part-routing matrices to identify families of parts with similar processing requirements. The reordering process can be as simple as listing which parts have four machines in common, then which have three in common, two in common, etc., or as sophisticated as pattern-recognition algorithms from the field of artificial intelligence. Figure 7.10 (see page 348) shows the results of reordering Figure 7.9. Now the part families and cell formations are clear. Cell 1, consisting of machines 1, 2, 4, 8, and 10, will process parts A, D, and F; Cell 2, consisting of machines 3, 6, and 9, will process products C and G; and Cell 3, consisting of machines 5, 7, 11, and 12, will process parts B, H, and E. A complete cellular layout showing the three cells feeding a final assembly line is given in Figure 7.11. The representative part flows for parts A, B, and C are much more direct than those in the process layout. There is no backtracking or crisscrossing of routes, and the parts travel a shorter distance to be processed. Notice that parts G and E cannot be completely processed within cells 2 and 3, to which they have been assigned. However, the two cells are located in such a fashion that the transfer of parts between the cells does not involve much extra movement.

Production flow analysis reorders part routing matrices to identify families of parts with similar processing requirements.

	Machines											
Parts	1	2	3	4	5	6	7	8	9	10	11	12
A	×	×		×				×		×		
B					×		×					×
C			×			×			×			
D	×	×		×				×		×		
E					×	×						×
F	×			×				×				
G			×			×			×			×
H							×				×	×

FIGURE 7.9 **Part Routing Matrix**

Parts	1	2	4	8	10	3	6	9	5	7	11	12
A	×	×	×	×	×							
D	×	×	×	×	×							
F	×		×	×								
C						×	×	×				
G						×	×	×				×
B									×	×		×
H										×	×	×
E							×		×			×

Cell 1: Parts A, D, F
Machines 1, 2, 4, 8, 10

Cell 2: Parts C, G
Machines 3, 6, 9

Cell 3: Parts B, H, E
Machines 5, 7, 11, 12

FIGURE 7.10 Part Routing Matrix Reordered to Highlight Cells

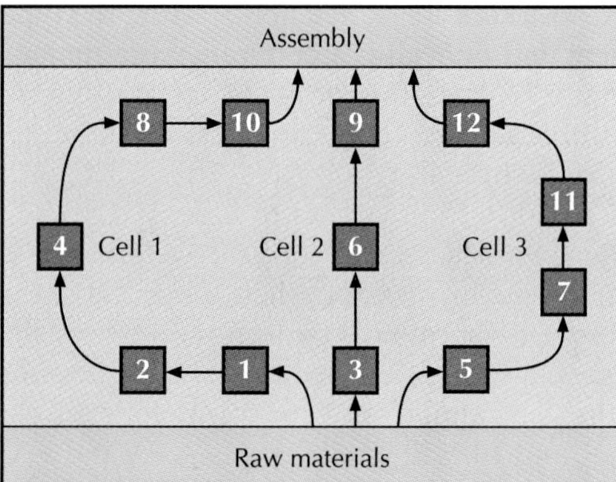

FIGURE 7.11 Revised Layout with Three Cells

The U shape of cells 1 and 3 is a popular arrangement for manufacturing cells because it facilitates the rotation of workers among several machines. Workers in a cellular layout typically operate more than one machine, as was true of the process layout. However, workers who are assigned to each cell must now be multifunctional—that is, skilled at operating many different kinds of machines, not just one type, as in the process layout. In addition, workers are assigned a *path* to follow among the machines that they operate, which may or may not coincide with the path the product follows through the cell. Figure 7.12 shows a U shaped manufacturing cell with worker paths highlighted.

The advantages of cellular layouts can be summarized as follows:

Cellular layouts reduce transit time set-up and in-process inventory.

- *Reduced material handling and transit time:* Material movement is more direct. Less distance is traveled between operations. Material does not accumulate or wait long periods of time to be moved. Within a cell, the worker is more likely to carry a partially finished item from machine to machine than wait for material handling equipment, as is characteristic of process layouts, where larger loads must be moved further distances.
- *Reduced setup time:* Since similar parts are processed together, the adjustments required to set up a machine should not be that different from item to item. If it

Transparency 7.7 A Cellular Layout

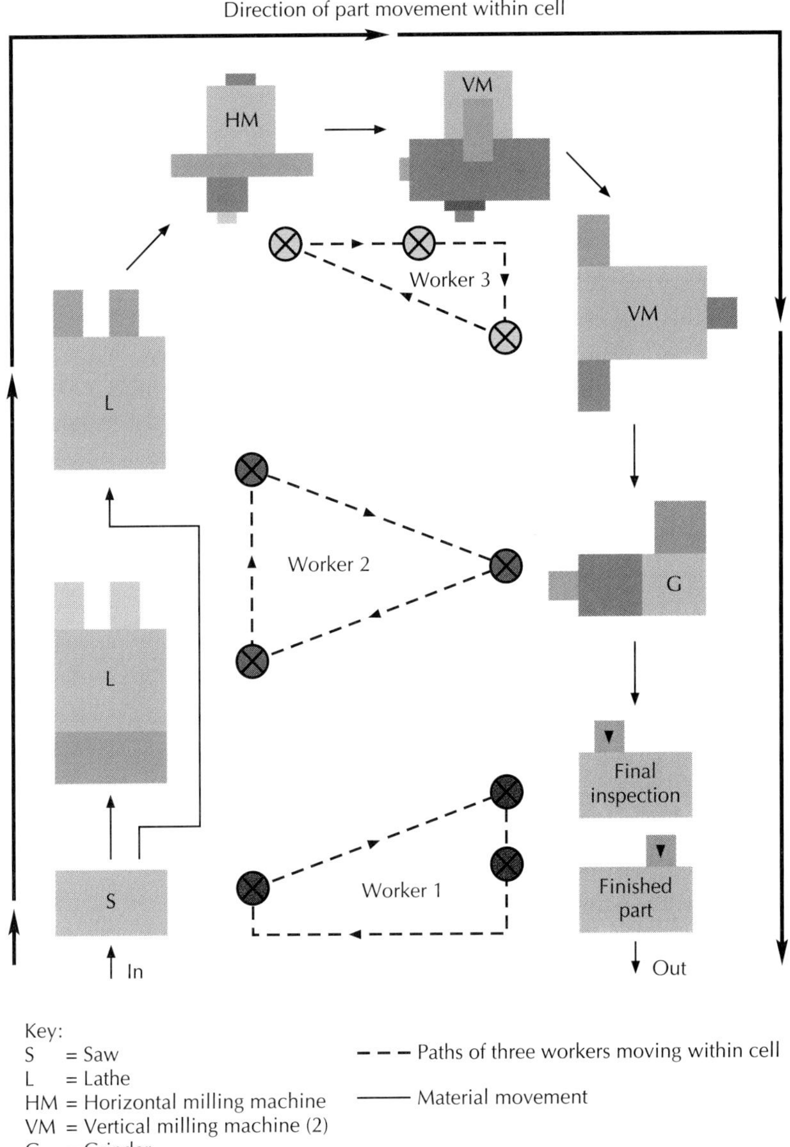

FIGURE 7.12 A Manufacturing Cell with Worker Paths

Source: J.T. Black, "Cellular Manufacturing Systems Reduce Setup Time, Make Small Lot Production Economical," *Industiral Engineering* (November 1983). Copyright 1983 Institute of Industrial Engineers.

doesn't take that long to change over from one item to another, then the changeover can occur more frequently, and items can be produced and transferred in very small batches or lot sizes.

- *Reduced work-in-process inventory:* In a work cell, as with assembly lines, the flow of work is balanced so that no bottlenecks or significant buildup of material occurs between stations or machines. Less space is required for storage of in-process inventory between machines, and machines can be moved closer together, thereby saving transit time and increasing communication.
- *Better use of human resources:* Typically, a cell contains a small number of workers responsible for producing a completed part or product. The workers act as a self-managed team, in most cases more satisfied with the work that they do

and more particular about the quality of their work. Labor in cellular manufacturing is a very flexible resource. Workers in each cell are multifunctional and can be assigned to different routes within a cell or between cells as demand volume changes.

Teaching Note 7.1 A Layout Experiment

- *Easier to control:* Items in the same part family are processed in a similar manner through the work cell. There is a significant reduction in the paperwork necessary to document material travel, such as where an item should be routed next, if the right operation has been performed, and the current status of a job. With fewer jobs processed through a cell, smaller batch sizes, and less distance to travel between operations, the progress of a job can be verified *visually* rather than by mounds of paperwork.
- *Easier to automate:* Automation is expensive. Rarely can a company afford to automate an entire factory all at once. Cellular layouts can be automated one cell at a time. Figure 7.13, on page 351, shows an automated cell with one robot in the center to load and unload material from several CNC machines and an incoming and outgoing conveyor. Automating a few workstations on an assembly line will make it difficult to balance the line and achieve the increases in productivity expected. Introducing automated equipment in a job shop has similar results, because the "islands of automation" speed up only certain processes and are not integrated into the complete processing of a part or product.

GAINING THE COMPETITIVE EDGE

Cellular Layout Improves Washing Tub Assembly

Mid Central Plastics, located in Des Moines, Iowa, employs 230 people in the production of custom parts using plastic injection molding machines. The company decided to investigate whether reorganizing into manufacturing cells would improve the production of one of its higher-volume parts, washing machine tubs.

In the original system, inner and outer washing machine tubs were produced on injection molding machines located side by side. The tubs were then stacked individually on pallets with 0.80 spacers between each layer and moved 300 feet by forklift to a storage area to wait for assembly. During the process, press operators typically experienced considerable idle time, whereas forklift operators and assemblers were overtaxed.

In the new layout, two injection molding machines are dedicated to tub production and connected by a conveyor. The assembly area is located at the end of the conveyor. Outer tubs produced at one molding machine are placed on the conveyor headed toward the second molding machine, which produces inner tubs. The operator/assembler at the second machine attaches the inner tub to the outer tub and stacks the assembly on a pallet. Pallets of assembled tubs are moved by forklift to the storage area.

On a small scale, this new arrangement represents a conversion from a process layout to a cellular layout. The creation of a washer tub cell saved Mid Central $10,000 a month in labor costs, eliminated the need for the stacking spacers, reduced preassembly storage space by 7,000 cubic feet, and significantly reduced reject rates. The higher quality resulted from defects being discovered and corrected immediately, since the tubs were assembled right after production. One unfavorable result, from an accounting point of view (but one that did not affect overall costs), was the necessity to slow down the production rate of inner tubs to match the production rate of outer tubs. The reduced rate of output was more than offset by the increased quality and reduced time spent in transit, storage, and assembly.

Source: Based on "Software Assists Material Handling Analysis," *Industrial Engineering* (May 1992): 21–22.

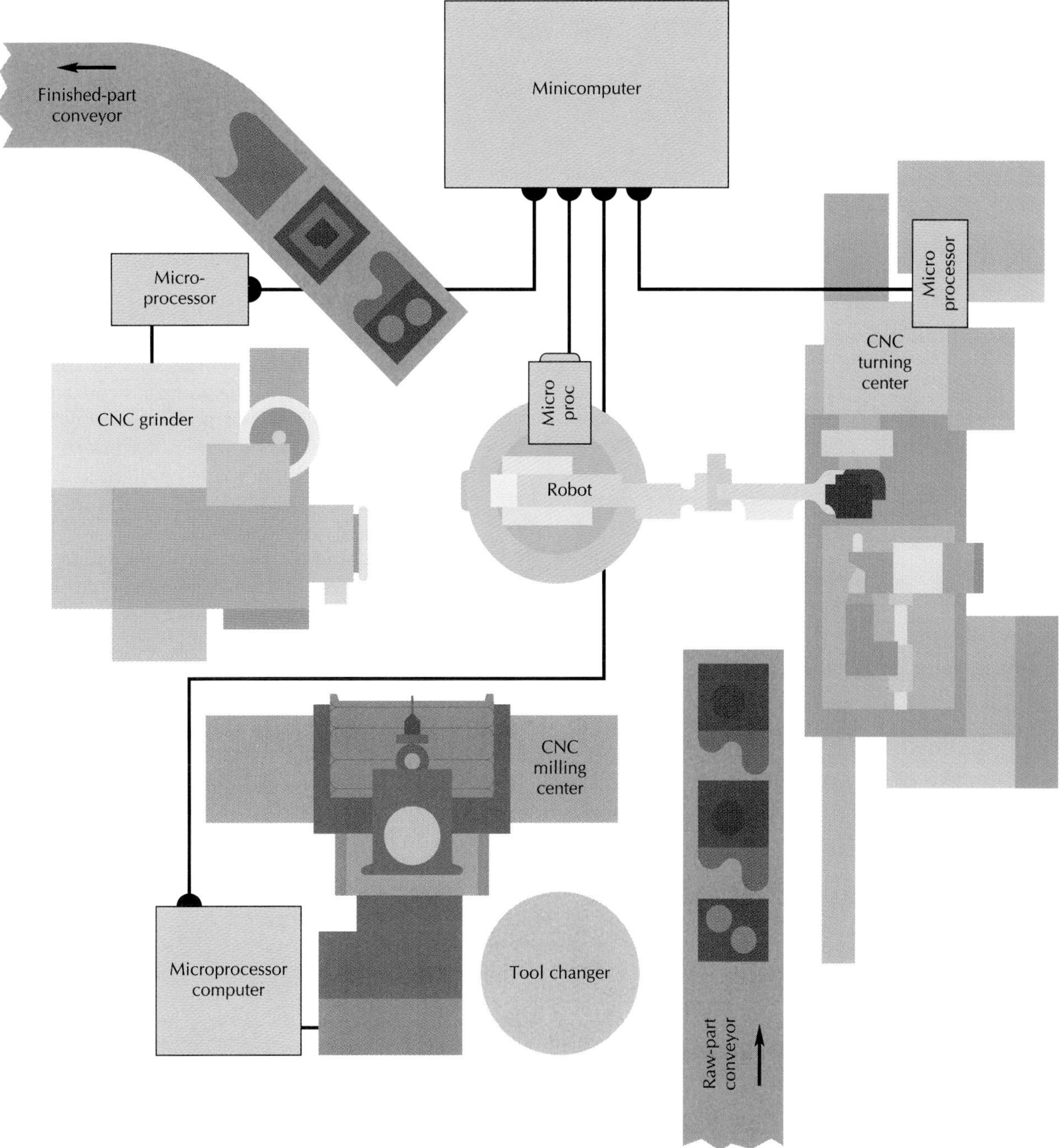

FIGURE 7.13 An Automated Manufacturing Cell

Source: J.T. Black, "Cellular Manufacturing Systems Reduce Setup Time, Make Small Lot Production Economical," *Industiral Engineering* (November 1983). Copyright 1983 Institute of Industrial Engineers.

Although the advantages of cellular layouts are impressive, there are several disadvantages that must also be considered:

- *Inadequate part families:* There must be enough similarity in the types of items processed to form distinct part families. Cellular manufacturing is appropriate for medium levels of product variety and volume. The formation of part families and the allocation of machines to cells is not always an easy task. Part families identified for design purposes may not be appropriate for manufacturing purposes.

Cellular layouts require distinct part families, careful balances, expanded worker training, and increased capital investment.

- *Poorly balanced cells:* It is more difficult to balance the flow of work through a cell than a single-product assembly line, because items may follow different sequences through the cell that require different machines or processing times. The sequence in which parts enter the cell can thus affect the length of time a worker or machine spends at a certain stage of processing. Poorly balanced cells can be very inefficient. It is also important to balance the workload among cells in the system, so that one cell is not overloaded while others are idle. This may be taken care of in the initial cellular layout, only to become a problem as changes occur in product designs or product mix. Severe imbalances may require the reformation of cells around different part families, and the cost and disruption that implies.
- *Expanded training and scheduling of workers:* Training workers to do different tasks is expensive and time-consuming and requires the worker's consent. Initial union reaction to multifunctional workers was not positive. Today, many unions have agreed to participate in the flexible assignment of workers in exchange for greater job security. Although flexibility in worker assignment is one of the advantages of cellular layouts, the task of determining and adjusting worker paths within or between cells can be quite complex.
- *Increased capital investment:* In cellular manufacturing, multiple smaller machines are preferable to single large machines. Implementing a cellular layout can be economical if new machines are being purchased for a new facility, but

GAINING THE COMPETITIVE EDGE

Chickahominy Middle School Uses the Cellular Concept

Middle schools educate students in grades 6, 7, and 8, during the in-between transitional period of preadolescence. Educators struggle with balancing the structure and freedom imposed on these students by the educational system. In elementary school, students stay in one class with one teacher for the duration of the year. In high school, students change classes and teachers, and each student has a different class schedule (or path through the school building). How should students, classes, and teachers interact in middle school?

Chickahominy Middle School, located in Hanover County, Virginia, designed its new school building to reflect the need for middle school students to exhibit independence but not be overwhelmed. Allowing each grade level its own section of the building is fairly standard, but Chickahominy goes one step further. Students within each grade level also have separate *home-base* areas consisting of a group of four classrooms and four teachers for the basic studies of language arts, science, social studies, and math. For example, this year's sixth graders are partitioned into four groups, the Alpha Aces, the Dream Team, the Explorers, and the Superstars. Four teachers (one from each specialty) have homerooms of 25 students in each hall. These students (a total of 100) change classes within their home-base area for their basic studies but venture outside of their area (and hall) for special courses such as gym, band, art, or music. The students rotate according to individual schedules, not as an entire class. That keeps the mixture of students and variety of classes interesting without being confusing. The mix between the Alpha Aces, for example, and the Explorers is accomplished in elective courses.

The grouping of teachers has been beneficial, too, allowing them to better coordinate instruction and monitor student progress. Although the school system doesn't call its school layout a cellular layout, that's exactly what it is. The controlled environments created for the Dream Team, the Superstars, and the others are miniature versions of high school and are what we would call *cells* of learning.

Source: Based on Chickahominy Middle School, Hanover County School System, Mechanicsville, VA 23111

it can be quite expensive and disruptive in existing production facilities where new layouts are required. Existing equipment may be too large to fit into cells or may be underutilized when placed in a single cell. Additional machines of the same type may have to be purchased for different cells. The cost and downtime required to move machines can also be high.

Cellular layouts have become popular in the past decade as the backbone of modern factories. Cells can differ considerably in size, in automation, and in the variety of parts processed. Regardless of the details, there is a definite trend towards smaller, interconnected layout units called cells. Cells are even becoming popular in service layouts.

Flexible Manufacturing Systems

A **flexible manufacturing system** can produce an enormous variety of items.

We discussed **flexible manufacturing systems (FMSs)** as an example of technology in the previous chapter. In this chapter, we examine the FMS as an alternative layout. The idea of an FMS was proposed in England in the 1960s as a flexible *machining* system called System 24 that could operate without human operators 24 hours a day under computer control. Thus, the emphasis from the beginning was on automation rather than the reorganization of work flow. Early FMSs were large and complex, consisting of dozens of CNC machines and sophisticated material handling systems. The systems were very automated, very expensive, and controlled by incredibly complex software. The FMS control computer operated the material handling system, maintained the library of CNC programs and downloaded them to the machines, scheduled the FMS, kept track of tool use and maintenance, and reported on the performance of the system.

There are only a limited number of industries that can afford the investment required for a traditional FMS as described. In fact, fewer than 400 FMSs are in operation around the world today. Currently, the trend in flexible manufacturing is toward smaller versions of the traditional FMS, sometimes called *flexible manufacturing cells.* It is not unusual in today's terminology for two or more CNC machines to be considered a flexible cell and two or more cells, an FMS.

The concept of building up an FMS with flexible cells is different than automating and tying together group technology cells that make up a cellular lay-

GAINING THE COMPETITIVE EDGE

Saturn Uses Flexible Machining Cells

General Motor's Saturn plant is one of the first U.S. automakers to use high-flexibility, high-volume machining cells. The five-cell system utilizes two operators per cell, fifty-nine pallets, and ten setup stations. Two of the cells machine front engine covers for two- and four-valve engines. Three additional cells machine transmission parts: upper and lower valve bodies, oil-pump housings, and rear covers. Each cell contains four machining centers serviced by a rail-guided automatic guided vehicle (AGV).

The flexible cell setup allows a number of different items to be processed and also accommodates changes in production volume. More machines can easily be added as needed, retooling is simplified, and operators can be shared across cells. Currently, the cells run constantly except for scheduled preventive maintenance. Operators are used only to load the system (the cells can run unattended), so that a small number of operators can be assigned to each cell rather than to individual machines. With flexible machining cells, Saturn was able to make more than 200 design revisions within a model year with only slight changes in CNC programs and no capital investment.

Source: Based on "Saturn Gets High Volume and Flexibility from LeBlond Makino Cells," *Industrial Engineering* (October 1992): 18.

out. To clarify, let's examine several different types of FMS layouts. FMS layouts differ based on the variety of parts that the system can process, the size of the parts processed, and the average processing time required for part completion. Figures 7.14 and 7.15 show four basic types of FMS layouts, 1. progressive, 2. closed loop, 3. ladder, and 4. open field.

The *progressive layout*, in which all parts follow the same progression through the machining stations is the most limited. This layout is appropriate for processing a family of parts and is the most similar to an automated group technology cell. The *closed-loop system* is arranged in the general order of processing for a much larger variety of parts. Parts can easily skip stations or can move around the loop to visit stations in an alternate order. Progressive and closed-loop systems are used for part sizes that are relatively large and that require longer processing times. The *ladder layout* is so named because the machine tools appear to be located on the steps of a ladder, allowing two machines to work on one item at a time. Programming the machines may be based on similarity concepts from group technology, but the types of parts processed are not limited to particular part families. Parts can be routed to any machine in any sequence. An *open-field system* is the most complex and flexible FMS layout. It allows material to move among the machine centers in any order and typically includes several support stations such as tool interchange stations, pallet or fixture build stations, inspection stations, and chip/coolant collection systems.

In group technology or cellular layouts, parts are assigned to families based on similar flow paths. Thus, the routing of parts through a manufacturing cell follows the arrangement of machines within the cell (i.e., the product layout concept).

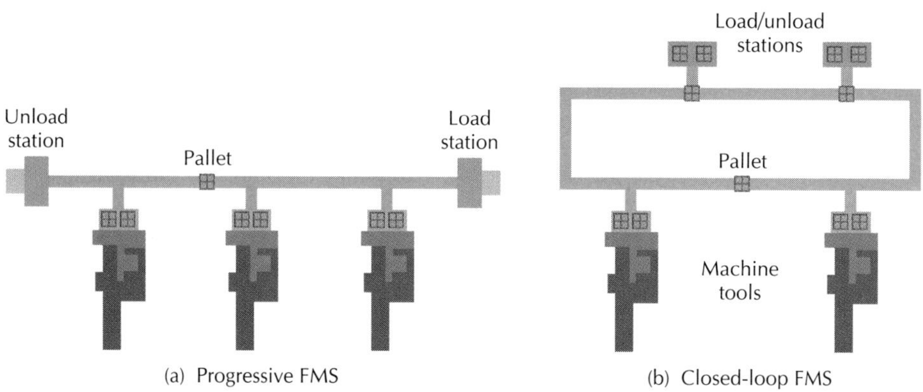

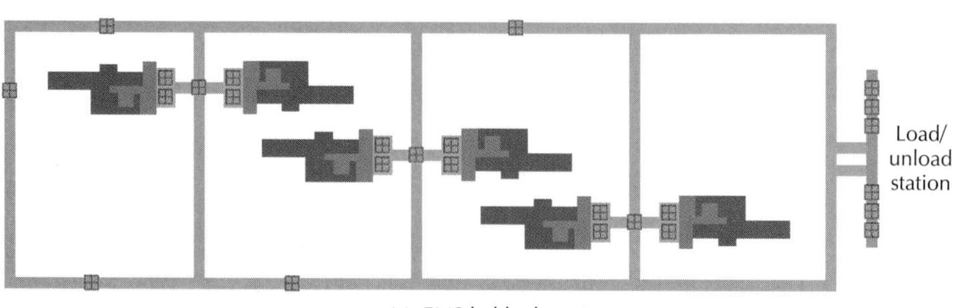

FIGURE 7.14 Alternative FMS Layouts

Source: W. Luggen, *Flexible Manufacturing Cells and Systems*, Englewood Cliffs, N.J.: Prentice-Hall, 1991, pp. 90–92.

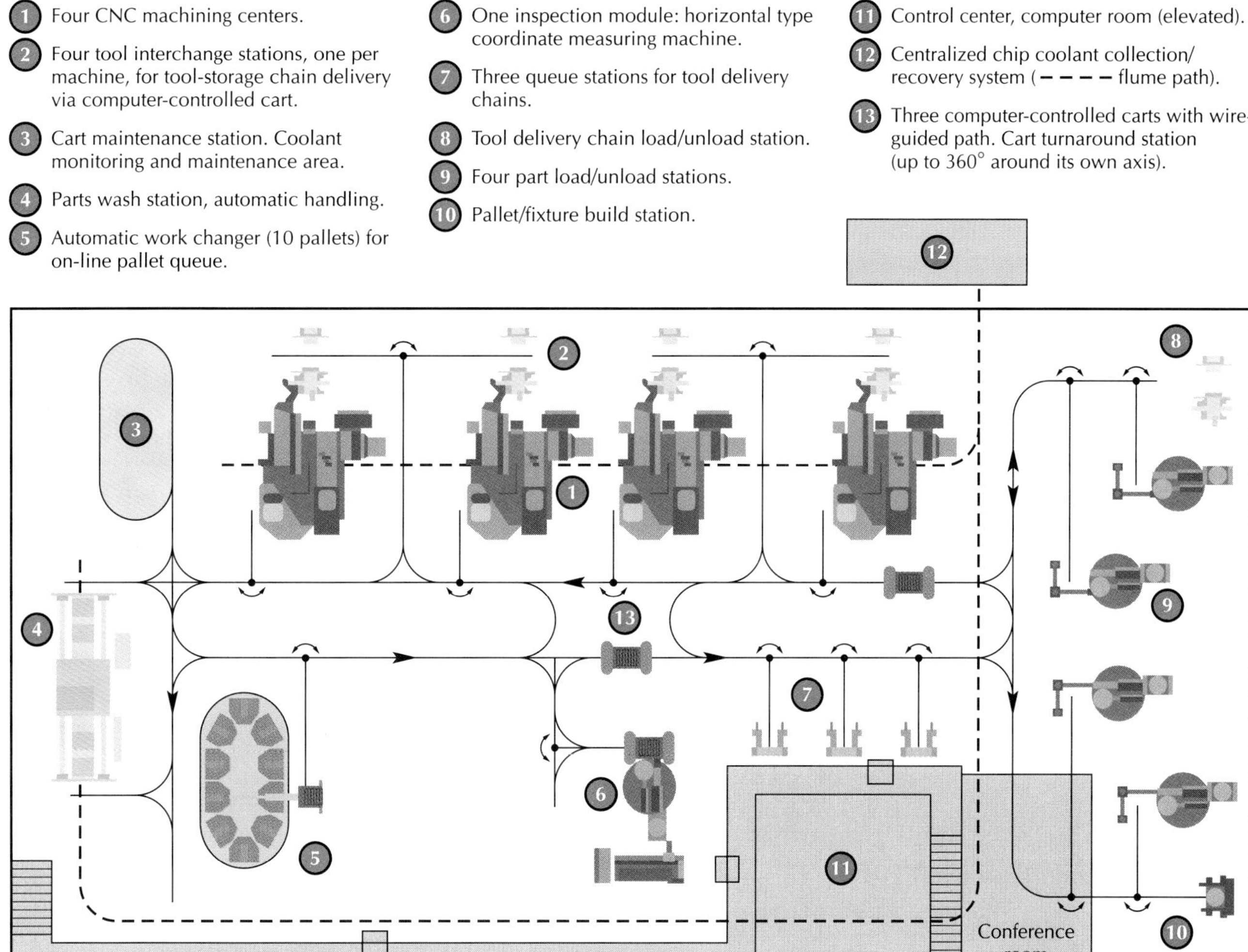

FIGURE 7.15 An Open Field FMS

Source: W. Luggen, *Flexible Manufacturing Cells and Systems,* Englewood Cliffs, N.J.: Prentice-Hall, 1991, p. 93.

Teaching Note 7.2 Flexibility

The routing of parts in an FMS is highly variable, often referred to as "random," like a job shop or process layout. Parts may rotate around the FMS on a conveyor or other material handling system device several times before a machine is available for processing. If more than one item requires the use of a particular machine, a priority system is enacted by the FMS controller. An FMS can produce an enormous variety of items efficiently because of the versatility of the machine centers in the FMS, the speed with which machines can be set up for different processing requirements, and the speed and flexibility of material transport between centers. The system is just as efficient at producing one item at a time as one hundred at a time.

Views on the effectiveness of the FMS concept differ. Some analysts view FMS as part of the "supermachine" syndrome and as no more efficient than an automated job shop. Others consider FMS to represent the factory of the future, with highly efficient production and unlimited flexibility. Both cellular layouts and FMS provide efficient, flexible manufacturing. Currently, the cellular layout is more common because for most types of manufacturing it provides sufficient flexibility at a much lower cost than an FMS.

Video 7.2 *LTV's Flexible Manufacturing Cell*

GAINING THE COMPETITIVE EDGE

An FMS at LTV

Vought Aircraft Company constructed an advanced flexible manufacturing systems to date to machine the 2,000 parts needed for the B-1 bomber. Using conventional techniques, machining the 2,000 parts would require more than 900,000 hours of machine time. With flexible machining, Vought can do the job in fewer than 32,000 hours.

The system consists of eight Cincinnati Milicron CNC machining centers, each with the capacity to use 90 different tools and to withstand a workpiece weight of 5,000 pounds. Most parts are machined from plate stock and pass through the system at least three times. The machining sequence begins at the fixture buildup area, where an operator loads the riser and fixture onto a standard pallet. A build schedule for the operator to follow is displayed on a terminal at the work site. The fixtures are loaded onto one of two load/unload carousels, where operators, in turn, load the appropriate blank stock. One of four automatic guided vehicles (AGVs) takes the pallet to the appropriate machining center and then on to an automated parts washer that flushes chips from the part and prepares the part for inspection. The parts washer separates ferrous and nonferrous chips for easier recycling.

The part is then moved to a coordinate measuring machine for inspection. If the part is out of tolerance, it is sent to a second coordinate measuring machine for reinspection. If the second inspection confirms the problem, the part is automatically routed to the material review station, and the machine that produced the out-of-tolerance part is shut down. In addition, operating personnel are instructed as to possible causes of the problem.

When a part passes inspection, it is routed back to the load/unload carousel to be refixtured and to enter the system again if necessary. Fixtures are either reloaded or torn down.

Vought's FMS stands out because of the number and diversity of parts processed on the system and its virtually closed-loop quality control features.

Source: Based on Goetsch, David, *Advanced Manufacturing Technology*, Albany, N.Y.: Delmar Publishers, 1990, pp. 320–323.

The only manual operations in LTV's FMS are performed at the load/unload stations in the center of the photograph. Blank stock to be machined is shown in the foreground. The items rotating on the carousel are different fixturing devices that the workers build up and tear down to hold the various blanks in place for machining. Automated guided vehicles transport items to and from machining centers and the load/unload stations. Notice the computers (in blue) at each machining center and the main control room in the rear. Nearly 1,200 CNC part programs and 900 verification programs for part geometry are contained in the system.

Mixed-Model Assembly Lines

Traditional assembly lines are designed to process a single model or type of product. You may recall from our earlier discussion that these lines are efficient but not very flexible. **Mixed-model assembly lines** are widely used in just-in-time (JIT) production systems. Prior to the proven success of these systems by the Japanese, U.S. firms had used assembly lines to process more than one type of product, but they were not used efficiently. In the U.S. version, models of the same type were produced in long production runs, sometimes lasting for months, and then the line was shut down and changed over for the next model. The next model was also run for an extended time, producing perhaps half a year to a year's supply; then the line was shut down again and changed over for yet another model, and so on. The problem with this arrangement was the difficulty in responding to changes in customer demand. If a certain model was selling well and customers wanted more of it, they would have to wait until the next batch of that model was scheduled to be produced. On the other hand, if demand was disappointing for models that had already been produced, the manufacturer was stuck with high stocks of unwanted inventory.

A **mixed-model assembly line** processes more than one product model.

Recognizing that this mismatch of production and demand was a problem, U.S. analysts concentrated on devising more sophisticated forecasting techniques. However, the Japanese changed the manner in which the mixed-model line was laid out and operated. First, they reduced the time needed to change over the line to produce different models. Then they trained their workers to perform a variety of tasks and allowed them to work at more than one workstation on the line, as needed. Finally, they changed the way in which the line was arranged and scheduled. Let's look at the differences between single-model and mixed-model assembly lines in more detail.

Single-model and mixed-model assembly lines differ in layout and operation.

- *Line balancing:* In a mixed-model line, element times can vary from model to model. Instead of using the element times from one model to balance the line, a distribution of possible element times from the array of models must be considered. In most cases, the expected value, or average, element times are used in the balancing procedure. Otherwise, mixed-model lines are balanced in much the same way as single-model lines.
- *U-shaped line:* In order to compensate for the different work requirements of assembling different models, it is necessary to have a flexible workforce and to arrange the line so that workers can assist one another as needed. Figure 7.15 gives an example of improvements in line balancing efficiency when a U-shaped line is used.
- *Flexible workforce:* Although worker paths are predetermined to fit within a set cycle time, the use of average time values in mixed-model lines will obviously produce variations in worker performance. Hence, the lines are not paced, that is, run at a set speed. In fact, items move through the line at the pace of the slowest operation. This is not to say that production quotas are not important. If the cycle time (maximum time allowed if quota is to be met) is exceeded at any station on the line, other workers are notified by flashing lights or sounding alarms so that they can come to the aid of the troubled station. The assembly line is slowed or stopped until the work at the errant workstation is completed. This flexibility of workers helping other workers makes a tremendous difference in the ability of the line to adapt to the varied length of tasks inherent in a mixed-model line.
- *Model sequencing:* Since different models are produced on the same line, mixed-model scheduling involves an additional decision—the order, or sequence, of models to be run through the line. From a logical standpoint, it would be unwise to sequence two models back-to-back that require extra long processing

Precedence diagram:

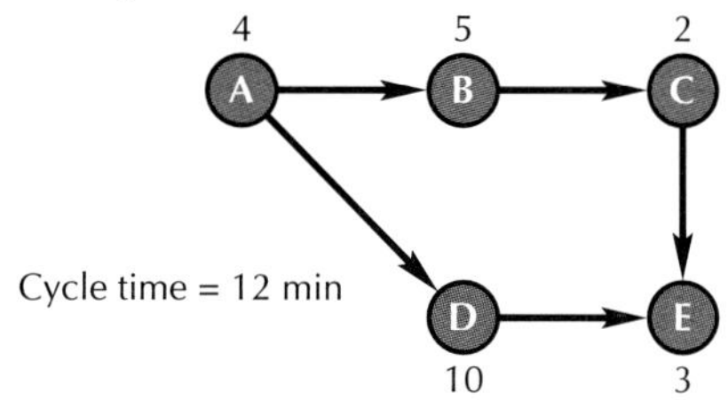

(a) Balanced for a straight line

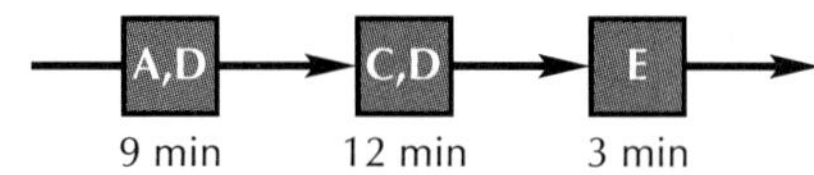

$$\text{Efficiency} = \frac{24}{3(12)} = \frac{24}{36} = .6666 = 66.7\%$$

(b) Balanced for a U-shaped line

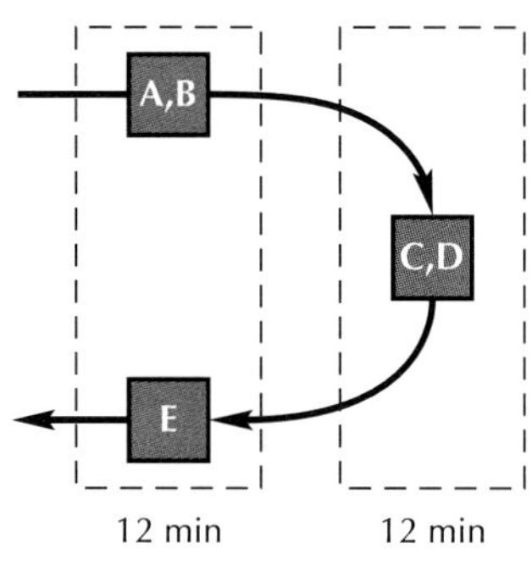

$$\text{Efficiency} = \frac{24}{2(12)} = \frac{24}{24} = 100\%$$

FIGURE 7.16 Balancing U-Shaped Lines

times. It would make more sense to mix the assembling of models so that a short model (requiring less than the average time) followed a long one (requiring more than the average time). With this pattern, workers could "catch up" from one model to the next.

Teaching Note 7.3 Mixed-Model Sequencing

Another objective in model sequencing is to spread out the production of different models as evenly as possible throughout the time period scheduled. We need to work through an example to illustrate how extensively the JIT mixes up production on the final assembly lines.

EXAMPLE 7.5

Mixed-Model Sequencing

Problem Statement:

Demand for the popular water toy Sudsy Soaker has far exceeded expectations. In order to increase the availability of different models of the toy, the manufacturer has decided to begin producing its most popular models as often as possible on its one assembly line. Given monthly requirements of 7,200, 3,600, and 3,600 units for Sudsy Soaker 50, Sudsy Soaker 100, and Sudsy Soaker 200, respectively, determine a model sequence for the final assembly line that will smooth out the production of each model. (Assume 30 working days per month and 8 working hours per day. Also assume that the time required to assemble each model is approximately the same.)

Solution:

First, convert monthly requirements to daily requirements. Then, calculate a cycle time in minutes for each model.

Model	*Monthly Requirements*	*Daily Requirements*	*Cycle Time*[a]
SS50	7,200	$\frac{7,200}{30} = 240$	$\frac{480}{240} = 2$
SS100	3,600	$\frac{3,600}{30} = 120$	$\frac{480}{120} = 4$
SS200	3,600	$\frac{3,600}{30} = 120$	$\frac{480}{120} = 4$
Total	14,400	480	

[a]Cycle time $= \frac{8 \text{ hrs} \times 60 \text{ min/hr}}{\text{daily output requirements}}$

In order to meet daily production requirements, the assembly line will need to produce a Sudsy Soaker every minute. Because the Sudsy Soakers are produced on a mixed-model assembly line, the individual models will be produced less often. An SS50 will be produced every 2 minutes, SS100, every 4 minutes, and SS200, every 4 minutes. During the course of a day, 240 SS50s, 120 SS100s, and 120 SS200s will be assembled. Thus, in the assembly sequence model SS50 will appear twice as often as either model SS100 or model SS200.

The following sequence meets those requirements and spreads out the production of each model evenly. It should be repeated 120 times a day to meet demand.

A — B — A — C

To U.S. manufacturers, this jellybean sequence of final assembly seems extreme. But this extreme mix of models also does a better job of responding to changes in market demand. Different model types are constantly available, and the overall schedule can be adjusted if demand shifts are detected.

SUMMARY

In this chapter, we discussed the characteristics and design of process layouts for batch production in job shop environments and product layouts for mass production on assembly lines. We also discussed fixed-position layouts, service layouts, cellular layouts, flexible manufacturing systems, and mixed-model assembly lines.

In the current manufacturing environment of new product introductions, rapidly changing technologies, and intense competition, the ability of a manufacturing system to adapt is essential. Therefore, layouts of all types are emphasizing flexibility. Setup times are being reduced so that it is feasible to produce more than one model on an assembly line. Flexible manufacturing systems are being designed to process any item that will fit the dimensions of the pallet on which it is transported and processed. Some companies with cellular layouts are placing wheels and casters on their machines so that manufacturing cells can easily be rearranged as needed. IBM is experimenting with a modular conveyor system that would allow an assembly line to be rearranged while workers are on their lunch break.

As important as flexibility is, the cost of moving material is still a primary consideration in layout design. Today, as in the past, layout decisions are concerned with minimizing material flow. However, with the trend toward reduced inventory levels, there has been a shift in emphasis from minimizing the *number* of loads moved to minimizing the *distance* they are moved. Instead of accumulating larger loads of material and moving them less often, machines are being shoved closer together to allow the frequent movement of smaller loads. Planners who used to devote a considerable amount of time to designing the location of storage areas and the movement of material into and out of storage areas are now more concerned with the rapid movement of material to and from the facility itself. Facility location and the logistics of material transportation are the topics of the next chapter.

SUMMARY OF KEY FORMULAS

Cycle Time

$$C = \frac{\text{production time available}}{\text{desired units of output}}$$

Theoretical Minimum Number of Workstations

$$N = \frac{\sum_{i=1}^{j} t_i}{C}$$

Efficiency

$$E = \frac{\sum_{i=1}^{j} t_i}{nC}$$

Balance Delay

$$1 - \text{efficiency}$$

SUMMARY OF KEY TERMS

balance delay: the total idle time of the line.

block diagram: a schematic layout diagram that includes the size of each work area.

cellular layout: a layout that groups dissimilar machines into cells that process parts with similar shapes or processing requirements.

cycle time: the maximum amount of time an item is allowed to spend at each workstation if the targeted production rate is to be achieved; also, the time between successive product completions.

facility layout: the arrangement of machines, departments, workstations, and other areas within a facility.

fixed-position layout: a layout in which the product remains at a stationary site for the entire manufacturing cycle.

flexible manufacturing system (FMS): programmable equipment connected by an automated material handling system and controlled by a central computer.

line balancing: a layout technique that attempts to equalize the amount of work assigned to each workstation on an assembly line.
mixed-model assembly line: an assembly line that processes more than one product model.
Muther's grid: a format for displaying manager preferences for department locations.
precedence requirements: physical restrictions on the order in which operations are performed.
process layout: a layout that groups similar machines together into work centers according to the process or function they perform.
product layout: a layout that arranges machines in a line according to the sequence of operations that are needed to assemble a particular product.
production flow analysis (PFA): a group technology technique that reorders part-routing matrices to identify families of parts with similar processing requirements.
relationship diagram: a schematic diagram that denotes location preference with different line thicknesses.
unit load: the quantity in which material is normally moved; it could represent a single unit, pallet, or bin of material.

SOLVED PROBLEMS

1. Process Layout

Problem Statement:
Mohawk Valley Furniture Warehouse has purchased a retail outlet with six departments, as shown in grid 1. The anticipated number of customers that move between the departments each week is given in the load summary chart.

a. Calculate the nonadjacent loads for the layout shown in grid 1.
b Revise Mohawk's layout such that nonadjacent loads are minimized.

Load Summary

From \ *To*	*DEPARTMENT*					
DEPARTMENT	*A*	*B*	*C*	*D*	*E*	*F*
A		70				50
B					100	
C		70				
D			80			
E	40					30
F		60			100	

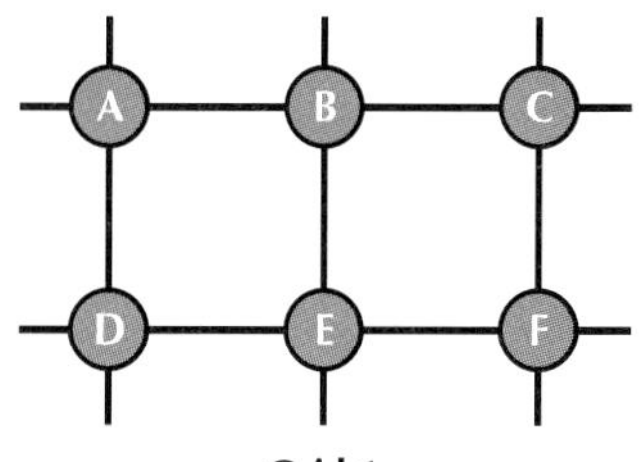

Grid 1

Solution:

Composite movements ranked from highest to lowest are as follows:

E ↔ F	130
B ↔ E	100
C ↔ D	80
A ↔ B	70
B ↔ C	70
B ↔ F	60
A ↔ F	50
A ↔ E	40

a. Nonadjacent loads for grid 1 are shown in the following art.

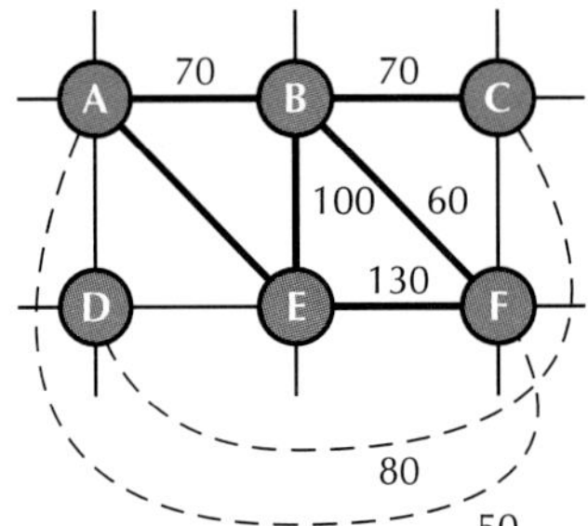

130 nonadjacent loads

b. To reduce the number of nonadjacent loads, try switching the location of D and F.

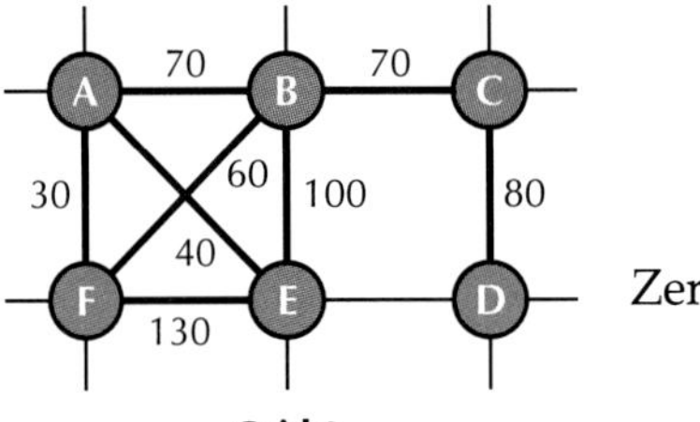

Zero nonadjacent loads

Grid 2

2. *Product Layout*

Problem Statement:

The Basic Block Company needs to produce 4,000 boxes of blocks per 40-hour week to meet upcoming holiday demand. The process of making blocks can be broken down into six work elements. The precedence and time requirements for each element are as follows. Draw and label a precedence diagram for the production process. Set up a balanced assembly line and calculate the efficiency of the line.

Work Element	*Predecessor*	*Performance Time (min)*
a	—	0.10
b	a	0.40
c	a	0.50
d	—	0.20
e	c, d	0.60
f	b, e	0.40

Solution:

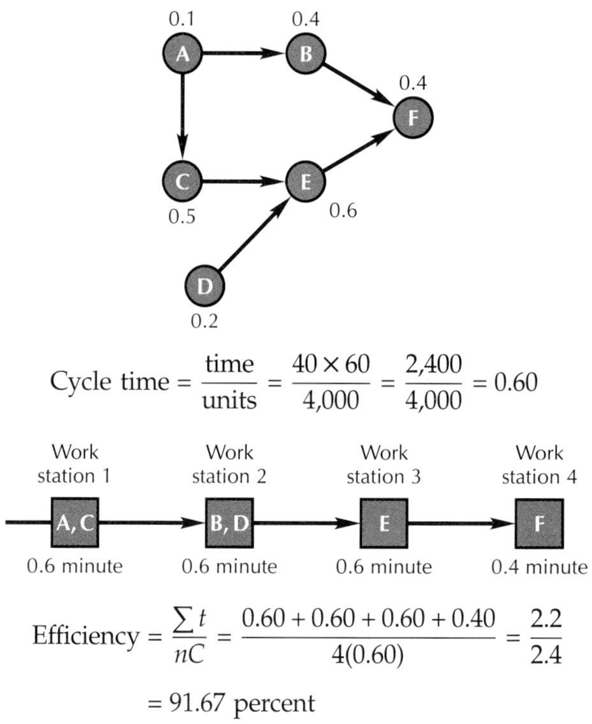

$$\text{Cycle time} = \frac{\text{time}}{\text{units}} = \frac{40 \times 60}{4{,}000} = \frac{2{,}400}{4{,}000} = 0.60$$

$$\text{Efficiency} = \frac{\sum t}{nC} = \frac{0.60 + 0.60 + 0.60 + 0.40}{4(0.60)} = \frac{2.2}{2.4}$$

$$= 91.67 \text{ percent}$$

QUESTIONS

7-1. List five or more objectives of facility layout. How does layout affect efficiency?

7-2. Distinguish between a process and product layout.

7-3. Give an example of a fixed-position layout for producing a product and providing a service.

7-4. What type of layout(s) would be appropriate for each?
   a. A grocery store
   b. Home construction
   c. Electronics assembly
   d. A university

7-5. How do the cost functions differ for the three basic types of layout?

7-6. What is the difference between block diagramming and relationship diagramming?

7-7. How do service layouts differ from manufacturing layouts?

7-8. What are the objectives of line balancing?

7-9. Describe several heuristic approaches to line balancing.

7-10. What is group technology and how does it relate to cellular layouts?

7-11. How are manufacturing cells formed? How does the role of the worker differ in cellular manufacturing?

7-12. How does a cellular layout combine a product and process layout?

7-13. Discuss the advantages and disadvantages of cellular layouts.

7-14. Describe a flexible manufacturing system. How does it differ from a cellular layout?

7-15. How do mixed-model assembly lines differ from traditional assembly lines? What additional decisions are required?

7-16. What are the advantages of a jellybean sequence for mixed-model assembly lines?

PROBLEMS

7-1. 30 nonadjacent loads

2	3	1
	4	

7-1. Spiffy Dry Cleaners recently underwent a change in management, and the new owners want to revise the current layout. The store performs four main services: 1. laundry, 2. dry cleaning, 3. pressing, and 4. alterations. Each is located in a separate department, as shown here. The load summary chart gives the current level of interaction between the departments. Calculate the number of nonadjacent loads for the current layout. Design an alternate layout to minimize the number of nonadjacent loads.

Load Summary Chart

	1	2	3	4
1	—	0	125	40
2	0	—	45	75
3	85	235	—	20
4	60	30	10	—

Current Layout

3	1	4
	2	

7-2. 65 nonadjacent loads

2	3	1
5	4	

7-2. Spiffy's has decided to add seasonal storage to its service offerings. A revised load summary chart is given next. Where should this fifth department be located? Calculate the number of nonadjacent loads for the new layout.

Load Summary Chart

	1	2	3	4	5
1	—	0	125	40	35
2	0	—	45	75	70
3	85	235	—	20	180
4	60	30	10	—	55
5	65	100	115	25	—

7-3.

1	2	3
4	6	5

7-3. Given the following load summary chart, design a layout on a 3×2 grid that will minimize nonadjacent loads.

Load Summary Chart

From \ *To*	*WORK CENTER*					
WORK CENTER	1	2	3	4	5	6
1		70		50		30
2	20		10			60
3		100			70	
4	25					50
5		40	10			
6	10		20		40	

7-4. Design a layout on a 3×2 grid that satisfies the preferences listed here.

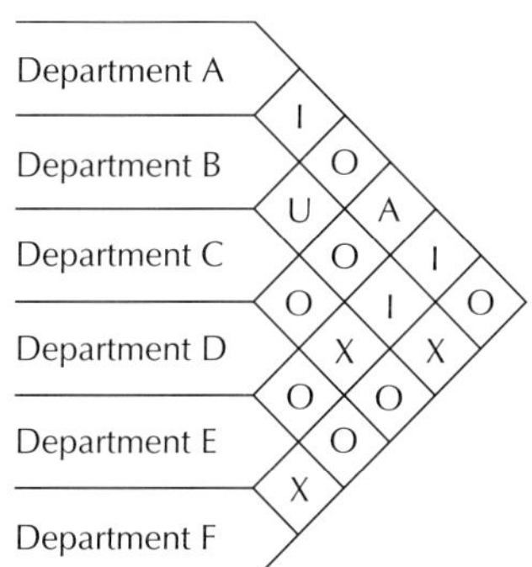

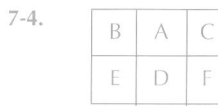

7-4.

B	A	C
E	D	F

7-5. Pratt's Department Store is opening a new store in The Center's Mall. Customer movement tracked in its existing stores shows the following pattern:

No. of Customers

From \ *To*	*Women's*	*Men's*	*Boy's*	*Girl's*	*Infants*	*Housewares*	*Accessories*
Women's		20	50	50	50	70	60
Men's			20	10	5	20	30
Boy's		20		20			
Girl's	30		50		30		
Infant's	30						
Housewares	40						30
Accessories	30					20	

7-5. a.

H	A	
M	W	
B	G	I

b. L-shaped

a. Design a layout for Pratt's new store on a 3×3 grid that will minimize nonadjacent customer movement.

b. If you eliminate the squares of the grid where there are no departments, what is the shape of your building?

7-6. State University's Liberty Hall has been fully renovated to house business school faculty. Each department is assigned to a separate floor. There are six offices per floor, three on each side of the hall. In their previous location, it seemed that those faculty who were located adjacent to each other tended to do more papers together. The accompanying matrix shows how many joint papers have been published between faculty members in one department.

Assume the department head wants to encourage the research productivity of the faculty by locating professors adjacent to each other who have previously coauthored papers together. Design a layout that will maximize the interaction between professors who have previously coauthored papers together.

7-6.

J	H	B
R	M	S

Number of Joint Papers Published

	Johnson	*Hill*	*Rider*	*Shapiro*	*Baker*	*Massie*
Johnson		2	1			1
Hill			1	2	1	3
Rider						1
Shapiro						1
Baker						2
Massie						

7-7.

Sue	Allen	Terry
Jorge	Ashley	Mike
Bobby	Johnny	Carrie
Kent	Jamil	Mary

7-7. Renae Podowski's second grade class is very rowdy. Every student in the class has been disruptive at one time or another. Over the past few weeks, she has kept a careful record of the number of times she has had to speak to students for talking to each other. The classroom is set up in three rows with four seats in each row. Given the following data, design a classroom layout for Mrs. Podowski that will reduce classroom disturbances.

Number of Times Students Have Been Disciplined for Talking to Each Other

	Johnny	*Mary*	*Sue*	*Terry*	*Jorge*	*Allen*	*Jamil*	*Mike*	*Ashley*	*Bobby*	*Kent*	*Carrie*
Johnny			10	7		10						
Mary			4	3	4	20		10	5	3	12	
Sue				6			3	12		10	5	2
Terry					10		4			5	8	5
Jorge							2	4			2	1
Allen										6	4	6
Jamil								2	15			
Mike										6	5	
Ashley											3	
Bobby												5
Kent												4
Carrie												

7-8. a. See Solutions Manual.
b. 48 min
c. 80 min
d. A, B → C, D, E, F
e. 83.3%; 16.7%
f. 2; no

7-8. Professional Image Briefcases is an exclusive producer of handcrafted, stylish cases. Priding itself on its earlier reputation, the company assembles each case with care and attention to detail. This laborious process requires the completion of six primary work elements, which are listed here.

Work Element	*Precedence*	*Time (min)*
A Tan leather	—	30
B Dye leather	A	15
C Shape case	B	10
D Mold hinges and fixtures	—	5
E Install hinges and fixtures	C, D	10
F Assemble case	E	10

a. Construct a precedence diagram for the manufacture of briefcases.
b. If the demand is 50 cases per 40-hour week, compute the cycle time for the process.
c. Compute the lead time required for assembling one briefcase.

d. How would you balance this assembly line?
e. Compute the line's efficiency and balance delay.
f. Calculate the theoretical minimum number of workstations. Can a better arrangement be determined?

7-9. Referring to Problem 7-8, suppose the demand for briefcases increases to 80 cases per week.

a. Calculate a new cycle time and rebalance the line
b. Calculate the efficiency and balance delay of the manufacturing process.
c. Calculate the theoretical minimum number of workstations. Can a better arrangement be determined?

7-9. a. 30 min [A] → [B, C, D] → [E, F]
b. 88.9%; 11.1%
c. 3; no

7-10. The TLB Yogurt Company has set a production quota of 600 party cakes per 40-hour workweek. Use the following information.

a. Draw and label a precedence diagram.
b. Compute cycle time.
c. Compute the theoretical minimum number of workstations.
d. Balance the assembly line by the trial-and-error technique.
e. Calculate the efficiency and balance delay of the assembly line.

7.10 a. See Solutions Manual.
b. 4 min
c. 4
d. [A, E] → [B, C] → [D] → [F]
e. 100%; 0%

Work Element	*Predecessor*	*Performance Time (min)*
A	—	1
B	A	2
C	B	2
D	A, E	4
E	—	3
F	C, D	4

7-11. The Speedy Pizza Palace is revamping its order processing and pizza-making procedures. In order to deliver fresh pizza fast, six elements must be completed.

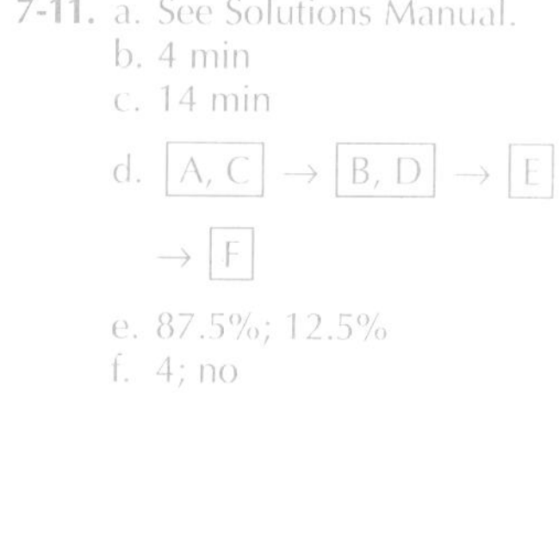
7-11. a. See Solutions Manual.
b. 4 min
c. 14 min
d. [A, C] → [B, D] → [E] → [F]
e. 87.5%; 12.5%
f. 4; no

Work Element	*Precedence*	*Time (min)*
A Receive order	—	2
B Shape dough	A	1
C Prepare toppings	A	2
D Assemble pizza	B, C	3
E Bake pizza	D	3
F Deliver pizza	E	3

a. Construct a precedence diagram.
b. If the demand is 120 pizzas per night (5:00 P.M. to 1:00 A.M.), compute the cycle time for the process.
c. Compute the lead time for the process.
d. How would you balance this line?
e. Compute the efficiency and balance delay of the line.
f. Calculate the theoretical minimum number of workstations. Is there a better way to arrange the line?

7-12. Referring to Problem 7-11, suppose demand increases to 160 pizzas per night.

a. How should the elements be arranged in order to balance the line?
b. Calculate the efficiency and balance delay of the process.
c. Calculate the theoretical minimum number of workstations. Can a better arrangement be determined?

7-12. a. [A] → [B, C] → [D] → [E] → [F]
b. 93.3%; 6.7%
c. 5; no

7-13. a. 4.8 min; 200
b. 240; 80%; 3
c. A, B, C → D, E ;
100%; 200
d. See Solutions Manual.

7-13. EyeCare, Inc., is a full-service optical supplier that sells eyeglasses, contact lenses, and protective eye apparel to opticians. Almonzo's job is to assemble custom-ordered lenses into eyeglasses for customers. Sales have been good lately, and Almonzo has been assembling 100 glasses a day. The manager of EyeCare asked Almonzo to write down the precedence requirements and approximate assembly times for each step in the assembly process. The data are shown here.

a. Assuming an 8-hour work day, how long does it take Almonzo to assemble one pair of glasses? If two workers were to work at Almonzo's pace, how many pairs of glasses could they assemble in one day?
b. EyeCare anticipates a surge in demand with the opening of its own retail outlets. If the assembly process is set up as an assembly line, what is the maximum number of eyeglasses that can be assembled in one day, regardless of the number of workers hired? What is the efficiency of the line? How many workers are needed?
c. The manager can afford to hire only one additional assembler. Set up the assembly process as an assembly line with two workers. Balance the line to produce as many units as it can. Calculate the efficiency of the line. How many pairs of eyeglasses can be assembled by two workers using an assembly line process?
d. Comment on the results of this problem.

Element	*Description*	*Precedence*	*Time (min)*
A	Inspect right and left lens for scratches and proper match.	—	1
B	Pop lens into frame.	A	1
C	Position right side piece and attach to frame.	B	0.4
D	Position left side piece and attach to frame.	B	0.4
E	Package.	C, D	2

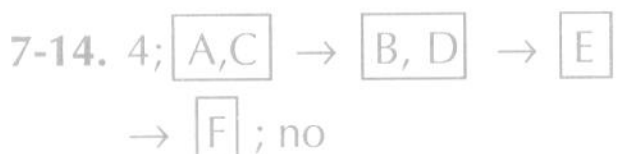

7-14. Professor Garcia has assigned 15 cases in his POM Seminar class to be completed in a 15-week semester. The students, of course, are moaning and groaning that the caseload cannot possibly be completed in the time allotted. Professor Garcia sympathetically suggests that the students work in groups and learn to organize their work efficiently. Knowing when a situation is hopeless, the students make a list of the tasks that have to be completed in preparing a case. These tasks are listed here, along with precedence requirements and estimated time in days. Assuming students will work 5 days a week on this assignment, how many students should be assigned to each group, and what is the most efficient allocation of tasks? Can 15 cases be completed in a semester? Explain your answer.

Element	*Description*	*Precedence*	*Time (days)*
a	Read case	—	1
b	Gather data	a	4
c	Search literature	a	3
d	Load in data	b	1
e	Run computer analysis	d	4
f	Write/type case	c, e	4

7-15. The precedence diagram and task times (in minutes) for assembling McCauley's Mystifier are shown here. Set up an assembly line to produce 125 mystifiers in a 40-hour week. Balance the line by trial and error, and calculate the efficiency of the line.

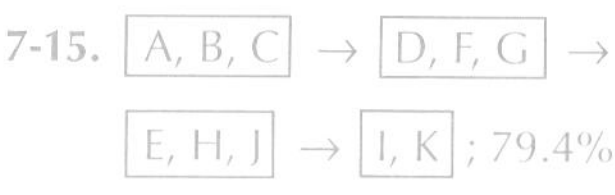

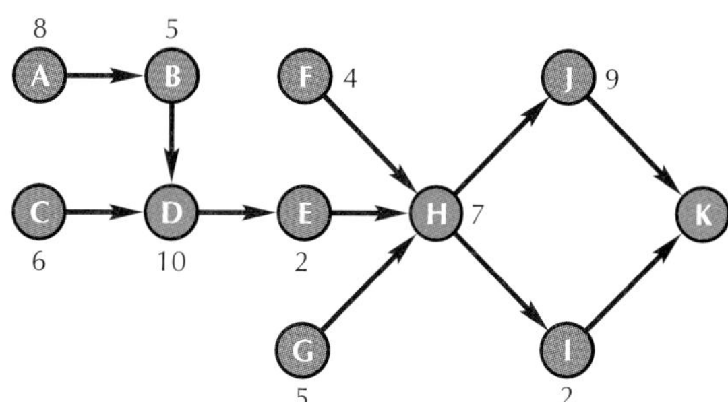

7-16. Balance the assembly line described in Problem 7-15 by: a. ranked positional weight, b. longest operation time, c. shortest operation time, d. most number of following tasks, and e. least number of following tasks. Comment on your results.

7-16. See Solutions Manual.

7-17. The work elements, precedence requirements, and time requirements to assemble a picture frame are shown here.

a. Construct a precedence diagram of the process and label task times.
b. Set up an assembly line capable of producing 1,600 frames per 40-hour week.
c. Calculate the efficiency and balance delay of the line.

7-17. a. See Solutions Manual.
b. A, B, C → D, E → F, G, H, I
c. 75.5%; 24.4%

Element	*Description*	*Precedence*	*Time (min)*
A	Attach left frame side to top of frame.	—	0.35
B	Attach right frame side to bottom of frame.	—	0.35
C	Attach left and right frame subassemblies.	A, B	0.70
D	Cut 8-inch × 10-inch glass.	—	0.50
E	Cut 8-inch × 10-inch cardboard.	—	0.50
F	Place glass into frame.	C, D	0.20
G	Place cardboard into frame.	C, E, F	0.20
H	Secure cardboard and glass.	F, G	0.50
I	Apply descriptive label to glass.	D	0.10

7-18. Refer to Problem 7-17.

a. Calculate the maximum number of frames that can be assembled each week.
b. Rebalance the line for maximum production. Assuming one worker per workstation, how many workers would be required?
c. Assume the company can sell as many frames as can be produced. If workers are paid $8 an hour and the profit per frame is $5, should the production quota be set to maximum?

7-18. a. 3,428
b. 5
c. yes

7-19. The precedence diagram and task times for assembling modular furniture are shown on page 370. Set up an assembly line to assemble 1,000 sets of modular furniture in a 40-hour week. Balance the line by trial and error, and calculate the efficiency of the line.

7-19. a. A, B, C → C, D, F, G, H → J → I, K
b. 75%

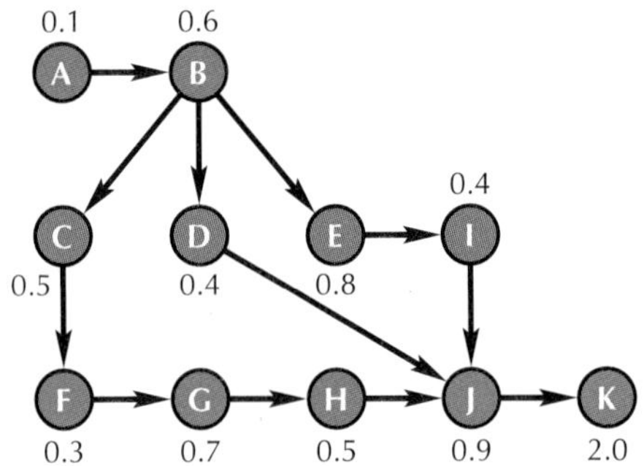

7-20. See Solutions Manual.

7-20. Balance the assembly line described in the previous problem by: a. ranked positional weight, b. longest operation time, c. shortest operation time, d. most number of following tasks, and e. least number of following tasks. Comment on your results.

7-21. B, Q, B, Q, B, I

7-21. As local developers prepare for an increase in housing starts, they must anticipate their demand for various materials. One such material is tile. Used in bathrooms, kitchens, and for decoration, tiles come in many shapes, colors, and sizes. In order to accommodate the varying needs, the tile manufacturer must schedule its production efficiently. Each month developers order 30,000 boxes of quarry tile, 15,000 boxes of Italian mosaic tile, and 45,000 boxes of 4-inch bathroom tile. Determine a mixed-model sequence that will efficiently meet these needs. Assume 30 days per month.

See Solutions Manual.

CASE PROBLEM

Arranging Darian's Gymnastics Center

Darian and Anita Rice looked around the office nervously as they waited for the architect to arrive. Building his own gymnastics center had been a dream of Darian's ever since childhood, and it was hard to believe the dream was so close to becoming a reality.

"Hello, folks. Sorry I'm late," Tom Armstead, the architect, said apologetically as he entered the room. "Now tell me all about this gym of yours."

"It's not a gym, it's a gymnastics center," smiled Darian. This fellow didn't seem formidable at all. Darian just hoped Mr. Armstead was competent and wouldn't waste their time. "We want a full-service gymnastics center to train children who enjoy gymnastics as a recreational activity as well as those who wish to compete. We need a facility that is flexible and inexpensive."

"Don't we all. What kind of equipment will you need?" asked Tom.

Anita, the more analytic of the two, handed him a prepared list: "A 40-foot by 40-foot floor-exercise mat, four or five balance beams, a set of even parallel bars, a set of uneven parallel bars, a large trampoline, a foam pit, a power strip or two, a vault, a pommel horse, a climbing rope, stall bars, a mushroom, a horizontal bar, and rings."

"Is that all?" teased Tom.

"It'll do for starters."

"And what size building do you think you'll need for the gymnastics center?"

"About 7,500 square feet, just a shell of a building really. We expect to train around 500 youngsters per session and hold meets in which 50 or so team members are in competition. We'll need a small space for an office—really just a counter would do. Other than that, the entire building should be one open floor area for gymnastics."

"It sounds like you've put a lot of thought into this project. What exactly do you want me to do?"

"Well, we want this facility to be well planned from the start. We want to have a basic layout in mind before the building is designed. From a financial viewpoint, we want to get the most use out of our space; the space must be functional. We're tired of haphazard arrangements that endanger the gymnasts and disrupt classes."

"Sounds fair. If you will explain to me some of your preferences on where each piece of equipment should be located in relation to another, then I can draw up a relationship diagram that will satisfy your needs. After that we can worry about the size and shape of the building."

"Do you need dimensions or space requirements for the equipment?"

"Not just yet. We're going to determine the *relative* location of the equipment first. Let me get out a new pad and pencil. . . . Okay, go to it."

Darian and Anita spoke rapidly, the ideas flying back and forth between the two entrepreneurs.

"The floor exercise area is for running and tumbling. It should not be located near any swinging apparatus, such as the bars, rope, or rings."

"Falls for the trampoline are potentially dangerous, so the trampoline should not be located where climbing or swinging activities take place."

"Sometimes the vault is used as a dismount aid, though."

"That's true . . . it's important the vault be near the trampoline. Speaking of the vault, we have to have a power strip[4] for the vault and for the pit, too. But we should keep the balance beams and uneven bars away from the power strip."

"The pit?"

"Yes, the pit. The pit is an 8-foot-deep concrete hole in the floor filled with big pieces of foam rubber. It's great for learning tumbling skills, and a pit fight is the kids' favorite activity."

"We need the horizontal bars next to the pit. It would be nice if the uneven bars and stall bars were located near there, too.

"And the climbing rope should be somewhere nearby—the kids love to swing on it and drop into the pit."

"I like to have a class working on different pieces of equipment at the same time. It would be helpful if related equipment were grouped together."

"Yes, like uneven parallel bars and balance beams for the girls."

"And pommel horse, mushroom, even bars, and rings for the boys."

"We'll want the office/reception desk near the front door. We also want to keep the trampoline, pit, and anything that involves chalk dust away from the office/reception area."

"Well, that's enough to get me started. Make an appointment for next week and I'll show you what I've come up with."

"No, he's not going to waste our time," thought Darian. "This gymnastics center is really going to happen."

1. Put Darian and Anita's preferences for equipment location into a Muther's grid.
2. Create a 3 × 5 layout in which you try to satisfy preferences. Draw a relationship diagram of the layout and look for opportunities for improvement.

[4]A power strip is a narrow, but lengthy, mat used to gain the speed necessary for certain tumbling stunts.

REFERENCES

Black, J. T., *The Design of the Factory with a Future,* New York: McGraw-Hill, 1991.

Flanders, R. E., "Design, Manufacture and Production Control of a Standard Machine," *Transactions of ASME* 46 (1925).

Goetsch, D., *Advanced Manufacturing Technology,* Albany, N.Y.: Delmar, 1990.

Jablonowski, J., "Reexamininig FMSs," *American Machinist,* Special Report 774 (March 1985).

Luggen, W. *Flexible Manufacturing Cells and Systems,* Englewood Cliffs, N.J.: Prentice Hall, 1991.

Monden, Y., *Toyota Production System,* 2nd ed, Atlanta, Ga.: IIE Press, 1993.

Muther, R., *Systematic Layout Planning,* Boston: Industrial Education Institute, 1961.

Russell, R. S., P. Y. Huang, and Y. Y. Leu, "A Study of Labor Allocation in Cellular Manufacturing," *Decision Sciences* 22, no. 3 (1991): 594–611.

Sumichrast, R. T., R. S. Russell, and B. W. Taylor, "A Comparative Analysis of Sequencing Procedures for Mixed-Model Assembly Lines in a Just-In-Time Production System," *International Journal of Production Research* 30, no. 1 (1992): 199–214.

Towards a New Era in Manufacturing Studies Board, Washington D.C.: National Academy Press, 1986.

8

LOCATION ANALYSIS AND LOGISTICS MANAGEMENT

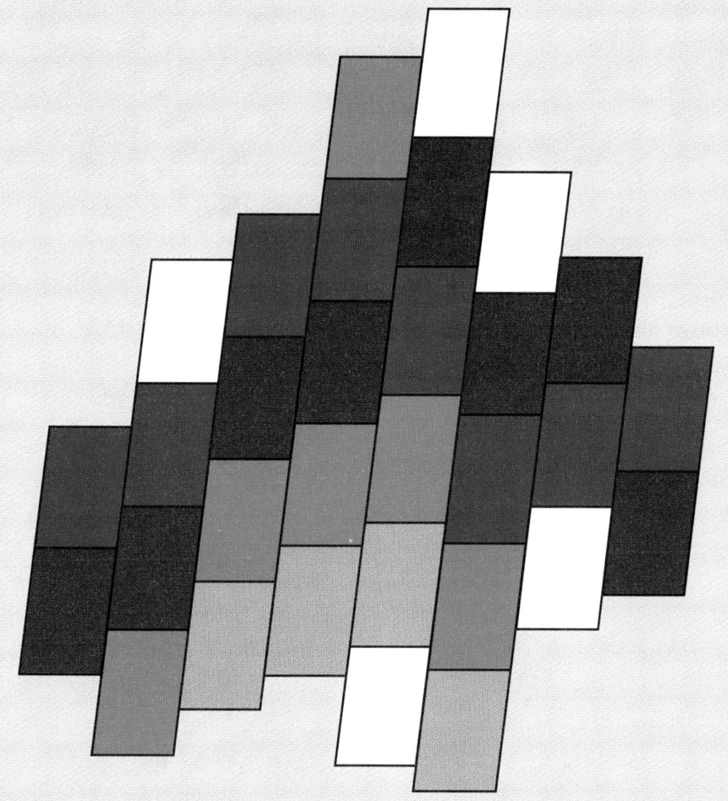

CHAPTER OUTLINE

This McDonald's in Pushkin Square in Moscow, Russia, religiously adheres to founder Ray Kroc's creed of QSC&V (quality, service, cleanliness, and value) just as any other McDonald's in the United States or around the world does. In order to achieve their expected level of quality and service in Moscow, McDonald's developed an entire logistical support system for growing, processing, and distributing food, part of which is the $60 million food plant shown here. This follows McDonald's overall approach to logistics, which is to construct a strong logistical chain from suppliers to customers with no weak links, especially among suppliers. McDonald's makes sure everyone along the supply chain clearly understands its expectations for performance, and, closely monitors this performance for all logistical elements.

SUPPLIER LOCATION FOR THE MOSCOW McDONALD'S

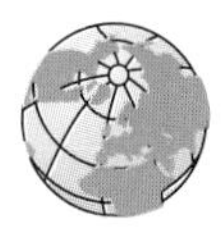

Around the world, McDonald's operates more than 11,000 restaurants in 51 countries, 4,000 outside the United States. One of the most unique is the initial 700-seat McDonald's in Moscow. McDonald's insists that a Big Mac must taste the same in Moscow as it does in New York, Paris, or Sydney, yet all food products used to supply their restaurant in Russia must be secured locally. McDonald's prepared for this challenge by planning the supply and distribution system for the Moscow restaurant six years in advance, when McDonald's experts began to work with Russians to upgrade their production standards to supply the desired quality of meat, wheat, potatoes, milk, and other necessary basic ingredients.

Supplier location has always been recognized as an important part of the logistics function at McDonald's, and past experience has shown that what works best was to combine a number of independently owned food-processing plants dedicated solely to supplying McDonald's restaurants. This type of centralized system, called a *food town,* reduced both transportation and material handling costs. A $60 million food town was established in Russia that combined a bakery, meat plant, chicken plant, lettuce plant, fish plant, and distribution center. Each of these processing facilities is independently managed, but all share cooling and freezing facilities with the distribution center. Locating dedicated processing facilities together is the only way McDonald's could ensure the standards of quality and service they require in their Moscow restaurant. However, the system also results in savings from reduced capital setup costs, inventory and material handling costs, and distribution costs.[1]

[1]Ritchie, P., "McDonald's: A Winner Through Logistics," *International Journal of Physical Distribution and Logistics Management* 20, no. 3 (1990): 21–24.

Decisions regarding where to locate a business facility or plant are not made as often as other operating decisions; however, they tend to be crucial in terms of the profitability and long-term survival of a firm. A mistake in location is not easily overcome. An old saying frequently used to describe individual or business success is, "They were in the right place at the right time." For a service operation such as a restaurant, hotel, or retail store, being in the right place usually means in a location that is convenient and easily accessible to their customers.

Fast-food restaurants are typically found clustered in shopping malls, at interstate highway interchanges, and, in general, wherever there are heavy customer traffic flows. Department stores also locate in upscale shopping malls; however, discount stores tend to be isolated or located in shopping centers with other stores offering lower or discount prices. Pharmacies are often found near hospitals and clinics, as are doctor's offices, whereas law offices are typically located near banks and other financial institutions. Such operations tend to be in locations that have a critical mass of customers in their particular market. Location decisions for service-oriented firms tend to be an important part of the overall market strategy for the delivery of their products or services to their customers. However, a business cannot simply survey the demographic characteristics of a geographic area and build a facility at the location with the greatest potential for customer traffic; other factors, particularly financial considerations, must be part of the location decision. Obviously, a site on Fifth Avenue in New York would be attractive for a McDonald's restaurant, but can enough hamburgers and french fries be sold to pay the rent? In this case, the answer is yes.

Location decisions are made more frequently for service operations than manufacturing facilities. Facilities for service-related businesses are smaller and less costly. They depend upon a certain degree of market saturation; the location is actually part of their product. The decision where to locate and build a manufacturing facility is equally important, but for different reasons, not the least of which is the very high expense of building a plant or factory. Although the primary location criteria for a service-related business is usually access to customers, for a manufacturing facility a different set of criteria is important. These include the labor climate and wage rates, proximity to suppliers and markets, distribution and transportation costs, energy availability and cost, and proximity to other company facilities.

At one time most manufacturing in the United States was located in the Midwest and in the Great Lakes region. However, during the past two decades companies and plants have steadily migrated to the south and west (the region known popularly as the Sunbelt) to take advantage of cheaper and less organized labor and a warmer climate. Often these relocations are in response to aggressive marketing tactics by towns, localities, and communities that offer favorable incentive packages, including lower land prices, tax breaks, less stringent environmental restrictions, roads, and so on. Improved modes of transportation, including the expansion of the interstate highway system, nationwide rail transport, and convenient air service as well as advances in computer and communications technology, have removed previous geographic barriers to what were once considered to be remote business environments. Companies now typically evaluate locations across the country and even around the world. U.S. firms more and more frequently are locating facilities outside the United States in Mexico, Europe, and Asia to be closer to new, international markets and to benefit from lower wage rates, whereas many European and Asian firms are locating plants in the United States to be closer to their markets.

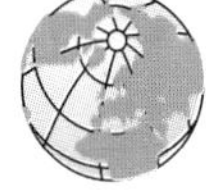

In this chapter we discuss the important considerations and factors involved in making location decisions. However, a large portion of this chapter focuses on a closely related topic to facility location, the distribution of goods and services, which is known as logistics management. As we mentioned in the preceding brief discussion, important factors in determining a facility location are distribution routes and modes of transportation. Also, quick receipt and delivery of materials and products is becoming a measure of quality customer service. In fact, a recent trend begun by Japanese manufacturers is to have their suppliers of parts and materials in very close proximity to a plant in order to receive quick service and to minimize inventory and shipping costs. The ability to distribute and receive materials, goods, and services in a timely, efficient, and low-cost manner has become an increasingly important customer service and quality consideration for many firms. Our discussion of this topic includes the presentation of several mathematical modeling approaches, including transportation models and network flow models for determining cost- and time-efficient distribution routes.

TYPES OF FACILITIES

As we mentioned in the introduction, the type of facility is a major determinant of its location. The factors that are important for determining the location of a manufacturing plant are usually different from those that are important in locating a service facility or a warehouse. In this section we discuss the major categories of facilities and the different factors that are important in the location decision.

Heavy Manufacturing

Heavy-manufacturing facilities are large, require a lot of space, and are expensive.

Heavy-manufacturing facilities are primarily plants that are relatively large and require a lot of space and, as a result, are expensive to construct. Examples include automobile plants, steel mills, and oil refineries. Important factors in the location decision for plants include construction costs, land costs, modes of transportation for shipping heavy manufactured items and receiving bulk shipments of raw materials, proximity to raw materials, utilities, means of waste disposal, and labor availability. Sites for manufacturing plants are normally selected where construction and land costs can be kept at a minimum and raw material sources are nearby in order to reduce transportation costs. Access to railroads is frequently a major factor in locating a plant. Environmental issues have increasingly become a major factor in plant location decisions. Plants can create various forms of pollution, including raw material wastes, burning and air pollution, noise pollution, and traffic pollution. These plants must be located where the harm to the environment is minimized. Although proximity to customers is an important factor for some facility types, it is less so for manufacturing plants.

Light Industry

Light-industry facilities are smaller, cleaner plants and are usually less costly.

Light-industry facilities are typically perceived as smaller, cleaner plants that produce electronic equipment and components, parts used in assemblies, or assembled products. Examples might include plants making stereos, TVs, or computers, tool and die shops, breweries, or pharmaceutical firms. Several of the factors that are important for heavy-manufacturing facilities are less important for light industry. Land and construction costs are not generally as crucial, because the plants tend to be smaller and require less engineering. It is not as important to be near raw materials, since they are not received in large bulk quantities, nor is storage capacity required to as great a degree. As a result, transportation costs are somewhat less important. Many parts and material suppliers fall into this category, and, as such, proximity to customers can be an important factor. (This is a point we discuss in greater detail later in the section "Facility Location and Quality Management.") Alternatively, many light industries ship directly to regional warehouses or distributors, making it less important to be near customers. Environmental issues are less important in light industry, since burning raw materials is not normally part of their production processes, nor are there large quantities of waste. Important factors include the labor pool, especially the availability of skilled workers, the community environment, access to commercial air travel, government regulation, and zoning requirements.

Warehouses and Distribution Centers

Warehouses are a category of their own. Products are not manufactured or assembled within their confines, nor are they sold from them. They represent an intermediate point in the logistical inventory system where products are held in storage. Normally a warehouse is simply a building that is used to receive, handle, and then ship products. They generally require only moderate environmental conditions and security and little labor, although some specialized warehouses require a more controlled environment, such as refrigeration or security for precious metals or drugs. Because of their role as intermediate points in the movement of products from the manufacturer to the customer, transportation and shipping costs are the most important factors in the location decision for warehouses. The proximity to customers can also be an important consideration, depending on the delivery requirements, including frequency of delivery required by the customer. Construction and land costs tend to be of less importance as does labor availability. Since warehouses require no raw materials, have no production processes, and create no waste, factors such as proximity to raw materials, utilities, and waste disposal are of almost no importance.

Warehouses are buildings or shells for receiving, storing, handling, and shipping products.

Retail and Service

Retail and service operations generally require the smallest and least costly facilities. Examples include such service facilities as restaurants, banks, hotels, cleaners, clinics, and law offices and retail facilities such as groceries and department stores, among many others. The single most important factor for locating a service or retail facility is proximity to customers. It is usually critical that a service facility be near the customers it serves, and a retail facility must be near the customers who buy from it. Construction costs are generally less important (especially when compared with a manufacturing plant); however, land or leasing costs can be important. For retail operations, for which the saying "location is everything" is very meaningful, site costs can be very high. Other location factors that are important for heavy- and light-manufacturing facilities, such as proximity to raw materials, zoning, utilities, transportation, and labor, are less important or not important at all for service and retail facilities.

Service facilities are the smallest and least costly but are more dependent on customer traffic.

SITE SELECTION: WHERE TO LOCATE

When we see on the television news or read in the newspaper that a company has selected a site for a new plant, the decision can appear to be almost trivial. Usually it is reported that a particular site was selected from among two or three alternatives, and a few reasons are provided, such as good community or available land. However, such media reports conceal the long, detailed process for selecting a site for a major manufacturing facility. When General Motors selected Spring Hill, Tennessee, as the location for their new Saturn Plant in 1985, it culminated a selection process that required several years and the evaluation of hundreds of potential sites.

When the site selection process is initiated, the pool of potential locations for a manufacturing facility is, literally, global. Since proximity to customers is not normally an important location factor for a manufacturing plant, countries around the world become potential sites. As such, the site selection process is one of gradually and methodically narrowing down the pool of alternatives until the final location is determined. In the following discussion we identify some of the more important factors that companies consider when determining the country, region, community, and site at which to locate a facility.

Site selection requires determination of country, region, community, and site.

Country

Transparency 8.1 Site Selection Factors (Country and Region)

Some U.S. companies constructed facilities overseas because of lower labor costs.

Until recent years companies almost exclusively tended to locate within their national borders. This has changed somewhat in recent years as U.S. companies began to locate outside the continental United States to take advantage of lower labor costs. This was largely an initial reaction to the competitive edge gained by overseas firms, especially Far Eastern countries, in the 1970s and 1980s. U.S. companies too quickly perceived that foreign competitors were gaining a competitive edge primarily because of lower labor costs. They failed to recognize that the real reason was often a new managerial philosophy based on quality and the reduction of all production-related costs. High transportation costs for overseas shipping, the lack of skilled labor, unfavorable foreign exchange rates, and changes in an unstable government have often combined to negate any potential savings in labor costs gained by locating overseas. Ironically, some German companies, such as Mercedes-Benz, are now locating plants in the United States because of lower labor costs. An overseas location is also attractive to some companies who need to be closer to their customers, especially many suppliers.

Location factors that are often considered for an overseas site include the following:

- Government stability
- Government regulations
- Political and economic systems
- Economic stability
- Exchange rates
- Culture
- Climate
- Export and import regulations, duties and fees
- Raw material availability
- Number and proximity of suppliers
- Transportation system
- Labor pool and cost
- Available technology
- Commercial travel
- Technical expertise

Region

In the United States the most popular regions for manufacturing facilities are the Sunbelt regions in the SE and SW.

The next stage in the site selection process is to determine the part of the country or the state in which to locate the facility. In the United States the Southeast and Southwest are generally most preferable, and the upper Midwest is least preferable for manufacturing facilities. This reflects a general migration of industry from the Midwest to the Sunbelt regions during the last two decades. The factors that influence in what part of the country to locate are more focused and area-specific than the general location factors for determining a country.

Factors that are considered when selecting the part of the country for a facility include the following:

- Labor (availability, cost, and unions)
- Proximity of customers
- Number of customers
- Construction/leasing costs
- Land cost
- Modes and quality of transportation
- Transportation costs
- Government regulations
- Environmental regulations
- Raw material availability
- Commercial travel
- Climate
- Utilities

Community

The site selection process further narrows the pool of potential locations for the facility down to several communities or localities. Many of the same location factors that are considered in selecting the country or region in which to locate are also considered at this level of the process. Location factors include the following:

Transparency 8.2 Site Selection Factors (Community and Site)

- Community government
- Local business regulations
- Environmental regulations
- Government services (Chamber of Commerce, etc.)
- Business climate
- Community services
- Transportation system
- Proximity of customers
- Concentration of customers
- Taxes
- Construction/leasing costs
- Land cost
- Availability of sites
- Financial services
- Labor pool
- Community inducements
- Proximity of suppliers

Site

The site selection process eventually narrows down to the determination of the best location within a community. In many cases a community may have only one or a few acceptable sites, so that once the community is selected the site selection is an easy decision. Alternatively, if many potential sites exist, a thorough evaluation is required of sites that are potentially very similar. For service and retail operations, customer concentrations become a very important consideration in selecting a site within a community, as does cost. These and other factors in the selection of a site are included among the following:

- Customer base
- Construction/leasing cost
- Land cost
- Site size
- Transportation
- Utilities
- Zoning restrictions
- Traffic
- Safety/security
- Competition
- Area business climate
- Income level

The Site Evaluation Process

In the previous sections we have identified the important factors that companies often consider when determining where to locate a facility. In the site selection process these factors and others are evaluated by a search team or individual from the company. Sometimes a consulting firm is hired that specializes in site selection for different types of facilities. For example, there are consulting firms that specialize solely in selecting sites for bookstores in university communities. Similarly, there are site location firms that travel around the world evaluating locations for plants for large companies. However, whoever conducts the search, the evaluation process requires large amounts of data and information relative to the different location factors. The cost data alone for different factors such as construction, land, labor, and transportation can be voluminous. National, state, and community governments generally have departments or offices that specialize in attracting businesses and have data and information useful in the site selection process. Government agencies also publish numerous documents with data and information about potential business sites in their jurisdiction. These offices will also usually provide assistance in gathering relevant data from publications, brochures, reports, or a computerized information system. They will also help to gather information that is not readily available. Chambers of commerce for different cities are excellent sources of information about communities and potential facility sites.

A voluminous amount of data and information is required to evaluate sites.

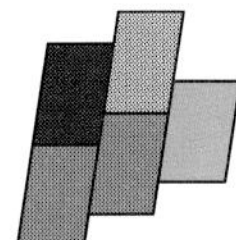

CRITICAL FACTORS IN LOCATION ANALYSIS

In the previous section we identified some of the factors that impact on the location decision for a new facility. These factors included some that tend to be critical regardless of the type of facility or location, such as labor, transportation, access to customers and markets, and community environment. In this section we discuss these factors and others in more detail.

Labor

Cost and availability of labor, work force skills, and labor unions are important factors in the location decision.

The labor climate is one of the most important overall factors in the location decision, particularly for manufacturing operations and even to a certain extent for service operations. Labor climate includes the cost of labor, embodied in wage rates and salaries, the availability of labor, the work ethic of the labor population, the possibility of labor conflict and problems with organized labor, and the general skill level of the labor pool.

Wage rates have traditionally been lower in the Southeast and Southwest than in other geographic regions, especially the Northeast and Midwest. This has contributed to the relocation of many manufacturing companies to the Sunbelt region. However, as the Sunbelt region has become more industrialized and populated and the average per capita income has risen in these regions, foreign countries now sometimes offer more inviting labor situations.

Individual communities will often reflect different work ethics in terms of absenteeism, commitment, and productivity. This sometimes results from the fact that a new plant in a town where few plants are located often offers a welcome, desirable work experience with higher-paying jobs.

Labor conflict is anathema to many companies, and they will avoid union contamination of their work force at almost any cost. Alternatively, many local unions are able to assist in attracting new plants or keep plants from relocating by their willingness to work with management and make attractive labor compromises and concessions.

Transportation and Logistics

Facilities need to have access to modes of transport: rails, trucking, waterways, and air transport.

The proximity of suppliers and markets are both important considerations in the location decision. For many heavy-manufacturing companies it is essential to be close to raw material sources, such as forestry and wood products companies, mining operations, and food-processing plants. Although it is not necessary for some companies to be in close proximity to their source of raw materials, it is important that they be near one of the five primary modes of transportation, railroads, highways/trucking, waterways, air transport, or pipelines that is adequate to meet their shipping and receiving needs. Distribution and supply routes and modes of transportation are also important for many service-related businesses. Fast-food operations, retail stores, groceries, and service stations are examples of businesses that use materials or products that must be transported to them from a warehouse or distributor.

The costs associated with transporting materials and finished products can be significant for businesses, especially when frequent deliveries over long distances are required or the items being distributed are large. The magnitude of these costs is often the primary reason that a business will locate near its customers, its suppliers, or both. The closeness of suppliers can also determine the amount of inventory a firm will be required to keep in stock. If a supplier is very near a plant or business, then items can be received quickly, negating the necessity to keep large stocks of materials, supplies, or parts on hand, thus reducing inventory costs. As the distance from suppliers increases, the variability of the timing of deliveries increases. This fact magnifies the uncertainties inherent in a company's usage rate, which requires even larger stocks of inventory to guard against stockouts and work stoppages resulting from late deliveries. The same problems can occur in reverse if a company is far from its customers. Uncertainty in delivery schedules caused by long distances can cause customers to maintain larger-than-desired inventory stocks. This situation generally decreases the level of customer service that can be provided. The supplier-customer relationship is discussed in greater detail in the section "Facility Location and Quality Management."

Customers and Markets

Service facilities generally require high customer-traffic volume.

We have already noted how important it is for service-related businesses to be located near their customers. Many businesses simply look for a high volume of customer traffic as the main determinant of location, regardless of the potential competition. An interstate highway exit onto a major thoroughfare will almost always include a number of competing service stations and fast-food restaurants. Shopping malls are an example of a location in which a critical mass of customer traffic is sought to support a variety of similar and dissimilar businesses. For example, a shopping mall typically has numerous restaurants (sometimes grouped

The Bourse mall in Philadelphia is one of the approximately 38,000 shopping centers that operated in the United States during the first part of this decade. These shopping centers accounted for over $717 billion in annual sales and included a gross leasable area of over $4^1/_2$ billion square feet, or 19 square feet for every person in the United States. Three hundred and sixty-five of these centers encompassed over a million square feet each and included an average of 155 stores and businesses, which is more stores than many small towns and communities have. In fact, some of these mega-malls seem like small cities. Shopping centers and malls attract a mass of customers that will support a multitude of different stores and businesses, that on their own could not attract a sufficiently profitable number of customers to a single location. Many retail business chains now locate almost exclusively in shopping centers and malls, thus their location decision becomes one of center selection and where within a center they want to be located. Demographic and geographic considerations are left to the center developers.

into food courts), several large department stores, and a variety of smaller specialty stores that sell similar products. In fact, a large department store in a mall will stock almost every product (not brand) that virtually every one of the smaller stores around it also stocks. Instead of seeking a location away from large competitors these smaller retail stores cluster together to feed off the customer traffic created by the larger anchor stores. Alternatively, businesses that rely on a steady customer clientele, such as doctors, dentists, lawyers, barber shops and hair salons, and health clubs often tend to seek locations with limited competition, which minimizes customer turnover.

Although it is important to be located where customers are in order to make sales, it is also important to be near enough to customers to provide a high level of customer service. This is especially true given the current emphasis and expectations regarding quality service. As a result, it has become increasingly important for manufacturing firms to be near their customers, especially if they are suppliers of parts or materials used to produce finished goods. As we have already mentioned on several occasions, there is pressure on suppliers to locate near their customers in order to reduce the uncertainty of delivery schedules and provide better (i.e., quicker) customer service. As international markets have opened up, a number of major manufacturing companies have located plants overseas for similar reasons—that is, to minimize transportation costs and be closer to their customers.

Community Environment

A number of specific factors associated with the local community where a business might locate can be important to the location decision. These factors include the following:

- Climate
- Available housing in different price ranges
- Taxes
- Financial health and institutions
- Universities and research parks
- System of local government
- Cultural and entertainment activities
- Recreational programs and facilities
- Zoning regulations and ordinances
- Educational system
- Crime rates
- Medical, fire, and police services
- Local population and available labor pool
- Distance to convenient air service
- Local road system and traffic
- Shopping
- Environmental, noise, and pollution regulations
- Local attitudes toward business

Communities often try to attract new businesses.

Communities will often aggressively seek out new businesses to locate in their area by enhancing many of these factors, including providing tax breaks and low-interest loans; easing construction, easing zoning and environmental regulation and ordinances; improving and building roads; and issuing bonds to support site preparation and construction of the facility. Alternatively, communities will occasionally work to keep out undesirable businesses that might foul the environment or increase the demand on community services without providing acceptable long-term benefits.

Site Characteristics

When locating at a new site, a business can either purchase or lease an existing building or select a parcel of land and construct a new facility. Service-related businesses often rent or purchase existing facilities, for example, in shopping malls or office buildings. It is usually more difficult for manufacturing operations to find a building that is suitable for their specific needs, and so construction is usually required.

If a new facility is built, a range of factors must be considered, many of which are the same as for a person building a house. These include the size of the space,

GAINING THE COMPETITIVE EDGE

Selecting Hotel Sites

La Quinta Motor Inns is a midsized chain of moderately priced hotels headquartered in San Antonio, Texas, that is oriented toward business travelers. Location is one of the two most important marketing considerations (along with product) for a hotel chain, and thus site selection is an extremely important decision. Good site selection for its hotels can provide a chain with a competitive advantage and increase market share. Quick selection of good locations is also important, since competitive chains are often interested in the same sites.

A regression model was developed for La Quinta to predict the success (i.e., profitability) of a potential site based on characteristics that normally make a hotel location attractive to potential guests. To construct the model, data were collected from 57 existing La Quinta hotels during a two-year period. The model was based on a list of location characteristics (variables) classified into five categories: competitive, demand generators, demographic, market awareness, and physical. Examples of competitive factors include room rates and proximity of competitors; demand generators encompass eighteen variables, including presence of a military base, local college enrollments, proximity of office spaces, airport passengers, tourists, and traffic count; examples of demographic factors are family income and residential population; among the market awareness factors are distance to nearest hotel and time in operation; and physical characteristics included accessibility, proximity to major traffic artery, and distance to downtown, among others. The model indicated that important factors in achieving profitability tended to be market awareness, hospital space, local population, and low unemployment rates in the area. Other important factors included accessibility to downtown office space, traffic count, college students, presence of a military base, median income, and competitive room rates. The model was used to predict whether a potential hotel site would be profitable or unprofitable (i.e., good or bad) and, thus, to enable La Quinta to minimize the selection of bad sites.

Source: Based on Kimes, S. E., and J. A. Fitzsimmons, "Selecting Profitable Hotel Sites at La Quinta Motor Inns," *Interfaces* 20, no. 2, (March–April, 1990): 12–20.

potential for expansion, soil stability and content, neighborhood, drainage, direct access to roads, sewer and water connections, utilities, and cost. When evaluating a site for lease or purchase, other considerations (that would be built into a new facility) include structural integrity of the facility, the ability to make alterations to the structure, existing parking and the potential for additional parking, neighborhood, loading-dock facilities, storage, maintenance and utility expenses, the lease rate (or purchase cost), and, if leasing, the length of the lease.

A recent trend in site locations has been a proliferation of industrial and office parks, in which many of the special use needs of businesses have been planned for. Industrial parks usually have a combination of available parcels of land and existing structures that cater to service operations or vendors with storage requirements and light manufacturing. Office parks typically have a number of existing buildings and office suites that are attractive to white-collar service operations such as insurance companies, lawyers, doctors, real estate, and financial institutions.

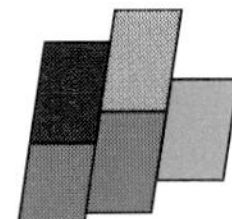

FACILITY LOCATION AND QUALITY MANAGEMENT

Many of the factors that are related to the decision about where to locate a facility have traditionally been considered in terms of their cost impact. A factor such as a facility's proximity to suppliers and customers has been important because of shipping costs. The labor pool at a potential location was important because of the cost of labor or the presence of organized labor. However, as we discussed in Chapter 3, "Quality Management," the traditional economic cost trade-off relationship, in which decisions correspond to the lowest point on the total cost curve, has been altered in the modern total quality management (TQM) approach. The driving force for decision making in TQM is continuous quality improvement. Companies subscribing to this philosophy will often forego cost effectiveness in the short run in order to improve quality and the production process, which will result in greater profits in the long run. This can mean making a facility location decision based on its impact on quality rather than on other factors related to cost.

Prompt customer service is an important principle of TQM.

The supplier-customer relationship is an important aspect of TQM. The acquisition of quality parts and materials is a fundamental principle of TQM and is essential in a TQM operation. However, the quality of parts and materials does not completely define the supplier-customer relationship. Another important aspect of this relationship is customer service, which to the customer often means prompt, on-time delivery. In a TQM environment customers insist not only that quality items be supplied, but also that these items be provided on time and in the right amount. As a result, location, transportation, and, particularly, supplier location become important variables in the TQM equation.

Companies that use JIT as part of TQM sometimes require suppliers to locate near them.

The impact of the supplier-customer relationship on location is especially pronounced for those companies who employ the just-in-time (JIT) inventory system in conjunction with their TQM program. For the supplier, JIT means contracting to deliver small quantities of items to their customers just in time for production. This can often result in deliveries on a daily basis or even several deliveries per day. For example, every part used on the production line at the Honda Marysville, Ohio, plant is delivered on a daily basis.[2] When deliveries must be made this frequently and on-time delivery is so crucial to the customer's TQM-driven production process, proximity to the customer can be a critical factor. Ansari and Modarress[3] in their book *Just-In-Time Purchasing* list geographic location of the supplier as one of the five criteria used by JIT companies for selecting and evaluating suppliers. Another of the criteria is on-time delivery performance. They note that a local supplier is preferred, and if that is not possible, suppliers that are close are often given preference.

Other studies bear out the importance of supplier location for companies using JIT. Schonberger and Gilbert[4] list "nearby suppliers"as one of the characteristics of JIT purchasing, and Dowst[5] cites delivery as the second of the five most important supplier performance characteristics (next to quality) among customers.

Companies often suggest that potential suppliers relocate nearer the company if they want to be considered for business and are not close. Some larger manufacturing companies, such as in the automobile industry, have informed their suppliers that if they wish to continue supplying the company, they must relocate closer in order to provide the quality delivery performance and customer service expected. For example, more than 75 percent of the U.S. suppliers for Honda are within a 150-mile radius of their Marysville, Ohio, assembly plant. All the suppliers for Buick City in Flint, Michigan, are within 300 miles, or 8 hours. Similarly, 75 percent of the suppliers for Ford's Lincoln Continental plant in

[2]Raia, E., "JIT in Detroit,"*Purchasing* (1988): 68–77.

[3]Ansari, A., and B. Modarress, *Just-In-Time Purchasing*, New York: The Free Press, 1990.

[4]Schonberger, R. J., and J. P. Gilbert, "Just-In-Time Purchasing: A Challenge for U.S. Industry," *California Management Review* (1983): 58.

[5]Dowst, S., "Quality Suppliers: The Search Goes On," *Purchasing* (September 15, 1988): 94A4–94A12.

Wixom, Michigan, are within this same radius. Most suppliers of seats are within 20 miles of the automobile plants they serve. Kasle Steel built a new mill within the gates of Buick City.[6]

Since the contemporary relationship between suppliers and customers is a function of an increasing commitment to quality improvement, location decisions can often be viewed as a direct result of TQM. In such instances the supplier locates near the customer to provide quality service consistent with the customer's (and their own) TQM effort, in lieu of other potential location factors. Of course, it is not always possible for suppliers to locate in close proximity to their customers. In today's global business community, suppliers can be overseas. However, in such cases—and even in the United States—it is not unheard of for companies to locate production facilities near their suppliers.

Besides the importance of supplier location to customer's for delivery performance, location can also be important to the quality improvement effort in other areas. If they are geographically close, suppliers and their customers can work closely together in the areas of product and process design and quality control.

Close proximity enables suppliers and customers to work together to improve quality.

In many cases, the supplier is an internal part of the company, and quality customer service means meeting the demands of the overall production process. For example, the *Gaining the Competitive Edge* box on McDonald's Australian distribution system on page 386 describes a situation where the location of a food-distribution warehouse was determined by quality standards rather than operational costs. The most cost-effective location in Sydney was too far from the western Australian McDonald's to meet quality delivery standards. These standards include delivering food products to restaurants twice a week within 2 days after order placement and within 15 minutes of a specified time. Location decisions like this that are not cost-effective are made in order to achieve long-term strategic goals for quality improvement according to the basic TQM philosophy. The impetus for the location decision is quality, and short-term cost is secondary.

Another important factor in the location decision has traditionally been the available labor pool, specifically the cost of labor. Although labor cost is still a major consideration, other labor characteristics related to TQM have become important in the location decision. Labor skills and diversity, experience, and workers' traits, such as work ethic and values, are important aspects of a TQM program. Prior to the general focus on quality, the initial reaction of some companies was to locate plants overseas to take advantage of cheaper labor in order to compete with the Japanese strictly on a cost basis. Although many companies still pursue this strategy, others have discovered that low cost was only a part of the more encompassing Japanese and European approach to quality management. In this approach a skilled, diverse, highly trained and motivated work force was more important than a cheap labor force.

TQM requires access to skilled labor.

Location decisions do not always have a direct impact on quality management, as with the supplier-customer relationship. The construction of facilities that can cause environmental damage or community problems and result in negative media attention can be as harmful to a company's reputation for quality as a 20 percent defective rate. Quality is, to a large extent, a matter of perception in the minds of consumers. If a company constructs a manufacturing plant in a formerly pristine woodland and invokes the wrath of environmentalists or if a fast-food chain opens a restaurant in a quiet residential area, generating neighborhood hostility, a perception of poor quality based on poor citizenship can result whether the company's products are of good quality or not. As such, companies generally

Environmental responsibility is an important aspect of TQM philosophy.

[6]Rain, E., "JIT in Detroit," *Purchasing* (September 15, 1988): 68–77.

GAINING THE COMPETITIVE EDGE

McDonald's Distribution System in Australia

Around the world McDonald's operates more than 11,000 restaurants in fifty-one countries, 4,000 outside the United States. In 1971 the first McDonald's opened in Australia in Sydney, and by 1992 they numbered over 300. In most areas of operation, the Australia McDonald's function the same as their U.S. counterparts, except for supply and distribution. The unique geography of Australia—with large unpopulated expanses and relatively small population concentrations—has forced the location of restaurants in different patterns from the United States and has resulted in different logistical challenges.

Most of the Australia McDonald's are operated by independent businesspeople, with McDonald's having corporate responsibility for purchasing food on behalf of the operators and arranging delivery to the restaurants. Initially, the first McDonald's restaurants in Sydney, Melbourne, and Brisbane were supplied directly by individual suppliers, selected and approved by McDonald's. However, in 1974 a central distribution system was established, with F. J. Walker Foods as the primary distributor. By 1990 Walker Foods distributed all food, paper, and supplies for all McDonald's across Australia, although McDonald's still selects all suppliers and negotiates food prices. When the centralized distribution system was started, Walker Foods supplied interstate restaurants in Victoria, Queensland, and South Australia directly from Sydney. As the number of restaurants grew in each market, distribution center warehouses were opened in these markets to serve local restaurants. This logistics system encompasses three functions: the procurement and shipment of 2,000 different ingredients, or raw materials, from forty-eight food and packaging plants to suppliers, the shipment of more than 200 types of finished products from suppliers to the interstate distribution centers, the ordering of products by the restaurants, and delivery. F. J. Walker Foods annually delivers approximately six million cases of food and paper products plus 500 different operating supply items to restaurants across Australia.

An exception to the system was the simultaneous opening of a western Australia restaurant and a serving warehouse in this market. Although it would have been more cost-efficient to make deliveries from the central distribution facility in Sydney to Perth (in western Australia), the 4,000-kilometer distance would have made it impossible to meet McDonald's expected standards of customer service. These standards include delivering frozen, dry, and chilled food products twice a week to each restaurant 98 percent of the time within 15 minutes of a specified time and delivery of complete orders 99.8 percent of the time within 2 days of the order being placed. Although McDonald's concentrates on minimizing inventory stock levels at distribution warehouses, it has not gone to a just-in-time system because of their standards for delivery and quality customer service. Stockouts are absolutely prohibited at distribution centers, and no expense is spared to ensure that every menu item is always available at every restaurant.

Source: Based on Ritchie, P., "McDonald's: A Winner Through Logistics," *International Journal of Physical Distribution and Logistics Management* 20, no. 3 (1990): 21–24.

must carefully consider image and reputation as important considerations in their TQM program when making location decisions.

In general, location decisions are increasingly being made based on how they fit in with a company's quality management program and not so much on other factors, such as short-run cost-effectiveness. Customer service performance as part of a company's continuous quality improvement effort overrides other location determinants.

LOCATION ANALYSIS TECHNIQUES

A number of quantitative techniques are available to assist in making a location decision. In this section we will discuss three of these techniques, the location rating factor, the center-of-gravity technique, and, the load-distance technique. The location factor rating is a system for mathematically evaluating important location factors, such as those identified in the previous section. The last two methods, the center-of-gravity and load-distance techniques, are examples of a class of quantitative models that seek to minimize transportation costs between a proposed location and existing facilities.

Location Factor Rating

The decision where to locate is basically subjective, based on a variety of different types of information and inputs. There is no single model or technique that will select "the best" location from a group. However, there are techniques available that help to organize location information and that can be used as a basis for comparing different locations according to specific criteria.

One of the more popular methods for evaluating and comparing different locations is the **location factor rating** system. In this procedure the factors that are important in the location decision are identified. Each factor is assigned a weight from 0 to 1.00 that prioritizes the factor and reflects its importance. A score is assigned (usually between 0 and 100) to each factor based on its attractiveness compared to other locations, and the weighted scores are summed.

A **location factor rating** involves identifying and weighting the important factors in the location decision.

EXAMPLE 8.1

Location Factor Rating

Alternate Example 8.1

Problem Statement:

The Dynaco Manufacturing Company is going to build a new plant to manufacture ring bearings (used in automobiles and trucks). The site selection team is evaluating three potential sites, and they have scored the important factors for each site as follows. They want to use these ratings to compare the locations.

Transparency 8.3 Example 8.1. Location Factor Rating

		SCORES (0 To 100)		
LOCATION FACTOR	Weight	Site 1	Site 2	Site 3
Labor pool and climate	0.30	80	65	90
Proximity to suppliers	0.20	100	91	75
Wage rates	0.15	60	95	72
Community environment	0.15	75	80	80
Proximity to customers	0.10	65	90	95
Shipping modes	0.05	85	92	65
Air service	0.05	50	65	90

Solution:

The weighted scores for each site are computed by multiplying the factor weights by the score for that factor. For example the weighted score for "labor pool and climate" for site 1 is

$$(0.30)\,(80) = 24 \text{ points}$$

The weighted scores for each factor for each site and the total scores are summarized as follows.

	WEIGHTED SCORES		
LOCATION FACTOR	*Site 1*	*Site 2*	*Site 3*
Labor pool and climate	24.00	19.50	27.00
Proximity to suppliers	20.00	18.20	15.00
Wage rates	9.00	14.25	10.80
Community environment	11.25	12.00	12.00
Proximity to customers	6.50	9.00	9.50
Shipping modes	4.25	4.60	3.25
Air service	2.50	3.25	4.50
Total score	77.50	80.80	82.05

Site 3 has the best factor rating compared to the other locations; however, this evaluation would have to be used with other information, particularly a cost analysis, before making a decision.

Center-of-Gravity Technique

The **center of gravity** is the center of movement in a geographic area based on transport weight and distance.

Transparency 8.4 Center-of-Gravity Technique

In general, transportation costs are a function of distance, weight, and time. The **center-of-gravity,** or *weight center,* technique is a quantitative method for locating a facility such as a warehouse at the center of movement in a geographic area based on weight and distance. This method identifies a set of coordinates designating a central location on a map that minimizes the weighted average of the weight transported to all other locations. As such, it implicitly assumes that by minimizing the weight shipped, costs are also minimized.

The starting point for this method is a grid map set up on a Cartesian plane, as shown in Figure 8.1. Note that there are three locations identified as 1, 2, and 3, each at a set of coordinates (x_i, y_i) identifying its location in the grid. The value W_i is the annual weight shipped from that location. The objective is to determine a central location for a new facility that minimizes the distance these weights are shipped.

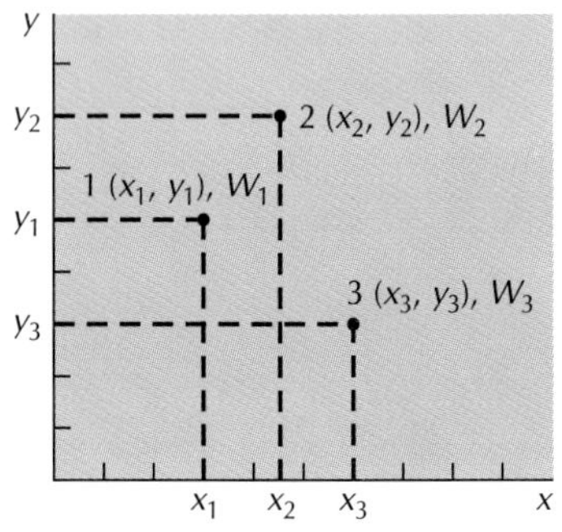

FIGURE 8.1 Grid-Map Coordinates

The coordinates for the location of the new facility are computed using the following formulas:

$$x = \frac{\sum_{i=1}^{n} x_i W_i}{\sum_{i=1}^{n} W_i}, \qquad y = \frac{\sum_{i=1}^{n} y_i W_i}{\sum_{i=1}^{n} W_i}$$

where

x, y = coordinates of the new facility at center of gravity
x_i, y_i = coordinates of existing facility i
W_i = annual weight shipped from facility i

Alternate Example 8.2

EXAMPLE 8.2
The Center-of-Gravity Technique

Problem Statement:

The Burger Doodle restaurant chain purchases ingredients from four different food suppliers. The company wants to construct a new central distribution center to process and package the ingredients before shipping them to their various restaurants. The suppliers transport ingredient items in 40-foot truck trailers, each with a capacity of 38,000 pounds. The locations of the four suppliers, A, B, C, and D, and the annual number of trailers that will be transported to the distribution center are shown in the following figure.

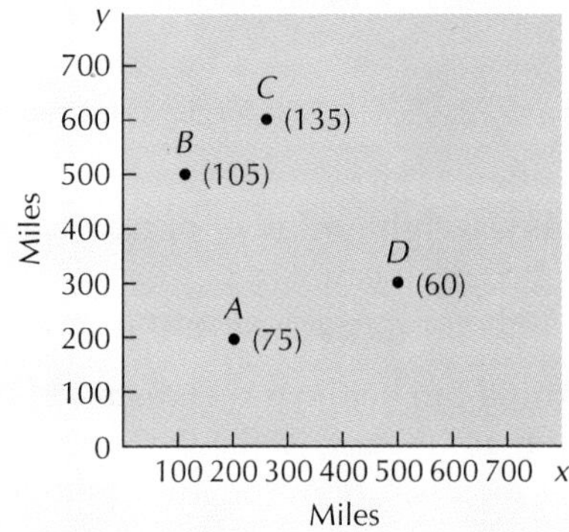

Using the center-of-gravity method, determine a possible location for the distribution center.

Solution:

A	B	C	D
$x_A = 200$	$x_B = 100$	$x_C = 250$	$x_D = 500$
$y_A = 200$	$y_B = 500$	$y_C = 600$	$y_D = 300$
$W_A = 75$	$W_B = 105$	$W_C = 135$	$W_D = 60$

$$x = \frac{\sum_{i=A}^{D} x_i W_i}{\sum_{i=A}^{D} W_i}$$

$$= \frac{(200)(75) + (100)(105) + (250)(135) + (500)(60)}{75 + 105 + 135 + 60}$$

$$= 238$$

$$y = \frac{\sum_{i=A}^{D} y_i W_i}{\sum_{i=A}^{D} W_i}$$

$$= \frac{(200)(75) + (500)(105) + (600)(135) + (300)(60)}{75 + 105 + 135 + 60}$$

$$= 444$$

Thus, the suggested coordinates for the new distribution center location are $x = 238$ and $y = 444$. However, it should be kept in mind that these coordinates are based on straight-line distances, and in a real situation actual roads might follow more circuitous routes.

Transparency 8.5 Load-Distance Technique

Load-Distance Technique

Load-distance technique is a method of evaluating different locations based on the load being transported and the distance.

A variation of the center-of-gravity method for determining the coordinates of a facility location is the **load-distance technique.** In this method, a single set of location coordinates is not identified. Instead, various locations are evaluated using a load-distance value that is a measure of weight and distance. For a single potential location, a load-distance value is computed as follows:

$$LD = \sum_{i=1}^{n} l_i d_i$$

where

LD_i = the load-distance value
l_i = the load expressed as a weight, number of trips, or units being shipped from the proposed site and location i
d_i = the distance between the proposed site and location i

The distance d_i in this formula can be the travel distance, if that value is known or can be determined from a map. It can also be computed using the following formula for the straight-line distance between two points, which is also the hypotenuse of a right triangle.

$$d_i = \sqrt{(x_i - x)^2 + (y_i - y)^2}$$

where

(x,y) = coordinates of proposed site
(x_i, y_i) = coordinates of existing facility

The load-distance technique is applied by computing a load-distance value for each potential facility location. The implication is that the location with the lowest value would result in the minimum transportation cost and thus would be preferable.

Alternate Example 8.3

EXAMPLE 8.3

The Load-Distance Technique

Problem Statement:

The Burger Doodle restaurant chain described in Example 8.2 wants to evaluate three different sites it has identified as being potentially good locations for its new distribution center relative to the four suppliers identified in Example 8.1. Referring to the figure in Example 8.2, the coordinates of the three sites under consideration are as follows:

Site 1: $x_1 = 360, y_1 = 180$
Site 2: $x_2 = 420, y_2 = 450$
Site 3: $x_3 = 250, y_3 = 400$

Solution:

First, the distances between the proposed sites (1, 2, and 3) and each existing facility (A, B, C, and D), are computed using the straight-line formula for d_i:

$$\text{Site 1}: \quad d_A = \sqrt{(x_A - x_1)^2 + (y_A - y_1)^2}$$

$$= \sqrt{(200 - 360)^2 + (200 - 180)^2}$$

$$= 161.2$$

$$d_B = \sqrt{(x_B - x_1)^2 + (y_B - y_1)^2}$$

$$= \sqrt{(100 - 360)^2 + (500 - 180)^2}$$

$$= 412.3$$

$$d_C = \sqrt{(x_C - x_1)^2 + (y_C - y_1)^2}$$
$$= \sqrt{(250 - 360)^2 + (600 - 180)^2}$$
$$= 434.2$$
$$d_D = \sqrt{(x_D - x_1)^2 + (y_D - y_1)^2}$$
$$= \sqrt{(500 - 360)^2 + (300 - 180)^2}$$
$$= 184.4$$

Site 2 : $d_A = 333,\ d_B = 323.9,\ d_C = 226.7,\ d_D = 170$

Site 3 : $d_A = 206.2,\ d_b = 180.3,\ d_C = 200,\ d_D = 269.3$

Next, the formula for load distance is computed for each proposed site.

$$\text{LD (site 1)} = \sum_{i=1}^{D} l_i d_i$$
$$= (75)(161.2) + (105)(412.3) + (135)(434.2) + (60)(184.4)$$
$$= 125{,}063$$
$$\text{LD (site 2)} = (75)(333) + (105)(323.9) + (135)(226.7) + (60)(170)$$
$$= 99{,}789$$
$$\text{LD (site 3)} = (75)(206.2) + (105)(180.3) + (135)(200) + (60)(269.3)$$
$$= 77{,}555$$

Since site 3 has the lowest load-distance value, it would be assumed that this location would also minimize transportation costs. Notice that site 3 is very close to the location determined using the center-of-gravity method in Example 8.2.

Computerized Location Analysis

The AB:POM computer software package used elsewhere in this text has a "Plant Location"module capable of performing location factor rating and the center-of-gravity technique. The computer output for these two techniques is illustrated for Examples 8.1 and 8.2.

Transparency 8.6 AB:POM Location Factor Rating and Center-of-Gravity Technique

```
                          Plant Location            Solution
Number of factors (1-99) 7      Number of locations (1-6) 3
                            Example 8.1
FACTORS                   Weight   city 1   city 2   city 3
Labor pool/climate          0.30    80.00    65.00    90.00
Proximity to supply         0.20   100.00    91.00    75.00
Wage rates                  0.15    60.00    95.00    72.00
Community environm't        0.15    75.00    80.00    80.00
Customer proximity          0.10    65.00    90.00    95.00
Shipping modes              0.05    85.00    92.00    65.00
Air service                 0.05    50.00    65.00    90.00

Weighted score                      77.50    80.80    82.05
The location with the best (highest) score is city 3
```

EXHIBIT 8.1

```
                              Plant Location                          Solution
Number of sites (1-99) 4
                               Example 8.2
                                                       Weighted Coordinates
SITES            Weight/trips     x coord      y coord      X-coord      Y-coord
Supplier A              75.00      200.00       200.00      15000.0      15000.0
Supplier B             105.00      100.00       500.00      10500.0      52500.0
Supplier C             135.00      250.00       600.00      33750.0      81000.0
Supplier D              60.00      500.00       300.00      30000.0      18000.0
TOTAL                  375.00     1050.00      1600.00      89250.0       166500
AVERAGE                            262.50       400.00       238.00       444.00
The unweighted mean is x = 262.5 y = 400
The weighted mean is   x = 238   y = 444
The median trip is trip/weight 188 and occurs at x = 250 y = 500
```

EXHIBIT 8.2

LOGISTICS MANAGEMENT

In the previous section we noted on several occasions that the transportation and distribution of items to and from a facility was one of the most important location factors. For some manufacturing firms, transportation costs can be as much as 20 percent of total production costs. For firms involved in the distribution of items such as catalog sales, it can be even higher. For example, in one year L.L. Bean shipped approximately 11 million packages, 650,000 in one week alone, which is about 195 tractor trailers. During the Christmas season they will fill a 40-foot UPS trailer every 20 minutes.[7] The different modes of transportation include railroads, highway trucking, air transport, waterways, and pipelines. Transportation costs will vary according to the type of transportation used, the distance traveled, and, the size, volume, and weight of the items being transported.

Logistics management involves managing and controlling the transport and distribution of goods and services.

Logistics is the movement of materials, parts, and goods from suppliers to customers.

Logistics management is the process of managing and controlling the transportation and distribution of items. **Logistics** is defined as the movement of materials, parts, and finished goods from suppliers, between distribution sites, and to customers. The objective of logistics management is to deliver the correct amount of goods (i.e., products or materials) to the location where they are needed on time and at the lowest possible cost. Activities commonly associated with logistics management include facility location, transportation, inventory and handling, and storage. Virtually every type of business, service, and manufacturing requires some form of logistical support to operate.

In the following section we focus on transport and distribution systems since we discussed facility location previously in this chapter, and we discuss inventory management in other parts of the text. We describe each of the major transport and distribution systems used to ship parts, products, and materials from their sources to users. We also describe one of the most effective and popular quantitative techniques for determining transportation and distribution routes, the transportation method.

[7] Day, Thomas C., *Allocating Telecommunications Resources*, Video 90.06, Franz Edelman Video Library, TIMS, Providence, R.I., 1990

TRANSPORT AND DISTRIBUTION SYSTEMS

The five principal systems of transportation and distribution within the United States and between countries are railroads, highways, water, air, and pipelines. In the United States the greatest volume of freight is shipped by railroads (approximately one-third of the total), followed by trucking, pipelines, and inland waterways. By far the smallest volume of freight is carried by air. In this section we discuss each of these systems, noting their advantages and disadvantages and their primary uses.

Five major systems of transport are rails, highways, water, air, and pipelines.

Railroads

There are more than 150,000 miles of railroad lines in the United States, most of which are concentrated in the East and Midwest. Railroads generally provide the lowest-cost means of shipping. They are particularly good for transporting low-value, high-density, bulk products such as raw materials over long distances between major distribution centers. Such products generally require little sorting or classification. Of the total annual rail freight tonnage, a little more than half comprises coal, minerals, and ores, with coal accounting for over 40 percent.

rails: low cost, high-volume transport

In general, railroads are not economical for shipping small loads over short distances because of the high cost of terminal handling and the inflexibility of rail lines. Railroads also operate on less flexible schedules than trucks, and they usually cannot go directly from one business location or plant to another as trucks can; trains operate from terminal to terminal. Rail transport is also usually slower than trucking, since shipments spend some amount of time being put together as trains

Rail quality is the worst of all major freight-transport modes.

In a piggyback system trucks collect goods and bring them to a central terminal where the truck trailers are loaded onto the back of railroad cars. These railcars are then hauled over long distances to other terminals or ports where the trailers are distributed by trucks or ships to their ultimate destinations. Piggybacks combine the flexibility of trucking for pickup and delivery with the low cost of long haul rail service. Through the 1980's and into the 1990's over four million trailer loads were moved annually in the United States by piggyback. Norfolk & Southern uses piggyback cars (such as the double stack cars shown here) extensively to meet JIT manufacturing demands of automotive industry customers in the Detroit area. On the west coast the Southern Pacific Railroad originates thirty-five eastbound double stack trains per week from Southern California alone.

at terminals. In a 1992 survey by Andersen Consulting on transportation quality, rail freight service had by far the worst record of quality performance of all modes of freight transport. Railroads had more than 17 percent late deliveries, almost ten times that of trucking, plus approximately 9 percent billing errors and 5 percent damage claims.[8]

Railroads have made several innovations in recent years to help overcome some of these disadvantages and allow them to compete more effectively with trucking for smaller loads. Piggyback cars haul truck trailers or containers on their flatcars. They combine the low-cost, long-distance travel of trains with the flexible delivery and pickup capabilities of trucking. An even more recent innovation is the Road-Railer, essentially a truck trailer with steel wheels for rail travel and rubber tires for road travel. These cars can swiftly change from highway to rails and back again, allowing for more scheduling flexibility, faster deliveries, and smaller loads. Norfolk Southern railroad has approximately 1,600 Road-Railers in its fleet that it uses to meet the JIT shipment demands of its automotive industry customers in the Detroit area.[9] These forms of *intermodal shipping* also have demon-

Intermodal shipping combines rail and truck cars.

GAINING THE COMPETITIVE EDGE

Meeting JIT Delivery Schedules at Roadway Express, Inc.

Roadway Express, Inc., of Akron, Ohio, is one of the nation's largest LTL common carriers. Trucking common carriers are traditionally divided into two categories, general freight and specialized carriers. Specialized carriers transport freight primarily in full truckloads and specialize in such products as liquid petroleum, petroleum products, refrigerated products, and processed agricultural products. General freight carriers are dominated by LTL, or "less-than-truckload,"shipments. An LTL carrier like Roadway Express generally operates a network of trucks and terminals. A fleet of trucks pick up and deliver smaller, LTL shipments. After these shipments are picked up, they are consolidated at terminals into full truckloads, which are carried to centralized destination terminals. There, the shipments are unloaded for delivery by LTL trucks.

With the recent proliferation of total quality management programs incorporating JIT among its customers, Roadway Express has had to adapt to provide the absolute on-time delivery of small lots of goods on the frequent basis that is required by JIT. Roadway Express has accomplished this by being more flexible in its service. In order to meet JIT schedules between suppliers in Texas and auto plants in Michigan, they establish specific shipping days with suppliers for Michigan LTL shipments. At its El Paso terminal, Roadway consolidates these LTL shipments into full truckloads that then travel directly to the Michigan plant without breaking down the load at an intermediate central terminal. The transit time using this flexible system is 72 hours, compared to the 6 days normally required for LTL shipments. Another tactic used to meet JIT schedules is to establish progressive pickups, or "milk runs."A trailer truck travels from supplier to supplier picking up shipments according to a scheduled day and time. When the pickup run is complete, the truck goes directly to the auto plant in Michigan, eliminating all intermediate terminal handling. The coordination required by a progressive pickup system between the suppliers, Roadway, and the plant is facilitated by the use of a computerized information and communications system. This system is able to track and control the movement of freight using bar-code technology.

Source: Based on Raia, E., "JIT in Detroit,"*Purchasing* (September 15, 1988): 68–77.

[8]Bradley, P., "Carriers Pursue Great Leaps Along Road to Better Service,"*Purchasing* (January 4, 1993): 83–87.

[9]Raia, E., "JIT in Detroit,"*Purchasing* (September 15, 1988): 68–77.

strated a much higher level of quality performance than traditional rail freight service, comparing favorably with trucking.

Trucking

trucking: flexible, small loads, good quality

Trucking is the primary mode of freight transportation in the United States. Trucks provide flexible point-to-point service, delivering small loads over short to long distances over widely dispersed geographic areas. The trucking system is extensive, with thousands of firms in the United States, and service is typically fast, reliable, and less damage-prone than rail shipping. However, although the ability to handle small loads efficiently is an advantage, the inability to carry large loads economically is trucking's most serious disadvantage. In addition, trucks lose their cost advantage over railroads over long distances when terminal handling costs are proportionally less of the total transport bill.

Trucking has become part of the TQM supplier-customer relationship.

Companies that have adopted TQM programs and JIT systems have put increased pressure on truck carriers in recent years to improve performance. Specifically this means picking up and delivering orders complete and free from damage, on time, with the paperwork in order, at a low cost. Carriers are now being looked at as part of the TQM chain from the supplier to the purchaser/processor to the eventual customer. An effective TQM relationship between suppliers and their customers/purchasers can be disrupted by a carrier that is unable to meet tight JIT schedules and damages parts during transit. As a result many companies have reduced the number of truck carriers they have traditionally employed to a select few. By concentrating their shipments with a select few carriers, companies have more control over the carriers, and their business becomes more important to individual carriers. Trucking firms also get the message that if they do not measure up to a company's quality standards, they will be let go.

Airfreight

air transport: quick but expensive

Airfreight used to be carried almost exclusively as cargo on scheduled passenger airlines. Since passenger service is the primary business of airlines, freight was carried only on a space-available basis. This severely limited the volume of freight that could be carried and made scheduled delivery less than reliable. However, in recent years there has been a proliferation of air freight carriers, including UPS, Federal Express, and Purolator. Passenger airlines have virtually been eliminated as freight carriers. As a result, even though air transport is the least utilized of all shipping modes, it is the fastest growing. The type of products shipped by airfreight tend to be light, such as electronic components or medical supplies, highly

GAINING THE COMPETITIVE EDGE

The Federal Express Superhub

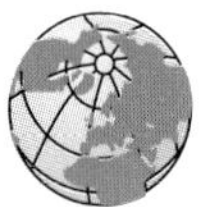

The central component in Federal Express's global airfreight system is an airline terminal it constructed in Memphis, Tennessee, called the *superhub.* This facility is the nerve center of Federal Express's vast distribution network. Packages from around the world are routed to the superhub to be sorted and sent on to their destinations. The support network includes sorting operations in Los Angeles, Oakland, Chicago, Indianapolis, Newark, London, Brussels, and the Far East. Each night, in less than 3 hours, the superhub sorts and transfers more than a million packages between connecting flights encompassing more than 100 planes. The superhub, pioneered by Federal Express, has subsequently been copied by every other airfreight express service.

Source: Based on *The Allyn and Bacon Plant Tour Video,* Program 1: "Federal Express: Setting the Pace for the 90s," copyright 1988 by Federal Express, distributed by Allyn and Bacon.

Video 8.1 *The Allyn and Bacon Plant Tour Video,* Program 1: "Federal Express"

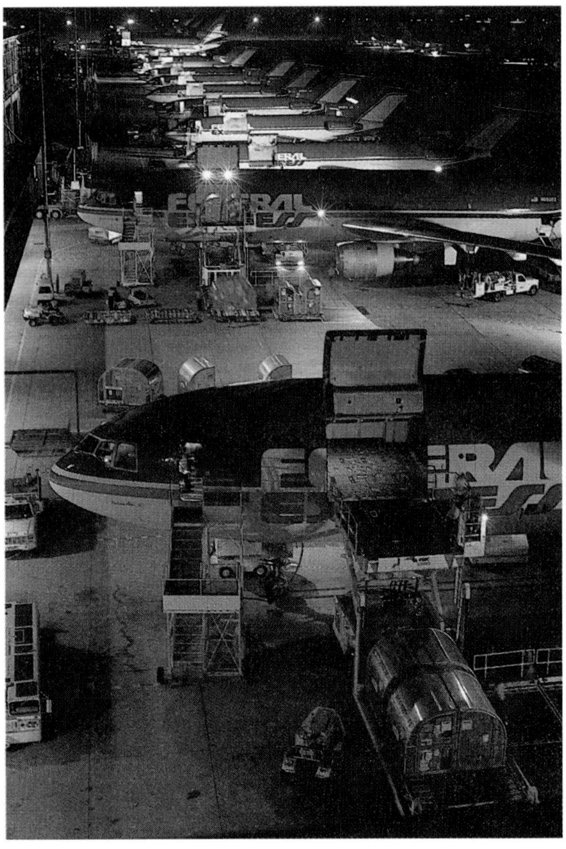

The Federal Express Superhub in Memphis, Tennessee, is the headquarters of Federal Express. Federal Express, the industry leader in overnight mail service, began to see its market share and profitability erode during the mid-1980s from fierce competition, a burgeoning fax business, and electronic mail. In reaction Federal Express strategically shifted its focus from overnight letter service to the higher margin package delivery business. Federal Express has alwys been a leader in the use of technology. Hand-held Cosmos trackers and computer terminals in their vans allow drivers to track customer packages and quickly access customer data. Federal Express is using the same technology to manage customer inventories for high priced goods in warehouses at its hubs. With an expanded truck fleet and second day package delivery, Federal Express has become a just-in-time deliverer for companies like IBM who want to get out of warehousing and depoting parts.

perishable products, such as flowers or fruit, or emergency items, where rapid delivery outweighs all transport costs.

The obvious major advantages of airfreight are quickness and reliability. It is an efficient and economical means of transport for high-value, lightweight products that need to be shipped over long distances. It can be particularly advantageous for overseas transit, where the alternative is substantially slower water transport. However, air transport is so much more expensive than other transport systems that it is cost-prohibitive for most types of products. In addition, airfreight is part of a terminal-to-terminal logistics system that requires handling, loading, and unloading at the origin and destination, combined with truck pickup and delivery. Air freight companies have become very adept at combining air and trucking systems, resulting in reliable and rapid delivery in diverse geographic areas and over short distances. However, it is still very costly, and for short distances of less than 500 miles, or a single day's road travel, it may not be much quicker than a point-to-point truck carrier.

Water

water transport: low-cost, high-volume, slow

Water is one of the oldest means of freight transport in the United States, beginning with the construction of the Erie Canal between 1817 and 1825. Over the years an intricate system of waterways, canals, and lock systems has been developed in the United States and abroad. As a result, water transport is still a significant and viable means for transporting certain types of products between specific locations, although it is less visible and publicized than other transport modes. The three primary water transport systems for the United States are inland waterways, consisting of the nation's river systems, canals, and the Great Lakes, the nation's coastlines, and the oceans that connect the United States with the rest of the world.

Water transport is a very low cost form of shipping, however, it is also slow. It is also tied to a fixed system of river and coastal ports that serve as terminals and distribution points. As a result, it is limited to heavy, bulk items such as raw materials, minerals, ores, grains, chemicals, and petroleum products. If speed of delivery is not a factor, water transport becomes very competitive with railroads for shipping these kinds of bulk products because of its comparatively lower cost.

Teaching Note 8.1 Inland Waterways and Floods

Water transport is virtually the only means of international shipping between countries separated by oceans for most products, since air transport is limited to a very narrow range of freight items. Transoceanic shipping companies have been very effective in developing intermodal transport systems. They combine trucks, railroads, and ships to connect markets, customers, and suppliers around the world. The most successful and visible example is the use of container systems and container ships. Standardized containers that fit on rail flat cars and can be converted to truck trailers have proved to be a very effective and economical means of transporting products across long distances that encompass land and water.

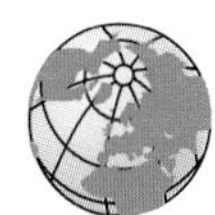

Pipelines

In the United States pipelines are used primarily for transporting crude oil and natural gas as well as some petroleum products, chemicals, and sherry coal. However, since the volume of shipments of these items is so great in the United States, pipelines are a major form of freight transport. It is obviously a very specialized form of transport and is limited to products in liquid form. Although pipelines require a very high initial capital investment to construct, once in place they have a long life and are low-cost in terms of operation, maintenance, and labor.

pipelines: liquid transport; high initial investment but low operating costs

THE TRANSPORTATION METHOD

An important decision in logistics management is determining the lowest cost means of transport from among several alternatives. In many cases it is possible to transport items from a plant or warehouse to a retail outlet or distributor via truck, rail, or air. The best means of transport is often the one with the lowest cost. Sometimes the modes of transport may be the same, but the company must decide between different transport providers, for example, different trucking firms. A quantitative technique that is used for determining the least cost means of transporting goods or services is the *transportation method.*

A **transportation model** is formulated for a class of problems with the following characteristics: 1. A product is *transported* from a number of sources to a number of destinations at the minimum possible cost, and 2. each source is able to supply a fixed number of units of the product and each destination has a fixed demand for the product. The following example demonstrates the formulation of the transportation model.

A **transportation model** involves transporting items from sources with fixed supply to destinations with fixed demand at lowest cost.

EXAMPLE 8.4

A Transportation Problem

Teaching Note 8.2 The Transportation Problem Formulated as a Linear Programming Model

Transparency 8.7 Transportation Model Formulation

Problem Statement:

Grain is harvested in the Midwest and stored in grain elevators in three cities—Kansas City, Omaha, and Des Moines. These grain elevators supply three mills, operated by the Heartland Bread and Cereal Company, located in Chicago, St. Louis, and Cincinnati. Grain is shipped to the mills in railroad cars. Each grain elevator is able to supply the following number of tons of grain to the mills on a monthly basis.

Grain Elevator	*Supply*
1. Kansas City	150
2. Omaha	175
3. Des Moines	275
	600 tons

Each mill demands the following number of tons of wheat per month.

Mill	*Demand*
A. Chicago	200
B. St. Louis	100
C. Cincinnati	300
	600 tons

The cost of transporting one ton of wheat from each grain elevator (source) to each mill (destination) differs according to the distance and rail system. These costs are shown next. For example, the cost of shipping 1 ton of wheat from the grain elevator at Omaha to the mill at Chicago is $7.

	MILL		
GRAIN ELEVATOR	*Chicago* A	*St. Louis* B	*Cincinnati* C
Kansas City	$6	$8	$10
Omaha	7	11	11
Des Moines	4	5	12

The problem is to determine how many tons of wheat to transport from each grain elevator to each mill on a monthly basis in order to minimize the total cost of transportation. A diagram of the different transportation routes with supply, demand, and cost figures is given in Figure 8.2.

Transportation models are solved within the context of a *tableau,* which for our example model is shown in the following table. Each cell in the tableau represents the amount transported from one source to one destination. The smaller box within each cell contains the unit transportation cost for that route. For example, in cell 1A the value $6 is the cost of transporting 1 ton of wheat from Kansas City to Chicago. Along the outer rim of the tableau are the supply and demand constraint quantity values, which are referred to as *rim requirements.*

The Transportation Tableau

To / *From*	*Chicago*	*St. Louis*	*Cincinnati*	*SUPPLY*
Kansas City	6	8	10	150
Omaha	7	11	11	175
Des Moines	4	5		275
DEMAND	200	100	300	600

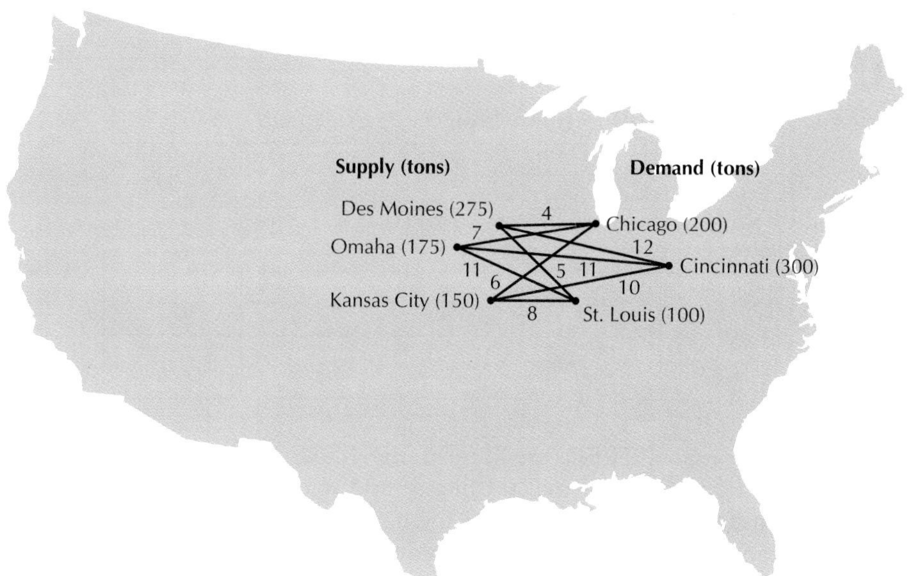

FIGURE 8.2 Network of Transportation Routes

There are two basic methods available for solving transportation models manually, the *stepping-stone method* and the *modified distribution method.* Both methods require a number of computational steps and are very time-consuming if done by hand. We will not present the detailed solution procedure for either method here. The stepping-stone method is described in the Chapter 8 Supplement, following this chapter. Instead, we will focus on computer solution of the transportation model.

Manual solution methods for transportation problems are tedious and time-consuming; see Chapter 8S.

Computer Solution of a Transportation Model

Modules to solve transportation models are generally available in most quantitative software packages. The transportation problem can be solved using the transportation module of AB:POM, the computer software program that we have used previously in this text. We will demonstrate the transportation program in AB:POM using the grain shipping problem from Example 8.4. The program input requires that the number of sources and destinations be indicated, which establishes the basic dimensions of the model. The remaining inputs are the supply and demand values and the individual costs for each potential route. The program output is shown as follows.

Transparency 8.8 AB:POM Transportation Problem Solution

```
                       Transportation                Solution
Number of sources (2-99) 3   Number of destinations (2-99) 3
                        Example 8.4
Options -> NO steps Comptr PrntOFF
SHIPMENTS      dest 1       dest 2       dest 3        Supply
srce 1                                     150            150
srce 2            25                       150            175
srce 3           175          100                         275
Demand           200          100          300
The minimum total cost =             $4,525
                   NOTE: alternate optimal solutions exist
```

EXHIBIT 8.3

This solution is shown in tableau format as follows:

From \ To	Chicago	St. Louis	Cincinnati	SUPPLY
Kansas City	6	8	10	150
Omaha	7	11	11	175
Des Moines	4 175	5 100		275
DEMAND	200	100	300	600

Interpreting this solution, 150 tons are shipped from Kansas City to Cincinnati, 25 tons are shipped from Omaha to the mill at Chicago, and so on. The total shipping cost is $4,525. The Heartland Company could use these results to make decisions about how to ship wheat and to negotiate new rate agreements with railway shippers.

In the computer output there is a note that alternate optimal solutions exist. This note means that there is a second solution reflecting a different shipping distribution but with the same total cost of $4,525. Manual solution is required to identify this alternate; however, it would provide a different shipping pattern that the company might view as advantageous.

In a *unbalanced transportation problem,* supply exceeds demand or vice versa.

In Example 8.4 the unique condition occurred where there were the same number of sources as destinations, three, and the supply at all three sources equaled the demand at all three destinations, 600 tons. This is the simplest form of transportation model, however, solution is not restricted to these conditions. Sources and destinations can be unequal, and total supply does not have to equal total demand, which is called an *unbalanced* problem. A model with these characteristics is provided in Example 8.5, along with a **prohibited route.** If a route is prohibited, units cannot be transported from a particular source to a particular destination.

A **prohibited route** is a transportation route over which goods cannot be transported.

EXAMPLE 8.5

An Unbalanced Transportation Model With a Prohibited Route

Problem Statement:

Tobacco purchased by Cooperative Tobacco Farmers, Inc., is stored in warehouses in four cities at the end of each growing season.

Location	*Capacity (tons)*
A. Charlotte	90
B. Raleigh	50
C. Lexington	80
D. Danville	60
	280

These warehouses supply the following amounts of tobacco to companies in three cities.

Plant	*Demand (tons)*
1. Richmond	120
2. Winston-Salem	100
3. Durham	110
	330

The railroad shipping costs per ton of tobacco are shown below.

	To		
From	*1*	*2*	*3*
A	$ 70	$100	$ 50
B	120	90	40
C	70	30	110
D	90	50	70

Because of railroad construction, shipments are presently prohibited from Charlotte to Richmond.

Solution:

The transportation tableau for this problem summarizing the model parameters for each route is as follows:

From \ To	*Richmond*	*Winston-Salem*	*Durham*	***SUPPLY***
Charlotte	[500]	[100]	[50] 90	90
Raleigh	[120] 30	[90]	[40] 20	50
Lexington	[70]	[30] 80	[110]	80
Danville	[90] 40	[50] 20	[70]	60
DEMAND	120	100	110	

The AB:POM program input has basically the same requirements as with Example 8.4. The number of sources is designated as 4, the number of destinations is 3, and, no special adjustment is required for the difference between supply and demand. However, an adjustment is required to reflect the prohibited route from Charlotte to Richmond. This is accomplished by assigning a cost to this route that is several times as great as the other shipping cost in the model, for example, $500. Since the objective of the model is to determine the minimum-cost shipping routes, a high cost will assure this route is not selected.

The solution output is as follows:

```
                        Transportation                Solution
Number of sources (2-99) 4   Number of destinations (2-99) 3
                         Example 8.5
Options-> NO steps Comptr PrntOFF
srce 1                                      90          90
srce 2             30                       20          50
srce 3                         80                       80
srce 4             40          20                       60
Demand            120         100          110
The minimum total cost = $15,900
NOTE: Dummy row has been added
                   NOTE: alternate optimal solutions exist
```

EXHIBIT 8.4

The solution in tableau format is as follows:

From \ To	Richmond	Winston-Salem	Durham	SUPPLY
Charlotte	[500]	[100]	[50] 90	90
Raleigh	[120] 30	[90]	[40] 20	50
Lexington	[70]	[30] 80	[110]	80
Danville	[90] 40	[50] 20	[70]	60
DEMAND	120	100	110	

The total cost of these distribution routes is $15,900.

SUMMARY

Where to locate an operational facility is one of the most important, strategic decisions an organization can make, and the logistics and distribution function is one of the most important factors in making the location decision. The location decision has long-term implications for a business and it is not an easy decision to reverse if it is a bad one. For a service-related operation, the wrong location can mean an insufficient number of customers to be profitable, whereas for a manufacturing operation, a wrong location can mean excessive costs, especially for transportation and distribution, and less-than-desired customer service, which can result in a loss of business.

There is no foolproof method for ensuring a correct location decision. The decision is basically subjective, based on a careful consideration of all relevant factors and especially the costs involved. We have identified some of the most important factors in deciding where to locate, however, weighing these factors against each other and determining which are most important is a difficult process.

As we have noted, among the most important factors in the location decision are modes and routes of distribution and transportation. This is a potentially high-cost function related directly to the location decision. In this chapter we have discussed several quantitative techniques, including the transportation method, that assist in determining efficient transportation routes.

SUMMARY OF KEY FORMULAS

Center-of-Gravity Coordinates

$$x = \frac{\sum_{i=1}^{n} x_i W_i}{\sum_{i=1}^{n} W_i}, \qquad y = \frac{\sum_{i=1}^{n} y_i W_i}{\sum_{i=1}^{n} W_i}$$

Load-Distance Technique

$$\text{LD} = \sum_{i=1}^{n} l_i d_i$$

$$d_i = \sqrt{(x_i - x)^2 + (y_i - y)^2}$$

SUMMARY OF KEY TERMS

center-of-gravity technique: a quantitative method for locating a facility at the center of movement in a geographic area based on weight and distance.

load-distance technique: a quantitative method for evaluating various facility locations using a value that is a measure of weight and distance.

location factor rating: a system for weighting the importance of different factors in the location decision, scoring the individual factors, and then developing an overall location score that enables a comparison of different location sites.

logistics: the movement of materials, parts, and finished goods from suppliers, between distribution sites, and to customers.

prohibited route: a transportation route over which items cannot be transported.

transportation model: a method for determining the route to transport from sources to destinations at the minimum cost.

SOLVED PROBLEM

Transportation Model

Problem Statement:

A manufacturing firm ships its finished products from three plants to three distribution warehouses. The supply capacities of the plants, the demand requirements at the warehouses, and the transportation costs per ton are as follows:

	WAREHOUSES			
Plant	*A*	*B*	*C*	*Supply (units)*
1	$ 8	5	6	120
2	15	10	12	80
3	3	9	10	80
Demand (units)	150	70	60	280

Solve this problem using a computer.

Solution:

The solution output for this model is as follows:

```
                         Transportation                  Solution
Number of sources (2-99) 3   Number of destinations (2-99) 3
minimize
                      Solved Problem #1
Options -> NO steps Comptr PrntOFF
SHIPMENTS             dest 1      dest 2      dest 3      Supply
srce 1                    70                      50         120
srce 2                                70          10          80
srce 3                    80                                  80
Demand                   150          70          60
The minimum total cost =          $1,920
```

EXHIBIT 8.5

QUESTIONS

8-1. How are the location decisions for service operations and manufacturing operations similar and how are they different?

8-2. Indicate what you perceive to be general location trends for service operations and manufacturing operations.

8-3. What factors make the Sunbelt region of the United States an attractive location for service and manufacturing businesses?

8-4. Describe the positive and negative factors for a company contemplating locating in a foreign country.

8-5. What would be the important location factors that McDonald's might consider before opening up a new restaurant?

8-6. The following businesses are considering locating in your community:
a. A pizza delivery service
b. A sporting goods store
c. A small brewery
d. A plant making aluminum cans
Describe the positive and negative location factors for each of these businesses.

8-7. The transportation method is thought of as a technique for logistics management. Describe how it might be used to help make facility location decisions.

PROBLEMS

8-1. Mall 4, 77.75

8-1. Sweats and Sweaters is a small chain of stores specializing in casual cotton clothing. The company currently has five stores in Georgia, South Carolina, and North Carolina, and it wants to open a new store in one of four new mall locations in the Southeast. A consulting firm has been hired to help the company decide where to locate their new store. The store has indicated five factors that are important to their decision, including proximity of a college, community median income, mall vehicle traffic flow and parking, quality and number of stores in the mall, and proximity of other malls or shopping areas. The consulting firm had the company weight the importance of each factor. The consultants visited each potential location and rated them according to each factor, as follows.

		SCORE			
LOCATION FACTOR	*Weight*	*Mall 1*	*Mall 2*	*Mall 3*	*Mall 4*
College proximity	0.30	40	60	90	60
Median income	0.25	75	80	65	90
Vehicle traffic	0.25	60	90	79	85
Mall quality and size	0.10	90	100	80	90
Proximity of other shopping	0.10	80	30	50	70

Given that all sites have basically the same leasing costs and labor and operating costs, recommend a location based on the rating factors.

8-2. a. $x = 233.33$, $y = 241.67$ ★
b. See Solutions Manual.

8-2. The Burger Doodle restaurant chain uses a distribution center to prepare the food ingredients it provides its individual restaurants. The company is attempting to determine the location for a new distribution center that will service five restaurants. The grid-map coordinates of the five restaurants and the annual number of 40-foot trailer trucks transported to each restaurant is shown.

RESTAURANT	COORDINATES x	y	Annual Truck Shipments
1	100	300	30
2	210	180	25
3	250	400	15
4	300	150	20
5	400	200	18

a. Determine the least cost location using the center-of-gravity method.

b. Plot the five restaurants and the proposed new distribution center on a grid map.

8-3. The Burger Doodle restaurant chain in Problem 8-2 is considering three potential sites, with the following grid-map coordinates, for its new distribution center; *A*(350, 300), *B*(150, 250), and *C*(250, 300). Determine the best location using the load-distance formula, and plot this location on a grid map with the five restaurants. How does this location compare with the location determined in Problem 8-2.

★ 8-3. Site B

8-4. A development company is attempting to determine the location for a new outlet mall. The region where the outlet mall will be constructed includes four towns, which together have a sizable population base. The grid map coordinates of the four towns and the population of each are given.

★ 8-4. a. $x = 30$, $y = 53.5$
b. See Solutions Manual.

TOWN	COORDINATES x	y	Population (10,000s)
Four Corners	30	60	6.5
Whitesburg	50	40	4.2
Russellville	10	70	5.9
Whistle Stop	40	30	3.5

a. Determine the best location for the outlet mall using the center-of-gravity method.

b. Plot the four towns and the location of the new mall on a grid map.

★ 8-5. Site A

8-5. Using a location factor rating, the development company in Problem 8-4 has identified three good sites, with the following grid map coordinates, for their new outlet mall: A(20, 50), B(30, 30), and, C(35, 10). Determine the best location for the new outlet mall using the load-distance technique, and plot this location on a grid map with the four towns. How does this location compare with the location determined in Problem 8-4?

★ 8-6. St. Louis–Chicago = 250, Richmond–Chicago = 50, Richmond–Atlanta = 350, TC = 24,000

8-6. Green Valley Mills produces carpet at plants in St. Louis and Richmond. The carpet is then shipped to two outlets located in Chicago and Atlanta. The cost per ton of shipping carpet from each of the two plants to the two warehouses is as follows:

From	To: Chicago	Atlanta
St. Louis	$40	$65
Richmond	70	30

The plant at St. Louis can supply 250 tons of carpet per week; the plant at Richmond can supply 400 tons per week. The Chicago outlet has a demand of 300 tons per week, and the outlet at Atlanta demands 350 tons per week. The company wants to know the number of tons of carpet to ship from each plant to each outlet in order to minimize the total shipping cost. Solve this transportation problem using a computer.

8-7. 1–3 = 2, 1–4 = 10, 2–2 = 9, 2–3 = 8, 3–1 = 10, 5–2 = 1, TC = $20,200

8-7. A transportation problem involves the following costs, supply, and demand.

	To				
From	*1*	*2*	*3*	*4*	***SUPPLY***
1	$500	$750	$300	$450	12
2	650	800	400	600	17
3	400	700	500	550	11
DEMAND	10	10	10	10	

Solve this model using a computer.

8-8. 1–2 = 500, 1–3 = 300, 2–1 = 150, 2–3 = 350, 3–1 = 600, TC = 28,750

8-8. Solve the following transportation problem using a computer.

	To			
From	*1*	*2*	*3*	***SUPPLY***
1	$40	$10	$20	800
2	15	20	10	500
3	20	25	30	600
DEMAND	1,050	500	650	

8-9. A–2 = 20, A–3 = 60, B–2 = 70, C–1 = 80, C–2 = 20, TC = $1,290

8-9. Solve the following transportation problem using a computer.

	To			
From	*1*	*2*	*3*	***SUPPLY***
A	$ 6	$9	$7	130
B	12	3	5	70
C	4	8	11	100
DEMAND	80	110	60	

8-10. A–2 = 70, A–4 = 80, B–1 = 50, B–4 = 160, C–1 = 80, C–3 = 180, TC = $82,600

8-10. Steel mills in three cities produce the following amounts of steel.

Location	*Weekly Production (tons)*
A. Bethlehem	150
B. Birmingham	210
C. Gary	320
	680

These mills supply steel to four cities, where manufaturing plants have the following demand.

Location	*Weekly Demand (tons)*
1. Detroit	130
2. St. Louis	70
3. Chicago	180
4. Norfolk	240
	620

Shipping costs per ton of steel are as follows.

From	To 1	2	3	4
A	$140	$ 90	$160	$180
B	110	80	70	160
C	160	120	100	220

Because of a truckers' strike, shipments are prohibited from Birmingham to Chicago. Solve this problem using a computer.

8-11. In Problem 8-10, what would be the effect of a reduction in production capacity at the Gary location from 320 tons to 290 tons per week?

8-11. No effect

8-12. Oranges are grown, picked, and then processed and packaged at distribution centers in Tampa, Miami, and Fresno. These centers supply oranges to markets in New York, Philadelphia, Chicago, and Boston. The following table shows the shipping costs per truckload ($100s), supply, and demand.

8-12. T–NY = 100, T–C = 100, M–NY = 30, M–P = 120, F–P = 50, F–B = 150, TC = $5,080

From	To New York	Philadelphia	Chicago	Boston	SUPPLY
Tampa	$ 9	$14	$12	$17	200
Miami	11	10	6	10	200
Fresno	12	8	15	7	200
DEMAND	130	170	100	150	

Because of an agreement between distributors, shipments are prohibited from Miami to Chicago. Solve this problem using a computer.

8-13. In Example 8.5 shipments are prohibited from Charlotte to Richmond because of railroad construction. Once the rail construction is completed, what will be the effect on the optimal shipping routes?

8-13. A–1 = 70, A–3 = 20, B–3 = 50, C–2 = 80, D–2 = 20, D–3 = 40, TC = $14,100

8-14. A manufacturing firm produces diesel engines in four cities—Phoenix, Seattle, St. Louis, and Detroit. The company is able to produce the following numbers of engines per month:

8-14. 1–C = 5, 2–C = 10, 3–B = 20, 4–A = 10, TC = $19,500

Plant	*Production*
1. Phoenix	5
2. Seattle	25
3. St. Louis	20
4. Detroit	25

Three trucking firms purchase the following numbers of engines for their plants in three cities:

Firm	*Demand*
A. Greensboro	10
B. Charlotte	20
C. Louisville	15

The transportation costs per engine ($100s) from sources to destinations are as shown.

	To		
From	*A*	*B*	*C*
1	$ 7	$ 8	$ 5
2	6	10	6
3	10	4	5
4	3	9	11

However, the Charlotte firm will not accept engines made in Seattle, and the Louisville firm will not accept engines from Detroit; therefore, these routes are prohibited. Solve this problem using a computer.

8-15. 1–A = 70, 2–B = 25, 2–C = 90, 3–A = 10, 3–B = 25, 3–D = 25, TC = $13,200

8-15. The Interstate Truck Rental firm has accumulated extra trucks at three of its truck leasing outlets, as shown.

Leasing Outlet	*Extra Trucks*
1. Atlanta	70
2. St. Louis	115
3. Greensboro	60
	245

The firm also has four outlets with shortages of rental trucks, as follows.

Leasing Outlet	*Truck Shortage*
A. New Orleans	80
B. Cincinnati	50
C. Louisville	90
D. Pittsburgh	25
	245

The firm wants to transfer trucks from those outlets with extras to those with shortages at the minimum total cost. The following costs of transporting these trucks from city to city have been determined.

	To			
From	*A*	*B*	*C*	*D*
1	$ 70	$80	$45	$90
2	120	40	30	75
3	110	60	70	80

Solve this problem using a computer.

8-16. 1–C = 25, 2–B = 50, 2–C = 65, 3–D = 25, TC = $7,075

8-16. ★ In Problem 8-15, what would be the effect on the optimal solution if there were no shortage of rental trucks at the New Orleans outlet?

8-17. A–2 = 1,800, A–4 = 950, B–1 = 1,600, B–3 = 1,150, B–5 = 2,250, C–3 = 350, C–6 = 1,400, TC = $3,260

8-17. ★ The Shotz Beer Company has breweries in three cities; the breweries can supply the following numbers of barrels of draft beer to the company's distributors each month.

Brewery	*Monthly Supply (barrels)*
A. Tampa	3,500
B. St. Louis	5,000
C. Milwaukee	2,500
	11,000

The distributors, spread throughout six states, have the following total monthly demand:

Distributor	*Monthly Demand (barrels)*
1. Tennessee	1,600
2. Georgia	1,800
3. North Carolina	1,500
4. South Carolina	950
5. Kentucky	2,250
6. Virginia	1,400
	9,500

8-18. No change

The company must pay the following shipping costs per barrel:

	To					
From	*1*	*2*	*3*	*4*	*5*	*6*
A	\$0.50	\$0.35	\$0.60	\$0.45	\$0.80	\$0.75
B	0.25	0.65	0.40	0.55	0.20	0.65
C	0.40	0.70	0.55	0.50	0.35	0.50

Determine the minimum cost shipping routes for the company.

8-18. In Problem 8-17 the Shotz Beer Company management has negotiated a new shipping contract with a trucking firm between its Tampa brewery and its distributor in Kentucky that reduces the shipping cost per barrel from \$0.80 per barrel to \$0.65 per barrel. How will this cost change affect the optimal solution?

8-19. 1–B = 250, 1–D = 170, 2–A = 520, 2–C = 90, 3–C = 130, 3–D = 210, TC = \$21,930

8-19. Computers Unlimited sells microcomputers to universities and colleges on the East Coast and ships them from three distribution warehouses. The firm is able to supply the following numbers of microcomputers to the universities by the beginning of the academic year:

Distribution Warehouse	*Supply (microcomputers)*
1. Richmond	420
2. Atlanta	610
3. Washington, D.C.	340
	1,370

Four universities have ordered microcomputers that must be delivered and installed by the beginning of the academic year:

University	*Demand (microcomputers)*
A. Tech	520
B. A and M	250
C. State	400
D. Central	380
	1,500

The shipping and installation costs per microcomputer from each distributor to each university are as follows:

	To			
From	*A*	*B*	*C*	*D*
1	$22	17	30	18
2	15	35	20	25
3	28	21	16	14

Solve this problem using a computer.

8-20. Add a warehouse at Charlotte.

8-20. In Problem 8-19, Computers Unlimited wants to meet demand more effectively at the four universities it supplies. It is considering two alternatives: 1. expand its warehouse at Richmond to a capacity of 600 at a cost equivalent to an additional $6 in handling and shipping per unit or 2. purchase a new warehouse in Charlotte that can supply 300 units with shipping costs of $19 to Tech, $26 to A and M, $22 to State, and $16 to Central. Which alternative should management select based on solely transportation costs (i.e., no capital costs)?

8-21. 1–B = 60, 2–A = 45, 2–B = 25, 2–C = 35, 3–B = 5, TC = 1,605 units

8-21. A large manufacturing company is closing three of its existing plants and intends to transfer some of its more skilled employees to three plants that will remain open. The number of employees available for transfer from each closing plant is as follows:

Closing Plant	*Transferable Employees*
1	60
2	105
3	70
	235

The following number of employees can be accommodated at the three plants remaining open:

Open Plants	*Employees Demanded*
A	45
B	90
C	35
	170

Each transferred employee will increase product output per day at each plant as follows:

	TO		
From	*A*	*B*	*C*
1	5	8	6
2	10	9	12
3	7	6	8

Determine the best way to transfer employees in order to ensure the maximum increase in product output.

8-22. See Solutions Manual.

8-22. The Sav-Us Rental Car Agency has six lots in Nashville, and they want to have a certain number of cars available at each lot at the beginning of each day for local rental. The agency would like a model they could quickly solve at the end of each day that would tell them how to redistribute the cars among the six lots at the minimum total mileage. The distances between the six lots are as follows:

	To (Miles)					
From	*1*	*2*	*3*	*4*	*5*	*6*
1	—	12	17	18	10	20
2	14	—	10	19	16	15
3	14	10	—	12	8	9
4	8	16	14	—	12	15
5	11	21	16	18	—	10
6	24	12	9	17	15	—

The agency would like the following number of cars at each lot at the end of the day. Also shown is the number of available cars at each lot at the end of a particular day.

Lot	*1*	*2*	*3*	*4*	*5*	*6*
Available	37	20	14	26	40	28
Desire	30	25	20	40	30	20

Determine the optimal reallocation of rental cars that will minimize the total mileage.

8-23. The Roadnet Transport Company has expanded its shipping capacity by purchasing 90 trailer trucks from a competitor that went bankrupt. The company subsequently located 30 of the purchased trucks at each of its shipping warehouses in Charlotte, Memphis, and Louisville. The company makes shipments from each of these warehouses to terminals in St. Louis, Atlanta, and New York. Each truck is capable of making one shipment per week. The terminal managers have each indicated their capacity for extra shipments. The manager at St. Louis can accommodate 40 additional trucks per week, the manager at Atlanta can accommodate 40 additional trucks, and the manager at New York can accommodate 50 additional trucks. The company makes the following profit per truckload shipment from each warehouse to each terminal. The profits differ as a result of differences in products shipped, shipping costs, and transport rates.

8-23. C–A = 30, M–S = 30, L–NY = 30, TP = $159,000

	TERMINAL		
WAREHOUSE	*St. Louis*	*Atlanta*	*New York*
Charlotte	$1,800	$2,100	$1,600
Memphis	1,000	700	900
Louisville	1,400	800	2,200

Determine how many trucks to assign to each route (i.e., warehouse to terminal) to maximize profit.

8-24. Brooks City has three consolidated high schools each with a capacity of 1,200 students. The school board has partitioned the city into five busing districts—north, south, east, west, and central—each with different high school student populations. The three schools are located in the central, west, and south districts. Some students must be bused outside of their district, and the school board wants to minimize the total bus distance traveled by these

★ 8-24. N–C = 700, S–S = 300, E–S = 900, W–W = 600, C–C = 500, TM = 14,600

students. The average distances from each district to the three schools and the total student population of each district are as follows:

	DISTANCE (MILES)			
DISTRICT	Central School	West School	South School	Student Population
North	8	11	14	700
South	12	9	—	300
East	9	16	10	900
West	8	—	9	600
Central	—	8	12	500

The school board wants to determine the number of students to bus from each district to each school in order to minimize the total busing miles traveled. Formulate a transportation model for this problem and solve.

8-25. A–2 = 1, C–1 = 1, D–1 = 1, E–3 = 1, F–3 = 1, G–2 = 1, H–1 = 1, TC = $1,070 ★

8-25. The Vanguard Publishing Company hires eight college students as salespeople to sell encyclopedias during the summer. The company desires to distribute them to three sales territories. Territory 1 requires three salespeople, and territories 2 and 3 require two salespeople each. It is estimated that each salesperson will be able to generate the following amounts of dollar sales per day in each of the three territories:

	TERRITORY		
SALESPERSON	1	2	3
A	$110	$150	$130
B	90	120	80
C	205	160	175
D	125	100	115
E	140	105	150
F	100	140	120
G	180	210	160
H	110	120	70

Determine which salespeople to allocate to the three territories so that sales will be maximized.

8-26. 1–K = 1, 2–A = 1, 3–K = 1, 4–A = 1, 5–C = 1, 6–C = 1, TM = 15.0 ★

8-26. The Southeastern Athletic Conference has six basketball officials who must be assigned to three conference games, two to each game. The conference office wants to assign the officials so that the total distances they travel time will be minimized. The hours each official would have to travel to each game is given in the following table.

	GAME		
OFFICIAL	Athens	Columbia	Knoxville
1	2.0	4.5	1.0
2	4.0	9.0	7.0
3	6.0	7.0	3.0
4	3.0	6.0	4.0
5	7.0	1.5	5.0
6	8.0	2.5	3.5

Determine the optimal game assignments that will minimize the total time traveled by the officials.

CASE PROBLEM

★ See Solutions Manual.

Scheduling at Hawk Systems, Inc.

Jim Huang and Roderick Wheeler were sales representatives in a computer store at a shopping mall in Arlington, Virginia, when they got the idea of going into business in the burgeoning and highly competitive microcomputer market. Jim went to Taiwan over the summer to visit relatives and made a contact with a new firm producing display monitors for microcomputers that was looking for an East Coast distributor in the United States. Jim made a tentative deal with the firm to supply a maximum of 500 monitors per month and called Rod to see if he could find a building out of which they could operate and some potential customers.

Rod went to work. The first thing he did was send bids to several universities in Maryland, Virginia, and Pennsylvania for contracts to be an authorized vendor for monitors at the schools. Next he started looking for a facility to use. Jim and his operation would include minor physical modifications to the monitors, including some labeling, testing, packaging, and storage, in preparation for shipping. He knew he needed a building with good security, air conditioning, and a loading dock. However, his search proved to be more difficult than he anticipated. Building space of the type and size he needed was limited in the area and was very expensive. Rod began to worry that he would not be able to find a suitable facility at all. He decided to look for space in the Virginia and Maryland suburbs and countryside, and although he found some good locations, the shipping costs to these locations were extremely high.

Disheartened by his lack of success, Rod sought help from his sister-in-law, Miriam, a local real estate agent. Rod poured out the details of his plight to Miriam over dinner at his mother's house, and she was sympathetic. She told Rod that she owned a building in Arlington that might be just what he was looking for, and she would show it to him the next day. She actually showed him the ground floor of the building, and it was perfect. It had plenty of space, good security, and a nice office, plus it was in a nice, upscale shopping area with lots of good restaurants. Rod was elated; it was just the type of environment he had envisioned in which to set up their business. However, his joy soured when he asked Miriam what the rent was. She said she had not worked out the details, but it would be around \$100,000 per year. Rod was shocked, so Miriam said she would offer him an alternative: a storage fee of \$10 per monitor for every monitor purchased and in stock the first month of operation, with an increase of \$2 per month per unit for the remainder of the year. Miriam explained that based on what he told her about the business, they would not have any sales until universities started around the end of August or the first of September and that their sales would fall off to nothing in May or June. She said her offer meant that she would share in their success or failure. If they ended up with some university contracts, she would reap a reward along with them, and if they did not sell many monitors, she could lose on the deal; additionally, in the summer months after school ended, if they had no monitors in stock, they would pay her nothing.

Rod mulled this over; it sounded fair, and he liked the building. Also, he liked the idea that they would not be indebted for a flat lease payment, since the rent was essentially on a per-unit basis. If they failed, at least they would not be stuck with a huge lease. So, he reluctantly agreed.

When Jim returned from Taiwan, he was pretty skeptical about Rod's lease arrangement with Miriam. He was chagrined that Rod didn't perform a more thorough analysis of the costs, but Rod explained that it was pretty hard to do an analysis when he did not know their costs, potential sales, or selling price. Jim said he had a point, and his concern was somewhat offset by the fact that Rod had gotten contracts with five universities as an authorized vendor for monitors at a selling price of $180 per unit. So, the two sat down to begin planning their operation.

First, Jim said he had thought of a name for their enterprise, Hawk Systems, Inc., which he said stood for Huang and Wheeler Computers. When Rod asked how Jim got a "K"out of "Computers," Jim cited poetic license.

Jim said that he had figured that the total cost of the units for them, including the purchase of the units, shipping, and their own material, labor, and administrative costs, would be $100 per unit during the first 4 months but would then drop to $90 per month for the following 4 months and, finally to $85 per month for the remainder of the year. Jim said that the Taiwan firm was anticipating being able to lower the purchase price, since their production costs would go down as they gained experience.

Jim thought their own costs would go down too. He also explained that they would not be able to return any items, so it was important they they develop a good order plan that would minimize costs. This goal was now much more important than Jim had originally thought because of their peculiar lease agreement based on their inventory level. Rod said that he had done some research on past computer sales at the universities with whom they had contracted and came up with the following sales forecast for the 9 months of the academic year (from September through May):

September	340	February	550
October	650	March	390
November	420	April	580
December	200	May	120
January	660		

Rod explained to Jim that computer equipment purchases at universities go up in the fall and then drop until January, when they peak again in April just before university budgets are exhausted at the end of the academic year.

Jim then asked Rod what kind of monthly ordering schedule from Taiwan they should develop to meet demand while minimizing their costs. Rod said that it was a difficult question, but he remembered seeing a distribution model developed once using a transportation model in an operations management course when he was in college. Jim suggested he get out his old textbook and get busy, or they would be turning over all their profits to Miriam.

However, before Rod was able to develop a schedule, Jim got a call from the Taiwan firm saying that they had gotten some more business later in the year and they could no longer supply up to 500 units per month. Instead they could supply 700 monitors for the first 4 months and 300 for the next 5. Jim and Rod worried what this would do to their inventory costs.

1. Formulate and solve a transportation model that will determine an optimal monthly ordering and distribution schedule for Hawk Systems that will minimize costs.
2. If Hawk Systems has to borrow approximately $200,000 to start up their business, will they end up making anything the first year?
3. What will the change in the supply pattern from the Taiwan firm cost Hawk Systems?
4. How did Miriam fare with her alternative lease arrangement? Would she have been better off with a flat $100,000 lease payment?

REFERENCES

Bowersox, D. J., *Logistics Management,* 2d ed., New York: Macmillan, 1978.

Davis, G. M., and S. W. Brown, *Logistics Management,* Lexington, Mass.: Lexington Books, 1974.

Francis, R. L., and J. A. White, *Facilities Layout and Location: An Analytical Approach,* Englewood Cliffs, N.J.: Prentice-Hall, 1987.

Fulton, M., "New Factors in Plant Location,"*Harvard Business Review* (May–June 1971): 4–17, 166–168.

Hitchcock, F. L. "The Distribution of a Product from Several Sources to Numerous Localities."*Journal of Mathematics and Physics* 20 (1941): 224, 230.

Magee, J. F., W. C. Copacino, and D. B. Rosenfield, *Modern Logistics Management,* New York: John Wiley, 1985.

Moore, Laurence J., Sang M. Lee, and Bernard W. Taylor, *Management Science,* 4th ed., Boston: Allyn and Bacon, 1993.

Schmenner, R. W., *Making Business Location Decisions,* Englewood Cliffs, N.J.: Prentice Hall, 1982.

Taylor, B. W., *Introduction to Management Science,* 4th ed., Boston: Allyn and Bacon, 1993.

SUPPLEMENT 8

TRANSPORTATION MODEL SOLUTION METHODS

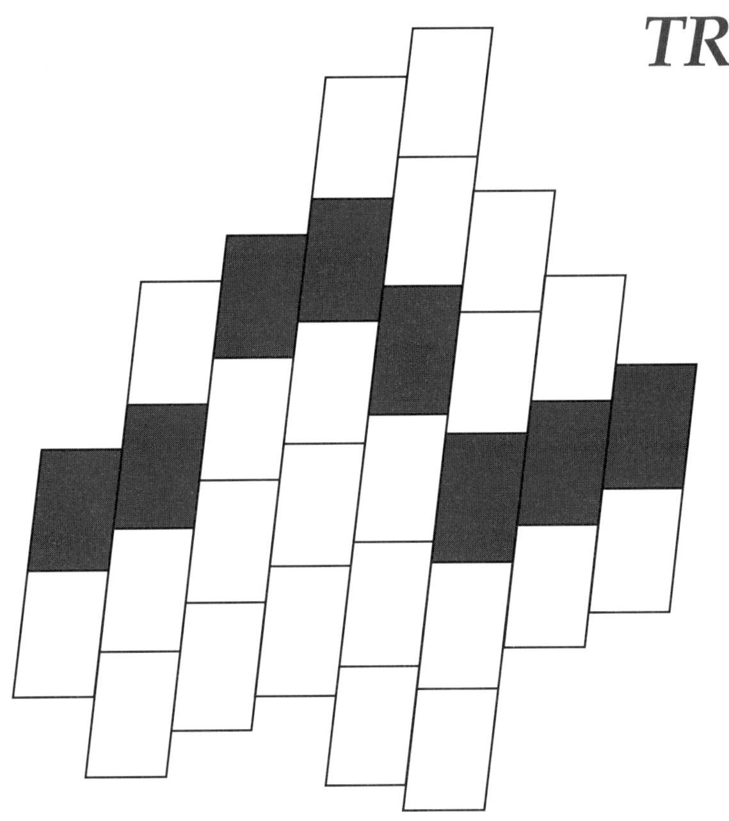

CHAPTER OUTLINE

A **transportation model** is a method for determining the route to transport at the minimum cost.

The **stepping-stone method** is an approach that evaluates the cost of unused routes.

In Chapter 8 we demonstrated how to formulate a **transportation model** and solve it using a computer, specifically the Transportation module in the AB:POM software package. In this supplement we show how to solve a transportation model manually. The solution technique we use for solving a transportation model is called the **stepping-stone method.** In order to show how the stepping-stone method works we will use Example 8.4. You will recall that the problem was to ship grain from three grain elevators in 1. Kansas City, 2. Omaha, and 3. Des Moines to three mills at A. Chicago, B. St. Louis, and C. Cincinnati at the minimum total shipping cost. We set up the problem within the context of a *tableau,* which is shown in Table S8.1.

Each cell in the tableau represents the amount transported from one source to one destination. The smaller box within each cell contains the unit transportation cost for that route. For example, in cell 1A the value $6 is the cost of transporting 1 ton of wheat from Kansas City to Chicago. Along the outer rim of the tableau are the supply and demand constraint quantity values, which are referred to as *rim requirements.*

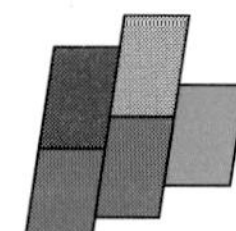

INITIAL SOLUTION METHODS

Prior to applying the stepping-stone solution technique, an initial starting point must be found. In a transportation model an initial solution can be found by several alternative methods, including the *northwest corner method,* the *minimum cell cost method,* and *Vogel's approximation method.*

The Northwest Corner Method

In the **northwest corner method** allocate the maximum amount to the NW corner and then the maximum to adjacent cells.

With the **northwest corner method,** an initial allocation is made to the cell in the upper left-hand corner of the tableau (i.e., the "northwest corner"). The amount allocated is the most possible *subject* to the supply and demand constraints for that cell. In our example, we first allocate as much as possible to cell 1A (the northwest corner). This amount is 150 tons, since that is the maximum that can be supplied by grain elevator 1 at Kansas City, even though 200 tons are demanded by mill A at Chicago. This initial allocation is shown in Table S8.2.

We next allocate to a cell *adjacent* to cell 1A, in this case either cell 2A or cell 1B. Since cell 1B no longer represents a feasible allocation, 50 tons are allocated to cell 2A. This allocation is also shown in Table S8.2.

Subsequent allocations are made using the same logic: 100 tons are allocated to cell 2B, 25 tons are allocated to cell 2C, and, finally, 275 tons are allocated to cell

Transparency S8.1 NW Corner Initial Solution

TABLE S8.1 The Transportation Tableau

From \ To	A	B	C	SUPPLY
1	[6]	[8]	[10]	150
2	[7]	[11]	[11]	175
3	[4]	[5]	[12]	275
DEMAND	200	100	300	600

TABLE S8.2 The NW Corner Initial Solution

From \ To	A	B	C	SUPPLY
1	[6] 150	[8]	[10]	150
2	[7] 50	[11] 100	[11] 25	175
3	[4]	[5]	[12] 275	275
DEMAND	200	100	300	600

3C, which are shown in Table S8.2. Notice that all the row and column allocations add up to the appropriate rim requirements.

The transportation cost of this solution is computed by multiplying the cell allocations (i.e., the amounts transported) by the cell costs:

$$\begin{aligned} TC &= \$6(150) + 8(0) + 10(0) + 7(50) + 11(100) + 11(25) + 4(0) + 5(0) + 12(275) \\ &= \$5{,}925 \end{aligned}$$

The steps of the northwest corner method are summarized as follows:

steps of NW corner method

1. Allocate as much as possible to the cell in the upper left-hand corner, subject to the supply and demand constraints.
2. Allocate as much as possible to the next adjacent feasible cell.
3. Repeat step 2 until all rim requirements have been met.

The Minimum Cell Cost Method

With the **minimum cell cost method** the basic logic is to allocate to the cells with the lowest costs. The initial allocation is made to the cell in the tableau having the lowest cost, which for our example problem is cell 3A, with a minimum cost of $4. As much as possible is allocated to this cell, which is 200 tons, since only 200 tons are demanded. This allocation is shown in Table S8.3.

In the **minimum cell cost method,** allocate the maximum amount to cells with lowest cost.

Notice that all the cells in column A have now been eliminated, since all the wheat demanded at destination A, Chicago, has been supplied by source 3, Des Moines.

The subsequent allocations are made using the same logic to the cells that have the minimum cost and are also feasible. Cell 3B is allocated 75 tons, cell 1B is allocated 25 tons, cell 1C receives the fourth allocation of 125 tons, and cell 2C receives the last allocation of 175 tons. These allocations, which complete the initial minimum cell cost solution, are shown in Table S8.4, on page 420.

The total cost of this initial solution is $4,550, as compared to a total cost of $5,925 for the initial northwest corner solution. It is not a coincidence that a lower total cost is derived using the minimum cell cost method; it is a logical occurrence. Since the northwest corner method does not consider cost at all in making allocations and the minimum cell cost method does, it is natural that a lower initial cost will be attained using the latter method. Thus, the initial solution achieved by using the minimum cell cost method is usually better in that, since it has a lower cost, it is closer to the optimal solution. As a result, fewer subsequent solution iterations will be required to achieve the optimal solution.

The steps of the minimum cell cost method are as follows:

steps of the minimum cell cost method

1. Allocate as much as possible to the feasible cell with the minimum transportation cost, and adjust the rim requirements.
2. Repeat step 1 until all rim requirements have been met.

Transparency S8.2 Minimum Cell Cost Initial Solution

TABLE S8.3 The Initial Minimum Cell Cost Allocation

From \ To	A	B	C	SUPPLY
1	[6]	[8]	[10]	150
2	[7]	[11]	[11]	175
3	[4] 200	[5]	[12]	275
DEMAND	200	100	300	600

TABLE S8.4 The Initial Minimum Cell Cost Solution

From \ To	A	B	C	SUPPLY
1	[6]	[8] 25	[10] 125	150
2	[7]	[11]	[11] 175	175
3	[4] 200	[5] 75	[12]	275
DEMAND	200	100	300	600

TABLE S8.5 The VAM Penalty Costs

From \ To	A	B	C	SUPPLY	
1	6	8	10	150	2
2	7	11	11	175	4
3	4	5	12	275	1
DEMAND	200	100	300	600	
	2	3	1		

TABLE S8.6 The VAM Allocation

From \ To	A	B	C	SUPPLY	
1	6	8	10	150	2
2	175 (7)	11	11	175	4
3	4	5	12	275	1
DEMAND	200	100	300	600	
	2	3	1		

Vogel's Approximation Method

In **Vogel's approximation method,** allocate to cells according to the magnitude of row and column penalty costs.

The third method for determining an initial solution, **Vogel's approximation method** (also called **VAM**), is based on the concept of *penalty cost*, or *regret*. If a decision maker incorrectly chooses from several alternative courses of action, a penalty may be suffered (and the decision maker may regret the decision that was made). In a transportation problem, the courses of action are the alternative routes, and a wrong decision is allocating to a route (cell) that does not contain the lowest cost.

Transparency S8.3 VAM Initial Solution

In the VAM method, the first step is to develop a penalty cost for each source and destination. For example, consider column A in Table S8.5. Destination A, Chicago, can be supplied by Kansas City, Omaha, and Des Moines. The best decision would be to supply Chicago from source 3, because cell 3A has the minimum cost of $4. If a wrong decision were made and the next higher cost of $6 were selected at cell 1A, a "penalty" of $2 per ton would result (i.e., $6 – 4 = $2). This demonstrates how the penalty cost is determined for each row and column of the tableau. The general rule for computing a penalty cost is to subtract the minimum cell cost from the next-higher cell cost in each row and column. The penalty costs for our example are shown at the right and at the bottom of Table S8.5.

Allocate maximum amount to cells in row or column with greatest penalty.

The initial allocation in the VAM method is made in the row or column that has the highest penalty cost. In Table S8.5, row 2 has the highest penalty cost, $4. We allocate as much as possible to the feasible cell in this row with the minimum cost, which is 175 tons to cell 2A, with a cost of $7. With this allocation the greatest penalty cost of $4 has been avoided, since the best course of action has been selected. The allocation is shown in Table S8.6.

After the initial allocation is made, *all* penalty costs must be recomputed. In some cases the penalty costs will change; in other cases they will not.

We repeat the previous steps and allocate 100 tons to cell 3B. Following these steps and recomputing the penalty costs after each allocation results in subsequent allocations of 25 tons to 3A, 150 tons to 1C, and, finally, 150 tons to 3C. These allocations are shown in Table S8.7.

The total cost of this initial solution is $5,125, which is neither as high as the northwest corner initial solution of $5,925 nor as low as the minimum cell cost solution of $4,550. As with the minimum cell cost method, VAM typically results in a lower cost for the initial solution than does the northwest corner method.

steps of VAM

The steps of Vogel's approximation method can be summarized as follows:

1. Determine the penalty cost for each row and column by subtracting the lowest cell cost in the row or column from the next lowest cell cost in the same row or column.
2. Select the row or column with the highest penalty cost.

TABLE S8.7 The Initial VAM Solution

From \ To	A	B	C	SUPPLY
1	[6]	[8]	[10] 150	150
2	[7] 175	[11]	[11]	175
3	[4] 25	[5] 100	[12] 150	275
DEMAND	200	100	300	600

3. Allocate as much as possible to the feasible cell with the lowest transportation cost in the row or column with the highest penalty cost.
4. Repeat steps 1, 2, and 3 until all rim requirements have been met.

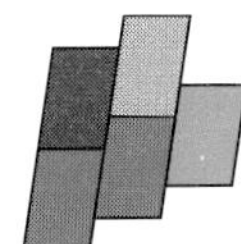

THE STEPPING-STONE SOLUTION METHOD

Teaching Note S8.1 The Stepping-Stone Method Versus MODI

Once an initial solution has been determined by any of the previous three methods, the next step is to solve the model for the optimal (i.e., minimum total cost) solution using the *stepping-stone solution method*. Since the initial solution obtained by the minimum cell cost method had the lowest total cost of the three initial solutions, we will use it as the starting solution (Table S8.8, page 422).

The logic of the stepping-stone method is to determine if a cell not in use will lower transport cost if used.

The basic solution principle in a transportation problem is to determine whether a transportation route not presently being used (i.e., an empty cell) would result in a lower total cost if it were used. For example, Table S8.8 shows four empty cells (1A, 2A, 2B, 3C) representing unused routes. Our first step in the stepping-stone method is to evaluate these empty cells to see whether the use of any of them would reduce total cost. If we find such a route, then we will allocate as much as possible to it. This will require that we change other route allocations in order to balance the problem again.

First, let us consider allocating 1 ton of wheat to cell 1A. If 1 ton is allocated to cell 1A, cost will be increased by $6—the transportation cost for cell 1A. However, by allocating one ton to cell 1A, we increase the supply in row 1 to 151 tons, as shown on page 422 in Table S8.9.

Since the supply and demand constraints of the problem cannot be violated, if we add 1 ton to cell 1A, we must subtract 1 ton from another allocation along that row. Cell 1B is a logical candidate, since it contains 25 tons. By subtracting 1 ton from cell 1B, we now have 150 tons in row 1, and we have satisfied the supply constraint again. At the same time, subtracting 1 ton from cell 1B has reduced total cost by $8.

However, by subtracting 1 ton from cell 1B, we now have only 99 tons allocated to column B, where 100 tons are demanded. In order to compensate for this constraint violation, 1 ton must be added *to a cell that already has an allocation*. Since cell 3B has 75 tons, we will add one ton to this cell, which again satisfies the demand constraint of 100 tons.

A requirement of this solution method is that units can be added to and subtracted from only those cells that already have allocations. That is why 1 ton was added to cell 3B and not to cell 2B. It is from this requirement that the method derives its name. The process of adding and subtracting units from allocated cells is analogous to crossing a pond by stepping on stones (i.e., only allocated-to cells).

TABLE S8.8 The Minimum Cell Cost Solution

From \ To	A	B	C	SUPPLY
1	[6]	[8] 25	[10] 125	150
2	[7]	[11]	[11] 175	175
3	[4] 200	[5] 75	[12]	275
DEMAND	200	100	300	600

TABLE S8.9 The Allocation of 1 Ton to Cell 1A

From \ To	A	B	C	SUPPLY	
1	[6] +1	[8] 25	[10] 125	150	151
2	[7]	[11]	[11] 175	175	
3	[4] 200	[5] 75	[12]	275	
DEMAND	200	100	300	600	

Transparency S8.4 The Stepping-Stone Solution

By allocating one extra ton to cell 3B, we have increased cost by $5, the transportation cost for that cell. However, we have also increased the supply in row 3 to 276 tons, a violation of the supply constraint for this source. As before, this violation can be remedied by subtracting 1 ton from cell 3A, which contains an allocation of 200 tons. This action again satisfies the supply constraint for row 3, and it also reduces the total cost by $4, the transportation cost for cell 3A. These allocations and deletions are shown in Table S8.10.

Notice in Table S8.10 that by subtracting 1 ton from cell 3A, we did not exceed the demand at destination A, since we previously added 1 ton to cell 1A.

Now let us review the increases and reductions in costs resulting from this process. We initially increased cost by $6 at cell 1A, then reduced cost by $8 at cell 1B, then increased cost by $5 at cell 3B, and, finally, reduced cost by $4 at cell 3A:

$$1A \rightarrow 1B \rightarrow 3B \rightarrow 3A = +6 - 8 + 5 - 4 = -\$1$$

In other words, for each ton allocated to cell 1A (a route presently not used), total cost will be reduced by $1. This indicates that the initial solution is not optimal, since a lower cost can be achieved by allocating additional tons of wheat to cell 1A.

Start with an empty cell and form a closed path of occupied cells, alternately adding to and subtracting from cells to meet rim requirements.

Before testing the remaining empty cells, let us identify a few of the general characteristics of the stepping-stone process. First, we always start with an empty cell and form a *closed path* of cells that presently have allocations. In developing the path, it is possible to skip over both unused and used cells. In any row or column, there must be *exactly one* addition and *one* subtraction. (For example, in row 1, wheat is added to cell 1A and is subtracted at cell 1B.)

Let us test cell 2A to see if it results in a cost reduction. The stepping-stone closed path for cell 2A is shown in Table S8.11. Notice that the path for cell 2A is slightly more complex than the path for cell 1A. Notice also that the path crosses

TABLE S8.10 The Addition of 1 Ton to Cell 3B and the Subtraction of 1 Ton from Cell 3A

From \ To	A	B	C	SUPPLY
1	+1 [6]	−1 [8] 25	[10] 125	150
2	[7]	[11]	[11] 175	175
3	−1 [4] 200	+1 [5] 75	[12]	275
DEMAND	200	100	300	600

TABLE S8.11 The Stepping-Stone Path for Cell 2A

From \ To	A	B	C	SUPPLY
1	[6]	− [8] 25	+ [10] 125	150
2	+ [7]	[11]	− [11] 175	175
3	− [4] 200	+ [5] 75	[12]	275
DEMAND	200	100	300	600

2A→2C→1C→1B→3B→3A
+$7 – 11 + 10 – 8 + 5 – 4 = –$1

itself at one point, which is perfectly acceptable. An allocation to cell 2A will reduce cost by $1, as shown in the computation in Table S8.11. Thus, we have located another possible entering variable, although it is no better than cell 1A.

The remaining stepping-stone paths and the resulting computations for cells 2B and 3C are shown in Tables S8.12 and S8.13, respectively. Notice that after all four unused routes are evaluated, there is a tie for the lowest-cost routes, cells 1A and 2A. Both show a reduction in cost of $1 per ton allocated to that route. The tie can be broken arbitrarily, and so we select cell 1A as a new route.

Since the total cost of the model will be reduced by $1 for each ton we can reallocate to cell 1A, we naturally want to reallocate as much as possible. In order to determine how much to allocate, we need to look at the path for cell 1A again, as shown in Table S8.10. The stepping-stone path for 1A shows that tons of grain must be subtracted at cells 1B and 3A in order to meet the rim requirements and thus satisfy the model constraints. Since we cannot subtract more than is available in a cell, we are limited by the 25 tons in cell 1B. In other words, if we allocate more than 25 tons to cell 1A, we must subtract more than 25 tons from 1B, which is impossible, since only 25 tons are available. Therefore, 25 tons is the amount we reallocate to cell 1A according to our path. That is, 25 tons are added to 1A, subtracted from 1B, added to 3B, and subtracted from 3A. This reallocation is shown on page 424 in Table S8.14.

The process culminating in Table S8.14 represents one *iteration* of the stepping-stone method. Now we must check to see whether this solution is, in fact, optimal. We do this by plotting the paths for the unused routes (i.e., empty cells 2A, 1B, 2B, and 3C) in Table S8.14, just as we did in the previous iteration.

The paths and cost reduction for each empty cell are summarized as follows.

2A: $2A \rightarrow 2C \rightarrow 1C \rightarrow 1A$ = + $7 – 11 + 10 – 6 = $0
1B: $1B \rightarrow 3B - 3A \rightarrow 1A$ = + $8 – 5 + 4 – 6 = $1
2B: $2B \rightarrow 3B \rightarrow 3A \rightarrow 1A \rightarrow 1C \rightarrow 2C$ = $11 – 5 + 4 – 6 + 10 – 11 = $3
3C: $3C \rightarrow 3A \rightarrow 1A \rightarrow 1C$ = $12 – 4 + 6 – 10 = $4

Our evaluation of the four paths indicates no cost reductions; therefore, this solution is optimal. The total minimum cost is

TC = $6(25) + 8(0) + 10(125) + 7(0) + 11(0) + 11(175) + 4(175) + 5(100) + 12(0)
= $4,525

However, notice that the path for cell 2A resulted in a cost change of $0. In other words, allocating to this cell would neither increase nor decrease total cost. This situation indicates that the problem has *more than one optimal solution.* Thus, 2A could be entered into the solution as a route, and there would be no change in the total minimum cost of $4,525. To identify the alternate solution, we would

TABLE S8.12 The Stepping-Stone Path for Cell 2B

From \ *To*	*A*	*B*	*C*	*SUPPLY*
1	[6]	[8] – 25	[10] + 125	150
2	[7]	[11] +	[11] – 175	175
3	[4] 200	[5] 75	[12]	275
DEMAND	200	100	300	600

2B→2C→1C→1B
+$11 – 11 + 10 – 8 = +$2

TABLE S8.13 The Stepping-Stone Path for Cell 3C

From \ *To*	*A*	*B*	*C*	*SUPPLY*
1	[6]	[8] + 25	[10] – 125	150
2	[7]	[11]	[11] 175	175
3	[4] 200	[5] – 75	[12] +	275
DEMAND	200	100	300	600

3C→1C→1B→3B
+$12 – 10 + 8 – 5 = +$5

TABLE S8.14 The Second and Optimal Iteration of the Stepping-Stone Method

From \ To	A	B	C	SUPPLY
1	[6] 25	[8]	[10] 125	150
2	[7]	[11]	[11] 175	175
3	[4] 175	[5] 100	[12]	275
DEMAND	200	100	300	600

TABLE S8.15 The Alternate Optimal Solution

From \ To	A	B	C	SUPPLY
1	[6]	[8]	[10] 150	150
2	[7] 25	[11]	[11] 150	175
3	[4] 175	[5] 100	[12]	275
DEMAND	200	100	300	600

allocate as much as possible to cell 2A, which in this case is 25 tons of wheat. The alternate solution is shown in Table S8.15.

Steps of the stepping-stone method

Teaching Note S8.2 The MODI Solution

Teaching Note S8.3 Integer Solution

The steps of the stepping-stone method are summarized next:

1. Determine the stepping-stone paths and cost changes for each empty cell in the tableau.
2. Allocate as much as possible to the empty cell with the greatest net decrease in cost.
3. Repeat steps 1 and 2 until all empty cells have positive cost changes that indicate an optimal solution.

The Unbalanced Transportation Model

Thus far, the methods for determining an initial solution and an optimal solution have been demonstrated for a problem where supply equals demand, which is referred to as a *balanced* transportation model. Realistically, however, an *unbalanced problem*, where supply exceeds demand or vice versa, is a more likely occurrence. Consider our example with the supply at Des Moines increased to 375 tons. This increases total supply to 700 tons, whereas total demand remains at 600 tons. To compensate for this imbalance, we add a dummy column, as shown in Table S8.16.

The dummy column is assigned a demand of 100 tons to balance the model. The additional 100 tons available but not demanded will be allocated to a cell in the dummy row. The transportation costs for the cells in the dummy row are zero, since the amounts allocated to those cells are not really transported.

Add a dummy row or column to compensate for an unbalanced condition.

The addition of a dummy column has no effect on the initial solution methods or on the methods for determining an optimal solution. The cells are treated the same as any other tableau cell. For example, in the minimum cell cost method,

TABLE S8.16 An Unbalanced Model (Supply > Demand)

From \ To	A	B	C	Dummy	SUPPLY
1	[6]	[8]	[10]	[0]	150
2	[7]	[11]	[11]	[0]	175
3	[4]	[5]	[12]	[0]	375
DEMAND	200	100	300	100	700

three cells would be tied for the minimum cost cell, each with a cost of zero. In this case (or any time there is a tie between cells) the tie is broken arbitrarily.

In the case where demand exceeds supply, a dummy row is added.

Degeneracy

In all the tableaus showing a solution to our example transportation problem, the following condition was met.

Teaching Note S8.4 Degeneracy

$$m \text{ rows} + n \text{ columns} - 1 = \text{the number of cells with allocations}$$

For example, in any of the balanced tableaus for wheat transportation, the number of rows was 3 (i.e., $m = 3$) and the number of columns was 3 (i.e., $n = 3$); thus,

$$3 + 3 - 1 = 5 \text{ cells with allocations}$$

These tableaus always had five cells with allocations; thus, our condition for normal solution was met. When this condition is not met and fewer than $m + n - 1$ cells have allocations, the tableau is said to be **degenerate.**

In a **degeneracy,** not enough cells are occupied to form stepping-stone paths.

Consider the wheat transportation example with the supply values changed to the amounts shown in Table S8.17. The initial solution shown in this tableau was developed using the minimum cell cost method. The tableau shown in Table S8.17 does not meet the condition $m + n - 1$ = the number of cells with allocations, since there are only four cells with allocations. The difficulty resulting from a degenerate basic feasible solution is that the stepping-stone method will not work unless the preceding condition is met (there is an appropriate number of cells with allocations). When the tableau is degenerate, a closed path cannot be completed for all cells in the stepping-stone method, for example, cell 1A in Table S8.17.

To create a closed path, one of the empty cells must be artificially designated as a cell with an allocation. Cell 1A in Table S8.18 is designated arbitrarily as a cell with an artificial allocation of ϕ. This indicates that this cell will be treated as a cell with an allocation in determining the stepping-stone paths, although there is no real allocation in this cell. Notice that the location of ϕ was *arbitrary,* since there is no general rule for allocating the artificial cell. Allocating ϕ to a cell does not guarantee that all the stepping-stone paths can be determined.

For example, if ϕ had been allocated to cell 2B instead of to cell 1A, none of the stepping-stone paths could have been determined, even though technically the tableau would no longer be degenerate. In such a case, the ϕ must be reallocated to another cell, and all paths must be determined again. This process must be repeated until an artificial allocation has been made that will enable the determination of all paths. In most cases, however, there is more than one possible cell to which such an allocation can be made.

Transparency S8.5 Degeneracy

TABLE S8.17 The Minimum Cell Cost Initial Solution

From \ To	A	B	C	SUPPLY
1	[6]	[8] 100	[10] 50	150
2	[7]	[11]	[11] 250	250
3	[4] 200	[5]	[12]	200
DEMAND	200	100	300	600

TABLE S8.18 The Corrected Initial Solution

From \ To	A	B	C	SUPPLY
1	[6] ϕ	[8] 100	[10] 50	150
2	[7]	[11]	[11] 250	250
3	[4] 200	[5]	[12]	200
DEMAND	200	100	300	600

TABLE S8.19 The Second Stepping-Stone Iteration

From \ *To*	*A*	*B*	*C*	*SUPPLY*
1	6 100	8	10 50	150
2	7	11	11 250	250
3	4 100	5 100	12	200
DEMAND	200	100	300	600

2A: $2A \rightarrow 2C \rightarrow 1C \rightarrow 1A = 7 - 11 + 10 - 6 = 0$
2B: $2B \rightarrow 2C \rightarrow 1C \rightarrow 1B = 11 - 11 + 10 - 8 = +2$
3B: $3B \rightarrow 1B \rightarrow 1A \rightarrow 3A = 5 - 8 + 6 - 4 = -1$
3C: $3C \rightarrow 1C \rightarrow 1A \rightarrow 3A = 12 - 10 + 6 - 4 = +4$

Since cell 3B shows a $1 decrease in cost for every ton of wheat allocated to it, we will allocate 100 tons to cell 3B. This results in the tableau shown in Table S8.19. Notice that the solution in Table S8.19 now meets the condition $m + n - 1 = 5$. Thus, in applying the stepping-stone method to this tableau, it is not necessary to make an artificial allocation to an empty cell. It is quite possible to begin the solution process with a normal tableau and have it become degenerate or begin with a degenerate tableau and have it become normal. If it had been indicated that the cell with the ϕ should have units subtracted from it, no actual units could have been subtracted. In that case the ϕ would have been moved to the cell that represents the entering variable. (The solution shown in Table S8.19 is optimal; however, an alternate optimal solution exists at cell 2A.)

Prohibited Routes

A *prohibited route* is one over which goods cannot be transported.

Sometimes one or more of the routes in the transportation model are *prohibited routes.* That is, units cannot be transported from a particular source to a particular destination. When this situation occurs, we must make sure that no units in the optimal solution are allocated to the cell representing this route. A value of M representing a large cost is assigned as the transportation cost for a cell that represents a prohibited route. Thus, when the prohibited cell is evaluated, it will always contain a large positive cost change of M, which will keep it from being selected as a new route.

SUMMARY

In *MODI,* use mathematical formulas that replicate stepping-stone paths to determine the cost of unused routes.

In this supplement we have described and demonstrated the stepping-stone method for solving transportation problems. There are other manual techniques for solving transportation models one of which is the modified distribution method, also known as MODI. MODI is actually a modified version of the stepping-stone method, except that it uses mathematical equations to determine the cost increase or reduction for an empty cell instead of stepping-stone paths. Transportation problems are a form of linear programming problems and as such can be solved using linear programming solution techniques. The student interested in these alternate solution methods for the transportation problem should consult the references at the end of this supplement.

SUMMARY OF KEY TERMS

degeneracy: a transportation tableau that does not have sufficient cell allocations to enable solution.

minimum cell cost method: a method for determining the initial solution to a transportation problem by successively allocating to the lowest-cost cells.

northwest corner method: a method for determining the initial solution to a transportation problem by allocating as much as possible to the cell in the upper left-hand corner of the tableau and successively filling adjacent cells.

stepping-stone method: an approach for solving a transportation problem by evaluating the cost of unused routes.

transportation model: a method for determining the route to transport from sources to destinations at the minimum cost.

Vogel's approximation method (VAM): a method for determining the initial solution to a transportation problem by allocating to cells according to the magnitude of row and column penalty costs.

SOLVED PROBLEM

Transportation Model

Problem Statement:

A manufacturing firm ships its finished products from three plants to three distribution warehouses. The supply capacities of the plants, the demand requirements at the warehouses, and the transportation costs per ton are shown as follows.

	WAREHOUSES			
PLANT	*A*	*B*	*C*	*SUPPLY (units)*
1	$ 8	5	6	120
2	15	10	12	80
3	3	9	10	80
DEMAND (units)	150	70	60	280

Determine the initial solution to this problem using the minimum cell cost method, and solve the problem using the stepping-stone method.

Solution:

Step 1: The initial solution

The initial solution, obtained using the minimum cell cost method, is shown in the following tableau.

The Minimum Cell Cost Initial Solution

From \ *To*	*A*	*B*	*C*	*SUPPLY*
1	[8]	[5] 70	[6] 50	120
2	[15] 70	[10]	[12] 10	80
3	[3] 80	[9]	[10]	80
DEMAND	150	70	60	280

Step 2: The stepping-stone solution

The steps of the stepping-stone method are illustrated in the following tableaus.

The First Stepping-Stone Iteration

From \ To	A	B	C	SUPPLY
1	−1 [8]	[5] 70	[6] 50	120
2	[15] 70	−1 [10]	[12] 10	80
3	[3] 80	+10 [9]	+10 [10]	80
DEMAND	150	70	60	280

Allocate 50 tons to cell 1A.

The Second Stepping-Stone Iteration

From \ To	A	B	C	SUPPLY
1	[8] 50	[5] 70	+1 [6]	120
2	[15] 20	−2 [10]	[12] 60	80
3	[3] 80	+9 [9]	+10 [10]	80
DEMAND	150	70	60	280

Allocate 20 tons to cell 2B.

The Third Stepping-Stone Iteration

From \ To	A	B	C	SUPPLY
1	[8] 70	[5] 50	−1 [6]	120
2	+2 [15]	[10] 20	[12] 60	80
3	[3] 80	+9 [9]	+8 [10]	80
DEMAND	150	70	60	280

Allocate 50 tons to cell 1C.

The Optimal Solution

From \ *To*	*A*	*B*	*C*	*SUPPLY*
1	[8] 70	+1 [5]	[6] 50	120
2	+1 [15]	[10] 70	[12] 10	80
3	[3] 80	+10 [9]	+9 [10]	80
DEMAND	150	70	60	280

The following solution is optimal: 1A = 70, 1C = 50, 2B = 70, 2C = 10, 3A = 80, and TC = $1,920

QUESTIONS

S8-1. Explain the difference between a balanced and an unbalanced transportation model.

S8-2. Why are the minimum cell cost method and VAM superior to the northwest corner method for determining an initial solution to a transportation problem?

S8-3. How are alternate optimal solutions identified in a transportation problem, and how are alternate optimal solutions determined?

S8-4. Explain what a penalty cost is.

S8-5. What is degeneracy in a transportation problem, and how is it remedied?

PROBLEMS

S8-1. Solve Problem 8-6.

S8-2. a. Determine the initial solution for Problem 8-7 using the northwest corner method, the minimum cell cost method, and Vogel's approximation method. Compute total cost for each.
b. Using the VAM initial solution, find the optimal solution using the stepping-stone method.

S8-3. Solve Problem 8-8.

S8-4. a. Determine the initial solution for Problem 8-9 using the minimum cell cost method.
b. Solve it using the stepping-stone method.

S8-5. a. Determine the initial solution for Problem 8-10 using any method.
b. Solve it using the stepping-stone method.
c. Is there an alternate optimal solution? Explain. If yes, identify it.

S8-6. a. Determine the initial solution for Problem 8-12 using the minimum cell cost method.
b. Solve it using the stepping-stone method.
c. Are there alternate optimal solutions? Explain. If so, identify them.

S8-1. 1–1 = 250, 2–1 = 50, 2–2 = 350, TC = 24,000

S8-2. a. See Solutions Manual.
b. 1–3 = 2, 1–4 = 10, 2–2 = 9, 2–3 = 8, 3–1 = 10, 3–2 = 1, TC =$20,200

S8-3. 1–2 = 500, 1–3 = 300, 2–1 = 150, 2–3 = 350, 3–1 = 600, D–1 = 300, TC = 28,750

S8-4. a. See Solutions Manual.
b. A–2 = 20, A–3 = 60, A–D = 50, B–2 = 70, C–1 = 80, C–2 = 20, TC = $1,290

★

S8-5. a. See Solutions Manual.
b. A–2 = 70, A–4 = 80, B–1 = 50, B–4 = 160, C–1 = 80, C–3 = 180, C–D = 60, TC = $82,600
c. Yes

★

S8-6. a. See Solutions Manual.
b. T–NY = 100, T–C = 100, M–NY = 30, M–P = 120, M–D = 50, F–P = 50, F–B = 150, TC = $5,080
c. No.

★ S8-7. a. See Solutions Manual. b. 1–C = 5, 2–C = 10, 2–D = 15, 3–B = 20, 4–A = 10, 4–D = 15, TC = $19,500

S8-7. a. Determine the initial solution for Problem 8-14 using VAM.
b. Solve using the stepping-stone method and compute total minimum cost.

S8-8. (a) and (b) 1–A = 70, 2–B = 25, 2–C = 90, 3–A = 10, 3–B = 25, 3–D = 25, TC = $13,200

S8-8. a. Determine the initial solution for Problem 8-16 using the minimum cell cost method.
b. Solve it using the stepping-stone method and compute total minimum cost.

S8-9. See Solutions Manual.

S8-9. Solve Problem 8-17.

S8-10. a. See Solutions Manual. b. 1–B = 250, 1–D = 170, 2–A = 520, 2–C = 90, 3–C = 130, 3–D = 210, D–C = 180, TC = $21,930

S8-10. a. Determine the initial solution for Problem 8-19 using VAM.
b. Solve it using the stepping-stone method and compute total minimum cost.

S8-11. 1–B = 60, 2–A = 45, 2–B = 25, 2–C = 35, 3–B = 5, 3–D = 65, TQ = 1,605

S8-11. Solve Problem 8-21.

★ S8-12. See Solutions Manual.

S8-12. Solve Problem 8-22.

S8-13. C–A = 30, M–St. L = 30, L–NY = 30, D–St. L = 10, D–A = 10, D–NY = 20, TP = $159,000

S8-13. Solve Problem 8-23.

★ S8-14. N–C = 700, S–S = 300, E–S = 900, W–W = 600, C–C = 500, D–W = 600, TM = 14,600

S8-14. Solve Problem 8-24.

★ S8-15. A–2 = 1, B–D = 1, C–1 = 1, D–1 = 1, E–3 = 1, F-3 = 1, G–2 = 1, H–1 = 1, TC = $1,070

S8-15. Solve Problem 8-25.

★ S8-16. 1–C = 1, 2–A = 1, 3–C = 1, 4–A = 1, 5–B = 1, 6–B = 1, TM = 150

S8-16. Solve Problem 8-26.

REFERENCES

Hitchcock, F. L., "The Distribution of a Product from Several Sources to Numerous Localities," *Journal of Mathematics and Physics* 20 (1941): 224, 230.

Moore, Laurence J., Sang M. Lee, and Bernard W. Taylor, *Management Science,* 4th ed., Boston: Allyn and Bacon, 1993.

Taylor, B. W., *Introduction to Management Science,* 4th ed., Boston: Allyn and Bacon, 1993.

9

JOBS: DESIGN, ANALYSIS, AND MEASUREMENT

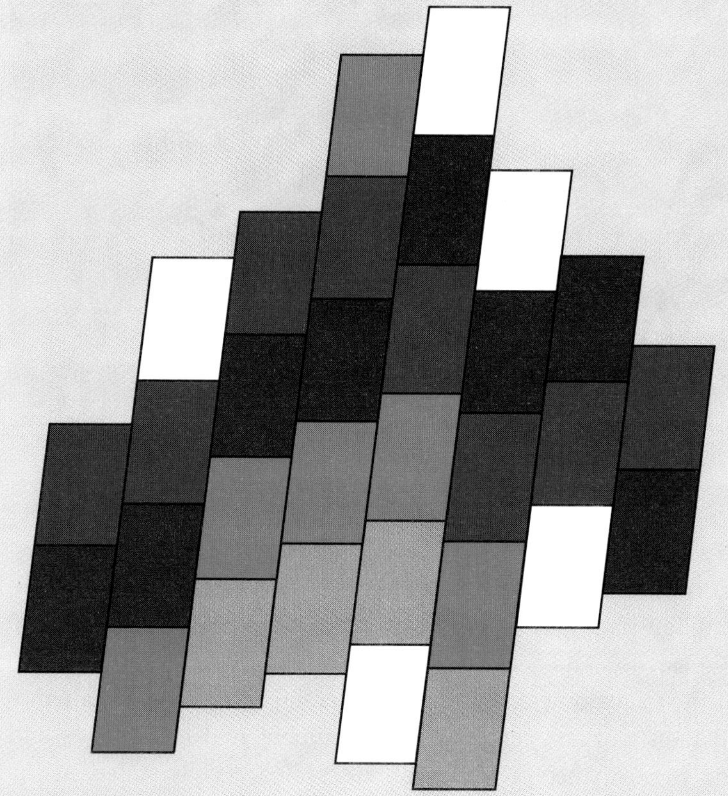

CHAPTER OUTLINE

Federal Express with its high payscale, positive working environment, philosophy of treating its employees like customers, is a much sought-after employer. As a result, it attracts and retains highly motivated, hard working employees.

EMPLOYEE SATISFACTION AT FEDERAL EXPRESS

Federal Express Corporation, a $7 billion operation with 85,000 employees, ships an average of 1.5 million packages daily. A key corporate goal is to achieve 100 percent customer satisfaction and service. The company believes employee satisfaction is a prerequisite to customer satisfaction. Federal Express hires highly motivated people and then works to create an environment that encourages and expects outstanding performance. Their corporate philosophy is stated in the phrase "People, Service, Profit (P-S-P)," which reflects their belief that if they put their employees' welfare first, they will provide excellent service and profits will follow. In effect, Federal Express attempts to treat its own employees as customers.

The employee-related programs and processes developed at Federal Express are designed to respond to three basic questions on the part of employees: What do you expect of me? What's in it for me? Where do I go with a problem? The answer to "What do you expect from me?" focuses on orientation and training, assuming that most employees want to do a good job and will, if shown how. The company has developed a wide variety of interactive video training programs. Every 6 months, couriers, customer service agents, and pilots are tested via interactive video, and their performance is appraised by their managers. Employees are also provided with the latest technology and trained in its use. Feedback is encouraged during the training process as well as during normal work, in the belief that the person closest to the job knows how to do it best. Providing such feedback is a reward in itself.

Although Federal Express provides excellent wages, benefits, and profit-sharing opportunities, it also answers the question "What is in it for me?" through a number of recognition programs and awards designed to reward extra effort. In conjunction with the company's high-performance expectations, the reward system includes extensive promotion from within Federal Express. More than 75 percent of all positions are filled internally.

In response to the third question, "Where do I go with a problem?" Federal Express has developed three programs: Guaranteed Fair Treatment, Survey Feedback Action, and Open Door. The first program is a process for employees to appeal any perceived wrongs up through the highest level of the organization. (This process is also used as a means for reviewing and revising employee-related policies). The Survey Feedback Action program is an annual employee attitude survey about the work environment (with anonymous responses). Survey results are distributed to managers, who are required to participate in feedback sessions with their immediate employees to seek corrective action for problems identified in the survey. The third program, Open Door, enables employees to question any company policy or procedure in writing without fear of reprisal or intimidation. Questions are forwarded to the most appropriate respondent, including the CEO, who must answer within 10 days.

All these programs and processes at Federal Express are aimed at creating an environment of open, candid, and trusting communication. To facilitate communication the company operates one of the world's largest private television networks, FXTV, to conduct training programs and provide up-to-date information and answers to employees.[1]

A job, in the context of operations management, is a defined set of tasks or steps that comprise the work performed by employees. These tasks contribute to the production of a product or delivery of a service. In general, a job is considered to be the "hands-on" activity directly connected to the making of a product. It is not managerial or supervisory in nature, but rather it is at the lowest level of the organization. The design of jobs has traditionally been an integral and very important aspect of production and operations management. Many years ago the production of goods and services was achieved almost entirely by artisans working independently with tools. Later, production consisted primarily of people working with equipment, machinery, and other labor-saving devices in a more organized, coordinated effort. Thus, it is no surprise that production management has focused on the design and management of work embodied in jobs performed by labor.

The development of the concepts of scientific management by F. W. Taylor around the turn of the century was a revolutionary and pivotal occurrence in manufacturing management. Scientific management was one of the first systematic approaches to the design and management of work. Many of the approaches to operations management that followed either grew out of refinements or variations in scientific management or grew from theories and approaches that disagreed with scientific management. Behavioralist, or humanistic, approaches to job design and management are examples of the latter case. They are based on the premise that the repetitive job operations and specialization of labor necessary to create work efficiency, as espoused by Taylor and his followers, is dehumanizing, boring, and ultimately counterproductive.

In the last two decades, job (and work) design has taken on even increased significance and importance. One prominent reason is the pervasive attention now

[1] Smith, F. W., "Our Human Side of Quality," *Quality Progress,* 23, no. 10 (1990): 19–21; Karabatsos, N., "Absolutely, Positively Quality," *Quality Progress* 23, no. 5 (1990): 24–28.

focused on product quality. In Chapter 3, "Quality Management," we discussed the importance of job design and worker involvement in achieving product quality. Quality is now considered to be a primary criterion and motivating force in job design. Employee commitment to continuous quality improvement and effective, ongoing job training is recognized as a key factor in the success of a total quality management (TQM) program.

Quality is a crucial aspect in job design.

Another reason for the increased interest in job design is the changing nature of work and the workplace. The rapid technological advances in equipment and machinery have resulted in jobs that are more technically sophisticated. They require greater skill levels, greater technical expertise, and a greater degree of responsibility from workers. Jobs in certain industries that did not change for five or six decades now change on virtually a continuing basis. This change is a result of changing technologies and international market conditions, competition that emphasizes diverse product lines (instead of mass production), and an emphasis on product quality.

Present-day technically sophisticated jobs require greater skills.

In this chapter we discuss both the traditional aspects of job design and the recent changes in the nature of job design. We also discuss work measurement in the latter part of the chapter. Work measurement, an area closely associated with job design, is the act of determining the time required to perform a job or the elements of a job in order to generate a unit of output. Work measurement was historically a necessary component in the establishment of incentive and piece-rate wage systems. Although such systems have recently fallen into disfavor because they are viewed as being detrimental to quality improvement efforts, work measurement in itself is still a very useful management tool for job evaluation and analysis. The time required to perform jobs is an essential input for determining labor needs, scheduling work, estimating labor costs and budgeting, and planning product output.

THE CHANGING NATURE OF JOBS AND JOB DESIGN

As we just mentioned, the principles of scientific management developed by F. W. Taylor in the 1880s and 1890s were the dominant factors in job design and operations management during the first part of the twentieth century. Although dramatic changes in the approach to job design have taken place in the last two decades, prior to discussing these changes it will be useful to gain a historical perspective on that from which job design is being changed.

Scientific Management

Teaching Note 9.1 Frederick W. Taylor

When F. W. Taylor began the work in the 1880s and 1890s that led to his development of scientific management, his "laboratory" was the machine shop, which was the basic factory of that age. The work force was made up of skilled machinists, who were subcontracted by owners and were provided with tools, resources, materials, and a workplace, and semiskilled laborers hired by the machinists. The skilled machinists were, in effect, the shop managers, planning and supervising the work, which they also performed, and controlling the production process. The shop owner had very little real control over the work area, which was mostly left to the skilled artisans/machinists.

This system was effective for small, provincial markets and limited technologies. However, as markets grew and owners invested greater sums of money in more sophisticated, heavier machinery and larger factories, they correspondingly became more cost-conscious and eager to expand production.

It was in this changing environment that F. W. Taylor began his development of the *scientific management* approach to job design. The primary tenets of Taylor's approach were to break jobs down into their most elemental activities for design purposes and to simplify job designs to the extent that only very limited skills were required to learn a job, thus minimizing the time required for learning. This approach further divided the jobs directly involved with making the product (requiring less skill) from the work required to set up machinery and maintain it, that is, the jobs requiring greater skill. Taylor's purpose in this scheme was to have all machines in the work area run by people who were of "small calibre and attainment" and, thus, cheaper than the skilled artisans/workers in the previous system.

Scientific management involves breaking down jobs into elemental activities and simplifying job design.

Figure 9.1 provides the general breakdown of jobs in the Taylor system. In this framework, a **job** is the set of all the tasks performed by a worker, whereas **tasks** are individual activities consisting of one or more *elements.* Elements, in turn, encompass several **job motions,** or basic physical movements. As an example, consider sewing machine operators whose job is to make baseball-style caps. The tasks of the job are sewing together the individual wedges of material forming the crown, attaching the cap bill, and stitching the cap logo. An element of a task might be positioning and sewing two wedges of material together or threading the sewing machine. The individual motions that make up the element are reaching for a wedge of material, grasping the material, positioning it, and releasing it.

Jobs comprise a set of **tasks,** *elements,* and **job motions** (*basic physical movements*).

Scientific management sought to break down a job into its simplest elements and motions, to render the elements as efficient as possible by eliminating unnecessary motions, and then to divide the tasks among several workers so that each task would require only minimal skill. The basic tool for performing this form of motion analysis was the stopwatch, and time was the sole measure of task and job efficiency. This system enabled the owner to hire large numbers of cheap, unskilled laborers, who were basically interchangeable and easily replaced. If a worker were fired or were to quit, another could easily be found and placed on

Traditionally, time has been a measure of job efficiency.

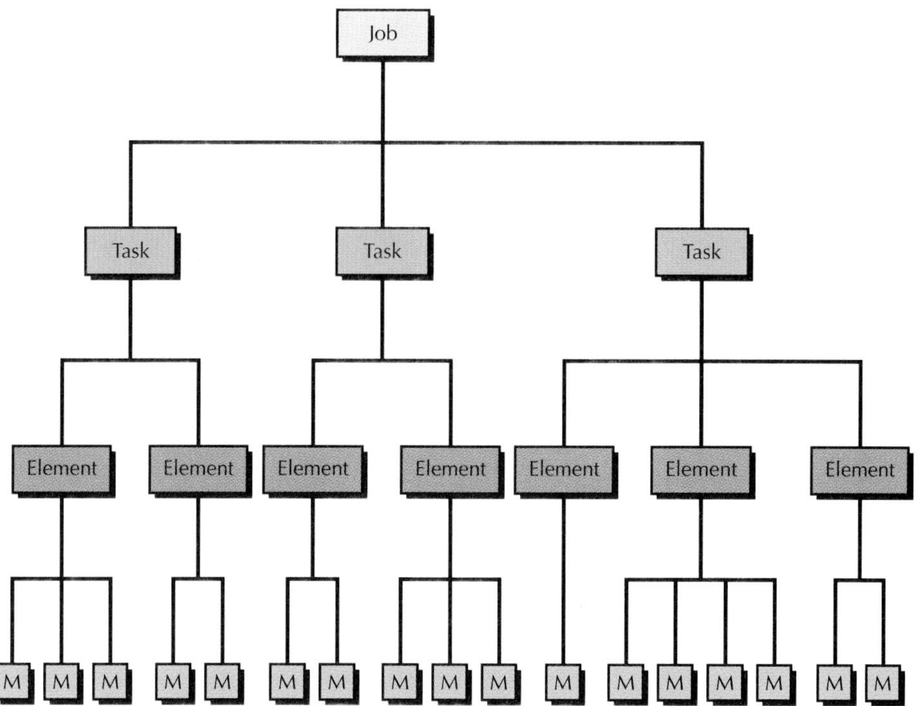

FIGURE 9.1 Basic Job Structure

Transparency 9.1 Basic Job Structure

the job with virtually no training expense. Further, in this system, the timing of job elements (by stopwatch) enabled management to develop *standard times* for a job for producing one unit of output. Workers were paid according to their total output in a *piece-rate system*. A worker was paid "extra" wages according to the amount he or she exceeded the "standard" daily output. Such a wage system is based on the premise that the single motivating factor for a worker to increase output is monetary reward (a narrow view of worker motivation that was later successfully challenged by numerous behavioralists).

In a *piece-rate wage system*, pay is based on output.

F. W. Taylor's work was not immediately accepted or implemented. By the mid-1910s there existed no factory or shop that had fully implemented scientific management principles. Certainly Taylor's approach was resisted by the skilled artisans/managers who controlled most shops at that time. However, the major hindrance was the lack of mass product markets that would make economical the fragmentation of jobs and the breakdown of work into elemental tasks. This system required high volumes of output to make the large number of workers needed for the expanded number of jobs cost-effective. The scenario that brought the principles of scientific management and mass production together was Henry Ford and the assembly line production of automobiles.

Scientific management was not immediately accepted by U.S. companies.

The Assembly Line

The adoption of scientific management at Ford was the catalyst for its subsequent widespread acceptance.

Between 1908 and 1929 Ford Motor Company created and maintained a mass market for the Model-T automobile, over 15 million of which were eventually produced. During this period, Ford achieved an expanded level of production output by combining the elements of standardized parts and product design, constrained machine tool technology, continuous-flow production, and the extensive implementation of Taylor's principles of scientific management to job design, which reduced work to simple tasks. These elements were encompassed in the assembly line production process.

Assembly line production meshed with the principles of scientific management.

On an assembly line, workers no longer moved from place to place to perform tasks, as they had in the factory/shop. Instead they remained stationary at a single workplace and the work was conveyed to them along the assembly line. Machine tool technology had advanced from the general-purpose machinery available at the turn of the century, which required the abilities of a skilled machinist, to highly specialized, semiautomatic machine tools, which required less skill to feed parts into or perform repetitive tasks. These machines, 15,000 of which were installed at Ford's Highland Park plant, remained stationary along the assembly line. The pace of work was established mechanically by the line and not by the worker or management. The jobs along the line were broken down to an extreme level, with highly repetitive, simple tasks.

The assembly line process at Ford was enormously successful. The amount of labor time required to assemble a Model-T chassis was reduced from more than 12 hours in 1908 to a little less than 3 hours by 1913. Prior to the development of the assembly line in 1908, the average task time in the manufacture of chassis's was more than 8 hours. By 1914 jobs and tasks had been broken down along the assembly line to such an extent that the average time for some tasks was as low as $1\frac{1}{2}$ minutes. The basic assembly line structure and many job designs that existed in 1914 remained virtually unchanged for the next fifty years.

The success of the assembly line at Ford greatly popularized the principles of job design encompassed in Taylor's scientific management. Numerous U.S. industrial firms imitated Ford's assembly line system and its extreme levels of task specialization in hopes of emulating their success. Between the two World Wars, the assembly line system and its associated approaches to job design were exported overseas as Ford opened plants in Great Britain, Germany, and other European countries. Westinghouse, a strong advocate of the Taylor system, provided

After WW I, scientific management spread to Europe.

several German electrical companies with technical expertise on assembly line manufacturing. This further spread these approaches to job design throughout the western industrialized nations. For a large part of the industrial world the concepts of job fragmentation, task specialization, closely defined job descriptions, and repetitive work espoused in the principles of scientific management became the predominant approach to job design.

It is interesting to note that Taylor's principles of job design did not gain popularity in Japan or many other Far Eastern nations. Industrialization occurred much more rapidly in Japan and essentially bypassed the skilled industrial artisan phase that engendered Taylor's work. Factory work teams that included both management and maintenance functions were a tradition in Japanese industry, and job flexibility—as opposed to rigidity and specialization—was the cultural norm. Mitsubishi Electric of Japan attempted to adopt Westinghouse assembly line production concepts; Ford opened a plant in Yokohama in 1925, and General Motors opened another in Osaka in 1926. However, these efforts were largely unsuccessful in promoting the job design characteristics that had become popular in the West. U.S. tariff barriers caused both automobile plants to close by 1939. Ironically, many of the employees from these plants later formed the nucleus of the initial Toyota Company work force.

Scientific management was not adopted in Japan.

Limitations and Failures of Traditional Job Design Approaches

The traditional principles of job design characterized by job fragmentation and task specialization had obvious advantages to management. They resulted in the successes we have already mentioned, such as the increased level of production output and the lowering of labor costs at Ford and other companies. Jobs were designed that required minimal skills, so workers could easily be replaced and trained at low cost, taking advantage of a large pool of cheap unskilled labor shifting from farms to industry. Because low-cost mass production was possible, the U.S. standard of living was increased enormously and became the envy of the rest of the world. Also, the positive features of this type of job design were not all on the side of management. It allowed unskilled, uneducated workers to gain employment based almost solely on their willingness to work hard physically at jobs that were mentally undemanding.

Advantages of task specialization include high output, low costs, and minimal training.

However, over time the traditional approaches to job design proved to have serious disadvantages and limitations as well. Soon after the achievement of the successes of assembly lines at Ford, behavioral research began to uncover flaws in the scientific management principles of job design. Workers frequently became bored and dissatisfied with the numbing repetition of simple job tasks that required little thought, ingenuity, or responsibility.

Disadvantages of task specialization include boredom, lack of motivation, and mental fatigue.

F. W. Taylor perceived that wages were the primary motivating force for work, but behavioral scientists have proven rather conclusively that the psychological content of work can be a more powerful motivational force for increasing productivity than pay. In task specialization, each worker contributes so little to the overall completed product that there is no gratification, intrinsic reward, or sense of pride in the work itself. The skill level required in repetitive, specialized tasks is so low that workers do not have the opportunity to prove their worth or abilities in order to seek advancement. Repetitive tasks requiring the same monotonous physical motions can result in unnatural physical and mental fatigue. And despite the best efforts of work methods engineers and job designers, workers frequently return to their own way of performing a task, regardless of the detail of the job design. There is only minimal opportunity for workers to interact with other workers and discuss their work. These negative factors subsequently lead to tardiness, turnover, absenteeism, and a general feeling of dissatisfaction. When these factors are combined with abusive supervisory tactics and management practices motivated solely by production output goals, they can lead to belligerence and antagonism between labor and management.

Behavioral Influences on Job Design

Quality of Work Life: Program introduced at GM

Because of indications of widespread worker dissatisfaction and deep-seated antagonisms between workers and management reflected in union-management conflicts, a movement toward new approaches to job design and management practices began during the late 1960s and early 1970s. This change in philosophy regarding job design specifically promoted by a growing number of union leaders, government officials, and academics was typified by the "Quality of Work Life" program popularized at General Motors and tried by several other companies. These programs had a strong behavioral, or humanistic, focus and promoted principles of "good" job design, which, for the most part, were the complete antithesis of the principles of F. W. Taylor. Although these programs differed from organization to organization and among individual proponents, they generally included the following precepts for job design.

Transparency 9.2 General Precepts of "Quality of Work Life" Job Design

Horizontal job enlargement involves expanding the scope of a job to include more tasks.

1. The scope of a job should include all the tasks necessary to complete a product or process, thus providing the worker with a sense of closure and achievement. This is also referred to as **horizontal job enlargement,** in the sense that the number of tasks encompassed by a redesigned job are expanded at the same level of skill and responsibility as the original job. This not only makes a job more interesting because of the greater variety of tasks that are required, but it also provides the worker with a sense that he or she has actually made something. For example, consider again the sewer making a baseball-style cap. The original process of making a cap might include three separate sequential jobs performed by three separate workers: sewing the cloth wedges together to make the crown, stitching the logo, and then attaching the cap bill. Combining all three jobs into a single job for one worker is an example of horizontal enlargement.

Vertical job enlargement allows workers more responsibility.

2. Job design should allow workers some degree of self-determination of their own work methods and the ability to exercise some control over their own work. In effect, some of the supervisory responsibilities for a job are transferred to the worker from management. This is referred to as **vertical job enlargement,** also called *job enrichment.* Expanding a job in this direction provides the worker with a greater sense of job satisfaction.

worker responsibility for quality

3. Job design should incorporate some individual responsibility for job reliability and quality. This is actually another aspect of vertical job enlargement in that it shares a responsibility previously held solely by management.

Job rotation involves the capability of workers to move to different jobs.

4. Workers should be trained for a variety of jobs so that they develop greater skill levels, have a more complete understanding of the overall production process, and are capable of performing different jobs, also known as **job rotation.** By allowing workers to periodically change jobs, it can break the monotony of boring or repetitive jobs. By enhancing the skill level of workers, it provides them with a greater sense of self-worth, and enhances their opportunities for job movement.

communication between workers

5. The organizational structure of jobs should enable and promote interaction and communication among workers and between workers and management. This encourages workers to seek ways to improve their own jobs and to share this knowledge among their colleagues.

Although behavioral approaches to job design and the quality of work life programs that encompassed these principles were widely praised and encouraged and some isolated cases of success resulted, they were not widely adopted. Job design generally remained under the predominant influence of the traditional principles of Taylor. There was no strong movement toward a widespread change in

GAINING THE COMPETITIVE EDGE

Worker Training in the German Trumpf Company

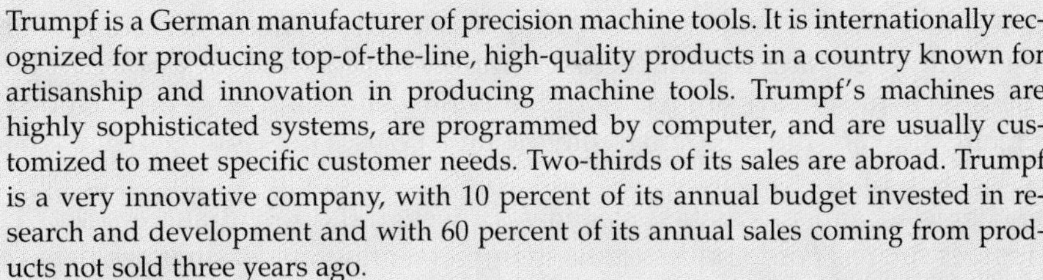

Trumpf is a German manufacturer of precision machine tools. It is internationally recognized for producing top-of-the-line, high-quality products in a country known for artisanship and innovation in producing machine tools. Trumpf's machines are highly sophisticated systems, are programmed by computer, and are usually customized to meet specific customer needs. Two-thirds of its sales are abroad. Trumpf is a very innovative company, with 10 percent of its annual budget invested in research and development and with 60 percent of its annual sales coming from products not sold three years ago.

However, despite its technological sophistication and innovations, a primary reason for Trumpf's success is its highly skilled workers, which is a trait of German manufacturing. Each Trumpf worker goes through a $3\frac{1}{2}$-year apprentice program. An apprentice spends 4 days each week at the Trumpf plant and 1 day at a state-run industrial school. A similar program is employed by manufacturing companies throughout Germany. This dual state-industry educational program ensures that German industry will have a large, skilled, flexible work force.

At Trumpf an apprentice spends the first 6 months of the program doing nothing but filing steel by hand. Trumpf believes that mastery of manual skills is a necessity for learning basic machine work, as a preliminary to developing sophisticated machine tool systems. This emphasis on manual skills also teaches self-discipline and instills self-confidence, which will result in a high level of artisanship and quality. Germany has a long, historical tradition of manual artisanship which is reflected in their machine tool industry. Workers are perceived as aritsans and enjoy a high social status in Germany and throughout Western Europe. Alternatively, in the United States, industry historically relied on immigrant workers for manual skills and did not develop extensive training programs on a national scale to the extent that Germany has. Further, the social status of manual workers in the United States has historically been lower than in Germany and Europe, making it a less attractive occupation. The result for U.S. manufacturing companies in recent years has often been a shortage of skilled workers that would allow them to compete effectively in international markets with European companies.

Trumpf has a U.S. plant, which produces the same high-quality work as its German plants, indicating that Trumpf quality and artisanship can be replicated with properly trained U.S. workers. In fact, most of Trumpf's Japanese sales come from products it makes in America.

Source: Based on Peters, Tom (narrator), "Germany's Quality Obsession." Video co-produced by The Tom Peters Group, KERA, and Video Publishing House, Inc., copyright Video Publishing House, Inc., and Excell, A California partnership, 1991.

the philosophy of job design. However, a dramatic turning point in the approach to job design was rapidly approaching.

CONTEMPORARY TRENDS IN JOB DESIGN

Transparency 9.3 Contemporary Trends in Job Design

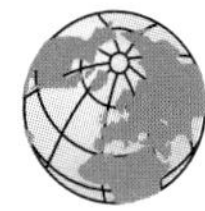

During the 1980s and 1990s the competitive advantage gained by many Japanese companies in international markets, and especially in the automobile industry, caused U.S. firms to reevaluate their management practices vis-à-vis those of the Japanese. The nature of jobs and job design is one particular area where there was a striking difference between Japanese and U.S. approaches and results. For example, one Japanese automobile company was able to assemble a car with half the blue-collar labor as a comparable U.S. auto company—about 14 hours in Japan, as opposed to 25 hours in the United States. As we previously mentioned, for various cultural and historical reasons, Japan did not adopt the traditional Western approaches to job design with a high degree of work simplification and task specialization. Instead Japanese job structure allowed for more individual worker responsibility and less supervision, group work activity and interaction, higher worker skill levels, and training across a variety of tasks and jobs. Some of these job design characteristics are recognizable as the behavioral precepts included in the quality of work life programs from the mid-1970s. There is a tendency among Americans to think that these job characteristics are unique to the Japanese culture, character, and production systems. However, the recent successes of U.S. companies such as Ford and Motorola in implementing quality management programs as well as successful Japanese companies operating in America, such as Nissan and Honda, show that cultural factors are less important than management practices.

Japanese successes are due less to cultural factors than to management practices.

In this section we explore some of the recent trends in job design that emanate primarily from Japan. We emphasize the Japanese approaches to jobs and job design because that is where the attention of U.S. companies has been focused as they attempt to emulate Japanese successes. Also, the Japanese approach to job design has been so markedly different from the U.S. approach that every feature invites comparison.

Job and Task Flexibility

Japanese management has greater flexibility in labor deployment than their U.S. counterparts as a result of extensive cross training. This practice has created a more skilled and integrated work force in Japan and enables workers to move across a variety of different jobs and tasks. This versatility is especially important given the changing nature of product markets. Companies now have to respond to changing consumer tastes that are more diverse, more fragmented, and more concerned with quality. Mass, standardized production has been supplemented by the production of smaller production batches to reflect the consumer's desire for product variety. Advances in technology, machinery, and equipment have also occurred at a more rapid pace. Companies must be able to react quickly to these factors in order to remain competitive. To do so requires that job designs, jobs, and workers be adaptable to new and changing products and production processes. The traditional approach of designing jobs with clearly defined, simple, repetitive tasks so that workers can be treated as replaceable parts is effective in a mass production system but is too rigid for the dynamics of international competition.

Japanese train workers to do a variety of jobs and tasks.

Alternatively, Japanese companies design jobs and train workers to achieve the flexibility to move workers between jobs as the need arises, which is well suited to the dynamics of new markets, product diversity, and new technologies. This flexibility is also necessary for the Japanese production system, with its goal of very low work-in-process inventories, as typified by the just-in-time (JIT) system. Buffer inventories are normally kept in stock at stages of the production process in order to offset irregularities and problems in the system and keep the production flow moving smoothly. However, Japanese companies seek to eliminate these buffer inventories completely by having the workers identify the causes of process problems and solve them. At Toyota, for example, as production problems are corrected, managers respond by progressively reducing the in-process buffer inventories, constantly seeking to drive them to zero. If irregularities do threaten to stop production, the workers are simply expected to work harder to avoid stoppages. Further, the Japanese do not maintain surplus labor to offset absenteeism, illness, or vacation time; other workers are expected to fill in where needed to maintain the normal work level. Japanese companies frequently operate on an understaffed basis, with the difference made up by extra effort from workers. Japanese companies also use warning lights to signify problems in assembly lines. When no lights are on, it is a signal to management that the work force can be reduced further. These management practices are feasible only if there is a high degree of job flexibility and workers are capable of moving from one job to another as other workers are taken from the production line.

Quality Improvement Responsibility

In the traditional U.S. approach, quality is management's responsibility, whereas Japanese approach says quality is the responsibility of the worker.

Extreme task specialization, as reflected in traditional U.S. job designs, is clearly a hindrance in achieving product quality. A worker's individual contribution to the overall production of a product or service is so slight that the worker has no perspective on what good or bad quality is. Workers in this system do not feel a responsibility for product quality, nor has U.S. management traditionally sought to instill a sense of responsibility for quality as part of the job design. The monitoring and control of quality has been perceived as a management responsibility and prerogative that was not shared with workers. Quality was traditionally achieved through inspection, after the fact.

The Japanese perspective on the relationship of quality and the worker is completely different. Part of a worker's job responsibility is product quality and quality improvement. Achieving product quality at the job level—that is, quality at the source—is fundamental to the Japanese approach to quality management. An important aspect of this approach is the concept of **empowerment,** wherein the worker has the authority and responsibility to alert management to quality problems and to act individually to correct problems without fear of reprisal. The authority of Japanese workers to halt an entire production operation or line on their own initiative if they discover a quality problem is well documented.

Empowerment is giving workers the authority to alert management to problems.

One important result of the responsibility for quality being transferred to the worker is the elimination of the need for quality inspectors and inspection, thus reducing the total cost of quality and the number of personnel required for this activity.

Increased Skill and Ability Levels

In order to perform in a variety of jobs, to monitor product quality, and to operate more sophisticated machinery and equipment, a greater job skills, training, and

Video 9.1 *CNN Work in Progress*

GAINING THE COMPETITIVE EDGE

Worker Empowerment at Harley-Davidson

In 1981 Harley-Davidson Company, the only U.S. manufacturer of motorcycles, was facing bankruptcy. Over a decade later the company is so successful that it cannot make motorcycles fast enough, and there is a waiting list of customers. One of the major factors in Harley-Davidson's turnaround was the increased job responsibility for machining centers on the shop floor. Machinists, besides operating their complex, computerized, machining centers, also bargain directly with vendors and suppliers, set up their own workplace, set their budgets, and monitor in control quality. The workers essentially have responsibility for designing the work process. In so doing they have raised the quality of Harley-Davidson motorcycles to a level that provides the company with an international competitive edge.

Source: Based on *CNN Work in Progress,* video documentary produced by CNN, hosted by Bernard Shaw, and narrated by Stephen Frazier; distributed by Allyn and Bacon, 1993.

ability are required than has traditionally been the case for workers in U.S. companies. We have mentioned on several occasions that the U.S. approach to work has been to design jobs that require minimal skills and abilities so that workers could easily and cheaply be replaced and trained. However, for even the simplest production jobs in Japan, the equivalent of a U.S. high school diploma is a minimum requirement, and the job applicant must go through a rigorous selection process with qualifying exams.

Teaching Note 9.2 Job Training at Yomazaki Machinery UK Ltd.

Once a worker joins a Japanese company, job training is extensive and varied. Since the ability level of workers is higher to begin with, expectations for performance and advancement from both the employee and management are also higher. Numerous courses are typically available for training in different jobs and functions. Job training is considered part of a structured career-development system that includes job rotation. This system of training and job rotation enhances the flexibility of the production process we mentioned earlier. It creates talent reserves that can be used as the need arises when products or processes change or the work force is reduced.

Extensive job training and job rotation are characteristic of Japanese system.

Employee Involvement

Employee involvement is a key feature of Japanese production systems, and involvement is typically realized through groups or teams, which are the basic organizational work unit in the Japanese company. The most well known example of the Japanese work team is the *quality circle,* in which a group of eight to ten workers plus their supervisor address and solve problems in their immediate work area. These groups have a formal structure and methodology for selecting and solving problems. (A more detailed discussion of quality circles is included in Chapter 3, "Quality Management.")

quality circles: group problem solving

Video 9.2 *CNN Work in Progress*

Video 9.3 1992 *Malcolm Baldrige Awards, Quest for Excellence V*

GAINING THE COMPETITIVE EDGE

Employee Training at Quad Graphics, Inc.

Quad Graphics, Inc., near Milwaukee, is a $500,000-a-year company that prints most of the different magazines found on newsstands in the United States. Employees at Quad Graphics work either three 12-hour days or four 10-hour days per week. They come back to work one day per week without pay to learn or teach about refinements in the company's state-of-the-art presses. Everyone in the company must learn and everyone must instruct. In fact, no one is promoted unless they have trained a successor. The employees experiment with the company's equipment in order to redesign and refine jobs. During the past decade 6,000 new jobs were created at the company; however, the jobs are not easy or routine. The employees must use their one day of learning to keep up with job changes.

A similar commitment to worker training is characteristic of other companies that have achieved success with TQM programs. For example, 1992 Malcolm Baldrige National Quality Award winner, AT&T Universal Card Services, provides 84 hours of employee training annually. Another 1992 Baldrige Award winner, the Ritz Carlton Hotel, provides 136 hours of training annually, and the Granite Rock Company, also a 1992 Baldrige Award winner, spends three times the industry average on employee training. At all these companies and at Quad Graphics, the employers want a work force capable of being retrained again and again as jobs evolve and change.

Source: Based on *CNN Work in Progress,* video documentary produced by CNN, hosted by Bernard Shaw, and narrated by Stephen Frazier; distributed by Allyn and Bacon, 1993. *Malcolm Baldrige Awards, Quest for Excellence V,* video presented by U.S. Department of Commerce, the Technology Administration, the National Institute of Standards and Technology, and the American Society for Quality Control, produced by Image Associates; distributed by Allyn and Bacon, 1993.

GAINING THE COMPETITIVE EDGE

Employee Involvement at Xerox

In the early 1980s Xerox Corporation's revenue share of the copier business declined from 90 to 43 percent as a result of increased competition from Ricoh, Sharp, and Canon in Japan and Kodak and IBM in the United States. In order to reduce costs, Xerox developed plans to subcontract component parts to other companies. One such plan at the components' manufacturing operations (CMO) plant in Webster, New York, would save $3.2 million and eliminate the entire wire harness department and its 180 employees. However, the local chapter of the Amalgamated Clothing and Textile Workers Union (ACTWU) asked management to establish a joint labor-management *study action team,* to study the problem and see if solutions could be discovered that would reduce costs by $3.2 million without resulting in employee layoffs.

The study action team consisted of eight employees selected jointly by union officials and management, including one manager, one industrial engineer, and six hourly employees (from each area in the department). The team members were relieved of their normal work duties and studied the problem for 6 months, and at the end of this period they had developed a set of recommendations that would save $3.7 million and the 180 jobs. The recommendations included purchasing new, more efficient equipment, developing work groups where each employee would perform several operations, and redesigning the department's work flow.

As a result of this success, other study action teams were developed to address problems at Xerox. These successes altered the labor-management relationship at Xerox and led to other changes in the work environment and employee involvement. Work groups were established that restructured the functions and responsibilities of employees in each work area to fit tasks together in order to achieve efficient production flows. Groups with like responsibilities meet biweekly to set work schedules, identify customer needs, review area performance, and identify problems. At the Webster CMO plant 36 groups were established, each with 15 to 40 members, responsible for planning, scheduling, making changes, and solving problems in their work area; that is, each became a minibusiness within the larger organization. The study action teams and work area groups created a new, flexible job environment at Xerox in which change in work practices and new technologies are readily accepted by employees.

Source: Based on Lazes, P., L. Rumpeltes, A. Hoffner, L. Pace, and A. Costanza, "Xerox and the ACTWU: Using Labor-Management Teams to Remain Competitive," *National Productivity Review* 10, no. 3 (1991): 339–49.

Quality circles are an extremely important component of Japanese total quality management programs. They are best known in the United States for their role in improving product quality. However, work groups such as quality circles solve problems and attempt to improve productivity and efficiency in all areas, not just quality (although efforts for improvement in one area invariably lead to quality improvement as well). Quality circles have been especially effective in job redesign and improvement and in job training. In many instances, the solution to a quality problem is discovered by the work group to be a problem in job design. However, it should be noted that the quality circle is not a democratic group that supersedes supervisory authority; employee involvement does not mean worker authority. In fact, the ratio of supervisors to workers is generally greater in Japan than America and supervisors are at least as authoritative, if not more.

Quality circles solve problems in all areas of production process.

Evaluation and Reward

Even though group participation is a key component in the Japanese production system, individual achievement is highly valued and rewarded. Japanese companies typically invest much more on personnel evaluation and have larger personnel departments than U.S. companies. Individual workers participate in self-evaluation and set personal goals, and their performances are rated by superiors. These individual evaluations are important when determining pay and advancement.

Job security is a key factor in Japanese reward system.

A key factor in the Japanese reward system is the lifelong job security provided by many companies. This security results in a very high degree of employee loyalty to the company, which, in turn, heightens the worker's willingness to accept job rotation, responsibility for job improvement, and the constant pressure of providing extra effort to offset process irregularities. These and other unique features of the Japanese management system require the "sacrifice of self" for the good for the organizational whole. This personnel system is dramatically different from the traditional U.S. system, in which jobs are designed in such a way that the occupants are treated as replaceable parts.

Worker Compensation

Earlier in this chapter we mentioned that in the traditional approaches to work and jobs, typified by Taylor's scientific management, financial incentive was believed to be the sole motivating force for workers. Although behavioralists later showed that wages are not the *sole* impetus for work and worker satisfaction, they are still a very important aspect of work.

Traditional forms of worker payment are hourly wages and incentive pay systems.

The two basic forms of worker payment are the hourly wage and the individual incentive, or piece-rate, wage, both of which are tied to time. The well-known hourly wage is self-explanatory; the longer someone works, the more he or she is paid. In a strict piece-rate system, workers are paid for the number of units they produce during the work day. The faster the worker performs, the more output

GAINING THE COMPETITIVE EDGE

An Incentive Compensation Program at Viking Freight

All employees at Viking Freight Systems, Inc., participate in an incentive compensation program that financially rewards them for their combined contributions to the achievement of corporate objectives. Employees are divided into groups with shared job characteristics and objectives. For example, workers at each of the company's 47 terminal sites are considered groups, as well as all truck drivers, salespeople, maintenance personnel, and so on. A group's performance is measured every four weeks according to specific criteria. The primary criterion (common to all groups) is that the company's operating ratio (operating expenses divided by revenues) must be less than 95 percent for the month. The remaining performance criteria are group-specific. For example, the criteria for the forty-seven terminal groups are revenue attainment, percent of performance, on-time service, and claims ratio. Specific objectives are set by engineering for each criterion—for example, at least 98 percent on-time service—and, in order to receive incentive payments, the terminal groups must reach these targets. Payments are made by separate check in group meetings, and the frequency of the payments (every four weeks) continually maintains focus on the program. When the program was started in 1986, employees achieved 84.8 percent of company performance goals, and by 1991 performance against standards was 103.1 percent. In 1991 employees earned incentive payments in twelve of thirteen 4-week periods, averaging 5.5 percent of their gross pay, or approximately $125 to $200 per period.

Source: Based on Stambaugh, T., "An Incentive Pay Success Story," *Personnel Journal* 71, no. 7 (1992): 48–54.

that is generated and the greater the pay. These two forms of payment are also frequently combined with a guaranteed base hourly wage, and additional incentive piece-rate payments based on the number of units produced above a standard hourly rate of output. Other basic forms of compensation include straight salary, the most common form of payment for management, and commissions, a payment system usually applied to sales and salespeople.

Piece-rate systems can be detrimental to quality.

Although an individual piece-rate system does provide incentive to increase output, it does not ensure high quality. In fact, it can do just the opposite and be detrimental to quality. In an effort to produce as much as possible, the worker will become sloppy, take shortcuts, and pay less attention to detail. As a result, there has been a move in recent years away from individual wage incentive systems based on output and time. In its place there has been a trend toward compensation systems based on other measures of performance, such as quality, productivity, cost reduction, and the achievement of organizational goals. These systems usually combine an hourly base payment with some form of incentive payment. However, incentives are typically not individual but are tied to group or company performance.

In *profit sharing*, employees receive a share of company profits.

Profit-sharing plans, in which employees receive a portion of company profits, are found in most Japanese companies and are becoming increasingly popular in the U.S. Other plans provide bonuses or incentive payments on top of hourly wages based on formulas that include cost reduction, the percentage of defective items or good-quality items, and/or productivity. However, such compensation plans base bonuses or incentive payments on group activity rather than individual effort; that is, a department's or plant's performance triggers incentive payments. This type of compensation is generally consistent with the Japanese team and participative approaches to jobs and work.

Technology and Automation

Technology has broadened the scope of job design in the United States and overseas.

The worker-machine interface is a crucial—and possibly the most crucial—aspect of job design, particularly in manufacturing but also in many other industries and services. Thus, the rapid development of new technologies results in new, more sophisticated machinery. Also, the development and proliferation of computer

Robots do not necessarily perform a job faster than humans, but they can tolerate hostile environments, work longer hours, and do a job more consistently. Robots are used for a wide range of manufacturing jobs including material handling, machining, assembly and inspection. For example, at Ford over 98 percent of the welding for the Taurus is performed by robots; at General Dynamics holes are drilled for F-16 fighter planes with robots, and disk drives are installed in the manufacture of IBM personal computers with robots. The use of robotics in the United States has been limited primarily to larger industries, with the automobile industry accounting for over half the robots used in this country.

technology and systems has greatly broadened the scope of job design and heightened the need for workers with better skills and abilities and more job training.

During the 1970s and 1980s the Japanese investment in new plants and equipment was substantially greater than in the United States. Japanese companies developed and installed a new generation of automated equipment and robotics that enhanced their abilities to achieve higher output and lower costs. This new equipment also reduced the manual labor necessary to perform jobs and improve safety. Computer systems provided workers with an expanded array of information that increased their ability to identify and locate problems in the production process and monitor product quality. New job designs and redesigns of existing jobs were required that reflected these new technologies.

Job Satisfaction

The cumulative effect of these new trends in job and work design outlined in the preceding discussion has been a greater level of worker satisfaction with jobs in Japan than in the United States. Jobs with these characteristics are more challenging, varied, and interesting, require more skill, and include more individual responsibility. Workers take greater pride in their jobs and have a more clearly delineated perspective of the contribution their job makes to the success of the organization. The reward system is more effective; as a result, employee loyalty is greater. Because of the team approach, there is greater interaction with supervisory management, which reduces potential employee-management conflict.

U.S. Adaptation of Trends in Job Design

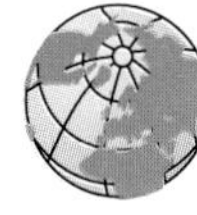

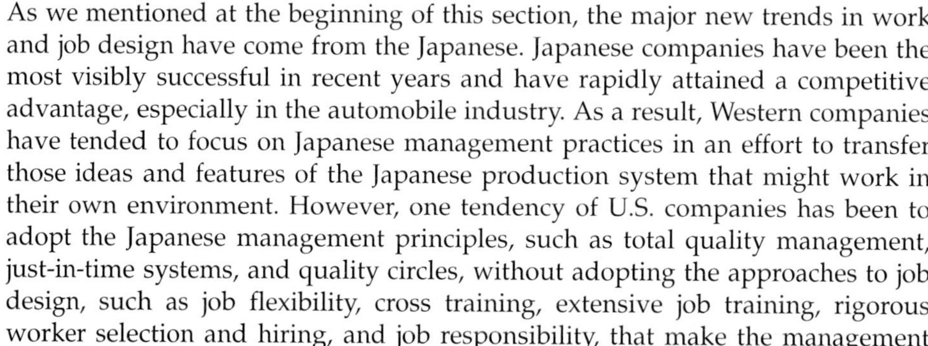

U.S. companies have tended to adopt TQM practices without adopting new approaches to job design.

As we mentioned at the beginning of this section, the major new trends in work and job design have come from the Japanese. Japanese companies have been the most visibly successful in recent years and have rapidly attained a competitive advantage, especially in the automobile industry. As a result, Western companies have tended to focus on Japanese management practices in an effort to transfer those ideas and features of the Japanese production system that might work in their own environment. However, one tendency of U.S. companies has been to adopt the Japanese management principles, such as total quality management, just-in-time systems, and quality circles, without adopting the approaches to job design, such as job flexibility, cross training, extensive job training, rigorous worker selection and hiring, and job responsibility, that make the management systems effective.

Job design features of the Japanese are transferable to the United States despite cultural differences.

Some of the features of Japanese job design and the work environment have cultural aspects that make it seem that direct adaptation by U.S. companies is not possible or, at least, would be difficult. However, there have been enough successes in recent years among U.S. companies to suggest that with proper management practices, job design features are transferable. A number of U.S. companies, especially those that have a strong commitment to a total quality management program, have had success with employee-involvement programs and quality circles. Jobs have been designed to include more individual responsibility and worker empowerment. The increased use of automated equipment and robotics by American manufacturing firms has forced them to redesign jobs to reflect the greater skill levels and abilities that this new technology requires. The movement away from mass production to smaller batch production in order to meet changing consumer preferences has forced American companies to redesign job structures to create more flexibility to broaden the scopes of jobs, and to reduce the degree of task specialization. Many American companies have also come to realize that work-job satisfaction and pride can have a significant impact on both quality and productivity.

Transparency 9.4 The Evolution of Job Design

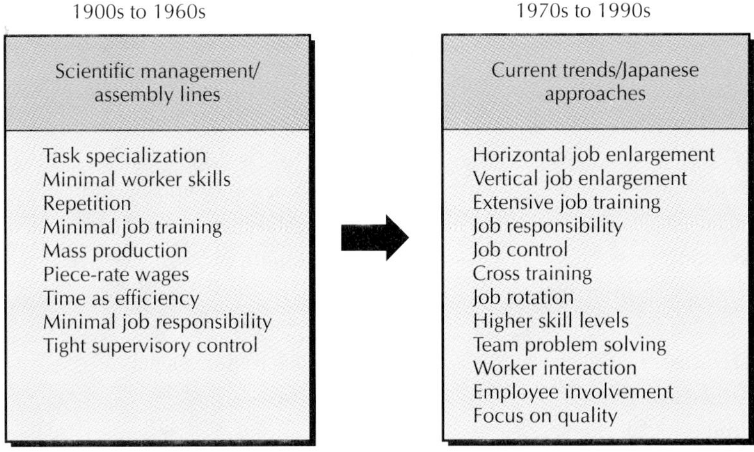

1900s to 1960s
Scientific management/ assembly lines
Task specialization
Minimal worker skills
Repetition
Minimal job training
Mass production
Piece-rate wages
Time as efficiency
Minimal job responsibility
Tight supervisory control
1970s to 1990s
Current trends/Japanese approaches
Horizontal job enlargement
Vertical job enlargement
Extensive job training
Job responsibility
Job control
Cross training
Job rotation
Higher skill levels
Team problem solving
Worker interaction
Employee involvement
Focus on quality

FIGURE 9.2 The Evolution of Job Design

Our discussion on job design in this section has tended to concentrate on manufacturing-related industries, such as the automobile industry. These industries are the most visible and have generated the most print and media exposure. This result is not unusual because the dominant principles and approaches to job design and the nature of work have traditionally come from the manufacturing sector. However, most of the recent trends in job design are just as applicable to nonmanufacturing and service industries. In fact, it is ironic to note that the greatest degree of routine work and task specialization now appears to be in service industries and in clerical jobs rather than in manufacturing. For example, fast-food operations have adopted many of the job-design and task-specialization principles of assembly lines to produce hamburgers. Such jobs tend to be low-paying and repetitive, and workers are easily replaced; familiar characteristics of traditional job-design principles we discussed at the beginning of this chapter.

Contemporary service jobs often exhibit characteristics of scientific management.

Figure 9.2 summarizes our discussion of both the traditional approaches and the current trends in job design and highlights the differences between them.

THE ELEMENTS OF JOB DESIGN

In our discussion of job design to this point, we have considered jobs and work in a broad context and have reviewed the various approaches to job design and work from traditional and current perspectives. In this section we focus on the specific elements of designing jobs, including the various factors that must be considered. The elements of job design generally fall into three major categories, which we discuss separately: an analysis of the tasks that are included in the job, the worker requirements, and the environment in which the job takes place. These categories essentially address the questions of how the job is performed, who does it, and where it is done. Table 9.1, on page 448, summarizes a selection of individual elements that would generally be considered in the job design process.

elements of job design: analysis of tasks, worker requirements, and job environment

Task Analysis

Earlier in this chapter we defined tasks as the individual activities in a job. Task analysis is basically a determination of how to do each task and how all the tasks fit together to form a job. It includes such elements as defining and describing the individual tasks and determining their proper and most efficient sequence, their duration, their relationship with other tasks, and their frequency. Task analysis should be sufficiently detailed so that it results in a step-by-step procedure for the

task analysis: how tasks fit together to form a job

TABLE 9.1 Elements of Job Design

Task Analysis	*Worker Analysis*	*Environmental Analysis*
• Description of tasks to be performed • Task sequence • Function of tasks • Frequency of tasks • Criticality of tasks • Relationship with other jobs/tasks • Performance requirements • Information requirements • Control requirements • Error possibilities • Task duration(s) • Equipment requirements	• Capability requirements • Performance requirements • Evaluation • Skill level • Job training • Physical requirements • Mental stress • Boredom • Motivation • Number of workers • Level of responsibility • Monitoring level • Quality responsibility • Empowerment level	• Workplace location • Process location • Temperature and humidity • Lighting • Ventilation • Safety • Logistics • Space requirements • Noise • Vibration

Transparency 9.5 The Elements of Job Design

job. The sequence of tasks in some jobs is a logical ordering; for example, the wedges of material used in making a baseball cap must be cut before they can be sewn together, and they must all be sewn together before the cap bill can be attached. However, the cap logo can be stitched either before or after the bill has been sewn on, although it would probably be easier (and less cumbersome) to do it before the bill is attached.

Some tasks are more critical than others, and the consequences of the more critical tasks not performed correctly must be assessed; that is, will the entire production process be affected, will a safety hazard result, or will quality be affected? The performance requirements of a task can be the time required to complete the task, the accuracy in performing the task to specifications, the output level or productivity yield, or quality performance. The performance of some tasks require information such as a measurement (cutting furniture pieces), temperature (food processing), weight (filling bags of fertilizer), or a litmus test (for a chemical process).

performance requirements of a task: time, accuracy, productivity, quality

Consideration of error possibilities is a form of what-if? analysis determining everything that can go wrong with the task. The possibility (and probability) of error also determines how much task control and monitoring there must be and the level of preventive maintenance.

Worker Analysis

determining worker capabilities and responsibilities for a job

Worker analysis is a determination of who performs the job. More precisely, what characteristics must the worker possess to meet the job requirements, what responsibilities will the worker have in the job, and how will the worker be rewarded? Jobs require worker capabilities and skill levels; however, the two can be different. Although a worker may have the skill to perform individual tasks, he or she may not have the capability to react to task errors or control and monitor the task adequately.

Some jobs require manual labor and a certain degree of physical strength, whereas others require virtually no physical characteristics. Such physical requirements are assessed not only to make sure the right worker is placed in the job, but also to determine if the physical requirements are excessive, necessitating redesign. The same type of design questions must be addressed for mental stress.

Environmental Analysis

Environmental analysis refers to the physical position of the job in the production or service facility and the environmental conditions that must exist. These conditions include such things as proper temperature, lighting, ventilation, and noise. For example, the production of microchips requires an extremely clean, climatically controlled, enclosed environment. Detail work, such as engraving or sewing, requires proper lighting; some jobs that create dust levels, such as lint in textile operations, require proper ventilation. Some jobs require a large amount of space around the immediate job area. The logistics of getting the job output to the next stage in the production process is part of design consideration.

job environment: the physical characteristics and location of a job

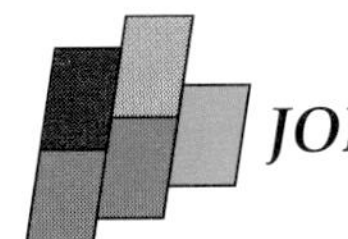

JOB ANALYSIS

Part of the design process for a job is to study the *methods* used in the work included in the job to see how the job is done or should be done. As a result, this area of job design has traditionally been referred to as *methods analysis,* or simply *work methods.* Methods analysis is typically an activity conducted by someone trained in the study of work methods, such as an industrial engineer or a methods analyst.

work methods: studying how a job is done

The most frequent application of methods analysis is for the redesign or improvement of existing jobs. An analyst will study an existing job to see how the work is accomplished in order to determine if the tasks are performed in the most efficient manner possible, if all the present tasks are necessary, or if new tasks should be added. The analyst might also want to see how the job fits in with other jobs—that is, how well a job is integrated into the overall production process or a sequence of jobs.

Earlier in this chapter, in the section "Contemporary Trends in Job Designs," we talked about the impact of product diversity, technological changes, and quality on job design. All these factors can necessitate methods analysis. The development and installation of new machinery or equipment, new products or product changes, and changes in quality standards can all require that a job be analyzed for redesign.

Methods analysis is also used to develop new jobs. In this case the analyst must work with a description or outline of a proposed job and attempt to develop a mental picture of how the job will be performed.

The primary tools of methods analysis are a variety of charts that illustrate in different ways how a job or a work process is done. A primary benefit of these charts is that they are more easily understood by supervisors, managers, and workers than a written description might be. The charts enable the methods analyst to show these individuals how a job is accomplished and get their input and feedback on the design or redesign process. We will describe two of the more popular charts, the *process flowchart* and the *worker-machine chart.*

Process Flowchart

A **process flowchart** is frequently used to analyze the sequential steps of a job or how a set of jobs fit together into the overall flow of the production process. Examples might include the flow of a product through a manufacturing assembly process, the making of a pizza, the activities of a surgical team in an operating room, or the processing of a catalog mail or telephone order.

A **process flowchart** is a graph of the steps of a job.

○	Operation: An activity directly contributing to the product or service.
⇨	Transportation: Moving of the product or service from one location to another.
□	Inspection: Examing the product or service for completeness, irregularities, or quality.
D	Delay: The process having to wait.
▽	Storage: Storing of the product or service.

FIGURE 9.3 Symbols for a Process Flowchart

A process flowchart employs some basic symbols to describe the various tasks or steps in a job or a series of jobs. These symbols are described in Figure 9.3. The symbols are subsequently connected by lines on the chart to show the flow of the process.

EXAMPLE 9.1

Developing a Job Process Flowchart

Problem Statement:

The QuikCopy Store does copying jobs for walk-in customers. When a customer comes into the store with a copy job, a desk operator fills out a work order (name, number of copies, quality of paper, etc.) and places it in a box. An operator subsequently picks up the job, makes the copies, and returns the completed job to the cashier, where the job transaction is completed. The store would like a job process flowchart that describes this sequence of tasks.

Solution:

The process flowchart for the steps in the copying job are shown in Figure 9.4. Although the process encompasses several operators and jobs, it focuses primarily on the tasks of the copy machine operator, who actually makes the copies.

Figure 9.4 is recognizable as a flowchart of the work process, much like a flowchart that describes the steps of a computer programming model. It helps the analyst to consider a number of different aspects of a job or process that may result in improvement, including the following:

- The nature and importance of the tasks
- Task relationships
- Task sequence
- Worker assignment to tasks
- Frequency of delays
- Movement between tasks

Often a process flowchart is used in combination with other types of methods analysis charts and a written job description to form a comprehensive and detailed picture of a job. Essentially, the methods analyst is a "job detective," who wants to get as much evidence as possible about a job from as many perspectives as possible in order to improve the job.

Worker-Machine Chart

A **worker-machine chart** determines if worker and machine time are used efficiently.

A **worker-machine chart** illustrates the amount of time a worker and a machine are working or idle in a job. This type of chart is occasionally used in conjunction

Transparency 9.6 Process Flowchart of Copying Job

Process Flowchart

Job Copying Job — Date 9/11
Analyst Calvin
Page 1

Process Description	Process Symbols
Desk operator fills out work order	O ⇨ □ D ▽
Work order placed in "waiting job" box	O ⇨ □ D ▽
Job picked up by operator and read	O ⇨ □ D ▽
Job carried to appropriate copy machine	O ⇨ □ D ▽
Operator waits for machine to vacate	O ⇨ □ D ▽
Operator loads paper	O ⇨ □ D ▽
Operator sets machine	O ⇨ □ D ▽
Operator performs and completes job	O ⇨ □ D ▽
Operator inspects job for irregularities	O ⇨ □ D ▽
Job filed alphabetically in completed work shelves	O ⇨ □ D ▽
Job waits for pickup	O ⇨ □ D ▽
Job moved by cashier for pickup	O ⇨ □ D ▽
Cashier completes transaction	O ⇨ □ D ▽
Cashier packages job (bag, wrap, or box)	O ⇨ □ D ▽
	O ⇨ □ D ▽
	O ⇨ □ D ▽

FIGURE 9.4 Process Flowchart of Copying Job

with a process flowchart when the job process includes equipment or machinery. The primary purpose of the worker-machine chart is to see if the worker's time and the machine time are being used efficiently—that is, if the worker or machine is idle an excessive amount of time.

EXAMPLE 9.2

Developing a Worker-Machine Chart

Problem Statement:

The QuikCopy Store described in Example 9.1 also makes photo identification cards for college students and business and factory workers. An operator types in data about the customer on a card, submits this to the photo machine, positions the customer for the photo, and takes the photograph. Then the machine processes the final photo identification card. The store would like to develop a worker-machine chart for this job.

Solution:

Figure 9.5, on page 452, shows the worker-machine chart for the job of making photo ID cards.

Notice that the chart is drawn according to a time scale along the left side of the chart. This enables the analyst, the operator, and the supervisor to get a visual perspective of the amount of work and idle time in the job process. For this job, the summary at the bottom of Figure 9.5 indicates that the operator and machine were both working and idle approximately the same amount of time.

Another type of worker-machine chart is the *gang process chart,* which illustrates a job in which a team of workers are interacting with a piece of equipment or a machine. Examples of this type of job might include workers at a coal furnace in a steel mill or a military gunnery team on a battleship or in the field. A gang chart is constructed in basically the same way as the chart in Figure 9.5, except

Worker-Machine Chart

Job: Photo-ID Cards — Date: 10/14

Time (min)	Operator	Time (min)	Photo Machine
1–2	Key in customer data on card	2.6	Idle
3	Feed data card in	0.4	Accept card
	Position customer for photo	1.0	Idle
4	Take picture	0.6	Begin photo process
5–7	Idle	3.4	Photo/card processed
8–9	Inspect card and trim edges	1.2	Idle
10			

Summary

	Operator Time	%	Photo Machine Time	%
Work	5.8	63	4.8	52
Idle	3.4	37	4.4	48
Total	9.2 min	100%	9.2 min	100%

FIGURE 9.5 Worker-Machine Chart

there are multiple columns for the different operators. The primary purpose of a gang process chart is to determine if the interaction between the workers is efficient and coordinated.

Motion Study

Motion study is used to ensure efficiency of motion in a job.

The most detailed form of job analysis is **motion study,** which is the study of the individual human motions that are used in a job task. The purpose of motion study is to make sure that a job task does not include any unnecessary motion or movement by the worker and to select the sequence of motions that ensure that the task is being performed in the most efficient manner possible.

Frank and Lillian Gilbreth developed motion study.

Motion study originated with the work of Frank Gilbreth, a colleague of F. W. Taylor at the turn of the century. Gilbreth employed a systematic approach to the study of human motions to arrive at the "one best way" to perform a work task. F. W. Taylor's approach to the study of work methods was to select the one best worker among a group of workers and use that worker's methods as the standard by which other workers were trained. Alternatively, Gilbreth studied many workers and from among them picked the best way to perform each activity. Then he combined these elements to form the one best way to perform a task.

Gilbreth and his wife, Lillian, used movies to study individual work motions in slow motion and frame by frame, which is called *micromotion analysis.* Using these motion pictures of workers performing tasks and humans performing normal physical activities, the Gilbreths carefully analyzed and categorized the basic physical elements of motion used in work. They called these basic elements of motion **therbligs**, which is Gilbreth spelled backwards with the *t* and *h* reversed. Examples of therbligs (i.e., basic elemental motions) include *search* (look or feel for an item), *select* (choose from a group of items), *grasp* (enclose an item), *hold* (retain an item after grasping), *position* (move an item), and *release* (let go of the item).

Therbligs are basic physical elements of motion.

The Gilbreth's motion study research and analysis eventually evolved into a set of widely adopted *principles of motion study,* which companies have used as general guidelines for the efficient design of work. These principles are generally categorized according to the efficient use of the *human body,* the efficient arrangement of the *workplace,* and the efficient use of *equipment and machinery.* The principles of motion study usually include about twenty or twenty-five rules for conserving motion. Table 9.2 summarizes these rules by categorizing them into a general set of guidelines.

principles of motion study: guidelines for work design

Motion study originated at approximately the same time that F. W. Taylor developed the principles of scientific management, and these two concepts complemented each other. Motion study was particularly effective for designing the repetitive, simplified, assembly line–type jobs with extreme task specialization that were characteristic of manufacturing operations at that time. Frank Gilbreth's first subject was a bricklayer; through his study and improvement of this worker's motions, he was able to improve the bricklayer's productivity three-fold. However, in Gilbreth's day, bricklayers were paid on the basis of how many bricks they could lay in an hour in a piece-rate wage system. Who would be able to find a bricklayer today that would be paid according to such a system! In general, this

TABLE 9.2 Summary of General Guidelines for Motion Study

Efficient Use of the Human Body
• Work should be simplified, rhythmic, and symmetric.
• Hand/arm motions should be coordinated and simultaneous.
• The full extent of physical capabilities should be employed; all parts of the body should perform; the hand should never be idle.
• Energy should be conserved by letting machines perform tasks when possible, minimizing the distance of movements, and physical momentum should be in favor of the worker.
• Tasks should be simple, requiring minimal eye contact and minimal muscular effort, with no unnecessary motions, delays, or idelness.
Efficient Arrangement of the Workplace
• All tools, materials, and equipment should have a designated, easily accessible location that minimizes the motions required to get them.
• Seating and the general work environment should be comfortable and healthy.
Efficient Use of Equipment
• Equipment and mechanized tools enhance worker abilities.
• The use of foot-operated mechanized equipment that relieves the hand/arms of work should be maximized.
• Equipment should be constructed and arranged to fit worker use.

reflects the decline in the use of motion study during the last several decades. As we discussed in our section on job design, there is a movement away from extreme task specialization and simplified, repetitive jobs in lieu of greater job responsibility and a broader range of tasks, which in turn has reduced the use of motion study. Nevertheless, motion study is still employed for certain types of repetitive jobs, especially in the service industries, such as postal workers in mailrooms, who process and route thousands of pieces of mail.

pioneers in the field of industrial engineering

Teaching Note 9.3 Frank and Lillian Gilbreth

The Gilbreth's made significant and lasting contributions to the study of work methods; together with F. W. Taylor and Henry Gantt, they are considered as pioneers and founders of the field of industrial engineering. Frank Gilbreth is known as the father of motion study, whereas Lillian Gilbreth is referred to as the first lady of engineering. Their use of motion pictures is still popular today as means of studying human motion. Computer-generated images are used to analyze an athlete's movements in order to enhance performance, and video cameras are widely used to study everything from surgical procedures in the operating room to telephone operators and machine operators.

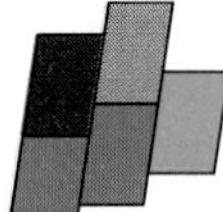

WORK MEASUREMENT

In work measurement, the unit of measure is *time*. Specifically, work measurement is the determination of an estimate of the time required to do a job. The traditional means for determining a time estimate has been the time study method, in which a stopwatch is used to time the individual elements of a job. These elemental times are summed to get a time estimate for a job and then adjusted by a performance rating of the worker and an allowance factor for unavoidable delays, resulting in a **standard time.** The standard time is the time required by an "average" worker to perform one cycle of a job under normal circumstances and conditions.

Standard time is the time required by an average worker to perform a job.

As is the case for many of the other topics related to work and jobs in this chapter, work measurement and time study were introduced by Frederick W. Taylor in the late 1880s and 1890s. One of the main objectives of his efforts was to determine a "fair" method of job performance evaluation and payment, which at that time was frequently a matter of contention between management and labor. The basic form of wage payment was an incentive piece-rate system, in which workers were paid a wage rate per unit of output instead of an hourly wage rate; the more workers produced, the more they earned. The problem with this system at the time was that there was no way to determine a "normal," or "fair," rate of output. It was to management's advantage to make the normal rate of output high, and it was to labor's advantage to have it low. Since management normally made such decisions, the piece rate was usually "tight," making it hard for the worker to make the expected, or fair, output rate. Thus, the workers earned less. This was the scenario in which Taylor introduced his time study approach in order to develop an equitable piece-rate wage system based on fair standard job times.

incentive piece-rate wage system based on time study

The stopwatch time study approach for work measurement was extremely popular and widespread during the first half of the twentieth century. Many union contracts in the automotive, textile, and other manufacturing industries for virtually every production job in a company were based almost entirely on standard times developed from time studies. However, the basic principle underlying an incentive wage system is that pay is the sole motivation for work. We have pointed out on several occasions earlier in this chapter that this principle has been successfully disproved. In fact, in recent years incentive wage systems have been shown to inhibit quality improvement efforts. As a result, the use of stopwatch time study for performance evaluation has dramatically declined, especially in manufacturing industries.

stopwatch time study used for work measurement

However, performance evaluation represents only one use for time study and work measurement. It is also extremely useful—and often is a necessity—for planning purposes in order to predict the level of output and performance a company might achieve in the future. Thus, work measurement and time study remain very useful for operations management and are subjects warranting further discussion.

Stopwatch Time Study

The result of a time study, as we mentioned in the previous section, is a *standard time* for performing one cycle of a repetitious job. The basic component of the standard time is the average job time computed from a number of cycle observations for a worker. As such, time study is a statistically based technique that is most accurate and useful for jobs that include tasks that are repeated in each job cycle, that is, highly repetitive tasks.

The basic steps required to perform a time study are as follows.

Transparency 9.7 Basic Steps of a Time Study

steps of a stopwatch time study

1. *Establish the standard job method.* The job should be analyzed using methods analysis to make sure the best method is being used. If, after a time study has been done and standard time has been developed, it is determined the job method(s) can be improved, then the standard time is no longer valid.

2. *Break down the job into elements.* The job is broken down into short, elemental tasks with obvious "break points" between them. The more detailed the elements, the easier it is to eliminate elemental times that are not normally included in each job cycle and might abnormally affect the standard time. Also, a worker may be more or less proficient at different tasks, and the elemental breakdown enables the engineer/analyst to reflect such differences more accurately.

3. *Study the job.* Time studies have traditionally been conducted using a stopwatch attached to a clipboard, although, hand-held electronic time-study machines (similar to an electronic calculator) are now available that store elemental times in a memory that can be transferred to a computer for processing. To conduct a time study with a stopwatch, the industrial engineer or technician takes a position near the worker and records each elemental time on an observation sheet designed for time studies. A time study requires the use of both hands, one to write down the observations and the other to work the stopwatch, and the ability to maintain continuous visual observation of the worker while also reading the times from the stopwatch and writing them down. The stopwatch is read in hundredths of a minute, and individual elemental times are frequently only a few hundredths of a minute in duration, or almost the time required to start and stop the watch. In recent years, videocameras have been used to videotape jobs, with the time study conducted outside of the workplace at a later time.

Teaching Note 9.4 Performance Rating

determining the average time for a job

4. *Rate the worker's performance.* As the time study is being conducted, the worker's performance is also rated by the person doing the study. The objective of the study is to determine a "normal," or average time for the job, so the engineer/technician must adjust the elemental times up or down with a rating factor to achieve a normal time. A performance rating factor of 100 percent reflects normal work performance, whereas a factor below 100 percent represents a below-average performance (and time) and one above 100 percent indicates performance better than normal. Rating factors usually range between 80 percent and 120 percent.

judging job performance

The observer conducting the study must, in effect, "judge" the difficulty of the job and mentally assess what normal performance is, primarily in terms of *speed.* Effort, or physical exertion, can also be a characteristic of performance; however, it must be viewed with caution, since a poor worker might exhibit a lot of exertion, whereas a good worker might exhibit little exertion in doing the same job. Some rating systems use description terms for rating, such as excellent, good, fair, and poor, or a letter grade, such as A, B, C, D, or F, to describe elements and then assign a predetermined, set numeral value to each descriptive term. For example, a "good" rating might result in a numerical rating of 1.07, or 107 percent.

The performance rating factor is a crucial component of the time study, and it is also subjective. The person conducting the study must be very familiar with the job in order to rate accurately the worker's performance. Industrial engineers and time study technicians usually hold frequent rating training sessions, where all individuals in the group will rate the same worker and then compare their results in order to reach a consensus as to what constitutes normal job performance. In addition, films and videos are available that show different levels of performance, effort, and speed for a variety of motions, tasks, and jobs. Even then it is often difficult to evaluate performance during an actual study.

Workers are not always cooperative, and they sometimes resent time studies, especially if they know they are being used to set wages. They will purposely slow or speed up their normal work rate, make frequent mistakes, or alter the normal work methods, all designed to disrupt the work study. The author recalls an incident while conducting a time study in a textile plant. During the study one of the authors briefly glanced at his stopwatch, and when he looked back up the worker had disappeared. The subject had leapt up, grabbed the metal superstructure above the workplace, and quickly pulled himself up. He was barely able to suppress his laughter as he watched the author frantically search for him on the floor below. Given this type of climate for conducting time studies, it is easy to understand why quality consultants and teachers perceive incentive wage systems and work measurement to be detrimental to quality improvement.

5. *Compute the average time.* Once a sufficient number of job cycles have been observed, an average time for each element is calculated. We talk more about the appropriate number of cycles to include in the study a little later.

Normal time is the elemental average time multiplied by a performance rating.

6. *Compute the normal time.* The **normal time** is calculated by multiplying the elemental average time by the performance rating factor according to the following formula:

$$\text{Normal time} = (\text{elemental average time})(\text{rating factor})$$

or

$$Nt = (\bar{t})(RF)$$

The normal cycle time (NT) is computed by summing the elemental normal times,

$$NT = \Sigma Nt$$

allowing for abnormal factors

7. *Compute the standard time.* The standard time is computed by adjusting the normal cycle time by an allowance factor for unavoidable work delays (such as a machine breakdown), personal delays (such as using the restroom), and normal mental or physical fatigue. The allowance factor is designated as a percentage increase in the normal cycle time for the jobs. The standard time is calculated according to the following formula:

$$\text{Standard time} = (\text{normal cycle time})(1 + \text{allowance factor})$$

or

$$ST = (NT)(1 + AF)$$

Alternate Example 9.1

EXAMPLE 9.3

Performing a Time Study and Developing a Standard Time

Problem Statement:

The Metro Food Services Company delivers fresh sandwiches each morning to vending machines throughout the city. Workers work through the night to prepare the sandwiches for morning delivery. A worker normally makes several different kinds of sandwiches. A time study for a worker making ham and cheese sandwiches is shown in Figure 9.6 (see page 458). Notice that each element has two readings. Row t includes the individual elemental times, whereas the R row contains a cumulative (running) clock reading recorded going down the column. In this case the individual elemental times are determined by subtracting the cumulative times between sequential readings. (However, several different types of stopwatch arrangements are available. One contains multiple watches with one stopped and read while the other is timing the next element. Another is a watch with two hands, where one hand stops at the element time when pushed and the other hand restarts at zero for the next element.)

Solution:

In Figure 9.6 the average element times are first computed as

$$\bar{t} = \frac{\sum t}{10}$$

For element 1 the average time is

$$\bar{t} = \frac{0.53}{10} = 0.053$$

The normal elemental times are computed by adjusting the average time, $\bar{t}$, by the performance rating factor, RF. For element 1 the normal time is

$$\begin{aligned} Nt &= (\bar{t})(\text{RF}) \\ &= (0.053)(1.05) \\ &= 0.056 \end{aligned}$$

The normal cycle time, NT, is computed by summing the normal times for all elements, which for this example is 0.387. The standard time is computed by adjusting the normal cycle time by an allowance factor,

$$\begin{aligned} \text{ST} &= (\text{NT})(1 + \text{AF}) \\ &= (0.387)(1 + 0.15) \\ &= 0.445 \text{ min} \end{aligned}$$

If, for example, the company wants to know how many ham and cheese sandwiches can be produced in a 2-hour period, they could simply divide the standard time into 120 minutes:

$$\frac{120 \text{ min}}{0.445 \text{ min/sandwich}} = 269.7 \text{ or } 270 \text{ sandwiches}$$

EXAMPLE 9.4

An Incentive Piece-Rate System

Problem Statement:

If the Metro Food Services Company in Example 9.3 pays workers a piece rate of \$0.04 per sandwich, what would an average worker be paid per hour, and what would the subject of the time study in Example 9.3 expect to be paid?

Solution:

The average worker would produce the following number of sandwiches in an hour:

$$\frac{60 \text{ min}}{0.445 \text{ min/sandwich}} = 134.8 \text{ or } 135 \text{ sandwiches}$$

The hourly wage rate would thus average

$$(135)(0.04) = \$5.40$$

Alternatively, the worker from Example 9.3 would produce at the average cycle time not adjusted by the rating factor, or 0.361 minutes. Adjusting this time by the allowance time results in a time of

$$(0.361)(1 + 0.15) = 0.415 \text{ min}$$

This worker could be expected to produce the following number of sandwiches per hour:

$$\frac{60 \text{ min}}{0.415 \text{ min/sandwich}} = 144.6 \text{ or } 145 \text{ sandwiches}$$

The average hourly wage rate for this worker would be

$$(145)(0.04) = \$5.80$$

or $0.40 more per hour.

Transparency 9.8 Time Study Observation Sheet

Time Study Observation Sheet

Identification of operation	Sandwich Assembly		Date 5/17
	Operator Smith	Approval Jones	Observer Russell

			Cycles										Summary			
			1	2	3	4	5	6	7	8	9	10	Σt	$\bar{t}$	RF	Nt
1	Grasp and lay out bread slices	t	0.04	0.05	0.05	0.04	0.06	0.05	0.06	0.06	0.07	0.05	0.53	0.053	1.05	0.056
		R	0.04	0.38	0.72	1.05	1.40	1.76	2.13	2.50	2.89	3.29				
2	Spread mayonaise on both slices	t	0.07	0.06	0.07	0.08	0.07	0.07	0.08	0.10	0.09	0.08	0.77	0.077	1.00	0.077
		R	0.11	0.44	0.79	1.13	1.47	1.83	2.21	2.60	2.98	3.37				
3	Place ham, cheese and lettuce on bread	t	0.12	0.11	0.14	0.12	0.13	0.13	0.13	0.12	0.14	0.14	1.28	0.128	1.10	0.141
		R	0.23	0.55	0.93	1.25	1.60	1.96	2.34	2.72	3.12	3.51				
4	Place top on sandwich, slice and stack	t	0.10	0.12	0.08	0.09	0.11	0.11	0.10	0.10	0.12	0.10	1.03	0.103	1.10	0.113
		R	0.33	0.67	1.01	1.34	1.71	2.07	2.44	2.82	3.24	3.61				
5		t														
		R														
6		t														
		R														
7		t														
		R														
8		t														
		R														
9		t														
		R														
10		t														
		R														

Normal cycle time 0.387 + Allowance 15% = Std. time 0.445 min.

FIGURE 9.6 Time Study Observation Sheet

Number of Cycles

In Example 9.3 the time study was conducted for ten cycles. However, was this sufficient for us to have confidence that the standard time was accurate? The time study is actually a statistical sample distribution, where the number of cycles is the sample size.

determining the statistically appropriate number of job cycles to study

Assuming that this distribution of sample times is normally distributed (a traditional assumption for time study), we can use the following formula to determine the sample size, n, for a time study:

$$n = \left(\frac{zs}{e\overline{T}}\right)^2$$

where

z = the number of standard deviations from the mean in a normal distribution reflecting a level of confidence

$s = \sqrt{\frac{\sum(x_i - \bar{x})^2}{n-1}}$ = sample standard deviation from the sample time study

$\overline{T}$ = the average job cycle time from the sample time study

e = the degree of error from the true mean of the distribution

EXAMPLE 9.5

Determining the Number of Cycles for a Time Study

Problem Statement:

In Example 9.3 the Metro Food Services Company conducted a time study for ten cycles of a job assembling ham and cheese sandwiches, which we will consider to be a sample. The average cycle time, $\overline{T}$, for the job was 0.361 minutes, and the standard deviation of the sample was 0.03 minutes. The company wants to determine the number of cycles for a time study such that they can be 95 percent confident that the average time computed from the time study is within 5 percent of the true average cycle time.

Solution:

The sample size is computed using $Z = 1.96$ for a probability of 0.95, as follows

$$\begin{aligned} n &= \left(\frac{zs}{e\overline{T}}\right)^2 \\ &= \left[\frac{(1.96)(0.03)}{(0.05)(0.361)}\right]^2 \\ &= 10.61, \text{ or } 11 \end{aligned}$$

The time study should include 11 cycles in order to be 95 percent confident that the time study average job cycle time is within 5 percent of the true average job cycle time. Thus, the ten cycles that were used in our time study were just about right.

Elemental Time Files

In our discussion of time study, we alluded to several of the difficulties associated with conducting time studies. Workers often do not like to be the subject of a time study and will not cooperate, and rating workers can be a difficult, subjective task. In addition, time studies can be very time-consuming and costly. As an alternative, many companies have accumulated large files of time study data over time for elements that are common to many jobs throughout their organization. Instead of conducting an actual time study, these **elemental standard time files** can be accessed to derive the standard time, or the elemental times in the files can be used in conjunction with current time study data, reducing the time and cost required for the study.

Elemental standard time files are predetermined job element times.

However, the use of elemental time files has several disadvantages. It is difficult to put together a standard time in the abstract without the benefit of a time study. The engineer/technician is left wondering if anything was left out or if the environment or job conditions have changed enough since the data were collected to alter the original elemental times. Also, the individuals developing the current standard time must have a great deal of confidence in their predecessor's abilities and competence.

Predetermined Motion Times

The use of elemental standard times from company files is one way to construct a standard time without a time study, or before a task or job is even in effect yet. Another approach for developing time standards without a time study is to use a system of **predetermined motion times.** A predetermined motion time system provides normal times for basic, generic micromotions, such as reach, grasp, move, position, and release, that are common to many jobs. These basic motion times have been developed in a laboratory-type environment from studies of workers across a variety of industries and, in some cases, from motion pictures of workers. As might be guessed, predetermined motion systems were the evolutionary culmination of Frank Gilbreth's micromotion study begun in the early 1900s.

Predetermined motion times are predetermined times for basic micromotions.

In order to develop a standard time using predetermined motion times, a job must be broken down into the basic micromotions just described. Then the appropriate motion time is selected from a set of motion time tables (or a computerized data base), taking into account job conditions such as the weight of an object moved and the distance it might be moved. The standard time is determined by summing all the motion times. As might be suspected, even a very short job can have many motions; a job of only 1 minute can have more than 100 basic motions. As a result, the individual developing the time standard from a predetermined motion time system must be skilled in its use and is generally required to undertake extensive training.

As mentioned, several systems of predetermined motion times exist, the two most well known being methods time measurement (MTM) and basic motion time study (BMT). MTM was developed in the late 1940s and has been used extensively during the last half-century. Table 9.3 provides an example of an MTM table for the motion *move.* The motion times are measured in *time measurement units,* or *TMUs,* where one TMU equals 0.0006 minutes and 100,000 *TMUs* equal one hour.

advantage of predetermined motion times: worker cooperation necessary, workplace uninterrupted, performance ratings unnecessary, consistent

disadvantages of predetermined motion times: ignore job context, may not reflect skills and abilities of local workers, useful for highly repetitive, simple jobs

There are several advantages of using a predetermined motion time system. It enables a standard time to be developed for a new job before the job is even part of the production process. Worker cooperation and compliance are not required, and the workplace and environment is not disrupted. Since performance ratings are included in the motion times, they are not needed, thus eliminating this subjective part of developing standard times. Predetermined motion times are consistent and not subject to as much uncertainty as elemental standard data files.

There are also certain disadvantages with predetermined motion time systems. The use of such a system ignores the job context within which a single motion takes place—that is, where each motion is considered independently of all

TABLE 9.3 MTM Table for MOVE

Distance moved (inches)	Time (TMU)				Weight Allowance			Case and description
	A	B	C	Hand in motion B	Weight (lb) up to:	Dynamic factor	Static constant TMU	
¾ or less	2.0	2.0	2.0	1.7				
1	2.5	2.9	3.4	2.3	2.5	1.00	0	
2	3.6	4.6	5.2	2.9				A. Move object to other hand or against stop.
3	4.9	5.7	6.7	3.6	7.5	1.06	2.2	
4	6.1	6.9	8.0	4.3				
5	7.3	8.0	9.2	5.0	12.5	1.11	3.9	
6	8.1	8.9	10.3	5.7				
7	8.9	9.7	11.1	6.5	17.5	1.17	5.6	
8	9.7	10.6	11.8	7.2				
9	10.5	11.5	12.7	7.9	22.5	1.22	7.4	B. Move object to approximate or indefinite location.
10	11.3	12.2	13.5	8.6				
12	12.9	13.4	15.2	10.0	27.5	1.28	9.1	
14	14.4	14.6	16.9	11.4				
16	16.0	15.8	18.7	12.8	32.5	1.33	10.8	
18	17.6	17.0	20.4	14.2				
20	19.2	18.2	22.1	15.6	37.5	1.39	12.5	
22	20.8	19.4	23.8	17.0				C. Move object to exact location.
24	22.4	20.6	25.5	18.4	42.5	1.44	14.3	
26	24.0	21.8	27.3	19.8				
28	25.5	23.1	29.0	21.2	47.5	1.50	16.0	
30	27.1	24.3	30.7	22.7				
Additional	0.8	0.6	0.85		TMU per inch over 30 in.			

Source: MTM Association for Standards and Research.

others. What the hand comes from doing when it reaches for an object may effect the motion time as well as the overall sequence of motion. Also, although predetermined motion times are generally determined from a broad sample of workers across several industries, they still may not reflect the skill level, training, or abilities of workers in a specific company. Finally, predetermined motion times are useful only for highly repetitive, simple jobs that can be broken down into basic motions. These are job characteristics that, as we explained in an earlier section on job design, are on the wane.

Work Sampling

Teaching Note 9.5 The Origination of Work Sampling

Work sampling is a work measurement technique that does not employ time study or require that the job be broken down into individual elements, or motions. It is a method for determining the proportion of time a worker or machine spends on various activities. The general procedure for work sampling is to make brief, random observations of a worker or machine over a period of time and record the

Work sampling determines the proportion of time a worker spends on activities.

activity in which they are involved. An estimate of the proportion of time that is being spent on an activity is determined by dividing the number of observations recorded for that activity by the total number of observations. For example, a work sample can indicate the proportion of time a worker is busy or idle or performing one task or another or how frequently a machine is idle or in use. A secretary's work can be sampled to determine what portion of the day is spent typing, answering the telephone, filing, and so on. It also can be used to determine the allowance factor that was used to calculate the standard time for a time study. (You will recall that the allowance factor was a percentage of time reflecting worker delays and idle time for machine breakdowns, personal needs, etc.)

analyzing jobs with nonrepetitive tasks

The primary uses of work sampling are to determine *ratio delay,* which is the percentage of time a worker or machine is delayed or idle, and to analyze jobs that have *nonrepetitive tasks*—for example, a secretary, a nurse, or a police officer. The information from a work sample in the form of the percentage of time spent on each job activity or task can be very useful in designing or redesigning jobs, developing job descriptions, and determining the level of work output that can be expected from a worker for use in planning.

The steps in work sampling are summarized as follows.

steps of work sampling

1. *Define the job activities.* The activities that are to be observed must be complete—for example, mutually exclusive and exhaustive—so that any time an observation is made, an activity is clearly indicated. For example, if the activities of interest are "worker idle" and "worker not idle," this clearly defines all possible activities for the work sample.

2. *Determine the number of observations in the work sample.* As we indicated, the purpose of the work sample is to calculate a proportion of time that a worker is performing a specific job activity. The degree of accuracy of the work sample depends on the number of observations, or sample size. The larger the sample size, the more accurate the proportion estimate will be. The accuracy of the proportion, p, is usually expressed in terms of an allowable degree of error, e (for example, 3 or 4 percent), with a degree of confidence of, for example, 95 to 98 percent. Using these parameters and assuming the sample is approximately normally distributed, the sample size can be determined using the following formula:

$$n = \left(\frac{z}{e}\right)^2 p(1-p)$$

where

n = the sample size (number of sample observations)

z = the number of standard deviations from the mean for the desired level of confidence

e = the degree of allowable error in the sample estimate

p = the proportion of time spent on a work activity estimated prior to the work sample

3. *Determine the length of the sampling period.* The length of the work sampling study must be sufficient to record the number of observations for the work activity as determined in Step 2. The observations cannot be taken one after another; the schedule of observations must be random. (If the worker knew that an observation would be taken every half hour, he or she might alter their normal work activity.) The most direct way to achieve randomness is to tie the observation schedule to a table or computer program of random numbers. For example, if a table of three-digit random numbers is used, the first one or two random numbers in the digit could specify the time in minutes between observations. A number of similar schemes are possible for developing a schedule of observations using random numbers.

4. *Conduct the work sampling study and record the observations.* The final step in the work sampling process is the actual study. The observations are tallied and the proportion, p, is computed by dividing the number of activity observations by the total number of observations.

5. *Periodically recompute the number of observations.* Recall from Step 2 that p is actually an estimate of the proportion of time spent on a work activity made prior to the sample. As the work sample is actually conducted it may be discovered that the actual proportion appears to be different than what was originally estimated. Therefore, it is beneficial periodically to recompute the sample size, n, based on preliminary values of p to see if more or less observations are needed than first determined.

EXAMPLE 9.6

Conducting a Work Sampling Study

Problem Statement:

The Northern Lights Company is a retail catalog operation specializing in outdoor clothing. The company has a pool of 28 telephone operators to take catalog orders during the business hours of 9:00 A.M. to 5:00 P.M. (The company uses a smaller pool of operators for the remaining 16 off-peak hours.) The company has recently been experiencing a larger number of lost calls because operators are busy, and they suspect it is because the operators are spending around 30 percent of their time describing products to customers. The company believes that if operators knew more about the products instead of having to pull up a description screen on the computer each time a customer asked a question about a product, they could save a lot of operator time, so they are thinking about instituting a product awareness training program. However, first the company wants to perform a work sampling study to determine the proportion of time operators are answering product-related questions. The company wants the proportion of this activity to be accurate within ± 2 percent, with a 95 percent degree of confidence.

Solution:

The person conducting the work sample must first determine the number of observations to take, as follows:

$$\begin{aligned} n &= \left(\frac{z}{e}\right)^2 pq \\ &= \left(\frac{1.96}{0.02}\right)^2 (0.3)(0.7) \\ &= 2{,}016.84, \quad \text{or} \quad 2{,}017 \end{aligned}$$

This is a large number of observations, however, since there are 28 operators, only 2,017/28, or 72, observation trips need to be taken. Actually, the observations could be made by picking up a one-way phone line to listen in on the operator-customer conversation. The "conversation" schedule was set up using a two-digit random number table (similar to Table S12.2). The random numbers are the minutes between each observation, and since the random numbers ranged from 00 to 99, the average time between observations is about 50 minutes. As such, the study was expected to take about 8 days (with slightly over 9 observations per day).

In fact, after 10 observation trips and a total of 280 observations, the portion of time the operators spent answering the customers' product-related questions was 38 percent, so the random sample size was recomputed,

$$n = \left(\frac{1.96}{0.02}\right)^2 (0.38)(0.62)$$
$$= 2{,}263$$

This number of observations is 246 more than originally computed, or almost 9 additional observation trips, resulting in a total of 81. (As noted previously, it is beneficial periodically to recompute the sample size based on preliminary results in order to ensure that the final result will reflect the degree of accuracy and confidence originally specified.)

Work sampling is a cheaper, easier approach to work measurement.

Work sampling is an easier, less formal approach to work measurement than time study. Because time study is not required, work sampling is usually cheaper, requires less time, and requires less skill and training on the part of the analyst/technician conducting the study. Another distinct advantage of work sampling is that it tends to be less disruptive of the workplace and less annoying to workers, because it requires much less time to sample than time study. Also, the worker is not being timed; that is, the "symbolic" stopwatch is absent. In addition, the worker has less opportunity to affect the results, intentionally or unintentionally. If the worker or something else interrupts the work sampling study, the effect is minimal. However, a disadvantage is the large number of observations required to obtain an accurate sample estimate, sometimes requiring the study to span several days or weeks. There is also much less detail about the job methods and elements; a time study can also be a job study and can often identify a need for job redesign or an irregularity in the work methods that needs correction.

Learning Curves

A **learning curve** illustrates the improvement rate of workers as a job is repeated.

A **learning curve,** or an *improvement curve,* as it is sometimes called, is a graph that reflects the fact that as workers repeat their tasks, they will improve performance. The learning curve effect was introduced in 1936 in an article in the *Journal of Aeronautical Sciences* by T. P. Wright, who described how the direct labor cost for producing airplanes decreased as the number of planes produced increased. This observation and the rate of improvement were found to be strikingly consistent across a number of airplane manufacturers. The basic premise of the learning curve is that improvement occurs because workers learn how to do a job better as they produce more and more units. However, it is generally recognized that other production-related factors also improve performance over time, such as methods analysis and improvement, job redesign, retooling, and worker motivation.

As workers produce more items they become better at their job.

Figure 9.7 illustrates the general relationship defined by the learning curve; as the number of cumulative units produced increases, the labor time per unit decreases. More specifically, the learning curve reflects the fact that each time the number of units produced doubles, the processing time per unit decreases by a constant percentage.

The processing time per unit decreases by a constant percentage each time output doubles.

The decrease in processing time per unit as production doubles will normally range from 10 to 20 percent. The traditional convention is to describe a learning curve in terms of 1 minus the percentage rate of improvement. For example, an 80 percent learning curve describes an improvement rate of 20 percent each time production doubles, a 90 percent learning curve indicates a 10 percent improvement

Transparency 9.9 Learning Curves

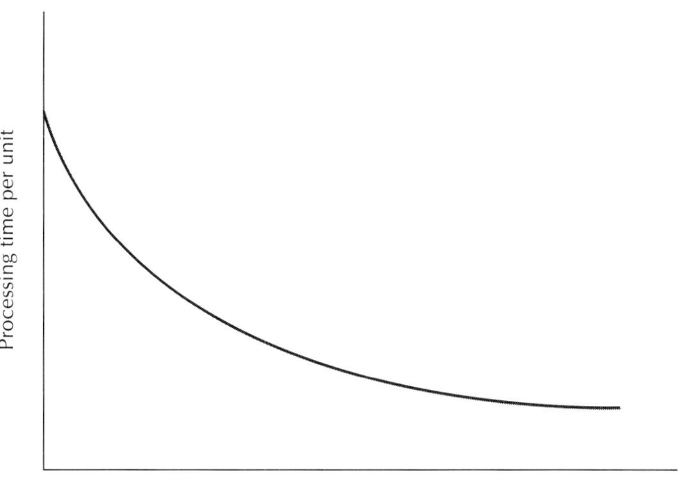

FIGURE 9.7 Learning Curve

rate, and a 100 percent learning curve signifies that no improvement results as production increases.

You will notice that the learning curve in Figure 9.4 is similar to an exponential distribution. The corresponding learning curve formula for computing the time required for the nth unit produced is

$$t_n = t_1 n^b$$

where

t_n = the time required for the nth unit produced
t_1 = the time required for the first unit produced
n = the cumulative number of units produced
b = in r/in 2, where r is the percentage rate of improvement

EXAMPLE 9.7

Determining the Learning Curve Effect

Problem Statement:

Paulette Taylor and Maureen Becker, two undergraduates at State University, produce customized personal computer systems at night in their apartment (hence the name of their enterprise, PM Computer Services). They shop around and purchase cheap components and then put together generic personal computers, which have various special features, for faculty, students, and local businesses. Each time they get an order, it takes them quite a while to assemble the first unit, but they learn as they go along, and they reduce the assembly time as they produce more units. They have recently received their biggest order to date from the statistics department at State for 36 customized personal computers. However, it is near the end of the university's fiscal year, and the computers are needed very quickly in order to charge them on this year's budget. Paulette and Maureen assembled the first unit as a trial and found that it took them 18 hours of direct labor. In order to determine if they can fill the order in the time allotted, they want to apply the learning curve effect to determine how much time the 9th, 18th and 36th units will require to assemble. Based on past experience they believe their learning curve is 80 percent.

Solution:

The time required for the 9th unit is computed using the learning curve formula as follows:

$$
\begin{aligned}
t_n &= t_1 n_b \\
t_9 &= (18)(9)^{\text{in}(0.8)/\text{in } 2} \\
&= (18)(9)^{\text{in}(0.8)/\text{in } 2} \\
&= (18)\ (0.493) \\
&= 8.874 \text{ hr}
\end{aligned}
$$

The time required for the 18th and 36th units are computed similarly:

$$
\begin{aligned}
t_{18} &= (18)(18)^{\text{in}(0.8)/\text{in } 2} \\
&= (18)(0.394) \\
&= 7.092 \text{ hr}
\end{aligned}
$$

and

$$
\begin{aligned}
t_{36} &= (18)(36)^{\text{in}(0.8)/\text{in } 2} \\
&= (18)(0.315) \\
&= 5.67 \text{ hr}
\end{aligned}
$$

Aircraft manufacturers like Boeing shown here have long relied on learning curves for production planning. Learning curves were first recognized in the aircraft industry in 1936 by T.P. Wright. Aircraft production at that time required a very large amount of direct labor for assembley work, thus any marked increases in productivity were clearly recognizable. Based on empirical analysis, Wright discovered that on average when output doubled in the aircraft industry, labor requirements decreased by approximately 20 percent, that is, an 80 percent learning curve. During World War II when aircraft manufacturing proliferated the learning curve became a particularly important tool for planning and an integral part of military aircraft contracts. Studies during these years demonstrated the existence of the learning curve in other industries as well. For example, studies of historical production figures at Ford Motor Company showed productivity improved for the Model T from 1909 to 1926 according to an 86 percent learning curve. The learning curve effect was subsequently shown to exist not only in labor-intensive manufacturing, but also in capital-intensive manufacturing industries such as petroleum refining, steel, paper, construction, electronics and apparel, as well as in clerical operations.

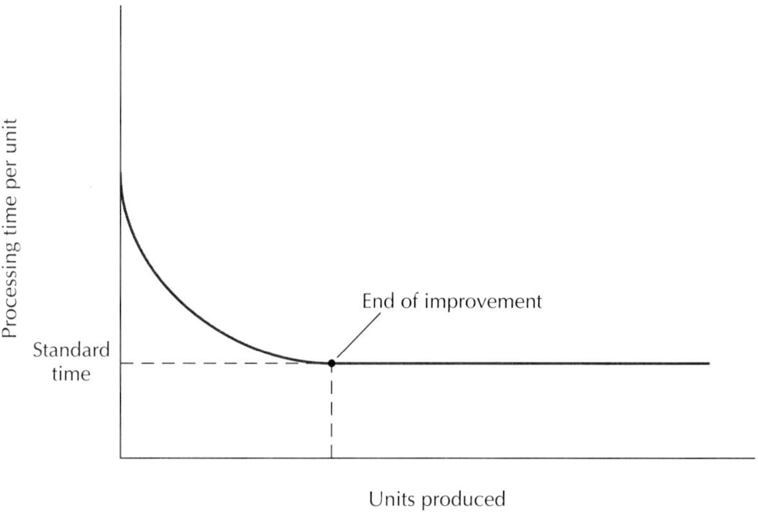

FIGURE 9.8 Learning Curve for Mass Production Job

Learning curves are useful primarily for measuring work improvement for nonrepetitive, complex jobs that require a relatively long time to complete, such as building airplanes. Alternatively, for short, repetitive, and routine jobs, there will be little relative improvement, and it will occur in a brief time span during the first (of many) job repetitions. For that reason, learning curves have limited use for mass production and assembly line-type jobs, although the learning curve can indicate the number of units produced before a standard time is likely to be achieved. A learning curve for this type of operation usually achieves any improvement early in the process and then flattens out and shows virtually no improvement, as reflected in Figure 9.8.

Learning curves are not effective for mass production jobs.

Learning curves have a variety of beneficial uses, chiefly for planning-related functions. They can help managers project labor and budgeting requirements in order to develop production scheduling plans. Knowing how many production labor hours will be required over time can enable managers to determine the number of workers to hire. Also, knowing how many labor hours will eventually be required for a product can help managers make overall product cost estimates to use in bidding for jobs and later for determining the product selling price. However, caution must also be displayed in the use of learning curves. Product modifications during the production process can negate the learning curve effect. As we mentioned at the beginning of this section, improvement can derive from a number of sources besides worker learning that can dramatically alter the conventional learning curve effect, such as modifications of work methods or new equipment. Also, industry-determined improvement rates may not always be applicable for individual companies. For example, if a particular company uses a lot of automated equipment relative to labor and the pace of the production process is determined mostly by equipment (instead of labor), then industry learning rates that were based on a higher ratio of labor to machinery might be misleading.

advantages of learning curves: planning labor, budget, and scheduling requirements

limitations of learning curves: product modifications negate lc effect, improvement can derive from sources besides learning, industry-derived lc rates may be inappropriate

Determining Learning Curves with the Computer

A number of computer software packages are available that have the capability to provide learning curve results and develop the actual learning curves. The AB:POM computer package that we have used elsewhere in this text has such a learning curve module. Exhibit 9.1, on the next page, shows the AB:POM learning curve module using the data from Example 9.7. The program requests the labor time for the first unit, the unit number of the last unit, and the learning coefficient (i.e., the improvement percentage), which results in the output showing the production time and cumulative time for selected units.

Notice that the values for the 9th, 18th, and 36th units are identical to those obtained in Example 9.7, except for a slight difference due to rounding. AB:POM will also generate the actual learning curve for this problem, as shown in Exhibit 9.2.

Transparency 9.10 AB:POM Learning Curves

Experience (learning) Curves — Solution

Example 9.7

		Unit Number	Production Time	Cumulative Time
		1	18.000	18.000
		3*	12.63787	43.27573
		6*	10.11029	73.60661
Labor time for first unit, Y1	18.000	9*	8.873094	100.2259
		12*	8.088235	124.4906
Unit number of last unit, N	36	15*	7.527586	147.0733
		18*	7.098475	168.3688
Learning coefficient	0.800	21*	6.754807	188.6332
		24*	6.470588	208.045
		27*	6.229832	226.7344
		30*	6.022069	244.8006
		33*	5.840099	262.3209
		36*	5.67878	279.3572

*units numbers have been skipped

EXHIBIT 9.1

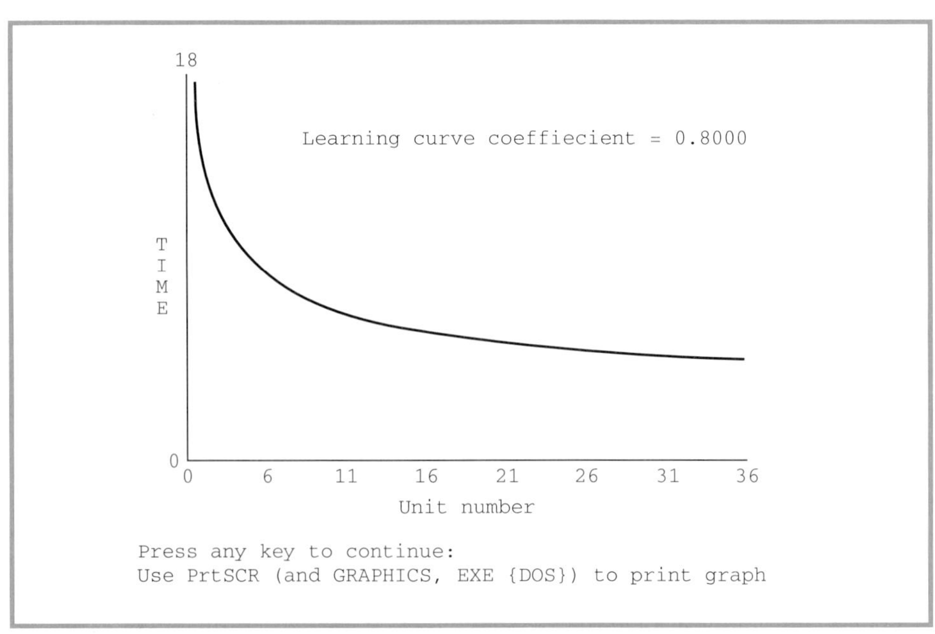

EXHIBIT 9.2

SUMMARY

As has been the case with many other areas in production and operations management, the quality movement and increased international competition have had a dramatic impact on job design and, subsequently, the analysis and measurement of jobs. Traditional approaches to job design in the United States that have focused on task specialization, simplification, and repetition are being supplemented by Japanese approaches that promote higher job skill levels, broader task responsibility, more worker involvement, and, most importantly, worker responsibility for quality. A number of U.S. manufacturing firms have attempted to adapt Japanese work methods, with varying degrees of success, to the extent that service-related industries now more commonly exhibit traditional job approaches than manufacturing.

As the nature of jobs and job design changes, the techniques and approaches to methods analysis and work measurement also change. The primary basis for time study has historically been to establish piece-rate incentive wage systems; however, as such systems are increasingly being perceived as counter to quality improvement efforts, work measurement and time study are being used less and less for that purpose. However, as we have discussed, work measurement techniques are still extremely useful and, many times, necessary for production planning, scheduling, and cost control.

SUMMARY OF KEY FORMULAS

Normal elemental time

$$\mathrm{N}t = (\bar{t})(R\mathrm{F})$$

Normal cycle time

$$\mathrm{NT} = \Sigma \mathrm{N}t$$

Standard job time

$$\mathrm{ST} = (\mathrm{NT})(1 + \mathrm{AF})$$

Time study sample size

$$n = \left(\frac{zs}{e\bar{T}}\right)^2$$

Work sampling sample size

$$n = \left(\frac{z}{e}\right)^2 p(1 \quad p)$$

Learning curve formula

$$t_n = t_1 n^{\mathrm{in}\, r/\mathrm{in}\, 2}$$

SUMMARY OF KEY TERMS

elemental standard time files: company files containing historical data of elemental time studies that can be used to develop a standard time.

empowerment: the authority and responsibility of the workers to alert management about job-related problems.

horizontal job enlargement: the scope of a job that includes all tasks necessary to complete a product or process.

job: a defined set of tasks that comprise the work performed by employees that contributes to the production of a product or delivery of a service.

job motions: basic physical movements that comprise a job element.

job rotation: the capability of workers to move to different jobs.

learning curve: a graph that reflects the improvement rate of workers as a job is repeated and more units are produced.

motion study: the study of the individual human motions used in a job task.

normal time: in a time study, the elemental average time multiplied by a performance rating.

predetermined motion times: normal times for basic, generic micromotions developed by an outside organization in a laboratory-type environment.

process flowchart: a flowchart that illustrates, with symbols, the sequence of steps for a job or how several jobs fit together within the flow of the production process.

standard time: the time required by an average worker to perform one cycle of a job under normal circumstances and conditions.

tasks: individual, defined job activities that consist of one or more elements.

therbligs: a term for the basic physical elements of motion.

vertical job enlargement: the degree of self-determination and control allowed workers over their own work; also referred to as job enrichment.

worker-machine chart: a chart that illustrates on a time scale the amount of time an operator and a machine are working or are idle in a job.

work sampling: a work-measurement technique for determining the proportion of time a worker or machine spends on job activities.

SOLVED PROBLEMS

1. *Standard Job Time*

Problem Statement

An industrial engineer at a manufacturing company has conducted a time study for ten cycles of a job. The job has five elements and the total elemental times (minutes) for each element and performance rating factors are as follows.

Element	Σt *(min)*	*RF*
1	3.61	1.05
2	4.84	0.90
3	2.93	1.00
4	4.91	1.10
5	1.78	0.95

The engineer wants to compute the standard time using an allowance factor of 18 percent.

Solution:

Step 1: Determine the normal elemental times by multiplying the average elemental times by the rating factors.

Element	Σt	$\bar{t}$	RF	Nt
1	3.61	0.361	1.05	0.379
2	4.84	0.484	0.90	0.436
3	2.93	0.293	1.00	0.293
4	4.91	0.491	1.10	0.542
5	1.78	0.178	0.95	0.169

Step 2: Compute the normal cycle time.

$$\begin{aligned} \text{NT} &= \Sigma \text{N}t \\ &= 1.819 \text{ min} \end{aligned}$$

Step 3: Compute the standard time.

$$\begin{aligned} \text{ST} &= \text{NT}\,(1 + \text{AF}) \\ &= 1.819(1 + 0.18) \\ &= 2.146 \text{ min} \end{aligned}$$

2. *Time Study Sample Size*

Problem Statement:

The industrial engineer in the previous problem wants to determine the sample size, n, for a time study so that she is 98 percent confident that the average time computed from the time study is within 4 percent of the actual average cycle time. The sample standard deviation is 0.23.

Solution:

Step 1: Determine the value of z for a probability of 0.98 from the normal table (B.3 in Appendix B) and $\bar{t}$.

$$\begin{aligned} \bar{T} &= \Sigma t = 1.807 \text{ min} \\ z &= 2.33 \end{aligned}$$

Step 2: Compute the sample size.

$$\begin{aligned} n &= \left(\frac{zs}{e\bar{T}}\right)^2 \\ &= \left[\frac{(2.33)(0.23)}{(0.04)(1.807)}\right]^2 \\ &= 54.97, \text{ or } 55 \text{ cycles} \end{aligned}$$

3. *Work Sampling*

Problem Statement:

A technician has been assigned to conduct a work sampling study of a machine maintenance worker to determine the portion of the time the worker spends in one particular department. Management has indicated that they believe that repairs in this department consume 50 percent of the maintenance worker's time, and they want the estimate to be within ±5 percent of the true proportion, with a 95 percent degree of confidence.

Solution:

Determine the number of observations in the sample.

$$n = \left(\frac{z}{e}\right)^2 p(1-p)$$

$$= \left(\frac{1.96}{0.05}\right)^2 (0.5)(0.5)$$

$$= 384.16, \text{ or } 385 \text{ observations}$$

4. Learning Curve

Problem Statement:

A military contractor is manufacturing an electronic component for a weapons system. It is estimated from the production of a prototype unit that 176 hours of direct labor will be required to produce the first unit. The industrial standard learning curve for this type of electronic component is 90 percent. The contractor wants to know the labor hours that will be required for the 144th (and last) unit produced.

Solution:

Determine the time for the 144th unit.

$$t_n = t_1 n^b$$

$$t_{144} = (176)(144)^{\text{in}(0.9)/\text{in } 2}$$

$$= (176)(4.69)$$

$$= 82.69 \text{ hr}$$

QUESTIONS

9-1. Describe the characteristics of job design according to the scientific management approach.

9-2. Describe the contributions of F. W. Taylor and the Gilbreths to job design and analysis and work measurement.

9-3. Explain the difference between horizontal and vertical job enlargement.

9-4. What is the difference between tasks, elements, and motions in a basic job structure?

9-5. How did the development of the assembly line production process at Ford Motor Company popularize the scientific management approach to job design?

9-6. Why were the principles of scientific management not adopted in Japan during the first half of the twentieth century as they were in the United States and other western nations?

9-7. Contrast the Japanese approaches to job design with the traditional U.S. approach based on scientific management.

9-8. What are the advantages of the scientific management approach to job design (specifically, task specialization, simplicity, and repetition) to both management and the worker?

9-9. Describe the primary characteristics of the behavioral approach to job design.

9-10. How has the increased emphasis on quality improvement affected job design in the United States and Japan?

9-11. How successful have companies in the United States been in adapting new trends in job design that mostly have originated in Japan?

9-12. Describe the three major categories of the elements of job design.

9-13. Describe the differences between a process flowchart and a worker-machine chart and what they are designed to achieve.

9-14. Compare the use of predetermined motion times for developing time standards instead of using time study methods and discuss the advantages and disadvantages.

9-15. Describe the steps involved in conducting a time study, and discuss any difficulties you might envision at various steps.

9-16. What are some of the criticisms of work measurement, in general, and time study, specifically, that have caused its popularity to wane in recent years?

9-17. A traditional performance rating benchmark (or guideline) for "normal" effort, or speed, is dealing 52 cards into four piles, forming a square with each pile 1 foot apart, in 0.50 minute. Conduct an experiment with one or more fellow students, where one deals the cards and the others rate the dealer's performance, and then compare these subjective ratings with the actual time of the dealer.

9-18. When is work sampling a more appropriate work-measurement technique than time study?

9-19. Describe the steps involved in conducting a work sample.

9-20. Select a job that you are conveniently able to observe, such as a secretary, store clerk, or custodian, and design a work sampling study for a specific job activity. Indicate how the initial estimate of the proportion of time for the activity would be determined and how the observation schedule would be developed. (However, do not conduct the actual study).

9-21. For what type of jobs are learning curves most useful?

9-22. What does a learning curve specifically measure?

9-23. Discuss some of the uses and limitations of learning curves.

PROBLEMS

9-1. A time study technician at the Southern Textile Company has conducted a time study of a spinning machine operator that spins rough cotton yarn into a finer yarn on bobbins for use in a weaving operation. The time study was requested as the result of a union grievance. The average cycle time for the operator to replace all the full bobbins on the machine with empty bobbins was 3.62 minutes. The technician assigned an overall performance rating for the job of 100 percent, and the allowance factor specified by the union contract is 15 percent. Compute the standard time for this job. **9-1.** ST = 4.163 min

9-2. A sewing operator at the Gameday Sportswear Company assembles baseball-style caps with a team logo from precut wedges of material that form the crown, a precut bill, and additional precut pieces of material for the headband and reinforcing. The job encompasses seven basic elements. A time technician for the company has conducted a time study of the job for 20 cycles and accumulated the following elemental times and assigned performance ratings. ★ **9-2.** ST = 3.25 min

Element	*Σhr t*	*RF*
1	3.15	1.10
2	8.67	1.05
3	14.25	1.10
4	11.53	1.00
5	6.91	0.95
6	5.72	1.05
7	5.38	1.05

Determine the standard time for this job using an allowance factor of 12 percent.

9-3. a. ST = 2.39 min
b. Ave. hourly wage = $4.52; subject hourly wage = $4.82

★ 9-3. The Braykup China Company makes an assortment of gift and commemorative items with team and college logos, such as plates, bowls, and mugs. One popular item is a commemorative stein. The steins are all physically identical, with the only style change being the team colors, name, and logo. The stein parts include a porcelain mug, a hinged pewter top that is opened up when someone drinks from the mug, and a bracket that attaches the top to the mug handle. The bracket is soldered together from two matching parts; on one end, the bracket encircles the handle and the other end attaches to the lid mechanism. The stein is assembled from these parts in one job. A time study chart for this job with the elements of the job and the time observations obtained from a stopwatch time study are as follows.

Time Study Observation Sheet																
Identification of operation		Stein assembly											Date 7/15			
		Operator Smith				Approval Jones							Observer Russell			
		Cycles											Summary			
			1	2	3	4	5	6	7	8	9	10	Σ*t*	$\bar{t}$	*RF*	*Nt*
1	Place mug in vice/ holder upside down	*t*														
		R	0.12	2.05	4.04	5.92	7.86	9.80	11.73	13.65	15.64	17.59			1.05	
2	Press both bracket sides around handle	*t*														
		R	0.19	2.12	4.09	6.01	7.94	9.88	11.81	13.72	15.7	17.66			1.00	
3	Solder bracket seam on inside of handle	*t*														
		R	1.05	3.01	4.91	6.87	8.81	10.71	12.66	14.56	16.52	18.50			1.10	
4	Turn stein right side up	*t*														
		R	1.13	3.08	4.98	6.93	8.90	10.79	12.74	14.66	16.63	18.59			1.10	
5	Solder lid top to bracket	*t*														
		R	1.75	3.76	5.65	7.60	9.56	11.45	13.36	15.34	17.31	19.28			1.05	
6	Remove stein from holder and place in box	*t*														
		R	1.91	3.90	5.79	7.75	9.70	11.61	13.53	15.49	17.46	19.44			1.00	
7		*t*														

a. Using an allowance factor of 15 percent, determine the standard time for this job.

b. If the company pays workers a piece rate of $0.18 per stein, what wage would an average worker make per hour and what would the subject of this time study make per hour?

9-4. a. ST = 0.5148
b. ave. wage = $3.50/hr; subject wage = $3.41/hr

★ 9-4. Puff'n Stuff Services is a small company that assembles mailings for clients in the Atlanta area. Different-size envelopes are stuffed with various items such as coupons, advertisements, political messages, and so on, by a staff of workers, who are paid on a piece-rate basis. A time study of a job has been conducted by an engineering consulting firm using a subject stuffing manila envelopes. The observations from the time study for 10 cycles of the five-element job and the performance rating for each element are given next.

	ELEMENTAL TIMES (MIN)										
ELEMENT	1	2	3	4	5	6	7	8	9	10	RF
1	0.09	0.10	0.12	0.09	0.08	0.07	0.09	0.06	0.10	0.09	1.10
2	0.08	0.09	0.08	0.07	0.10	0.10	0.08	0.06	0.11	0.09	0.95
3	0.15	0.13	0.14	0.16	0.12	0.15	0.16	0.15	0.15	0.14	0.90
4	0.10	0.09	0.09	0.08	0.11	0.08	0.09	0.10	0.10	0.09	1.00
5	0.06	0.05	0.09	0.06	0.07	0.05	0.08	0.05	0.09	0.07	0.95

a. Using an allowance factor of 10 percent, compute the standard time for this job.
b. If the firm pays workers a piece rate of $0.03 per envelope for this job, what would the average worker make per hour, and what would the subject of the study make per hour?

9-5. The Konishi Electronics Company manufacturers computer microchips. A particular job that has been under analysis as part of a quality improvement program was the subject of a time study. The time study encompassed twenty job cycles, and the results include the following cumulative times and performance rating factors for each element.

9-5. a. ST = 4.52 min
b. n = 31 cycles

Element	Σt (min)	RF
1	10.52	1.15
2	18.61	1.10
3	26.20	1.10
4	16.46	1.05

a. Compute the standard time for this job using an allowance factor of 15 percent.
b. Using a sample standard deviation of 0.51 minutes, determine the number of cycles for this time study such that the company would be 95 percent confident that the average time from the time study is within 5 percent of the true average cycle time.

9-6. Data Products, Inc., packages and distributes a variety of personal computer–related products. A time study has been conducted for a job packaging 3.5-inch personal computer diskettes for shipment to customers. The job requires a packager to place 20 diskettes in a rectangular plastic bag, close the bag with a twist tie, and place the filled bag into a bin, which is replaced by another worker when it is filled. The job can be broken into four basic elements. The following elemental times (in minutes) were obtained from the time study for ten job cycles.

★ 9-6. a. ST = 2.13 min
b. n = 9 cycles

	ELEMENTAL TIMES										
ELEMENT	1	2	3	4	5	6	7	8	9	10	RF
1	0.36	0.31	0.42	0.35	0.38	0.30	0.41	0.42	0.35	0.35	1.05
2	0.81	0.95	0.76	0.85	1.01	1.02	0.95	0.90	0.87	0.88	0.90
3	0.56	0.38	0.42	0.45	0.51	0.48	0.50	0.52	0.39	0.46	1.00
4	0.19	0.12	0.16	0.21	0.15	0.16	0.18	0.19	0.19	0.15	1.05

a. Using an allowance factor of 16 percent, determine the standard time for this job.

b. Determine the number of cycles for this time study such that the company would be 95 percent confident that the average time from the time study is within ±4 percent of the true average cycle time.

9-7. $n = 12.2$ cycles

9-7. In Problem 9-2, a time study was conducted for the job of sewing baseball-style caps. Using a sample standard deviation of 0.25, determine the number of cycles for the time study such that the company would be 98 percent confident that the average cycle time for the job is within 6 percent of the actual average cycle time.

9-8. $n = 3$ cycles

9-8. Determine the sample size for the time study of the stein assembly operation described in Problem 9-3. The Braykup China Company wants to be 95 percent confident that the average cycle time from the study is within 2 percent of the true average.

9-9. a. ST = 1.383 min
b. $n = 8$ cycles
c. May reduce quality

★ 9-9. Sonichi Electronics manufacturers small electronic consumer items such as portable clocks, calculators, and radios. The company is concerned about the high cost of their product-inspection operation. As a result they had their industrial engineering department conduct a time study of an inspector who inspects portable radios. The operation consists of seven elements, as follows: 1. The package is opened and the radio is removed, 2. the battery casing cover is removed, 3. two AA batteries are inserted, 4. the radio is turned on, and the inspector turns the station-selector dial and listens briefly to at least two stations, 5. the radio is turned off and the batteries are removed, 6. the battery cover is replaced, and 7. the radio is repackaged. The time study observations (in minutes) for ten cycles are shown in the following table.

	ELEMENTAL TIMES										
ELEMENT	*1*	*2*	*3*	*4*	*5*	*6*	*7*	*8*	*9*	*10*	*RF*
1	0.23	0.20	0.19	0.20	0.18	0.18	0.24	0.25	0.17	0.20	1.05
2	0.12	0.10	0.08	0.09	0.10	0.10	0.13	0.14	0.10	0.11	1.00
3	0.16	0.18	0.17	0.17	0.17	0.20	0.16	0.15	0.18	0.18	1.05
4	0.26	0.28	0.32	0.19	0.35	0.33	0.22	0.28	0.28	0.27	0.95
5	0.10	0.08	0.09	0.10	0.11	0.11	0.09	0.12	0.12	0.12	1.00
6	0.06	0.08	0.08	0.08	0.07	0.06	0.10	0.08	0.09	0.11	1.05
7	0.20	0.28	0.25	0.36	0.17	0.22	0.33	0.19	0.20	0.16	1.05

a. The allowance factor for this job is 15 percent. Determine the standard time.
b. If management wants the estimate of the average cycle time to be within ±0.03 minute with a 95 percent level of confidence, how many job cycles should be observed?
c. Management is considering putting inspectors on a piece-rate wage system in order to provide them with greater incentive to inspect more items. What affect might this have on the quality inspection function?

9-10. $n = 1{,}843$, or 62 trips

9-10. Baker Street Stereo is a catalog ordering operation. The company maintains an ordering staff of 30 telephone operators, who take orders from customers. Management wants to determine the proportion of time that operators are idle. A work sampling study was conducted at random over a 4-day period, and the following random observations were recorded.

Observation		*Operators Idle*	*Observation*		*Operators Idle*
10/15:	1	6		11	4
	2	5	10/17:	12	7
	3	4		13	3
	4	7		14	3
	5	5		15	6
	6	2		16	5
10/16:	7	4		17	7
	8	3		18	4
	9	5	10/19:	19	5
	10	6		20	6

If management wants the proportion of time from the work sampling study to be ±2 percent accurate with a confidence level of 98 percent, how many additional sample observations should be taken?

9-11. The associate dean of the college of business at Tech has succumbed to faculty pressure to purchase a new fax machine, although she has always contended that the machine would have minimal use. She has estimated that the machine will be used only 20 percent of the time. Now that the machine has been installed, she has asked the students in the introductory POM course to conduct a work sampling study to see what proportion of time the new fax machine is used. She wants the estimate to be within 3 percent of the actual proportion, with a confidence level of 95 percent. Determine the sample size for the work sample.

9-11. $n = 683$ observations

9-12. The Rowntown Cab Company has 26 cabs. The local manager wants to conduct a work sampling study to determine what proportion of the time a cab driver is sitting idle, which he estimates is about 30 percent. The cabs were observed at random during a 5-day period by the dispatcher, who simply called each cab and checked on its status. The manager wants the estimate to be within ±3 percent of the actual proportion, with a 95 percent level of confidence.

9-12. a. $n = 897$ observations
b. $n = 580$ observations

a. Determine the sample size for this work sampling study.
b. The results of the first twenty observations of the work sampling study are shown as follows.

Observation	*Idle Cabs*	*Observation*	*Idle Cabs*
1	4	11	6
2	3	12	4
3	5	13	3
4	8	14	5
5	7	15	2
6	5	16	0
7	3	17	3
8	6	18	4
9	4	19	5
10	3	20	4

What is the revised estimate of the sample size based on these initial results?

9-13. a. 88.8%
b. n = 451, so 151 additional observations are needed.

9-13. The head of the department of management at State University has noticed that the four secretaries in the departmental office seem to spend a lot of time answering questions from students that could better be answered by the college advising office, by faculty advisors, or simply from the available literature, that is, course schedules, catalogs, the student handbook, and so on. As a result the department head is considering remodeling the office with cubicles so students do not have easy access to the secretaries. However, before investing in this project the head has decided to conduct a work sampling study to determine the proportion of time the secretaries spend assisting students. The head arranged for a graduate assistant to make observations for the work sample, but the graduate student's schedule enabled her to make only 300 random observations in the time allotted for the study. The results of the work sampling study showed that the secretaries assisted students 12 percent of the time, somewhat less than the head anticipated.

a. Given the number of observations that were included in the work sampling study, how confident can the department head be that the sample result is within 3 percent of the actual proportion?
b. How many fewer or additional observations would be required for the department head to be 95 percent confident in the work sampling results?

9-14. $n = 914$, so 814 additional observations are needed.

9-14. In Problem 9-11, the POM students have completed 100 observations of the work sampling study and have a preliminary result showing the fax machine is in use 31 percent of the time. How many additional observations are required based on this result?

9-15. ST = 3.946 min/call

9-15. Northwoods Backpackers is a catalog ordering operation specializing in outdoor camping and hiking equipment and clothing. In addition to its normal pool of telephone operators to take customer orders, the company has a group of customer service operators to respond to customer complaints and product-related inquiries. The time required for customer service operators to handle customer calls differs, based on an operator's ability to think fast and quickly recall from memory product information (without using product description screens on the computer). The company wants to determine the standard time required for a customer service operator to complete a call without having to resort to a time study. Instead, management had a work sampling study of an operator conducted during an 8-hour workday that included 160 observations. The study showed the operator was talking to customers only 78 percent of the time, and call records indicated that the operator handled 120 customer calls during the day. The customer service manager has indicated that the particular operator that was studied performs at about 110 percent compared to a normal operator. Company policy allows 15 percent personal time on the job for lunch, breaks, and so on. Determine the standard time per customer call.

9-16. 77.75%; $n = 413$, so 253 additional observations are needed.

★ 9-16. In Problem 9-15 how confident can Northwoods Backpackers be in the standard time they computed if they assumed that the proportion of time that an operator is busy determined from the work sampling study is accurate within ±4 percent? How many additional observations might be needed for them to be 95 percent confident in the standard time per customer call?

9-17. $t_{60} = 32.92$ hr, $t_{120} = 27.99$ hr

9-17. Nite-Site, Inc., manufactures image intensification devices used in products such as night-vision goggles and aviator's night-vision imaging systems. The primary customer for these products is the U.S. military. The military requires that learning curves be employed in the bid process for awarding military contracts. The company is planning to make a bid for 120 image intensifiers to be used in a military vehicle. The company estimates the first unit will require 86 hours of direct labor to produce. The industry learning curve for this particular type of product is 85 percent. Determine how many hours will be required to produce the 60th and 120th units.

9-18. Jericho Vehicles manufactures special-purpose all-terrain vehicles primarily for the military and government agencies in the United States and for foreign governments. The company is planning to bid on a new all-terrain vehicle specially equipped for desert military action. The company has experienced an 80 percent learning curve in the past for producing similar vehicles. Based on a prototype model, they estimate the first vehicle produced will require 1,600 hours of direct labor. The order is for 60 all-terrain vehicles. Determine the time that will be required for the 30th and 60th units.

9-18. t_{30} = 535.29 hr, t_{60} = 428.23 hr

9-19. Jericho Vehicles is considering making a bid for a mobile rocket-launching system for the U.S. military. However, the company has almost no experience in producing this type of vehicle. In an effort to develop a learning curve for the production of this new mobile weapon system, management has called contacts from several former competitors who went bankrupt. Although management could not obtain direct learning curve rates, it did learn from one contact that for a system with similar features, the first unit required 2,200 hours of direct labor to produce and the 30th and final unit required 810 hours to produce. Determine the learning curve rate for this vehicle.

★ **9-19.** 0.8158

9-20. PM Computer Services (described in Example 9.7) has received an order for 120 specially configured personal computers for a local business. Paulette and Maureen have so many orders that they can no longer perform the work themselves, and they must hire extra labor to assemble the units for this new order. They have hired 8 students from the university to work part time, 20 hours per week, to assemble the computers. Paulette and Maureen assembled a prototype unit and it required 26 hours of direct labor; from experience they know their computer assembly operation has an 84 percent learning curve. Approximately when will PM Services be able to deliver the completed order?

★ **9-20.** 7.38 weeks

CASE PROBLEM

Measuring Faculty Work Activity at State University

See Solutions Manual.

At several recent meetings of the faculty senate at State University, one of the primary agenda items has been discussion of various media reports that college faculty are more concerned about their research than about teaching and, specifically, that faculty don't spend enough time working with students, which should be their main task. These media reports also imply that faculty work only during the time they are in class, which for most faculty is between 6 and 12 hours per week. The faculty believes this information is very misleading and potentially dangerous to higher education in general. The faculty representatives on the senate claim that the time they spend in class is only a small portion of their actual workload, and although they spend some amount of time on their research, they also dedicate a very large portion of their time outside of class to class preparation and meeting with students. Unfortunately, few people outside of the faculty appear to believe this argument, including—most prominently—the students, parents, certain legislators, and, recently, even several highly placed university administrators.

In an attempt to educate the students more about what faculty actually do with their time, the senate invited several student leaders to one of its meetings, where they discussed the issue. Among the students invited to this meeting was Mary Shipley, editor of *The Daily State*, the student newspaper. Subsequently Mary wrote an editorial in the paper about how faculty members spent their time.

Mary was a student in the college of business at State; coincidentally, the topic currently under discussion in her production and operations management class was "Job Design and Work Measurement." The day after her editorial appeared, she was asked the following question in her class by a fellow student, Art Cohen.

"Mary, it looks like to me that all you did in your editorial was repeat what you had been told by the faculty at the faculty senate meeting. I don't really believe you have any idea about what faculty do, anymore than the rest of us!"

Before Mary could respond, another student, Angela Watts broke in, "Well it shouldn't be too hard to check out. That's what we are studying in class right now—how to measure work. Why don't we check out how much time the faculty work at different tasks?"

At this point their teacher, Dr. Larry Moore, broke into the discussion. "That's a good idea, Angela. It sounds like to me as if you just resolved our problem of a class project for this term. I'm going to break you all into teams and let each team monitor a specific faculty member, using work sampling to determine the amount of time the faculty member spends with students outside of the classroom."

"That's not really going to provide any relevant information," interrupted Bobby Jenkins. "That will just provide us with a percentage of time faculty work with students. If a professor spends 90 percent of his or her time working with students, that sounds great, but if they are only in their office 2 hours a day, 90 percent of 2 hours is not very much."

"I see what you mean," Dr. Moore replied. "That's a good point. Somehow we need to determine how many hours a day a faculty member devotes to his or her job in order to have a frame of reference."

"The way it looks to me, a professor works only about 3 or 4 hours a day," said Rodney Jefferson. This drew general laughter from the class and Dr. Moore.

"I don't think that's really true," responded Mary Shipley. "One of the things the faculty pointed out to me and I indicated in my editorial was that even though faculty members may not be in their offices all the time, they may still be working, either at home or in the library. And a lot of times they have committee work at various locations around campus." A lot of the class seemed to be in general agreement with this. "Anyway," Mary continued, "I don't think the issue with which we are really concerned is how much a professor works. I believe we all agree that they probably put in a full 7- or 8-hour day like almost anyone else. The point as I see it is, what do they do with that time? Do they spend it all on their own research and writing or are they working with students?"

"Okay then," said Dr. Moore. "If we can all agree that the number of hours of work is a moot point, then let's set up our work sampling experiment as follows. We'll break down the activities outside of classroom teaching as 'working with students,' or 'not working with students,' which could include anything else the faculty member is working on, such as research, making out tests, preparing for class, and so on. That should be all-inclusive. What proportion of time do you think a faculty member spends with students outside the classroom, to use a starting point? Ten percent? Twenty percent?"

The class seemed to mull this over for a few minutes and someone shouted from the back of the room, "20 percent." Someone else said 30 percent, and after a few seconds people were simply talking back and forth.

"Okay, okay," said Dr. Moore, "everyone calm down. Let's say 20 percent. That sounds like a reasonable number to me, and you can always adjust it in the course of your experiment. Let's allow for an error of 3 percent and use a confidence level of 95 percent. Does this sound okay to everybody?" He waited a few moments for any negative reaction, but there seemed to be general agreement.

"Good, I'll post teams on my office door by tomorrow, and I'll let each team select the faculty member they want to study. Let me know by the end of the week and I'll alert the faculty members so they will know what to expect. Also, it's possible someone might not want to participate, and I'll let you know that too so you can select someone else. Please be as unobtrusive as possible and try not to bother anybody. Okay, if there are no other questions, that's it. Get busy."

Describe how you would set up this work sampling experiment at your school, and, if your teacher is agreeable, carry out this project. Also, describe how you might alter the work sample to analyze other faculty work activities.

REFERENCES

Barnes, R. M., *Motion and Time Study: Design and Measurement of Work,* 8th ed., New York: John Wiley, 1980.
Belkaoui, A., *The Learning Curve,* Westport, Conn.: Quorum Books, 1986.
Emerson, H. P., and D.C.E. Maehring, *Origins of Industrial Engineering,* Atlanta, Ga.: Institute of Industrial Engineers, 1988.
Gilbreth, F., *Motion Study,* New York: D. Van Nostrand Co., 1911.
Knights, D., H. Willmott, and D. Collinson, eds., *Job Redesign: Critical Perspectives on the Labor Process,* Hants, England: Gower, 1985.
Mundel, M. E., *Motion and Time Study: Improving Productivity,* 6th ed., Englewood Cliffs, N.J.: Prentice Hall, 1985.
Smith, G. L., Jr., *Work Measurement: A Systems Approach,* Columbus, Ohio: Grid Publishing, 1978.
Taylor, F. W., *The Principles of Scientific Management,* New York: Harper and Brothers, 1911.
Wood, S., ed., *The Transformation of Work,* London: Unwin Hyman, 1989.

10
FORECASTING

CHAPTER OUTLINE

American Airlines jets at the airline's Dallas/Fort Worth hub. American Airlines forecasts everything from airplane parts to passengers. An accepted airline practice is overbooking on flights, that is, setting rseservation levels higher than aircraft capacity in order to compensate for passenger cancellations and no-shows. Overbooking allows airlines to significantly reduce the number of empty seats on its flights it might experience otherwise. A key factor in setting the correct number of overbookings so that passengers will not have to be bumped because there are no seats, is an accurate forecast of passenger demand.

FORCASTING AIRCRAFT PARTS DEMAND AT AMERICAN AIRLINES

To support the operation of its fleet of more than 400 aircraft, American Airlines must maintain an extensive inventory of expendable and repairable (rotatable) parts. Although expendable parts are of low value and are discarded when replaced, rotatable parts are of much higher value (i.e., an average price of $5,000); thus, maintaining an adequate inventory is costly. American Airlines has an inventory of more than 5,000 different types of rotatable parts, including such items as landing gear, wing flaps, altimeters, and coffee makers. Rotatable parts are allocated to different airports based upon anticipated demand. The airline developed the rotatables allocation and planning system (RAPS) to manage the inventory of rotatable parts. Critical components of RAPS are forecasts of expected demand for total parts across all airports and for demand at each individual airport. The forecast for total system demand is calculated using linear regression, which establishes the relationship between monthly parts usage and monthly flying hours. Each month the system updates an 18-month history of parts usage and flying hours using the most recent month's data. The process of generating the forecast using linear regression is completely automated, requiring only a few hours. It is estimated that RAPS has provided a one-time savings of $7 million and a recurring annual savings of almost $1 million.[1]

Teaching Note 10.1 Use of Forecasting

A forecast is a prediction of what will occur in the future. Meteorologists forecast the weather, sportscasters and gamblers predict the winners of football games, and

[1]Tedone, M. J., "Repairable Part Management," *Interfaces* 19, no. 4 (July–August 1989): 61–68.

managers of business firms attempt to predict how much of their product will be desired in the future. In fact, a forecast of product demand is the basis for most important management planning decisions. Production planning decisions regarding scheduling, inventory, process, facility layout and design, work force, material purchasing, and so on, are functions of how much the company plans to produce to meet customer demand. Financial planning decisions include the establishment of budgets and capital expenditures that will support the demand driven production process. Long-range, strategic plans by top management are based on forecasts of the type of products consumers will demand in the future and the size of the product markets.

Forecasting is a precarious and uncertain endeavor. It is not possible to predict consistently what the future will be, even with the help of a crystal ball and a deck of tarot cards. Thus, management generally hopes to forecast demand with as much accuracy as possible, which is becoming increasingly difficult to do. In the current international business environment, consumers have more product choices and more information on which to base choices. They also demand and receive greater product diversity, made possible by rapid technological advances. This makes forecasting products and product demand more difficult. Consumers and markets have never been stationary targets, but they are moving more rapidly now than they ever have before.

Management sometimes uses **qualitative** methods based on judgment, opinion, past experience, or simply best guesses, to make forecasts. However, a number of **quantitative** forecasting methods are also available to aid management in making planning decisions. In this chapter we discuss two of the traditional types of mathematical forecasting methods, time series analysis and regression, as well as several nonmathematical, qualitative approaches to forecasting. Although, as we mentioned, no technique will result in a totally accurate forecast, these methods can provide reliable guidelines and a degree of accuracy in making decisions.

Qualitative forecast methods are based on mathematical formulas; **quantitative forecast methods** are subjective methods.

FORECASTING AND QUALITY MANAGEMENT

Accurate forecasting has always been an important operational function for companies. However, it is even more crucial in a total quality management (TQM) environment, for several reasons. TQM does not simply mean providing a good-quality product, it also means quality customer service. More and more, customers are perceiving good quality service to mean having a product when they demand it. This holds true for manufacturing firms as well as service companies. When a customer walks into a McDonald's to order a meal, they do not expect to have to wait long to place their order. They expect McDonald's to have the item they want, and they expect to receive their order within a short period of time. To the customer all these service characteristics relate to quality. Forecasting is an important aspect of all of these characteristics. An accurate forecast of customer traffic flow and product demand enables McDonald's to schedule enough servers, to stock enough food, and to schedule food production to provide high-quality service. An inaccurate forecast causes service to break down, resulting in poor quality. Similar service characteristics are present for manufacturing operations, especially for suppliers. Customers expect parts to be provided when demanded. Accurately forecasting customer demand is a crucial part of providing the high-quality service that complements a high-quality product.

Forecasting customer demand is an important factor in providing quality customer service.

Many companies have adopted the just-in-time (JIT) approach to inventory management as part of their TQM program. The two naturally complement each other. JIT is basically an inventory system wherein parts or materials are not provided at a stage in the production process until they are needed. This procedure eliminates the need for buffer inventory, which, in turn, reduces both waste and inventory costs, a primary goal of TQM. In order for JIT to work, there must be a smooth, uninterrupted process flow with no defective items. Traditionally inventory was held at in-process stages to compensate for defects, but with TQM the goal is to eliminate defects, thus obviating the need for inventory. Accurate forecasting is critical for a company that adopts both JIT and TQM. It is especially important for suppliers of TQM companies that use JIT. The supplier is expected to be able to provide parts and materials rapidly as they are needed. Failure to meet these expectations violates the principles of TQM and is perceived as poor-quality service, which, as we mentioned, is as undesirable as a poor-quality product. As this discussion implies, TQM requires a finely tuned, efficient production process, with no defects, minimal or no inventory, and no waste. In this way costs are reduced. Accurate forecasting is essential for maintaining this type of process. If poor-quality information is provided for product demand, the entire TQM system functions less efficiently.

JIT requires accurate forecasting to be successful.

Forecasting that is not related to product demand is also very important for TQM companies. A critical function in the TQM approach is product design. A basic principle of TQM is that the company must understand the customer. It must know what the customer wants and needs in a product and the level of quality that is expected. As such, forecasting the type of products that customers will want in the future, what features these products should possess, and how much of the products will be demanded are very important considerations in the product-design process. Accurate forecasts of customer wants and needs provide a company with an important competitive edge. This competitive edge is reflected in the product design, which is the stage where quality is first built into the product. Product design subsequently determines process design and what kinds of new equipment and technologies will be required to meet design requirements. This makes the accurate forecasting of new technologies an important function as well.

Forecasting the quality features that customers want in products is an important part of TQM.

Forecasting product demand, new product features, and new products and technologies are examples of *reactive* forecasting. In other words, the company reacts to predictions about the future to meet demand or design new products. Alternatively, the purpose of forecasting is sometimes *proactive*. The company might use a forecast to develop a plan to influence demand, such as an advertising or media campaign to increase demand for a product. Letting customers know about product quality and making the customer aware of product value—that is, the features and quality provided for the cost—are important areas in the TQM approach. For proactive forecasting, the company uses a forecast to evaluate markets, assess potential demand, and determine the amount of advertising and the marketing effort required to educate customers about their products.

In general, forecasting is an important piece of the information flow that a TQM program needs to be successful. In TQM all operational and support functions in a company are dedicated to continuous quality improvement. Similarly, forecasting is a major component of the planning process that impacts on all of these same functions.

Transparency 10.1 Components of Forecasting Demand

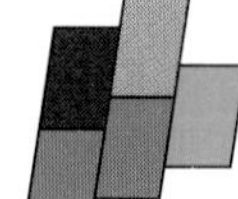

COMPONENTS OF FORECASTING DEMAND

The type of forecasting method depends on time frame, demand behavior, and causes of behavior.

The type of forecasting method to use depends on several factors including the time frame of the forecast (i.e., how far in the future is being forecasted), the *behavior* of demand, and the possible existence of patterns (trends, seasonality, etc.), and the *causes* of demand behavior. We discuss each of those factors separately.

Time Frame

Teaching Note 10.2 Forecasting Terminology

In general, forecasts can be classified according to three **time frames:** short-range, medium-range, and long-range.

The **time frame** indicates how far into the future one is forecasting.

Short-range forecasts typically encompass the immediate future. They are concerned with the daily operations of a company, dictated by daily or weekly demand such as production scheduling and resource requirements. A short-range forecast rarely goes beyond a couple of months into the future.

A **short-range forecast** is one encompassing the immediate future.

A **medium-range forecast** typically encompasses anywhere from 1 or 2 months to two years. A forecast of this length is normally used by management to develop such things as an annual production plan or an annual budget or the development of a project or program, such as the development of a new production line or the implementation of a quality circle program.

A **medium-range forecast** encompasses from 1 to 2 months up to 2 years.

A **long-range forecast** usually spans a period longer than 2 years. This type of forecast is normally used by management for strategic planning. It might include planning new products for changing markets, entry into new markets, the development of new production facilities, or the long-term implementation of a new program, such as a quality management program. In general, the further into the future management seeks to predict, the more difficult forecasting becomes.

A **long-range forecast** encompasses a period of time longer than 2 years.

These classifications should be considered as generalizations. The line of demarcation between short-, medium-, and long-range forecasts is often quite arbitrary and not always distinct. For some companies a medium-range forecast could be several years, and for other firms a long-range forecast could be in terms of months. The classification of a forecast depends to a large extent on how rapidly the product market changes and how susceptible the market is to technological changes.

Demand Behavior

Demand sometimes behaves in a random, irregular fashion, with no apparent patterns. However, it often exhibits predictable behavior, reflected by trends or repetitive patterns in which it is hoped the forecast will reflect. The three primary types of demand movement are *trends, cycles,* and *seasonal patterns.*

A **trend** is a gradual, long-term up or down movement of demand. For example, the demand for personal computers has generally followed an upward trend during the last few decades, without any sustained downward movement in the market. Trends are the easiest patterns of demand behavior to detect and are often the starting points for developing forecasts. Figure 10.1(a) illustrates a demand trend in which there is a general upward movement, or increase. Notice that Figure 10.1(a) also includes several random movements up and down. **Random variations** are movements that are not predictable and follow no pattern (and thus are virtually unpredictable).

A **trend** is a gradual, long-term up or down movement of demand.

Random variations are movements in demand that do not follow a pattern.

A **cycle** is an undulating movement in demand, up and down, that repeats itself over a lengthy time span (i.e., more than a year). For example, new housing starts and, thus, construction-related products tend to follow cycles in the economy. Automobile sales tend to follow cycles in the same fashion. The demand for winter sports equipment increases every four years before and after the Winter Olympics. Figure 10.1(b) shows the general behavior of a demand cycle.

A **cycle** is an up-and-down repetitive movement in demand.

A **seasonal pattern** is an oscillating movement in demand that occurs periodically (in the short run) and is repetitive. Seasonality is often weather related. For example, every winter the demand for snowblowers and skis increases dramatically, and retail sales in general increase during the holiday season. However, a seasonal pattern can occur on a daily or weekly basis. For example, some restaurants are busier at lunch than at dinner, and shopping mall stores and theaters tend to have higher demand on weekends. Figure 10.1(c) illustrates a

A **seasonal pattern** is an up-and-down repetitive movement in demand trend occurring periodically.

Transparency 10.2 Forms of Forecast Movement

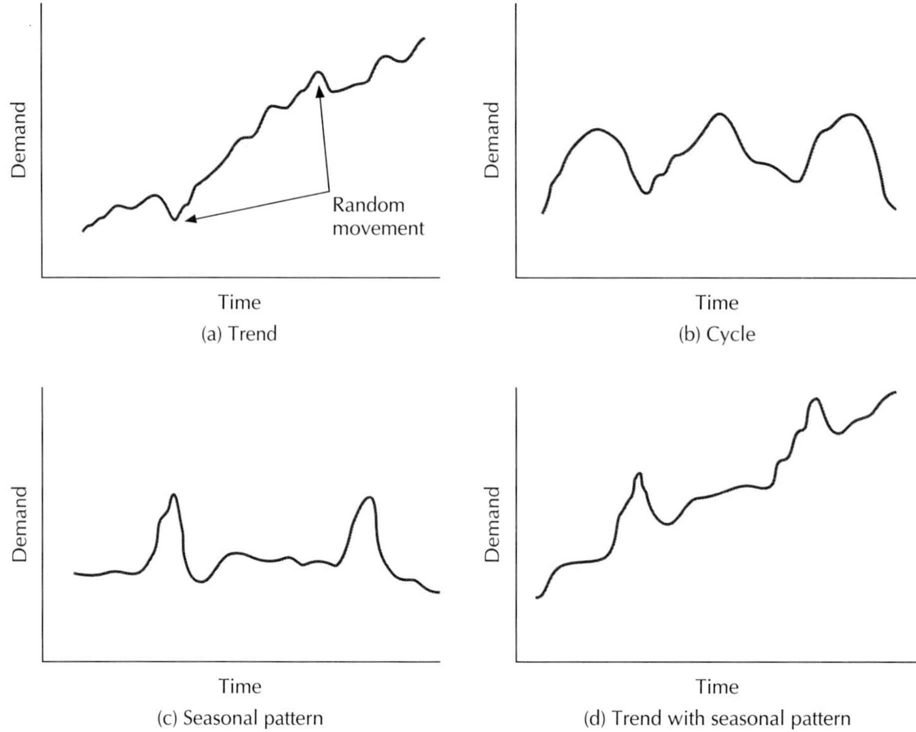

FIGURE 10.1 Forms of Forecast Movement

seasonal pattern in which the same demand behavior is repeated each year at the same time.

Of course, demand behavior frequently displays several of these characteristics simultaneously. Although housing starts display cyclical behavior, there has been an upward trend in new house construction over the years. As we noted, demand for skis is seasonal, however, there has been a general upward trend in the demand for winter sports equipment during the past two decades. Figure 10.1(d) displays the combination of two demand patterns, a trend with a seasonal pattern.

There are instances when demand behavior exhibits no pattern. These are referred to as *irregular movements,* or variations. For example, a local flood might cause a momentary increase in carpet demand, or negative publicity resulting from a lawsuit might cause product demand to drop for a period of time. Although this behavior is causal and, thus, not totally random, it still does not follow a pattern that can be reflected in a forecast.

Forecasting Methods

types of methods: time series, casual, and qualitative.

Causal forecasting methods relate demand to other factors that cause demand behavior.

The factors discussed previously in this section determine to a certain extent the type of forecasting method that can or should be used. In this chapter we are going to discuss the basic types of forecasting: *time series, causal methods,* and *qualitative methods.* Time series methods are statistical techniques that use historical demand data to predict future demand. **Causal forecasting methods** attempt to develop a mathematical relationship (in the form of a regression model) between demand and factors that cause it to behave the way it does. Qualitative methods employ managerial judgment, expertise, and opinions to make forecasts. Although all these types of forecasting methods can be used for any time frame, time series is most often used for short- and medium-range forecasts, whereas qualitative methods are frequently used for medium- and long-range forecasting. We begin our discussion of these methods with time series.

The Forecasting Process

Forecasting is not simply identifying and using a quantitative method to compute a numerical estimate of what demand will be in the future. Instead, it is a continuing process that requires constant monitoring and adjustment. The general steps in this process are illustrated in Figure 10.2.

Forecasting is a process that is continuous.

In the next few sections we present several different forecasting methods that are applicable for different patterns of demand behavior. Thus, one of the first steps in the forecasting process is to plot the available historical demand data and, by visually looking at it, attempt to determine the forecasting method that best

Transparency 10.3 The Forecasting Process

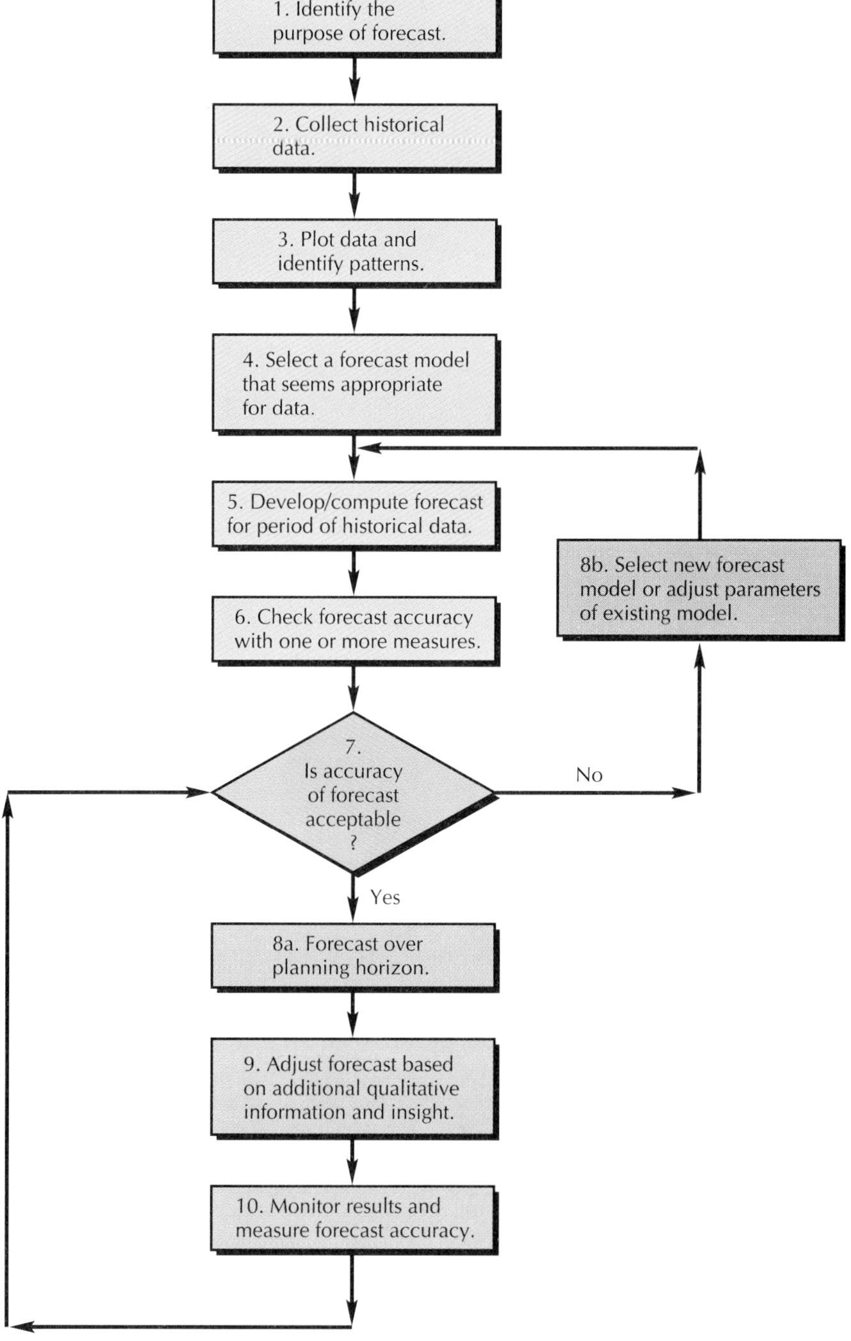

FIGURE 10.2 Steps of the Forecasting Process

seems to fit the patterns the data exhibits. Historical demand data often is simply past sales data; true product demand is usually not available. Once a method has been identified, there are several measures available for comparing the historical data with the forecast to see how accurate the forecast is. Following our discussion of the forecasting methods, we present several measures of forecast accuracy. If the forecast does not seem to be particularly accurate, another method can be tried until an accurate forecast method is identified. After the forecast is made over the desired planning horizon, it may be possible for the operations manager or analyst to use judgment, experience, knowledge of the market, or even intuition to adjust the forecast to enhance further its accuracy. Finally, as demand actually occurs over the planning period, it must be monitored and compared with the forecast in order to assess the performance of the forecast method. If the forecast is accurate, then it is appropriate to continue using the forecast method. If it is not accurate, then consideration must be given to selecting a new model or adjusting the existing one. As we proceed through the various forecasting methods and measures of accuracy in the following sections, it will be beneficial to keep this continuing process, as illustrated in Figure 10.2, in mind.

TIME SERIES METHODS

Time series methods use historical demand data over a period of time to predict future demand.

Teaching Note 10.3 Forecasting Techniques Used in This Chapter

Time series methods are statistical techniques that make use of historical data accumulated over a period of time. Time series methods assume that what has occurred in the past will continue to occur in the future. As the name time series suggests, these methods relate the forecast to only one factor—time. They tend to be most useful for short-range forecasting, although they can be used for longer-range forecasting. They are also some of the most popular and widely used forecasting techniques.

Moving Average

Transparency 10.4 Moving Average Forecasts

A time series forecast can be as simple as using demand in the current period to predict demand in the next period. For example, if demand is 100 units this week, the forecast for next week's demand would be 100 units; if demand turned out to be 90 units instead, then the following week's demand would be 90 units, and so on. However, this type of forecasting method does not take into account any type of historical demand *behavior;* it relies only on demand in the current period. As such, it reacts directly to the normal, random, and down movements in demand.

The **moving average** method uses average demand for a fixed sequence of periods.

Moving average is good for stable demand with no pronounced behavioral patterns.

Alternatively, the simple **moving average** method uses several demand values during the recent past to develop a forecast. (As we mentioned before, past sales is often used as a surrogate for demand.) This tends to *dampen,* or *smooth out,* the random increases and decreases of a forecast that uses only one period. As such, the simple moving average is particularly useful for forecasting demand that is relatively stable and does not display any pronounced demand behavior, such as a trend or seasonal pattern.

Moving averages are computed for specific periods, such as three months or five months, depending on how much the forecaster desires to "smooth" the demand data. The longer the moving average period, the smoother it will be. The formula for computing the simple moving average is as follows:

$$MA_n = \frac{\sum_{i=1}^{n} D_i}{n}$$

where

n = number of periods in the moving average
D_i = demand in period i

EXAMPLE 10.1
Computing a Simple Moving Average

Teaching Note 10.4 Data Collection

Alternate Example 10.1

Problem Statement:
The Instant Paper Clip Office Supply Company sells and delivers office supplies to various companies, schools, and agencies within a 50-mile radius of its warehouse. The office supply business is extremely competitive, and the ability to deliver orders promptly is an important factor in getting new customers and keeping old ones. (Offices typically order not when they run low on supplies, but when they completely run out. As a result, they need their orders immediately.) The manager of the company wants to be certain that enough drivers and delivery vehicles are available so that orders can be delivered promptly and they have adequate inventory in stock. Therefore, the manager wants to be able to forecast the number of orders that will occur during the next month (i.e., to forecast the demand for deliveries).

From records of delivery orders, management has accumulated the following data for the past 10 months, from which it wants to compute 3- and 5-month moving averages.

Month	*Orders*
January	120
February	90
March	100
April	75
May	110
June	50
July	75
August	130
September	110
October	90

Solution:
For this example we are assuming that it is presently the end of October. The forecast resulting from either the 3- or the 5-month moving average is typically for the next month in the sequence, which in this case is November. The moving average is computed from the demand for orders for the last 3 months in the sequence according to the following formula:

$$\begin{aligned} MA_3 &= \frac{\sum_{i=1}^{3} D_i}{3} \\ &= \frac{90 + 110 + 130}{3} \\ &= 110 \text{ orders} \end{aligned}$$

The 5-month moving average is computed from the last 5 months of demand data as follows:

$$MA_5 = \frac{\sum_{i=1}^{5} D_i}{5}$$

$$= \frac{90 + 110 + 130 + 75 + 50}{5}$$

$$= 91 \text{ orders}$$

The 3- and 5-month moving averages for all the months of demand data are shown in the table below. Notice that we have computed forecasts for all the months. Actually, only the forecast for November based on the most recent monthly demand would be used by the manager. However, the earlier forecasts for prior months allow us to compare the forecasting with actual demand to see how accurate the forecasting method is—that is, how well it does.

Three- and Five-Month Averages

Month	*Orders per Month*	*Three-Month Moving Average*	*Five-Month Moving Average*
January	120	—	—
February	90	—	—
March	100	—	—
April	75	103.3	—
May	110	88.3	—
June	50	95.0	99.0
July	75	78.3	85.0
August	130	78.3	82.0
September	110	85.0	88.0
October	90	105.0	95.0
November	—	110.0	91.0

Both moving average forecasts in Table 10.1 tend to smooth out the variability occurring in the actual data. This smoothing effect can be observed in the following figure in which the 3-month and 5-month averages have been superimposed on a graph of the original data. The extremes in the actual orders per month have been reduced. This is beneficial if these extremes simply reflect random fluctuations in orders per month, since our moving average forecast will not be strongly influenced by them.

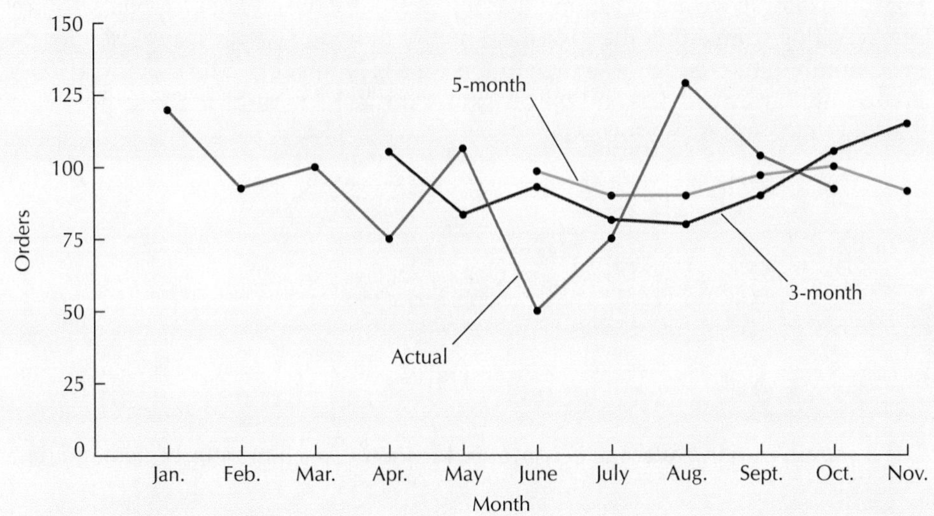

Notice that the 5-month moving average in the figure on page 492 smooths out fluctuations to a greater extent than the 3-month moving average. However, the 3-month average more closely reflects the most recent data available to the office supply manager. (The 5-month average forecast considers data back to June; the 3-month average goes back only to August.) In general, forecasts computed using the longer-period moving average are slower to react to recent changes in demand than would those made using shorter-period moving averages. The extra periods of data dampen the speed with which the forecast responds. Establishing the appropriate number of periods to use in a moving average forecast often requires some amount of trial-and-error experimentation.

Longer-period moving averages react more slowly to recent demand changes than shorter-period moving averages.

One additional point to mention relates to the period of the forecast. Sometimes a forecaster will need to forecast for a short planning horizon rather than just a single period. For both the 3- and 5-month moving average forecasts computed in Example 10.1 and shown in the accompanying table, the final forecast is for one period only in the future. Since the moving average includes multiple periods of data for each forecast and it is most often used to forecast in a stable demand environment, it would be appropriate to use the forecast for multiple periods in the future. It could then be updated as actual demand data become available.

Teaching Note 10.5 The Moving Average

The major disadvantage of the moving average method is that it does not react well to variations that occur for a reason, such as trends and seasonal effects (although this method does reflect trends to a moderate extent). Those factors that cause changes are generally ignored. It is basically a "mechanical" method, which reflects historical data in a consistent fashion. However, the moving average method does have the advantage of being easy to use, quick, and relatively inexpensive, although moving averages for a substantial number of periods for a lot of different items can result in the accumulation and storage of a large amount of data. In general, this method can provide a good forecast for the short run, but no attempt should be made to push the forecast too far into the distant future.

Weighted Moving Average

The moving average method can be adjusted to more closely reflect fluctuations in the data. This adjusted method is referred to as a **weighted moving average** method. In this method, weights are assigned to the most recent data according to the following formula:

In the **weighted moving average,** weights are assigned to the most recent data.

$$WMA_n = \sum_{i=1}^{n} W_i D_i$$

where

W_i = the weight for period i, between 0 and 100 percent.

$\sum W_i = 1.00$

EXAMPLE 10.2

Computing a Weighted Moving Average

Problem Statement:

The Instant Paper Clip Company in Example 10.1 wants to compute a 3-month weighted moving average with a weight of 50 percent for the October data, a weight of 33 percent for the September data, and a weight of 17 percent for the August data.

Solution:
The weighted moving average is computed as

$$\begin{aligned} WMA_3 &= \sum_{i=1}^{3} W_i D_i \\ &= (0.50)(90) + (0.33)(110) + (0.17)(130) \\ &= 103.4 \text{ orders} \end{aligned}$$

Notice that the forecast includes a fractional part, 0.4. Since 0.4 orders would be impossible, this number appears to be unrealistic. In general, the fractional parts need to be included in the computation to achieve mathematical accuracy, but when the final forecast is achieved, it must be rounded up or down.

This forecast is slightly lower than our previously computed 3-month average forecast of 110 orders, reflecting the lower number of orders in October (the most recent month in the sequence).

Determining the precise weights to use for each period of data frequently requires some trial-and-error experimentation, as does determining the exact number of periods to include in the moving average. If the most recent periods are weighted too heavily, the forecast might overreact to a random fluctuation in demand. If they are weighted too lightly, the forecast might underreact to actual changes in demand behavior.

Transparency 10.5 Exponential Smoothing Forecasts

Exponential smoothing is an averaging method that reacts more strongly to recent changes in demand.

Exponential Smoothing

The **exponential smoothing** forecasting technique is also an averaging method that weights the most recent past data more strongly. As such, the forecast will react more to immediate changes in the data. This is very useful if the recent changes in the data are the results of an actual change (e.g., a seasonal pattern) instead of just random fluctuations (for which a simple moving average forecast would suffice).

Exponential smoothing is one of the more popular and frequently used forecasting techniques, for a variety of reasons. Unlike moving averages, which can require a large amount of historical data, exponential smoothing requires minimal data. Only the forecast for the current period, the actual demand for the current period, and a weighting factor called a smoothing constant are necessary. Manual computation is simple, and the mathematics of the technique are easy to understand by management. However, virtually all POM and forecasting computer software packages include modules for exponential smoothing. Most importantly, exponential smoothing has a good track record of success. It has been employed over the years by many companies that have found it to be an accurate method of forecasting.

The exponential smoothing forecast is computed using the formula

$$F_{t+1} = \alpha D_t + (1 - \alpha)F_t$$

where

F_{t+1} = the forecast for the next period
D_t = actual demand in the present period
F_t = the previously determined forecast for the present period
α = a weighting factor referred to as the **smoothing constant**

A **smoothing constant** is the weighting factor given to the most recent data in exponential smoothing forecasts.

The smoothing constant, α, is between 0.0 and 1.0. It reflects the weight given to the most recent demand data. For example, if $\alpha = 0.20$,

$$F_{t+1} = 0.20D_t + 0.80F_t$$

which means that our forecast for the next period is based on 20 percent of recent demand (D_t) and 80 percent of past demand (in the form of the forecast F_t, since F_t is derived from previous demands and forecasts). If we go to one extreme and let $\alpha = 0.0$, then

$$F_{t+1} = 0D_t + 1F_t$$
$$= F_t$$

and the forecast for the next period is the same as for this period. In other words, *the forecast does not reflect the most recent demand at all.*

On the other hand, if $\alpha = 1.0$, then

$$F_{t+1} = 1D_t + 0F_t$$
$$= 1D_t$$

and we have considered only the most recent occurrence in our data (demand in the present period) and nothing else. Thus, we can conclude that the higher α is, the more sensitive the forecast will be to changes in recent demand, and the smoothing will be less. Alternatively, the closer α is to zero, the greater will be the dampening, or smoothing, effect. As α approaches zero, the forecast will react and adjust more slowly to differences between the actual demand and the forecasted demand. The most commonly used values of α are in the range 0.01 to 0.50. However, the determination of α is usually judgmental and subjective and is often based on trial-and-error experimentation. An inaccurate estimate of α can limit the usefulness of this forecasting technique.

The closer α is to 1.0, the greater the reaction to the most recent demand.

EXAMPLE 10.3

Alternate Example 10.2

Computing an Exponentially Smoothed Forecast

Problem Statement:

PM Computer Services assembles customized personal computers from generic parts. As was mentioned in a previous example, the company was formed and is operated by two part-time State University students, Paulette Tyler and Maureen Becker, and has had steady growth since it started. The company assembles computers mostly at night, using other part-time students for labor. Paulette and Maureen purchase generic computer parts in volume at discount from a variety of sources whenever they see a good deal. As such, it is important that they develop a good forecast of demand for their computers so that they will know how many computer component parts to purchase and stock.

The company has accumulated the demand data shown in the accompanying table for its computers for the past 12 months, from which it wants to compute exponential smoothing forecasts using smoothing constants (α) equal to 0.30 and 0.50.

Demand for Personal Computers

Period	*Month*	*Demand*
1	January	37
2	February	40
3	March	41
4	April	37
5	May	45
6	June	50
7	July	43
8	August	47
9	September	56
10	October	52
11	November	55
12	December	54

Solution:

In order to develop the series of forecasts for the data in the table on page 495, we will start with period 1 (January) and compute the forecast for period 2 (February) using $\alpha = 0.30$. The formula for exponential smoothing also requires a forecast for period 1, which we do not have, so we will use the demand for period 1 as both *demand* and *forecast* for period 1. Other ways to determine a starting forecast include averaging the first three or four periods or making a subjective estimate. Thus, the forecast for February is

$$\begin{aligned} F_2 &= \alpha D_1 + (1 - \alpha)F_1 \\ &= (0.30)(37) + (0.70)(37) \\ &= 37 \text{ units} \end{aligned}$$

The forecast for period 3 is computed similarly:

$$\begin{aligned} F_3 &= \alpha D_2 + (1 - \alpha)F_2 \\ &= (0.30)(40) + (0.70)(37) \\ &= 37.9 \text{ units} \end{aligned}$$

The remainder of the monthly forecasts are shown in the following table. The final forecast is for period 13, January, and is the forecast of interest to PM Computer Services:

$$\begin{aligned} F_{13} &= \alpha D_{12} + (1 - \alpha)F_{12} \\ &= (0.30)(54) + (0.70)(50.84) \\ &= 51.79 \text{ units} \end{aligned}$$

Exponential Smoothing Forecasts, α = .30 and α = .50

			Forecast, F_{t+1}	
Period	*Month*	*Demand*	$\alpha = 0.30$	$\alpha = 0.50$
1	January	37	—	—
2	February	40	37.00	37.00
3	March	41	37.90	38.50
4	April	37	38.83	39.75
5	May	45	38.28	38.37
6	June	50	40.29	41.68
7	July	43	43.20	45.84
8	August	47	43.14	44.42
9	September	56	44.30	45.71
10	October	52	47.81	50.85
11	November	55	49.06	51.42
12	December	54	50.84	53.21
13	January	—	51.79	53.61

This table also includes the forecast values using $\alpha = 0.50$. Both exponential smoothing forecasts are shown in Figure 10.3 together with the actual data.

In Figure 10.3, the forecast using the higher smoothing constant, $\alpha = 0.50$, reacts more strongly to changes in demand than does the forecast with $\alpha = 0.30$, although both smooth out the random fluctuations in the forecast. Notice that both forecasts lag behind the actual demand. For example, a pronounced downward change in demand in July is not reflected in the forecast until August. If these changes mark a change in trend (i.e., a long-term upward or downward movement) rather than just a random fluctuation, then the forecast will always lag behind this trend. We can see a general upward trend in delivered orders throughout the year. Both forecasts tend to be consistently lower than the actual demand; that is, the forecasts lag the trend.

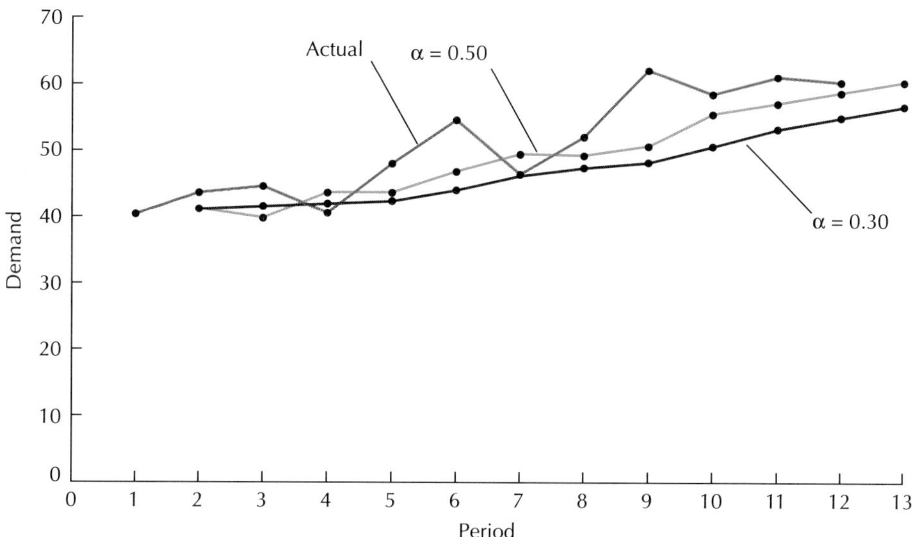

FIGURE 10.3 Exponential Smoothing Forecasts

Based on simple observation of the two forecasts in Figure 10.3, $\alpha = 0.50$ seems to be the more accurate of the two in the sense that it seems to follow the actual data more closely. (Later in this chapter we discuss several quantitative methods for determining forecast accuracy.) In general, when demand is relatively stable without any trend, a small value for α is more appropriate to simply smooth out the forecast. Alternatively, when actual demand displays an increasing (or decreasing) trend, as is the case in the figure, a larger value of α is generally better. It will react more quickly to the more recent upward or downward movements in the actual data. In some approaches to exponential smoothing, the accuracy of the forecast is monitored in terms of the difference between the actual values and the forecasted values. If these differences become larger, then α is changed (higher or lower) in an attempt to adapt the forecast to the actual data. However, the exponential smoothing forecast can also be adjusted for the effects of a trend.

As we noted with the moving average forecast, the forecaster sometimes needs a forecast for more than one period into the future. In Example 10.3, the final forecast computed was for 1 month, January. A forecast for 2 or 3 months could have been computed by grouping the demand data into the required number of periods and then using these values in the exponential smoothing computations. For example, if a 3-month forecast were needed, demand for January, February, and March could be summed and used to compute the forecast for the next 3-month period, and so on, until a final 3-month forecast results. Alternatively, if a trend is present the final period forecast can be used for an extended forecast by adjusting it by a trend factor.

Adjusted Exponential Smoothing

The **adjusted exponential smoothing** forecast consists of the exponential smoothing forecast with a trend adjustment factor added to it. The formula for the adjusted forecast is

An **adjusted exponential smoothing forecast** is an exponential smoothing forecast with an adjustment for a trend added to it.

$$AF_{t+1} = F_{t+1} + T_{t+1}$$

where

β = a smoothing constant for trend
T = an exponentially smoothed trend factor

The closer β is to 1.0, the stronger a trend is reflected.

Teaching Note 10.6 Selecting α and β

As is α, β is a value between 0.0 and 1.0. It reflects the weight given to the most recent trend data. Also, β is often determined subjectively based on the judgment of the forecaster, as is α. A high β reflects trend changes more than a low β. It is not uncommon for β to equal α in this method.

The trend factor is computed much the same as the exponentially smoothed forecast. It is, in effect, a forecast model for trend.

$$T_{t+1} = \beta(F_{t+1} - F_t) + (1 - \beta)T_t$$

where

$$T_t = \text{the last period's trend factor}$$

Notice that this formula for the trend factor reflects a weighted measure of the increase (or decrease) between the current forecast, F_{t+1}, and the previous forecast, F_t.

Alternate Example 10.3

EXAMPLE 10.4

Computing an Adjusted Exponentially Smoothed Forecast

Problem Statement:

PM Computer Services (Example 10.3), now wants to develop an adjusted exponentially smoothed forecast using the same 12 months of demand shown in the table on page 495. They will use the exponentially smoothed forecast with $\alpha = 0.5$ computed in Example 10.3 with a smoothing constant for trend, β, of 0.30.

Solution:

The formula for the adjusted exponential smoothing forecast requires an initial value for T_t to start the computational process. This initial trend factor is most often an estimate determined subjectively or based on past data by the forecaster. In this case, since we have a relatively long sequence of demand data (i.e., 12 months) we will start with the trend, T_t, equal to zero. By the time the forecast value of interest, F_{13}, is computed, we should have a relatively good value for the trend factor.

The adjusted forecast for February, AF_2, is the same as the exponentially smoothed forecast, since the trend computing factor will be zero (i.e., F_1 and F_2 are the same and $T_2 = 0$). Thus, we compute the adjusted forecast for March, AF_3, as follows, starting with the determination of the trend factor, T_3:

$$\begin{aligned} T_3 &= \beta(F_3 - F_2) + (1 - \beta)T_2 \\ &= (0.30)(38.5 - 37.0) + (0.70)(0) \\ &= 0.45 \end{aligned}$$

and

$$\begin{aligned} AF_3 &= F_3 + T_3 \\ &= 38.5 + 0.45 \\ &= 38.95 \end{aligned}$$

This adjusted forecast value for period 3 is shown in the accompanying table, with all other adjusted forecast values for the 12-month period plus the forecast for period 13, computed as follows.

$$\begin{aligned} T_{13} &= \beta(F_{13} - F_{12}) + (1 - \beta)T_{12} \\ &= (0.30)(53.61 - 53.21) + (0.70)(1.77) \\ &= 1.36 \end{aligned}$$

and

$$\begin{aligned} AF_{13} &= F_{13} + T_{13} \\ &= 53.61 + 1.36 \\ &= 54.96 \text{ units} \end{aligned}$$

Adjusted Exponential Smoothing Forecast Values

Period	Month	Demand	*Forecast* F_{t-1}	*Trend* T_{t+1}	*Adjusted Forecast* AF_{t+1}
1	January	37	37.00	—	—
2	February	40	37.00	0.00	37.00
3	March	41	38.50	0.45	38.95
4	April	37	39.75	0.69	40.44
5	May	45	38.37	0.07	38.44
6	June	50	41.68	1.04	42.73
7	July	43	45.84	1.97	47.82
8	August	47	44.42	0.95	45.37
9	September	56	45.71	1.05	46.76
10	October	52	50.85	2.28	53.13
11	November	55	51.42	1.76	53.19
12	December	54	53.21	1.77	54.98
13	January	—	53.61	1.36	54.96

The adjusted exponentially smoothed forecast values shown in the table are compared with the exponentially smoothed forecast values and the actual data in the figure below. Notice that the adjusted forecast is consistently higher than the exponentially smoothed forecast and is thus more reflective of the generally increasing trend of the actual data. However, in general, the pattern, or degree of smoothing, is very similar for both forecasts.

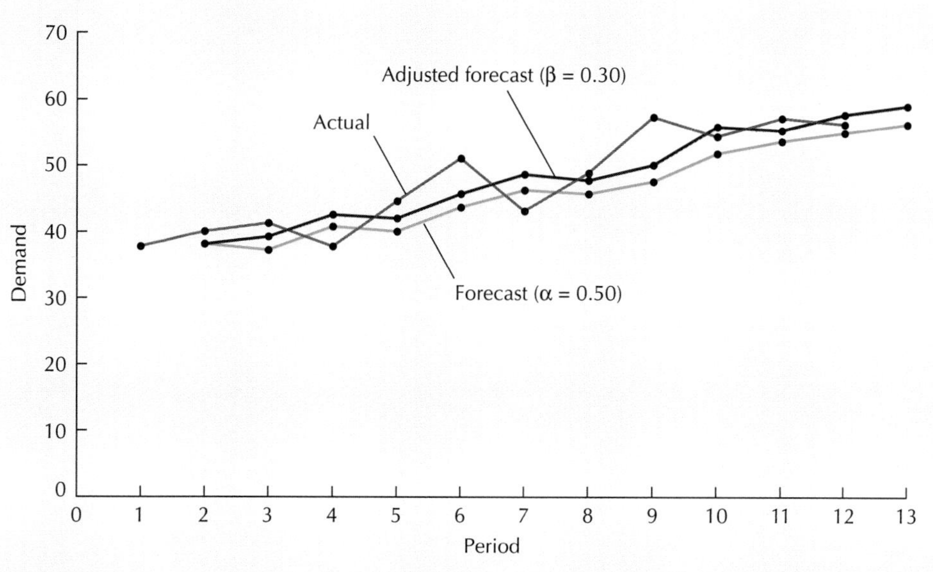

Linear Trend Line

Transparency 10.6 Linear Trend Line

Linear regression is most often thought of as a causal method of forecasting in which a mathematical relationship is developed between demand and some other factor that causes demand behavior. However, when demand displays an obvious trend over time, a least squares regression line, or **linear trend line,** can be used to forecast demand.

A **linear trend line** is a linear regression model relating demand to time.

A linear trend line relates a dependent variable, which for our purposes is demand, to one independent variable, time, in form of a linear equation:

$$y = a + bx$$

where

$$a = \text{intercept (at period 0)}$$
$$b = \text{slope of the line}$$
$$x = \text{the time period}$$
$$y = \text{forecast for demand for period } x$$

These parameters of the linear trend line can be calculated using the least squares formulas for linear regression,

$$b = \frac{\sum xy - n\bar{x}\bar{y}}{\sum x^2 - n\bar{x}^2}$$

$$a = \bar{y} - b\bar{x}$$

where

$$n = \text{number of periods}$$

$$\bar{x} = \frac{\sum x}{n}$$

$$\bar{y} = \frac{\sum y}{n}$$

Alternate Example 10.4

EXAMPLE 10.5

Computing a Linear Trend Line

Problem Statement:

The demand data for PM Computer Services (shown in the table for Example 10.3) appears to follow an increasing linear trend. As such, the company wants to compute a linear trend line as an alternative to the exponential smoothing and adjusted exponential smoothing forecasts developed in Examples 10.3 and 10.4.

Solution:

The values that are required for the least squares calculations are shown in the accompanying table.

Least Squares Calculations

x *(period)*	y *(demand)*	xy	x^2
1	37	37	1
2	40	80	4
3	41	123	9
4	37	148	16
5	45	225	25
6	50	300	36
7	43	301	49
8	47	376	64
9	56	504	81
10	52	520	100
11	55	605	121
12	54	648	144
78	557	3,867	650

Using these values for $\bar{x}$ and $\bar{y}$ and the values from the table, the parameters for the linear trend line are computed as follows,

$$\bar{x} = \frac{78}{12} = 6.5$$

$$\bar{y} = \frac{557}{12} = 46.42$$

$$b = \frac{\Sigma xy - n\bar{x}\bar{y}}{\Sigma x^2 - n\bar{x}^2}$$

$$= \frac{3{,}867 - (12)(6.5)(46.42)}{650 - 12(6.5)^2}$$

$$= 1.72$$

$$a = \bar{y} - b\bar{x}$$

$$= 46.42 - (1.72)(6.5)$$

$$= 35.2$$

Therefore, the linear trend line is

$$y = 35.2 + 1.72x$$

In order to calculate a forecast for period 13, $x = 13$ is substituted in the linear trend line:

$$y = 35.2 + 1.72(13)$$
$$= 57.56$$

The figure below shows the linear trend line in comparison to the actual data. The trend line appears to reflect closely the actual data—that is, to be a "good fit"—and would thus be a good forecast model for this problem. However, a disadvantage of the linear trend line is that it will not adjust to a change in the trend, as the exponential smoothing forecast methods will; that is, it is assumed that all future forecasts will follow a straight line. This limits the use of this method to a shorter time frame in which you can be relatively certain that the trend will not change.

A linear trend line will not adjust to a change in trend as will exponential smoothing.

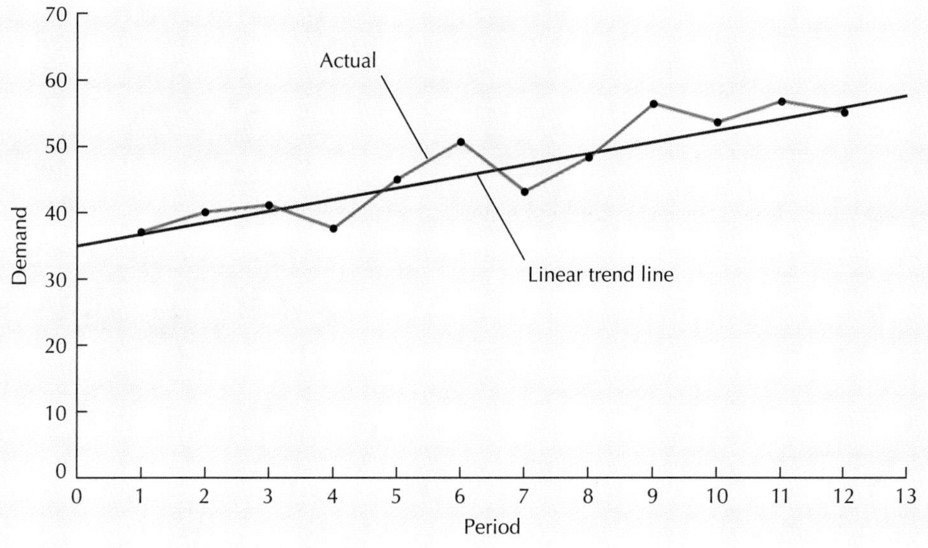

Seasonal Adjustments

As we mentioned at the beginning of this chapter, a seasonal pattern is a repetitive up-and-down movement in demand. Many demand items exhibit seasonal behavior. Clothing sales follow annual seasonal patterns, with demand for warm clothes increasing in the fall and winter and declining in the spring and summer as the demand for cooler clothing increases. Demand for many retail items, including toys, sports equipment, clothing, electronic appliances, hams, turkeys, wine, and fruit, increase during the holiday season. Greeting card demand increases in conjunction with various special days, such as Valentine's Day and Mother's Day. Seasonal patterns can also occur on a monthly, weekly, or even a daily basis. Some restaurants have higher demand in the evening time than at lunch or on weekends as opposed to weekdays. Traffic—and hence sales—at shopping malls picks up on Friday and Saturday.

There are several methods available for reflecting seasonal patterns in a time series forecast. In this section we will describe one of the simpler methods using a *seasonal factor.* A **seasonal factor** is a numerical value that is multiplied by the normal forecast in order to get a seasonally adjusted forecast.

Adjusting for seasonality by multiplying the normal forecast by a **seasonal factor.**

One method for developing a demand for seasonal factors is to divide the actual demand for each seasonal period by total annual demand, according to the following formula:

$$S_i = \frac{D_i}{\Sigma D}$$

The resulting seasonal factors between 0 and 1.0 are, in effect, the portion of total annual demand assigned to each season. These seasonal factors are thus multiplied by the annual forecasted demand to yield seasonally adjusted forecasts for each period.

Snow skiing is an industry that exhibits several different patterns of demand behavior. It is primarily a seasonal (i.e., winter) industry, thus any forecasts of the demand for skiing-related products and services should include a seasonal adjustment. In addition, over a long period of time the snow skiing industry has exhibited a generally increasing growth trend. As such, the technique used to forecast demand for skiing products and services should also include an adjustment for trend, as well as a seasonal adjustment. Other, more random factors, can cause variations, or abrupt peaks and valleys, in demand. For example, demand for skiing products showed a pronounced increase after the success of the U.S. ski team in the 1994 Winter Olympics in Lilliehammer, Norway. Conversely, warm weather and a lack of snow in some regions of the U.S. during several winters in the late 1980s and early 1990s depressed the skiing industry resulting in decreased product demand.

EXAMPLE 10.6

Computing a Forecast with Seasonal Adjustments

Problem Statement:

Wishbone Farms grows turkeys, which it sells to a meat-processing company throughout the year. However, their peak season is obviously during the fourth quarter of the year, from October to December. Wishbone Farms has experienced the demand for turkeys for the past 3 years shown in the accompanying table.

Demand for Turkeys at Wishbone Farms

	DEMAND (1,000s) PER QUARTER				
Year	*1*	*2*	*3*	*4*	*Total*
1991	12.6	8.6	6.3	17.5	45.0
1992	14.1	10.3	7.5	18.2	50.1
1993	15.3	10.6	8.1	19.6	53.6
Total	42.0	29.5	21.9	55.3	148.7

Solution:

Because we have three years of demand data, we can compute the seasonal factors by dividing total quarterly demand for the three years by total demand across all three years.

$$S_1 = \frac{D_1}{\sum D} = \frac{42.0}{148.7} = 0.28$$

$$S_2 = \frac{D_2}{\sum D} = \frac{29.5}{148.7} = 0.20$$

$$S_3 = \frac{D_3}{\sum D} = \frac{21.9}{148.7} = 0.15$$

$$S_4 = \frac{D_4}{\sum D} = \frac{55.3}{148.7} = 0.37$$

Next, we want to multiply the forecasted demand for the next year, 1994, by each of the seasonal factors to get the forecasted demand for each quarter. However, in order to accomplish this, we need a demand forecast for 1994. In this case, since the demand data in the table seem to exhibit a generally increasing trend, we compute a linear trend line for the three years of data in the table to get a rough forecast estimate.

$$\begin{aligned} y &= 40.97 + 4.30x \\ &= 40.97 + 4.30(4) \\ &= 58.17 \end{aligned}$$

Thus, the forecast for 1994 is 58.17, or 58,170 turkeys.

Using this annual forecast of demand, the seasonally adjusted forecasts, SF_i, for 1994 are

$$\begin{aligned} SF_1 &= (S_1)(F_5) = (0.28)(58.17) = 16.28 \\ SF_2 &= (S_2)(F_5) = (0.20)(58.17) = 11.63 \\ SF_3 &= (S_3)(F_5) = (0.15)(58.17) = 8.73 \\ SF_4 &= (S_4)(F_5) = (0.37)(58.17) = 21.53 \end{aligned}$$

Comparing these quarterly forecasts with the actual demand values in the table, they would seem to be relatively good forecast estimates, reflecting both the seasonal variations in the data and the general upward trend.

Transparency 10.7 Measures of Forecast Accuracy

FORECAST ACCURACY

Forecast error is the difference between the forecast and actual demand.

Teaching Note 10.7 Forecast Accuracy

It is not possible for a forecast to be completely accurate; forecasts will always deviate from the actual demand. This difference between the forecast and the actual is referred to as the **forecast error.** Although some amount of forecast error is inevitable, the objective of forecasting is that the error be as slight as possible. Of course, a degree of error that is not small may indicate to management that either the forecasting technique being used is the wrong one or the technique needs to be adjusted by changing its parameters (for example, α in the exponential smoothing forecast). In our discussion of the relationship between quality management and forecasting at the beginning of this chapter, we emphasized the importance of accurate forecasts for a company using TQM. High-quality forecasts are as important to continuous quality improvement as is quality in any other operation or business function.

There are a variety of different measures of forecast error, and in this section we will discuss several of the more popular ones: mean absolute deviation (MAD), mean absolute percentage deviation (MAPD), cumulative error, or bias (E), and, average error ($\bar{E}$).

Mean Absolute Deviation

MAD is the average, absolute difference between the forecast and demand.

The **mean absolute deviation,** or **MAD,** as it is more commonly known, is one of the most popular and simplest to use measures of forecast error. MAD is an average of the difference between the forecast and actual demand, as computed by the following formula:

$$\text{MAD} = \frac{\Sigma\,|D_t - F_t|}{n}$$

where

t = the period number
D_t = demand in period t
F_t = the forecast for period t
n = the total number of periods
$|\ |$ = absolute value

Alternate Example 10.5

EXAMPLE 10.7

Measuring Forecast Accuracy with MAD

Problem Statement:

In Examples 10.3, 10.4, and 10.5, forecasts were developed using exponential smoothing, ($\alpha = 0.30$ and $\alpha = 0.50$), adjusted exponential smoothing ($\alpha = 0.50$, $\beta = 0.30$), and a linear trend line, respectively, for the demand data for PM Computer Services. The company wants to compare the accuracy of these different forecasts using MAD.

Solution:

We will compute MAD for all four forecasts, however we will present the computational detail for the exponential smoothing forecast only with $\alpha = 0.30$. The accompanying table shows the values necessary to compute MAD for the exponential smoothing forecast.

Computational Values for MAD

Period	*Demand, D_t*	*Forecast $F_t(\alpha = 0.30)$*	*Error $(D_t - F_t)$*	$\lvert D_t - F_t \rvert$
1	37	37.00	—	—
2	40	37.00	3.00	3.00
3	41	37.90	3.10	3.10
4	37	38.83	–1.83	1.83
5	45	38.28	6.72	6.72
6	50	40.29	9.69	9.69
7	43	43.20	–0.20	0.20
8	47	43.14	3.86	3.86
9	56	44.30	11.70	11.70
10	52	47.81	4.19	4.19
11	55	49.06	5.94	5.94
12	54	50.84	3.15	3.15
	557		49.31	53.39[a]

[a]The computation of MAD will be based on eleven periods, periods 2 through 12, excluding the initial demand and forecast values, both of which equal 37.

Using the data in the table, MAD is computed as

$$\text{MAD} = \frac{\Sigma \lvert D_t - F_t \rvert}{n}$$
$$= \frac{53.39}{11}$$
$$= 4.85$$

In general, the smaller the value of MAD, the more accurate the forecast, although viewed alone, MAD is difficult to access. In this example, the data values were relatively small and the MAD value of 4.85 should be judged accordingly. Overall it would seem to be a "low" value; that is, the forecast appears to be relatively accurate. However, if the magnitude of the data values were in the thousands or millions, then a MAD value of a similar magnitude might not be bad either. The point is, you cannot compare a MAD value of 4.85 with a MAD value of 485 and say the former is good and the latter is bad, they depend to a certain extent on the relative magnitude of the data.

The lower the value of MAD, relative to the magnitude of the data, the more accurate the forecast.

One benefit of MAD is to compare the accuracy of several different forecasting techniques, as we are doing in this example. The MAD values for the remaining forecasts are as follows.

Exponential smoothing (α = 0.50):	MAD = 4.04
Adjusted exponential smoothing (α = 0.50, β = 0.30):	MAD = 3.81
Linear trend line:	MAD = 2.29

Comparing all four forecasts, because the linear trend line has the lowest MAD value of 2.29, it would seem to be the most accurate, although it does not appear to be significantly better than the adjusted exponential smoothing forecast. Further, we can deduce from these MAD values that increasing α from 0.30 to 0.50 enhanced the accuracy of the exponentially smoothed forecast. The adjusted forecast is even more accurate.

MAPD is the absolute error as a percentage of demand.

A variation of MAD is the **mean absolute percent deviation (MAPD)**. It measures the absolute error as a percentage of demand rather than per period. As a result, it eliminates the problem of interpreting the measure of accuracy relative to the magnitude of the demand and forecast values, as MAD does. The mean percent deviation is computed according to the following formula:

$$\text{MAPD} = \frac{\sum |D_t - F_t|}{\sum D_t}$$

Using the data from the table in Example 10.7 for the exponential smoothing forecast ($\alpha = 0.30$) for PM Computer Services, MAPD is computed as

$$\text{MAPD} = \frac{53.39}{520}$$
$$= 0.096, \quad \text{or} \quad 9.6 \text{ percent}$$

A lower percent deviation implies a more accurate forecast. The MAPD values for our other three forecasts are

Exponential smoothing ($\alpha = 0.50$): MAPD = 8.5 percent
Adjusted exponential smoothing ($\alpha = 0.50$, $\beta = 0.30$): MAPD = 8.1 percent
Linear trend line: MAPD = 4.9 percent

Cumulative Error

Cumulative error is the sum of the forecast errors.

Cumulative error is computed simply by summing the forecast errors, as shown in the following formula.

$$E = \Sigma e_t$$

Large $+E$ indicates forecast is biased low; large $-E$, forecast is biased high.

A relatively large positive value indicates that the forecast is probably consistently lower than the actual demand, or is biased low. A large negative value implies that the forecast is consistently higher than actual demand, or is biased high. Also, when the errors for each period are scrutinized, if there appears to be a preponderance of positive values, this shows that the forecast is consistently less than the actual value and vice versa.

The cumulative error for the exponentially smoothing forecast ($\alpha = 0.30$) for PM Computer Services can be read directly from the table in Example 10.7; it is simply the sum of the values in the "Error" column:

$$E = \Sigma e_t$$
$$= 49.31$$

This relatively large value positive error for cumulative error, plus the fact that the individual errors for each period in the table are positive, indicates that this forecast is consistently below the actual demand. A quick glance back at the plot of the exponential smoothing ($\alpha = 0.30$) forecast in the figure on page 497 visually verifies this result.

The cumulative error for the other forecasts are

Exponential smoothing ($\alpha = 0.50$): $E = 33.21$
Adjusted exponential smoothing ($\alpha = 0.50$, $\beta = 0.30$): $E = 21.14$

We did not show the cumulative error for the linear trend line. E will always equal zero for the linear trend line, thus, it is not a good measure on which to base comparisons with forecast methods.

A measure closely related to cumulative error is the **average error,** or *bias.* It is computed by averaging the cumulative error over the number of time periods,

Average error is the per-period average of cumulative error.

$$\bar{E} = \frac{\sum e_t}{n}$$

For example, the average error for the exponential smoothing forecast ($\alpha = 0.30$) is computed as follows. (Notice a value of 11 was used for n, since we used actual demand for the first-period forecast, resulting in no error, that is, $D_1 = F_1 = 37$.)

$$\bar{E} = \frac{49.31}{11} = 4.48$$

The average error is interpreted similarly to the cumulative error. A positive value indicates low bias and a negative value indicates high bias. A value close to zero implies a lack of bias.

Table 10.1 summarizes the measures of forecast accuracy we have discussed in this section for the four example forecasts we developed in the previous section for PM Computer Services. The results are consistent for all four forecasts, indicating that for the PM Computer Services example data, a larger value of α is preferable for the exponential smoothing forecast. The adjusted forecast is more accurate than the exponential smoothing forecasts, and the linear trend is more accurate than all the others. Although these results are example specific, it does indicate how the different forecast measures for accuracy can be used to adjust a forecasting method or select the best method.

Forecast Control

There are several techniques available for monitoring the amount of forecast error over time to make sure that the forecast is performing correctly—that is, the forecast is in control. Forecasts can go "out of control" and start providing inaccurate forecasts for several reasons, including a change in trend, the unanticipated appearance of a cycle, or an irregular variation such as unseasonable weather or a political event that distracts consumers.

A **tracking signal** indicates if the forecast is consistently biased high or low. It is computed by dividing the cumulative error by MAD, according to the formula

A **tracking signal** monitors the forecast to see if it is biased high or low.

$$\text{Tracking signal} = \frac{\Sigma(D_t - F_t)}{\text{MAD}} = \frac{E}{\text{MAD}}$$

The tracking signal is recomputed each period, with updated, "running" values of cumulative error and MAD. The movement of the tracking signal is compared to control limits; as long as the tracking signal is within these limits, the forecast is in control.

TABLE 10.1 Comparison of Forecasts for PM Computer Services

Forecast	*MAD*	*MAPD*	*E*	$\bar{E}$
Exponential smoothing ($\alpha = 0.30$)	4.85	9.6%	49.31	4.48
Exponential smoothing ($\alpha = 0.50$)	4.04	8.5%	33.21	3.02
Adjusted exponential smoothing ($\alpha = 0.50$, $\beta = 0.30$)	3.81	8.1%	21.14	1.92
Linear trend line	2.29	4.9%	—	—

Forecast errors are typically normally distributed, which results in the following relationship between MAD and the standard deviation of the distribution of error, σ:

$$\text{MAD} \cong 0.8\sigma$$

This enables us to establish statistical control limits for the tracking signal that corresponds to the more familiar normal distribution. For example, statistical control limits of ±3 standard deviations, corresponding to 99.7 percent of the errors, would translate to ± 3.75 MADs; that is, $3\sigma \div 0.8 = 3.75$ MADs. In general, control limits of ± 2 to ± 5 MADs are used most frequently.

EXAMPLE 10.8

Developing a Tracking Signal

Problem Statement:

In Example 10.7, the mean absolute deviation was computed for the exponential smoothing forecast ($\alpha = 0.30$) for PM Computer Services. Using a tracking signal, monitor the forecast accuracy using control limits of ± 3 MADs.

Solution:

In order to use the tracking signal, we must recompute MAD each period as the cumulative error is computed.

Using MAD = 3.00, the tracking signal for period 2 is

$$TS_2 = \frac{E}{\text{MAD}} = \frac{3.00}{3.00} = 1.00$$

The tracking signal for period 3 is

$$TS_3 = \frac{6.10}{3.05} = 2.00$$

The remaining tracking signal values are shown in the accompanying table.

Tracking Signal Values

Period	*Demand,* D_t	*Forecast,* F_t	*Error,* $D_t - F_t$	$\Sigma E = \Sigma(D_t - F_t)$	*MAD*	*Tracking Signal*
1	37	37.00	—	—	—	—
2	40	37.00	3.00	3.00	3.00	1.00
3	41	37.90	3.10	6.10	3.05	2.00
4	37	38.83	−1.83	4.27	2.64	1.62
5	45	38.28	6.72	10.99	3.66	3.00
6	50	40.29	9.69	20.68	4.87	4.25
7	43	43.20	−0.20	20.48	4.09	5.01
8	47	43.14	3.86	24.34	4.06	6.00
9	56	44.30	11.70	36.04	5.01	7.19
10	52	47.81	4.19	40.23	4.92	8.18
11	55	49.06	5.94	46.17	5.02	9.20
12	54	50.84	3.15	49.32	4.85	10.17

The tracking signal values in the table above move outside ± 3 MAD control limits (i.e., ± 3.00) in period 5 *and* continue increasing. This suggests that the forecast is not performing accurately, or, more precisely, is consistently biased low (i.e., actual demand consistently exceeds the forecast). This is illustrated in Figure 10.6. Notice that the tracking signal moves beyond the upper limit of 3 following period 6 and continues to rise. For the sake of comparison, the tracking signal for the linear trend line forecast computed in Example 10.5 is also plotted on this graph. Notice that it remains within the limits (touching the upper limit in period 3), indicating a lack of consistent bias.

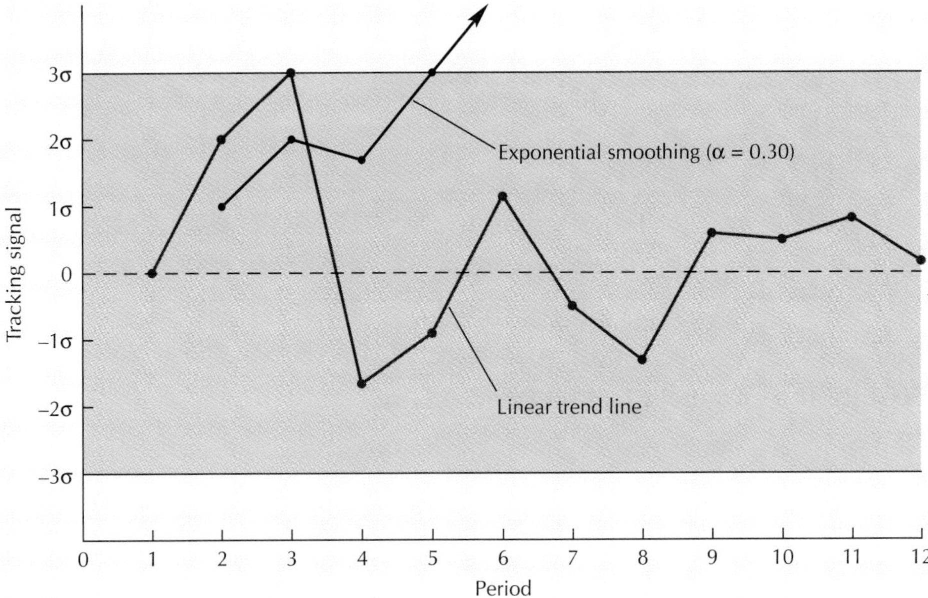

Another method for monitoring forecast error is the use of statistical control charts. For example, $\pm 3\sigma$ control limits would reflect 99.7 percent of the forecast errors (assuming they are normally distributed). The standard deviation, σ, also called the standard error, is computed as follows,

$$\sigma = \sqrt{\frac{\Sigma(D_t - F_t)^2}{n-1}}$$

This formula without the square root is known as the **mean squared error** (**MSE**), and it is sometimes used as a measure of forecast error. It reacts to forecast error much like MAD.

MSE is the average of the squared forecast errors.

Using the same example for the exponential smoothing forecast ($\alpha = 0.30$) for PM Computer Services, the standard deviation is computed as

$$\sigma = \sqrt{\frac{375.68}{10}} = 6.12$$

Using this value of σ we can compute statistical control limits for forecast errors for our exponential smoothing forecast ($\alpha = 0.30$) example for PM Computer Services. Plus or minus 3σ control limits, reflecting 99.7 percent of the forecast errors, give $\pm$ 3(6.12), or $\pm$ 18.39. Although it can be observed from the table on page 508

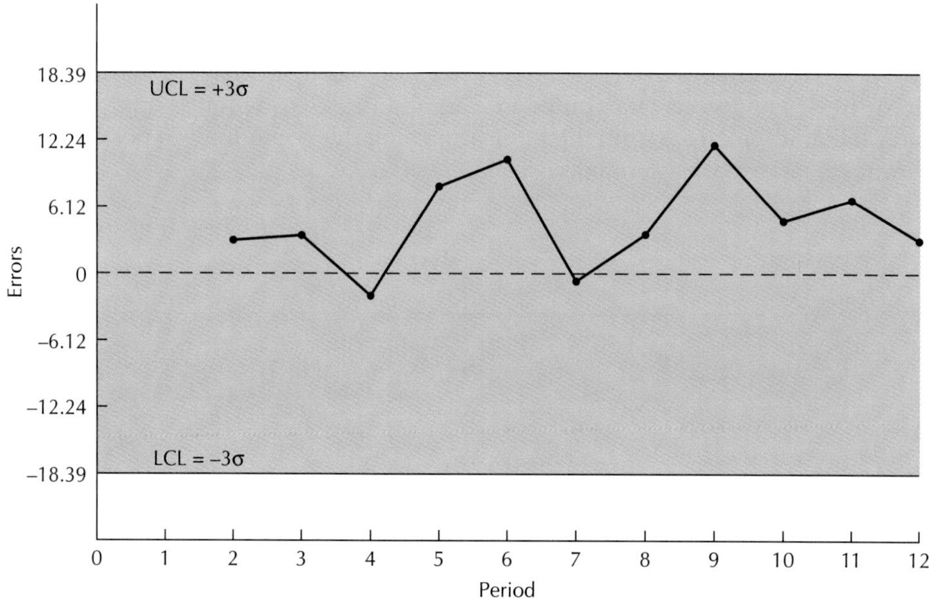

FIGURE 10.4 Control Chart for Forecast Error

that all the error values are within the control limits, we can still detect that most of the errors are positive, indicating a low bias in the forecast estimates. This is illustrated in a graph of the control chart in Figure 10.4 with the errors plotted on it.

TIME SERIES FORECASTING USING A COMPUTER

The AB:POM personal computer software package that we have used on many previous occasions in the text has the capability of performing forecasting for all the time series methods we have described so far. AB:POM has modules for moving averages, exponential smoothing and adjusted exponential smoothing, and linear regression.

In order to demonstrate the forecasting capability of AB:POM, we generate the exponential smoothing ($\alpha = 0.30$) forecast computed manually in Example 10.3. The solution output is shown in Exhibit 10.1

Notice that the computer output includes the forecast per period and the forecast for the next period (13) as well as two of the measures of forecast accuracy we presented, cumulative and average error (bias) and mean absolute deviation (MAD). A third measure of forecast error, mean squared error (MSE), which we briefly mentioned, is also computed. All these values are the same as those in Table 10.1, which we computed manually for this forecast.

The AB:POM will also generate a graph of exponential smoothing forecasts. The graph of the exponential smoothing ($\alpha = 0.30$) forecast from Example 10.4 is shown in Exhibit 10.2.

AB:POM also has a linear regression module that can be used to develop a linear trend line forecast. The solution output for the linear trend line forecast we developed in Example 10.5 is shown in Exhibit 10.3 on page 512.

```
                                  Forecasting                    Solution
Number of past data periods (2-99) 12
                                  Example 10.3
Method→Exponential Smoothing
alpha(α)    0.300

            Demand(y)    Forecast      Error     |Error|     Error^2
Jan           37.00       37.00
Feb           40.00       37.00        3.00        3.00        9.00
Mar           41.00       37.90        3.10        3.10        9.61
Apr           37.00       38.83       -1.83        1.83      3.3489
May           45.00      38.281       6.719       6.719      45.145
Jun           50.00     40.2967      9.7033      9.7033      94.154
Jul           43.00     43.2077     -0.2077     .207691     .043136
Aug           47.00     43.1454     3.85462     3.85462      14.858
Sep           56.00     44.3018     11.6982     11.6982     136.849
Oct           52.00     47.8112     4.18876     4.18876     17.5457
Nov           55.00     49.0679     5.93213     5.93213     35.1902
Dec           54.00     50.8475      3.1525      3.1525     9.93821
TOTALS       557.00                 49.3108     53.3862     375.682
AVERAGE     46.4167                  4.4828      4.8533     34.1529
                                     (Bias)       (MAD)       (MSE)
        Next period forecast= 51.7933       Standard error= 6.12929

                         Forecasting Summary Table
Method used: Exponential Smoothing α= .3
Bias  = 4.482803
MAD   = 4.853293
MSE   = 34.15289 Standard Error = 6.129288 Using n-1 in denominator
Forecast for next period = 51.79325
```

EXHIBIT 10.1

Transparency 10.8 AB:POM Exponential Smoothing Forecasting

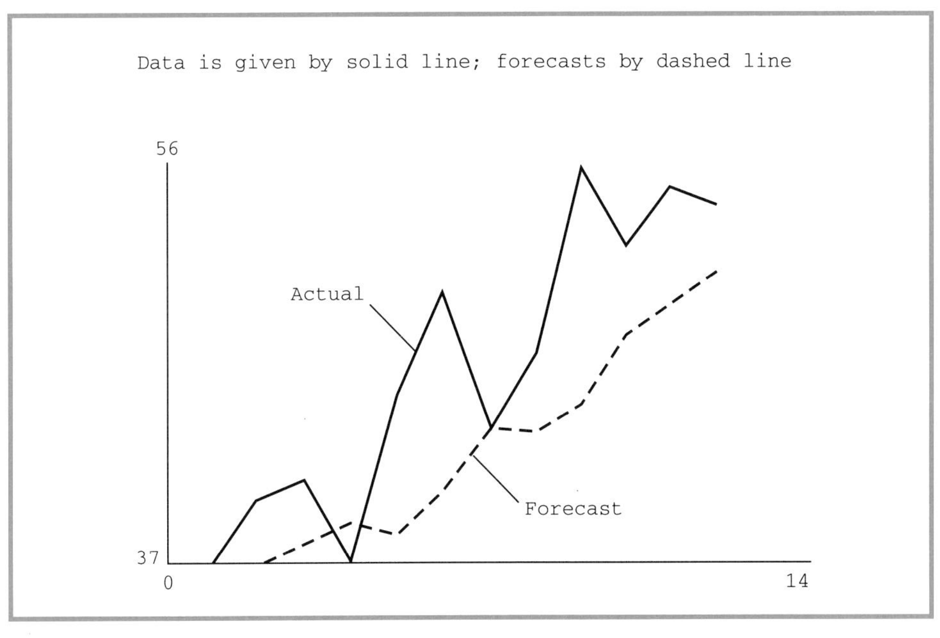

EXHIBIT 10.2

```
                                    Forecasting                           Solution
Number of past data periods (2-99) 12      Number of independ. variables (1-6) 1

                                    Example 10.5
Method --> Least Squares - Simple and Multiple Regression
             B 0       B 1
Coef --->    35.2121   1.72378
             Dpnd (y)        X1   Forecast      Error     |Error|     Error^2

Jan             37.00      1.00     36.936    .064102    .064102     0.00411
Feb             40.00      2.00    38.6597    1.34033    1.34033     1.79648
Mar             41.00      3.00    40.3834    0.61655    0.61655     .380134
Apr             37.00      4.00    42.1072    -5.1072    5.10722     26.0837
May             45.00      5.00     43.831      1.169      1.169     1.36656
Jun             50.00      6.00    45.5548    4.44522    4.44522       19.76
Jul             43.00      7.00    47.2786    -4.2786    4.27855      18.306
Aug             47.00      8.00    49.0023    -2.0023    2.00233     4.00933
Sep             56.00      9.00    50.7261     5.2739     5.2739      27.814
Oct             52.00     10.00    52.4499    -.44988    .449883     .202394
Nov             55.00     11.00    54.1737    0.82634    0.82634     .682837
Dec             54.00     12.00    55.8974    -1.8974    1.89743     3.60026
TOTALS                                        .000011    27.4709     104.006
AVERAGE                                          0.00    2.28924     8.66715
                                               (Bias)      (MAD)       (MSE)

Regression line: See summary table

Correlation coefficient = 0.8963039                       Standard error = 3.07491
                              Forecasting Summary Table
Method used: Multiple Regression               Regression line:
                                               Dpnd(y) = 35.2121
Bias =    0.000                                       +1.723776*X1

MAD = 2.289238                                   Correlation coefficient = 0.8963039

MSE = 8.667151

Standard Error = 3.07491 Using n-1 in denominator
```

EXHIBIT 10.3

Transparency 10.9 AB:POM Linear Trend Line Forecast

Video 10.1 *TIMS Edelman Awards Tape,* Program 2: "Citgo Petroleum"

GAINING THE COMPETITIVE EDGE

Forecasting Wholesale Prices and Product Volume at Citgo Petroleum

In 1983 Southland Corporation, the parent company of the 7-Eleven convenience store chain, acquired Citgo Petroleum Corporation, one of the largest industrial companies in the nation. However, prior to their acquisition, Citgo had lost money for several years, including a pretax loss of $50 million in 1984. Thus, a primary objective of Southland was to implement new management procedures to improve Citgo's profitability. In order to achieve this objective, Southland made extensive use of forecasting methods employed in an on-line "production acquisition and supply system" referred to as PASS. This system contained current operational information on sales, inventory, and trades and exchanges for all refined products for the past, present, and future. Historically, Citgo had forecast only total product volume and prices necessary for monthly and quarterly budgets, but with the development of PASS, forecasting techniques, including regression analysis, were used to provide wholesale

Box continues

price forecasts and wholesale volume forecasts, by product and by line of business, for an 11-week planning horizon for all company departments. This has helped to improve interdepartmental coordination. Forecasts for retail sales volume for 7-Eleven stores are also generated, as well as spot market price forecasts for different regions of the country. By using a single forecasting system, all parts of Citgo were better coordinated, and operational control was significantly improved. In 1985 Citgo achieved a pretax profit of more than $70 million; the improved forecasting models were a significant factor in this turnaround in performance.

Source: Based on Klingman, D., et al., "The Successful Deployment of Management Science Throughout Citgo Petroleum Corporation," *Interfaces*, no. 1 (January–February 1987): 4–25.

REGRESSION METHODS

Regression is used for forecasting by attempting to establish a mathematical relationship between two or more variables. For our purposes we are interested in identifying relationships between variables and demand. In other words, if we know that something has caused demand to behave in a certain way in the past, we would like to identify that relationship so if the same thing happens again in the future, we can predict what demand will be. For example, there is a well-known relationship between increased demand in new housing and lower interest rates. Correspondingly, a whole myriad of building products and services display increased demand if new housing starts increase. It is apparent that the rapid increase in sales of VCRs has resulted in an increase in demand for video movies.

The simplest form of regression is linear regression, which you will recall we used previously to develop a linear trend line for forecasting. In the following section we will show how to develop a regression model for variables related to demand other than time.

Linear Regression

Linear regression is a mathematical technique that relates one variable, called an *independent variable,* to another, referred to as the *dependent variable,* in the form of an equation for a straight line. A linear equation has the following general form:

Linear regression is a mathematical technique that relates a dependent variable to an independent variable in the form of a linear equation.

Transparency 10.10 Linear Regression

$$y = a + bx$$

where

y = the dependent variable
a = the intercept
b = the slope of the line
x = the independent variable

Because we want to use linear regression as a forecasting model for demand, the dependent variable, y, represents demand, and x is an independent variable that causes demand to behave in a linear manner.

Linear regression relates demand (dependent variable) to an independent variable.

In order to develop the linear equation, the slope, b, and the intercept, a, must first be computed using the following least squares formulas:

$$a = \bar{y} - b\bar{x}$$

$$b = \frac{\sum xy - n\bar{x}\bar{y}}{\sum x^2 - n\bar{x}^2}$$

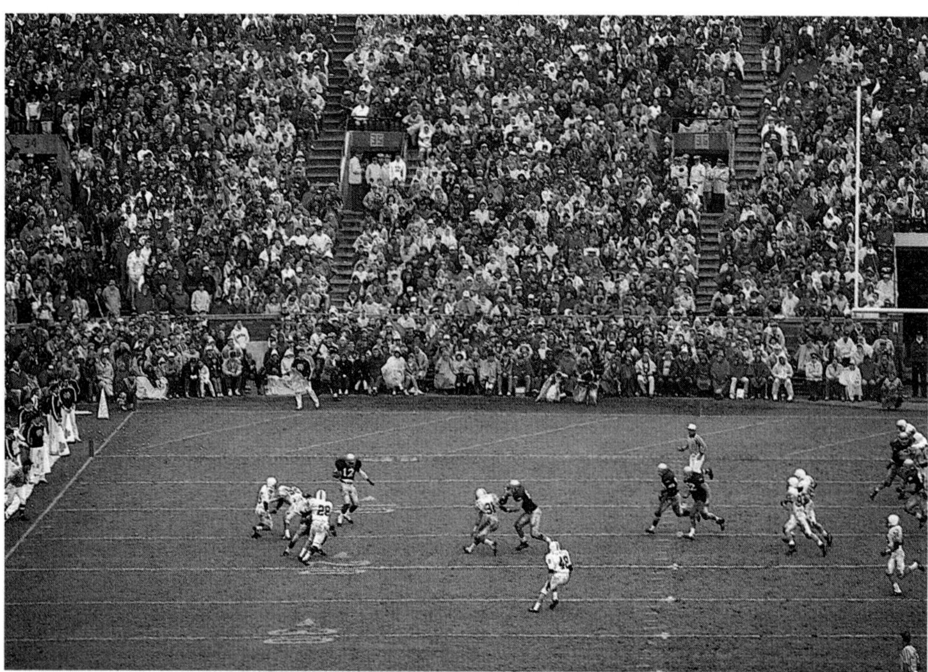

Intercollegiate athletics has become a big business at many schools like Notre Dame and Penn State, the opposing teams in this football game at South Bend. In 1990 Notre Dame signed a five-year television contract with NBC for a reported $37.5 million, and some of the major New Year's Day football games pay as much as $3 million apiece to the participants; the Rose Bowl pays over $6 million each. The annual athletic budget at the University of Michigan is reported to be over $20 million. Revenues from athletics are generated not only from ticket sales, but also from private donations, television and radio fees, and an assortment of school and team related publications, clothing and paraphernalia. These revenues are dependent upon a number of critical variables and like any business, athletic departments would like to be able to forecast demand for their products based on these variables. For example, ticket sales to athletic events, television fees, and clothing sales are all dependent on how well the athletic teams perform, the quality of the opponents, marketing and advertising, and even the weather, among other things.

where

$$\overline{x} = \frac{\Sigma x}{n} = \text{mean of the } x \text{ data}$$

$$\overline{y} = \frac{\Sigma y}{n} = \text{mean of the } y \text{ data}$$

EXAMPLE 10.9

Developing a Linear Regression Forecast

Problem Statement:

The State University athletic department wants to develop its budget for the coming year using a forecast for football attendance. Football attendance accounts for the largest portion of its revenues, and the athletic director believes attendance is directly related to the number of wins by the team. The business manager has accumulated total annual attendance figures for the past eight years.

WINS	ATTENDANCE
4	36,300
6	40,100
6	41,200

Table continues

WINS	ATTENDANCE
8	53,000
6	44,000
7	45,600
5	39,000
7	47,500

Given the number of returning starters and the strength of the schedule, the athletic director believes the team will win at least seven games next year. Develop a simple regression equation for this data to forecast attendance for this level of success.

Solution:

The computations necessary to compute a and b using the least squares formulas are summarized in the accompanying table. (Note that the magnitude of y has been reduced to make manual computation easier.)

Least Squares Computations

x (wins)	y (attendance, 1,000s)	xy	x^2
4	36.3	145.2	16
6	40.1	240.6	36
6	41.2	247.2	36
8	53.0	424.0	64
6	44.0	264.0	36
7	45.6	319.2	49
5	39.0	195.0	25
7	47.5	332.5	49
49	346.9	2,167.7	311

$$\bar{x} = \frac{49}{8} = 6.125$$

$$\bar{y} = \frac{346.9}{8} = 43.36$$

$$b = \frac{\Sigma xy - n\bar{x}\bar{y}}{\Sigma x^2 - n\bar{x}^2}$$

$$= \frac{(2{,}167.7) - (8)(6.125)(43.36)}{(311) - (8)(6.125)^2}$$

$$= 4.06$$

$$a = \bar{y} - b\bar{x}$$

$$= 43.36 - (4.06)(6.125)$$

$$= 18.46$$

Substituting these values for a and b into the linear equation line, we have

$$y = 18.46 + 4.06x$$

Thus, for $x = 7$ (wins), the forecast for attendance is

$$y = 18.46 + 4.06(7)$$
$$= 46.88, \quad \text{or} \quad 46{,}880$$

The data points with the regression line are shown in the figure below. Observing the regression line relative to the data points, it would appear that the data follow a distinct upward linear trend, which would indicate that the forecast should be relatively accurate. In fact, the MAD value for this forecasting model is 1.41 which suggests an accurate forecast.

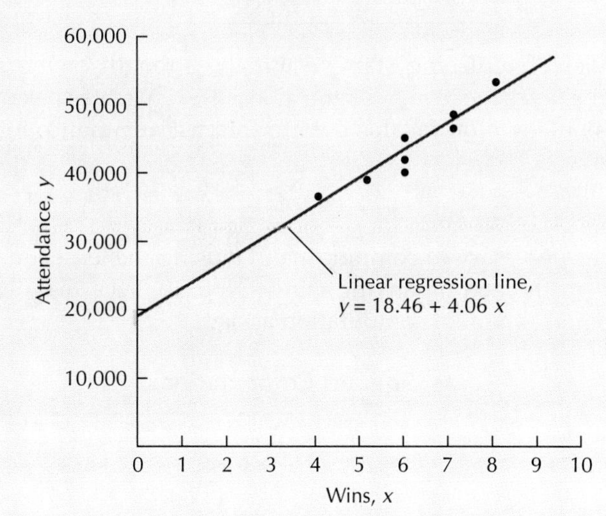

Correlation

Correlation is a measure of the strength of the relationship between independent and dependent variables.

Correlation in a linear regression equation is a measure of the strength of the relationship between the independent and dependent variables. The formula for the correlation coefficient is

$$r = \frac{n\sum xy - \sum x \sum y}{\sqrt{\left[n\sum x^2 - (\sum x)^2\right]\left[n\sum y^2 - (\sum y)^2\right]}}$$

The value of r varies between –1.00 and +1.00, with a value of ±1.00 indicating a strong linear relationship between the variables. If $r = 1.00$, then an increase in the independent variable will result in a corresponding linear increase in the dependent variable. If $r = -1.00$, an increase in the dependent variable will result in a linear decrease in the dependent variable. A value of r near zero implies that there is little or no linear relationship between variables.

We can determine the correlation coefficient for the linear regression equation determined in Example 10.9 by substituting most of the terms calculated for the least squares formula (except for Σy^2) into the formula for r:

$$r = \frac{(8)(2{,}167.7) - (49)(346.9)}{\sqrt{[(8)(311) - (49)^2][(8)(15{,}224.7) - (346.9)^2]}}$$

$$= 0.947$$

The **coefficient of determination** is the percentage of the variation in the dependant variable that results from the independent variable.

This value for the correlation coefficient is very close to 1.00 indicating a strong linear relationship between the number of wins and home attendance.

Another measure of the strength of the relationship between the variables in a linear regression equation is the **coefficient of determination.** It is computed by simply squaring the value of r. It indicates the percentage of the variation in the dependent variable that is a result of the behavior of the independent variable. For our example, $r = 0.947$; thus, the coefficient of determination is

$$\begin{aligned} r^2 &= (0.947)^2 \\ &= 0.897 \end{aligned}$$

This value for the coefficient of determination means that 89.7 percent of the amount of variation in attendance can be attributed to the number of wins by the team (with the remaining 10.3 percent due to other unexplained factors, such as weather, a good or poor start, or publicity). A value of 1.00 (or 100 percent) would indicate that attendance depends totally on wins. However, since 10.3 percent of the variation is a result of other factors, some amount of forecast error can be expected.

Multiple Regression

Multiple regression is a relationship of demand to two or more independent variables.

Another causal method of forecasting is **multiple regression,** a more powerful extension of linear regression. Linear regression relates demand to one other independent variable, whereas multiple regression reflects the relationship between a dependent variable and two or more independent variables. A multiple regression model has the following general form:

$$y = \beta_0 + \beta_1 x_1 + \beta_2 x_2 + \dots + \beta_k x_k$$

where

β_0 = the intercept

$\beta_1, \dots, \beta_k$ = parameters representing the contribution of the independent variables

$x_1, \dots, x_k$ = independent variables

For example, the demand for new housing (y) in a region or urban area might be a function of several independent variables, including interest rates, population, housing prices, and personal income. Development and computation of the multiple regression equation, including the compilation of data, is quite a bit more complex than linear regression. As such, the only viable means for forecasting using multiple regression is with a computer.

Regression Analysis with a Computer

The development of the simple linear regression equation and the correlation coefficient for our example was not too difficult because the amount of data was relatively small. However, manual computation of the components of simple linear regression equations can become very time-consuming and cumbersome as the amount of data increases. A number of different statistical software packages, such as SAS and MINITAB, and quantitative methods software packages, such as AB:QM and STORM, have modules for regression. Also, virtually all spreadsheet packages, such as Lotus 1-2-3, IFPS, and Excel, have regression capabilities. The software packages are generally easy to use and relieve the manager of the computational burden while increasing the opportunity for analysis.

The AB:POM package that we used previously in this chapter to develop time series forecasts also has the capability of performing linear regression, as we demonstrated earlier. To demonstrate this program module, we use Example 10.9. The program output, including the linear equation and correlation coefficient, is shown in Exhibit 10.4.

```
                                   Forecasting                          Solution
Number of past data periods (2-99) 8        Number of independ. variables (1-6) 1
                                   Example 10.9
Method --> Least Squares - Simple and Multiple Regression
              B 0          B 1
Coef --->    18464.4      4060.92
```

	Dpnd (y)	X1	Forecast	Error	|Error|	Error^2
obs 1	36300.0	4.00	34708.0	1591.95	1591.95	2534315
obs 2	40100.0	6.00	42829.9	-2729.9	2729.88	7452260
obs 3	41200.0	6.00	42829.9	-1629.9	1629.88	2656518
obs 4	53000.0	8.00	50951.7	2048.28	2048.28	4195440
obs 5	44000.0	6.00	42829.9	1170.12	1170.12	1369174
obs 6	45600.0	7.00	46890.8	-1290.8	1290.80	1666177
obs 7	39000.0	5.00	38769.0	231.035	231.035	53377.2
obs 8	47500.0	7.00	46890.8	609.195	609.195	371119
TOTALS				.007813	11301.1	%20298380
AVERAGE				.000977	1412.64	2537298
				(Bias)	(MAD)	(MSE)

```
Regression line: See summary table

Correlation coefficient = 0.9477996                  Standard error = 1702.871

                              Forecasting Summary Table

Method used: Multiple Regression                 Regression line:
                                                 Dpnd(y) = 18464.4
Bias = .00097656                                        +4060.919*X1

MAD = 1412.644                                    Correlation coefficient = 0.9477996

MSE = 2537297.5

Standard Error = 1702.871 Using n-1 in denominator
```

EXHIBIT 10.4

Transparency 10.11 AB:POM Linear Regression

QUALITATIVE METHODS

For the previous forecasting methods we have discussed in this chapter, quantitative forecasting models have been developed based on historical data that related demand to either time or other factors that caused demand. However, there are instances when historical data are not available or relevant for making forecasts. This statement is especially true for the long-range forecasting often required for strategic planning relative to the development of new products. Approaches to this type of nonquantitative, subjective forecasting include the judgment or opinion of individuals or groups within the organization, such as management, sales, and engineering; consumer research; structured expert opinion, as in the form of the Delphi method; and various consulting firms, specialists, government departments, and publications.

In-House Forecasting

Management, marketing and purchasing, and engineering are sources for internal qualitative forecasts.

There are normally individuals or groups within an organization whose judgments and opinions regarding future demand is as valid or more valid than outside experts or other structured approaches. Top management normally is the key group involved in the development of strategic plans. Through this planning process, they are generally most familiar with their firms' own capabilities and resources and the markets for their products.

The sales force of a company and the customer service area represent a direct point of contact with the consumer. This contact provides these staff members with information and awareness of consumer demand in the future that others may not possess. Engineering personnel have an innate understanding of the technological aspects of the products in their companies' markets and the type of products that might be feasible and likely in the future. Purchasing represents another point of contact with the outside, and staff within this function may be the first to learn of new product developments and trends within an industry. All these individuals and groups possess knowledge of their markets and products that can be used for long-range forecasting.

In-house knowledge, experience, and intuition also can be used to adjust forecasts determined by a quantitative method. You may recall in our discussion of the forecasting process relative to Figure 10.2 that one of the steps after a forecast has been developed is to make adjustments based on qualitative information. The fact that a forecast has been determined by a mathematical formula does not make it sacrosanct. It may well be that the astute and experienced operations manager or staff member can use their own knowledge or other information about future conditions to adjust a demand forecast up or down and improve its accuracy.

Consumer Research

Consumer, or market, research is an organized approach using surveys to determine what products and services customers want and will purchase. Consumer research is normally conducted by the marketing department within an organization, by industry organizations and groups, and by private marketing firms. Although market research can provide accurate and useful forecasts of product demand, it must be skillfully and correctly conducted, and it can be expensive. A market research study requires that a survey instrument be carefully designed by trained professionals. It must be administered through mailings, telephone contacts, or personal interviews; a sufficient response must be obtained. Also, the results must be summarized and interpreted correctly. Shortcomings in any of these steps can result in an erroneous forecast, which can do more harm than having no forecast at all.

In the section on quality management and forecasting at the beginning of this chapter, we emphasized the importance of forecasting in a TQM environment. Understanding the customer, including the customer's needs and wants in terms of product features and quality, is a fundamental requirement of TQM. Forecasting what the customer wants is a function of the marketing department and the outcome of consumer research.

Forecasting consumer needs and wants is a fundamental aspect of TQM.

The Delphi Method

The **Delphi method** involves soliciting forecasts about technological advances from experts.

The **Delphi method** is a procedure for acquiring informed judgments and opinions from knowledgeable individuals using a series of questionnaires in order to develop a consensus forecast about what will occur in the future. It was developed at the Rand Corporation shortly after World War II to forecast the impact of a hypothetical nuclear attack on the United States. Although the Delphi method has been used for a variety of applications, forecasting has been one of its primary uses since its inception. It has been especially useful for forecasting technological change and advances.

Technological forecasting has become increasingly crucial in order to compete in the modern international business environment. New, enhanced computer technology, new production methods, and advanced machinery and equipment are constantly being made available to companies. These advances, in turn, enable them to introduce more new products into the marketplace at a faster pace than ever before. The companies that succeed are those that manage to get a "technological" jump on their competitors by accurately predicting what technology will be available in the future and how it can be exploited. What new products and services will be technologically feasible, when they be can introduced, and what their demand will be are questions about the future for which answers cannot be predicted from historical data. Instead, the informed opinion and judgment of experts are necessary to make these types of single, long-term forecasts.

The Delphi method generally starts with a small organizing committee with a leader or coordinator. Their initial function is to design the study and specifically determine from whom to seek information and how to get the information. The means for soliciting information is a series of three or four questionnaires. The information from each new questionnaire uses the information from the previous one to focus progressively on important points and factors. The ultimate objective of the questionnaires is to reach a consensus on the forecast.

The participants in the Delphi method are normally a group of experts who may not know each other's identity. The group can be as small as a panel of four or five individuals. The group members respond anonymously to the questionnaires and provide reasons for their responses. Each successive questionnaire summarizes responses from the previous questionnaire, asks what-if? questions about the ideas generated to date, requests priorities and rankings, and summarizes arguments for and against. In this manner it is hoped that the experts will achieve a consensus opinion through conformance of thought.

The Delphi method is not always successful in generating a consensus or what is perceived to be a reliable forecast. In fact, it has never been shown that the forecasts produced using the Delphi method have achieved a high success rate. Nevertheless, it remains a logical alternative for making long-term subjective forecasts in the absence of any better approach.

The Forecasting Industry

The last decade has seen the proliferation of a variety of new sources of forecasts. Numerous business publications and subscription newsletters and reports, as well as popular magazines, regularly publish forecasts of economic, political, sociological, and technological conditions. In many instances they are based on public opinion polls or market research, however, more frequently they are derived from the well-known "panel of experts."

Some of these forecasts are the result of careful assessments of factors that will affect the future, which are made by knowledgeable individuals. However, such forecasts are often contradictory and occasionally are self-serving (designed to draw readers or subscribers to the publication instead of accurately informing the public). Nevertheless, these publications are frequently subscribed to by business executives in an attempt to predict what the demand for their product or service will be in the future. (If there were no market for them, they would not exist.)

Other sources of publications and reports that include forecasts, particularly about future economic conditions, are the U.S. Government, many universities, and publicly funded research groups, or "think tanks." Reports from such institutions also tend to be the result of the informed judgment and opinions of economists, academicians, business analysts, and other experts and can, similarly, be contradictory.

Another new phenomenon is consulting firms that specialize in forecasting demand for new products for the purpose of "venture capitalism." These firms assist (for a fee) companies or individual investors in determining what new

GAINING THE COMPETITIVE EDGE

Assessing the Forecasting Accuracy of the *Business Week* Industry Outlook

Since 1978 the magazine *Business Week* has published an industry outlook survey that predicts where industries are headed in the coming year. The survey is judgmental and is based on the expertise of editors and correspondents, combined with interviews conducted with industry leaders. The magazine claimed high reliability and accuracy for the forecast, but these claims were discounted by critics, especially academicians, who were skeptical of judgmental forecasting. A study was conducted of the surveys from 1978 to 1986 to assess the accuracy of the forecasts for the auto, steel, chemical, computer, and energy industries. The surveys were evaluated according to whether or not the general direction of the annual outlook was correct and if specific forecasts for sales, profit, market share, and so on, were accurate. Three measures of forecast accuracy were used: direction of forecast (either right or wrong), degree of optimism or pessimism, and mean absolute percentage error. The results of the evaluation showed that almost 80 percent of the outlooks correctly predicted the overall direction an industry would move in the coming year. Forecasts that predicted the direction, either a rise or decline, were usually correct. Although the direction was typically correct, the forecasts did tend to err most often on the side of optimism. For all five industries, 64 percent of the forecasts predicted events more favorable than those that occurred. The specific forecasts had an average error of only 19.6 percent (compared to an error of 27 percent for a forecast of no change at all). Given that the purpose of the annual outlook is to provide a general indication of where industries are headed in the coming year, *Business Week* seems to succeed nicely, despite the critics' skepticism regarding judgmental forecasts.

Source: Based on Schnaars, S. P., and I. Mohr, "The Accuracy of *Business Week*'s Industry Outlook Survey," *Interfaces* 18, no. 5 (September–October 1988): 31–38.

products can and should be introduced to the market and the demand that will likely result. These firms use consumer research methods and expert opinion, and they also pull together relevant information from a variety of perspectives, including technological, political, demographic, and economic aspects. Large investment firms also have staffs or departments that provide similar forecasts.

SUMMARY

As we mentioned at the beginning of this chapter, forecasts of product demand are a vital necessity for almost all aspects of operational planning. Short-range demand forecasts determine the daily resource requirements needed for production, including labor and material, as well as for developing work schedules and shipping dates and controlling inventory levels. Medium-range forecasts of demand are necessary to determine labor and staff requirements, skills, resources, purchasing contracts, and facilities. Long-range forecasts are needed to plan new products for development and changes in existing products and to acquire the plant, equipment, personnel, and resources necessary for future operations.

We have presented several methods of forecasting useful for different time frames. Time series and regression methods can be used to develop forecasts encompassing a time horizon of any length, although they tend to be used most frequently for short- and medium-range forecasts. These quantitative forecasting techniques are generally easy to understand, simple to use, and not especially costly unless the data requirements are substantial. They also have exhibited a good track record of performance for many companies that have used them. For these reasons, regression methods, and especially times series, are widely popular.

When managers and students are first introduced to forecasting methods, they are sometimes surprised and disappointed at the lack of exactness of the forecasts. However, they soon learn that forecasting is not easy, and exactness is not possible. However, those that have the skill and experience to obtain more accurate forecasts than their competitors will gain a competitive edge.

SUMMARY OF KEY FORMULAS

Moving average

$$MA_n = \frac{\sum_{i=1}^{n} D_i}{n}$$

Weighted moving average

$$WMA_n = \sum_{i=1}^{n} W_i D_i$$

Exponential smoothing

$$F_{t+1} = \alpha D_t + (1 - \alpha)F_t$$

Adjusted exponential smoothing

$$AF_{t+1} = F_{t+1} + T_{t+1}$$

Trend factor

$$T_{t+1} = \beta(F_{t+1} - F_t) + (1 - \beta)T_t$$

Linear trend line

$$y = a + bx$$

Least squares

$$a = \bar{y} - b\bar{x}$$

$$b = \frac{\sum xy - n\bar{x}\bar{y}}{\sum x^2 - n\bar{x}^2}$$

Seasonal factor

$$S_i = \frac{D_i}{\sum D}$$

Seasonally adjusted forecast

$$SF_i = (S_i)(F_t)$$

Mean absolute deviation

$$MAD = \frac{\sum |D_t - F_t|}{n}$$

Mean absolute percent deviation

$$MAPD = \frac{\sum |D_t - F_t|}{D_t}$$

Mean squared error

$$\text{MSE} = \frac{\Sigma(D_t - F_t)^2}{n-1}$$

Cumulative error

$$E = \Sigma e_t$$

Average error (Bias)

$$\bar{E} = \frac{\Sigma e_t}{n}$$

Tracking signal

$$\text{TS} = \frac{\Sigma(D_t - F_t)}{\text{MAD}}$$

Linear regression equation

$$y = a + bx$$

Correlation coefficient

$$r = \frac{n\Sigma xy - \Sigma x \Sigma y}{\sqrt{\left[n\Sigma x^2 - (\Sigma x)^2\right]\left[n\Sigma y^2 - (\Sigma y)^2\right]}}$$

Coefficient of determination

$$\text{Coefficient of determination} = r^2$$

SUMMARY OF KEY TERMS

adjusted exponential smoothing: an exponentially smoothing forecast adjusted for trend.

average error: the cumulative error averaged over the number of time periods.

causal forecasting methods: a class of mathematical techniques that relate demand to other factors that cause demand behavior.

coefficient of determination: the correlation coefficient squared; it measures the portion of the variation in the dependent variable that can be attributed to the independent variable.

correlation: a measure of the strength of the causal relationship between the independent and dependent variable in a linear regression equation.

cumulative error: a sum of the forecast errors, also known as bias.

cycle: an undulating up-and-down movement in demand over time.

Delphi method: a procedure for acquiring informal judgments and opinions from knowledgeable individuals to use as a subjective forecast.

exponential smoothing: a forecasting technique based on averaging data that weights more recent past data more strongly than more distant past data.

forecast error: the difference between actual and forecasted demand.

linear regression: a mathematical technique that relates a dependent variable to an independent variable in the form of a linear equation.

linear trend line: a forecast using the linear regression equation to relate demand to time.

long-range forecast: a forecast encompassing a period of time longer than two years.

mean absolute deviation (MAD): the per-period average of the absolute difference between actual and forecasted demand.

mean absolute percent deviation (MAPD): the absolute forecast error measured as a percent of demand.

mean squared error (MSE): the average of the squared forecast errors.

medium-range forecast: a forecast encompassing from 1 or 2 months up to 2 years.

moving average: average demand for a fixed sequence of periods including the most recent period.

multiple regression: a mathematical relationship that relates a dependent variable to two or more independent variables.

qualitative forecast methods: nonquantitative, subjective forecasts based on judgment, opinion, experience, and expert opinion.

quantitative forecast methods: forecasts derived from a mathematical formula.

random variations: movements in demand that are not predictable and follow no pattern.

seasonal factor: a numerical value that is multiplied times a normal forecast to get a seasonally adjusted forecast.

seasonal pattern: an oscillating movement in demand that occurs periodically in the short run and is repetitive.

short-range forecast: a forecast encompassing the immediate future, usually days or weeks, but up to several months.

smoothing constant: the weighting factor given to the most recent data in exponential smoothing forecasts.

time frame: how far into the future the forecast is done.

time series: a class of statistical methods that uses historical demand data over a period of time to predict future demand.

tracking signal: a measure computed by dividing the cumulative error by MAD; used for monitoring bias in a forecast.

trend: a gradual, long-term up-or-down movement of demand.

weighted moving average: a moving average with more recent demand values adjusted with weights.

SOLVED PROBLEMS

1. Moving Average

Problem Statement:

A manufacturing company has monthly demand for one of its products as follows,

Month	*Demand*
February	520
March	490
April	550
May	580
June	600
July	420
August	510
September	610

Develop a three-period average forecast and a three-period weighted moving average forecast with weights of 0.50, 0.30, and 0.20 for the most recent demand values, in that order. Calculate MAD for each forecast, and indicate which would seem to be most accurate.

Solution:

Step 1: Compute the 3-month moving average using the formula

$$MA_3 = \sum_{i=1}^{3} \frac{D_i}{3}$$

For May, the moving average forecast is

$$MA_3 = \frac{520 + 490 + 550}{3} = 520$$

Step 2: Compute the 3-month weighted moving average using the formula

$$WMA_3 = \Sigma W_i D_i$$

For May, the weighted average forecast is

$$WMA_3 = (0.50)(520) = (0.30)(490) + (0.20)(550)$$
$$= 526.00$$

The values for both moving averages forecasts are shown in the following table.

Month	*Demand*	MA_3	WMA_3
February	520	—	—
March	490	—	—
April	550	—	—
May	580	520.00	526.00
June	600	540.00	553.00
July	420	576.67	584.00
August	510	533.33	506.00
Septbember	610	510.00	501.00
October	—	513.33	542.00

Step 3: Compute the MAD value for both forecasts:

$$MAD = \frac{\Sigma |D_t - F_t|}{n}$$

The MAD value for the 3-month moving average is 80.0, and the MAD value for the 3-month weighted moving average is 75.6, indicating there is not much difference in accuracy between the two forecasts, although the weighted moving average is slightly better.

2. *Exponential Smoothing*

Problem Statement:

A computer software firm has experienced the following demand for its "Personal Finance" software package

Period	*Units*
1	56
2	61
3	55
4	70
5	66
6	65
7	72
8	75

Develop an exponential smoothing forecast using $\alpha = 0.40$ and an adjusted exponential smoothing forecast using $\alpha = 0.40$ and $\beta = 0.20$. Compare the accuracy of the two forecasts using MAD and cumulative error.

Solution:

Step 1: Compute the exponential smoothing forecast with $\alpha = 0.40$ using the following formula:

$$F_{t+1} = \alpha D_t + (1 - \alpha)F_t$$

For period 2, the forecast (assuming $F_1 = 56$) is

$$\begin{aligned} F_2 &= \alpha D_1 + (1 - \alpha)F_1 \\ &= (0.40)(56) + (0.60)(56) \\ &= 56 \end{aligned}$$

For period 3, the forecast is

$$\begin{aligned} F_3 &= (0.40)(61) + (0.60)(56) \\ &= 58 \end{aligned}$$

The remaining forecasts are computed similarly and are shown in the accompanying table.

Step 2: Compute the adjusted exponential smoothing forecast with $\alpha = 0.40$ and $\beta = 0.20$ using the formula

$$\begin{aligned} AF_{t+1} &= F_{t+1} + T_{t+1} \\ T_{t+1} &= \beta(F_{t+1} - F_t) + (1 - \beta)T_t \end{aligned}$$

Starting with the forecast for period 3 (since $F_1 = F_2$, and we will assume $T_2 = 0$),

$$\begin{aligned} T_3 &= \beta(F_3 - F_2) + (1 - \beta)T_2 \\ &= (0.20)(58 - 56) + (0.80)(0) \\ &= 0.40 \\ AF_3 &= F_3 + T_3 \\ &= 58 + 0.40 \\ &= 58.40 \end{aligned}$$

The remaining adjusted forecasts are computed similarly and are shown in the following table.

Period	D_t	F_t	AF_t	$D_t - F_t$	$D_t - AF_t$
1	56	—	—	—	—
2	61	56.00	56.00	5.00	5.00
3	55	58.00	58.40	–3.00	–3.40
4	70	56.80	56.88	13.20	13.12
5	66	62.08	63.20	3.92	2.80
6	65	63.65	64.86	1.35	0.14
7	72	64.18	65.26	7.81	6.73
8	75	67.31	68.80	7.68	6.20
9	—	70.39	72.19	—	—
				35.97	30.60

Step 3: Compute the MAD value for each forecast.

$$\text{MAD}(\text{F}_t) = \frac{\Sigma\,|D_t - F_t|}{n}$$
$$= \frac{41.97}{7}$$
$$= 5.99$$
$$\text{MAD}(\text{AF}_t) = \frac{37.39}{7}$$
$$= 5.34$$

Step 4: Compute the cumulative error for each forecast:

$$E(F_t) = 35.97$$
$$E(\text{AF}_t) = 30.60$$

Because both MAD and the cumulative error are less for the adjusted forecast, it would appear to be the most accurate.

3. *Linear Regression*

Problem Statement:

A local building products store has accumulated sales data for 2 × 4 lumber (in board feet) and the number of building permits in its area for the past ten quarters.

Quarter	*Building permits* x	*Lumber sales (1,000s of board feet)* y
1	8	12.6
2	12	16.3
3	7	9.3
4	9	11.5
5	15	18.1
6	6	7.6
7	5	6.2
8	8	14.2
9	10	15.0
10	12	17.8

Develop a linear regression model for these data and determine the strength of the linear relationship using correlation. If the model appears to be relatively strong, determine the forecast for lumber given ten building permits in the next quarter.

Solution:

Step 1: Compute the components of the linear regression equation, $y = a + bx$, using the least squares formulas,

$$\bar{x} = \frac{92}{10} = 9.2$$

$$\bar{y} = \frac{128.6}{10} = 12.86$$

$$b = \frac{\sum xy - n\bar{x}\bar{y}}{\sum x^2 - n\bar{x}^2}$$

$$= \frac{(1{,}170.3) - (10)(9.2)(12.86)}{(932) - (10)(9.2)^2}$$

$$b = 1.25$$

$$a = \bar{y} - b\bar{x}$$

$$= 12.86 - (1.25)(9.2)$$

$$a = 1.36$$

Step 2: Develop the linear regression equation.

$$y = a + bx$$

$$y = 1.36 + 1.25x$$

Step 3: Compute the correlation coefficient.

$$r = \frac{n\sum xy - \sum x \sum y}{\sqrt{\left[n\sum x^2 - (\sum x)^2\right]\left[n\sum y^2 - (\sum y)^2\right]}}$$

$$= \frac{(10)(1{,}170.3) - (92)(128.6)}{\sqrt{[(10)(932) - (92)^2][(10)(1{,}810.48) - (128.6)^2]}}$$

$$= 0.925$$

Thus, there appears to be a strong linear relationship.

Step 4: Calculate the forecast for $x = 10$ permits.

$$y = a + bx$$
$$= 1.36 + 1.25(10)$$
$$= 13.86, \quad \text{or} \quad 13{,}860 \text{ board feet}$$

QUESTIONS

10-1. List some of the operations and functions in a company that are dependent on a forecast for product demand.

10-2. What is the difference between quantitative forecast methods and qualitative forecast methods?

10-3. Describe the difference between short-, medium-, and long-range forecasts.

10-4. What is the difference between a trend and a cycle and a seasonal pattern?

10-5. How is the moving average method similar to exponential smoothing?

10-6. In the chapter examples for time series methods, the starting forecast was always assumed to be the same as actual demand in the first period. Suggest other ways that the starting forecast might be derived in actual use.

10-7. What effect on the exponential smoothing model will increasing the smoothing constant have?

10-8. How does adjusted exponential smoothing differ from exponential smoothing?

10-9. What determines the choice of the smoothing constant for trend in an adjusted exponential smoothing model?

10-10. How does the linear trend line forecasting model differ from a linear regression model for forecasting?

10-11. Of the time series models presented in this chapter, including the moving average and weighted moving average, exponential smoothing and adjusted exponential smoothing, and linear trend line, which one do you consider the best? Why?

10-12. What advantages does adjusted exponential smoothing have over a linear trend line for forecasted demand that exhibits a trend?

10-13. Describe how a forecast is monitored to detect bias.

10-14. Explain the relationship between the use of a tracking signal and statistical control limits for forecast control.

10-15. Selecting from MAD, MAPD, MSE, E, and $\bar{E}$, which measure of forecast accuracy do you consider superior? Why?

10-16. What is the difference between linear and multiple regression?

10-17. Define the different components (y, x, a, and b) of a linear regression equation.

10-18. A company that produces video equipment, including VCRs, video cameras, and televisions, is attempting to forecast what new products and product innovations might be technologically feasible and that customers might demand ten years into the future. Speculate on what type of qualitative methods they might use to develop this type of forecast.

PROBLEMS

10-1. The Saki motorcycle dealer in the Minneapolis–St. Paul area wants to be able to forecast accurately the demand for the Saki Super TX II motorcycle during the next month. Because the manufacturer is in Japan, it is difficult to send motorcycles back or reorder if the proper number is not ordered a month ahead. From sales records, the dealer has accumulated the following data for the past year.

10-1. a. and b. See Solutions Manual. c. MAD(3)=1.89, MAD(5)=2.43; 3-month MA

Month	*Motorcycle Sales*
January	9
February	7
March	10
April	8
May	7
June	12
July	10
August	11
September	12
October	10
November	14
December	16

a. Compute a 3-month moving average forecast of demand for April through January (of the next year).
b. Compute a 5-month moving average forecast for June through January.
c. Compare the two forecasts computed in parts (a) and (b) using MAD. Which one should the dealer use for January of the next year?

10-2. The manager of the Carpet City outlet needs to be able to forecast accurately the demand for Soft Shag carpet (its biggest seller). If the manager does not order enough carpet from the carpet mill, customers will buy their carpets from one of Carpet City's many competitors. The manager has collected the following demand data for the past 8 months.

10-2. a. and b. See Solutions Manual. c. MAD(3)=1.6, MAD(W3)=2.15; 3-month MA

Month	*Demand for Soft Shag Carpet (1,000 yd)*
1	8
2	12
3	7
4	9
5	15
6	11
7	10
8	12

a. Compute a 3-month moving average forecast for months 4 through 9.
b. Compute a weighted 3-month moving average forecast for months 4 through 9. Assign weights of 0.55, 0.33, and 0.12 to the months in sequence, starting with the most recent month.
c. Compare the two forecasts using MAD. Which forecast appears to be more accurate?

10-3. a., b., and c. See Solutions Manual.
d. $E(3\text{ qtr}) = 32$, $E(5\text{ qtr}) = 36.4$, $E(W\ 3\text{ qtr}) = 26.26$; weighted 3-quarter; low bias

★ 10-3. The Fastgro Fertilizer Company distributes fertilizer to various lawn and garden shops. The company must base its quarterly production schedule on a forecast of how many tons of fertilizer will be demanded from it. The company has gathered the following data for the past three years from its sales records.

Year	*Quarter*	*Demand for Fertilizer (tons)*
1	1	105
	2	150
	3	93
	4	121
2	5	140
	6	170
	7	105
	8	150
3	9	150
	10	170
	11	110
	12	130

a. Compute a 3-quarter moving average forecast for quarters 4 through 13 and compute the forecast error for each quarter.
b. Compute a 5-quarter moving average forecast for quarters 6 through 13 and compute the forecast error for each quarter.
c. Compute a weighted 3-quarter moving average forecast using weights of 0.50, 0.33, and 0.17 for the most recent, next recent, and most distant data, respectively, and compute the forecast error for each quarter.
d. Compare the forecasts developed in parts (a), (b), and (c) using cumulative error. Which forecast appears to be most accurate? Do any exhibit any bias?

10-4. See Solutions Manual; slight upward trend and pronounced seasonal pattern.

10-4. Graph the demand data in Problem 10-3. Can you identify any trends, cycles, and/or seasonal patterns?

10-5. a. and b. See Solutions Manual.
c. 3-semester MA is more accurate.

10-5. The chairperson of the department of management at State University wants to forecast the number of students who will enroll in production and operations management next semester in order to determine how many sections to schedule. The chair has accumulated the following enrollment data for the past eight semesters.

Semester	*Students Enrolled in POM*
1	400
2	450
3	350
4	420
5	500
6	575
7	490
8	650

a. Compute a three-semester moving average forecast for semesters 4 through 9.
b. Compute the exponentially smoothed forecast ($\alpha = 0.20$) for the enrollment data.
c. Compare the two forecasts using MAD and indicate the most accurate.

10-6. The manager of the Petroco Service Station wants to forecast the demand for unleaded gasoline next month so that the proper number of gallons can be ordered from the distributor. The owner has accumulated the following data on demand for unleaded gasoline from sales during the past 10 months. ★

10-6. a. and b. See Solutions Manual.
c. Adjusted exponentially smoothed forecast is slightly more accurate.

Month	*Gasoline Demanded (gal)*
October	800
November	725
December	630
January	500
February	645
March	690
April	730
May	810
June	1,200
July	980

a. Compute an exponentially smoothed forecast using an α value of 0.30.
b. Compute an adjusted exponentially smoothed forecast ($\alpha = 0.30$ and $\beta = 0.20$).
c. Compare the two forecasts using MAPD and indicate which seems to be the most accurate.

10-7. The Victory Plus Mutual Fund of growth stocks has had the following average monthly price for the past 10 months. ★

10-7. Linear trend line is the most accurate.

Month	*Fund Price*
1	62.7
2	63.9
3	68.0
4	66.4
5	67.2

Table continues

Month	*Fund Price*
6	65.8
7	68.2
8	69.3
9	67.2
10	70.1

Compute the exponentially smoothed forecast with $\alpha = 0.40$, the adjusted exponential smoothing forecast with $\alpha = 0.40$ and $\beta = 0.30$, and the linear trend line forecast. Compare the accuracy of the three forecasts using cumulative error and MAD, and indicate which forecast appears to be most accurate.

10-8. Linear trend line is the most accurate.

★ 10-8. The Bayside Fountain Hotel is adjacent to County Coliseum, a 24,000-seat arena that is home to the city's professional basketball and ice hockey teams and that hosts a variety of concerts, trade shows, and conventions throughout the year. The hotel has experienced the following occupancy rates for the nine years since the coliseum opened.

Year	*Occupancy Rate*
1986	83%
1987	78
1988	75
1989	81
1990	86
1991	85
1992	89
1993	90
1994	86

Compute an exponential smoothing forecast with $\alpha = 0.20$, an adjusted exponential smoothing forecast with $\alpha = 0.20$ and $\beta = 0.20$, and a linear trend line forecast. Compare the three forecasts using MAD and average error ($\bar{E}$), and indicate which forecast seems to be most accurate.

10-9. $\bar{E} = 26.30$, $E = 289.336$; biased low

★ 10-9. The Whistle Stop Cafe in Weems, Georgia, is well known for its popular homemade ice cream, which it makes in a small plant in back of the cafe. People drive all the way from Atlanta and Macon to buy the ice cream. The two ladies who own the cafe want to develop a forecasting model so they can plan their ice cream production operation and determine the number of employees they need to sell ice cream in the cafe. They have accumulated the following sales records for their ice cream for the past 12 quarters.

Year/Quarter		*Ice Cream Sales (gal)*
1992:	1	350
	2	510
	3	750
	4	420
1993:	5	370
	6	480
	7	860
	8	500

Table continues

Year/Quarter	*Ice Cream Sales (gal)*
1994: 9	450
10	550
11	820
12	570

Develop an adjusted exponential smoothing model with $\alpha = 0.50$ and $\beta = 0.50$ to forecast demand, and assess its accuracy using cumulative error (E) and average error ($\bar{E}$). Does there appear to be any bias in the forecast?

10-10. For the demand data in Problem 10-9, develop a seasonally adjusted forecast for 1995. (Use a linear trend line model to develop a forecast estimate for 1995.) Which forecast model do you perceive to be the most accurate, the exponential smoothing model from Problem 10-9 or the seasonally adjusted forecast?

10-10. Qtr. 1=462.6, Qtr. 2=591.1, Qtr. 3=950.9, Qtr. 4=565.4; seasonal forecast is most accurate.

10-11. Develop a seasonally adjusted forecast for the demand data for fertilizer in Problem 10-3. Use a linear trend line model to compute a forecast estimate for demand in year 4.

10-11. Qtr. 1=155.6, Qtr. 2=192.9, Qtr. 3=118.2, Qtr. 4=155.6

10-12. Monaghan's Pizza delivery service has randomly selected eight weekdays during the past month and recorded orders for pizza at four different time periods per day, as follows.

★ 10-12. 10 A.M.–3 P.M. = 45.87; 3 P.M.–7 P.M. = 67.88; 7 P.M.–11 P.M. = 38.52; 11 P.M.–2 A.M. = 31.18

	DAYS							
TIME PERIOD	*1*	*2*	*3*	*4*	*5*	*6*	*7*	*8*
10:00 A.M. – 3:00 P.M.	62	49	53	35	43	48	56	43
3:00 P.M. – 7:00 P.M.	73	55	81	77	60	66	85	70
7:00 P.M. – 11:00 P.M.	42	38	45	50	29	37	35	44
11:00 P.M. – 2:00 A.M.	35	40	36	39	26	25	36	31

Develop a seasonally adjusted forecasting model for daily pizza demand and forecast demand for each of the time periods for a single upcoming day.

10-13. The Cat Creek Mining Company mines and ships coal. It has experienced the following demand for coal during the past eight years.

★ 10-13. Linear trend line forecast is most accurate.

Year	*Coal sales (tons)*
1987	4,260
1988	4,510
1989	4,050
1990	3,720
1991	3,900
1992	3,470
1993	2,890
1994	3,100

Develop an adjusted exponential smoothing model ($\alpha = 0.30$, $\beta = 0.20$) and a linear trend line model and compare the forecast accuracy of the two using MAD. Indicate which forecast seems to be most accurate.

10-14. The Northwoods Outdoor company is a catalog sales operation that specializes in outdoor recreational clothing. Demand for its items is very seasonal, peaking during the holiday season and during the spring. It has

★ 10-14. a. and b. See Instructor's Section. c. Linear trend line forecast is slightly more accurate.

accumulated the following data for order per "season" (quarter) during the past five years.

QUARTER	ORDERS (1000s) 1990	1991	1992	1993	1994
January–March	18.6	18.1	22.4	23.2	24.5
April–June	23.5	24.7	28.8	27.6	31.0
July–September	20.4	19.5	21.0	24.4	23.7
October–December	41.9	46.3	45.5	47.1	52.8

a. Develop a seasonally adjusted forecast model for these order data. Forecast demand for each quarter for 1996 (using a linear trend line forecast estimate for orders in 1996).
b. Develop a separate linear trend line forecast for each of the four seasons and forecast each season for 1996.
c. Which of the two approaches used in parts (a) and (b) appear to be the most accurate? Use MAD to verify your selection.

10-15. No

10-15. Aztec Industries has developed a forecasting model that was used to forecast during a 10-month period. The forecasts and actual demand are shown as follows.

Month	*Actual Demand*	*Forecast Demand*
1	160	170
2	150	165
3	175	157
4	200	166
5	190	183
6	220	186
7	205	203
8	210	204
9	200	207
10	220	203

Measure the accuracy of the forecast using MAD, MAPD, and cumulative error. Does the forecast method appear to be accurate?

10-16. Yes, biased low

10-16. Monitor the forecast in Problem 15 for bias using a tracking signal and a control chart with ± 3 MAD. Does there appear to be any bias in the forecast?

10-17. No bias

10-17. Develop a statistical control chart for the forecast error in Problem 10-9 using $\pm 3\sigma$ control limits, and indicate if the forecast seems to be biased.

10-18. Forecast is not accurate, biased high.

10-18. Monitor the adjusted exponential smoothing forecast in Problem 10-13 for bias using a tracking signal and a control chart with ±3 MAD.

10.19. a. Relatively accurate
b. 3-mo MA more accurate
c. Biased low

10-19. ★ RAP Computers assembles minicomputers from generic parts it purchases at discount and sells the units via phone orders it receives from customers responding to their ads in trade journals. The business has developed an exponential smoothing forecast model to forecast future computer demand. Actual demand for their computers for the past 8 months is as follows.

Month	Demand	Forecast
March	120	—
April	110	120.0
May	150	116.0
June	130	129.6
July	160	129.7
August	165	141.8
September	140	151.1
October	155	146.7
November	—	150.0

a. Using the measure of forecast accuracy of your choice, ascertain if the forecast appears to be accurate.
b. Determine if a 3-month moving average would provide a better forecast.
c. Use a tracking signal to monitor the forecast in part (a) for bias.

10-20. Develop an exponential smoothing forecast with $\alpha = 0.20$ for the demand data in Problem 10-1. Compare this forecast with the 3-month moving average computed in 10-1(a) using MAD and indicate which forecast seems to be most accurate.

10-20. 3-mo MA most accurate

10-21. The Jersey Dairy Products Company produces cheese which it sells to supermarkets and food processing companies. Because of concerns about cholesterol and fat in cheese, the company has seen demand for its products decline during the past decade. They are now considering introducing some alternative lowfat dairy products and want to determine how much available plant capacity they will have next year. They have developed an exponential smoothing forecast with $\alpha = 0.40$ to forecast cheese. The actual demand and the forecasts from their model are shown as follows.

10-21. Biased high; linear trend line forecast is more accurate.

YEAR	DEMAND (1,000 lbs)	Forecast
1	16.8	—
2	14.1	16.8
3	15.3	15.7
4	12.7	15.5
5	11.9	14.4
6	12.3	13.4
7	11.5	12.9
8	10.8	12.4

Assess the accuracy of the forecast model using MAD and cumulative error, and determine if the forecast error reflects bias using a tracking signal and ±3 MAD control limits. If the exponential smoothing forecast model is biased, determine if a linear trend model would provide a more accurate forecast.

10-22. The manager of the Ramona Inn Hotel near Cloverleaf Stadium believes that how well the local Blue Sox professional baseball team is playing has an impact on the occupancy rate at the hotel during the summer months. Following are the number of victories for the Blue Sox (in a 162-game schedule) for the past eight years and the hotel occupancy rates.

10-22. $y = 0.69 + 0.0022x$, 0.884 occupancy rate

Year	Number of Blue Sox Wins	Occupancy Rate
1	75	83%
2	70	78
3	85	86
4	91	85
5	87	89
6	90	93
7	87	92
8	67	91

Develop a linear regression model for these data, and forecast the occupancy rate for next year if the Blue Sox win 88 games.

10.23. a. $y = 2.36 + 0.267x$; 10.40
b. 0.699

10-23. Carpet City wants to develop a means to forecast its carpet sales. The store manager believes that the store's sales are directly related to the number of new housing starts in town. The manager has gathered data from county records of monthly house construction permits and from store records on monthly sales. These data are as follows.

Monthly Carpet Sales (1,000 yd)	Monthly Construction Permits
5	21
10	35
4	10
3	12
8	16
2	9
12	41
11	15
9	18
14	26

a. Develop a linear regression model for this data and forecast carpet sales if thirty construction permits for new homes are filed.
b. Determine the strength of the causal relationship between monthly sales and new home construction using correlation.

10.24. a. $y = -113.40 + 2.986x$; 140.43 gal
b. 0.929

★

10-24. The manager of Gilley's Ice Cream Parlor needs an accurate forecast of the demand for ice cream. The store orders ice cream from a distributor a week ahead, and if too little is ordered the store loses business. If they order too much, it must be thrown away. The manager believes that a major determinant of ice cream sales is temperature; that is, the hotter it is, the more ice cream people buy. Using an almanac, the manager has determined the average daytime temperature for 10 weeks selected at random and then, from store records, has determined the ice cream consumption for the same 10 weeks. The data are summarized as follows.

Week	Temperature	(Gallons Sold)
1	73º	110
2	65	95
3	81	135
4	90	160

Table continues

Week	Temperature	(Gallons Sold)
5	75	97
6	77	105
7	82	120
8	93	175
9	86	140
10	79	121

a. Develop a linear regression model for this data and forecast the ice cream consumption if the average weekly daytime temperature is expected to be 85°.
b. Determine the strength of the linear relationship between temperature and ice cream consumption using correlation.

10-25. Compute the coefficient of determination for the data in Problem 24 and explain its meaning.

10-25. 0.863

10-26. Administrators at State University believe that decreases in the number of freshmen applications that they have experienced are directly related to tuition increases. They have collected the following enrollment and tuition data for the last decade.

10.26. a. $y = 6{,}541.66 - 0.448x$; $y(9{,}000) = 2{,}503.2$; $y(7{,}000) = 3{,}400.6$
b. –0.754
c. See Solutions Manual.

Year	Freshman Applications	Annual Tuition ($)
1	6,050	3,600
2	4,060	3,600
3	5,200	4,000
4	4,410	4,400
5	4,380	4,500
6	4,160	5,700
7	3,560	6,000
8	2,970	6,000
9	3,280	7,500
10	3,430	8,000

a. Develop a linear regression model for these data and forecast the number of applications for State University if tuition increases to $9,000 per year and if tuition is lowered to $7,000 per year.
b. Determine the strength of the linear relationship between freshmen applications and tuition using correlation.
c. Describe the various planning decisions for State University that would be impacted by the forecast for freshmen applications.

10-27. Develop a linear trend line model for the freshmen applications data at State University in Problem 10-26.

a. Does this forecast appear to be more or less accurate than the linear regression forecast developed in Problem 10-26? Justify your answer.
b. Compute the correlation coefficient for the linear trend line forecast and explain its meaning.

10-27. $y = 5582 - 260.36x$
a. Linear trend line forecast more accurate.
b. –0.843

10-28. Explain what the numerical value of the slope of the linear regression equation in Problem 10-24 means.

10-28. See Solutions Manual.

10-29. Some members of management of the Fairface Cosmetics Firm believe that demand for its products is related to the promotional activities of local department stores where their cosmetics are sold. However, others in

 ★ 0-29. No, correlation coefficient = –0.201.

management believe that other factors, such as local demographics, are stronger determinants of demand behavior. The following data for local annual promotional expenditures for Fairface products and local annual unit sales for Fairface lip gloss have been collected form 20 stores selected at random from different localities.

Store	*Annual Unit Sales ($1,000s)*	*Annual Promotional Expenditures ($1,000s)*
1	3.5	12.6
2	7.2	15.5
3	3.1	10.8
4	1.6	8.7
5	8.9	20.3
6	5.7	21.9
7	6.3	25.6
8	9.1	14.3
9	10.2	15.1
10	7.3	18.7
11	2.5	9.6
12	4.6	12.7
13	8.1	16.3
14	2.5	8.1
15	3.0	7.5
16	4.8	12.4
17	10.2	17.3
18	5.1	11.2
19	11.3	18.5
20	10.4	16.7

Based on these data, does it appear that the strength of the relationship between sales and promotional expenditures is sufficient to warrant using a linear regression forecasting model? Explain your response. (Computer solution is suggested.)

10-30. See Solutions Manual.

★ 10-30. The Gametime Hat company manufactures baseball-style caps with various team logos. The caps come in an assortment of designs and colors. The company has had monthly sales for the past 24 months as follows.

Month	*Demand (1,000s)*	*Month*	*Demand (1,000s)*
1	8.2	13	10.3
2	7.5	14	10.5
3	8.1	15	11.7
4	9.3	16	9.8
5	9.1	17	10.8
6	9.5	18	11.3
7	10.4	19	12.6
8	9.7	20	11.5
9	10.2	21	10.8
10	10.6	22	11.7
11	8.2	23	12.5
12	9.9	24	12.8

Develop a forecast model using the method you believe best, and justify your selection using a measure (or measures) of forecast accuracy. (Computer solution recommended.)

CASE PROBLEM

See Solutions Manual.

Forecasting at State University

During the last few years the legislature has severely reduced funding for State University. In reaction, the administration at State has significantly raised tuition each year for the past five years. Perceived as a bargain five years ago, State is now considered to be one of the more expensive state-supported universities. This has led some parents and students to question the value of a State education, and applications for admission have declined. Since a portion of state educational funding is based on a formula tied to enrollments, State has maintained its enrollment levels by going deeper into its applicant pool and accepting less qualified students.

On top of these problems, a substantial increase in the college-age population is expected in the next decade, resulting from a "baby boom" in the early 1980s. Key members of the state legislature have told the university administration that State will be expected to absorb additional students during the next decade. However, because of the economic outlook and the budget situation, they should not expect any funding increases for additional facilities, classrooms, dormitory rooms, or faculty. The university already has a classroom deficit in excess of 25 percent, and class sizes are above the average of their peer institutions.

The president of the university, Tanisha Lindsey, established several task forces consisting of faculty and administrators to address these problems. These groups made several wide-ranging general recommendations, including the implementation of appropriate total quality management (TQM) practices and more in-depth, focused planning.

Discuss in general terms how forecasting might be used for university planning to address these specific problem areas and the role of forecasting in initiating a TQM approach. Include in your discussion the types of forecasting methods that might be used.

CASE PROBLEM

See Solutions Manual.

Tech Bookstore Warehouse Expansion

The Tech Bookstore is owned and operated by the university through an independent corporation with its own board of directors. Don Williams, manager of the Tech Bookstore, has been developing a proposal to submit to the Board of Directors for some capital improvements in the bookstore in order better to serve the students and faculty customers at Tech. One area that required particular attention was the limited space currently devoted to computer equipment and software. He estimates that he really needs to triple the size of the existing space of the computer department in order to provide the products and services needed. Unfortunately, the bookstore is located in an area of the campus that prohibits physical expansion of the store. The store is bounded on one side by the library, on another by the continuing education center, and on the other two sides by roads. As such, any additional space for the computer department must come from inside the store walls, and there is no other department with surplus space.

Mr. Williams concluded that the only legitimate means of expanding retail operations is to use most of the existing in-store storage space in the building. Doing so requires that he obtain additional storage space off the bookstore premises. Thus, he began to investigate the possibility of leasing or perhaps purchasing a warehouse within convenient driving distance of the bookstore so that he could bring items to the store on demand by truck.

Mr. Williams worked with a local realtor to identify several local properties that looked promising. However, as he prepared his proposal for the board of directors, Mr. Williams discovered that he could arrange a number of different types of mortgages for a warehouse, very similar to the mortgages an individual might arrange to purchase a home. He discovered that he could get a fixed-rate mortgage or three- or five-year adjustable-rate mortgages. An adjustable-rate mortgage has constant payments over the first three or five years of the mortgage life, and then the interest rate is adjusted every third or fourth year based on government long-term (three- to five-year) treasury note rates. In addition, the length of the mortgage can vary.

Mr. Williams knew he needed to analyze these mortgage alternatives further before making his proposal. He decided the first thing he needed to do was get some idea of how U.S. treasury notes might behave and attempt to forecast what their rates would be like in the future. He went to the university library and got the following data for three- to five-year treasury note interest rates from 1960 to 1991.

Year	*Rate*	*Year*	*Rate*
1960	3.21	1977	6.69
1961	3.40	1978	8.29
1962	3.57	1979	9.71
1963	3.72	1980	11.55
1964	4.06	1981	14.44
1965	4.22	1982	12.92
1966	5.16	1983	10.45
1967	5.07	1984	11.89
1968	5.59	1985	9.64
1969	6.85	1986	7.06
1970	7.37	1987	7.68
1971	5.77	1988	8.26
1972	5.85	1989	8.55
1973	6.92	1990	8.26
1974	7.82	1991	6.80
1975	7.49	1992	6.12
1976	6.77		

Develop an appropriate forecast model for Don Williams to use to forecast treasury note rates in the future and indicate how accurate it appears to be based on historical data. What patterns in interest rate behavior might Mr. Williams logically predict in the next decade, if any? What other types of forecasts might be of interest to Mr. Williams relative to his decision to lease or purchase a warehouse?

REFERENCES

Box, G .E .P., and G. M. Jenkins, *Time Series Analysis: Forecasting and Control,* 2d ed., Oakland, Calif.: Holden-Day, 1976.

Brown, R. G., *Statistical Forecasting for Inventory Control,* New York: McGraw-Hill, 1959.

Chambers, J. C., K. M. Satinder, and D. D. Smith, "How to Choose the Right Forecasting Technique," *Harvard Business Review* (July–August 1971): 45–74.

Gardner, E. S., "Exponential Smoothing: The State of the Art," *Journal of Forecasting* 4, no. 1 (1985).

Gardner, E. S., and D. G. Dannenbring, "Forecasting With Exponential Smoothing: Some Guidelines for Model Selection," *Decision Sciences* 11, no. 2 (1980) 370–83.

Makridakis, S., S. C. Wheelwright, and V. E. McGee, *Forecasting: Methods and Applications,* 2d ed., New York: John Wiley, 1983.

Tersine, R. J., and W. Riggs, "The Delphi Technique: A Long-Range Planning Tool," *Business Horizons* 19, no. 2 (1976).

11

AGGREGATE PRODUCTION AND CAPACITY PLANNING

CHAPTER OUTLINE

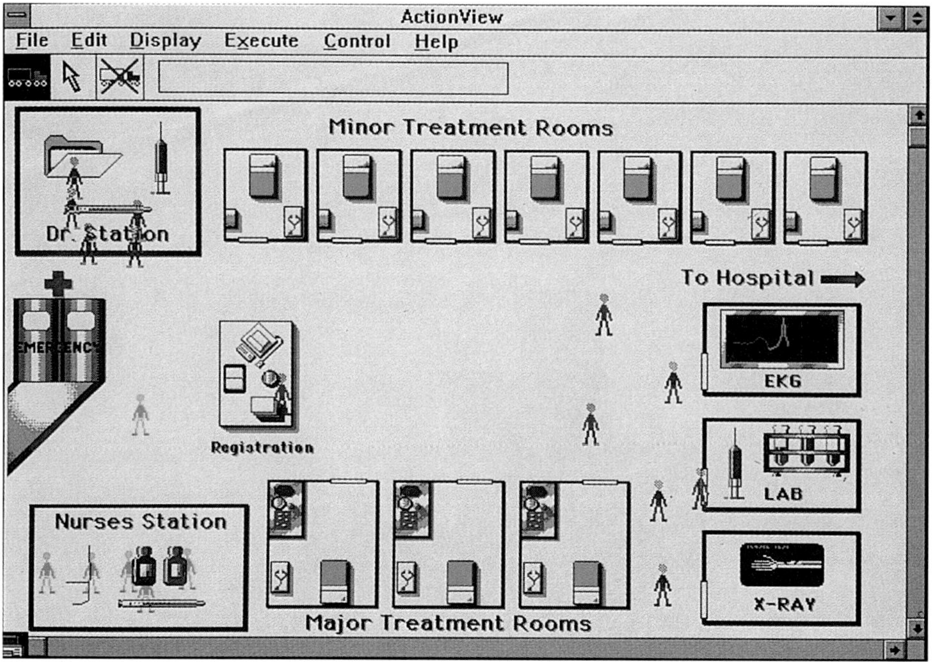

Increased life expectancy, improved health care, and shifting demographics have alternate demand for hospital resources. Tight budgets have intensified the problem. Capacity decisions related to staffing, expansion, priority of care, and space utilization are part of aggregate planning. The computer program shown here is being used to simulate different alternatives for alleviating overcrowding of an outpatient facility.

PLANNING HOSPITAL NEEDS

The Henry Ford Health System, located in southeast Michigan, consists of a 903-bed tertiary care hospital and research facility, thirty-five ambulatory care centers, three additional inpatient centers, a 400,000-member HMO, and 920 salaried physicians. The hospital houses thirty different nursing units, ranging from an eight-bed neurosurgical intensive care unit to a forty-four-bed general medicine unit. Over the past ten years, more and more complex medical procedures are being performed with little if any requirements for inpatient care. As a result, the overall demand for hospital beds has declined, and many communities have set about to reduce their excess capacity. Further attempts to control health-care costs have centered on staffing requirements, especially nursing staff, which accounts for 40 percent of personnel costs. The problem that hospital administrators are facing is basically an aggregate planning problem of varying demand and resource requirements with associated costs and demand penalties.

Henry Ford Hospital (HFH) exhibits many of the characteristics that make aggregate planning a difficult process:

- *Rapid demand changes:* The average turnover rate at HFH is 100 beds per day. A different mix of patients requires different resources, so even if overall demand is steady, the specific resources required by patient demand can be diverse. In addition to the high turnover, demand at HFH is sporadic. It is not unusual for the number of occupied beds to vary as much as 150 in a 2-week period.
- *High penalty costs:* If a patient is not admitted to the hospital due to lack of space, the HFH system is doubly penalized. It loses the revenue it would have received

from the patient, but also, as an HMO, it must pay another hospital to provide the required care. If the care is unsatisfactory, the potential for malpractice can be quite expensive.

- *Limited resources:* The labor market for RNs is tight. It can take from 3 to 4 months to recruit and train a new RN and it costs $7,600 per nurse.
- *High carrying costs:* The cost of staffing an unoccupied patient module (defined as an eight-bed unit) is in excess of $35,000 per month.

The problems of matching resources to demand became apparent when HFH made a decision to reduce the nursing staff by several positions, only to reopen those positions and recruit more staff a short time later. To avoid a recurrence of such short-sighted decision making, HFH created a "bed model" to better understand the changing demand patterns, the points and magnitude of changes in demand, and the costs and other consequences of resource adjustments. Based on sophisticated control charts of patient demand, the model helped hospital administrators formulate policies on resource usage. Demand conditions identified as out of control required increases or decreases in resources.

From the analysis, HFH determined the following:

- Although an average change in demand of fifty patients may affect the revenue of the hospital as a whole, when it is spread across twelve different medical units, the change in terms of resources required may be negligible. For example, it may not even result in the loss of one full-time position.
- Organizing nurses into "pods" of two to four nursing units that require similar nursing skills allows resources to be utilized more effectively. Nurses can float or be temporarily reassigned to any of the nursing units in their pod without retraining or reduction in performance.
- Permanent staff reduction should not be considered for fewer than fifteen positions at a time. Typically, an overstaffed situation cannot be corrected in less than 4 weeks. The estimated cost of operating overstaffed is $14,600 per week.
- Increases in permanent staff should not be considered until at least five extra personnel are needed. In the interim, the cost of using overtime and temporary agency staff is $6,300 per week.
- Before reducing resources, a check should be made of the demand over the last 60 days in any unit or pod to make sure it did not exceed 90 percent of capacity in any one day.

These types of decision rules helped HFH better manage its resources and more effectively respond to demand. Currently, the hospital is considering ways to improve its aggregate planning process by finding a forecasting method that can reasonably predict demand 6 to 8 weeks into the future, refining the forecast to include demand changes assignable to special causes (such as holidays), and establishing procedures for rapidly opening beds for sudden surges in demand.[1]

[1]Schramm, William R., and Louis E. Freund, "Application of Economic Control Charts by a Nursing Modeling Team," *Industrial Engineering* (April 1993): 27–31.

Aggregate production planning determines the resource capacity needed to meet demand.

Aggregate production planning (APP) determines the resource capacity that a firm will need to meet its demand. It plans the production of goods or services over an intermediate time horizon, from 6 to 18 months in the future. Within this time frame, it is usually not feasible to increase capacity by building new facilities or purchasing new equipment; however, it *is* feasible to hire or lay off workers, increase or reduce the workweek, add an extra shift, subcontract out work, use overtime, or build up and deplete inventory levels. Thus, aggregate production planning is also concerned with determining, allocating, and adjusting resource capacity to meet demand. For this reason, it is often referred to as *aggregate capacity planning* or, simply, *aggregate planning*.[2]

The term *aggregate* is used because the plans are developed for product lines or product families rather than individual products. For example, an aggregate production plan might specify how many bicycles are to be produced but would not identify them by color, size, tires, or type of brakes. Resource capacity is also expressed in aggregate terms, typically as labor or machine hours. Average labor hours are used, without regard to the type of labor. Similarly, machine hours are not identified by type of machine or may be given only for critical work centers. As a service example, we might determine that a correctional facility can house 100 inmates, without differentiating by sex or type of offender.

The production plan itself is usually expressed in *units* of aggregate production per month or quarter, but that figure may be converted to *sales dollars* for use by top management. The size of the work force, inventory levels, and number of units or sales dollars subcontracted, back ordered, or lost may also be specified in the production plan.

APP evaluates alternative capacity sources to find an economic strategy for satisfying demand.

The objectives of aggregate production planning are twofold: 1. to develop an economic strategy for meeting demand, and 2. to establish a companywide game plan for the allocation of resources. In terms of the first objective, we discuss several quantitative techniques that help the decision maker select the most cost-effective methods of adjusting capacity. We also discuss some alternatives for managing demand that might better utilize existing capacity.

The second objective refers to the long-standing battle between the marketing and production functions within a firm. Marketing personnel who are evaluated solely on sales volume have the tendency to make unrealistic sales commitments (either in terms of quantity or timing) that production is expected to meet, sometimes at an exorbitant price. On the other hand, production personnel, who are evaluated on keeping manufacturing costs down, may refuse to accept orders that would require more expensive resources (such as overtime wage rates) or hard-to-meet completion dates. The job of production planning is to match forecasted demand with available capacity. If capacity is inadequate, it can usually be expanded, but at a cost. The company needs to determine if the extra cost is worth the increased revenue from the sale and if the sale is consistent with the strategy of the firm. Thus, the aggregate production plan should not be determined by manufacturing personnel alone; rather, it should be agreed upon by top management from all the functional areas of the firm—manufacturing, marketing, and finance. Furthermore, it should reflect company policy (such as avoiding layoffs, limiting inventory levels, or maintaining a specified customer service level) and strategic objectives (such as capturing a certain share of the market or achieving targeted levels of quality or profit). Because of the various factors and viewpoints that are considered, the production plan is often referred to as the company's *game plan* for the coming year, and deviations from the plan are carefully monitored. Figure 11.1 shows the various inputs to and outputs from aggregate production planning.

A company *game plan:* Don't promise what you can't deliver.

[2]We use the terms aggregate production planning, aggregate capacity planning, aggregate planning, production planning, and capacity planning interchangeably in this chapter.

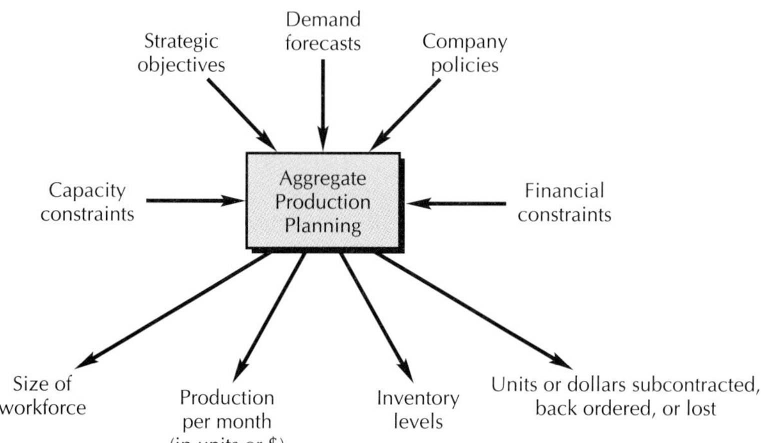

FIGURE 11.1 Inputs and Outpus to Aggregate Production Planning

Transparency 11.1 Aggregate Production Planning

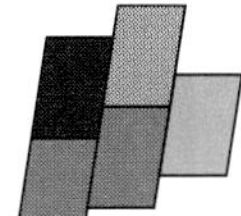

STRATEGIES FOR MEETING DEMAND

If demand for a company's products or services are stable over time or its resources are unlimited, then aggregate planning is trivial. Normally, demand forecasts are converted to resource requirements, the resources necessary to meet demand are acquired and maintained over the time horizon of the plan, and minor variations in demand are handled with overtime or undertime. Aggregate production planning becomes a challenge when demand fluctuates over the planning horizon. A seasonal demand pattern is a good example. In those cases, variations in demand could be met by the following strategies:

Meeting demand is a challenge when it fluctuates.

1. Producing at a constant rate and using inventory to absorb fluctuations in demand (level production)
2. Hiring and firing workers to match demand (chase demand)
3. Maintaining resources for high demand levels
4. Increasing or decreasing working hours (overtime and undertime)
5. Subcontracting work to other firms
6. Using part-time workers
7. Providing the service or product at a later time period (back ordering)

When one of these alternatives is selected, a company is said to have a **pure strategy** for meeting demand. When two or more are selected, a company has a **mixed strategy.** Figure 11.2, on page 548, shows two pure strategies in graphical form, 1. level production, and 2. chase demand.

A **pure strategy** involves only one capacity factor; a **mixed strategy** involves more than one.

The **level production** strategy sets production at a fixed rate (usually to meet average demand) and uses inventory to absorb variations in demand. During periods of low demand, overproduction is stored as inventory, to be depleted in periods of high demand. The cost of this strategy is the cost of holding inventory, including the cost of obsolete or perishable items that may have to be discarded.[3] Many U.S. firms have been criticized for relying too heavily on this strategy and for underestimating the high costs of holding inventory.

Level production involves producing at a constant rate and using inventory as needed to meet demand.

The **chase demand** strategy matches the production plan to the demand pattern and absorbs variations in demand by hiring and firing workers. During

Chase demand involves changing workforce levels so that production matches demand.

[3]We discuss inventory costs and policies further in the next chapter. At this point, we consider the costs only in aggregate terms.

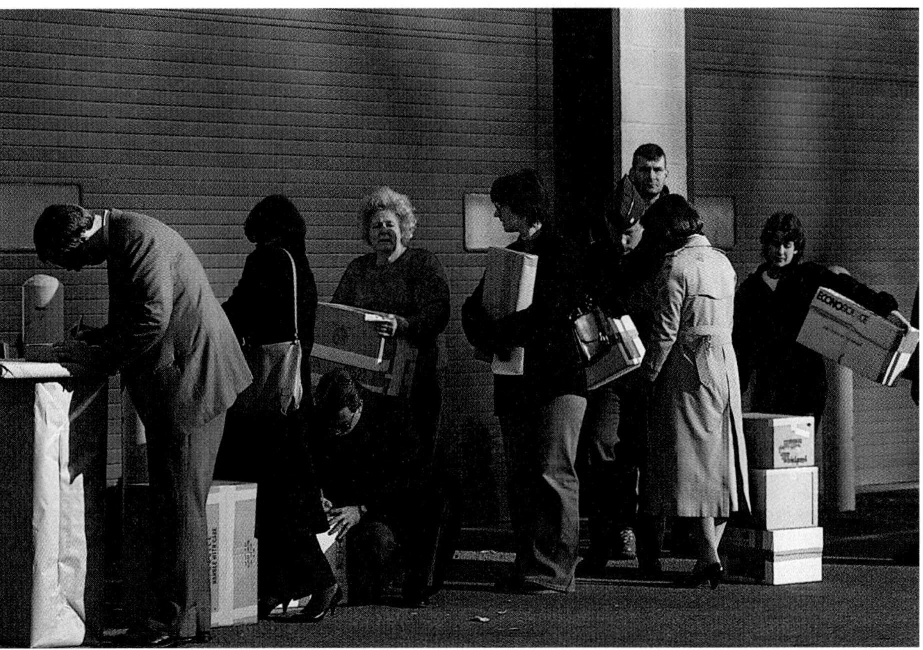

Products and services with seasonal demand patterns present challenges for planners, schedulers, and workers. In this photo, a long line of customers wait to mail their holiday packages. Should more workers be hired to handle the increased demand? Should the facility extend its hours? Should temporary mailing facilities be opened elsewhere? What incentives can be provided for mailing early? Aggregate planning examines the trade-offs, costs, and benefits of alternative strategies for meeting demand.

periods of low demand, production is cut back and workers are laid off. During periods of high demand, production is increased and additional workers are hired. The cost of this strategy is the cost of hiring and firing workers. Obviously, this approach would not work for industries in which worker skills are scarce or competition for labor is intense. On the other hand, during periods of high unemployment or for low-skilled workers, this approach may be quite cost-effective.

Maintaining resources for high-demand levels ensures high levels of customer service but can be very costly in terms of the investment in extra workers and machines that remain idle during low-demand periods. This strategy is used when superior customer service is important (such as Nordstrom's department store) or when customers are willing to pay extra for the availability of critical staff or equipment. Professional services trying to generate more demand may keep staff levels high, defense contractors may be paid to keep extra capacity "available," child-care facilities may elect to maintain staff levels for continuity when attendance is low, and full-service hospitals may invest in specialized equipment that is rarely used but is critical for the care of a small number of patients.

Overtime and undertime are common strategies when demand fluctuations are not extreme. In this way, a competent staff is maintained, hiring and firing

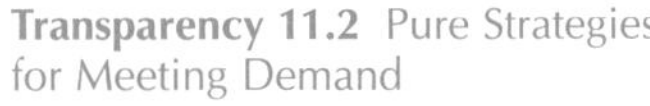

Transparency 11.2 Pure Strategies for Meeting Demand

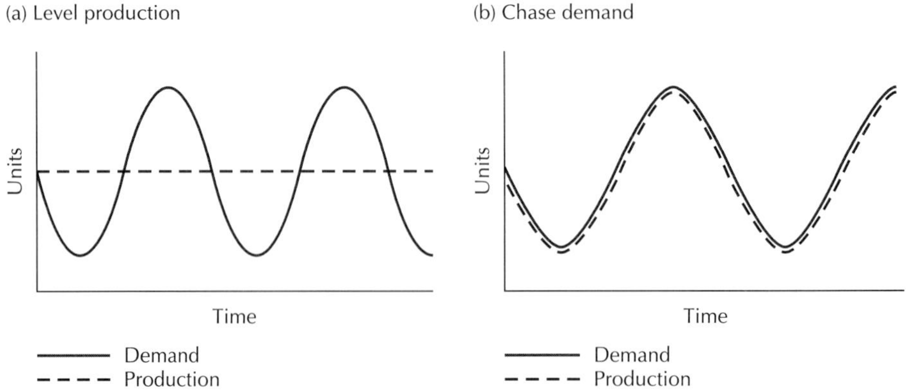

FIGURE 11.2 Pure Strategies for Meeting Demand

costs are avoided, and demand is met temporarily without investing in permanent resources. Disadvantages include the premium paid for overtime work, a tired and potentially less efficient work force, and the possibility that overtime alone may be insufficient to meet peak demand periods.

Mixed strategies: a combination of overtime/undertime, subcontracting, hiring/firing, part-time workers, inventory, back ordering

Subcontracting is a feasible alternative if a suitable subcontractor can be found who can reliably meet quality and time requirements. This is a common solution for component parts when demand exceeds expectations for the final product. The subcontracting decision requires maintaining strong ties with possible subcontractors and first-hand knowledge of their work. Disadvantages of subcontracting include reduced profits, loss of control over production, long leadtimes, and the potential that the subcontractor may end up being a competitor one day (a prediction for the aerospace industry).

Transparency 11.3 Mixed Strategies for Meeting Demand

Using part-time workers works well for unskilled jobs and in areas with large temporary labor pools (such as students, housewives, or retirees). Part-time workers are less costly than full-time workers (no health care or retirement benefits) and

Teaching Note 11.1 Contingent Workers

Video 11.1 *TIMS Edelman Awards Tape,* Program 3: "L.L. Bean"

Teaching Note 11.2 Tracking Peak Demand

GAINING THE COMPETITIVE EDGE

Meeting Peak Holiday Demand at Neiman Marcus

Neiman Marcus operates a 377,000-square-foot mail-order distribution center in Irving, Texas. Forty percent of its business is accounted for by the 2.8 million "Christmas Book" catalogs mailed out in mid-September. A flurry of orders is received immediately after the catalogs are mailed out; then volume drops off and levels out until early November. The sales volume then begins a steep ascent that peaks early in December. September demand represents 52 percent of peak shipments, and October represents 91 percent of peak shipments. Demand in November and December is in excess of 100,000 shipments per week. The peak demand volume of 28,000 orders per day is more than double normal sales. Despite these numbers, Neiman Marcus ships 90 percent of holiday orders within 1 day and 99 percent within 2 days, with 99.4 percent accuracy. How do they achieve such performance levels?

For one thing, they plan in advance. Although it's hard to predict which items will be hot sellers each year, close relations with suppliers and an early analysis of September's demand pattern (within 10 days of the catalog mailing) can make back ordering large volumes feasible. Fast-moving items are moved to a prominent place in the warehouse, and work flow is prioritized so that customer back orders receive immediate attention. A new conveyor system sports color-coded conveyors that identify flow patterns from different sources to shipping (from apparel to shipping, for example, versus toys or small gifts). It also utilizes bar codes extensively to route cartons to special areas for gift wrapping, Federal Express shipment, or special attention. Customers are given options for when their order is shipped. They can order now for shipment at a later date or receive Federal Express second-day service on any item in the catalog at no extra cost.

Another key to success is dedicated people with a great attitude. Neiman Marcus hires 300 extra people in their distribution center during the holiday season. Twenty percent of these workers return each year. To allow sufficient time for training, the company begins hiring temporaries when the catalogs are mailed out in September and gradually builds up their numbers over the next 2 months. Permanent staff personnel train the new hires, and the system of work is purposely designed to be simple and easy to learn.

Incentive pay, based on productivity and quality and reinforced with prizes and awards, adds fun and excitement to the work environment. With Neiman Marcus, as with many other retailers, making people happy during the holiday season ensures that the year will be a profitable one.

Source: Based on Auguston, Karen, "Neiman Marcus Plans Picking to Meet Peak Holiday Demands," *Modern Material Handling* (December 1992): 44–48.

are more flexible (their hours can and usually do vary considerably). Part-time workers have been the mainstay of retail, fast-food, and other services for some time and are becoming more accepted in manufacturing and government jobs. Japanese manufacturers traditionally use a large percentage of part-time or temporary workers. IBM staffs its entire third shift at Research Triangle Park, North Carolina, with temporary workers (college students). Part-time and temporary workers now account for about one-third of our nation's work force. Problems with part-time workers include high turnover, accelerated training requirements, less commitment to the company, and scheduling difficulties.

Back ordering is a viable alternative only if the customer is willing to wait for the product or service. For some restaurants, you may be willing to wait an hour for a table; for others you may not. Currently, customers of GM are willing to wait several months for the high-quality Saturn automobile. It will be interesting to see how long this trend lasts.

One aggregate planning strategy is not always preferable to another. The most effective strategy depends on the demand distribution, competitive position, and cost structure of each individual firm or product line. Fortunately, several quantitative techniques are available to help with the aggregate planning decision.

AGGREGATE PRODUCTION AND CAPACITY PLANNING TECHNIQUES

Transparency 11.4 Aggregate Production Planning Techniques

There are several quantitative techniques for aggregate planning.

The following quantitative techniques have been successfully applied to aggregate production and capacity planning. We discuss each of them in this section.

1. Trial and error (pure and mixed strategies)
2. General linear programming models
3. Transportation method of linear programming
4. Linear decision rule (LDR)
5. Search decision rule (SDR)
6. Management coefficients model

Trial-and-Error Techniques

Trial-and-error techniques involve formulating several strategies for meeting demand, constructing production plans from those strategies, determining the cost and feasibility of each plan, and selecting the lowest cost plan from among the feasible alternatives. Although an optimum solution may result, it is not guaranteed by the procedure. The effectiveness of trial-and-error strategies is directly related to management's understanding of the cost variables involved and the reasonableness of the scenarios tested. Example 11.1 compares the cost of two pure strategies, and then Example 11.2 uses AB:POM to compare several pure and mixed strategies for a more extensive problem.

Alternate Example 11.1

EXAMPLE 11.1

Production Planning Using Pure Strategies

Problem Statement:

The Good and Rich Candy Company makes a variety of candies in three factories worldwide. Its line of chocolate candies exhibits a highly seasonal demand pattern, with peaks during the winter months (for the holiday season and Valentine's Day) and valleys during the summer months (when chocolate tends to melt and customers are watching their weight). Given the following costs and quarterly sales forecasts, determine whether a level production or chase demand production strategy would more economically meet the demand for chocolate candies.

Quarter	*Sales Forecast (lb)*
Spring	80,000
Summer	50,000
Fall	120,000
Winter	150,000

Hiring cost = \$100 per worker
Firing cost = \$500 per worker
Inventory carrying cost = \$0.50 pound per quarter
Production per employee = 1,000 pounds per quarter
Beginning work force = 100 workers

Solution:
For the level production strategy, we first need to calculate average quarterly demand.

$$\frac{(50{,}000 + 120{,}000 + 150{,}000 + 80{,}000)}{4} = \frac{400{,}000}{4} = 100{,}000 \text{ pounds}$$

This becomes our planned production for each quarter. Since each worker can produce 1,000 pounds a quarter, 100 workers will be needed each quarter to meet the production requirements of 100,000 pounds. Production in excess of demand is stored in inventory, where it remains until it is used to meet demand in a later period. Demand in excess of production is met by using inventory from the previous quarter. The production plan and resulting inventory costs are summarized in the following table.

Level Production Strategy

Quarter	*Sales Forecast*	*Production Plan*	*Inventory*
Spring	80,000	100,000	20,000
Summer	50,000	100,000	70,000
Fall	120,000	100,000	50,000
Winter	150,000	100,000	0
			140,000

Cost = (140,000 pounds of inventory x 0.50 per pound) = \$70,000

For the chase demand strategy, production each quarter matches demand. To accomplish this, workers are hired and fired at a cost of \$100 for each one hired and \$500 for each one fired. Since each worker can produce 1,000 pounds per quarter, we divide the sales forecast by 1,000 to determine the required work force size. We begin with 100 workers and hire and fire as needed. The production plan and resulting hiring and firing costs are summarized in the accompanying table.

Chase Demand Strategy

Quarter	*Sales Forecast*	*Production Plan*	*Workers Needed*	*Workers Hired*	*Workers Fired*
Spring	80,000	80,000	80		20
Summer	50,000	50,000	50		30
Fall	120,000	120,000	120	70	
Winter	150,000	150,000	150	30	—
				100	50

Cost = (100 workers hired x \$100) + (50 workers fired x \$500)
= \$10,000 + \$25,000 = \$35,000

Comparing the cost of level production with chase demand, it is obvious that chase demand is the best strategy for the Good and Rich line of chocolate candies.

Although the chase demand strategy may be the best choice from an economic point of view, it may also seem unduly harsh on the company's work force. An example of a good "fit" between a company's chase demand strategy and the needs of the work force is a candy manufacturer located in rural Pennsylvania with a demand and cost structure much like that of Example 11.1. The location of the manufacturing facility is essential to the effectiveness of the company's production plan. During the winter months, when demand for candy is high, the company hires farmers from surrounding areas, who are basically idle that time of year. The farmers are let go during the spring and summer months, when they are anxious to return to their fields and the demand for candy falls. The plan is cost-effective and the extra help is content with the sporadic hiring and firing practices of the company.

The most common APP approach is trial and error using spreadsheets.

Probably the most common approach to production planning is trial and error using mixed strategies and computers (usually spreadsheets) to evaluate different options quickly. Mixed strategies can incorporate management policies, such as "no more than *x* percent of the work force can be laid off in one quarter" or "inventory levels cannot exceed *x* dollars." They can also be adapted to the particular quirks of a company or industry. For example, many industries that experience a slowdown during part of the year may elect simply to shut down the manufacturing facility at some point during the low-demand season and schedule everyone's vacation during that time. Furniture manufacturers typically close down for the month of July each year, and shipbuilders close down for the month of December. For some industries, the production planning task revolves around the supply of raw materials, not the demand pattern. Consider, for example, the applesauce manufacturer whose raw material is available only 40 days during a year. The work force size at its peak is 1500 workers, but it normally consists of around 350 workers. Almost 10 percent of the company's payroll is made up of unemployment benefits—the price of doing business in that particular industry.

Alternate Example 11.2

EXAMPLE 11.2

Trial-and-Error Production Planning Using Pure and Mixed Strategies

Problem Statement:

Demand for Quantum Corporation's action toy series follows a seasonal pattern—growing through the fall months and culminating in December, with smaller peaks in January (for after-season markdowns, exchanges, and accessory purchases) and July (for Christmas-in-July specials). The regular work force can produce on average 500 cases of action toys each month. Overtime is limited to 250 cases, and subcontracting is theoretically unlimited (i.e., equal to the highest monthly demand). Fifty cases of action toys are currently in inventory. The wage rate is \$10 per case for regular production, \$15 for overtime production, and \$25 for subcontracting. No stockouts are allowed. Increasing the work force costs approximately \$10 for every extra case produced. Decreasing the work force costs \$20 per case.

Management wishes to test the following scenarios for planning production:

1. Level production over the 12 months. Do not allow overtime or subcontracting.
2. Produce to meet demand each month. Absorb variations in demand by changing the size of the work force. Do not allow overtime, subcontracting, or inventory.

3. Keep the work force at its current level. Allow variations in demand to be absorbed first by overtime, then by subcontracting.
4. Create a production plan of your own design that allows overtime, subcontracting, inventory, and a changing work force.

Solution:

The first two strategies suggested are pure strategies, level production and chase demand, respectively. The last two strategies are mixed. AB:POM was used to evaluate the four planning scenarios. The solution printouts are shown in Exhibits 11.1 and 11.2 on pages 554 and 555, respectively.

Teaching Note 11.3 AB:POM for Aggregate Planning

The results in terms of average cost are summarized in the following table.

Scenario	*Cost*
1. Level production	$150,726
2. Chase demand	$177,500
3. Constant work force; then OT and subcontracting	$175,600
4. Mixed strategy (user-defined)	$158,600

From the scenarios tested, level production is the best strategy. It calls for a one-time increase in production to 984 cases per month that is basically maintained throughout the year (983 cases are produced during the latter half of the year). Inventory is held 11 months of the year. No overtime or subcontracting is used.

The mixed strategy designed by the user (your design may be different) increases regular production by hiring more workers in July and again in September. Overtime and subcontracting are used in January, November, and December. Inventory is held 9 months of the year.

Chase demand, in which work force size is varied each month to match demand, is the worst strategy for this data. Maintaining the original work force and then relying on overtime and subcontracting only slightly improves overall costs.

General Linear Programming Model

Pure and mixed strategies for production planning are easy to evaluate, but they do not necessarily provide an optimum solution. Consider the Good and Rich Company of Example 11.1. The *optimum* production plan is probably some combination of inventory and work force adjustment. We could simply try different combinations and compare the costs (i.e., the trial-and-error approach), or we could find the optimum solution by using *linear programming*.[4] Example 11.3 develops an optimum aggregate production plan for Good and Rich chocolate candies using linear programming.

Linear programming gives an optimum solution, but demand and costs must be linear.

Alternate Example 11.3

EXAMPLE 11.3

Aggregate Production Planning using Linear Programming

Problem Statement:

Formulate a linear programming model for Example 11.1 that will satisfy demand for Good and Rich chocolate candies at minimum cost. Solve the model with available linear programming software.

[4] Students unfamiliar with linear programming are referred to Chapter 2 Supplement for review.

METHOD -> Smooth production (let inventory vary)
SHORTAGES: Lost sales - Shortages not carried from period to period

All pds -->		3000	0	0	$10.0	$15.0	$20.0	$1.00	$5.00	$10.0	$20.0
		CAPACITIES						UNITS			
Pd	Demnd	Regtm	Ovrtm	Subcn	Regtim	Ovrtim	Subcon	Holdng	Shortg	Incres	Decres
Init	50	500	0	0							
Jan	1000	3000	0	0	984	0	0	34	0	484	0
Feb	250	3000	0	0	984	0	0	768	0	0	0
Mar	200	3000	0	0	984	0	0	1552	0	0	0
Apr	300	3000	0	0	984	0	0	2236	0	0	0
May	400	3000	0	0	983	0	0	2819	0	0	1
Jun	500	3000	0	0	983	0	0	3302	0	0	0
Jul	800	3000	0	0	983	0	0	3485	0	0	0
Aug	400	3000	0	0	983	0	0	4068	0	0	0
Sep	1000	3000	0	0	983	0	0	4051	0	0	0
Oct	1500	3000	0	0	983	0	0	3534	0	0	0
Nov	2500	3000	0	0	983	0	0	2017	0	0	0
Dec	3000	3000	0	0	983	0	0	0	0	0	0
TOTL	11800	36000	0	0	11800	0	0	27866	0	484	1
SUBTOTAL COSTS ->					118000	0	0	27866	0	4840	20

TOTAL COSTS = 150726

METHOD -> Produce to demand (let workforce vary)
SHORTAGES: Lost sales - Shortages not carried from period to period

All pds -->		3000	0	0	$10.0	$15.0	$20.0	$1.00	$25.0	$10.0	$20.0
		CAPACITIES						UNITS			
Pd	Demnd	Regtm	Ovrtm	Subcn	Regtim	Ovrtim	Subcon	Holdng	Shortg	Incres	Decres
Init	50	500	0	0							
Jan	1000	3000	0	0	950	0	0	0	0	450	0
Feb	250	3000	0	0	250	0	0	0	0	0	700
Mar	200	3000	0	0	200	0	0	0	0	0	50
Apr	300	3000	0	0	300	0	0	0	0	100	0
May	400	3000	0	0	400	0	0	0	0	100	0
Jun	500	3000	0	0	500	0	0	0	0	100	0
Jul	800	3000	0	0	800	0	0	0	0	300	0
Aug	400	3000	0	0	400	0	0	0	0	0	400
Sep	1000	3000	0	0	1000	0	0	0	0	600	0
Oct	1500	3000	0	0	1500	0	0	0	0	500	0
Nov	2500	3000	0	0	2500	0	0	0	0	1000	0
Dec	3000	3000	0	0	3000	0	0	0	0	500	0
TOTL	11800	36000	0	0	11800	0	0	0	0	3650	1150
SUBTOTAL COSTS ->					118000	0	0	0	0	36500	23000

EXHIBIT 11.1 AB:POM Solutions for Quantum Toys—Pure Strategies

METHOD -> Constant Reg time, then OT and sub
SHORTAGES: Lost sales - Shortages not carried from period to period

All pds -->		500	250	3000	$10.0	$15.0	$20.0	$1.00	$25.0	$10.0	$20.0
			CAPACITIES					UNITS			
Pd	Demnd	Regtm	Ovrtm	Subcn	Regtim	Ovrtim	Subcon	Holdng	Shortg	Incres	Decres
Init	50	500	0	0							
Jan	1000	500	250	3000	500	250	200	0	0	0	0
Feb	250	500	250	3000	500	0	0	250	0	0	0
Mar	200	500	250	3000	500	0	0	550	0	0	0
Apr	300	500	250	3000	500	0	0	750	0	0	0
May	400	500	250	3000	500	0	0	850	0	0	0
Jun	500	500	250	3000	500	0	0	850	0	0	0
Jul	800	500	250	3000	500	0	0	550	0	0	0
Aug	400	500	250	3000	500	0	0	650	0	0	0
Sep	1000	500	250	3000	500	0	0	150	0	0	0
Oct	1500	500	250	3000	500	250	600	0	0	0	0
Nov	2500	500	250	3000	500	250	1750	0	0	0	0
Dec	3000	500	250	3000	500	250	2250	0	0	0	0
TOTL	11800	6000	3000	36000	6000	1000	4800	4600	0	0	0
SUBTOTAL COSTS ->					60000	15000	96000	4600	0	0	0

TOTAL COSTS = 175600

METHOD -> User defined
SHORTAGES: Lost sales - Shortages not carried from period to period

All pds -->		500	250	0	$10.0	$15.0	$20.0	$1.00	$25.0	$10.0	$20.0
			SCHEDULE					UNITS			
Pd	Demnd	Regtm	Ovrtm	Subcn	Regtim	Ovrtim	Subcon	Holdng	Shortg	Incres	Decres
Init	50	500	0	0							
Jan	1000	500	250	200	500	250	200	0	0	0	0
Feb	250	500	0	0	500	0	0	250	0	0	0
Mar	200	500	0	0	500	0	0	550	0	0	0
Apr	300	500	0	0	500	0	0	750	0	0	0
May	400	500	0	0	500	0	0	850	0	0	0
Jun	500	500	0	0	500	0	0	850	0	0	0
Jul	800	800	0	0	800	0	0	850	0	300	0
Aug	400	800	0	0	800	0	0	1250	0	0	0
Sep	1000	1000	0	0	1000	0	0	1250	0	200	0
Oct	1500	1000	0	0	1000	0	0	750	0	0	0
Nov	2500	1000	250	500	1000	250	500	0	0	0	0
Dec	3000	1000	250	1750	1000	250	1750	0	0	0	0
TOTL	11800	8600	750	2450	8600	750	2450	7350	0	500	0
SUBTOTAL COSTS ->					86000	11250	49000	7350	0	5000	0

EXHIBIT 11.2 AB:POM Solutions for Quantum Toys—Mixed Strategies

Solution:

Model formulation:

$$\text{Minimize } Z = \$100(H_1 + H_2 + H_3 + H_4) + \$500(F_1 + F_2 + F_3 + F_4) + \$0.50(I_1 + I_2 + I_3 + I_4)$$

subject to

Demand constraints

$$P_1 - I_1 = 80{,}000 \quad (1)$$
$$I_1 + P_2 - I_2 = 50{,}000 \quad (2)$$
$$I_2 + P_3 - I_3 = 120{,}000 \quad (3)$$
$$I_3 + P_4 - I_4 = 150{,}000 \quad (4)$$

Production constraints

$$P_1 - 100W_1 = 0 \quad (5)$$
$$P_2 - 100W_2 = 0 \quad (6)$$
$$P_3 - 100W_3 = 0 \quad (7)$$
$$P_4 - 100W_4 = 0 \quad (8)$$

Work force constraints

$$W_1 - H_1 + F_1 = 100 \quad (9)$$
$$W_2 - W_1 - H_2 + F_2 = 0 \quad (10)$$
$$W_3 - W_2 - H_3 + F_3 = 0 \quad (11)$$
$$W_4 - W_3 - H_4 + F_4 = 0 \quad (12)$$

where H_t = number of workers hired for period t
F_t = number of workers fired for period t
I_t = units in inventory at the end of period t
P_t = units produced in period t
W_t = work force size for period t

- *Objective function:* The objective function seeks to minimize the cost of hiring workers, firing workers, and holding inventory. Cost values are provided in the problem statement for Example 11.1. The number of workers hired and fired each quarter and the amount of inventory held are variables whose values are determined by solving the linear programming (LP) problem.
- *Demand constraints:* The first set of constraints ensure that demand is met each quarter. Demand can be met from production in the current period and/or inventory from the previous period. Units produced in excess of demand remain in inventory at the end of the period. In general form, the demand equations are constructed as

$$I_{t-1} + P_t = D_t + I_t$$

where D_t is the demand in period t, as specified in the problem.

To express the equation in standard LP format, the value on the right-hand side must be a constant. Leaving demand on the right-hand side, we have

$$I_{t-1} + P_t - I_t = D_t$$

There are four demand constraints, one for each quarter. Since there is no beginning inventory, $I_0 = 0$, and it can be dropped from the first demand constraint.

- *Production constraints:* The four production constraints convert the work force size to the number of units that can be produced. Each worker can produce 1,000 units a quarter, so the production each quarter is 1,000 times the number of workers employed, or

$$P_t = 1{,}000W_t$$

In standard LP format, the equation becomes:

$$P_t - 1{,}000W_t = 0$$

- *Work force constraints:* The work force constraints limit the work force size in each period to the previous period's work force plus the number of workers in the current period minus the number of workers fired.

  $$W_t = W_{t-1} + H_t - F_t$$

  Bringing all the variables to the left-hand side, the equation becomes

  $$W_t - W_{t-1} - H_t + F_t = 0$$

  Notice the first work force constraint appears slightly different. Since the beginning work force size of 100 is known, it remains on the right-hand side of the equation.

- *Additional constraints:* Additional constraints can be added to the LP formulation as needed to limit such options as subcontracting or overtime. The cost of those options is then added to the objective function.

The LP formulation is solved using AB:POM to yield the solution in Exhibit 11.3. Notice that the variables from H_1 to W_4 appear as x_1 through x_{20} in the AB:POM solution. The cost of the optimum solution is $32,000, an improvement of $3,000 over the chase demand strategy and $38,000 over the level production strategy. This reduced cost figure was achieved by doing the following:

- *Firing twenty workers in the first quarter:* This brought the work force size down from one hundred to eighty workers. The eighty workers produced 80,000 pounds of chocolate, which exactly met demand. In the second quarter, no workers were hired or fired, 80,000 pounds were produced, 50,000 pounds were used to meet demand, and 30,000 pounds were placed into inventory.

Example 11.3 - Good and Rich Co.

Solution value = 32000

		Optimal Value	Reduced Cost	Original Coeficnt	Lower Limit	Upper Limit
x1	H_t	0.00	600.00	100.00	-500.00	Infinity
x2		0.00	500.00	100.00	-400.00	Infinity
x3		10.00	0.00	100.00	50.00	350.00
x4		60.00	0.00	100.00	-350.00	200.00
x5	F_t	20.00	0.00	500.00	-100.00	1400.00
x6		0.00	100.00	500.00	400.00	Infinity
x7		0.00	600.00	500.00	-100.00	Infinity
x8		0.00	600.00	500.00	-100.00	Infinity
x9	I_t	0.00	0.90	0.50	-0.40	Infinity
x10		30000.00	0.00	0.50	0.05	0.60
x11		0.00	0.40	0.50	0.1	Infinity
x12		0.00	0.60	0.50	-0.10	Infinity
x13	P_t	80000.00	0.00	0.00	-0.90	Infinity
x14		80000.00	0.00	0.00	-0.50	0.10
x15		90000.00	0.00	0.00	-0.10	0.45
x16		150000.0	0.00	0.00	-0.60	0.40
x17	W_t	80.00	0.00	0.00	-900.00	Infinity
x18		80.00	0.00	0.00	-500.00	100.00
x19		90.00	0.00	0.00	-100.00	450.00
x20		150.00	0.00	0.00	-600.00	400.00

EXHIBIT 11.3

- *Hiring ten workers in the third quarter:* The work force rose to ninety workers, and 90,000 pounds of chocolate candies were produced. The 90,000 pounds produced plus the 30,000 pounds in inventory were sufficient to meet the demand of 120,000 pounds.
- *Hiring sixty workers in the fourth quarter:* The resulting work force of 150 workers produced 150,000 pounds of chocolate candies, which exactly met demand.

Transportation Method of Linear Programming

Teaching Note 11.4 The Transportation Method of APP

Use the transportation method when hiring and firing is not an option.

For those cases in which changing the size of the work force over the planning horizon is not an issue in developing the aggregate production plan (i.e., the decision has already been made or is prohibited), the transportation method of linear programming provides a straightforward, optimal solution procedure. First proposed by E. H. Bowman in 1965, the technique gathers all the cost information into one matrix and plans production based on the lowest-cost alternatives. Example 11.4 illustrates the procedure. Table 11-1 shows a blank transportation tableau for aggregate planning.

Transparency 11.5 Transportation Tableau

TABLE 11.1 Transportation Tableau for Aggregate Production Planning

		PERIOD OF PRODUCTION				
PERIOD OF USE		*1*	2	3	4	*Capacity*
1	Beginning Inventory					
	Regular					
	Overtime					
	Subcontract					
2	Regular					
	Overtime					
	Subcontract					
3	Regular					
	Overtime					
	Subcontract					
4	Regular					
	Overtime					
	Subcontract					
	Demand					

Alternate Example 11.4

EXAMPLE 11.4

APP by the Transportation Method of Linear Programming

Problem Statement:

Burruss Manufacturing Company uses overtime, inventory, and subcontracting to absorb fluctuations in demand. An annual production plan is devised and updated quarterly. Cost data, expected demand, and available capacities in units for the next four quarters are given here. Demand must be satisfied in the period it occurs; that is, no back-ordering is allowed. Design a production plan that will satisfy demand at minimum cost.

Quarter	*Expected Demand*	*Regular Capacity*	*Overtime Capacity*	*Subcontract Capacity*
1	900	1000	100	500
2	1500	1200	150	500
3	1600	1300	200	500
4	3000	1300	200	500

Regular production cost per unit	\$20
Overtime production cost per unit	\$25
Subcontracting cost per unit	\$28
Inventory holding cost per unit per period	\$ 3
Beginning inventory	300 units

Solution:

The problem is solved using the transportation tableau shown in Table 11.2 on page 561.

The tableau is a worksheet that is completed as follows:

- To set up the tableau, demand requirements for each quarter are listed on the bottom row and capacity constraints for each type of production (i.e., regular, overtime, or subcontracting) are placed in the far right column.
- Next, cost figures are entered into the small square at the corner of each cell. Reading across the first row, the beginning inventory values can be interpreted as follows. Inventory on hand in period 1 that is used in period 1 incurs zero cost. Inventory on hand in period 1 that is not used until period 2 incurs \$3 holding cost. If the inventory is held until period 3, the cost is \$3 more, or \$6. Similarly, if the inventory is held until period 4, the cost is an additional \$3, or \$9.
- Interpreting the cost entries in the second row, if a unit is produced under regular production in period 1 and used in period 1, it costs \$20. If a unit is produced under regular production in period 1 but is not used until period 2, it incurs a production cost of \$20 plus an inventory cost of \$3, or \$23. If the unit is held until period 3, it will cost \$3 more, or \$26. If it is held until period 4, it will cost \$29. The cost calculations continue in a similar fashion for overtime and subcontracting, beginning with production costs of \$25 and \$28, respectively.
- The costs for production in periods 2, 3, and 4 also are determined in a similar fashion, with one exception. Half of the remaining transportation tableau is blocked out as infeasible. This occurs because no back ordering is allowed for this problem, and production cannot take place in one period to satisfy demand that occurs in previous periods.
- Now that the tableau is set up, we can begin to allocate units to the cells and develop our production plan. The procedure is to assign units to the lowest-cost cells in a column so that demand requirements for the column are met, yet capacity constraints of each row are not exceeded. Beginning with the first de-

mand column for period 1, we have 300 units of beginning inventory available to us at no cost. If we use all 300 units in period 1, there is no inventory left for use in later periods. We indicate this fact by putting a dash in the remaining cells of the beginning inventory row. We can satisfy the remaining 600 units of demand for period 1 with regular production at a cost of $20 per unit.

- In period 2, the lowest-cost alternative is regular production in period 2. We assign 1,200 units to that cell and, in the process, use up all the capacity for that row. Dashes are placed in the remaining cells of the row to indicate that they are no longer feasible choices. The remaining units needed to meet demand in period 2 are taken from regular production in period 1 that is inventoried until period 2, at a cost of $23 per unit. We assign 300 units to that cell.
- Continuing to the third period's demand of 1,600 units, we fully utilize the 1,300 units available from regular production in the same period and 200 units of overtime production. The remaining 100 units are produced with regular production in period 1 and held until period 3, at a cost of $26 per unit. As noted by the dashed line, period 1's regular production has reached its capacity and is no longer an alternative source of production.
- Of the fourth period's demand of 3,000 units, 2,000 come from regular production, overtime, and subcontracting in the same period. Then 650 more units can be provided at a cost of $31 per unit from overtime production in period 2 and subcontracting in period 3. The next-lowest alternative is $34 from overtime in period 1 or subcontracting in period 3. At this point, we can make a judgment call as to whether our own workers want overtime or whether it would be easier to subcontract out the entire amount. As shown in Table 2, we decide to use overtime to its full capacity and fill the remaining demand from subcontracting.

For this example, our initial solution to the aggregate production problem happens to be optimal. In other cases, it may be necessary to iterate to additional transportation tableaux before an optimum solution is reached.[5] The optimum production plan, derived from the transportation tableau, is given in Table 11-3.

The values in the production plan are taken from the transportation tableau one row at a time. For example, the 1,000 units of regular production for period 1 is the sum of 600 + 300 + 100 from the second row of the transportation tableau. Ending inventory is calculated by summing beginning inventory and all forms of production for that period and then subtracting demand. For example, the ending inventory for period 1 is

$$(300 + 1{,}000 + 100) - 900 = 500$$

The cost of the production plan can be determined directly from the transportation tableau by multiplying the units in each cell times the cost in the corner of the cell and summing them. Alternatively, the cost can be determined from the production plan by multiplying the total units produced in each production category or held in inventory by their respective costs and summing them, as follows:

$$(4{,}800 \times \$20) + (650 \times \$25) + (1{,}250 \times \$28) + (2{,}100 \times \$3) = \$153{,}550$$

Although linear programming models will yield an optimum solution to the aggregate planning problem, there are some limitations. The relationships among variables must be linear, the model is deterministic, and only one objective is allowed (usually minimizing cost).

[5]The transportation method of LP is discussed in more detail in the supplement to Chapter 8.

TABLE 11.2 Completed Transportation Tableau for Burruss Manufacturing

PERIOD OF PRODUCTION		PERIOD OF USE 1	2	3	4	Capacity
1	Beginning Inventory	[0] 300	[3] —	[6] —	[9] —	300
	Regular	[20] 600	[23] 300	[26] 100	[29] —	1,000
	Overtime	[25]	[28]	[31]	[34] 100	100
	Subcontract	[28]	[31]	[34]	[37]	500
2	Regular		[20] 1,200	[23] —	[26] —	1,200
	Overtime		[25]	[28]	[31] 150	150
	Subcontract		[28]	[31]	[34] 250	250
3	Regular			[20] 1,300	[23] —	1,300
	Overtime			[25] 200	[28] —	200
	Subcontract			[28]	[31] 500	500
4	Regular				[20] 1,300	1,300
	Overtime				[25] 200	200
	Subcontract				[28] 500	500
	Demand	900	1,500	1,600	3,000	

TABLE 11.3 Production Plan for Burruss Manufacturing

		STRATEGY VARIABLES			
Period	*Demand*	*Regular Production*	*Overtime*	*Subk*	*Ending Inventory*
1	900	1,000	100	0	500
2	1,500	1,200	150	250	600
3	1,600	1,300	200	500	1,000
4	3,000	1,300	200	500	0
Total	7,000	4,800	650	1,250	2,100

Linear Decision Rule

The **linear decision rule** (LDR) solves a set of quadratic cost equations for an optimum solution.

The **linear decision rule (LDR)** is an optimizing technique developed in the 1950s for aggregate planning of a paint factory. A set of four cost equations was used to describe the major capacity-related cost variables in the factory: 1. payroll costs, 2. hiring and firing costs, 3. overtime and undertime costs, and 4. inventory costs. Figure 11.3, on page 563, shows a rough graph of these functions.

With the exception of payroll costs, which vary directly with the number of people employed, the cost functions are quadratic. This is a more realistic assumption for most companies. For example, consider the cost of hiring workers. When a few extra workers are hired, the cost is not very significant, but when hundreds or thousands of workers are hired, more support staff and supervisors are needed, services or facilities may have to be expanded, and the incremental contribution of the additional employees may decrease as less qualified or less experienced workers are hired. In terms of firing workers, major reorganizations are needed for large layoffs, and the cost of unemployment payments increases more rapidly as the percentage of workers fired increases.

When overtime is used, the first overtime workers can be placed at bottleneck work centers to boost productivity quickly. As more overtime is added, it is less productive. Workers whose performance may be excellent for the first few hours of overtime may find their performance deteriorating at the end of a 12-, 16-, or 20-hour day. Undertime follows a similar pattern. If a few hours of undertime are used (i.e., workers work 6 hours a day instead of 8), productivity remains relatively stable. However, if workers are called in for only 2 or 4 hours of work, they tend not to be as productive—they may just be getting up to speed when the day is over.

The inventory cost function in LDR attempts to balance the cost of ordering inventory with the cost of holding inventory. The bowl-shaped curve shown in Figure 11.3(d) is identical to the one we discuss in detail in the next chapter.

You may wonder at this point why this technique is called the *linear* decision rule if most of the costs are quadratic. That discrepancy can be explained by the procedure that is used to derive a solution. The four cost equations are summed and then differentiated, first with respect to the work force level and then with respect to the production rate. The differentiation of a curve yields a line. Thus, two

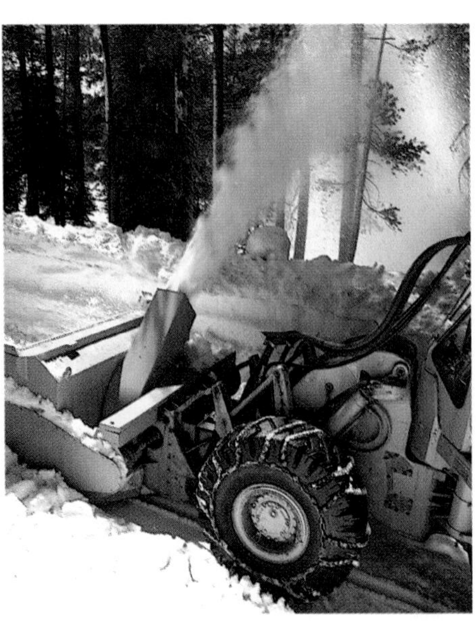

A carefully planned product mix can smooth out resource requirements. Existing products or services with cyclical demand patterns may be coupled with new products or services that exhibit countercyclical patterns in demand. One common example is a company that keeps its employment levels steady by removing snow in the wintertime and maintaining lawns during the summer.

Teaching Note 11.5 Linear Decision Rule

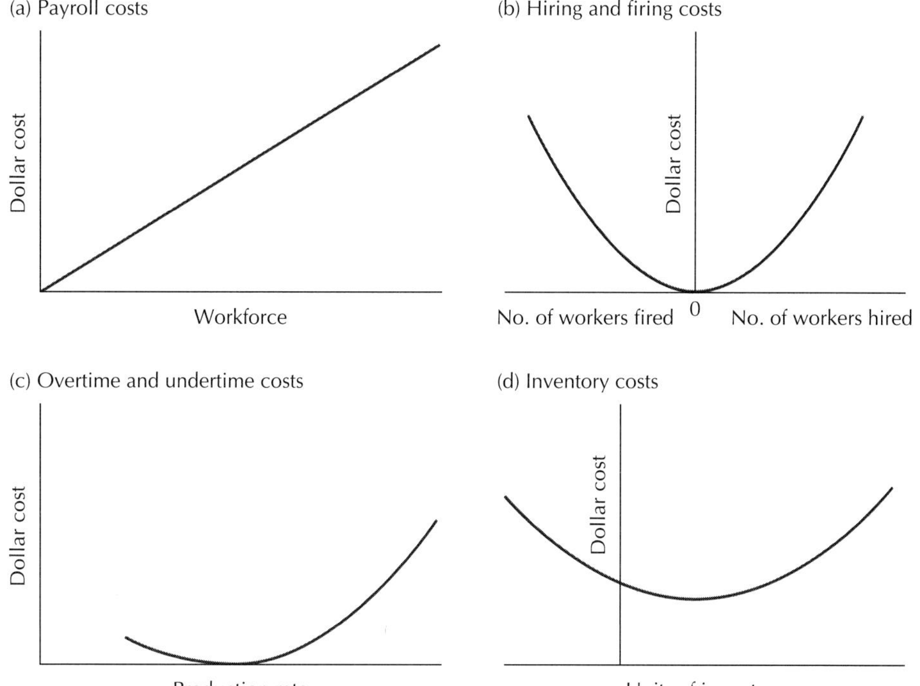

FIGURE 11.3 Cost Functions for the Linear Decision Rule

linear equations are produced (one for work force size and one for production rate), which are solved simultaneously to reach an optimum work force size and production rate for each period.

Although the cost equations developed for LDR may not match every company's needs, the procedure for deriving a solution is useful. Individual firms will need to construct their own cost functions from which to derive an optimal production plan. This process can be difficult. In addition, many companies are intimidated by the math involved with LDR. Thus, although LDR comes highly recommended in academic literature, it is rarely used in industry.

Search Decision Rule

SDR is sophisticated trial-and-error by computer.

The **search decision rule (SDR)** developed by W. H. Taubert in 1968 is a pattern search algorithm that tries to find the minimum cost combination of various work force levels and production rates. Any type of cost function can be used. The search is performed by a computer and may involve the evaluation of thousands of possible solutions, but an optimum solution is not guaranteed. Because of its ability to accept a variety of cost functions, SDR has enjoyed widespread use in industry.

Management Coefficients Model

The **management coefficients model** uses regression to improve the consistency of production planning decisions; expert systems are more common today.

The **management coefficients model** was developed by E. H. Bowman in the 1960s. A precursor to the expert systems of today, this approach assumes that managers have made good production planning decisions in the past and need only a reminder of how those decisions were made to continue to make good decisions. In other words, managers tend to have a problem with *consistency* in decision making, which can be corrected by using the management coefficients model. No cost functions are required for the model to operate. Instead, regression analysis is used on past planning decisions to develop an equation that minimizes deviations from average behavior. The equation can be used to determine work force levels, inventory levels, and production rates for future periods.

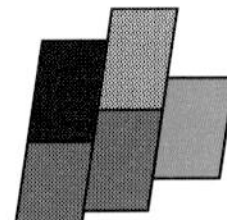

STRATEGIES FOR MANAGING DEMAND

The strategies and production planning techniques we have discussed thus far in this chapter have concentrated on adjusting capacity to meet demand. Another approach to aggregate planning involves actively *managing demand* rather than passively reacting to it. There are basically two approaches to managing demand: 1. demand can be shifted to other time periods that are easier to service with pricing incentives, sales promotions, and advertising campaigns, or 2. the product or service mix can be altered to include products or services with countercyclical demand patterns.

Aggregate planning can be used to "manage" demand, too.

Transparency 11.6 Strategies for Managing Demand

We are all familiar with attempts to shift demand into different time periods. Witness the winter coat specials in July, bathing suit sales in January, early-bird discounts on dinner, lower long-distance rates in the evenings, and get-away weekends at hotels during the off-season. Promotions can also be used to extend high demand into low-demand seasons. Holiday gift buying is encouraged earlier each year, and beach resorts plan festivals in September and October.

Shift demand into other periods

The second approach to managing demand involves examining the idleness of resources and creating a demand for those resources. Thus, McDonald's offers breakfast to keep its kitchens busy during the prelunch hours, pancake restaurants serve lunch and dinner, and heating firms also sell air conditioners. An example of a firm that has done an especially good job of finding "countercyclical" products to smooth the load on its manufacturing facility is a small U.S. manufacturer of peanut-harvesting equipment. The company is a job shop that has general-purpose equipment, 50 highly skilled workers, and a talented engineering staff. With these flexible resources, the company can make just about anything its engineers can design. Inventories of finished goods are frowned upon because they represent a significant investment in funds and because the product is so large that it takes up too much storage space. Peanut-harvesting equipment is generally purchased on an as-needed basis from August to October, so during the spring and early summer, the company makes bark-scalping equipment for processing mulch and pine nuggets used by landscaping services. Demand for peanut-harvesting equipment is also affected by the weather each growing season, so during years of extensive drought, the company produces and sells irrigation equipment. The company also decided to market its products internationally with a special eye toward countries whose growing seasons are opposite to that of the United States. Thus, many of its sales are made in China and India during the very months when demand in the United States is low.

Create demand for idle resources

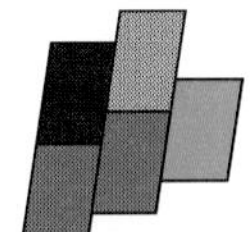

DISAGGREGATION

By determining a strategy for meeting and managing demand, aggregate planning provides a framework within which shorter-term production and capacity decisions can be made. In production planning, the next level of detail is a *master production schedule,* in which weekly (not monthly or quarterly) production plans are specified by individual final product (not product line). At another level of detail, we find a *material requirements plan* that plans the production of the components that go into the final products. In capacity planning, we might develop a *rough-cut capacity plan* as a quick check to see if the master production schedule is feasible. One level down, we would develop a much more detailed *capacity requirements plan* that matches the factory's machine and labor resources to the the material requirements plan. Finally, we would use a *shop floor control plan* to schedule and monitor the production that takes place at individual machines or work centers. At each level, decisions are made within the parameters set by the higher-level

Teaching Note 11.6 Customer Expectations

GAINING THE COMPETITIVE EDGE

Fine Furniture on Demand

In the recessionary times of recent years, keeping large inventories of fine furniture for low volumes of demand has become cost-prohibitive for furniture retailers. At the same time, customers who are hesitant about investing in big-ticket discretionary items, such as furniture, may easily be convinced to forego a purchase if they must wait several months for delivery of an item. Delivery cycles of 90 to 120 days, which used to be the norm for the furniture industry, are clearly unacceptable in today's tight market. Furniture is a zero-sum industry, meaning that to increase sales, market share must be taken away from a competitor. Obviously, deciding what customers want and having it available when they want it is essential to a company's success.

Furniture is somewhat like fashion; more that 10 percent of a manufacturer's line is new every year. Purchases are heavily skewed toward new items. Prototype products are displayed at semiannual market events, during which time almost 25 percent of the year's orders are placed by furniture dealers. Orders decrease significantly after the market events, when customers are purchasing from dealer stock. As a result, it may be 12 months or more before true customer demand at the retail level becomes apparent.

Henredon Furniture Industries makes fine wood furniture known for its intricate inlaid wood designs and handcrafted precision. The company sells its wares in more than 600 retail outlets, varying from chain stores to mom-and-pop operations. More than 1,000 items are offered to its customers at any given time, including dining room furniture, bedroom furniture, and occasional pieces. Production is typically performed in small lots of 100 pieces or less. In the past, Henredon managed its business by reacting to market conditions. Production schedules specifying which items to produce or cut were based on the previous 4 months' average sales. This often resulted in the wrong items being produced and large backlogs of other items subsequently requested by customers.

Recently, Henredon tried a new approach to production planning that is more proactive and better suited to the varying demand patterns of the furniture industry. The planning process begins with a forecast designed specifically for the furniture industry that smooths out seasonal variations and allows different demand patterns for new products. The forecast is then passed to a Lotus spreadsheet for production planning of 150 classes of furniture. The production plan is converted to a plant scheduling model to verify resource availability and then dropped into another Lotus spreadsheet to estimate shipments, backlogs, and inventories. What-if? scenarios are conducted to determine how long an item can afford to be out of stock before customer demand is lost.

Closer ties with the ultimate customer have helped Henredon manage demand and better understand its customers. Wine and cheese parties at dealer showrooms to promote specific furniture lines have helped to stimulate demand and make it more predictable. A "reserve stock program" for selected dealers guarantees ship-to-order service for items the dealer displays on the floor. As a result of these efforts, Henredon reduced its average order backlog from 11 weeks to 4 weeks. The inventory mix has significantly improved, and sales are up 3 percent.

Source: Based on Jenkins, Carolyn, "Accurate Forecasting Reduces Inventory and Increases Output at Henredon," *APICS —The Performance Advantage,* September 1992, pp. 37–39.

decisions. The process of moving from the aggregate plan to the next level down is called **disaggregation.** We discuss each of these levels of production and capacity planning later in the text.

Disaggregation is the process of breaking an aggregate plan into more-detailed plans.

AGGREGATE PLANNING FOR SERVICES

The aggregate planning process is different for services in the following ways:

Characteristics of aggregate planning for services

1. *Most services can't be inventoried.* It is impossible to store an airline seat, hotel room, or hair appointment for use in later periods when demand may be higher. When the goods that accompany a service can be inventoried, they typically have a very short life. Newspapers are good for only a day, flowers, at most a week, and cooked hamburgers, only 10 minutes.
2. *Demand for services is difficult to predict.* Demand variations occur frequently and are often severe. The exponential distribution is commonly used to simulate the erratic demand for services—high demand peaks over short periods of time with long periods of low demand in between. *Customer service levels* established by management express the percentage of demand that must be met and, sometimes, how quickly demand must be met. This is an important input to aggregate planning for services.
3. *Capacity is also difficult to predict.* The variety of services offered and the individualized nature of services make capacity difficult to predict. The "capacity" of a bank teller depends on the number and type of transactions requested by the customer. Units of capacity can also vary. Should a hospital define capacity in terms of numbers of beds, numbers of patients, size of the nursing or medical staff, or number of patient hours?
4. *Service capacity must be provided at the appropriate place as well as time.* Many services have a number of branches or outlets widely dispersed over a geographic region. Determining the range of services and staff levels at each location is part of aggregate planning.
5. *Labor is usually the most constraining resource for services.* This situation is an advantage in the aggregate planning process because labor is very flexible. Variations in demand can be handled by hiring temporary workers, using part-time workers, or using overtime. Summer recreation programs and theme parks typically hire teenagers out of school for the summer. Federal Express staffs its peak hours of midnight to 2 A.M. with area college students. McDonald's, Wal-Mart, and other retail establishments are wooing senior citizens as reliable part-time workers.

   Workers can also be cross-trained to perform a variety of jobs and can be called upon as needed. A common example is the sales clerk who also stocks inventory. Less common are the police officers in a suburb of Detroit who are cross-trained as firefighters and paramedics.

There are several services that have unique aggregate planning problems. Doctors, lawyers, and other professionals have emergency or priority calls for their service that must be meshed with regular appointments. Hotels and airlines routinely *overbook* their capacity in anticipation of customers who do not show up. The pricing structure for different classes of customers adds an extra factor to the aggregate planning decision. Pricing structures for airlines are especially complex. As part of the aggregate planning process, planners must determine the percentage of seats or rooms to be allocated to different fare classes in order to maximize profit or yield. This process is called **yield management.**

Yield management is a process for determining the percentage of seats or rooms to be allocated to different fare classes.

GAINING THE COMPETITIVE EDGE

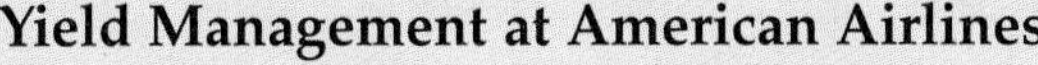

Yield Management at American Airlines

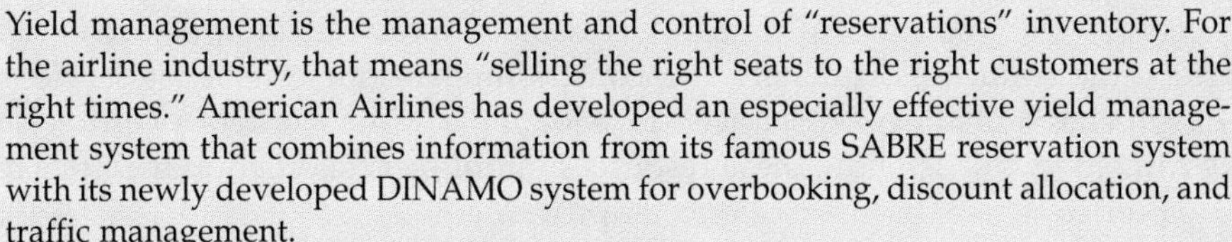

Yield management is the management and control of "reservations" inventory. For the airline industry, that means "selling the right seats to the right customers at the right times." American Airlines has developed an especially effective yield management system that combines information from its famous SABRE reservation system with its newly developed DINAMO system for overbooking, discount allocation, and traffic management.

Overbooking is the practice of intentionally selling more tickets for a flight than there are seats. Without overbooking, American estimates that 15 percent of the seats on sold-out flights would fly empty. The DINAMO overbooking model considers the probability that a passenger will cancel or not show up (estimated with exponential smoothing), the probability that a passenger who is turned away will choose another American flight (estimated by a passenger choice model), and the cost of overselling a flight (e.g., providing lodging and extra airline tickets to those "bumped").

Discount allocation is the process of determining the number of discount fares to offer on a flight. It is more concerned with the quality than the quantity of fares sold. At deep discount levels, even a full flight would lose money. At full fare, too many seats would remain empty. DINAMO provides a middle ground between the two with a concept called virtual nesting. Virtual nesting groups similar priced seats into eight or so buckets. Seats are sold from the lowest-valued buckets first. Full-fare seating is closed only if the flight is overbooked. For example, a flight of one hundred seats might reserve thirty seats for deep discount, sixty seats for moderate discount, and ten seats for full fare.

Traffic management changed dramatically with deregulation of the airline industry. Hub-and-spokes systems with connecting flights became the norm. Flights that once served a single market now serve thirty or more markets. DINAMO determines revenue targets for each market/fare class based on the fare and the probability that a connecting passenger will displace local traffic on each segment of the flight. As you might guess, the number of market/fare classes can be huge—American has 150,000 to manage.

Yield management allows airlines more effectively to match demand to supply. American's sophisticated yield management system saved the airlines $1.4 billion over its first three years of operation and is expected to generate $500 million annually in the coming years.

Source: Based on Smith, Barry, John Leimkuhler, and Ross Darrow, "Yield Management at American Airlines," *Interfaces* (January–February 1992): 8–31.

Teaching Note 11.7 Video Suggestion

SUMMARY

This chapter discussed the concept and process of aggregate production planning. To summarize, aggregate production planning does the following:

- Determines the resource capacity needed to meet demand
- Matches market demand to company resources
- Plans production 6 months to 18 months in advance
- Expresses demand, resources, and capacity in general terms
- Develops a strategy for economically meeting demand
- Establishes a companywide game plan for allocating resources

Aggregate planning is trivial in companies where demand is stable or resources are abundant, but it is critical for companies with seasonal demand patterns and for most services. Although there are several sophisticated techniques for aggregate planning, practitioners seem to prefer the trial-and-error approach using spreadsheets and what-if? analysis.

Aggregate planning for services is somewhat different than for manufacturing because the variation in demand is usually more severe and occurs over shorter time frames. Fortunately, the constraining resource in most services is labor, which is quite flexible. Services use a lot of part-time workers, overtime, and undertime. We will see how these resources might be scheduled more efficiently in Chapter 16 which discusses service improvement.

Production and capacity plans are developed at several levels of detail. In this chapter, we discussed the aggregate plan as the "game plan" for the company. The process of deriving more detailed production and capacity plans from the aggregate plan is called disaggregation.

The next chapter addresses one of the options we have discussed for absorbing variations in demand, inventory management.

SUMMARY OF KEY TERMS

aggregate production planning: the process of determining the quantity and timing of production over an intermediate time frame.

chase demand: a production planning strategy that schedules production to match demand and absorbs variations in demand by adjusting the size of the work force.

disaggregation: the process of breaking down the aggregate plan into more detailed plans.

level production: a production planning strategy that produces units at a constant rate and uses inventory to absorb variations in demand.

linear decision rule (LDR): a mathematical technique that solves a set of simultaneous equations to determine the optimum work force size and production rate.

management coefficients model: an analysis approach to aggregate production planning that uses regression analysis to improve the consistency of production planning decisions.

mixed strategy: a planning strategy that varies two or more capacity factors to determine a feasible production plan.

pure strategy: a planning strategy that varies only one capacity factor in determining a feasible production plan.

search decision rule (SDR): a pattern search algorithm for aggregate production planning.

yield management: a term used in the airline and hotel industries to describe the process of determining the percentage of seats or rooms to be allocated to different fare classes.

SOLVED PROBLEMS

1. The Transportation Method

Problem Statement:

Vultex Fibers produces a line of sweatclothes that exhibits a varying demand pattern. Given the following demand forecasts, production costs, and constraints, design a production plan for Vultex using the transportation method of LP. Also, calculate the cost of the production plan.

Period	*Demand*
September	100
October	130
November	200
December	300

Maximum regular production	100 units/month
Maximum overtime production	50 units/month
Maximum subcontracting	50 units/month
Regular production costs	$10/unit
Overtime production costs	$25/unit
Subcontracting costs	$35/unit
Inventory holding costs	$5/unit/month
Beginning inventory	0

Solution:

		PERIOD OF USE				
PERIOD OF PRODUCTION		*1*	*2*	*3*	*4*	*Capacity*
	Beginning Inventory	— [0]	— [5]	— [10]	— [15]	0
1	Regular	100 [10]	— [15]	— [20]	— [25]	100
	Overtime	[25]	[30]	[35]	50 [40]	50
	Subcontract	[35]	[40]	[45]	[50]	50
2	Regular		100 [10]	— [15]	— [20]	100
	Overtime		30 [25]	20 [30]	— [35]	50
	Subcontract		[35]	[40]	30 [45]	50
3	Regular			100 [10]	— [15]	100
	Overtime			50 [25]	— [30]	50
	Subcontract			30 [35]	20 [40]	50
4	Regular				100 [10]	100
	Overtime				50 [25]	50
	Subcontract				50 [35]	50
	Demand	100	130	200	300	

Period	*Demand*	*PRODUCTION PLAN* *Regular Production*	*Overtime Production*	*Sub-contracting*	*Ending Inventory*
Sept	100	100	50	0	50
Oct	130	100	50	30	100
Nov	200	100	50	50	100
Dec	300	100	50	50	0
Total	730	400	200	130	250

Cost = (400 x \$10) + (200 x \$25) + (130 x \$35) + (250 x \$5)
= 4,000 + 5,000 + 4,550 + 1,250
= \$14,800

2. *Trial and Error vs. Linear Programming*

Problem Statement.

Ollie Auto Company is a small manufacturer of cars, vans, and trucks in Eastern Europe. Demand for each of Ollie's three product lines has been healthy in recent months, but an impending labor strike threatens to slow down production. Ollie's data on forecasted demand, labor requirements, and profit for each product line are shown here. He estimates that even if the workers strike next month, the company can maintain a core of 75 workers, giving a maximum of 3,000 hours per week, or 12,000 hours per month. Ollie has been studying capitalism and has decided that if the strike occurs, he will absorb the reduced labor hours by decreasing production of those product lines that yield the least profit.

a. Generate a new production plan using Ollie's logic.
b. How much projected profit will be lost next month if the strike materializes?
c. Given that Ollie cannot possibly sell more than the demand forecast, recommend a product mix that will maximize profits during the strike.

Product Line	*Monthly Demand*	*Labor Required per Unit*	*Profit per Unit*
Cars	500	6 hours	\$1,000
Vans	100	4 hours	\$ 500
Trucks	200	2 hours	\$ 400

Solution:

a. Ollie wants to produce as much as possible of the high-profit products—in this case, cars. It would take (6 x 500) = 3,000 hours to completely meet the demand for cars, but producing 500 cars would use up the available labor hours. Ollie would produce *no* vans or trucks.
b. If Ollie had the capacity to meet demand, he would make a profit of:

(500 x \$1,000) + (100 x \$500) + (200 x \$400) = 500,000 + 50,000 + 80,000
= \$630,000

```
                        Linear Programming                    Solution
Number of constraints (2-99) 4        Number of variables (2-99) 3
maximize
                        Ollie Auto Company
Options→ NO step Cmputr PrtOFF
                  x1        x2          x3                 RHS
maximize        1000       500         400                          Shadow
const 1            1         0           0    <        500.00         0.00
const 2            0         1           0    <        100.00         0.00
const 3            0         0           1    <        200.00      66.6667
const 4            6         4           2    <       3000.00      166.667
Values →      433.33      0.00      200.00         $513,333.34
             Phase 2            Iteration 5                   0.06 seconds
```

Exhibit 11.4

If Ollie produced only cars, his profit would be reduced to

$$(500 \times \$1,000) = \$500,000$$

Thus, Ollie Auto stands to loose $130,000 per month as the labor strike continues.

c. First, we should note that although cars yield the highest profit for Ollie, they also use up the most labor resources. To find the optimum resource allocation, we can solve this problem with linear programming.

Model formulation:

$$x_1 = \text{number of cars produced}$$
$$x_2 = \text{number of vans produced}$$
$$x_3 = \text{number of trucks produced}$$

Maximize $Z = 1,000x_1 + 500x_2 + 400x_3$

subject to

$$x_1 \le 500$$
$$x_2 \le 100$$
$$x_3 \le 200$$
$$6x_1 + 4x_2 + 2x_3 \le 3,000$$

The AB:POM solution is given in Exhibit 11.4.

Ollie can produce 433 cars and 200 trucks during the labor strike, for a profit of $513,000. This strategy yields $13,000 more in profit than Ollie's initial strategy of producing cars alone.

QUESTIONS

11-1. What is the purpose of aggregate production planning?
11-2. When is aggregate production planning most useful?
11-3. List several alternatives for adjusting capacity.
11-4. What is the difference between a pure and mixed strategy?
11-5. Describe the output of aggregate production planning.
11-6. How do the following techniques differ in terms of the types of cost functions used and the type of solution produced?
   a. Linear programming
   b. Linear decision rule

c. Search decision rule
d. Management coefficients model

11-7. What options are available for altering the capacity of each of the following?
a. An elementary school
b. A prison
c. An airline

11-8. Discuss the advantages and disadvantages of the following strategies for meeting demand:
a. Use part-time workers.
b. Subcontract work.
c. Build up and deplete inventory.

11-9. Discuss several strategies for managing demand.

11-10. How is the aggregate planning process different when used for services rather than for manufacturing?

PROBLEMS

11-1. 120,000 regular production, periods 1–3
50,000 regular production, period 4
40,000 OT, period 3
$23,830,000

11-1. The Wetski Water Ski Company is the world's largest producer of water skis. As you might suspect, water skis exhibit a highly seasonal demand pattern, with peaks during the summer months and valleys during the winter months. Given the following costs and quarterly sales forecasts, use the transportation method to design a production plan that will economically meet demand.

Quarter	*Sales Forecast*
1	50,000
2	150,000
3	200,000
4	50,000

Inventory carrying cost = $3.00 per ski pair per quarter
Production per employee = 1,000 pairs of skis per quarter
Regular work force = 120 workers
Overtime capacity = 50,000 pairs of skis
Subcontracting capacity = 30,000 pairs of skis
Cost of regular production = $50 per pair of skis
Cost of overtime production = $75 per pair of skis
Cost of subcontracting = $85 per pair of skis

11-2. Chase demand

11-2. The CEO of Wetski Water Ski has just received a memo from the personnel manager complaining about the high cost and consequences of the company's erratic employment policies. Recalculate the cost of the aggregate production plan designed for Wetski in the previous problem. This time, include the cost of hiring and firing workers at the rate of $100 per worker hired and $400 per worker fired. Try a level production or chase demand production strategy. If necessary, allow back ordering at $10 per pair of skis per quarter. Which production plan more economically meets demand?

11-3. User-designed (mixed)

11-3. Rowley Apparel, manufacturer of the famous "Race-A-Rama" swimwear line, needs help planning production for next year. Demand for swimwear follows a seasonal pattern, as shown here. Given the following costs and demand forecasts, test these three strategies for meeting demand: a. level production, b. chase demand, and c. a user-designed plan (regular production at its capacity from April through September and then as much regular production and inventory in the other months as needed to meet annual demand). Which strategy would you recommend?

Month	*Demand Forecast*
January	1,000
February	500
March	500
April	2,000
May	3,000
June	4,000
July	5,000
August	3,000
September	1,000
October	500
November	500
December	3,000

Regular capacity per month	3,000 units
Overtime capacity per month	1,500 units
Subcontracting capacity per month	1,000 units
Regular wage rate	\$15 per unit
Overtime wage rate	\$25 per unit
Subcontracting	\$30 per unit
Holding cost	\$0.50 per unit
Lost sales cost	\$40 per unit
No beginning inventory	

11-4. In Problem 11-3, assume increasing the workforce costs \$1.00 per unit and decreasing the workforce \$2.00 per unit. Which strategy is the best now?

11-4. User-designed (mixed)

11-5. In Problem 11-3, suppose the market for Race-A-Rama swimwear has increased 2,000 units per month. Consider these three strategies: a. level production, b. chase demand, and c. constant production supplemented by overtime and subcontracting. Which strategy would you recommend?

11-5. Constant production, then overtime & subtracting

11-6. College Press publishes textbooks for the college market. The demand for college textbooks is high during the beginning of each semester and then tapers off during the semester. The unavailability of books can cause a professor to switch adoptions, but the cost of storing books and their rapid obsolescence must also be considered. Given the demand and cost factors shown here, use the transportation method to design an aggregate production plan for College Press that will economically meet demand. What is the cost of the production plan?

11-6. 10,000 regular production each period
5,000 overtime each period
4,000 subcontracting in period 3
6,000 subcontracting in period 4
\$1,808,000

Months	*Demand Forecast*
Feb.–Apr.	5,000
May–July	10,000
Aug.–Oct.	30,000
Nov.–Jan.	25,000

Regular capacity per month	10,000 books
Overtime capacity per month	5,000 books

Subcontracting capacity per month	6,000 books
Regular production rate	$20 per book
Overtime wage rate	$30 per book
Subcontracting	$35 per book
Holding cost	$2.00 per book
No beginning inventory	

11-7. a. $1,492,500
b. $1,507,500
c. $1,447,500

11-7. Mama's Stuffin' is a popular food item during the fall and winter months, but it is marginal in the spring and summer. Use the following demand forecasts and costs to test the following production planning strategies for Mama's Stuffin':

a. Level production over the 12 months. Use regular production and overtime to capacity.
b. Produce to meet demand each month. Absorb variations in demand by changing the size of the work force. Use subcontracting as needed.
c. Keep the work force at its current level. Allow variations in demand to be absorbed first by overtime and inventory, then by subcontracting.

Month	*Demand Forecast*
April	1,000
May	1,000
June	1,000
July	1,000
August	500
September	2,500
October	3,000
November	9,000
December	7,000
January	4,000
February	3,000
March	2,000

Regular capacity per month	2,000 pallets
Overtime capacity per month	1,000 pallets
Subcontracting capacity per month	unlimited
Regular production cost	$30 per pallet
Overtime production cost	$40 per pallet
Subcontracting	$50 per pallet
Holding cost	$5 per pallet
No beginning inventory	
Beginning work force	10 workers
Production rate	200 pallets per worker per month
Hiring cost	$5,000 per worker or $25 per pallet
Firing cost	$8,000 per worker or $40 per pallet

11-8. $1,139,250

★ 11-8. Quik-Fix Tax Service prepares taxes for customers year round. However, demand is heaviest during March, April, and May. Quik-Fix increases its work force several times over during those months and uses as much overtime (half of the regular time) as is available. In rare cases, Quik-Fix subcontracts out some work, but that practice really eats into profits. Subcontracting is limited to 1,000 customers per month. The average cost to prepare a customer's taxes is $50. Customers whose taxes are completed late pay a reduced rate. Use the following data to help Quik-Fix design an economical service strategy.

Month	*Demand Forecast*
January	1,000
February	1,000
March	3,000
April	10,000
May	5,000
June	400
July	400
August	200
September	200
October	300
November	300
December	500

Regular preparation cost	$50 per customer
Overtime production cost	$75 per customer
Subcontracting	$100 per customer
Backordering cost	$25 per customer per month
No beginning inventory	
Hiring cost	$50 per worker or $0.25 per customer
Firing cost	$50 per worker or $0.25 per customer
Beginning work force	2 workers
Preparation rate	200 customers per worker per month

11-9. Marc Klein is a manufacturer of rock-climbing equipment in Bohn, Germany. Demand for each of Marc's four product lines has been steady in recent months; however, government caps on worker hours threaten to slow down production. Marc's data on forecasted demand, labor requirements, and profit for each product line is shown. Marc estimates that his twenty-seven workers will be able to work a maximum of 1,080 hours per week, or 4,320 hours per month.

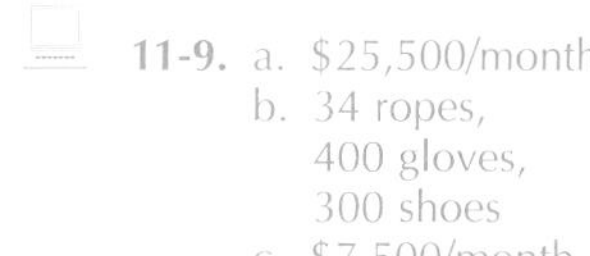

Product Line	*Monthly Demand*	*Labor Required per Unit*	*Profit per Unit*
Safety rope	200 units	15 hr	$30
Safety harness	100 units	20 hr	$25
Gloves	400 units	2 hr	$ 5
Shoes	300 units	10 hr	$50

a. What is the maximum profit Marc can earn per month, assuming he has the capacity to meet the monthly demand?
b. What product mix will maximize profit should the work-hour restrictions be put into effect?
c. How much profit per month does Marc expect to lose with the new regulations?

CASE PROBLEM

An Aggregate Plan for Darian's Gymnastics Center

Darian's Gymnastics Center has been extremely successful in its first two years of operation. During peak demand season, approximately 500 youngsters per week are taught gymnastics from the fundamentals to level 8 competition. Initially, Darian and Anita (his wife and partner) concentrated on generating enough demand for classes to keep their investment solvent. Now, they find themselves bursting at the seams, but only during the last half of the day. Anita does all the hiring and scheduling of employees and classes. She describes her dilemma as follows:

- Most of our students are school-age, so our classes are scheduled from 4:00 P.M. to 9:00 P.M. weekdays and 8:00 A.M. to 6:00 P.M. on Saturdays. The gym is crowded during those times and even though we maintain an 8 to 1 ratio of teachers to students, parents seem bothered by the current level of activity. I'd like to keep it down to a maximum of 5 classes using the gym at any one time.
- Most of our instructors are college students who have top-notch skills and identify well with the children. However, because of their age and other responsibilities, turnover is high. This is not popular with parents either. It's hard on me, too.
- We currently have around 20 individuals in each of our three competitive programs: women's gymnastics team, men's gymnastics team, and preteam. The competitive programs are based on a 10-month contract, with charges of $200/month, $100/month, and $100/month, respectively. The preteam and men's team practice for 5 hours a week, and the women's team practices 10 hours a week. These programs provide financial stability for the center and are the basis for our reputation and, thus, class enrollments. However, the center cannot survive on competitive programs alone. The recreational programs "feed" the competitive programs and generate a lot of excitement at the center and in the community. I'd like at least to maintain our current level of enrollment. Besides, several "Romp and Run" facilities (basically indoor playsets) have recently opened up in the city and that takes customers away from us.
- Students sign up for the recreational program in 6-week blocks of time. Each class meets for an hour once a week. The classes are broken up into beginners, intermediates, and advanced. Within each level, there are boys and girls classes, classes grouped by age, and accelerated classes. The fee per 6-week class is $60. Our enrollment is fairly steady throughout the year. The center is not air conditioned, so we only teach a few classes over the summer. We're basically closed down during July and August.
- Full time is 40 hours per week. Part-time employees generally work 30 hours a week, although we have had some work as few as 10 hours a week. I would like to staff the center with a core of full-time people and supplement with part-timers.
- I need some ideas for utilizing the center better and generating more revenue. I really don't know how to evaluate the trade-offs between expanding the competitive program and expanding the recreational program. We could easily take 20 more students in each team category, but I'm not sure that would be wise.

1. Calculate the capacity of Darian's Gymnastics Center in terms of student hours. How close is the center to capacity?
2. Should Anita accept more team members? Expand the number of recreational classes? Recommend avenues for increasing capacity and revenue.
3. What staffing pattern should Anita use?

1. 1,400 hr, 60%
2. Double team size, add 20 more rec. classes. See Solutions Manual.
3. At capacity, 12 FT, 3 PT.

REFERENCES

Bowman, E. H., "Production Planning by the Transportation Method of Linear Programming," *Journal of Operations Research Society* (February 1956): 100–103.

Bowman, E. H., "Consistency and Optimality in Managerial Decision Making," *Management Science* (January 1963): 310–21.

Buffa, E. S., and J. G. Miller, *Production-Inventory Systems: Planning and Control,* 3d ed., Homewood, Ill.: Irwin, 1979.

Holt, C., F. Modigliani, J. Muth, and H. Simon, *Planning Production, Inventories and Work Force,* Englewood Cliffs, N.J.: Prentice Hall, 1960.

Murdick, R., B. Render, and R. Russell, *Service Operations Management,* Boston: Allyn and Bacon, 1990.

Taubert, W., "A Search Decision Rule for the Aggregate Scheduling Problem," *Management Science* (February 1968): B343–59.

Tersine, R., *Production/Operations Management: Concepts, Structure, and Analysis,* New York: Elsevier-North Holland, 1985.

Vollmann, T., W. Berry, and D. C. Whybark, *Manufacturing Planning and Control Systems,* Homewood, Ill.: Irwin, 1991.

12

INVENTORY MANAGEMENT

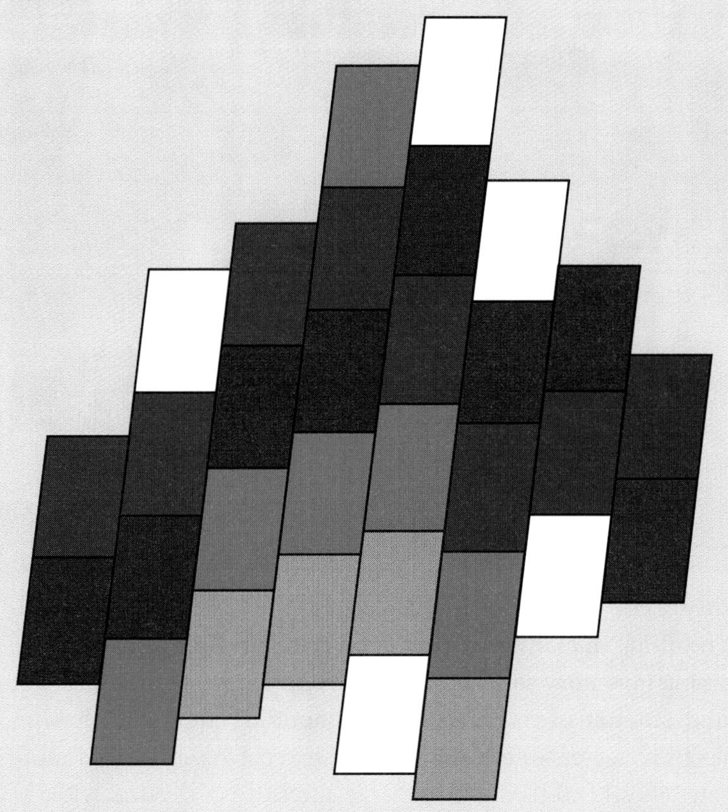

CHAPTER OUTLINE

This IBM employee is handling items for shipment at an IBM warehouse facility. Large companies like IBM maintain millions of dollars worth of product and parts inventories, which represent a significant overall cost to the company. Companies ranging from IBM to the local grocery store continually attempt to reduce inventory levels in order to save money.

PARTS INVENTORY MANAGEMENT AT IBM

The computer industry has expanded dramatically in the last decade, with enhanced technology resulting in many new products. This trend has also led to the necessity of maintaining inventory service systems to support these products. For IBM the number and amount of machines and computing equipment has increased, and this has in turn created a need for more extensive service and more spare parts. Approximately 1,000 IBM products are currently in service, with installed units numbering in excess of tens of millions, and IBM has more than 200,000 part numbers to support these products. For IBM to compete effectively in the information processing industry, it is essential that they maintain a service parts inventory system to support the products they sell and install.

IBM's National Service Division (NSD) has developed an extensive and sophisticated parts inventory management system (PIMS) to provide prompt and reliable customer service. This system manages a parts distribution network consisting of 2 central warehouses, 21 field distribution centers, located in metropolitan areas, 64 parts stations, and 15,000 outside locations. NSD employs more than 15,000 customer engineers to repair and maintain its installed products. The parts inventory maintained in this system is valued in the billions of dollars. PIMS employed economic order quantity (EOQ) formulas to determine parts and replenishment batch sizes and to set service priority goals. Recently IBM made dramatic improvements to its parts inventory management system, embodied in a modeling framework called Optimizer. This system contained four basic modules: a forecasting system that estimates part failure rates; a system to provide inventory data; a decision model that determines a stock control policy at each location and for each part in the system and that minimizes the expected costs and satisfies service constraints; and a system that interfaces the output of the decision module and PIMS. The new system resulted in a reduction in inventory investment, improved service, greater flexibility in responding to changes in service requirements, better planning capabilities, and better understanding of the impact of parts operations on customer service. The Optimizer system recommended a reduction in the time-averaged value of inventory by approximately 25 percent—more than a half billion dollars in inventory investment. However, some of the proposed inventory reduction was reallocated to improve service levels, resulting in an annual total inventory reduction of a quarter of a billion dollars. Using the new system, IBM also made several strategic changes in its inventory network, including decreasing the number of field distribution centers, increasing parts stations, and increasing the replenishment rate at these stations. These changes resulted in a 10 percent improvement in parts availability and a $20 million annual savings in operating efficiency.[1]

Two topics in operations management that have received close attention in recent years are quality and inventory. The impetus for the enhanced interest in these two traditional operations management topics has been their highly publicized role in a new, dynamic international business environment. In particular, the success of Japanese businesses in their innovative approaches to quality and inventory management, which has contributed to their competitive advantage, has popularized these topics. The most recognizable feature of the Japanese Just-in-Time production system (to which Chapter 16 is devoted) is its emphasis on achieving small inventory lot sizes and reducing inventory to extremely low levels during the production process. This basic philosophy of minimizing inventory has subsequently spread to all aspects of inventory management. It has become a fundamental principle of the total quality management (TQM) philosophy.

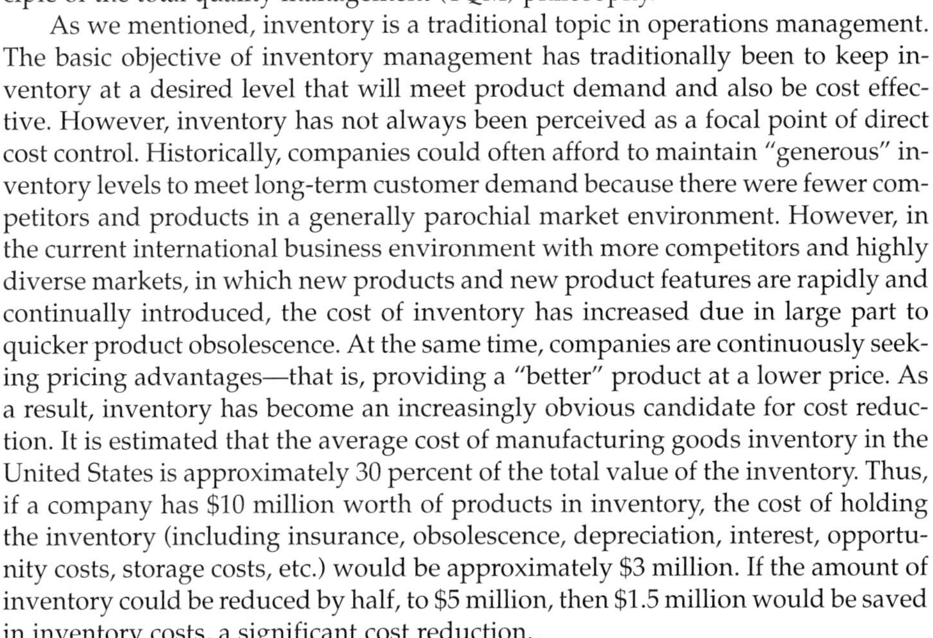

As we mentioned, inventory is a traditional topic in operations management. The basic objective of inventory management has traditionally been to keep inventory at a desired level that will meet product demand and also be cost effective. However, inventory has not always been perceived as a focal point of direct cost control. Historically, companies could often afford to maintain "generous" inventory levels to meet long-term customer demand because there were fewer competitors and products in a generally parochial market environment. However, in the current international business environment with more competitors and highly diverse markets, in which new products and new product features are rapidly and continually introduced, the cost of inventory has increased due in large part to quicker product obsolescence. At the same time, companies are continuously seeking pricing advantages—that is, providing a "better" product at a lower price. As a result, inventory has become an increasingly obvious candidate for cost reduction. It is estimated that the average cost of manufacturing goods inventory in the United States is approximately 30 percent of the total value of the inventory. Thus, if a company has $10 million worth of products in inventory, the cost of holding the inventory (including insurance, obsolescence, depreciation, interest, opportunity costs, storage costs, etc.) would be approximately $3 million. If the amount of inventory could be reduced by half, to $5 million, then $1.5 million would be saved in inventory costs, a significant cost reduction.

As a result of the traditionally high cost of inventory, a prominent tenet of Japanese management philosophy is that inventory is an "evil" that is

[1]Cohen, M. "Optimizer: IBM's Multi-Echelon Inventory System for Managing Service Logistics," *Interfaces* 20, no. 1 (January–February 1990): 65–82.

unnecessary and should be eliminated. This is the fundamental philosophy on which the JIT system of inventory management is based. In JIT, products are moved from one stage to the next in the manufacturing process as they are needed, without any buffer inventories between stages. Many U.S. manufacturing firms maintain in-process, buffer inventories between work stages to offset irregularities and problems in the production process and keep production flowing smoothly. Alternatively, Japanese manufacturing companies perceive buffer inventories to be a crutch that masks production problems, primarily poor quality. They attempt to eliminate these buffers completely by having their workers identify the causes of the problems and solving them. At Toyota, for example, as production problems are corrected, managers respond by progressively reducing in-process inventories, constantly driving them to zero. The Japanese have also learned that they can demand and receive orders for parts and materials from suppliers frequently and quickly, sometimes within an hour or less. Suppliers are often located within close geographic proximity to major Japanese manufacturers so that orders can be received quickly. If the time to receive an order is short and constant, then buffer stocks are unnecessary for the manufacturer, and the costs associated with this inventory are eliminated. Thus, the Japanese approach to inventory management is to eliminate inventory and inventory costs altogether.

The Japanese approach to inventory management in manufacturing is to eliminate inventory.

Because of the enthusiasm for JIT, some adherents of quality management view the traditional approach to inventory management to be out of step with current management practices. From this perspective there is no good level of inventory; the operational goal should be no inventory at all. However, the JIT approach is effective primarily for a production or manufacturing process. For the retailer who sells finished goods directly to the consumer or the supplier who sells parts or materials to the manufacturer, inventory is a virtual necessity. Few shoe stores, discount stores, or department stores can stay in business with only one or two items on their shelves or racks. Thus, for these operations the traditional inventory decisions of how much to order and when to order continue to be important. In addition, for many companies that have not adopted JIT practices for one reason or another, the traditional approaches to inventory management remain viable and important.

Despite JIT influence, inventory stocks are still required for retailers and suppliers.

In this chapter we review the basic elements of traditional inventory management and discuss several of the more popular models and techniques for making cost-effective inventory decisions. These decisions are basically *how much to order* and *when to order* in order to replenish inventory to an optimal level.

THE ELEMENTS OF INVENTORY MANAGEMENT

Inventory is a stock of items kept on hand to meet demand.

Teaching Note 12.1 Real-World Examples

Inventory is defined as a stock of items kept on hand by an organization to use to meet customer demand. Virtually every type of organization maintains some form of inventory. Department stores carry inventories of all the retail items they sell; a nursery has inventories of different plants, trees, and flowers; a rental-car agency has inventories of cars; and a major league baseball team maintains an inventory of players on its minor league teams. Even a family household maintains inventories of items such as food, clothing, medical supplies, and personal hygiene products.

In general, most people think of inventory as a final product waiting to be sold to a retail customer—for example, a new car or a can of tomatoes at the grocery store. This is certainly one of its most important uses. However, especially in a manufacturing firm, inventory can take on a number of different forms besides finished goods, including the following:

- Raw materials
- Purchased parts and supplies
- Labor
- In-process (partially completed) products
- Component parts
- Working capital
- Tools, machinery, and equipment
- Finished goods

The purpose of *inventory management* is to determine the amount of inventory to keep in stock (i.e., how much to order) and when to replenish, or order, inventory. In this chapter we describe several different inventory systems and techniques that are useful in making these determinations.

Inventory management: how much and when to order

The Role of Inventory

A company or organization keeps stocks of inventory for a variety of important reasons. The most prominent is holding inventories of finished goods to meet customer demand for a product, especially in a retail operation. However, customer demand can also be a secretary going to a storage closet to get a printer ribbon or paper, or a carpenter getting a board or nail from a storage shed. A level of inventory is normally maintained that will meet anticipated or expected customer or user demand.

However, since demand is usually not known with certainty, additional amounts of inventory, called safety, or buffer, stocks, are often kept on hand to meet unexpected variations in excess of expected demand.

Additional stocks of inventories are sometimes built up to meet demand that is seasonal or cyclical in nature. Companies will produce items when demand is low in order to meet high seasonal demand for which their production capacity is insufficient. For example, toy manufacturers produce large inventories during the summer and fall to meet anticipated demand during the holiday season. Doing so enables them to maintain a relatively smooth production flow throughout the year. They would not normally have the production capacity or logistical support to produce enough to meet all of the holiday demand during that season. Correspondingly, retailers might find it necessary to keep large stocks of inventory on their shelves to meet peak seasonal demand, or for display purposes to attract buyers.

At the other end of the production process from finished goods inventory, suppliers might keep large stocks of parts and material inventory to meet variations in customer demand. This is especially true of manufacturing suppliers who are under pressure to meet the exacting demands of JIT-motivated, frequent, on-time delivery of small lots. When JIT was introduced in the automobile industry, it was reported that suppliers created a boom in the warehousing business in Detroit, creating huge stocks of inventory in order to meet JIT schedules.[2]

A company will often purchase large amounts of inventory to take advantage of price discounts, as a hedge against anticipated price increases in the future, or because they can get a lower price by purchasing in volume. For example, Wal-Mart Stores have long been known to purchase an entire manufacturer's stock of soap powder or other retail item because they can get a very low price, which they subsequently pass on to their customers. Companies will often purchase large stocks of items when a supplier liquidates because of a low price. In some cases large orders will be made simply because the cost of an order may be very high and it is more cost-effective to have higher inventories than to order frequently.

[2]Raia, E., "JIT in Detroit," *Purchasing* (September 15, 1988): 68–77.

In-process (buffer) inventories are partially completed items kept between stages of a production process.

The basic premise of the popular JIT approach to inventory management is to reduce inventory levels at all stages of the production process. However, many companies still find it necessary to maintain **buffer inventories** at different stages in a manufacturing process to provide independence between operations and to avoid work stoppages or delays. Inventories of raw materials and purchased parts are kept on hand so that the production process will not be delayed as a result of missed or late deliveries or shortages from a supplier. Work-in-process inventories are kept between stages in the manufacturing process so that production can continue smoothly if there are temporary machine breakdowns or other work stoppages. Similarly, a stock of finished parts or products allows customer demand to be met in the event of a work stoppage or problem with the production process.

Demand

A crucial component and the basic starting point for the management of inventory is customer demand. Inventory exists for the purpose of meeting the demand of customers who can be inside the organization, such as a machine operator waiting for a part or partially completed product to work on. Customers can also be external to the organization—for example, an individual purchasing groceries or a new stereo. As such, an essential determinant of effective inventory management is an accurate forecast of demand. For this reason the topics of forecasting (Chapter 10) and inventory management are directly interrelated.

Dependent demand items are used internally to produce a final product.

Teaching Note 12.2 Dependent Versus Independent Demand

In general, the demand for items in inventory is classified as dependent or independent. **Dependent demand** items are typically component parts or materials used in the process of producing a final product. For example, if an automobile company plans to produce 1,000 new cars, then it will need 5,000 wheels and tires (including spares). In this case the demand for wheels is dependent on the production of cars; that is, the demand for one item is a function of demand for another item.

Tires like these stored at a Goodyear plant are an example of a dependent demand item. The number of tires demanded by an automobile manufacturer like Ford is dependent upon the number of cars it produces. Other automotive products that reflect dependent demand include windshields, seats, steering wheels, and various engine parts. Cars are an example of independent demand, as are appliances, computers, and houses.

Alternatively, cars are an example of an **independent demand** item. In general, independent demand items are final or finished products that are not a function of, or dependent upon, internal production activity. Independent demand is usually external and, thus, is beyond the direct control of the organization. In this chapter we focus on the management of inventory for independent demand items; the following chapter is devoted to inventory management for dependent demand items.

Independent demand items are final products demanded by external customers.

Inventory and Quality Management

The primary reason for maintaining inventory is for an organization to meet its own and customer demands for items. The ability to meet effectively internal organizational demand or external customer demand in a timely, efficient manner is referred to as the *level of customer service.* One of the fundamental principles of quality management is to provide as high a level of customer service as possible. This is especially important in today's highly competitive business environment, in which quality is such an important and visible product characteristic. Customers for finished goods usually perceive quality service as availability of goods they want when they want them. (This is equally true of internal customers, such as company departments or employees.) In order to provide this level of quality customer service, the tendency is to maintain large stocks of all types of items. However, there is a cost associated with carrying items in inventory, which creates a cost trade-off situation between the quality level of customer service and the cost of that service. This cost trade-off is described graphically in Figure 12.1.

Inventory must be sufficient to provide high quality customer service in TQM.

Teaching Note 12.3 Quality Service

The trade-off situation described in Figure 12.1 is similar to the quality-cost trade-off relationship in Figure 3.3. As the level of inventory increases in Figure 12.1, which is perceived as better customer service, inventory costs increase, whereas quality-related customer service costs, such as lost sales and loss of customers, decreases, resulting in a total cost curve. The conventional approach to inventory management is to maintain a level of inventory that coincides with the minimum point on the total cost curve, reflecting a compromise between inventory costs and customer service. However, it should be noted that the basic contemporary philosophy of quality management is to provide a level of quality (or customer service) somewhere to the right of the optimal point in Figure 12.1. This corresponds to the "zero defects" philosophy of quality management, which holds that the long-term benefits of absolute quality in terms of larger market share outweigh lower short-run production-related costs, such as inventory costs. Attempting to apply this philosophy to inventory management is obviously complex, since it has already been mentioned that one means of competing in today's

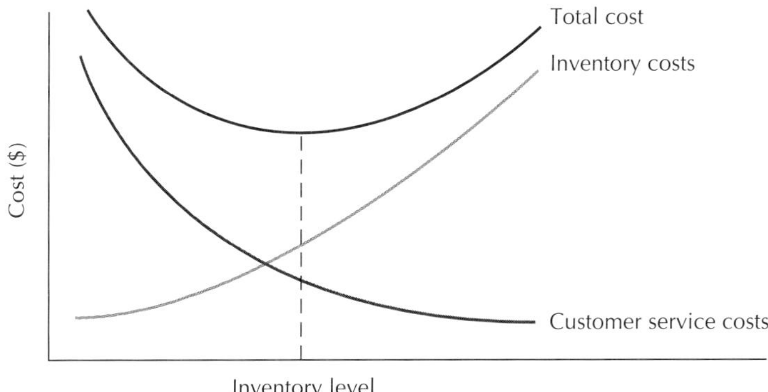

FIGURE 12.1 The Inventory-Customer Service Cost Trade-Off

Transparency 12.1 The Inventory–Customer Service Cost Trade-off diverse business environment is to reduce prices through reduced inventory costs. Nevertheless, it is an area where the traditional approach requires scrutiny in light of contemporary trends relative to TQM.

Inventory Costs

Inventory costs: carrying, ordering, and shortage costs.

There are three basic costs associated with inventory: carrying, or holding, costs; ordering costs; and shortage costs.

Carrying costs are the costs of holding an item in inventory.

Carrying costs are the costs of holding items in storage. These costs vary with the level of inventory and occasionally with the length of time an item is held; that is, the greater the level of inventory over time, the higher the carrying costs. Carrying costs can include the cost of losing the use of funds tied up in inventory; direct storage costs such as rent, heating, cooling, lighting, security, refrigeration, record keeping, and logistics; interest on loans used to purchase inventory; depreciation; obsolescence as markets for products in inventory diminish; product deterioration and spoilage; breakage; taxes; and pilferage.

Carrying costs are normally specified in one of two ways. The most general form is to assign total carrying costs, determined by summing all the individual costs just mentioned, on a per-unit basis per time period, such as a month or year. In this form, carrying costs are commonly expressed as a per-unit dollar amount on an annual basis, for example, $10 per year. Alternatively, carrying costs are sometimes expressed as a percentage of the value of an item or as a percentage of average inventory value. It is generally estimated that carrying costs range from 10 to 40 percent of the value of a manufactured item.

Ordering costs are the costs of replenishing inventory.

Ordering costs are the costs associated with replenishing the stock of inventory being held. These are normally expressed as a dollar amount per order and are independent of the order size. Thus, ordering costs vary with the number of orders made; that is, as the number of orders increases, the ordering cost increases. Costs incurred each time an order is made can include requisition and purchase orders, transportation and shipping, receiving, inspection, handling and storage, and accounting and auditing costs.

Ordering costs generally react inversely to carrying costs. As the size of orders increases, fewer orders are required, thus reducing ordering costs. However, ordering larger amounts results in higher inventory levels and higher carrying costs. In general, as the order size increases, ordering costs decrease and carrying costs increase.

Shortage costs are temporary or permanent loss of sales when demand cannot be met.

Shortage costs, also referred to as *stockout costs,* occur when customer demand cannot be met because of insufficient inventory on hand. If these shortages result in a permanent loss of sales for items demanded but not provided, shortage costs include the loss of profits. Shortages can also cause customer dissatisfaction and a loss of goodwill that can result in a permanent loss of customers and future sales. In some instances, the inability to meet customer demand or lateness in meeting demand results in specified penalties in the form of price discounts or rebates. When demand is internal, a shortage can cause work stoppages in the production process and create delays, resulting in downtime costs and the cost of lost production (including indirect and direct production costs).

Costs resulting from immediate or future lost sales because demand cannot be met are more difficult to determine than carrying or ordering costs. As a result, shortage costs are frequently subjective estimates and many times are no more than an educated guess.

Shortages occur because it is costly to carry inventory in stock. As a result, shortage costs have an inverse relationship to carrying costs; as the amount of inventory on hand increases, the carrying cost increases, whereas shortage costs decrease.

The objective of inventory management is to employ an inventory control system that will indicate how much should be ordered and when orders should take place in order to minimize the sum of the three inventory costs just described.

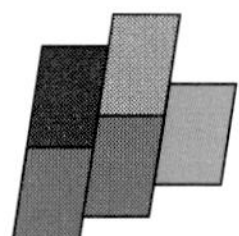

INVENTORY CONTROL SYSTEMS

An inventory system is a structure for controlling the level of inventory by determining how much to order (the level of replenishment), and when to order. There are two basic types of inventory systems: a *continuous* (or *fixed-order-quantity*) *system* and a *periodic* (or *fixed-time-period*) *system*. The primary difference between the two systems is that in a continuous system, an order is placed for the same constant amount whenever the inventory on hand decreases to a certain level, whereas in a periodic system, an order is placed for a variable amount after an established passage of time.

Continuous Inventory Systems

In a **continuous inventory system,** alternatively referred to as a *perpetual system* and a **fixed-order-quantity system,** a continual record of the inventory level for every item is maintained. Whenever the inventory on hand decreases to a predetermined level, referred to as the *reorder point,* a new order is placed to replenish the stock of inventory. The order that is placed is for a fixed amount that minimizes the total inventory carrying, ordering, and shortage costs. This fixed-order amount is called the *economic order quantity;* its determination is discussed in greater detail in a later section.

In a **continuous inventory (or fixed-order-quantity) system,** a constant amount is ordered when inventory declines to a predetermined level.

A positive feature of a continuous system is that the inventory level is closely and continuously monitored, so that management always knows the inventory status. This is especially advantageous for critical inventory items such as replacement parts or raw materials and supplies. However, the cost of maintaining a continual record of the amount of inventory on hand can also be a disadvantage of this type of system.

A simple example of a continuous inventory system is a ledger-style checkbook that many of us use on a daily basis. Our checkbook comes with 300 checks; after the 200th check has been used (and there are 100 left), there is an order form for a new batch of checks that has been inserted by the printer. This form, when turned in at the bank, initiates an order for a new batch of 300 checks from the printer. Many office inventory systems use *reorder cards* that are placed within stacks of stationery or at the bottom of a case of pens or paper clips to signal when a new order should be placed. If you look behind the items on a hanging rack in a K-Mart store, there will be a card indicating it is time to place an order for the item for an amount indicated on the card.

A more sophisticated example of a continuous inventory system is the computerized checkout system with a laser scanner used by many supermarkets and retail stores. In this system a laser scanner reads the universal product code (UPC), or bar code, from the product package; the transaction is instantly recorded, and the inventory level's updated. Such a system is not only quick and accurate, it also provides management with continuously updated information on the status of inventory levels. Although not as publicly visible as supermarket systems, many manufacturing companies suppliers and distributors also use bar-code systems and hand-held laser scanners to inventory materials, supplies, equipment, in-process parts, and finished goods.

To consumers the most familiar type of bar code scanners are used with cash registers at retail stores. These scanners not only register the price of the product but also keep a record of the sale for inventory purposes. The traditional bar code is a single line with 11 digits, the first six identifying the manufacturer and the last five assigned to a specific product by the manufacturer. This employee is using a portable hand-held bar code scanner to scan a two-dimensional bar code for inventory control. A 2-D bar code can store approximately 100 times more information (the equivalent of about 2 pages of text) than the traditional retail bar code and works just as fast. It contains as much information as a 20-foot strip of the familiar supermarket bar code. It is actually a stack of 90 one-dimensional bar codes that the scanner reads downward as well as across. In addition to identifying the product, it can indicate where a product came from, where it's supposed to go, and how the product should be handled in transit. It also can include emergency information for hazardous products and corrective information in case part of the code has been torn off or destroyed.

Because continuous inventory systems are much more common than periodic systems, models that determine fixed-order quantities and the time to order garner most of our attention in this chapter.

Periodic Inventory Systems

In a **periodic inventory (or fixed-time-period) system,** an order is placed for a variable amount after a fixed passage of time.

In a **periodic inventory system,** also referred to as a **fixed-time-period system** or a *periodic review system,* the inventory on hand is counted at specific time intervals, for example, every week or at the end of each month. After the amount of inventory in stock is determined, an order is placed for an amount that will bring inventory back up to a desired level. In this system the inventory level is not monitored at all during the time interval between orders, so it has the advantage of little or no required record keeping. However, it also has the disadvantage of less direct control. This typically results in larger inventory levels for a periodic inventory system than in a continuous system to guard against unexpected stockouts early in the fixed period. Such a system also requires that a new order quantity be determined each time a periodic order is made.

An example of a periodic inventory system is often found at the bookstore at a college or university. Textbooks are normally ordered according to a periodic system, wherein a count of textbooks in stock (for every course) is made after the first few weeks of a semester or quarter. An order for new textbooks for the next semester is then made according to estimated course enrollments for the next term (i.e., demand) and the amount remaining in stock. Smaller retail stores, drugstores, grocery stores, and offices often use periodic systems; the stock level is checked every week or month, often by a vendor, to see how much (if anything) should be ordered.

The ABC Classification System

The **ABC system** is a method for classifying inventory according to its dollar value to the firm. Typically thousands of items are held in inventory by a company, especially in manufacturing, but only a small percentage is of such a high dollar value to warrant close inventory control. In general, about 5 to 15 percent of all inventory items account for 70 to 80 percent of the total dollar value of inventory. These are classified as *A*, or *Class A*, items. *B* items typically represent approximately 30 percent of total inventory units but only about 15 percent of total inventory dollar value. The last class of items, *C*, generally account for 50 to 60 percent of all inventory units but represent only a modest 5 to 10 percent of total dollar value. For example, a discount store such as Wal-Mart normally stocks only a few television sets, a somewhat larger number of bicycles or sets of sheets, and hundreds of boxes of soap powder, bottles of shampoo, and AA batteries.

An **ABC system** is an inventory classification system in which a small percentage of (A) items account for most of the inventory value.

An underlying principle of ABC analysis is that each class of inventory requires different levels of inventory control; that is, the higher the value of the inventory, the tighter the control. Thus, class A items should experience tight inventory control, whereas B and C require more relaxed (and perhaps minimal) attention.

A items require close inventory control because of their high value; B and C items less control.

The first step in applying ABC analysis is to classify all inventory items as either A, B, or C. This requires that each item in inventory be assigned a dollar value, which is computed by multiplying the dollar cost of one unit by the annual demand for that item. All items are then ranked according to their dollar value, with, for example, the top 10 percent classified as A items, the next 30 percent, as B items, and the last 60 percent, as C items. These classifications will not be exact, but they have been found to be close to the actual occurrence in firms with remarkable frequency.

The next step in ABC analysis is to determine the level of inventory control for each classification. Class A items require very tight inventory control because they represent such a large percentage of the total dollar value of inventory. Efforts should be made to keep inventory levels as low as possible, and safety stocks should be minimized. This typically requires accurate demand forecasts and more detailed record keeping. The appropriate inventory control system and inventory modeling procedure to determine order quantity should be applied. In addition, close attention should be given to purchasing policies and procedures if the inventory items are acquired from outside the firm. B and C items typically require less stringent inventory control. Since carrying costs are usually lower for C items, higher inventory levels can sometimes be maintained with larger safety stocks. It may not even be necessary to apply sophisticated inventory management principles to controlling C items; simple manual observation may be sufficient. In general, A items frequently require a continuous control system, where the inventory level is continuously monitored, whereas a periodic review system with less monitoring will suffice for C items.

EXAMPLE 12.1

ABC System Classification

Problem Statement:

The maintenance department for a small manufacturing firm has responsibility for maintaining an inventory of spare parts for the machinery it services. The parts inventory, unit cost, and annual usage are as follows.

Part	Unit Cost	Annual Usage
1	$ 60	90
2	350	40
3	30	130
4	80	60
5	30	100
6	20	180
7	10	170
8	320	50
9	510	60
10	20	120

The department manager wants to classify the inventory parts according to the ABC system in order to determine which stocks of parts should most closely be monitored.

Solution:

The first step is to rank the items according to their total value and also compute each item's percentage value and quantity.

Part	Total Value	% Value	% Quantity	% Cumulative
9	$30,600	35.9	6.0	6.0
8	16,000	18.7	5.0	11.0
2	14,000	16.4	4.0	15.0
1	5,400	6.3	9.0	24.0
4	4,800	5.6	6.0	30.0
3	3,900	4.6	10.0	40.0
6	3,600	4.2	18.0	58.0
5	3,000	3.5	13.0	71.0
10	2,400	2.8	12.0	83.0
7	1,700	2.0	17.0	100.0
	$85,400			

Making an intuitive judgment, it appears that the first three items form a group with the highest value, the next three items form a second group, and the last four items constitute a group. Thus, the ABC classification for these items is as follows.

Class	Items	% value	% quantity
A	9, 8, 2	71.0%	15.0%
B	1, 4, 3	16.5	25.0
C	6, 5, 10, 7	12.5	60.0

ECONOMIC ORDER QUANTITY MODELS

In a continuous, or fixed-order-quantity, system when inventory reaches a specific level, referred to as the *reorder point*, a fixed amount is ordered. The most widely used and traditional means for determining how much to order in a continuous system is the **economic order quantity (EOQ)** model, also referred to as the economic lot-size model. The earliest published derivation of the basic EOQ model formula occurred in 1915 and is credited to Ford Harris, an employee at Westinghouse.

EOQ is the optimal order quantity that will minimize total inventory costs.

The function of the EOQ model is to determine the optimal order size that minimizes total inventory costs. There are several variations of the EOQ model, depending on the assumptions made about the inventory system. In this section we will describe three model versions, including the basic EOQ model, the EOQ model with noninstantaneous receipt, and the EOQ model with shortages.

The Basic EOQ Model

The simplest form of the economic order quantity model on which all other model versions are based is called the *basic EOQ model.* It is essentially a single formula for determining the optimal order size that minimizes the sum of carrying costs and ordering costs. The model formula is derived under a set of simplifying and restrictive assumptions, as follows:

assumptions of EOQ model

- Demand is known with certainty and is relatively constant over time.
- No shortages are allowed.
- Lead time for the receipt of orders is constant.
- The order quantity is received all at once.

The graph in Figure 12.2 reflects these basic model assumptions.

Figure 12.2 describes the continuous-inventory **order cycle** system inherent in the EOQ model. An order quantity, Q, is received and is used up over time at a constant rate. When the inventory level decreases to the reorder point, R, a new order is placed; a period of time, referred to as the *lead time,* is required for delivery. The order is received all at once just at the moment when demand depletes the entire stock of inventory (and the inventory level reaches 0), thus allowing no shortages. This cycle is repeated continuously for the same order quantity, reorder point, and lead time.

The **order cycle** is the time between receipt of orders in an inventory cycle.

EOQ is a continuous inventory system.

As we mentioned earlier, the economic order quantity is the order size that minimizes the sum of carrying costs and ordering costs. These two costs react inversely to each other in response to an increase in the order size. As the order size increases, fewer orders are required, causing the ordering cost to decline, whereas the average amount of inventory on hand will increase, resulting in an increase in

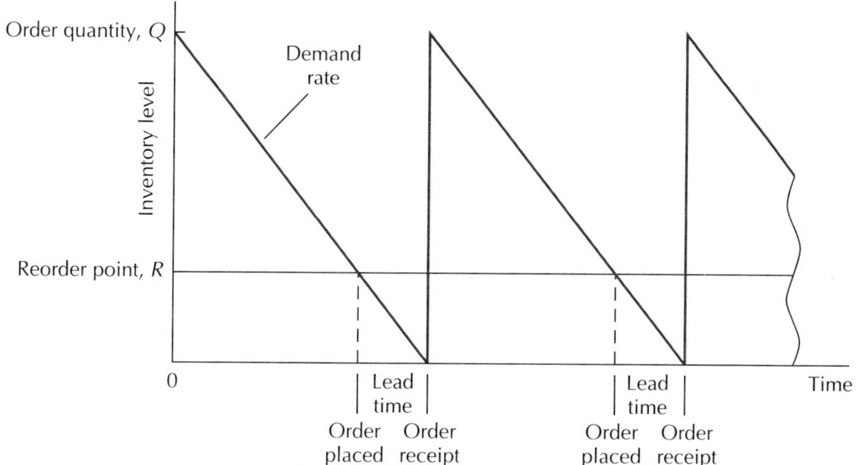

Transparency 12.2 The EOQ Model

FIGURE 12.2 The Inventory Order Cycle

carrying costs. Thus, in effect, the optimal order quantity represents a compromise between these two conflicting costs.

The total annual ordering cost is computed by simply multiplying the cost per order, designated as C_o, times the number of orders per year. Since annual demand is assumed to be known and to be constant, the number of orders will be D/Q, where Q is the order size and

$$\text{Annual ordering cost} = \frac{C_oD}{Q}$$

The only variable in this equation is Q; both C_o and D are constant parameters. Thus, the relative magnitude of the ordering cost is dependent upon the order size.

Total annual carrying cost is computed by multiplying the annual per-unit carrying cost, designated as C_c, times the average inventory level, determined by dividing the order size, Q, by 2: $Q/2$;

$$\text{Annual carrying cost} = \frac{C_cQ}{2}$$

The total annual inventory cost is simply the sum of the ordering and carrying costs:

$$\text{TC} = \frac{C_oD}{Q} + \frac{C_cQ}{2}$$

These three cost functions are shown in Figure 12.3. Notice the inverse relationship between ordering cost and carrying cost, resulting in a convex total cost curve.

Optimal Q corresponds to the lowest point on the total cost curve.

The optimal order quantity occurs at the point in Figure 12.3 where the total cost curve is at a minimum, which also coincides exactly with the point where the carrying cost curve intersects with the ordering cost curve. This enables us to determine the optimal value of Q by equating the two cost functions and solving for Q, as follows.

$$\frac{C_oD}{Q} = \frac{C_cQ}{2}$$

$$Q^2 = \frac{2C_oD}{C_c}$$

$$Q_{\text{opt}} = \sqrt{\frac{2C_oD}{C_c}}$$

Alternatively the optimal value of Q can be determined by differentiating the total cost curve with respect to Q, setting the resulting function equal to zero (the slope at the minimum point on the total cost curve), and solving for Q, as follows:

$$\text{TC} = \frac{C_oD}{Q} + \frac{C_cQ}{2}$$

$$\frac{\partial \text{TC}}{\partial Q} = -\frac{C_oD}{Q^2} + \frac{C_c}{2}$$

$$0 = -\frac{C_oD}{Q^2} + \frac{C_c}{2}$$

$$Q_{\text{opt}} = \sqrt{\frac{2C_oD}{C_c}}$$

Transparency 12.3 The EOQ Cost Model

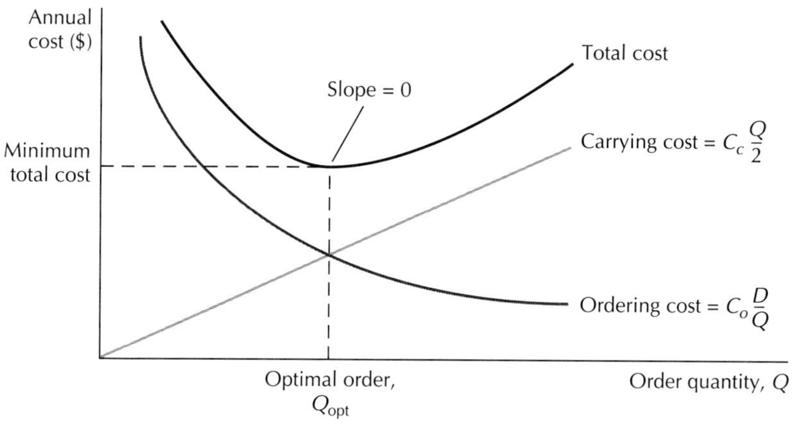

FIGURE 12.3 The EOQ Cost Model

The total minimum cost is determined by substituting the value for the optimal order size, Q_{opt}, into the total cost equation,

$$TC_{min} = \frac{C_o D}{Q_{opt}} + \frac{C_c Q_{opt}}{2}$$

EXAMPLE 12.2

Alternate Example 12.1

The Economic Order Quantity

Problem Statement:

The I-75 Carpet Discount Store in North Georgia stocks carpet in its warehouse and sells it through an adjoining showroom. The store keeps several brands and styles of carpet in stock, however, its biggest seller is Super Shag carpet. The store wants to determine the optimal order size and total inventory cost for this brand of carpet given an estimated annual demand of 10,000 yards of carpet, an annual carrying cost of \$0.75 per yard, and an ordering cost of \$150. The store would also like to know the number of orders that will be made annually and the time between orders (i.e., the order cycle) given that the store is open every day except Sunday, Thanksgiving Day, and Christmas Day (which is not on a Sunday).

Solution:

$$C_c = \$0.75$$
$$C_o = \$150$$
$$D = 10{,}000 \text{ yards}$$

The optimal order size is computed as follows:

$$Q_{opt} = \sqrt{\frac{2C_o D}{C_c}}$$
$$= \sqrt{\frac{2(150)(10{,}000)}{(0.75)}}$$
$$= 2{,}000 \text{ yards}$$

The total annual inventory cost is determined by substituting Q_{opt} into the total cost formula:

$$TC_{min} = \frac{C_o D}{Q_{opt}} + \frac{C_c Q_{opt}}{2}$$

$$= \frac{(150)(10{,}000)}{2{,}000} + \frac{(0.75)(2{,}000)}{2}$$

$$= \$750 + 750$$

$$= \$1{,}500$$

The number of orders per year is computed as follows.

$$\text{Number of orders per year} = \frac{D}{Q_{opt}}$$

$$= \frac{10{,}000}{2{,}000}$$

$$= 5 \text{ orders per year}$$

Given that the store is open 311 days annually (365 days minus 52 Sundays, Thanksgiving, and Christmas) the order cycle is determined as follows:

$$\text{Order cycle time} = \frac{311 \text{ days}}{D\ Q_{opt}}$$

$$= \frac{311}{5}$$

$$= 62.2 \text{ store days}$$

It should be noted that the optimal order quantity determined in this example and in general is an approximate value, since it is based on estimates of carrying and ordering costs as well as uncertain demand (although all of these parameters are treated as known, certain values in the EOQ model). Thus, in practice it is acceptable to round the Q values off to the nearest whole number. The precision of a decimal place is generally not necessary, nor is it appropriate. In addition, because the optimal order quantity is computed from a square root, errors or variations in the cost parameters and demand tend to be dampened. For instance, in Example 12.2, if the order cost had actually been 30 percent higher, or \$200, the resulting optimal order size would have varied only by a little under 10 percent (i.e., 2,190 yards instead of 2,000 yards). In addition, variations in both inventory costs will tend to offset each other, since they have an inverse relationship. As a result, the EOQ model is relatively resilient to errors in the cost estimates and demand, or is *robust*, which has tended to enhance its popularity.

The EOQ model is *robust;* because Q is a square root, errors in the estimation of D, C_c, and C_o are dampened.

The EOQ Model with Noninstantaneous Receipt

relaxing the assumption that Q is received all at once.

The **noninstantaneous receipt model** is an inventory system in which an order is received gradually, as inventory is depleted.

A variation of the basic EOQ model is achieved when the assumption that orders are received all at once is relaxed. This version of the EOQ model is known as the **noninstantaneous receipt model,** also referred to as the *gradual usage* and *production lot-size model.* In this EOQ model variation the order quantity is received gradually over time, and the inventory level is depleted at the same time it is being replenished. This is a situation most commonly found when the inventory user is also the producer, as, for example, in a manufacturing operation where a part is produced to use in a larger assembly. This situation also can occur when orders are delivered gradually over time or the retailer and producer of a product are one in the same.

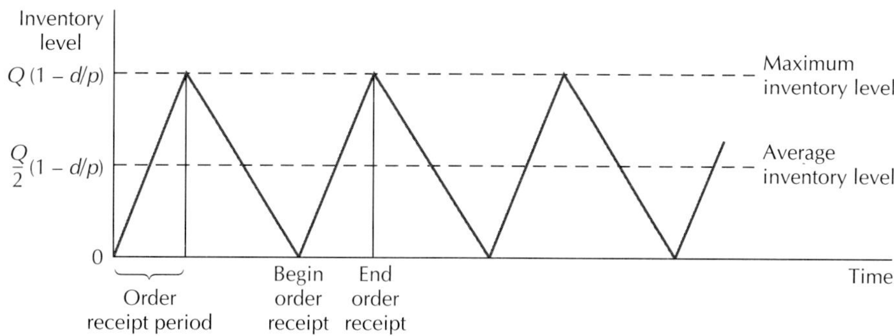

Transparency 12.4 The EOQ Model with Noninstantaneous Receipt

FIGURE 12.4 The EOQ Model with Noninstantaneous Order Receipt

The noninstantaneous receipt model is illustrated graphically in Figure 12.4, which highlights the difference between this variation and the basic EOQ model.

The ordering cost component of the basic EOQ model does not change as a result of the gradual replenishment of the inventory level, since it is dependent only on the number of annual orders. However, the carrying-cost component is not the same for this model variation because average inventory is different. In the basic EOQ model, average inventory was half the maximum inventory level, or $Q/2$, but in this model variation, the maximum inventory level is not simply Q; it is an amount somewhat lower than Q, adjusted for the fact the order quantity is depleted during the order receipt period.

In order to determine the average inventory level, we define the following parameters unique to this model.

p = daily rate at which the order is received over time, also known as the *production rate*
d = the daily rate at which inventory is demanded

The demand rate cannot exceed the production rate, since we are still assuming that no shortages are possible, and, if $d = p$, then there is no order size, since items are used as fast as they are produced. Thus, for this model the production rate must exceed the demand rate, or $p > d$.

Observing Figure 12.4, the time required to receive an order is the order quantity divided by the rate at which the order is received, or Q/p. For example, if the order size is 100 units and the production rate, p, is 20 units per day, the order will be received in 5 days. The amount of inventory that will be depleted or used up during this time period is determined by multiplying by the demand rate: $(Q/p)d$. For example, if it takes 5 days to receive the order and during this time inventory is depleted at the rate of 2 units per day, then a total of 10 units is used. As a result, the maximum amount of inventory that is on hand is the order size minus the amount depleted during the receipt period, computed as follows and shown in Figure 12.4:

$$\text{Maximum inventory level} = Q - \frac{Q}{p}d$$
$$= Q\left(1 - \frac{d}{p}\right)$$

Since this is the maximum inventory level, the average inventory level is easily determined by dividing this amount by 2:

$$\text{Average inventory level} = \frac{1}{2}\left[Q\left(1 - \frac{d}{p}\right)\right]$$

$$= \frac{Q}{2}\left(1 - \frac{d}{p}\right)$$

The total carrying cost using this function for average inventory is

$$\text{Total carrying cost} = \frac{C_cQ}{2}\left(1 - \frac{d}{p}\right)$$

Thus the total annual inventory cost is determined according to the following formula:

$$TC = \frac{C_oD}{Q} + \frac{C_cQ}{2}\left(1 - \frac{d}{p}\right)$$

Solving this function for the optimal value Q results in

$$Q_{\text{opt}} = \sqrt{\frac{2C_oD}{C_c\left(1 - \frac{d}{p}\right)}}$$

EXAMPLE 12.3

The EOQ Model with Noninstantaneous Receipt

Problem Statement:

For Example 12.2, we now assume that the I-75 Outlet Store has its own manufacturing facility in which it produces Super Shag carpet. We further assume that the ordering cost, C_o, is the cost of setting up the production process to make Super Shag carpet. Recall that C_c = \$0.75 per yard and D = 10,000 yards per year. The manufacturing facility operates the same days the store is open (i.e., 311 days) and produces 150 yards of the carpet per day. Determine the optimal order size, total inventory cost, the length of time to receive an order, the number of orders per year, and the maximum inventory level.

Solution:

$$C_o = \$150$$

$$C_c = \$0.75 \text{ per unit}$$

$$D = 10{,}000 \text{ yards}$$

$$d = \frac{10{,}000}{311} = 32.2 \text{ yards per day}$$

$$p = 150 \text{ yards per day}$$

The optimal order size is determined as follows:

$$Q_{\text{opt}} = \sqrt{\frac{2C_oD}{C_c\left(1 - \frac{d}{p}\right)}}$$

$$= \sqrt{\frac{2(150)(10{,}000)}{0.75\left(1 - \frac{32.2}{150}\right)}}$$

$$= 2{,}256.8 \text{ yards}$$

This value is substituted into the following formula to determine total minimum annual inventory cost:

$$TC_{\min} = \frac{C_o D}{Q} + \frac{C_c Q}{2}\left(1 - \frac{d}{p}\right)$$

$$= \frac{(150)(10{,}000)}{2{,}256.8} + \frac{(0.75)(2{,}256.8)}{2}\left(1 - \frac{32.2}{150}\right)$$

$$= \$1{,}329$$

The length of time to receive an order for this type of manufacturing operation is commonly called the length of the *production run.* It is computed as follows.

$$\text{Production run length} = \frac{Q}{p}$$

$$= \frac{2{,}256.8}{150}$$

$$= 15.05 \text{ days per order}$$

The number of orders per year is actually the number of production runs that will be made:

$$\text{Number of production runs (from orders)} = \frac{D}{Q}$$

$$= \frac{10{,}000}{2{,}256.8}$$

$$= 4.43 \text{ runs per year}$$

Finally, the maximum inventory level is

$$\text{Maximum inventory level} = Q\left(1 - \frac{d}{p}\right)$$

$$= 2{,}256.8\left(1 - \frac{32.2}{150}\right)$$

$$= 1{,}772 \text{ yards}$$

The EOQ Model with Shortages

relaxing the EOQ assumption that shortages cannot exist

One of the assumptions of our basic EOQ model is that shortages and back ordering are not allowed. The third model variation that we describe, the EOQ model with shortages, relaxes this assumption. However, we do assume that all demand not met because of inventory shortage can be back ordered and delivered to the customer later. Thus, all demand is eventually met. The EOQ model with shortages is illustrated in Figure 12.5 on page 598.

Since back-ordered demand, or shortages, S, are filled when inventory is replenished, the maximum inventory level does not reach Q, but instead reaches a level equal to $Q - S$. It can be seen from Figure 12.5 that the amount of inventory on hand $(Q - S)$ decreases as the amount of the shortage increases and vice versa. As such, the cost associated with shortages, which we described earlier in this chapter as primarily the cost of lost sales and customer goodwill, has an inverse

Transparency 12.5 The EOQ Model with Shortages

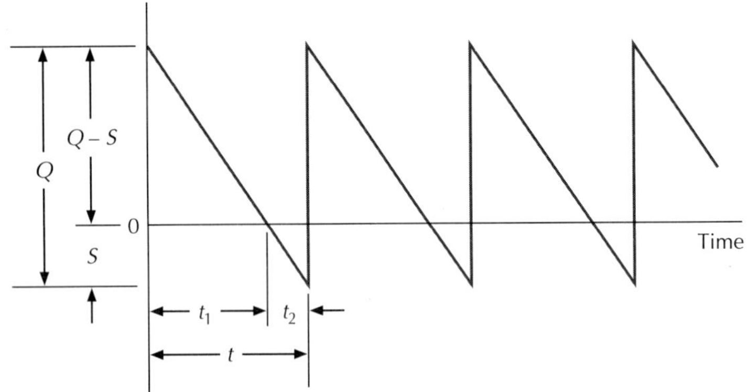

FIGURE 12.5 The EOQ Model with Shortages

relationship to carrying costs. As the order size, Q, increases, the carrying cost increases and the shortage cost declines. This relationship between carrying and shortage cost as well as ordering cost is shown in Figure 12.6.

We forego the lengthy derivation of the individual cost components of the EOQ model with shortages, which requires the application of plane geometry to the graph in Figure 12.5. The individual cost functions are provided as follows, where S = the shortage level and C_s = the annual per unit cost of shortages.

$$\text{Total shortage costs} = \frac{C_s S^2}{2Q}$$

$$\text{Total carrying cost} = \frac{C_s(Q-S)^2}{2Q}$$

$$\text{Total ordering cost} = \frac{C_o D}{Q}$$

Combining these individual cost components results in the total inventory cost formula:

$$TC = \frac{C_s S^2}{2Q} + \frac{C_c(Q-S)^2}{2Q} + \frac{C_o D}{Q}$$

You will notice from Figure 12.6 that the three cost-component curves do not intersect at a common point, as was the case in the basic EOQ model. As a result, the only way to determine the optimal order size *and the optimal shortage level, S,* is to use calculus to differentiate the total cost function with respect to Q and S, set the two resulting equations equal to zero, and solve them simultaneously. Doing so results in the following formulas for the optimal order quantity and shortage level.

$$Q_{\text{opt}} = \sqrt{\frac{2C_o D}{C_c}\left(\frac{C_s + C_c}{C_s}\right)}$$

$$S_{\text{opt}} = Q_{\text{opt}}\left(\frac{C_c}{C_c + C_s}\right)$$

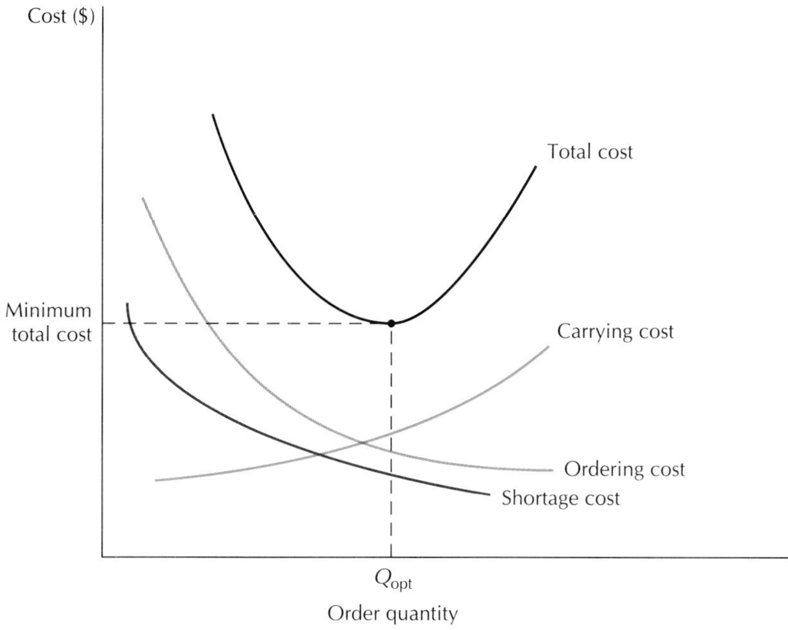

FIGURE 12.6 The EOQ Cost Model with Shortages

Several interesting aspects about these optimal values should be noted. In the first formula for the optimal order quantity, the first term under the square root is the same as the basic EOQ model, $2C_0D/C_c$. The second term, by which the first term is multiplied, is a ratio with the shortage cost in both the numerator and denominator. Therefore, as the shortage cost becomes large relative to the carrying cost, the fraction $\frac{(C_s + C_c)}{C_s}$ approaches 1 and the formula for Q_{opt} becomes the same as the basic EOQ model without shortages. In other words, as the cost of shortages increases, allowable shortages are decreased to the point where they are not allowed at all.

This leads us to a second interesting observation: the EOQ model with shortages will always result in a lower total cost than the basic EOQ model without shortages (assuming C_o and C_c are the same for both models). But what if the shortage cost is enormously high; won't the total inventory cost with shortages be higher? The answer is no. As we have already pointed out, when C_s, the shortage cost, becomes large compared to the carrying cost, the EOQ model with shortages converges toward the basic EOQ model without shortages, and shortages are simply eliminated. We might then ask why we don't simply always allow shortages. The reason is that it does not require a very high shortage cost relative to the carrying cost to make the EOQ model with shortages revert to the basic EOQ model without shortages.

The EOQ model with shortages will always have lower total cost than the basic EOQ model.

EXAMPLE 12.4

The EOQ Model with Shortages

Alternate Example 12.2

Problem Statement:

For Example 12.2, we now assume that the I-75 Carpet Outlet Store allows shortages and the shortage cost, C_s, is \$2 per yard per year. All other costs and demand remain the same (C_c = \$0.75, C_o = \$150, and D = 10,000 yards). Determine the optimal order size and shortage level and total minimum annual inventory cost.

Solution:

$$C_o = \$150$$
$$C_c = \$0.75 \text{ per yard}$$
$$C_s = \$2 \text{ per yard}$$
$$D = 10{,}000 \text{ yards}$$

$$Q_{\text{opt}} = \sqrt{\frac{2C_oD}{C_c}\left(\frac{C_s + C_c}{C_s}\right)}$$
$$= \sqrt{\frac{2(150)(10{,}000)}{(0.75)}\left(\frac{2 + 0.75}{2}\right)}$$
$$= 2{,}345.2 \text{ yards}$$

$$S_{\text{opt}} = Q_{\text{opt}}\left(\frac{C_c}{C_c + C_s}\right)$$
$$= 2{,}345.2\left(\frac{0.75}{2 + 0.75}\right)$$
$$= 639.6 \text{ yards}$$

$$\text{TC}_{\text{min}} = \frac{C_sS^2}{2Q} + \frac{C_c(Q - S)^2}{2Q} + \frac{C_oD}{Q}$$
$$= \frac{(2)(639.6)^2}{2(2{,}345.2)} + \frac{(0.75)(1{,}705.6)^2}{2(2{,}345.2)} + \frac{(150)(10{,}000)}{2{,}345.2}$$
$$= \$174.44 + 465.16 + 639.60$$
$$= \$1{,}279.20$$

You will notice that the total cost with shortages is, in fact, lower than the total cost without shortages computed in Example 12.2 (\$1,500), as we anticipated. Also notice that the sum of the total shortage cost, \$174.44, and the total carrying cost, \$465.16, or \$639.60, equals the total ordering cost, \$639.60; a result that always occurs in this model.

Several additional parameters of the EOQ model with shortages can be computed for this example:

$$\text{Number of orders} = \frac{D}{Q}$$
$$= \frac{10{,}000}{2{,}345.2}$$
$$= 4.26 \text{ orders per year}$$

$$\text{Maximum inventory level} = Q - S$$
$$= 2{,}345.2 - 639.6$$
$$= 1{,}705.6 \text{ yards}$$

The time between orders, identified as t in Figure 12.5, is

$$t = \frac{\text{days per year}}{\text{number of orders per year}}$$
$$= \frac{311}{4.26}$$
$$= 85.7 \text{ days between orders}$$

The time during which inventory is on hand, t_1 in Figure 12.5, and the time during which there is a shortage during each order cycle, t_2 in Figure 12.5, can be computed using the following formulas.

$$t_1 = \frac{Q - S}{D}$$
$$= \frac{2{,}345.2 - 639.6}{10{,}000}$$
$$= 0.171 \text{ year, or 62.4 days without shortages per order}$$
$$t_2 = \frac{S}{D}$$
$$= \frac{639.6}{10{,}000}$$
$$= 0.064 \text{ year, or 27.3 days with shortages per order}$$

Computer Analysis of EOQ Models

The AB:POM computer package has a module for performing EOQ analysis for a variety of models, including the basic model, the noninstantaneous receipt model, and the model with shortages. In order to demonstrate the capabilities of this program we will use Examples 12.2, 12.3, and 12.4, for which the solution output is given in Exhibit 12.1 on page 602.

Teaching Note 12.4 EOQ Experimentation with the Computer

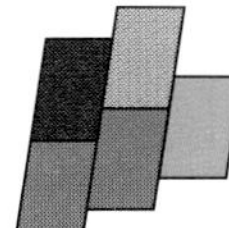

QUANTITY DISCOUNTS

It is often possible for a customer to receive a price discount on an item if predetermined numbers of units are ordered, called a **quantity discount.** For example, in the back of a magazine you might see an advertisement for a firm that states that it will produce a coffee mug (or hat) with a company or organizational logo on it, and the price will be $5 per mug if you purchase 100, $4 per mug if you purchase 200, or $3 per mug if you purchase 500 or more. Many manufacturing companies receive price discounts for ordering materials and supplies in high volume, and retail stores receive price discounts for ordering merchandise in large quantities.

A **quantity discount** is given for specific higher order quantities.

The basic EOQ model can be used to determine the optimal order size with quantity discounts; however, the application of the model is slightly altered. The total inventory cost function must now include the purchase price for the order:

determining if an order size with a discount is more cost-effective than optimal Q

$$\text{TC} = \frac{C_o D}{Q} + \frac{C_c Q}{2} + PD$$

where

P = per unit price of the item
D = annual demand

Purchase price was not considered as part of our basic EOQ formulation earlier because it had no real impact on the optimal order size. In the preceding formula PD is a constant value that would not alter the basic shape of the total cost curve; that is, the minimum point on the cost curve would still be at the same location, corresponding to the same value of Q. Thus, the optimal order size is the same no matter what the purchase price is. However, when a discount price is available, it is associated with a specific order size, which may be different from the optimal

```
                                        Inventory                         Solution
Economic Order Quality (EOQ) Model
                                       Example 12.2
Demand rate (D)         10000.00      Optimal order quantity (Q*)          2000.00
Setup cost (S)            150.00      Maximum Inventory Level (Imax)       2000.00
Holding cost (H)            0.75
Unit cost                   0.00      Orders per period (year)                5.00
                                      Inventory $$ (Hold, Setup, Short)  $1,500.00
                                      Unit costs (PD)                        $0.00
                                      Total Cost                         $1,500.00

                                        Inventory                         Solution
Production Order Quantity Modcl
                                       Example 12.3
Demand rate (D)         10000.00      Optimal order quantity (Q*)          2256.41
Setup cost (S)            150.00      Maximum Inventory Level (Imax)       1772.72
Holding cost (H)            0.75
Production rate (p)       150.00      Orders per period (year)                4.43
Days per year             311.00      Inventory $$ (Hold, Setup, Short)  $1,329.54
  OR
Daily demand rate (d)   32.15434      Unit costs (PD)                        $0.00
Unit cost                   0.00      Total cost                         $1,329.54

                                        Inventory                         Solution
Back Order Inventory Model
                                       Example 12.4
Demand rate (D)         10000.00      Optimal order quantity (Q*)          2345.21
Setup cost (S)            150.00      Maximum Inventory Level (Imax)       1705.61
Holding cost (H)            0.75      Maximum Inventory Shortage (B)        639.60
Back order cost (B)         2.00      Orders per period (year)                4.26
Unit cost                   0.00      Inventory $$ (Hold, Setup, Short)  $1,279.20
                                      Unit costs (PD)                        $0.00
                                      Total Cost                         $1,279.20
```

EXHIBIT 12.1

Transparency 12.6 AB:POM EOQ Models

order size, and the customer must evaluate the trade-off between possibly higher carrying costs with the discount quantity versus EOQ cost. As a result, the purchase price does impact on the order-size decision when a discount is available.

quantity discounts evaluated with constant C_c and as a percentage of price

Quantity discounts can be evaluated using the basic EOQ model under two different scenarios—with constant carrying costs and with carrying costs as a percentage of the purchase price. It is not uncommon for carrying costs to be determined as a percentage of purchase price, although it was not considered as such in our previous basic EOQ model. Carrying cost could have very well been a percentage of purchase price, but it was reflected as a constant value, C_c, in the basic EOQ model because the purchase price was not part of the EOQ formula. However, in the case of a quantity discount, carrying cost will vary with the change in price if it is computed as a percentage of purchase price.

Quantity Discounts with Constant Carrying Cost

The EOQ cost model with constant carrying costs for a pricing schedule with two discounts, d_1 and d_2, for example, is illustrated in Figure 12.7 for the following discounts.

Order Size	*Price*
0–99	$10
100–199	8 (d_1)
200+	6 (d_2)

Notice that the optimal order size, Q_{opt}, is the same regardless of the discount price. Although the total cost curve decreases with each discount in price (i.e., d_1 and d_2), since ordering and carrying cost are constant, the optimal order size Q_{opt}, does not change.

The graph in Figure 12.7 also reflects the *three-tiered* total cost curve resulting from the two quantity discounts. Only the first portion of the top total cost curve (without a discount) is valid. The remainder of this curve, identified by the dashed line, is superseded by the middle portion of the total cost curve for the first discount, TC(d_1). The effective part of this curve is between the first discount, $Q(d_1) = 100$, and the beginning of the second discount, $Q(d_2) = 200$. At the second discount order size, $Q(d_2) = 200$, the effective portion of the total cost curve is the last section of TC(d_2). Thus, the effective total cost curve is a stairstep, starting with the original total cost curve, dropping down to the next cost curve for the first discount, and finally dropping to the third total cost curve for the next discount. Notice that the optimal order size, Q_{opt}, is feasible only for TC(d_1); that is, it is not on the effective part of either TC or TC(d_2). If the EOQ optimal order size, Q_{opt}, had coincided with the effective portion of the *lowest total cost curve,* it would have been the optimal order size for the discount price schedule. Since it is not, the total cost with Q_{opt} must be compared to the lower total cost curve with $Q(d_2)$ to see which is the minimum.

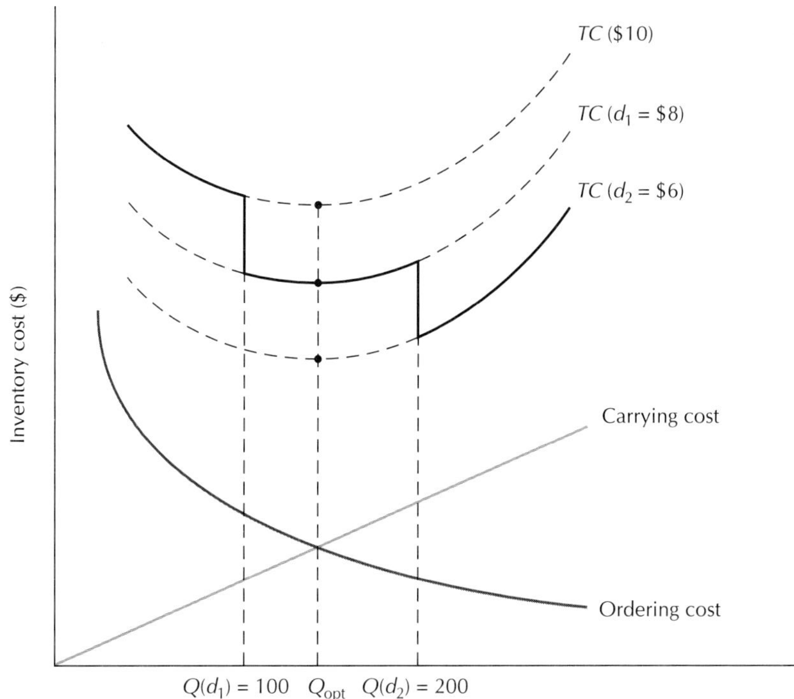

FIGURE 12.7 Quantity Discounts with Constant Carrying Cost

Transparency 12.7 Quantity Discounts with Constant Carrying Cost

Alternate Example 12.3

EXAMPLE 12.5

A Quantity Discount with Constant Carrying Cost

Problem Statement:

Comptek Computers wants to reduce a large stock of microcomputers it is discontinuing. It has offered the University Bookstore at Tech a quantity discount pricing schedule if they will purchase the microcomputers in volume, as follows.

Quantity	*Price*
1–49	$1,400
50–89	1,100
90+	900

The annual carrying cost for the bookstore for a microcomputer is $190, the ordering cost is $2,500, and annual demand for this particular model is estimated to be 200 units. The bookstore wants to determine if it should take advantage of this discount or order the basic EOQ order size.

Solution:

First determine the optimal order size and total cost with the basic EOQ model.

$$C_o = \$2{,}500$$

$$C_c = \$190 \text{ per unit}$$

$$D = 200$$

$$Q_{opt} = \sqrt{\frac{2C_oD}{C_c}} = \sqrt{\frac{2(2{,}500)(200)}{190}} = 72.5$$

Although we will use $Q_{opt} = 72.5$ in the subsequent computations, realistically the order size would be 73 computers. This order size is eligible for the first discount of $1,100; therefore, this price is used to compute total cost as follows.

$$TC = \frac{C_oD}{Q_{opt}} + \frac{C_cQ_{opt}}{2} + PD = \frac{(2{,}500)(200)}{72.5} + \frac{(190)(72.5)}{2} + (1{,}100)(200)$$

$$TC_{min} = \$233{,}784$$

Since there is a discount for a larger order size than 50 (i.e., there is a lower cost curve), this total cost of $233,784 must be compared with total cost with an order size of 90 and a price of $900, as follows.

$$TC = \frac{C_oD}{Q} + \frac{C_cQ}{2} + PD = \frac{(2{,}500)(200)}{90} + \frac{(190)(90)}{2} + (900)(200) = \$194{,}105$$

Since this total cost is lower ($194,105 < $233,784) the maximum discount price should be taken, and 90 units should be ordered. (Note that we know that there is no order size larger than 90 that would result in a lower cost, since the minimum point on this total cost curve has already been determined to be 50.)

Transparency 12.8 Quantity Discounts with Carrying Cost as a Percentage of Price

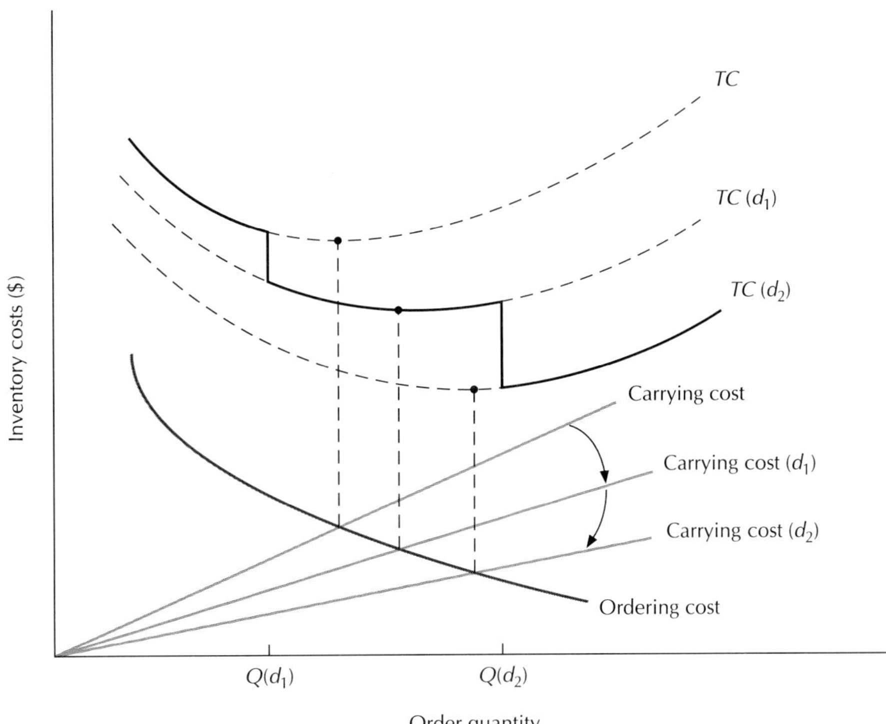

FIGURE 12.8 Quantity Discounts with Carrying Cost as a Percentage of Price

Quantity Discounts with Carrying Cost as a Percentage of Price

The difference between the model in the previous section and the quantity discount model with carrying cost as a percentage of price can be observed in Figure 12.8. Notice that the carrying cost is no longer constant; the carrying cost function shifts downward as the price decreases (since carrying cost is a percentage of price). The result is three total cost curves that do not have a common optimal order size, Q_{opt}. Thus, the optimal order size with a discount must be determined slightly differently than the case for a constant carrying cost.

The optimal order size and total cost are determined using the basic EOQ model for the case with no quantity discount. This total cost value is then compared to the various discount-quantity order sizes to determine the minimum-cost order size. However, once this minimum-cost order size is determined, it must be compared to the EOQ-determined order size for the specific discount price, since the EOQ order size, Q_{opt}, changes for every discount level.

EXAMPLE 12.6

Quantity Discount with Carrying Cost as a Percentage of Price

Problem Statement:

Reconsider Example 12.5, except now assume that annual carrying cost for a microcomputer at the University Bookstore is 15 percent of the purchase price. Using the same discount pricing schedule, determine the optimal order size.

Solution:

The annual carrying cost is determined as follows.

Quantity	*Price*	*Carrying Cost*
0–49	$1,400	1,400 (0.15) = $210
50–89	1,100	1,100 (0.15) = 165
90+	900	900 (0.15) = 135

$C_o = \$2{,}500$
$D = 200$ microcomputers per year

First compute the optimal order size for the purchase price without a discount and with $C_c = \$210$, as follows:

$$Q_{\text{opt}} = \sqrt{\frac{2C_oD}{C_c}}$$
$$= \sqrt{\frac{2(2{,}500)(200)}{210}}$$
$$= 69$$

Since this order size exceeds 49 units, it is not feasible for this price, and a lower total cost will automatically be achieved with the first price discount of $1,100. However, the optimal order size will be different for this price discount, since carrying cost is no longer constant. Thus, the new order size is computed as follows.

$$Q_{\text{opt}} = \sqrt{\frac{2(2{,}500)(200)}{165}}$$
$$= 77.8$$

This order size is the true optimum for this price discount instead of the 50 units required to receive the discount price. Thus, it will result in the minimum total cost, computed as follows:

$$\text{TC} = \frac{C_oD}{Q} + \frac{C_cQ}{2} + PD$$
$$= \frac{(2{,}500)(200)}{77.8} + \frac{(165)(77.8)}{2} + (1{,}100)(200)$$
$$= \$232{,}845$$

This cost must still be compared with the total cost for lowest discount price ($900) and order quantity (90 units), computed as follows.

$$\text{TC} = \frac{(2{,}500)(200)}{90} + \frac{(135)(90)}{2} + (900)(200)$$
$$= \$191{,}630$$

Since this total cost is lower ($191,630 < $232,845), the maximum discount price should be taken and 90 units ordered. However, as before we still must check to see if there is a new optimal order size for this discount that will result in an even lower cost. The optimal order size with $C_c = \$135$ is

$$Q_{\text{opt}} = \sqrt{\frac{2(2{,}500)(200)}{135}}$$
$$= 86.1$$

Since this order size is less than the 90 units required to receive the discount, it is not feasible; thus, the optimal order size is 90 units.

Computer Analysis of the EOQ Model with Quantity Discounts

The AB:POM computer package also has the capability to perform EOQ analysis with quantity discounts. Exhibit 12.2 shows the computer output for Example 12.5

```
                                 Inventory                        Solution
Quantity Discount (EOQ) Model
                                Example 12.5

Demand rate (D)          200.00   Optimal order quantity (Q*)          90.00
Setup cost (S)          2500.00   Maximum Inventory Level (Imax)       90.00
Holding cost (H)         190.00
Price Ranges                      Orders per period (year)              2.22
   From        To        Price    Inventory $$ (Hold, Setup, Short)  $14,105.56
      1        49      1400.00    Unit costs (PD)                   $180,000.00
     50        89      1100.00    Total Cost                        $194,105.56
     90    999999       900.00
1000000         0         0.00    ← This price range was not used

                                 Inventory                        Solution
Quantity Discount (EOQ) Model
                                Example 12.5

Demand rate (D)          200.00   Optimal order quantity (Q*)          90.00
Setup cost (S)          2500.00   Maximum Inventory Level (Imax)       90.00
Holding cost (H)         15.00%
Price Ranges                      Orders per period (year)              2.22
   From        To        Price    Inventory $$ (Hold, Setup, Short)  $11,630.56
      1        49      1400.00    Unit costs (PD)                   $180,000.00
     50        89      1100.00    Total Cost                        $191,630.56
     90    999999       900.00
1000000         0         0.00    ← This price range was not used
```

EXHIBIT 12.2

Transparency 12.9 AB:POM EOQ Model with Quantity Discount

(with constant carrying costs) and Example 12.6 (with carrying costs as a percentage of price).

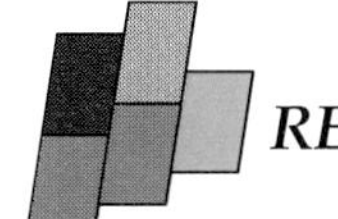

REORDER POINT

In our description of the various EOQ models in the previous sections, we addressed one of the two primary questions related to inventory management, how much should be ordered. In this section we will discuss the other aspect of inventory management, when to order. The determinant of when to order in a continuous inventory system is the **reorder point,** the inventory level at which a new order is placed.

The **reorder point** is the level of inventory at which a new order should be placed.

The reorder point for our basic EOQ model with constant demand and a constant lead time to receive an order is relatively straightforward. It is simply equal to the amount demanded during the lead time period, computed using the formula

$$R = dL$$

where

d = demand rate per time period (e.g., daily)
L = lead time

EXAMPLE 12.7

Reorder Point for the Basic EOQ Model

Problem Statement:

The I-75 Discount Carpet Store described in Example 12.2 is open 311 days per year. If annual demand is 10,000 yards of Super Shag Carpet and the lead time to receive an order is 10 days, determine the reorder point for carpet.

Solution:

$$
\begin{aligned}
R &= dL \\
&= \left(\frac{10{,}000}{311}\right)(10) \\
&= 321.54
\end{aligned}
$$

Thus, when the inventory level falls to approximately 321 yards of carpet, a new order is placed. Notice that the reorder point is not related to the optimal order quantity or any of the inventory costs.

Safety Stocks

In Example 12.7, an order is made when the inventory level reaches the reorder point. During the lead-time period, the remaining inventory in stock will be depleted at a constant demand rate, such that the new order quantity will arrive at exactly the same moment as the inventory level reaches zero. However, realistically demand—and, to a lesser extent lead time—are uncertain. As a result, the inventory level might be depleted at a slower or faster rate during the lead-time period. This situation is depicted in Figure 12.9 for uncertain demand and a constant lead time.

A **stockout** is an inventory shortage.

Safety stock is a buffer added to the inventory on hand during lead time.

Notice in the second order cycle that a **stockout** occurs when demand exceeds the available inventory in stock. As a hedge against stockouts when demand is uncertain, a **safety** (or *buffer*) **stock** of inventory is frequently added to the expected demand during lead time. The addition of a safety stock to the stockout occurrence shown in Figure 12.9 is displayed in Figure 12.10.

Service Level

There are several approaches to determining the amount of the safety stock. One of the more popular methods is to establish a safety stock that will meet a speci-

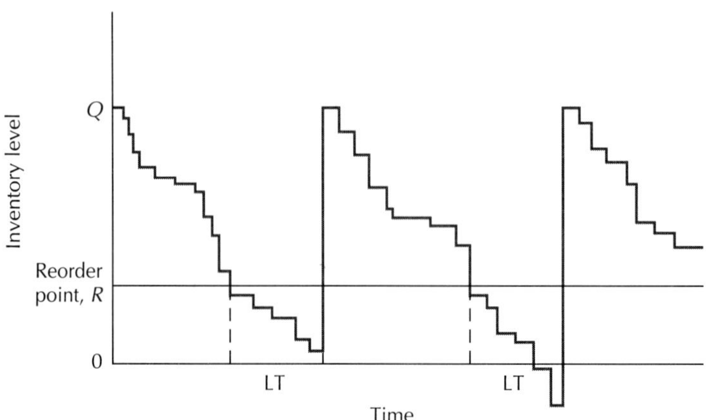

FIGURE 12.9 Variable Demand with a Reorder Point

Transparency 12.10 Reorder Point with a Safety Stock

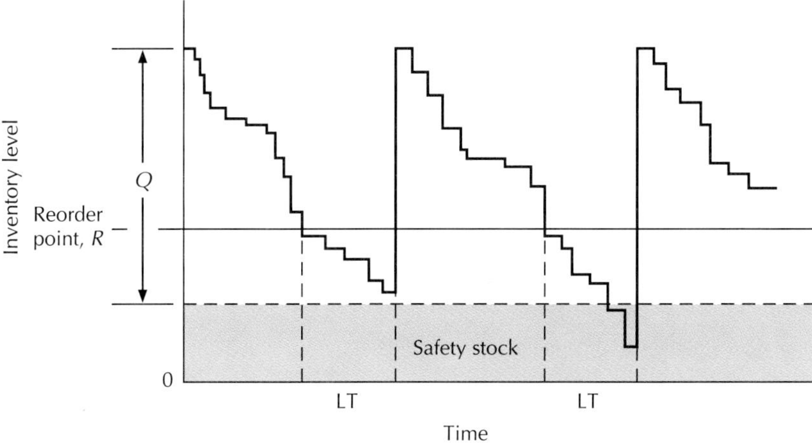

FIGURE 12.10 Reorder Point with a Safety Stock

Service level is the probability that the inventory available during lead time will meet demand.

fied **service level.** The service level is defined as the probability that the amount of inventory on hand during the lead time is sufficient to meet expected demand—that is, the probability that a stockout will not occur. The term *service* is used, since the higher the probability that inventory will be on hand, the more likely that customer demand will be met, that is, that the customer can be served. For example, a service level of 90 percent means that there is a 0.90 probability that demand will be met during the lead-time period, and the probability that a stockout will occur is 10 percent. The specification of the service level is typically a policy decision based on a number of factors, including carrying costs for the extra safety stock and present and future lost sales if customer demand cannot be met.

Reorder Point with Variable Demand

In order to compute the reorder point with a safety stock that will meet a specific service level, we will assume that the individual demands during each day of lead time are uncertain, independent, and can be described by a normal distribution. The average demand for the lead-time period is the sum of the average daily demands for the days of the lead time, which is also the product of the average daily demands multiplied by the lead time. Likewise, the variance of the distribution is the sum of the daily variances for the number of days in the lead-time period. Using these parameters the reorder point to meet a specific service level can be computed as follows:

$$R = \bar{d}L + z\sigma_d\sqrt{L}$$

where

$\bar{d}$ = average daily demand

L = lead time

σ_d = the standard deviation of daily demand

z = number of standard deviations corresponding to the service level probability

$z\sigma_d\sqrt{L}$ = safety stock

The term $\sigma_d\sqrt{L}$ in this formula for the reorder point is the square root of the sum of the daily variances during lead time:

Transparency 12.11 Reorder Point for a Service Level

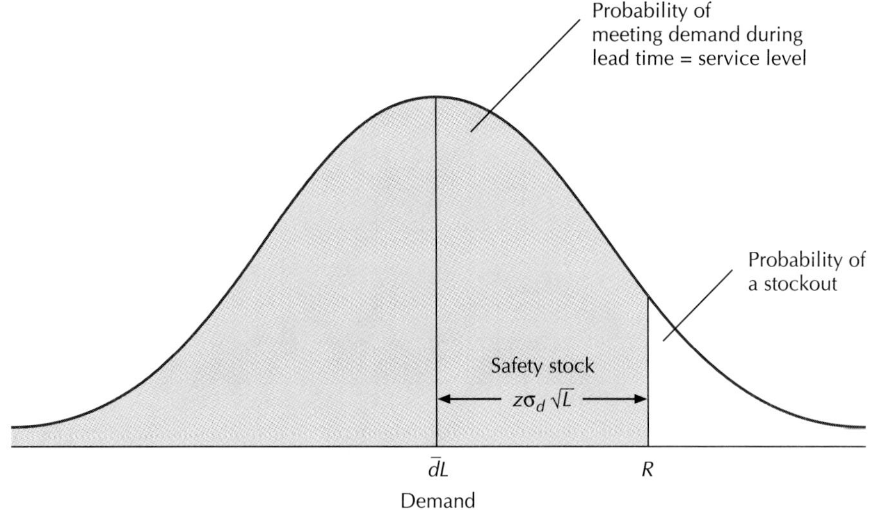

FIGURE 12.11 Reorder Point for a Service Level

$$\text{Variance} = (\text{daily variances})\ (\text{number of days of lead time})$$
$$= \sigma_d^2 L$$
$$\text{Standard deviation} = \sqrt{\sigma_d^2 L}$$
$$= \sigma_d\sqrt{L}$$

The reorder point relative to the service level is shown in Figure 12.11. The service level is the shaded area, or probability, to the left of the reorder point, R.

EXAMPLE 12.8

Reorder Point for Variable Demand

Problem Statement:

Recall the I-75 Discount Carpet Store first introduced in Example 12.2. We will now assume that daily demand for Super Shag carpet stocked by the store is normally distributed with an average daily demand of 30 yards and a standard deviation of 5 yards of carpet per day. The lead time for receiving a new order of carpet is 10 days. Determine the reorder point and safety stock if the store wants a service level of 95 percent with the probability of a stockout equal to 5 percent.

Solution:

$$\bar{d} = 30 \text{ yards per day}$$
$$L = 10 \text{ days}$$
$$\sigma_d = 5 \text{ yards per day}$$

For a 95 percent service level, the value of z (from Table B.3 in Appendix B) is 1.97. The reorder point is computed as follows:

$$R = \bar{d}L + z\sigma_d\sqrt{L}$$
$$= 30(10) + (1.97)(5)(\sqrt{10})$$
$$= 300 + 31.1$$
$$= 331.1 \text{ yards}$$

The safety stock is the second term in the reorder point formula:

$$\begin{aligned} \text{Safety stock} &= z\sigma_d\sqrt{L} \\ &= (1.97)(5)(\sqrt{10}) \\ &= 31.1 \text{ yards} \end{aligned}$$

Reorder Point with Variable Lead Time

In the model in the previous section for determining the reorder point, we assumed a variable demand rate and a constant lead time. In the case where demand is constant and the lead time varies, we can use a similar formula:

$$R = d\bar{L} + zd\sigma_L$$

where

$$\begin{aligned} d &= \text{constant daily demand} \\ \bar{L} &= \text{average lead time} \\ \sigma_L &= \text{standard deviation of lead time} \\ d\sigma_L &= \text{standard deviation of demand during lead time} \\ zd\sigma_L &= \text{safety stock} \end{aligned}$$

EXAMPLE 12.9

Reorder Point with Constant Demand and Variable Lead Time

Problem Statement:

For Example 12.8 and the I-75 Discount Carpet Store, we will now assume that daily demand for Super Shag carpet is a constant 30 yards. Lead time is normally distributed with a mean of 10 days and a standard deviation of 3 days. Determine the reorder point and safety stock corresponding to a 95 percent service level.

Solution:

$$\begin{aligned} d &= 30 \text{ yards per day} \\ \bar{L} &= 10 \text{ days} \\ \sigma_L &= 3 \text{ days} \\ z &= 1.97 \quad \text{(for a 95 percent service level)} \\ R &= d\bar{L} + zd\sigma_L \\ &= (30)(10) + (1.97)(30)(3) \\ &= 300 + 177.3 \\ &= 477.3 \text{ yards} \end{aligned}$$

Reorder Point with Variable Demand and Lead Time

The final reorder point case we will consider is where both demand and lead time are variables. The reorder point formula for this model is as follows:

$$R = \bar{d}\,\bar{L} + z\sqrt{\sigma_d^2\bar{L} + \sigma_L^2\bar{d}^2}$$

where

$$\bar{d} = \text{average daily demand}$$

$$\bar{L} = \text{average lead time}$$

$$\sqrt{\sigma_d^2\bar{L} + \sigma_L^2\bar{d}^2} = \text{standard deviation of demand during lead time}$$

$$z\sqrt{\sigma_d^2\bar{L} + \sigma_L^2\bar{d}^2} = \text{safety stock}$$

EXAMPLE 12.10

Reorder Point with Variable Demand and Lead Time

Problem Statement:

We again consider the I-75 Carpet Discount Store used in Examples 12.8 and 12.9. In this case daily demand is normally distributed with a mean of 30 yards and a standard deviation of 5 yards. Lead time is also assumed to be normally distributed with a mean of 10 days and a standard deviation of 3 days. Determine the reorder point and safety stock for a 95 percent service level.

Solution:

$$\bar{d} = 30 \text{ yards per day}$$

$$\sigma_d = 5 \text{ yards per day}$$

$$\bar{L} = 10 \text{ days}$$

$$\sigma_L = 3 \text{ days}$$

$$z = 1.97 \quad \text{(for a 95 percent service level)}$$

$$\begin{aligned} R &= \bar{d}\,\bar{L} + z\sqrt{\sigma_d^2\bar{L} + \sigma_L^2\bar{d}^2} \\ &= (30)(10) + (1.97)\sqrt{(5)^2(10) + (3)^2(30)^2} \\ &= 300 + 180 \\ &= 480 \text{ yards} \end{aligned}$$

Thus, the reorder point is 480 yards with a safety stock of 180 yards. Notice that this reorder point encompasses the largest safety stock of our three reorder point examples, which would be anticipated given the increased variability resulting from variable demand and lead time.

ORDER QUANTITY FOR A PERIODIC INVENTORY SYSTEM

Earlier in this chapter we defined a continuous, or fixed-order-quantity, inventory system as one which the order quantity was constant and the time between orders varied. So far this type of inventory system has been the primary focus of our discussion. The less common *periodic,* or *fixed-time-period, inventory system* is one in which the time between orders is constant and the order size varies. Drugstores are one example of a business that sometimes uses a fixed-period inventory system. Drugstores stock a number of personal hygiene- and health-related products such as shampoo, toothpaste, soap, bandages, cough medicine, and aspirin.

Normally, the vendors who provide these items to the store will make periodic visits—for example, every few weeks or every month—and count the stock of inventory on hand for their product. If the inventory is exhausted or at some predetermined reorder point, a new order will be placed for an amount that will bring the inventory level back up to the desired level. The drugstore managers will generally not monitor the inventory level between vendor visits, but instead will rely on the vendor to take inventory at the time of the scheduled visit.

A limitation of this type of inventory system is that inventory can be exhausted early in the time period between visits, resulting in a stockout that will not be remedied until the next scheduled order. Alternatively, when inventory reaches a reorder point in a fixed-order-quantity system, an order is made that minimizes the time during which a stockout might exist. As a result of this drawback, a larger safety stock is normally required for the fixed-interval system.

A periodic inventory system normally requires a larger safety stock.

Order Quantity with Variable Demand

If the demand rate and lead time are constant, then the fixed-period model will have a fixed-order quantity that will be made at specified time intervals, which is the same as the fixed-quantity (EOQ) model under similar conditions. However, as we have already explained, the fixed-period model reacts significantly differently than the fixed-order model when demand is a variable.

The order size for a fixed-period model given variable daily demand that is normally distributed is determined by the following formula:

$$Q = \bar{d}(t_b + L) + z\sigma_d\sqrt{t_b + L} - I$$

where

$$\bar{d} = \text{average demand rate}$$
$$t_b = \text{the fixed time between orders}$$
$$L = \text{lead time}$$
$$\sigma_d = \text{standard deviation of demand}$$
$$z\sigma_d\sqrt{t_b + L} = \text{safety stock}$$
$$I = \text{inventory in stock}$$

The first term in this formula, $\bar{d}(t_b + L)$, is the average demand during the order cycle time plus the lead time. It reflects the amount of inventory that will be needed to protect against the entire time from this order to the next and the lead time until the order is received. The second term, $z\sigma_d\sqrt{t_b+L}$, is the safety stock for a specific service level, determined in much the same way as previously described for a reorder point. The final term, I, is the amount of inventory on hand when the inventory level is checked and an order is made.

EXAMPLE 12.11

Order Size for Fixed-Period Model with Variable Demand

Problem Statement:

The Corner Drug Store stocks a popular brand of sunscreen. The average demand for the sunscreen is 6 bottles per day, with a standard deviation of 1.2 bottles. A vendor for the sunscreen producer checks the drugstore stock every 60 days. During one visit the drugstore had 8 bottles in stock. The lead time to receive an order is 5 days. Determine the order size for this order period that will enable the drugstore to maintain a 95 percent service level.

Solution:

$$\bar{d} = 6 \text{ bottles per day}$$
$$\sigma_d = 1.2 \text{ bottles}$$
$$t_b = 60 \text{ days}$$
$$L = 5 \text{ days}$$
$$I = 8 \text{ bottles}$$
$$z = 1.97 \text{ (for a 95 percent service level)}$$
$$Q = \bar{d}(t_b + L) + z\sigma_d\sqrt{t_b + L} - I$$
$$= (6)(60 + 5) + (1.97)(1.2)\sqrt{60 + 5} - 8$$
$$= 401 \text{ bottles}$$

SUMMARY

Teaching Note 12.5 Single-Period Model for Limited Demand

In this chapter we described the two types of systems for managing inventory, continuous and periodic, and we presented several models for determining how much to order and when to order for each system. However, we focused our attention primarily on the more commonly used continuous, fixed-order-quantity systems with EOQ models for determining order size and reorder points for determining when to order.

The objective of these order quantity models was to determine the optimal trade-off between inventory carrying costs and ordering costs that would minimize total inventory cost. However, a drawback of approaching inventory management in this manner is that it can delude management into thinking that if they determine the minimum cost order quantity, they have achieved all they can in reducing inventory costs, which is not the case. Management should continually strive both to accurately assess and to reduce individual inventory costs. If management has accurately determined carrying and order costs, then they can seek ways to lower them that will reduce overall inventory costs regardless of the order size and reorder point.

SUMMARY OF KEY FORMULAS

Basic EOQ model

$$Q_{\text{opt}} = \sqrt{\frac{2C_oD}{C_c}}$$

$$\text{TC} = \frac{C_oD}{Q} + \frac{C_cQ}{2}$$

EOQ model with noninstantaneous receipt

$$Q_{\text{opt}} = \sqrt{\frac{2C_oD}{C_c\left(1 - \frac{d}{p}\right)}}$$

$$\text{TC} = \frac{C_oD}{Q} + \frac{C_cQ}{2}\left(1 - \frac{d}{p}\right)$$

EOQ model with shortages

$$Q_{\text{opt}} = \sqrt{\frac{2C_oD}{C_c}\left(\frac{C_s + C_c}{C_s}\right)}$$

$$S_{\text{opt}} = Q_{\text{opt}}\left(\frac{C_c}{C_c + C_s}\right)$$

$$\text{TC} = \frac{C_sS^2}{2Q} + \frac{C_c(Q - S)^2}{2Q} + \frac{C_oD}{Q}$$

Inventory cost for quantity discounts

$$\text{TC} = \frac{C_oD}{Q} + \frac{C_cQ}{2} + PD$$

Reorder point with constant demand and lead time

$$R = dL$$

Reorder point with variable demand

$$R = \bar{d}L + z\sigma_d\sqrt{L}$$

Reorder point with variable lead time

$$R = \bar{d}L + zd\sigma_L$$

Reorder point with variable demand and lead time

$$R = \bar{d}\,\bar{L} + z\sqrt{\sigma_d^2\bar{L} + \sigma_L^2\bar{d}^2}$$

Fixed-time-period order quantity with variable demand

$$Q = \bar{d}(t_b + L) + z\sigma_d\sqrt{t_b + L} - I$$

SUMMARY OF KEY TERMS

ABC system: a method for classifying inventory items according to their dollar value to the firm based on the principle that only a few items account for the greatest dollar value of total inventory.

carrying costs: the cost of holding an item in inventory including lost opportunity costs, storage, rent, cooling, lighting, interest on loans, and so on.

continuous inventory system: a system in which the inventory level is continually monitored; when it decreases to a certain level, a fixed amount is ordered.

dependent demand: typically component parts or materials used in the process to produce a final product.

economic order quantity: a fixed order quantity that minimizes total inventory costs.

fixed-order-quantity system: also known as a continuous system; an inventory system in which a fixed, predetermined amount is ordered whenever inventory in stock falls to a certain level called the reorder point.

fixed-time-period system: also known as a periodic system; an inventory system in which a variable amount is ordered after a predetermined, constant passage of time.

independent demand: final or finished products that are not a function of, or dependent upon, internal production activity.

inventory: a stock of items kept on hand by an organization to use to meet customer demand.

in-process (buffer) inventory: stocks of partially completed items kept between stages of a production process.

noninstantaneous receipt model: also known as the production lot-size model; an inventory system in which an order is received gradually and the inventory level is depleted at the same time it is being replenished.

order cycle: the time between the receipt of orders in an inventory system.

ordering costs: the cost of replenishing the stock of inventory including requisition cost, transportation and shipping, receiving, inspection, handling, etc.

periodic inventory system: a system in which the inventory level is checked after a specific time period and a variable amount is ordered, depending on the inventory in stock.

quantity discount: a pricing schedule in which lower prices are provided for specific (higher) order quantities.

reorder point: a level of inventory in stock at which a new order is placed.

safety stock: an amount added to the expected amount demanded during the lead-time period (the reorder point level) as a hedge against a stockout.

service level: the probability that the amount of inventory on hand during the lead-time period is sufficient to meet expected demand.

shortage costs: temporary or permanent loss of sales that will result when customer demand cannot be met.

stockout: an inventory shortage occurring when demand exceeds the inventory in stock.

SOLVED PROBLEMS

1. Basic EOQ Model

Problem Statement:

Electronic Village stocks and sells a particular brand of personal computer. It costs the store \$450 each time it places an order with the manufacturer for the personal computers. The annual cost of carrying the PCs in inventory is \$170. The store manager estimates that annual demand for the PCs will be 1,200 units. Determine the optimal order quantity and the total minimum inventory cost.

Solution:

$$D = 1{,}200 \text{ personal computers}$$

$$C_c = \$170$$

$$C_o = \$450$$

$$Q_{\text{opt}} = \sqrt{\frac{2C_oD}{C_c}}$$

$$= \sqrt{\frac{2(450)(1{,}200)}{170}}$$

$$= 79.7 \text{ personal computers}$$

$$\text{TC} = \frac{C_oD}{Q_{\text{opt}}} + \frac{C_cQ_{\text{opt}}}{2}$$

$$= 450\left(\frac{1{,}200}{79.7}\right) + 170\left(\frac{79.7}{2}\right)$$

$$= \$13{,}549.91$$

2. *EOQ Model with Shortages*

Problem Statement:

Assume in the first solved problem that Electronic Village allows shortages and the shortage cost is \$600 per unit per year. Compute the optimal order quantity and the total minimum inventory cost.

Solution:

$$C_s = \$600$$

$$Q_{\text{opt}} = \sqrt{\frac{2C_oD}{C_c}\left(\frac{C_s + C_c}{C_s}\right)}$$

$$= \sqrt{\frac{2(150)(1{,}200)}{170}\left(\frac{600 + 170}{600}\right)}$$

$$= 90.3 \text{ personal computers}$$

$$S_{\text{opt}} = Q\left(\frac{C_c}{C_c + C_s}\right)$$

$$= 90.3\left(\frac{170}{170 + 600}\right)$$

$$= 19.9 \text{ personal computers}$$

$$\text{TC} = \frac{C_sS^2}{2Q} + \frac{C_c(Q - S)^2}{2Q} + \frac{C_oD}{Q}$$

$$= \frac{(600)(19.9)^2}{2(90.3)} + 170\frac{(90.3 - 19.9)^2}{2(90.3)} + 450\left(\frac{1{,}200}{90.3}\right)$$

$$= \$1{,}315.65 + \$4{,}665.27 + 5{,}980.07$$

$$= \$11{,}960.98$$

3. *Quantity Discount*

Problem Statement:

A manufacturing firm has been offered a particular component part it uses according to the following discount pricing schedule provided by the supplier.

1–199	\$65
200–599	59
600+	56

The manufacturing company uses 700 of the components annually, the annual carrying cost is \$14 per unit, and the ordering cost is \$275. Determine the amount the firm should order.

Solution:

First, determine the optimal order size and total cost with the basic EOQ model.

$$C_o = \$275$$

$$C_c = \$14$$

$$D = 700$$

$$Q_{\text{opt}} = \sqrt{\frac{2C_oD}{C_c}}$$

$$= \sqrt{\frac{2(275)(700)}{14}}$$

$$Q_{opt} = 165.83$$

$$TC = \frac{C_o D}{Q_{opt}} + \frac{C_c Q_{opt}}{2} PD$$

$$= \frac{(275)(700)}{165.83} + \frac{(7)(165.83)}{2} + (\$65)(700)$$

$$= \$47{,}821$$

Next, compare the order size with the second level quantity discount with an order size of 200 and a discount price of \$59.

$$TC = \frac{(275)(700)}{200} + \frac{(14)(200)}{2} = (59)(700)$$

$$= \$43{,}662.50$$

This discount results in a lower cost.

Finally, compare the current discounted order size with the fixed-price discount for $Q = 600$.

$$TC = \frac{(275)(700)}{600} + \frac{(14)(600)}{2} = (56)(700)$$

$$= \$43{,}720.83$$

Since this total cost is higher, the optimal order size is 200 with a total cost of \$43,662.50.

4. *Reorder Point with Variable Demand*

Problem Statement:

A computer products store stocks color graphics monitors, and the daily demand is normally distributed with a mean of 1.6 monitors and a standard deviation of 0.4 monitors. The lead time to receive an order from the manufacturer is 15 days. Determine the reorder point that will achieve a 98 percent service level.

Solution:

$$\bar{d} = 1.6 \text{ monitors per day}$$

$$L = 15 \text{ days}$$

$$\sigma_d = 0.4 \text{ monitors per day}$$

$$z = 2.05 \text{ (for a 98 percent service level)}$$

$$R = \bar{d}L + z\sigma_d\sqrt{L}$$

$$= (1.6)(15) + (2.05)(0.4)\sqrt{15}$$

$$= 24 + 3.18$$

$$= 27.18 = 28 \text{ monitors}$$

QUESTIONS

12-1. Describe the difference between independent and dependent demand and give an example of each for a pizza restaurant such as Domino's or Pizza Hut.

12-2. Distinguish between a fixed-order-quantity system and fixed-time-period system and give an example of each.

12-3. Discuss customer service level for an inventory system within the context of quality management.

12-4. Explain the ABC inventory classification system and indicate its advantages.

12-5. Identify the two basic decisions addressed by inventory management and discuss why the responses to these decisions differ for continuous and periodic inventory systems.

12-6. Describe the major cost categories used in inventory analysis and their functional relationship to each other.

12-7. Explain how the order quantity is determined using the basic EOQ model.

12-8. What are the assumptions of the basic EOQ model and to what extent do they limit the usefulness of the model?

12-9. How are the reorder point and lead time related in inventory analysis?

12-10. Describe how the noninstantaneous receipt model differs from the basic EOQ model.

12-11. What will be the effect on the EOQ model with shortages if the shortage cost is very high?

12-12. How must the application of the basic EOQ model be altered in order to reflect quantity discounts?

12-13. Why do the basic EOQ model variations not include the price of an item?

12-14. By performing several mathematical manipulations, we can express the total cost equation for the general EOQ model as

$$\text{Total annual inventory cost} = \sqrt{2C_oC_cD}$$

Performing similar mathematical manipulations on the EOQ model with shortages and back ordering will result in the following total cost equation for that model:

$$\text{Total annual inventory cost} = \sqrt{2C_oC_cD} \cdot \sqrt{\frac{C_s}{C_c + C_s}}$$

Comparing these two total cost equations, what can you infer about the general relationship between the EOQ model with shortages and the model without shortages?

12-15. In the noninstantaneous-receipt EOQ model, what would be the effect of the production rate becoming increasingly large as the demand rate became increasingly small, until the ratio d/p was negligible?

12-16. Explain in general terms how a safety stock level is determined using customer service level.

PROBLEMS

12-1. Hayes Electronics stocks and sells a particular brand of microcomputer. It costs the firm $450 each time it places an order with the manufacturer for the microcomputers. The cost of carrying one microcomputer in inventory

12-1. a. $Q = 79.7$
b. TC = $13,550
c. 15.05 orders
d. 24.18 d

for a year is $170. The store manager estimates that total annual demand for the computers will be 1,200 units, with a constant demand rate throughout the year. Orders are received within minutes after placement from a local warehouse maintained by the manufacturer. The store policy is never to have stockouts of the microcomputers. The store is open for business every day of the year except Christmas Day. Determine the following:

a. Optimal order quantity per order
b. Minimum total annual inventory costs
c. The number of orders per year
d. The time between orders (in working days)

12-2. See Solutions Manual.

12-2. Hayes Electronics (Problem 12-1) assumed with certainty that the ordering cost is $450/order and the inventory carrying cost is $170/unit/year. However, the inventory model parameters are frequently only estimates that are subject to some degree of uncertainty. Consider four cases of variation in the model parameters as follows: a. both ordering cost and carrying cost are 10 percent less than originally estimated, b. both ordering cost and carrying cost are 10 percent higher than originally estimated, c. ordering cost is 10 percent higher and carrying cost is 10 percent lower than originally estimated, and d. ordering cost is 10 percent lower and carrying cost is 10 percent higher than originally estimated. Determine the optimal order quantity and total inventory cost for each of the four cases. Prepare a table with values from all four cases and compare the sensitivity of the model solution to changes in parameter values.

12-3. a. $Q = 240$ yd
b. TC = $4,800
c. 80 orders
d. 4 d

12-3. A firm is faced with the attractive situation in which it can obtain immediate delivery of an item it stocks for retail sale. The firm has therefore not bothered to order the item in any systematic way. However, recently profits have been squeezed due to increasing competitive pressures, and the firm has retained a management consultant to study its inventory management. The consultant has determined that the various costs associated with making an order for the item stocked are approximately $30 per order. She has also determined that the costs of carrying the item in inventory amount to approximately $20 per unit per year (primarily direct storage costs and foregone profit on investment in inventory). Demand for the item is reasonably constant over time, and the forecast is for 19,200 units per year. When an order is placed for the item, the entire order is immediately delivered to the firm by the supplier. The firm operates 6 days a week plus a few Sundays, or approximately 320 days per year. Determine the following:

a. Optimal order quantity per order
b. Total annual inventory costs
c. Optimal number of orders to place per year
d. Number of operating days between orders, based on the optimal ordering

12-4. $Q = 10{,}000$; TC = $3,500; 3.5 orders; 104.3 d

12-4. The Western Jeans Company purchases denim from Cumberland Textile Mills. The Western Company uses 35,000 yards of denim per year to make jeans. The cost of ordering denim from the textile company is $500 per order. It costs Western $0.35 per yard annually to hold a yard of denim in inventory. Determine the optimal number of yards of denim the Western Company should order, the minimum total annual inventory cost, the optimal number of orders per year, and the optimal time between orders.

12-5. a. $Q = 190{,}918.8$ yd
b. TC = $15,273.51
c. 6.36 orders
d. 54.4 d

12-5. The Metropolitan Book Company purchases paper from the Atlantic Paper Company. Metropolitan produces magazines and paperbacks that require 1,215,000 yards of paper per year. The cost per order for the company is

$1,200; the cost of holding 1 yard of paper in inventory is $0.08 per year. Determine the following:

a. Economic order quantity
b. Minimum total annual cost
c. Optimal number of orders per year
d. Optimal time between orders

12-6. The Simple Simon Bakery produces fruit pies for freezing and subsequent sale. The bakery, which operates 5 days a week, 52 weeks a year, can produce pies at the rate of 64 pies per day. The bakery sets up the pie-production operation and produces until a predetermined number (Q) have been produced. When not producing pies, the bakery uses its personnel and facilities for producing other bakery items. The setup cost for a production run of fruit pies is $500. The cost of holding frozen pies in storage is $5 per pie per year. The annual demand for frozen fruit pies, which is constant over time, is 5,000 pies. Determine the following:

a. The optimum production run quantity (Q)
b. Total annual inventory costs
c. The optimum number of production runs per year
d. The optimum cycle time (time between run starts)
e. The run length in working days

12-6. a. $Q = 1{,}195.6$ b. TC = $4,181.86 c. 4.18 orders d. 62.2 d e. 18.68 d

12-7. The Pedal Pusher Bicycle Shop operates 364 days a year, closing only on Christmas Day. The shop pays $300 for a particular bicycle purchased from the manufacturer. The annual holding cost per bicycle is estimated to be 25 percent of the dollar value of inventory. The shop sells an average of 25 bikes per week. Frequently, the dealer does not have a bike in stock when a customer purchases it and the bike is back ordered. The dealer estimates her shortage cost per unit back ordered, on an annual basis, to be $250 due to lost future sales (and profits). The ordering cost for each order is $100. Determine the optimal order quantity and shortage level and the total minimum cost.

12-7. $Q = 67.13$; $S = 15.49$; TC = $3,872.98

12-8. The Petroco Company uses a highly toxic chemical in one of its manufacturing processes. It must have the product delivered by special cargo trucks designed for safe shipment of chemicals. As such, ordering (and delivery) costs are relatively high, at $2,600 per order. The chemical product is packaged in 1-gallon plastic containers. The cost of holding the chemical in storage is $50 per gallon per year. The annual demand for the chemical, which is constant over time, is 2,000 gallons per year. The lead time from time of order placement until receipt is 10 days. The company operates 310 workings days per year. Compute the optimal order quantity, total minimum inventory cost, and the reorder point.

12-8. $Q = 456.07$ gal; TC = $22,803.51; $R = 64.5$ gal

12-9. The Big Buy Supermarket stocks Munchies Cereal. Demand for Munchies is 4,000 boxes per year (365 days). It costs the store $60 per order of Munchies, and it costs $0.80 per box per year to keep the cereal in stock. Once an order for Munchies is placed, it takes 4 days to receive the order from a food distributor. Determine the following:

a. Optimal order size
b. Minimum total annual inventory cost
c. Reorder point

12-9. a. $Q = 774.6$ boxed b. TC = $619.68 c. $R = 43.84$ boxes

12-10. The Wood Valley Dairy makes cheese to supply to stores in its area. The dairy can make 250 pounds of cheese per day, and the demand at area stores is 180 pounds per day. Each time the dairy makes cheese, it costs $125 to set up the production process. The annual cost of carrying a pound of

12-10. $Q = 2{,}211$; TC = $7,428

cheese in a refrigerated storage area is $12. Determine the optimal order size and the minimum total annual inventory cost.

12-11. $Q = 23{,}862$; TC = $298,276

12-11. The Rainwater Brewery produces Rainwater Light Beer, which it stores in barrels in its warehouse and supplies to its distributors on demand. The demand for Rainwater is 1,500 barrels of beer per day. The brewery can produce 2,000 barrels of Rainwater per day. It costs $6,500 to set up a production run for Rainwater. Once it is brewed, the beer is stored in a refrigerated warehouse at an annual cost of $50 per barrel. Determine the economic order quantity and the minimum total annual inventory cost.

12-12. a. $Q = 1{,}200$ tons
b. TC = $2,880
c. $R = 300$ tons

12-12. The purchasing manager for the Atlantic Steel Company must determine a policy for ordering coal to operate 12 converters. Each converter requires exactly 5 tons of coal per day to operate, and the firm operates 360 days per year. The purchasing manager has determined that the ordering cost is $80 per order, and thc cost of holding coal is 20 percent of the average dollar value of inventory held. The purchasing manager has negotiated a contract to obtain the coal for $12 per ton for the coming year.

a. Determine the optimal quantity of coal to receive in each order.
b. Determine the total inventory-related costs associated with the optimal ordering policy (do not include the cost of the coal).
c. If 5 days' lead time is required to receive an order of coal, how much coal should be on hand when an order is placed?

12-13. a. $Q = 2{,}529.8$ logs
b. TC = $12,649.61
c. $T_b = 63.3$ d
d. 303.7

12-13. The Pacific Lumber Company and Mill processes 10,000 logs annually, operating 250 days per year. Immediately upon receiving an order, the logging company's supplier begins delivery to the lumber mill at the rate of 60 logs per day. The lumber mill has determined that the ordering cost is $1,600 per order, and the cost of carrying logs in inventory before they are processed is $15 per log on an annual basis. Determine the following:

a. The optimal order size
b. The total inventory cost associated with the optimal order quantity
c. The number of operating days between orders
d. The number of operating days required to receive an order

12-14. $Q = 1{,}598$; $S = 486.3$; TC = $1,945.17

12-14. The Roadking Tire Store sells a brand of tire called the Roadrunner. The annual demand from the store's customers for Roadrunner tires is 3,700 per year. The cost to order tires from the tire manufacturer is $420 per order. The annual carrying cost is $1.75 per tire. The store allows shortages, and the annual shortage cost per tire is $4. Determine the optimal order size, maximum shortage level, and minimum total annual inventory cost.

12-15. $Q = 17{,}544.2$; $S = 4{,}616.90$; TC = $3,231.83

12-15. The Laurel Creek Lawn Shop sells Fastgro Fertilizer. The annual demand for the fertilizer is 270,000 pounds. The cost to order the fertilizer from the Fastgro company is $105 per order. The annual carrying cost is $0.25 per pound. The store operates with shortages, and the annual shortage cost is $0.70 per pound. Compute the optimal order size, minimum total annual inventory cost, and the maximum shortage level.

12-16. a. $Q = 142.21$ sets
b. $S = 60.95$ sets
c. TC = $3,656.70

12-16. Videoworld is a discount television store that sells color televisions. The annual demand for color television sets is 400. The cost per order from the manufacturer is $650. The carrying cost is $45 per set each year. The store has an inventory policy that allows shortages. The shortage cost per set is estimated at $60. Determine the following:

a. Optimal order size
b. Maximum shortage level
c. Minimum total annual inventory cost

12-17. The I-75 Carpet Discount Store has annual demand of 10,000 yards of Super Shag Carpet. The annual carrying cost for a yard of this carpet is $0.75, and the ordering cost is $150. The carpet manufacturer normally charges the store $8 per yard for the carpet. However, the manufacturer has offered a discount price of $6.50 per yard if the store will order 5,000 yards. How much should the store order, and what will be the total annual inventory cost for that order quantity?

12-17. Select discount; $Q = 5{,}000$.

12-18. The Fifth Quarter Bar buys Old World draft beer by the barrel from a local distributor. The bar has an annual demand of 900 barrels, which it purchases at a price of $205 per barrel. The annual carrying cost is 12 percent of the price, and the cost per order is $160. The distributor has offered the bar a reduced price of $190 per barrel if it will order a minimum of 300 barrels. Should the bar take the discount?

12-18. Select discount; $Q = 300$.

12-19. The bookstore at State University purchases sweatshirts emblazoned with the school name and logo from a vendor. The vendor sells the sweatshirts to the store for $38 apiece. The cost to the bookstore for placing an order is $120, and the annual carrying cost is 25 percent of the cost of a sweatshirt. The bookstore manager estimates that 1,700 sweatshirts will be sold during the year. The vendor has offered the bookstore the following volume discount schedule.

★ 12-19. Select $Q = 500$; TC = $64,704.

Order Size	*Discount*
1–299	0%
300–499	2%
500–799	4%
800+	5%

The bookstore manager wants to determine the bookstore's optimal order quantity, given this quantity discount information.

12-20. Determine the optimal order quantity of sweatshirts and total annual cost in Problem 12-19 if the carrying cost is a constant $8 per shirt per year.

★ 12-20. Select $Q = 500$; TC = $64,424.

12-21. The office manager for the Gotham Life Insurance Company orders letterhead stationery from an office products firm in boxes of 500 sheets. The company uses 6,500 boxes per year. Annual carrying costs are $3 per box, and ordering costs are $28. The following discount price schedule is provided by the office supply company.

★ 12-21. Select $Q = 6{,}000$; TC = $87,030.33.

Order Quantity (boxes)	*Price per box*
200– 999	$16
1,000–2,999	14
3,000–5,999	13
6,000+	12

Determine the optimal order quantity and the total annual inventory cost.

12-22. Determine the optimal order quantity and total annual inventory cost for boxes of stationery in problem 21 if the carrying cost is 20 percent of the price of a box of stationery.

★ 12-22. Select $Q = 6{,}000$; TC = $85,230.33.

12-23. The 23,000 seat City Coliseum houses the local professional ice hockey, basketball, indoor soccer, and arena football teams as well as various trade shows, wrestling and boxing matches, tractor pulls, and circuses. Coliseum vending annually sells large quantities of soft drinks and beer in plastic

★ 12-23. Select $Q = 20{,}000$; TC = $893,368.

cups with the name of the coliseum and the various team logos on them. The local container cup manufacturer that supplies the cups in boxes of 100 has offered coliseum management the following discount price schedule for cups.

Order Quantity (boxes)	*Price per box*
2,000– 6,999	$47
7,000–11,999	43
12,000–19,999	41
20,000+	38

The annual demand for cups is 2.3 million, the annual carrying cost per box of cups is $1.90, and ordering cost is $320. Determine the optimal order quantity and total annual inventory cost.

12-24. Select Q = 20,000; TC = $893,368.

★ 12-24. Determine the optimal order quantity and total annual inventory cost for cups in Problem 12-23 if the carrying cost is 5 percent of the price of a box of cups.

12-25. Q = $371,842.26; TC = $150,128.30; N = 14/year; R = $255,000

★ 12-25. The A to Z Office Supply Company operates by stocking a large volume of items in its warehouses and then supplying customer orders. It maintains its inventory levels by borrowing cash from a local bank. The company estimates that its demand for borrowed cash is $17,000 per day, and there are 305 working days per year. Any money borrowed during the fiscal year must be repaid with interest by the end of the current year. The annual interest rate charged by the bank is currently 9 percent. Any time a loan is obtained from the bank, it charges the company a loan-origination fee of $1,200 plus $2\frac{1}{4}$ points (i.e., 2.25 percent of the amount borrowed). Determine the optimal amount of a loan for the company, the total annual cost of the company's borrowing policy, and the number of loans the company will obtain during the year. Also, determine the level of cash on hand at which the company should apply for a new loan given that it takes 15 days for a loan to be processed by the bank.

12-26. Accept alternate option.

★ 12-26. In Problem 12-25, the local bank has offered the A to Z Office Supply Company a discount; on any loan amount greater than or equal to $500,000, the bank will lower the number of points charged on the loan origination fee from 2.25 percent to 2 percent. What should the company's optimal loan amount be?

12-27. Safety stock = 2,410.29 yd

12-27. The amount of denim used daily by The Western Jeans Company in its manufacturing process to make jeans is normally distributed with an average of 3,000 yards of denim and a standard deviation of 600 yards. The lead time required to receive an order of denim from the textile mill is a constant 6 days. Determine the safety stock and reorder point if The Western Company wants to limit the probability of a stockout and work stoppage to 5 percent.

12-28. 91% service level

★ 12-28. In Problem 12-27, what level of service would a safety stock of 2,000 yards provide?

12-29. R = 82,368 lb

12-29. The Atlantic Paper Company produces paper from wood pulp ordered from a lumber products firm. The paper company's daily demand for wood pulp is a constant 8,000 pounds. Lead time is normally distributed with an average of 7 days and a standard deviation of 1.6 days. Determine the reorder point if the paper company wants to limit the probability of a stockout and work stoppage to 2 percent.

12-30. The Uptown Bar and Grill Serves Rainwater draft beer to its customers. The daily demand for beer is normally distributed with an average of 18 gallons and a standard deviation of 4 gallons. The lead time required to receive an order of beer from the local distributor is normally distributed with a mean of 3 days and a standard deviation of 0.8 days. Determine the safety stock and reorder point if the restaurant wants to maintain a 90 percent service level. What would be the increase in the safety stock if a 95 percent service level was desired?

★ **12-30.** Increase safety stock to 26.37 gal

12-31. In Problem 12-30, the manager of the Uptown Bar and Grill has negotiated with the beer distributor for the lead time to receive orders to be a constant 3 days. What effect does that have on the reorder point developed in problem 12-30 for a 90 percent service level?

12-31. $R = 62.94$ gal

12-32. The daily demand for Sunlight paint at the Rainbow Paint Store in East Ridge is normally distributed with a mean of 26 gallons and a standard deviation of 10 gallons. The lead time for receiving an order of paint from the Sunlight distributor is 9 days. Since this is the only paint store in East Ridge, the manager is interested in maintaining only a 75 percent service level. What reorder point should be used to meet this service level? The manager subsequently learned that a new paint store would open soon in East Ridge, which has prompted her to increase the service level to 95 percent. What reorder point will maintain this service level?

12-32. 295.8 gal

12-33. PM Computers assembles microcomputers from generic components. It purchases its color monitors from a manufacturer in Taiwan; thus, there is a long and uncertain lead time for receiving orders. Lead time is normally distributed with a mean of 25 days and a standard deviation of 10 days. Daily demand is also normally distributed with a mean of 2.5 monitors and a standard deviation of 1.2 monitors. Determine the safety stock and reorder point corresponding to a 90 percent service level.

12-33. 33.17 monitors

12-34. PM Computers (Problem 12-33) is considering purchasing monitors from a U.S. manufacturer that would guarantee a lead time of 8 days, instead of from the Taiwanese company. Determine the new reorder point given this lead time and identify the factors that would enter into the decision to change manufacturers.

★ **12-34.** $R = 24.38$

12-35. The Corner Drug Store fills prescriptions for a popular children's antibiotic, Amoxycilin. The daily demand for Amoxycilin is normally distributed with a mean of 200 ounces and a standard deviation of 80 ounces The vendor for the pharmaceutical firm that supplies the drug calls the drug store pharmacist every 30 days and checks the inventory of Amoxycilin. During a call the druggist indicated the store had 60 ounces of the antibiotic in stock. The lead time to receive an order is 4 days. Determine the order size that will enable the drugstore to maintain a 95 percent service level.

12-35. $Q = 7{,}509.69$ oz

12-36. The Fast Service Food Mart stocks frozen pizzas in a refrigerated display case. The average daily demand for the pizzas is normally distributed with a mean of 8 pizzas and a standard deviation of 2.5 pizzas. A vendor for a packaged food distributor checks the market's inventory of frozen foods every 10 days; during a particular visit there were no pizzas in stock. The lead time to receive an order is 3 days. Determine the order size for this order period that will result in a 99 percent service level. During the vendor's following visit there were 5 frozen pizzas in stock. What is the order size for the next order period?

12-36. 120 pizzas

12-37. The Impanema Restaurant stocks a red Brazilian table wine it purchases from a wine merchant in a nearby city. The daily demand for the wine at the restaurant is normally distributed with a mean of 18 bottles and a stan-

12-37. $Q = 609.83$ bottles

dard deviation of 4 bottles. The wine merchant sends a representative to check the restaurant's wine cellar every 30 days, and during a recent visit there were 25 bottles in stock. The lead time to receive an order is 2 days. The restaurant manager has requested an order size that will enable him to limit the probability of a stockout to 2 percent.

12-38. See Solutions Manual.

12-38. The Dynaco Company stocks a variety of parts and materials it uses in its manufacturing processes. Recently, as demand for their finished goods has increased, management has had difficulty managing parts inventory; they frequently run out of some crucial parts and seem to have an endless supply of others. In an effort to control inventory more effectively they would like to classify their inventory of parts according to the ABC approach. Following is a list of selected parts and the annual usage and unit value for each.

Item Number	*Annual Usage*	*Unit Cost*	*Item Number*	*Annual Usage*	*Unit Cost*
1	36	$ 350	16	60	$ 610
2	510	30	17	120	20
3	50	23	18	270	15
4	300	45	19	45	50
5	18	1,900	20	19	3,200
6	500	8	21	910	3
7	710	4	22	12	4,750
8	80	26	23	30	2,710
9	344	28	24	24	1,800
10	67	440	25	870	105
11	510	2	26	244	30
12	682	35	27	750	15
13	95	50	28	45	110
14	10	3	29	46	160
15	820	1	30	165	25

Classify the inventory items according to the ABC approach using dollar value of annual demand.

See Solutions Manual.

CASE PROBLEM

The Northwoods General Store

The Northwoods General Store in Vermont sells a variety of outdoor clothing items and equipment and several food products at its modern, but rustic-looking, retail store. Its food products include salmon and maple syrup. The store also runs a lucrative catalog order operation. One of its most popular products is maple syrup, which is in metal half-gallon cans with a picture of its store on the front.

Maple syrup was one of the first products the store made and sold, and the store continues to produce it virtually on the premises. Setting up the syrup-making equipment to produce a batch of syrup costs $450. Storing the syrup for sales throughout the year is a tricky process, since it must be stored in a temperature-controlled facility. The annual cost of carrying a gallon of the syrup is $15. Based on past sales data the store has forecasted a demand of 7,500 gallons of maple syrup for the coming year. The store can produce approximately 100 gallons of syrup per day during the maple syrup season, which runs from November through February.

Because of the short season when the store can actually get syrup out of trees, it must obviously produce enough during the 4-month season to meet demand for the whole year. Specifically, store management would like a production and inventory schedule that minimizes their costs and indicates when during the year they need to start operating the syrup-making facility full time on a daily basis to meet demand for the remaining 8 months.

Develop a syrup production and inventory schedule for the Northwoods General Store.

REFERENCES

Brown, R. G., *Decision Rules for Inventory Management*, New York: Holt, Rinehart and Winston, 1967.

Buchan, J., and E. Koenigsberg, *Scientific Inventory Management*, Englewood Cliffs, N.J.: Prentice Hall, 1963.

Buffa, E. S., and Jefferey Miller, *Production-Inventory Systems: Planning and Control*. Rev. ed., Homewood, Ill.: Richard D. Irwin, 1979.

Churchman, C. W., R. L. Ackoff, and E. L. Arnoff, *Introduction to Operations Research*, New York: John Wiley, 1957.

Fetter, R. B., and W. C. Dalleck, *Decision Models for Inventory Management*, Homewood, Ill.: Richard D. Irwin, 1961.

Greene, J. H., *Production and Inventory Control*, Homewood, Ill.: Richard D. Irwin, 1974.

Hadley, G., and T. M. Whitin, *Analysis of Inventory Systems*, Englewood Cliffs, N.J.: Prentice Hall, 1963.

MaGee, J. F., and D. M. Boodman, *Production Planning and Inventory Control*, 2d ed., New York: McGraw-Hill, 1967.

Monden, Y., *Toyota Production System*, Norcross, Ga.: Industrial Engineering and Management Press, 1983.

Starr, M. K., and D. W. Miller, *Inventory Control: Theory and Practice*, Englewood Cliffs, N.J.: Prentice Hall, 1962.

Wagner, H. M., *Statistical Management of Inventory Systems*, New York: John Wiley, 1962.

Whitin, T. M., *The Theory of Inventory Management*, Princeton, N.J.: Princeton University Press, 1957.

SUPPLEMENT 12 SIMULATION

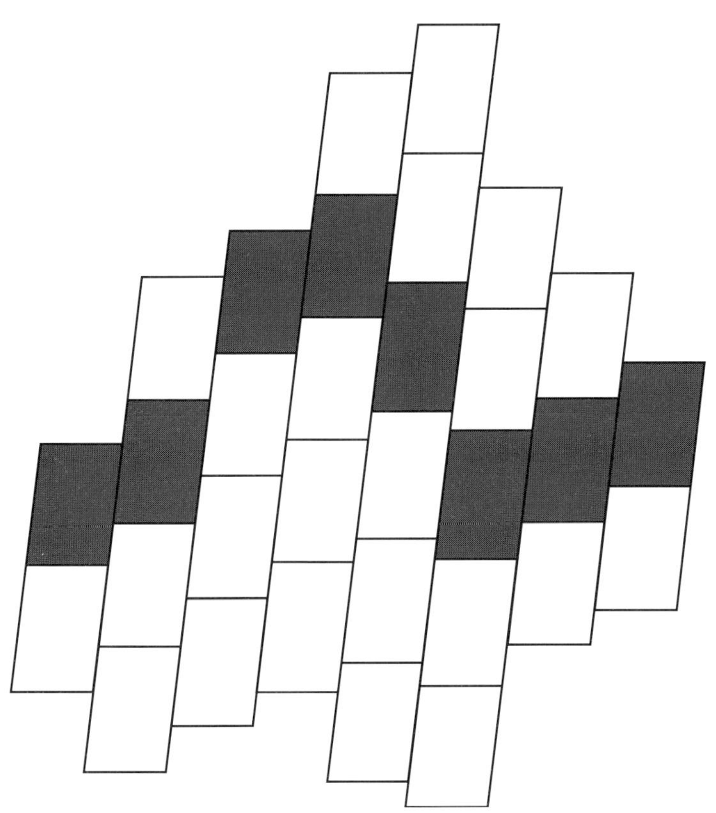

CHAPTER OUTLINE

Simulation is a mathematical and computer modeling technique for replicating real-world problem situations.

Teaching Note S12.1 Popularity of Simulation

Teaching Note S12.2 Examples of Simulation

Simulation is a very popular modeling approach because it can be applied to virtually any type of problem. It can frequently be used when there is no other applicable quantitative method; it is the technique of last resort for many problems. It differs from other quantitative methods such as linear programming, in that it is a modeling approach primarily used to analyze probabilistic problems. It does not normally provide a solution; instead it provides information that is used to make a decision.

Analogue simulation is a form of simulation familiar to most people. In analogue simulation, an original physical system is replaced by an analogous physical system that is easier to manipulate. Much of the experimentation in astronaut-controlled space flight was conducted using physical simulation that re-created the conditions of space. For example, conditions of weightlessness were simulated using rooms filled with water. Other examples include wind tunnels that simulate the conditions of flight and treadmills that simulate automobile tire wear in a laboratory instead of on the road.

This chapter supplement is concerned with an alternative type of simulation, *computerized mathematical simulation.* In this form of simulation, systems are replicated with mathematical models, which are analyzed with a computer. This type of simulation has become a very popular technique that has been applied to a wide variety of operational problems.

THE MONTE CARLO PROCESS

One characteristic of some systems that makes them difficult to solve analytically is that they consist of random variables represented by probability distributions. Thus, a large proportion of the applications of simulations are for probabilistic models.

The **Monte Carlo technique** is a method for selecting numbers randomly from a probability distribution for use in a simulation.

Teaching Note S12.3 History of the Monte Carlo Method

The term *Monte Carlo* has become synonymous with probabilistic simulation in recent years. However, the **Monte Carlo technique** can be more narrowly defined as a technique for selecting numbers *randomly* from a probability distribution (i.e., sampling) for use in a *trial* (computer) run of a simulation. As such, the Monte Carlo technique is not a type of simulation model but rather a mathematical process used within a simulation.

The name Monte Carlo is appropriate, since the basic principle behind the process is the same as in the operation of a gambling casino in Monaco. In Monaco such devices as roulette wheels, dice, and playing cards are used. These devices produce numbered results at random from well-defined populations. For example, a 7 resulting from thrown dice is a random value from a population of eleven possible numbers (i.e., 2 through 12). This same process is employed, in principle, in the Monte Carlo process used in simulation models.

The Monte Carlo process of selecting random numbers according to a probability distribution is demonstrated using the following example. The manager of a supermarket must decide how many cases of milk to order each week which is a random variable (which we will define as x) that ranges from 14 to 18 every week. From past records, the manager has determined the frequency of demand for cases of milk for the past 100 weeks. From this frequency distribution, a probability distribution of demand can be developed, as shown in Table S12.1.

The purpose of the Monte Carlo process is to generate the random variable, demand, by "sampling" from the probability distribution, $P(x)$. The demand per week could be randomly generated according to the probability distribution by spinning a roulette wheel that is partitioned into segments corresponding to the probabilities, as shown in Figure S12.1.

TABLE S12.1 Probability Distribution of Demand

Cases Demanded per Week, x	*Frequency of Demand*	*Probability of Demand P(x)*
14	20	0.20
15	40	0.40
16	20	0.20
17	10	0.10
18	10	0.10
	100	1.00

Transparency S12.1 Monte Carlo Simulation

There are 100 numbers from 0 to 99 on the outer rim of the wheel, and they have been partitioned according to the probability of each demand value. For example, 20 numbers from 0 to 19 (i.e., 20 percent of the total 100 numbers) correspond to a demand of 14 cases of milk. Now we can determine the value of demand by seeing at which number the wheel stops as well as by looking at the segment of the wheel.

When the manager spins this new wheel, the demand for cases of milk will be determined by a number. For example, if the number 71 comes up on a spin, the demand is 16 cases per week; the number 30 indicates a demand of 15. Since the manager does not know which number will come up prior to the spin and there is an equal chance of any of the 100 numbers occurring, the numbers occur at random. That is, they are **random numbers.**

Random numbers each have an equal likelihood of being selected at random.

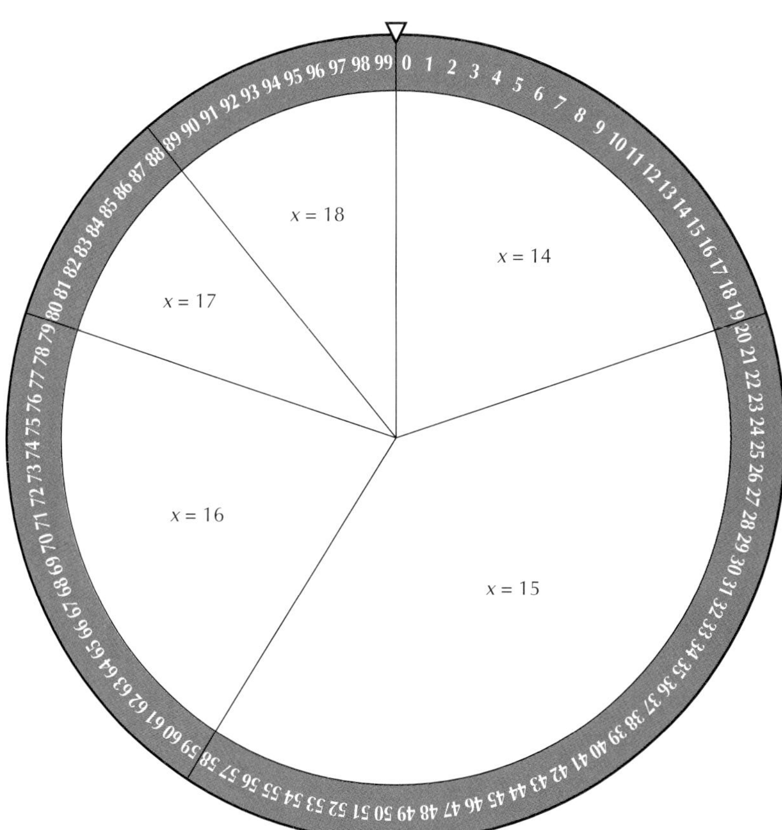

FIGURE S12.1 A Roulette Wheel of Demand

Obviously, it is not generally practical to predict weekly demand for milk by spinning a wheel. Alternatively, the process of spinning a wheel can be replicated using random numbers alone.

First, we will transfer the ranges of random numbers for each demand value from the roulette wheel to a table, as in Table S12.2. Next, instead of spinning the wheel to get a random number, we will select a random number from Table S12.3, which is referred to as a *random number table*. (These random numbers have been generated by computer so that they are *equally likely to occur*, just as if we had spun a wheel.) As an example, let us select the number 39 in Table S12.3. Looking again at Table S12.2, we can see that the random number 39 falls in the range 20–59, which corresponds to a weekly demand of 15 cases of milk.

By repeating this process of selecting random numbers from Table S12.3 (starting anywhere in the table and moving in any direction but not repeating the same sequence) and then determining weekly demand from the random number, we can simulate demand for a period of time. For example, following is demand for a period of 15 consecutive weeks.

Week	*r*	*Demand (x)*
1	39	15
2	73	16
3	72	16
4	75	16
5	37	15
6	02	14
7	87	17
8	98	18
9	10	14
10	47	15
11	93	18
12	21	15
13	95	18
14	97	18
15	69	16
		$\Sigma = 241$

These data can now be used to compute the estimated average weekly demand.

$$\text{Estimated average demand} = \frac{241}{15}$$
$$= 16.1 \text{ cases per week}$$

Transparency S12.2 Generating Demand from Random Numbers

TABLE S12.2 Generating Demand from Random Numbers

Demand *x*		*Ranges of Random Numbers* *r*		
14		0–19		
15	←	20–59	←	$r = 39$
16		60–79		
17		80–89		
18		90–99		

TABLE S12.3 Random Number Table

Transparency S12.3 Random Number Table

39 65 76 45 45	19 90 69 64 61	20 26 36 31 62	58 24 97 14 97	95 06 70 99 00
73 71 23 70 90	65 97 60 12 11	31 56 34 19 19	47 83 75 51 33	30 62 38 20 46
72 18 47 33 84	51 67 47 97 19	98 40 07 17 66	23 05 09 51 80	59 78 11 52 49
75 12 25 69 17	17 95 21 78 58	24 33 45 77 48	69 81 84 09 29	93 22 70 45 80
37 17 79 88 74	63 52 06 34 30	01 31 60 10 27	35 07 79 71 53	28 99 52 01 41
02 48 08 16 94	85 53 83 29 95	56 27 09 24 43	21 78 55 09 82	72 61 88 73 61
87 89 15 70 07	37 79 49 12 38	48 13 93 55 96	41 92 45 71 51	09 18 25 58 94
98 18 71 70 15	89 09 39 59 24	00 06 41 41 20	14 36 59 25 47	54 45 17 24 89
10 83 58 07 04	76 62 16 48 68	58 76 17 14 86	59 53 11 52 21	66 04 18 72 87
47 08 56 37 31	71 82 13 50 41	27 55 10 24 92	28 04 67 53 44	95 23 00 84 47
93 90 31 03 07	34 18 04 52 35	74 13 39 35 22	68 95 23 92 35	36 63 70 35 33
21 05 11 47 99	11 20 99 45 18	76 51 94 84 86	13 79 93 37 55	98 16 04 41 67
95 89 94 06 97	27 37 83 28 71	79 57 95 13 91	09 61 87 25 21	56 20 11 32 44
97 18 31 55 73	10 65 81 92 59	77 31 61 95 46	20 44 90 32 64	26 99 76 75 63
69 08 88 86 13	59 71 74 17 32	48 38 75 93 29	73 37 32 04 05	60 82 29 20 25
41 26 10 25 03	87 63 93 95 17	81 83 83 04 49	77 45 85 50 51	79 88 01 97 30
91 47 14 63 62	08 61 74 51 69	92 79 43 89 79	29 18 94 51 23	14 85 11 47 23
80 94 54 18 47	08 52 85 08 40	48 40 35 94 22	72 65 71 08 86	50 03 42 99 36
67 06 77 63 99	89 85 84 46 06	64 71 06 21 66	89 37 20 70 01	61 65 70 22 12
59 72 24 13 75	42 29 72 23 19	06 94 76 10 08	81 30 15 39 14	81 33 17 16 33
63 62 06 34 41	79 53 36 02 95	94 61 09 43 62	20 21 14 68 86	84 95 48 46 45
78 47 23 53 90	79 93 96 38 63	34 85 52 05 09	85 43 01 72 73	14 93 87 81 40
87 68 62 15 43	97 48 72 66 48	53 16 71 13 81	59 97 50 99 52	24 62 20 42 31
47 60 92 10 77	26 97 05 73 51	88 46 38 03 58	72 68 49 29 31	75 70 16 08 24
56 88 87 59 41	06 87 37 78 48	65 88 69 58 39	88 02 84 27 83	85 81 56 39 38
22 17 68 65 84	87 02 22 57 51	68 69 80 95 44	11 29 01 95 80	49 34 35 36 47
19 36 27 59 46	39 77 32 77 09	79 57 92 36 59	89 74 39 82 15	08 58 94 34 74
16 77 23 02 77	28 06 24 25 93	22 45 44 84 11	87 80 61 65 31	09 71 91 74 25
78 43 76 71 61	97 67 63 99 61	30 45 67 93 82	59 73 19 85 23	53 33 65 97 21
03 28 28 26 08	69 30 16 09 05	53 58 47 70 93	66 56 45 65 79	45 56 20 19 47
04 31 17 21 56	33 73 99 19 87	26 72 39 27 67	53 77 57 68 93	60 61 97 22 61
61 06 98 03 91	87 14 77 43 96	43 00 65 98 50	45 60 33 01 07	98 99 46 50 47
23 68 35 26 00	99 53 93 61 28	52 70 05 48 34	56 65 05 61 86	90 92 10 70 80
15 39 25 70 99	93 86 52 77 65	15 33 59 05 28	22 87 26 07 47	86 96 98 29 06
58 71 96 30 24	18 46 23 34 27	85 13 99 24 44	49 18 09 79 49	74 16 32 23 02
93 22 53 64 39	07 10 63 76 35	87 03 04 79 88	08 13 13 85 51	55 34 57 72 69
78 76 58 54 74	92 38 70 96 92	52 06 79 79 45	82 63 18 27 44	69 66 92 19 09
61 81 31 96 82	00 57 25 60 59	46 72 60 18 77	55 66 12 62 11	08 99 55 64 57
42 88 07 10 05	24 98 65 63 21	47 21 61 88 32	27 80 30 21 60	10 92 35 36 12
77 94 30 05 39	28 10 99 00 27	12 73 73 99 12	49 99 57 94 82	96 88 57 17 91

The manager can then use this information to determine the number of cases of milk to order each week.

Although this example is convenient for illustrating how simulation works, the average demand could have been more appropriately calculated *analytically* using the formula for expected value. The *expected value,* or average, for weekly demand can be computed analytically from the probability distribution, $P(x)$, as follows.

$$E(x) = (0.20)(14) + (0.40)(15) + (0.20)(16) + (0.10)(17) + (0.10)(18)$$
$$= 15.5 \text{ cases per week}$$

The analytical result of 15.5 cases is close to the simulated result of 16.1 cases, but clearly there is some difference. The margin of difference (0.6 case) between the simulated value and the analytical value is a result of the number of periods over which the simulation was conducted. The results of any simulation study are subject to the number of times the simulation occurred (i.e., the number of *trials*). Thus, the more periods for which the simulation is conducted, the more accurate the result. For example, if demand were simulated for 1,000 weeks, in all likelihood an average value exactly equal to the analytical value (15.5 cases of milk per week) would result.

Steady-state result is an average result that remains constant after enough trials.

Once a simulation has been repeated enough times, it reaches an average result that remains constant, called a **steady-state result.** For this example, 15.5 cases is the long-run average or steady-state result, but we have seen that the simulation would have to be repeated more than 15 times (i.e., weeks) before this result was reached.

Teaching Note S12.4 Manual Versus Computer Simulation

The simulation we performed manually for the milk-demand example was not too difficult. However, if we had performed the simulation for 1,000 weeks, it would have taken several hours. On the other hand, this simulation could be done on the computer in several seconds. Also, our simulation example was not very complex. As simulation models get progressively more complex, it becomes virtually impossible to perform them manually, thus making the computer a necessity.

The following example presents a simulation model that is slightly more complex but still not too difficult to analyze manually.

EXAMPLE S12.1

Simulation of an Inventory System with Uncertain Demand and Lead Time

Problem Statement:

The Videotech Store has the following probability distribution of weekly VCR demand.

Demand for VCRs	*Probability*
0	0.10
1	0.15
2	0.30
3	0.25
4	0.20
	1.00

The time it takes for the store to receive an order of VCRs from its distributor (i.e., the lead time) is defined by the following distribution.

Lead Time (weeks)	*Probability*
1	0.35
2	0.45
3	0.20
	1.00

When the number of VCRs in stock falls to a certain level (called the reorder point), the store manager makes an order from the distributor. (The reorder point is considered to be the number of units in stock plus the number on order.) The store manager wants to simulate this inventory system for 10 weeks using an order size of five and a reorder point of three VCRs to see how many units of lost sales (i.e., VCRs demanded but not in stock) will result and the average number of units in stock.

Solution:

The first step is to develop a range of random number values of each probability distribution as follows.

Demand	*Probability*	*RN Range*
0	0.10	1–10
1	0.15	11–25
2	0.30	26–55
3	0.25	56–80
4	0.20	81–99, 00

Lead time	*Probability*	*RN Range*
1	0.35	1–35
2	0.45	36–80
3	0.20	81–99, 00

Next the inventory system is simulated for 10 weeks, as shown in the following table.

Simulation for Inventory System

Transparency S12.4 Simulation for Inventory System

Time Period	*Beginning Inventory*	*RN*	*Demand*	*Ending Sold*	*Lost Inventory*	*Place Sale*	*Order*	*Lead RN*	*Time*
1	5	44	2	2	3	0	Yes	17	1
2	3	92	4	3	0	1	No	—	0
3	5	02	0	0	5	0	No	—	0
4	5	12	1	1	4	0	No	—	0
5	4	25	1	1	3	0	Yes	53	2
6	3	93	4	3	0	1	No	—	0
7	0	46	2	0	0	2	No	—	0
8	5	34	2	2	3	0	Yes	21	1
9	3	22	1	1	2	0	No	—	0
10	7	79	3	3	4	0	No	—	0

The simulation works as follows.

1. The simulation is started with 5 units in stock, selected arbitrarily.
2. A random number is selected, 44, which results in a demand of 2 units. Since 2 units are available, they are sold.
3. The amount sold is subtracted from the beginning inventory, which results in an ending inventory of 3 units. Since all items demanded were sold there were no lost sales.
4. Since the ending inventory level is at the reorder point of 3 units, a new order is placed.
5. A random number is selected, 53, which results in a lead time of 1 week. This means that a new order will arrive in week 3.

This same process is repeated for week 2. Notice that demand, 4, exceeds the inventory stock, 3, so there is one lost sale. An order is not placed during week 2 because the amount on order, 5, plus the ending inventory, 0, exceeds the reorder point (of 3).

For the 10-week simulation the following statistics are determined.

$$\text{Average lost sales} = \frac{4}{10} = 0.4 \text{ units}$$

$$\text{Average ending inventory} = \frac{24}{10} = 2.4 \text{ units}$$

It is obvious that the simulation was not conducted for enough time periods to generate steady-state statistics. However, this brief simulation does illustrate how a simulation model is constructed. For a more complex inventory problem of this type, where the demand might vary between 1 and 100 units and the lead times might vary between 1 and 10 weeks, computer simulation is the only means of analysis.

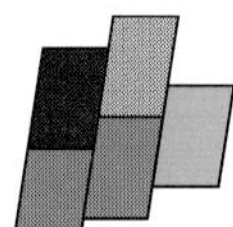

SIMULATION LANGUAGES AND SOFTWARE

Teaching Note S12.5 Computer Software for Simulation

The computer programming aspects of simulation can be quite difficult. Fortunately, generalized simulation languages have been developed to perform many of the functions of a simulation study. Each of these languages requires at least some knowledge of a scientific or business-oriented programming language.

Video S12.1 *TIMS Edelman Awards Tape,* Program 1: "Reynolds Metals"

GAINING THE COMPETITIVE EDGE

Simulating the Dispatching of Freight Carriers At Reynolds Metals Company

Reynolds Metals Company is decentralized into twelve operating divisions encompassing sixty domestic manufacturing facilities. The company incurs more than $80 million annually in truck freight expenses for approximately 75,000 truck shipments across its network of plants, warehouses, suppliers, and customers. Consistent with its decentralized operating philosophy, each of the company's divisions and plants has historically been responsible for managing its own freight operation, including the selection of independent carriers and their dispatchment for shipments. However, because of high costs and concern about service quality, in 1987 Reynolds Metals created a central dispatch system located in Richmond, Virginia, to centralize the management and operation of its interstate truck shipping. A key component in the development of this system was a simulation model for carrier selection and deployment at central dispatch. Because of the uncertainty in the number and timing of daily shipments, it was not possible to use an optimization technique. The model simulated daily freight operations and truck movements over time and was specifically used to finalize the number of carriers, select a group of "core" carriers (to be used exclusively by the company), assign carriers to locations, establish the carriers' fixed and variable truck commitments at each location, communicate expected shipping volumes and equipment commitment to carriers, and estimate costs and savings. The simulation basically replicates the daily central dispatching activity at a plant, warehouse, or supplier, which includes the identification of shipments, dispatching trucks, and shipping. The model was constructed using SLAM network simulation software and FORTRAN. The central dispatch system allowed Reynolds Metals to reduce its number of carriers from more than 200 to 14 and resulted in annual freight cost savings of more than $7 million. In addition, service was improved from 80 percent on-time deliveries to 95 percent, resulting in the attraction of new customers.

Source: Based on Moore, E. W., Jr., "The Indispensable Role of Management Science in Centralizing Freight Operations at Reynolds Metals Company," *Interfaces* 21, no. 1 (January–February 1991): 107–29.

Some of these simulation languages are GPSS, GASP, DYNAMO, SIMSCRIPT, SIMULA, and SLAM. Each of the languages is more applicable to certain problems than others. For example, DYNAMO is useful when the random variables change over time (i.e., when they are dynamic); GPSS and GASP are useful languages for queuing problems; SLAM "network" simulation packages, applicable to systems that can be represented as networks.

Some of the most popular programming languages used for simulation applications include FORTRAN, BASIC, APL, and COBOL. Also, simulation can now be conducted within many spreadsheet packages such as LOTUS, IFPS, and EXCEL as well as in a number of management science software packages.

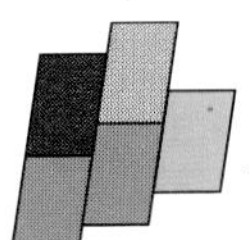

AREAS OF SIMULATION APPLICATION

Transparency S12.5 Areas of Simulation Application

Simulation can be used to address many types of operational problems.

Teaching Note S12.6 Areas of Application

Teaching Note S12.7 Student Simulation

Simulation is one of the most useful of all quantitative techniques. The reason for this popularity is that simulation can be applied to a number of operational problems that are too difficult to model and solve analytically. Some analysts feel that complex systems should be studied via simulation whether or not they can be analyzed analytically, because it provides such an easy vehicle for experimenting on the system. As a result, simulation has been applied to a wide range of problems. Surveys conducted during the 1980s indicate that a large majority of major corporations use simulation in such functional areas as production, planning, engineering, financial analysis, research and development, information systems, and personnel. Following are descriptions of some of the more common applications of simulation.

Waiting Lines/Service

A major application of simulation has been in the analysis of waiting line, or queuing, systems. As will be indicated in Chapter 16, the assumptions required to solve the operating characteristic formulas for waiting line systems are relatively restrictive. For the more complex queuing systems (which result from a relaxation of these assumptions), it is not possible to develop analytical formulas, and simulation is often the only available means of analysis. For example, for a busy supermarket with multiple waiting lines, some for express service and some for regular service, simulation may be the only form of analysis to determine how many registers and servers are needed to meet customer demand.

Inventory Management

Product demand is an essential component in determining the amount of inventory a commercial enterprise should keep. Many of the traditional mathematical formulas used to analyze inventory systems make the assumption that this demand is certain (i.e., not a random variable). In practice, however, demand is rarely known with certainty. Simulation is one of the best means for analyzing inventory systems in which demand is a random variable. Simulation has been used to experiment with new, innovative inventory systems such as just-in-time (JIT). Companies use simulation to see how effective and costly a JIT system would be in their own manufacturing environment without having physically to implement the system.

Production and Manufacturing Systems

Simulation is often applied to production problems, such as production scheduling, production sequencing, assembly line balancing (of in-process inventory), plant layout, and plant location analysis. It is surprising how often various production processes can be viewed as queuing systems that can be analyzed only by using simulation. Since machine breakdowns typically occur according to some probability distributions, maintenance problems are also frequently analyzed using simulation.

In the past few years, several software packages for the personal computer have been developed to simulate all aspects of manufacturing operations. Two examples are SIMFACTORY and XCELL. SIMFACTORY is written in the SIMSCRIPT 11.5 simulation language, a highly acclaimed and powerful language. This package is very user-friendly and requires no programming by the user; it has exceptional modeling and graphics capabilities. Applications of SIMFACTORY can be placed into two categories: evaluation of proposed systems (such as when an expansion of operations or a new manufacturing facility is contemplated) and evaluation of changes in existing operating policies, product mixes, scheduling strategies, and capacity. XCELL, although not as powerful as SIMFACTORY, is nevertheless an excellent package that enables the user to design a model of a factory, which can then be evaluated. While the model is being run, the "factory" can be changed to simulate different scenarios.

Capital Investment and Budgeting

Capital budgeting problems require estimates of cash flows, which are often a result of many random variables. Simulation has been used to generate values of the various contributing factors to derive estimates of cash flows. Simulation has also been used to determine the inputs into rate-of-return calculations, where the inputs are random variables such as market size, selling price, growth rate, and market share.

Logistics

Logistics problems typically include numerous random variables, such as distance, different modes of transport, shipping rates, and schedules. Simulation can be used to analyze different distribution channels to determine the most efficient logistics system.

Service Operations

The operations of police departments, fire departments, post offices, hospitals, court systems, airports, and other public service systems have been analyzed using simulation. Typically, such operations are so complex and contain so many random variables that no technique except simulation can be employed for analysis.

Environmental and Resource Analysis

Some of the more recent innovative applications of simulation have been directed at problems in the environment. Simulation models have been developed to ascertain the impact of projects such as manufacturing plants, waste-disposal facilities, and nuclear power plants. In many cases, these models include measures to analyze the financial feasibility of such projects. Other models have been developed to simulate waste and population conditions. In the area of resource analysis, numerous simulation models have been developed in recent years to simulate energy systems and the feasibility of alternative energy sources.

SUMMARY

Simulation has become an increasingly important quantitative technique for solving problems in operations in recent years. Various surveys have shown

GAINING THE COMPETITIVE EDGE

Simulating a Queuing Problem at a Security Gate

The Westinghouse Hanford Company is a secured work facility, which vehicles enter in the morning on a four-lane road and leave in the afternoon on a two-lane road. An average of 7 buses and approximately 285 private vehicles and vanpools entered in the morning at a gate where normally two security guards checked vehicles, drivers, and passengers. The vehicles formed a single line at the gate that extended past the available queue space of 40 vehicles and out onto the highway, which resulted in a major safety hazard. Buses formed a separate line. The situation was not only a safety hazard, but the waiting time was excessive. In the afternoon the vehicles exited in one lane and buses in the other, but vanpools picked up passengers in the bus lane, causing delays for the buses while they waited for the vanpools to merge into the vehicle lane. The objective in the morning was to minimize the queue length while also minimizing the number of security guards, and the afternoon goal was to move the buses through the gate as early as possible while also minimizing the number of security guards. An analytical queuing model did not fit this particular queuing scenario, so a simulation model was used instead. The first objective was to validate that the simulation model replicated the actual system. This was accomplished by comparing the simulation results to actual results for a 3-day period. Next, two morning scenarios were tested, with the simulation model first increasing the number of guards to three while maintaining the single lane of traffic and then forming two traffic lines, each with a security guard.

The second scenario proved to be an excellent solution at no additional cost. It was implemented, and for most of the time fewer than five vehicles waited in line. The maximum number at any time was twenty-one vehicles for both lines combined. For the afternoon exiting problem, several scenarios were also tested, with the best assigning one security guard to each of the two lanes and having the vanpools remain in the bus lane and not changing lanes after passenger pickup. With this solution buses exited 5 to 7 minutes earlier than in the original system, and the safety problem of passengers crossing traffic lanes to get to vanpools was eliminated. In both the morning and afternoon cases, effective no-cost solutions were achieved.

Source: Based on Landaver, E., and L. Becker, "Reducing Waiting Time at Security Checkpoints," *Interfaces* 19, no. 5 (September–October 1989): 57–65.

simulation to be one of the techniques most widely applied to real-world problems. Evidence of this popularity is the number of specialized simulation languages that have been developed by the computer industry and academia to deal with complex problem areas.

The popularity of simulation is due in large part to the flexibility it allows in analyzing systems, compared to more confining analytical techniques. In other words, the problem does not have to fit the model (or technique)—the simulation model can be constructed to fit the problem. Simulation is popular also because it is an excellent experimental technique, enabling systems and problems to be tested within a laboratory setting.

However, in spite of its versatility, simulation has limitations and must be used with caution. One limitation is that simulation models are typically unstructured and must be developed for a system or problem that is also unstructured. Unlike some of the structured techniques presented in this text, the models cannot simply be applied to a specific type of problem. As a result, developing simulation models often requires a certain amount of imagination and intuitiveness that is not required by some of the more straightforward solution techniques we have presented. In addition, the validation of simulation models is an area of serious concern. It is often impossible to validate simulation results realistically or to know if they accurately reflect the system under analysis. This problem has become an area of such concern that *output analysis* of simulation results is a field of study in its own right. Another limiting factor in simulation is the cost in terms of money and time of model building. Because simulation models are developed for unstructured systems, they often take large amounts of staff, computer time, and money to develop and run. For many business companies, these costs can be prohibitive.

SUMMARY OF KEY TERMS

simulation: an approach to operational problem solving in which a real-problem situation is replicated within a mathematical model.

Monte Carlo technique: a technique for selecting numbers randomly from a probability distribution for use in a simulation model.

random numbers: numbers in a table, each of which has an equal likelihood of being selected at random.

steady-state result: an average model result that approaches constancy after a sufficient passage of time or enough repetitions or trends.

SOLVED PROBLEM

Simulation

Problem Statement:

Members of the Willow Creek Emergency Rescue Squad know from past experience that they will receive between zero and six emergency calls each night, according to the following discrete probability distribution.

Calls	*Probability*
0	0.05
1	0.12
2	0.15
3	0.25
4	0.22
5	0.15
6	0.06
	1.00

The rescue squad classifies each emergency call into one of three categories: minor, regular, or major emergency. The probability that a particular call will be each type of emergency is as follows.

Emergency Type	*Probability*
Minor	0.30
Regular	0.56
Major	0.14
	1.00

The type of emergency call determines the size of the crew sent in response. A minor emergency requires a two-person crew, a regular call requires a three-person crew, and a major emergency requires a five-person crew.

Simulate the emergency calls received by the rescue squad for ten nights, compute the average number of each type of emergency call each night, and determine the maximum number of crew members that might be needed on any given night.

Solution:

Step 1: Develop random number ranges for the probability distributions.

Calls	*Probability*	*Cumulative Probability*	*Random Number Range,* r_1
0	0.05	0.05	1–5
1	0.12	0.17	6–17
2	0.15	0.32	18–32
3	0.25	0.57	33–57
4	0.22	0.79	58–79
5	0.15	0.94	80–94
6	0.06	1.00	95–99, 00
	1.00		

Emergency Types	*Probability*	*Cumulative Probability*	*Random Number Range,* r_2
Minor	0.30	0.30	1–30
Regular	0.56	0.86	31–86
Major	0.14	1.00	87–99, 00
	1.00		

Step 2: Set up a tabular simulation. Use the second column of random numbers in Table S12.3.

Night	r_1	*Number of Calls*	r_2	*Emergency Type*	*Crew Size*	*Total per Night*
1	65	4	71	Regular	3	
			18	Minor	2	
			12	Minor	2	
			17	Minor	2	9
2	48	3	89	Major	5	
			18	Minor	2	
			83	Regular	3	10
3	08	1	90	Regular	3	3
4	05	0	—	—	—	—
5	89	5	18	Minor	2	
			08	Minor	2	
			26	Minor	2	
			47	Regular	3	
			94	Major	5	14
6	06	1	72	Regular	3	3
7	62	4	47	Regular	3	
			68	Regular	3	
			60	Regular	3	
			88	Major	5	14
8	17	1	36	Regular	3	3
9	77	4	43	Regular	3	
			28	Minor	2	
			31	Regular	3	
			06	Minor	2	10
10	68	4	39	Regular	3	
			71	Regular	3	
			22	Minor	2	
			76	Regular	3	11

Step 3: Compute the results.

$$\text{Average number of minor emergency calls per night} = \frac{10}{10} = 1.0$$

$$\text{Average number of regular emergency calls per night} = \frac{14}{10} = 1.4$$

$$\text{Average number of major emergency calls per night} = \frac{3}{10} = 0.30$$

If all the calls came in at the same time, the maximum number of squad members required during any one night would be 14.

QUESTIONS

S12-1. Explain what the Monte Carlo technique is and how random numbers are used in a Monte Carlo process.

S12-2. How are steady-state results achieved in a simulation?

S12-3. What type of information for decision making does simulation typically provide?

PROBLEMS

S12-1. See Solutions Manual.

S12-1. The Hoylake Rescue Squad receives an emergency call every 1, 2, 3, 4, 5, or 6 hours, according to the following probability distribution.

Time Between Emergency Calls (hours)	*Probability*
1	0.05
2	0.10
3	0.30
4	0.30
5	0.20
6	0.05
	1.00

The squad is on duty 24 hours per day, 7 days per week.

a. Simulate the emergency calls for 3 days (note that this will require a "running," or cumulative, hourly clock) using the random number table.
b. Compute the average time between calls and compare this value with the expected value of the time between calls from the probabilistic distribution. Why are the results different?
c. How many calls were made during the 3-day period? Can you logically assume that this is an average number of calls per 3-day period? If not, how could you simulate to determine such an average?

S12-2. a. 2.95 breakdowns/wk b. 5.55 hr/wk c. $277.50/wk d. No

★ S12-2. The Dynaco Manufacturing Company produces a product in a process consisting of operations of five machines. The probability distribution of the number of machines that will break down in a week is as follows.

Machine Breakdowns per Week	*Probability*
0	0.10
1	0.10
2	0.20
3	0.25
4	0.30
5	0.05
	1.00

Every time a machine breaks down at the Dynaco Manufacturing Company, either 1, 2, or 3 hours are required to fix it, according to the following probability distribution.

Repair Time (hours)	*Probability*
1	0.30
2	0.50
3	0.20
	1.00

a. Simulate the repair time for 20 weeks and compute the average weekly repair time.
b. If the random numbers that are used to simulate breakdowns per week are also used to simulate repair time per breakdown, will the results be affected in any way? Explain.
c. If it costs $50 per hour to repair a machine when it breaks down (including lost productivity), determine the average weekly breakdown cost.
d. The Dynaco Company is considering a preventive maintenance program that would alter probabilities of machine breakdowns per week as follows.

Machine Breakdowns per Week	*Probability*
0	0.20
1	0.30
2	0.20
3	0.15
4	0.10
5	0.05
	1.00

The weekly cost of the preventive maintenance program is $150. Using simulation, determine whether the company should institute the preventive maintenance program.

S12-3. The Stereo Warehouse in Georgetown sells stereo sets, which it orders from Fuji Electronics in Japan. Because of shipping and handling costs, each order must be for five stereos. Because of the time it takes to receive an order, the warehouse outlet places an order every time the present stock drops to five stereos. It costs $100 to place an order. It costs the warehouse $400 in lost sales when a customer asks for a stereo and the warehouse is

★ S12-3. $\mu = \$25.10$

out of stock. It costs $40 to keep each stereo stored in the warehouse. If a customer cannot purchase a stereo when it is requested, the customer will not wait until one comes in but will go to a competitor. The following probability distribution for demand for stereos has been determined.

Demand per Month	*Probability*
0	0.04
1	0.08
2	0.28
3	0.40
4	0.16
5	0.02
6	0.02
	1.00

The time required to receive an order once it is placed has the following probability distribution.

Time to Receive and Order (months)	*Probability*
1	0.60
2	0.30
3	0.10
	1.00

The warehouse presently has five stereos in stock. Orders are always received at the beginning of the week. Simulate the Stereo Warehouse's ordering and sales policy for 20 months, using the first column of random numbers in Table S12.3. Compute the average monthly cost.

S12-4. See Solutions Manual.

★ S12-4. A baseball game consists of plays that can be described as follows.

Play	*Description*
No advance	An out where no runners advance. This includes strikeouts, pop ups, short flies, and the like.
Groundout	All runners can advance one base.
Possible double play	Double play if there is a runner on first base and fewer than two outs. The lead runner can be forced out; runners not out advance one base. If there is no runner on first or there are two outs, this play is treated as a "no advance."
Long fly	A runner on third base can score.
Very long fly	Runners on second and third base advance one base.
Walk	Includes a hit batter.
Infield single	All runners advance one base.
Outfield single	A runner on first base advances one base, but a runner on second or third base scores.
Long single	All runners can advance a maximum of two bases.
Double	Runners can advance a maximum of two bases.
Long double	All runners score.
Triple	
Home run	

Note: Singles also include a factor for errors, allowing the batter to reach first base.

Distributions for these plays for two teams, the White Sox (visitors) and the Yankees (home), are as follows.

Team: White Sox

Play	*Probability*
No advance	0.03
Groundout	0.39
Possible double play	0.06
Long fly	0.09
Very long fly	0.08
Walk	0.06
Infield single	0.02
Outfield single	0.10
Long single	0.03
Double	0.04
Long double	0.05
Triple	0.02
Home run	0.03
	1.00

Team: Yankees

Play	*Probability*
No advance	0.04
Groundout	0.38
Possible double play	0.04
Long fly	0.10
Very long fly	0.06
Walk	0.07
Infield single	0.04
Outfield single	0.10
Long single	0.04
Double	0.05
Long double	0.03
Triple	0.01
Home run	0.04
	1.00

Simulate a nine-inning baseball game using this information.[1]

REFERENCESS

Banks, J., and J. S. Carson, *Discrete-Event System Simulation,* Englewood Cliffs, N.J.: Prentice Hall, 1984.

Christy, D., and H. Watson, "The Applications of Simulation: A Survey of Industry Practice," *Interfaces* 13, no. 5 (October 1983): 47–52.

[1]This problem was adapted from Trueman, R. E., "A Computer Simulation Model of Baseball: With Particular Application to Strategy Analysis," in R. E. Machol, S. P. Ladany, and D. G. Morrison, eds., *Management Science in Sports,* New York: North Holland Publishing, Co., 1976, pp. 1–14.

Hammersly, J. M., and D. C. Handscomb, *Monte Carlo Methods,* New York: John Wiley, 1984.

Law, A. M., and W. D. Kelton, *Simulation Modeling and Analysis,* New York: McGraw-Hill, 1982.

Meier, R. C., W. T. Newell, and H. L. Pazer, *Simulation in Business and Economics,* Englewood Cliffs, N.J.: Prentice Hall, 1969.

Naylor, T. H., J. L. Balintfy, D. S. Burdinck, and K. Chu, *Computer Simulation Techniques,* New York: John Wiley, 1966.

Payne, J. A., *Introduction to Simulation,* New York: McGraw-Hill, 1982.

Pritsker, A. A. B., C. E. Sigal, and R. D. Hammesfahr, *SLAM II: Network Models for Decision Support,* Englewood Cliffs, N.J.: Prentice Hall, 1989.

Taha, H. A., *Simulation Modeling and Simen,* New York: McGraw-Hill, 1988.

Taylor, B. W., *Introduction to Management Science,* 4th ed., Boston: Allyn and Bacon, 1993.

13

MATERIAL REQUIREMENTS PLANNING

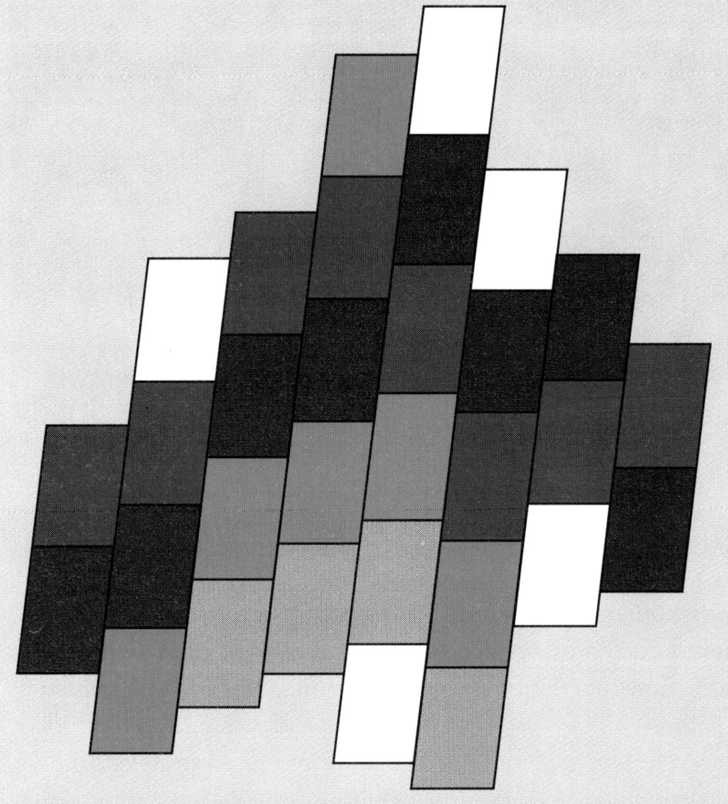

CHAPTER OUTLINE

Many U.S. manufacturers use a computerized production planning and inventory control system called material requirements planning (MRP). MRP is especially useful in industries with complex products, varying due dates, and fluctuating demand.

FIVE MILLION POSSIBILITIES AT HUBBELL LIGHTING

Quality for some customers refers to more than the physical product received. For many customers, quality of service (which includes prompt delivery) is equally as important. Consider Hubbell Lighting, a manufacturer of industrial lighting products. Although the company has always had a reputation for good-quality products, it has not always met the due dates promised to its customers. Hubbell's customers are a diverse group, including schools, shopping malls, amusement parks, football franchises, and even NASA. The work is specialized for each customer, involves little automation, and can generally be described as a "glorified job shop." Its complexity is derived from the sheer size of the manufacturing task—the hundreds of different products produced, the thousands of parts needed to make up a typical product, the tremendous number of scheduling decisions required on a day-to-day basis, and the vast amount of information that is necessary to support those decisions. For example, one of Hubbell's factories, which employs around 425 workers, develops an aggregate production plan for 63 product families and weekly schedules for the production of 3,200 end items. These end items consist of 15,000 components that may be assembled into 5 million possible final product configurations. The factory (and the company as a whole) uses a computerized inventory control and production planning system called *material requirements planning* (MRP) to help plan and coordinate the various stages of production. Without an MRP system, a factory of this type simply could not function. Prior to implementing MRP, the factory completed fewer than 75 percent of its orders on time. After MRP implementation, on-time delivery rose to 97 percent, with an additional 2 percent completed within 1 or 2 days of promised completion.

Material requirements planning (MRP) was introduced in the 1970s as a computerized inventory control system that would calculate the demand for component items, keep track of when they are needed, and generate work orders and purchase orders that take into account the lead time required to make the items in-house or buy them from a supplier. Much of the credit for introducing MRP and educating industry about its benefits goes to three individuals, Joseph Orlicky, George Plossl, and Oliver Wight, and to a professional society they endorsed, known as the American Production and Inventory Control Society (APICS). Basically an information system, MRP was quite revolutionary in its early days, because it brought computers and systematic planning to the manufacturing function. Since its introduction, the system has undergone several revisions that reflect the increased power and accessibility of computers and the changing role of manufacturing. The latest version, dubbed MRP II for *manufacturing resource planning,* is much broader in scope than the original material planner, incorporating marketing and financial functions as well. In today's modern factories, MRP II is the standard for management information systems and an important component of computer-integrated manufacturing (CIM).

MRP is a computerized inventory control and production planning system.

We begin this chapter with a discussion of the objectives and applicability of MRP. Then, we carefully examine the major inputs and outputs to the system and work through a simple MRP problem. Next, we present several advanced topics and extensions to MRP, including capacity requirements planning (CRP), use of safety stock, lot sizing, and processing frequency. Finally, we discuss MRP II and the problems and prospects of MRP/MRP II.

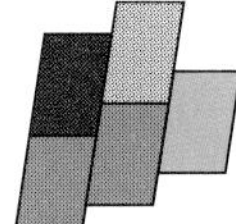

OBJECTIVES AND APPLICABILITY OF MRP

The main objective of any inventory system is to ensure that material is available when it is needed. However, left unchecked, this can lead to a tremendous investment of funds in unnecessary inventory. Therefore, an equally important objective of MRP is to maintain the lowest possible level of inventory. MRP does this by determining *when* component items are needed and scheduling them to be ready at that time, no earlier and no later.

MRP was the first inventory system to recognize that inventories of raw materials, components, and finished goods may need to be handled differently. In the process of planning inventory levels for these various types of goods, the system also planned purchasing activities (for raw materials and purchased components), manufacturing activities (for component parts and assemblies), and delivery schedules (for finished products). Thus, the system was more than an inventory control system; it became a production scheduling system as well.

MRP schedules component items when they are needed—no earlier and no later.

Teaching Note 13.1 The Beginnings of MRP

One of the few certainties in a manufacturing environment is that things rarely go as planned—orders arrive late, machines break down, workers are absent, designs are changed, and so on. With its computerized data base, MRP is able to keep track of the relationship of job orders so that if a delay in one aspect of production is unavoidable, other related activities can be rescheduled, too. MRP systems have the ability to keep schedules valid and up-to-date.

When to Use MRP

Managing component demand inventory requires a different approach than managing finished goods inventory. For one thing, the demand for component parts does not have to be forecasted, it can be derived from the demand for the finished product. For example, suppose demand for a table, consisting of four legs and a table top, is 100 units per week. Then, demand for table tops would also be 100 per week and demand for table legs would be 400 per week. Demand for table legs is totally *dependent* on the demand for tables. The demand for tables may be forecasted, but the demand for table legs is calculated. The tables are an example of *independent demand,* whereas the table top and table legs exhibit *dependent demand.*

Another difference between finished products and component parts is the continuity of their demand. For the inventory control systems we discussed in the previous chapter, we assumed that demand occurred at a constant rate. The inventory systems were designed to keep some inventory on hand at all times, enough, we hoped, to meet each day's demand. With component items, demand does not necessarily occur on a continuous basis. Let's assume in our table example that table legs are the last items to be assembled onto the tables before shipping. Also assume that it takes 1 week to make a batch of tables and that table legs are assembled onto the table tops every Friday. If we were to graph the demand for table legs, as shown in Figure 13.1, it would be zero for Monday, Tuesday, Wednesday, and Thursday, but on Friday the demand for table legs would jump to 400. The same pattern would repeat the following week. With this scenario, we do not need to keep an inventory of table legs available on Monday through Thursday of any week. We need table legs only on Fridays. Looking at our graph, demand for table legs occurs in *lumps;* it is *discrete,* not continuous. Using an inventory system such as EOQ for component items would result in inventory being held that we know we won't need until a later date. The excess inventory takes up space, soaks up funds, and requires additional resources for counting, sorting, storing, and moving.

MRP is useful for dependent and discrete demand items, complex products, job shop production, and assemble-to-order environments.

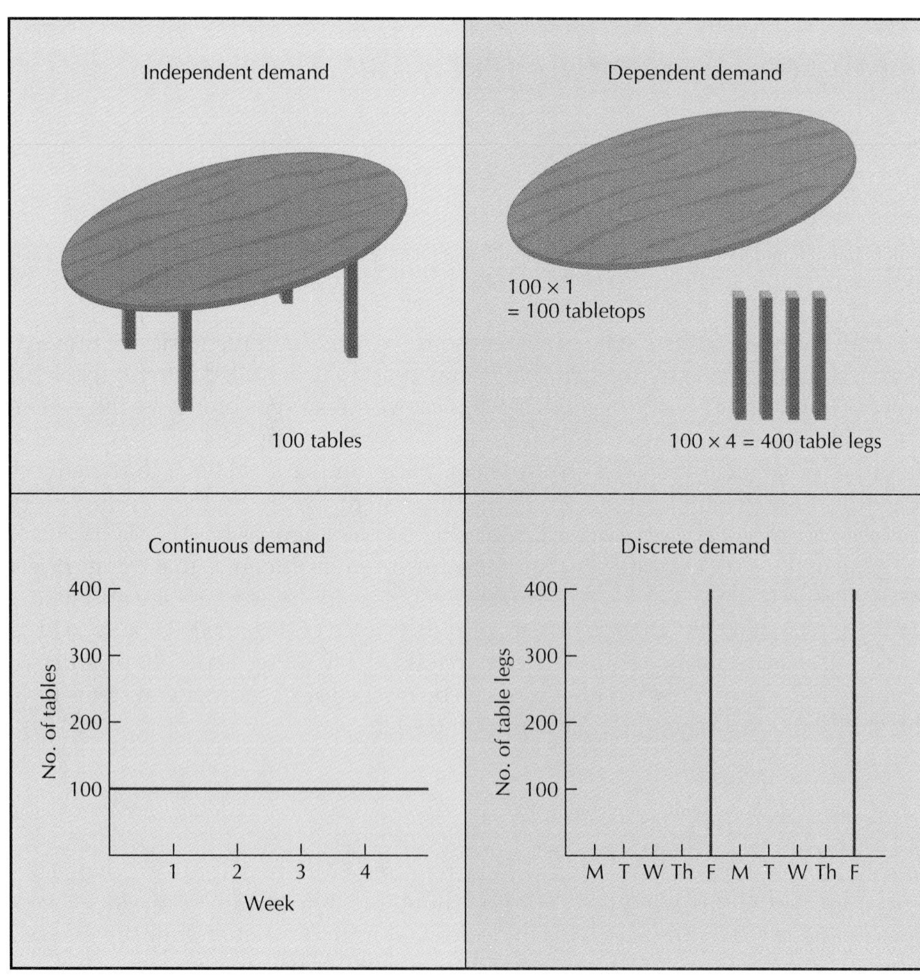

FIGURE 13.1 Demand Characteristics for Finished Products and Their Components

Industries that manufacture complex products, in which the coordination of component production is important, find MRP especially useful. A complex product may have hundreds of component parts, dozens of assemblies, and several levels of assembly. MRP tries to ensure that multiple components of an assembly are ready at the same time so that they can be assembled together. Products with simple structures do not need the sophistication of MRP to plan production or monitor inventory levels.

The advantages of MRP are more evident when the manufacturing environment is complex and uncertain. Manufacturing environments in which customer orders are erratic, each job takes a different path through the system, lead time is uncertain, and due dates vary need an information system such as MRP to keep track of the different jobs and coordinate their schedules. The type of environment we are describing is characteristic of *intermittent*, or *job shop*, processes.[1] Although MRP is currently available for continuous and repetitive manufacturing, it was designed primarily for systems that produce goods in batches.

Finally, MRP systems are very useful in industries that offer a variety of finished products where the customer is allowed to choose among many different options. These products typically have many common components and are inventoried in some form before the customer order is received. For example, customers of a well-known electronics firm routinely expect delivery in 6 weeks on goods that take 28 weeks to manufacture. The manufacturer copes with this seemingly unrealistic demand by producing major assemblies and subassemblies in advance of the customer order and then finalizing the product upon receipt of the order. This type of operation is called **assemble-to-order.**

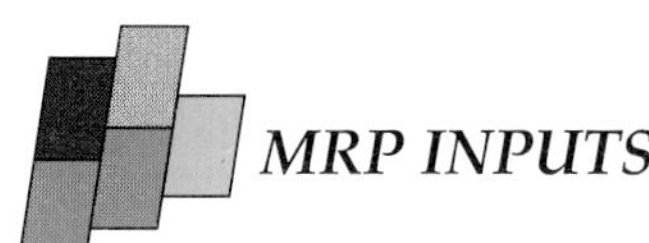

MRP INPUTS

Assemble-to-order is a manufacturing environment in which previously completed subassemblies are configured to order

As shown in Figure 13.2 on page 652, there are three major inputs to the MRP process: 1. the master production schedule, 2. the product structure file, and 3. the inventory master file.

Transparency 13.1 Material Requirements Planning

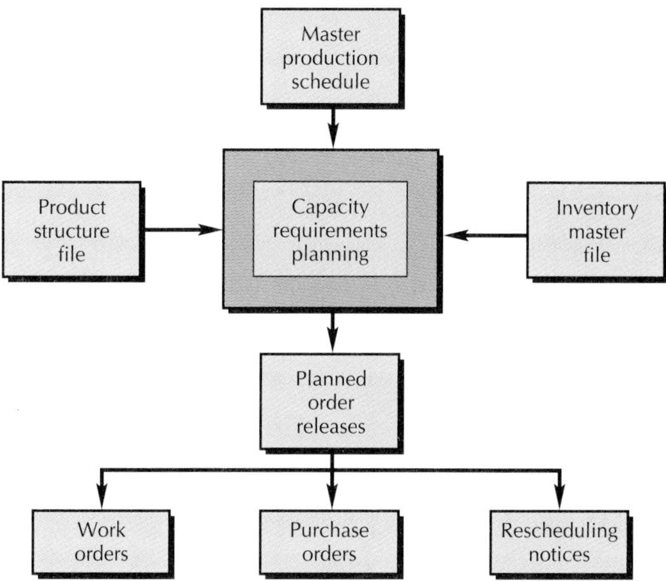

FIGURE 13.2 Material Requirements Planning

[1]For a more thorough discussion of types of processes, see Chapter 6.

Master Production Schedule

The **master production schedule** drives the MRP process with a schedule of finished products.

The **master production schedule (MPS)**, also called the *master schedule*, specifies which end items or finished products a firm is to produce, how many are needed, and when they are needed. You may recall that aggregate production planning creates a similar schedule for product lines or families, given by months or quarters of a year. The master production schedule works within the constraints of the production plan but produces a more specific schedule by individual products. The time frame is more specific, too. An MPS is usually expressed in days or weeks and extends over several months or at least long enough to cover the complete manufacture of the items contained in the MPS. The total length of time required to manufacture a product is called its **cumulative lead time.**

Cumulative lead time is the total length of time needed to manufacture a product.

Table 13.1 shows a sample master production schedule consisting of four end items produced by a manufacturer of specialty writing accessories. Several comments should be made concerning the quantities contained in the MPS:

- *The quantities represent production, not demand.* As we saw in the aggregate production planning chapter, production does not necessarily have to match demand. The strategy decisions made in the production planning stage filter down to the master production schedule. The steady production pattern of lap boards and pencil cases in Table 13.1 is probably the result of different production planning strategies.
- *The quantities may consist of a combination of customer orders and demand forecasts.* In other words, some of the figures are confirmed, but others are predictions. As might be expected, the quantities in the more recent time periods are more firm, whereas the quantities further in the future may need to be revised several times before the schedule is completed. Some companies set a **time fence,** within which no more changes to the master schedule are allowed. This helps to stabilize the production environment.

  The MPS for clipboards and lapboards shown in Table 13.1 illustrates two approaches to future scheduling. For clipboards, demand beyond period 3 is forecasted at an even 100 units per period. Projecting these requirements now based on past demand data helps in planning for the availability of resources. For lap desks, demand beyond period 3 appears sparse, probably because it is based on actual customer orders received. We can expect those numbers to increase as the future time periods draw nearer. Evidently, a lengthy lead time is not necessary to gather the resources for producing lap desks.
- *The quantities represent what needs to be produced, not what can be produced.* Because the MPS is derived from the production plan, it is relatively close with its requirements, but until the MRP system considers the specific resource needs and the timing of those needs, the feasibility of the MPS cannot be guaranteed. Thus, the MRP system is often used to *simulate* production to verify that the MPS is feasible or, in more specific cases, to confirm that a particular order can be completed by a certain date before the quote is given to the customer.

A **time fence** is a management-specified date beyond which no changes in the master schedule are allowed.

Teaching Note 13.2 MPS and FAS

TABLE 13.1 Master Production Schedule

MPS Item	*Period*							
	1	2	3	4	5	6	7	8
Clipboard	86	93	119	100	100	100	100	100
Lapboard	0	50	0	50	0	50	0	50
Lap Desk	75	120	47	20	17	10	0	0
Pencil Case	125	125	125	125	125	125	125	125

The master production schedule drives the MRP process. The schedule of finished products provided by the master schedule is needed before the MRP system can do its job of generating production schedules for component items.

The Product Structure File

The **product structure file** contains a **bill of material** for every item produced.

Once the MPS is set, the MRP system accesses the **product structure file** to determine which component items need to be scheduled. The product structure file contains a **bill of material (BOM)** for every item produced. The bill of material for a product lists the items that go into the product, includes a brief description of each item, and specifies when and in what quantity each item is needed in the assembly process.

When each item is needed can best be described in the form of a product structure diagram, as shown in Figure 13.3 for a clipboard. An assembled item is sometimes referred to as a *parent* and a component, as a *child.* The parent-child relationship should be obvious in the diagram. The number in parenthesis beside each item is the quantity of a given component needed to make *one* parent. Thus, one clip assembly, two rivets, and one board are needed to make each clipboard. The clip assembly, rivets, and board appear at the same level of the product structure because they are to be assembled together.

Recall from our discussion in Chapter 6 that a diagram can be converted to a computerized bill of material by labeling the levels in the product structure. The final product, or end item, at the top of the structure—in this case, the clipboard—is always labeled level 0. The level number increases as we move down the product structure. The clipboard has three levels of assembly. The first bill of material listed in Table 13.2 shows some levels indented underneath others. This specifies which components belong to which parents and can easily be matched to the product structure diagram.

The bill of material generated from the product structure file can take different forms, depending on its intended use. Table 13.2 shows four common BOM formats, which can be described as follows:

- *Multilevel indented explosion:* The multilevel indented explosion is the most common BOM format because it provides extensive information about the product and reinforces the explosion logic. The indented levels are designed to clearly show the sequence of assembly.

Transparency 13.2 Product Structure Diagram

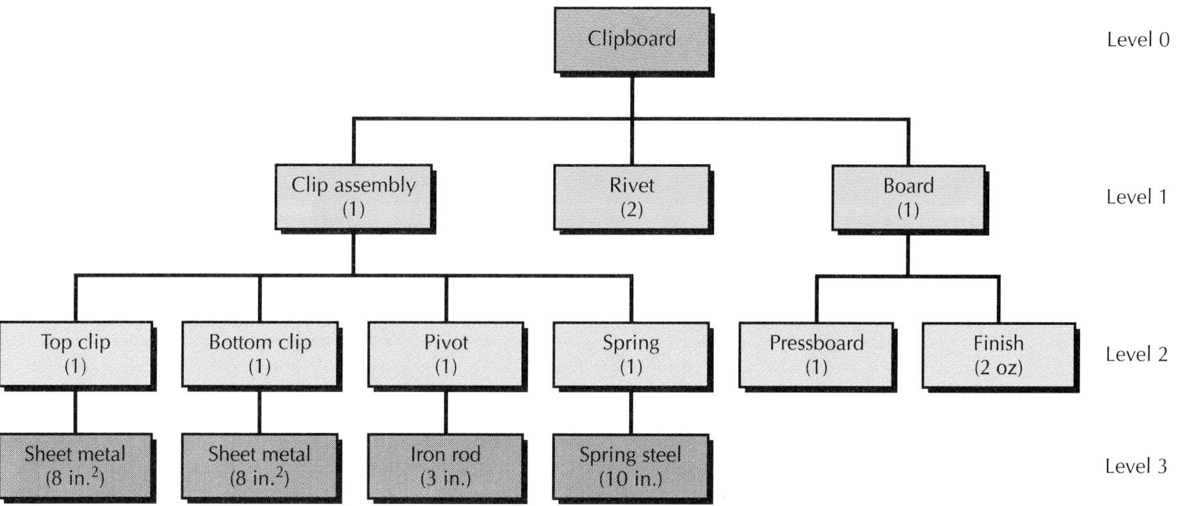

FIGURE 13.3 Product Structure Diagram for a Clipboard

Transparency 13.3 Bill of Material Formats

TABLE 13.2 Bill of Material Formats

(a) Multi-Level Indented Explosion

Level	Item	UM	Quantity
0 - - - -	Clipboard	Ea	1
- 1 - - -	Clip Assembly	Ea	1
- - 2 - -	Top Clip	Ea	1
- - - 3 -	Sheet metal	in^2	8
- - 2 - -	Bottom Clip	Ea	1
- - - 3 -	Sheet Metal	in^2	8
- - 2 - -	Pivot	Ea	1
- - - 3 -	Iron Rod	in	3
- - 2 - -	Spring	Ea	1
- - - 3 -	Spring Steel	in	10
- 1 - - -	Rivet	Ea	2
- 1 - - -	Board	Ea	1
- - 2 - -	Press Board	Ea	1
- - 2 - -	Finish	oz	2

(b) Single-Level Bill of Material

Level	Item	UM	Quantity
0 - - - -	Clipboard	Ea	1
- 1 - - -	Clip Assembly	Ea	1
- 1 - - -	Rivet	Ea	1
- 1 - - -	Board	Ea	1

(c) Summarized Bill of Material

Level	Item	UM	Quantity
	Clip Board	Ea	1
	Clip Assembly	Ea	1
	Rivet	Ea	2
	Board	Ea	1
	Top Clip	Ea	1
	Bottom Clip	Ea	1
	Pivot	Ea	1
	Spring	Ea	1
	Pressboard	Ea	1
	Finish	oz	2
	Sheet Metal	in^2	16
	Iron Rod	in	3
	Spring Steel	in	10

(d) Where-Used Bill of Material

Level	Item	UM	Quantity
0 + + + +	Pressboard	Ea	1
+ 1 + + +	Board	Ea	1
+ + 2 + +	Clipboard	Ea	1
+ 1 + + +	Board	Ea	3
+ + 2 + +	Lap Board	Ea	1

Multiple levels indicate that the product is exploded completely down its product structure. By providing both assembly level and contents, a component can be traced upward or downward in a given product. The principal disadvantage of this format is the cost of maintaining the large files. An item may appear several times in a product's structure at different levels, and each appearance is kept tract of separately.

- *Single-level bill of material:* The single-level bill of material specifies only those components required at a particular level of assembly. It is useful for 1. issuing subassembly orders and parts requisitions, 2. maintaining assembly routing information and standards, 3. preparing different output formats from the same basic information, and 4. reducing computer file size and facilitating file maintenance. File size is significantly reduced if BOMs are stored in single-level format and indexed so that several single bills can be linked together to create a complete bill for a given product.

BOMs can be expressed in different formats.

- *Summarized bill of material:* The summarized bill of material lists the *total* quantity of each component required to make a product without regard to level of assembly. Thus, Table 13.2(c) shows 16 square inches of sheet metal required for each clipboard rather than two requirements for 8 square inches each. Summarized bills are used for planning simple products with no subassembly levels or for make-to-stock items assembled on a continuous basis. They are also commonly used in fields that interface with production, such as cost accounting (for product costing and analysis) and sales (for parts and price lists).
- *Where-used bill of material:* A where-used BOM inverts the product structure to identify in what subassembly, assembly, or final product the item is used. It links, or "pegs," a component with its parent item. In Table 13.2(d), one pressboard is used to make one board. One board, in turn, may be used to make one clipboard, or three boards may be used to make one lapboard. Notice the levels are indented with pluses rather than minuses, as seen in the previous BOMs. Pluses communicate to the user immediately that this is an inverted BOM, tracing up rather than down the product structure.

  Where-used bills are useful in analyzing the effects of changes in engineering design, the availability of components, demand requirements, or available capacity. A complete where-used bill is the most costly format to maintain; thus, it is usually avoided or prepared only for one-time, special-purpose requests. More commonly, the user requests a **pegging** report, which identifies the parent item one level at a time. By using the pegging report several times in succession, the user actually links several single-level where-used bills together until the desired information is reached. A component-parent relationship traced completely up the product structure will reach the master production schedule. Some MRP systems will even identify a master schedule item as a customer order (with the specific order number), a forecast of demand, or a service requirement (which will be inventoried for later use).

Pegging is the ability to trace through a product structure.

Several specialized bills of material have been designed to simplify information requirements, clarify relationships, and reduce computer processing time. We will describe three of them, 1. phantom bills, 2. K-bills, and 3. modular bills.

- *Phantom bills* are used for transient subassemblies that never see a stockroom because they are immediately consumed in the next stage of manufacture. These items have a lead time of zero and a special code so that no orders for them will be released. Phantom bills are becoming more common as companies are adopting JIT and cellular manufacturing concepts that speed products through the manufacturing and assembly process.

Teaching Note 13.3 Adjusting Bills of Material for JIT

- Kit numbers, or K-bills, group small, loose parts such as fasteners, nuts, and bolts together under one psuedoitem number. In this way, requirements for the items are processed only once (for the group), rather than for each individual item. K-bills reduce the paperwork, processing time, and file space required in generating orders for small, inexpensive items that are usually ordered infrequently in large quantities.

Modular bills of material are used to plan the production of products with many optimal features.

Phantom bills, k-bills, and modular bills simplify planning.

- **Modular bills of material** are appropriate when the product is manufactured in major subassemblies or modules that are later assembled into the final product with customer-designated options. With this approach, the end item in the master production schedule is not the finished product, but a major option or module. This reduces the number of bills of material that need to be input, maintained, and processed by the MRP system. Consider the options available on the X10 automobile, partially diagrammed in Figure 13.4. The customer has a choice between three engine types, eight exterior colors, three interiors, eight interior colors, and four car bodies. Thus, there are $3 \times 8 \times 3 \times 8 \times 4 = 2{,}304$ possible model configurations—and the same number of bills of material—unless modular bills are used. By establishing a bill of material for each option rather than each combination of options, the entire range of options can be accounted for by $3 + 8 + 3 + 8 + 4 = 26$ modular bills of material.

  Modular bills of material also simplify forecasting and planning. The quantity per assembly for an option is given as a decimal figure, interpreted as a percentage of the requirements for the parent item. For example, from Figure 13.4, in preparation for an anticipated demand of 1,000 X10 automobiles, 1,000 engines are needed. Of those 1,000 engines, the master production schedule would generate requirements for 40 percent, or 400, four-cylinder engines, 50 percent, or 500, six-cylinder engines, and 10 percent or 100, eight-cylinder engines.

The creation of a product structure file can take a considerable amount of time. Accurate bills of material are essential to an effective MRP system. The bill of material must specify how a product is actually manufactured rather than how it was *designed* to be manufactured. Redundant or obsolete part numbers must be purged from the system. This may not seem like a big task, but in some companies every time a part is purchased from a different supplier, it is assigned a different part number. One firm in the process of implementing MRP was able to eliminate 6,000

Transparency 13.4 Modular Bills of Material

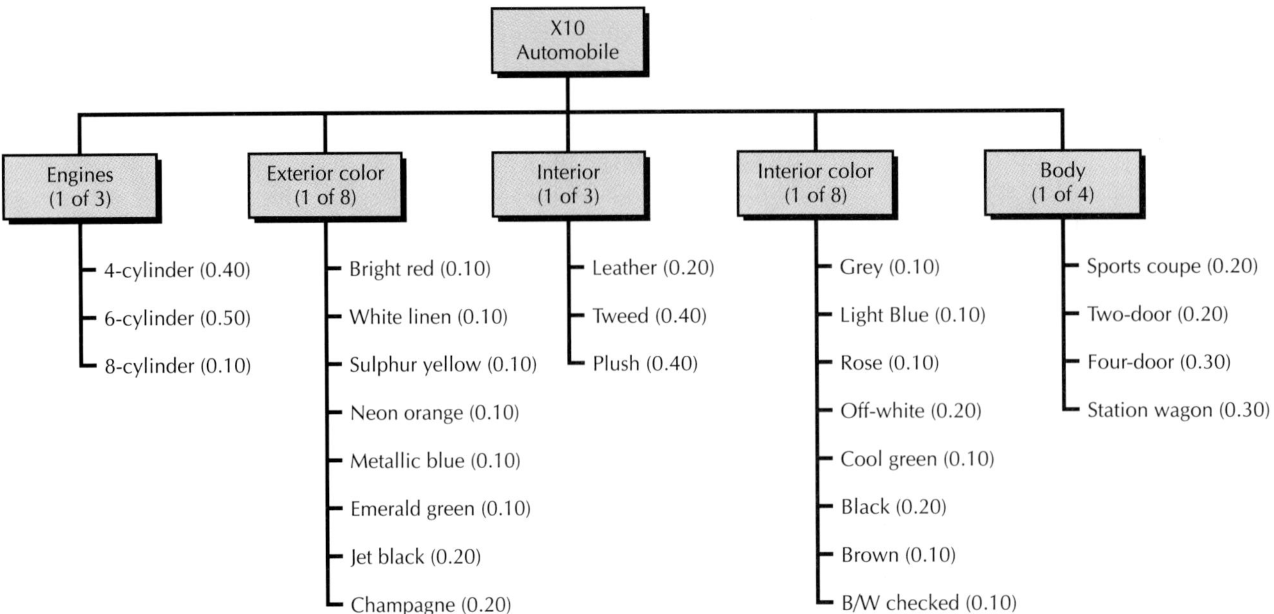

FIGURE 13.4 Modular Bills of Material

extra part numbers from its data base and dispose of thousands of dollars of obsolete inventory that had not previously been identified as such.

Inventory Master File

The **inventory master file** contains an extensive amount of information on every item that is produced, ordered, or inventoried in the system. It includes such data as on-hand quantities, on-order quantities, lot sizes, safety stock, lead time, and past usage figures. Table 13.3 shows a representative record from an inventory master file that provides a detailed description of the item, specifies the inventory policy, updates the physical inventory count, summarizes the item's year-to-date or month-to-date usage, and provides internal codes to link this file with other related information in the MRP data base.

The **inventory master file** is a data base of information on every item produced, ordered, or inventoried.

The inventory master file is updated whenever items are withdrawn from or added to inventory or whenever an order is released, revised, or completed. Accuracy of inventory transactions is essential to MRP's ability to keep inventory levels at a minimum. It is estimated that 95 percent inventory accuracy is a prerequisite for an effective MRP system. Although technologies such as bar codes, voice-activated systems, and automated "picking" equipment can improve inventory accuracy considerably, a general overhaul of inventory procedures is often needed. This involves

1. Maintaining orderly stockrooms;
2. Controlling access to stockrooms;

TABLE 13.3 Inventory Master File

DESCRIPTION		*INVENTORY POLICY*	
Item	Water Pump	Lead time	2
Item no.	7341	Annual demand	1,000
Item type	Manuf.	Holding cost	1
Product/sales class	Ass'y	Ordering/setup cost	50
Value class	B	Safety stock	25
Buyer/planner	RSR	Reorder point	39
Vendor/drawing	07142	EOQ	316
Phantom code	N	Minimum order qty.	100
Unit price/cost	10.25	Maximum order qty.	500
Pegging	Y	Multiple order qty	100
LLC	3	Policy code	3
PHYSICAL INVENTORY		*USAGE/SALES*	
On hand	100	YTD usage/sales	1,100
Location	W142	MTD usage/sales	75
On order	50	YTD receipts	1,200
Allocated	75	MTD receipts	0
Cycle	3	Last receipt	8/25
Last count	9/5	Last issue	10/5
Difference	–2		
		CODES	
		Cost acct.	00754
		Routing	00326
		Engr.	07142

Accurate inventory counts are essential to a successful MRP system. Access to stockrooms is limited so that the withdrawal of inventory can be carefully monitored. Cycle counting, in which inventory is counted continuously during the year on a specified cycle, can improve operations by reconciling differences as they occur instead of waiting for end-of-the-year physical inventories.

3. Establishing and enforcing procedures for inventory withdrawal;
4. Ensuring prompt and accurate entry of inventory transactions;
5. Taking physical inventory count on a regular basis; and
6. Reconciling inventory discrepancies in a timely manner.

GAINING THE COMPETITIVE EDGE

MRP Improves Customer Service

Courtaulds Films makes coextruded oriented polypropylene, the plastic film that covers food products in your supermarket. Courtauld has two manufacturing plants, one in Swindon, England, and the other in Mantes, France. The plants run 24 hours a day, 7 days a week. After the chemical process of making a film base, the film is extruded, gripped by a fast-moving chain, heated, and stretched lengthwise by 500 percent and sideways by 1,000 percent. That means the final product is five times longer and ten times wider than when it began the extruding process. Prior to MRP, Courtaulds met delivery promises only 75 percent of the time. The company had difficulty scheduling the 60 types of raw materials, 40 types of films, and 12,500 make-to-order end products. Courtauld visited neighbor Formica, a class A MRP user, to learn the secret of their 95 percent on-time deliveries. Courtauld implemented MRP and quickly became a class A user themselves.

The most beneficial aspect of MRP for Courtauld is its master scheduling component. Courtauld can instruct the system to keep 5 to 10 percent of the master schedule uncommitted until 1 week before production. This leaves space for "orders of opportunity." The system also reserves capacity in advance for major customers and treats all other customers on a first-come, first-served basis.

The *available-to-promise* (ATP) capability is especially useful in make-to-order environments. ATP displays the status of the four manufacturing lines in England and France and responds to inquiries about capacity that is available to promise to customers. With this information, Courtauld can make better decisions on whether to accept new orders and can quote more realistic delivery dates for orders that are accepted.

Source: Based on Goddard, Walter, "Getting a Grip on Customer Service," *Modern Materials Handling* (September 1992): 41.

If you have taken part in an end-of-year inventory count, you can verify the wide discrepancies that are commonly found between what the records say is in inventory and what is physically there. Unfortunately, by the time the errors are discovered, it is really too late to correct them or find out why they occurred. The slate is merely cleaned for next year's record, with the hope or promise that next time will be better.

Cycle counting is a procedure that involves taking physical counts of at least some inventory items daily and reconciling differences as they occur. The system specifies which items are to be counted each day on a computer printout and may tie the frequency of the count to the frequency of orders for the item within the MRP system. Thus, items that are used more often are counted more often. The cycle counting system may also be related to the ABC classification system discussed in the last chapter. A items would be counted more often than B items. C items may still be counted only once a year. Approved cycle counting systems are accepted by the accounting standards board as valid replacements for end-of-year physical inventories.

Cycle counting improves inventory accuracy.

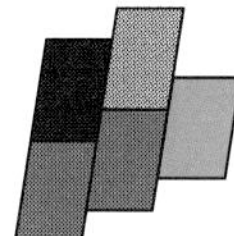

THE MRP PROCESS

The MRP system is responsible for scheduling the production of all items beneath the end item level. It explodes end item requirements into component requirements, nets out on-hand inventory, offsets for lead times, and recommends the release of work orders and purchase orders. It also maintains the validity of existing schedules by issuing rescheduling notices when necessary.

The MRP process includes explosion, netting, and lead-time offsetting.

The MRP process is best explained through an example. We will use a worksheet called the MRP matrix to record the calculations that are made. Table 13.4 shows the matrix and provides a brief description of the entries that are required. As you go through Example 13.1, be sure to identify the basic steps in the MRP process of 1. explosion, 2. netting, and 3. lead-time offsetting.

TABLE 13.4 The MRP Matrix

Transparency 13.5 The MRP Matrix

Item: *Lot Size:*	*LLC:* *LT:*	*PD*	*1*	*2*	*3*	*4*	*5*	*6*	*7*	*8*	*9*	*10*
Gross requirements												
Scheduled receipts												
Projected on hand												
Net requirements												
Planned order receipts												
Planned order releases												

Item: the name or number that identifies the item being scheduled.

LLC: low-level code; the lowest level at which the item appears in a product structure.

Lot size: normally, an order will be placed in *multiples* of this quantity, but it can also represent a *minimum* or *maximum* order quantity or the type of lot-sizing technique.

LT: lead time; the time from when an order is placed until it is received.

PD: past-due time bucket. If an order appears in the PD time bucket, the schedule is infeasible and an error message will be generated.

Gross requirements: the demand for an item by time period. For an end item, this quantity is obtained from the master production schedule. For a lower-level item, it is derived from the *planned order releases* of its parents.

Teaching Note 13.4 The MRP Matrix

Scheduled receipts: the quantity of material that is already ordered (from work orders or purchase orders) and when it is expected to arrive. Once a planned order is released, it becomes a scheduled receipt.

Projected on hand: the expected quantity in inventory at the end of a period that will be available for demand in subsequent periods. It is calculated by subtracting the *gross requirements* in the period from the sum of *scheduled receipts* for the same period, *projected on hand* from the previous period, and *planned order releases* from the $t - l$ period (where t represents the current period and l is the lead time).

Net requirements: the net number of items that must be provided and when they are needed. It is calculated by subtracting the *scheduled receipts* in the period plus the *projected on hand* in the previous period from *gross requirements*. It appears in the same time period as gross requirements.

Planned order receipts: the same as net requirements adjusted for lot sizing. If lot sizing is seldom used or lead time is negligible, this row can be deleted from the matrix.

Planned order releases: planned order receipts offset for lead times. It shows when an order should be placed (i.e., released) so that items are available when needed. *Planned order releases* at one level generate *gross requirements* at the next lower level.

Alternate Example 13.1

EXAMPLE 13.1

The Alpha Beta Company

Problem Statement:

The Alpha Beta Company produces two products, A and B, that are made from components C and D. Given the following product structures, master scheduling requirements, and inventory information, determine when orders should be released for A, B, C, and D and the size of those orders.

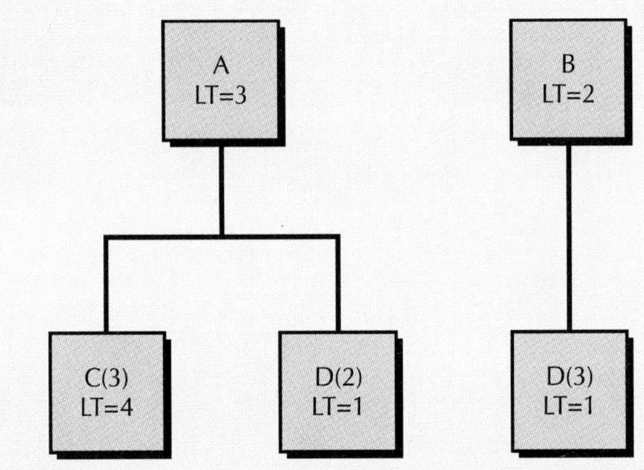

	On Hand	Scheduled Receipts	Lot Size	MPS
A	10	0	1	100, period 8
B	5	0	1	200, period 6
C	140	0	150	—
D	200	250, period 2	250	—

Solution:

Table 13.5, on page 662, shows a completed MRP matrix for each of the four items shown in the product structure diagram. The matrices were completed first for the level 0 items, A and B, then for the level 1 items, C and D.

Netting is the process of subtracting on-hand quantities from gross requirements to produce net requirements.

- *Item A:* First, we fill in the *gross requirements* for A, 100 units in period 8. Since A is an end item, we read this information from the master production schedule. In the *projected on-hand row,* we begin with 10 units of A in inventory and continue with 10 units on hand until we need to use it. At the end of period 7, we have 10 units of A in inventory. We need 100 A's in period 8. We can use the 10 A's we have on hand and make 90 more. The subtraction of the on-hand quantity from the gross requirements is called **netting.** The net requirement of

90 A's is the gross requirement *net* of inventory. It appears in the same time period as the gross requirement. There are no lot sizing requirements (A's are ordered in lots of 1), so the planned order receipts are the same as the net requirements.

If we need to receive 90 A's by period 8 and it takes 3 periods to make A, we need to release an order for A in period 5. Thus, the quantity of 90 appears in period 5 of the planned order release row. This process of subtracting the lead time from the due date is called **lead time offsetting,** or *time phasing,* of requirements. The planned order release row is the result, or *output,* of the MRP calculations for item A. Only the entries in the final row of the matrix will be used in subsequent MRP calculations for component items.

Lead time offsetting is the process of subtracting an item's lead time from its due date.

- *Item B:* Item B's matrix is completed in the same fashion as item A's. The gross requirement of 200 B's in period 6 is given in the master production schedule. Since there are 5 units of B on hand, the net requirement for B is 195 in period 6. There are no scheduled receipts for B and no lot-sizing requirements. If 195 B's are needed in period 6 and it takes 2 weeks to make B's, we need to release an order to begin production of B's in period 4.
- *Item C:* For all level 1 items, we need to *calculate* the gross requirements by multiplying the quantity per assembly given in parentheses on the product structure diagram times the planned order release (POR) of the parent item. This multiplication process is called **explosion.**

  An order for 90 A's is set to be released in period 5. Three C's are needed for every A, so we place a gross requirement for 270 C's in period 6. We have 140 C's in inventory. They remain in inventory until period 5, when we use them to satisfy partially the demand for C's. The net requirement for C is thus 130 units, but instead of ordering the net requirement of 130, we order the lot-size quantity of 150. If 130 C's need to be received by period 5 and it takes 4 weeks to make C's, we need to release the order for C in period 1. The 150 C's will arrive in period 6. We will use 130 of them to meet A's demand for C's. The remaining 20 units will be placed into inventory.

Explosion is the process of determining requirements for lower-level items.

- *Item D:* Item D has two parents, A and B. We need to gather all the gross requirements for D first before completing the rest of the matrix. Item A has a planned order release of 90 units in period 5. Two D's are required for every A, so (90 x 2) = 180 D's need to be available by period 5. D's other parent, item B, has a planned order release of 195 units scheduled in period 4. Every B requires three D's, so (195 x 3) = 585 D's are also needed by period 4.

  We have 200 D's on hand at the end of period 1. An order of 250 D's is scheduled to be received in period 2. By the end of period 2, we project that (200 + 250) = 450 D's will be on hand. We plan to use those 450 D's to fill partially the first gross requirement entry, leaving a net requirement of (585 – 450) = 135 D's in period 4. D's are ordered in lots of 250, so even though we only need 135 D's, we will place an order for 250. It takes 2 weeks to make D's. Since they are needed in period 4, we will plan to release the order in period 2. When the order arrives, 135 D's will go toward making B's, and the remaining (250 – 135) = 115 will be placed into inventory.

  The 115 D's projected to be on hand by the end of period 4 can be used to satisfy partially the gross requirement for 180 D's, leaving a net requirement of (180 – 115) = 65 D's in period 5. Because of lot-sizing requirements, we will order 250 D's. Item D has a lead time of two periods. If we need to receive D's by period 5, we need to release an order for D in period 3. We plan the order release for 250 and project that (250 – 65) = 185 units will be left over and placed into inventory at the end of period 5.
- We have now completed the MRP calculations. To summarize the results, we construct a *planned order report* from the planned order release row of each matrix, as follows:

Planned Order Report

Period	*Item*	*Quantity*
1	C	150
2	D	250
3	D	250
4	B	195
5	A	90

TABLE 13.5 MRP Matrices for Example 13.1

Item: A ***Lot Size: 1***	***LLC: 0*** ***LT: 3***	***PD***	***1***	***2***	***3***	***4***	***5***	***6***	***7***	***8***
Gross requirements										100
Scheduled receipts										
Projected on hand		10	10	10	10	10	10	10	10	0
Net requirements										90
Planned order receipts										90
Planned order releases							90			

Item: B ***Lot Size: 1***	***LLC: 0*** ***LT: 2***	***PD***	***1***	***2***	***3***	***4***	***5***	***6***	***7***	***8***
Gross requirements								200		
Scheduled receipts										
Projected on hand		5	5	5	5	5	5	0	0	0
Net requirements								195		
Planned order receipts								195		
Planned order releases						195				

90 × 3 = 270}

Item: C ***Lot Size: 150***	***LLC: 1*** ***LT: 4***	***PD***	***1***	***2***	***3***	***4***	***5***	***6***	***7***	***8***
Gross requirements							270			
Scheduled receipts										
Projected on hand		140	140	140	140	140	20	20	20	20
Net requirements							130			
Planned order receipts							150			
Planned order releases			150							

195 × 3 = 585} {90 × 2 = 180

Item: D ***Lot Size: 250***	***LLC: 1*** ***LT: 2***	***PD***	***1***	***2***	***3***	***4***	***5***	***6***	***7***	***8***
Gross requirements						585	180			
Scheduled receipts				250						
Projected on hand		200	200	450	450	115	185	185	185	185
Net requirements						135	65			
Planned order receipts						250	250			
Planned order releases				250	250					

The MRP matrices are the worksheets that determine the planned orders for each inventory item. They are generally not printed out unless requested by the MRP planner. Looking at the MRP matrix for item D, it appears that the objective of maintaining the lowest possible level of inventory has been violated. This is due to the lot-sizing requirement that orders item D in multiples of 250 and the scheduled receipt for D that arrives before it is needed. The MRP system will issue an error message for the scheduled receipt, as indicated beneath D's matrix as part of an exception report, but it will not comment on the excess inventory due to lot sizing because the user has input those requirements. Unless there is some problem in obtaining the two orders for item D, the planner will probably never notice the excess inventory of item D either. This illustrates one of the problems with MRP systems. Users tend to input policies that undermine the basic objectives of the system, and the logic of the system is often hidden from the user.

If the MRP calculations seem tedious, remember that the system is computerized and no manual calculations are required. AB:POM can be used to solve simple MRP problems. Exhibit 13.1, on page 664, shows the AB:POM input and solution matrices for Example 13.1, the Alpha Beta Company.

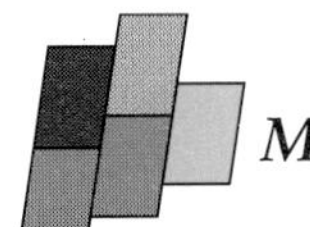

MRP OUTPUTS

The outputs of the MRP process are planned orders from the planned order release row of the MRP matrix. As shown in Figure 13.2, these can represent *purchase orders* to be sent to outside suppliers or *work orders* to be released to the shop floor for in-house production. MRP output can also recommend changes in previous plans or existing schedules. These *action notices*, or *rescheduling notices*, are issued for items that are no longer needed as soon as planned or for quantities that may have changed. Recall that one of the advantages of the MRP system is its ability to show the effect of a change in one part of the production process on the rest of the system. It simulates the ordering, receiving, and usage of raw materials, components, and assemblies into future time periods and issues warnings to the MRP planner of impending stockouts or missed due dates.

Table 13.6, on page 665, shows a monthly *planned order report* for an individual item, in this case, item #2740. The report maps out the material orders planned and released orders scheduled to be completed in anticipation of demand. Notice that safety stock is treated as a quantity not to be used and that a problem exists on 10-1, where projected on hand first goes negative. To correct this problem, the system suggests that the scheduled receipt of 200 units due on 10-8 be moved forward to 10-1. The MRP system will not generate a new order if a deficit can be solved by expediting existing orders. It is up to the MRP planner to assess the feasibility of expediting the scheduled receipt and to take appropriate action. Table 13.7, also on page 665, shows an *MRP action report* for a family of items for which a particular MRP planner is responsible. It summarizes the action messages that have been compiled for individual items. Indeed, on 10-1, we see the action message for the water pump that appeared on the previous report. Notice the variety of action messages listed. Some suggest that planned orders be moved forward or backward. Others suggest that scheduled receipts be expedited or de-expedited.

MRP outputs include purchase orders, work orders, and various reports.

It is now the planner's job to respond to the actions contained in the action report. For example, if a planner decides to **expedite** an order—that is, have it completed in less than its average lead time—he or she might call up a supplier or a shop supervisor and ask for priority treatment. Giving one job higher priority may involve reducing the priority of other jobs. This is possible if the MRP action report indicates that some jobs are not needed as early as anticipated. The process of moving some jobs *forward* in the schedule (expediting) and moving other jobs

To **expedite** an order is to speed it up so it is completed in less than its lead time.

Example 13.1 - Alpha Beta Company
Indented Bill of Materials

Item ID	Leadtime	Number per parent	On hand Inventory	Lot Size (if not lot for lot)
A	3	1	10	
C	4	3	140	150
D	2	2	200	250
B	2	1	5	
D	2	3		250

Item A

	Week 1	Week 2	Week 3	Week 4	Week 5	Week 6	Week 7	Week 8
TOT. REQ.	0	0	0	0	0	0	0	100
ON HAND	10	10	10	10	10	10	10	10
ORD REC.	0	0	0	0	0	0	0	0
NET REQ.	0	0	0	0	0	0	0	90
ORD REL.	0	0	0	0	90	0	0	0

Item C

	Week 1	Week 2	Week 3	Week 4	Week 5	Week 6	Week 7	Week 8
TOT. REQ.	0	0	0	0	270	0	0	0
ON HAND	140	140	140	140	140	20	20	20
ORD REC.	0	0	0	0	0	0	0	0
NET REQ.	0	0	0	0	130	0	0	0
ORD REL.	150	0	0	0	0	0	0	0

Item D

	Week 1	Week 2	Week 3	Week 4	Week 5	Week 6	Week 7	Week 8
TOT REQ.	0	0	0	585	180	0	0	0
ON HAND	200	200	450	450	115	185	185	185
ORD REC.	0	250	0	0	0	0	0	0
NET REQ.	0	0	0	135	65	0	0	0
ORD REL.	0	250	250	0	0	0	0	0

Item B

	Week 1	week 2	Week 3	Week 4	Week 5	Week 6	Week 7	Week 8
TOT. REQ.	0	0	0	0	0	200	0	0
ON HAND	5	5	5	5	5	5	0	0
ORD REC.	0	0	0	0	0	0	0	0
NET REQ.	0	0	0	0	0	195	0	0
ORD REL.	0	0	0	195	0	0	0	0

EXHIBIT 13.1 AB:POM Solution to Example 13.1—Alpha Beta Company

backward (de-expediting) allows the material planner, with the aid of the MRP system, to fine-tune the material plan. Temporary lead time adjustments through overtime or outside purchases of material can also fix a timing problem in the MRP plan, but at a cost. An MRP action report that is exceedingly long or does not strike a balance between speeding up some orders and slowing down others can signify trouble. Action messages that recommend only the expediting of orders indicate an overloaded master schedule and an ineffective MRP system.

TABLE 13.6 Planned Order Report

Item	#2740			Date	9-25-95
On hand	100			Lead time	2 weeks
On order	200			Lot size	200
Allocated	50			Safety stock	50

Date	*Order No.*	*Gross Reqs.*	*Scheduled Receipts*	*Projected On Hand*	*Action*
				50	
9-26	AL 4416	25		25	
9-30	AL 4174	25		0	
10-01	GR 6470	50		–50	
10-08	SR 7542		200	150	Expedite SR 10-1
10-10	CO 4471	75		75	
10-15	GR 6471	50		25	
10-23	GR 6471	25		0	
10-27	GR 6473	50		–50	Release PO 10-13

Key: AL = allocated
CO = customer order
PO = purchase order
WO = work order
SR = scheduled receipt
GR = gross requirements

TABLE 13.7 MRP Action Report

Current date: 9-25-95

Item	*Date*	*Order No.*	*Qty.*	*Action*	
#2740	10-08	7542	200	Expedite	SR 10-1
#3616	10-09			Move forward	PO 10-7
#2412	10-10			Move forward	PO 10-5
#3427	10-15			Move backward	PO 10-25
#2516	10-20	7648	100	De-expedite	SR 10-10
#2740	10-27		200	Release	PO 10-13
#3666	10-31		50	Release	WO 10-24

The MRP system, as the name implies, ensures that *material* requirements are met. However, material is not the only resource necessary to produce goods—a certain amount of labor and machine hours are also required. Thus, the next step in the planning process is to verify that the MRP plan is "feasible" by checking for the availability of labor and/or machine hours. This process is called *capacity requirements planning* and is similar to MRP.

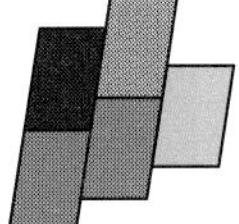

CAPACITY REQUIREMENTS PLANNING

CRP creates a load profile that identifies underloads and overloads.

Capacity requirements planning (**CRP**) is a computerized system that projects the load from a given material plan onto the capacity of a system and identifies underloads and overloads. It is then up to the MRP planner to *level the load,*—that is, smooth out the resource requirements so that capacity constraints are not violated. This can be accomplished by shifting requirements, reducing requirements, or temporarily expanding capacity.

There are three major inputs to CRP, as shown in Figure 13.5: 1. the *planned order releases* from the MRP process, 2. a *routing file,* which specifies which machines are required to complete an order from the MRP plan, in what order the operations are to be conducted, and the length of time each operation should take, and 3. an *open orders file,* which contains information on the status of jobs that have already been released to the shop, but have not yet been completed. With this information, CRP can produce a **load profile** for each machine or work center in the shop. The load profile compares released orders and planned orders with work center capacity.

A **load profile** compares released orders and planned orders with work center capacity.

Capacity is productive capability. Utilization and efficiency are used to calculate capacity.

Capacity, usually expressed as standard machine hours or labor hours,[2] is calculated as follows:

$$\text{Capacity} = (\text{no. machines or workers}) \times (\text{no. shifts}) \times (\text{utilization}) \times (\text{efficiency})$$

Utilization is the percentage of available working time that a worker spends working or a machine is running. **Efficiency** is how well a machine or worker performs compared to a standard output level.

Utilization refers to the percentage of available working time that a worker actually works or a machine actually runs. Scheduled maintenance, lunch breaks, and setup time are examples of activities that reduce actual working time. **Efficiency** refers to how well a machine or worker performs compared to a standard output level. Standards can be based on past records of performance or can be developed from the work-measurement techniques discussed in Chapter 10. An efficiency of 100 percent is considered normal or standard performance, 125 percent is above normal, and 90 percent is below normal. Efficiency is also dependent on product mix. Some orders obviously will take longer than others to process, and some machines or workers may be better at processing certain types of orders. **Load** is the standard hours of work (or equivalent units of production) assigned to a production facility. After load and capacity have been determined, a **load percent** can be calculated as

Load refers to the standard hours of work assigned to a facility.

$$\text{Load percent} = \frac{\text{capacity}}{\text{load}}$$

Load percent is the ratio of capacity to load.

Transparency 13.6 Capacity Requirements Planning

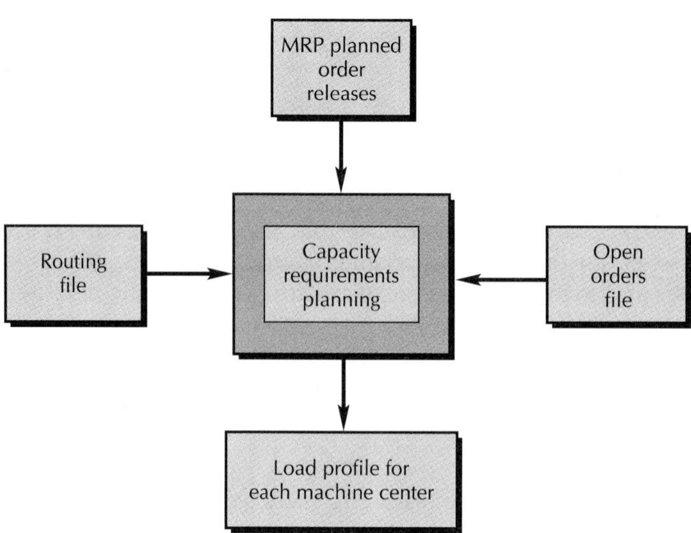

FIGURE 13.5 Capacity Requirements Planning

[2]Alternatively, capacity can be expressed as units of output.

Centers loaded above 100 percent will not be able to complete the scheduled work without some adjustment in capacity or reduction in load.

EXAMPLE 13.2

Alternate Example 13.2

Determining Loads and Capacities

Problem Statement:

Copy Courier is a fledging copy center located in downtown Richmond and run by two college students. Currently, the equipment consists of two high-speed copiers that can be operated by one operator. If the students work alone, it is conceivable that two shifts per day can be staffed. The students each work 8 hours a day, 5 days a week. They do not take breaks during the day, but they do allow themselves 30 minutes for lunch or dinner. In addition, they service the machines for about 30 minutes at the beginning of each shift. The time required to set up for each order varies by the type of paper, use of color, number of copies, and so on. Estimates of setup time are kept with each order. Since the machines are new, their efficiency is estimated at 100 percent.

Due to some fancy advertising and new customer incentives, orders have been pouring in. The students need help determining the capacity of their operation and the current load on their facility. Use the following information to calculate the normal daily capacity of Copy Courier and to project next Monday's load profile and load percent.

Job No.	*No. of Copies*	*Setup Time (min)*	*Run Time (min/unit)*
10	500	5.2	0.08
20	1,000	10.6	0.10
30	5,000	3.4	0.12
40	10,000	11.2	0.14
50	2,000	15.3	0.10

Solution:

The machines and/or operators at Copy Courier are out of service for 1 hour each shift for maintenance and lunch. Utilization is, thus, 7/8, or 87.5 percent. Daily copy shop capacity is

2 machines × 2 shifts × 8 hours/shift × 100 percent efficiency × 87.5 percent utilization = 28 hours, or 1,680 minutes

The projected load for Monday of next week is as follows.

Job no.	*Total time*
10	5.2 + (500 x 0.08) = 45.2
20	10.6 + (1,000 x 0.10) = 110.6
30	3.4 + (5,000 x 0.12) = 603.4
40	11.2 + (10,000 x 0.14) = 1,411.2
50	15.3 + (2,000 x 0.10) = 215.3
	2,385.7 minutes

$$\text{Load percent} = \frac{2{,}385.7}{1{,}680} = 1.42 = 142\%$$

Copy Courier is loaded 42% over capacity next Monday. Increasing utilization (even to 100%) would not be sufficient to get the work done. In order to complete all of the customer orders on time, another shift could be added (i.e., another person hired). With this adjustment, the copy shop's daily capacity would increase to

2 machines × 3 shifts × 8 hours/shift × 100 percent efficiency × 87.5 percent utilization = 42 hours, or 2,520 minutes

The revised load percent is:

$$\frac{2385.7}{2520} = 0.9467 = 94.67\%$$

In the future, Copy Courier will want to determine if it has enough capacity to complete a job by the customer's requested due date *before* the job is accepted.

Load profiles can also be displayed graphically, as shown in Figure 13.6. The dashed line represents the normal capacity of machine 32A, which in this case is 40 hours per week. We can see that the machine is *underloaded* in periods 1, 5, and 6, and *overloaded* in periods 2, 3, and 4.

Underloaded conditions can be leveled by

remedies for underloads

1. Acquiring more work;
2. *Pulling work ahead* that is scheduled for later time periods; or
3. Reducing normal capacity.

Additional work can be acquired by transferring similar work from other machines in the same shop that are near or over capacity, by making components in-house that are normally purchased from outside suppliers, or by seeking work from outside sources. Pulling work ahead seems like a quick and easy alternative to alleviate both underloads and overloads. However, we must remember that the MRP plan was devised based on an interrelated product structure, so the feasibility of scheduling work in an earlier time period is contingent on the availability of required materials or components. In addition, work completed prior to its due date must be stored in inventory and thus incurs a holding cost. When work is shifted to other time periods, the MRP plan should be rerun to check the feasibility of the proposed schedule.

If an underloaded condition continues for some time, reducing the size of the work force may be a viable alternative. Smaller underloads can be handled by re-

Transparency 13.7 A Load Profile

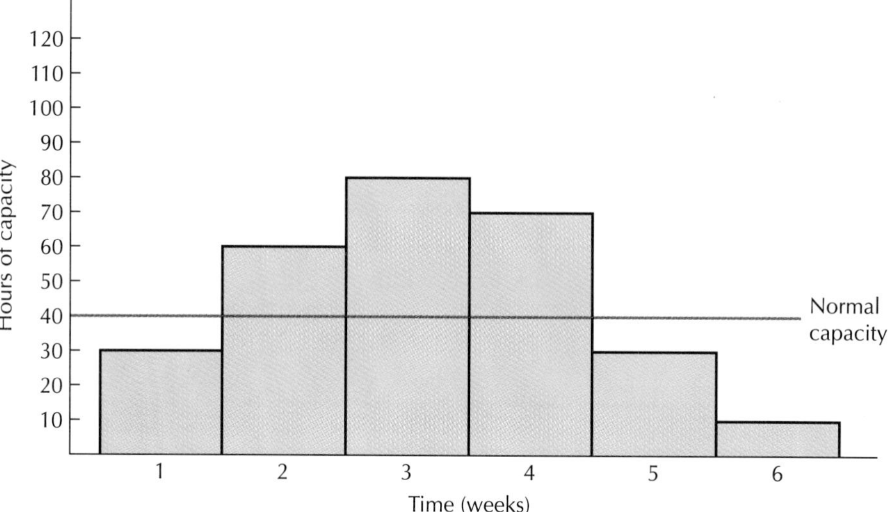

FIGURE 13.6 Initial Load Profile for Machine 32A

ducing the length of the working day or workweek, by scheduling idled workers for training sessions or vacations, or by transferring workers to other positions at machine centers or departments where overloads are occurring.

Overloaded conditions are the primary concern of the MRP planner because an overloaded schedule, left unchecked, cannot possibly be completed as planned. Overloads can be reduced by

remedies for overloads

1. Eliminating unnecessary requirements;
2. Rerouting jobs to alternative machines or work centers;
3. Splitting lots between two or more machines;
4. Increasing normal capacity;
5. Subcontracting;
6. Increasing the efficiency of the operation;
7. *Pushing work back* to later time periods; or
8. Revising the master schedule.

Some capacity problems are generated from an MRP plan that includes nonvital requirements for lot sizes or safety stock or unsubstantiated requirements for service parts or forecasted demand. To verify that a capacity overload is caused by "real" need, the planner might examine the MRP matrices of the items processed through a machine center during an overloaded period as well as the matrices of the parents of those items processed, all the way up the product structure to the master schedule. Alternatively, the MRP system could be rerun with lot sizes temporarily set to one and safety stock to zero to see if the capacity problem is eliminated.

MRP systems assume that an entire lot of goods is processed at one machine. Given the job shop environment in which most MRP systems are installed, there are usually several machines that can perform the same job (although perhaps not as efficiently). With CRP, load profiles are determined with jobs assigned to the preferred machine first, but when capacity problems occur, jobs can certainly be reassigned to alternate machines. In addition, if two or more similar machines are available at the same time, it may be possible to *split* a batch—that is, assign part of an order to one machine and the remainder to another machine.

EXAMPLE 13.3

Alternate Example 13.3

Splitting Orders

Problem Statement:

Duffy's Machine Shop has a shortage of lathes. Next week's schedule, for example, has given the lathe department a load of 125 percent. Management's usual response is to schedule overtime, but the company is in a tight financial bind and wants to evaluate other options. The shop supervisor, who has been reading about methods for reducing processing time, suggests something called **order splitting.**

Order splitting is the simultaneous processing of a single order in separate batches at several machines.

It turns out that some of the lathe work can actually be performed on a milling machine, but it's rarely done that way because the process takes longer and the setup is more involved. More precisely, the setup time for lathes averages 30 minutes, whereas the setup for milling machines averages 45 minutes. Processing time per piece is 5 minutes on the lathe, compared to 10 minutes on the milling machine. Management is wondering what the effect would be of producing an entire order of 100 pieces on the lathe or splitting the order in half between the lathe and milling machine. Further, if the objective is to complete the order as soon as possible, is there an optimum split between the two types of machines?

Solution:

If the order were processed on lathe alone, it would take

$$30 + 5(100) = 530 \text{ minutes to complete}$$

If the order were equally split between lathe and milling machine, the processing time at each machine would be:

$$30 + 5\,(50) = 280 \text{ minutes on lathe}$$
$$45 + 10\,(50) = 545 \text{ minutes on milling machine}$$

Assuming that the lathe and milling machine are run simultaneously, the completion time for the entire order of 100 units is calculated by determining the completion time at each machine and taking the largest number, in this case, 545 minutes. Thus, if the order were equally split between the two machines, it would actually take longer to complete.

Determining the *optimal* split between machines involves the use of algebra. We want each machine to finish processing at approximately the same time, so we need to equate the processing-time equations for each machine and solve for the optimum number of units processed. If we let x represent the number of units processed on the lathe, then $(100 - x)$ is the number of units processed on the milling machine.

$$30 + 5x = 45 + 10(100 - x)$$
$$5x = 15 + 1{,}000 - 10x$$
$$15x = 1{,}015$$
$$x = 67.66, \text{ or } 68 \text{ units}$$
$$100 - x = 100 - 68 = 32 \text{ units}$$

Thus, the optimal split would process 68 units on the lathe and 32 units on the milling machine. Completion time for the optimal split is calculated as follows:

$$30 + 5(68) = 370 \text{ minutes}$$
$$45 + 10(32) = 365 \text{ minutes}$$

By splitting the order, it can be completed in 370 minutes, versus the 530 minutes on the lathe alone. That is a 39 percent reduction in processing time. Applied to the weekly demand, the 25 percent overload could be alleviated by splitting orders.

Normal capacity can be increased by adding extra hours to the day, extra days to the week, or extra shifts. Temporary overloads are usually handled with overtime. More extensive overloads may require hiring additional workers. Work can also be subcontracted out.

In effect, improving the efficiency of an operation increases its capacity. Assigning the most efficient workers to an overloaded machine, improving the operating procedures or tools, or decreasing the percentage of items that need to be reworked or scrapped increases efficiency and allows more items to be processed in the same amount of time. Because output increases with the same amount of input, *productivity* increases. This is especially useful for alleviating chronic overloads at bottleneck operations, but it could take some time to put into effect.

If later time periods are underloaded, it may be possible to push work back to those periods, so that the work is completed but at a later date than originally scheduled. There are two problems with this approach. First, postponing some jobs could throw the entire schedule off, meaning customers will not receive the goods when promised. This could involve a penalty for late delivery, loss of an order, or loss of a customer. Second, filling up the later time periods may preclude accepting new orders in those periods. It is normal for time periods further in the future to be underloaded. As the time period draws nearer, customer orders accelerate and begin taking up more of the system's capacity.

If all the preceding approaches to remedying overloads have been tried, but an overloaded situation still exists, the only option is to revise the master schedule. That solution means that some customer will not receive goods as previously promised. The planner, in conjunction with someone from marketing, should determine which customer has the lowest priority and whether their order should be postponed or canceled.

There are, of course, cost consequences associated with each of these alternatives, but there is usually no attempt to derive an optimum solution. More than likely, the MRP planner will use the options that are most familiar to him or her and that produce a feasible solution quickly. In many manufacturing environments, new customer orders arrive daily, and feasible MRP plans can become infeasible overnight.

Figure 13.7 shows one possible remedy for the overloads shown in Figure 13.6. Ten hours of work are pulled ahead from period 2 to period 1. Ten hours of overtime are assigned in period 2. An entire 40-hour shift is added in period 3. Ten hours of work from period 4 are pushed back to period 5, and 20 hours are pushed back to period 6.

From this discussion, it should be obvious that CRP *identifies* capacity problems, but it is up to the planner to *solve* the problems. With experience, the task of shifting work and leveling loads is not as formidable as it appears. However, it is very helpful if the initial load profile is as accurate as possible and if previous planning stages (i.e., aggregate production planning and master production scheduling) have considered capacity constraints. Some companies formalize capacity planning at each stage of production planning. **Resource requirements planning** is associated with an aggregate production plan, and **rough-cut capacity planning** is performed prior to the approval of a master schedule. Capacity requirements planning may still be performed on the material requirements plan, but its role is to fine-tune existing resources, rather than to find or develop new resources.

Resource requirements planning is a check of aggregate capacity before executing a production plan; **rough-cut capacity planning** is a check of capacity before executing a master schedule.

Once the feasibility of an MRP plan has been verified by CRP, the plan can be executed by releasing orders in the time periods indicated. Early MRP systems had no mechanism for monitoring the success of their plans. Today's MRP systems include elaborate capacity and reporting modules for scheduling and monitoring daily work requirements. A later section on computerized MRP systems and MRP II discusses these enhanced systems in more detail.

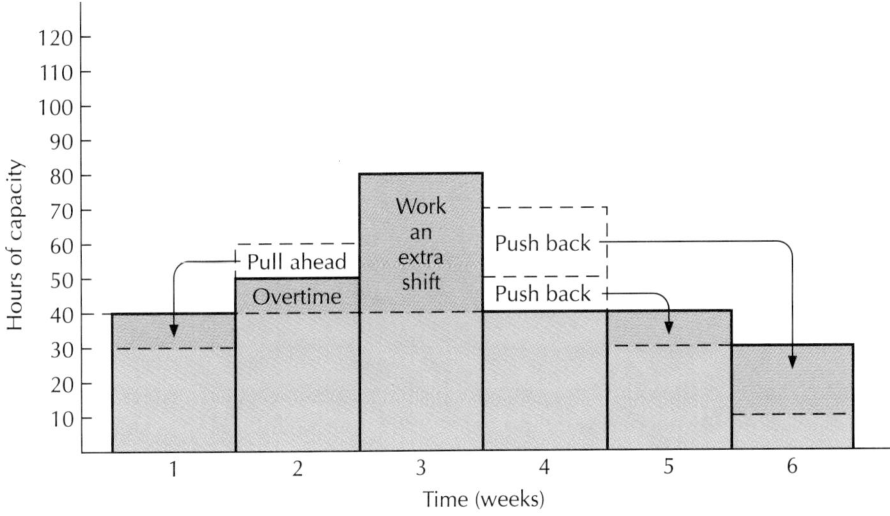

FIGURE 13.7 Adjusted Load Profile for Machine 32A

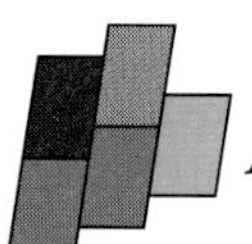

ADVANCED TOPICS IN MRP

An MRP system is large and complex. We do not have the space in this text to explore all the functions of the system or the options available. Instead, we have concentrated on the basics of MRP that are common to the majority of MRP software. However, there are a few advanced issues that we feel ought to be mentioned, including the use of safety stock and safety lead time, lot-sizing techniques, and processing frequency.

Safety Stock and Safety Lead Time

Safety stock is extra inventory held to guard against uncertainties.

Safety stock, as we learned in Chapter 12, is extra units held in inventory to hedge against a possible stockout. The trick with safety stock is holding enough extra inventory to keep the production system operational but not too much to clog the system with inventory support activities, such as moving, counting, storing, and retrieving. Safety stock becomes a greater issue in MRP systems because safety stock held at one level in a product structure has a cascading effect on all subsequent levels of the product. In other words, requirements for a small amount of extra stock high up in a product structure can "explode" into large amounts of component inventory requirements. The extra inventory from safety stock can completely negate any reductions in inventory gained from tighter MRP schedules. To prevent safety stock from getting out of hand, it is recommended that safety stock be held only in response to a specific problem (such as uncertain demand, quality problems, or vendor unreliability), and that those problems try to be worked out *before* relying on the cushion of extra inventory. Also, safety stock should be held as low in the product structure as possible to prevent unforeseen ballooning of inventory levels. Records should also be kept on the cost of safety stock and how often it is actually used.

Safety lead time is extra time added to an item's lead time.

Use safety stock and safety lead time judiciously.

Safety lead time is the addition of extra time in the lead time quoted for a part or product to guard against delays or uncertain occurrences (i.e., late deliveries, machine breakdowns, unexpected orders, etc.). As in the case of safety stock, management should try to solve these problems *before* adding extra time to lead-time figures. In addition, the cascading effect of lead-time inflation throughout a product structure should be recognized. Data on lead times are usually based on past performance. If a due date is not met, it is commonplace to increase the lead time for the items involved so that future due dates will not be missed. Unfortunately, some laws of human nature come into play, such as "work expands to fill the time allotted to it."[3] Inflated lead times become expected lead times until another incident occurs in which a due date is not met, and lead times are again increased. Some bizarre results of this unfortunate cycle have been reported. One ball bearing manufacturer carried a lead time of 48 weeks for an item that could be manufactured in 3 weeks. Similarly, an iron foundry routinely quoted a 30-week lead time for castings that require only 5 days to make.[4] The lesson here is that lead times should be *calculated,* not determined based on past scheduling performance.

Lot Sizing

Lot sizing is the process of determining the quantities in which orders are placed; **lot-for-lot (L4L)** is a sizing technique that orders the exact amount needed.

Lot sizing refers to the quantities in which orders are placed. If orders are placed for the exact amount needed (i.e., the net requirements), lot sizing is said to be **lot-for-lot (L4L).** This approach to lot sizing is consistent with the objective of MRP of

[3]This is known as Parkinson's law.

[4]Wight, O., *Production Planning and Inventory Control in the Computer Age,* Boston: Cahners Books International, 1974.

minimizing inventory levels. However, there are circumstances when it may be wise to order an amount different from what is needed. For example, minimum order quantities are typically used to take advantage of purchase discounts, maximum order quantities are useful for large items or when space is limited, and multiple order quantities may be necessary to accommodate packaging restrictions (such as gallon containers, bundles, or pallet loads). Lot sizing also reduces the number of setups or changeovers required on a machine, in effect increasing its capacity to process more items.

Transparency 13.8 Lot-Sizing Techniques

Several sophisticated lot-sizing techniques are available with most MRP systems. These include the economic order quantity (EOQ), periodic order quantity (POQ), part-period balancing (PPB), and Wagner-Whitin (WW).

Lot-sizing techniques available with MRP include EOQ, POQ, PPB, and WW.

We discussed EOQ in Chapter 12. EOQ can be used in conjunction with MRP, but it requires some adjustment. In the EOQ formula, annual demand is replaced with average demand per period. Further, the EOQ is viewed as a minimum order quantity. That is, if requirements are less than the EOQ, the EOQ is ordered, but if requirements exceed the EOQ, the amount needed is ordered. The EOQ is really designed for products with stable, continuous demand. It does not perform well for component items and is normally used only for finished goods in MRP systems.

A variation of the EOQ created for use in MRP systems is the **periodic order quantity, or POQ.** The POQ, based on the fixed-order-interval model in traditional inventory systems, is calculated by dividing the EOQ by average demand. The result is a figure that represents the number of demand periods between each order. Thus, if the POQ were three, an order would be placed every three periods. The quantity of the order would be determined by summing up the requirements until the next order period, three periods away. The following example illustrates the use of EOQ and POQ. For simplicity, the techniques are applied only to end items, and lead time is assumed to be negligible.

Periodic order quantity is a lot-sizing technique that places orders at set time periods.

EXAMPLE 13.4

Lot Sizing with EOQ and POQ

Alternate Example 13.4

Problem Statement:

The Boswitch Company, a local manufacturer of sports equipment, has been using an MRP system successfully for about 2 years. Recently, Bob Sage, the plant manager, decided to investigate the use of lot sizing for MRP-generated orders. As a test case, Bob selected a typical product in their line of fishing rods and gathered data each week over a month's time. Using the weekly requirements and cost data given here, help Bob determine if the EOQ or POQ lot-sizing technique is more appropriate.

Period	1	2	3	4
Requirements	50	30	10	40

Ordering or setup cost = \$20 per order
Holding cost = \$1 per unit per week
Lead time = 0
Beginning inventory = 0

Solution:

$$C_o = 20$$

$$C_c = 1$$

$$D = \frac{(50 + 30 + 10 + 40)}{4} = \frac{130}{4} = 32.5$$

We use the average demand requirements per week in our EOQ formula and holding cost per week instead of per year. Holding cost and demand must be expressed in the same time units. The EOQ is calculated as follows.

$$Q_{\text{opt}} = \sqrt{\frac{2C_oD}{C_c}} = \sqrt{\frac{2(20)(32.5)}{1}} = 36 \text{ rods}$$

Thus, every time an order is placed, 36 rods will be ordered. The following chart maps out the ordering and holding costs involved with this inventory policy.

Item: Fishing Rod *Lot Size: EOQ 36*	*LLC: 0* *LT: 0*	*PD*	1	2	3	4
Gross requirements			50	30	10	40
Scheduled receipts						
Projected on hand		36	22	28	18	14
Net requirements			14	8		22
Planned order releases			36	36		36

The EOQ inventory policy results in an order being placed in weeks 1, 2, and 4, for an ordering cost of (3 x \$20) = \$60. Holding cost is calculated by summing the projected on-hand quantities over the 4 weeks and multiplying by the holding cost per unit per week of \$1. Thus, the holding cost of the EOQ policy is (22 + 28 + 18 + 14) x \$1 = \$82. The total cost of the EOQ inventory policy is (\$60 + \$82) = \$142. Notice that the EOQ maintains some inventory at all times.

The POQ is calculated as follows.

$$T_{\text{opt}} = \frac{Q_{\text{opt}}}{D} = \frac{36}{32.5} = 1.1 = 1 \text{ week}$$

Thus, an order will be placed every week, for a total ordering cost of \$20 x 4 = \$80. The size of each order is the weekly demand, so holding cost in this case is zero. The total cost of using the POQ inventory policy is \$80 + \$0 = \$80. The following MRP matrix shows the ordering process.

Item: Fishing Rod *Lot Size: POQ 1*	*LLC: 0* *LT: 0*	*PD*	1	2	3	4
Gross requirements			50	30	10	40
Scheduled receipts						
Projected on hand						
Net requirements			50	30	10	40
Planned order releases			50	30	10	40

Comparing the two lot-sizing techniques, POQ is more appropriate for these data. It saves approximately \$62 per month over the EOQ technique.

Part-period balancing is a technique designed for variable demand data.

The part-period balancing and Wagner-Whitin algorithms were specially designed for variable-demand data (i.e., demand that is very "lumpy"). These lot-sizing techniques allow both the quantity and timing of orders to vary. **Part-period balancing (PPB)** was introduced in the 1970s by IBM as part of their MRP software. It divides demand requirements into order periods such that ordering costs and holding costs are balanced. A *part period* is equivalent to one unit of inventory carried for one period. Although the technique does not guarantee an optimum solution, it does produce a very good solution. Refinements to part-period balancing that look ahead or look backward to adjust the orders initially generated often do reach optimality.[5]

The procedure for PPB is as follows:

1. Calculate an *economic part period,* or EPP, for the problem. This value expresses the relationship between ordering costs and holding costs as a ratio. It is used as a measuring tool to determine when to place an order.

$$\text{EPP} = \frac{\text{ordering cost}}{\text{holding cost}} = \frac{C_o}{C_c}$$

2. Beginning with the first period's requirements, assume an order is placed to cover demand over a number of periods. The exact number of periods is determined by calculating a *generated part period,* GPP, for each period and accumulating the GPPs until they exceed the EPP just calculated.

$$\text{GPP} = (\text{no. units in inventory})\ (\text{no. periods held})$$

   When cumulative GPP > EPP, place an order.
3. After the order period has been determined, the process of generating part-period values begins again. When all the order periods have been identified, the size of each order can be calculated by accumulating the demand requirements between order periods.

EXAMPLE 13.5

Alternate Example 13.5

Lot Sizing with Part-Period Balancing

Problem Statement:

Use the part-period balancing lot-sizing technique to generate orders for the fishing rod requirements given in Example 13.4.

Solution:

First, we calculate the economic part-period value.

$$\text{EPP} = \frac{20}{1} = 20$$

Then, we begin calculating generated part periods and accumulating them. The results are shown in the following table. Refer to the completed table as you follow this discussion.

Period	1	2	3	4
Requirements	50	30	10	40
GPP	0(50) 0	1(30) 30	1(10) 10	2(40) 80
CGPP	0	30	10	90
Order period	*	*		*
Order quantity	50	40		40

[5]For more information on part-period balancing and its refinements, refer to DeMatteis, J. J., and A. G. Mendoza, "An Economic Lot-Sizing Technique: The Part-Period Algorithm," *IBM Systems Journal* (1968): 30–46.

We know an order must be placed in period 1 because we have no inventory available to meet the requirements. (The asterisk in the order period row of the table indicates that an order will be placed in that period.) The order must at least cover period 1's demand of 50 units. Since we will use the 50 units ordered in period 1 in period 1, we will not be placing any of those units into inventory. Thus, the GPP for period 1 is (50 units) (0 periods held) = 0. If period 1's order also covers demand in period 2, then the GPP for period 2 is (30 units) (1 period held) = 30. The cumulative GPP at the end of period 2 is (0 + 30) = 30. Since the CGPP of 30 exceeds the EPP of 20, we should place an order in period 2. We indicate that decision with an asterisk. We are not sure at this point how large the order will be.

If we order in period 2 to meet period 3's demand, we will need to hold the 10 units demanded in period 3 in inventory for one period. Thus, GPP = (10 units) (1 period held) = 10. The cumulative GPP is also 10. *Note:* Each time an order is placed, the CGPP reverts to 0. Because 10 is not greater than the EPP of 20, we continue calculating GPPs. If we order in period 2 to meet period 4's demand, we will need to hold the 40 units demanded in period 4 in inventory for 2 periods. Thus, the GPP for period 4 is (40 units) (2 periods held) = 80. The cumulative GPP is 10 + 80 = 90. Since 90 exceeds the EPP of 20, an order should be placed in period 4.

According to the PPB technique, we should place orders in periods 1, 2, and 4. The final step of the algorithm is to determine the size of each order. To do that, we simply sum up the requirements between order periods. Therefore, we order 50 units in period 1 to meet period 1's demand, we order 40 units in period 2 to meet the demand in periods 2 and 3, and we order 40 units in period 4 to meet period 4's demand.

At $20 per order, the ordering cost of this plan is (3 x $20) = $60. To determine holding costs, we multiply the CGPP in the nonorder periods by the holding cost per unit. In this problem, period 3 is the only period in which an order is not placed. Thus, the holding cost can be calculated as (10 units x $1) = $10. The total cost of the PPB ordering plan is $60 + $10 = $70.

Wagner-Whitin is an optimizing lot-sizing technique for variable demand data.

Wagner-Whitin is an optimizing lot-sizing technique based on dynamic programming. It tries all possible combinations of orders in a sequential systematic manner, while reducing the size of the problem by eliminating alternatives proven to be inferior to others. Wagner-Whitin begins with the first period in the planning horizon and evaluates all possible combinations of orders to meet demand in that period. It then proceeds to period 2 and does the same, and so on, until the optimal method for meeting demand in all periods has been determined. Although we don't have the space in this text to explore thoroughly dynamic programming, the following example will give you a feel for the technique. To simplify the discussion of the technique, a table has been prepared that shows the alternatives, their cost, and the options eliminated at each step of the analysis. Parentheses are used to designate the scope of one order. For example, (1, 2) means that an order is placed in period 1 to meet the demand for periods 1 and 2.

Of the lot-sizing techniques we have discussed, only the Wagner-Whitin algorithm *guarantees* an optimum solution. AB:POM will perform lot-for-lot, EOQ, PPB, and Wagner-Whitin lot sizing. To determine the costs of a POQ solution, calculate POQ by hand and then input the resulting orders into the user-defined lot-sizing option of AB:POM.

Alternate Example 13.6

EXAMPLE 13.6
Lot Sizing Using Wagner-Whitin[6]

Problem Statement:

Use the Wagner-Whitin lot-sizing technique to generate orders for the fishing rod requirements given in Example 13.4.

Solution:

Period	*Alternatives*	*Ordering cost*	*Holding cost*	*Total cost*	*Optimal policy*
1	(1)	20	0	20	(1)

The only option available to meet period 1's demand is to order in period 1.

2	(1)(2)	40	0	40	(1)(2)
	(1, 2)	20	30	50	

To meet period 2's demand, we could order in period 1 and again in period 2, or we could order enough in period 1 to cover the demand in both periods. From our analysis, we observe that orders placed in periods 1 and 2 will always be preferred to an order placed in period 1 to cover demand in 1 and 2. Thus, we can eliminate all future options that combine 1 and 2. In effect, we are dropping period 1 from the planning horizon.

3	(1)(2)(3)	60	0	60	
	(1)(2, 3)	40	10	50	(1)(2, 3)

Now we see that ordering to meet demand in periods 2 and 3 combined is preferred to ordering in periods 2 and 3 separately. Thus, we can eliminate all future options that order separately for period 3.

4	(1)(2, 3)(4)	60	10	70	(1)(2, 3)(4)
	(1)(2, 3, 4)	40	90	130	
	(1)(2)(3, 4)	60	40	100	

The optimal ordering policy is (1) (2, 3) (4); that is, we will place an order in period 1 for 50 units, in period 2 for 40 units, and in period 4 for 40 units, for a total inventory cost of $70.

The dangers from using lot sizing in MRP systems are similar to the dangers of safety stock or safety lead time; that is, a decision that seems appropriate for one item at one level of a product structure may not be appropriate for other items that derive their demand from that item. Consider product A shown in Figure 13.8 on page 678, assembled from components B and C. A has a lot size of 100, B's is 500, and C's is 400. Currently there are no A's in inventory, 100 B's, and 90 C's. A customer order of 85 A's would cause a planned order release of 100 A's and 400 C's, even though we need only 10 more C's. That seems wasteful and contrary to the objectives of MRP. Further, if no lot sizing is used, we actually have enough components on hand to assemble the order from stock. No outside order is needed.

[6]This problem is adapted from the original publication on the algorithm: Wagner, H. M., and T. M. Whitin, "Dynamic Version of the Economic Lot Size Model," *Management Science* (October 1958): 89–96.

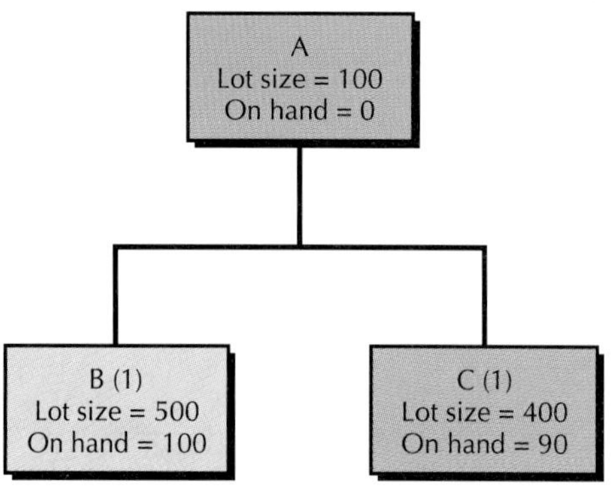

FIGURE 13.8 Practical Aspects of Multilevel Lot Sizing

Given a customer order for 85 A's, what manufacturing or purchase orders should be issued?

Several studies have been conducted to examine the effect of using different lot-sizing techniques at different levels of a product structure.[8] From these studies we can generally conclude the following:

1. *Fixed-quantity techniques, if necessary, should be used for items at the top of the product structure.* Lot-sizing techniques that allow the timing of orders to vary with demand will cause far too many changes in material and capacity requirements as top-level requirements are exploded down the product structure.
2. *Lot-for-lot should be used at intermediate levels.* It is just too difficult to predict the effect of lot-sizing decisions at one level of a product structure on subsequent levels. Lot sizing, other than lot-for-lot, encourages excessive amounts of inventory and unnecessary capacity problems.
3. *POQ or PPB should be reserved for the lowest levels in a product structure.* Any cost advantages from larger-quantity orders would be greatest for those items purchased from outside suppliers, that is, at the bottom of the product structure. Further, the lot-sizing "effect" of these techniques is not passed down to other items.
4. *Lot sizing should be viewed as an enhancement to a well-run MRP system.* Novice MRP users are better off ignoring the lot-sizing options in MRP software. They can create more problems than they solve!

Processing Frequency

MRP systems have enormous data bases. Although the values in the various data bases may be updated frequently (basically on-line), it would be folly to generate new production and purchasing schedules each time a change occurs in the data base. The question then becomes, how often should a new schedule be generated? Most MRP systems have two forms of processing, *net change* and *regenerative.* **Net change MRP** processes only those records affected by a change in data. The changes are usually accumulated and run through the system together, typically overnight. **Regenerative MRP** re-explodes the entire data base, collecting all changes that have occurred since the last schedule has been generated. This is the most error-proof approach, but it can take a considerable amount of time (i.e., an entire weekend) and dramatically increase data processing costs. Although the

Net change MRP partially explodes the BOM only for those items affected by change.

Regenerative MRP re-explodes the entire master schedule throughout the entire BOM.

[8]See, for example, Yelli, L. E., "Material Requirements Lot Sizing: A Multi-Level Approach," *International Journal of Production Research* 17, no. 3 (1979): 223–32; Steinberg, E., and A. Napier, "Optimal Multilevel Lot Sizing for Requirements Planning Systems," *Management Science* 26, no. 12 (December 1980): 1258–72.

frequency of processing differs by industry and size of company, most MRP users are able to perform net change daily and regenerative weekly.

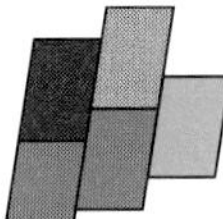

MANUFACTURING RESOURCE PLANNING (MRP II)

The MRP systems on the market today are composed of many different modules that can be purchased separately. Typically, the modules include the following:

- Forecasting
- Customer order entry
- Production planning/master production scheduling
- Product structure/bill-of-material processor
- Inventory control
- Material requirements planning
- Capacity planning
- Shop floor control
- Purchasing
- Accounting
- Financial analysis

MRP systems are usually implemented in modules.

We can recognize some of these modules as inputs to or outputs from the basic MRP process. Others represent a broadened scope of MRP-related activities, beginning with forecasting demand and ending with a financial analysis of the firm.

Companies differ in their approach to implementing MRP, but seldom will a company purchase an entire MRP system at one time. Most firms opt for installing the product structure/bill-of-material processor first and then add the inventory module, followed by the MRP module. The BOM and inventory modules have the largest data bases of the modules and serve as major inputs to the rest of the process. Purchasing is also brought on-line early, usually shortly after the BOM module is installed. Also, assemble-to-order companies tend to thrive on the customer order entry module and will implement that one as soon as possible.

Teaching Note 13.5 The MRP II Award

It may be some time before the master schedule module or higher-level planning modules are added. How, you may wonder, does the MRP system run without a master schedule? Actually, a master production schedule is used, but it is not generated or maintained by the MRP system; it is input by hand. The capacity planning module is important for a well-run MRP system, and its absence often separates the successful MRP user from the unsuccessful user. Shop floor control is a difficult module to implement and is probably the most disappointing one in practice. Chapter 14 discusses shop floor control in more detail.

As MRP evolved and more modules and features were added in the areas of capacity planning, marketing, and finance, it became clear that the name *material* requirements planning was no longer adequate to describe the full range of activities this system could coordinate. In keeping with the MRP acronym, the new and improved MRP became known as **MRP II,** for **manufacturing resource planning.** Figure 13.9, on page 680, shows approximately how the various MRP II functions interact. The term *closed-loop* has been used to describe the numerous feedback loops between plans for production and available capacity and between planned and actual occurrences.

MRP II, an extension of MRP, plans all the resources needed for running a business.

It is interesting to note that *manufacturing* resource planning is already a misnomer because MRP II software is also used in services, such as education, architecture, health care, distribution, and the like. Thus, systems such as SRP (service requirements planning) and DRP (distribution requirements planning) are also available.

Transparency 13.9 Manufacturing Resource Planning (MRP II)

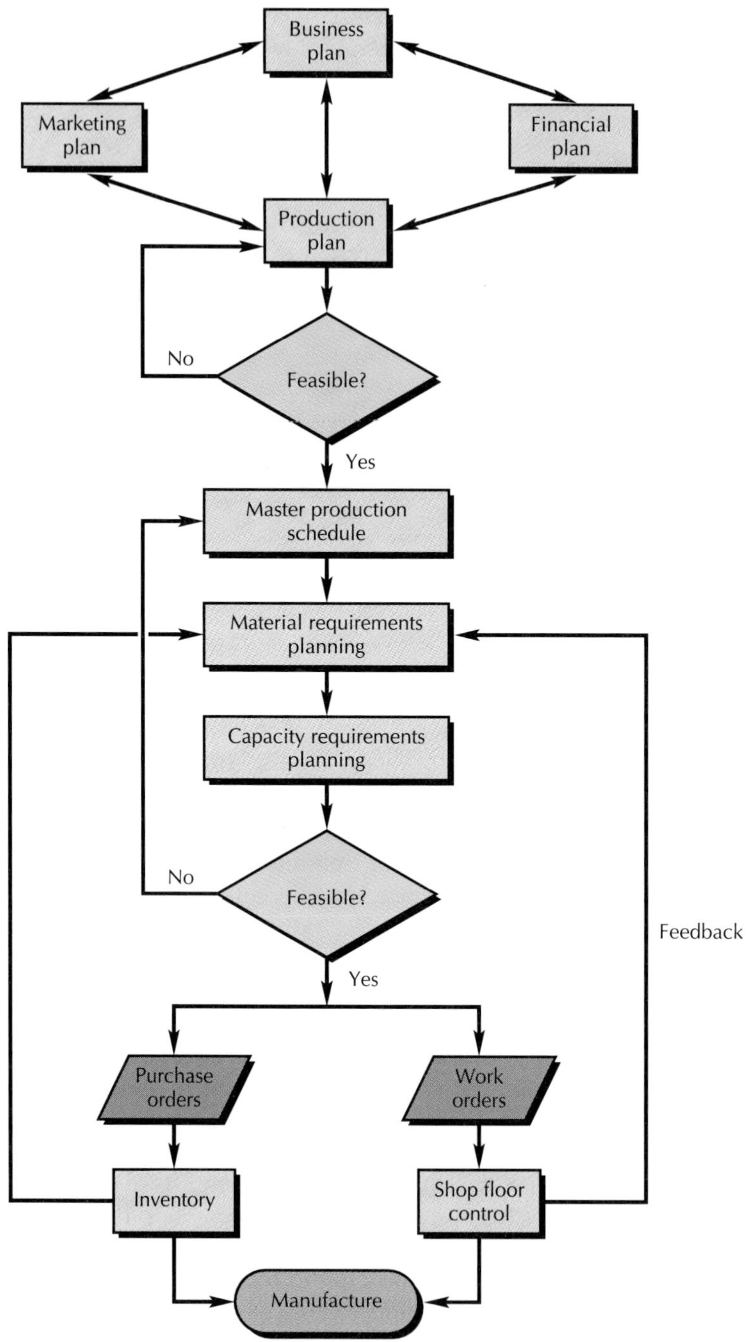

FIGURE 13.9 Manufacturing Resource Planning (MRP II)

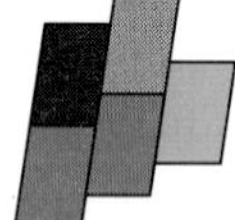

PROBLEMS AND PROSPECTS OF MRP/MRP II

MRP has never fully achieved the successes that were promised in the early 1970s, when the concept was first introduced. Many of its problems have been associated with poor implementation strategies, lack of support by top management, and lack of commitment by other company personnel. Expectations for what MRP could accomplish were inflated by software vendors and consultants, who seemed to assure managers that the "problem" of manufacturing could be solved if they

GAINING THE COMPETITIVE EDGE

MRP Works for Small Companies, Too

MRP is usually reserved for large manufacturers with more than $25 million in sales, but Clarkson Co., a manufacturer of industrial valves, with sales of $5 million, says MRP can work for small companies, too. Using MRP as a common information data base helped to make the decision-making process in the company more consistent. As a result, Clarkson was able to reduce its inventory investment by 30 percent, cut its lead time from 8 weeks to 2 weeks, increase its on-time delivery to 95 percent or better, and double sales.

The market for lightweight fly reels has increased in recent years due to larger trout, better technology (such as rim control and disk drag), and more sophisticated trout fishers. British Fly Reels, a small manufacturer located in Falmouth, UK, was set to capitalize on the expanded market with its popular RimFly and DragonFly fishing reels. However, as in many small but growing companies, their operations expertise existed in the memories of certain individuals, not in a central computer system. Material shortages were rampant, shop floor scheduling was reactive instead of proactive, and delivery dates were missed. An MRP system was brought on-line to remedy the situation. It operated on a local area network with 10 PC workstations. The most difficult task of MRP implementation was creating the data for 1,800 part numbers from scratch. This involved developing a part-numbering system, defining a bill of material for each product, estimating lead times, and maintaining accurate on-hand inventory counts. It became obvious that previous attempts to calculate material requirements by hand had failed, and needed purchase orders were simply not being placed. The MRP system generated schedules and supporting purchase orders quickly and efficiently.

Athey Products Corporation employs about 240 workers in its Raleigh, North Carolina, plant to produce street sweepers and refuse haulers. Although not as glamorous as automobiles, their products are just as complex, involving more than 20,000 components and 1,400 vendors. Athey recently installed a tailored MRP II system to streamline order entry, product costing, component inventory, and financial operations. They completely restructured their bill of material and revised their product costing based on manufacturing operations. Account delinquencies and customer histories were managed more efficiently. Inventory transactions became real-time, and the annual physical inventory count was replaced with cycle counting. Purchasing enjoyed increased access to and control of inventory and vendor order data, and sales could quickly configure each order and quote customized prices. As a result, inventory shrank by 33 percent, productivity rose by 63 percent, and Athey was able to handle a 100 percent increase in its parts business.

Sources: Based on "Small Company, Big Benefits with MRP II," *Modern Materials Handling* (September 1992): 65; Huckerby, Marilyn, "Reeling in the Benefits," *Computerized Manufacturing,* (April/May 1992): 50; Jernigan, Jeff, "Comprehensiveness, Cost-Effectiveness Sweep Aside Operations Challenges," *APICS—The Performance Advantage* (March 1993): 44–45.

purchased certain hardware and software products. Money was thrown at the problem, in the form of MRP-related purchases, without an understanding of actual manufacturing needs. We all know that automated systems, especially those dealing with large amounts of information, are only as good as the input provided to them. Inaccurate data, by default or design, has ruined many an MRP system. Adding fancy options, such as lot sizing and safety stock, and unrealistic assessments of capacity are other common sources of problems. As a common data base for the entire firm, MRP tends to be perceived initially by those in different functional areas as an intrusion into their turf. For example, with MRP, marketing can look at the production figures and determine whether manufacturing has scheduled enough production to meet demand, production can monitor the accuracy of

Implementation problems have plagued MRP systems.

Teaching Note 13.6 MRP Implementation

marketing's demand forecasts by comparing planned against actual figures, and salespersons can access the status of customer orders themselves without relying on promises of service from production. Eventually, the common access to information improves managerial decision making, but there is an adjustment period while managers learn to work together instead of at odds.

MRP was the first computerized system to experience widespread use on the factory floor, and as such, it was quite disruptive. Shop supervisors, whose jobs for the last 20 years had consisted of making daily schedules for their workers, were handed a computer printout on Monday mornings that laid out worker assignments for a week in advance. Workers accustomed to long queues of work waiting to be processed instinctively slowed down their production rate as the results of tight MRP scheduling began to take effect and queues dwindled. These examples are representative of the behavioral problems that faced MRP in its early stages of development. As with many new technologies or concepts, the technical issues of MRP were solved far in advance of the behavioral issues. Fortunately, the passage of time and the educational efforts associated with a broadened MRP concept have helped to smooth the way for effective implementation of MRP II. U.S. industry is again experiencing the discomfort of changing "the way work is done" in the midst of the current quality revolution. Even though new processes may be simple, *changing* to new processes is not simple.

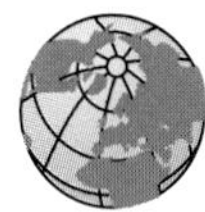

This discussion is not meant to imply that MRP systems have not been successful. Companies who have carefully implemented the system have seen dramatic improvements in performance and reductions in cost. Reports of 40 percent reductions in inventory levels, 33 percent improvements in customer service levels, and 20 percent reductions in production costs are common. However, the fact cannot be ignored that in the 1980s the Japanese JIT production systems produced spectacular results, whereas MRP-led U.S. firms were struggling. With implementation problems no longer at the forefront, practitioners and academicians alike have begun to search for the "real" problems inherent with MRP. They have found that some aspects of the MRP concept do not match the realities of manufacturing. In summary, these mismatches include the following:

MRP causes problems by considering capacity last, using fixed lead times, and requiring excessive reporting.

- *MRP plans for material requirements first; capacity is an afterthought.* As you may have noticed, the iterative procedure described in this chapter for leveling the load on a machine center and making an MRP schedule workable is not very efficient. Too many manual adjustments are required. Furthermore, in some industries, the approach is obviously wrong. If there is a particular process that constrains the system or other capacity constraints that are difficult to relax, then they should drive the schedule rather than the availability of materials.
- *Lead time in an MRP system is fixed.* This fact assumes that either lot sizes will continue unchanged or that they have no bearing on lead time. Under this assumption, the lead time necessary to process an order would remain the same whether that order consisted of one unit or one hundred units. In addition, the lead time figures that are used in MRP are typically averages of past practice, whether that practice produced good or bad manufacturing performance. Finally, fixed lead times ignore current shop loads. The fact is, lead times are as much a result of the scheduling system as an input to it. Consider two jobs whose processing time is 5 hours each. If these jobs require different resources and the resources are available, then the lead time will indeed be 5 hours for each job. If, however, both jobs require the same resource (which is currently available), then one job will have a lead time of 5 hours, and the other will have a lead time of 10 hours. Thus, lead time is a function of both capacity and priority. Most experts agree that the shop floor control problems experienced by MRP users are directly related to the issue of accurately predicting lead times.

GAINING THE COMPETITIVE EDGE

What-if? Planning at John Deere & Co.

The Waterloo, Iowa, tractor works of John Deere & Co. employs 5,000 workers in a 7.5 million–square-foot facility. More than 60,000 parts are managed daily in the production of farm tractors. Recently, an interactive advanced planning system was purchased as an add-on to the existing MRP system. The planning system uses an off-line copy of the MRP data base to perform what-if? simulated MRP runs. Deere has used the system to level demand and fine-tune labor requirements, evaluate inventory requirements for varying customer response times, and quickly adjust its manufacturing plan when crises occur. As a result of the what-if? enhancement to its MRP system, Deere:

1. Found a cost-saving balance between overtime and inventory for a period of gradually increasing demand;
2. Reduced the lead time required to restock its dealers from 12 weeks to 5 weeks; and
3. Kept production going, while shipping priority items on time, during a labor strike at a parts supplier.

Source: Based on "System Helps Deere & Co. Weather Market Fluctuations," *Industrial Engineering* (June 1992): 16–17.

- *The reporting requirements of MRP are excessive.* MRP tries to keep track of the status of all jobs in the system and reschedules jobs as problems occur. In the new manufacturing environment of speed and small lot sizes, this is cumbersome. It might take as long to *record* the processing of an item at a workstation as it does to process the item. Bar-code technology has helped alleviate this problem somewhat, but the issues still remain: How much processing detail is really needed in the common data base? How much control is enough?

With these basic problems, what then, are the prospects for MRP/MRP II in the future? Actually, they are quite good, but in a modified form. Some industries,

John Deere runs a Class A MRP II system. Shown here are two workers putting the finishing touches on a combine attachment. A completed combine contains thousands of different parts, most of them made in-house. MRP II can coordinate the production and assembly of these components, and adjust schedules quickly to deal with unexpected occurrences. Customer-specific options can also be readily accomodated.

MRP II is an effective planning tool.

Teaching Note 13.7 MRP and CIM

primarily companies that produce goods in standard batches, can successfully use MRP/MRP II as is. However, for most companies, the real benefits of MRP II are obtained from its ability to coordinate a company's strategy among different functional areas—that is, to "plan." The common data base and simulation capabilities are very useful in responding quickly to what-if? questions at various levels of detail. BOM processors, purchasing modules, and customer order entry are standard requirements for manufacturing information systems. They are especially helpful in monitoring design quality, vendor quality, and customer service. The transparency of MRP-related decisions to different areas of the firm is invaluable in building trust, teamwork, and better decisions. The financial tie-ins can produce superior fine-tuning of cash flow planning and profit/cost projections. In sum, MRP does a great job of planning and coordinating until it hits the shop floor. We hope to shed some light on that problem in the next chapter on scheduling.

SUMMARY

Material requirements planning (MRP) is a computerized inventory control and production planning system. It has enjoyed widespread use in U.S. industry (primarily for batch manufacturing) as an information system that improves manufacturing decision making. MRP began as a system for ensuring that sufficient *material* was available when needed. However, in application, it became clear that material was not the only resource in short supply. Planning capabilities for machine and labor resources were added to the system in the form of capacity requirements planning (CRP).

MRP requires input from other functional areas of a firm, such as marketing and finance. As these areas began to see the power of a common data base system, they encouraged the expansion of MRP into areas such as demand forecasting, demand management, customer order entry, accounts payable, accounts receivable, budgets, and cash-flow analysis. Clearly, this enhanced version was more powerful than the original MRP systems that ordered material and scheduled production. It provided a common data base that the entire company could use. Its what-if? capability proved invaluable in evaluating trade-offs, and the easy access to information encouraged more sophisticated planning. The "new" MRP, called MRP II, for manufacturing resource planning, has become a standard component for companies entering the age of computer-integrated manufacturing (CIM).

As wonderful as MRP II sounds, there are some drawbacks to the system. The system requires a lot of information, and the information must be accurate and timely. The reporting requirements are sometimes overwhelming, especially as manufacturers move toward more rapid production and shorter cycle times. Perhaps the biggest problem with MRP/MRP II has been its limited success in the execution of shop floor schedules at a time when the Japanese have excelled in this endeavor. Manufacturing experts are now encouraging managers to take advantage of the planning capabilities of MRP II and the execution capabilities of the Japanese production system, JIT. We explore the topics of scheduling and JIT in the next two chapters.

SUMMARY OF KEY FORMULAS

Capacity Requirements

$$\text{Utilization} = \frac{\text{time working}}{\text{total time available}}$$

Capacity Requirements

$$\text{Capacity} = (\text{no. machines}) \times (\text{no. shifts}) \times (\text{utilization}) \times (\text{efficiency})$$

$$\text{Load percent} = \frac{\text{capacity}}{\text{load}}$$

Economic order quantity for MRP

$$Q_{\text{opt}} = \max\left(\sqrt{\frac{2C_oD}{C_c}}, \text{net requirements}\right)$$

Periodic order quantity

$$T_{\text{opt}} = \frac{Q_{\text{opt}}}{D}$$

Part-period balancing

$$\text{EPP} = \frac{C_o}{C_c}$$

$$\text{GPP} = (\text{no. units in inventory})(\text{no. periods held})$$

SUMMARY OF KEY TERMS

assemble-to-order: a manufacturing environment in which major subassemblies are produced in advance of a customer's order and are then configured to order.

bill-of-material: a list of all the materials, parts, and assemblies that make up a product, including quantities, parent-component relationships, and order of assembly.

capacity: the productive capability of a worker, machine, work center, or system.

capacity requirements planning (CRP): a computerized system that projects the load from a given material plan onto the capacity of a system and identifies underloads and overloads.

cumulative lead time: the total length of time required to manufacture a product; also, the longest path through a product structure.

cycle counting: a method for auditing inventory accuracy that counts inventory and reconciles errors on a cyclical schedule rather than once a year.

efficiency: how well a machine or worker performs compared to a standard output level.

expediting: the process of speeding up orders so that they are completed in less than their average lead time.

explosion: the process of determining requirements for lower-level items by multiplying the planned orders for parent items by the quantity per assembly of component items.

inventory master file: a file that contains inventory status and descriptive information on every item in inventory.

lead time offsetting: the process of subtracting an item's lead time from its due date to determine when an order should be released; also called time-phasing.

load: refers to the standard hours of work assigned to the facility.

load percent: the ratio of capacity to load.

load profile: a chart that compares released orders and planned orders with work center capacity.

lot-for-lot (L4L): a lot-sizing technique that orders the exact amount needed.

lot sizing: the process of determining the quantities in which orders are placed.

manufacturing resource planning (MRP II): an extension of MRP that plans all the resources necessary for manufacturing; includes financial and marketing analysis, feedback loops, and an overall business plan.

master production schedule: a schedule for the production of end items (usually final products). It drives the MRP process that schedules the production of component parts.

material requirements planning (MRP): a computerized inventory control and production planning system for generating purchase orders and work orders of materials, components, and assemblies.

modular bill of material: a special bill of material used to plan the production of products with many optional features.

net change MRP: an approach to MRP processing that partially explodes the bill of material only for those items that are affected by a change.

netting: the process of subtracting on-hand quantities from gross requirements to produce net requirements.

order splitting: the processing of a single order in separate batches at multiple machines simultaneously.

part-period balancing (PPB): a lot-sizing technique designed for variable demand data.

pegging: the ability to trace through a product structure to identify the source of requirements.

periodic order quantity (POQ): a lot-sizing technique designed for variable demand that places orders at set time periods.

product structure file: a file that contains computerized bills of material for all products.

regenerative MRP: an approach to MRP processing that re-explodes the master schedule throughout the entire bill of material.

resource requirements planning: a check of aggregate capacity before executing a production plan.

rough-cut capacity planning: a check of capacity in general terms prior to the approval of a master schedule.

safety lead time: extra time added to an item's lead time to guard against delays or uncertain occurrences.

time fence: a date specified by management beyond which no changes in the master schedule are allowed.

utilization: the percentage of available working time that a worker spends working or a machine is running.

Wagner-Whitin (WW): an optimizing lot-sizing technique for variable demand data based on dynamic programming.

SOLVED PROBLEMS

1. MRP Calculations

Problem Statement:

Complete the following MRP matrix for item X.

Item: X *LLC: 1* *LT: 2* *Lot Size: Min 50*	*PD*	*1*	*2*	*3*	*4*	*5*	*6*	*7*	*8*
Gross requirements		20	30	50	50	60	90	40	60
Scheduled receipts			50						
Projected on hand	40								
Net requirements									
Planned order receipts									
Planned order releases									

a. In what periods should orders be released and what should be the size of those orders?
b. How would the planned order releases change with lot-for-lot (L4L) lot sizing?
c. How would the planned order releases change if lot-for-lot lot sizing and a safety stock of 20 were required?

Solution:

a.

Item: X *LLC: 1* *Lot Size: Min 50* *LT: 2*	*PD*	*1*	*2*	*3*	*4*	*5*	*6*	*7*	*8*
Gross requirements		20	30	50	50	60	90	40	60
Scheduled receipts			50						
Projected on hand	40	20	40	40	40	30	0	10	0
Net requirements				10	10	20	60	40	50
Planned order receipts				50	50	50	60	50	50
Planned order releases		50	50	50	60	50	50		

Orders should be released in periods 1, 2, 3, 4, 5, and 6 for quantities of 50, 50, 50, 60, 50, and 50, respectively.

b.

Item: X *LLC: 1* *Lot Size: L4L* *LT: 2*	*PD*	*1*	*2*	*3*	*4*	*5*	*6*	*7*	*8*
Gross requirements		20	30	50	50	60	90	40	60
Scheduled receipts			50						
Projected on hand	40	20	40	0	0	0	0	0	0
Net requirements				10	50	60	90	40	60
Planned order receipts				10	50	60	90	40	60
Planned order releases		10	50	60	90	40	60		

Orders would be released in periods 1 through 6 and for the quantities of 10, 50, 60, 90, 40, and 60 units, respectively.

c.

Item: X *LLC: 1* *Lot Size: L4L* *LT: 2*	*PD*	*1*	*2*	*3*	*4*	*5*	*6*	*7*	*8*
Gross requirements		20	30	50	50	60	90	40	60
Scheduled receipts			50						
Projected on hand	40	20	40	20	20	20	20	20	20
Net requirements				30	50	60	90	40	60
Planned order receipts				30	50	60	90	40	60
Planned order releases		30	50	60	90	40	60		

Orders would be placed in periods 1 through 6 in quantities of 30, 50, 60, 90, 40, and 60, respectively. The initial order quantity would be increased by 20 units to serve as safety stock, and that amount would remain in inventory throughout the planning horizon. An alternative way to handle safety stock is to delete it from the initial projected on-hand quantity before the MRP matrix is completed. Thus, the analysis would begin showing 20 units initially on hand.

2. Lot Sizing

Problem Statement:

Files and More, Inc. (F & M) is a manufacturer of office equipment that uses the economic order quantity to schedule its production. Due to the current recession and the need to cut costs, F & M has targeted its inventory as a prime area of cost reduction. However, the company does not want to reduce its customer service level in the process. F & M has called in a student consultant group from the local university and asked them to evaluate its inventory policy. As a test case, demand and cost data have been prepared for a basic two-drawer file cabinet. It is your task as part of the student consultant group to evaluate several lot-sizing techniques with which you are familiar and compare their performance against the EOQ policy that is currently used at F & M.

Period	1	2	3	4	5
Demand	20	40	30	10	45

Ordering cost = \$100 per order
Holding cost = \$1 per cabinet per week
Assume lead time = 0

Solution:

We will evaluate the EOQ, POQ, PPB, and WW lot-sizing techniques.

EOQ:

$$\text{Average demand} = \frac{20 + 40 + 30 + 10 + 45}{5} = \frac{145}{5} = 29$$

$$Q_{\text{opt}} = \sqrt{\frac{2C_oD}{C_c}} = \sqrt{\frac{2(100)(29)}{1}} = \sqrt{5{,}800} = 76.15$$

Item: File Cabinet *Lot Size: EOQ 76*	*LLC: 0* *LT: 0*	*PD*	*1*	*2*	*3*	*4*	*5*
Gross requirements			20	40	30	10	45
Scheduled receipts							
Projected on hand			56	16	62	52	7
Net requirements			20		14		
Planned order releases			76		76		

Ordering cost = (2 orders × \$100/order) = \$200
Holding cost = (56 + 16 + 62 + 52 + 7) × \$1 = \$193
Total cost = \$393

POQ:

$$\text{Order interval} = \frac{Q_{\text{opt}}}{D} = \frac{76}{29} = 2.62, \quad \text{or} \quad 3 \text{ periods}$$

Item: File Cabinet *LLC: 0* *Lot Size: POQ 3* *LT: 0*	*PD*	*1*	*2*	*3*	*4*	*5*
Gross requirements		20	40	30	10	45
Scheduled receipts						
Projected on hand		70	30	0	45	0
Net requirements						
Planned order releases		90			55	

Ordering costs = (2 orders x $100/order) = $200
Holding costs = (70 + 30 + 45) x $1 = $145
Total cost = $345

PPB:

$$PP = \frac{100}{1} = 100$$

Period	*1*	*2*	*3*	*4*	*5*
Demand	20	40	30	10	45
GPP	0(20) 0	1(40) 40	2(30) 60	3(10) 30	1(45) 45
CGPP	0	40	100	130	45
Order period	*			*	
Order quantity	90			55	

Order cost = (2 orders x $100/order) = $200
Holding cost = (100 + 45) x $1 = $145
Total cost = $345

WW:

	Ordering Policy	*Ordering Cost*	*Holding Cost*	*Total Cost*
Period 1	(1)	$100	$0	$100*
Period 2	(1)(2)	$200	$0	$200
	(1, 2)*	$100	$20	$120*
Period 3	(1, 2) (3)	$200	$40	$240
	(1, 2, 3)*	$100	40 + 60 = $100	$200*
Period 4	(1, 2, 3)(4)	$200	40 + 60 = $100	$300
	(1, 2, 3, 4)	$100	40 + 60 + 30 = $130	$230*
	(1, 2) (3, 4)	$200	40 + 0 + 10 = $50	$250
Period 5	(1, 2, 3, 4) (5)	$200	40 + 60 + 30 = $130	$330*
	(1, 2, 3, 4, 5)	$100	40 + 60 + 30 + 180 = $310	$410
	(1, 2, 3) (4, 5)	$200	40 + 60 + 0 + 45 = $145	$345

Order 100 units in period 1 and 45 in period 5, for a total cost of $330.

Summary of Lot-Sizing Results	
EOQ	$393
POQ	$345
PPB	$345
WW	$330
Lot-for-lot	$500

The best lot-sizing policy, provided by Wagner-Whitin, would save approximately $65 per month in inventory costs for the basic file cabinet, without reducing customer service. Over a year's time, approximately $780 could be saved for this product alone.

QUESTIONS

13-1. Describe a production environment in which MRP would be useful.
13-2. Explain with an example the difference between dependent and independent demand.
13-3. What are the objectives of an MRP system?
13-4. What are the three major inputs to MRP? What are the three forms of output?
13-5. How is a master production schedule created and how is it used?
13-6. Describe several bill-of-material formats. What special type of information does each provide?
13-7. What is the purpose of phantom bills, K-bills, and modular bills of material?
13-8. What type of information is included in the inventory master file?
13-9. Describe cycle counting. How does it improve inventory performance?
13-10. Describe the MRP process, including netting, explosion, and lead time offsetting.
13-11. How does a planned order report differ from an MRP action report?
13-12. What are the inputs to capacity requirements planning?
13-13. Discuss several alternatives for leveling the load on a facility.
13-14. How can capacity planning be incorporated at each stage of production planning?
13-15. What kinds of decisions does an MRP planner make?
13-16. What is the purpose of safety stock? Safety lead time? Give some recommendations on their use.
13-17. Discuss several lot-sizing techniques that are used with MRP systems. In general, when should each be used?
13-18. What processing alternatives are available for MRP systems? How frequently are most MRP plans updated?
13-19. List some typical modules available from MRP software vendors. Which modules are usually applied first? Last?
13-20. How does MRP II differ from MRP?
13-21. Why has MRP been difficult to implement?
13-22. What are the major benefits from MRP/MRP II?
13-23. What are the major drawbacks of MRP/MRP II?
13-24. Interview production managers at three plants in your area about their use of MRP/MRP II. How have their experiences been similar? What accounts for the similarities and differences?
13-25. Find out if there is a local APICS chapter in your area. Attend a meeting and write a summary of the speaker's comments.

PROBLEMS

13-1. a. 6
b. 7
c. 3
d. See Solutions Manual.

13-1. Refering to the product structure diagram on page 691, determine:
a. How many K's are needed for each A?
b. How many E's are needed for each A?
c. What is the low-level code for item E?
d. Construct a multilevel bill of material for product A.

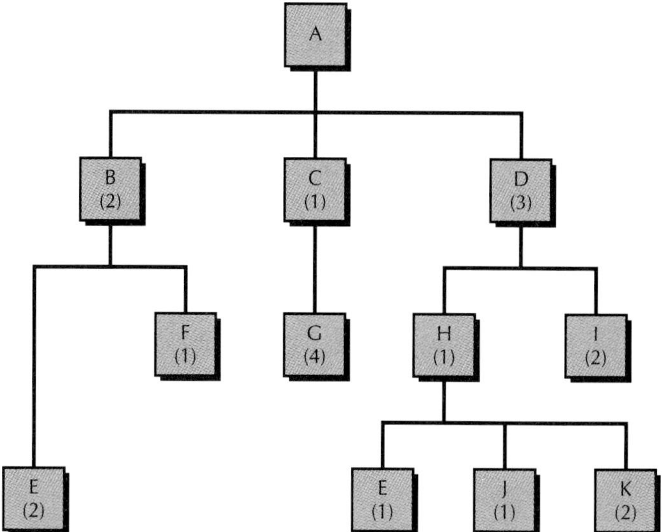

13-2. The classic One-Step step stool is assembled from a prefabricated seat, one bottom leg, one top leg, five nuts, and four leg tips. From the accompanying parts list and assembly instructions, construct a product structure diagram for the One-Step step stool.

13-2. See Solutions Manual.

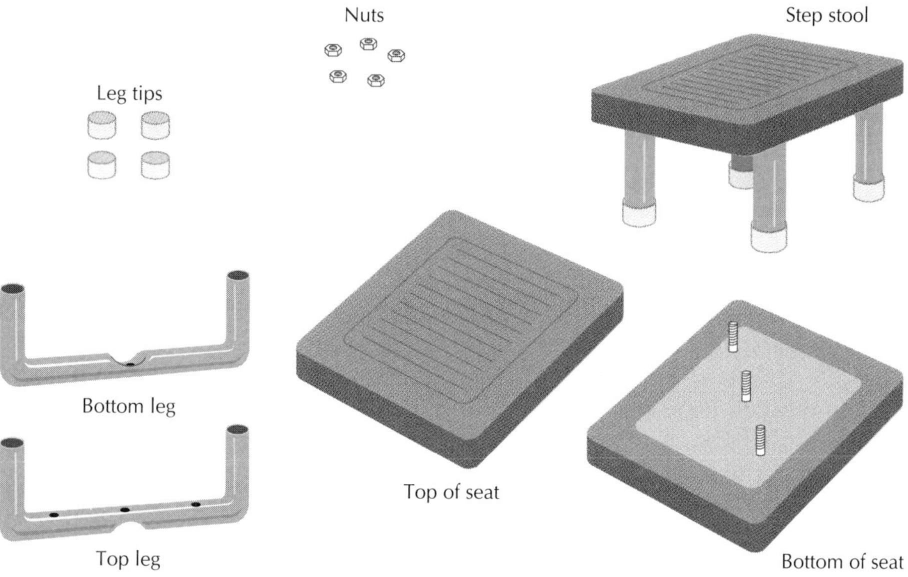

Assembly Instructions:

Step 1: Push leg tips on legs.

Step 2: Position the bottom leg in the seat, as illustrated, so the bolt protrudes through hole A. Attach nuts to bolts indicated by A.

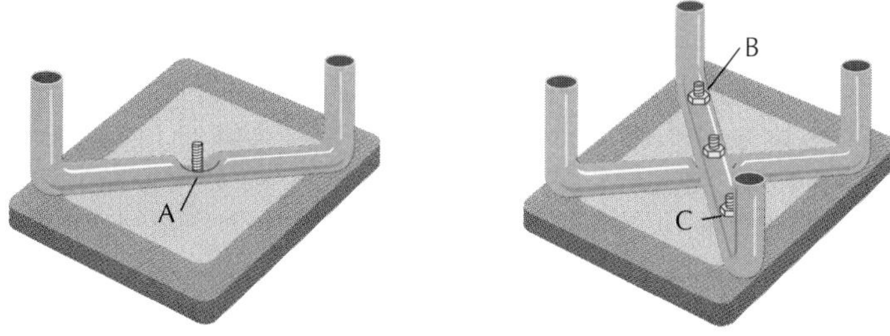

Step 3: Position the top leg in the seat, as illustrated, so bolts protrude through holes in leg. Attach nuts to bolts indicated by A, B and C.

13-3. a. See Solutions Manual. b. 4, 16, 16

13-3. Kid's World sells outside play equipment for children. One of their most popular items is a 5-foot by 7-foot wooden sandbox. General assembly instructions, lead times, and lot-sizing information are given.

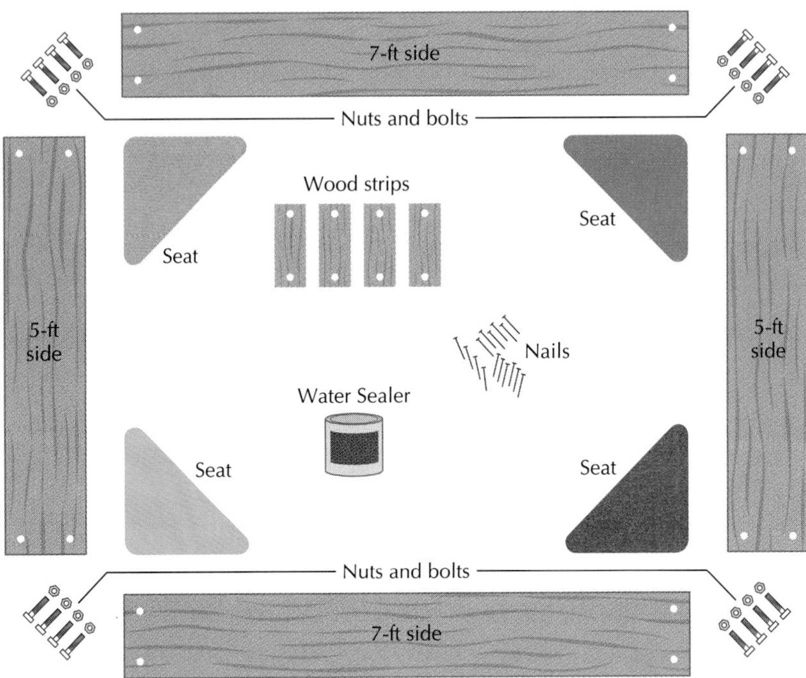

Assembly Instructions:

The wood pieces for the sandbox are ordered precut and treated. Kid's World sands the wood, drills several holes in each piece as required for assembly, and coats each piece with 2 ounces of watersealer. The sides are then assembled one corner at a time by attaching a 1-foot wood strip catercorner between a 5-foot and 7-foot side. Four bolts are inserted through the predrilled holes and secured with nuts. After the left and right corners of the sandbox have been assembled, the two pieces are joined in a similar manner to form the box assembly. A triangular-shaped wooden seat is attached to each corner of the box assembly with four flat-headed nails for each seat. The sandbox is now complete.

The hardware and wood pieces are purchased from a local lumber yard and, in most cases, can be delivered with 3 days notice. Nails are purchased in boxes of 200; nuts and bolts, by the dozen.

a. Prepare a multilevel bill of material for the 5-foot by 7-foot sandbox.
b. How many 1-foot wood strips are needed to make one sandbox? How many nails? How much water sealer?

13-4. See Solutions Manual.

13-4. Avery's Robotics manufactures small assembly robots to customer order. Avery's current policy of maintaining a separate bill of material for each possible combination of customer options has become unmanageable. Avery has heard of modular bills of material but is having difficulty understanding the concept. He has gathered some data on customer preference and knows that 60 percent of his customers choose controller A and 80 percent choose end effector 2. He is wondering whether or not to drop controller B and end effector 1 altogether. Explain the concept of modular

BOMs to Avery by restructuring the following four individual bills into one modular bill of material.

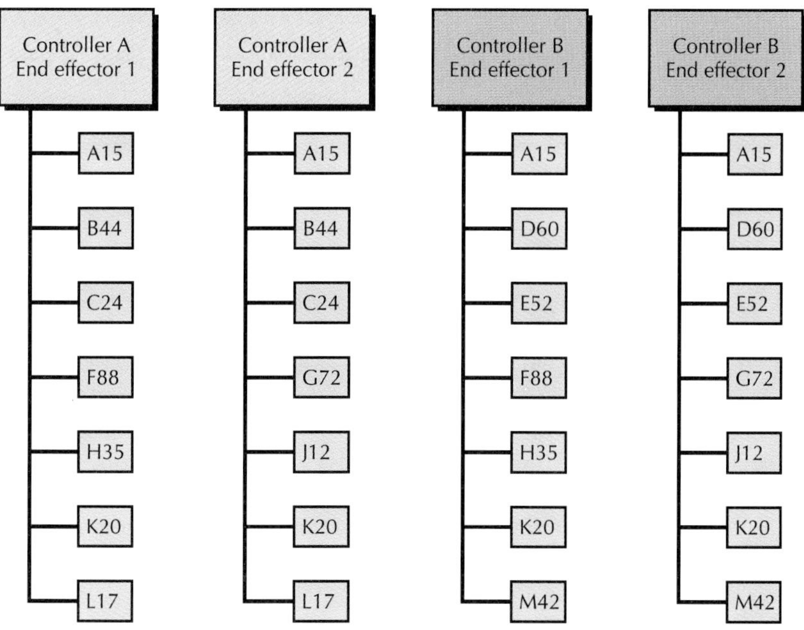

Hint: Determine which components are unique to the type of controller, which components are unique to the type of end effector, and which components are common to the robot regardless of controller or end effector option.

13-5. Tilco Toys makes the popular Battle Axe action figures. To maintain market share, Tilco has discovered it must introduce a new batch of Battle Axes (consisting of five figures) every three months. Careful data are maintained on the figures that sell the best so that their characteristics can be repeated in subsequent product offerings. In order to reduce the time and cost of development and production of each new batch of figures, the designers simply choose different combinations of options from the following list:

13-5. a. See Solutions Manual.
b. 8, 6, 2
c. 0.192%

Group	*Force*	*Clothing*	*Weapons*	*Transportation*
Falcons (40%)	Knights (30%)	Armor (20%)	Sword (30%)	Horse (40%)
Hawks (40%)	Slayers (20%)	Cloth (40%)	Crossbow (20%)	Wagon (20%)
Woodsmen (20%)	Archers (30%)	Fur (10%)	Spear (10%)	Catapult (10%)
	Engineers (20%)	Leather (30%)	Longbow (10%)	Battering Ram (10%)
			Battle Axe (20%)	Dragon (10%)
			Throwing Star (10%)	Boat (10%)

a. Assuming the usage percentages shown above are an accurate reflection of the product offerings last year, describe the twenty figures that *could* have been introduced.
b. How many Black Falcons were introduced last year? How many Knights? How many Dragons?
c. What is the probability that an armored Falcon engineer with a horse and sword was introduced?

13-6. Complete the following MRP matrix for item A:

13-6. See Solutions Manual.

Item: A LLC: 1 *LT: 2 Lot Size: Mult 25*	*PD*	*1*	*2*	*3*	*4*	*5*	*6*	*7*	*8*
Gross requirements		10	15	50	75	60	85	45	60
Scheduled receipts			50						
Projected on hand	20								
Net requirements									
Planned order receipts									
Planned order releases									

13-7. See Solutions Manual.

13-7. Camp's Inc. produces two products, X and Z, with product structures as shown. An order for 200 units of X has been received for period 8, and 350 units of Z are scheduled to be shipped in the eighth period. An inquiry of available stock reveals 25 units of X on hand, 40 of Z, 30 of R, 100 of S, 90 of T, 120 of U, 150 of V, and 160 of W. Of the T's on order, 250 are due in by period 2; 75 S's should arrive in period 1. For economy reasons, U is never made in quantities under 500. Similarly, V and W have multiple order quantities of 900 and 1,500, respectively.

Determine when orders should be released for each item and the size of those orders.

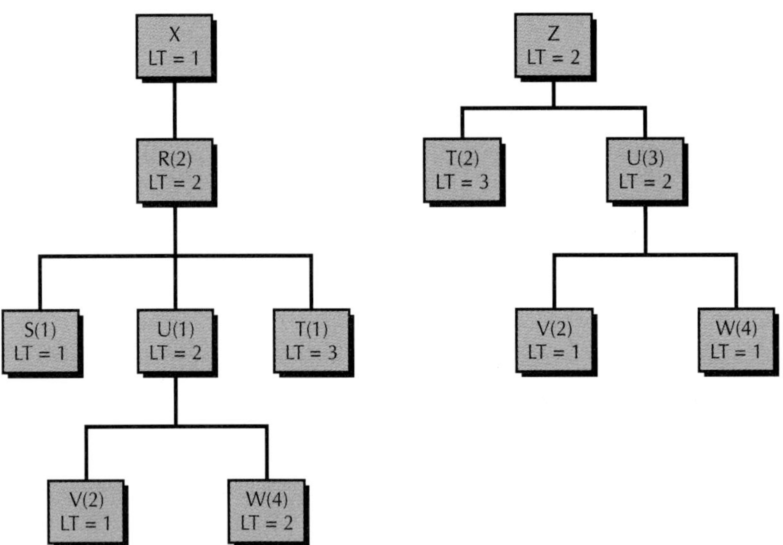

13-8. See Solutions Manual.

★ 13-8. Low Crawl, Inc. is a well-known manufacturer of quality barbed wire. The firm's newest team of management consultants has recommended MRP as an efficient alternative to the present haphazard scheduling and inventory system. Using the following information, help the company initiate its MRP system by:

a. Drawing a product structure diagram for a standard bale of barbed wire;
b. Creating a multilevel bill of material from the diagram; and
c. Generating orders necessary to deliver 10 bales of barbed wire to a new correctional facility on the east coast by period 8.

Description of the Production Process

Each bale of barbed wire is made up of 30 strands of barbed wire. A barbed wire consists of four barbs attached to a 1-foot strand of coated wire. Each strand has been coated with two fluid ounces of galvanizing fluid. The strand is produced by combining eight 1-foot lengths of metal bead into a single strand of the same length. The lengths are cut from a 50-foot roll of metal bead. Barbs are 1-inch lengths of metal bead that have been cut from the 50-foot roll and then sharpened.

Metal bead can be ordered only in 50-foot rolls. The galvanizing fluid is purchased in 5-gallon containers.

Inventory Master File

Description	*Unit of Measure*	*On Hand*	*On Order*	*Scheduled Receipt Date*	*Lead Time*
Bale	Ea	0	—	—	1
Barbed Wire	Ea	20	—	—	2
Barb	Ea	150	—	—	1
Coated Strand	Ea	50	—	—	1
Strand	Ea	10	—	—	1
Galvanized fluid	Oz	140	—	—	2
1-in bead length	Ea	350	—	—	1
1-ft bead length	Ea	300	—	—	1
Metal bead	Ft	150	50	Period 1	1

13-9. Spark, Short, & Fry, Inc. has been manufacturing electrical equipment since the early 1950s. The firm's most popular alternator, the famous "Zappo" model, has recently been restructured for assembly purposes. Because of favorable labor conditions, component parts are assembled in batch runs. At any given time each level of production has several partially assembled components. Given the following assembly and inventory information, construct a product structure diagram for the Zappo alternator, and plan the order releases necessary to assemble 400 alternators for period 10. 13-9. See Solutions Manual.

Description of the Production Process

Production of an alternator begins with the armature. The armature is placed and secured in a housing. Magnetic brushes are then installed on opposing sides of the armature housing. The rear armature cover is fitted on and held while the front cover is secured with longitudinal bolts. Next the pulley assembly is connected. Finally, contact wires are screwed on and the alternator is checked before shipping.

Inventory Master File

Item Description	*Lead Time*	*On Order*	*Scheduled Receipt Date*	*On Hand*	*Lot Size (multiples)*
Alternator	1	—	—	0	1
Contact wire	2	—	—	60	50
SA-410	1	—	—	80	1
Pulley assembly	3	100	Period 2	180	50
SA-310	1	—	—	20	1
Longitudinal bolt	3	—	—	210	100
Front cover	2	—	—	85	100
Rear cover	2	100	Period 1	0	100
SA-210	1	—	—	0	1
Magnetic brush	3	100	Period 1	180	100
SA-110	1	—	—	100	1
Armature	3	50	Period 2	75	50
Armature housing	4	50	Period 2	70	50

13-10. See Solutions Manual.

13-10. Valley's Hand-Vac is a small, portable vacuum cleaner that has become very popular in recent years. Attached is a page from Valley's parts manual. The Hand-Vac is made up of two major assemblies, the forward housing assembly and rear housing assembly. The rear housing assembly includes items 1 through 7 on the diagram. The front housing assembly consists of a front-end subassembly (items 12 through 15 on the diagram) and a completed fan subassembly (items 9 through 11 on the diagram). The Hand-Vac, three tools, and the packaging material make up the final product, a packaged Hand-Vac, ready for shipment.

Valley's production control staff would like to use an MRP system to plan its purchase and production orders. They have decided to start with the BOM module but are not sure how to structure a bill of material. Help them out by creating a product structure diagram for the Hand-Vac. Be sure to include assemblies and subassemblies that may not be listed in the parts list.

Parts List for Valley's Hand-Vac

No.	Part No.	Part name	Price	No.	Part No.	Part name	Price
1	51292	Outlet End	0.45	10	51488	Rotary Fan & Spacer Ass'y	0.45
2	51284	Handle	0.70	11	51281	Front Fan Cover	0.40
3	52043	Switch & Insulator	1.05	12	51272	Forward Housing	2.85
4	51576	Electric Cord	4.10	13	51286	Air Filter	0.40
5	51265	Rear Housing	2.05	14	52388	Reusable Bag	1.95
6	51268	Motor Mounting Plate	0.35	15	51288	Inlet End Ass'y	1.05
7	51495	Motor Ass'y & Fan Spacer	19.85	16	51642	Upholstery Tool	1.50
8	51270	Screw & Lock Washer Ass'y	0.05	17	52074	Crevice Tool	0.95
9	51273	Stationary Fan	0.45	18	50815	Dusting Tool	1.80
				19	57432	Packaging Material	2.00

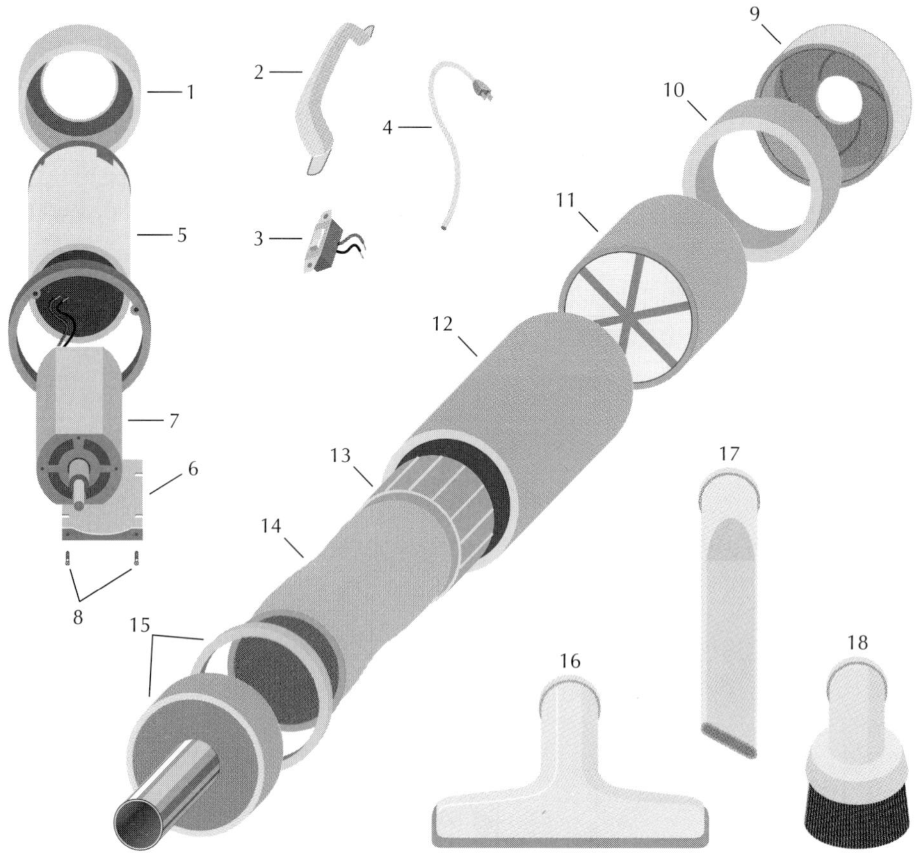

13-11. Given an ordering cost of $400 per order and a holding cost of $2 per unit per period, determine which lot-sizing technique(s) will result in the lowest total cost.

13-11. WW $3,240

Period	1	2	3	4	5	6	7	8	9	10
Demand	100	90	85	70	150	200	300	250	100	80

13-12. Given an ordering cost of $200 per order and a holding cost of $2 per unit per period, examine the following demand patterns and predict which lot-sizing technique(s) will result in the lowest total cost. Verify your predictions.

13-12. a. WW and EOQ
b. WW
c. WW and PPB
d. WW and PPB

a.

Period	1	2	3	4
Requirements	50	50	50	50

b.

Period	1	2	3	4
Requirements	50	10	50	10

c.

Period	1	2	3	4
Requirements	50	50	10	10

d.

Period	1	2	3	4
Requirements	50	10	10	50

13-13. Daily demand for an item over a 2-week time period is shown here. Assume a holding cost of $0.50 per unit per day, a setup cost of $100 per setup, and no units on hand or on order. Determine when a work order should be released for the item and the size of the order using any three of the lot-sizing techniques discussed in this chapter. Which technique produces the lowest total cost?

13-13. L4L $1,400, EOQ $941.50, PPB $730, WW* $700

Period	1	2	3	4	5	6	7	8	9	10	11	12	13	14
Demand	50	30	25	35	40	50	35	45	70	75	50	30	25	10

13-14. Given the following data, determine when orders should be released and the quantity of those orders using the part-period balancing lot-sizing technique. Also, calculate the total cost of the inventory policy. Does it provide any cost savings over lot-for-lot ordering?

13-14. $290; savings $70

LT = 0
Holding cost per unit per week = $1
Setup cost per setup = $60

Period	1	2	3	4	5	6
Requirements	10	60	20	30	10	60
GPP						
CGPP						
Order Period						
Order Size						

13-15. See Solutions Manual.

★ 13-15. Product A is assembled from one B and two C's. Each item requires one or more operations, as indicated by the circles in the product structure diagram. Assume lead time is negligible. From the information given:

a. Develop a load profile chart for each of the three work centers.
b. What would you recommend as normal capacity at each work center? How would you handle the overloads?

Product Structure Diagram

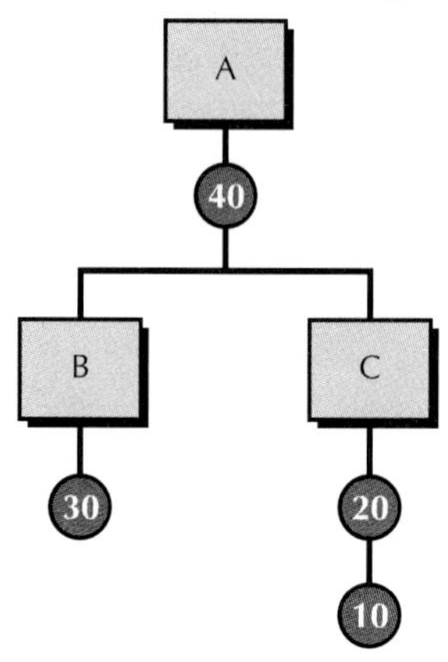

Master Production Schedule

Period	1	2	3	4	5	6
Product A	100	150	100	200	125	100

Routing and Work Standards File

Operation	*Item*	*Work Center*	*Standard Time per Unit (hr)*
10	C	Machining	0.50
20	C	Heat treat	2.00
30	B	Machining	1.00
40	A	Assembly	0.50

13-16. a. 12
b. See Solutions Manual.
c. 6,666; 4,000

13-16. The Best Wheel's Bicycle Company produces bicycles in different styles for boys and girls, in heights of 26 inches or 20 inches, and with ten speeds, three speeds, or one speed.

a. How many different kinds of bicycles does Best Wheels make?
b. Construct a modular bill of material for Best Wheels (one level). Assume that bike sales are equally split between boys and girls, 26-inch bikes are preferred two-to-one to 20-inch bikes, and three-speed bikes account for only 20 percent of sales. The remaining sales are divided equally between ten-speed and one-speed bikes.
c. If bicycle sales are expected to reach 10,000 over the holiday shopping season, how many 26-inch bikes should Best Wheels plan to produce? How many ten-speed bikes?

13-17. See Solutions Manual.

13-17. The Best Wheels Bicycle Company has scheduled the production of the following bicycles this month.

	Model	Week 1	2	3	4
(B2610)	Boy's 26-inch 10-speed	50	100	200	150
(G2610)	Girl's 26-inch 10-speed	50	100	200	150
(B2003)	Boy's 20-inch 3-speed	15	30	60	45
(G2003)	Girl's 20-inch 3-speed	15	30	60	45
(B2001)	Boy's 20-inch 1-speed	20	40	80	60
(G2001)	Girl's 20-inch 1-speed	20	40	80	60

The two critical work centers for producing these bikes are welding and assembly. Welding has an efficiency of 95 percent and a utilization of 90 percent. Assembly has an efficiency of 90 percent and a utilization of 92 percent. The time required (in hours) by each bike in the two work centers is as follows:

	Welding	*Assembly*
B2610	0.20	0.18
G2610	0.22	0.18
B2003	0.15	0.15
G2003	0.17	0.15
B2001	0.07	0.10
G2001	0.09	0.10

a. Assume 40 hours is available per week for each work center. Calculate the capacity and load percent per work center per week and construct a load profile chart for each work center.
b. If any number of hours could be scheduled for each work center, how many hours should be scheduled so that the work center loads do not exceed 100 percent?
c. If utilization and efficiency for both work centers can be increased to 99 percent, how many hours should be scheduled so that work center loads are still under 100 percent?

13-18. Jones' Dry Cleaning has just purchased a new machine that can press an entire shirt in 1 minute. The machine requires no setup beyond an initial warmup of 15 minutes at the beginning of a day. The old machine takes 4 minutes to press a shirt plus 1 minute to reposition the shirt during the process. If 250 shirts are waiting to be pressed, how long will it take to finish the day's work in each case?

a. On the old machine alone
b. On the new machine alone
c. If the shirts are split evenly between the new machine and old machine
d. If the optimal split between the old and new machine is used

13-18. a. 20.8 hr
b. 4.4 hr
c. 10.4 hr
d. 3.75 hr

13-19. Consider the following products manufactured by Kidstyle International, their master schedule, and inventory records. Assume all quantities per assembly are one. Generate MRP matrices for all items. It should be apparent that some rescheduling must take place.

Use the MRP matrices, the attached scheduling notes, and policies provided by Kidstyles, and your knowledge as an MRP planner to identify the options in meeting the prospective shortages. What are the ramifications of

★ 13-19. See Solutions Manual.

Teaching Note 13.8 Advanced MRP Problem

each option? Which option would you recommend and why? Your report should include a printout of the MRP matrices as they would appear after your recommendations have been enacted.

Bill of Material

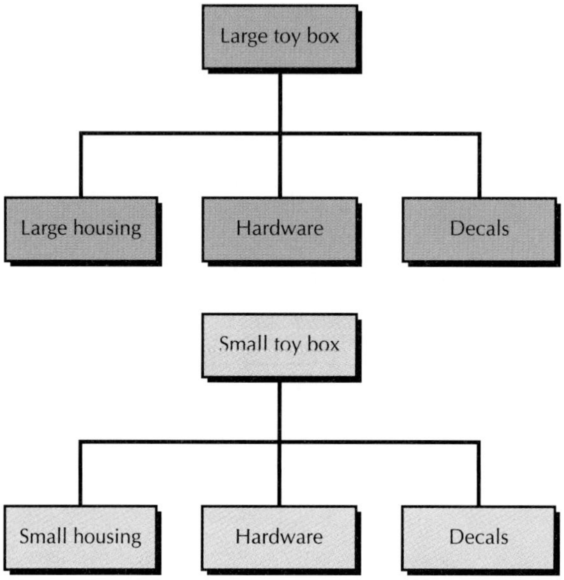

Large toy box
- Large housing
- Hardware
- Decals

Small toy box
- Small housing
- Hardware
- Decals

Master Production Schedule

Item	1	2	3	4	5	6	7	8
Large toy box		30		60		30		
Small toy box	25		45	60		30		

Item Master File

Item	*On Hand*	*Safety Stock*	*LT*	*Lot Size*	*Scheduled Receipt Period*	*Scheduled Receipt Quantity*	*Unit Value*
Large toy box	30	0	2	Mult 50	—	—	$50.00
Small toy box	25	0	2	L4L	—	—	30.00
Large housing	35	0	2	Mult 100	—	—	15.00
Small housing	45	0	2	Mult 75	—	—	10.00
Hardware	55	0	2	Mult 40	2	40	5.00
Decals	50	0	2	L4L	2	50	5.00

Kidstyle's Scheduling Notes and Policies

1. Monthly sales forecasts should be met within plus or minus 10 percent.
2. Delay of a customer's order costs 10 percent of the value of the order per week.
3. Customer orders may be delayed a maximum of 2 weeks.
4. It is possible to halve lead time, but the cost of producing or ordering the item increases by 50 percent (e.g., workers get paid time and a half for overtime.)

Pegging Report

REQUIREMENTS			SOURCE		
Item	*Period*	*Quantity*	*Type*	*Reference*	*Period*
Small toy box	1	25	MS-CO	B070002	1
	3	45	MS-CO	B070002	3
	4	30	MS-CO	B064444	4
		30	MS-FO	Z842009	
	6	30	MS-FO		6
Large toy box	2	30	MS-CO	A080100	2
	4	30	MS-CO	B064444	4
		30	MS-FO	Z900620	
	6	30	MS-FO		6

TYPE codes: MS-FO—forecasts from master schedule
MS-CO—customer order from master schedule
MS-SP—service parts from master schedule

CASE PROBLEM

See Solutions Manual.

Renovating the Grand Palms Hotel

Myra's hand ached from all the notes she had taken on her tour of the Grand Palms Hotel with the corporate renovation team. She sat at her desk trying to make sense of all the changes that had to be made. The Grand Palms is an older, eight-floor hotel consisting of 36 efficiency rooms and 64 one-bedroom apartments. Its guests, mainly D.C. lobbyists, typically stay months at a time while Congress is in session. The renovation is to be conducted during a 2-month recess at the rate of one floor per week.

The renovation of each efficiency requires new pad and carpet (145 square feet), new blackout draperies and sheers (50 yards of material), new window blinds (2 sets), a reupholstered sofa (12 yards of material), reupholstered dining chairs (4 chairs, 1 yard of material each), a new floor lamp, a new desk lamp, a new end table, new artwork (one still life), and a new evacuation plaque (in four languages).

Each one-bedroom apartment requires new pad and carpet (300 square feet), new blackout draperies and sheers (78 yards of material), new window blinds (2 sets), a reupholstered sofa (22 yards of material), reupholstered dining chairs (5 chairs, 1 yard of material each), a new floor lamp, a new desk lamp, a new end table, new artwork (two landscapes—coventry and reflections), and a new evacuation plaque (in four languages). The dining chairs are covered in a single solid color, while the sofa and bedspread are covered in the same material as the drapes.

Forty-two units will be decorated in a pink/gray motif (floors 2, 5, and 8), and fifty-eight will be done in a blue/green motif (floors 1, 3, 4, 6, and 7). Floor 1 has 10 units, floors 2 and 8 have 15 units, and the remaining floors each have 12 units. The efficiencies are located on the odd-numbered floors, and the one-bedroom apartments are on the even-numbered floors. Each floor has a different evacuation plaque.

"It'll take me a week to put this together into some kind of schedule," sighed Myra.

1. How would an MRP system help in scheduling the renovation process (and make Myra's job easier)?
2. Show how a bill of material could be constructed for renovation of the Grand Palms Hotel. (Choose one floor as an illustration.)
3. Assuming the work begins on the top floor and proceeds downward, determine the requirements for 1 week of the renovation.

See Solutions Manual.

CASE PROBLEM

Three Long Years

Bob Bryant looked at the reports in front of him and the five managers seated at the table. He wondered how his staff was going to explain this month's factory performance. Bob was the plant manager at Taylor Scientific Equipment, whose main customers were universities and the U.S. government. About 3 years ago, at the suggestion of the Department of Defense, the company had purchased an MRP II system to satisfy the government's record-keeping requirements. Bob had supported the move in hopes that the MRP system would solve the plant's efficiency problems as well. But things had not exactly turned out as planned. So far as he could tell, only two of the system's ten modules were up and running, shipping and sales. It was time for some answers.

"John, let's go through the process again. Tell me what happens when an order is received."

"Since each customer order is unique, we sit down and develop a bill of material for the order."

"Sit down where—at the computer terminal?"

"No, actually we develop the bill by hand and then input it into the MRP system."

"But once the BOM is in the system, it generates routings and a schedule?"

"We wish. Right now the routings are also developed manually and then input into the system, and the work standards, too."

"I suppose capacity planning is out of the question."

"We do that manually, but its more like capacity control. We evaluate how well we've used the shop's capacity at the end of each week."

"And how are the lessons learned incorporated into next week's schedule?"

John squirmed, "I just remember them."

"I see. Fred, how is the inventory system coming along?"

"Great. We have this new bar-coded inventory information system that gives us more accurate information on what inventory is where. It's very fast and . . . "

"And it feeds this information directly into the MRP system?"

"Well, no. . . . "

"I know, WE DO THAT MANUALLY," chorused Bob in unison with Fred. His frustration was beginning to show.

"I have some good news to report," volunteered Donna from data processing. "In our preliminary test of the shop floor control module, Department 074 says the daily schedules we provide them with are the best thing we've done for them in years. In fact, they even came up with some suggestions for improving the report format to make it easier to use, which we took care of that very day. Right, Terry?"

"I hate to burst your bubble, Donna," spoke up Terry from 074, "but in all honesty, we asked you to triple-space the schedule so we could write our own one in beneath it. It saves us a lot of time having the work orders, machine centers, and workers listed on one page like you've done."

Bob threw up his hands in disgust, "Well, fellas, it looks like our company has invested $100,000 in a fancy report generator."

1. Why do you think Taylor Scientific is having so much difficulty implementing an MRP system?
2. What can Bob do, as plant manager, to remedy the situation?

REFERENCES

DeMatteis, J. J., "An Economic Lot-Sizing Technique: The Part-Period Algorithm," *IBM Systems Journal* (1968): 30–38.

Fox, R. E., "MRP, Kanban or OPT, What's Best?" *Inventories and Production,* (January–February 1982).

Garwood, D., "Stop Before You Use the Bill Processor . . . ," *Production and Inventory Management* (2nd Quarter, 1970): 73–75.

Kanet, J. J., "MRP 96: Time to Rethink Manufacturing Logistics," *Production and Inventory Management,* (Second Quarter, 1988): 57–61.

Orlicky, J., *Material Requirements Planning,* New York: McGraw-Hill, 1975.

Steinberg, E., and A. Napier, "Optimal Multilevel Lot Sizing for Requirements Planning Systems," *Management Science* 26, no. 12 (December 1980): 1258–72.

Tersine, R. J., *Production/Operations Management: Concepts, Structure, and Analysis,* New York: Elsevier North Holland, 1985.

Vollman, T. E., W. L. Berry, and D. C. Whybark, *Manufacturing Planning and Control Systems,* 3rd ed., Homewood, Ill.: Irwin, 1992.

Wallace, T. F., *MRP II: Making It Happen,* Essex Junction, Vt.: Oliver Wight Limited Publications, 1985.

Wight, O., *Production Planning and Inventory Control in the Computer Age,* Boston: Cahners Books International, 1974.

Yelle, L. E., "Material Requirements Lot Sizing: A Multi-Level Approach," *International Journal of Production Research* 17, no. 3 (1979): 223–232.

14

SCHEDULING

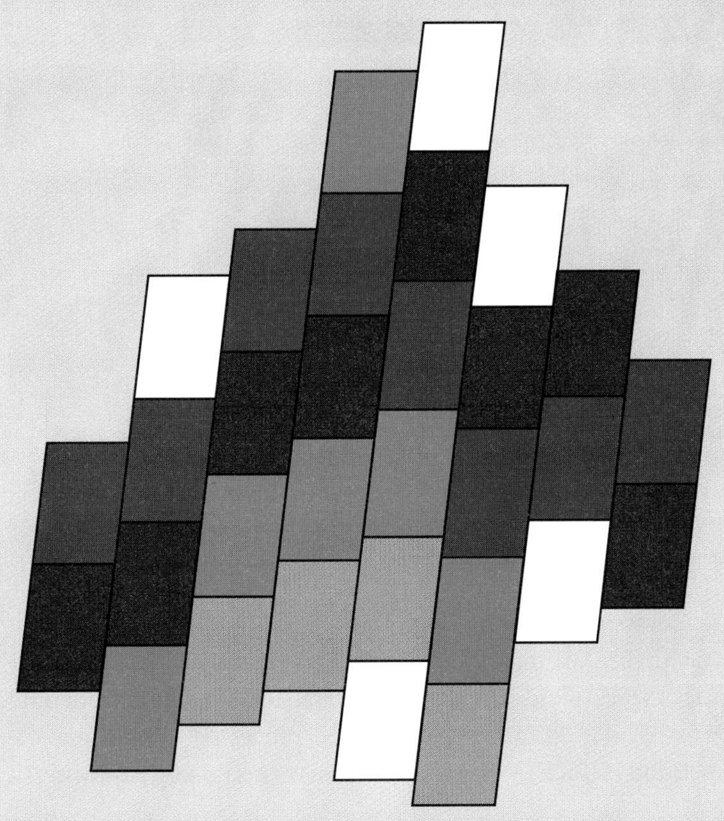

CHAPTER OUTLINE

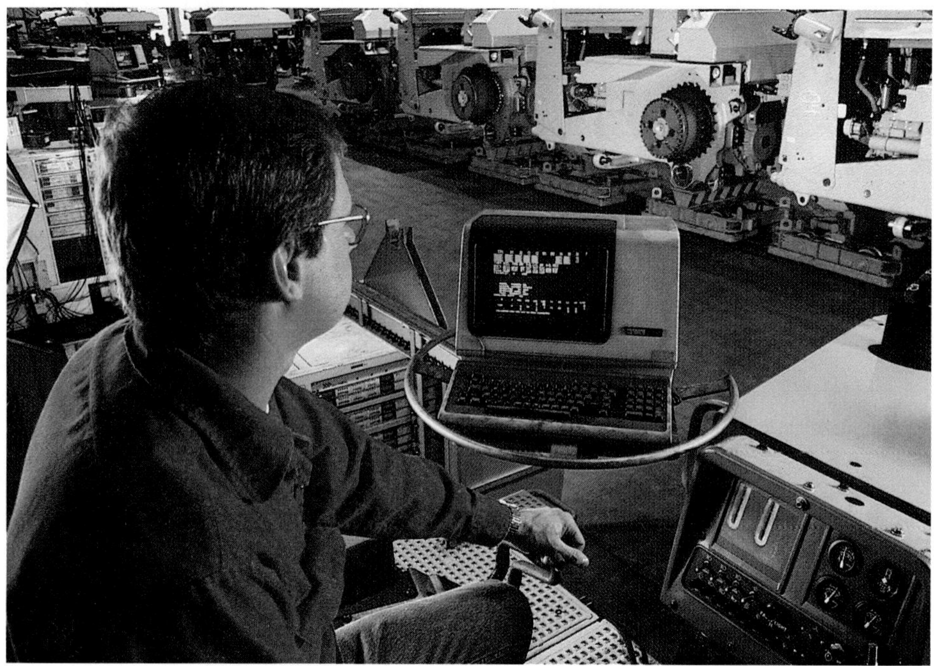

Scheduling decisions involve a wide range of activities including worker and machine assignment, job sequencing, and the coordination of material handling and maintenance support. In this picture a material handler examines a computerized dispatch list and receives on-line information about pickups and deliveries.

HOT, WARM, AND COLD AT TCONA

The TCONA (Truck Components Operations North American) Division of Eaton Corporation manufactures transmissions, axles, and brake components for medium to heavy trucks worldwide. The plant has 700 machine tools divided into five departments. More than 75 different parts can be processed in each department, and between 600 and 700 active part numbers are in production in any given month.

With the advent of JIT, TCONA customers are no longer satisfied with lengthy lead times; they place their orders in smaller volumes more frequently. This makes the task of scheduling more critical. For example, machinists can find themselves tearing down and setting up new jobs of ten to fifteen parts several times a day. This is no problem for those work centers that have been automated by CNC machines, but for older machines, it can significantly delay production. When this occurred at TCONA, Eaton quickly realized that it could not afford the capital investment required to automate operations completely. It's a good thing they did not have the resources to automate because as it turns out, they didn't need to. What they needed was a more effective scheduling system.

Scheduling is the last stage of planning before production.

They chose FACTOR, a computerized scheduling system that allows the user to select from among eighteen different scheduling rules or create their own. Eaton created a priority sequencing rule that divides a 30-day schedule into three categories: hot, warm, and cold. Customer orders due in less than 10 days are placed in the "hot" category and processed according to earliest due date. Customer orders due in 10 to 20 days are placed in the "warm" category and prioritized by minimum setup time, unless it causes the job to become "hot," in which case it reverts to earliest due date. The remaining customer orders are classified as "cold" orders and are processed by minimum setup alone.

Within 6 months of using the new scheduling system, Eaton TCONA's shaft department had reduced setups and increased output by almost 30 percent. Late shipments to customers were entirely eliminated.[1]

Scheduling specifies *when* labor, equipment, and facilities are needed to produce a product or provide a service. It is the last stage of planning before production takes place.

The scheduling function differs considerably based on the type of operation. In process industries, such as chemicals and pharmaceuticals, scheduling might consist of determining the mix of ingredients that goes into a vat or when the system should stop producing one type of mixture, clean out the vat, and start producing another. Linear programming can find the lowest-cost mix of ingredients, and the economic production quantity (EPQ) can determine the optimum length of a production run. These techniques are described in detail in Chapters 2 Supplement and Chapter 12, respectively.

For mass production, the schedule of production is pretty much determined when the assembly line is laid out. Products simply flow down the assembly line from one station to the next in the same prescribed, nondeviating order every time. Day-to-day scheduling decisions consist of determining how fast to feed items into the line and how many hours per day to run the line. On a mixed-model assembly line, the order of products assembled also has to be determined.

The scheduling function differs by type of process.

For projects, the scheduling decisions are so numerous and interrelated that specialized project-scheduling techniques such as PERT and CPM have been devised. Chapter 17 is devoted to these planning and control tools for project management.

For batch or job shop production, scheduling decisions can be quite complex. In previous chapters, we discussed *aggregate planning,* which plans for the production of product lines or families; *master scheduling,* which plans for the production of individual end items or finished goods; and *material requirements planning* (MRP) and *capacity requirements planning* (CRP), which plan for the production of components and assemblies. Scheduling determines to which machine a part will be routed for processing, which worker will operate a machine that produces a part, and the order in which the parts are to be processed. Scheduling also determines which patient to assign to an operating room, which doctors and nurses are to care for a patient during certain hours of the day, the order in which a doctor is to see patients, and when meals should be delivered or medications dispensed. What makes scheduling so difficult in a job shop is the variety of jobs (or patients) that are processed, each with distinctive routing and processing requirements. In addition, although the volume of each customer order may be small, there are probably a great number of different orders in the shop at any one time. This necessitates planning for the production of each job as it arrives, scheduling its use of limited resources, and monitoring its progress through the system.

This chapter concentrates on scheduling issues for job shop production. We will discuss several objectives for scheduling, the role of scheduling, and different scheduling techniques. We will also examine problems associated with poor scheduling performance and some commonsense approaches to scheduling. We will conclude by considering two specific scheduling applications, maintenance scheduling and personnel scheduling.

[1]Credle, Russell, "Finite Scheduling Helps Eaton Cut Line Setups and Increase Line Throughput," *APICS—The Performance Advantage* (January 1993): 30–32.

OBJECTIVES IN SCHEDULING

There are many possible objectives in constructing a schedule, including

- Meeting customer due dates;
- Minimizing job lateness;
- Minimizing response time;
- Minimizing completion time;
- Minimizing time in the system;
- Minimizing overtime;
- Maximizing machine or labor utilization;
- Minimizing idle time; and
- Minimizing work-in-process inventory.

Transparency 14.1 Objectives in Scheduling

Managers have multiple, conflicting scheduling objectives.

Shop floor control is the scheduling and monitoring of day-to-day production in a job shop.

Job shop scheduling is also known as **shop floor control** (**SFC**), *production control*, and *production activity control* (PAC). Regardless of their primary scheduling objective, manufacturers will typically have a **production control department** whose responsibilities consist of the following:

Transparency 14.2 Production Control

Loading is the process of assigning work to limited resources, and **load leveling** is the process of smoothing out the work assigned.

The **dispatch list** is a shop paper that specifies the sequence in which jobs should be processed.

1. *Checking the availability of material, machines, and labor.* The MRP system plans for material availability. CRP converts the material plan into machine and labor requirements and projects resource overloads and underloads. Production control assigns work to individual workers or machines and then attempts to smooth out the load to make the MRP schedule "doable." These activities are called **loading** and **load leveling,** respectively.
2. *Releasing work orders to the shop and issuing dispatch lists for individual machines.* MRP recommends when orders should be released (hence the name, *planned* order releases). After verifying their feasibility, production control actually releases the orders. When several orders are released to one machine center, they must be prioritized so that the worker will know which ones to do first. The **dispatch list** contains the sequence in which jobs should be processed. This sequence is often based on certain *sequencing rules.*
3. *Maintaining progress reports on each job until it is completed.* This monitoring function of production control is an important activity because items may need to be rescheduled as changes occur in the system. In addition to timely data collection, it involves the use of Gantt charts and input/output control charts.

LOADING

Transparency 14.3 Loading

Many times an operation can be performed by various persons, machines, or work centers but with varying efficiencies. If there is enough capacity, it would, of course, be wisest to assign each worker to the task that he or she performs best and each job to the machine that can process it most efficiently. In effect, that is what happens when CRP generates a load profile for each machine center. The routing file used by CRP lists the machine that can perform the job most efficiently first. If no overloads appear in the load profile, then production control can proceed to the next task of sequencing the work at each center. However, when resource constraints produce overloads in the load profile, production control must examine the list of jobs initially assigned and decide which jobs to reassign elsewhere. The problem of determining how best to allocate jobs to machines or workers to tasks can be solved with heuristics, such as the *index method,* or with mathematical programming techniques, such as the *assignment method* of linear programming.

Index Method

The index method is a heuristic that will provide a good solution to a problem but does not guarantee an optimum solution. The procedure is as follows:

1. Construct a table with the jobs to be assigned listed along the side and the machine centers or other resources listed across the top. If machine center capacities are given, list them across the bottom of the table. Fill in the table with the cost or time required to process each job at each machine center.
2. Calculate an *index* for each job at each machine by dividing the smallest value in a row into every other value in the row.
3. Find the lowest index in each column. An index of 1.00 represents the best assignment for a particular job. Assign the job with the lowest index to the machine represented by that column.
4. Continue until no more jobs can be allocated or no more capacity is available.

The *index method* of loading is a simple heuristic.

EXAMPLE 14.1

The Index Method of Shop Loading

Alternate Example 14.1

Problem Statement:

Southern Cans packages processed food into cans for a variety of customers. The factory has four multipurpose cookers and canning lines that can pressure-cook, vacuum-pack, and apply labels to just about any type of food or size of can. However, the processing equipment was purchased some years apart and some of the cookers are faster and more efficient than others. The scheduler at Southern Cans, Tom Clark, has four orders that need to be run today for a particular customer: canned beans, canned peaches, canned tomatoes, and canned corn. The customer is operating under a just-in-time production system and needs the mixed order of canned food tomorrow. Tom has estimated the number of hours required to pressure-cook, process, and can each type of food by type of cooker as follows:

	COOKER			
FOOD	1	2	3	4
Beans	10	5	6	10
Peaches	6	2	4	6
Tomatoes	7	6	5	6
Corn	9	5	4	10

Due to time constraints imposed by lengthy changeover procedures, only one job can be assigned to each cooker. How should the jobs be assigned to the cookers in order to process the food most efficiently (i.e., in the least amount of time)?

Solution:

- *Matrix of row indices:* First we prepare a matrix of row indices by dividing the entries in row 1 by 5, in row 2 by 2, in row 3 by 5, and in row 4 by 4.

2.00	1.00	1.20	2.00
3.00	1.00	2.00	3.00
[1.40]	1.20	1.00	1.20
2.25	1.25	1.00	2.50

- *Assignment by column:* Next, we look for the lowest value in each column, beginning with column 1. The lowest index in column 1 is 1.40, so we assign tomatoes to cooker 1. Row 3 and column 1 can now be eliminated from the matrix.

1.00	1.20	2.00
1.00	2.00	3.00
1.25	[1.00]	2.50

There is a tie for lowest value in column 2, so we proceed to column 3 and assign corn to cooker 3. The matrix is reduced further by eliminating row 4 and column 3.

1.00	[2.00]
[1.00]	3.00

The lowest value in column 4 is 2.00, so we assign beans to cooker 4. That leaves peaches to be assigned to cooker 2.

Referring back to our original matrix, the assignment is as follows:

	COOKER			
FOOD	*1*	*2*	*3*	*4*
Beans	10	5	6	[10]
Peaches	6	[2]	4	6
Tomatoes	[7]	6	5	6
Corn	9	5	[4]	10

The total machine time required to process all four jobs is 10 + 2 + 7 + 4 = 32 hours. However, given that the four cooking/canning lines can operate simultaneously, the customer's order will be completed in the maximum time required to process any one of the four jobs, that is, 10 hours.

Assignment Method

The *assignment method* of loading is a form of linear programming.

The *assignment method* is a specialized linear programming solution procedure that is much simpler to apply than the simplex method discussed in Chapter 2 Supplement. Given a table of jobs and machines, it develops an *opportunity cost matrix* for assigning particular jobs to particular machines. With this technique, only one job may be assigned to each machine. The procedure is as follows:

1. Perform *row reductions* by subtracting the minimum value in each row from all other row values.
2. Perform *column reductions* by subtracting the minimum value in each column from all other column values.
3. The resulting table is an *opportunity cost matrix.* Cross out all zeros in the matrix using the minimum number of horizontal or vertical lines.

4. If the number of lines equals the number of rows in the matrix, an optimum solution has been reached and assignments can be made where the zeros appear. Otherwise, *modify the matrix* by subtracting the minimum uncrossed value from all other uncrossed values and adding this same amount to all cells where two lines intersect. All other values in the matrix remain unchanged.
5. Repeat steps 3 and 4 until an optimum solution is reached.

EXAMPLE 14.2

Alternate Example 14.2

The Assignment Method of Loading

Problem Statement:

Solve the loading problem described in Example 14.1 by the assignment method. Compare the results with the index method.

Solution:

Row reduction:

$$\begin{matrix} 5 & 0 & 1 & 5 \\ 4 & 0 & 2 & 4 \\ 2 & 1 & 0 & 1 \\ 5 & 1 & 0 & 6 \end{matrix}$$

Column reduction:

$$\begin{matrix} 3 & 0 & 1 & 4 \\ 2 & 0 & 2 & 3 \\ 0 & 1 & 0 & 0 \\ 3 & 1 & 0 & 5 \end{matrix}$$

Cover all zeros:

$$\begin{matrix} 3 & 0 & 1 & 4 \\ 2 & 0 & 2 & 3 \\ \text{—}0 & \text{—}1\text{—} & 0\text{—} & 0\text{—} \\ 3 & 1 & 0 & 5 \end{matrix}$$

Since the number of lines does not equal the number of rows, continue.
Modify the matrix:

$$\begin{matrix} 1 & 0 & 1 & 2 \\ 0 & 0 & 2 & 1 \\ 0 & 3 & 2 & 0 \\ 1 & 1 & 0 & 3 \end{matrix}$$

Cover all zeros:

$$\begin{matrix} 1 & 0 & 1 & 2 \\ 0 & 0 & 2 & 1 \\ 0 & 3 & 2 & 0 \\ 1 & 1 & 0 & 3 \end{matrix}$$

Since the number of lines equals the number of rows, we have reached the optimum solution.

Make assignments:

FOOD	COOKER 1	2	3	4
Beans	1	[0]	1	2
Peaches	[0]	0	2	1
Tomatoes	0	3	2	[0]
Corn	1	1	[0]	5

The first row has only one zero, so beans are assigned to cooker 2. The last row has only one zero, so corn is assigned to cooker 3. The second row has two zeros, but cooker 2 is already occupied, so peaches are assigned to cooker 1. That leaves cooker 4 for tomatoes. Referring back to our original matrix,

FOOD	COOKER 1	2	3	4
Beans	10	[5]	6	10
Peaches	[6]	2	4	6
Tomatoes	7	6	5	[6]
Corn	9	5	[4]	10

the total time to process all four jobs is 5 + 6 + 6 + 4 = 21 hours. Given that the four cooker/canning lines can operate simultaneously, we can complete the customer's order in 6 hours.

Notice that this solution completes the customer's order 4 hours sooner than the index method solution. Also, 11 fewer hours of machine time are required for the assignment model solution.

Assignment models can be solved with AB:POM. Solutions are given in terms of minimizing cost or maximizing profit, although the solution could represent minimized time or maximized quality levels or other such variables. Also, the solution can be provided for minimizing the sum of assignment values or minimizing the worst value. The latter case, called the *bottleneck problem,* is useful in situations like Example 14.2 where machines may be operating simultaneously. In that case the completion time of a group of jobs is the *maximum* completion time of the individual jobs rather than the sum of completion times. The assignment method does not guarantee optimality in minimizing a maximum value.

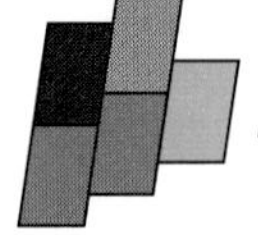

SEQUENCING

Sequencing prioritizes jobs that have been assigned to a resource.

Transparency 14.4 Sequencing

When more than one job is assigned to a machine, the operator needs to know the order in which he or she is to process the jobs. The process of prioritizing jobs is called **sequencing.** If no particular order is specified, the operator would probably process the job that arrived first to the machine. This default sequence is called *first-come, first-served* (FCFS). Or, if jobs are stacked upon arrival to a machine, it might be easier to process the job first that arrived last and is now on top of the stack. This is called *last-come, first-served* (LCFS) sequencing.

Another common approach is to process the job first that is due the soonest or the job that has the highest customer priority. These are known as *earliest due date*

(DDATE) and *highest customer priority* (CUSTPR) sequencing, respectively. Operators may also look through a stack of jobs to find one with a *similar setup* to the job that is currently being processed (SETUP). That would minimize the downtime of the machine and make the operator's job easier.

Variations on the DDATE rule include *minimum slack* (SLACK) and *smallest critical ratio* (CR). SLACK considers the work remaining to be performed on a job as well as the time remaining (until the due date) to perform that work. Jobs are processed first that have the least difference (or slack) between the two, as follows:

a sampling of heuristic sequencing rules

$$\text{SLACK} = (\text{due date} - \text{today's date}) - (\text{remaining processing time})$$

The critical ratio uses the same information as SLACK but arranges it in ratio form so that scheduling performance can be easily assessed. Mathematically, the CR is calculated as follows:

$$\text{CR} = \frac{\text{time remaining}}{\text{work remaining}} = \frac{\text{due date} - \text{today's date}}{\text{remaining processing time}}$$

If the work remaining is greater than the time remaining, the critical ratio will be less than 1. Conversely, if the time remaining is greater than the work remaining, the critical ratio will be greater than 1. Of course, if time remaining equals work remaining, the critical ratio exactly equals 1. Thus, the critical ratio allows us to make the following statements about our schedule:

If CR > 1, then the job is *ahead of schedule.*
If CR < 1, then the job is *behind schedule.*
If CR = 1, then the job is exactly *on schedule.*

Other sequencing rules examine processing time and order the work either by shortest processing time (SPT) or longest processing time (LPT). LPT operates on the implicit assumption that long jobs are important jobs and is analogous to the strategy of doing larger tasks first to get them out of the way. SPT focuses instead on shorter jobs and is able to complete many more jobs earlier than LPT. With either rule, some jobs may be inordinately late because they are always put at the back of a queue.

All these "rules" for arranging jobs in a certain order for processing seem reasonable. We might wonder which methods are best or if it really matters which jobs are processed first anyway. Perhaps a few examples will help answer those questions.

Teaching Note 14.1 AB:POM for Scheduling

Sequencing Jobs Through One Machine

The simplest sequencing problem consists of a queue of jobs at one machine. No new jobs arrive to the machine during the analysis, processing times and due dates are fixed, and setup time is considered negligible. For this scenario, the *completion time* (also called **flow time**) of each job will differ depending on its place in the sequence, but the overall completion time for the set of jobs (called the **makespan**), will not change. **Tardiness** measures the difference between a job's due date and its completion time for those jobs completed after their due date. Even in this simple case, there is no sequencing rule that optimizes both processing efficiency and due date performance. Let's consider an example.

Flow time is the time it takes a job to flow through the system; **makespan** is the time it takes for a group of jobs to be completed.

Tardiness is the difference between the late job's due date and its completion time.

EXAMPLE 14.3

Simple Sequencing Rules

Video 14.1 *COMAP,* Program 3: "Juggling Machines"

Alternate Example 14.3

Problem Statement:

Today is the morning of October 1. Because of the approaching holiday season, Joe Palotty is scheduled to work 7 days a week for the next 2 months. October's work for Joe consists of five jobs, A, B, C, D, and E. Job A takes 5 days to complete and is due October 10, job B takes 10 days to complete and is due October 15, job C takes 2 days to process and is due October 5, job D takes 8 days to process and is due October 12, and job E, which takes 6 days to process, is due October 8.

There are 120 possible sequences for the five jobs. Clearly, enumeration is impossible. Let's try some simple sequencing rules. Sequence the jobs by: a. first-come, first-served (FCFS), b. earliest due date (DDATE), c. minimum slack (SLACK), d. smallest critical ratio (CR), and e. shortest processing time (SPT). Determine the completion time and tardiness of each job under each sequencing rule. Should Joe process his work as is, that is, first-come, first-served? If not, what sequencing rule would you recommend to Joe?

Solution:

a. FCFS: Process the jobs in order of their arrival, A, B, C, D, E.

Sequence	*Processing Time*	*Completion Time*	*Due Date*	*Tardiness*
A	5	5	10	0
B	10	15	15	0
C	2	17	5	12
D	8	25	12	13
E	6	31	8	23
Average		18.60		9.6

b. DDATE: Sequence the jobs by earliest due date.

Sequence	*Processing Time*	*Completion Time*	*Due Date*	*Tardiness*
C	2	2	5	0
E	6	8	8	0
A	5	13	10	3
D	8	21	12	9
B	10	31	15	16
Average		15.00		5.6

c. SLACK: Sequence the jobs by minimum slack. The slack for each job is calculated as: (due date – today's date) – processing time.

Job	
Job A	(10 – 1) – 5 = 4
B	(15 – 1) – 10 = 4
C	(5 – 1) – 2 = 2
D	(12 – 1) – 8 = 3
E	(8 – 1) – 6 = 1

Sequence	*Processing Time*	*Completion Time*	*Due Date*	*Tardiness*
E	6	6	8	0
C	2	8	5	3
D	8	16	12	4
A	5	21	10	11
B	10	31	15	16
Average		16.40		6.8

d. CR: Sequence the jobs by smallest critical ratio, calculated as:

$$CR = \frac{\text{time remain}}{\text{work remain}}$$

Job	*CR*
A	$\frac{(10-1)}{5} = 1.80$
B	$\frac{(15-1)}{10} = 1.40$
C	$\frac{(5-1)}{2} = 2.00$
D	$\frac{(12-1)}{8} = 1.37$
E	$\frac{(8-1)}{6} = 1.16$

Sequence	*Processing Time*	*Completion Time*	*Due Date*	*Tardiness*
E	6	6	8	0
D	8	14	12	2
B	10	24	15	9
A	5	29	10	19
C	2	31	5	26
Average		20.8		11.2

e. SPT: Sequence the jobs by smallest processing time.

Sequence	*Processing Time*	*Completion Time*	*Due Date*	*Tardiness*
C	2	2	5	0
A	5	7	10	0
E	6	13	8	5
D	8	21	12	9
B	10	31	15	16
Average		14.80		6

Summary

Rule	*Average Completion Time*	*Average Tardiness*	*No. of Jobs Tardy*	*Maximum Tardiness*
FCFS	18.60	9.6	3*	23
DDATE	15.00	5.6*	3*	16*
SLACK	16.40	6.8	4	16*
CR	20.80	11.2	4	26
SPT	14.80*	6.0	3*	16*

*Best Value

All the sequencing rules complete the month's work by October 31, as planned. However, no sequencing rule is able to complete *all* jobs on time. FCFS requires an average of 18.6 days to complete each job, compared to 15 days for DDATE, 16.4 days for SLACK, 20.8 days for CR, and 14.8 days for SPT. FCFS, DDATE, and SPT complete three jobs after their due date, whereas SLACK and CR complete four jobs tardy. The maximum tardiness for FCFS is 23 days (for job E). That's better than the maximum tardiness of 26 days for CR (for job C), but worse than the maximum tardiness of 16 days for DDATE, SLACK, and SPT (for job B).

DDATE has the lowest mean tardiness of 7 days, compared to an average of 8.5 days tardy for SLACK, 10 days tardy for SPT, 14 days tardy for CR, and 16 days for FCFS. From these results, it is clear that the performance of FCFS is either met or exceeded by DDATE and SPT. Thus, Joe should take the time to sequence this month's work.

Whether Joe sequences his work by DDATE, SLACK, or SPT depends on the objectives of the company for whom he works. DDATE produces the lowest mean tardiness but has more jobs tardy than SPT. The particular jobs that are tardy may also make a difference. SPT completes more jobs faster than DDATE or SLACK but takes longer to complete the tardy jobs.

There is no one sequencing rule that optimizes both processing efficiency and due date performance.

Are the preceding results a function of this particular example, or are they indicative of the types of results we will get whenever these rules are applied? Analytically, we can prove that for a set number of jobs to be processed on *one* machine, the SPT sequencing rule will minimize mean job completion time (also known as flowtime) and minimize mean number of jobs in the system. On the other hand, the DDATE sequencing rule will minimize mean tardiness and maximum tardiness. No definitive statements can be made concerning the performance of the other sequencing rules.

Sequencing Jobs Through Two Serial Machines

Johnson's rule gives an optimum sequence for jobs processed serially through two machines.

Since few factories consist of just one machine, we might wonder if techniques exist that will produce an optimal sequence for any number of jobs that must be processed through more than one machine. **Johnson's rule** finds the fastest way to process a series of jobs through a two-machine system where every job follows the same sequence on the two machines. Based on a variation of the SPT rule, it requires that the sequence be "mapped out" to determine the final completion time, or makespan, for the set of jobs. The procedure is as follows:

Teaching Note 14.2 Example of Johnson's Rule for More Than Two Machines

1. List the time required to process each job at each machine center. Set up a one-dimensional matrix to represent the desired sequence with the number of slots equal to the number of jobs.
2. Select the smallest processing time at either machine. If that time occurs at machine center 1, put the associated job as near to the *beginning* of the sequence as possible.
3. If that time occurs at machine center 2, put the associated job as near to the *end* of the sequence as possible.
4. Remove the job from the list.
5. Repeat steps 2–4 until all slots in the matrix have been filled or all jobs have been sequenced.

Alternate Example 14.4

EXAMPLE 14.4

Johnson's Rule

Problem Statement:

Johnson's job shop has five jobs that must be sanded first at machine center 1 and then painted at machine center 2. Given the following processing times, determine the sequence that will allow the set of five jobs to be completed as soon as possible. Calculate the final completion time for the set of jobs and the idle time of each machine center.

Job	*Machine Center 1*	*Machine Center 2*
A	6	8
B	11	6
C	7	3
D	9	7
E	5	10

Solution:

The smallest processing time, 3 hours, occurs at machine center 2 for job C, so we place job C as near to the end of the sequence as possible. C is now eliminated from the job list.

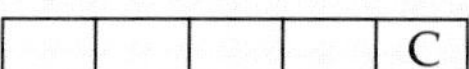

The next smallest time is 5 hours. It occurs at machine center 1 for job E, so we place job E as near to the beginning of the sequence as possible. Job E is eliminated from the job list.

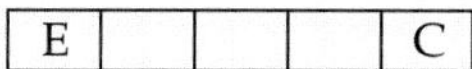

The next smallest time is 6 hours. It occurs at machine center 1 for job A and at machine center 2 for job B. Thus, we place job A as near to the beginning of the sequence as possible and job B as near to the end of the sequence as possible. Jobs A and B are eliminated from the job list.

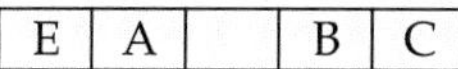

The only job remaining is job D. It is placed in the only available slot, in the middle of the sequence.

E	A	D	B	C

This sequence will complete these jobs more quickly than any other arrangement. The following bar charts (called *Gantt charts*) are used to determine the makespan or final completion time for the set of five jobs. Notice that the sequence of jobs (E, A, D, B, C) is the same for both machine centers and that a job cannot begin at machine center 2 until it has been completed at machine center 1. Also, a job cannot begin at machine center 2 if another job is currently in process. Time periods during which a job is being processed are labeled with the job's letter. The shaded areas represent idle time.

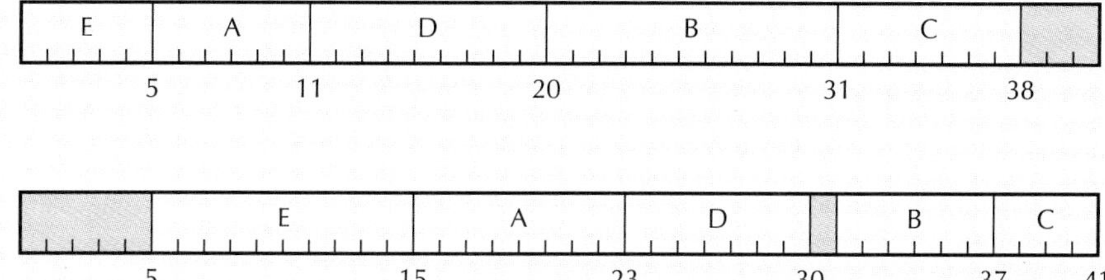

The completion time for the set of five jobs is 41 hours. Of those 41 hours, machine center 1 is idle 3 hours and machine center 2 is idle 7 hours. Note that although Johnson's rule minimizes makespan and idle time, it does not consider job due dates in constructing a sequence, so there is no attempt to minimize job tardiness.

As sequencing problems grow in size and complexity, they become difficult to solve by hand. AB:POM performs FCFS, SPT, LPT, SLACK, and CR sequencing for one-machine problems and Johnson's rule sequencing for two-machine problems.

Sequencing Jobs Through Any Number of Machines in Any Order

In a realistic job shop, jobs follow different routes through a facility that consists of many different machine centers or departments. A small job shop may have three or four departments; a large job shop may have fifty or more. From several to several hundred jobs may be circulating the shop at any given time. New jobs are released into the shop daily and placed in competition with existing jobs for priority in processing. Queues form and dissipate as jobs move through the system. A dispatch list that shows the sequence in which jobs are to be processed at a particular machine may be valid at the beginning of a day or week but may become outdated as new jobs arrive to the system. Some jobs may have to wait to be assembled with others before continuing to be processed. Delays in completing operations can cause due dates to be revised and schedules changed.

Video 14.2 *TIMS Edelman Awards Tape,* Program 1: "Reynolds Metals"

In this enlarged setting, the types of sequencing rules used can be expanded, too. We can still use simple sequencing rules such as SPT, FCFS, and DDATE, but we can also conceive of more complex, or *global,* rules. We may use FCFS to describe the arrival of jobs to a particular machine but *first-in-system, first-served* (FISFS) to differentiate the job's release into the system. Giving a job top priority at one machine only to have it endure a lengthy wait at the next machine seems fruitless, so we might consider looking ahead to the next operation and sequencing the jobs in the current queue by smallest *work-in-next-queue* (WINQ).

We can create new rules such as *fewest number of operations remaining* (NOPN) or slack per remaining operation (S/OPN), which require updating as jobs progress through the system. *Remaining work* (RWK) is a variation of SPT that processes jobs by the smallest total processing time for *all* remaining operations, not just the current operation. Any rule that has a remaining work component, such as SLACK or CR, needs to be updated as more operations of a job are completed. Thus, we need a mechanism for keeping track of and recording job progress. Recall that MRP systems can be used to change due dates, release orders, and, in general, coordinate production. Many of the rules described in this section are options in the shop floor module of standard MRP packages. Critical ratio is especially popular for use in conjunction with MRP.

More complicated production systems and more complicated sequencing rules are evaluated with simulation.

The complexity and dynamic nature of the scheduling environment precludes the use of analytical solution techniques. The most popular form of analysis for these systems is *simulation.* Academia has especially enjoyed creating and testing sequencing rules in simulations of hypothetical job shops. One early simulation study alone examined ninety-two different sequencing rules. Although no optimum solutions have been identified in these simulation studies, they have produced some general guidelines for *when* certain sequencing rules may be appropriate. Here are a few of their suggestions:

guidelines for selecting a sequencing rule

1. *SPT is most useful when the shop is highly congested.* SPT tends to minimize mean flow time, mean number of jobs in the system (and thus work-in-process inventory), and percent of jobs tardy. By completing more jobs quickly, it theoretically satisfies a greater number of customers than the other rules. However, with SPT some long jobs may be completed *very* late, resulting in a small number of very unsatisfied customers.

For this reason, when SPT is used in practice, it is usually truncated (or stopped), depending on the amount of time a job has been waiting or the nearness of its due date. For example, many mainframe computer systems process jobs by SPT. Jobs that are submitted are placed in several categories (A, B, or C) based on expected CPU time. The shorter jobs, or A jobs, are processed first, but every couple of hours the system stops processing A jobs and picks the first job from the B stack to run. After the B job is finished, the system returns to the A stack and continues processing. C jobs may be processed only once a day. Other systems that have access to due date information will keep a long job waiting until it's SLACK is zero or its due date is within a certain range.

2. *Use SLACK or S/OPN for periods of normal activity.* When capacity is not severely restrained, a SLACK-oriented rule that takes into account both due date and processing time will produce good results.

3. *Use DDATE when only small tardiness values can be tolerated.* DDATE tends to minimize mean tardiness and maximum tardiness. Although more jobs will be tardy under DDATE than SPT, the degree of tardiness will be much less.

4. *Use LPT if subcontracting is anticipated* so that larger jobs are completed in-house, and smaller jobs are sent out as their due date draws near.

5. *Use FCFS when operating at low-capacity levels.* FCFS allows the shop to operate essentially without sequencing jobs. When the workload at a facility is light, any sequencing rule will do, and FCFS is certainly the easiest to apply.

6. *Do not use SPT to sequence jobs that have to be assembled with other jobs at a later date.* For assembly jobs, a sequencing rule that gives a common priority to the processing of different components in an assembly, such as *assembly DDATE,* produces a more effective schedule.

MONITORING

Transparency 14.5 Monitoring

In a job shop environment where jobs follow different paths through the shop, visit many different machine centers, and compete for similar resources, it is not always easy to keep track of the status of a job. When jobs are first released to the shop, it is relatively easy to observe the queue that they join and predict when their initial operations might be completed. As the job progresses, however, or the shop becomes more congested, it becomes increasingly difficult to follow the job through the system. Competition for resources (resulting in long queues), machine breakdowns, quality problems, and setup requirements are just a few of the things that can delay a job's progress.

A **work package** is shop paperwork that travels with a job.

Shop paperwork, sometimes called a **work package,** travels with a job to specify what work needs to be done at a particular work center and where the item should be routed next. After workers complete their tasks, they are usually required to sign off on the work they have performed either manually on the work package or electronically through a PC located on the shop floor. Bar-code technology has made this task easier by eliminating much of the tedium and errors of entering the information by computer keyboard. In its simplest form, the bar code is attached to the work package, which the worker reads with a wand at the beginning and end of his or her work on the job. In other cases, the bar code is attached to the pallet or crate that carries the items from work center to work center. In this instance, the bar code is read automatically as it enters and leaves the work area. The time a worker spends on each job, the results of quality checks or inspections, and the utilization of resources can also be recorded in a similar fashion.

For the information gathered at each work center to be valuable, it must be up to date, accurate, and accessible to operations personnel. The monitoring function performed by production control takes this information and transforms it into various reports for workers and managers to use. Progress reports can be generated to show the status of individual jobs, the availability or utilization of certain resources, and the performance of individual workers or work centers. Exception reports may be generated to highlight deficiencies in certain areas, such as scrap, rework, shortages, anticipated delays, and unfilled orders. *Hot lists* show which jobs receive the highest priority and must be done immediately. A well-run facility will produce fewer *exception reports* and more *progress reports.* In the next two sections we describe two such progress reports, the Gantt chart and input/output control chart.

Gantt Charts

Gantt charts show both planned and completed activities against a time scale.

Gantt charts, introduced previously in this chapter to plan, or map out, work activities, can also be used to monitor a job's progress against the plan. As shown in Figure 14.1, on page 720, Gantt charts can display both planned and completed activities against a time scale. In this figure, the arrow indicating today's date crosses over the schedules for job 12A, job 32B, and job 23C.

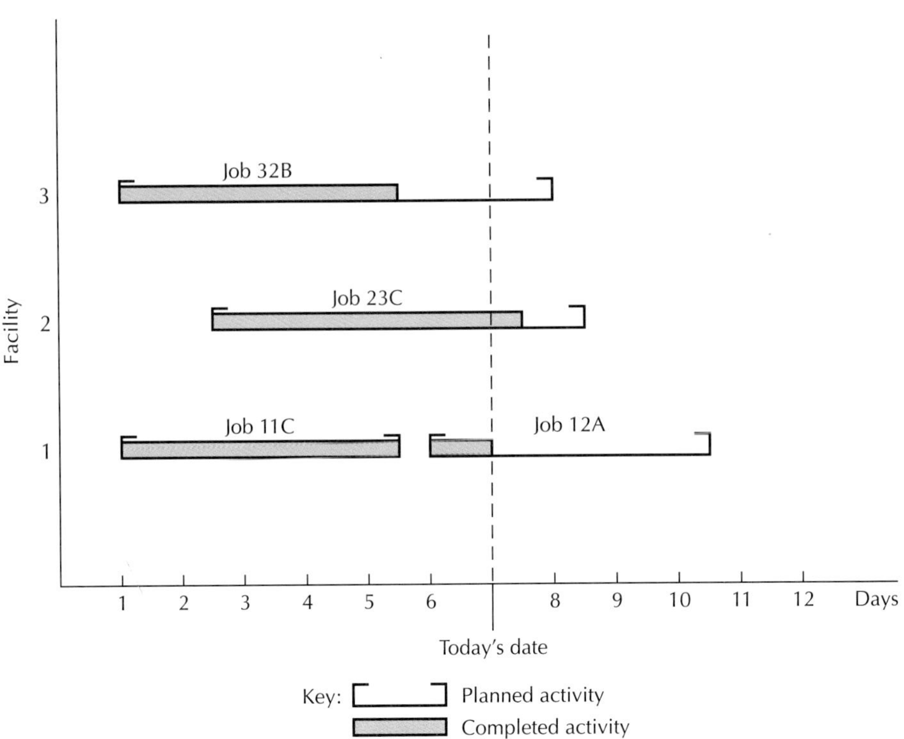

FIGURE 14.1 A Gantt Chart

From the chart we can quickly see that job 12A is exactly on schedule because the bar monitoring its completion exactly meets the line for the current date. Similarly, job 32B is behind schedule and job 23C is ahead of schedule.

Gantt charts, designed by Henry Gantt, have been used since the early 1900s and are still popular today. They may be created and maintained by computer or by hand. In some facilities, Gantt charts consist of large scheduling boards (the size of several bulletin boards) with magnetic strips, pegs, or string of different colors to mark clearly job schedules and job progress for the benefit of an entire plant.

Input/Output Control

I/O control monitors the input and output from each work center.

Input/output (I/O) control monitors the input to and output from each work center. Prior to such analysis, it was common to examine only the output from a work center and to compare the actual output with the output planned in the shop schedule. Using that approach in a job shop environment in which the performance of different work centers is interrelated may result in erroneous conclusions about the source of a problem. Reduced output at one point in the production process may be caused by problems at the current work center, but it may also be caused by problems at previous work centers that *feed* the current work center. Thus, in order to identify more clearly the source of a problem, the *input* to a work center must be compared to the *planned input*, and the *output* must be compared to the *planned output*. Deviations between planned and actual values are calculated, and their cumulative effects are observed. The resulting backlog or queue size is monitored to ensure that it stays within a manageable range.

The input rate to a work center can really be controlled only for the initial operations of a job. These first work centers are often called *gateway* work centers, because the majority of jobs must pass through them before subsequent operations are performed. Input to later operations, performed at *downstream* work centers, is difficult to control because it is a function of how well the rest of the shop is operating—that is, where queues are forming and how smoothly jobs are progressing through the system. The deviation of planned to actual input for downstream

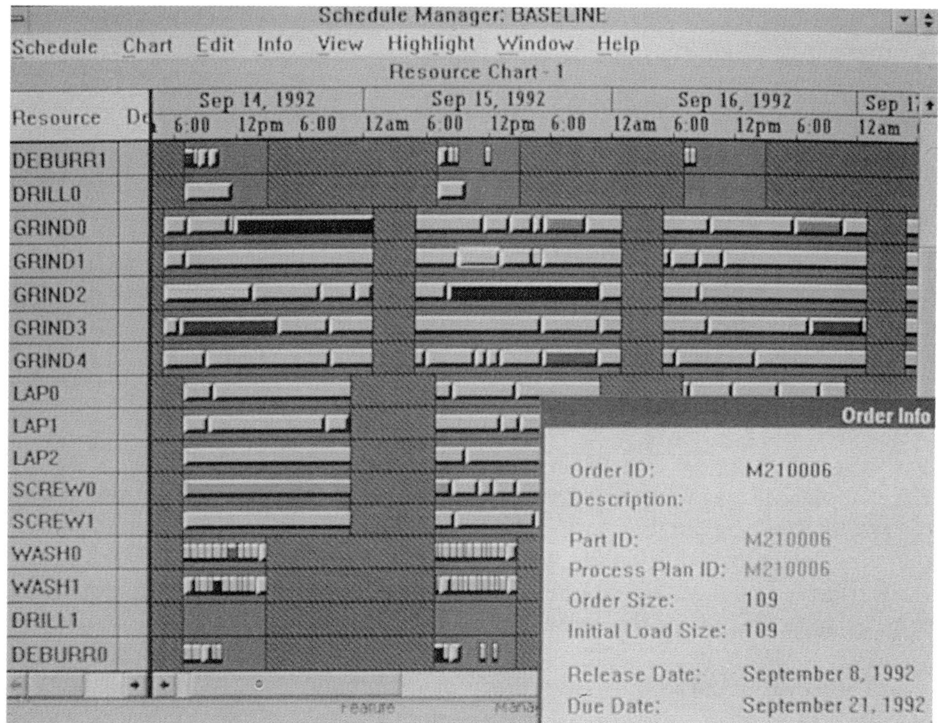

Gantt charts have been used for over 75 years to plan and monitor schedules. Today Gantt charts are more widely used than ever, often as part of the action plan from a quality improvement team. In some factories, Gantt charts appear on large magnetic boards, displaying the plant's daily progress for everyone to see. Computerized versions chart time, resources, and precedence requirements in an easy-to-read visual format.

work centers can be minimized by controlling the output rates of feeding work centers. The use of input/output reports can best be illustrated with an example.

EXAMPLE 14.5

Input/Output Control

Problem Statement:

The following information has been compiled in an input/output report for work center 5. Complete the report and interpret the results.

Input/Output Report

Period		1	2	3	4	*Total*
Planned input		60	65	70	75	
Actual input		60	60	65	65	
Deviation						
Planned output		75	75	75	75	
Actual output		70	70	65	65	
Deviation						
Backlog	30					

Solution:

The input/output report has planned a level production of 75 units per period for work center 5. This is to be accomplished by working off the backlog of work and steadily increasing the input of work.

The report is completed by calculating the deviation of (actual – planned) for both inputs and outputs and then summing the values in the respective planned, actual, and deviation rows. The initial backlog (at the beginning of period 1) is 30 units. Subsequent backlogs are calculated by subtracting each period's actual output from its actual input plus previous backlog.

Completed Input/Output Report

Period		1	2	3	4	*Total*
Planned input		60	65	70	75	270
Actual input		60	60	65	65	250
Deviation		0	–5	–5	–10	–20
Planned output		75	75	75	75	300
Actual output		70	70	65	65	270
Deviation		–5	–5	–10	–10	–30
Backlog	30	20	10	10	10	

The completed input/output report shows that work center 5 did not process all the jobs that were available during the four periods; therefore, the desired output rate was not achieved. This can be attributed to a lower-than-expected input of work from feeding work centers. The I/O reports from those work centers need to be examined to locate the source of the problem.

Input/output control provides the information necessary to regulate the flow of work to and from a network of work centers. Increasing the capacity of a work center that is processing all the work available to it will not increase output. The source of the problem needs to be identified. Excessive queues, or *backlogs*, is one indication that *bottlenecks* exist. To alleviate bottleneck work centers, the problem causing the backlog can be worked on, the capacity of the work center can be adjusted, or input to the work center can be reduced. Increasing the input to a bottleneck work center will not increase the center's output. It will merely clog the system further and create longer queues of work-in-process.

FINITE SCHEDULING

Infinite scheduling loads without regard to capacity, then levels the load and sequences the jobs.

Finite scheduling sequences jobs as part of the loading decision. Resources are never loaded beyond capacity.

The process for scheduling that we have described thus far in this chapter, loading work into work centers, leveling the load, sequencing the work, and monitoring its progress, is called **infinite scheduling.** The term *infinite* is used because the initial loading process assumes infinite capacity. Leveling and sequencing decisions are made after overloads or underloads have been identified. This iterative process is time-consuming and is not very efficient.

An alternative approach to scheduling called **finite scheduling** assumes a fixed maximum capacity and will not load the resource beyond its capacity. Loading and sequencing decisions are made at the same time, so that the first jobs loaded onto a work center are of highest priority. Any jobs remaining after the capacity of the work center or resource has been reached are of lower priority and are scheduled for later time periods. This approach is easier than the infinite scheduling approach, but it will be successful only if the criteria for choosing the work to be performed, as well as capacity limitations, can be expressed accurately and concisely.

Finite scheduling systems use a variety of methods to develop their schedules, including mathematical programming, network analysis, simulation, and expert systems or other forms of artificial intelligence. Because the scheduling system is making the decisions and not the human scheduler, companies may find it difficult to purchase a system off the shelf that can embody their specific manufacturing environment or can be readily updated as changes in the environment occur. Finite schedulers are becoming more popular as software systems become more adaptable and easier to use and as manufacturing environments are simplified and are better understood. There are several finite schedulers available. One of the oldest is IBM's CAPOSS (Capacity Planning and Operations Sequencing System). ISIS, developed by a graduate student at Carnegie-Mellon, was one of the first schedulers to use artificial intelligence. Another prominent finite scheduler is called OPT (for Optimized Production Technology). We discuss OPT and its derivatives in the next section because the assumptions on which this system are based can help us better to understand how manufacturing systems operate.

OPT and Synchronous Production

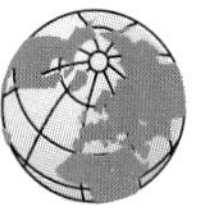

Teaching Note 14.3 *The Goal*

OPT is a software system for shop floor scheduling developed in the 1970s by an Israeli physicist named Eliyahu Goldratt in response to a friend's request for help in scheduling his chicken coop business. Lacking a background in manufacturing or production theory, Dr. Goldratt took a commonsense, intuitive approach to the scheduling problem. He developed a software system that used mathematical programming and simulation to create a schedule that realistically considered the constraints of the manufacturing system. The software produced good schedules quickly and was marketed in the early 1980s in the United States. After more than 100 firms had successfully used OPT, the creator sold the rights to the software and began marketing the theory behind the software instead. He called his approach to scheduling the *theory of constraints.* General Motors and other manufacturers call its application **synchronous production.** We discuss two of the major precepts of synchronous production.

OPT, or **synchronous production,** concentrates on scheduling the bottleneck resource.

We have mentioned before that decision making in manufacturing is often difficult because of the size and complexity of the problems faced. Dr. Goldratt's first insight into the scheduling problem led him to simplify the number of variables considered. He learned early that manufacturing resources typically are not used evenly. Instead of trying to balance the capacity of the manufacturing system, he decided that most systems are inherently unbalanced and that he would try to balance the *flow* of work through the system instead. He identified resources as bottleneck or nonbottleneck and observed that the flow through the system is controlled by the bottleneck resources. These resources should always have material to work on, should spend as little time as possible on nonproductive activities (e.g., setups, waiting for work), should be fully staffed, and should be the focus of improvement or automation efforts. Goldratt pointed out that an hour's worth of production lost at a bottleneck reduces the output of the system by the same amount of time, whereas an hour lost at a nonbottleneck may have no effect on system output.

From this realization, Goldratt was able to simplify the scheduling problem significantly. He concentrated initially on scheduling production at bottleneck resources and then scheduled the nonbottleneck resources to support the bottleneck activities. Thus, production is synchronized, or "in sync," with the needs of the bottleneck and the system as a whole.

Goldratt's second insight into manufacturing concerned the concept of lot sizes or batch sizes. Goldratt saw no reason for fixed batch sizes. He differentiated between the quantity in which items are produced, called the *process batch,* and the quantity in which the items are transported, called the *transfer batch.* Ideally, items should be transferred in lot sizes of one. The process batch size for bottlenecks should be large, to eliminate the need for setups. The process batch size for nonbottlenecks can be small because time spent in setups for nonbottlenecks does not

Process batch sizes and transfer batch sizes do not have to match.

affect the rest of the system. Let's consider an example to illustrate the use of these concepts.

EXAMPLE 14.6

Synchronous Production

Problem Statement:

Teaching Note 14.4 The $5,000 Problem

The following diagram contains the product structure, routing, and processing time information for product A. The process flows from the bottom of the diagram upward. Assume one unit of items B, C, and D are needed to make each A. The manufacture of each item requires three operations at machine centers 1, 2, or 3. Each machine center contains only one machine. A machine setup time of 60 minutes occurs whenever a machine is switched from one operation to another (within the same item or between items).

Design a schedule of production for each machine center that will produce 100 A's as quickly as possible. Show the schedule on a Gantt chart of each machine center.

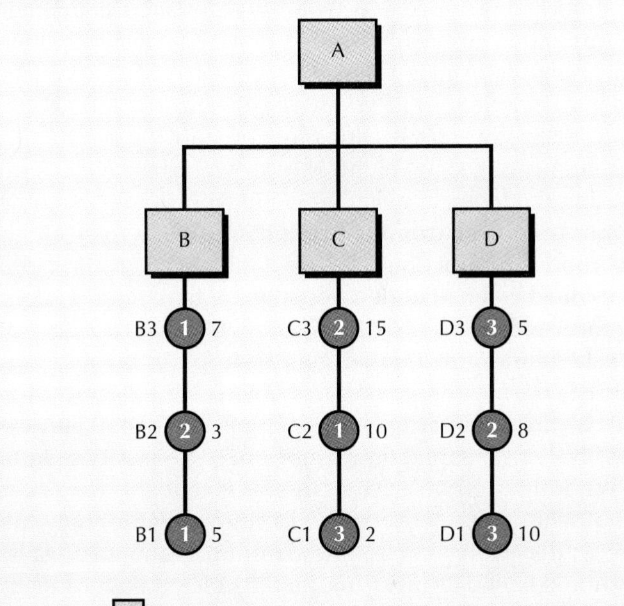

Solution:

In developing a schedule, we will use the following concepts from OPT:

1. Identify the bottleneck machine.
2. To keep the bottleneck busy, schedule the item first whose lead time to the bottleneck is less than or equal to the bottleneck processing time.
3. Forward schedule the bottleneck machine.
4. Backward schedule the other machines to sustain the bottleneck schedule.
5. Remember that the transfer batch size does not have to match the process batch size.

- The bottleneck machine is calculated by summing the processing times of all operations to be performed at a machine.

Machine 1		*Machine 2*		*Machine 3*	
B1	5	B2	3	C1	2
B3	7	C3	15	D3	5
C2	10	D2	8	D1	10
	22		26*		17

*Bottleneck

- Machine 2 is identified as the bottleneck, so we schedule machine 2 first. From the product structure diagram, we see three operations that are performed at machine 2—B2, C3, and D2. If we schedule item B first, a B will reach machine 2 every 5 minutes (since B has to be processed through machine 1 first), but each B takes only 3 minutes to process at machine 2, so the bottleneck will be idle for 2 minutes of every 5 minutes. That's not keeping our bottlenecks busy. A similar result occurs if we schedule item D first on machine 2. The bottleneck will be idle for 2 minutes out of every 10 minutes until D has finished processing. The best alternative is to schedule item C first. The first C won't reach machine 2 until time 12, but after that a C will be waiting for the bottleneck machine, because it takes longer for C to be processed through machine 2 than through the first two machines in C's routing sequence combined.
- We begin our Gantt charts by processing item C through the three machine centers. Before we continue, a few comments about the Gantt charts are needed. The charts will look different from our earlier Gantt charts because we will allow each item to be transferred to the next operation immediately after it is completed at the current operation (i.e., the transfer batch size is 1). We will process the items in batches of 100 to match our demand requirements. The diagonal lines represent idle time between operations due to setup time requirements or because a feeding operation has not yet been completed. Refer to the Gantt charts in Figure 14.2 (see page 726) for the remainder of the discussion.
- C3 is completed at machine center 2 at time 1512. After setup, it is ready for a new item at time 1572. We have a choice between B2 and D2, since both B1 and D1 can be completed by 1572. Completion time at machine center 2 will be the same regardless of whether B2 or D2 is processed first; however, the completion time at the other machine centers (and thus for product A) will be affected by the bottleneck sequence. From the product structure diagram, we note that B3 can be completed more quickly than D3 because D3 must wait 3 minutes for D2 to be completed, whereas B3 will always have a queue of items from B2 to work on. Thus, we schedule B2 and then D2 on machine center 2.
- With the bottleneck sequence of C3, B2, D2 established, we can now schedule machine center 1 (C2, B1, B3) and machine center 3 (C1, D1, D3). The completion time for producing 100 A's is 2,737 minutes. The total idle time at the three machine centers is 994 minutes.
- For comparison purposes, alternate bottleneck sequences and their resulting completion times and idle times are given next.

Bottleneck Sequence	*Completion Time for 100 A's (min)*	*Total Idle Time (min)*
C3, B2, D2	2,737	994
C3, D2, B2	3,135	1,447

It is obvious that the bottleneck sequence determines how soon the order for 100 A's can be completed. In addition to the idea of transferring work as soon as it is completed, synchronous production is different from previous sequencing methods we have discussed in that it focuses on *where* an operation is performed and the pattern or interrelationships among operations and resources.

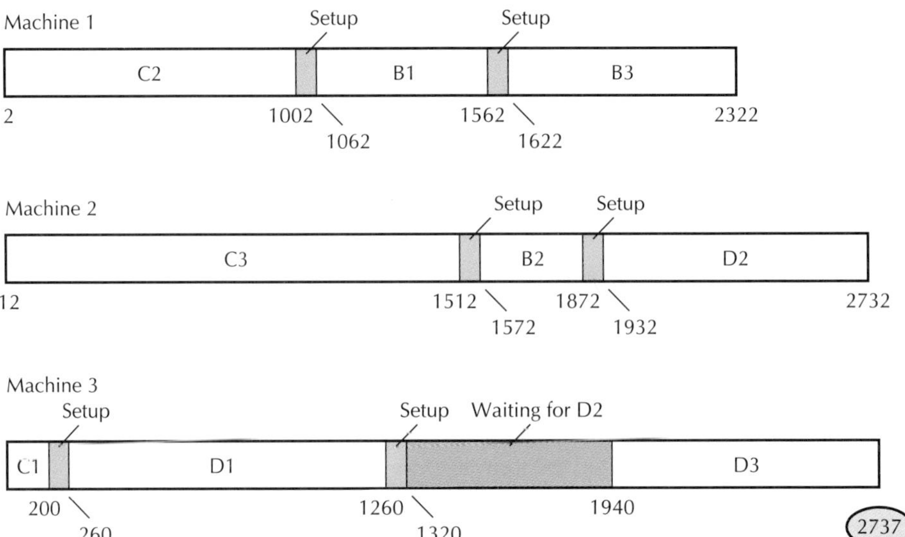

FIGURE 14.2 Gantt Chart Solution to Example 14.6

GAINING THE COMPETITIVE EDGE

Quaker Furniture Gets in Sync

Business for Quaker Furniture was disturbing—sales were up, but profits were down. With sales running \$8 million a year, Quaker could hardly keep up with the demand. When customers complained about the normal lead time of 8 weeks, Quaker set up a "quick-ship" program to deliver special orders in 3 weeks; however, they could only handle 15 percent of their customers as "special." No matter how hard the company tried, they could not seem to get orders out fast enough for their customers, profits were not as high as they should be, and the employees were exhausted trying to meet the hectic schedules. The factory was caught in a cycle of "bumping" some customer orders ahead of others, which satisfied the customer but drove efficiency down. More inventory was ordered, produced, and held to try to speed up production, but instead, the extra inventory slowed things down. Higher efficiencies at individual operations were not increasing overall plant efficiency.

In response, the vice president of operations for Quaker decided to try a new approach for coordinating the flow of material through the factory, *synchronous manufacturing*. One of the concepts of synchronous manufacturing that he found most useful is called the *drum-buffer-rope* (DBR). The *drum* is the master schedule. Control points identified in the process serve as "drumbeats" for when material should be released to the shop. A *buffer* is set up at the least-capacity resources (i.e., bottlenecks) to smooth disruptions to the flow of work. The *rope* ties the release of materials to each operation's drumbeat. DBR ensures that bottleneck resources are fully utilized and that nonbottleneck resources process work in the proper sequence for supporting the bottleneck resources.

Since implementing synchronous manufacturing, Quaker has cut work-in-process inventory (WIP) by 39 percent, improved delivery performance by 25 percent, decreased normal lead time to 6 weeks, and increased the percentage of quick-ship orders to 40 percent. These improvements were made concurrently with an increase in the number of models and fabric options, a 16 percent decrease in the work force, and a 19 percent reduction in break-even volume. Quaker's new goal is to eliminate its quick-ship program and ship all orders within 3 weeks.

Source: Based on Libby, William, "Quaker Furniture Manages Materials Using Synchronous Manufacturing," *APICS—The Performance Advantage* (March 1992): 24–26.

MAINTENANCE SCHEDULING

Schedules of equipment usage are affected by the demand for the equipment, the capacity of the equipment, and the availability of the equipment. Availability refers to how much of the time the machine can be used for productive activities. Nonproductive activities include setting up the machine to process a different type of item, tearing down the machine, maintaining the machine, repairing the machine, and waiting for workers, material, or service.

Machines cannot operate continuously without some attention. Maintenance activities can be performed when a machine breaks down to restore the machine to its original operating condition or at different times during regular operation of the machine in an attempt to prevent a breakdown from occurring. The first type of activity is referred to as **breakdown maintenance;** the second is called **preventive maintenance.** Costs are associated with each approach, and certain trade-offs apply. Breakdowns seldom occur at convenient times, and repair personnel are not always available when needed. Workers can be idled by breakdowns, and entire assembly lines can be stopped. Customer orders can be delayed, and sales can be lost. Lost production, poor quality, and missed deadlines from an inefficient or broken down machine can represent a significant expense. In addition, the cost of breakdown maintenance is usually much greater than preventive maintenance. (Most of us know that to be true from our own experience at maintaining an automobile. Regular oil changes cost pennies compared to replacing a car engine.) For these reasons, most companies do not find it cost-effective to rely solely on breakdown maintenance. The question then becomes, how much preventive maintenance is necessary and when should it be performed? Preventive maintenance cannot entirely eliminate equipment failure; breakdowns can still occur, but it is hoped they will occur with less frequency. Although we can't predict with certainty when breakdowns will occur, if we keep good records on machine operations and maintenance, we can construct a history of the times between breakdowns and the frequency of their occurrence. From that information and the estimated cost of breakdown and preventive maintenance, we can recommend an appropriate maintenance schedule.

Breakdown maintenance involves the repairs needed to make a failed machine operational; **preventive maintenance** is a system of periodic inspection and maintenance designed to keep a machine in operation.

breakdown maintenance versus preventive maintenance

With no preventive maintenance, the expected time between breakdowns is a simple expected value calculated from historical records, as follows:

$$\text{EV}(n) = \sum_{n} nP_n$$

where n = time period in which a breakdown may occur

P_n = probability of a breakdown in time period n

The expected *number* of breakdowns is the reciprocal of the time between breakdowns, or $\frac{1}{EV(n)}$. The expected breakdown cost per period can be calculated as the cost of a breakdown times the number of machines maintained times the expected number of breakdowns, or

$$\text{TC}_b = \frac{Nc_b}{\text{EV}(n)}$$

where TC_b = total cost of breakdown maintenance

N = the number of machines in a group to be maintained

c_b = cost of breakdown maintenance on a single machine

$\frac{1}{\text{EV}(n)}$ = expected number of breakdowns

The expected cost of breakdowns per period with preventive maintenance includes both the preventive maintenance cost and the breakdown maintenance cost of those units that fail even though preventive maintenance has been applied, or

$$\text{TC}_\text{p} = \frac{C_p + B_n c_b}{n}$$

where TC_p = total cost of preventative maintenance

C_p = cost of preventive maintenance

B_n = expected number of breakdowns with preventive maintenance performed every n time periods

$= N(P_1 + \cdots + P_n) + B_1 P_{n-1} + B_2 P_{n-2} + \cdots + B_{n-1} P_1$

c_b = cost of breakdown maintenance on a single machine

The following example illustrates how these formulas can be used.

EXAMPLE 14.7

Preventive Maintenance

Problem Statement:

Adele Sharp is in charge of maintaining Fidelity Bank's twenty ATM machines located throughout the city. Repairing a broken ATM costs approximately $500 per machine. Adele has found that preventive maintenance, at a cost of $50 per machine, can reduce but not eliminate breakdowns. From her maintenance records on the ATM network, she has constructed the following breakdown frequencies:

Weeks until breakdown	1	2	3	4	5
Number of breakdowns	20	25	30	20	5

a. Calculate the weekly maintenance cost if no preventive maintenance is allowed.
b. If preventive maintenance is performed, how often should the ATM machines be serviced?
c. What maintenance schedule would you recommend?

Solution:

From the frequency distribution, calculate the following probabilities:

Weeks until Breakdown, n	*No. of Breakdowns*	*Probability of Breakdown, P_n*
1	20	0.20
2	25	0.25
3	30	0.30
4	20	0.20
5	5	0.05
	100	1.00

a. With no preventive maintenance, the expected time between breakdowns for a machine is

$$\text{EV}(n) = \sum_{n=1}^{5} nP_n$$
$$= (1)(0.20) + (2)(0.25) + (3)(0.30) + (4)(0.20) + (5)(0.05)$$
$$= 0.20 + 0.50 + 0.90 + 0.80 + 0.25 = 2.65 \text{ weeks}$$

The weekly cost of breakdown maintenance is:

$$\text{TC}_b = \frac{Nc_b}{\text{EV}(n)}$$
$$= \frac{(20 \text{ machines} \times \$500/\text{machine})}{2.65 \text{ weeks}}$$
$$= \frac{\$10{,}000}{2.65} = \$3{,}773.58$$

b. The expected number of breakdowns with preventive maintenance performed every n weeks, B_n, is

$B_1 = NP_1 = 20(0.20) = 4$
$B_2 = N(P_1 + P_2) + B_1P_1 = 20(0.20 + 0.25) + 4(0.20) = 9 + 0.8 = 9.8$
$B_3 = N(P_1 + P_2 + P_3) + B_1P_2 + B_2P_1 = 20\ (0.20 + 0.25 + 0.30) + 4(0.25) + 9.8(0.20)$
$= 15 + 1 + 1.96 = 17.96$
$B_4 = N(P_1 + P_2 + P_3 + P_4)\ B_1P_3 + B_2P_2 + B_3P_1 = 20(0.20 + 0.25 + 0.30 + 0.20)$
$+ 4(0.30) + 9.8(0.25) + 17.96(0.20) = 19 + 1.2 + 2.45 + 3.59 = 26.24$
$B_5 = N(P_1 + P_2 + P_3 + P_4)\ B_1P_4 + B_2P_3 + B_3P_2 + B_4P_1 = 20(0.20 + 0.25 + 0.30 + 0.20$
$+ 0.05) + 4(0.20) + 9.8(0.30) + 17.96(0.25) + 26.24(0.20)$
$= 20 + 0.80 + 2.94 + 4.49 + 5.25 = 33.48$

The number of breakdowns is multiplied by the breakdown cost and added to the preventive maintenance cost. Table 14.1 summarizes the cost of preventive maintenance every n weeks.

c. For every alternative considered, preventive maintenance is preferable to breakdown maintenance. Preventive maintenance every 2 weeks is the best alternative, saving ($3,773 – $2,950) = $823 a week over breakdown maintenance.

Total productive maintenance combines the U.S. practice of preventative maintenance with the Japanese concepts of total quality and employee involvement.

With the advent of such philosophies as JIT and TQM, management attitudes toward maintenance are changing. A concept called **total productive maintenance (TPM)** has emerged; it combines the American practice of preventive maintenance with the Japanese approach to total quality and employee involvement. TPM acknowledges an expanded role for preventive maintenance. Preventive maintenance is viewed as three related activities:

TABLE 14.1 The Cost of Preventive Maintenance Alternatives

(1) *Preventive Maint. Every n Weeks*	(2) *Expected Breakdowns in n Weeks* B_n	(3) *Expected Breakdowns per Week,* B_n/n	(4) *Expected Breakdowns Cost per Week* $(B_n/n \cdot \$500)$	(5) *Preventive Maint. Cost per Week* $(20 \cdot \$50)/n$	*Expected Total Maintenance Cost per Week Col. (4) + (5)*
1	4.00	4/1 = 4.00	4.00 × $500 = $2,000	$1,000/1 = $1,000	$3,000
2	9.80	9.80/2 = 4.90	4.90 × $500 = $2,450	$1,000/2 = $500	$2,950*
3	17.96	17.96/3 = 5.99	5.99 × $500 = $2,995	$1,000/3 = $333	$3,328
4	26.24	26.24/4 = 6.56	6.56 × $500 = $3,280	$1,000/4 = $250	$3,530
5	33.48	33.48/5 = 6.70	6.70 × $500 = $3,350	$1,000/5 = $200	$3,550

*Lowest cost.

Motorola is known for innovation, quality, and speed-to-market. This photo shows a manufacturing environment that is well-organized, spotless, and clear from clutter. How does cleanliness affect quality or competitiveness? Keeping the work area shining is part of a preventive maintenance effort in which unusual occurrences (such as drips and abrasions) are detected quickly. An orderly environment also encourages workers to replace tools and materials in prescribed locations and to take more care in their work.

Transparency 14.6 Maintenance

1. *Daily maintenance* to prevent equipment deterioration, such as lubricating, cleaning, adjusting, and inspecting a machine. These activities should normally be performed by the equipment operator.
2. *Periodic inspection* of the equipment to measure deterioration of performance and diagnose problems. This may also be performed by the equipment operator but is often reserved for maintenance personnel. These inspections are usually planned at regular time intervals and can lead to a revised daily maintenance routine, more frequent inspections, or to the third type of preventive maintenance.
3. *Preventive repairs* in advance of a breakdown as early treatment to repair machines whose deterioration has reached a certain level. This activity is normally reserved for maintenance personnel but ideally would be performed by equipment operators.

TPM takes a broader view than preventive maintenance. It tries to maximize the productive potential of each machine over its lifespan.

Thus, the TPM approach to preventive maintenance emphasizes the machine operator's role in maintaining the equipment (referred to in Japan as *autonomous maintenance*). It also considers preventive maintenance to be more than preventive repairs. Damage to a machine due to untidy environments, sloppy operation, or lack of daily care can cause a machine's performance to deteriorate. Preventive maintenance involves ensuring an optimal working environment. In order to accomplish this, maintenance and operating data on each machine must be carefully compiled, and machine operators must be trained in designing maintenance remedies based on the data collected. The process of collecting data and identifying the signs of deterioration prior to failure is referred to as *predictive maintenance.*

Even with this expanded view of preventive maintenance, Japanese managers found that machine breakdowns could not be *eliminated* with preventive maintenance alone. Total productive maintenance goes further by including such activities as designing products that can easily be produced on existing machines, designing machines for easier operation, changeover, and maintenance, training and retraining workers to operate and maintain machines properly, purchasing machines that, in concert, maximize productive potential, and designing a preventive maintenance plan that spans the entire life of each machine. The goal of TPM is zero breakdowns (and zero defects). Does it work? One Deming

Teaching Note 14.5 TPM

GAINING THE COMPETITIVE EDGE

DockPlan Saves American Airlines Big Bucks

American Airlines has a fleet of 600 aircraft, including Boeing models 727, 737, 747, 757, and 767, McDonnell Douglas models Super 80, DC-10, and MD-11, and Airbus models 300 and Fokker 100. The aircraft are in various stages of maturity and have their own unique utilization and maintenance profiles. More than 30 different types of maintenance checks are required on a periodic basis to ensure the airworthiness of the fleet. The most costly of these is the overhaul check, ranging from $100,000 to $1 million every 1 to 5 years, depending on the type and age of the aircraft. American Airlines uses a 5-year planning horizon for its maintenance activities and an in-house decision support system called DockPlan.

The capacity of the maintenance facility is limited by the number of hangars, mechanics, and equipment, the type of aircraft, and the type of maintenance required. From experience, American has found that it is most efficient to process similar fleet types and similar maintenance programs at the same time. DockPlan takes this information into account when generating maintenance schedules. DockPlan's initial schedule is based on a computerized scheduling heuristic, but the system allows input from experienced planners so that the final schedule is a result of iterative decisions between people and machines.

DockPlan's schedules are not guaranteed to be optimal, but the results are very good. In one 6-month period, DockPlan saved American more than $3 million in maintenance labor costs. The schedule it produced for 727 overhauls has effectively given back the use of one aircraft for an entire year. American estimates that DockPlan will save $454 million in overhaul maintenance cost over the active life of its widebody aircraft.

Source: Based on Gray, Douglas, "Airworthy—Decision Support for Aircraft Overhaul Maintenance Planning," *OR/MS Today* (December 1992): 24–29.

Prize-winning company, Aishin Seiki, has not experienced an equipment breakdown in more than 4 years. Prior to TPM, they had more than 700 breakdowns per month!

EMPLOYEE SCHEDULING

Employee scheduling has lots of options because labor is a very flexible resource.

Labor is one of the most flexible resources. Workers can be hired and fired more easily than equipment can be purchased or sold. Labor-limited systems can expand capacity through overtime, expanded workweeks, extra shifts, or part-time workers. This flexibility is a valuable asset, but it tends to make scheduling a difficult task. Service firms especially spend an inordinate amount of time developing employee schedules. It would not be uncommon for a supervisor to spend an entire week making up the next month's employee schedule. The task becomes even more daunting for facilities that operate on a 24-hour basis with multiple shifts.

The assignment method of linear programming discussed earlier in this chapter was designed for the employee-scheduling problem of assigning workers with different performance ratings to available jobs. Large-scale linear programming is currently used by McDonald's to schedule its large contingent of part-time workers. American Airlines uses a combination of integer linear programming and expert systems for scheduling ticket agents to coincide with peak and slack demand periods and for the complicated scheduling of flight crews. Although mathematical programming certainly has found application in employee scheduling, most scheduling problems are solved by heuristics (i.e., rules of thumb) that develop a repeating pattern of work assignments. Often, heuristics are imbedded in a decision support system to facilitate their use and increase their flexibility. One such heuristic, adapted from Baker and Magazine,[2] is used for scheduling full-time workers with two days off per week. The procedure is given next and is illustrated with an example.

Employee Scheduling Heuristic:

1. Let N = no. of workers available
   D_i = demand for workers on day i
   X = day working
   O = day off
2. Assign the first $N - D_1$ workers day 1 off. Assign the next $N - D_2$ workers day 2 off. Continue in a similar manner until all days have been scheduled.
3. If the number of workdays for a full-time employee is less than 5, assign the remaining workdays so that consecutive days off are possible or where unmet demand is highest or arbitrarily.
4. Assign any remaining work to part-time employees, subject to maximum hour restrictions.
5. If consecutive days off are desired, consider switching schedules among days with the same demand requirements.

EXAMPLE 14.8

Employee Scheduling

Problem Statement:

Diet-Tech employs five workers to operate its weight-reduction facility in Southside Richmond. Demand for service each week (in terms of minimum number of workers required) is given in the following table. Create an employee schedule that will meet the demand requirements and guarantee each worker 2 days off per week.

Day of Week	*M*	*T*	*W*	*Th*	*F*	*Sa*	*Su*
Min. No. of Workers Required	3	3	4	3	4	5	3
Taylor							
Smith							
Simpson							
Allen							
Dickerson							

Solution:

The completed employee schedule matrix is shown next.

[2] Baker, Kenneth R., and Michael J. Magazine, "Workforce Scheduling with Cyclic Demands and Days-Off Constraints," *Management Science* 24, no. 2 (October 1977): 161–7.

Day of Week	*M*	*T*	*W*	*Th*	*F*	*Sa*	*Su*
Min. No. of Workers Required	*3*	*3*	*4*	*3*	*4*	*5*	*3*
Taylor	O	X	X	O	X	X	X
Smith	O	X	X	O	X	X	X
Simpson	X	O	X	X	O	X	X
Allen	X	O	X	X	X	X	O
Dickerson	X	X	O	X	X	X	O

Following the heuristic, the first (5 – 3) = 2 workers, Taylor and Smith, are assigned Monday off. The next (5 – 3) = 2 workers, Simpson and Allen, are assigned Tuesday off. The next (5 – 4) = 1 worker, Dickerson, is assigned Wednesday off. Returning to the top of the roster, the next (5 – 3) = 2 workers, Taylor and Smith, are assigned Thursday off. The next (5 – 4) = 1 worker, Simpson, is assigned Friday off. Everyone works on Saturday, and the next (5 – 3) = 2 workers, Allen and Dickerson, get Sunday off.

The resulting schedule meets demand and has every employee working 5 days a week with 2 days off. Unfortunately, none of the days off are consecutive. By switching the initial schedules for Tuesday and Thursday (both with a demand of 3) and the schedules for Wednesday and Friday (both with a demand of 4), the following schedule results:

Day of Week	*M*	*T*	*W*	*Th*	*F*	*Sa*	*Su*
Min. No. of Workers Required	*3*	*3*	*4*	*3*	*4*	*5*	*3*
Taylor	O	O	X	X	X	X	X
Smith	O	O	X	X	X	X	X
Simpson	X	X	O	O	X	X	X
Allen	X	X	X	O	X	X	O
Dickerson	X	X	X	X	O	X	O

In this revised schedule, the first three workers have consecutive days off. The last two workers have one weekend day off and one day off during the week.

The heuristic just illustrated can be adapted to ensure that the two days off per week are consecutive days. In addition, Baker and Magazine have developed other heuristics for facilities that schedule workers 2 weeks at a time. In this analysis, workers are given schedules with every other weekend off and two days off every 2 weeks, consecutive or nonconsecutive. These heuristics were used in a decision support system called SuperSchedule[3] to

Decision support systems are popular for scheduling.

- Generate a scheduling pattern to be followed cyclically throughout the year;

[3]Xudong, H., R. Russell, and J. Dickey, "Workload Analysis Expert System and Optimizer," *Proceedings of the Seventh International Congress of Cybernetics and Systems*, Vol. 1, London (September 1987): 68–72.

- Determine whether a 40-hour or 80-hour base for overtime is more cost-effective;
- Examine the effect of alternate-days-off patterns;
- Determine the appropriate breakdown of part-time versus full-time employees;
- Justify the use of additional staff;
- Assess the feasibility of vacation or other leave requests; and
- Determine the benefit of cross training employees in certain positions.

Teaching Note 14.6 Decision Support Systems for Scheduling

It is obvious that scheduling systems of this type can be very useful in enhancing both the scheduling process and the quality of the resulting schedule.

GAINING THE COMPETITIVE EDGE

You Can Choose Your Own Hours at McDonald's

Employee scheduling for small businesses is a headache. It is not unusual for a manager to spend more than 8 hours manually preparing work schedules each week. In addition to the length of time required, scheduling in fast-food restaurants has the following problems:

- *Sales volume and, thus, employee requirements, vary dramatically over the day.* Fast-food restaurants do 17% of their business during the noon hour. Worker requirements in the grill and counter areas can vary from one to eight or more employees.
- *There are no standard workdays or workweeks.* Shifts vary from three to eight hours. Legal restrictions on the length of the workday are watched carefully due to the number of teenage employees.
- *Employees differ in the times they are available to work.* This is especially true because most of the workers are part-timers.
- *Employee skills and performance levels vary considerably.* Workers qualified to work the drive-through are not necessarily the best workers behind the counter or at the grill.

A typical fast-food restaurant has 3 work areas, 150 employees, and 30 work shifts. This presents a very large scheduling problem. (If formulated as a linear programming model, it would contain approximately 100,000 variables and 3,000 constraints.) The system used by McDonald's generates employee schedules that

- Satisfy half-hourly personnel requirements with a minimum of surplus scheduled hours;
- Give each employee the same number of workdays and work hours (marginal work days are given to employees with the best skill ratings);
- Assign employees to work areas where they perform the best;
- Schedule each employee during his or her preferred work times as much as possible;
- Schedule every employee to work around the same time each workday;
- Provide adequate skill coverage during each half-hour time period in each work area.

What-if? analysis can also be performed to handle adjustments in workforce size, modifications of sales and labor requirements, changes in desired work shifts, and changes in other operating parameters. All in all, the scheduling system has standardized the scheduling process at McDonald's, reduced the time to prepare a schedule by 90 percent, and produced higher-quality schedules from the perspective of both management and labor.

Source: Based on Love, Robert, Jr., and James Hoey, "Management Science Improves Fast-Food Operations," *Interfaces* (March–April 1990): 21–29.

SUMMARY

In this chapter, we have discussed the objectives of scheduling, the scheduling activities of loading, sequencing, and monitoring, finite scheduling approaches, and maintenance and employee scheduling. We have dealt primarily with a job shop environment in which jobs arrive at varying time intervals, require different resources and sequences of operations, and are due at different times. This lowest level of scheduling is often referred to as *shop floor control* or *production control.* It involves assigning jobs to machines or workers (called loading), specifying the order in which operations are to be performed, and monitoring the work as it progresses. Techniques such as the index method or assignment method are used for loading, various rules whose performance varies according to the scheduling objective are used for sequencing, and Gantt charts and input/output control charts are used for monitoring.

Realistic schedules must reflect capacity limitations. *Infinite scheduling* initially assumes infinite capacity and then manually "levels the load" of resources that have exceeded capacity. *Finite scheduling* loads jobs in priority order and delays those jobs for which current capacity is exceeded. *Synchronous production* is a finite scheduling approach that schedules bottleneck resources first and then schedules other resources to support the bottleneck schedule. It also allows items to be transferred between resources in lot sizes that differ from the lot size in which the item is produced.

Maintenance scheduling typically involves determining how much preventive maintenance is needed and when it should be performed. Expected values can be used to analyze the cost trade-offs between breakdown and preventive maintenance at various intervals given certain probabilities of breakdowns. New approaches to maintenance include the concept of *total productive maintenance* (TPM). TPM expands the view of preventive maintenance to incorporate more worker involvement, better record keeping on machine performance, and daily machine upkeep routines. TPM further extends into the areas of product design, equipment design, and worker training in an effort to completely eliminate breakdowns.

Employee scheduling is often difficult because of the variety of options available and the special requirements for individual workers. Scheduling heuristics are typically used to develop patterns of worker assignment. Decision support systems for employee scheduling (and other types of scheduling) are becoming more commonplace.

SUMMARY OF KEY FORMULAS

Minimum slack

$$\text{SLACK} = (\text{Due date} - \text{today's date}) - (\text{remaining processing time})$$

Critical ratio

$$\text{CR} = \frac{\text{due date} - \text{today's date}}{\text{remaining processing time}}$$

Expected breakdown cost without preventive maintenance

$$\text{TC}_b = \frac{Nc_b}{\text{EV}(n)}$$

Expected number of breakdowns with maintenance performed every n *weeks*

$$B_n = N(P_1 + \cdots + P_n) + B_1P_{n-1} + B_2P_{n-2} + \cdots + B_{n-1}P_1$$

Expected breakdown cost with preventive maintenance

$$\text{TC}_\text{p} = \frac{C_p + B_n c_b}{n}$$

SUMMARY OF KEY TERMS

breakdown maintenance: the repairs required to make a machine operational after it has failed, or broken down.

dispatch list: a shop paper that specifies the sequence in which jobs should be processed; it is often derived from specific sequencing rules.

finite scheduling: an approach to scheduling that loads jobs in priority order and delays those jobs for which current capacity is exceeded.

flow time: the time that it takes for a job to "flow" through the system; that is, its completion time.

Gantt chart: a bar chart designed by Henry Gantt in the early 1900s to show a job's progress graphically or to compare actual against planned performance.

infinite scheduling: an approach to scheduling that initially assumes infinite capacity and then manually "levels the load" of resources that have exceeded capacity.

input/output (I/O) control: a procedure for monitoring the input to and output from a work center in order to regulate the flow of work through a system.

Johnson's rule: an algorithm for sequencing any number of jobs through two serial operations in order to minimize makespan.

loading: the process of assigning work to individual workers or machines.

load leveling: the process of smoothing out the work assigned across time and the available resources.

makespan: the time that it takes for a group of jobs to be completed–that is, the completion time of the last job in a group.

preventive maintenance: a system of daily maintenance, periodic inspection, and preventive repairs designed to reduce the probability of machine breakdown.

production control department: a department within the manufacturing function responsible for loading, sequencing, and monitoring jobs.

scheduling: the determination of *when* labor, equipment, and facilities are needed to produce a product or provide a service.

sequencing: the process of assigning priorities to jobs so that they are processed in a particular order.

shop floor control: scheduling and monitoring day-to-day production in a job shop; also known as production control or production activity control.

synchronous production: a finite scheduling approach that differentiates between bottleneck and nonbottleneck resources and between transfer batches and process batches.

tardiness: the difference between a job's due date and its completion time for those jobs completed after their due date.

total productive maintenance (TPM): an approach to machine maintenance that combines the U.S. practice of preventive maintenance with the Japanese concepts of total quality and employer involvement.

work package: shop paperwork that travels with a job to specify what work needs to be done at a particular machine center and where the item should be routed next.

SOLVED PROBLEMS

1. *Assignment Problem*

Problem Statement:

Wilkerson Printing has four jobs waiting to be run this morning. Fortunately, they have four printing presses available. However, the presses are of different vintage and operate at different speeds. The approximate times (in minutes) required to process each job on each press are given next. Assign jobs to presses so that the batch of jobs can be completed as soon as possible.

	PRESS			
JOB	*1*	*2*	*3*	*4*
A	20	90	40	10
B	40	45	50	35
C	30	70	35	25
D	60	45	70	40

Solution:

Row reduction:

10	80	30	0
5	10	15	0
5	45	10	0
20	5	30	0

Column reduction:

5	75	20	0
0	5	5	0
0	40	0	0
15	0	20	0

Cover all zeros:

```
5     75    20     0
|            |     |
0      5     5     0
|            |     |
0     40     0     0
|            |     |
15 —   0  — 20  —  0
```

The number of lines equals the number of rows, so this is the optimal solution.

Make assignments:

5	75	20	[0]
[0]	5	5	0
0	40	[0]	0
15	[0]	20	0

Assign job A to press 4, job B to press 1, job C to press 4, and job D to press 2. Since the jobs can be run concurrently, the entire batch will be completed by the maximum completion time of the individual jobs, or job D's time of 45 minutes. The total machining time required is (10 + 40 + 35 + 45) = 130 minutes.

Here is the AB:POM solution to this problem:

```
                         Assignment                      Solution
Number of jos (2-99) 4           Number of machines (2-99) 4
minimize
                       Wilkerson Press
ASSGNMNTS         mach 1        mach 2        mach 3      mach 4
job 1                                                          1
job 2                  1
job 3                                             1
job 4                              1
      The bottleneck is            $45

                     NOTE: alternate optimal solutions exist
```

EXHIBIT 14.1

2. *Johnson's Rule*

Problem Statement:

Clean and Shine Car Service has five cars waiting to be washed and waxed. The time required (in minutes) for each activity is given next. In what order should the cars be processed through the facility? When will the batch of cars be completed?

Car	*Wash*	*Wax*
1	5	10
2	7	2
3	10	5
4	8	6
5	3	5

Solution:

We will use Johnson's rule to sequence the cars. The lowest processing time is 2 minutes for waxing car 2. Since waxing is the second operation, we place car 2 as near to the end of the sequence as possible, in last place. The next-lowest time is 3 minutes for washing car 5. Since washing is the first operation, we place car 5 as near to the front of the sequence as possible, in first place. The next-lowest time is 5 minutes for washing car 1 and waxing car 3. Car 1 is scheduled in second place, and car 3 is put in next-to-last place (i.e., fourth). That leaves car 4 for third place.

Sequence:

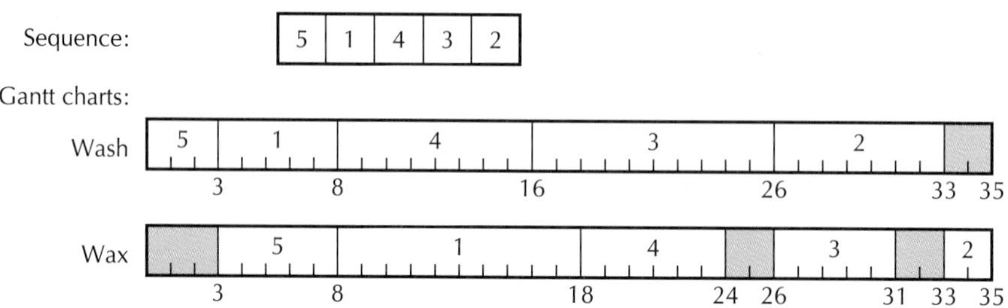

The completion time for washing and waxing the five cars is 35 minutes. The washing facility is idle for 2 minutes at the end of the cycle. The waxing facility is idle for 3 minutes at the beginning of the cycle and 4 minutes during the cycle.

Here is the AB:POM solution for this problem:

```
                    Job Shop Sequencing            Solution
Number of jobs (1-99) 5          Number of machines (1-2) 2
                Clean and Shine Car Service
Johnson   mach 1  mach 2   Order  Done 1  Done 2 (flow time)
job 1          5      10  second      8       18
job 2          7       2   fifth     33       35
job 3         10       5  fourth     26       31
job 4          8       6   third     16       24
job 5          3       5   first      3        8
                           Makespan (maximum flow time) = 35
SEQUENCE
job 5, job 1, job 4, job 3, job 2
```

EXHIBIT 14.2

QUESTIONS

14-1. How do scheduling activities differ for projects, mass production, and process industries?

14-2. Why is scheduling a job shop so difficult?

14-3. What three functions are typically performed by a production control department?

14-4. Give examples of four types of operations (manufacturing or service) and suggest which scheduling objectives might be appropriate for each.

14-5. How can the success of a scheduling system be measured?

14-6. Describe the process of loading and load leveling. What quantitative techniques are available to help in this process?

14-7. What is the purpose of dispatch lists? How are they usually constructed?

14-8. When should the following sequencing rules be used?
   a. SPT
   b. Johnson's rule
   c. DDATE
   d. FCFS

14-9. What is the difference between local and global sequencing rules? Give several examples of each.

14-10. What information is provided by the critical ratio sequencing rule? How does it differ from SLACK?

14-11. How are work packages, hot lists, and exception reports used in a job shop?

14-12. What are Gantt charts and why are they used so often?

14-13. Explain the concept behind input/output control.

14-14. Describe how gateway work centers, downstream work centers, and backlog affect shop performance.

14-15. Explain the difference between infinite and finite scheduling.

14-16. How does synchronized production differ from traditional scheduling methods?

14-17. How should bottleneck resources and nonbottleneck resources be scheduled?

14-18. Why should transfer batches and process batches be treated differently?

14-19. What factors should be considered in scheduling maintenance activities?

14-20. What costs are involved in breakdown maintenance? In preventive maintenance?

14-21. What is meant by autonomous maintenance? Predictive maintenance?
14-22. What three types of activities comprise preventive maintenance?
14-23. How can a balance be struck between the cost of breakdown maintenance and the cost of preventive maintenance?
14-24. Explain the concept of total productive maintenance.
14-25. Preventive maintenance can be viewed as the process of maintaining the "health" of a machine. Using health care as an analogy, explain the differences and trade-offs between breakdown maintenance, preventive maintenance, and total productive maintenance.
14-26. What are some typical issues involved in employee scheduling?
14-27. What quantitative techniques are available to help develop employee schedules?

PROBLEMS

14-1. Nurse 1 to Jones, Nurse 2 to Hathaway, Nurse 3 to Sweeney, Nurse 4 to Bryant; 3 hours

14-1. At Valley Hospital, nurses beginning a new shift report to a central area to receive their primary patient assignments. Not every nurse is as efficient as another with particular kinds of patients. Given the following patient roster, care levels, and time estimates, assign nurses to patients to optimize efficiency. Also, determine how long it will take for the nurses to complete their routine tasks on this shift.

		TIME REQUIRED (HOURS) TO COMPLETE ROUTINE TASKS			
PATIENT	*CARE LEVEL*	*Nurse 1*	*Nurse 2*	*Nurse 3*	*Nurse 4*
M. Jones	A2-Recovery	3	5	4	3
B. Hathaway	B2-Therapy	2	1	3	2
D. Bryant	B1-Testing	3	4	2	2
C. Sweeney	A1-Recovery	4	3	3	4

14-2. Nurse 1 to Bryant, Nurse 2 to Jones, Nurse 3 to Hathaway, Nurse 4 to Sweeney; 93

14-2. Valley Hospital (from Problem 14-1) wants to focus on customer perceptions of quality, so it has asked its patients to evaluate the nursing staff and indicate preferences for assignment. Reassign the nursing staff to obtain the highest customer approval rating possible (a perfect score is 100).

	RATING			
PATIENT	*Nurse 1*	*Nurse 2*	*Nurse 3*	*Nurse 4*
M. Jones	89	95	83	84
B. Hathaway	88	80	96	85
D. Bryant	87	92	82	84
C. Sweeney	93	82	86	94

Compare the results with those from Problem 14-1. What is the average rating of the assignment? What other criteria could be used to assign nurses?

14-3. Product 1 to Machine 2, Product 2 to Machine 4, Product 3 to Machine 1, Product 4 to Machine 3, Product 5 to Machine 5

14-3. Fibrous Incorporated makes products from rough tree fibers. Its product line consists of five items processed mainly through one of five machines. The machines are not identical, and some products are better suited to some machines. Given the following production time (in minutes) per unit determine an optimal assignment of product to machine.

PRODUCT	MACHINE A	B	C	D	E
1	17	10	15	16	20
2	12	9	16	9	14
3	11	16	14	15	12
4	14	10	10	18	17
5	13	12	9	15	11

14-4. Sunshine House received a contract this year as a supplier of Girl Scout cookies. Sunshine currently has five production lines, each of which will be dedicated to a particular kind of cookie. The production lines differ by sophistication of machines, site, and experience of personnel. Given the following estimates of processing times (in hours), assign cookies to lines so that the order can be completed as soon as possible.

14-4. CM to 5, PB to 4, SB to 1, FD to 3, MC to 2; 22 hr

COOKIES	PRODUCTION LINE 1	2	3	4	5
Chocolate Mint	30	18	26	17	15
Peanut Butter	23	22	32	25	30
Shortbread	17	31	24	22	29
Fudge Delight	28	19	13	18	23
Macaroons	23	14	16	20	27

14-5. Evan Schwartz has six jobs waiting to be processed through his machine. Today is November 1. Processing time (in days) and due date information for each job is given below.

14-5. DDATE or SPT

Job	Processing Time	Due date
A	2	11-3
B	1	11-2
C	4	11-12
D	3	11-4
E	4	11-8
F	5	11-10

Sequence the jobs by a. FCFS, b. SPT, c. SLACK, and d. DDATE. Calculate the average completion time and average tardiness of the six jobs under each sequencing rule. Which rule would you recommend?

14-6. College students always have a lot of work to do, but this semester, Katie Lawrence is overwhelmed. Listed next are the assignments she faces, the estimated completion times (in days), and due dates.

14-6. FCFS, SPT, SLACK, or DDATE; SPT, SLACK, or DDATE

Assignment	Estimated Completion Time	Due date
1. Management case	5	10-20
2. Marketing survey	10	11-3
3. Financial analysis	4	10-25
4. Term project	21	11-15
5. Computer program	14	11-2

a. Help Katie prioritize her work so that she completes as many assignments on time as possible. Today is October 1.
b. Would your sequence of assignments change if Katie were interested in minimizing the average tardiness of her assignments?

14-7. SPT

14-7. Today is day 4 of the planning cycle. Sequence the following jobs by a. FCFS, b. SPT, c. SLACK, d. CR, and e. DDATE. Calculate the mean completion time and mean tardiness for each sequencing rule. Which rule would you recommend?

Job	*Processing Time (in days)*	*Due date*
A	3	Day 10
B	10	12
C	2	25
D	4	8
E	5	15
F	8	18
G	7	20

14-8. SPT or DDATE

14-8. Alice's Alterations has eight jobs to be completed and only one sewing machine (and sewing machine operator). Given the processing times and due dates as shown here, prioritize the jobs by a. SPT, b. DDATE, c. SLACK, and d. CR.

Task	*Processing Time (in days)*	*Due Date*
A	5	10
B	8	15
C	6	15
D	3	20
E	10	25
F	14	40
G	7	45
H	3	50

Today is day 5. Calculate mean flow time, mean tardiness, maximum tardiness, and number of jobs tardy for each sequence. Which sequencing rule would you recommend? Why?

14-9. 6, 5, 4, 2, 1, 3; 5 hr 35 min

14-9. Tracy has six chapters on her desk that must be typed and proofed as soon as possible. Tracy does the typing; the author does the proofing. Some chapters are easy to type but more difficult to proof. The estimated time (in minutes) for each activity is given here. In what order should Tracy type the chapters so that the entire batch can be finished as soon as possible? When can Tracy expect to be finished?

Chapter	*Typing*	*Proofing*
1	30	20
2	90	25
3	60	15
4	45	30
5	75	60
6	20	30

14-10. Claims received by Healthwise Insurance Company are reviewed at one station, adjudicated, and sent to another station for entry into the data base. The processing time (in minutes) required for each general type of claim is shown here. Currently, Bill Frazier has ten claims to be reviewed. In what order should he process the claims so that the entire batch can get into the system as soon as possible? How long will it take to process completely the ten claims?

14-10. 8, 4, 6, 5, 9, 2, 3, 1, 10, 7; 1 hr 45 min

	PROCESSING TIME	
CLASSIFICATION	Review	Data Entry
1. Medicare I	8	5
2. Physician 24	15	10
3. Medicare II	6	5
4. Physician 4	5	10
5. HMO I	17	15
6. Physician 17	10	10
7. Emergency II	5	3
8. HMO II	4	15
9. Physician 37	12	10
10. Emergency I	20	3

14-11. Jobs processed through Percy's machine shop pass through three operations, 1. milling, 2. grinding, and 3. turning. The times requested at each of these operations by the current queue of jobs is shown below.

14-11. SPT

Job	Milling	Grinding	Turning
A	5	1	4
B	2	2	5
C	3	2	1
D	0	3	0
E	4	1	2

Sequence the jobs by a) the shortest processing time (in hours) of each operation (SPT), and b) the shortest processing time of the sum of the remaining operations (RWK). Make a Gantt chart for each machine and each rule. Which sequencing rule would you recommend?

14-12. The following data have been compiled for an input/output report at work center 7. Complete the report and analyze the results.

14-12. Backlog 30, 20, 10, 5, 5, 10

Period		1	2	3	4	5	Total
Planned input		50	55	60	65	65	
Actual input		50	50	55	60	65	
Deviation							
Planned output		65	65	65	65	65	
Actual output		60	60	60	60	60	
Deviation							
Backlog	30						

14-13. The input/output report for work center 6 is as follows. Complete the report and comment on the results.

14-13. Backlog 10, 0, 0, 0, 0

Period		1	2	3	4	5	*Total*
Planned input		50	55	60	65	65	
Actual input		40	50	55	60	65	
Deviation							
Planned output		50	55	60	65	65	
Actual output		50	50	55	60	65	
Deviation							
Backlog	10						

14-14. See Solutions Manual.

14-14. Kim Johnson, R.N., the charge nurse of the antepartum ward of City Hospital in Burtonsville, Maryland, needs help in scheduling the nurse workforce for next week.

a. Create an employee schedule that will meet the demand requirements and guarantee each nurse 2 days off per week.
b. Revise the schedule so that the 2 days off are consecutive.

Days of Week	*M*	*T*	*W*	*Th*	*F*	*Sa*	*Su*
Min. no. of nurses	3	3	4	5	4	3	3
Kim Johnson							
Tom Swann							
Flo Coligny							
Shelley Betts							
Phuong Truong							

14-15. See Solutions Manual.

14-15. Rosemary Haynes needs help in scheduling the volunteers working at the local crisis pregnancy center. Create a work schedule that will meet the demand requirements, given that a volunteer will only work 2 days per week. Try to make the work days consecutive.

Days of Week	*M*	*T*	*W*	*Th*	*F*	*Sa*	*Su*
Min. no. of volunteers	4	3	2	3	6	4	2
Rosemary Hayhes							
Albert Taglieri							
Richard White							
Gail Cooke							
Shelly Black							
Karen Romero							
Jamie Dixson							
Susie Deyo							
Peter Bradley							
Rachel Hatcher							
C. J. Adams							
Sally Beck							

14-16. Allied needs to improve the reliability of its machines in order to support JIT manufacturing. Maintenance records show the following frequencies of breakdowns for its group of 10 CNC machines:

★ 14-16. Preventive maintenance every week.

Weeks Until Breakdown	*No. of Breakdowns*
1	6
2	10
3	12
4	15
5	7

The cost of fixing a broken machine (including the cost of down time) is approximately $2,000 per breakdown. The cost of preventive maintenance is $100 per machine. Construct a table comparing the cost of different maintenance strategies. Which maintenance strategy do you recommend?

14-17. Millard Manufacturing makes sealants for household and industrial use. Whenever any of its four huge mixing machines are down, the company stands to lose $20,000. However, preventive maintenance also takes away from productive time and can easily cost $5,000 per week. Given the following frequencies of breakdowns, determine a cost-effective maintenance strategy for Millard.

★ 14-17. Preventive maintenance every week.

Weeks until Breakdown	*No. of Breakdowns*
1	5
2	6
3	4
4	10

CASE PROBLEM

★ 1204 min

From a Different Perspective

"And do you have the answer to Problem 6, Pete?" asked Professor Grasso.

"Yes sir, I have the answer according to the textbook, but I'm not sure I get it," replied Pete.

"You don't understand how to get the solution?"

"Oh, I understand the numbers, but I don't know what they're good for. Where I work, nobody ever "sequences" anything. You don't have time to calculate things like slack and critical ratio. You do what's next in line or on top of the stack, unless you see a red tag on something that needs to be rushed through. Or maybe you run what's most like what you've just finished working on so the machine doesn't have to be changed. Or you run what can get done the fastest because when you produce more you get paid more."

"Pete, it sounds to me like you *are* using sequencing rules—FCFS, highest priority, minimum setup, and SPT."

"Maybe you're right, but there's still something that bothers me. If you're going to go to all the trouble to rearrange a stack of jobs, you'd want more information than what we're working with."

"What do you mean?"

"I mean, there's no use rushing a job at one station to let it sit and wait at the next. It's like those maniacs who break their neck to pass you on the road, but they never get anywhere. A few minutes later you're right behind them at a stoplight."

"I see."

"You need some way of looking at the entire job, where it's going next, what resources it's going to use, if it has to be assembled with something else, things like that."

"You've got a point, Pete. Why don't you give us a 'real' example we can work with? You talk, I'll write it on the board."

Pete talked for about 20 more minutes, and when he was finished, Professor Grasso had the following diagram on the board:

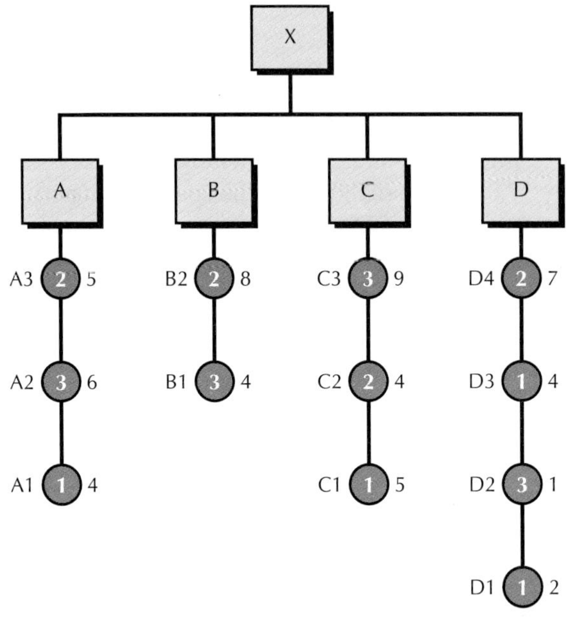

"OK, class, let's take this home and work on it. You have one of each machine type 1, 2, and 3. There's no inventory on hand and nothing on order. See how quickly you can produce 50 units of product X. Best schedule gets 5 extra points on the final exam."

REFERENCES

Baker, K., and M. Magazine, "Workforce Scheduling with Cyclic Demands and Days-Off Constraints," *Management Science* 24, no. 2 (October 1977): 161–7.

Conway, R., W. Maxwell, and L. Miller, *Theory of Scheduling,* Reading, Mass.: Addison-Wesley, 1967.

Goldratt, E. *What Is This Thing Called Theory of Constraints and How Should It Be Implemented?* Croton-on-Hudson, N.Y.: North River Press, 1990.

Goldratt, E., and J. Cox, *The Goal: Excellence in Manufacturing,* Croton-on-Hudson, N.Y.: North River Press, 1984.

Huang, P., L. Moore, and R. Russell, "Workload versus Scheduling Policies in a Dual-Resource Constrained Job Shop," *Computers and Operations Research* 11, no. 1 (1984): 37–47.

Nakajima, S., *Introduction to TPM,* Cambridge, Mass.: Productivity Press, 1988.

Russell, R., and B. W. Taylor, "An Evaluation of Sequencing Rules for an Assembly Shop," *Decision Sciences* 16, no. 2 (1985): 196–212.

Tersine, R. J., *Production/Operations Management: Concepts, Structure, and Analysis,* New York: Elsevier-North Holland, 1985.

Umble, M., and M. L. Srikanth, *Synchronous Manufacturing: Principles for World Class Excellence,* Cincinnati: South-Western Publishing Co., 1990.

Vollman, T., W. Berry, and D. C. Whybark, *Manufacturing Planning and Control Systems,* Homewood, Ill.: Irwin, 1992.

Xudong, H., R. Russell, and J. Dickey, "Workload Analysis Expert System and Optimizer," *Proceedings of the Seventh International Congress of Cybernetics and Systems,* Vol. 1, London (September 1987): 68–72.

15

JUST-IN-TIME AND CONTINUOUS IMPROVEMENT

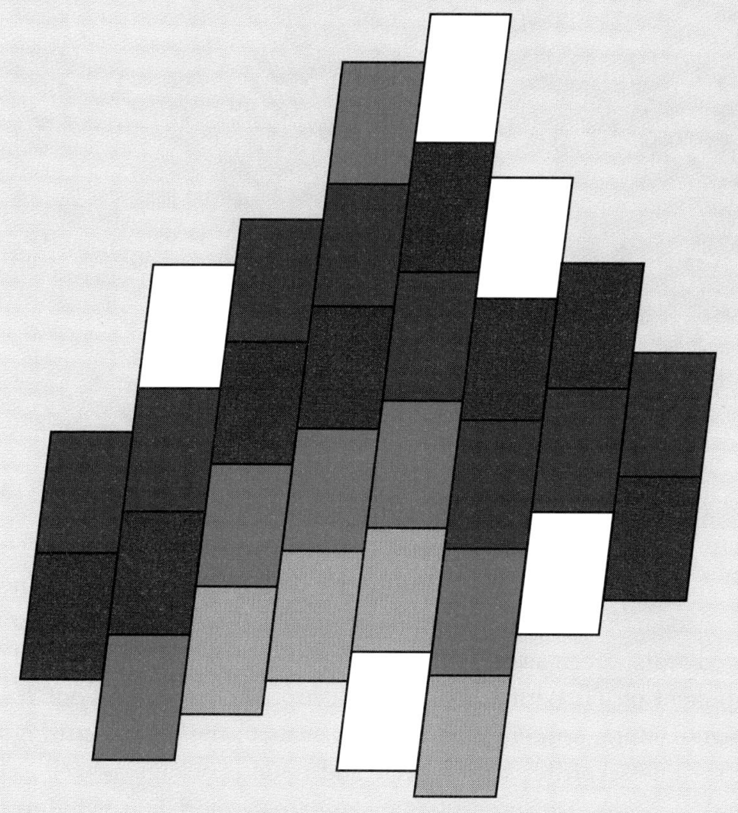

CHAPTER OUTLINE

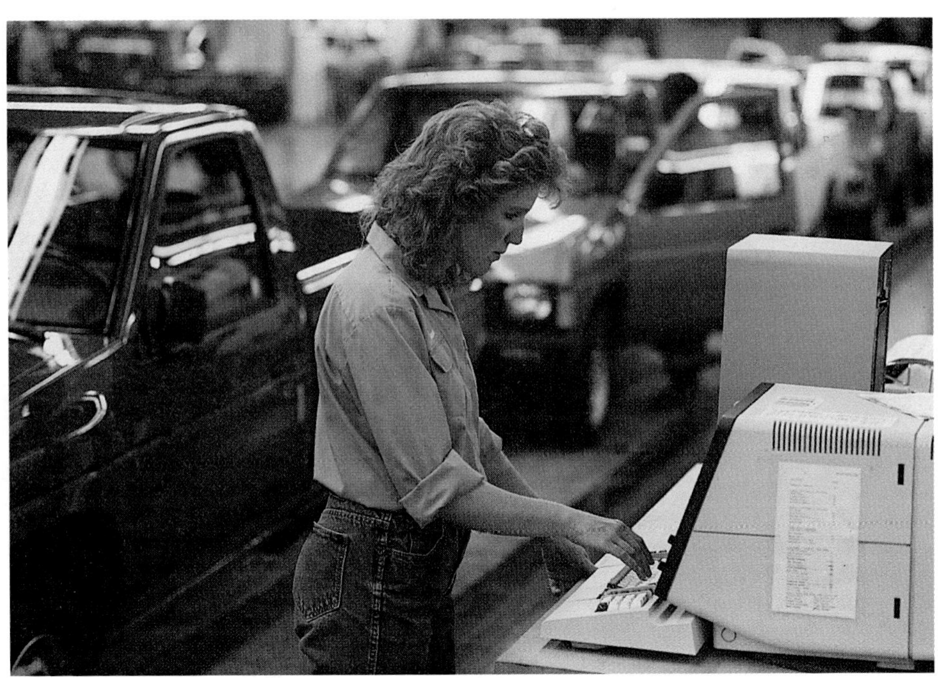

Assembly lines traditionally were set up to process only one product model at a time. The machines and workers could then be specialized to the item produced. Production of another model would require the line to shut down and retool. With the advent of JIT, mixed models could be produced on the same assembly line at the same time. This required reductions in changeover times from one model to another and more flexible workers and machines. Notice the different color trucks coming off this mixed-model assembly line at Nissan's Smyrna, Tennessee plant.

JIT IN DETROIT

A blue car leaves the painting room, followed by a red car, followed by a green car. An hour later, seats arriving from a supplier are off-loaded in the following order: blue seats, red seats, green seats. Is this a coincidence? No, it's sequenced delivery, one component of JIT. With 3 hours' notice suppliers, located about 20 miles away, can manufacture, sequence, and deliver seats to the manufacturing plant. Sequencing is done according to seat style and option package as well as color. Tires, wiring harnesses, struts, door panels, carpets, and rear window shelves also arrive in sequence. Seats and tires arrive every hour; struts arrive about every 4 hours. In Japan, you say? No, in Detroit!

What about suppliers who aren't located so near? The NUMMI plant in Fremont, California, has systems called COPS (California orderly pickup system) and MOPS (Midwest orderly pickup system). Suppliers work from a 2-week production schedule provided by the manufacturer. They ship the same amount of parts at the same time every day. Ten trucks begin a "milk run" each day, picking up parts from suppliers in the midwest and bringing them to consolidation points in Detroit and Chicago. Supplies consolidated in Detroit are trucked to a rail station in Chicago and loaded onto flatbed railroad cars for daily deliveries to NUMMI. The total cycle time from pickup to delivery is 4 days.[1]

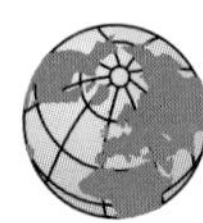

JIT involves producing only what is needed, when it is needed.

Taiichi Ohno, a former shop manager and eventual vice president of Toyota Motor Company, is the individual most credited with the development of just-in-time. **Just-in-time (JIT)** is a U.S. term coined to describe the Toyota production system, widely recognized today as one of the most efficient manufacturing operations in

[1]Raia, Ernest, "JIT in Detroit," *Purchasing* (September 15, 1988): 68–77.

the world. In its simplest form, JIT requires that only the necessary units be provided in the necessary quantities at the necessary times. Producing one unit extra is as bad as being one unit short. Completing production 1 day early is as bad as finishing 1 day late. In other words, all items should be supplied just as they are needed, or "just in time."

This hardly seems to be the basis of a revolution in manufacturing, but the concept is deceptively simple. If you produce only what you need when you need it, then there is no room for error. For JIT to work, many fundamental elements must be in place—steady production, flexible resources, extremely high quality, no machine breakdowns, reliable suppliers, quick machine setups, and lots of discipline to maintain the other elements.

Teaching Note 15.1 Ford's Rouge Plant, the Original JIT?

Just-in-time is both a philosophy and an integrated system for production management that evolved slowly through a trial-and-error process over a span of more than 15 years. There was no master plan or blueprint for JIT. Ohno describes the development of JIT as follows:

JIT is a philosophy and an integrated management system.

> By actually trying, various problems became known. As such problems became gradually clear, they taught me the direction of the next move. I think that we can only understand how all of these pieces fit together in hindsight.[2]

In this chapter, we explore the pieces of JIT and try to discover how they came to be a part of Ohno's integrated management system, known as just-in-time. We also explore JIT in the broader context of continuous improvement, the benefits of JIT, and JIT implementation. We conclude the chapter with a discussion of JIT in services.

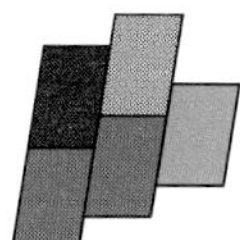

BASIC ELEMENTS OF JIT

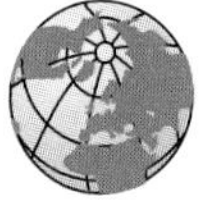

In the 1950s, the entire Japanese automobile industry produced 30,000 vehicles, fewer than 1fi days' production for U.S. automakers. With such low levels of demand, the principles of mass production that worked so well for U.S. manufacturers could not be applied in Japan. Further, the Japanese were short on capital and storage space. So it seems natural that efforts to improve performance (and stay solvent) would center on reducing that asset that soaks up both funds and space—inventory. What is significant is that a system originally designed to reduce inventory levels eventually became a system for continually improving all aspects of manufacturing operations. The stage was set for this evolution by the president of Toyota, Eiji Toyoda, who gave a mandate to his people to "eliminate waste." **Waste** was defined as "anything other than the minimum amount of equipment, materials, parts, space, and time which are absolutely essential to add value to the product."[3] Examples of waste in operations are shown in Figure 15.1.

JIT's mandate: Eliminate waste.

Waste is anything other than that which adds value to the product or service.

The JIT production system is the result of the mandate to eliminate waste. It is composed of the following basic elements:

1. Flexible resources
2. Cellular layouts
3. Pull production system
4. Kanban production control
5. Small-lot production
6. Quick setups
7. Uniform production

Transparency 15.1 Elements of JIT

Teaching Note 15.2 Elements of JIT

basic elements of JIT

[2]Suzaki, K., *The New Manufacturing Challenge*, New York: The Free Press, 1985, p. 250.

[3]Suzaki, *The New Manufacturing Challenge*, pp. 8–9.

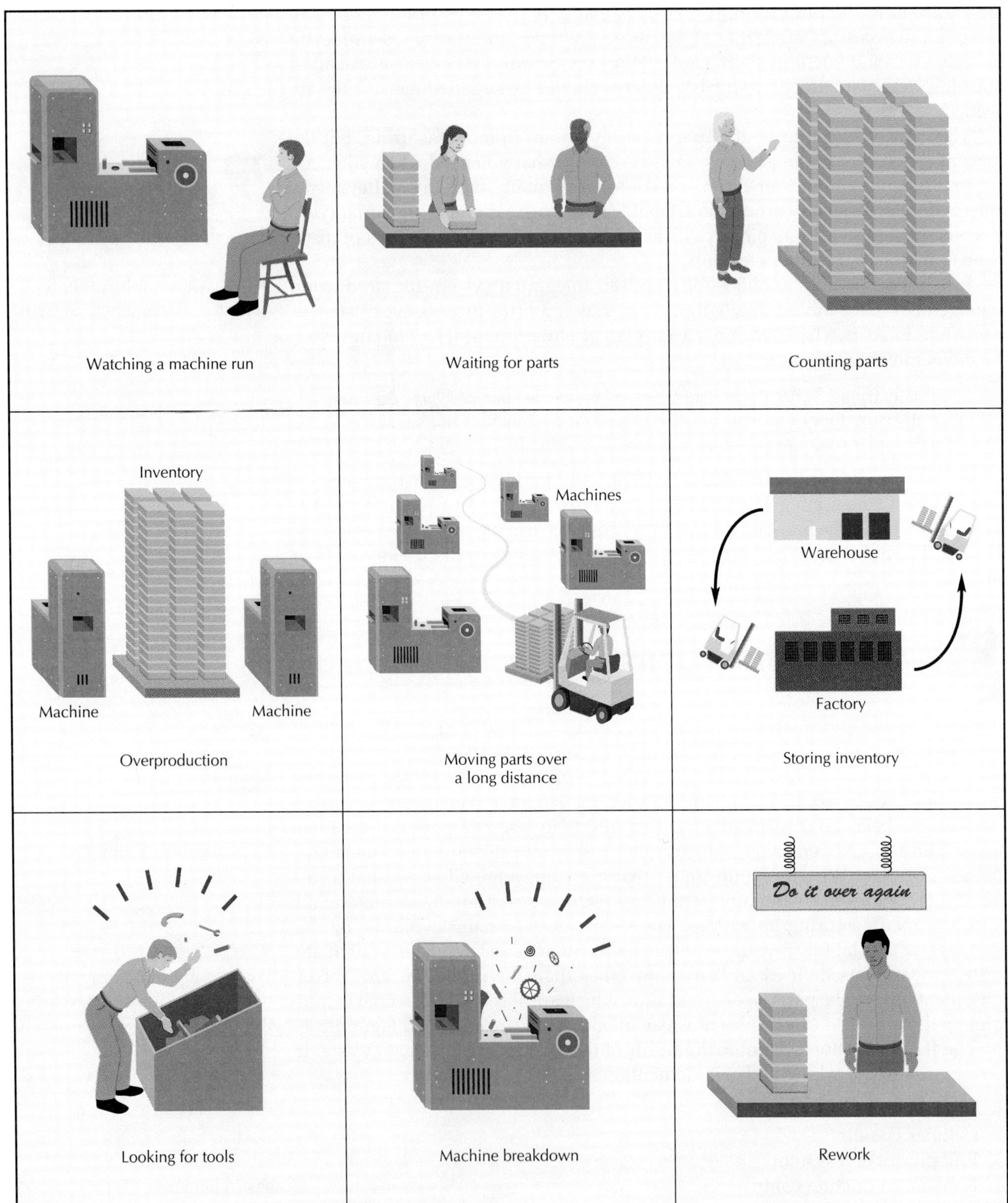

FIGURE 15.1 Waste in Operations

Transparency 15.2 Waste in Operations

8. Quality at the source
9. Supplier networks
10. Continuous improvement

Let's explore each of these elements and determine how they work in concert.[4]

Teaching Note 15.3 Big JIT and Little jit

Flexible Resources

The concept of flexible resources, in the form of **multifunctional workers** and **general-purpose machines,** is recognized as a key element of JIT, but most people do not realize that it was one of the first elements to fall into place. Taiichi Ohno had transferred to Toyota from Toyoda textile mills with no knowledge of (or preconceived notions about) automobile manufacturing. His first attempt to eliminate waste (not unlike U.S. managers) concentrated on worker productivity. Borrowing heavily from U.S. time and motion studies, he set out to analyze every job and every machine in his shop. He quickly noted a distinction between the operating time of a machine and the operating time of the worker. Initially, he asked each worker to operate two machines rather than one. To make this possible, he located the machines in parallel lines or in L-formations. After a time, he asked workers to operate three or four machines arranged in a U-shape. The machines were no longer of the same type (as in a job shop layout) but represented a series of processes common to a group of parts (i.e., a cellular layout).

Multifunctional workers perform more than one job; **general-purpose machines** perform several basic functions.

The operation of different, multiple machines required additional training for workers and specific rotation schedules. Figure 15.2 shows a standard operating routine for an individual worker. The solid lines represent operator processing time (e.g., loading, unloading, or setting up a machine), the dashed lines represent machine processing time, and the squiggly lines represent walking time for the operator from machine to machine. The time required for the worker to complete one pass through the operations assigned is called the operator *cycle time.*

With single workers operating multiple machines, the machines themselves also required some adjustments. Limit switches were installed to turn off machines automatically after each operation was completed. Changes in jigs and

multifunctional workers

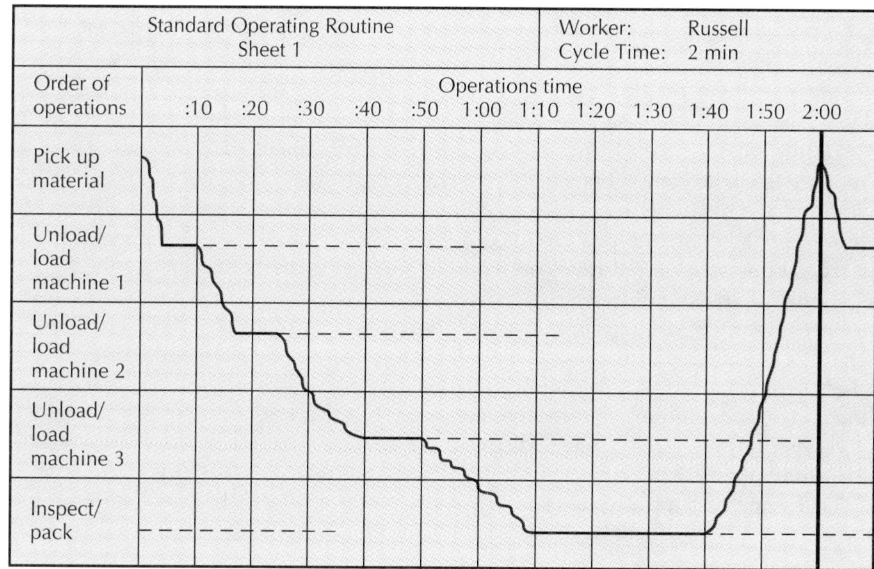

FIGURE 15.2 Standard Operating Routine for a Worker

[4]Much of the material in these sections is adapted from Chapter 5 in Michael Cusomano's text *The Japanese Automobile Industry,* Cambridge, Mass.: Howard University Press, 1985.

fixtures allowed machines to hold a workpiece in place, rather than rely on the presence of an operator. Extra tools and fixtures were purchased and placed at their point of use so that operators didn't have to leave their stations to retrieve them when needed. By the time Ohno was finished with this phase of his improvement efforts, it was possible for one worker to operate as many as seventeen machines (the average was five to ten machines).

The flexibility of labor brought about by Ohno's changes prompted a switch to more flexible machines. Thus, although other manufacturers were interested in purchasing more specialized automated equipment, Toyota preferred small, general-purpose machines. A general-purpose lathe, for example, might be used to bore holes in an engine block and then do other drilling, milling, and threading operations at the same station. The waste of movement to other machines, setting up other machines, and waiting at other machines was eliminated.

GAINING THE COMPETITIVE EDGE

Changes at Corning

Until recently, Corning held the patents for an important component of catalytic converters, a honeycombed ceramic part. Typical of many American firms, Corning could create innovative designs but could not manufacture them competitively. So, for years, production of the part had been licensed to a Japanese company, NGK Insulators. With the patent due to expire in the early 1990s, Corning decided it wanted to challenge NGK for the catalytic converter market. Corning reopened a mothballed plant and used JIT principles to set up a new manufacturing system.

Typically, each automobile factory orders catalytic components of its own design, so the volume of each order is not large. That means machines need to change over quickly from one model to another, and workers on the assembly lines need to perform different tasks. This requirement for flexibility of both machines and labor led to radically different job structures for Corning workers and management.

Imagine a plant with no time clocks, one manager per 60 employees, and blanket authority for all employees to sign purchase orders up to $500. The workers, classified only as operations associates or maintenance engineers, work in self-managed teams. (This is in contrast to Corning's other plants, which have 50 or so job classifications.) They learn multiple skills, rotate through as many as 15 different jobs, and are paid based on the skills they have acquired, rather than their hourly production. They are also eligible for bonuses based on plant performance.

Corning decided to lean more on employee involvement than manufacturing technology. Says the plant manager, "There were places we could have robotized, but we decided against it, because we wanted humans to give us the critical feedback." For example, the extrusion process for ceramics uses computers and sensors to display crucial information but relies on workers to decide whether to change the kiln temperature or speed of flow.

The company is striving for a no-layoff policy and has contracted out such jobs as security and custodial care so those jobs can serve as a backup for production workers should sales fall. Job training includes statistical process control, machine maintenance, and shipping and receiving procedures. Workers who fail to complete the two-year training program face dismissal.

Corning pursued an aggressive strategy based on resource flexibility, and it paid off. The company currently supplies catalytic components to Japanese and U.S. automakers.

Source: Based on "Beating Japan at Its Own Game," *The New York Times,* July 16, 1989, and Naj, Amal Kumar, "Some Manufacturers Drop Efforts to Adopt Japanese Techniques," *The Wall Street Journal,* May 7, 1993.

Sometimes what appears to be a cellular layout is actually a traditional process layout. This photo shows four CNC lathes and their operators. A manufacturing cell would consist of different machines arranged in a flow pattern and probably fewer workers than machines. The work-in-process inventory would also be less.

Cellular Layouts

As noted before, Ohno first reorganized his shop into **manufacturing cells** to utilize labor more efficiently. However, the flexibility of the new layout proved to be fundamental to the effectiveness of JIT as a whole. The concept of cellular layouts did not originate with Ohno. It was first described by a U.S. engineer in the 1920s. As with many other techniques, it was Ohno's inspired application of the idea that brought it to the attention of the world. We discussed cellular layouts (and the concept of group technology on which it is based) in Chapter 7. Let's review some of that material here.

Manufacturing cells are comprised of dissimilar machines brought together to manufacture a family of parts.

Cells group dissimilar machines together to process a family of parts with similar shapes or processing requirements. The layout of machines within the cell resembles a small assembly line and is usually U-shaped. Work is moved within the cell, ideally one unit at a time, from one process to the next by a worker as he or she walks around the cell in a prescribed path. Figure 15.3, on page 754, shows a typical manufacturing cell with worker routes.

Most cells are U-shaped.

Work normally flows through the cell in one direction and experiences little waiting. In a one-person cell, the cycle time of the cell is determined by the time it takes for the worker to complete his or her path through the cell. This means that, although different items produced in the cell may take different amounts of time to complete, the time between successive items leaving the cell remains virtually the same because the worker's path remains the same. Thus, changes of product mix within the cell are easy to accommodate. Changes in volume can be handled by adding or subtracting workers to the cell and adjusting their walking routes accordingly. Figure 15.4, on page 755, shows how worker routes can be adjusted in a system of integrated cells.

Cycle time is adjusted by changing worker paths.

Because cells produce similar items, setup time requirements are low and lot sizes can be reduced. Movement of output from the cells to subassembly or assembly lines occurs in small lots and is controlled by kanbans (which we discuss later). Cellular layouts, because of their manageable size, work flow, and flexibility, facilitate another element of JIT, pull production.

Transparency 15.3 Cellular Layout

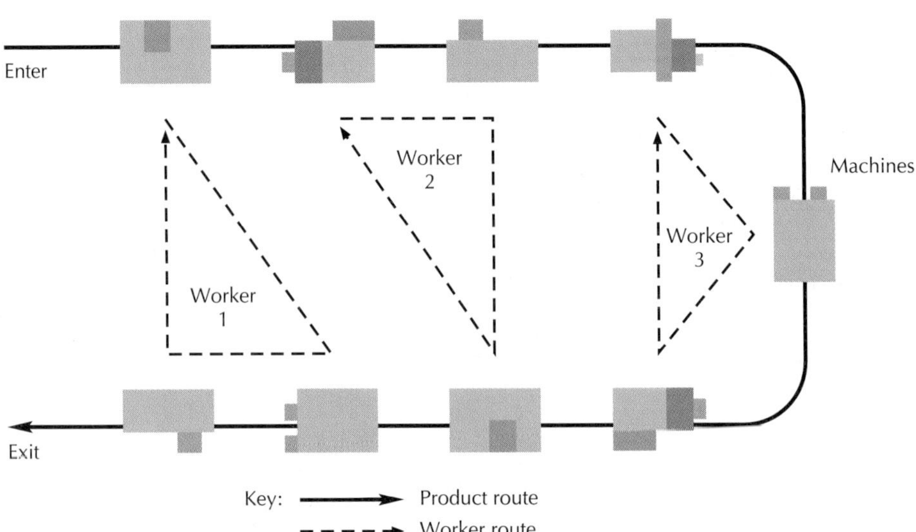

FIGURE 15.3 Manufacturing Cell with Worker Routes

The Pull System

A major problem in automobile manufacturing is the coordination of the production and delivery of materials and parts with the production of subassemblies and the requirements of the final assembly line. It is a complicated process, not because of the technology involved, but because of the thousands of large and small components produced by thousands of workers for a single automobile. Traditionally, inventory has been used to cushion against laxes in coordination, and these inventories can be quite large. Ohno struggled for five years trying to come up with a system to improve the coordination between processes and thereby eliminate the need for large amounts of inventory. He finally got the idea for his famous *pull* system from another American classic, the supermarket. Ohno read (and later observed) that Americans do not keep large stocks of food at home. Instead, they make frequent visits to nearby supermarkets to purchase items as they need them. The supermarkets, in turn, carefully control their inventory by replenishing items on their shelves only as they are removed. Customers actually "pull through" the system the items they need, and supermarkets do not order more items than can be sold.

Push systems rely on a predetermined schedule.

Pull systems rely on customer requests.

Teaching Note 15.4 A Video Suggestion

Applying this concept to manufacturing requires a reversal of the normal process/information flow, called a *push* system. In a **push system,** a schedule is prepared in advance for a series of workstations, and each workstation pushes the work they have completed to the next station. With the **pull system,** workers go back to previous stations and take only those parts or materials they need and can process immediately. When their output has been taken, workers at the previous station know it is time to start producing more, and they replenish the exact quantity that the subsequent station just took away. If their output is not taken, workers at the previous station simply stop production; no excess is produced. This system forces operations to work in coordination with one another. It prevents overproduction and underproduction; only necessary quantities are produced. "Necessary" is not defined by a schedule that specifies what ought to be needed; rather, it is defined by the operation of the shop floor, complete with unanticipated occurrences and variations in performance.

Although the concept of pull production seems simple, it can be difficult to implement because it is so different from normal scheduling procedures. After several years of experimenting with the pull system, Ohno found it necessary to introduce *kanbans* to exercise more control over the pull process on the shop floor.

Transparency 15.4 Worker Routes

Cell 1
Cell 2
Worker
1
Worker
2
Worker
3
Cell 3
Cell 4
Cell 5

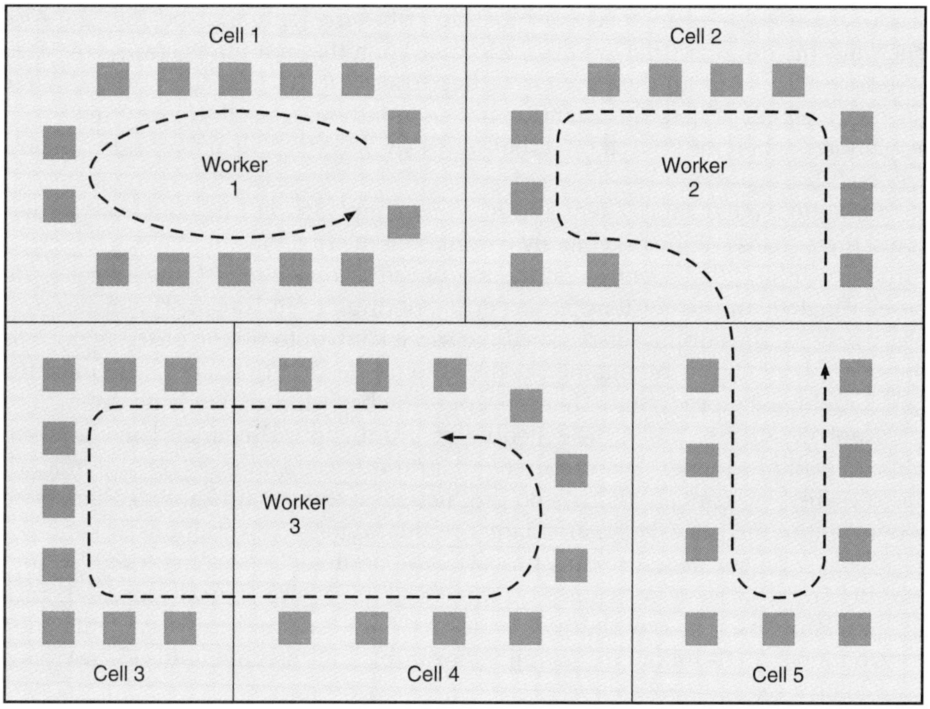

FIGURE 15.4 Worker Routes Lengthened As Volume Decreases

Kanban Production Control System

Kanban is the Japanese word for card. In the pull system, each kanban corresponds to a standard quantity of production or size of container. A kanban contains basic information such as the part number, a brief description, type of container, unit load (i.e., quantity per container), preceding station (where it came from), and subsequent station (where it goes to). Sometimes the kanban is color-coded to indicate raw materials or other stages of manufacturing. The information on the kanban does not change during production. The same kanban can rotate back and forth between preceding and subsequent workstations. A sample kanban is shown in Figure 15.5.

A **kanban** is a card that corresponds to a standard quantity of production (usually a container size).

Kanbans are closely associated with the fixed-quantity inventory system we discussed in Chapter 12. Recall that in the fixed-quantity system, a certain quantity, Q, is ordered whenever the stock on hand falls below a reorder point. The reorder point is determined so that demand can be met while an order for new material is being processed. Thus, the reorder point corresponds to demand during lead time. A visual fixed-quantity system, called the *two-bin system,* illustrates the concept nicely. Referring to Figure 15.6, on page 756, two bins are maintained for each item. The first (and usually larger bin) contains the order quantity minus the reorder point, the second bin contains the reorder point quantity. At the bot-

Kanbans were derived from the two-bin inventory system.

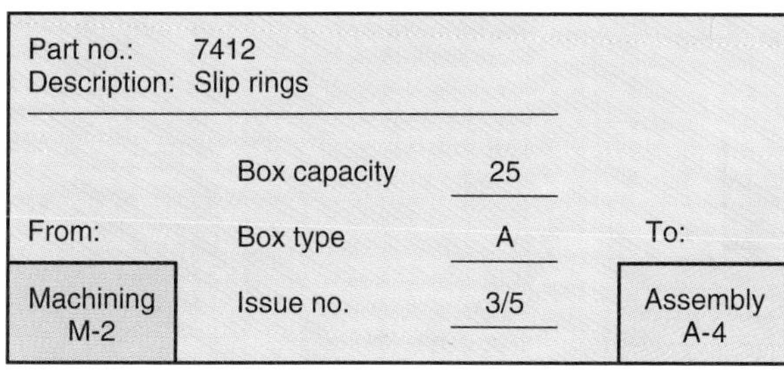

Part no.: 7412
Description: Slip rings
Box capacity 25
From:
Box type A
To:
Machining
M-2
Issue no. 3/5
Assembly
A-4

FIGURE 15.5 A Sample Kanban

tom of the first bin is an order card that describes the item and specifies the supplier and the quantity that is to be ordered. When the first bin is empty, the card is removed and sent to the purchasing department to order a new supply. While the order is being filled, the quantity in the second bin is used. If everything goes as planned, when the second bin is empty, the new order will arrive and both bins will be filled again.

Ohno looked at this system and liked its simplicity, but he could not understand the purpose of the first bin. By eliminating the first bin and placing the order card (which he called a *kanban*) at the top of the second bin, Q-R inventory could be eliminated. In this system, an order is continually in transit. When the new order arrives, the supplier is reissued the same kanban to fill the order again. The only inventory that is maintained is the amount needed to cover usage until the next order can be processed. This concept is the basis for the kanban system.

Kanbans maintain the discipline of pull production.

Teaching Note 15.5 A Kanban Demonstration

Kanbans do not make the schedule of production; they maintain the discipline of pull production by authorizing the production and movement of materials. If there is no kanban, there is no production. If there is no kanban, there is no movement of material. There are many different types and variations of kanbans. The most sophisticated system is probably the dual kanban system used by Toyota. In a dual kanban system, two types of kanbans are typically used, 1. production kanbans, and 2. withdrawal kanbans. Each kanban is physically attached to a container. Let's follow the simplified example outlined in Figure 15.7(a) to explain their use.

A **production kanban** is a card authorizing production of goods.

1. Process B receives a **production kanban.** It must produce enough of the item requested to fill the empty container to which the production kanban is attached.
2. To complete the requirements of production, process B uses a container of inputs and generates a request for more input from the preceding workstation, process A.

Two-bin Inventory System

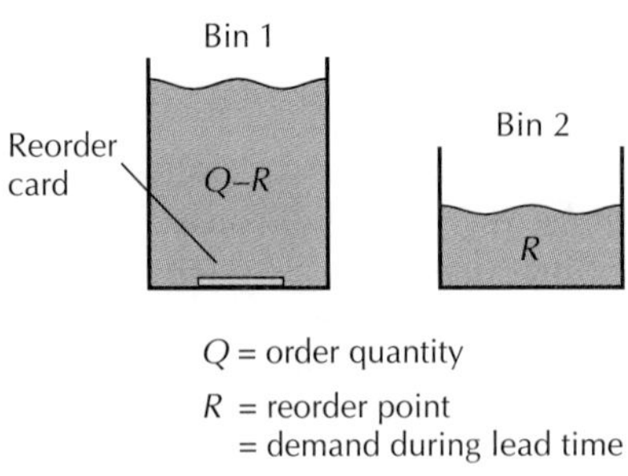

Q = order quantity
R = reorder point
= demand during lead time

Kanban Inventory System

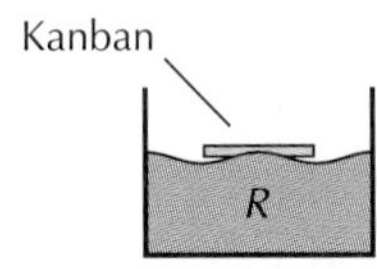

FIGURE 15.6 The Origin of Kanban

Transparency 15.5 Types of Kanbans

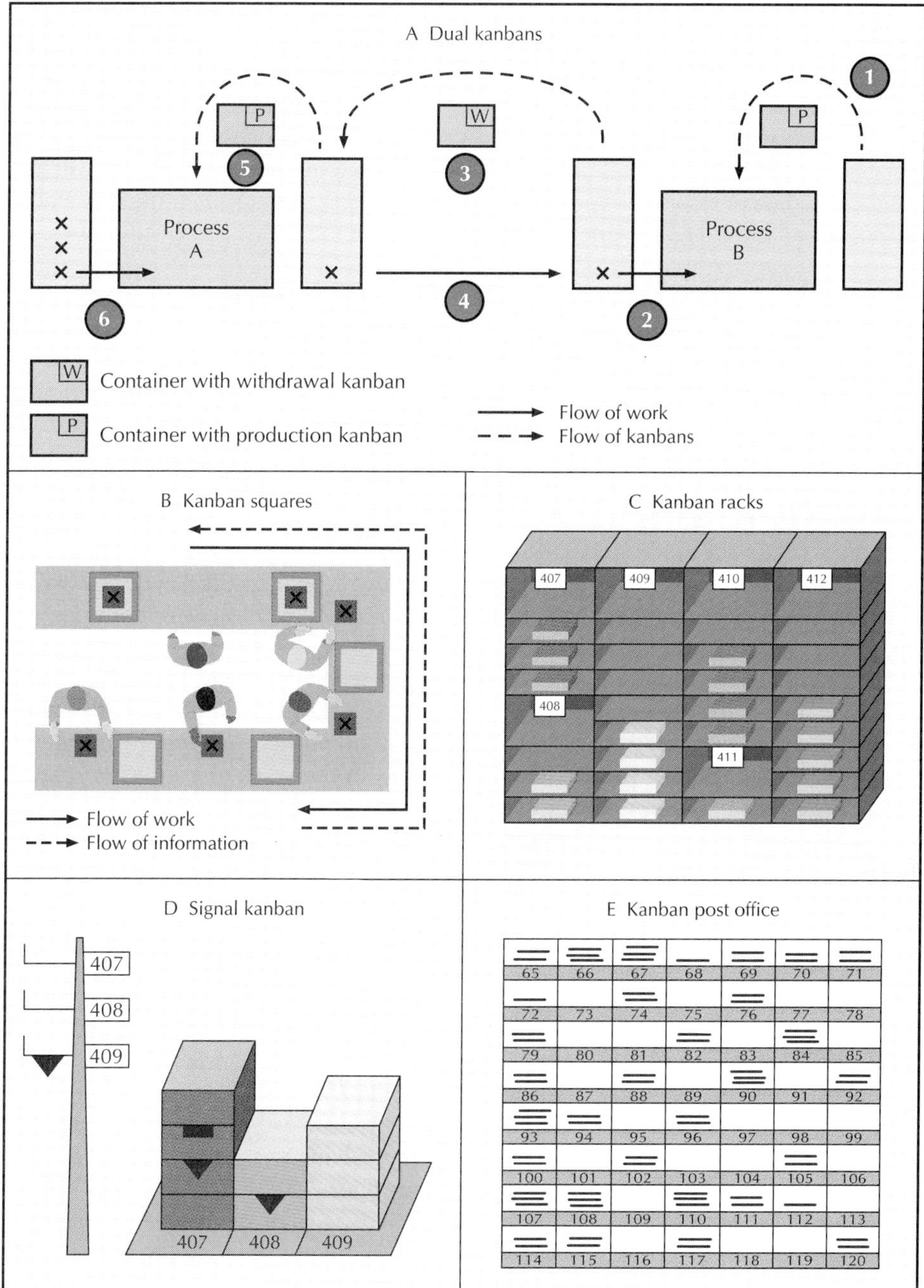

FIGURE 15.7 Types of Kanbans

3. The request for more input items takes the form of a **withdrawal kanban** sent to process A.
4. Since process A has some output available, it attaches the withdrawal kanban to the full container and sends it immediately to process B.
5. The production kanban that originally accompanied the full container is removed and placed on the empty container, thereby generating production at process A.
6. Production at process A requires a container of inputs. No new order is generated because three containers of input are already on hand.

A **withdrawal kanban** authorizes the movement of goods.

There are many variations of kanbans.

The dual kanban approach is used when material is not necessarily moving between two consecutive processes or when there is more than one input to a process and the inputs are dispersed throughout the facility (as for an assembly process). If the processes are tightly linked, a single kanban can be used. For example, in Figure 15.7(a), if process B always followed process A, the output for process A would also be the input for process B. A kanban could be permanently attached to the containers that rotate between A and B. An empty container would be the signal for more production, and the distinction between production and withdrawal kanban would no longer be necessary.

To take this concept one step further, if two processes are physically located near each other, the kanban system can be implemented *without* physical cards. Figure 15.7(b) shows the use of kanban squares placed between successive work stations. A **kanban square** is a marked area that will hold a certain number of output items (usually one or two). If the kanban square following his or her process is empty, the worker knows it is time to begin production again. *Kanban racks,* illustrated in Figure 15.7(c), can be used in a similar manner. When the allocated slots on a rack are empty, workers know it is time to begin a new round of production to fill up the slots. If the distance between stations prohibits the use of kanban squares or racks, the signal for production can be a colored golf ball rolled down a tube, a flag on a post, a light flashing on a board, or an electronic or verbal message requesting more.

A **kanban square** is a marked area designated to hold items.

Signal kanbans are used when inventory between processes is still necessary. It closely resembles the reorder point system. As shown in Figure 15.7(d), a triangular marker is placed at a certain level of inventory. When the marker is reached (a visual reorder point), it is removed from the stack of goods and placed on an order post, thereby generating a replenishment order for the item. The square-shaped kanban in the diagram is called a **material kanban.** In some cases it is necessary to order the *material* for a process in advance of the initiation of the process.

A **signal kanban** is a triangular kanban used to signal production at the previous workstation.

A **material kanban** is used to order material in advance of a process.

Kanbans can also be used outside the factory to order material from suppliers. The supplier brings the order (e.g., a filled container) directly to its point of use in the factory and then picks up an empty container with kanban to fill and return later. It would not be unusual for 5,000 to 10,000 of these *supplier kanbans* to rotate between the factory and suppliers. To handle this volume of transactions, a kind of kanban "post office" can be set up, with kanbans sorted by supplier. The supplier then checks his or her "mailbox" to pick up new orders before returning to the factory. Bar-coded kanbans and electronic kanbans can also be used to facilitate communication between customer and supplier.

Supplier kanbans rotate between the factory and suppliers.

It is easy to get caught up with the technical aspects of kanbans and lose sight of the objective of the pull system, which is to reduce inventory levels. We have noted that the kanban system is actually very similar to the reorder point system. The difference is in application. The reorder point system attempts to create a permanent ordering policy, whereas the kanban system encourages the continual reduction of inventory. We can see how that occurs by examining the formula for determining the number of kanbans needed to control the production of a particular item.

The number of kanbans needed can be calculated from demand and lead time information.

$$\text{No. of kanbans} = \frac{\text{average demand during lead time} + \text{safety stock}}{\text{container size}}$$

$$N = \frac{dL + S}{C}$$

where

N = number of kanbans or containers

d = average number of units demanded over some time period

L = lead time; the time it takes to replenish an order (expressed in the same time terms as demand)

S = safety stock; usually given as a percentage of demand during lead time but can be based on service level and variance of demand during lead time (as in Chapter 12)

C = container size

To force the improvement process, the container size is usually much smaller than the demand during lead time. At Toyota, containers can hold at most 10 percent of a day's demand. This allows the number of kanbans (i.e., containers) to be reduced one at a time. The fewer number of kanbans (and corresponding lower level of inventory) causes problems or bottlenecks in the system to become visible. Workers and managers then attempt to solve the problems that have been identified.

EXAMPLE 15.1

Alternate Example 15.1

Determining the Number of Kanbans

Problem Statement:

Julie Hurling works in a cosmetic factory filling, capping, and labeling bottles. She is asked to process an average of 150 bottles per hour through her work cell. If one kanban is attached to every container, a container holds 25 bottles, it takes 30 minutes to receive new bottles from the previous workstation, and the factory uses a safety stock factor of 10 percent, how many kanbans are needed for the bottling process?

Solution:

Given:

$$d = 150 \text{ bottles per hour}$$
$$L = 30 \text{ minutes} = 0.5 \text{ hour}$$
$$S = 0.10\ (150 \times 0.5) = 7.5$$
$$C = 25 \text{ bottles}$$

Then,

$$N = \frac{dL + S}{C} = \frac{(150 \times 0.5) + 7.5}{25}$$
$$= \frac{75 + 7.5}{25} = 3.3 \text{ kanbans or containers}$$

We can round either up or down (3 containers would force us to improve operations, and 4 would allow some slack).

Small-Lot Production

Small-lot production provides many benefits.

Small-lot production requires less space and capital investment than systems that incur large inventories. By producing small amounts at a time, processes can be physically moved closer together and transportation between stations can be simplified. In small-lot production, quality problems are easier to detect and workers show less tendency to let poor quality pass (as they might in a system that is producing huge amounts of an item anyway). Lower inventory levels make processes more dependent on each other. This is beneficial because it reveals errors and bottlenecks more quickly and gives workers an opportunity to solve them.

The analogy of water flowing over a bed of rocks is useful here. As shown in Figure 15.8, the inventory level is like the level of water. It hides problems but allows for smooth sailing. When the inventory level is reduced, the problems (or rocks) are exposed. After the exposed rocks are removed from the river, the boat can again progress, this time more quickly than before.

Although it is true that a company can produce in small lot sizes without using the pull system or kanbans, from experience we know that small-lot

Transparency 15.6 JIT Making Problems Visible

(a) Inventory hides problems.

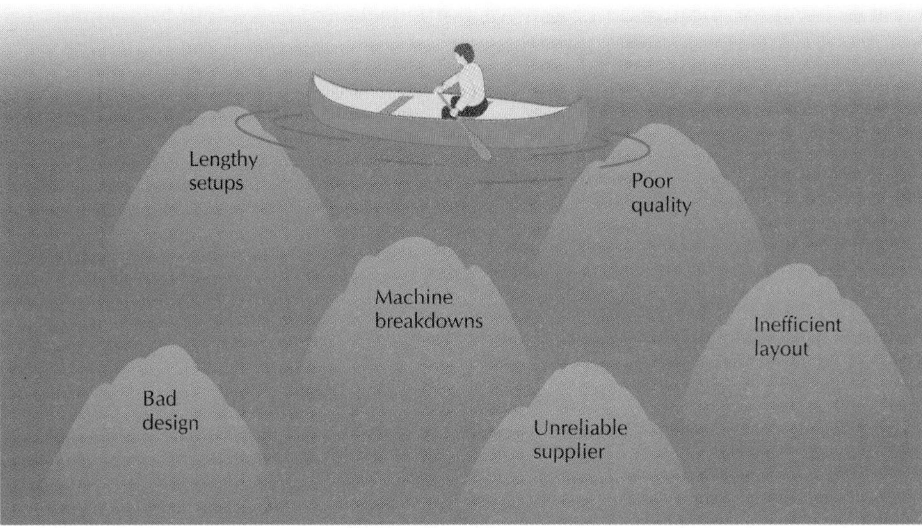

(b) Lower levels of inventory expose problems.

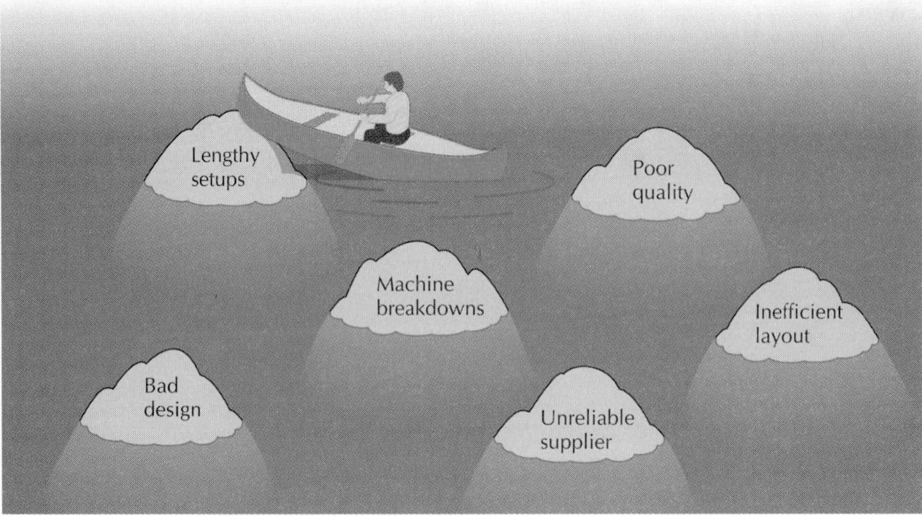

FIGURE 15.8 JIT Making Problems Visible

production in a push system is difficult to coordinate. Similarly, using large lot sizes with a pull system and kanbans would be not be advisable. Let's look more closely at the relationship between small lot sizes, the pull system, and kanbans.

From the kanban formula, it becomes clear that a reduction in the number of kanbans (given a constant container size) requires a corresponding reduction in safety stock or in lead time itself. The need for safety stock can be reduced by making demand and supply more certain. Flexible resources allow the system to adapt more readily to unanticipated changes in demand. Demand fluctuations can also be controlled through closer contact with customers and better forecasting systems. Deficiencies in supply can be controlled through eliminating mistakes, producing only good units, and reducing or eliminating machine breakdowns.

Lead time is typically made up of four components: 1. processing time, 2. move time, 3. waiting time, and 4. setup time. *Processing time* can be reduced by reducing the number of items processed and the efficiency or speed of the machine or worker. *Move time* can be decreased if machines are moved closer together, the method of movement is simplified, routings are standardized, or the need for movement is eliminated. *Waiting time* can be reduced through better scheduling of materials, workers, and machines and sufficient capacity. In many companies, however, lengthy *setup times* are the biggest bottleneck. Reduction of setup time is an important part of JIT.

Quick Setups

Several processes in automobile manufacturing defy production in small lots because of the enormous amount of time required to set up the machines. Stamping is a good example. First, a large roll of sheet steel is run through a blanking press to produce stacks of flat blanks slightly larger than the size of the desired parts. Then, the blanks are inserted into huge stamping presses that contain a matched set of upper and lower dies. When the dies are held together under thousands of pounds of pressure, a three-dimensional shape emerges, such as a car door or fender. Because the dies weigh several tons each and have to be aligned with exact precision, die changes typically take an entire day to complete.

Obviously, manufacturers are reluctant to change dies often. Ford, for example, might produce 500,000 right door panels and store them in inventory before switching dies to produce left door panels. Some Western manufacturers have found it easier to purchase several sets of presses and dedicate them to stamping out a specific part for months or years. Due to capital constraints, that was not an option for Toyota. Instead, Ohno began simplifying die-changing techniques. Convinced that major improvements could be made, a consultant, Shigeo Shingo, was hired to study die setup systematically, to reduce changeover times further, and to teach these techniques to production workers and Toyota suppliers.

Shingo proved to be a genius at the task. He reduced setup time on a 1000-ton press from 6 hours to 3 minutes using a system he called **SMED** (single-minute exchange of dies). SMED is based on the following principles, which can be applied to any type of setup:

SMED delineates principles for quick setups.

1. *Separate internal setup from external setup.* **Internal setup** has to be performed while the machine is stopped; it cannot take place until the machine has finished with the previous operation. **External setup,** on the other hand, can be performed in advance, while the machine is running. By the time a machine has finished processing its current operation, the worker should have completed the external setup and be ready to perform the internal setup for the next operation. Applying this concept alone can reduce setup time by 30 percent to 50 percent.
2. *Convert internal setup to external setup.* This process involves making sure that the operating conditions, such as gathering tools and fixtures, preheating an

Internal setup can be performed only when the machine is stopped; **external setup** can be done while the machine is operating.

In this photo, a worker sets up a drill press for the next job while the machine is stopped. This is known as an internal setup. In an external setup, the process is not interrupted by setup activities. Setup time can be significantly reduced by converting internal setups to external setups.

injection mold, centering a die, or standardizing die heights, are prepared in advance.

3. *Streamline all aspects of setup.* External setup activities can be reduced by organizing the workplace properly, locating tools and dies near their points of use, and keeping machines and fixtures in good repair. Internal setup activities can be reduced by simplifying or eliminating adjustments. Examples include precoding desired settings, using quick fasteners and locator pins, preventing misalignment, eliminating tools, and making movements easier. Figure 15.9 provides some common analogies for these improvements.
4. *Perform setup activities in parallel or eliminate them entirely.* Adding an extra person to the setup team can reduce setup time considerably. In most cases, two people can perform a setup in less than half the time needed by a single person. In addition, standardizing components, parts, and raw materials can reduce and sometimes eliminate setup requirements.

In order to view the setup process objectively, it is useful to assign the task of setup-time reduction to a team of workers and engineers. Videotaping the setup in progress often helps the team generate ideas for improvement. Time and motion study principles (like those we discussed in Chapter 9) can be applied. After the new setup procedures have been agreed upon, they need to be practiced until they are perfected. One only has to view the pit crews at the Indy 500 to realize that quick changeovers have to be orchestrated and practiced.

Uniform Production

Uniform production results from smoothing production requirements.

In addition to eliminating waste, JIT systems attempt to maintain **uniform production** levels by smoothing the production requirements on the final assembly line. Changes in final assembly often can have dramatic effects on component production upstream. When this happens in a kanban system, kanbans for certain parts will circulate very quickly at some times and very slowly at others. Adjustments of plus or minus 10 percent in monthly demand can be absorbed by the kanban system, but wider demand fluctuations cannot be handled without substantially increasing inventory levels or scheduling large amounts of overtime.[5]

Reduce variability with more accurate forecasts.

One way to reduce variability in production is to guard against unexpected demand through more accurate forecasts. To accomplish this, the sales division of

[5]Huang, P. Y., L. P. Rees, and B. W. Taylor, "A Simulation Analysis of the Just-in-Time Technique (with Kanbans) for a Multiline, Multistage Production System," *Decision Sciences* (July 1983).

Transparency 15.7 Reducing Setup Time

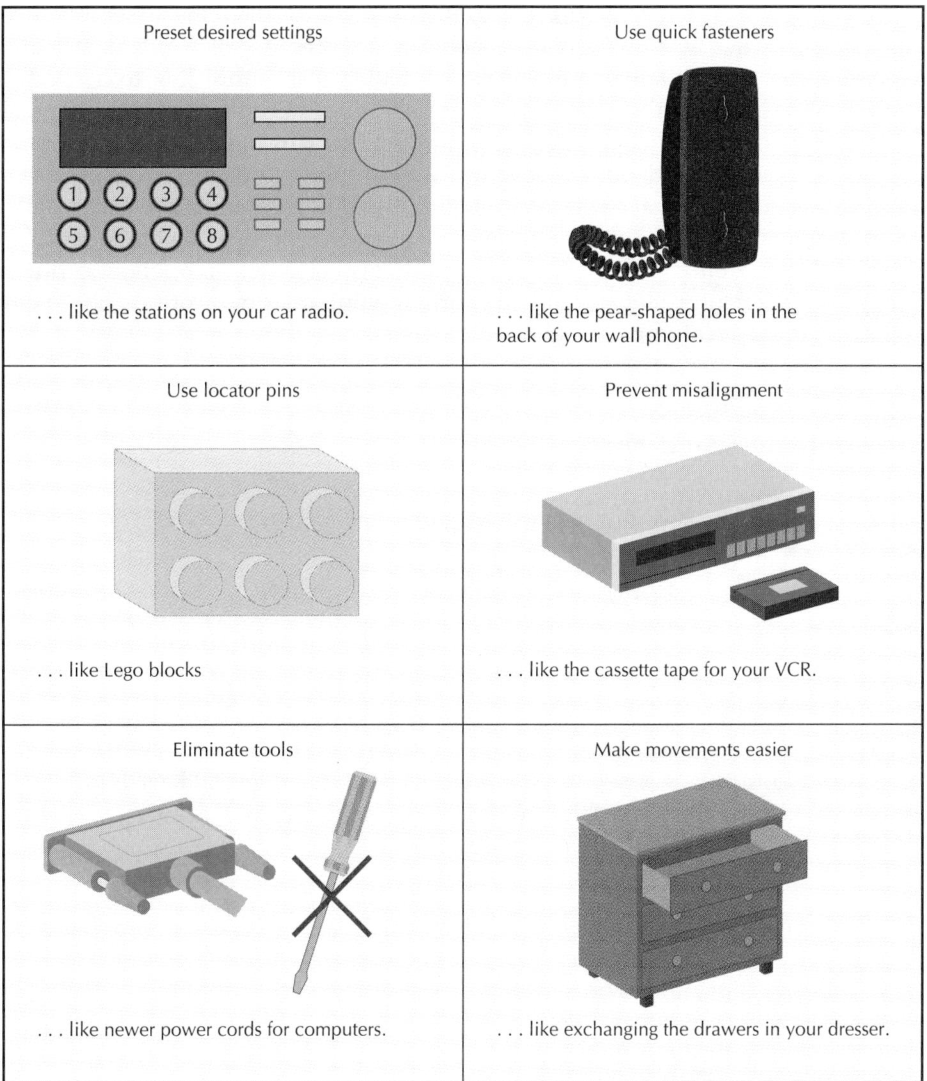

Preset desired settings
. . . like the stations on your car radio.
Use quick fasteners
. . . like the pear-shaped holes in the back of your wall phone.
Use locator pins
. . . like Lego blocks
Prevent misalignment
. . . like the cassette tape for your VCR.
Eliminate tools
. . . like newer power cords for computers.
Make movements easier
. . . like exchanging the drawers in your dresser.

FIGURE 15.9 Some Common Techniques for Reducing Setup Time

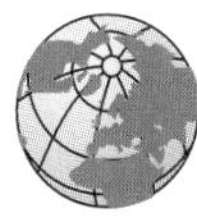

Toyota was given the lead in production planning. Toyota Motor Sales began to do more than receive orders from dealers. They conducted surveys of tens of thousands of people twice a year to estimate demand for Toyota cars and trucks. When followed by five or six smaller surveys, the demand forecasts became more accurate. Monthly production schedules were drawn up from these forecasts 2 months in advance. The plans were reviewed 1 month in advance and then again 10 days in advance. Daily production schedules, which by then included firm orders from dealers, were finalized 4 days from the start of production. Model mix changes could still be made the evening before or the morning of production. This flexibility was possible because schedule changes were communicated only to the final assembly line. Kanbans took care of dispatching revised orders to the rest of the system.

Reduce variability by smoothing demand.

Another approach to achieving uniform production is to level or smooth demand across the planning horizon. Demand is divided into small increments of time and spread out as evenly as possible throughout the time periods. *Leveling* refers to more than producing the same amount of each item each day; item production is *mixed* throughout the day as well, in very small quantities. The mix is controlled by the sequence of models on the final assembly line.

Mixed-model assembly steadies component production.

Toyota assembles several different vehicle models on each final assembly line. The assembly lines were initially designed this way because of limited space and resources and lack of sufficient volume to dedicate an entire line to a specific model. However, the mixed-model concept has since become an integral part of JIT. As we discussed in Chapter 7, daily production is arranged in the same ratio as monthly demand, and jobs are distributed as evenly as possible across the day's schedule. This means that at least some quantity of every item is produced daily, and the company will always have some quantity of an item available to respond to variations in demand. The mix of assembly also steadies component production, reduces inventory levels, and supports the pull system of production. Let's review an example of mixed-model sequencing.

Alternate Example 15.2

EXAMPLE 15.2

Mixed-Model Sequencing

Problem Statement:

If Toyota receives a monthly demand estimate of 1,200 small cars (S), 2,400 midsize cars (M), and 2,400 luxury cars (L), how should the models be produced in order to smooth production as much as possible? (Assume 30 days in a month).

Solution:

Our first step is to convert monthly demand to a daily schedule by dividing by the number of days in a month. As a result, we need to produce 40, 80, and 80 of each model, respectively, per day. In mixing the production of models as much as possible throughout the day, we want to produce twice as many midsize and luxury cars as small cars. One possible final assembly sequence is L-M-S-M-L. This sequence would be repeated 40 times a day.

If the preceding example sounds extreme, it is not. Toyota assembles three models in 100 variations on a single assembly line at its Tahara plant, and the mix is jiggled daily with almost no warning.[6] The plant is highly automated, and each model carries with it a small yellow disc that transmits instructions to the next workstation. Cars roll off the final assembly line in what looks like unit production—a black Lexus sedan, a blue Camry, a red Lexus sports coupe, a white Camry with left-hand drive, and so on.

This is in sharp contrast to the large lots of similar items produced by mass-production factories, in which 2,400 luxury cars might be produced the first week and a half of the month, 2,400 midsize cars, the second week and a half, and 1,200 small cars, the final week. Under this system, it would be difficult to change product mix midway through the month, and small-car customers would have to wait 3 to four weeks before their order would be available.

Quality at the Source

Smaller lot sizes encourage quality.

For a JIT system to work well, quality has to be extremely high. There is no extra inventory to buffer against defective units. Producing poor-quality items and then having to rework or reject them is a waste that should be eliminated. Quality improvement efforts at Toyota accelerated as processes were being streamlined and the JIT system was formulated. It soon became obvious that smaller lot sizes actually encouraged better quality. Workers can observe quality problems more easily; when problems are detected, they can be traced to their source and remedied without reworking too many units. Also, by inspecting the first and the last unit

[6] Hiatt, Fred, "Japan Creating Mass-Produced Customization," *Washington Post*, March 25, 1990.

in a small batch or by having a worker make a part and then use the part, virtually 100 percent inspection can be achieved.

Toyota's quality objective is zero defects (just as its inventory objective is zero inventory). In pursuit of zero defects the company seeks to identify quality problems at their source, to solve them, and *never* to pass on a defective item. To this end, Ohno was determined that the workers, not inspectors, should be responsible for product quality. To go along with this responsibility, he also gave workers the unprecedented authority of **jidoka**—the authority to stop the production line if quality problems were encountered.

Jidoka is authority to stop the production line.

To encourage jidoka, each worker is given access to a switch that can be used to activate call lights or to halt production. The call lights, called **andons,** flash above the workstation and at several andon boards throughout the plant. Green lights indicate normal operation, yellow lights show a call for help, and red lights indicate a line stoppage. Supervisors, maintenance personnel, and engineers are summoned to troubled workstations quickly by flashing lights on the andon board. At Toyota, the assembly line is stopped for an average of 20 minutes a day because of jidoka. Each jidoka drill is recorded on easels kept at the work area. A block of time is reserved at the end of the day for workers to go over the list and work on solving the problems raised. For example, an 8-hour day might consist of 7 hours of production and 1 hour of problem solving.

Andons are call lights that signal quality problems.

This concept of allocating extra time to a schedule for nonproductive tasks is called **undercapacity scheduling.** Another example of undercapacity scheduling is producing for two shifts each day and reserving the third shift for preventive maintenance activities. Making time to plan, train, solve problems, and maintain the work environment is an important part of JIT's success.

Undercapacity scheduling leaves time for planning, problem-solving, and maintenance.

We discussed quality management and statistical quality control in Chapters 3 and 4. Many of the philosophies and methods discussed earlier apply to quality in JIT systems. Toyota's companywide quality control (CWQC) is one of the first examples of total quality in action. Included in their quality effort is total productive maintenance (TPM), which we discussed in the previous chapter. Worker involvement, zero defects, and continuous improvement are hallmarks of JIT's quality system.

Supplier Networks

A network of reliable suppliers is also essential to JIT. Toyota mastered this element by selecting a small number of suppliers (around 200, in contrast to Ford's 2,000)[7] and developing strong, long-term working relationships with them. Twelve Toyota plants are located near Toyota City, in an area two-thirds the size of Connecticut. Suppliers encircle the plants, most within a 50-mile radius. This enables parts to be delivered several times a day. Bulky parts, such as engines and transmissions, are delivered every 15 to 30 minutes. Supplier kanbans and JIT at supplier plants are used to accomplish this feat.

Use fewer suppliers.

Toyota began working with its suppliers in 1962 to improve responsiveness and quality. By 1970, 60 percent of them were using kanbans and by 1982, 98 percent were. Suppliers who met stringent quality standards could forgo inspection of incoming goods. This meant goods could be brought right to the assembly line or area of use without being counted, inspected, tagged, or stocked. Because of geography, manufacturers in the United States can probably never match the frequency of delivery enjoyed by Toyota, but they can reduce the number of suppliers, work more closely with them in the design of parts and the quality of parts, and expect prompt—even daily—deliveries.

[7]Ford now uses about 300 suppliers.

GAINING THE COMPETITIVE EDGE

Material Handling Innovations Support JIT

Ford produces vans, minivans, and club wagons at its assembly plant in Avon Lake, Ohio. In a product-sharing venture with Nissan, the Mercury Villager minivan is also sold as Nissan's Quest. Nissan provides the engineering and Ford builds the vehicle. Production at the plant follows JIT principles, and so does material handling.

Levels of inventory are limited to a few hours on some items and a few days on others. Sixty-five dock doors are strategically located around the building for delivery of material as close to its point of use as possible. Sheet metal from Nissan's plant in Smyrna, Tennessee, is delivered on a variety of customized collapsible racks. The racks fold down to one-fourth their loaded size.

Tires and wheels are a major inventory and handling problem during automobile assembly. Ford receives its wheels with the tires already mounted. Bridgestone/Firestone creates the assemblies (sometimes using General and Goodyear tires) and delivers them floor-stacked in a tractor-trailer several times a day. Tires are removed from the trailer by lift trucks fitted with clamp attachments and placed into one of four lanes of a special "destacking" machine. The machine automatically unstacks the tires and arranges them in the sequence they will be used. An electronic broadcast from the trim department in the production area specifies the sequence of assembly. Every fifth tire is a spare. Tires are delivered to the assembly area at the proper height for installation. When the worker is ready to assemble tires to the vehicle, he or she has only to tilt the tire up and apply the bolts; no lifting or multiple steps of assembly are needed.

Seats are manufactured by a company named Vintec, located about 25 miles away. Ford broadcasts the build sequence to the supplier, and the supplier assigns a sequence number to each delivery. Bar coding each seat is unnecessary. The driver delivers a trailer with enough seats for 22 vehicles, about 1 hour's worth of production. The truck is unloaded by an automated process that verifies the load's sequence number, locks the trailer into the dock, positions the dock board, and begins moving the seats off the truck onto a roller conveyor. The seats arrive already fixed to special pallets that are used until the seats are transferred to an overhead conveyor at the assembly line. Seats are fed from the truck by conveyors to the assembly line in perfect style and color sequence, with no human intervention. A photo sensor determines when the last seat has been unloaded and when to begin loading empty pallets back onto the empty trailer.

Tires and seats are in constant use. Their only storage time is on the delivery truck. Smaller parts are stored by the assembly line in small vertical lift automatic storage and retrieval systems (ASRS). The mini-ASRS is computer controlled to "expose" automatically the parts needed at a workstation for the particular assembly the workers have in front of them. The entire material handling system supports the continuous flow of material through the plant JIT-style.

Source: Based on Witt, C. E., "Quality Manufacturing Drives New Minivan Plant," *Material Handling Engineering* (July 1992): 37–39.

One of the common misconceptions about JIT is that inventory is pushed back to the suppliers. That is true only if producers are not really using JIT or if suppliers try to meet JIT demand requirements without practicing JIT themselves. Otherwise, suppliers can benefit from the guaranteed demand, steadiness of demand, advanced notice of volume changes, minimal design changes, engineering and management assistance, and sharing of profits characteristic of the close vendor-producer partnerships of JIT. That said, JIT has certainly changed the manner in which suppliers are chosen and goods are supplied to producers. The following is a list of trends in supplier policies since the advent of JIT:

Supplier policies have changed with JIT.

1. *Locate near to the customer.* Although this is not possible in all cases, it does occur, as evidenced by the circle of suppliers that surrounds the Tennessee valley

where the Nissan and Saturn plants are located. Nissan receives deliveries of vehicle seats four times an hour and notifies the supplier 2 hours in advance the exact sequence (i.e., type and color) in which the seats are to be unloaded.

2. *Use small, side-loaded trucks and ship mixed loads.* These trucks are easier to load and can be loaded in the sequence that the customer will be using the items. Several suppliers may combine their loads on one truck that will tour the supplier plants to pick up items for delivery to the customer.
3. *Consider establishing small warehouses near to the customer or consolidating warehouses with other suppliers.* The small warehouses could be used for frequently delivered items, and the consolidation warehouses could become *load-switching points* when geographic distances between supplier and customer prohibit daily deliveries. Yellow Freight has been very successful with this approach.
4. *Use standardized containers and make deliveries according to a precise delivery schedule.* Exchanging containers makes deliveries and replenishment move along quickly. Delivery windows are becoming very short, and penalties for missing them are high. Chrysler penalizes its trucking firm $32,000 for each hour a delivery is late.
5. *Become a certified supplier and accept payment at regular intervals rather than upon delivery.* This eliminates much of the paperwork and waiting time associated with traditional delivery. Certified suppliers are subjected to a limited amount of quality and quantity checks or may be exempt from them altogether.

CONTINUOUS IMPROVEMENT

JIT is a practical system for production created from trial and error experiences in eliminating waste and simplifying production. The final element of JIT, continuous improvement, is the focus of the system and impacts on every other element. JIT continually looks for ways to reduce inventory, quicken setups, improve quality, and react faster to customer demand. Thus, we could say that JIT is a system of continuous improvement. This is fitting since the system evolved through a process of continuous improvement. What better way to illustrate the effectiveness of an approach!

JIT is a system of continuous improvement.

There are several aspects of continuous improvement that we have alluded to in previous discussions, but have not addressed explicitly. In this section we discuss visual control, poka-yoke devices, total employee involvement (TEI), and principles for continuous improvement.

Visual Control

Visual control is concerned with making problems visible and making workers aware of their environment. The first step, *visibility,* requires maintaining a clean and orderly workplace in which unneeded items are discarded, useful items are assigned a specific location, and workers scrupulously maintain their equipment, tools, and workspace. In Japan, this is referred to as the five S's (seiri, seiton, seiso, seiketsu, and shitsuke), roughly translated as organization, tidiness, cleanliness, maintenance, and discipline. In this type of environment, tools and materials are seldom misplaced or lost, and unusual occurrences become noticeable. For example, oil spots on a clean floor may indicate a machine problem, whereas oil spots on a dirty floor would go undetected.

Visual control makes problems visible.

The second step, *awareness,* involves clear expectations, including visible instructions for worker or machine action, and direct feedback on the results of that action. Examples include kanbans, standard operation sheets, andons, process control charts, and tool boards. A factory with visual control will look different than other factories. You may find machines or stockpoints in each section painted different colors, material handling routes marked clearly on the floor, demonstration stands and instructional photographs placed near machines, graphs of quality or performance data displayed at each workstation, and explanations and pictures of recent improvement efforts posted by work teams. Figure 15.10 shows several examples of visual control.

Poka-Yoke

Poka-yokes prevent defects from occurring.

Teaching Note 15.6 Poka-Yokes

A **poka-yoke** is any foolproof device or mechanism that prevents defects from occurring. Although it may be considered a type of visual control, it goes one step further. For example, a dial on which desired ranges are marked in different colors is an example of visual control. A dial that shuts off a machine whenever the instrument needle falls above or below the desired range is a poka-yoke. Machines

Transparency 15.8 Visual Control

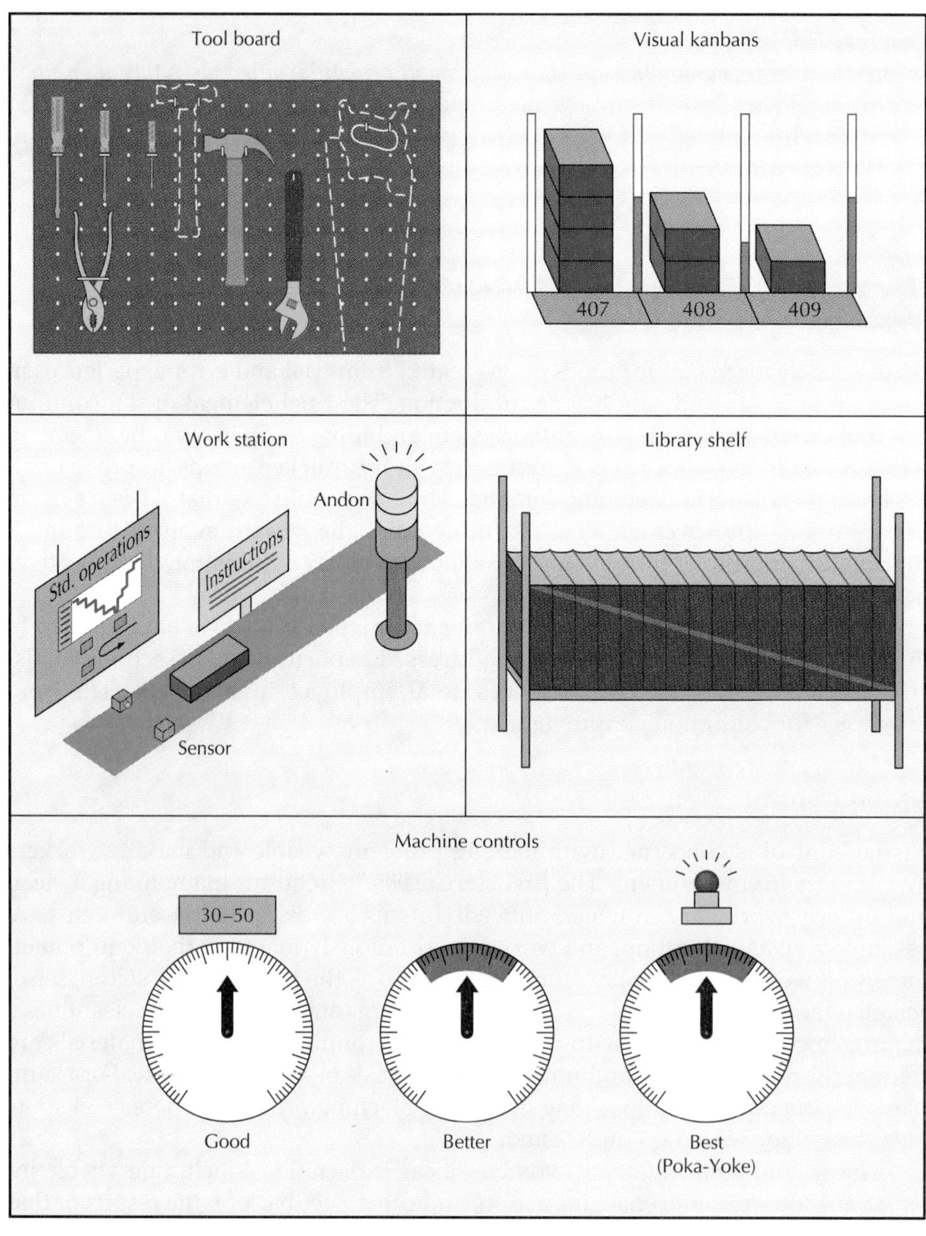

FIGURE 15.10 Examples of Visual Control

set to stop after a certain amount of production are poka-yokes, as are sensors that prevent the addition of too many items into a package or the misalignment of components for an assembly.

Total Employee Involvement

Continuous improvement is not something that can be delegated to a department or a staff of experts. It calls for **total employee involvement**—that is, it must involve every individual at every level of the organization. Contrary to what you may read in the popular press, kanbans haven't revolutionized manufacturing. It's the continual improvements to the system by individuals and teams who manage and operate it on a day-to-day basis that have created the revolution. The essence of JIT success is the willingness of workers to spot quality problems, halt production when necessary, generate ideas for improvements, analyze processes, perform different functions, and adjust their working routine. In Japanese companies, recognition of the importance of workers is called *respect for humanity* and includes giving workers proper training. Nissan, for example, spent more than $30,000 to train each assembly line worker at its plant in Smyrna, Tennessee, before they ever started on the job.

Total employment involvement is a system that involves every employee at every level.

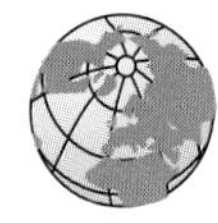

Continuous improvement goes by the name of **kaizen** in Japan. With the collective involvement and creativity of all employees, kaizen can be an extremely powerful force. Japanese companies have been very successful in achieving the total involvement of employees in operations improvement. In 1 year, Canon employees generated over 900,000 suggestions, an average of 78 suggestions per employee. That seems incredible until we realize that Canon's suggestion program ranked thirteenth among Japanese companies that year. Toyota's legendary employee involvement system generated more than 5 million suggestions (hundreds per employee), but Matsushita won first place with 6.5 million suggestions.[8] Even if each suggestion saves only $1 a year, that's quite an advantage.

Kaizen is continuous improvement.

Teaching Note 15.7 An Idea Fair

Inevitably, when data are presented on the large number of employee suggestions characteristic of Japanese firms, the ability of the workers to do their jobs effectively is questioned. How do they have time to think up so many new ideas and do their jobs too? But that's the point, the worker's job *is* to think up ideas.

In order to achieve such high levels of participation, companies have to set high expectations for worker involvement and create a corporate culture for participation. This requires training employees in problem-solving techniques (such as those we discussed in Chapter 4) and giving them plenty of opportunity to use the techniques. It also involves implementing a good portion of the ideas generated, or else the ideas may stop flowing.

Principles of Continuous Improvement

The following principles may be helpful in initiating and following through on continuous improvement efforts:[9]

1. *Create a mind-set for improvement.* Totally deny the status quo. Do not be limited by traditional concepts. Think of how the new method *will* work, not how it won't. Don't accept excuses.
2. *Try and try again.* Don't seek perfection. Small improvements will give you ideas for larger ones. Act and then assess the results. Correct mistakes the moment they are identified.

[8] Shingo, S., *Modern Approaches to Manufacturing Improvement*, Cambridge, Mass.: Productivity Press, 1990, pp. 12–13.

[9] These are adapted from ten principles given in Hirano, Hiroyuki, *JIT Factory Revolution*, Cambridge, Mass: Productivity Press, 1988, Chapter 2.

3. *THINK.* Don't "buy" improvements. Give your brain a chance to work. Ask why? five times.
4. *Work in teams.* The ideas of ten people are better than the knowledge of one person. Brainstorm. Bounce ideas off one another.
5. *Recognize that improvement knows no limits.* Never be satisfied. Get in the habit of looking for better ways of doing things. Accept the challenge.

GAINING THE COMPETITIVE EDGE

Large and Small Improvements at Xaloy

Xaloy, located in Pulaski, Virginia, supplies bimetallic cylinders to *original equipment manufacturer* (OEM) companies that produce ejection and injection molding machines. In the 1980s the company was hit hard by the recession and stiff foreign competition. After applying JIT principles, they were able to increase sales by 70 percent with only a 10 percent increase in their workforce and could begin operating at a profit.

The production process for cylinders is straightforward. Logs of steel are sawed to a specified length, bored out, and filled with a special metal alloy. The alloy is heated to 2,000º F to coat the inside with molten alloy. The interior is then ground smooth and the exterior is machined several times. Finally, fixtures are added to attach the cylinder to the extruding machine. Xaloy might produce 4,000 cylinders a year, with individual orders of five or fewer like cylinders. The operation is a typical make-to-order job shop.

The first benefits from JIT came from reducing inventory and adjusting the layout. Steel was cut only when needed and machines were grouped by product size. Before JIT, 2,000 cylinders might be stacked on the floor as in-process inventory to meet a monthly demand for 200 cylinders. After JIT, a monthly shipment of 400 cylinders would be supported with 350 or fewer WIP cylinders. The distance a unit traveled during manufacturing was cut by 50 percent, 25 percent of the floor space was freed, and the lead time required to produce one cylinder was cut in half, from 13 weeks to 6 1/2 weeks.

Xaloy worked with its vendors to coordinate the delivery of steel to the plant. It provided 6-month forecasts of its need for steel by amount, type, and length. Monthly orders were placed to be delivered weekly. Weekly shipments averaged one truckload of two to three different items. The revised ordering procedure reduced raw material inventory from $525,000 to $300,000.

On the marketing side, Xaloy became a JIT supplier to machine tool manufacturers. Instead of individual orders being placed throughout the year, one customer signed a 1-year contract with Xaloy and provided them with 8-week production schedules. Some deliveries were expected in as little as 2 weeks.

Continuous improvement activities yielded both large and small benefits. Tables were built to hold a limited number of cylinders and avoid the tendency to stack them indiscriminantly on the floor. Tools that had been scattered all around were organized into cabinets, a simple go/no-go gauging system was designed for measuring counterbore dimensions, and new methods for disposing of metal chips and waste oil were explored. Workers redesigned machine boring heads to save more than 250 hours a year in setups and used new clamping systems to cut setups on five honing machines by 50 percent. One of the biggest savings came from a single change that reduced the labor content of the product by 20 percent. Instead of spending hours straightening the cylinders after they had been heated and cooled, cylinders were hung vertically in a specially designed cooling pit to prevent bending.

These and other JIT pursuits positioned Xaloy to compete for a share of the foreign OEM market as the U.S. machine tool industry faltered.

Source: Based on Waters, C., "Profit and Loss," *INC.* (April 1985): 103–12.

Benefits of JIT

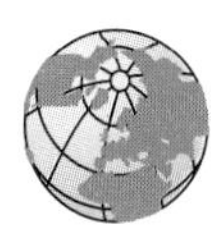

The introductory chapter of this text showed statistics from several industries in which U.S. manufacturers were significantly outperformed by Japanese competitors who used JIT. Similar performances by Japanese-owned plants operating in the United States dispelled the myths that their excellence in manufacturing can be attributed to differences in technology or culture. A study of the average benefits accrued to U.S. manufacturers over a 5-year period from implementing JIT are equally impressive: 90 percent reductions in manufacturing cycle time, 70 percent to 90 percent reductions in inventory, 50 percent reductions in labor costs, and 80 percent reductions in space requirements.[10] Statistics such as these have led experts to predict that JIT will become the standard global production system of the twenty-first century (with mass production and job shop production as the exceptions).

The *Gaining the Competitive Edge* boxes in this chapter will give you a good feel for the diversity of JIT applications in the United States and the range of benefits JIT can provide. To summarize, the main benefits of JIT are as follows:

JIT provides a wide range of benefits.

1. Reduced inventory
2. Improved quality
3. Lower costs
4. Reduced space requirements
5. Shorter lead time
6. Increased productivity
7. Greater flexibility
8. Better relations with suppliers
9. Simplified scheduling and control activities
10. Increased capacity
11. Better use of human resources
12. More product variety

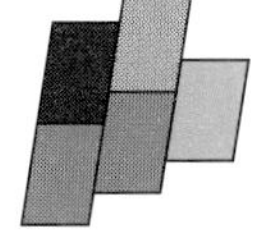

JIT IMPLEMENTATION

JIT is perceived as a Japanese approach to manufacturing. Although steel processing and shipbuilding were early adopters of JIT, in reality, the majority of Japanese industry did not embrace JIT until the mid-1970s, after they observed Toyota's superior ability to withstand the 1973 oil crisis. Many U.S. firms, in turn, adopted JIT in some form in the 1980s. Those firms that tried to implement JIT by slashing inventory and demanding that their suppliers make frequent deliveries missed the power of the system. Supplier deliveries and kanbans are some of the last elements of JIT to implement.

The firms that were most successful in implementing JIT understood the breadth and interrelatedness of the concepts and adapted them to their own particular environment. This makes sense when you consider the essence of JIT—eliminate waste, speed up changeovers, work closely with suppliers, streamline the flow of work, use flexible resources, pay attention to quality, expose problems, and use worker teams to solve problems. None of these concepts or techniques are new or particularly revolutionary. How they are applied can differ considerably from company to company. What is unique and remarkable is how the pieces are

Use JIT to finely tune an operating system.

[10]Plossl, G.W., *Just-in-Time: A Special Roundtable*, Atlanta, Ga.: George Plossl Educational Services, 1985.

tied together into a finely tuned operating system and how synchronized that system can be with both the external and internal business environments.

Companies often become frustrated when implementing JIT because the system exposes problems that have been hidden for a long time. Some people mistakenly assume that JIT *caused* those problems, when, in fact, JIT merely *exposed* existing problems. For example, in 1992 General Motors was forced to close nine plants (including its renowned Saturn assembly plant) and idle 43,000 workers, after a 9-day strike at its Lordstown parts plant.[11] The Saturn plant held a 1-day supply of key parts and was closed within 17 hours of the strike. Although some observers saw this as an indictment of JIT, others said it highlighted GM's policy of vertical integration (the component plant was a GM plant) as outdated and a poor match with the requirements of JIT.

Lean production is a term used to describe JIT and the Toyota production system.

Many firms have their own name for their version of just-in-time. JIT is called stockless production at Hewlett-Packard, material as needed (MAN) at Harley-Davidson, continuous-flow manufacturing (CFM) at IBM, zero inventory production system (ZIPS) at Omark Industries, and **lean production** in the landmark book *The Machine That Changed the World* by Womack, Jones, and Roos that chronicles the automobile industry.

JIT applications on U.S. soil, whether in Japanese- or U.S.-run plants, differ somewhat from the original Japanese versions. U.S. JIT plants are typically larger, deliveries from suppliers are less frequent, more buffer inventory is held (because of the longer delivery lead times), and kanbans, if used at all, are very simple. Worker-designed feedback systems are different, too. Instead of alarms and flashing lights when things go wrong, workers at the Saturn plant hear a recording of "The Pink Panther." At the Nissan plant, workers are reminded to change workstations along an S-shaped assembly line by the changing tempo of piped-in music (from country to rock). Morning calesthentics are out for most U.S. plants, but the placement of ping-pong tables and basketball hoops alongside the assembly line for exercise during worker-designated breaks is popular.

JIT is still evolving.

As might be expected, JIT is still evolving. Toyota has learned from its U.S. plants that the stress of arbitrarily reducing inventory to reveal problems does not necessarily make workers more creative in improving the system.[12] To the contrary, creating an environment that is receptive to change, without forcing it, seems to work just as well. Shorter work days and longer breaks during the day do not seriously impede productivity either. In Japan, Toyota's practice of clustering plants and suppliers in geographic proximity to one another has worked well for frequent deliveries and small-lot production, but it has also used up the available labor in the area. Toyota's new plants are more dispersed, like U.S. plants, and require more inventory. They are also more automated. The Tahara plant, for example, is almost entirely automated, with buffers of inventory between the seven major sections of the final assembly line.[13] Although this seems to be a divergence from the principles of JIT, it may merely reflect that JIT, like other management systems, must be adapted to the manufacturing environment.

JIT isn't for everyone!

We should note that JIT is not appropriate for every type of operation. For high-volume, repetitive items, mass production is still the best process to use. Even Toyota produces high-demand components (typically small items that require stamping and forging) in lots as large as 10,000 units, sending them to subsequent processes in small batches only when requested. Similarly, JIT is inappropriate for very low volume items or unique orders. Recall that for JIT to be successful, there must be some stability of demand. A true make-to-order shop

[11]"Strike at GM points up JIT's Risks, Rewards," *Modern Materials Handling* (November 1992): 14–15.

[12]Hilltop, Jean, "Just-In-Time Manufacturing: Implications for the Management of Human Resources," *European Management Journal* (March 1992): 49–54.

[13]Taylor, Alex, "How Toyota Copes with Hard Times," *Fortune* (January 25, 1993): 78–81.

GAINING THE COMPETITIVE EDGE

How Hewlett-Packard Implemented JIT

Hewlett-Packard was one of the first U.S. companies to implement JIT. It is interesting to study the order in which they applied the many concepts of JIT to operations at their electronics plant in Boise, Idaho.

1. *Design a flow process.* Their first step was to concentrate on designing the flow process. This step involved analyzing their processes, rearranging their facility into work cells, reducing setup times, reducing lot sizes, emphasizing preventive maintenance, linking operations, and balancing workstation capacities.
2. *Implement total quality control.* The second area of attention was total quality. Hewlett-Packard trained workers in problem-solving methods, formed improvement teams, and practiced process control. They also implemented poka-yoke devices and other automatic inspection systems.
3. *Stabilize the schedule.* The third area of application was production planning. They leveled production, froze their master schedule, and instituted undercapacity scheduling.
4. *Introduce kanban pull.* Only after all these elements were in place did HP attempt kanbans and the pull system. This resulted in further reductions in lot sizes.
5. *Work with vendors.* After kanban implementation, HP began working with their vendors to reduce lead times, to project requirements, to make more frequent deliveries, and to meet quality expectations.
6. *Reduce inventory more.* Then, HP went back and analyzed processes again, looking for improvement opportunities. Transit, storage and retrieval, and transportation operations were targeted, and further reductions in inventory were achieved.
7. *Improve product design.* Finally, HP analyzed the design process itself, standardizing product configurations, reducing the number of parts, attacking product and process design simultaneously, and increasing quality expectations.

These advances in JIT were implemented over the course of two years, with the following results:

- Cycle time was reduced from 5 days to less than 2 days.
- Inventory turns doubled, raw material inventory was reduced from 1 month to 10 days, and rework went from 25 percent to none.
- Space requirements were reduced by 2,400 square feet.
- Suppliers delivered daily, delivery was 100 percent on time, and 100 percent incoming quality was achieved.

Source: Based on Sepehri, M., *Just-in-Time, Not Just in Japan,* Falls Church, Va.: APICS, 1986, pp. 6–7; Chase, R., and N. Aquilano, *Production and Operations Management,* Homewood, Ill.: Irwin, 1992, p. 279.

would find it difficult to operate under JIT. Even in make-to-order businesses, however, there are usually some parts or processes that are common or repetitive and can benefit from JIT concepts. What we are finding is that there are more operations that can benefit from JIT than cannot.

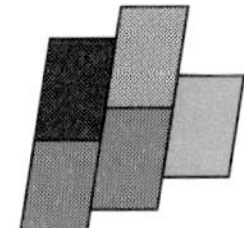

JIT IN SERVICES

Most people who think of JIT as a system for reducing inventory do not consider the system to be applicable to services. However, you know from reading this chapter that JIT consists of more than low inventory levels. It eliminates waste, streamlines operations, promotes fast changeovers and close supplier relations, and adjusts quickly to changes in demand. As a result, products (or services) can be provided quickly, at less cost, and in more variety. Although it is rarely referred to as such, we can readily observe some of the basic elements of JIT in service operations. Think about:

Many services use JIT concepts.

- McDonald's, Domino's, and Federal Express, who compete on speed and still provide their products and services at low cost and with increasing variety;
- Construction firms that coordinate the arrival of material "just as it is needed" instead of stockpiling them at the site;
- Multifunctional workers in department stores that work the cash register, stock goods, arrange displays, and make sales;
- Work cells at fast-food restaurants that allow workers to be added during peak times and reduced during slow times;
- "Dollar" stores that price everything the same and simply count the number of items purchased as the customer leaves;
- Process mapping that has streamlined operations and eliminated waste in many services (especially in terms of paper flow and information processing);
- Medical facilities that have the flexibility to fill prescriptions, perform tests, and treat patients without routing them from one end of the building to another;
- Just-in-time publishing that allows professors to choose material from a variety of sources and construct a custom-made book in the same amount of time off-the-shelf books can be ordered and at competitive prices;
- Lens providers, cleaners, and car-repair services that can turn around customer orders in an hour;
- Cleaning teams that follow standard operations routines in quickly performing their tasks; and
- Supermarkets that replenish their shelves according to what the customer withdraws.

In a broader sense, then, JIT concepts are flourishing in services.

Services have also been dramatically affected by JIT in manufacturing. Trucking firms, railroads, and delivery services have increased the speed at which their services are performed and increased their reliability in response to JIT. Retail stores can provide customers with more choices faster than ever before. Milliken promises custom-ordered carpets within two weeks, Benetton can create and ship new product lines within 10 days of redesign, and Motorola can provide customized pagers overnight. With this type of rapid response, stores can order and receive goods faster from the manufacturer than they can retrieve them from their warehouses.

Finally, much of the emphasis of JIT comes from being close to the customer, close to the supplier, and close to the worker. Services have traditionally excelled in those areas.

SUMMARY

Just-in-time (JIT) has truly changed the face of manufacturing and transformed the global economy. JIT originated at Toyota Motor Company as an effort to eliminate waste (particularly inventories), but it evolved into a system for the continuous improvement of all aspects of manufacturing operations. JIT is both a philosophy and a collection of management methods and techniques. The main advantage of the system is derived from the integration of the techniques into a focused, smooth-running management system.

In JIT systems, workers are multifunctional and are required to perform different tasks, as well as aid in the improvement process. Machines are also multifunctional and are arranged in small, U-shaped work cells that enable parts to be processed in a continuous flow through the cell. Workers produce parts one at a time within the cells and transport parts between cells in small lots as called for by subassembly lines, assembly lines, or other work cells. The work environment is kept clean, orderly, and free of waste so that unusual occurrences are visible.

Schedules are prepared only for the final assembly line, in which several different models are assembled on the same line. Requirements for component parts and subassemblies are then pulled through the system with kanbans. The principle of the pull system is not to make anything until requested to do so by the next station. The "pull" element of JIT will not work unless production is uniform, setups are quick, and lot sizes are low.

The pull system and kanbans are also used to order materials from outside suppliers. Suppliers are fewer in number and must be very reliable. They may be requested to make multiple deliveries of the same item in the same day, so their manufacturing system must be flexible, too. Deliveries are made directly to the factory floor, eliminating stockrooms and the waste of counting, inspecting, recording, storing, and transporting.

Just-in-time, as the name implies, does not produce in anticipation of need. It produces only the necessary items in the necessary quantities at the necessary times. Inventory is viewed as a waste of resources and an obstacle to improvement. Because there is little buffer inventory between workstations, quality must be extremely high, and every effort is made to prevent machine breakdowns.

When all these elements are in place, JIT systems produce high quality goods, quickly and at low cost. These systems also are able to respond to changes in customer demand. JIT systems are most effective in repetitive environments, but elements of JIT can be applied to almost any operation, including service operations. Successful applications of JIT abound in every corner of the world.

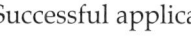

SUMMARY OF KEY FORMULAS

Determining the Number of Kanbans

$$N = \frac{dL + S}{C}$$

SUMMARY OF KEY TERMS

andons: call lights installed at work stations to notify management and other workers of a quality problem in production

external setup: setup activities that can be performed in advance while the machine is operating.

general-purpose machines: machines that perform basic functions such as turning, drilling, and milling.

internal setup: setup activities that can be performed only when the machine is stopped.

jidoka: authority given to the workers to stop the assembly line when quality problems are encountered.

just-in-time: both a philosophy and an integrated system for production management that emphasizes the elimination of waste and the continuous improvement of operations.

kaizen: a Japanese term for a system of continuous improvement.

kanban: a card corresponding to a standard quantity of production (or size container) used in the pull system to authorize the production or withdrawal of goods.

kanban square: a marked area designated to hold a certain amount of items; an empty square is the signal to produce more items.
lean production: a term used to describe JIT and the Toyota production system.
manufacturing cell: a group of dissimilar machines brought together to manufacture a family of parts with similar shapes or processing requirements.
material kanban: a square-shaped kanban used to order material in advance of a process.
multifunctional workers: workers who have been trained to perform more than one job or function.
poka-yoke: any foolproof device or mechanism that prevents defects from occurring.
production kanban: a card authorizing the production of a container of goods.
pull system: a production system in which items are manufactured only when called for by the users of those items.
push system: a production system in which items are manufactured according to a schedule prepared in advance.
signal kanbans: a triangular kanban used as a reorder point to signal production at the previous workstation.
total employee involvement: a system that involves every employee at every level in continuous improvement efforts.
undercapacity scheduling: the allocation of extra time in a schedule for nonproductive tasks such as problem solving or maintenance.
uniform production: the result of smoothing production requirements on the final assembly line.
visual control: procedures and mechanisms for making problems visible.
waste: anything other than the minimum amount of equipment, materials, parts, space, and time that are absolutely essential to add value to the product.
withdrawal kanban: a card authorizing the withdrawal and movement of a container of goods.

QUESTIONS

15-1. What is the purpose of JIT?
15-2. How did JIT evolve into a system of continuous improvement?
15-3. Why are flexible resources essential to JIT?
15-4. What does a cellular layout contribute to JIT?
15-5. Differentiate between a push and a pull production system.
15-6. How was the concept of kanban developed from the two-bin inventory system?
15-7. How are the kanban system and the reorder point system similar? How are they different?
15-8. Describe how the following kanbans operate:
a. Production and withdrawal kanbans
b. Kanban squares
c. Signal kanbans
d. Material kanbans
e. Supplier kanbans
15-9. What are the advantages of small lot sizes?
15-10. Why do large lot sizes not work well with pull systems?
15-11. Why are small lot sizes not as effective in a push system?
15-12. Explain the principles of SMED. What does SMED try to achieve?
15-13. Why is uniform production important to JIT? How is it achieved?

15-14. What are the advantages of mixed-model sequencing?
15-15. How are JIT and TQC related? Which should be implemented first?
15-16. How are suppliers affected by JIT?
15-17. Suggest several ways that JIT requirements can be made easier for suppliers.
15-18. Give examples of visual control. How does visual control affect quality?
15-19. What is the difference between visual control and poka-yoke?
15-20. Why is worker involvement important to continuous improvement?
15-21. List several principles of continuous improvement.
15-22. What are some typical benefits from implementing JIT?
15-23. Which elements of JIT do you think would be difficult for U.S. firms to implement?
15-24. Design a strategy for JIT implementation.
15-25. In what type of environment is JIT most successful?
15-26. Can JIT be applied to services? How?

PROBLEMS

15-1. An assembly station is asked to process 100 circuit boards per hour. It takes 20 minutes to receive the necessary components from the previous workstation. Completed circuit boards are placed in a rack that will hold 10 boards. The rack must be full before it is sent on to the next workstation. If the factory uses a safety factor of 10 percent, how many kanbans are needed for the circuit board assembly process?

15-1. 3.63, or 4

15-2. Referring to Problem 15-1, how many kanbans would be needed in each case?

a. Demand is increased to 200 circuit boards per hour.
b. The lead time for components is increased to 30 minutes.
c. The rack size is halved.
d. The safety factor is increased to 20 percent.

15-2. a. 7.26, or 8
b. 5.5, or 6
c. 7.26, or 8
d. 3.96, or 4

15-3. It takes Aaron 15 minutes to produce 10 widgets to fill a container and 5 minutes to transport the container to the next station, where Maria works. Maria's process takes about 30 minutes. The factory uses a safety factor of 20 percent. Currently, 5 kanbans rotate between Aaron and Maria's stations. What is the approximate demand for widgets?

15-3. 126/hr

15-4. Stan Weakly can sort a bin of 100 letters in 10 minutes. He typically sorts 500 letters an hour. A truck arrives with more bins every 30 minutes. The office uses a safety factor of 10 percent. How many kanbans are needed for the letter-sorting process?

15-4. 2.7, or 3

15-5. The office administrator wishes to decrease the number of kanbans in the letter-sorting process described in Problem 15-4. Which of the following alternatives has the greatest effect on reducing the number of kanbans?

a. Eliminating the safety factor
b. Receiving truck deliveries every 15 minutes
c. Increasing the bin capacity to 200 letters

What is the effect on inventory levels of decreasing the number of kanbans?

15-5. b, decreases

15-6. Sandy is asked to produce 250 squidgets an hour. It takes 30 minutes to receive the necessary material from the previous workstation. Each output container holds 25 squidgets. The factory currently works with a safety factor of 10 percent. How many kanbans should be circulating between Sandy's process and the previous process?

15-6. 6

15-7. a. 8.25, or 9
b. 2.75, or 3
c. 13.75, or 14

15-7. Referring to Problem 15-6, what happens to the number of kanbans and to inventory levels in each case?

a. The time required to receive material is increased to 45 minutes.
b. Output expectations decrease to 125 squidgets an hour.
c. The size of the container is cut to 10 squidgets.

15-8. A to assembly, 3; B to assembly, 9

★ 15-8. In a large microelectronics plant, the assembly cell for circuit boards has a demand for 200 units an hour. Two feeder cells supply parts A and B to the assembly cell (one A and one B for each board). Standard containers that look like divided trays are used. A container will hold 20 A's or 10 B's. It takes 10 minutes to fill up a container with A's and 20 minutes to fill up a container with B's. Transit time to the assembly cell is 5 minutes for both A and B. No safety factor is used. Set up a kanban control system for the assembly process.

See Solutions Manual.

CASE PROBLEM

JIT Woes

B&B Electronics, a supplier in the telecommunications industry, has a problem. Demand is down, but competitive pressures for better quality at a reduced price are up. Customers who used to order in large lots with plenty of lead time now want daily deliveries of small quantities. Contracts use terms such as "statistical evidence of quality" and "just-in-time delivery." More and more customers are requiring supplier certification with standards that B&B cannot meet. Plant manager John Walters has to take action.

"If JIT is good enough for our customers, it's good enough for us," he declared, and called in one of his managers, Kelly Thompson.

"Kelly, I can always rely on you to get us out of a jam, so don't let me down this time. I want you to implement JIT on the circuit board assembly line. Create a success story to show other employees how great this JIT stuff is. You've got free rein. . . . not much money, but free rein to change anything you want in the system. Oh, and I want some results by next month."

"Okay, boss," replied Kelly shakily. "What's your philosophy on JIT? I mean what do you consider its most important points?"

"My philosophy? JIT is cutting inventory, squeezing your suppliers, and using those kanban card things. My philosophy is just do it!"

"I get the picture," said Kelly as she retreated to her office cubby to study up on JIT.

1. What do you think of the plant manager's view of JIT?
2. If you were Kelly, how would you go about the task ahead of you? What parts of JIT would you try to implement first? Last? How would you gain worker support?

REFERENCES

Black, J. T., *The Design of the Factory with a Future,* New York: McGraw-Hill, 1991.

Chase, R., and N. Aquilano, *Production and Operations Management,* Homewood, Ill.: Irwin 1992.

Cusomano, Michael, *The Japanese Automobile Industry,* Cambridge, Mass.: Harvard University Press, 1985.

Hall, Robert, *Zero Inventories,* Homewood, Ill.: Dow Jones-Irwin, 1983.

Heard, Julie, "JIT for White Collar Work—The Rest of the Story," Chapter 12 in *Strategic Manufacturing: Dynamic New Directions for the 1990's,* P. Moody, ed. Homewood, Ill.: Irwin, 1990.

Hilltop, Jean, "Just-In-Time Manufacturing: Implications for the Management of Human Resources," *European Management Journal,* (March 1992): 49–54.

Hirano, H., *JIT Factory Revolution,* Cambridge, Mass: Productivity Press, 1988.

Huang, P. Y., L. P. Rees, and B. W. Taylor, "A Simulation Analysis of the Just-in-Time Technique (with Kanbans) for a Multiline, Multistage Production System," *Decision Sciences* (July 1983).

Monden, Yasuhiro, ed., *Applying Just-In-Time: The American/Japanese Experience,* Atlanta, Ga.: Industrial Engineering and Management Press, 1986.

Monden, Yasuhiro, *Toyota Production System,* 2d ed., Atlanta, Ga.: Industrial Engineering and Management Press, 1993.

Sepehri, M. *Just-in-Time, Not Just in Japan,* Falls Church, Va.: APICS, 1986.

Shingo, S., *Modern Approaches to Manufacturing Improvement,* Cambridge, Mass.: Productivity Press, 1990.

Suzaki, Kiyoshi, *The New Manufacturing Challenge,* New York: The Free Press, 1985.

Womack, James, Daniel Jones, and Daniel Roos, *The Machine That Changed the World,* New York: Macmillan, 1990.

16

WAITING LINE MODELS AND SERVICE IMPROVEMENT

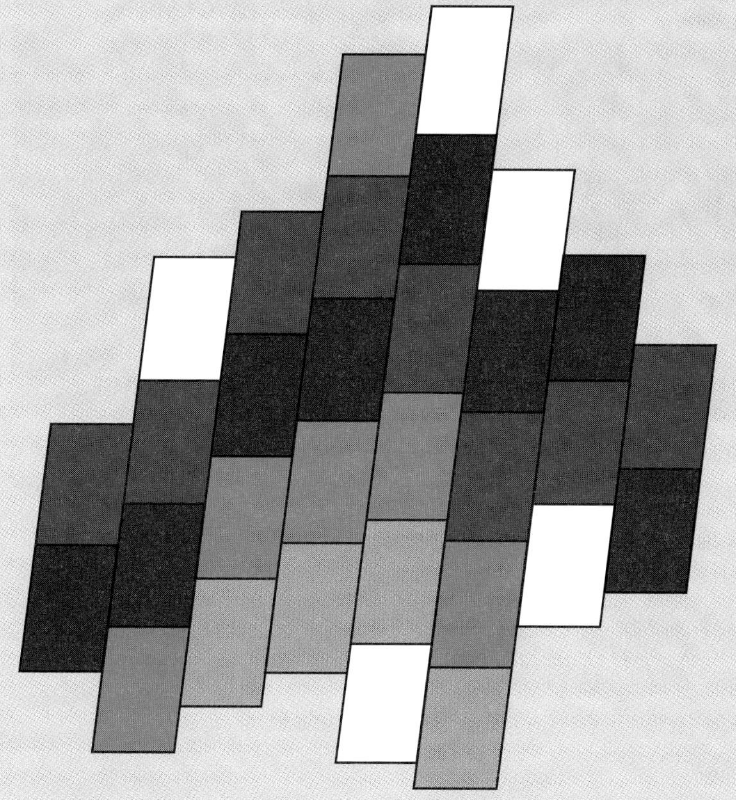

CHAPTER OUTLINE

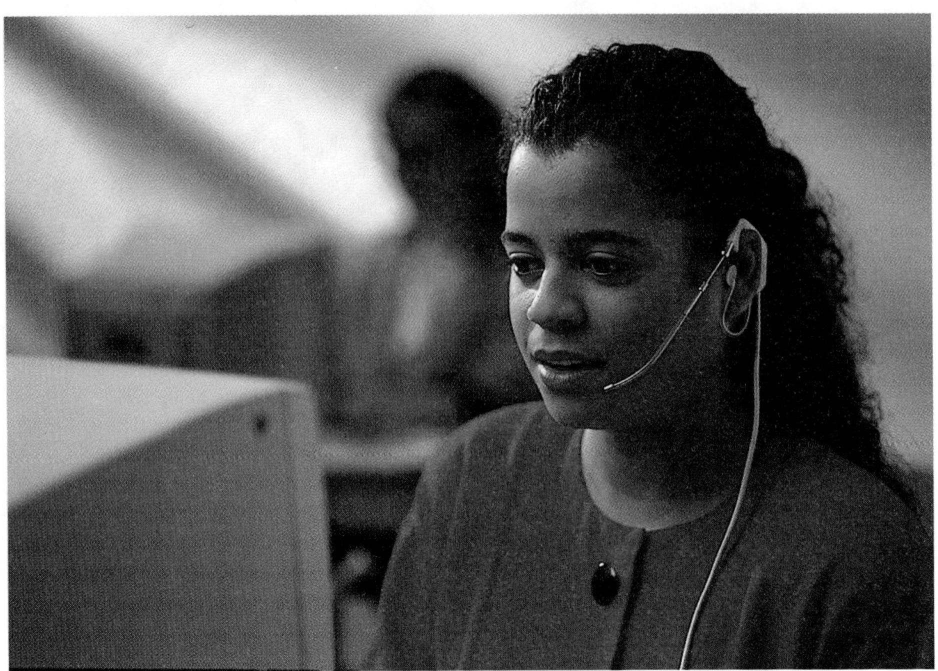

Annually over 13.6 billion catalogs are sent out to consumers by more than 10,000 mail-order companies. Each year over 100 million customers, or about 55 percent of the adult population in the United States, buys more than $50 billion worth of goods from these catalogs. During the 1980s and early 1990s the catalog mail-order business grew three times faster than most traditional retail operations. Catalogs represent over one-third of the total volume of mail handled annually by the U.S. Postal Service and generate over $7 billion in postal revenues. The impetus for this increase in mail order business has come from a variety of reasons such as the introduction of ZIP codes and the spread of credit cards, and including most prominently, the evolution of computer systems and the introduction of toll-free telephone numbers. A major portion of the orders taken by mail-order companies like J. Crew, Eddie Bauer, L.L. Bean, Spiegel, Inc., and J.C. Penney Co., Inc. are by telephone. These telephone ordering systems are in effect, large scale waiting line systems where telephone operators, such as the one shown here, serve customers who "wait in line" over the phone for service. A key ingredient for the success of catalog companies is to provide quality service, which to the customer usually means knowledgeable, pleasant, and fast service. Fast service in a telephone ordering system is determined by the number of customer calls coming in, the length of the calls, and the number of operators available to answer the calls and take orders.

Video 16.1 *TIMS Edelman Awards Tape,* Program 3: "L.L. Bean"

PROVIDING OPTIMAL TELEPHONE ORDER SERVICE AT L.L. BEAN

L.L. Bean is a popular retailer of outdoor clothing and equipment, with more than 65 percent of its sales in 1989 generated through 800-service telephone orders. Long-term decisions in their telemarketing operation relate to the number of telephone (trunk) lines to install and the number of agent positions and support equipment needed, whereas short-term decisions must be made on daily staff scheduling and the capacity needed to handle waiting calls. Intermediate decisions include the number of agents that are hired and trained. Although these decisions are normally routine, the situation changes dramatically during the 3-week period prior to Christmas, at which time 18 percent of the annual phone-order volume occurs. At this time management must make rapid, critical decisions about daily schedules, the number of agents on duty, the number of temporary agents to hire and train, the number of workstations, the number of telephone trunk lines, and other operational capacity considerations. At the other extreme, following this peak period, the system must gear down to reflect a reduction in call volume.

By 1988 L.L. Bean felt that decisions in this scenario were not optimal and customer service levels had become unacceptable. On sales of $580 million in 1988, the company estimated a loss of $10 million in profit due to the suboptimal allocation of resources and unacceptable customer service. In some time periods 80 percent of calls received a busy signal, and customers who connected might have waited 10 minutes for an agent. On very busy days the total lost orders because of busy signals and caller abandonment while waiting for an agent approached $500,000 in gross revenues.

To address this problem a decision-making model, called the economic optimization model (EOM), was developed using queuing analysis. The purpose of the model was to determine the optimal number of telephone trunks for incoming calls, the number of agents scheduled, and the queue capacity (the maximum number of customers who are put on hold to wait for an agent). The model objective was to minimize expected cost rather than simply to achieve a specific service level, which is frequently the basis of queuing analysis. In general, the EOM balanced the cost of the resources (i.e., trunk lines and agents) against the sum of queuing costs and the cost of lost orders at a point where total costs are minimized. Multiple-server and finite queue models were used to estimate operating characteristics for the trunk lines and agents, respectively, which were then used to determine the economic impact of busy signals, customer waiting time, and lost orders. The model was implemented in 1989; for the 3-week peak holiday season, the number of telephone agents was increased from 500 to 1,275, and the number of telephone trunk lines was increased from 150 to 576. Comparing this 3-week period in 1989 (with EOM) and the same period in 1988 (without EOM) showed a 24 percent increase in calls answered, a 16.7 percent increase in orders taken, an increase in revenues of 16.3 percent (approximately $15 million), an 81.3 percent reduction in the number of callers who abandoned, and a reduction in the average answer speed from 93 seconds to 15 seconds. Annual profits increased by approximately $10 million and the cost savings was estimated at approximately $1.6 million. The model also had the effect of improving agent morale and alleviating customer dissatisfaction due to long waits. The cost for this project was $40,000.[1]

Waiting in line is a common occurrence in everyone's life. Anyone who has gone shopping or to a movie has experienced the inconvenience of waiting in line to make purchases or buy a ticket. However, not only do people spend a significant portion of their time waiting in lines, but parts and products queue up prior to a manufacturing operation and wait to be worked on, machinery waits in line to be serviced or repaired, trucks line up to be loaded or unloaded at a shipping terminal, and planes wait to take off and land. Waiting in some form takes place in virtually every productive process or service. Since the time spent by people and things waiting in line is a valuable resource, the reduction of waiting time is an important aspect of operations management.

Teaching Note 16.1 Waiting Lines in Everyday Life

[1]Quinn, P., et al., "Allocating Telecommunications Resources at L.L. Bean, Inc." *Interfaces* 21, no. 1, (January–February 1991): 75–91.

Providing quick service is an important aspect of quality customer service and TQM.

The improvement of service with respect to waiting time has also become more important in recent years because of the increased emphasis on quality, especially in service-related operations. When customers go into a bank to take out a loan, cash a check, or make a deposit, take their car into a dealer for service or repair, or shop at a grocery store, they increasingly equate quality service with rapid service. Aware of this, more and more companies focus on reducing waiting time as an important component of quality improvement. In general, companies are able to reduce waiting time and provide faster service by increasing their service capacity, which usually means adding more servers—that is, more tellers at a bank, more mechanics at a car dealer, or more checkout clerks at a store. However, increasing service capacity in this manner has a monetary cost, and therein lies the basis of waiting line analysis, the trade-off between the cost of improved service and the cost of making customers wait.

The analysis of waiting lines is achieved through a set of mathematical formulas which comprise a field of study called *queuing theory*. The origin of queuing theory is found in telephone-network congestion problems and the work of A. K. Erlang. Erlang (1878–1929), a Danish mathematician, was the scientific advisor for the Copenhagen Telephone Company. In 1917 he published a paper outlining the development of telephone traffic theory, in which he was able to determine the probability of different numbers of calls waiting and the waiting time when the system was in equilibrium. Erlang's work provided the stimulus and formed the basis for the subsequent development of queuing theory.

A number of different queuing models and mathematical formulas exist to deal with a variety of types of waiting line systems. Although we discuss several of the most common types of queuing systems, we do not investigate the mathematical derivation of the various queuing formulas. They are generally complex and not really pertinent to our understanding of the use of queuing theory to improve service.

ELEMENTS OF WAITING LINE ANALYSIS

Waiting lines form because people or things arrive at the servicing function, or server, faster than they can be served. However, this does not mean that the service operation is understaffed or does not have the overall capacity to handle the influx of customers. In fact, most businesses and organizations have sufficient serving capacity available to handle its customers *in the long run*. Waiting lines result because customers do not arrive at a constant, evenly paced rate, nor are they all served in an equal amount of time. Customers arrive at random times, and the time required to serve each individually is not the same. Thus, a waiting line is continually increasing and decreasing in length (and is sometimes empty) and approaches an average rate of customer arrivals and an average time to serve the customer in the long run. For example, the checkout counters at a grocery store may have enough clerks to serve an average of 100 customers in an hour, and in a particular hour only 60 customers might arrive. However, at specific points in time during the hour, waiting lines may form because more than an average number of customers arrive and they have larger than average purchases.

Operating characteristics are average values for characteristics that describe the performance of a waiting line system.

Decisions about waiting lines and the management of waiting lines are based on these averages for customer arrivals and service times. They are used in queuing formulas to compute **operating characteristics** such as the average number of customers waiting in line and the average time a customer must wait in line. Different sets of formulas are used, depending on the type of waiting line system being investigated. For example, a bank drive-in teller window at which one bank clerk serves a single line of customers in cars is different than a single line of passengers at an airport ticket counter that are served by three or four airline agents. In this section we present the different elements and components that make up waiting lines prior to looking at queuing formulas in the following sections.

Basic Components of a Waiting Line

Transparency 16.1 Elements of Waiting Line Analysis

The basic components of a waiting line, or **queue,** are arrivals, servers, and the waiting line. The relationship between these components are shown in Figure 16.1 for the simplest type of *waiting line system,* a single server with a single queue. This is commonly referred to as a *single-channel* queuing system. Following is a brief description of each of these waiting line components.

A **queue** is a single waiting line.

A *waiting line system* consists of arrivals, servers, and waiting line structure.

The Calling Population

In our discussions of queuing, a customer is a person or thing that wants service from an operation. The **calling population** is the source of the customers to the queuing system, and it can be either *infinite* or *finite.* An infinite calling population assumes that there is such a large number of potential customers that it is always possible for one more customer to arrive to be served. For example, a grocery store, a bank, and a service station are assumed to have infinite calling populations, that is, the whole town or geographic area. Alternatively, a finite calling population has a specific, countable number of potential customers. It is possible for all the customers to be served or waiting in line at the same time; that is, it may occur that there is not one more customer to be served. Examples of a finite calling population are a repair facility in a shop, where there is a fixed number of machines available to be worked on, a trucking terminal that services a fleet of a specific number of trucks, or a nurse assigned to attend to a specific number of patients.

The **calling population** is the source of customers; *infinite* or *finite.*

The Arrival Rate

Teaching Note 16.2 Poisson and Exponential Distributions

The **arrival rate** is the rate at which customers arrive at the service facility during a specified period of time. This rate can be estimated from empirical data derived from studying the system or a similar system, or it can be an average of these empirical data. For example, if 100 customers arrive at a store checkout counter during a 10-hour day, we could say the arrival rate averages 10 customers per hour. However, although we might be able to determine a rate for arrivals by counting the number of customers during a specific time period, we would not know exactly when these customers would arrive. In other words, it might be that no customers would arrive during one hour and 20 customers would arrive during another hour. In general, these arrivals are assumed to be independent of each other and to vary randomly over time.

The **arrival rate** is the frequency at which customers arrive at a waiting line according to a probability distribution.

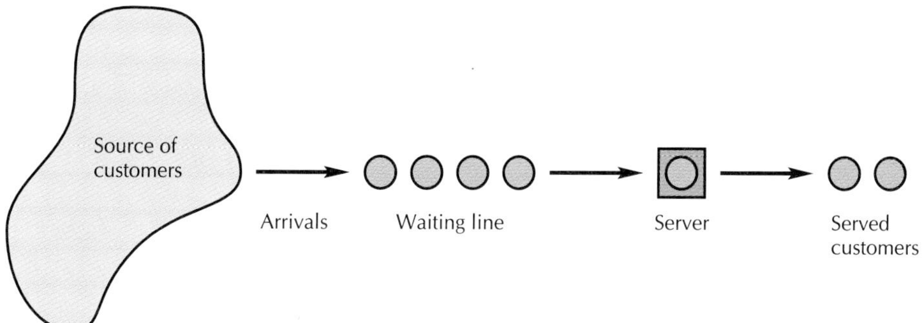

FIGURE 16.1 Components of a Queuing System

Arrival rate (λ) is most frequently described by a Poisson distribution.

Given these assumptions, it is further assumed that arrivals at a service facility conform to some probability distribution. Arrivals could be described by many distributions, but it has been determined (through years of research and the practical experience of people in the field of queuing) that the number of arrivals per unit of time at a service facility can frequently be defined by a *Poisson distribution.* The general model (formula) for the Poisson probability distribution is

$$P(r) = \frac{e^{-\lambda}(\lambda)^r}{r!}$$

where r is the number of arrivals in a prescribed time period, and λ is the mean arrival rate.

The Poisson distribution assumes random arrivals; that is, each arrival is assumed to be independent of other arrivals. An interesting characteristic of a Poisson distribution, which makes it easier to work with than some other distributions, is that the mean is equal to the variance. Thus, by specifying the mean of a Poisson distribution, we can define the entire distribution.

The Poisson distribution is a *discrete* probability distribution, since it reflects the number of arrivals per unit time. Figure 16.2 portrays the Poisson distribution graphically for several different values of the mean, λ, and different numbers of arrivals, r. It can be seen that as the mean becomes larger, the distribution becomes flatter and more symmetric.

An interesting feature of the Poisson process is that if the number of arrivals per unit time is Poisson distributed with a mean rate of λ, then the time between arrivals (interarrival time) is distributed as a negative exponential, or simply ex-

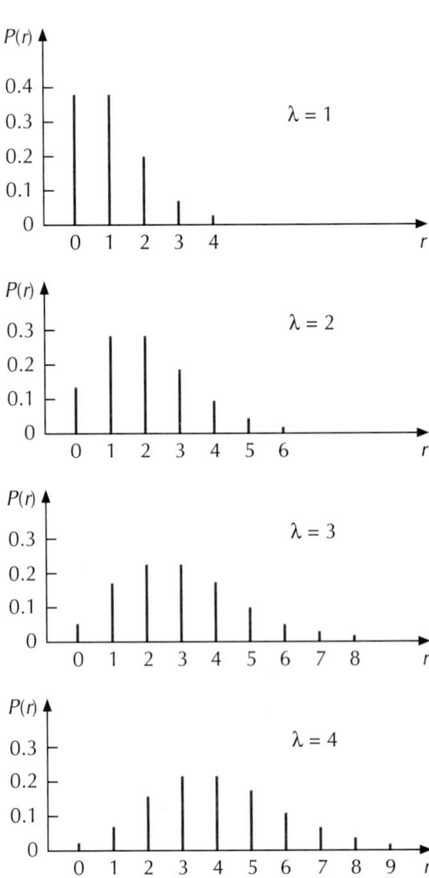

FIGURE 16.2 The Poisson Distribution

ponential, probability distribution with a mean of $1/\lambda$. This relationship has further implications for the service time of a queuing system.

Service Times

The convention in queuing theory is to describe arrivals in terms of a *rate* and service in terms of *time*. **Service times** in a queuing process may also be any one of a large number of different probability distributions. The distribution most commonly assumed for service times is the *negative exponential distribution*. From the preceding discussion of the relationship between the Poisson and negative exponential distributions, if service times follow a negative exponential distribution, the service rate follows a Poisson distribution.

Service time, the time required to serve a customer, is most frequently described by the negative exponential distribution.

Empirical research has shown that the assumption of negative exponentially distributed service times is not valid nearly as often as is the assumption of Poisson-distributed arrivals. Therefore, for actual applications of queuing analysis, this assumption would have to be carefully checked before this distribution was used. The formula for the negative exponential density function is

$$f(t) = \mu e^{-\mu t}$$

where t is the service time and μ equals the mean service rate.

As in the case of the Poisson arrival rate, the negative exponential service time corresponds to the assumption that service times are completely random. The probability of completing a service for a customer in any subsequent time period after service is begun is independent of how much time has already elapsed on the service for that customer.

The negative exponential distribution is a continuous probability distribution, since it relates to time of service. Figure 16.3 illustrates graphically the negative exponential distribution. It can be seen that short service times have the highest probability of occurrence. As service time increases, the probability function tails off (exponentially) toward zero probability.

Arrival Rate Less Than Service Rate

It is logical to assume that the rate at which services are completed must exceed the arrival rate of customers. If this is not the case, the waiting line will simply continue to grow, and there will be no "average" solution. Thus, it is generally assumed that the service rate does exceed the arrival rate.

Customers must be served faster than they arrive or an infinitely large queue will build up.

An interesting relationship among arrival rates, service rates, and expected queue lengths is illustrated in Figure 16.4. If the arrival rate must be less than the service rate, then the ratio of arrival rate to service rate will be less than 1. As that ratio approaches 1, the expected queue length will approach infinity. In Figure

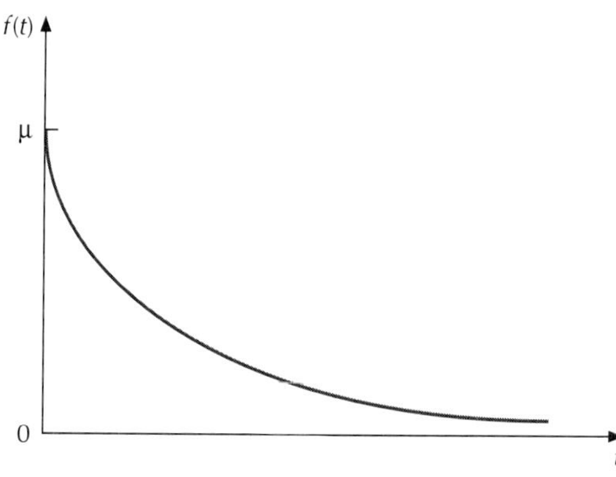

FIGURE 16.3 The Negative Exponential Distribution

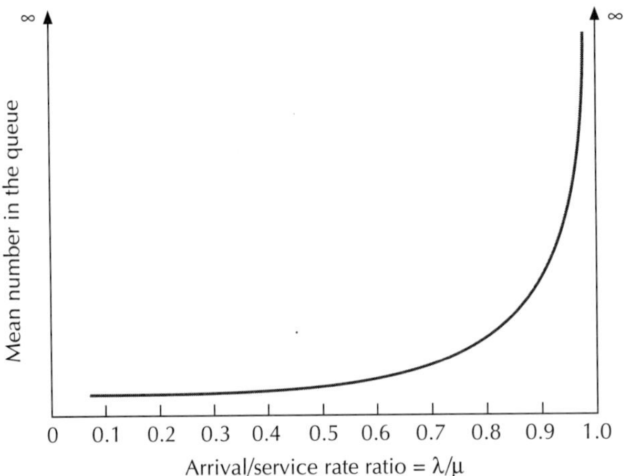

FIGURE 16.4 Relationship Between Arrival and Service Rates

16.4, λ represents the mean arrival rate and μ represents the mean service rate. It can be seen that once the ratio of λ to μ exceeds 0.7, the expected queue length increases very rapidly. This relationship of queue length to arrival rate and service rate assumes infinite (or at least very large) possible queue lengths.

Queue Discipline and Length

Queue discipline is the order in which customers are served.

The most common service rule is first come, first served.

The **queue discipline** is the order in which waiting customers are served. The most common type of queue discipline is service on a *first-come, first-served* basis. That is, the first person or item in line waiting is served first. However, other disciplines are possible. For example, a machine operator might stack in-process parts beside a machine so that the last part is on top of the stack and will be selected first. This queue discipline would be referred to as *last in, first out*. Or, the machine operator might simply reach into a box full of parts and select one at random. In this case the queue discipline is random. Often customers are scheduled for service according to a predetermined appointment, such as patients at a doctor's or dentist's office or diners at a restaurant where reservations are required. In this case the customers are taken according to a prearranged schedule regardless of when they arrive at the facility. Another example of the many types of queue disciplines is when customers are processed alphabetically according to their last names, such as at school registration or at job interviews.

An **infinite queue** can be of any length; the length of a **finite queue** is limited.

Queues can also be of an infinite or finite size or length. An **infinite queue** can be of any size with no upper limit and is the most common queue structure. For example, it is assumed that the waiting line at a movie theater could stretch through the lobby and out the door if necessary. Alternatively, a **finite queue** is limited in size. An example of a finite queue is the driveway at a bank teller window that can accommodate only a limited number of cars, or a waiting list to buy season tickets to the opera that is limited to only 20 names.

Basic Waiting Line Structures

Transparency 16.2 Basic Waiting Line Structures

Channels are the number of parallel servers; **phases** denote the number of sequential servers a customer must go through to receive service.

Waiting line processes are generally categorized into four basic structures, according to the nature of the service facilities: single-channel, single-phase; multiple-channel, single-phase; single-channel, multiple-phase; and multiple-channel, multiple-phase processes. Each of the four categories of queuing processes is illustrated graphically in Figure 16.5.

The number of **channels** in a queuing process is simply the number of parallel servers for servicing arriving customers. The number of **phases,** on the other

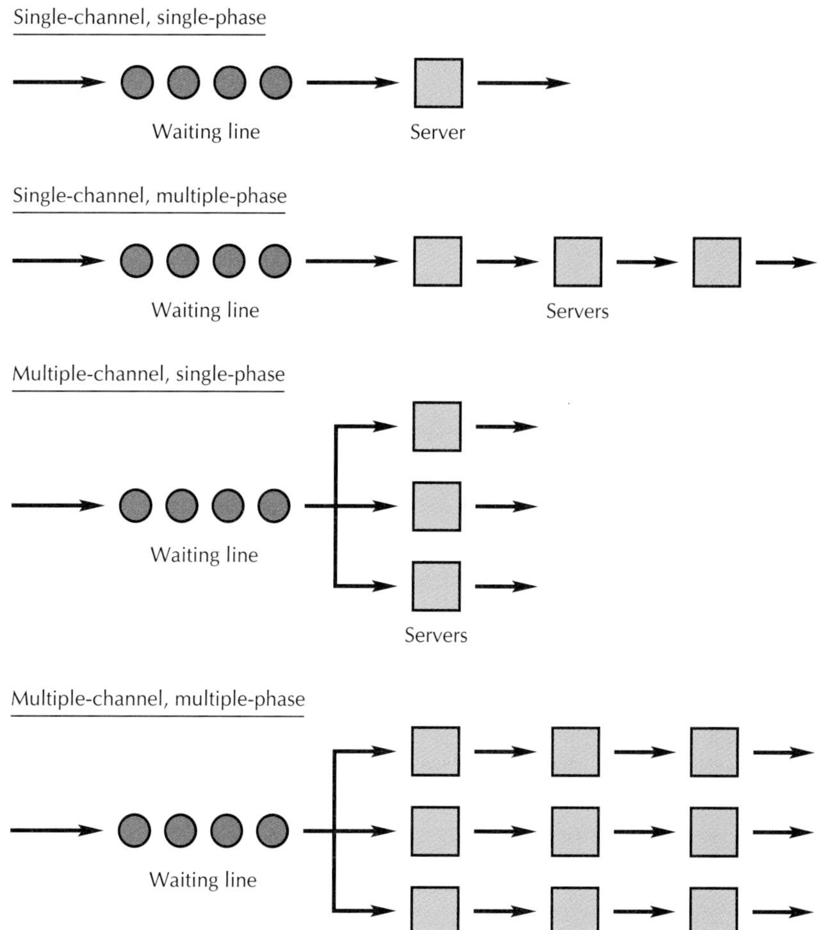

FIGURE 16.5 Basic Waiting Line Structures

hand, denotes the number of sequential servers each customer must go through in order to complete service. An example of a single-channel, single-phase queuing operation is a post office with only one postal clerk waiting on a single line of customers. A post office with several postal clerks waiting on a single line of customers is an example of a multiple-channel, single-phase operation.

When patients go to a doctor for treatment or check into a hospital, they often wait in a reception room prior to entering the treatment facility. Then, upon being seated in the treatment room, the patients receive an initial checkup or treatment from a nurse followed by treatment from a doctor. This sort of arrangement constitutes a single-channel, multiple-phase queuing process. If there are several doctors and nurses, the process is a multiple-channel, multiple-phase process.

An example of another multiple-phase system is a manufacturing assembly operation in which a product is worked on at several sequential machines or operators at a workstation. An additional example of a single-channel, multiple-phase system is a manufacturing assembly-line type operation in which in-process product units are fed to several sequential machines or operators at workstations to be worked on. Two or more of these lines operating in tandem and being fed by a single line of product units are an example of a multi-channel, multi-phase system.

You may immediately visualize a familiar waiting situation that fits none of these categories of waiting line structures. The four categories of queuing processes presented are simply the four basic categories; numerous variations can be described. For example, rather than a single queue preceding the multiple-channel, single-phase case, there might be a separate queue preceding each server. In the multiple-channel, multiple-phase case, items might switch back and forth from one channel to the other between each of the various service phases. It is readily apparent that queuing models can become quite complex. However, the fundamentals of basic queuing theory are relevant to the analysis of all queuing problems, regardless of their complexity.

Operating Characteristics

Transparency 16.3 Operating Characteristics

Teaching Note 16.3 Queuing Results

A *steady state* is a constant, average value for performance characteristics that the system will attain after a long time.

The mathematics that are used in queuing theory do not provide an optimal, or "best," solution. Instead they generate measures referred to as *operating characteristics* that describe the performance of the queuing system and that management uses to evaluate the system and make decisions. It is assumed that these operating characteristics will approach constant, average values after the system has been in operation for a long time, which is referred to as a *steady state.* These basic operating characteristics that are used in a waiting line analysis are defined in Table 16.1.

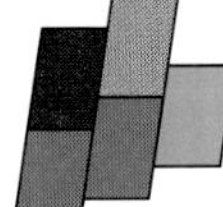

WAITING LINE COST ANALYSIS AND QUALITY

The Traditional Cost Relationships in Waiting Line Analysis

A queuing system's operating characteristics are actually inputs into a broader conceptual framework, within which most waiting line systems are analyzed. The analysis of waiting lines essentially reduces to determining the level of service (which usually means the number of servers) that minimizes total cost, where total cost is the sum of the cost of providing service and the cost of customers waiting. There is generally an inverse relationship between service cost and the cost of waiting, as reflected in the cost curves in Figure 16.6. As the level of service, reflected by the number of servers, goes up, the cost of service increases, whereas waiting cost decreases. The level of service provided should coincide with the minimum point on the total cost curve.

As the level of service improves, the cost of service increases.

Better service requires more servers.

The cost of providing the service is usually reflected in the cost of the servers, such as the cost of the tellers at a bank, postal workers at a post office counter, or the repair crew in a plant or shop. As the number of servers is increased to reduce waiting time, service cost goes up. Service cost is normally direct and relatively easy to compute. Alternatively, the cost of waiting is not as easy to determine. The

TABLE 16.1 Queuing System Operating Characteristics

Notation	*Operating Characteristic*
L	Average number of customers in the system (waiting and being served)
L_q	Average number of customers in the waiting line
W	Average time a customer spends in the system (waiting and being served)
W_q	Average time a customer spends waiting in line
P_0	Probability of no (zero) customers in the system
P_n	Probability of n customers in the system
ρ	Utilization rate; the proportion of time the system is in use

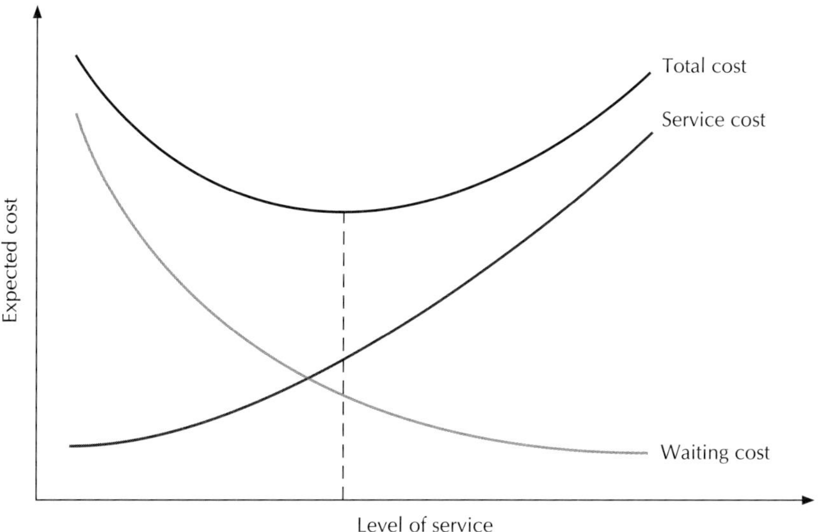

FIGURE 16.6 The Cost Relationship in Waiting Line Analysis

major determinant of waiting cost is the loss of business that might result because customers get tired of waiting and leave; then, they may purchase the product or service elsewhere. This business loss can be temporary (a single event) or permanent (the customer never comes back). The cost due to a loss of business is especially difficult to determine, since it is not part of normal accounting records, although some trade organizations for businesses and industries occasionally provide such data. Other types of waiting costs include the loss of production time and salary for employees waiting to use machinery or equipment, load or unload vehicles, etc. In general, as the level of service increases (and the number of servers is increased) the waiting cost decreases, as shown in Figure 16.6.

Waiting Line Costs and Quality Service

The traditional waiting line cost relationship is similar to the traditional quality-cost relationship.

It is interesting to compare the waiting line cost relationship in Figure 16.6 with the traditional quality-cost relationship in Figure 3.4 (from Chapter 3). These cost curves are shown side by side in Figure 16.7, on page 792. Note that the total quality-cost curve is a sum of the decreasing costs resulting from poor quality (including loss of business) and the increasing cost of preventing poor quality. This relationship is, in fact, very similar to the waiting line cost curve that sums decreasing waiting cost (including loss of business), which is a quality-related cost, and the increasing cost of better-quality service. In the case of both cost curves, the traditional approach is to provide a level of quality, or service, that minimizes total cost. However, in our discussion of quality management in Chapter 3, we noted that the contemporary approach to quality cost, is to seek "zero defects," or a level of quality significantly farther to the right of the minimum point on the total cost curve.

The traditional approach is to provide a level of service that minimizes service-related costs.

The modern approach to quality management is to assume that the traditional quality-cost relationship is a short-run perspective that understates the potential long-term loss of business from poor quality. In the long run, a higher level of quality will gain market share and increase business and thus is more cost effective. Further, as the company focuses on improving quality service, the cost of achieving good quality will be less because of the innovations in processes and work design that will result. This viewpoint is reflected in the modified version of the quality-cost trade-off curve shown in Figure 16.8, on page 792, which corresponds to Figure 3.5 in Chapter 3. Note that in this figure the cost of achieving good service does not rise as rapidly as it does in Figure 16.6. As a result, the total cost curve has a different shape, and the minimum cost point occurs at the 100 percent

The TQM approach is that absolute quality service will be the most cost-effective in the long run.

Transparency 16.4 Traditional Quality and Waiting Line Costs

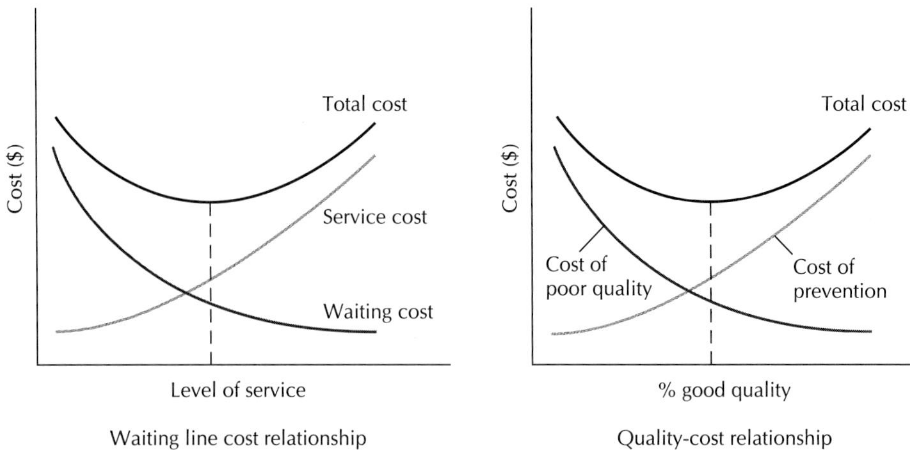

FIGURE 16.7 A Comparison of Traditional Quality and Waiting Line Costs

quality service level. This is the point corresponding to zero defects. This level of "better-quality" (i.e., quicker) service will, in the long run, increase business and be more cost effective, according to the modern view of quality management.

As an alternative to improving service quality by reducing waiting time, companies frequently attempt to make waiting more palatable by providing diversions. For example, many waiting rooms, such as at a doctor's office, provide magazines and newspapers for customers to read while waiting. Televisions are occasionally available in auto repair waiting areas, in airport terminals, or in bars and lounges of restaurants where customers wait for a table for dinner. At Disney World costumed characters entertain park visitors while they wait in line for rides. Mirrors are purposely located near elevators to distract people while they wait. A common practice at supermarkets is to locate magazines and other "impulse-purchase" items at the checkout counter, not only as a diversion while waiting but as potential purchases. All these tactics are designed to improve the quality of service that requires waiting without actually incurring the cost of reducing waiting time.

Transparency 16.5 The Cost Relationship for Quality Service

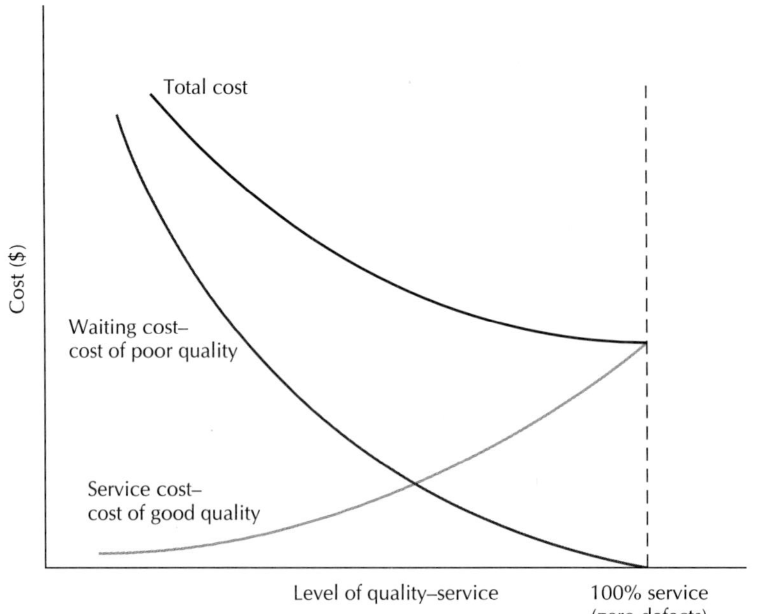

FIGURE 16.8 The Cost Relationship for Quality Service

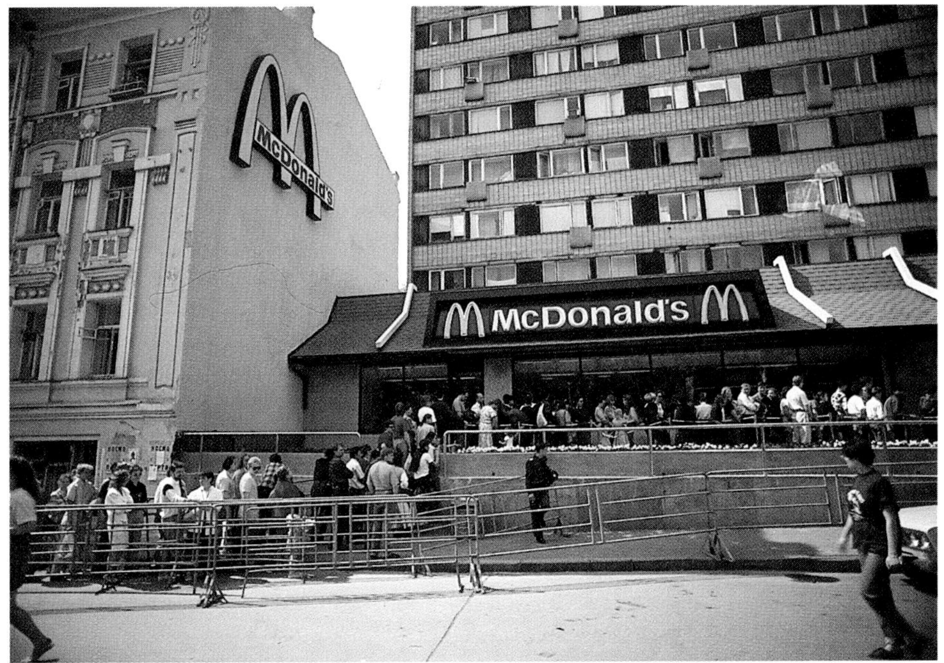

"Good" operating characteristics for a waiting line system, and hence good service, are relative and must have some basis for comparison. For example, the waiting time at this McDonald's in Pushkin Square in Moscow averages about 45 minutes. For Americans this level of service would be considered dismal. However, to Muscovites used to waiting in lines that often consume the better part of a day, the waiting time at this McDonald's is amazingly short. It represents good service.

SINGLE-CHANNEL, SINGLE-PHASE MODELS

The simplest, most basic of the waiting line structures illustrated in Figure 16.5 is the single-channel, single-phase—or, simply, *single-server*—model. There are several variations of the single-server waiting line system, and in this chapter we present several of the more frequently used variations, including the following:

variations of the basic single-server model

- Poisson arrival rate, exponential service times
- Poisson arrival rate, general (or unknown) distribution of service times
- Poisson arrival rate, constant service times
- Poisson arrival rate, exponential service times with a finite queue
- Poisson arrival rate, exponential service times with a finite calling population

The Basic Single-Server Model

In our presentation of the basic single server model we will assume the following:

assumptions of the basic single-server model

- Poisson arrival rate
- Exponential service times
- First-come, first-served queue discipline
- Infinite queue length
- Infinite calling population

The basic operating characteristics of this single-server model are computed using the following formulas, where λ = mean arrival rate, μ = mean service rate, and n = the number of customers in the waiting line system.

λ = mean arrival rate; μ = mean service rate.

The probability that no customers are in the queuing system (either in the queue or being served) is

Transparency 16.6 Queuing Formulas for Basic Single-Server Model

basic single-server queueing formulas

$$P_0 = \left(1 - \frac{\lambda}{\mu}\right)$$

The probability of exactly n customers in the queuing system is

$$P_n = \left(\frac{\lambda}{\mu}\right)^n \cdot P_0$$
$$= \left(\frac{\lambda}{\mu}\right)\left(1 - \frac{\lambda}{\mu}\right)$$

The average number of customers in the queuing system (i.e., the customers being serviced and in the waiting line) is

$$L = \frac{\lambda}{\mu - \lambda}$$

The average number of customers in the waiting line is

$$L_q - \frac{\lambda^2}{\mu(\mu - \lambda)}$$

The average time a customer spends in the queuing system (i.e., waiting and being served) is

$$W = \frac{1}{\mu - \lambda}$$
$$= \frac{L}{\lambda}$$

The average time a customer spends waiting in line to be served is

$$W_q = \frac{\lambda}{\mu(\mu - \lambda)}$$

The probability that the server is busy and a customer has to wait, known as the utilization factor, is

$$\rho = \frac{\lambda}{\mu}$$

The probability that the server is idle and a customer can be served is

$$I = 1 - \rho$$
$$= 1 - \frac{\lambda}{\mu} = P_0$$

Alternate Example 16.1

EXAMPLE 16.1

A Single-Server Model

Problem Statement:

The Fast Shop Drive-In Market has one checkout counter and one employee, who operates the cash register at the checkout counter. The combination of the cash register and the operator is the server (or service facility) in this queuing system; the customers who line up at the counter to pay for their selections form the waiting line.

Customers arrive at a rate of 24 per hour according to a Poisson distribution, and service times are exponentially distributed with a mean rate of 30 customers per hour. The market manager wants to determine the operating characteristics for this waiting line system.

Solution:

The operating characteristics are computed using the queuing formulas for the single-server model as follows.

$$P_0 = \left(1 - \frac{\lambda}{\mu}\right)$$
$$= \left(1 - \frac{24}{30}\right)$$
$$= 0.20 \text{ probability of no customers in the system}$$

$$L = \frac{\lambda}{\mu - \lambda}$$
$$= \frac{24}{30 - 24}$$
$$= 4 \text{ customers on the average in the queuing system}$$

$$L_q = \frac{\lambda^2}{\mu(\mu - \lambda)}$$
$$= \frac{(24)^2}{30(30 - 24)}$$
$$= 3.2 \text{ customers on the average in the waiting line}$$

$$W = \frac{1}{\mu - \lambda}$$
$$= \frac{1}{30 - 24}$$
$$= 0.167 \text{ hour (10 minutes) average time in the system per customer}$$

$$W_q = \frac{\lambda}{\mu(\mu - \lambda)}$$
$$= \frac{24}{30(30 - 24)}$$
$$= 0.133 \text{ hour (8 minutes) average time in the waiting line per customer}$$

$$\rho = \frac{\lambda}{\mu}$$
$$= \frac{24}{30}$$
$$= 0.80 \text{ probability that the server will be busy and the customer must wait}$$

$$I = 1 - \rho$$
$$= 1 - 0.80$$
$$= 0.20 \text{ probability that the server will be idle and a customer can be served}$$

Remember that these operating characteristics are averages that result over a period of time; they are not absolutes. In other words, customers who arrive at the Fast Shop Drive-In Market checkout counter will not find 3.2 customers in line. There could be no customers or 1, 2, 3, or 4 customers, for example. The value 3.2 is simply an average that occurs over time, as are the other operating characteristics.

EXAMPLE 16.2

Waiting Line Cost Analysis

Problem Statement:

At the Fast Shop Market in Example 16.1, the arrival rate of 24 customers per hour means that, on the average, a customer arrives about every 2.5 minutes (i.e., $\frac{1}{24} \times$ 60 minutes). This indicates that the store is very busy. Because of the nature of the store, customers purchase a few items and expect quick service. Customers expect to spend a relatively greater amount of time in a supermarket, since typically they make larger purchases, but customers who shop at a drive-in market do so, at least in part, because it is quicker than a supermarket.

Given customer's expectations, the store's manager believes that it is unacceptable for a customer to wait 8 minutes and spend a total of 10 minutes in the queuing system (not including the actual shopping time). The manager wants to test several alternatives for reducing customer waiting time: 1. the addition of another employee to pack up the purchases; and 2. the addition of an additional checkout counter.

Solution:

Alternative I: The Addition of an Employee

The addition of an extra employee will cost the market manager $150 per week. With the help of the market's national office's marketing research group, the manager has determined that for each minute that customer waiting time is reduced, the store avoids a loss in sales of $75 per week. (That is, the store loses money when customers leave prior to shopping because of the long line or when customers do not return.)

If a new employee is hired, customers can be served in less time. In other words, the service rate, which is the number of customers served per time period, will increase. The previous service rate was

$$\mu = 30 \text{ customers served per hour}$$

The addition of a new employee will increase the service rate to

$$\mu = 40 \text{ customers served per hour}$$

It will be assumed that the arrival rate will remain the same ($\lambda = 24$ per hour), since the increased service rate will not increase arrivals but instead will, it is hoped, minimize the loss of customers. (However, it is not illogical to assume that an increase in service might eventually increase arrivals in the long run.)

Given the new λ and μ values, the operating characteristics can be recomputed as follows.

$P_0 = 0.40$ probability of no customers in the system
$L = 1.5$ customers on the average in the queuing system
$L_q = 0.90$ customer on the average in the waiting line
$W = 0.063$ hour (3.75 minutes) average time in the system per customer
$W_q = 0.038$ hour (2.25 minutes) average time in the waiting line per customer
$\rho = 0.60$ probability that the customer must wait
$I = 0.40$ probability that the server will be idle and a customer can be served

The average waiting time per customer has been reduced from 8 minutes to 2.25 minutes, a significant amount. The savings (that is, the decrease in lost sales) is computed as follows.

$$8.00 \text{ minutes} - 2.25 \text{ minutes} = 5.75 \text{ minutes}$$
$$5.75 \text{ minutes} \times \$75/\text{minute}/\text{week} = \$431.25 \text{ per week}$$

Since the extra employee costs management \$150 per week, the total savings will be

$$\$431.25 - \$150 = \$281.25 \text{ per week}$$

The market manager would probably welcome this savings and consider the preceding operating statistics preferable to the previous ones for the condition where the market had only one employee.

Alternative II: The Addition of a New Checkout Counter

Next we will consider the manager's alternative of constructing a new checkout counter. The total cost of this project would be \$6,000, plus an extra \$200 per week for an additional cashier.

The new checkout counter would be opposite the present counter (so that the servers would have their backs to each other in an enclosed counter area). There would be several display cases and racks between the two lines, so that customers waiting in line would not move back and forth between lines. (Such movement, called **jockeying,** would invalidate the queuing formulas for this model.) We will assume that the customers would divide themselves equally between both lines, so the arrival rate for each line would be half of the prior arrival rate for a single checkout counter, or

$$\lambda = 12 \text{ customers per hour}$$

The service rate remains the same for each of the counters:

$$\mu = 30 \text{ customers served per hour}$$

Substituting this new arrival rate and the service rate into our queuing formulas results in the following operating characteristics:

$P_0 = 0.60$ probability of no customers in the system
$L = 0.67$ customer in the queuing system
$L_q = 0.27$ customer in the waiting line
$W = 0.055$ hour (3.33 minutes) per customer in the system
$W_q = 0.022$ hour (1.33 minutes) per customer in the waiting line
$\rho = 0.40$ probability that a customer must wait
$I = 0.60$ probability that a server will be idle and a customer can be served

Using the same sales savings of \$75 per week for each minute's reduction in waiting time, we find that the store would save

$$8.00 \text{ minutes} - 1.33 \text{ minutes} = 6.67 \text{ minutes}$$
$$.67 \text{ minutes} \times \$75/\text{minute} = \$500.00 \text{ per week}$$

Next we subtract the \$200 per week cost for the new cashier from this amount saved.

$$\$500 - 200 = \$300$$

Since the capital outlay of this project is \$6,000, it would take about 20 weeks (\$6,000/\$300 = 20 weeks) to recoup the initial cost (ignoring the possibility of interest on the \$6,000). Once the cost has been recovered, the store would save \$18.75 (\$300.00 – 281.25) more per week by adding a new checkout counter rather than simply hiring an extra employee. However, we must not disregard the fact that during the 20-week cost recovery period, the \$281.25 savings incurred by simply hiring a new employee would be lost.

For the market manager both of these alternatives seem preferable to the original conditions, which resulted in a lengthy waiting time of 8 minutes per customer. However, the manager might have a difficult time selecting between the two alternatives. It might be appropriate to consider other factors besides waiting time. For example, the portion of time the employee is idle is 40 percent with the first alternative and 60 percent with the second, which seems to be a significant difference. An additional factor is the loss of space resulting from a new checkout counter.

However, the final decision must be based on the manager's own experience and perceived needs. As we have noted previously, the results of queuing analysis simply provide information for decision making.

These two alternatives illustrate the cost trade-offs associated with improved service. As the level of service increases, the corresponding cost of this service also increases. For example, when we added an extra employee in alternative I, the service was improved, but the cost of providing service also increased. But when the level of service was increased, the costs associated with customer waiting decreased.

Computer Analysis of the Single-Server Model

Transparency 16.7 AB:POM Analysis of Single-Server Model

Teaching Note 16.4 Computer Software

A feature of the AB:POM computer software package used in different chapters in this text, is the capability to perform queuing analysis. As an illustration of the computerized analysis of the single-server queuing system, we will use AB:POM to determine the operating characteristics for the Fast Shop Market in Example 16.1. The solution output with input data is shown in Exhibit 16.1.

Constant Service Times

Constant service times occur with machinery and automated equipment.

The single-server model with Poisson arrivals and *constant service times* is a queuing variation that is of particular interest in operations management, since the most frequent occurrence of constant service times is with automated equipment and machinery. As such, this type of queuing model has direct application for many manufacturing operations.

Constant service times are a special case of the single-server model with *undefined* service times.

The constant service time model is actually a special case of a more general variation of the single-server model in which service times cannot be assumed to be exponentially distributed. As such, service times are said to be *general,* or *undefined.* The basic queuing formulas for the operating characteristics of the undefined service time model are as follows.

Transparency 16.8 Single-Server Model with Constant Service Times

$$P_0 = 1 - \frac{\lambda}{\mu}$$

$$L_q = \frac{\lambda^2\sigma^2 + (\lambda/\mu)^2}{2(1 - \lambda/\mu)}$$

$$L = L_q + \frac{\lambda}{\mu}$$

$$W_q = \frac{L_q}{\lambda}$$

$$W = W_q + \frac{1}{\mu}$$

$$\rho = \frac{\lambda}{\mu}$$

```
                        Waiting Line Models                            Solution
M/M/1 - single server, exponential service
                           Example 16.1
arrival rate (lambda)     24.00     Average server utilization              0.8000
service rate (mu)         30.00     Average number in the queue(Lq)         3.2000
number of servers             1     Average number in the system (L)        4.0000
                                    Average time in the queue (Wq)        .1333333
                                        Answer * 60                           8.00
                                    Average time in the system (W)        .1666667
                                        Answer * 60                          10.00
```

EXHIBIT 16.1

The key formula for undefined service times is for L_q, the number of customers in the waiting line. In this formula μ and σ are the mean and standard deviation, respectively, for any general probability distribution with independent service times. Recall that in our discussion of the Poisson distribution in the section on arrival rates, we noted that the mean is equal to the variance. This same relationship is true for Poisson service rates if service times are exponentially distributed. Thus, if we let $\sigma = \mu$ in the preceding formula for L_q for undefined service times, it becomes the same as our basic formula with exponential service times. In fact all the queuing formulas become the same as the basic single-server model.

In the case of constant service times, there is no variability in service times (i.e., service time is the same constant value for each customer); thus, $\sigma = 0$. Substituting $\sigma = 0$ into the undefined service time formula for L_q results in the following formula for constant service times.

$$\begin{aligned} L_q &= \frac{\lambda^2\sigma^2 + (\lambda/\mu)^2}{2(1-\lambda/\mu)} \\ &= \frac{\lambda^2(0) + (\lambda/\mu)^2}{2(1-\lambda/\mu)} \\ &= \frac{(\lambda/\mu)^2}{2(1-\lambda/\mu)} \\ &= \frac{\lambda^2}{2\mu(\mu-\lambda)} \end{aligned}$$

Notice that this new formula for L_q for constant service times is simply the basic single-server formula for L_q divided by 2. All the remaining formulas for the single-server model are the same.

EXAMPLE 16.3

Alternate Example 16.2

A Single-Server Model with Constant Service Times

Problem Statement:

The Petrolco Service Station has an automatic car wash, and cars purchasing gas at the station receive a discounted car wash, depending on the number of gallons of gas they buy. The car wash can accommodate one car at a time, and it requires a constant time of 4.5 minutes for a wash. Cars arrive at the car wash at an average rate of 10 per hour (Poisson distributed). The service station manager wants to determine the average length of the waiting line and the average waiting time at the car wash.

Solution:

First determine λ and μ such that they are expressed as rates:

$$\lambda = 10 \text{ per hour}$$

$$\mu = \frac{60}{4.5} = 13.3 \text{ per hour}$$

Substituting λ and μ into the queuing formulas for constant service time gives

$$L_q = \frac{\lambda^2}{2\mu(\mu - \lambda)}$$

$$= \frac{(10)^2}{2(13.3)(13.3 - 10)}$$

$$= 1.14 \text{ cars waiting}$$

$$W_q = \frac{L_q}{\lambda}$$

$$= \frac{1.14}{10}$$

$$= 0.117 \text{ hour, or } 7.02 \text{ minutes, waiting in line}$$

Finite Queue Length

For some waiting line systems, the length of the queue may be limited by the physical area in which the queue forms; space may permit only a limited number of customers to enter the queue. Such a waiting line is referred to as a *finite queue;* it results in another variation of the single-phase, single-channel queuing model.

Transparency 16.9 Single-Server Model with Finite Queue Length

The basic single-server model must be modified to consider the finite queuing system. It should be noted that for this case the service rate does not have to exceed the arrival rate ($\mu > \lambda$) in order to obtain steady-state conditions. The resultant operating characteristics, where M is the maximum number in the system, are as follows:

$$P_0 = \frac{1 - \lambda/\mu}{1 - (\lambda/\mu)^{M+1}}$$

$$P_n = (P_0)\left(\frac{\lambda}{\mu}\right)^n \qquad \text{for } n \leq M$$

$$L = \frac{\lambda/\mu}{1 - \lambda/\mu} - \frac{(M+1)(\lambda/\mu)^{M+1}}{1 - (\lambda/\mu)^{M+1}}$$

Since P_n is the probability of n units in the system, if we define M as the maximum number allowed in the system, then P_M (the value of P_n for $n = M$) is the probability that a customer will not join the system. The remaining equations are

$$L_q = L - \frac{\lambda(1 - P_M)}{\mu}$$

$$W = \frac{L}{\lambda(1 - P_M)}$$

$$W_q = W - \frac{1}{\mu}$$

Alternative Example 16.3

EXAMPLE 16.4

A Single-Server Model with Finite Queue

Problem Statement:

Slick's Quick Lube is a one-bay service facility located next to a busy highway in a metropolitan area. The facility has space for only one vehicle in service and three vehicles lined up to wait for service. There is no space for cars to line up on the busy adjacent highway, so if the waiting line is full (3 cars), prospective customers must drive on.

The mean time between arrivals for customers seeking lube service is 3 minutes. The mean time required to perform the lube operation is 2 minutes. Both the interarrival times and the service times are exponentially distributed. As stated previously, the maximum number of vehicles in the system is four. Determine the average waiting time, the average queue length, and the probability that a customer will have to drive on.

Solution:

$$\lambda = 20$$
$$\mu = 30$$
$$M = 4$$

First, we will compute the probability that the system is full and the customer must drive on, P_M. However, this first requires the determination of P_0, as follows:

$$P_0 = \frac{1 - \lambda/\mu}{1 - (\lambda/\mu)^{M+1}}$$
$$= \frac{1 - 20/30}{1 - (20/30)^5}$$
$$= 0.38 \text{ probability of no cars in the system}$$

$$P_M = (P_0)\left(\frac{\lambda}{\mu}\right)^{n=M}$$
$$= (0.38)\left(\frac{20}{30}\right)^4$$
$$= 0.076 \text{ probability that 4 cars are in the system and it is full.}$$

Next, in order to compute the average queue length, L_q, the average number of cars in the system, L, must be computed as follows.

$$L = \frac{\lambda/\mu}{1 - \lambda/\mu} - \frac{(M+1)(\lambda/\mu)^{M+1}}{1 - (\lambda/\mu)^{M+1}}$$
$$= \frac{20/30}{1 - 20/30} - \frac{(5)(20/30)^5}{1 - (20/30)^5}$$
$$= 1.24 \text{ customers in the system.}$$

$$L_q = L - \frac{\lambda(1 - P_M)}{\mu}$$
$$= 1.24 - \frac{20(1 - 0.076)}{30}$$
$$= 0.62 \text{ customers waiting}$$

In order to compute the average waiting time W_q, the average time in the system, W, must be computed first.

$$W = \frac{L}{\lambda(1 - P_M)}$$

$$= \frac{1.24}{20(1 - 0.076)}$$

$$= 0.067 \text{ hour (4.03 minutes) in the system}$$

$$W_q = W - \frac{1}{M}$$

$$= 0.067 - \frac{1}{30}$$

$$= 0.033 \text{ hour (2.03 minutes) waiting in line}$$

Computer Analysis of the Finite Queue Model

Transparency 16.10 AB:POM Solution of Finite Queue and Finite Calling Population Models

The single-server model with a finite queue can also be analyzed using the AB:POM software package. Exhibit 16.2 shows the model input and program solution results for Example 16.4.

Finite Calling Populations

The population of customers from which arrivals originate is limited, such as the number of police cars at a station to answer calls.

The single-server model with a Poisson arrival and exponential service times and a finite calling population has the following set of formulas for determining operating characteristics.

$$P_0 = \frac{1}{\sum_{n=0}^{N} \frac{N!}{(N-n)!}\left(\frac{\lambda}{\mu}\right)^n}, \quad \text{where } N = \text{population size}$$

$$P_n = \frac{N!}{(N-n)!}\left(\frac{\lambda}{\mu}\right)^n P_0, \quad \text{where } n = 1,2,\ldots,N$$

$$L_q = N - \frac{\lambda - \mu}{\lambda}(1 - P_0)$$

$$L = L_q + (1 - P_0)$$

$$W_q = \frac{L_q}{(N - L)\lambda}$$

$$W = W_q + \frac{1}{\mu}$$

```
                        Waiting Line Models                                Solution
M/M/1 - with a finite queue

                          Example 16.4
arrival rate (lambda)     20.00   Average server utilization            .6161137
service rate (mu)         30.00   Average number in the queue(Lq)       .6255924
number of servers             1   Average number in the system(L)       1.241706
maximum system size           4   Average time in the queue(Wq)         .0338462
                                      Answer * 60                         2.0308
                                  Average time in the system(W)         .0671795
                                      Answer * 60                         4.0308
                                  Effective arrival rate                18.48341
```

EXHIBIT 16.2

The formulas for P_0 and P_n are both relatively complex and can be cumbersome to compute manually. As a result tables are often used to compute these values, given λ and μ. Alternatively, a number of computer software packages with queuing modules have the capability of solving the finite calling population model, which we demonstrate with AB:POM in the next section.

EXAMPLE 16.5

Alternate Example 16.4

A Single-Server Model with Finite Calling Population

Problem Statement:

The Wheelco Manufacturing Company operates a job shop that has 15 machines. Due to the type of work performed in the shop, there is a lot of wear and tear on the machines, and they require frequent repair. When a machine breaks down, it is tagged for repair, with the date of breakdown noted. The company has one senior repair person, with an assistant who repairs the machines based on an oldest-date-of-breakdown rule (i.e., a FIFO queue discipline). The mean time between machine breakdowns is 40 hours, and the mean repair time is 3.6 hours. Both the breakdown interarrival times and the service times are exponentially distributed. The company would like an analysis performed of machine idle time due to breakdowns in order to determine if the present repair staff is sufficient.

Solution:

$$\lambda = \frac{1}{40 \text{ hour}} = 0.0250 \text{ per hour}$$

$$\mu = \frac{1}{3.6 \text{ hour}} = 0.2778 \text{ per hour}$$

$$N = 15 \text{ machines}$$

$$P_0 = \frac{1}{\sum_{n=0}^{N} \frac{N!}{(N-n)!}\left(\frac{\lambda}{\mu}\right)^n}$$

$$= \frac{1}{\sum_{n=0}^{15} \frac{15!}{(15-n)!}\left(\frac{0.0250}{0.2778}\right)^n}$$

$$= 0.0616$$

$$L_q = N - \frac{\lambda - \mu}{\lambda}(1 - P_0)$$

$$= 15 - \frac{0.0250 + 0.2778}{0.0250}(1 - 0.0616)$$

$$= 3.63 \text{ machines waiting}$$

$$L = L_q + (1 - P_0)$$

$$= 3.63 + (1 - 0.0616)$$

$$= 4.57 \text{ machines in the system}$$

$$W_q = \frac{L_q}{(N-L)\lambda}$$

$$= \frac{3.63}{(15 - 4.57)(0.0250)}$$

$$= 13.94 \text{ hours time waiting for repair}$$

$$W = W_q + \frac{1}{\mu}$$
$$= 13.94 + \frac{1}{0.2778}$$
$$= 17.54 \text{ hours time in the system}$$

These results show that the repairperson and assistant are busy 94 percent of the time repairing machines. Of the 15 machines, an average of 4.57, or 30 percent, are broken down waiting for repair or under repair. Each broken-down machine is idle (broken down waiting for repair or under repair) an average of 17.54 hours, or more than two working days; this amount is 44 percent of a 5-day working week. Obviously, this is not adequate. The company cannot afford to have an average of 30 percent of their machines idle, with an average idle time of 44 percent of a working week. Their initial feeling was that with an average of 40 hours between machine breakdowns (one every 5 days) and only 3.6 hours to repair a broken-down machine, one repair team should be more than adequate. Their intuitive reasoning is not reliable in this case, and a second repair team is necessary.

Computer Analysis of the Finite Calling Population Model

As mentioned previously, manual solutions of some of the finite calling population formulas can be time-consuming and tedious. However, a number of computer software packages have the capability to solve this type of queuing model, including AB:POM. Exhibit 16.3 shows the solution output for Example 16.5.

MULTIPLE-CHANNEL, SINGLE-PHASE MODELS

A large number of operational waiting line systems include multiple servers. However, these models can become very complex, so in this section we present only the most basic multiple-server (or channel) waiting line structure. This system includes a single waiting line and a service facility with several independent servers in parallel, as shown in Figure 16.3. An example of a multiple-server system is an airline ticket and check-in counter, where passengers line up in a roped-off, single line waiting for one of several agents for service. The same waiting line structure is frequently found at the post office, where customers in a single line wait for service from several postal clerks.

```
                          Waiting Line Models                          Solution
M/M/1 with a finite population
                               Example 16.5
arrival rate (lambda)    0.025    Average server utilization           .9383925
service rate (mu)       0.2778    Average number in the queue(Lq)      3.634193
number of servers            1    Average number in the system(L)      4.572586
population                  15    Average time in the queue(Wq)        13.94092
                                  Average time in the system(W)        17.54063
                                  Effective arrival rate               .2606854
```

EXHIBIT 16.3

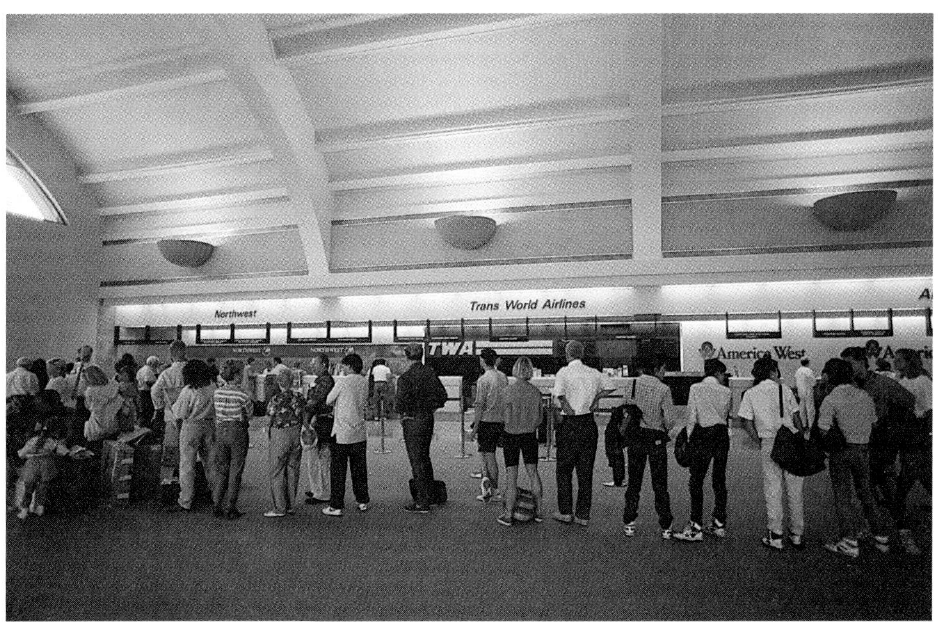

These passengers waiting in line to purchase tickets or check baggage and get a boarding pass at the Orange County, California airport are part of a waiting line system with multiple servers. Passengers are cordoned into a single line to wait for one of several airline agents to serve them. The number of agents scheduled for duty at the check-in counter is determined by waiting line operating characteristics based on different passenger arrival rates during the day and for different days. For example, on New Year's Day only one agent might be on duty, while on the Wednesday before Thanksgiving, one of the busiest airline travel days of the year, the maximum number of agents would be used.

The Basic Multiple-Server Model

The formulas that we present for determining the operating characteristics for the *multiple-server model* are based on the same assumptions as the single-server model—Poisson arrival rate, exponential service times, infinite calling population and queue length, and FIFO queue discipline. Also, recall that in the single-server model, $\mu > \lambda$, however, in the multiple-server model, $s\mu > \lambda$, where s is the number of servers. The operating characteristics formulas are as follows.

With *multiple-server models,* two or more independent servers in parallel serve a single waiting line.

$s\mu > \lambda$: The total number of servers must be able to serve customers faster than they arrive.

Transparency 16.11 Basic Multiple-Server Model

The probability that there are no customers in the system (all servers are idle) is

$$P_0 = \frac{1}{\left[\sum_{n=0}^{n=s-1} \frac{1}{n!}\left(\frac{\lambda}{\mu}\right)^n\right] + \frac{1}{s!}\left(\frac{\lambda}{\mu}\right)^s\left(\frac{s\mu}{s\mu - \lambda}\right)}$$

The probability of n customers in the queuing system is

$$P_n = \begin{cases} \frac{1}{s!\, s^{n-s}}\left(\frac{\lambda}{\mu}\right)^n P_0, & \text{for } n > s \\ \frac{1}{n!}\left(\frac{\lambda}{\mu}\right)^n P_0, & \text{for } n \le s \end{cases}$$

The probability that a customer arriving in the system must wait for service (i.e., the probability that all the servers are busy) is

$$P_w = \frac{1}{s!}\left(\frac{\lambda}{\mu}\right)^s \frac{s\mu}{s\mu - \lambda} P_0$$

$$L = \frac{\lambda\mu(\lambda/\mu)^s}{(s-1)!(s\mu - \lambda)^2} P_0 + \frac{\lambda}{\mu}$$

$$W = \frac{L}{\lambda}$$

$$L_q = L - \frac{\lambda}{\mu}$$

TABLE 16.2 Selected Values of P_0 for the Multiple-Server Model

$\rho = \lambda / s\mu$					*Number of Channels: s*					
ρ	2	3	4	5	6	7	8	9	10	15
0.02	0.96079	0.94177	0.92312	0.90484	0.88692	0.86936	0.85215	0.83527	0.81873	0.74082
0.04	0.92308	0.88692	0.85215	0.81873	0.78663	0.75578	0.72615	0.69768	0.67032	0.54881
0.06	0.88679	0.83526	0.78663	0.74082	0.69768	0.65705	0.61878	0.58275	0.54881	0.40657
0.08	0.85185	0.78659	0.72615	0.67032	0.61878	0.57121	0.52729	0.48675	0.44983	0.30119
0.10	0.81818	0.74074	0.67031	0.60653	0.54881	0.49659	0.44933	0.40657	0.36788	0.22313
0.12	0.78571	0.69753	0.61876	0.54881	0.48675	0.43171	0.38289	0.33960	0.30119	0.16530
0.14	0.75439	0.65679	0.57116	0.49657	0.43171	0.37531	0.72628	0.28365	0.24660	0.12246
0.16	0.72414	0.61838	0.52720	0.44931	0.38289	0.32628	0.27804	0.23693	0.20190	0.09072
0.18	0.69492	0.58214	0.48660	0.40653	0.33959	0.28365	0.23693	0.19790	0.16530	0.06721
0.20	0.66667	0.54795	0.44910	0.36782	0.30118	0.24659	0.20189	0.16530	0.13534	0.04979
0.22	0.63934	0.51567	0.41445	0.33277	0.26711	0.21437	0.17204	0.13807	0.11080	0.03688
0.24	0.61290	0.48519	0.38244	0.30105	0.23688	0.18636	0.14660	0.11532	0.09072	0.02732
0.26	0.58730	0.45640	0.35284	0.27233	0.21007	0.16200	0.12492	0.09632	0.07427	0.02024
0.28	0.56250	0.42918	0.32548	0.24633	0.18628	0.14082	0.10645	0.08045	0.06081	0.01500
0.30	0.53846	0.40346	0.30017	0.22277	0.16517	0.12241	0.09070	0.06720	0.04978	0.01111
0.32	0.51515	0.37913	0.27676	0.20144	0.14644	0.10639	0.07728	0.05612	0.04076	0.00823
0.34	0.49254	0.35610	0.25510	0.18211	0.12981	0.09247	0.06584	0.04687	0.03337	0.00610
0.36	0.47059	0.33431	0.23505	0.16460	0.11505	0.08035	0.05609	0.03915	0.02732	0.00452
0.38	0.44928	0.31367	0.21649	0.14872	0.10195	0.06981	0.04778	0.03269	0.02236	0.00335
0.40	0.42857	0.29412	0.19929	0.13433	0.09032	0.06065	0.04069	0.02729	0.01830	0.00248
0.42	0.40845	0.27559	0.18336	0.12128	0.07998	0.05267	0.03465	0.02279	0.01498	0.00184
0.44	0.38889	0.25802	0.16860	0.10944	0.07080	0.04573	0.02950	0.01902	0.01225	0.00136
0.46	0.36986	0.24135	0.15491	0.09870	0.06265	0.03968	0.02511	0.01587	0.01003	0.00101
0.48	0.35135	0.22554	0.14221	0.08895	0.05540	0.03442	0.02136	0.01324	0.00826	0.00075
0.50	0.33333	0.21053	0.13043	0.08010	0.04896	0.02984	0.01816	0.01104	0.00671	0.00055
0.52	0.31579	0.19627	0.11951	0.07207	0.04323	0.02586	0.01544	0.00920	0.00548	0.00041
0.54	0.29870	0.18273	0.10936	0.06477	0.03814	0.02239	0.01311	0.00767	0.00448	0.00030
0.56	0.28205	0.16986	0.09994	0.05814	0.03362	0.01936	0.01113	0.00638	0.00366	0.00022
0.58	0.26582	0.15762	0.09119	0.05212	0.02959	0.01673	0.00943	0.00531	0.00298	0.00017
0.60	0.25000	0.14599	0.08306	0.04665	0.02601	0.01443	0.00799	0.00441	0.00243	0.00012
0.62	0.23457	0.13491	0.07550	0.04167	0.02282	0.01243	0.00675	0.00366	0.00198	0.00009
0.64	0.21951	0.12438	0.06847	0.03715	0.01999	0.01069	0.00570	0.00303	0.00161	0.00007
0.66	0.20482	0.11435	0.06194	0.03304	0.01746	0.00918	0.00480	0.00251	0.00131	0.00005
0.68	0.19048	0.10479	0.05587	0.02930	0.01522	0.00786	0.00404	0.00207	0.00106	0.00004
0.70	0.17647	0.09569	0.05021	0.02590	0.01322	0.00670	0.00338	0.00170	0.00085	0.00003
0.72	0.16279	0.08702	0.04495	0.02280	0.01144	0.00570	0.00283	0.00140	0.00069	0.00002
0.74	0.14943	0.07875	0.04006	0.01999	0.00986	0.00483	0.00235	0.00114	0.00055	0.00001
0.76	0.13636	0.07087	0.03550	0.01743	0.00846	0.00407	0.00195	0.00093	0.00044	0.00001
0.78	0.12360	0.06335	0.03125	0.01510	0.00721	0.00341	0.00160	0.00075	0.00035	0.00001
0.80	0.11111	0.05618	0.02730	0.01299	0.00610	0.00284	0.00131	0.00060	0.00028	0.00001
0.82	0.09890	0.04933	0.02362	0.01106	0.00511	0.00234	0.00106	0.00048	0.00022	0.00000
0.84	0.08696	0.04280	0.02019	0.00931	0.00423	0.00190	0.00085	0.00038	0.00017	0.00000
0.86	0.07527	0.03656	0.01700	0.00772	0.00345	0.00153	0.00067	0.00029	0.00013	0.00000
0.88	0.06383	0.03060	0.01403	0.00627	0.00276	0.00120	0.00052	0.00022	0.00010	0.00000
0.90	0.05263	0.02491	0.01126	0.00496	0.00215	0.00092	0.00039	0.00017	0.00007	0.00000
0.92	0.04167	0.01947	0.00867	0.00377	0.00161	0.00068	0.00028	0.00012	0.00005	0.00000
0.94	0.03093	0.01427	0.00627	0.00268	0.00113	0.00047	0.00019	0.00008	0.00003	0.00000
0.96	0.02041	0.00930	0.00403	0.00170	0.00070	0.00029	0.00012	0.00005	0.00002	0.00000
0.98	0.01010	0.00454	0.00194	0.00081	0.00033	0.00013	0.00005	0.00002	0.00001	0.00000

$$W_q = W - \frac{1}{\mu}$$

$$= \frac{L_q}{\lambda}$$

$$\rho = \frac{\lambda}{s\mu}$$

The key formula in this set is for P_0, which can be time-consuming to compute manually. Table 16.2 provides values for P_0 selected values of the server utilization factor, ρ, and the number of servers, s.

EXAMPLE 16.6

A Multiple-Server Waiting Line System

Alternate Example 16.5

Problem Statement:

The customer service department of the Biggs Department Store has a waiting room in which chairs are placed along a wall, in effect forming a single waiting line. Customers come to this area with questions or complaints or to clarify matters regarding credit-card bills. The customers are served by three store representatives, each located in a partitioned stall. Customers are treated on a first-come, first-served basis.

The store management wants to analyze this queuing system because excessive waiting times can make customers angry enough to shop at other stores. Typically, customers who come to this area have some problem and thus are impatient anyway. Waiting a long time serves only to increase their impatience.

A study of the customer service department for a 6-month period shows that an average of 10 customers arrive per hour (according to a Poisson distribution), and an average of 4 customers can be served per hour by a customer service representative (Poisson distributed).

Solution:

$\lambda = 10$ customers per hour

$\mu = 4$ customers per hour per service representative

$s = 3$ customer service representatives

$s\mu = (3)(4) = 12 \quad (> \lambda = 10)$

Using the multiple-server model formulas, we can compute the following operating characteristics for the service department.

$$P_0 = \frac{1}{\left[\sum_{n=0}^{n=s-1} \frac{1}{n!}\left(\frac{\lambda}{\mu}\right)^n\right] + \frac{1}{s!}\left(\frac{\lambda}{\mu}\right)^s \left(\frac{s\mu}{s\mu - \lambda}\right)}$$

$$= \frac{1}{\left[\frac{1}{0!}\left(\frac{10}{4}\right)^0 + \frac{1}{1!}\left(\frac{10}{4}\right)^1 + \frac{1}{2!}\left(\frac{10}{4}\right)^2\right] + \frac{1}{3!}\left(\frac{10}{4}\right)^3 \frac{3(4)}{3(4) - 10}}$$

$= 0.045$ probability that no customers are in the service department

Notice that this value could have been estimated from Table 16.2 using $\rho = 0.833$ (i.e., $\rho = \lambda/s\mu = 10/12 = 0.833$) and $s = 3$. ρ is read from the lefthand column and s across the top.

$$L = \frac{\lambda\mu(\lambda/\mu)^s}{(s-1)!(s\mu-\lambda)^2}P_0 + \frac{\lambda}{\mu}$$

$$= \frac{(10)(4)(10/4)^3}{(3-1)![3(4)-10]^2}(0.045) + \frac{10}{4}$$

= 6 customers in the service department

$$W = \frac{L}{\lambda}$$

$$= \frac{6}{10}$$

= 0.60 hour (36 minutes) in the service department

$$L_q = L - \frac{\lambda}{\mu}$$

$$= 6 - \frac{10}{4}$$

= 3.5 customers waiting to be served

$$W_q = \frac{L_q}{\lambda}$$

$$= \frac{3.5}{10}$$

= 0.35 hour (21 minutes) waiting in line

$$P_w = \frac{1}{s!}\left(\frac{\lambda}{\mu}\right)^s \frac{s\mu}{s\mu-\lambda}P_0$$

$$= \frac{1}{3!}\left(\frac{10}{4}\right)^3 \frac{3(4)}{3(4)-10}(.045)$$

= 0.703 probability that a customer must wait for service
(i.e., that there are three or more customers in the system)

The department store's management has observed that customers are frustrated by the relatively long waiting time of 21 minutes and the 0.703 probability of waiting. To try to improve matters, management has decided to consider the addition of an extra service representative. The operating characteristics for this system must be recomputed with $s = 4$ service representatives.

Substituting this value along with λ and μ in the queuing formulas results in the following operating characteristics:

$P_0 = 0.073$ probability that no customers are in the service department
$L = 3.0$ customers in the service department
$W = 0.30$ hour, or 18 minutes, in the service department
$L_q = 0.5$ customer waiting to be served
$W_q = 0.05$ hour, or 3 minutes, waiting in line
$P_w = 0.31$ probability that a customer must wait for service

These results are significantly better; waiting time has been reduced from 21 minutes to 3 minutes. Of course this improvement in the quality of the service would have to be compared to the cost of adding an extra service representative in order to make a decision.

GAINING THE COMPETITIVE EDGE

Local Area Network Service at Merrill Lynch

Merrill Lynch and Company is the largest retail stock broker in the United States, with more than 450 branch offices and 10,000 brokers (or financial consultants). In 1987, the company was using a communication and information network that provided brokers with information through terminals at the branch offices connected to remote mainframe and minicomputers. The company wanted to replace this terminal-based system with local area networks (LANS) at each branch, at a cost of tens of millions of dollars. Each branch LAN would access from local data bases that were updated nightly via downloads from a remote mainframe, with one common database being updated continually during business hours. The data would reside locally on from one to four microcomputers acting as database servers. Several critical issues were related to the planning of this new system, including the overall cost of installation (i.e., the economic feasibility of the system), and the capacity of the database servers to handle the volume of transaction/inquiries from the brokers during business hours. A general multiple-server queuing model approach was developed to evaluate potential server response time under different levels of user demand (Poisson distributed). The modeling analysis showed that at most two database servers would be needed at any Merrill Lynch branch office (regardless of the size of the office and number of brokers) to provide adequate response time to brokers using the LAN system. This allowed Merrill Lynch to determine a maximum required capital expenditure for the system that proved to be economically feasible and allowed them to proceed with conversion to the new LAN system.

Source: Based on Berman, L., and R. Nigum, "Optimal Partitioning of Data Bases Across Multiple Servers in a LAN," *Interfaces* 22, no. 2 (March–April 1992): 18–27.

Computer Analysis of the Multiple-Server Model

The AB:POM software package for the personal computer used to analyze the single-server queuing system can also be used to analyze the multiple-server system. The solution output for Example 16.6 is shown in Exhibit 16.4.

Although more complex multiple-server models with a finite queue or finite calling population are not presented in this chapter, the AB:POM software package does have the capability to "solve" waiting line systems with these structural variations.

```
                          Waiting Line Models                         Solution
M/M/s - multiple server, exponential service
                             Example 16.6
arrival rate (lambda)     10.00     Average server utilization          .8333333
service rate (mu)          4.00     Average number in the queue(Lq)     3.511235
number of servers             3     Average number in the system(L)     6.011235
                                    Average time in the queue(Wq)       .3511235
                                        Answer * 60                     21.06741
                                    Average time in the system(W)       .6011235
                                        Answer * 60                     36.06741
```

EXHIBIT 16.4

MULTIPLE-PHASE MODELS

Transparency 16.12 AB:POM Solution of Multiple-Server Models

Multiple-phase queuing models are not analyzed in detail in this chapter, since they can become extremely complex. However, one unique case is briefly discussed. If the multiple-phase system satisfies all the assumptions of Poisson arrivals, exponential service times, infinite calling population, infinite possible queues, and service rate(s) exceeding arrival rate(s), then the multiple-phase system can be analyzed rather easily.

If a service facility has a Poisson input with parameter λ and an exponential service time distribution with parameter μ (where $\mu > \lambda$), then the steady-state output of this service facility is also a Poisson process with parameter λ. Thus, each successive facility in a multiple-phase system will have a Poisson input with parameter λ. This condition will hold for the single-channel model and for the multiple-channel model just discussed (if $s\mu > \lambda$).

This enables the individual phases to be evaluated independently of one another, and the aggregate operating characteristics can be obtained by summing the corresponding values obtained at the respective facilities. The operating characteristics are total expected waiting time, total expected time in the system, total expected number in queues, and total expected number in the overall system. It is important to note here that the intermediate queues are also assumed to be allowed to build up to any length.

Figure 16.9 illustrates three structures for multiple-phase models that can be analyzed by this procedure, if the previously stated assumptions are met. The first is simply a single-channel, multiple-phase model. The two phases are evaluated independently, and the individual phase characteristics summed. The second represents two stages of a multiple-channel, single-phase process. Thus, each stage is evaluated independently according to the multiple-channel, single-phase formulas, and the resulting operating characteristics are summed. The third structure

(a) Single-channel, multiple-phase

(b) Multiple-channel, single-phase with stages

(c) Multiple-channel, multiple-phase

FIGURE 16.9 Multiple-Phase Waiting Line Structures

represents a multiple-channel, single-phase equation for the first stage; one of the following stages is solved as a single-channel, single-phase process, with $\lambda_i = \lambda/3$ (where λ_i = mean arrival rate at the second stage for channel *i* server). Recall that the multiple-channel, single-phase model assumes that the service rate is identical for each server, yielding the assumption that $\lambda_i = \lambda/3$. Since the results are the same for each of the three second-stage servers, only one of these needs to be evaluated.

Multiple-phase models involve servers in sequence.

SUMMARY

Since waiting is an integral part of many service-related operations, it is an important area of analysis, especially relative to achieving improved-quality service. In this chapter we presented a selection of different mathematical formulas for analyzing a variety of waiting line structures. These formulas provide operating characteristics that are the basis for designing and improving waiting line systems.

However, although the queuing models presented in this chapter describe a wide variety of realistic waiting line systems, the number of conceivable waiting line structures is almost infinite, and many are so complex that no specific queuing model or formula is directly applicable. Examples of such complex queuing systems include a network of queues in which the leaving customers from several queuing systems provide the arrivals for succeeding queuing systems. A manufacturing system in which the in-process output from several production areas or production lines is the input to subsequent production areas or lines is an example of such a network. For such complex systems, a specific analytical model, such as those presented in this chapter, is not available, and simulation is the only alternative.

SUMMARY OF KEY FORMULAS

Single-Server Model

$$P_0 = 1 - \frac{\lambda}{\mu} \qquad W = \frac{1}{\mu - \lambda}$$

$$P_n = \left(\frac{\lambda}{\mu}\right)^n \left(\frac{1-\lambda}{\mu}\right) \qquad W_q = \frac{\lambda}{\mu(\mu - \lambda)}$$

$$L = \frac{\lambda}{\mu - \lambda} \qquad \rho = \frac{\lambda}{\mu}$$

$$L_q = \frac{\lambda^2}{\mu(\mu - \lambda)} \qquad I = 1 - \frac{\lambda}{\mu}$$

Single-Server Model with Undefined Service Times

$$P_0 = 1 - \frac{\lambda}{\mu} \qquad W_q = \frac{L_q}{\lambda}$$

$$L_q = \frac{\lambda^2\sigma^2 + (\lambda/\mu)^2}{2(1 - \lambda/\mu)} \qquad W = W_q + \frac{1}{\mu}$$

$$L = L_q + \frac{\lambda}{\mu} \qquad \rho = \frac{\lambda}{\mu}$$

Single-Server Model with Constant Service Times

$$P_0 = 1 - \frac{\lambda}{\mu} \qquad W_q = \frac{L_q}{\lambda}$$

$$L_q = \frac{\lambda^2}{2\mu(\mu - \lambda)} \qquad W = W_q + \frac{1}{\mu}$$

$$L = L_q + \frac{\lambda}{\mu} \qquad \rho = \frac{\lambda}{\mu}$$

Single-Server Model with Finite Queue

$$P_0 = \frac{1 - \lambda/\mu}{1 - (\lambda/\mu)^{M+1}} \qquad W = \frac{L}{\lambda(1 - P_M)}$$

$$P_N = (P_0)(\lambda/\mu)^n, \qquad n \le M \qquad W_q = W - \frac{1}{\mu}$$

$$L = \frac{\lambda/\mu}{1 - \lambda/\mu} - \frac{(M+1)(\lambda/\mu)^{M+1}}{1 - (\lambda/\mu)^{M+1}}$$

$$L_q = L - \frac{\lambda(1 - P_M)}{\mu}$$

Single-Server Model with Finite Calling Population

$$P_0 = \frac{1}{\sum_{n=0}^{N} \frac{N!}{(N-n)!}\left(\frac{\lambda}{\mu}\right)^n} \qquad W_q = \frac{L_q}{(N-L)\lambda}$$

$$P_n = \frac{N!}{(N-n)!}\left(\frac{\lambda}{\mu}\right)^n P_0 \qquad W = W_q + \frac{1}{\mu}$$

$$L_q = N - \frac{\lambda - \mu}{\lambda}(1 - P_0)$$

$$L = L_q + (1 - P_0)$$

Multiple-Server Model

$$P_0 = \frac{1}{\left[\sum_{n=0}^{n=s-1} \frac{1}{n!}\left(\frac{\lambda}{\mu}\right)^n\right] + \frac{1}{s!}\left(\frac{\lambda}{\mu}\right)^s \left(\frac{s\mu}{s\mu - \lambda}\right)}$$

$$P_n = \begin{cases} \frac{1}{s!s^{n-s}}\left(\frac{\lambda}{\mu}\right)^n P_0, & \text{for } n > s \\ \frac{1}{n!}\left(\frac{\lambda}{\mu}\right)^n P_0, & \text{for } n \le s \end{cases}$$

$$P_w = \frac{1}{s!}\left(\frac{\lambda}{\mu}\right)^s \frac{s\mu}{s\mu - \lambda} P_0$$

$$L = \frac{\lambda\mu(\lambda/\mu)^s}{(s-1)!(s\mu - \lambda)^2} P_0 + \frac{\lambda}{\mu}$$

$$W = \frac{L}{\lambda}$$

$$L_q = L - \frac{\lambda}{\mu}$$

$$W_q = W - \frac{1}{\mu}$$

SUMMARY OF KEY TERMS

arrival rate: the rate at which customers arrive at a service facility during a specified period of time.
calling population: the source of customers to a waiting line.
channels: the number of parallel servers.
finite queue: a waiting line that has a limited capacity.
infinite queue: a waiting line that grows to any length.
operating characteristics: measures of waiting line performance expressed as averages.
phases: the number of sequential servers a customer must go through to receive service.
queue: a single waiting line that forms prior to a service facility.
queue discipline: the order in which customers are served.
service time: the time required to serve a customer.

SOLVED PROBLEMS

1. *Single-Server Model*

Problem Statement:

The new-accounts officer at the Citizens Northern Savings Bank enrolls all new customers in checking accounts. During the 3-week period in August encompassing the beginning of the new school year at State University, the bank opens a lot of new accounts for students. The bank estimates that the arrival rate during this period will be Poisson distributed with an average of 4 customers per hour. The service time is exponentially distributed with an average of 12 minutes per customer to set up a new account. The bank wants to determine the operating characteristics for this system in order to determine if the current person is sufficient to handle the increased traffic.

Solution:

Determine operating characteristics for the single-server system:

$\lambda = 4$ customers per hour arrive

$\mu = 5$ customers per hour are served

$$P_0 = \left(1 - \frac{\lambda}{\mu}\right) = \left(1 - \frac{4}{5}\right)$$

$= 0.20$ probability of no customers in the system

$$L = \frac{\lambda}{\mu - \lambda} = \frac{5}{5 - 4}$$

$= 4$ customers on average in the queuing system

$$L_q = \frac{\lambda^2}{\mu(\mu - \lambda)} = \frac{(4)^2}{5(5 - 4)}$$

$= 3.2$ customers on average waiting

$$W = \frac{1}{\mu - \lambda} = \frac{1}{5 - 4}$$

$= 1$ hour average time in the system

$$W_q = \frac{\lambda}{\mu(\mu - \lambda)} = \frac{5}{5(5-4)}$$

$= 0.80$ hour (48 minutes) average time waiting

$$P_w = \frac{\lambda}{\mu} = \frac{4}{5}$$

$= 0.80$ probability that the new-accounts officer will be busy and that a customer must wait

The average waiting time of 48 minutes and the average time in the system are excessive, and the bank needs to add an extra employee during the busy period.

2. *Multiple-Server Model*

Problem Statement:
The Citizens Northern Bank in the preceding problem wants to compute the operating characteristics if an extra employee was added to assist with new accounts enrollments.

Solution:
Determine the operating characteristics for the multiple-server system:

$\lambda = 4$ customers per hour arrive

$\mu = 5$ customers per hour are served

$s = 2$ servers

$$P_0 = \frac{1}{\left[\sum_{n=0}^{n=s-1} \frac{1}{n!}\left(\frac{\lambda}{\mu}\right)^n\right] + \frac{1}{s!}\left(\frac{\lambda}{\mu}\right)^s\left(\frac{s\mu}{s\mu - \lambda}\right)}$$

$$= \frac{1}{\left[\frac{1}{0!}\left(\frac{4}{5}\right)^0 + \frac{1}{1!}\left(\frac{4}{5}\right)^1\right] + \frac{1}{2!}\left(\frac{4}{5}\right)^2 \frac{(2)(5)}{(2)(5) - 4}}$$

$= 0.429$ probability that no customers are in the system

$$L = \frac{\lambda\mu\left(\frac{\lambda}{\mu}\right)^s}{(s-1)!(s\mu - \lambda)^2} P_0 + \frac{\lambda}{\mu}$$

$$= \frac{(4)(5)\left(\frac{4}{5}\right)^2}{1![(2)(5) - 4]^2}(0.429) + \frac{4}{5}$$

$= 0.952$ customer on average in the system

$$L_q = L - \frac{\lambda}{\mu} = 0.952 - \frac{4}{5}$$

$= 0.152$ customer on average waiting to be served

$$W = \frac{L}{\lambda} = \frac{0.952}{4}$$

$= 0.238$ hour (14.3 minutes) average time in the system

$$W_q = \frac{L_q}{\lambda} = \frac{0.152}{4}$$

$= 0.038$ hour (2.3 minutes) average time spent waiting in line

$$P_W = \frac{1}{c!}\left(\frac{\lambda}{\mu}\right)^s \frac{s\mu}{s\mu - \lambda} P_0$$

$$= \frac{1}{2!}\left(\frac{4}{5}\right)^2 \frac{(2)(5)}{(2)(5) - 4}(0.429)$$

$= 0.229$ probability that a customer must wait for service

The waiting time with the multiple server model is 2.3 minutes, which is a significant improvement over the previous system; thus the bank should add the second new-accounts officer.

QUESTIONS

16-1. Identify ten real-life examples of queuing systems with which you are familiar.

16-2. Why must the utilization factor in a single-server model be less than 1?

16-3. Give five examples of real-world queuing systems with finite calling populations.

16-4. List the elements that define a queuing system.

16-5. How can the results of queuing analysis be used by a decision maker for making decisions?

16-6. What is the mean effective service rate in a multiple-server model, and what must be its relationship to the arrival rate?

16-7. For each of the following queuing systems, indicate if it is a single- or multiple-server model, the queue discipline, and if its calling population is infinite or finite.

a. Hair salon
b. Bank
c. Laundromat
d. Doctor's office
e. Advisor's office
f. Airport runway
g. Service station
h. Copy center
i. Team trainer
j. Mainframe computer

16-8. In Example 16.2 in this chapter, the second alternative was to add a new checkout counter at the market. This alternative was analyzed using the single-server model. Why was the multiple-server model not used?

16-9. Discuss briefly the relationship between waiting line cost analysis and quality improvement.

16-10. Define the four basic waiting line structures and give an example of each.

16-11. Describe the traditional cost relationship in waiting line analysis.

16-12. a. Is the following statement true or false? The single-phase, single-channel model with Poisson arrivals and undefined service times will always have larger (i.e., greater) operating characteristic values (i.e., W, W_q, L, L_q) than the same model with exponentially distributed service times. Explain your answer.

b. Is the following statement true or false? The single-phase, single-channel model with Poisson arrivals and constant service times will always have smaller (i.e., lower) operating characteristic values (i.e., W, W_q, L, L_q) than the same model with exponentially distributed service times. Explain your answer.

16-13. Under what conditions can the basic single-server and multiple-server models be used to analyze a multiple-phase waiting line system?

16-14. Why do waiting lines form at a service facility even though there may be more than enough service capacity to meet normal demand in the long run?

16-15. Provide an example of when a first-in, first-out (FIFO) rule for queue discipline would not be appropriate.

16-16. Under what conditions will the single-channel, single-phase queuing model with Poisson arrivals and undefined service times provide the same operating characteristics as the basic model with exponentially distributed service times?

16-17. What types of waiting line systems have constant service times?

Teaching Note 16.5 Homework Assignments

PROBLEMS

16-1. $P_0 = 0.33$, $P_3 = 0.099$, $L = 2.0$, $L_q = 1.33$, $W = 0.125$ hr, $W_q = 0.083$ hr, $\rho = 0.67$

16-1. A single-server queuing system with an infinite calling population and a first-come, first-served queue discipline has the following arrival and service rates:

$$\lambda = 16 \text{ customers per hour}$$
$$\mu = 24 \text{ customers per hour}$$

Determine P_0, P_3, L, L_q, W, W_q, and P_w.

16-2. $W_q = 0.417$ hr, $\rho = 0.833$

16-2. The ticket booth on the Tech campus is operated by one person, who is selling tickets for the annual Tech versus State football game on Saturday. The ticket seller can serve an average of 12 customers per hour; on average, 10 customers arrive to purchase tickets each hour. Determine the average time a ticket buyer must wait and the portion of time the ticket seller is busy.

16-3. a. $L_q = 0.9$, $W = 0.25$ hr, $W_q = 0.15$ hr
b. Infinite queue

16-3. The Whistle Stop Market has one pump for gasoline, which can service 10 customers per hour. Cars arrive at the pump at a rate of 6 per hour.

a. Determine the average queue length, the average time a car is in the system, and the average time a car must wait.
b. If, during the period from 4:00 P.M. to 5:00 P.M., the arrival rate increases to 12 cars per hour, what will be the effect on the average queue length?

16-4. $L_q = 3.2$, $\rho = 0.80$, $I = 0.20$

16-4. The Dynaco Manufacturing Company produces a particular product in an assembly line operation. One of the machines on the line is a drill press that has a single assembly line feeding into it. A partially completed unit arrives at the press to be worked on every 7.5 minutes, on the average, according to an exponential distribution. The machine operator can process an average of 10 parts per hour (Poisson distributed). Determine the average number of parts waiting to be worked on, the percentage of time the operator is working, and the percentage of time the machine is idle.

16-5. 1 part every 6.67 min ★

16-5. The management of Dynaco Manufacturing Company (Problem 16-4) likes to have its operators working 90 percent of the time. What must the assembly line arrival rate be in order for the operators to be as busy as management would like?

16-6. a. $L_q = 3.2$
b. $W_q = 0.8$ hr
c. $W = 1$ hr
d. Yes

16-6. The Peachtree Airport in Atlanta serves light aircraft. It has a single runway and one air-traffic controller to land planes. It takes an airplane 12 minutes to land and clear the runway (exponentially distributed). Planes arrive at the airport at the rate of 4 per hour (Poisson distributed).

a. Determine the average number of planes that will stack up waiting to land.
b. Find the average time a plane must wait in line before it can land.
c. Calculate the average time it takes a plane to clear the runway once it has notified the airport that it is in the vicinity and wants to land.
d. The FAA has a rule that an air-traffic controller can, on the average, land planes a maximum of 45 minutes out of every hour. There must be 15 minutes of idle time available to relieve the tension. Will this airport have to hire an extra air-traffic controller?

16-7. The First American Bank of Rapid City presently has one outside drive-up teller. It takes the teller an average of 4 minutes (exponentially distributed) to serve a bank customer. Customers arrive at the drive-up window at the rate of 12 per hour (Poisson distributed). The bank operations officer is currently analyzing the possibility of adding a second drive-up window at an annual cost of \$20,000. It is assumed that arriving cars would be equally divided between both windows. The operations officer estimates that each minute's reduction in customer waiting time would increase the bank's revenue by \$2,000 annually. Should the second drive-up window be installed?

★ 16-7. Yes, install second window.

16-8. During registration at State University every quarter, students in the College of Business must have their courses approved by the college advisor. It takes the advisor an average of 2 minutes (exponentially distributed) to approve each schedule, and students arrive at the advisor's office at the rate of 28 per hour (Poisson distributed).

a. Compute L, L_q, W, W_q, and ρ.
b. The dean of the college has received a number of complaints from students about the length of time they must wait to have their schedules approved. The dean feels that waiting 10 minutes to get a schedule approved is not unreasonable. Each assistant the dean assigns to the advisor's office will reduce the average time required to approve a schedule by 0.25 minute, down to a minimum time of 1.0 minute to approve a schedule. How many assistants should the dean assign to the advisor?

★ 16-8. a. $L = 14$, $L_q = 13.1$, $W = 0.5$ hr, $W_q = 0.47$ hr, $\rho = 0.93$
b. One

16-9. All trucks traveling on Interstate 40 between Albuquerque and Amarillo are required to stop at a weigh station. Trucks arrive at the weigh station at a rate of 200 per 8-hour day (Poisson distributed), and the station can weigh, on the average, 220 trucks per day (Poisson distributed).

a. Determine the average number of trucks waiting, the average time spent at the weigh station by each truck, and the average waiting time before being weighed for each truck.
b. If the truck drivers find out they must remain at the weigh station longer than 15 minutes on the average, they will start taking a different route or traveling at night, thus depriving the state of taxes. The state of New Mexico estimates it loses \$10,000 in taxes per year for each extra minute that trucks must remain at the weigh station. A new set of scales would have the same service capacity as the present set of scales, and it is assumed that arriving trucks would line up equally behind the two sets of scales. It would cost \$50,000 per year to operate the new scales. Should the state install the new set of scales?

★ 16-9. a. $L_q = 9.09$, $W = 0.05$ d, $W_q = 0.045$ d
b. Yes

16-10. In Problem 16-9, suppose arriving truck drivers look to see how many trucks are waiting to be weighed at the weigh station. If they see four or more trucks in line, they will pass by the station and risk being caught and ticketed. What is the probability that a truck will pass by the station?

16-10. 0.685

16-11. In Problem 16-8, the dean of the College of Business at State University is considering the addition of a second advisor in the college advising office

★ 16-11. $L = 1.19$, $L_q = 0.26$, $W = 0.043$ hr, $W_q = 0.009$ hr

to serve students waiting to have their schedules approved. This new advisor could serve the same number of students per hour as the present advisor. Determine L, L_q, W, and W_q for this altered advising system. As a student, would you recommend adding the advisor?

16-12. a. 0.2
b. $L_q = 1$
c. $W_q = 1.25$
d. 0.1825

★ 16-12. The Acme Machine Shop has five machines that periodically break down and require service. The average time between breakdowns is 4 days, distributed according to an exponential distribution. The average time to repair a machine is 1 day, distributed according to an exponential distribution. One mechanic repairs the machines in the order in which they break down.

a. Determine the probability of the mechanic being idle.
b. Determine the mean number of machines waiting to be repaired.
c. Determine the mean time machines wait to be repaired.
d. Determine the probability that three machines are not operating (are being repaired or waiting to be repaired).

16-13. Yes

★ 16-13. A to Z Publishers has a large number of employees who use the company's single fax machine. Employees arrive randomly to use the fax machine at an average rate of 20 per hour. This arrival process is approximated by a Poisson distribution. Employees spend an average of 2 minutes using the fax machine, either transmitting or receiving items. The time spent using the machine is distributed according to a negative exponential distribution. Employees line up in single file to use the machine, and they obtain access to it on a first-come, first-served basis. There is no defined limit to the number who can line up to use the machine.

Management has determined that by assigning an operator to the fax machine rather than allowing the employees to operate the machine themselves, it can reduce the average service time from the current 2 minutes to 1.5 minutes. However, the fax operator's salary is $8 per hour, which must be paid 8 hours per day even if there are no employees wishing to use the fax machine part of the time. Management has estimated the cost of employee time spent waiting in line and at the fax machine during service to be 17¢ per minute (based on an average salary of $10.20 per hour per employee). Should the firm assign an operator to the fax machine?

16-14. $L = 5.44$, $L_q = 3.77$,
$W = 0.054$ hr,
$W_q = 0.038$ hr

16-14. The Dynaco Manufacturing Company has an assembly line that feeds two drill presses. As partially completed products come off the line, they are lined up to be worked on as drill presses become available. The units arrive at the work station (containing both presses) at the rate of 100 per hour (Poisson distributed). Each press operator can process an average of 60 units per hour (Poisson distributed). Compute L, L_q, W, and W_q.

16-15. Yes

★ 16-15. In Problem 16-14, the Dynaco Company has found that if more than three units (average) are waiting to be processed at any one workstation, then too much money is being tied up in in-process inventory (i.e., units waiting to be processed). The company estimates that (on the average) each unit waiting to be processed costs $50 per day. Alternatively, operating a third press would cost $150 per day. Should the company operate a third press at this workstation?

16-16. No

16-16. Cakes baked by the Freshfood Bakery are transported from the ovens to be packaged by one of three wrappers. Each wrapper can wrap an average of 200 cakes per hour (Poisson distributed). The cakes are brought to the wrappers at the rate of 500 per hour (Poisson distributed). If a cake sits longer than 5 minutes before being wrapped, it will not be fresh enough to meet the bakery's quality control standards. Does the bakery need to hire another wrapper?

16-17. The Riverview Clinic has two general practitioners who see patients daily. An average of six patients arrive at the clinic per hour (Poisson distributed). Each doctor spends an average of 15 minutes (exponentially distributed) with a patient. The patients wait in a waiting area until one of the two doctors is able to see them. However, since patients typically do not feel well when they come to the clinic, the doctors do not believe it is good practice to have a patient wait longer than an average of 15 minutes. Should this clinic add a third doctor, and, if so, will this alleviate the waiting problem? ★ **16-17.** Yes

16-18. The Footrite Shoe Company is going to open a new branch at a mall, and company managers are attempting to determine how many salespeople to hire. Based on an analysis of mall traffic, the company estimates that customers will arrive at the store at the rate of 10 per hour (Poisson distributed), and from past experience at its other branches, the company knows that salespeople can serve an average of 6 customers per hour (Poisson distributed). How many salespeople should the company hire in order to maintain a company policy that on average a customer should have to wait for service no more than 30 percent of the time? ★ **16-18.** Three

16-19. When customers arrive at Gilley's Ice Cream Shop, they take a number and wait to be called to purchase ice cream from one of the counter servers. From experience in past summers, the store's staff knows that customers arrive at the rate of 40 per hour (Poisson distributed) on summer days between 3:00 P.M. and 10:00 P.M. and a server can serve 15 customers per hour on average (Poisson distributed). Gilley's wants to make sure that customers wait no longer than 10 minutes for service. Gilley's is contemplating keeping 3 servers behind the ice cream counter during the peak summer hours. Will this number be adequate to meet the waiting time policy? **16-19.** Yes

16-20. Moore's television-repair service receives an average of 6 TV sets per 8-hour day to be repaired. The service manager would like to be able to tell customers that they can expect their TV back in 4 days. What average repair time per set will the repair shop have to achieve to provide 4-day service on the average? (Assume that the arrival rate is Poisson distributed and repair times are exponentially distributed.) ★ **16-20.** 1.14 hr

16-21. Partially completed products arrive at a workstation in a manufacturing operation at a mean rate of 40 per hour (Poisson distributed). The processing time at the workstation averages 1.2 minutes per unit (exponentially distributed). The manufacturing company estimates that each unit of in-process inventory at the workstation costs $31 per day (on the average). However, the company can add extra employees and reduce the processing time to 0.90 minute per unit at a cost of $52 per day. Determine whether the company should continue the present operation or add extra employees. ★ **16-21.** Add employees

16-22. The Atlantic Coast Shipping Company has a warehouse terminal in Spartanburg, South Carolina. The capacity of each terminal dock is three trucks. As trucks enter the terminal, the drivers receive numbers, and when one of the three dock spaces becomes available, the truck with the lowest number enters the vacant dock. Truck arrivals are Poisson distributed, and the unloading and loading times (service times) are exponentially distributed. The average arrival rate at the terminal is 5 trucks per hour, and the average service rate per dock is 2 trucks per hour (30 minutes per truck).

a. Compute L, L_q, W, and W_q.

b. The management of the shipping company is considering adding extra employees and equipment to improve the average service time per terminal dock to 25 minutes per truck. It would cost the company $18,000 per year to achieve this improved service. Management estimates that it

★ **16-22.** a. $L = 6.0$, $L_q = 3.5$, $W_q = 0.7$ hr, $W = 1.2$ hr
b. Yes, invest.
c. Alternative 1, add fourth dock.

will increase its profit by $750 per year for each minute it is able to reduce a truck's waiting time. Determine whether management should make the investment.

c. Now suppose that the managers of the shipping company have decided that truck waiting time is excessive and they want to reduce the waiting time. They have determined that there are two alternatives available for reducing the waiting time. They can add a fourth dock, or they can add extra employees and equipment at the existing docks, which will reduce the average service time per location from the original 30 minutes per truck to 23 minutes per truck. The costs of these alternatives are approximately equal. Management desires to implement the alternative that reduces waiting time by the greatest amount. Which alternative should be selected?

16-23. $L_q = 1.13$, $W_q = 0.112$ hr

16-23. Drivers who come to get their licenses at the department of motor vehicles have their photograph taken by an automated machine that develops the photograph onto the license card and laminates the complete license. The machine requires a constant time of 4.5 minutes to develop a completed license. If drivers arrive at the machine at the mean rate of 10 per hour (Poisson distributed), determine the average length of the waiting line and the average waiting time.

16-24. $L_q = 0.083$, $W_q = 0.083$ min.

16-24. A vending machine at City Airport dispenses hot coffee, hot chocolate, or hot tea in a constant service time of 20 seconds. Customers arrive at the vending machine at a mean rate of 60 per hour, Poisson distributed. Determine the average length of the waiting line and the average time a customer must wait.

16-25. 0.281

★ 16-25. In Problem 16-20 suppose that Moore's television-repair service cannot accommodate more than 30 TV sets at a time. What is the probability that the number of TV sets on hand (under repair and waiting for service) will exceed the shop capacity?

16-26. Yes

★ 16-26. Norfolk, Virginia, a major seaport on the East coast, has a ship coal-loading facility. Coal trucks filled with coal presently arrive at the port facility at the mean rate of 149 per day (Poisson distributed). The facility operates 24 hours a day. The coal trucks are unloaded one at a time on a first-come, first-served basis by automated mechanical equipment that empties the trucks in a constant time of 8 minutes per truck, regardless of truck size. The port authority is negotiating with a coal company for an additional 30 trucks per day. However, the coal company will not use this port facility unless the port authority can assure them that their coal trucks will not have to wait to be unloaded at the port facility for more than 12 hours per truck on the average. Can the port authority provide this assurance?

16-27. 7 A.M. – 9 A.M.: 5; 9 A.M. – noon: 2; noon – 2 P.M.: 6; 2 P.M. – 5 P.M.: 4

★ 16-27. The Waterfall Buffet in the lower level of the National Art Gallery serves food cafeteria-style daily to visitors and employees. The buffet is self-service. From 7:00 A.M. to 9:00 A.M. customers arrive at the buffet at a rate of 10 per minute; from 9:00 A.M. to noon, at 4 per minute; from noon to 2:00 P.M., at 14 per minute; and from 2:00 P.M. to closing at 5:00 P.M., at 8 per minute (Poisson distributed). All the customers take about the same amount of time to serve themselves and proceed to the buffet. Once a customer goes through the buffet, it takes an average of 0.4 minute (exponentially distributed) to pay the cashier. The gallery does not want a customer to have to wait longer than 4 minutes to pay. How many cashiers should be working at each of the four times during the day?

16-28. a. $L = 4.197$, $L_q = 1.28$, $W_q = 0.256$ hr
b. Waiting time reduced to 0.061 hr

★ 16-28. The Clip Joint is a hair-styling salon at University Mall. Four stylists are always available to serve customers on a first-come, first-served basis. Customers arrive at an average rate of 5 per hour (Poisson distributed), and the stylists spend an average of 35 minutes (exponentially distributed) on each customer.

a. Determine the average number of customers in the salon, the average time a customer must wait, and the average number waiting to be served.

b. The salon manager is considering adding a fifth stylist. Would this have a significant impact on waiting time?

16-29. The Bay City Police Department has eight patrol cars that are on constant call 24 hours per day. A patrol car requires repairs every 3 days, on average, according to an exponential distribution. When a patrol car is in need of repair it is driven into the motor pool, which has a repairperson on duty at all times. The average time required to repair a patrol car is 12 hours (exponentially distributed). Determine the average time a patrol car is not available for use and the average number of patrol cars out of service at any one time, and indicate if the repair service seems adequate.

★ 16-29. $L = 2.71$, $W = 37.15$ hr

16-30. The Rowntown Cab Company has four cabs on duty during normal business hours. The cab company dispatcher receives requests for service every 8 minutes, on average, according to an exponential distribution. The average time to complete a trip is 20 minutes (exponentially distributed). Determine the average number of customers waiting for service and the average time a customer must wait for a cab.

16-30. $L_q = 0.533$, $W_q = 4.26$ min

16-31. The Northwoods retail catalog operation employs a bank of six telephone operators, who process orders using computer terminals. When a terminal breaks down, it must be disconnected and taken to a nearby electronics repair shop, where it is repaired. The mean time between terminal breakdowns is 6 working days, and the mean time required to repair a terminal is 2 working days (both exponentially distributed). As a result of lost sales, it costs the mail-order operation an estimated $50 per day in lost profits each day a terminal is out for repair. The company pays the electronics repair shop $3,000 per year on a service agreement to repair the terminals. The company is considering the possibility of signing a new service agreement with another electronics repair shop that will provide substitute terminals while the broken ones are at the repair shop. However, the new service agreement would cost the mail-order operation $15,000 per year. Assuming that there are 250 working days in a year, determine what the mail-order operation should do.

★ 16-31. Select the new service agreement.

16-32. The Riverton Post Office has four stations for service. Customers line up in single file for service on a FIFO basis. The mean arrival rate is 40 per hour, Poisson distributed, and the mean service time per server is 4 minutes, exponentially distributed. Compute the operating characteristics for this operation. Does the operation appear to be satisfactory in terms of: a. postal worker's (servers) idle time; b. customer waiting time and/or the number waiting for service; and c. the percentage of the time can a customer walk in and get served without waiting at all?

★ 16-32. a. 0.33
b. $L_q = 0.756$, $W_q = 0.019$ hr
c. 6%

CASE PROBLEM

★ See Solutions Manual.

The College of Business Copy Center

The copy center in the College of Business at State University has become an increasingly contentious item among the college administrators. The department heads have complained to the associate dean about the long lines and waiting times for their secretaries at the copy center. They claim that it is a waste of scarce resources for the secretaries to stand in line talking when they could be doing more productive work in the office. Alternatively, Hanford Burris, the associate dean, says the limited operating budget will not allow the college to purchase a new copier or copiers to relieve the problem. This standoff has been going on for several years.

In order to make her case for improved copying facilities, Lauren Moore, a teacher in Operations Management, assigned the students in one of her classes to gather some information about the copy center as a class project. The students were to record the arrivals at the center and the length of time it took to do a copy job once the secretary actually reached a copy machine. In addition, the students were to describe how the copy center system worked.

When the students completed the project, they turned in a report to Professor Moore. The report described the copy center as containing two machines. When secretaries arrive for a copy job, they join a queue, which looked more like milling around to the students, but they acknowledged that each secretary knew when it was his or her turn, and, in effect, the secretaries formed a single queue for the first available copy machine. Also, since copy jobs are assigned tasks, secretaries always stayed to do the job no matter how long the line was or how long they had to wait. They never left the queue.

From the data the students gathered, Professor Moore was able to determine that secretaries arrived every 8 minutes for a copy job and that the arrival rate was Poisson distributed. Further, she was able to determine that the average time it takes to complete a job was 12 minutes, and this is exponentially distributed.

Using her department's personnel records and some data from the university personnel office, Dr. Moore determined that a secretary's average salary is $8.50 per hour. From her academic calendar she added up the actual days in the year when the college and departmental offices were open and found there were 247. However, as she added up working days, it occurred to her that during the summer months the workload is much less, and the copy center would also probably get less traffic. The summer included about 70 days, during which she expected the copy center traffic would be about half of what it is during the normal year, but she speculated that the average time of a copying job would remain about the same.

Professor Moore next called a local office supply firm to check the prices on copiers. A new copier of the type in the copy center now would cost $36,000. It would also require $8,000 per year for maintenance and would have a normal useful life of 6 years.

Do you think Dr. Moore will be able to convince the associate dean that a new copy machine will be cost-effective?

REFERENCES

Cooper, R. B., *Introduction to Queuing Theory,* 2d ed., New York: North Holland, 1981.
Gross, D., and C. Harris, *Fundamentals of Queuing Theory,* 2d ed., New York: John Wiley, 1985.
Hillier, F. S., and O. S. Yu, *Queuing Tables and Graphics,* New York: North Holland, 1981.
Kleinrock, L., *Queuing Systems,* vols. 1 and 2, New York: John Wiley, 1975.
Lee, A., *Applied Queuing Theory,* New York: St. Martin's Press, 1966.
Morse, P. M., *Queues, Inventories, and Maintenance,* New York: John Wiley, 1958.
Saaty, T. L., *Elements of Queuing Theory with Applications,* New York: Dover, 1983.
Solomon, S. L., *Simulation of Waiting Line Systems,* Englewood Cliffs, N.J.: Prentice Hall, 1983.
White, J. A., J. W. Schmidt, and G. K. Bennett, *Analysis of Queuing Systems,* New York: Academic Press, 1975.

17
PROJECT MANAGEMENT

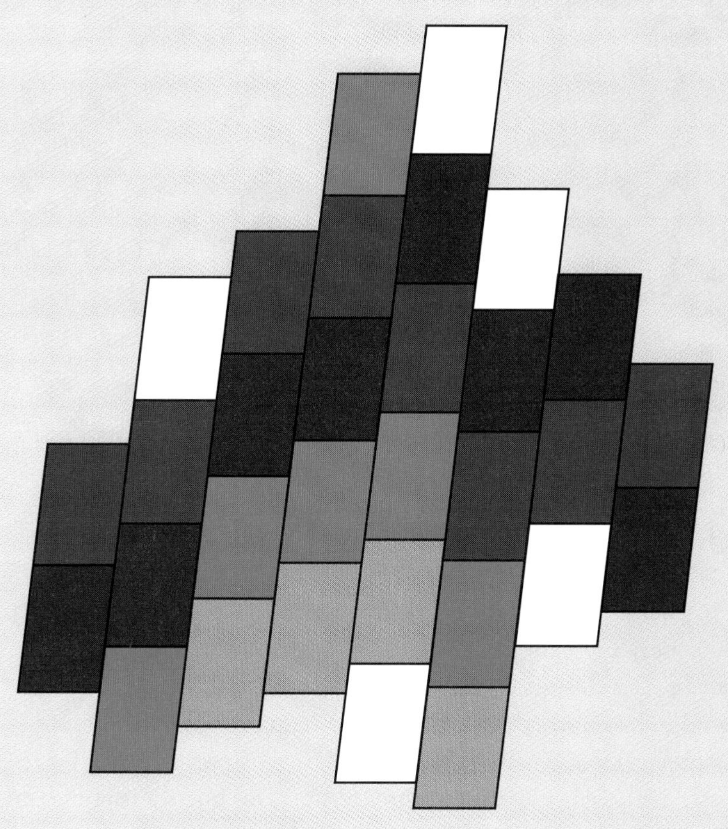

CHAPTER OUTLINE

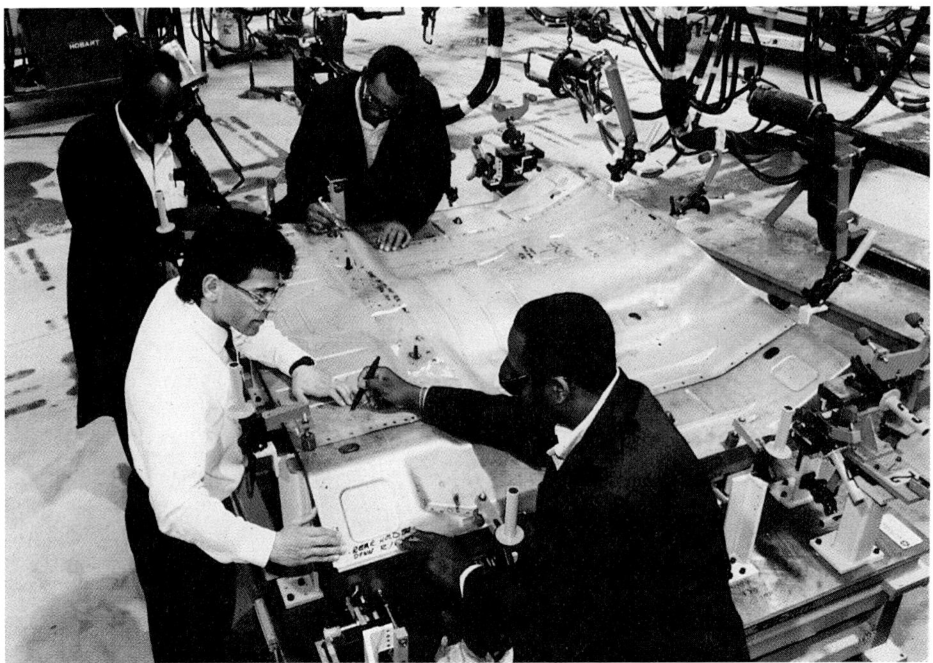

This group is part of the design team working on the LH project at the Chrysler Technology Center at Auburn Hills, Michigan. The overall design team is referred to as a platform group, where platform refers to one of four car classifications at Chrysler, that is, small cars, large cars, jeeps and trucks, and minivans. The platform team is a self-contained entity consisting of buyers, suppliers, designers and engineers that has total responsibility for the development of each car assigned to its platform. The platform group for LH cars (such as the Dodge Intrepid) at Chrysler included over 800 members. Chrysler embraced the team concept for car design and development in order to reduce project time and budget. For the LH project, the development time was only 39 months compared to the previous norm for a new car of 5 years.

PRODUCT DESIGN TEAMS AT CHRYSLER AND FORD

Video 17.1 COMAP, Program 4: "Trains, Planes, and Critical Paths"

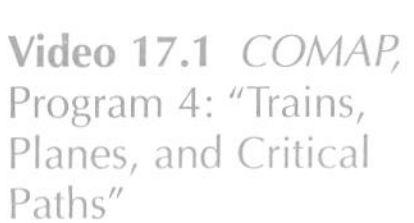

In the late 1980s Chrysler created a product design team called a *platform* group for the design of their new LH cars including the Dodge Intrepid, Eagle Vision, and Chrysler Concorde. The design teams evolved primarily from a need to reduce the time required to develop new cars. The time required for U.S. automakers to develop a new product was frequently as long as five years, whereas the best Japanese automakers developed new cars in three years. The initial design team concept was used for the development of the Viper, Chrysler's $50,000 sports car. The project design team consisted of approximately 80 members, and the company's goal was to develop the car in less than four years. Introduced in early 1992, the Viper was put into production in only 36 months. Ultimately the same design team approach was applied to the LH cars, and they reached production in 39 months.[1]

When the Ford Mustang was introduced in 1964, it was an immediate hit, with sales over 417,000 within 12 months. However, annual sales, which were around 500,000 through the 1960s, had dropped to only 86,000 by 1992. In 1989 Ford management almost decided to discontinue the Mustang when a study showed the cost for redesigning it would be $1 billion. However, a group of Ford employees and Mustang loyalists persuaded the company to let them take on the redesign project, promising a lower cost. Operating with more independence than most project teams, the 400-member group brought the car on-line after three years in 1994 for $700 million, 25 percent faster and 30 percent cheaper than any other comparable design project at Ford.[2]

[1] Raia, E., "LH Story," *Purchasing* (February 18, 1993): 55–57.

[2] Kennedy, J., "Pony Express," *Roanoke Times and World News*, October 15, 1993, pp. Extra 1,4.

In other chapters in this text we have discussed the scheduling of repetitive operations and activities, such as work scheduling and job scheduling, as an important aspect of managing an operation. Operational schedules are established using various techniques in order to keep the flow of products or services through the production process on time. However, not all operational activities are repetitive; some are unique, occurring only once within a specified time frame. Such unique, one-time activities are referred to as **projects.**

A **project** is a unique, one-time operational activity or effort.

A project is an innovation or change in operations. *Project management* is the management of the project work effort to develop and implement the innovation or change to the existing operation. It encompasses planning the project and controlling the project activities, subject to resource and budget constraints, in order to keep the project on schedule. Examples of projects include constructing all kinds of facilities and buildings, such as houses, factories, a shopping mall, an athletic stadium, or an arena; developing a military weapons system, a new aircraft, or a new ship; launching a satellite system; constructing an oil pipeline; developing and implementing a new computer system; planning a rock concert, football bowl game, or basketball tournament; and introducing new products into the market, among many others.

Projects have become increasingly more pervasive in operating environments in recent years, as opposed to routine or status quo activities. This is a result of the diversity of new products and product markets and the shorter life span of products, combined with rapid technological changes. The nature of the international business environment is such that new machinery and equipment, as well as new production processes and computer support systems, are constantly evolving. This provides the capability of developing new products and services, which in turn has generated consumer demand for even greater product diversity. As a result of this accelerated pace of change, a larger proportion of total organizational effort now goes toward project-oriented activities than in the past. Thus, the planning and management of projects has taken on a more crucial role in operations management.

In this chapter we focus on project management using CPM and PERT, a popular set of network scheduling techniques. Their popularity is in part due to the fact that they use networks, and as such, provide a graph or visual representation of the interrelationship and sequence of individual project activities, rather than simply a verbal or mathematical description. However, prior to our presentation of the CPM/PERT technique, we will discuss the elements of project management.

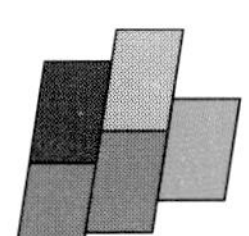

THE ELEMENTS OF PROJECT MANAGEMENT

Transparency 17.1 The Elements of Project Planning

Management is generally perceived to be concerned with the planning, organization and control of an ongoing process or activity such as the production of a product or delivery of a service. Project management is different in that it reflects a commitment of resources and people to a typically important activity for a relatively short time frame, after which the management effort is dissolved. There is not the continuity of supervision associated with projects that is normally the case in the management of a production process. As such, the features and characteristics of project management tend to be somewhat unique. In this section, we will discuss the three primary elements of project management: the project team, project planning, and project control.

Project teams are made up of individuals from various areas and departments within a company.

The Project Team and TQM

The project team typically consists of a group of individuals selected from other areas in the organization or from consultants outside the organization because of their special skills, expertise, and experience related to the project activities. Members of the engineering staff, particularly industrial engineering, are often assigned to project work because of their technical skills, especially if the project is related to production processes or equipment. The project team may also include various managers and staff personnel from specific areas related to the project. Even workers can be involved on the project team if their job is a function of the project activity. For example, a project team for the construction of a new loading dock facility at a plant might logically include truck drivers, forklift operators, dock workers, and staff personnel and managers from purchasing, shipping, receiving, and packaging, as well as engineers to assess vehicle flow, routes, and space considerations. An important principle of TQM is that the employees who work in an area be part of the "problem-solving," or project, team in order to take advantage of their unique perspective and expertise.

Matrix organization is a team structure with members from functional areas, depending on the skills required.

The term **matrix organization** refers to a team approach to special projects. The team is developed from members of different functional areas or departments in the company. For example, team members might come from engineering, production, marketing, or personnel, depending on the specialized skills required by the project. The team members are, in effect, on loan from their home departments to work on a project. The term *matrix* is derived from the two-dimensional characteristics of this type of organizational structure. On one dimension, the vertical, is the company's normal organizational structure for performing jobs, whereas the horizontal dimension is the special functional structure (i.e., the functional team members) required by the project.

Projects related to product design require a team approach in TQM.

In recent years a team approach to product design has developed as part of many companies' commitment to total quality management (TQM). In a TQM environment the purpose of the product design team is to bring together different functional representatives and specialists from inside and outside the company that will successfully design quality into a product. An additional objective of the project design team is to get a new product to the market before competitors. A typical product design team might include members from marketing, engineering, purchasing, manufacturing, quality management, and suppliers. Note the inclusion of suppliers from outside the company in order to make sure the desired quality features are designed into parts and that parts and materials are available when needed (i.e., quality service).

Assignment to a project team is usually temporary and thus can have both positive and negative repercussions. The temporary loss of workers and staff from their permanent jobs can be disruptive for both the employee and the work area. The employee must sometimes "serve two masters" in a sense, reporting to both the project manager and a regular supervisor. Alternatively, since projects are usually exciting, they provide an opportunity to do work that is new and innovative, although the employee may be reluctant to report back to a more mundane, regular job after the project is completed.

The most important member of the project team is the *project manager*. The job of managing a project is subject to a great deal of uncertainty and the distinct possibility of failure. Since a project is unique and usually has not been attempted previously, the outcome is not as certain as the outcome of an ongoing process would be. A degree of security is attained in the supervision of a continuing process that is not present in project management. The project team members are often from diverse areas of the organization and possess different skills, which must be coordinated into a single, focused effort to complete the project successfully. In addition, the project is invariably subject to time and budgetary constraints that are not the same as normal work schedules and resource consumption in an ongoing process. Overall, there is usually more perceived and real pressure associated with project management than in a normal management position. However, there are potential rewards, including the ability to demonstrate one's management abili-

The project manager is often under greater pressure.

ties in a difficult situation, the challenge of working on a unique project, and the excitement of doing something new.

Project Planning

Planning a project requires that the objectives of the project be clearly defined so that the manager and the team know what is expected. Sometimes this takes the form of a formal written description of what is to be accomplished, the work to be done, and the project time frame, called a **statement of work.** All activities (or steps) in the project must then be completely identified. This is not a simple task, since the work involved in the project is new, without a great deal of experiential references to draw upon. An **activity** is the performance of an individual job or work effort that requires labor, resources, and time and that is subject to managerial control or supervision. Once the activities have been identified, their sequential relationship to each other, called a **precedence relationship,** must be determined, that is, it must be decided which activities come first, which follow, and so on. In the CPM/PERT technique we discuss later in the chapter, the precedence relationship is visually displayed in the form of a network of activities.

A **statement of work** is a written description of the goals, work, and time frame of a project.

An **activity** requires labor, resources, and time.

A **precedence relationship** is the sequential relationship of activities in a project.

Once the activities of the project have been identified and their relationship to each other has been determined in the form of a network or other project planning device, the project activities must be scheduled. Scheduling is accomplished by determining estimates of the time required by each activity and then using these estimates to develop an overall project schedule and time to project completion. The estimated project time must be compared to the project objective; if the project time estimate is too long, then means must be sought to reduce project time. This is usually accomplished by assigning more resources or work effort to individual activities in order to reduce the time they require. This is a topic we discuss in greater detail in the section on time-cost trade-offs.

To summarize, the elements of the project planning process are as follows:

elements of project planning.

- Define project objective(s).
- Identify activities.
- Establish precedence relationships.
- Make time estimates.
- Determine project completion time.
- Compare project schedule objectives.
- Determine resource requirements to meet objectives.

Project Control

Project management consists of two distinct phases, planning and control. Once the project planning process is completed, the project can physically be initiated, that is, the work involved in the activities can begin. At this point the focus of project management becomes the control of the actual work involved in the project. Control includes making sure all activities are identified and included and making sure the activities are completed in the sequence they are supposed to be. Also, resource needs must be identified as work is initiated and completed, and the schedule must be adjusted to reflect time changes and corrections. However, in most cases the primary focus of control is on maintaining the project schedule and making sure the project is completed on time.

The **work breakdown structure (WBS)** is an important methodology for project planning and control. In a WBS a project is broken down into its major subcomponents, referred to as modules. These subcomponents are then subdivided into more detailed components, which are further broken down into activities and, finally, individual tasks. The end result is a project organizational structure made

WBS breaks down a project into subcomponents, components, activities, and tasks.

GAINING THE COMPETITIVE EDGE

Project Management Teams at IBM

Within the Commercial Data Processing Products Division at IBM, new computer-based systems are developed for internal operational and management information needs. The Information Systems Department within this division used their own experiences in project management while developing these systems to establish a training/project development program for project management teams.

A systems development project for creating an information system consists of five generic steps: project initiation (prioritize needs), system design, planning and scheduling, system development, system test, and system implementation and evaluation. When projects are first initiated, managers transferred from operations (such as manufacturing) to project management teams must be reoriented to the differing management styles, including the difference in time frames (i.e., daily operations versus 6-month to 2-year project planning). The project development program structure includes a 5-(nonconsecutive) day workshop in which the project team develops the project schedule for actual ongoing projects. The starting point in the workshop for developing the project schedule plan is a *project phase structure chart,* a graphic display that divides the project into four basic phases (initiation, planning, development, and implementation) and describes the basic activities for each. Next, project milestones and completion criteria for each are developed. These are targets around which the project schedule is constructed. The project phases are then divided into *work breakdown structure outlines,* which show all activities for the project and include time estimates and resource requirements. This document is subsequently used to build the project network. The actual project network is constructed using "adhesive" notes for activities and laying out precedence relationships on a wall chart. The network development includes the following steps: build the initial network chart, input time estimates and print schedules, replan the critical path to meet the acceptable finish date, level person resources within the time constraint of the critical path, and develop a project control action plan. This last item is an effort to brainstorm the final schedule plan to expose possible risky critical and near-critical activities that might delay the project. Team members are assigned to investigate potential problem activities and develop an action plan to avoid the problem. This process is repeated at the completion of each project milestone.

Source: Based on Rogers, L. A., "Project Team Training: A Proven Key to Organizational Teamwork and a Breakthrough in Planning Performances," *Project Management Journal* 21, no. 2 (June 1990): 9–18.

up of different levels, with the overall project at the top of the structure and the individual tasks for each activity at the bottom level. The WBS format is a good way to identify activities and to determine the individual task, module, and project workloads and resources required. Further, it helps to identify relationships between modules and activities. It also identifies unnecessary duplication of activities. The modules in the WBS are sometimes used to put together the project network.

THE GANTT CHART

A **Gantt chart** is a graph or bar chart with a bar for each project activity that shows the passage of time.

A **Gantt chart** is a traditional management technique for scheduling and planning small projects with relatively few activities and precedence relationships. The scheduling technique (also called a *bar chart*) was developed by Henry Gantt. He was a pioneer in the field of industrial engineering and was at the artillery ammunition shops of the Frankford Arsenal in 1914 when World War I was declared.

The Gantt chart has been a popular project scheduling tool since its inception and is still widely used today. In addition, it is the direct precursor of the CPM/PERT technique, which we discuss in the following sections.

The Gantt chart is a graphical technique with a bar or time line displayed for each activity in the project being analyzed. Figure 17.1 illustrates a Gantt chart for a simplified project description for building a house. The project contains only seven very general activities, such as designing the house, laying the foundation, ordering materials, etc. The first activity in the project is "design house and obtain financing," and it requires 3 months to complete; this time is shown by the bar running from left to right across the chart. After the first activity is finished, the next two activities, "lay foundation" and "order materials," can start simultaneously. This set of activities demonstrates how a precedence relationship works; the design of the house and the financing must precede the next two activities.

The activity "lay foundation" requires 2 months to complete, so it will be finished, at the earliest, at the end of month 5. "Order and receive materials" requires 1 month to complete, and it could be finished after month 4. However, observe

Transparency 17.2 A Gantt Chart

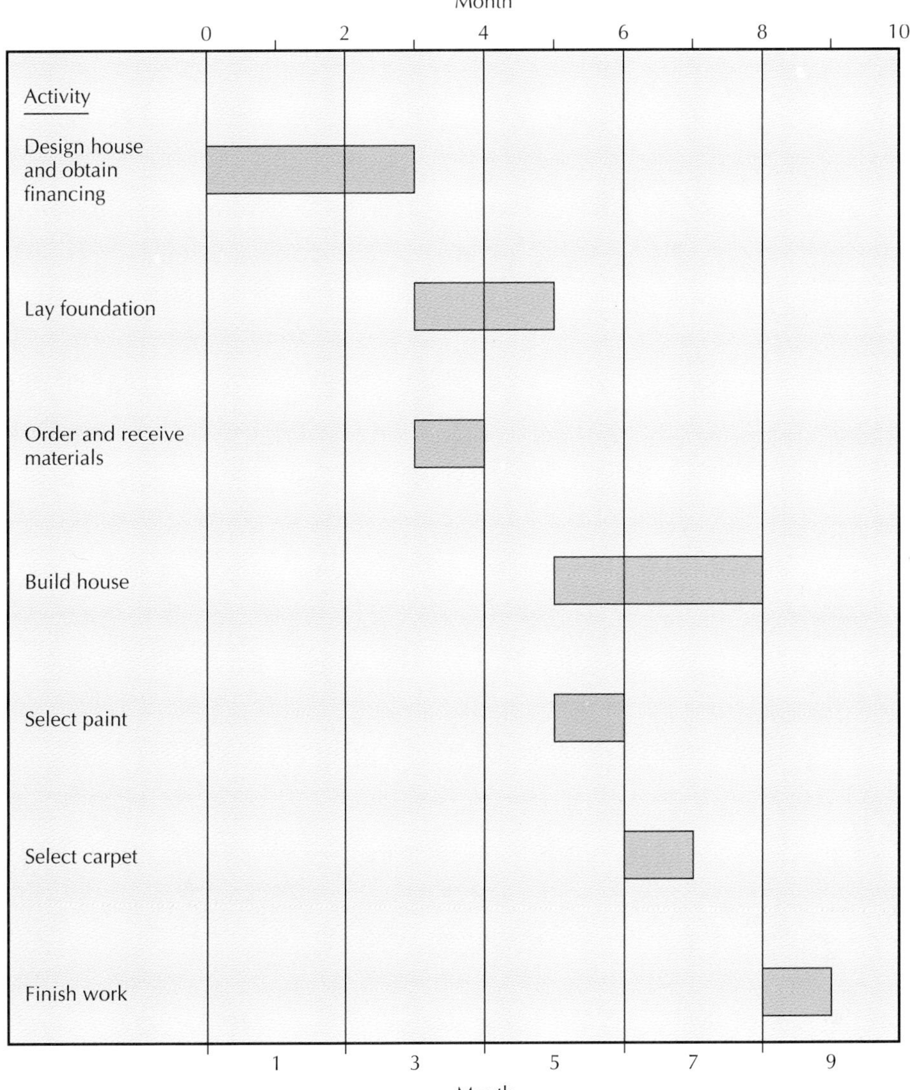

FIGURE 17.1 A Gantt Chart

that it is possible to delay the start of this activity 1 month until month 4. This delay would still enable the activity to be completed by the end of month 5, when the next activity, "build house," is scheduled to start. This extra time for the activity "order materials" is called *slack*. **Slack** is the amount by which an activity can be delayed without delaying any of the activities that follow it or the project as a whole. The remainder of the Gantt chart is constructed in a similar manner, and the project is scheduled to be completed at the end of month 9.

Slack is the amount of time an activity can be delayed without delaying the project.

The Gantt chart provides a visual display of the project schedule, indicating when activities are scheduled to start, when they will be finished, and where extra time is available and activities can be delayed. The project manager can use the chart to monitor the progress of the activities and see which ones are ahead of schedule and which ones are behind schedule. The Gantt chart also indicates the precedence relationships between activities; however, these relationships are not always easily discernible. This problem is one of the disadvantages of the Gantt chart method, and it limits the chart's use to smaller projects with relatively few activities. Alternatively, the CPM/PERT network technique does not suffer this disadvantage.

Teaching Note 17.1 CPM/PERT Use in the Real World

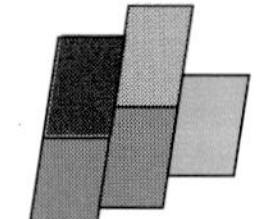

CPM/PERT

In 1956 a research team at E. I. du Pont de Nemours & Company, Inc., led by a du Pont engineer, Morgan R. Walker, and a Remington-Rand computer specialist, James E. Kelley, Jr., initiated a project to develop a computerized system to improve the planning, scheduling, and reporting of the company's engineering programs (including plant maintenance and construction projects). The resulting network approach is known as the **critical path method (CPM)**. At virtually the same time the U.S. Navy established a research team composed of members of the Navy Special Projects Office, Lockheed (the prime contractor), and the consulting firm of Booz, Allen, and Hamilton, led by D. G. Malcolm. They developed a similar network approach for the design of a management control system for the development of the Polaris Missle Project (a ballistic missile-firing nuclear submarine). This network scheduling technique was named the **project evaluation and review technique,** or **PERT.** The Polaris project eventually included 23 PERT networks encompassing 3,000 activities.

In **CPM** activities are shown as a network of precedence relationships using activity-on-node network construction.

In **PERT** activities are shown as a network of precedence relationships using activity-on-arrow network construction.

Both CPM and PERT are derivatives of the Gantt chart and, as a result, are very similar. There were originally two primary differences between CPM and PERT. With CPM a single, or deterministic, estimate for activity time was used, whereas with PERT, probabilistic time estimates were employed. The other difference was related to the mechanics of drawing the project network. In PERT activities were represented as arcs, or arrowed lines, between two nodes, or circles, whereas in CPM activities were represented as the nodes or circles. However, these were minor differences, and over time CPM and PERT have been effectively merged into a single technique, conventionally referred to as CPM/PERT.

CPM/PERT uses a network to depict the precedence relationships among activities.

The primary advantage of CPM/PERT over the Gantt chart is in the use of a network to depict the precedence relationships between activities. Recall in our earlier discussion of the Gantt chart that we mentioned that it did not clearly show precedence relationships, which was a disadvantage that limited its use to small projects. Alternatively, the use of a network in CPM/PERT is a much more efficient and direct means of displaying precedence relationships. In other words, in a network it is visually easier to see the precedence relationships, which makes CPM/PERT a popular technique with managers and other users, especially for large projects with many activities.

The Lafayette, the nuclear powered ballistic missile submarine shown here, is a direct descendent of the Polaris, the first nuclear submarine of this type. In the late 1950s the Polaris Fleet Ballistic Missile Project was a massive undertaking that was a cornerstone of the United States' defense program. The project included over 250 prime contractors and 9,000 subcontractors. A failure by any of these subcontractors could have resulted in a significant delay in the project, which was considered a risk to national security. As such, a method was sought to coordinate the work of these subcontractors, anticipate and avoid bottlenecks, to forecast target completion dates, and in general to coordinate the work of hundreds of thousands of persons, into the finished weapon system. PERT, originally called the Program Evaluation Research Task and later changed to Program Evaluation and Review Technique, was the method developed to achieve this task. The Navy Department subsequently credited PERT with bringing the Polaris missile submarine to combat readiness approximately two years ahead of the originally scheduled completion date.

The Project Network

A CPM/PERT network consists of two basic components, *branches* and *nodes,* as shown in Figure 17.2, on the next page. As we mentioned earlier, when CPM and PERT were first developed, they employed different conventions for constructing a network. With CPM the nodes, or circles in Figure 17.2, represented the project activities. The arrows in between the nodes indicated the precedence relationships between activities. For the network in Figure 17.2, activity 1, represented by node 1, precedes activity 2, and 2 precedes 3. This approach to network construction is called **activity-on-node** (**AON**). With PERT the opposite convention was taken. The branches, or arrowed arcs, represented the activities and the nodes, or circles, in between them reflected **events,** or points in time such as the end of one activity and the beginning of another. In this approach, referred to as **activity-on-arrow** (**AOA**), the activities are normally identified by the node numbers at the start and end of an activity; for example activity 1-2 precedes activity 2-3 in Figure 17.2. In this text we will employ the activity-on-arrow convention.

In **AON,** nodes represent activities and arrows show precedence relationships.

An **event** is the completion or beginning of an activity in a project.

In **AOA,** arrows represent activities and nodes are events for points in time.

Teaching Note 17.2 Event Versus Activity Scheduling

In order to demonstrate how these basic components are used to construct a network, we will use our example project of building a house employed to illustrate the Gantt chart in Figure 17.1. The comparable CPM/PERT network for this project is shown in Figure 17.3. The precedence relationships are reflected in this

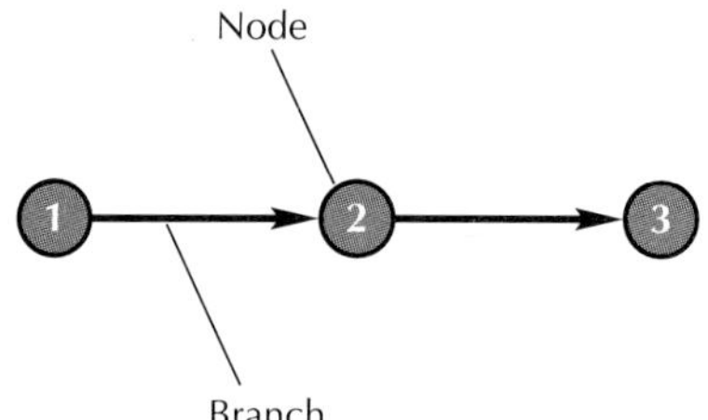

FIGURE 17.2 Network Components

network by the arrangement of the arrowed (or directed) branches in Figure 17.3. The first activity (1-2) in the project is to design the house and obtain financing. This activity must be completed before any subsequent activities can begin. Thus, activities 2-3, laying the foundation, and 2-4 , ordering and receiving materials, can start only when node 2 is *realized,* indicating the event that activity 1-2 is finished. (Notice in Figure 17.3 that a time estimate of 3 months has been assigned for the completion of this activity). Activity 2-3 and activity 3-4 can occur concurrently; neither depends on the other and both depend only on the completion of activity 1-2.

When the activities of laying the foundation (2-3) and ordering materials (2-4) are completed, then activities 4-5 and 4-6 can begin simultaneously. However, before discussing these activities further, notice activity 3-4, referred to in the network as a dummy.

Two or more activities cannot share the same start and end nodes; **dummy** required.

A **dummy** activity is inserted into the network to show a precedence relationship, but it does not represent any actual passage of time. Activities 2-3 and 2-4 have the precedence relationship shown in Figure 17.4(a). However, in a CPM/PERT network, two or more activities are not allowed to share the same starting and ending nodes. (The reason will become apparent later when we develop a schedule for the network.) Instead, activity (3-4) is inserted to give two activities separate end nodes and, thus, two separate identities as shown in figure 17.4(b). Notice, though, that a time of zero months has been assigned to activity 3-4. The dummy activity shows that activity 2-3 must be completed prior to any activities beginning at node 4, but it does not represent the passage of time.

Returning to the network in Figure 17.3, we see that two activities start at node 4. Activity 4-6 is the actual building of the house, and activity 4-5 is the search for and selection of the paint for the exterior and interior of the house. Activity 4-6 and activity 4-5 can begin simultaneously and take place concurrently. Following the selection of the paint (activity 4-5) and the realization of node 5, the carpet can be selected (since the carpet color depends on the paint color). This activity can also occur concurrently with the building of the house (activity 4-6). When the building is completed and the paint and carpet are selected, the house can be finished (activity 6-7).

The Critical Path

A network path is a sequence of connected activities that runs from the start node to the end node in the network. The network in Figure 17.3 has several paths through it. In fact, close observations of this network show four paths, identified as A, B, C, and D:

A: 1-2-3-4-6-7
B: 1-2-3-4-5-6-7
C: 1-2-4-6-7
D: 1-2-4-5-6-7

The minimum time in which the project can be completed (i.e., the house can be built) is equal to the length of time required by the longest path in the network.

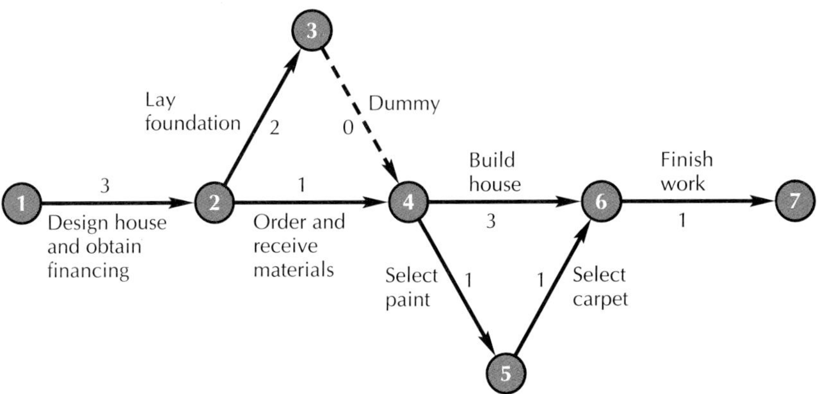

FIGURE 17.3 The Project Network for Building a House

Transparency 17.3 Project Network for House Construction and Activity Scheduling

The **critical path** is the longest path through a network; it is the minimum project completion time.

The longest path is referred to as the **critical path,** which is where the name *critical path method* comes from. To understand better the relationship between the minimum project time and the longest network path, we will determine the length of each of the four paths just listed.

By summing the activity times (shown in Figure 17.3) along each of the four paths, we can compute the length of each path, as follows:

Path A: 1-2-3-4-6-7
$3 + 2 + 0 + 3 + 1 = 9$ months

Path B: 1-2-3-4-5-6-7
$3 + 2 + 0 + 1 + 1 + 1 = 8$ months

Path C: 1-2-4-6-7
$3 + 1 + 3 + 1 = 8$ months

Path D: 1-2-4-5-6-7
$3 + 1 + 1 + 1 + 1 = 7$ months

Because path A is the longest path, it is also the critical path; thus the minimum completion time for the project is 9 months. Now let us analyze the critical path more closely. From Figure 17.5 we can see that activities 2-3 and 2-4 cannot start until 3 months have passed. It is also relatively easy to see that activity 3-4 will not start until 5 months have passed. The start of activities 4-5 and 4-6 is dependent

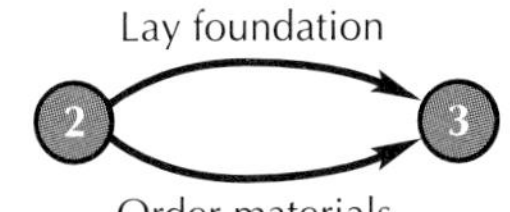

(a) Incorrect precedence relationship

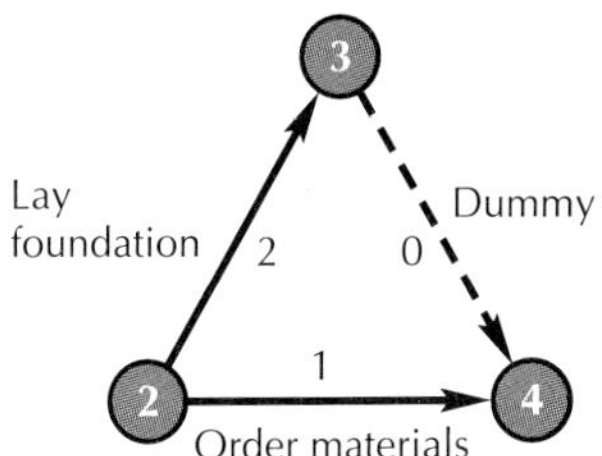

(b) Correct precedence relationship

FIGURE 17.4 Concurrent Activities

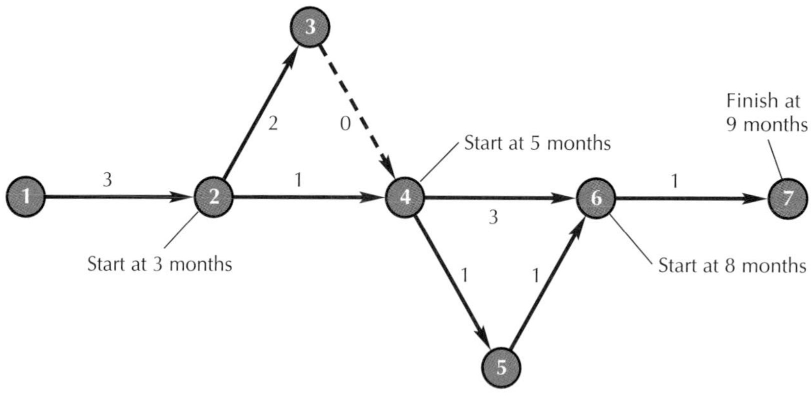

FIGURE 17.5 Activity Start Times

on two activities leading into node 4. Activity 3-4 is completed after 5 months (which we determine by adding the dummy activity time of zero to the time of 5 months until node 3 occurs), but activity 2-4 is completed at the end of 4 months. Thus, we have two possible start times for activities 4-5 and 4-6, 5 months and 4 months. However, since no activity starting at node 4 can occur until all preceding activities have been finished, the soonest node 4 can be realized is 5 months.

Now let us consider the activities leading from node 4. Using the same logic as before, we can see that activity 6-7 cannot start until after 8 months (5 months at node 4 plus the 3 months required by activity 4-6) or after 7 months (5 months at node 4 plus the 2 months required by activities 4-5 and 5-6). Because all activities ending at node 6 must be completed before activity 6-7 can start, the soonest they can occur is 8 months. Adding 1 month for activity 6-7 to the time at node 6 gives a project duration of 9 months. Recall that this is the time of the longest path in the network, or the critical path.

This brief analysis demonstrates the concept of a critical path and the determination of the minimum completion time of a project. However, this was a cumbersome method for determining a critical path. Next, we discuss a mathematical approach to scheduling the project activities and determining the critical path.

Activity Scheduling

ES is the earliest time an activity can start.

A **forward pass** starts at the beginning of a CPM/PERT network to determine earliest activity times.

EF is the earliest start time plus the activity time.

Transparency 17.4 Formulas for Activity Scheduling

In our analysis of the critical path, we determined the soonest time that each activity could be finished. For example, we found that the earliest time activity 4-5 could start was 5 months. This time is referred to as the **earliest start time,** and it is expressed symbolically as **ES.**

To determine the earliest start time for every activity, we make a **forward pass** through the network. That is, we start at the first node and move forward through the network. The earliest time for an activity is the maximum time in which all preceding activities have been completed—the time when the activity start node is realized.

The **earliest finish time, EF,** for an activity is simply the earliest start time plus the activity time estimate. For example, if the earliest start time for activity 1-2 is at time 0, then the earliest finish time is 3 months. In general, the earliest start and finish times for an activity *i-j* are computed according to the following mathematical relationship (where $i < j$).

$$ES_{ij} = \text{maximum } (EF_i)$$
$$EF_{ij} = ES_{ij} + t_{ij}$$

The earliest start and earliest finish times for all the activities in our project network are shown in Figure 17.6.

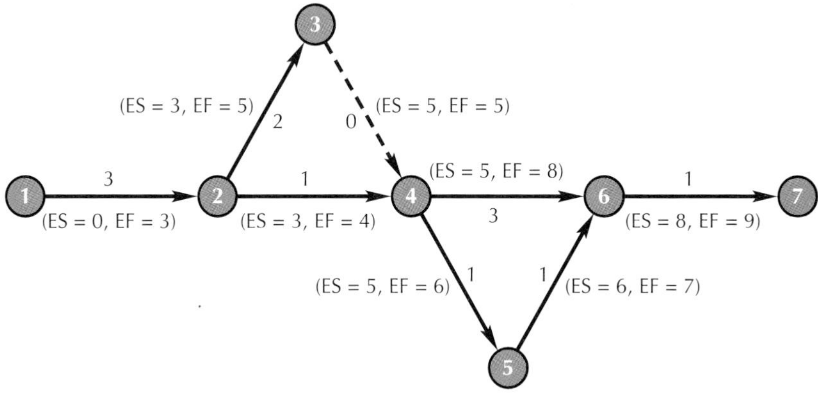

FIGURE 17.6 Earliest Activity Start and Finish Times

The earliest start time for the first activity in the network (for which there are no predecessor activities) is always 0, or, $ES_{12} = 0$. This enables us to compute the earliest finish time for activity 1-2 as

$$\begin{aligned} \text{EF}_{12} &= \text{EF}_{12} + t_{12} \\ &= 0 + 3 \\ &= 3 \text{ months} \end{aligned}$$

The earliest start for activity 2-3 is next computed:

$$\begin{aligned} \text{ES}_{23} &= \max \text{EF}_2 \\ &= 3 \text{ months} \end{aligned}$$

and the corresponding earliest finish time is

$$\begin{aligned} \text{EF}_{23} &= \text{ES}_{23} + t_{23} \\ &= 3 + 2 \\ &= 5 \text{ months} \end{aligned}$$

For activity 3-4 the earliest start time (ES_{34}) is 5 months and the earliest finish time (EF_{34}) is 5 months, and for activity 2-4 the earliest start time (ES_{24}) is 3 months and the earliest finish time (EF_{24}) is 4 months.

Now consider activity 4-5, which has two predecessor activities. The earliest start time is computed as

$$\begin{aligned} \text{ES}_{46} &= \max \text{EF}_4 \\ &= \max (5, 4) \\ &= 5 \text{ months} \end{aligned}$$

and the earliest finish time is

$$\begin{aligned} \text{EF}_{46} &= \text{ES}_{46} + t_{46} \\ &= 5 + 3 \\ &= 8 \text{ months} \end{aligned}$$

All the remaining earliest start and finish times are computed similarly. Notice in Figure 17.6 that the earliest finish time for activity 6-7, the last activity in the network, is 9, which is the total project duration, or critical path time.

Companions to the earliest start and finish are the **latest start** and **latest finish times, LS** and **LF.** The latest start time is the latest time an activity can start without delaying the completion of the project beyond the project critical path time. For our example, the project completion time (and earliest finish time) at node 7 is 9 months. Thus, the objective of determining latest times is to see how long each activity can be delayed without the project exceeding 9 months.

LS is the latest time an activity can start without delaying critical path time. **LF** is the latest time an activity can still be completed and still maintain the project critical path time.

In general, the latest start and finish times for an activity *i-j* are computed according to the following formulas:

$$LS_{ij} = LF_{ij} - t_{ij}$$
$$LF_{ij} = \min(LS_j)$$

A **backward pass** determines latest activity times by starting at the end of a CPM/PERT network and working forward.

The term $\min(LS_j)$ means the minimum latest start time for all activities leaving node *j*. Whereas a forward pass through the network is made to determine the earliest times, the latest times are computed using a **backward pass.** We start at the end of the network at node 7 and work backward, computing the latest times for each activity. Since we want to determine how long each activity in the network can be delayed without extending the project time, the latest finish time at node 7 cannot exceed the earliest finish time. Therefore, the latest finish time at node 7 is 9 months. This and all other latest times are shown in Figure 17.7.

Starting at the end of the network, the critical path time, which is also equal to the earliest finish time of activity 6-7, is 9 months. This automatically becomes the latest finish time for activity 6-7, or,

$$LF_{67} = 9 \text{ months}$$

Using this value, the latest start time for activity 6-7 can be computed:

$$\begin{aligned} LS_{67} &= LF_{67} - t_{67} \\ &= 9 - 1 \\ &= 8 \text{ months} \end{aligned}$$

The latest finish time for activity 5-6 is the minimum of the latest start times for the activities leaving node 6. Since activity 6-7 leaves node 6, the latest start time is computed as follows:

$$\begin{aligned} LF_{56} &= \min(LS_6) \\ &= 8 \text{ months} \end{aligned}$$

The latest start time for activity 5-6 is

$$\begin{aligned} LS_{56} &= LF_{56} - t_{56} \\ &= 8 - 1 \\ &= 7 \text{ months} \end{aligned}$$

For activity 4-6, the latest finish time (LF_{46}) is 8 months, and the latest start time (LS_{46}) is 5 months; for activity 4-5, the latest finish time (LF_{45}) is 7 months, and the latest start time (LS_{45}) is 6 months.

Now consider activity 2-4, which has two activities following it. The latest finish time is computed as follows:

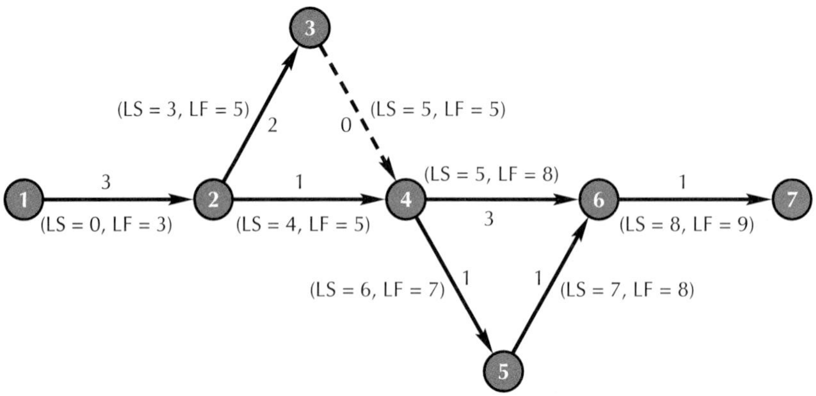

FIGURE 17.7 Latest Activity Start and Finish Times

$$
\begin{aligned}
LF_{24} &= \min(LF_4)\\
&= \min(5, 6)\\
&= 5 \text{ months}
\end{aligned}
$$

The latest start time is computed as

$$
\begin{aligned}
LS_{24} &= LF_{24} - t_{24}\\
&= 5 - 1\\
&= 4 \text{ months}
\end{aligned}
$$

All the remaining latest start and latest finish times are computed similarly. Figure 17.8 includes the earliest and latest start times, and earliest and latest finish times for all activities.

Activity Slack

The project network in Figure 17.8, with all activity start and finish times, highlights the critical path (1-2-3-4-6-7) we determined earlier by inspection. Notice that for the activities on the critical path, the earliest start times and latest start times are equal. This means that these activities on the critical path must start exactly on time and cannot be delayed at all. If the start of any activity on the critical path is delayed, then the overall project time will be increased. As a result, we now have an alternate way to determine the critical path besides simply inspecting the network. The activities on the critical path can be determined by seeing for which activities ES = LS or EF = LF. In Figure 17.8 the activities 1-2, 2-3, 3-4, 4-6 and 6-7 all have earliest start times and latest start times that are equal (and EF = LF); thus, they are on the critical path.

For those activities not on the critical path for which the earliest and latest start times (or earliest and latest finish times) are not equal, *slack* time exists. Recall that we introduced the concept of slack with our discussion of the Gantt chart in Figure 17.1. Slack is the amount of time an activity can be delayed without affecting the overall project duration. In effect, it is extra time available for completing an activity.

Slack, S, is computed using either of the following formulas:

$$S_{ij} = LS_{ij} - ES_{ij}$$

or

$$S_{ij} = LF_{ij} - EF_{ij}$$

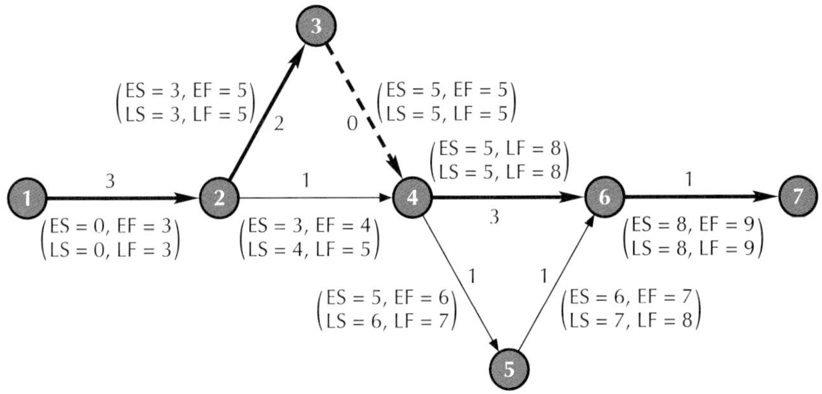

FIGURE 17.8 Earliest Activity Start and Finish Times

GAINING THE COMPETITIVE EDGE

Highway Construction at the Minnesota Department of Transportation

Highway-related construction is a prominent area of use of project management techniques. As an example, the Minnesota Department of Transportation (MN/DOT) generally has approximately 1,100 ongoing construction projects under development at any given time. These projects typically involve highway improvement, such as a new highway or freeway segment, a new bridge, or restoration of an existing facility, as well as projects involving airports, waterways, railroads, and so on. The highway department allows about 300 new project contracts each year.

This volume of project work requires an extensive project management organizational structure. Near the top of MN/DOT, the Office of Highway Programs Implementation coordinates project management teams located at the nine district offices in the system. Each district has between 5 and 15 project managers, each of whom is responsible for the design of several projects at one time.

An example of the use of critical path methods (CPM) at MN/DOT was for a $9.5 million flood-control project, which required a road segment less than 1 mile in length to be raised with flood walls and new bridges to be constructed. It was critical that the project be completed prior to the winter of the second year of the project. All construction activities were networked, and a critical path was determined. Bar charts were also used as a supplement to assist visualization of critical activities. Project control and the schedule were maintained through weekly meetings of the contractors. The project was completed on time, and the use of CPM was deemed successful.

Sources: Based on Pearson, R., "Project Management in the Minnesota Department of Transportation, Delivering Products: The Preconstruction Phase," *The PM Network* 2, no. 5 (November 1988): 7–18; Dirlan, G., "A View of Construction in MN/DOT Management," *The PM Network* 2, no. 5 (November 1988): 19.

For example, the slack for activity 2-4 is computed as follows.

$$\begin{aligned} S_{24} &= LS_{24} - ES_{24} \\ &= 4 - 3 \\ &= 1 \text{ month} \end{aligned}$$

If the start of activity 2-4 were delayed for 1 month, the activity could still be completed by month 5 without delaying the project completion time. The slack for each activity in our example project network is shown in Table 17.1 and Figure 17.9. Inspection of Table 17.1 shows that there is no slack for the activities on the critical path (marked with an asterisk). All other activities not on the critical path do have slack.

TABLE 17.1 Activity Slack

Activity	*LS*	*ES*	*LF*	*EF*	*Slack S*
* 1-2	0	0	3	3	0
2-3	3	3	5	5	0
2-4	4	3	5	4	1
* 3-4	5	5	5	5	0
4-5	6	5	7	6	1
* 4-6	5	5	8	8	0
5-6	7	6	8	7	1
* 6-7	8	8	9	9	0

* = critical path.

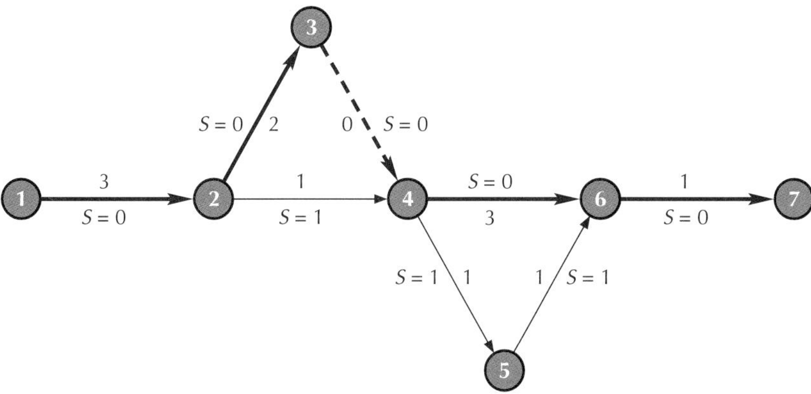

FIGURE 17.9 Activity Slack

Before we conclude our discussion of slack, we discuss one additional matter. Notice that activities 4-5 and 5-6 in Figure 17.9 can be delayed 1 month, but both activities cannot be delayed 1 month. If activity 4-5 starts at month 6 instead of 5, then it will be completed at month 7, which will not allow the start of activity 5-6 to be delayed. The opposite is also true. If 4-5 starts at month 5, activity 5-6 can be delayed 1 month. The slack on these two activities is referred to as *shared slack*. This means that the sequence of activities 4-5-6 can be delayed 1 month jointly without delaying the project.

Slack is obviously beneficial to the project manager, since it enables resources to be temporarily pulled away from activities with slack and used for other activities that might be delayed for various reasons or for which the time estimate has proved to be inaccurate.

The times for the network activities are simply estimates, for which there is usually not a lot of historical basis (since projects tend to be unique undertakings). As such, activity time estimates are subject to quite a bit of uncertainty. However, the uncertainty inherent in activity time estimates can be reflected to a certain extent by using probabilistic time estimates instead of the single, deterministic estimates we have used so far.

Since its inception a primary use of the CPM/PERT project management technique has been to manage and control construction projects of all types. Federal and state agencies often require contractors to develop and submit CPM/PERT networks for the construction of highways and roads, buildings, and other public facilities. Project management techniques provide an effective means to avoid delays and budget overruns for projects that may include hundreds or even thousands of subcontractors, such as the construction of this bridge across the Mississippi River at Alton, Illinois, near St. Louis.

PROBABILISTIC ACTIVITY TIMES

In the project network for building a house presented in the previous section, all the activity time estimates were single values. By using only a single activity time estimate, we are, in effect, assuming that activity times are known with certainty (i.e., they are deterministic). For example, in Figure 17.3, the time estimate for activity 2-3 (laying the foundation) is shown to be 2 months. Since only this one value is given, we must assume that the activity time does not vary (or varies very little) from 2 months. In reality, however, it is rare that activity time estimates can be made with certainty. Projects that are networked are likely to be unique. Thus there is little historical evidence that can be used as a basis to predict activity times. However, recall that we earlier indicated that one of the primary differences between CPM and PERT was that PERT used probabilistic activity times. It is this approach to estimating activity times for a project network that we will discuss in this section.

Probabilistic Time Estimates

Probabilistic time estimates reflect uncertainty of activity times.

A **beta distribution** is a probability distribution traditionally used in CPM/PERT.

Teaching Note 17.3 The Beta Distribution

In the PERT-type approach to estimating activity times, three time estimates for each activity are determined, which enables us to estimate the mean and variance of a **beta distribution** of the activity times.

We assume that the activity times can be described by a beta distribution for several reasons. The beta distribution mean and variance can be approximated with three time estimates. Also, the beta distribution is continuous, but it has no predetermined shape (such as the bell shape of the normal curve). It will take on the shape indicated—that is, be skewed—by the time estimates given. This is beneficial, since typically we have no prior knowledge of the shapes of the distributions of activity times in a unique project network. Although other types of distributions have been shown to be no more or less accurate than the beta, it has become traditional to use the beta distribution to estimate probabilistic activity times.

Time estimates for an activity are **optimistic** (*a*), **most likely** (*m*), and **pessimistic** (*b*) times.

The three time estimates for each activity are the **most likely time** (*m*), the **optimistic time** (*a*), and the **pessimistic time** (*b*). The most likely time is the time that would most frequently occur if the activity were repeated many times. The optimistic time is the shortest possible time within which the activity could be completed if everything went right. The pessimistic time is the longest possible time the activity would require to be completed assuming everything went wrong. In general, the person most familiar with an activity or the project manager makes these "subjective" estimates to the best of his or her knowledge and ability.

These three time estimates are subsequently used to estimate the mean and variance of a beta distribution, computed as follows:

Transparency 17.5 Estimates for Beta Distribution

$$\text{Mean (expected time):} \quad t = \frac{a + 4m + b}{6}$$

$$\text{Variance:} \quad \sigma^2 = \left(\frac{b - a}{6}\right)^2$$

where

a = optimistic time estimate

m = most likely time estimate

b = pessimistic time estimate

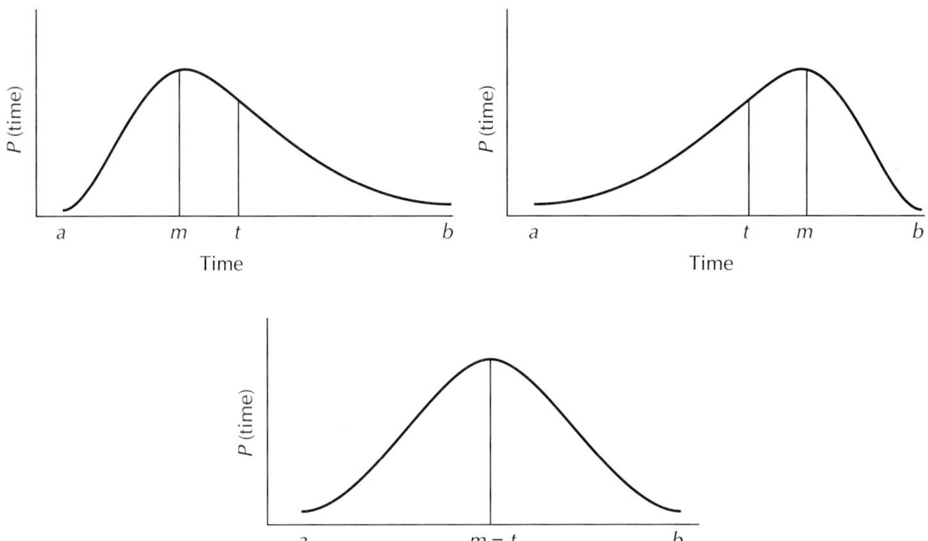

FIGURE 17.10 Examples of the Beta Distribution

These formulas provide a reasonable estimate of the mean and variance of the beta distribution, a distribution that is continuous and can take on various shapes, or exhibit skewness.

Figure 17.10 illustrates the general form of beta distributions for different relative values of *a*, *m*, and *b*.

EXAMPLE 17.1

A Project Network with Probabilistic Time Estimates

Alternate Example 17.1

Problem Statement:

The Southern Textile Company has decided to install a new computerized order-processing system. In the past, orders for the cloth the company produces were processed manually, which contributed to delays in delivering orders and resulted in lost sales. The new system will greatly enhance the quality of the service the company provides its customers. The company wants to develop a CPM/PERT network for the installation of the new system.

The network for the installation of the new order-processing system is shown in the accompanying figure. We briefly describe the activities. The network begins with three concurrent activities: the new computer equipment is installed (activity 1-2); the computerized order-processing system is developed (activity 1-3); and people are recruited to operate the system (activity 1-4). Once people are hired, they are trained for the job (activity 4-5), and other personnel in the company, such as marketing, accounting, and production personnel, are introduced to the new system (activity 4-8). Once the system is developed (activity 1-3) it is tested manually to make sure that it is logical (activity 3-5). Following activity 1-2, the new equipment is tested, any necessary modifications are made (activity 2-6), and the newly trained personnel begin training on the computerized system (activity 5-7). Also, event 5 begins the testing of the system on the computer to check for errors (activity 5-8). The final activities include a trial run and changeover to the system (activity 7-9), and final debugging of the computer system (activity 6-9).

Transparency 17.6 Project Network for Order-Processing System and Activity Scheduling

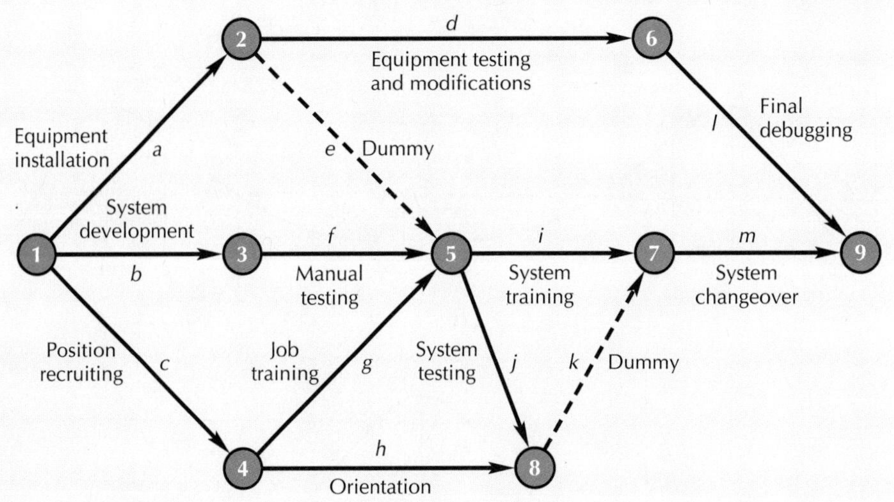

The three time estimates, the mean, and the variance for all the activities in the network as shown in the figure are provided in the table below.

Transparency 17.7 Activity Time Estimates for Project Network

Activity Time Estimates for Example 17.1

	Time Estimates (weeks)			*Mean Time*	*Variance*
Activity	*a*	*m*	*b*	*t*	σ^2
1-2	6	8	10	8	0.44
1-3	3	6	9	6	1.00
1-4	1	3	5	3	0.44
2-5	0	0	0	0	0.00
2-6	2	4	12	5	2.78
3-5	2	3	4	3	0.11
4-5	3	4	5	4	0.11
4-8	2	2	2	2	0.00
5-7	3	7	11	7	1.78
5-8	2	4	6	4	0.44
8-7	0	0	0	0	0.00
6-9	1	4	7	4	1.00
7-9	1	10	13	9	4.00

Solution:

As an example of the computation of the individual activity mean times and variance, consider activity 1-2. The three time estimates ($a = 6$, $m = 8$, $b = 10$) are substituted in the formulas as follows:

$$t = \frac{a + 4m + b}{6}$$

$$= \frac{6 + 4(8) + 10}{6}$$

$$= 8 \text{ weeks}$$

$$\sigma^2 = \left(\frac{b - a}{6}\right)^2$$

$$= \left(\frac{10 - 6}{6}\right)^2$$

$$= \frac{4}{9} \text{ week}$$

The other values for the mean and variance in the following table are computed similarly.

Once the expected times have been computed for each activity, we can determine the critical path the same way we did in the deterministic time network, except that we use the expected activity times, t. Recall that in the home building project network, we identified the critical path as the one containing those activities with zero slack. This requires the determination of earliest and latest start and finish times for each activity, as shown in the accompanying table and figure.

Activity Earliest and Latest Times and Slack

Activity	*t*	σ^2	*ES*	*EF*	*LS*	*LF*	*S*
1-2	8	0.44	0	8	1	9	1
1-3	6	1.00	0	6	0	6	0
1-4	3	0.44	0	3	2	5	2
2-5	0	0.00	8	8	9	9	1
2-6	5	2.78	8	13	16	21	8
3-5	3	0.11	6	9	6	9	0
4-5	4	0.11	3	7	5	9	2
4-8	2	0.00	3	5	14	16	11
5-7	7	1.78	9	16	9	16	0
5-8	4	0.44	9	13	12	16	3
8-7	0	0.00	13	13	16	16	3
6-9	4	1.00	13	17	21	25	8
7-9	9	4.00	16	25	16	25	0

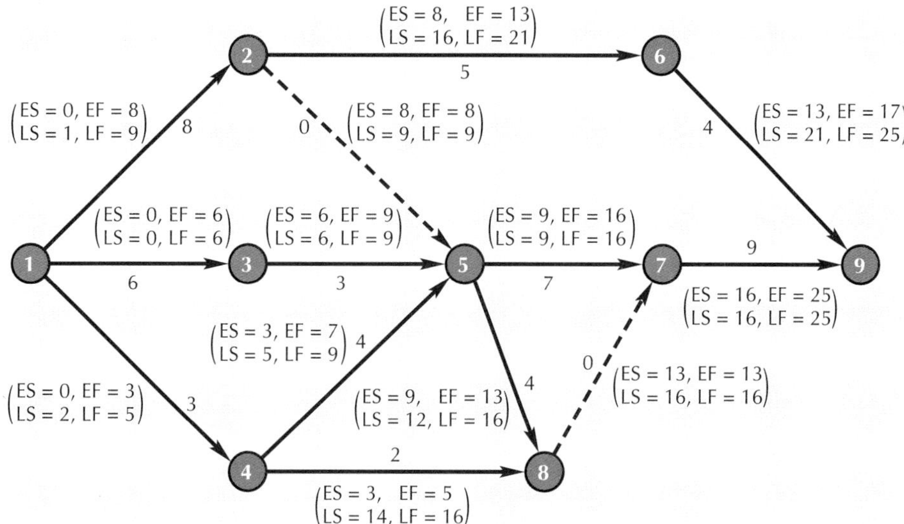

From the table, we can see that the critical path encompasses activities 1-3-5-7-9, since these activities have no available slack. We can also see that the expected project completion time (t_p) is the same as the earliest or latest finish for activity 7-9, or $t_p = 25$ weeks. To determine the project variance, we *sum the variances for those activities on the critical path.* Using the variances shown in the table above for the critical path activities, the total project variance can be computed as follows:

Project variance is the sum of variances on the critical path.

$$\begin{aligned}\sigma^2 &= \sigma_{13}^2 + \sigma_{35}^2 + \sigma_{57}^2 + \sigma_{79}^2 \\ &= 1.00 + 0.11 + 1.78 + 4.00 \\ &= 6.89 \text{ weeks}\end{aligned}$$

Probabilistic Network Analysis

The CPM/PERT method assumes that the activity times are statistically independent, which allows us to sum the individual expected activity times and variances in order to get an expected project time and variance. It is further assumed that the network mean and variance are normally distributed. This assumption is based on the central limit theorem of probability, which for CPM/PERT analysis and our purposes states that if the number of activities is large enough and the activities are statistically independent, then the sum of the means of the activities along the critical path will approach the mean of a normal distribution. For the small examples in this chapter, it is questionable whether there are sufficient activities to guarantee that the mean project completion time and variance are normally distributed. Although it has become conventional in CPM/PERT analysis to employ probability analysis using the normal distribution regardless of the network size, the prudent user should bear this limitation in mind.

Probabilistic analysis of a CPM/PERT network is the determination of the probability that the project will be completed within a certain time period given the mean and variance of a normally distributed project completion time. This is illustrated in Figure 17.11. The value Z is computed using the following formula:

$$Z = \frac{x - \mu}{\sigma}$$

where

$\mu = t_p$ = project mean time

x = the proposed project time

Z = number of standard deviations x is from the mean.

This value of Z is then used to find the corresponding probability in Table B.3 (Appendix B).

Transparency 17.8 Normal Distribution of Project Time

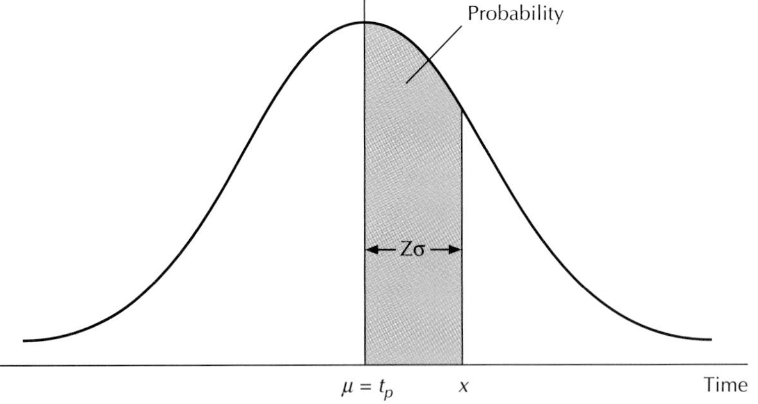

FIGURE 17.11 Normal Distribution of Project Time

EXAMPLE 17.2

Probabilistic Analysis of the Project Network

Problem Statement:

The Southern Textile Company introduced in Example 17.1 has told its customers that the new order-processing system will be completely operational in 30 weeks. What is the probability that the system will, in fact, be ready by that time?

Solution:
The probability that the project will be completed within 30 weeks is shown as the shaded area in the accompanying figure. To compute the Z value for a time of 30 weeks, we must first compute the standard deviation (σ) from the variance (σ^2).

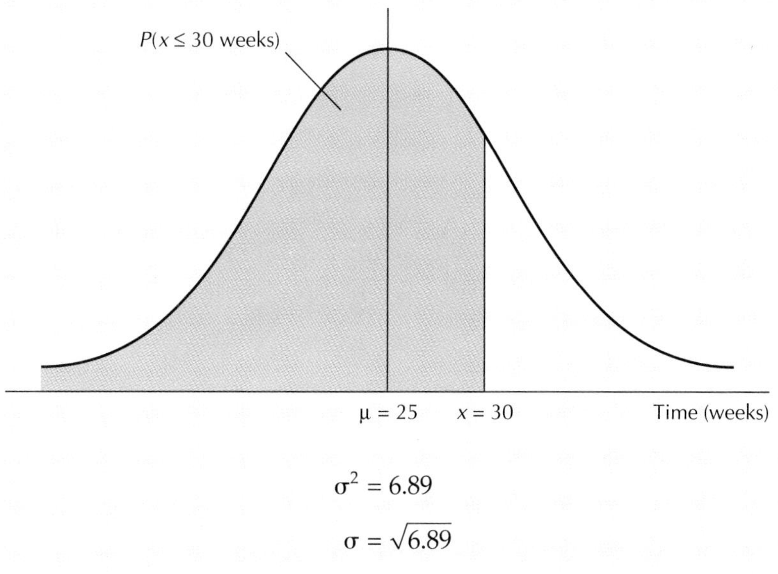

$$\sigma^2 = 6.89$$
$$\sigma = \sqrt{6.89}$$
$$= 2.62$$

Next we substitute this value for the standard deviation along with the value for the mean, 25 weeks, and our proposed project completion time, 30 weeks, into the following formula:

$$Z = \frac{x - \mu}{\sigma}$$
$$= \frac{30 - 25}{2.62}$$
$$= 1.91$$

A Z value of 1.91 corresponds to a probability of 0.4719 in Table B.3 in Appendix B. This means that there is a 0.9719 (0.5000 + 0.4719) probability of completing the project in 30 weeks or less.

EXAMPLE 17.3
Probabilistic Analysis of the Project Network

Problem Statement:
A customer of the Southern Textile Company in Example 17.1 has become frustrated with delayed orders and has told the company that if the new ordering system is not working within 22 weeks, they will not do any more business with the textile company. What is the probability the order processing system will be operational within 22 weeks?

Solution:
The probability that the project will be completed within 22 weeks is shown as the shaded area in the accompanying figure.

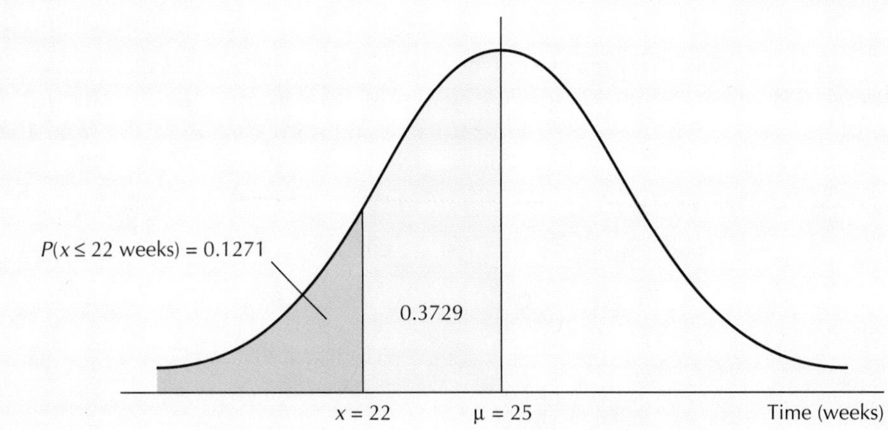

The probability of the project's being completed within 22 weeks is computed as follows:

$$\begin{aligned} Z &= \frac{22 - 25}{2.62} \\ &= \frac{-3}{2.62} \\ &= -1.14 \end{aligned}$$

A Z value of –1.14 corresponds to a probability of 0.3729 in Table B.3 of Appendix B. Thus, there is only a 0.1271 (i.e., 0.5000 – 0.3729) probability that the system will be operational in 22 weeks.

COMPUTER ANALYSIS OF CPM/PERT

The capability to perform CPM/PERT network analysis is a standard feature of most operations management software packages for the personal computer. To illustrate the application of such software to CPM/PERT analysis, we will employ the AB:POM package with our example of installing an order-processing system at the Southern Textile Company in Example 17.1. The program input and network output are shown in Exhibit 17.1. Note that the output is virtually identical to that of the table on page 843.

Project Management Software for the Personal Computer

Tens of commercial software packages are available for project management.

An article by Wasil and Assad[3] reported that during the period from 1985 to 1988, the number of commercially available project management software packages for personal computers increased from a few to more than 100, and the cost of these packages ranged from several hundred to several thousand dollars. Total sales for these packages were estimated at $51 million for 1987 alone. These figures indicate that project management with CPM/PERT has probably become the most visible and widely used project scheduling technique. Some of the more popular packages include Harvard Total Project Manager, Microsoft Project, Super Project Plus, and Time Line (all of which are at the lower end of the cost scale), MacProject, Project Manager Workbench, OPEN PLAN, and PROMIS. The types of projects to which such software packages have been applied include the construction of a sawmill, installation of software systems at hospitals, departmental reorganizations, development of a communications satellite, military projects, facility and employee re-

[3]Wasil, E., and A. Assad, "Project Management on the PC: Software, Applications, and Trends," *Interfaces* 18, no. 2 (March–April 1988): 75–84.

CPM/PERT Project Scheduling Solution

Number of Activities (1-99) 13

Example 17.1

Project completion time = 25 Project standard deviation - 2.624669

Start Node	End Node	Opt. Time	Likel Time	Pess. Time	Time	ES	EF	LS	LF	slack	sd (σ)
1	2	6	8	10	8	0	8	1	9	1	.66667
1	3	3	6	9	6	0	6	0	6	0	1
1	4	1	3	5	3	0	3	2	5	2	.66667
2	5	0	0	0	0	8	8	9	9	1	0
2	6	2	4	12	5	8	13	16	21	8	1.6667
3	5	2	3	4	3	6	9	6	9	0	.33333
4	5	3	4	5	4	3	7	5	9	2	.33333
4	8	2	2	2	2	3	5	14	16	11	0
5	7	3	7	11	7	9	16	9	16	0	1.3333
5	8	2	4	6	4	9	13	12	16	3	.66667
8	7	0	0	0	0	13	13	16	16	3	0
6	9	1	4	7	4	13	17	21	25	8	1
7	9	1	10	13	9	16	25	16	25	0	2

EXHIBIT 17.1

Transparency 17.9 AB:POM CPM/PERT Project Scheduling

location, and highway construction. In addition, several applications have incorporated the use of project management within management information systems. The availability of powerful, user-friendly project management software packages for the personal computer will only serve to increase the use of this technique.

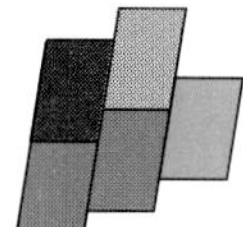

PROJECT CRASHING AND TIME-COST TRADE-OFF

To this point we have demonstrated the use of CPM/PERT network analysis for determining project schedules. This in itself is valuable to a project manager. However, in addition to scheduling projects, the project manager is frequently confronted with the problem of having to reduce the scheduled completion time of a project to meet a deadline. In other words, the manager must finish the project sooner than indicated by the CPM/PERT network analysis. Project duration can often be reduced by assigning more labor to project activities, often in the form of overtime, and by assigning more resources (material, equipment, etc.). However, additional labor and resources increase the overall project cost. Thus, the decision to reduce the project duration must be based on an analysis of the trade-off between time and cost. *Project crashing* is a method for shortening the project duration by reducing the time of one or more of the critical project activities to a time that is less than normal activity time. This reduction in the normal activity time is referred to as **crashing.** Crashing is achieved by devoting more resources, usually measured in terms of dollars, to the activities to be crashed.

Crashing is reducing project time by expending additional resources.

Project Crashing

To demonstrate how project crashing works, we will employ the CPM/PERT network for constructing a house first introduced in Figure 17.3. This network is repeated in Figure 17.12, except that the activity times previously shown as months have been converted to weeks. Although this example network encompasses only single-activity time estimates, the project crashing procedure can be applied in the same manner to PERT networks with probabilistic activity time estimates.

GAINING THE COMPETITIVE EDGE

Project Management Trends in the Utilities Industry

Electric power utilities have been active users of computer-based project management systems for more than 20 years. In many ways the use of project management in the utilities industry reflects the trends in the use of project management in general. Originally project management applications focused on large projects for constructing new generating plants and a primary tool was CPM networks. Since the mid-1970s virtually all power plant construction has included a computerized project management system. Utilities such as Northeast Utilities, Arkansas Power and Light, and Florida Power and Light all have their own project management staffs to oversee plant construction. For example, Northeast Utilities maintains a centralized project management staff of 700. In 1987 the project management teams of the Los Angeles Department of Water and Power used computerized CPM scheduling to develop a $1.6 billion coal-fired generating station.

Beginning in the late 1970s utilities began using project management techniques to control nuclear refueling outages at nuclear power plants. For example, Florida Power and Light has made extensive use of project management techniques, and specifically PROJECT/2 project management software, to control outages at their nuclear power plants. These efforts resulted in cost savings of $2.6 million during two outages and an average 4-day reduction in outage durations as well as timely execution of scheduled project work.

During the late 1980s and early 1990s, as construction of large nuclear power plants slowed, emphasis shifted from large construction projects to smaller "retrofit" projects to upgrade equipment and generally rejuvenate older plants. These smaller projects require control procedures to be more sophisticated, faster, and efficient. Another recent trend is toward *distributed project management* in which line management and supervisors are given responsibility for project planning, scheduling, and control. As an example, in a 1987 project by Combustion Engineering working closely with Korea Electric Power Company to design a new power plant, each of 20 supervisory engineers were provided with PC-based project management software packages to build their own networks. These networks were then uploaded to a scheduling system on a mainframe computer to create a single network of 17,000 activities, constraints, and resources. This example points out another trend in project management, the extensive use of personal computers for project management in the utilities industry. As an example, Pacific Gas and Electric Company, a large utility company with approximately 30,000 employees at 120 sites and offices, uses PC-based project management software on all projects with a value of $50,000 or more. Projects include design and construction of power plants, environmental studies, and research and development efforts.

Source: Based on Wallace, R. C., "History of the Project Management Applications in the Utility Industry," *Project Management Journal* 21, no. 3 (September 1990): 5–10.

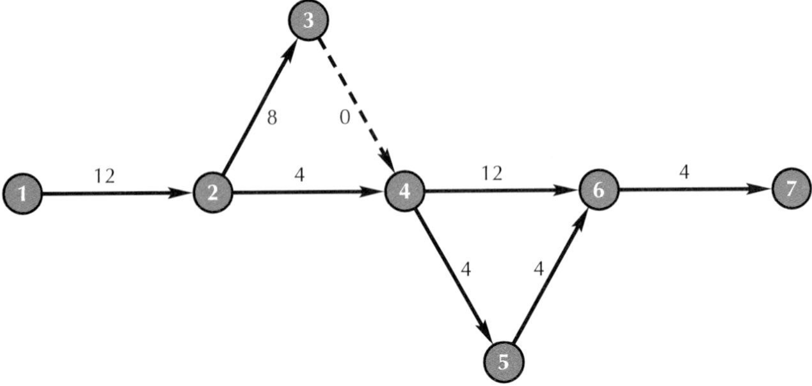

FIGURE 17.12 The Project Network for Building a House

In Figure 17.12, we will assume that the times (in weeks) shown on the network activities are the normal activity times. For example, 12 weeks are normally required to complete activity 1-2. Further, we will assume that the cost required to complete this activity in the time indicated is $3,000. This cost is referred to as the *normal activity cost.* Next, we will assume that the building contractor has estimated that activity 1-2 can be completed in 7 weeks, but it will cost $5,000 instead of $3,000 to complete the activity. This new estimated activity time is known as the **crash time,** and the cost necessary to achieve the crash time is referred to as the **crash cost.**

Crash time is an amount of time an activity is reduced; **crash cost** is the cost of reducing activity time.

Activity 1-2 can be crashed a total of 5 weeks (normal time – crash time = 12 – 7 = 5 weeks) at a total crash cost of $2,000 (crash cost – normal cost = $5,000 – 3,000 = $2,000). Dividing the total crash cost by the total allowable crash time yields the crash cost per week:

$$\frac{\text{Total crash cost}}{\text{Total crash time}} = \frac{\$2{,}000}{5} = \$400 \text{ per week}$$

If we assume that the relationship between crash cost and crash time is linear, then activity 1-2 can be crashed by any amount of time (not exceeding the maximum allowable crash time) at a rate of $400 per week. For example, if the contractor decided to crash activity 1-2 by only 2 weeks (for an activity time of 10 weeks), the crash cost would be $800 ($400 per week × 2 weeks). The linear relationships between crash cost and crash time and between normal cost and normal time are illustrated in Figure 17.13.

The objective of project crashing is to reduce project duration while minimizing the cost of crashing. Since the project completion time can be shortened only by crashing activities on the critical path, it may turn out that not all activities have to be crashed. However, as activities are crashed, the critical path may change, requiring crashing of previously noncritical activities to reduce the project completion time even further.

The goal of crashing is to reduce project duration at minimum cost.

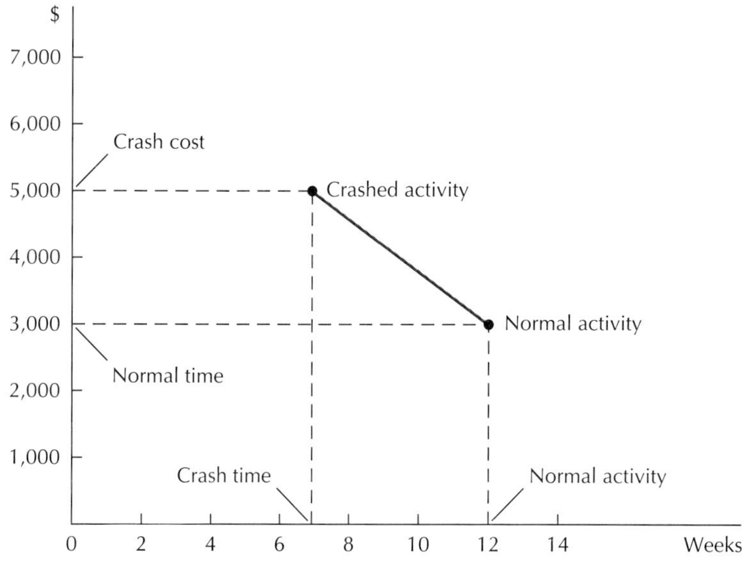

FIGURE 17.13 The Relationship Between Normal Time and Cost, and Crash Time and Cost

EXAMPLE 17.4

Project Crashing

Problem Statement:

Recall that the critical path for the house-building network in Figure 17.12 encompassed activities 1-2-3-4-6-7 and the project duration was 9 months, or 36 weeks. Suppose that the home builder needed the house in 30 weeks and wanted to know how much extra cost would be incurred to complete the house by this time.

The normal times and costs, the crash times and costs, the total allowable crash times, and the crash cost per week for each activity in the network in Figure 17.12 are summarized in the accompanying table.

Transparency 17.10 Project Network with Crashing

Normal Activity and Crash Data

Activity	*Normal Time (weeks)*	*Crash Time (weeks)*	*Normal Cost*	*Crash Cost*	*Total Allowable Crash Time (weeks)*	*Crash Cost per Week*
1-2	12	7	$ 3,000	$ 5,000	5	$ 400
2-3	8	5	2,000	3,500	3	500
2-4	4	3	4,000	7,000	1	3,000
3-4	0	0	0	0	0	0
4-5	4	1	500	1,100	3	200
4-6	12	9	50,000	71,000	3	7,000
5-6	4	1	500	1,100	3	200
6-7	4	3	15,000	22,000	1	7,000
			75,000	$110,700		

Solution:

We start the crashing process by looking at the critical path and seeing which activity has the minimum crash cost per week. Observing the table above and the figure below, we see that activity 1-2 has the minimum crash cost of $400 (excluding the dummy activity 3-4, which cannot be reduced). Thus, activity 1-2 will be reduced as much as possible. The table shows that the maximum allowable reduction for activity 1-2 is 5 weeks, but we can reduce activity 1-2 only to the point where another path becomes critical. When two paths simultaneously become critical, activities on both must be reduced by the same amount. If we reduce the activity time beyond the point where another path becomes critical, we may be incurring an unnecessary cost. This last stipulation means that we must keep up with all the network paths as we reduce individual activities, a condition that makes manual crashing very cumbersome. Later we demonstrate the use of the computer for project crashing; however, for the moment we pursue this example in order to demonstrate the logic of project crashing.

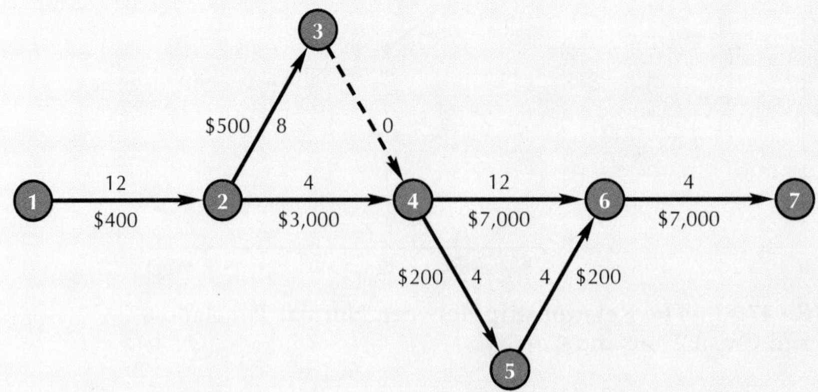

It turns out that activity 1-2 can be crashed by the total amount of 5 weeks without another path becoming critical, since activity 1-2 is included in all four paths in the network. Crashing this activity results in a revised project duration of 31 weeks at a crashing cost of $2,000. The revised network is shown in the figure on page 851.

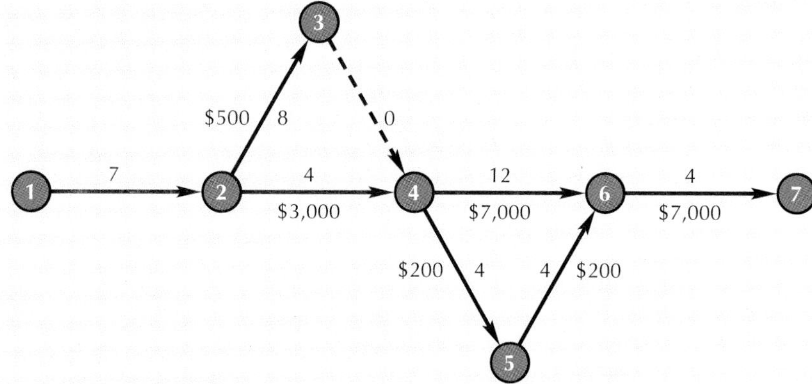

This process must now be repeated. The critical path in the figure above remains the same, and the minimum activity crash cost on the critical path is $500 for activity 2-3. Activity 2-3 can be crashed a total of 3 weeks, but since the contractor desires to crash the network only to 30 weeks, we need to crash activity 2-3 by only 1 week. Crashing activity 1-2 by 1 week does not result in any other path becoming critical, so we can safely make this reduction. Crashing activity 2-3 to 7 weeks (i.e., a 1-week reduction) costs $500 and reduces the project duration to 30 weeks.

The total cost of crashing the project to 30 weeks is $2,500. Thus, the contractor could inform the customer that an additional cost of only $2,500 would be incurred to finish the house in 30 weeks.

As indicated earlier, the manual procedure for crashing a network is very cumbersome and is generally unacceptable for project crashing. It is basically a trial-and-error approach that is useful for demonstrating the logic of crashing. However, it quickly becomes unmanageable for larger networks. This approach would have become difficult if we had pursued even the house-building example to a crash time greater than 30 weeks, with more than one path becoming critical.

When more than one path does become critical, all critical paths must be reduced by an equal amount. Since the possibility exists that an additional path might become critical each time the network is reduced by even one unit of time (i.e., 1 week, month, etc.) this means that a reduction of one time unit is the maximum amount that can be considered at each crashing step. This situation is addressed in the following example.

EXAMPLE 17.5

Project Crashing

Problem Statement:

A CPM/PERT project network for the construction of a loading dock facility at the Southern Textile Company is shown in the accompanying figure. The network

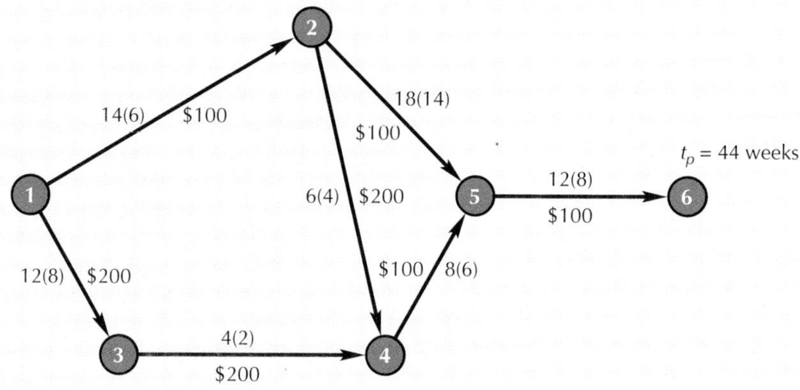

includes normal and crash times as well as crash costs, as shown in the table. The company wants to crash the network from the current critical path (1-2-5-6) project time of 44 weeks to 30 weeks.

Normal and Crash Times and Crash Costs

	Time (Weeks)		*Cost ($)*		
Activity	*Normal*	*Crash*	*Normal*	*Crash*	*Crash Cost per week*
1-2	14	6	1,400	2,200	100
1-3	12	8	1,000	1,800	200
2-5	18	14	1,600	2,000	100
2-4	6	4	800	1,200	200
3-4	4	2	400	800	200
4-5	8	6	400	600	100
5-6	12	8	800	1,200	100
			6,400	9,800	

Solution:

First, identify the activity on the critical path with the minimum crash cost per week. Since it is the same for each activity on the critical path, arbitrarily select activity (1-2) to crash. It can be crashed by 8 weeks to its lower limit of 6 weeks without another path becoming critical. The associated crashing cost is $800 ($100 × 8), yielding a total project cost of $7,200 ($6,400 + $800). The revised network is shown in the figure below. Note that there are now two critical paths, 1-2-5-6 and 1-3-4-5-6, each with a project time of 36 weeks.

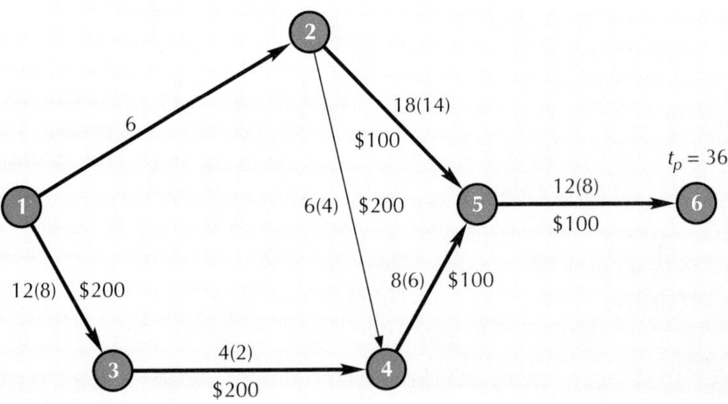

Next, select the activity or activities on the critical paths with the minimum crashing cost(s) that will reduce the total project time. By crashing activity 5-6, project time can be reduced without crashing more than one activity. If project time could be reduced at less cost by crashing two activities (on one or both of the two critical paths), this should be done. However, in this case, the least-cost option is to crash activity 5-6 by 4 weeks to its lower limit of 8 weeks at a cost of $400, resulting in a total project cost of $7,600. The revised network is shown in the following figure. Project time has been reduced to 32 weeks; however, the critical paths remain 1-2-5-6 and 1-3-4-5-6.

We repeat the same crashing process used before. Select the activity or activities that can be crashed at the minimum crashing cost and that result in a

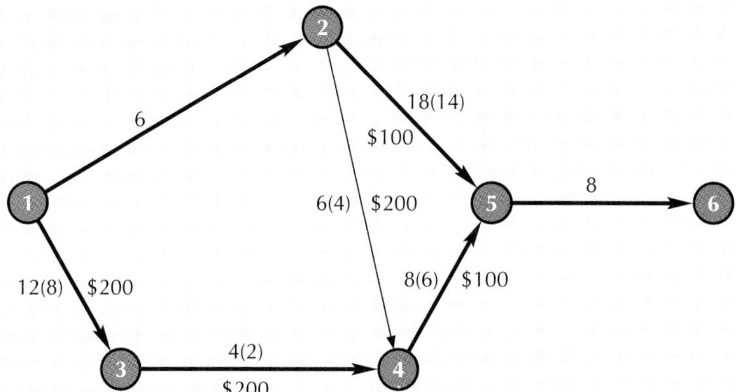

reduction in project time. Since there is no single activity shared by both critical paths that has not been crashed, select two activities (one from each critical path) to be crashed at minimum crashing cost. If only a single activity is crashed on one of the critical paths, the other critical path will remain critical (unshortened), and the total project time will remain unchanged. Therefore, select two activities (one from each critical path) that result in the minimum aggregate weekly crashing cost.

Activity 2-5 is selected from path 1-2-5-6, as it is the only remaining activity not crashed. Activity 4-5 is selected on path 1-3-4-5-6, since it has the least weekly crashing cost. Determine which of the two activities selected for crashing can be crashed by the least amount, and crash each activity by that amount. Although activity 2-5 can be crashed by 4 weeks, activity 4-5 can be crashed by only 2 weeks. Therefore, activity 4-5 is crashed by 2 weeks to its lower limit of 6 weeks, and activity 2-5 is crashed by 2 weeks to a duration of 16 weeks. Note that it makes no sense to crash 2-5 further, since it would not shorten the overall project time, because of critical path 1-3-4-5-6. The cost of crashing activities 2-5 and 4-5 is $200 each, yielding a total crashing cost of $400 and a total project cost of $8,000. The revised network with a total project time of 30 weeks, the company's objective, is shown in the figure below.

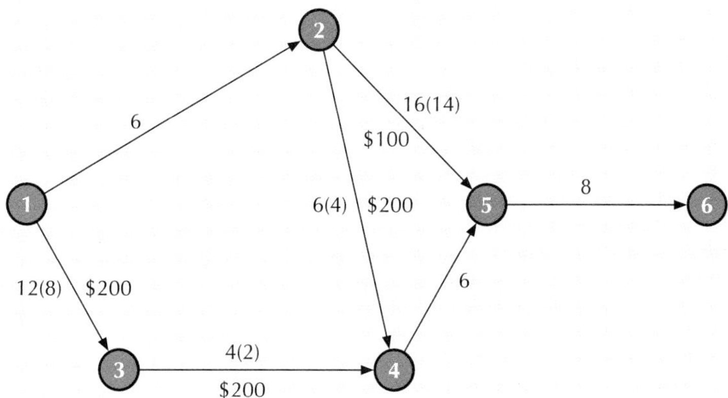

Project Crashing with the Computer

Manually crashing a network is a cumbersome and time-consuming process, even for small networks like our examples. As such, a computer program for project crashing is a virtual necessity for most realistically sized project networks. However, although almost all operations management and quantitative methods software packages have the capability of performing CPM/PERT network analysis,

Teaching Note 17.4 Project Crashing with Linear Programming

not all such packages have a project crashing module. An exception is the quantitative methods software package AB:QM version 3.0 by Lee Sang M., published by Allyn and Bacon. We will use this package to demonstrate the computer determination of project crashing.

The AB:QM project crashing program outputs for Examples 17.4 and 17.5 are shown in Exhibits 17.2 and 17.3.

The General Relationship of Time and Cost

Crashing costs increase as project time decreases; indirect costs increase as project time increases.

Transparency 17.11 AB:POM Project Crashing

In our discussion of project crashing, we demonstrated how the project critical path time could be reduced by increasing expenditures for labor and other direct resources. The implicit objective of crashing was to reduce the scheduled completion time for its own sake—that is, to reap the results of the project sooner. However, there may be other important reasons for reducing project time. As projects continue over time, they consume various *indirect costs*, including the cost of facilities, equipment, and machinery, interest on investment, utilities, labor, personnel costs, and the loss of skills and labor from members of the project team who are not working at their regular jobs. There also may be direct financial penalties for not completing a project on time. For example, many construction contracts and government contracts have penalty clauses for exceeding the project completion date.

In general, project crashing costs and indirect costs have an inverse relationship; crashing costs are highest when the project is shortened, whereas indirect

Program: CPM/PERT / CPM With Crashing

Problem Title: Example 17.4

***** Input Data *****

			TIME		COST	
Activity	Start	End	Normal	Crash	Normal	Crash
1	1	2	12.000	7.000	3000.000	5000.000
2	2	3	8.000	5.000	2000.000	3500.000
3	2	4	4.000	3.000	4000.000	7000.000
4	3	4	0.000	0.000	0.000	0.000
5	4	5	4.000	1.000	500.000	1100.000
6	4	6	12.000	9.000	50000.000	71000.000
7	5	6	4.000	1.000	500.000	1100.000
8	6	7	4.000	3.000	15000.000	22000.000

***** Program Output *****

Activity	Activity Nodes	Crash by	Crashing Cost	Activity Time	Activity Cost
1 *	1→2	5.000	2000.000	7.000	5000.000
2 *	2→3	1.000	500.000	7.000	2500.000
3	2→4	0.000	0.000	4.000	4000.000
4 *	3→4	0.000	0.000	0.000	0.000
5	4→5	0.000	0.000	4.000	500.000
6 *	4→6	0.000	0.000	12.000	50000.000
7	5→6	0.000	0.000	4.000	500.000
8 *	6→7	0.000	0.000	4.000	15000.000
(*: Critical Path Activities)			2500.000		77500.000

Expected Normal Completion Time: 36.000

Expected Crash Completion Time: 30.000

***** End of Output *****

EXHIBIT 17.2

costs increase as the project duration increases. This time-cost relationship is illustrated in Figure 17.14. The best, or optimal, project time is at the minimum point on the total cost curve.

```
Program: CPM/PERT / CPM With Crashing
Problem Title: Example 17.5
***** Input Data *****
```

Activity	Start	End	TIME Normal	TIME Crash	COST Normal	COST Crash
1	1	2	14.000	6.000	1400.000	2200.000
2	1	3	12.000	8.000	1000.000	1800.000
3	2	5	18.000	14.000	1600.000	2000.000
4	2	4	6.000	4.000	800.000	1200.000
5	3	4	4.000	2.000	400.000	800.000
6	4	5	8.000	6.000	400.000	600.000
7	5	6	12.000	8.000	800.000	1200.000

```
***** Program Output *****
```

Activity	Activity Nodes	Crash by	Crashing Cost	Activity Time	Activity Cost
1 *	1→2	8.000	800.000	6.000	2200.000
2 *	1→3	0.000	0.000	12.000	1000.000
3 *	2→5	2.000	200.000	16.000	1800.000
4	2→4	0.000	0.000	6.000	800.000
5 *	3→4	0.000	0.000	4.000	400.000
6 *	4→5	2.000	200.000	6.000	600.000
7 *	5→6	4.000	400.000	8.000	1200.000
(*: Critical Path Activities)			1600.000		8000.000

```
Expected Normal Completion Time:      44.000
Expected Crash Completion Time:       30.000

***** End of Output *****
```

EXHIBIT 17.3

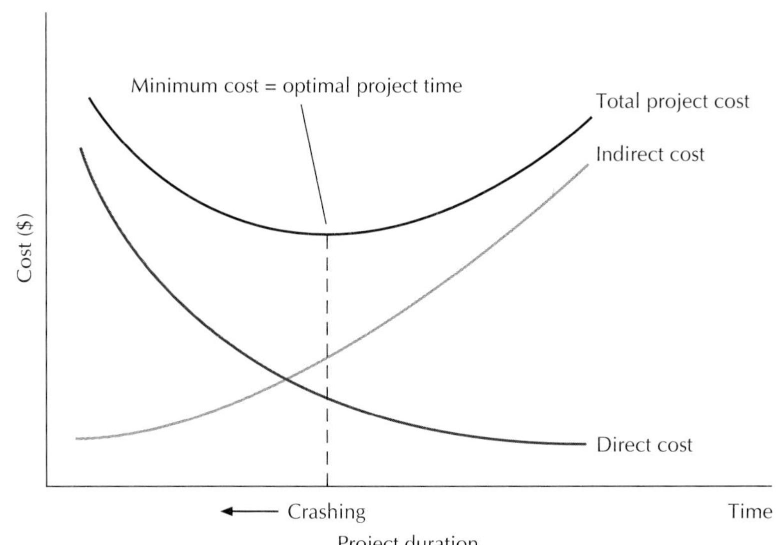

FIGURE 17.14 The Time-Cost Trade-off

Transparency 17.12 The General Relationship of Time and Cost

SUMMARY

Since the initial development of CPM/PERT in the 1950s, it has been applied in a variety of government agencies concerned with project control, including various military agencies, NASA, the Federal Aviation Agency (FAA), and the General Services Administration (GSA). These agencies are frequently involved in large-scale projects involving millions of dollars and many subcontractors. Examples of such governmental projects include the development of weapons systems, aircraft, and such NASA space-exploration projects as the space shuttle. It has become a common practice for these agencies to require subcontractors to develop and use a CPM/PERT analysis in order to maintain management control of the myriad of project components and subprojects.

CPM/PERT has also been widely applied in the private sector. Two of the major areas of application of CPM/PERT in the private sector have been research and development (R&D) and construction. CPM/PERT has been applied to various R&D projects, such as developing new drugs, planning and introducing new products, and developing new and more powerful computer systems. CPM/PERT analysis has been particularly applicable to construction projects. Almost every type of construction project—from building a house, to constructing a major sports stadium, to building a ship, to constructing the Alaska oil pipeline—has been the subject of network analysis.

One reason for this popularity is the fact that a network analysis provides a visual display of the project that is easy for managers and staff to understand and interpret. It is a powerful tool for identifying and organizing the activities in a project and controlling the project schedule. However, beyond that it provides an effective focal point for organizing the efforts of management and the project team.

Despite the popularity of CPM/PERT and its obvious advantages, it also has certain limitations. There tends to be such a heavy reliance by the project manager on the project network that errors in the precedence relationship or missing activities can be overlooked, until a point in time where these omissions become a problem. Attention to critical path activities can become excessive to the extent that other project activities may be neglected or they may be delayed to the point that other paths become critical. Obtaining accurate single-time estimates and even three probabilistic time estimates is difficult and subject to a great deal of uncertainty. Since persons directly associated with the project activity within the organization are typically the primary source for time estimates, they may be overly pessimistic if they have a vested interest in the scheduling process or overly optimistic if they do not. Personal interests aside, it is frequently difficult to define, within the context of an activity, what an optimistic or pessimistic time means. Also, since the inception of CPM/PERT, there has been considerable debate regarding the appropriateness of the beta distribution vis-à-vis other probability distributions for activity times and the resulting accuracy of the project time. Nevertheless, such reservations have not diminished the popularity of CPM/PERT, because most people feel its usefulness far outweighs any speculative or theoretical drawbacks.

SUMMARY OF KEY FORMULAS

Earliest Start and Finish Times

$$\mathrm{EF}_{ij} = \mathrm{ES}_{ij} + t_{ij}$$
$$\mathrm{ES}_{ij} = \max\,(\mathrm{EF}_i)$$

Latest Start and Finish Times

$$LS_{ij} = LF_{ij} - t_{ij}$$
$$LF_{ij} = \min (LS_j)$$

Activity Slack

$$S_{ij} = LS_{ij} - ES_{ij} = LF_{ij} - EF_{ij}$$

Mean Activity Time and Variance

$$t = \frac{a + 4m + b}{6}$$
$$\sigma^2 = \left(\frac{b-a}{6}\right)^2$$

 SUMMARY OF KEY TERMS

activity: performance of an individual job or work effort that requires labor, resources, and time and is subject to management control.

activity-on-arrow (AOA): a convention for constructing a CPM/PERT network in which the branches between nodes represent project activities.

activity-on-node (AON): a convention for constructing a CPM/PERT network in which the nodes represent project activities.

backward pass: starting at the end of a CPM/PERT network, a procedure for determining latest activity times.

beta distribution: a probability distribution traditionally used in CPM/PERT for estimating the mean and variance of project activity times.

crashing: a method for shortening the project duration by reducing the time of one or more critical activities at a cost.

crash cost: the cost of reducing the normal activity time.

crash time: the amount of time an activity is reduced.

critical path: the longest path through a CPM/PERT network, indicating the minimum time in which a project can be completed.

critical path method (CPM): a project scheduling technique in which activities are shown as a network of precedence relationships, traditionally using single-activity time estimates and activity-on-node network construction.

dummy: an activity in a network that shows a precedence relationship but represents no passage of time.

earliest finish time: the earliest time an activity can be completed.

earliest start time: the earliest time an activity can begin subject to preceding activities.

event: the completion or beginning of an activity in a project.

forward pass: starting at the beginning of a CPM/PERT network, a procedure for determining earliest activity times.

Gantt chart: a graphical display using bars (or time lines) to show the duration of project activities and precedence relationships.

latest finish time: the latest time an activity can be completed and still maintain the project critical path time.

latest start time: the latest time an activity can begin and not delay subsequent activities.

matrix organization: an organizational structure of project teams that includes members from various functional areas in the company.

most likely time: the activity that would occur most frequently if the activity were repeated many times.
optimistic time: the shortest possible activity time if everything went right.
pessimistic time: the longest possible activity time given that everything went wrong.
precedence relationship: the sequential relationship of project activities to each other.
project: a unique, one-time operational activity or effort.
project evaluation and review technique (PERT): a project scheduling technique in which activities are shown as a network of precedence relationships, traditionally using probabilistic time estimates and activity-on-arrow network construction.
slack: the amount by which a project activity can be delayed without delaying any of the activities that follow it or the project as a whole.
statement of work: a written description of the objectives of a project.
work breakdown structure (WBS): a methodology for subdividing a project into different hierarchical levels of components.

 *SOLVED PROBLEM*

CPM/PERT Network Analysis

Problem Statement:
Given the following network and activity time estimates, determine earliest and latest activity times, slack, the expected project completion time and variance, and the probability that the project will be completed in 28 days or less.

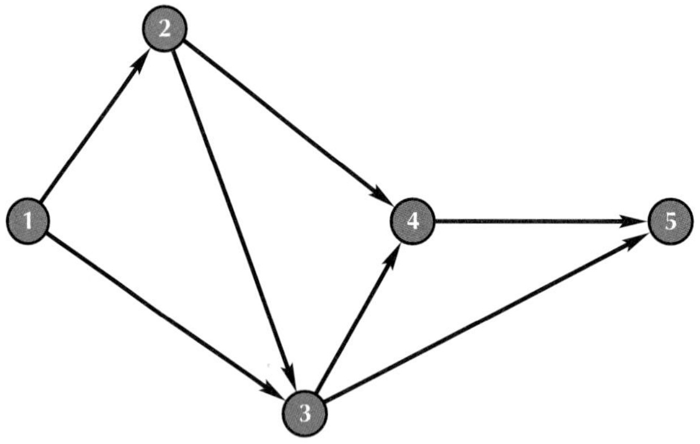

	Time Estimates (weeks)		
Activity	*a*	*m*	*b*
1-2	5	8	17
1-3	7	10	13
2-3	3	5	7
2-4	1	3	5
3-4	4	6	8
3-5	3	3	3
4-5	3	4	5

Solution:

Step 1: Compute the expected activity times and variances using the following formulas.

$$t = \frac{a + 4m + b}{6}$$

$$\sigma^2 = \left(\frac{b - a}{6}\right)^2$$

For example, the expected time and variance for activity 1-2 are

$$t = \frac{5 + 4(8) + 17}{6} = 9$$

$$\sigma^2 = \left(\frac{17 - 5}{6}\right)^2 = 4$$

These values and the remaining expected times and variances for each activity are shown in the following table.

Activity	*t*	σ^2
1-2	9	4
1-3	10	1
2-3	5	4/9
2-4	3	4/9
3-4	6	4/9
3-5	3	0
4-5	4	1/9

Step 2: Determine the earliest and latest activity times and activity slack. The earliest and latest times for all network activities and activity slack are shown in the following table and project network.

Activity	*t*	*ES*	*EF*	*LS*	*LF*	*S*
1-2	9	0	9	0	9	0
1-3	10	0	10	4	14	4
2-3	5	9	14	9	14	0
2-4	3	9	12	17	20	8
3-4	6	14	20	14	20	0
3-5	3	14	17	21	24	7
4-5	4	20	24	20	24	0

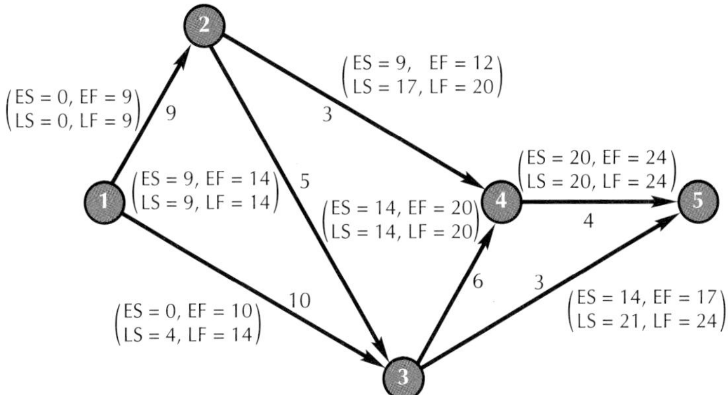

As an example, the earliest start and finish times for activity 1-2 are computed as follows.

$$\begin{aligned} ES_{ij} &= \max (EF_i) \\ ES_{12} &= \max (EF_1) \\ &= 0 \end{aligned}$$

$$\begin{aligned} EF_{ij} &= ES_{ij} + t_{ij} \\ EF_{12} &= ES_{12} + t_{12} \\ &= 0 + 9 \\ &= 9 \end{aligned}$$

The latest start and finish times for activity 4-5 are computed as follows.

$$\begin{aligned} LF_{ij} &= \min (LS_j) \\ LF_{45} &= \min (LS_5) \\ &= 24 \end{aligned}$$

$$\begin{aligned} LS_{ij} &= LF_{ij} - t_{ij} \\ LS_{45} &= LF_{45} - t_{45} \\ &= 24 - 4 \\ &= 20 \end{aligned}$$

Step 3: Identify the critical path and compute expected project completion time and variance. Observing the preceding table and those activities with no slack (i.e., $s = 0$), we can identify the critical path as 1-2-3-4-5. The expected project completion time (t_p) is 24 days. The variance is computed by summing the variances for the activities in the critical path:

$$\begin{aligned} v_p &= 4 + \frac{4}{9} + \frac{4}{9} + \frac{1}{9} \\ &= 5 \text{ days} \end{aligned}$$

Step 4: Determine the probability that the project will be completed in 28 days or less. The following normal probability distribution describes the probability analysis.

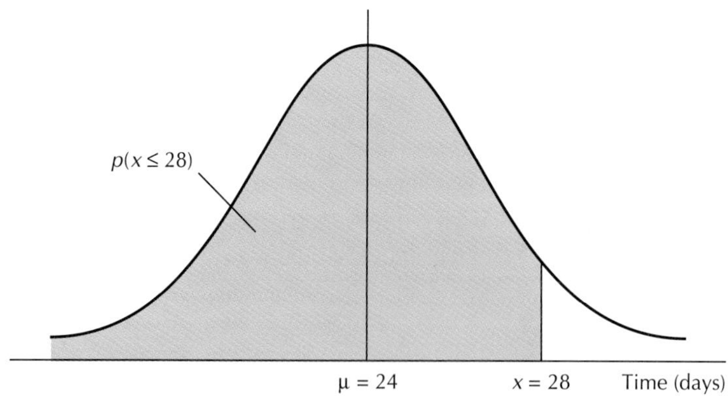

Compute Z using the following formula.

$$\begin{aligned} Z &= \frac{x - \mu}{\sigma} \\ &= \frac{28 - 24}{\sqrt{5}} \\ &= 1.79 \end{aligned}$$

The corresponding probability from Table B.3 (Appendix B) is 0.4633; thus,

$$P(x \leq 28) = 0.9633$$

QUESTIONS

17-1. Why is CPM/PERT a popular and widely applied project scheduling technique?
17-2. What is the purpose of a CPM/PERT network?
17-3. Why are dummy activities used in a CPM/PERT network?
17-4. What is the critical path and what is its importance in project planning?
17-5. What is slack and how is it computed?
17-6. How are the mean activity times and activity variances computed in probabilistic CPM/PERT analysis?
17-7. How is total project variance determined in CPM/PERT analysis?
17-8. What is the purpose of project crashing analysis?
17-9. Describe the process of manually crashing a project network.
17-10. Which method for determining activity time estimates, deterministic or probabilistic, do you perceive to be preferable? Explain.
17-11. Explain how a Gantt chart differs from a CPM/PERT network and indicate the advantage of the latter.
17-12. Discuss the relationship of direct and indirect costs in project management.
17-13. Describe the limitations and disadvantages of CPM/PERT.
17-14. Describe the difference between activity-on-node and activity-on-arrow project networks.
17-15. Identify and briefly describe the major elements of project management.

PROBLEMS

17-1. Construct a Gantt chart for the project described by the following set of activities, and indicate the project completion time.

17-1. See Solutions Manual.

Activity	*Time (weeks)*
1-2	5
1-3	4
2-4	3
3-4	6

17-2. Construct a Gantt chart for the project described by the following set of activities, and indicate the project completion time and the available slack for each activity.

17-2. 17 wk

Activity	*Time (weeks)*
1-2	3
1-3	7
2-4	2
3-4	5
3-5	6
4-6	1
5-6	4

17-3. Using the project activities shown on page 862, determine the following:

17-3. a. 23 wk
b. See Solutions Manual;

a. Construct a Gantt chart; indicate the project completion time and slack for each activity.
b. Construct the CPM/PERT network, compute the length of each path in the network, and indicate the critical path.

Activity	*Time (weeks)*
1-2	4
1-3	7
2-4	8
2-5	3
3-5	9
4-5	5
4-6	2
5-6	6
3-6	5

17-4. 1-3-4-5-6 → 20

17-4. Identify all the paths in the following network, compute the length of each, and indicate the critical path. (Activity times are in weeks.)

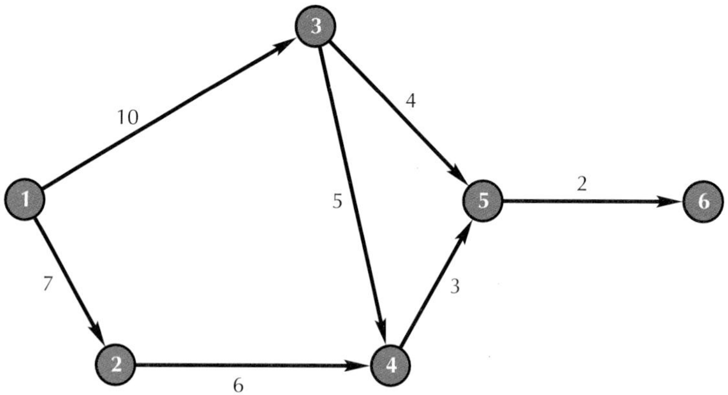

17-5. 1-3-4-5-6

17-5. For the network in Problem 17-4, determine the earliest start and finish times, latest start and finish times, and slack for each activity. Indicate how the critical path would be determined from this information.

17-6. 1-3-5-7-8-9 → 38 mo

17-6. Given the following network with activity times in months, determine the earliest start and finish times, latest start and finish times, and slack for each activity. Indicate the critical path and the project duration.

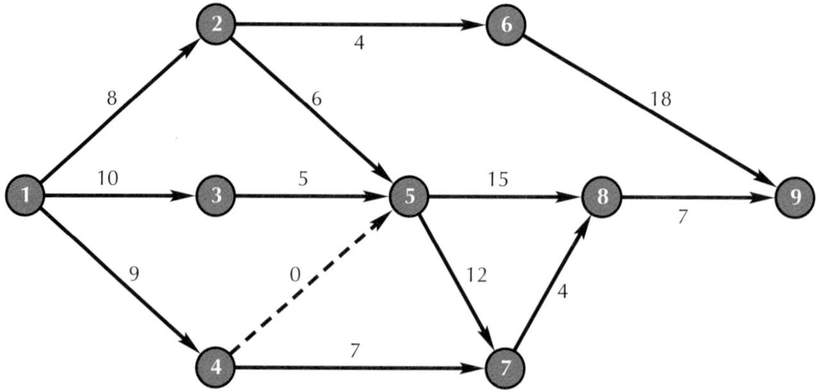

17-7. 1-2-6-7 → 34 wk

17-7. Given the following network with activity times in weeks, determine the earliest start and finish times, latest start and finish times, and slack for each activity. Indicate the critical path and the project duration.

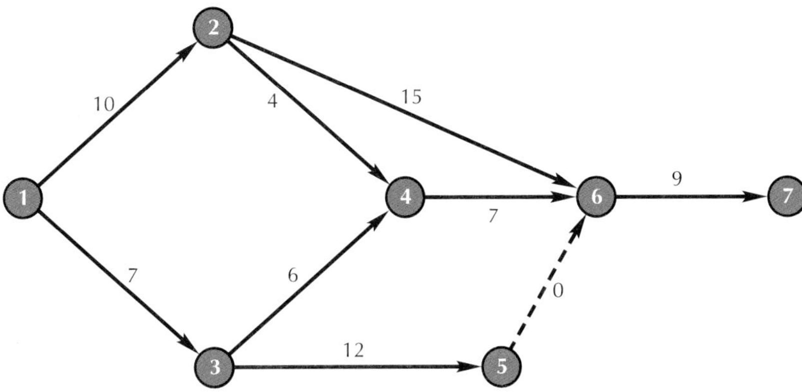

17-8. In one of the little-known battles of the Civil War, General Tecumseh Beuregard lost the Third Battle of Bull Run because his preparations were not complete when the enemy attacked. If the critical path method had been available, the general could have planned better. Suppose that the following project network with activity times in days had been available. Determine the earliest start and finish times, latest start and finish times, and activity slack for the network. Indicate the critical path and the time between the general's receipt of battle orders and the onset of battle. ★ 17-8. 15 d

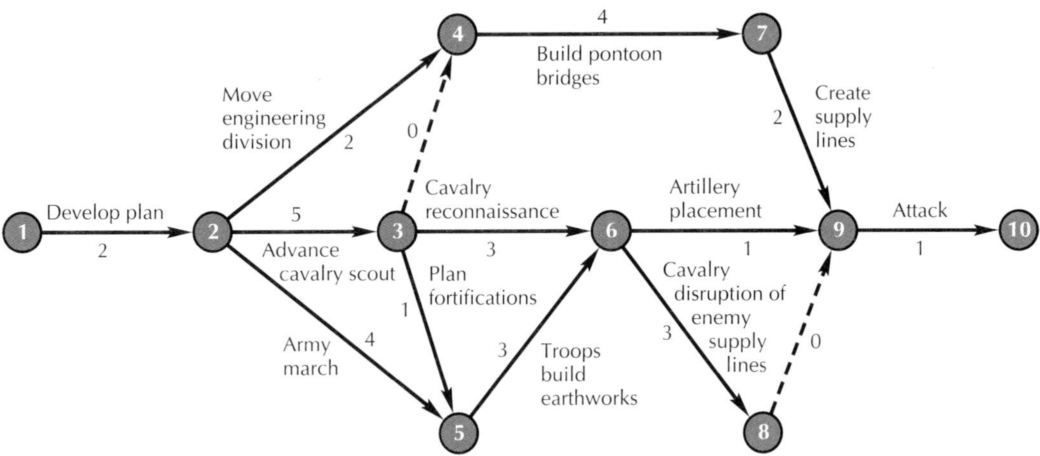

17-9. A group of developers is building a new shopping center. A consultant for the developers has constructed the following CPM/PERT network and assigned activity times in weeks. Determine the earliest start and finish times, latest start and finish times, activity slack, critical path, and duration for the project. ★ 17-9. 1-3-6-10-11-14-15 → 78 wk

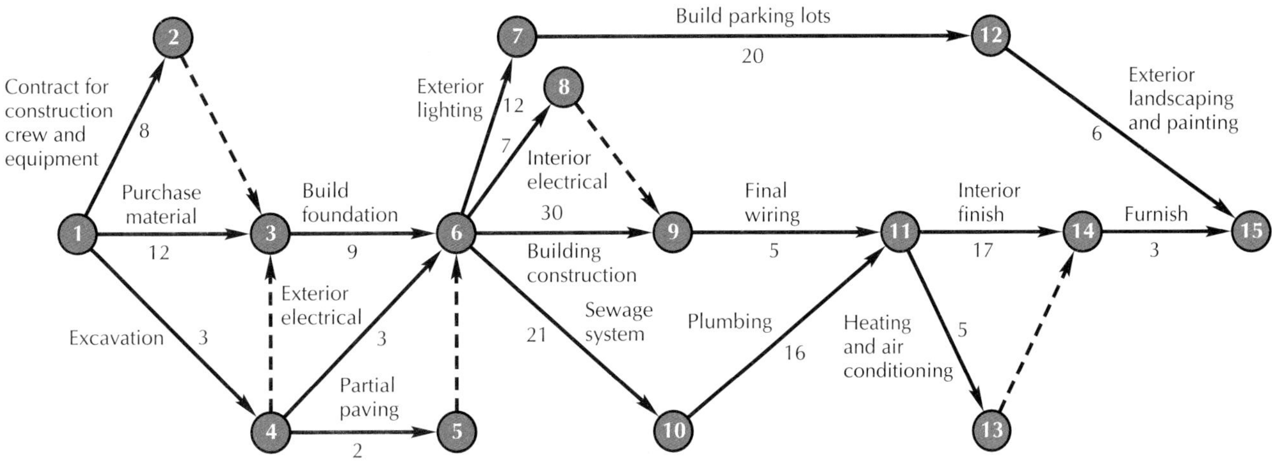

17-10. a-b-dummy-f-h → 15 wk

★ 17-10. The management of a factory is going to erect a maintenance building with a connecting electrical generator and water tank. The activities, activity descriptions, and estimated durations are given in the following table. (Notice that the activities are defined not by node numbers, but by activity descriptions. This alternate form of expressing activities and precedence relationships is sometimes used in CPM/PERT.)

Activity	*Activity Description*	*Activity Predecessor*	*Activity Duration (weeks)*
a	Excavate	—	2
b	Erect building	a	6
c	Install generator	a	4
d	Install tank	a	2
e	Install maintenance equipment	b	4
f	Connect generator and tank to building	b, c, d	5
g	Paint on a finish	b	3
h	Check out facility	e, f	2

Construct the network for this project, identify the critical path, and determine the project duration time.

17-11. 1-2-5-7; $\mu = 40.33$ wk, $\sigma = 5.95$

17-11. Given the following network and probabilistic activity time estimates, determine the expected time and standard deviation for each activity and indicate the critical path.

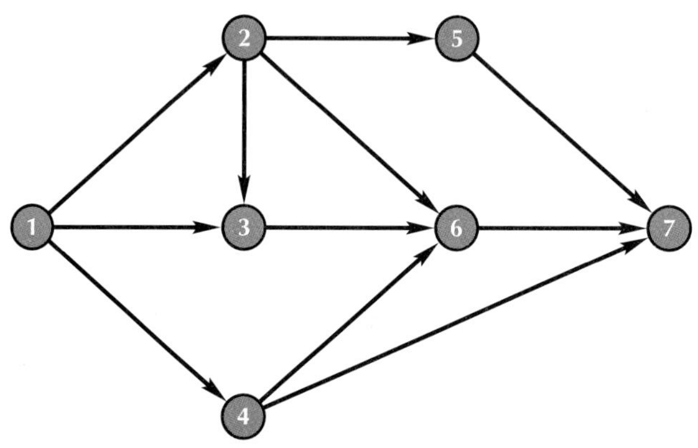

Activity	*Time Estimates (weeks)* *a*	*m*	*b*
1-2	6	10	15
1-3	2	7	16
1-4	4	8	11
2-3	3	10	15
2-5	7	9	20
2-6	4	12	15
3-6	3	6	9
4-6	5	9	16
5-7	3	20	35
4-7	4	12	16
6-7	2	9	14

17-12. The Farmer's American Bank of Leesburg is planning to install a new computerized accounts system. Bank management has determined the activities required to complete the project, the precedence relationships of the activities, and activity time estimates as follows:

★ 17-12. a-d-g-dummy-k; μ = 33 wk, σ = 3.87

Activity	*Description*	*Activity Predecessor*	*Time Estimates (weeks)*		
			a	*m*	*b*
a	Position recruiting	—	5	8	17
b	System development	—	3	12	15
c	System training	a	4	7	10
d	Equipment training	a	5	8	23
e	Manual system test	b, c	1	1	1
f	Preliminary system changeover	b, c	1	4	13
g	Computer-personnel interface	d, e	3	6	9
h	Equipment modification	d, e	1	2.5	7
i	Equipment testing	h	1	1	1
j	System debugging and installation	f, g	2	2	2
k	Equipment changeover	g, i	5	8	11

Determine the earliest and latest activity times, the expected completion time and standard deviation, and the probability that the project will be completed in 40 weeks or less.

17-13. The following probabilistic activity time estimates are for the network in Problem 17-6.

17-13. a, b, c, d. See Solutions Manual.
e. 1-3-5-7-8-9
f. μ = 46 mo, σ = 5

Activity	*Time Estimates (months)*		
	a	*m*	*b*
1-2	4	8	12
1-3	6	10	15
1-4	2	10	14
2-5	3	6	9
2-6	1	4	13
3-5	3	6	18
4-5	0	0	0
4-7	2	8	12
5-8	9	15	22
5-7	5	12	21
7-8	5	6	12
6-9	7	20	25
8-9	3	8	20

Determine the following:

a. Expected activity times
b. Earliest start and finish times
c. Latest start and finish times
d. Activity slack
e. Critical path
f. Expected project duration and standard deviation

17-14. a, b, c, d. See Solutions Manual.
e. 1-2-3-5-6-8-9-10
f. $\mu = 18$ d, $\sigma = 1.97$

17-14. The following probabilistic activity time estimates are for the CPM/PERT network in Problem 17-8.

	Time Estimates (months)		
Activity	*a*	*m*	*b*
1-2	1	2	6
2-4	1	3	5
2-3	3	5	10
2-5	3	6	14
3-4	0	0	0
3-5	1	1.5	2
3-6	2	3	7
4-7	2	4	9
5-6	1	3	5
7-9	1	2	3
6-9	1	1	5
6-8	2	4	9
8-9	0	0	0
9-10	1	1	1

Determine the following:

a. Expected activity times
b. Earliest start and finish times
c. Latest start and finish times
d. Activity slack
e. Critical path
f. Expected project duration and standard deviation

17-15. 0.2119

17-15. For the CPM/PERT network in Problem 17-13, determine the probability that the network duration will exceed 50 months.

17-16. a, b. See Solutions Manual.
c. b-f-dummy-j-k
d. $\mu = 28.17$, $\sigma = 3$
e. 0.0113

★ 17-16. The Stone River Textile Mill was inspected by OSHA and found to be in violation of a number of safety regulations. The OSHA inspectors ordered the mill to alter some existing machinery to make it safer (i.e., add safety guards, etc.); purchase some new machinery to replace older, dangerous machinery; and relocate some machinery to make safer passages and unobstructed entrances and exits. OSHA gave the mill only 35 weeks to make the changes; if the changes were not made by then, the mill would be fined $300,000.

The mill determined the activities in a PERT network that would have to be completed and then estimated the indicated activity times, as shown in the table. Construct the PERT network for this project and determine the following:

a. Expected activity times
b. Earliest and latest activity times and activity slack
c. Critical path
d. Expected project duration and variance
e. The probability that the mill will be fined $300,000

Activity	Description	Activity Predecessor	Time Estimates (weeks)		
			a	*m*	*b*
a	Order new machinery	—	1	2	3
b	Plan new physical layout	—	2	5	8
c	Determine safety changes in existing machinery	—	1	3	5
d	Receive equipment	a	4	10	25
e	Hire new employees	a	3	7	12
f	Make plant alterations	b	10	15	25
g	Make changes in existing machinery	c	5	9	14
h	Train new employees	d, e	2	3	7
i	Install new machinery	d, e, f	1	4	6
j	Relocate old machinery	d, e, f, g	2	5	10
k	Conduct employee safety orientation	h, i, j	2	2	2

17-17. In the Third Battle of Bull Run, for which a CPM/PERT network was developed in Problem 17-14, General Beauregard would have won if his preparations had been completed in 15 days. What would the probability of General Beauregard's winning the battle have been?

17-17. 0.0643

17-18. On May 21, 1927, Charles Lindbergh landed at Le Bourget Field in Paris, completing his famous transatlantic solo flight. The preparation period prior to his flight was quite hectic and time was very critical, since several other famous pilots of the day were also planning transatlantic flights. Once Ryan Aircraft was contracted to build the *Spirit of St. Louis*, it took only a little over $2^1/_2$ months to construct the plane and fly it to New York for the takeoff. If CPM/PERT had been available to Charles Lindbergh, it no doubt would have been useful in helping him plan this project. Use your imagination and assume that a CPM/PERT network, as shown on page 868, with the following estimated activity times, was developed for the flight.

★ 17-18. μ = 57.37 d, σ = 5.77; 0.9535

Activity	Time Estimates (days)		
	a	*m*	*b*
1-2	1	3	5
1-4	4	6	10
1-6	20	35	50
2-3	4	7	12
3-4	2	3	5
4-7	8	12	25
4-8	10	16	21
4-5	5	9	15
3-9	6	8	14
6-8	1	2	2
6-13	5	8	12
8-10	5	10	15
8-11	4	7	10
9-13	5	7	12
11-12	5	9	20
12-13	1	3	7

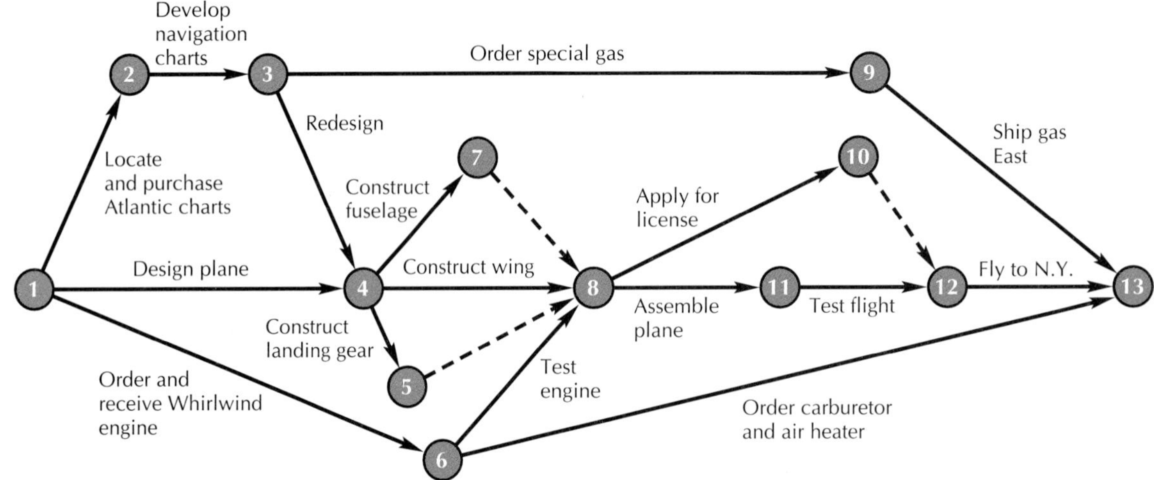

Determine the expected project duration and variance and the probability of completing the project in 67 days.

17-19. a-d-j-n-o; $\mu = 45$ wk, $\sigma = 4.10$; 50.3 wk

★ 17-19. RusTech Tooling, Inc., is a large job shop operation that builds machine tools and dies to manufacture parts for specialized items. The company bids primarily on contracts for government-related activities to produce parts for such things as military aircraft, weapons systems, and the space program. The company is bidding on a contract to produce a component part for the fuselage assembly in a new space shuttle. A major criterion for selecting the winning bid besides low cost is the time required to produce the part. However, if the company is awarded the contract it will be held strictly to the completion date specified in the bid, and any delays will result in severe financial penalties. In order to determine the project completion time to put in their bid, the company has identified the project activities, precedence relationships, and activity times shown in the following table.

		Time Estimates (weeks)		
Activity	*Activity Predecessor*	*a*	*m*	*b*
a	—	3	5	9
b	a	2	5	8
c	a	1	4	6
d	a	4	6	10
e	b	2	8	11
f	b	5	9	16
g	c	4	12	20
h	c	6	9	13
i	d	3	7	14
j	d	8	14	22
k	f, g	9	12	20
l	h, i	6	11	15
m	e	4	7	12
n	j	3	8	16
o	n	5	10	18

If RusTech, Inc., wants to be 90 percent certain that they can deliver the part without incurring a penalty, what time frame should they specify in the bid?

17-20. The following table provides the information necessary to construct a project network and project crash data.

17-20. See Solutions Manual.

	Activity Time (weeks)		Activity Cost ($)	
Activity	*Normal*	*Crash*	*Normal*	*Crash*
1-2	20	8	1,000	1,480
1-4	24	20	1,200	1,400
1-3	14	7	700	1,190
2-4	10	6	500	820
3-4	11	5	550	730

a. Construct the project network.
b. Compute the total allowable crash time per activity and the crash cost per week for each activity.
c. Determine the maximum possible crash time for the network and manually crash the network the maximum amount possible.
d. Compute the normal project cost and the cost of the crashed project.

17-21. The following table provides the information necessary to construct a project network and project crash data.

★ 17-21. See Solutions Manual.

		Activity Time (weeks)		Activity Cost ($)	
Activity	*Predecessor*	*Normal*	*Crash*	*Normal*	*Crash*
a	—	16	8	2,000	4,400
b	—	14	9	1,000	1,800
c	a	8	6	500	700
d	a	5	4	600	1,300
e	b	4	2	1,500	3,000
f	b	6	4	800	1,600
g	c	10	7	3,000	4,500
h	d, e	15	10	5,000	8,000

Construct the project network, and manually crash the network to 28 weeks.

17-22. For Solved Problem 1 at the end of this chapter, assume that the most likely times (m) are the normal activity times and the optimistic times (a) are the activity crash times. Further assume that the activities have the following normal and crash costs.

★ 17-22. See Solutions Manual; crash cost = $450

Activity	*Costs (normal cost, crash cost)*
1-2	($100, 400)
1-3	($250, 400)
2-3	($400, 800)
2-4	($200, 400)
3-4	($150, 300)
3-5	($100, 100)
4-5	($300, 500)

Crash the network to 18 weeks and indicate the total crash cost.

17-23. Crash cost = $5,100; 1-2-4-5-8-9 ★

17-23. The following table provides the crash data for the network project in Problem 17-12. The normal activity times are considered to be deterministic and not probabilistic.

	Activity Time (weeks)		*Activity Cost ($)*	
Activity	*Normal*	*Crash*	*Normal*	*Crash*
a	9	7	4,800	6,300
b	11	9	9,100	15,500
c	7	5	3,000	4,000
d	10	8	3,600	5,000
e	1	1	0	0
f	5	3	1,500	2,000
g	6	5	1,800	2,000
h	3	3	0	0
i	1	1	0	0
j	2	2	0	0
k	8	6	5,000	7,000

Crash the network to 26 weeks, indicate how much it would cost the bank, and identify the new critical path(s).

17-24. $2,633.33 ★

17-24. The following table provides the project crash data for the network in Problem 17-6.

	Activity Time (weeks)		*Activity Cost ($)*	
Activity	*Normal*	*Crash*	*Normal*	*Crash*
1–2	8	5	700	1,200
1–3	10	9	1,600	2,000
1–4	9	7	900	1,500
2–5	6	3	500	900
2–6	4	2	500	700
3–5	5	4	500	800
4–5	0	0	0	0
4–7	7	5	700	1,000
5–7	12	10	1,800	2,300
5–8	15	12	1,400	2,000
6–9	18	14	1,400	3,200
7–8	4	3	500	800
8–9	7	6	800	1,400

Crash the network to 32 months and indicate the new critical path activities and the cost of crashing the network.

See Solutions Manual. ★ 

CASE PROBLEM

The Bloodless Coup Concert

John Aaron had just called the meeting of the Programs and Arts Committee of the Student Government Association to order.

"Okay, okay, everybody, quiet down. I have an important announcement to make," he shouted above the noise. The room got quiet and John started again. "Well you guys, we can have the Coup."

His audience looked puzzled and Randy Jones asked, "What coup have we scored this time John?"

"The Coup, the Coup! You know, the rock group, the Bloodless Coup!"

Everyone in the room cheered and started talking excitedly. John stood up, waved his arms, and shouted, "Hey, calm down everybody and listen up." The room quieted again and everyone focused on John. "The good news is that they can come." He paused a moment. "The bad news is that they will be here in 18 days."

The students groaned and seemed to share Jim Hasting's feelings, "No way, man. It can't be done. Why can't we put it off for a couple of weeks?"

John answered, "They're just starting their new tour and are looking for some warm-up concerts. They will be traveling near here for their first concert date in D.C. and saw they had a letter from us, so they said they could come now—but that's it, now or never." He looked around the room at the solemn faces. "Look you guys, we can handle this. Let's think of what we have to do. Come on, perk up. Let's make a list of everything we have to do to get ready and figure out how long it will take. So somebody tell me what we have to do first!"

Anna Mendoza shouted from the back of the room, "We have to find a place; you know, get an auditorium somewhere. I've done that before, and it should take anywhere from 2 days up to 7 days, most likely about 4 days."

"Okay, that's great," John said as he wrote down the activity "secure auditorium" on the blackboard with the times out to the side. "What's next?"

"We need to print tickets and quick," Tracey Shea blurted. "It could only take a day if the printer isn't busy but it could take up to 4 days if they are. It should probably take about 2 days."

"But we can't print tickets until we know where the concert will be because of the security arrangement," Andy Taylor noted.

"Right," said John, "Get the auditorium first then print the tickets. What else?"

"We need to make hotel and transportation arrangements for the Coup and their entourage while they are here," Jim Hastings said. "But we better not do that until we get the auditorium. If we can't find a place for the concert, everything falls through."

"How long do you think it will take to make the arrangements?" John asked.

"Oh, between 3 and 10 days, probably about 5, most likely," Jim answered.

"We also have to negotiate with the local union for concert employees, stagehands, and whomever else we need to hire," said Reggie Wilkes. "That could take a day or up to 8 days, but 3 days would be my best guess."

"We should probably also hold off on talking to the union until we get the auditorium," John added. "That will probably be a factor in the negotiations."

"After we work things out with the union we can hire some stagehands," Reggie continued. "That could take as few as 2 days but as long as 7. I imagine it'll take about 4 days. We should also be able to get some student ushers at the same time once we get union approval. That could take only a day, but it has taken 5 days in the past; 3 days is probably the most likely."

"We need to arrange a press conference," said Art Cohen, leaning against a wall. "This is a heavy group, big-time."

"But doesn't a press conference usually take place at the hotel?" John asked.

"Yeah, that's right," said Art. "We can't make arrangements for the press conference until we work things out with the hotel. When we do that it should take about 3 days to set up a press conference, 2 days if we're lucky and 4 at the most."

The room got quiet as everyone thought.

"What else?" John said.

"Hey, I know," said Annie Roark. "Once we hire the stagehands they have to set up the stage. I think that could be done in a couple of days, but it could take up to 6 days, with 3 most likely." She paused for a moment before adding, "And we can also assign the ushers to their jobs once we hire them. That shouldn't take long, maybe only a day, 3 days worst. Probably 2 days would be a good time to put down."

"We also have to do some advertising and promotion if we want anyone to show for this thing," said Art nonchalantly. "I guess we need to wait until we print the tickets first so we'll have something to sell. That depends on the media, the paper, and radio stations. I've worked with this before. It could get done really quick, like 2 days, if we can make the right contacts, but it could take a lot longer, like 12 days if we hit any snags. We probably ought to count on 6 days as our best estimate."

"Hey, if we're going to promote this shouldn't we also have a preliminary act, some other group?" said Annie.

"Wow, I forgot all about that," said John. "Hiring another act will take me between 4 and 8 days; I can probably do it in 5. I can start on that right away at the same time you guys are arranging for an auditorium." He thought for a moment. "But we really can't begin to work on the promotion until I get the lead-in group. So what's left?"

"Sell the tickets," shouted several people at once.

"Right," said John, "we have to wait until they are printed; but I don't think we have to wait for the advertising and promotion to start do we?"

"No," said Jim, "but we should hire the preliminary act first so people will know what they're buying a ticket for."

"Agreed," said John. "The tickets could go quick; I suppose in the first day."

"Or," interrupted Mike Eggleston, "it could take longer. I remember two years ago it took 12 days to sell out for the Cosmic Modem."

"Okay, so it's between 1 and 12 days to sell the tickets," said John, "but I think about 5 days is more likely. Everybody agree?"

The group nodded in unison and they all turned at once to the list of activities and times John had written on the blackboard.

Use PERT analysis to determine the probability the concert preparations will be completed in time.

REFERENCES

Burman, P. J., *Precedence Networks for Project Planning and Control,* New York: McGraw-Hill, 1972.

Cleland, D. I., and W. R. King, *Project Management Handbook,* New York: Van Nostrand Reinhold, 1983.

Levy, F., G. Thompson, and J. Wiest, "The ABC's of the Critical Path Method," *Harvard Business Review* 41, no. 5 (October 1963).

Moder, J., C. R. Phillips, and E. W., Davis, *Project Management with CPM and PERT and Precedence Diagramming,* 3d ed., New York: Van Nostrand Reinhold, 1983.

O'Brian, J., *CPM in Construction Management,* New York: McGraw-Hill, 1965.

Wiest, J. D., and F. K. Levy, *A Management Guide to PERT/CPM,* 2d ed., Englewood Cliffs, N.J.: Prentice Hall, 1977.

EPILOGUE: CHANGE

The single most pervasive factor that has impacted on the field of production and operations management—and business in general—during the past two decades is change. Although we have focused on the impact of quality management on all facets of operations in this text and its effect on competitiveness, quality is just one manifestation of the rapid, mind-boggling changes that have occurred since the late 1970s. As the decade of the 1980s approached, we were keypunching cards for mainframe computers and the PC was still only in the planning steps at IBM. When one thought of Honda it was in terms of motorcycles, or boxlike little cars that people jokingly said were run by lawnmower engines. VCRs were unimaginable to most of the consuming public and televisions were made in America. JIT was the way they pronounced *jet* in Texas, not a revolutionary approach to inventory management, and strategic planning at many companies was nothing more than next years "management by objectives (MBO)" plan. Robots were found in science fiction movies, not on assembly lines, and good stereo speakers were only slightly smaller than a closet door. And quality was something that most U.S. consumers thought they could not afford.

Although technology progressed at a steady pace, markets remained parochial and were certainly not international. In retrospect, the changes in products often tended to be cosmetic rather than substantiative. Cars looked different in 1970 than they did in 1940; but to our fathers the only real difference was that they were higher-priced, broke down more frequently, and cost more to repair. They had the same basic features, traveled at the same speed, got the same gas mileage, and were about as comfortable. Basic operational principles and functions remained relatively consistent. Manufacturing was dominated by the assembly line, and workers and jobs conformed to norms that had gained credence at the turn of the century. The field of production and operations management was static, sustaining the basic principles and techniques of scheduling, inventory control, purchasing, and job design throughout the half decade. There was no need for dramatic change, as consumer demands and tastes seemed to remain essentially the same.

During the approximately half-century between the end of World War I and the late 1970s, the pace of change in manufacturing was slow and deliberate, seemingly almost creeping in comparison to the change of the last 15 years. A friend who worked at a textile mill that was a major manufacturer of denim in the early 1970s recounts that some of the machines in the plant dated back to just after the Civil War. Parts were simply replaced as they wore out, but the basic technology and products remained the same. Visiting the plant a little over a decade later, he found it unrecognizable. It had undergone not only a technological metamorphosis, but it was clean and safe as well. Unable to compete with foreign competitors under the old ground rules, the textile company adapted to change.

When change came in the late 1970s, it seemed to start with a low rumble, recognizable to only a few seers and visionaries. Then it gained momentum, like a giant snowball, going downhill fast through the 1980s and hurtling into the 1990s. Change became both the diagnosis for the failure of hundreds of businesses and enterprises and the prescription for success for many others. Technological change, change in modes of transportation, changes in communication, and, most importantly, the development of computer technology and electronics resulted in a new and expanded international market environment and new products to drive it. Consumer tastes and expectations, once static, undemanding and parochial, suddenly became eclectic, diverse, and discriminating.

If there is one consistent theme that seems to run through all the success stories reported in the media and described in the boxes and videos in this text, it is recognition of the need to adapt to change. Companies that have survived in this changing environment—so far—point to their ability to adapt to changes as the key to their success. However, they are also quick to point out that their future depends on their ability to recognize important changes in the future before they are overwhelmed by them and to react to them as rapidly as possible. Employers demand that employees be willing to accept change and to retrain and adapt or lose their jobs. Likewise, employees now look to companies for a commitment to invest in their training and education to help them withstand the onslaught of change in the future. There is a renewed commitment to research and new product development and to changing the way companies operate.

How has this affected the field of production and operations management and its teaching? Initially caught napping, POM educators and academicians are now riding the whirlwind and, like others, are reeducating themselves in order to teach a new generation of students the latest methods and techniques in POM. This text has attempted to reflect this era of change and provide a contemporary, up-to-date perspective on POM. This need explains why we have focused on quality management in this text. In our opinion it is the most pervasive and important change in production and operations management during the last decade. Unfortunately, parts of this text will probably be outdated by the time it reaches students and teachers. The interval between the time we started writing this book and the time when it was published was approximately three years, plenty of time for even more dramatic and significant changes to occur. So we apologize for our omissions and deficiencies in advance and assure you that they did not result from a lack of trying.

Yet as we speak of change, we are also reminded of a popular song of the 1970s, "Everything Old is New Again." A number of the most important reactions to change have been the rediscovery of things that worked in the past. We have recounted on several occasions how the basic principles of TQM, W. E. Deming's fourteen points and statistical process control, are not new but are simply rediscovered philosophies and tools from an earlier era. Worker empowerment, as described at Harley-Davidson in the Gaining the Competitive Edge Box in Chapter 9 seems like a throwback to the era before F. W. Taylor at the turn of the century. It does not appear that Harley-Davidson's machinists, who control their own work centers, deal with vendors, and are responsible for product quality, are much different from the skilled craftspeople/machinists of the early 1900s. They, likewise, controlled their own workplaces and were not subject to supervisory management. And to hear our grandfathers reminisce about this era, products were made to last and workers took pride in what they made—not so much different than today's emerging "new" philosophy of the workplace. Thus, adapting to change means not only trying the new, but also discovering the best of the old.

What change does the future hold? We are no more able to predict the changes of the next decade now than businesspeople and academicians were in the 1970s. However, it is certain that change will occur, and it is likely to be as rapid and powerful—or even more so—than the changes we have just experienced. Thus, the important lesson of the recent past is that to be successful in the future, companies must be ready, able, and willing to adapt to change. Likewise, to secure and retain jobs in the future, employees and students must be willing to retrain and educate themselves to adapt to change.

September, 1994
Roberta S. Russell
Bernard W. Taylor III

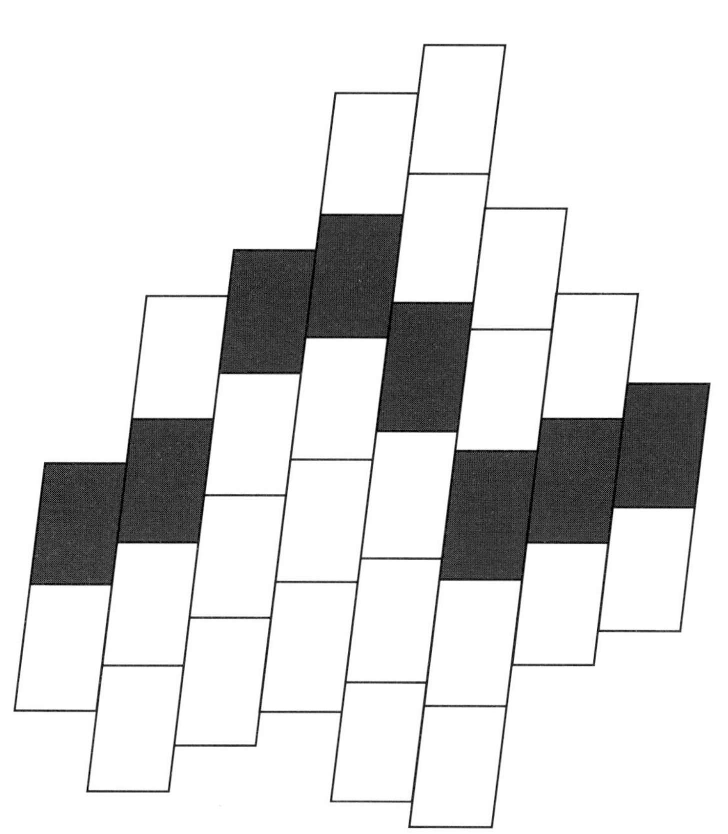

APPENDICES

A

STARTING AB:POM

B

TABLES

APPENDIX A STARTING AB:POM

AB:POM version 3.32 is a production and operations management software package developed and written by Howard J. Weiss and published by Allyn and Bacon, the publisher of this text. It has program modules for most of the topics in this text, and as a result, it is demonstrated in all but a few chapters. It is extremely user-friendly, requiring very little instruction to learn how to use. The purpose of this appendix is to provide the first-time user with some help in getting started with AB:POM; but with just a little experience, even the most novice computer user will become adept at its use. If AB:POM is purchased separately (from this text), it comes with a manual that contains much more detailed information than is included in this tutorial.

HARDWARE REQUIREMENTS

AB:POM runs with MS-DOS operating systems which includes IBM personal computers and a variety of IBM-compatible microcomputers. It requires less than 256K RAM to run all the program modules. Either a color or monochrome monitor can be used. A printer is not required to use AB:POM; however if you want a hard-copy printout, a printer is necessary. AB:POM can run with a single floppy disk drive, dual disk drives, or a hard disk. It comes in two versions: with two 5.25-inch floppy disks or one 3.5-inch disk.

STARTING AB:POM

AB:POM can be started from either a floppy disk system or a hard disk. If you are operating from a *floppy disk,* follow these steps.

1. Insert your DOS diskette in drive A and close the door.
2. Turn the computer on; if it is on, press **<CTRL>**, **<ALT>**, and **<DEL>** simultaneously to reboot.
3. You should see the A prompt (**A>**).
4. Remove your DOS diskette and insert either one of your 5.25-inch AB:POM disks or your single 3.5-inch AB:POM disk into the A drive (or the B drive).
5. Type **POM** and press the enter (or return) key (or if your AB:POM disk is in drive B, type **B:** and press the enter key; then type **POM** and press the enter key).

This series of steps should result in the AB:POM menu displayed on your screen (which we will discuss in a moment).

If you are using a *hard disk* system, the following steps should be followed.

1. Turn on the computer (making sure that nothing is in the A drive and the door is open).
2. Create a directory on the hard disk to store AB:POM (type **MD ABPOM**).
3. Using the copy *.* command, copy all the files from the AB:POM disk(s) to the hard disk (type **copy A: *.* C:\ABPOM**).
4. Enter the directory on your hard disk that contains the AB:POM files using the **CD**, or "change directory," command (type **CD ABPOM**).
5. Type **POM** and press the enter key.

Again, this will result in the AB:POM menu of programs. To run AB:POM in the future, execute steps 4 and 5.

THE OPENING SCREENS IN AB:POM

After the AB:POM program is started, the first screen appears as in Exhibit A.1.

Note that this is not simply a title screen, but it requires a decision on the part of the user regarding the appropriate version to use. The regular version of AB:POM is accessed by entering **A.** There are also versions for other Allyn and Bacon texts, including this one, that can be accessed. However, their differences are minor; essentially only a change in the order of presentation of the programming modules to coincide with the chapters in these other texts. For use with this text the user should enter either **A** or **T.**

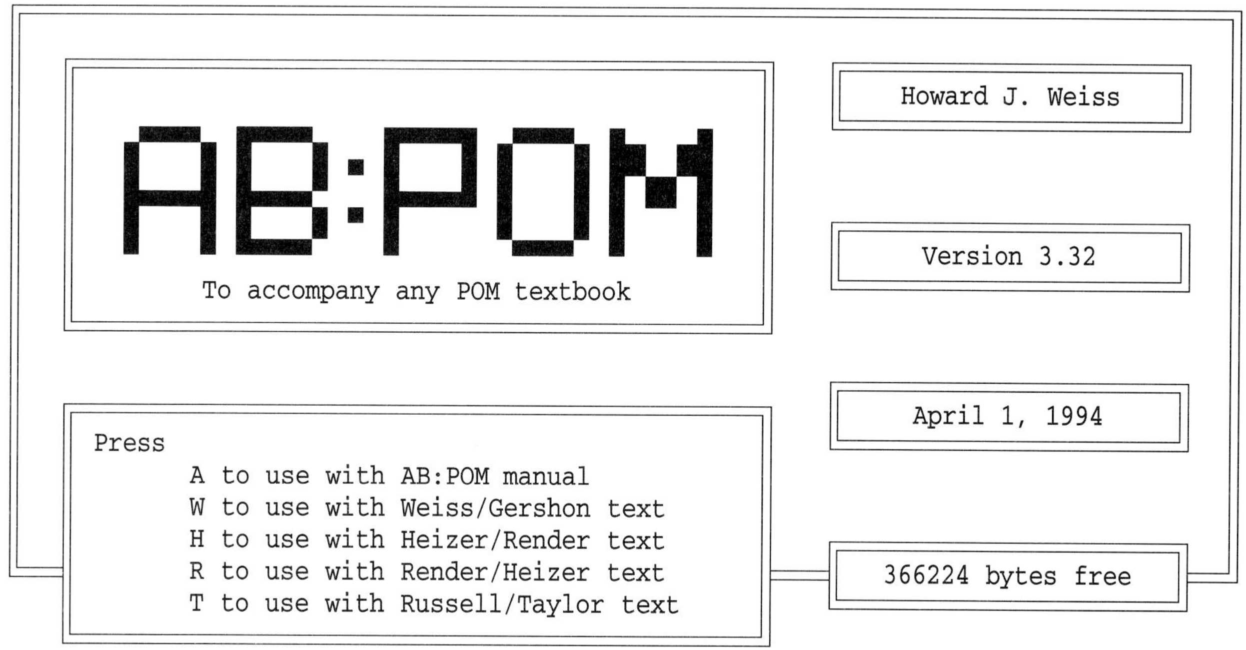

(C) Copyright Allyn & Bacon, 1991, 1992, 1993
Portions (C) Copyright Microsoft Corporation, 1982-1990

EXHIBIT A.1

The second screen to be displayed asks the user what type of color style should be employed, as shown in Exhibit A.2. Enter **M** for a single-color/monochrome screen, **1** for the color style shown (blue on black), or **2** for white on blue.

Screen type/color selection

Press 'm' if you have a single-color screen

Press '1' if you like this color style

Press '2' if you like this color style

Note: Press 'd' for some important comments if you are using DOS 2.1

EXHIBIT A.2

THE AB:POM MAIN MENU

Transparency A1 AB:POM Main Menu

The AB:POM menu is shown in Exhibit A.3 as it would appear on your computer screen, using the "T" version.

To access any of the program modules, toggle the cursor to the desired title and press the **enter** key. Alternatively, you can press the highlighted letter associated with each topic. (Remember that if you are using the AB:POM version with two 5.25-inch disks, you may need to replace the disk in the **A** drive with your other AB:POM disk to access some of the programs.)

Notice that the first option on the main menus is a **HELP** screen, which if entered will appear as shown in Exhibit A.4.

This **HELP** screen provides some general information about how to get started and how to seek help as you go through the different program modules. It is possible to access a **HELP** screen for the modules you may be in at virtually all times.

THE PROGRAM SETUP SCREEN

Transparency A2 Program Setup Screen

When you access a specific program from the main menu, a setup screen will be displayed. Exhibit A.5 shows the setup screen for the first program listed on the main menu, "Decision and Break-even Analysis."

This is essentially a blank screen with a set of program options at the bottom. All the setup screens for all program modules listed on the main menu look the same except for the program title at the top. There are six program options associated with the setup screen, which can be accessed by entering the designated **F** key or by entering the first (highlighted) letter for each option. Following is a brief explanation of each of these options.

F1 = Help

The **HELP** option provides a brief description of the program, the input data for the problem that the program requires, and any options available in the module.

F2 = New

Transparency A3 Decision and Breakdown Analysis Program Screen

This is the option that enables you to enter the data for a **new** problem. When you enter this option command for some programs, it will generate a list of optional modules corresponding to different problem types. For example, in the Decision and Break-even

```
                          Main menu

    Help                                  Forecasting
    Decision and Break-even Analysis      Aggregate Planning
    Linear Programming                    Inventory
    Quality Control                       Material Requirements Planning
    Reliability                           Sizing, Lot
    Operations Layout                     Assignment
    Balancing, Assembly line              Job Shop Sequencing
    Plant Location                        Waiting Line Models
    Transportation                        CPM/PERT Project Scheduling
    Experience (learning) Curves          Exit to DOS

          Select menu option by highlighted letter or point
           with arrow keys and then press ENTER (◄┘) key
```

EXHIBIT A.3

```
HELP

The main menu identifies the available modules. The
modules may be chosen by either pressing the highlighted letter
or by using the arrow keys to point to the option and then
pressing the ENTER (◄┘) key to select that item.

Help on the definition of the submenu options and the direction
keys can be found by pressing the F1 key or the S key or F2 or M.
A brief explanation of data types can be found by pressing the
F3 or D key. P can be used to print any help screen and the ESC
key should be pressed to exit the HELP screen.

Remember that the AB-POM diskette 1 contains a file named
README which contains useful information. The README file
is examined through DOS by using the TYPE or PRINT command.

NOTE: At almost all times, a message appears on the bottom two
rows giving instructions on what to do, or what keys are available.
When in doubt about what to do next, look to the bottom of the
screen for assistance.

F1=Submenu Options     F2=Movement Keys     F3=Data editing     F9=Print ESC=Done
Press s, m or d or 'F1', 'F2' or 'F3' for more help. Press ESC key to end help
```

EXHIBIT A.4

```
Decision and Break-even Analysis                Setup Screen

F1=Help  F2=New F3=Load F4=Main F5=Util F6=Quit
Use first letter or function key to select option - F2 key to start new problem
```

EXHIBIT A.5

```
Decision and Break-even Analysis                     Setup Screen

                  Decision Analysis Options

                      Decision Tables

                      Trees, Decision

                      Break-even Analysis

                      Return to submenu

        Select menu option by highlighted letter or point
         with arrow keys and then press ENTER (◄┘) key
```

EXHIBIT A.6

Analysis program, when the **F2** key is pressed, the list of optional subprograms is displayed, as shown in Exhibit A.6.

By entering any of these three subprogram options, we access a blank screen ready for data input for the specific problem type. In the next section we show how the data is input for an example problem.

F3 = Load

If you have problem data stored on a disk or in a file, it can be loaded into the program you are in with this command. Simply type in the data and the file name and press the **enter** key.

F4 = Main

This option allows you to return to the main menu and pass from one program module to another.

F5 = Util

This is a utilities subprogram that allows the user to customize colors, access DOS directly, delete files, send program output to a file, change AB:POM formatting procedures, turn off the beep when an error occurs, turn off the function keys at the bottom of the setup screen, and reset the number of lines on the screen depending on the type of monitor being used.

F6 = Exit

This subprogram option, when entered, will return you to DOS.

AN AB:POM EXAMPLE

In order to demonstrate AB:POM, we use Example 2.2 on decision analysis from Chapter 2. The same basic steps for inputting the problem data, solving the problem, and saving and/or printing the solution are followed in the other program modules. This problem had two states of nature, with probabilities of 0.70 and 0.30 respectively, and three decision alternatives. The outcomes, or payoffs, from these alternatives under each state of nature are shown as follows.

	STATES OF NATURE	
ALTERNATIVE	0.70	0.30
1	$ 800,000	$500,000
2	1,300,000	-150,000
3	320,000	320,000

The objective is to determine the correct decision that will result in the greatest profit using the expected value decision criterion.

The first step is to input the problem data onto the setup screen. The program begins by asking for a problem title; this query is followed by a few questions about the parameters of the problem dimensions in order to set up the basic input structure. The first inquiry is for the number of alternatives, and the response is 3. Next the program asks for the number of states of nature, which is 2, and then it asks whether the objective is to maximize profit or minimize cost and the answer is maximize profit. These responses result in the display in Exhibit A.7, called a *Data Screen*, with the basic structure of the problem set up.

The cursor is set at the first blank probability above state 1. After this value (0.70) is entered, the cursor automatically moves to the next adjacent value, until all the problem data have been entered. It stops at the final outcome value, corresponding to alternative 3 for state 2. Note that the titles for the states and alternatives can be changed to fit the problem description, although we did not do so here. The setup screen with all of the problem data is shown in Exhibit A.8.

Transparency A4 AB:POM Example Data Screen

```
═══════════════ Decision and Break-even Analysis ═══════════════ Data Screen
Number of alternatives (2-10) 3          Number of nature states (1-8) 2
Profits    - maximize profits

═══════════════════════ AB:POM Example ═══════════════════════

Probability->    0.000    0.000
                state 1  state 2
alternatv 1          0        0
alternatv 2          0        0
alternatv 3          0        0

F1=Help F2=New F3=Load F4=Main F5=Util F6=Quit F7=Save F9=Prnt F10=Run    Esc
Enter the probability for this state of nature
```

EXHIBIT A.7

```
Decision and Break-even Analysis                    Data Screen
Number of alternatives (2-10) 3          Number of nature states (1-8) 2
Profits      - maximize profits

                         AB:POM Example

Probability->      0.700      0.300
                 state 1    state 2
alternatv 1       800000     500000
alternatv 2      1300000    -150000
alternatv 3       320000     320000

End of data - use ESC key for menu

F1=Help F2=New F3=Load F4=Main F5=Util F6=Quit F7=Save F9=Prnt F10=Run    Esc
Enter the cost/profit for this alternative under this state of nature
```

EXHIBIT A.8

Once all the data have been input, the program stops; if you attempt to enter any more data it will beep. Notice that some new program options have been added at the bottom of the screen: **F7 = Save, F9 = Print,** and **F10 = Run.** For the moment the **F10** option is what we are interested in; to solve the problem we enter **F10.** The solution appears in Exhibit A.9.

SAVING, PRINTING, AND EDITING RESULTS

Once you have obtained the problem solution by entering **F10,** the input data can be saved in a file using the **F7** key. The solution can be printed by entering **F9.**

F7 = Save

When **F7** is entered, a screen will appear with the names of your existing AB:POM data files. You will be asked for the file name in which to store this set of data. After entering the file name, the data are saved.

F9 = Print

This program option allows you to print the problem solution as it appears on the display screen in Exhibit A.9 without all the outlines around the edge of the screen. If you would prefer to print the display screen exactly as it appears, then use **[SHIFT] - [PRTSC].** The program prints to the standard DOS printer file "lpt1." If your printer is not attached to

```
Decision and Break-even Analysis                                   Solution
Number of alternatives (2-10) 3              Number of nature states (1-8) 2
Profits     - maximize profits

                              AB:POM Example

Probability->    0.700     0.300
               state 1   state 2   EMV     Row Min  Row Max
alternatv 1     800000    500000 710000    500000   800000
alternatv 2    1300000   -150000 865000   -150000  1300000
alternatv 3     320000    320000 320000    320000   320000
               column maximum-> 865000    500000  1300000
The maximum expected monetary value is      865000 given by alternatv 2
The maximin is    500000 given by alternatv 1
The maximax is   1300000 given by alternatv 2

F1=Display Perfect Information                                F9=Prnt    Esc
Press <Esc> key to edit data or highlighted key or function key for options
```

EXHIBIT A.9

Transparency A5 AB:POM Solution Screen

lpt1, then you should use the **DOS MODE** statement to redirect the output to the desired location.

ESC

The **ESC** key will return control to the setup screen and allow you to toggle to any of the input data values in order to edit the problem. In the event you made an error when inputting the data, you can make corrections, or you can solve a new version of the problem.

HELP SCREENS

In each program module it is possible to access a series of **Help** screens. If you refer back to the original Data Screen for example, at the bottom of the screen an option is listed, **"F1 = Help"**. Entering **F1** will display the **Help** screen in Exhibit A.10.

Similar **Help** screens are available for all the program modules. At the bottom of this **Help** display screen are options for other **Help** screens. Entering the **F1** key will access a summary of all the different submenu options, from **F1** to **F10,** as shown in Exhibit A.11

The **F2** key accesses a **Help** screen that provides information about cursor movement around the display screens and between screens. The **F3** key accesses a **Help** screen that discusses the different type of data entries and how to edit the data. These two screens are shown in Exhibit A.12.

```
   This is the DECISION TABLES module. It is used to find expected values,
maximin (minimax) and maximax (minimin) when faced with a number of
decisions/options and a set of different scenarios.
   The initial input which is required is
 -> # of options/decisions which you have available
 -> # of scenarios
   When you begin you are asked whether you want to MAXIMIZE or MINIMIZE.
This can NOT be changed later.

   The data screen contains the following pieces of information.
   The major information required is the payoff, either profit or cost,
that occurs for each decision/scenario combination. In addition, you may
enter scenario probabilities. These are necessary for computing the
expected monetary value but not for the maximin, maximax, etc. Finally,
you have the opportunity to name the decisions (rows) and/or the
scenarios (columns).
   The program also can compute the Expected Value of Perfect Information
if you press the F1 key after the initial computations are complete.
```

```
F1=Submenu Options   F2=Movement Keys   F3=Data editing   F9=Print   ESC=Done
Press s, m or d or 'F1', 'F2' or 'F3' for more help. Press Esc key to end help
```

EXHIBIT A.10

```
                        Submenu Options
The submenu options will appear on the next to last line of the data
screen, after a module is chosen. The options are chosen by pressing
the highlighted letter. While you are editing data the only option
available is Esc. When you press the Esc key, the submenu options will
become available. It is also possible to access the submenu options by
using the function keys which are listed below.
 F1 - Help - Displays the module or submodule help screen
 F2 - New  - Use this to start a new problem
 F3 - Load - Use this to load a file from disk
 F4 - Main - This returns to the module menu
 F5 - Util - Customize colors, toggle sound, print to file, etc.
 F6 - Quit - Exit AB:POM and go to DOS
 F7 - Save - Save a problem/file on a diskette
*F8 - Titl - Change the problem title
 F9 - Prnt - Print the data or solution to a printer (or file)
F10 - Run  - Start the solution procedure
For most modules, ESC followed by the INSert key can be used to insert
a row (or column) or ESC followed by the DELete key to delete a row.

* not listed at bottom of data screen but always available
```

```
F1=Submenu Options   F2=Movement Keys   F3=Data editing   F9=Print   ESC=Done
Press s, m or d or 'F1', 'F2' or 'F3' for more help. Press Esc key to end help
```

EXHIBIT A.11

```
═══════════════ Cursor/Cell Movement Keys ═══════════════
↑   - move one cell up
↓   - move one cell down
→   - move one cell right
←   - move one cell left

TAB - move to far right column or move one screen to the right
SHIFT-TAB - move to far left column or move one screen to the left
PAGEUP - move to top row or move up one screen
PAGEDOWN - move to bottom row or move down one screen
HOME - move to beginning (upper left) of data
END - move to end (lower right) of data
ENTER - enter data and move to next cell
ESCAPE - turns on menu options or returns to previous screen

F1=Submenu Options    F2=Movement Keys    F3=Data editing    F9=Print ESC=Done
Press s, m or d or 'F1', 'F2' or 'F3' for more help. Press Esc key to end help
```

```
═══════════════ Data Entry/editing ═══════════════
There are three types of data which are entered onto the screen. The
three types require slightly different inputs. If you make a mistake
when pressing a key then a message will appear near the screen bottom.

NUMERICAL DATA
This is the most common, most standard type of data. In some cases
you will be restricted to positive numbers. In other cases you will
be restricted to integers.

CHARACTER DATA
In most modules you are allowed to name some of the variables. In
these cases you will be allowed to enter almost any character.

TOGGLED DATA
For some entries, the allowable responses have been preset for you.
In these cases you may press the space bar to switch from one to
another. Or, if you like, you may press ENTER to see all of the
allowable possibilities.
NOTE: On most modules if you move up to the title line you can change
the title. Pressing the F8 key will also allow for a title change.

F1=Submenu Options    F2=Movement Keys    F3=Data editing    F9=Print ESC=Done
Press s, m or d or 'F1', 'F2' or 'F3' for more help. Press Esc key to end help
```

EXHIBIT A.12

GRAPHICS

Some of the program modules will display a graph when appropriate. In order to print a graph, it is necessary to load the program **GRAPHICS.COM** from DOS prior to starting AB:POM.

GETTING OUT OF AB:POM

In order to exit AB:POM after a problem has been solved, use the **ESC** key to return to the setup screen and enter **Q** (for Quit) to return to DOS. Alternatively, you can return to the main menu and exit using the designated menu option for exiting.

APPENDIX B TABLES

TABLE B.1 Cumulative Binomial Probabilities: $P(c \leq x \mid n, p)$

n	x	p = 0.05	0.10	0.15	0.20	0.25	0.30	0.35	0.40	0.45	0.50
2	0	0.9025	0.8100	0.7225	0.6400	0.5625	0.4900	0.4225	0.3600	0.3025	0.2500
	1	0.9975	0.9900	0.9775	0.9600	0.9375	0.9100	0.8775	0.8400	0.7975	0.7500
	2	1.0000	1.0000	1.0000	1.0000	1.0000	1.0000	1.0000	1.0000	1.0000	1.0000
3	0	0.8574	0.7290	0.6141	0.5120	0.4219	0.3430	0.2746	0.2160	0.1664	0.1250
	1	0.9928	0.9720	0.9392	0.8960	0.8438	0.7840	0.7183	0.6480	0.5748	0.5000
	2	0.9999	0.9990	0.9966	0.9920	0.9844	0.9730	0.9571	0.9360	0.9089	0.8750
	3	1.0000	1.0000	1.0000	1.0000	1.0000	1.0000	1.0000	1.0000	1.0000	1.0000
4	0	0.8145	0.6561	0.5220	0.4096	0.3164	0.2401	0.1785	0.1296	0.0915	0.0625
	1	0.9860	0.9477	0.8905	0.8192	0.7383	0.6517	0.5630	0.4752	0.3910	0.3125
	2	0.9995	0.9963	0.9880	0.9728	0.9492	0.9163	0.8735	0.8208	0.7585	0.6875
	3	1.0000	0.9999	0.9995	0.9984	0.9961	0.9919	0.9850	0.9744	0.9590	0.9375
	4	1.0000	1.0000	1.0000	1.0000	1.0000	1.0000	1.0000	1.0000	1.0000	1.0000
5	0	0.7738	0.5905	0.4437	0.3277	0.2373	0.1681	0.1160	0.0778	0.0503	0.0313
	1	0.9774	0.9185	0.8352	0.7373	0.6328	0.5282	0.4284	0.3370	0.2562	0.1875
	2	0.9988	0.9914	0.9734	0.9421	0.8965	0.8369	0.7648	0.6826	0.5931	0.5000
	3	1.0000	0.9995	0.9978	0.9933	0.9844	0.9692	0.9460	0.9130	0.8688	0.8125
	4	1.0000	1.0000	0.9999	0.9997	0.9990	0.9976	0.9947	0.9898	0.9815	0.9688
	5	1.0000	1.0000	1.0000	1.0000	1.0000	1.0000	1.0000	1.0000	1.0000	1.0000
6	0	0.7351	0.5314	0.3771	0.2621	0.1780	0.1176	0.0754	0.0467	0.0277	0.0156
	1	0.9672	0.8857	0.7765	0.6554	0.5339	0.4202	0.3191	0.2333	0.1636	0.1094
	2	0.9978	0.9842	0.9527	0.9011	0.8306	0.7443	0.6471	0.5443	0.4415	0.3437
	3	0.9999	0.9987	0.9941	0.9830	0.9624	0.9295	0.8826	0.8208	0.7447	0.6563
	4	1.0000	0.9999	0.9996	0.9984	0.9954	0.9891	0.9777	0.9590	0.9308	0.8906
	5	1.0000	1.0000	1.0000	0.9999	0.9998	0.9993	0.9982	0.9959	0.9917	0.9844
	6	1.0000	1.0000	1.0000	1.0000	1.0000	1.0000	1.0000	1.0000	1.0000	1.0000
7	0	0.6983	0.4783	0.3206	0.2097	0.1335	0.0824	0.0490	0.0280	0.0152	0.0078
	1	0.9556	0.8503	0.7166	0.5767	0.4449	0.3294	0.2338	0.1586	0.1024	0.0625
	2	0.9962	0.9743	0.9262	0.8520	0.7564	0.6471	0.5323	0.4199	0.3164	0.2266
	3	0.9998	0.9973	0.9879	0.9667	0.9294	0.8740	0.8002	0.7102	0.6083	0.5000
	4	1.0000	0.9998	0.9988	0.9953	0.9871	0.9712	0.9444	0.9037	0.8471	0.7734
	5	1.0000	1.0000	0.9999	0.9996	0.9987	0.9962	0.9910	0.9812	0.9643	0.9375
	6	1.0000	1.0000	1.0000	1.0000	0.9999	0.9998	0.9994	0.9984	0.9963	0.9922
	7	1.0000	1.0000	1.0000	1.0000	1.0000	1.0000	1.0000	1.0000	1.0000	1.0000
8	0	0.6634	0.4305	0.2725	0.1678	0.1001	0.0576	0.0319	0.0168	0.0084	0.0039
	1	0.9428	0.8131	0.6572	0.5033	0.3671	0.2553	0.1691	0.1064	0.0632	0.0352
	2	0.9942	0.9619	0.8948	0.7969	0.6785	0.5518	0.4278	0.3154	0.2201	0.1445
	3	0.9996	0.9950	0.9786	0.9437	0.8862	0.8059	0.7064	0.5941	0.4770	0.3633
	4	1.0000	0.9996	0.9971	0.9896	0.9727	0.9420	0.8939	0.8263	0.7396	0.6367
	5	1.0000	1.0000	0.9998	0.9988	0.9958	0.9887	0.9747	0.9502	0.9115	0.8555
	6	1.0000	1.0000	1.0000	0.9999	0.9996	0.9987	0.9964	0.9915	0.9819	0.9648
	7	1.0000	1.0000	1.0000	1.0000	1.0000	0.9999	0.9998	0.9993	0.9983	0.9961
	8	1.0000	1.0000	1.0000	1.0000	1.0000	1.0000	1.0000	1.0000	1.0000	1.0000
9	0	0.6302	0.3874	0.2316	0.1342	0.0751	0.0404	0.0207	0.0101	0.0046	0.0020
	1	0.9288	0.7748	0.5995	0.4362	0.3003	0.1960	0.1211	0.0705	0.0385	0.0195
	2	0.9916	0.9470	0.8591	0.7382	0.6007	0.4628	0.3373	0.2318	0.1495	0.0898
	3	0.9994	0.9917	0.9661	0.9144	0.8343	0.7297	0.6089	0.4826	0.3614	0.2539
	4	1.0000	0.9991	0.9944	0.9804	0.9511	0.9012	0.8283	0.7334	0.6214	0.5000
	5	1.0000	0.9999	0.9994	0.9969	0.9900	0.9747	0.9464	0.9006	0.8342	0.7461

Table continues

TABLE B.1 (continued)

n	x	p 0.05	0.10	0.15	0.20	0.25	0.30	0.35	0.40	0.45	0.50
	6	1.0000	1.0000	1.0000	0.9997	0.9987	0.9957	0.9888	0.9750	0.9502	0.9102
	7	1.0000	1.0000	1.0000	1.0000	0.9999	0.9996	0.9986	0.9962	0.9909	0.9805
	8	1.0000	1.0000	1.0000	1.0000	1.0000	1.0000	0.9999	0.9997	0.9992	0.9980
	9	1.0000	1.0000	1.0000	1.0000	1.0000	1.0000	1.0000	1.0000	1.0000	1.0000
10	0	0.5987	0.3487	0.1969	0.1074	0.0563	0.0282	0.0135	0.0060	0.0025	0.0010
	1	0.9139	0.7361	0.5443	0.3758	0.2440	0.1493	0.0860	0.0464	0.0233	0.0107
	2	0.9885	0.9298	0.8202	0.6778	0.5256	0.3828	0.2616	0.1673	0.0996	0.0547
	3	0.9990	0.9872	0.9500	0.8791	0.7759	0.6496	0.5138	0.3823	0.2660	0.1719
	4	0.9999	0.9984	0.9901	0.9672	0.9219	0.8497	0.7515	0.6331	0.5044	0.3770
	5	1.0000	0.9999	0.9986	0.9936	0.9803	0.9527	0.9051	0.8338	0.7384	0.6230
	6	1.0000	1.0000	0.9999	0.9991	0.9965	0.9894	0.9740	0.9452	0.8980	0.8281
	7	1.0000	1.0000	1.0000	0.9999	0.9996	0.9984	0.9952	0.9877	0.9726	0.9453
	8	1.0000	1.0000	1.0000	1.0000	1.0000	0.9999	0.9995	0.9983	0.9955	0.9893
	9	1.0000	1.0000	1.0000	1.0000	1.0000	1.0000	1.0000	0.9999	0.9997	0.9990
	10	1.0000	1.0000	1.0000	1.0000	1.0000	1.0000	1.0000	1.0000	1.0000	1.0000
11	0	0.5688	0.3138	0.1673	0.0859	0.0422	0.0198	0.0088	0.0036	0.0014	0.0005
	1	0.8981	0.6974	0.4922	0.3221	0.1971	0.1130	0.0606	0.0302	0.0139	0.0059
	2	0.9848	0.9104	0.7788	0.6174	0.4552	0.3127	0.2001	0.1189	0.0652	0.0327
	3	0.9984	0.9815	0.9306	0.8389	0.7133	0.5696	0.4256	0.2963	0.1911	0.1133
	4	0.9999	0.9972	0.9841	0.9496	0.8854	0.7897	0.6683	0.5328	0.3971	0.2744
	5	1.0000	0.9997	0.9973	0.9883	0.9657	0.9218	0.8513	0.7535	0.6331	0.5000
	6	1.0000	1.0000	0.9997	0.9980	0.9924	0.9784	0.9499	0.9006	0.8262	0.7256
	7	1.0000	1.0000	1.0000	0.9998	0.9988	0.9957	0.9878	0.9707	0.9390	0.8867
	8	1.0000	1.0000	1.0000	1.0000	0.9999	0.9994	0.9980	0.9941	0.9852	0.9673
	9	1.0000	1.0000	1.0000	1.0000	1.0000	1.0000	0.9998	0.9993	0.9978	0.9941
	10	1.0000	1.0000	1.0000	1.0000	1.0000	1.0000	1.0000	1.0000	0.9998	0.9995
	11	1.0000	1.0000	1.0000	1.0000	1.0000	1.0000	1.0000	1.0000	1.0000	1.0000
12	0	0.5404	0.2824	0.1422	0.0687	0.0317	0.0138	0.0057	0.0022	0.0008	0.0002
	1	0.8816	0.6590	0.4435	0.2749	0.1584	0.0850	0.0424	0.0196	0.0083	0.0032
	2	0.9804	0.8891	0.7358	0.5583	0.3907	0.2528	0.1513	0.0834	0.0421	0.0193
	3	0.9978	0.9744	0.9078	0.7946	0.6488	0.4925	0.3467	0.2253	0.1345	0.0730
	4	0.9998	0.9957	0.9761	0.9274	0.8424	0.7237	0.5833	0.4382	0.3044	0.1938
	5	1.0000	0.9995	0.9954	0.9806	0.9456	0.8822	0.7873	0.6652	0.5269	0.3872
	6	1.0000	0.9999	0.9993	0.9961	0.9857	0.9614	0.9154	0.8418	0.7393	0.6128
	7	1.0000	1.0000	0.9999	0.9994	0.9972	0.9905	0.9745	0.9427	0.8883	0.8062
	8	1.0000	1.0000	1.0000	0.9999	0.9996	0.9983	0.9944	0.9847	0.9644	0.9270
	9	1.0000	1.0000	1.0000	1.0000	1.0000	0.9998	0.9992	0.9972	0.9921	0.9807
	10	1.0000	1.0000	1.0000	1.0000	1.0000	1.0000	0.9999	0.9997	0.9989	0.9968
	11	1.0000	1.0000	1.0000	1.0000	1.0000	1.0000	1.0000	1.0000	0.9999	0.9998
	12	1.0000	1.0000	1.0000	1.0000	1.0000	1.0000	1.0000	1.0000	1.0000	1.0000
13	0	0.5133	0.2542	0.1209	0.0550	0.0238	0.0097	0.0037	0.0013	0.0004	0.0001
	1	0.8646	0.6213	0.3983	0.2336	0.1267	0.0637	0.0296	0.0126	0.0049	0.0017
	2	0.9755	0.8661	0.6920	0.5017	0.3326	0.2025	0.1132	0.0579	0.0269	0.0112
	3	0.9969	0.9658	0.8820	0.7473	0.5843	0.4206	0.2783	0.1686	0.0929	0.0461
	4	0.9997	0.9935	0.9658	0.9009	0.7940	0.6543	0.5005	0.3530	0.2279	0.1334
	5	1.0000	0.9991	0.9925	0.9700	0.9198	0.8346	0.7159	0.5744	0.4268	0.2905
	6	1.0000	0.9999	0.9987	0.9930	0.9757	0.9376	0.8705	0.7712	0.6437	0.5000
	7	1.0000	1.0000	0.9998	0.9988	0.9944	0.9818	0.9538	0.9023	0.8212	0.7095
	8	1.0000	1.0000	1.0000	0.9998	0.9990	0.9960	0.9874	0.9679	0.9302	0.8666
	9	1.0000	1.0000	1.0000	1.0000	0.9999	0.9993	0.9975	0.9922	0.9797	0.9539
	10	1.0000	1.0000	1.0000	1.0000	1.0000	0.9999	0.9997	0.9987	0.9959	0.9888
	11	1.0000	1.0000	1.0000	1.0000	1.0000	1.0000	1.0000	0.9999	0.9995	0.9983

TABLE B.1 (continued)

n	x	ρ									
		0.05	**0.10**	**0.15**	**0.20**	**0.25**	**0.30**	**0.35**	**0.40**	**0.45**	**0.50**
	12	1.0000	1.0000	1.0000	1.0000	1.0000	1.0000	1.0000	1.0000	1.0000	0.9999
	13	1.0000	1.0000	1.0000	1.0000	1.0000	1.0000	1.0000	1.0000	1.0000	1.0000
14	0	0.4877	0.2288	0.1028	0.0440	0.0178	0.0068	0.0024	0.0008	0.0002	0.0001
	1	0.8470	0.5846	0.3567	0.1979	0.1010	0.0475	0.0205	0.0081	0.0029	0.0009
	2	0.9699	0.8416	0.6479	0.4481	0.2811	0.1608	0.0839	0.0398	0.0170	0.0065
	3	0.9958	0.9559	0.8535	0.6982	0.5213	0.3552	0.2205	0.1243	0.0632	0.0287
	4	0.9996	0.9908	0.9533	0.8702	0.7415	0.5842	0.4227	0.2793	0.1672	0.0898
	5	1.0000	0.9985	0.9885	0.9561	0.8883	0.7805	0.6405	0.4859	0.3373	0.2120
	6	1.0000	0.9998	0.9978	0.9884	0.9617	0.9067	0.8164	0.6925	0.5461	0.3953
	7	1.0000	1.0000	0.9997	0.9976	0.9897	0.9685	0.9247	0.8499	0.7414	0.6047
	8	1.0000	1.0000	1.0000	0.9996	0.9978	0.9917	0.9757	0.9417	0.8811	0.7880
	9	1.0000	1.0000	1.0000	1.0000	0.9997	0.9983	0.9940	0.9825	0.9574	0.9102
	10	1.0000	1.0000	1.0000	1.0000	1.0000	0.9998	0.9989	0.9961	0.9886	0.9713
	11	1.0000	1.0000	1.0000	1.0000	1.0000	1.0000	0.9999	0.9994	0.9978	0.9935
	12	1.0000	1.0000	1.0000	1.0000	1.0000	1.0000	1.0000	0.9999	0.9997	0.9991
	13	1.0000	1.0000	1.0000	1.0000	1.0000	1.0000	1.0000	1.0000	1.0000	0.9999
	14	1.0000	1.0000	1.0000	1.0000	1.0000	1.0000	1.0000	1.0000	1.0000	1.0000
15	0	0.4633	0.2059	0.0874	0.0352	0.0134	0.0047	0.0016	0.0005	0.0001	0.0000
	1	0.8290	0.5490	0.3186	0.1671	0.0802	0.0353	0.0142	0.0052	0.0017	0.0005
	2	0.9638	0.8159	0.6042	0.3980	0.2361	0.1268	0.0617	0.0271	0.0107	0.0037
	3	0.9945	0.9444	0.8227	0.6482	0.4613	0.2969	0.1727	0.0905	0.0424	0.0176
	4	0.9994	0.9873	0.9383	0.8358	0.6865	0.5155	0.3519	0.2173	0.1204	0.0592
	5	0.9999	0.9978	0.9832	0.9389	0.8516	0.7216	0.5643	0.4032	0.2608	0.1509
	6	1.0000	0.9997	0.9964	0.9819	0.9434	0.8689	0.7548	0.6098	0.4522	0.3036
	7	1.0000	1.0000	0.9994	0.9958	0.9827	0.9500	0.8868	0.7869	0.6535	0.5000
	8	1.0000	1.0000	0.9999	0.9992	0.9958	0.9848	0.9578	0.9050	0.8182	0.6964
	9	1.0000	1.0000	1.0000	0.9999	0.9992	0.9963	0.9876	0.9662	0.9231	0.8491
	10	1.0000	1.0000	1.0000	1.0000	0.9999	0.9993	0.9972	0.9907	0.9745	0.9408
	11	1.0000	1.0000	1.0000	1.0000	1.0000	0.9999	0.9995	0.9981	0.9937	0.9824
	12	1.0000	1.0000	1.0000	1.0000	1.0000	1.0000	0.9999	0.9997	0.9989	0.9963
	13	1.0000	1.0000	1.0000	1.0000	1.0000	1.0000	1.0000	1.0000	0.9999	0.9995
	14	1.0000	1.0000	1.0000	1.0000	1.0000	1.0000	1.0000	1.0000	1.0000	1.0000
20	0	0.3585	0.1216	0.0388	0.0115	0.0032	0.0008	0.0002	0.0000	0.0000	0.0000
	1	0.7358	0.3917	0.1756	0.0692	0.0243	0.0076	0.0021	0.0005	0.0001	0.0000
	2	0.9245	0.6769	0.4049	0.2061	0.0913	0.0355	0.0121	0.0036	0.0009	0.0002
	3	0.9841	0.8670	0.6477	0.4114	0.2252	0.1071	0.0444	0.0160	0.0049	0.0013
	4	0.9974	0.9568	0.8298	0.6296	0.4148	0.2375	0.1182	0.0510	0.0189	0.0059
	5	0.9997	0.9887	0.9327	0.8042	0.6172	0.4164	0.2454	0.1256	0.0553	0.0207
	6	1.0000	0.9976	0.9781	0.9133	0.7858	0.6080	0.4166	0.2500	0.1299	0.0577
	7	1.0000	0.9996	0.9941	0.9679	0.8982	0.7723	0.6010	0.4159	0.2520	0.1316
	8	1.0000	0.9999	0.9987	0.9900	0.9591	0.8867	0.7624	0.5956	0.4143	0.2517
	9	1.0000	1.0000	0.9998	0.9974	0.9861	0.9520	0.8782	0.7553	0.5914	0.4119
	10	1.0000	1.0000	1.0000	0.9994	0.9961	0.9829	0.9468	0.8725	0.7507	0.5881
	11	1.0000	1.0000	1.0000	0.9999	0.9991	0.9949	0.9804	0.9435	0.8692	0.7483
	12	1.0000	1.0000	1.0000	1.0000	0.9998	0.9987	0.9940	0.9790	0.9420	0.8684
	13	1.0000	1.0000	1.0000	1.0000	1.0000	0.9997	0.9985	0.9935	0.9786	0.9423
	14	1.0000	1.0000	1.0000	1.0000	1.0000	1.0000	0.9997	0.9984	0.9936	0.9793
	15	1.0000	1.0000	1.0000	1.0000	1.0000	1.0000	1.0000	0.9997	0.9985	0.9941
	16	1.0000	1.0000	1.0000	1.0000	1.0000	1.0000	1.0000	1.0000	0.9997	0.9987
	17	1.0000	1.0000	1.0000	1.0000	1.0000	1.0000	1.0000	1.0000	1.0000	0.9998
	18	1.0000	1.0000	1.0000	1.0000	1.0000	1.0000	1.0000	1.0000	1.0000	1.0000

TABLE B.2 Cumulative Poisson Probabilities: $P(c \le x \mid \lambda)$

x	λ = 0.1	0.2	0.3	0.4	0.5	0.6	0.7	0.8	0.9	1.0
0	0.9048	0.8187	0.7408	0.6703	0.6065	0.5488	0.4966	0.4493	0.4066	0.3679
1	0.9953	0.9825	0.9631	0.9384	0.9098	0.8781	0.8442	0.8088	0.7725	0.7358
2	0.9998	0.9989	0.9964	0.9921	0.9856	0.9769	0.9659	0.9526	0.9371	0.9197
3	1.0000	0.9999	0.9997	0.9992	0.9982	0.9966	0.9942	0.9909	0.9865	0.9810
4	1.0000	1.0000	1.0000	0.9999	0.9998	0.9996	0.9992	0.9986	0.9977	0.9963
5	1.0000	1.0000	1.0000	1.0000	1.0000	1.0000	0.9999	0.9998	0.9997	0.9994
6	1.0000	1.0000	1.0000	1.0000	1.0000	1.0000	1.0000	1.0000	1.0000	0.9999
7	1.0000	1.0000	1.0000	1.0000	1.0000	1.0000	1.0000	1.0000	1.0000	1.0000

x	λ = 1.1	1.2	1.3	1.4	1.5	1.6	1.7	1.8	1.9	2.0
0	0.3329	0.3012	0.2725	0.2466	0.2231	0.2019	0.1827	0.1653	0.1496	0.1353
1	0.6990	0.6626	0.6268	0.5918	0.5578	0.5249	0.4932	0.4628	0.4338	0.4060
2	0.9004	0.8795	0.8571	0.8335	0.8088	0.7834	0.7572	0.7306	0.7037	0.6767
3	0.9743	0.9662	0.9569	0.9463	0.9344	0.9212	0.9068	0.8913	0.8747	0.8571
4	0.9946	0.9923	0.9893	0.9857	0.9814	0.9763	0.9704	0.9636	0.9559	0.9473
5	0.9990	0.9985	0.9978	0.9968	0.9955	0.9940	0.9920	0.9896	0.9868	0.9834
6	0.9999	0.9997	0.9996	0.9994	0.9991	0.9987	0.9981	0.9974	0.9966	0.9955
7	1.0000	1.0000	0.9999	0.9999	0.9998	0.9997	0.9996	0.9994	0.9992	0.9989
8	1.0000	1.0000	1.0000	1.0000	1.0000	1.0000	0.9999	0.9999	0.9998	0.9998
9	1.0000	1.0000	1.0000	1.0000	1.0000	1.0000	1.0000	1.0000	1.0000	1.0000

x	λ = 2.1	2.2	2.3	2.4	2.5	2.6	2.7	2.8	2.9	3.0
0	0.1225	0.1108	0.1003	0.0907	0.0821	0.0743	0.0672	0.0608	0.0550	0.0498
1	0.3796	0.3546	0.3309	0.3084	0.2873	0.2674	0.2487	0.2311	0.2146	0.1991
2	0.6496	0.6227	0.5960	0.5697	0.5438	0.5184	0.4936	0.4695	0.4460	0.4232
3	0.8386	0.8194	0.7993	0.7787	0.7576	0.7360	0.7141	0.6919	0.6696	0.6472
4	0.9379	0.9275	0.9162	0.9041	0.8912	0.8774	0.8629	0.8477	0.8318	0.8153
5	0.9796	0.9751	0.9700	0.9643	0.9580	0.9510	0.9433	0.9349	0.9258	0.9161
6	0.9941	0.9925	0.9906	0.9884	0.9858	0.9828	0.9794	0.9756	0.9713	0.9665
7	0.9985	0.9980	0.9974	0.9967	0.9958	0.9947	0.9934	0.9919	0.9901	0.9881
8	0.9997	0.9995	0.9994	0.9991	0.9989	0.9985	0.9981	0.9976	0.9969	0.9962
9	0.9999	0.9999	0.9999	0.9998	0.9997	0.9996	0.9995	0.9993	0.9991	0.9989
10	1.0000	1.0000	1.0000	1.0000	0.9999	0.9999	0.9999	0.9998	0.9998	0.9997
11	1.0000	1.0000	1.0000	1.0000	1.0000	1.0000	1.0000	1.0000	0.9999	0.9999
12	1.0000	1.0000	1.0000	1.0000	1.0000	1.0000	1.0000	1.0000	1.0000	1.0000

x	λ = 3.1	3.2	3.3	3.4	3.5	3.6	3.7	3.8	3.9	4.0
0	0.0450	0.0408	0.0369	0.0334	0.0302	0.0273	0.0247	0.0224	0.0202	0.0183
1	0.1847	0.1712	0.1586	0.1468	0.1359	0.1257	0.1162	0.1074	0.0992	0.0916
2	0.4012	0.3799	0.3594	0.3397	0.3208	0.3027	0.2854	0.2689	0.2531	0.2381
3	0.6248	0.6025	0.5803	0.5584	0.5366	0.5152	0.4942	0.4735	0.4533	0.4335
4	0.7982	0.7806	0.7626	0.7442	0.7254	0.7064	0.6872	0.6678	0.6484	0.6288
5	0.9057	0.8946	0.8829	0.8705	0.8576	0.8441	0.8301	0.8156	0.8006	0.7851
6	0.9612	0.9554	0.9490	0.9421	0.9347	0.9267	0.9182	0.9091	0.8995	0.8893

TABLE B.2 (continued)

x	λ 3.1	3.2	3.3	3.4	3.5	3.6	3.7	3.8	3.9	4.0
7	0.9858	0.9832	0.9802	0.9769	0.9733	0.9692	0.9648	0.9599	0.9546	0.9489
8	0.9953	0.9943	0.9931	0.9917	0.9901	0.9883	0.9863	0.9840	0.9815	0.9786
9	0.9986	0.9982	0.9978	0.9973	0.9967	0.9960	0.9952	0.9942	0.9931	0.9919
10	0.9996	0.9995	0.9994	0.9992	0.9990	0.9987	0.9984	0.9981	0.9977	0.9972
11	0.9999	0.9999	0.9998	0.9998	0.9997	0.9996	0.9995	0.9994	0.9993	0.9991
12	1.0000	1.0000	1.0000	0.9999	0.9999	0.9999	0.9999	0.9998	0.9998	0.9997
13	1.0000	1.0000	1.0000	1.0000	1.0000	1.0000	1.0000	1.0000	0.9999	0.9999
14	1.0000	1.0000	1.0000	1.0000	1.0000	1.0000	1.0000	1.0000	1.0000	1.0000
	λ 4.1	**4.2**	**4.3**	**4.4**	**4.5**	**4.6**	**4.7**	**4.8**	**4.9**	**5.0**
0	0.0166	0.0150	0.0136	0.0123	0.0111	0.0101	0.0091	0.0082	0.0074	0.0067
1	0.0845	0.0780	0.0719	0.0663	0.0611	0.0563	0.0518	0.0477	0.0439	0.0404
2	0.2238	0.2102	0.1974	0.1851	0.1736	0.1626	0.1523	0.1425	0.1333	0.1247
3	0.4142	0.3954	0.3772	0.3595	0.3423	0.3257	0.3097	0.2942	0.2793	0.2650
4	0.6093	0.5898	0.5704	0.5512	0.5321	0.5132	0.4946	0.4763	0.4582	0.4405
5	0.7693	0.7531	0.7367	0.7199	0.7029	0.6858	0.6684	0.6510	0.6335	0.6160
6	0.8786	0.8675	0.8558	0.8436	0.8311	0.8180	0.8046	0.7908	0.7767	0.7622
7	0.9427	0.9361	0.9290	0.9214	0.9134	0.9049	0.8960	0.8867	0.8769	0.8666
8	0.9755	0.9721	0.9683	0.9642	0.9597	0.9549	0.9497	0.9442	0.9382	0.9319
9	0.9905	0.9889	0.9871	0.9851	0.9829	0.9805	0.9778	0.9749	0.9717	0.9682
10	0.9966	0.9959	0.9952	0.9943	0.9933	0.9922	0.9910	0.9896	0.9880	0.9863
11	0.9989	0.9986	0.9983	0.9980	0.9976	0.9971	0.9966	0.9960	0.9953	0.9945
12	0.9997	0.9996	0.9995	0.9993	0.9992	0.9990	0.9988	0.9986	0.9983	0.9980
13	0.9999	0.9999	0.9998	0.9998	0.9997	0.9997	0.9996	0.9995	0.9994	0.9993
14	1.0000	1.0000	1.0000	0.9999	0.9999	0.9999	0.9999	0.9999	0.9998	0.9998
15	1.0000	1.0000	1.0000	1.0000	1.0000	1.0000	1.0000	1.0000	0.9999	0.9999
16	1.0000	1.0000	1.0000	1.0000	1.0000	1.0000	1.0000	1.0000	1.0000	1.0000
	λ 5.1	**5.2**	**5.3**	**5.4**	**5.5**	**5.6**	**5.7**	**5.8**	**5.9**	**6.0**
0	0.0061	0.0055	0.0050	0.0045	0.0041	0.0037	0.0033	0.0030	0.0027	0.0025
1	0.0372	0.0342	0.0314	0.0289	0.0266	0.0244	0.0224	0.0206	0.0189	0.0174
2	0.1165	0.1088	0.1016	0.0948	0.0884	0.0824	0.0768	0.0715	0.0666	0.0620
3	0.2513	0.2381	0.2254	0.2133	0.2017	0.1906	0.1801	0.1700	0.1604	0.1512
4	0.4231	0.4061	0.3895	0.3733	0.3575	0.3422	0.3272	0.3127	0.2987	0.2851
5	0.5984	0.5809	0.5635	0.5461	0.5289	0.5119	0.4950	0.4783	0.4619	0.4457
6	0.7474	0.7324	0.7171	0.7017	0.6860	0.6703	0.6544	0.6384	0.6224	0.6063
7	0.8560	0.8449	0.8335	0.8217	0.8095	0.7970	0.7842	0.7710	0.7576	0.7440
8	0.9252	0.9181	0.9106	0.9026	0.8944	0.8857	0.8766	0.8672	0.8574	0.8472
9	0.9644	0.9603	0.9559	0.9512	0.9462	0.9409	0.9352	0.9292	0.9228	0.9161
10	0.9844	0.9823	0.9800	0.9775	0.9747	0.9718	0.9686	0.9651	0.9614	0.9574
11	0.9937	0.9927	0.9916	0.9904	0.9890	0.9875	0.9859	0.9840	0.9821	0.9799
12	0.9976	0.9972	0.9967	0.9962	0.9955	0.9949	0.9941	0.9932	0.9922	0.9912
13	0.9992	0.9990	0.9988	0.9986	0.9983	0.9980	0.9977	0.9973	0.9969	0.9964
14	0.9997	0.9997	0.9996	0.9995	0.9994	0.9993	0.9991	0.9990	0.9986	0.9986

Table continues

TABLE B.2 (continued)

x	λ 5.1	5.2	5.3	5.4	5.5	5.6	5.7	5.8	5.9	6.0
15	0.9999	0.9999	0.9999	0.9998	0.9998	0.9998	0.9997	0.9996	0.9996	0.9995
16	1.0000	1.0000	1.0000	0.9999	0.9999	0.9999	0.9999	0.9999	0.9999	0.9998
17	1.0000	1.0000	1.0000	1.0000	1.0000	1.0000	1.0000	1.0000	1.0000	0.9999
18	1.0000	1.0000	1.0000	1.0000	1.0000	1.0000	1.0000	1.0000	1.0000	1.0000
	λ 6.1	**6.2**	**6.3**	**6.4**	**6.5**	**6.6**	**6.7**	**6.8**	**6.9**	**7.0**
0	0.0022	0.0020	0.0018	0.0017	0.0015	0.0014	0.0012	0.0011	0.0010	0.0009
1	0.0159	0.0146	0.0134	0.0123	0.0113	0.0103	0.0095	0.0087	0.0080	0.0073
2	0.0577	0.0536	0.0498	0.0463	0.0430	0.0400	0.0371	0.0344	0.0320	0.0296
3	0.1425	0.1342	0.1264	0.1189	0.1119	0.1052	0.0988	0.0928	0.0871	0.0818
4	0.2719	0.2592	0.2469	0.2351	0.2237	0.2127	0.2022	0.1920	0.1823	0.1730
5	0.4298	0.4141	0.3988	0.3837	0.3690	0.3547	0.3407	0.3270	0.3137	0.3007
6	0.5902	0.5742	0.5582	0.5423	0.5265	0.5108	0.4953	0.4799	0.4647	0.4497
7	0.7301	0.7160	0.7018	0.6873	0.6728	0.6581	0.6433	0.6285	0.6136	0.5987
8	0.8367	0.8259	0.8148	0.8033	0.7916	0.7796	0.7673	0.7548	0.7420	0.7291
9	0.9090	0.9016	0.8939	0.8858	0.8774	0.8686	0.8596	0.8502	0.8405	0.8305
10	0.9531	0.9486	0.9437	0.9386	0.9332	0.9274	0.9214	0.9151	0.9084	0.9015
11	0.9776	0.9750	0.9723	0.9693	0.9661	0.9627	0.9591	0.9552	0.9510	0.9466
12	0.9900	0.9887	0.9873	0.9857	0.9840	0.9821	0.9801	0.9779	0.9755	0.9730
13	0.9958	0.9952	0.9945	0.9937	0.9929	0.9920	0.9909	0.9898	0.9885	0.9872
14	0.9984	0.9981	0.9978	0.9974	0.9970	0.9966	0.9961	0.9956	0.9950	0.9943
15	0.9994	0.9993	0.9992	0.9990	0.9988	0.9986	0.9984	0.9982	0.9979	0.9976
16	0.9998	0.9997	0.9997	0.9996	0.9996	0.9995	0.9994	0.9993	0.9992	0.9990
17	0.9999	0.9999	0.9999	0.9999	0.9998	0.9998	0.9998	0.9997	0.9997	0.9996
18	1.0000	1.0000	1.0000	1.0000	0.9999	0.9999	0.9999	0.9999	0.9999	0.9999
19	1.0000	1.0000	1.0000	1.0000	1.0000	1.0000	1.0000	1.0000	1.0000	0.9999
20	1.0000	1.0000	1.0000	1.0000	1.0000	1.0000	1.0000	1.0000	1.0000	1.0000
	λ 7.1	**7.2**	**7.3**	**7.4**	**7.5**	**7.6**	**7.7**	**7.8**	**7.9**	**8.0**
0	0.0008	0.0007	0.0007	0.0006	0.0006	0.0005	0.0005	0.0004	0.0004	0.0003
1	0.0067	0.0061	0.0056	0.0051	0.0047	0.0043	0.0039	0.0036	0.0033	0.0030
2	0.0275	0.0255	0.0236	0.0219	0.0203	0.0188	0.0174	0.0161	0.0149	0.0138
3	0.0767	0.0719	0.0674	0.0632	0.0591	0.0554	0.0518	0.0485	0.0453	0.0424
4	0.1641	0.1555	0.1473	0.1395	0.1321	0.1249	0.1181	0.1117	0.1055	0.0996
5	0.2881	0.2759	0.2640	0.2526	0.2414	0.2307	0.2203	0.2103	0.2006	0.1912
6	0.4349	0.4204	0.4060	0.3920	0.3782	0.3646	0.3514	0.3384	0.3257	0.3134
7	0.5838	0.5689	0.5541	0.5393	0.5246	0.5100	0.4956	0.4812	0.4670	0.4530
8	0.7160	0.7027	0.6892	0.6757	0.6620	0.6482	0.6343	0.6204	0.6065	0.5926
9	0.8202	0.8096	0.7988	0.7877	0.7764	0.7649	0.7531	0.7411	0.7290	0.7166
10	0.8942	0.8867	0.8788	0.8707	0.8622	0.8535	0.8445	0.8352	0.8257	0.8159
11	0.9420	0.9371	0.9319	0.9265	0.9208	0.9148	0.9085	0.9020	0.8952	0.8881
12	0.9703	0.9673	0.9642	0.9609	0.9573	0.9536	0.9496	0.9453	0.9409	0.9362
13	0.9857	0.9841	0.9824	0.9805	0.9784	0.9762	0.9739	0.9714	0.9687	0.9658
14	0.9935	0.9927	0.9918	0.9908	0.9897	0.9886	0.9873	0.9859	0.9844	0.9827

TABLE B.2 (continued)

x	λ 7.1	7.2	7.3	7.4	7.5	7.6	7.7	7.8	7.9	8.0
15	0.9972	0.9968	0.9964	0.9959	0.9954	0.9948	0.9941	0.9934	0.9926	0.9918
16	0.9989	0.9987	0.9985	0.9983	0.9980	0.9978	0.9974	0.9971	0.9967	0.9963
17	0.9996	0.9995	0.9994	0.9993	0.9992	0.9991	0.9989	0.9988	0.9986	0.9984
18	0.9998	0.9998	0.9998	0.9997	0.9997	0.9996	0.9996	0.9995	0.9994	0.9993
19	0.9999	0.9999	0.9999	0.9999	0.9999	0.9999	0.9998	0.9998	0.9998	0.9997
20	1.0000	1.0000	1.0000	1.0000	1.0000	0.9999	0.9999	0.9999	0.9999	0.9999
21	1.0000	1.0000	1.0000	1.0000	1.0000	1.0000	1.0000	1.0000	1.0000	1.0000
	λ 8.1	8.2	8.3	8.4	8.5	8.6	8.7	8.8	8.9	9.0
0	0.0003	0.0003	0.0002	0.0002	0.0002	0.0002	0.0002	0.0002	0.0001	0.0001
1	0.0028	0.0025	0.0023	0.0021	0.0019	0.0018	0.0016	0.0015	0.0014	0.0012
2	0.0127	0.0118	0.0109	0.0100	0.0093	0.0086	0.0079	0.0073	0.0068	0.0062
3	0.0396	0.0370	0.0346	0.0323	0.0301	0.0281	0.0262	0.0244	0.0228	0.0212
4	0.0941	0.0887	0.0837	0.0789	0.0744	0.0701	0.0660	0.0621	0.0584	0.0550
5	0.1822	0.1736	0.1653	0.1573	0.1496	0.1422	0.1352	0.1284	0.1219	0.1157
6	0.3013	0.2896	0.2781	0.2670	0.2562	0.2457	0.2355	0.2256	0.2160	0.2068
7	0.4391	0.4254	0.4119	0.3987	0.3856	0.3728	0.3602	0.3478	0.3357	0.3239
8	0.5786	0.5647	0.5508	0.5369	0.5231	0.5094	0.4958	0.4823	0.4689	0.4557
9	0.7041	0.6915	0.6788	0.6659	0.6530	0.6400	0.6269	0.6137	0.6006	0.5874
10	0.8058	0.7955	0.7850	0.7743	0.7634	0.7522	0.7409	0.7294	0.7178	0.7060
11	0.8807	0.8731	0.8652	0.8571	0.8487	0.8400	0.8311	0.8220	0.8126	0.8030
12	0.9313	0.9261	0.9207	0.9150	0.9091	0.9029	0.8965	0.8898	0.8829	0.8758
13	0.9628	0.9595	0.9561	0.9524	0.9486	0.9445	0.9403	0.9358	0.9311	0.9262
14	0.9810	0.9791	0.9771	0.9749	0.9726	0.9701	0.9675	0.9647	0.9617	0.9585
15	0.9908	0.9898	0.9887	0.9875	0.9862	0.9847	0.9832	0.9816	0.9798	0.9780
16	0.9958	0.9953	0.9947	0.9941	0.9934	0.9926	0.9918	0.9909	0.9899	0.9889
17	0.9982	0.9979	0.9976	0.9973	0.9970	0.9966	0.9962	0.9957	0.9952	0.9947
18	0.9992	0.9991	0.9990	0.9989	0.9987	0.9985	0.9983	0.9981	0.9978	0.9976
19	0.9997	0.9996	0.9996	0.9995	0.9995	0.9994	0.9993	0.9992	0.9991	0.9989
20	0.9999	0.9999	0.9998	0.9998	0.9998	0.9997	0.9997	0.9997	0.9996	0.9996
21	1.0000	0.9999	0.9999	0.9999	0.9999	0.9999	0.9999	0.9999	0.9998	0.9998
22	1.0000	1.0000	1.0000	1.0000	1.0000	1.0000	1.0000	0.9999	0.9999	0.9999
23	1.0000	1.0000	1.0000	1.0000	1.0000	1.0000	1.0000	1.0000	1.0000	1.0000
	λ 9.1	9.2	9.3	9.4	9.5	9.6	9.7	9.8	9.9	10.0
0	0.0001	0.0001	0.0001	0.0001	0.0001	0.0001	0.0001	0.0001	0.0001	0.0000
1	0.0011	0.0010	0.0009	0.0009	0.0008	0.0007	0.0007	0.0006	0.0005	0.0005
2	0.0058	0.0053	0.0049	0.0045	0.0042	0.0038	0.0035	0.0033	0.0030	0.0028
3	0.0198	0.0184	0.0172	0.0160	0.0149	0.0138	0.0129	0.0120	0.0111	0.0103
4	0.0517	0.0486	0.0456	0.0429	0.0403	0.0378	0.0355	0.0333	0.0312	0.0293
5	0.1098	0.1041	0.0987	0.0935	0.0885	0.0838	0.0793	0.0750	0.0710	0.0671
6	0.1978	0.1892	0.1808	0.1727	0.1650	0.1575	0.1502	0.1433	0.1366	0.1301
7	0.3123	0.3010	0.2900	0.2792	0.2687	0.2584	0.2485	0.2388	0.2294	0.2202
8	0.4426	0.4296	0.4168	0.4042	0.3918	0.3796	0.3676	0.3558	0.3442	0.3328

Table continues

TABLE B.2 (continued)

x	λ 9.1	9.2	9.3	9.4	9.5	9.6	9.7	9.8	9.9	10.0
9	0.5742	0.5611	0.5479	0.5349	0.5218	0.5089	0.4960	0.4832	0.4705	0.4579
10	0.6941	0.6820	0.6699	0.6576	0.6453	0.6330	0.6205	0.6080	0.5955	0.5830
11	0.7932	0.7832	0.7730	0.7626	0.7520	0.7412	0.7303	0.7193	0.7081	0.6968
12	0.8684	0.8607	0.8529	0.8448	0.8364	0.8279	0.8191	0.8101	0.8009	0.7916
13	0.9210	0.9156	0.9100	0.9042	0.8981	0.8919	0.8853	0.8786	0.8716	0.8645
14	0.9552	0.9517	0.9480	0.9441	0.9400	0.9357	0.9312	0.9265	0.9216	0.9165
15	0.9760	0.9738	0.9715	0.9691	0.9665	0.9638	0.9609	0.9579	0.9546	0.9513
16	0.9878	0.9865	0.9852	0.9838	0.9823	0.9806	0.9789	0.9770	0.9751	0.9730
17	0.9941	0.9934	0.9927	0.9919	0.9911	0.9902	0.9892	0.9881	0.9869	0.9857
18	0.9973	0.9969	0.9966	0.9962	0.9957	0.9952	0.9947	0.9941	0.9935	0.9928
19	0.9988	0.9986	0.9985	0.9983	0.9980	0.9978	0.9975	0.9972	0.9969	0.9965
20	0.9995	0.9994	0.9993	0.9992	0.9991	0.9990	0.9989	0.9987	0.9986	0.9984
21	0.9998	0.9998	0.9997	0.9997	0.9996	0.9996	0.9995	0.9995	0.9994	0.9993
22	0.9999	0.9999	0.9999	0.9999	0.9998	0.9998	0.9998	0.9998	0.9997	0.9997
23	1.0000	1.0000	1.0000	0.9999	0.9999	0.9999	0.9999	0.9999	0.9999	0.9999
24	1.0000	1.0000	1.0000	1.0000	1.0000	1.0000	1.0000	1.0000	0.9999	0.9999
25	1.0000	1.0000	1.0000	1.0000	1.0000	1.0000	1.0000	1.0000	1.0000	1.0000

x	λ 11.0	12.0	13.0	14.0	15.0	16.0	17.0	18.0	19.0	20.0
0	0.0000	0.0000	0.0000	0.0000	0.0000	0.0000	0.0000	0.0000	0.0000	0.0000
1	0.0002	0.0001	0.0000	0.0000	0.0000	0.0000	0.0000	0.0000	0.0000	0.0000
2	0.0012	0.0005	0.0002	0.0001	0.0000	0.0000	0.0000	0.0000	0.0000	0.0000
3	0.0049	0.0023	0.0011	0.0005	0.0002	0.0001	0.0000	0.0000	0.0000	0.0000
4	0.0151	0.0076	0.0037	0.0018	0.0009	0.0004	0.0002	0.0001	0.0000	0.0000
5	0.0375	0.0203	0.0107	0.0055	0.0028	0.0014	0.0007	0.0003	0.0002	0.0001
6	0.0786	0.0458	0.0259	0.0142	0.0076	0.0040	0.0021	0.0010	0.0005	0.0003
7	0.1432	0.0895	0.0540	0.0316	0.0180	0.0100	0.0054	0.0029	0.0015	0.0008
8	0.2320	0.1550	0.0998	0.0621	0.0374	0.0220	0.0126	0.0071	0.0039	0.0021
9	0.3405	0.2424	0.1658	0.1094	0.0699	0.0433	0.0261	0.0154	0.0089	0.0050
10	0.4599	0.3472	0.2517	0.1757	0.1185	0.0774	0.0491	0.0304	0.0183	0.0108
11	0.5793	0.4616	0.3532	0.2600	0.1847	0.1270	0.0847	0.0549	0.0347	0.0214
12	0.6887	0.5760	0.4631	0.3585	0.2676	0.1931	0.1350	0.0917	0.0606	0.0390
13	0.7813	0.6815	0.5730	0.4644	0.3632	0.2745	0.2009	0.1426	0.0984	0.0661
14	0.8540	0.7720	0.6751	0.5704	0.4656	0.3675	0.2808	0.2081	0.1497	0.1049
15	0.9074	0.8444	0.7636	0.6694	0.5681	0.4667	0.3714	0.2866	0.2148	0.1565
16	0.9441	0.8987	0.8355	0.7559	0.6641	0.5660	0.4677	0.3750	0.2920	0.2211
17	0.9678	0.9370	0.8905	0.8272	0.7489	0.6593	0.5640	0.4686	0.3784	0.2970
18	0.9823	0.9626	0.9302	0.8826	0.8195	0.7423	0.6549	0.5622	0.4695	0.3814
19	0.9907	0.9787	0.9573	0.9235	0.8752	0.8122	0.7363	0.6509	0.5606	0.4703
20	0.9953	0.9884	0.9750	0.9521	0.9170	0.8682	0.8055	0.7307	0.6472	0.5591
21	0.9977	0.9939	0.9859	0.9711	0.9469	0.9108	0.8615	0.7991	0.7255	0.6437
22	0.9989	0.9969	0.9924	0.9833	0.9672	0.9418	0.9047	0.8551	0.7931	0.7206
23	0.9995	0.9985	0.9960	0.9907	0.9805	0.9633	0.9367	0.8989	0.8490	0.7875
24	0.9998	0.9993	0.9980	0.9950	0.9888	0.9777	0.9593	0.9317	0.8933	0.8432

TABLE B.2 (continued)

x	λ 11.0	12.0	13.0	14.0	15.0	16.0	17.0	18.0	19.0	20.0
25	0.9999	0.9997	0.9990	0.9974	0.9938	0.9869	0.9747	0.9554	0.9269	0.8878
26	1.0000	0.9999	0.9995	0.9987	0.9967	0.9925	0.9848	0.9718	0.9514	0.9221
27	1.0000	0.9999	0.9998	0.9994	0.9983	0.9959	0.9912	0.9827	0.9687	0.9475
28	1.0000	1.0000	0.9999	0.9997	0.9991	0.9978	0.9950	0.9897	0.9805	0.9657
29	1.0000	1.0000	1.0000	0.9999	0.9996	0.9989	0.9973	0.9940	0.9881	0.9782
30	1.0000	1.0000	1.0000	0.9999	0.9998	0.9994	0.9985	0.9967	0.9930	0.9865
31	1.0000	1.0000	1.0000	1.0000	0.9999	0.9997	0.9992	0.9982	0.9960	0.9919
32	1.0000	1.0000	1.0000	1.0000	0.9999	0.9999	0.9996	0.9990	0.9978	0.9953
33	1.0000	1.0000	1.0000	1.0000	1.0000	0.9999	0.9998	0.9995	0.9988	0.9973
34	1.0000	1.0000	1.0000	1.0000	1.0000	1.0000	0.9999	0.9997	0.9994	0.9985
35	1.0000	1.0000	1.0000	1.0000	1.0000	1.0000	0.9999	0.9999	0.9997	0.9992
36	1.0000	1.0000	1.0000	1.0000	1.0000	1.0000	1.0000	0.9999	0.9998	0.9996
37	1.0000	1.0000	1.0000	1.0000	1.0000	1.0000	1.0000	1.0000	0.9999	0.9998
38	1.0000	1.0000	1.0000	1.0000	1.0000	1.0000	1.0000	1.0000	1.0000	0.9999
39	1.0000	1.0000	1.0000	1.0000	1.0000	1.0000	1.0000	1.0000	1.0000	0.9999
40	1.0000	1.0000	1.0000	1.0000	1.0000	1.0000	1.0000	1.0000	1.0000	1.0000

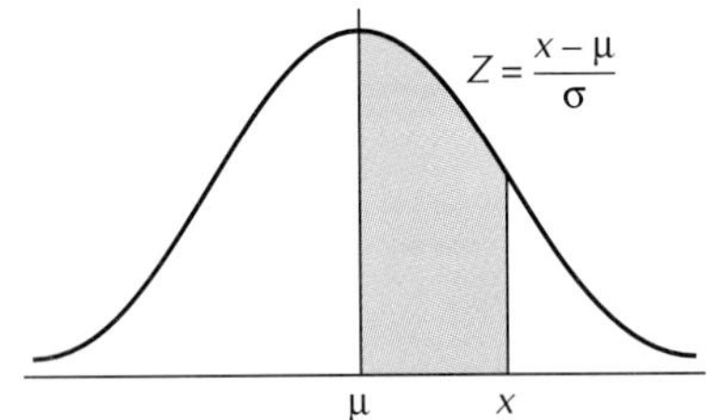

TABLE B.3 Normal Curve Areas

Z	0.00	0.01	0.02	0.03	0.04	0.05	0.06	0.07	0.08	0.09
0.0	0.0000	0.0040	0.0080	0.0120	0.0160	0.0199	0.0239	0.0279	0.0319	0.0359
0.1	0.0398	0.0438	0.0478	0.0517	0.0557	0.0596	0.0636	0.0675	0.0714	0.0753
0.2	0.0793	0.0832	0.0871	0.0910	0.0948	0.0987	0.1026	0.1064	0.1103	0.1141
0.3	0.1179	0.1217	0.1255	0.1293	0.1331	0.1368	0.1406	0.1443	0.1480	0.1517
0.4	0.1554	0.1591	0.1628	0.1664	0.1700	0.1736	0.1772	0.1808	0.1844	0.1879
0.5	0.1915	0.1950	0.1985	0.2019	0.2054	0.2088	0.2123	0.2157	0.2190	0.2224
0.6	0.2257	0.2291	0.2324	0.2357	0.2389	0.2422	0.2454	0.2486	0.2517	0.2549
0.7	0.2580	0.2611	0.2642	0.2673	0.2704	0.2734	0.2764	0.2794	0.2823	0.2852
0.8	0.2881	0.2910	0.2939	0.2967	0.2995	0.3023	0.3051	0.3078	0.3106	0.3133
0.9	0.3159	0.3186	0.3212	0.3238	0.3264	0.3289	0.3315	0.3340	0.3365	0.3389
1.0	0.3413	0.3438	0.3461	0.3485	0.3508	0.3531	0.3554	0.3577	0.3599	0.3621
1.1	0.3643	0.3665	0.3686	0.3708	0.3729	0.3749	0.3770	0.3790	0.3810	0.3830
1.2	0.3849	0.3869	0.3888	0.3907	0.3925	0.3944	0.3962	0.3980	0.3997	0.4015
1.3	0.4032	0.4049	0.4066	0.4082	0.4099	0.4115	0.4131	0.4147	0.4162	0.4177
1.4	0.4192	0.4207	0.4222	0.4236	0.4251	0.4265	0.4279	0.4292	0.4306	0.4319
1.5	0.4332	0.4345	0.4357	0.4370	0.4382	0.4394	0.4406	0.4418	0.4429	0.4441
1.6	0.4452	0.4463	0.4474	0.4484	0.4495	0.4505	0.4515	0.4525	0.4535	0.4545
1.7	0.4554	0.4564	0.4573	0.4582	0.4591	0.4599	0.4608	0.4616	0.4625	0.4633
1.8	0.4641	0.4649	0.4656	0.4664	0.4671	0.4678	0.4686	0.4693	0.4699	0.4706
1.9	0.4713	0.4719	0.4726	0.4732	0.4738	0.4744	0.4750	0.4756	0.4761	0.4767
2.0	0.4772	0.4778	0.4783	0.4788	0.4793	0.4798	0.4803	0.4808	0.4812	0.4817
2.1	0.4821	0.4826	0.4830	0.4834	0.4838	0.4842	0.4846	0.4850	0.4854	0.4857
2.2	0.4861	0.4864	0.4868	0.4871	0.4875	0.4878	0.4881	0.4884	0.4887	0.4890
2.3	0.4893	0.4896	0.4898	0.4901	0.4904	0.4906	0.4909	0.4911	0.4913	0.4916
2.4	0.4918	0.4920	0.4922	0.4925	0.4927	0.4929	0.4931	0.4932	0.4934	0.4936
2.5	0.4938	0.4940	0.4941	0.4943	0.4945	0.4946	0.4948	0.4949	0.4951	0.4952
2.6	0.4953	0.4955	0.4956	0.4957	0.4959	0.4960	0.4961	0.4962	0.4963	0.4964
2.7	0.4965	0.4966	0.4967	0.4968	0.4969	0.4970	0.4971	0.4972	0.4973	0.4974
2.8	0.4974	0.4975	0.4976	0.4977	0.4977	0.4978	0.4979	0.4979	0.4980	0.4981
2.9	0.4981	0.4982	0.4982	0.4983	0.4984	0.4984	0.4985	0.4985	0.4986	0.4986
3.0	0.4987	0.4987	0.4987	0.4988	0.4988	0.4989	0.4989	0.4989	0.4990	0.4990

SOLUTIONS TO SELECTED ODD-NUMBERED PROBLEMS

CHAPTER 2

1. a. drive-up window, \$20,000; b. breakfast, \$4,000; c. drive-up window, \$10,000; d. drive-up window, \$9,600; e. drive-up window, \$7,000
3. a. motel, \$20,000; b. theater, \$5,000; c. motel or restaurant, \$14,000; d. theater, \$5,400; e. motel, \$9,000
5. a. pass, 20 yd; b. off tackle or option, –2 yd; c. toss sweep, 6.8 yd; d. pass, toss sweep, off tackle, option, draw, screen, and toss sweep, 10.4, yd
7. a. 22 lb, \$21; b. maximax = 24 lb, \$24; maximin = 20 lb, \$20
9. Make a bid, \$142.0 million

CHAPTER 2 SUPPLEMENT

1. a. Maximize $Z = \$2.25x_1 + 3.10x_2$; s.t. $5.0x_1 + 7.5x_2 \leq 6{,}500$, $3.0x_1 + 3.2x_2 \leq 3{,}000$, $x_2 \leq 510$, $x_1 \geq 0$, $x_2 \geq 0$; b. and c. $x_1 = 456$, $x_2 = 510$, $Z = \$2{,}607$
3. Maximize $Z = 1{,}800x_{1a} + 2{,}100x_{1b} + 1{,}600x_{1c} + 1{,}000x_{2a} + 700x_{2b} + 900x_{2c} + 1{,}400x_{3a} + 800x_{3b} + 2{,}200x_{3c}$; s.t. $x_{1a} + x_{1b} + x_{1c} = 30$, $x_{2a} + x_{2b} + x_{2c} = 30$, $x_{3a} + x_{3b} + x_{3c} = 30$, $x_{1a} + x_{2a} + x_{3a} \leq 40$, $x_{1b} + x_{2b} + x_{3b} \leq 60$, $x_{1c} + x_{2c} + x_{3c} \leq 50$, $x_{ij} \geq 0$; $x_{1b} = 30$, $x_{2a} = 30$, $x_{3c} = 30$, $Z = 159{,}000$
5. Maximize $Z = 0.7x_{cr} + 0.6x_{br} + 0.4x_{pr} + 0.85x_{ar} + 1.05x_{cb} + 0.95x_{bb} + 0.75x_{pb} + 1.20x_{ab} + 1.55x_{cm} + 1.45x_{bm} + 1.25x_{pm} + 1.70x_{am}$; s.t. $x_{cr} + x_{cb} + x_{cm} \leq 200$, $x_{br} + x_{bb} + x_{bm} \leq 300$, $x_{pr} + x_{pb} + x_{pm} \leq 150$, $x_{ar} + x_{ab} + x_{am} \leq 400$, $0.90x_{br} + 0.90x_{pr} - 0.10x_{cr} - 0.10x_{ar} \leq 0$, $0.80x_{cr} + 0.20x_{br} - 0.20x_{pr} - 0.20x_{ar} \geq 0$, $0.25x_{bb} + 0.75x_{cb} - 0.75x_{pb} - 0.75x_{ab} \geq 0$, $x_{am} = 0$, $0.5x_{bm} + 5x_{pm} - 0.5x_{cm} - 5x_{am}$, $x_{ij} \geq 0$; $x_{cr} = 75$, $x_{ar} = 300$, $x_{bb} = 300$, $x_{ab} = 100$, $x_{cm} = 125$, $x_{pm} = 125$, $Z = 1{,}062.5$
7. a. Maximize $Z = 8x_1 + 10x_2$; s.t. $x_1 + x_2 \geq 400$, $x_1 \geq 0.4(x_1 + x_2)$, $x_2 \leq 250$, $x_1 = 2x_2$, $x_1 + x_2 \leq 500$, $x_i \geq 0$; b. $x_1 = 333.3$, $x_2 = 166.6$, $Z = 4{,}332.4$
9. Maximize $Z = 3x_{1R} + 5x_{2R} + 6x_{4R} + 9x_{1P} + 11x_{2P} + 6x_{3P} + 12x_{4P} + 1x_{1L} + 3x_{2L} + 4x_{4L} - 2x_{3L}$; s.t. $x_{1R} + x_{2R} + x_{3R} + x_{4R} \geq 3{,}000$, $x_{1P} + x_{2P} + x_{3P} + x_{4P} \geq 3{,}000$, $x_{1L} + x_{2L} + x_{3L} + x_{4L} \geq 3{,}000$, $x_{1R} + x_{1P} + x_{1L} \leq 5{,}000$, $x_{2R} + x_{2P} + x_{2L} \leq 2{,}400$, $x_{3R} + x_{3P} + x_{3L} \leq 4{,}000$, $x_{4R} + x_{4P} + x_{4L} \leq 1{,}500$, $0.6x_{1R} - 0.4x_{2R} - 0.4x_{3R} - 0.4x_{4R} \geq 0$, $-0.2x_{1R} + 0.8x_{2R} - 0.2x_{3R} - 0.2x_{4R} \leq 0$, $-0.3x_{1R} - 0.3x_{2R} + 0.7x_{3R} - 0.3x_{4R} \geq 0$, $-0.4x_{1P} - 0.4x_{2P} + 0.6x_{3P} - 0.4x_{4P} \geq 0$, $-0.5x_{1L} + 0.5x_{2L} - 0.5x_{3L} - 0.5x_{4L} \leq 0$, $0.9x_{1L} - 0.1x_{2L} - 0.1x_{3L} - 0.1x_{4L} \geq 0$, $x_{ij} \geq 0$; $x_{1R} = 2{,}000$, $x_{2R} = 100$, $x_{3R} = 900$, $x_{2P} = 2{,}300$, $x_{3P} = 3{,}100$, $x_{4L} = 1{,}500$, $x_{1L} = 3{,}000$, $Z = 71{,}400$ (multiple optimal solutions)
11. Minimize $Z = 10(x_1 + x_2 + x_3 + x_4 + x_5) + 15(y_1 + y_2 + y_3 + y_4 + y_5) + 2(w_1 + w_2 + w_3 + w_4)$; s.t. $x_i \leq 2{,}000$, $y_i \leq 600$, $x_1 + y_1 - w_1 = 1{,}200$, $x_2 + y_2 + w_1 - w_2 = 2{,}100$, $x_3 + y_3 + w_2 - w_3 = 2{,}400$, $x_4 + y_4 + w_3 - w_4 = 3{,}000$, $x_5 + y_5 + w_4 = 4{,}000$, $x_i \geq 0$, $y_i \geq 0$, $w_i \geq 0$; $x_1 = x_2 = x_3 = x_4 = x_5 = 2{,}000$, $y_1 = 300$, $y_2 = y_3 = y_4 = y_5 = 600$, $w_1 = 1{,}100$, $w_2 = 1{,}600$, $w_3 = 1{,}800$, $w_4 = 1{,}400$, $Z = 152{,}300$
13. Minimize $Z = x_1 + x_2 + x_3 + x_4 + x_5 + x_6$; s.t. $x_6 + x_1 \geq 90$, $x_1 + x_2 \geq 215$, $x_2 + x_3 \geq 250$, $x_3 + x_4 \geq 65$, $x_4 + x_5 \geq 300$, $x_5 + x_6 \geq 125$, $x_i \geq 0$; $x_1 = 90$, $x_2 = 250$, $x_4 = 175$, $x_5 = 125$, $Z = 640$
15. a. and b. $x_1 = 4$, $x_2 = 2$, $Z = 22$
17. a. $x_1 = 4$, $x_2 = 3$, $Z = 2{,}400$; b. no, 1 bracelet; c. \$600, $x_1 = 60$, $x_2 = 0$, $Z = 3{,}600$
19. a. $x_1 = 3.3$, $x_2 = 6.7$, $Z = 568$; b. steeper, changes optimal point
21. $x_1 = 2$, $x_2 = 3$, $Z = 17$

CHAPTER 3

1. a. 1990: 84.24%, 1991: 80.22%, 1992: 72.28%, 1993: 65.6%, 1994: 58.3%, decreasing trend; b. 1990: 1.71% and 14.04%, 1991: 5.3% and 14.48%, 1992: 13.32% and 14.4%, 1993: 21.97% and 12.43%, 1994: 29.96% and 11.74%; c. 1990: 6.93 and 44.48, 1991: 7.50 and 47.64, 1992: 7.85 and 50.04, 1993: 6.90 and 44.46, 1994: 5.79 and 38.32
3. a. 139.8; b. good = 91.6%
5. 1991: $12.49, 1992: $11.57, 1993: $11.15; 1991–92: – 7.37%, 1992–93: – 3.63%
7. a. Alternative 2, 203; b. alternative 2
9. a. 4.97; b. 4.97; c. 5.51; d. 5.14

CHAPTER 4

1. $\bar{p} = 0.151$, UCL = 0.258, LCL = 0.044; in control
3. $\bar{p} = 0.053$, UCL = 0.101, LCL = 0.005; in control
5. a. $\bar{c} = 24.73$, UCL = 39.65, LCL = 9.81; b. out of control
7. $\bar{c} = 10.67$, UCL = 17.20, LCL = 4.14; in control
9. a. $\bar{R} = 0.57$, UCL = 1.21, LCL = 0; b. in control
11. a. $\bar{R} = 2$, UCL = 4.56, LCL = 0; b. out of control
13. $\bar{\bar{x}} = 39.7$, UCL = 43.32, LCL = 36.08; in control
15. $Z_{A/B} = -0.603$, $Z_{U/D} = -0.50$, no pattern
17. $Z_{A/B} = 0.45$, $Z_{U/D} = 1.11$, no pattern
19. $Z_{A/B} = -3.71$, $Z_{U/D} = -2.08$, patterns exist
21. $P(c \le 2) = 0.2381$
23. a. $n = 131$, $c = 5$; b. AOQL = 0.0242
25. $n = 155$, $c \le 10$, $\alpha = 0.051$, $\beta = 0.085$
27. a. $c = 8$; b. $\beta = 0.155$
29. a. $\alpha = 0.183$, $\beta = 0.006$, unsatisfactory; b. AOQL = 0.015
31. 4.83 min
33. $n = 4$, $c = 97.78$ lb

CHAPTER 5

5. 0.998
7. a. 74%; b. Every 4 months
9. a. 20%, 34%; b. 97%, 98%
11. a. 90%; b. 39%
13. a. 10%, 16%, 18%; b. 63%; c. 50%, 69%, 75%; d. 26%
19. a. 27 weeks; c. 9 weeks
21. 0, 500, 2,000, 4,500

CHAPTER 6

5. 500; $7,500
7. 625
9. 22
11. > 150 make; ≤ 150, buy
13. pages > 100, A; 40 < pages ≤ 100, C pages ≤ 40; B
15. a. Buy; b. Supplier 2; c. Supplier 2, Make; d. ≤ 1,000, supplier 1, > 1,000 but < 4,900, supplier 2, ≥ 4,900, make

CHAPTER 7

1. 30 nonadjacent loads;

2	3	1
	4	

3.

1	2	3
4	6	5

5. a.

H	A	
M	W	
B	G	I

   b. L-shaped

7.

Sue	Allen	Terry
George	Ashley	Mike
Bobby	Johnny	Carrie
Kent	Don	Mary

9. a. 30 min, [A] → [B, C, D] → [E, F];
   b. 88.9%, 11.1%; c. 3, no
11. b. 4 min; c. 14 min;
   d. [A, C] → [B, D] → [E] → [F];
   e. 87.5%, 12.5%; f. 4, no
13. a. 4.8 min, 200; b.240, 80%, 3; c. [A, B, C] → [D, E], 100%, 200
15. [A, B, C] → [D, F, G] → [E, H, J] → [I, K], 79.4%
17. b. [A, B, C] → [D, E] → [F, G, H, I]; c. 75.5%; 24.4%
19. [a, b, c] → [c, d, f, g, h] → [j] → [i, k], 75%
21. B, Q, B, Q, B, I

CHAPTER 8

1. Mall 1 = 62.75, mall 2 = 73.50, mall 3 = 76.00, mall 4 = 77.75; mall 4
3. LD(A) = 19,405.35, LD(B) = 15,325.2, LD(C) = 15,569.49; site B
5. LD(A) = 455.61, LD(B) = 587.76, LD(C) = 932.17; site A
7. 3-1 = 10, 2-2 = 9, 3-2 = 1, 1-3 = 2, 2-3 = 8, 1-4 = 10, TC = 20,200
9. A2 = 20, A3 = 60, B2 = 70, C1 = 80, C2 = 20; TC = 1,290
11. No effect
13. A1 = 70, A3 = 20, B3 = 50, C2 = 80, D2 = 20, D3 = 40; TC = 14,100
15. 1A = 70, 2B = 25, 2C = 90, 3A = 10, 3B = 25, 3D = 25; TC = 13,200
17. A1 = 1,800, A4 = 950, B1 = 1,600, B3 = 1,150, B5 = 2,250, C3 = 350, C6 = 1,400; TC = 3,260 (with multiple optimal solutions)
19. 1B = 250, 1D = 170, 2A = 520, 2C = 90, 3C = 130, 3D = 210; TC = 21,930
21. 1B = 60, 2A = 45, 2B = 25, 2C = 35, 3B = 5; TC = 1,605
23. Charlotte – Atlanta = 30, Memphis – St. Louis = 30, Louisville – New York = 30; TP = 159,000
25. A2 = 1, C1 = 1, D1 = 1, E3 = 1, F3 = 1, G2 = 1, H1 = 1; TC = 1,070 (with multiple optimal solutions)

CHAPTER 8 SUPPLEMENT

1. 1-1 = 250, 2-1 = 50, 2-2 = 350; TC = 24,000
3. 1-2 = 500, 1-3 = 300, 2-1 = 150, 2-3 = 350, 3-1 = 600, 4-1 = 300; TC = 28,750
5. a. and b. VAM; A2 = 70, A4 = 80, B1 = 50, B4 = 160, C1 = 80, C3 = 180, C5 = 60; TC = 82,600; c. yes, A4 = 150, B1 = 120, B4 = 90, C1 = 10, C2 = 70, C3 = 180, C5 = 60; TC = 82,600
7. a. 1D = 5, 2D = 25, 3B = 5, 3C = 15, 4A = 10, 4B = 15; b. 1C = 5, 2C = 10, 2D = 15, 3B = 20, 3C = 0, 4A = 10, 4D = 15; TC = 19,500
9. A2 = 1,800, A4 = 950, A7 = 750, B1 = 1,600, B3 = 1,150, B5 = 2,250, C3 = 350, C6 = 1,400, C7 = 750; TC = 3,260
11. 1B = 60, 2A = 45, 2B = 25, 2C = 35, 3B = 5, 3D = 65; TC = 1,605
13. Charlotte – Atlanta = 30, Memphis – St. Louis = 30, Louisville – New York = 30, Dummy – St. Louis = 10, Dummy – Atlanta = 10, Dummy – New York = 20; TP = 159,000
15. A2 = 1, B4 = 1, C1 = 1, D1 = 1, E3 = 1, F3 = 1, G2 = 1, H1 = 1; TC = 1,070 (with multiple optimal solutions)

CHAPTER 9

1. 4.163 min
3. a. 2.39 min; b. avg. = \$4.52/hr, subject = \$4.82/hr
5. a. 4.52 min; b. $n = 31$
7. $n = 12.2$
9. a. 1.383 min; b. $n = 7.7$; c. poorer quality
11. $n = 683$
13. a. 88.8%; b. 151 more observations
15. 3.946 min
17. $t_{60} = 32.92$ hr, $t_{120} = 27.99$ hr
19. 0.8158

CHAPTER 10

1. a. Apr = 8.67, May = 8.33, Jun = 8.33, Jul = 9.00, Aug = 9.67, Sep = 11.0, Oct = 11.00, Nov = 11.00, Dec = 12.00, Jan = 13.33; b. Jun = 8.20, Jul = 8.80, Aug = 9.40, Sep = 9.60, Oct = 10.40, Nov = 11.00, Dec = 11.40, Jan = 12.60; c. MAD(3) = 1.89, MAD(5) = 2.43
3. a. $F_4 = 116.00$, $F_5 = 121.33$, $F_6 = 118.00$, $F_7 = 143.67$, $F_8 = 138.33$, $F_9 = 141.67$, $F_{10} = 135.00$, $F_{11} = 156.67$, $F_{12} = 143.33$, $F_{13} = 136.67$; b. $F_6 = 121.80$, $F_7 = 134.80$, $F_8 = 125.80$, $F_9 = 137.20$, $F_{10} = 143.00$, $F_{11} = 149.00$, $F_{12} = 137.00$, $F_{13} = 142.00$; c. $\mathrm{F}_4 = 113.85$, $\mathrm{F}_5 = 116.69$, $\mathrm{F}_6 = 125.74$, $\mathrm{F}_7 = 151.77$, $\mathrm{F}_8 = 132.4$, $\mathrm{F}_9 = 136.89$, $\mathrm{F}_{10} = 142.35$, $\mathrm{F}_{11} = 160.00$, $\mathrm{F}_{12} = 136.69$, $\mathrm{F}_{13} = 130.00$; d. 3 – qtr MA: $E = 32.0$, 5 – qtr MA: $E = 36.4$, weighted MA: $E = 28.09$
5. a. $F_4 = 400.00$, $F_5 = 406.67$, $F_6 = 423.33$, $F_7 = 498.33$, $F_8 = 521.67$, $F_9 = 571.67$; b. $F_2 = 400.00$, $F_3 = 410.00$, $F_4 = 398.00$, $F_5 = 402.40$, $F_6 = 421.92$, $F_7 = 452.53$, $F_8 = 460.00$, $F_9 = 498.02$; c. 3-sem MAD = 80.33, exp. smooth MAD = 87.16
7. F_{11} (exp. smooth) = 68.6, F_{11} (adjusted) = 69.17, F_{11} (linear trend) = 70.22; exp. smooth: $E = 14.75$, MAD = 1.89; adjusted: $E = 10.73$, MAD = 1.72; linear trend: MAD = 1.09
9. $F_{13} = 631.22$, $\bar{E} = 26.30$, $E = 289.33$, biased low
11. $F_1 = 155.6$, $F_2 = 192.9$, $F_3 = 118.2$, $F_4 = 155.6$
13. F_{95} (adjusted) = 3,313.19, F_{95} (linear trend) = 2,785.00; adjusted: MAD = 431.71, $E = -2{,}522$; linear trend: MAD = 166.25
15. $E = 86.00$, $\bar{E} = 8.60$, MAD = 15.00, MAPD = 0.08
17. UCL = 684.72, LCL = 684.72, no apparent bias
19. a. $\bar{E} = 10.73$, MAD = 16.76, MAPD = 0.37, E = 75.10; b. $\bar{E} = 8.00$, MAD = 12.67, MAPD = 0.24, $E = 39.99$; c. biased low
21. MAD = 1.78, E = 12.36, biased high; MAD (linear trend) = 0.688
23. $y = 2.36 + 0.267x$, y ($x = 30$) = 10.40; b. R = 0.699
25. 0.863
27. $y = 5582 - 260.36x$; a. MAD (linear regression) = 466.9, MAD (linear trend) = 372.1; b. –0.843
29. $r = 0.643$

CHAPTER 11

1. 120,000 regular production, periods 1–3; 50,000 regular production, period 4; 40,000 OT, period 3; $23,830,000
3. User designed (mixed)
5. Constant production, then OT σ sub.
7. a. $1,492,500; b. $1,507,500; c. $1,447,500
9. a. $25,500/month; b. 34 ropes, 400 gloves, 300 shoes; c. $7,500/month

CHAPTER 12

1. a. $Q = 79.7$; b. $13,550; c. 15.05 orders; d. 24.18 days
3. a. $Q = 240$; b. $4,800; c. 80 orders; d. 4 days
5. a. $Q = 190{,}918.8$ yd; b. $15,273.51; c. 6.36 orders; d. 57.4 days
7. $Q = 67.13$, $S = 15.49$, TC = $3,872.98
9. a. $Q = 774.6$ boxes, TC = $619.68, $R = 43.84$ boxes
11. $Q = 23{,}862$, TC = $298,276
13. a. $Q = 2{,}529.8$ logs; b. TC = $12,649.11; c. $T_b = 63.3$ days; d. 303.7 days
15. $Q = 17{,}544.2$; $S = 4{,}616.94$; TC=$3,231.83
17. $Q = 5{,}000$; TC = $67,175

19. $Q = 500$
21. $Q = 6{,}000$; TC = \$87,030.33
23. $Q = 20{,}000$; TC \$893,368
25. $Q =$ \$371,842.26; TC = \$150,128.30; 13.944 loans/yr; reorder pt. = \$255,000
27. $R = 20{,}410.30$; safety stock = 2,410.29 yd
29. $R = 82{,}368$ lb
31. $R = 62.94$
33. $R = 95.67$, safety stock = 33.17
35. $Q = 7{,}509.69$ oz
37. $Q = 609.83$ bottles

CHAPTER 12 SUPPLEMENT

1. b. $\mu = 3.48$, EV = 3.65, not enough simulations; c. 21 calls, no, repeat simulation
3. $\mu =$ \$250

CHAPTER 13

1. a. 6; b. 7; c. 3
3. b. 4, 16, 16
5. b. 8, 6, 2; c. 0.192%
7. Release orders for 175 *X*'s in period 7, 310 *Z*'s in period 6, 320 *R*'s in period 5, 630 *U*'s, and 145 *S*'s in period 4, 600 *T*'s, 500 *U*'s, and 1210 *V*'s in period 3, 90 *V*'s and 2520 *W*'s in period 2, and 1840 *W*'s in period 1.
9. Release orders for 100 armature housings in period 1; 100 armatures in period 2; 400 magnetic brushes in period 3; 400 longitudinal bolts in period 4; 50 pully assemblies and 200 *SA* 110 in period 5; 300 *SA* 310's, 300 front covers, 200 rear covers, and 300 *SA* 210's in period 6; 750 contact wires in period 7; 320 *SA* 410's in period 8; and 400 alternators in period 9.
11. Wagner-Whitin \$3,240
13. LFL \$1,400; EOQ \$941.50; PPB \$730; WW* \$700
    WW orders: 140 in period 1, 125 in period 5, 115 in period 8, 190 in period 10
15. b. normal capacity of 250 hours for machining, 500 hours for heat treat, and 50 hours for assembly
17. a. Load percent: 84.8%, 170%, 295%, 254% at welding; 80%, 160%, 320%, 240% at assembly; b. 34, 68, 136, 102 hours at welding; 32, 64, 128, 96 hours at assembly; c. 30, 59, 118, 89 hours at welding; 27, 54, 108, 81 hours at assembly

CHAPTER 14

1. Jones to Nurse 1, Hathaway to Nurse 2, Sweeney to Nurse 3, Bryant to Nurse 4
3. Product 1 to machine 2, product 2 to machine 4, product 3 to machine 1, product 4 to machine 3, product 5 to machine 5
5. DDATE or SPT
7. SPT
9. 6, 5, 4, 2, 1, 3; 5 hr 35 min
11. SPT
13. Backlog 10, 0, 0, 0, 0
15. One worker does not have two consecutive work days.
17. Preventive maintenance every week

CHAPTER 15

1. 3.63, or 4
3. 126/hr
5. b. decreases
7. a. 8.25 or 9; b. 2.75 or 3; c. 13.75 or 14

CHAPTER 16

1. $P_0 = 0.33$, $P_3 = 0.099$, $L = 2.0$, $L_q = 1.33$, $W = 0.125$ hr, $W_q = 0.083$ hr, $P_w = .67$
3. a. $L_q = 0.9$, $W = 0.25$ hr, $W_q = 0.15$ hr; b. $\lambda > \mu$
5. $\lambda = 9$/hr
7. yes
9. a. $L_q = 9.09$ trucks, $W = 0.05$ days, $W_q = 0.045$ days; b. yes
11. $L = 1.19$, $L_q = 0.26$, $W = 0.043$ hr, $W_q = 0.009$ hr; yes
13. Yes, assign an operator
15. Yes, add third press
17. Yes, hire a third doctor
19. 3 servers should be sufficient
21. Add additional employees; expected savings = \$25.50/days
23. $L_q = 1.13$, $W_q = 0.112$ hr
25. $P_{n \geq 31} = 0.281$
27. 7:00 A.M. – 9:00 A.M. = 5, 9:00 A.M. – noon = 2, noon – 2:00 P.M. = 6, 2:00 P.M. – 5:00 P.M. = 4
29. L = 2.71 cars out of service, $W = 37.15$ hr
31. Select new service agreement, savings = \$1,813.50

CHAPTER 17

1. Time = 10 weeks
3. a. 23 wk; $s_{12} = 0$, $s_{13} = 1$, $s_{24} = 0$, $s_{25} = 10$, $s_{35} = 1$, $s_{45} = 0$, $s_{46} = 9$, $s_{56} = 0$, $s_{36} = 11$; b. 1-2-4-5-6
5. 1-2: ES = 0, EF = 7, LS = 2, LF = 9, S = 2; 1-3: ES = 0, EF = 10, LS = 0, LF = 10, S = 0; 2-4: ES = 7, EF = 13, LS = 9, LF = 15, S = 2; 3-4: ES = 10, EF = 15, LS = 10, LF = 15, S = 0; 3-5: ES = 10, EF = 14, LS = 14, LF = 18, S = 4; 4-5: ES = 15, EF = 18, LS = 15, LF = 18, S = 0; 5-6: ES = 18, EF = 20, LS = 18, LF = 20, S = 0; CP = 1-3-4-5-6
7. 1-2: ES = 0, EF = 10, LS = 0, LF = 10, S = 0; 1-3: ES = 0, EF = 7, LS = 5, LF = 12, S = 5; 2-4: ES = 10, EF = 14, LS = 14, LF = 18, S = 4; 2-6: ES = 10, EF = 25, LS = 10, LF = 25, S = 0; 3-4: ES = 7, EF = 13, LS = 12, LF = 18, S = 5; 3-5: ES = 17, EF = 19, LS = 13; LF = 25, S = 6; 4-6: ES = 14, EF = 21, LS = 18, LF = 25, S = 4; 5-6: ES = 19, EF = 19, LS = 25, LF = 25, S = 6; 6-7: ES = 25, EF = 34, LS = 25, LF = 34, S = 0; CP = 1-2-6-7 = 34
9. CP = 1-3-6-10-11-14-15 = 78 wk
11. CP = 1-2-5-7 = 40.33, $\sigma = 5.95$
13. e. CP = 1-3-5-7-8-9; f. time = 46 mo, $\sigma = 5$ mo
15. 0.2119
17. 0.0643
19. At least 50.3 weeks
21. Total crash cost = \$3,200
23. CP = 1-2-4-5-8-9; crash cost = \$5,100; total cost = \$33,900

INDEX

PHOTO CREDITS

CHAPTER 1. Page 2: Courtesy of AT&T Archives; 11: Courtesy of Harley-Davidson Inc.; 14: Chris Sorensen; 19: Courtesy of Allen-Bradley Company; 21: Courtesy of Motorola Inc.

CHAPTER 2. Page 30: Courtesy of Reynolds Metal Company (left and right); 33: Courtesy of Motorola Inc.

CHAPTER 3. Page 86: Courtesy of National Institute of Standards and Technology (left), Courtesy of IBM Corporation (right); 95: Courtesy of Chrysler Corporation (left and right); 116: Jose Fernmandez/Woodfin Camp & Associates, Inc.; 118: William Strode/Woodfin Camp & Associates, Inc.

CHAPTER 4. Page 146: Richard Pasley; 152: Courtesy of Ford Motor Company; 162: Ken Rogers/Black Star.

CHAPTER 5. Page 210: Courtesy of Titleist and Foot-Joy Worldwide (left and right); 250: Courtesy of IBM Corporation; 252: Wayne Eastep/The Stock Market (left), Courtesy of AutoDesk, Inc. (right); 254: Richard Pasley (left), Dale E. Boyer/Photo Researchers, Inc. (right).

CHAPTER 6. Page 276: John Chiasson/The Gamma Liaison Network; 285: Courtesy of Newport News & Shipbuilding (top) Judi Baldwin/Newport News & Shipbuilding (right), E. Mirsch/Newport News & Shipbuilding (left); 286: Courtesy of Nissan Motor Manufacturing Corporation U.S.A.; 287: Jodi Buren/Woodfin Camp & Associates, Inc. (left), Rob Crandall/Stock Boston (right); 305: Courtesy of Nissan Motor Manufacturing Corporation U.S.A. (left), P. Shambroom/Photo Researchers, Inc. (right).

CHAPTER 7. Page 324: John A. Wee; 328: Junebug Clark/Photo Researchers, Inc. (left), Courtesy of Martin Marietta Corporation (right); 330: Matthew McVay/Stock Boston; 356: Courtesy of Vought Aircraft Company.

CHAPTER 8. Page 374: J. Nicholl/Katz/Woodfin Camp & Associates, Inc. (left), Frank Siteman/Stock Boston (right); 381: Dimaggio/Kalish/The Stock Market; 393: Courtesy of Triple Crown Services, Inc.; 396: Chris Sorensen.

CHAPTER 9. Page 432: Chris Sorensen; 445: Ted Horowitz/The Stock Market; 466: Matthew McVay/Stock Boston.

CHAPTER 10. Page 484: Courtesy of American Airlines; 502: David Brownell/The Image Bank; 514: Jake Rajis/The Image Bank.

CHAPTER 11. Page 544: Courtesy of Micro Analysis & Design, Inc.; 548: Sue Klemens/Stock Boston; 562: Ted Mahieu/The Stock Market (left), Robert E. Daemmrich/Stock Boston (right).

CHAPTER 12. Page 580: Courtesy of IBM Corporation; 584: Courtesy of The Goodyear Tire & Rubber Company; 588: Courtesy of Symbol Technology.

CHAPTER 13. Page 648: Tom Carroll; 658: Robert E. Daemmrich/Tony Stone Worldwide Ltd.; 683: Courtesy of Deere & Company.

CHAPTER 14. Page 706: Courtesy of Catepillar Inc.; 721: Courtesy of Pritsker Corporation; 730: Courtesy of Motorola Inc.

CHAPTER 15. Page 748: Stacy Pick/Stock Boston; 753: Stacy Pick/Stock Boston; 762: David Ulmer/Stock Boston.

CHAPTER 16. Page 782: Don Mason/The Stock Market; 793: Jack Reznicki/The Stock Market; 805: Spencer Grant/Stock Boston.

CHAPTER 17. Page 824: Courtesy of Chrysler Corporation; 831: Photri; 839: Terry Farmer/Tony Stone Worldwide Ltd.